A Flexible Organization for Instructors

1 The Winning Hand of Entrepreneurship

– TRUE/FALSE QUESTIONS

T p. 4 C — 1. An entrepreneurial career can provide an exciting life and substantial personal rewards while also contributing to the welfare of society.

1 Discuss the availability of entrepreneurial opportunities and give examples of successful businesses started by entrepreneurs.

F p. 6 A — 2. When Jonathan F. Johnson founded Marketplace Holdings by buying out a chain of rundown supermarkets, he decided it was best for his enterprise to compete against rivals based on price.

Justification: Johnson couldn't beat his competitors on price, so he decided to focus on service.

T p. 8 A — 3. Annie Beiler founded Aunt Annie's by first developing a better-tasting pretzel and then building a successful, growing, and profitable business on that foundation.

F p. 9 A — 4. Robert Kopras's Roto Zip Spiral Saw has been a success because major tool companies recognized the potential of this tool and quickly moved to capitalize on Kopras's invention.

Justification: Major tool companies rejected Kopras's ideas, saying it would be too costly.

2 Explain the entrepreneurial challenges presented by e-business and global changes.

F p. 11 C — 5. Globalization is an important economic trend, but not for small firms since they have been excluded from participating in it.

Justification: Large corporations have been the dominant players in international business, but small firms have also participated; further, their presence in global markets is growing.

T p. 12 C — 6. Even though small firms are typically situated in one locality, many of them now export or import products internationally.

3 Explain the nature of entrepreneurship and how it is related to small business.

F p. 12 D — 7. The term *entrepreneur* is understood in this text to refer only to founders of small businesses.

Justification: According to the text, *entrepreneur* refers to founders, franchisees, second-generation members of family-owned firms, and owner-managers who buy out the founders of existing firms.

Test Bank Questions are grouped by learning objective, so that you can thoroughly test all objectives — or emphasize the ones that you feel are most important. Correlation tables at the beginning of each chapter make it easy to prepare tests that cover the objectives at the level of difficulty appropriate for your students.

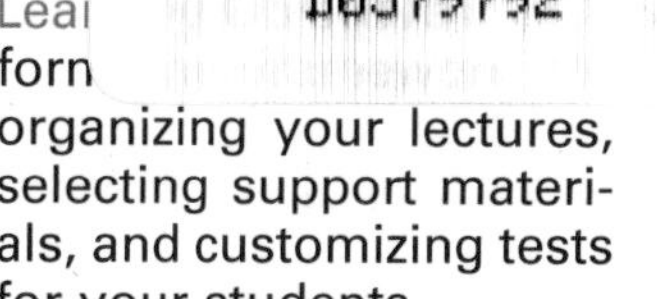

Text
Lea
forn
organizing your lectures, selecting support materials, and customizing tests for your students.

Testing Software

Longenecker • Moore • Petty • Palich

ess
t
hasis

Chapter 1

Looking Ahead

After studying this chapter, you should be able to

1 *Discuss the availability of entrepreneurial opportunities and give examples of successful businesses started by entrepreneurs.*

2 *Explain the nature of entrepreneurship and how it is related to small business.*

3 *Identify some motivators or rewards of entrepreneurial careers.*

4 *Describe the various types of entrepreneurs and entrepreneurial ventures.*

5 *Identify five potential advantages of small entrepreneurial firms.*

6 *Discuss factors related to readiness for entrepreneurship and getting started in an entrepreneurial career.*

7 *Explain the concept of an entrepreneurial legacy and the challenges involved in crafting a worthy legacy.*

Would you like to become an entrepreneur, to start and operate a small business of your own? Perhaps you wonder whether such dreams can come true today. The good news is that thousands of individuals start such businesses every year. You are living in a world of entrepreneurial opportunity!

You are about to embark on a course of study that will prove invaluable if you elect to pursue a career in entrepreneurship or small business. An entrepreneurial career can provide an exciting life and substantial personal rewards, while also contributing to the welfare of society. This book is designed to give you an understanding of entrepreneurship and to help prepare you for the life of an entrepreneur.

ENTREPRENEURIAL OPPORTUNITIES

Entrepreneurial opportunities exist for those who can produce products or services desired by customers. A promising entrepreneurial opportunity is more than just an interesting idea. It involves a product or service that is so attractive to customers that they are willing to pay their hard-earned money for it. In other words, an entrepreneur must find a way to create value for customers.

Our working definition of **entrepreneurial opportunity**, as a desirable and timely innovation that creates value for interested buyers or end users, distinguishes between opportunities and ideas. It is important to note, however, that a given opportunity will not be equally attractive to everyone. Because of differences in experiences and perspectives, one person may see an opportunity where others do not. But, in any case, a true opportunity exists only for the entrepreneur who has the interest, resources, and capabilities required to succeed.

Entrepreneurial opportunities exist today in a business world that differs markedly from the business world of yesterday. In this section, we will discuss the paths to successful entrepreneurial ventures taken by some present-day entrepreneurs.

1 *Discuss the availability of entrepreneurial opportunities and give examples of successful businesses started by entrepreneurs.*

entrepreneurial opportunity
A value-creating innovation with market potential

Three Success Stories

We hope that you will receive inspiration from the three interesting stories of entrepreneurial success that follow. Perhaps you, too, will soon be part of a success story—one to be written in the days ahead! In addition, you will see that entrepreneurship takes many forms. These stories suggest a few of the numerous possibilities you can consider for your own career. Some of your own opportunities, of course, may be drastically different from those described.

3

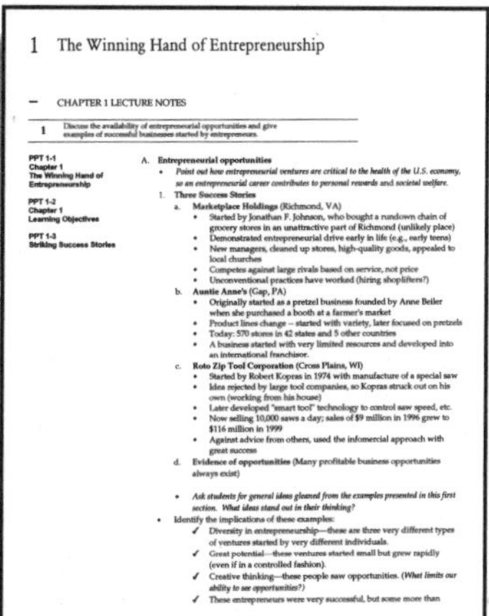

1 The Winning Hand of Entrepreneurship

– CHAPTER 1 LECTURE NOTES

1 Discuss the availability of entrepreneurial opportunities and give examples of successful businesses started by entrepreneurs.

PPT 1-1 Chapter 1 The Winning Hand of Entrepreneurship

PPT 1-2 Chapter 1 Learning Objectives

PPT 1-3 Striking Success Stories

A. **Entrepreneurial opportunities**
- *Point out how entrepreneurial ventures are critical to the health of the U.S. economy, so an entrepreneurial career contributes to personal rewards and societal welfare.*

1. **Three Success Stories**
   a. **Marketplace Holdings** (Richmond, VA)
      - Started by Jonathan F. Johnson, who bought a rundown chain of grocery stores in an unattractive part of Richmond (unlikely place)
      - Demonstrated entrepreneurial drive early in life (e.g., early teens)
      - New managers, cleaned up stores, high-quality goods, appealed to local churches
      - Competes against large rivals based on service, not price
      - Unconventional practices have worked (hiring shoplifters?)

   b. **Auntie Anne's** (Gap, PA)
      - Originally started as a pretzel business founded by Anne Beiler when she purchased a booth at a farmer's market
      - Product lines change – started with variety, later focused on pretzels
      - Today: 570 stores in 42 states and 5 other countries
      - A business started with very limited resources and developed into an international franchisor.

   c. **Roto Zip Tool Corporation** (Cross Plains, WI)
      - Started by Robert Kopras in 1974 with manufacture of a special saw
      - Idea rejected by large tool companies, so Kopras struck out on his own (working from his house)
      - Later developed "smart tool" technology to control saw speed, etc.
      - Now selling 10,000 saws a day; sales of $9 million in 1996 grew to $116 million in 1999
      - Against advice from others, used the infomercial approach with great success

   d. **Evidence of opportunities** (Many profitable business opportunities always exist)

- *Ask students for general ideas gleaned from the examples presented in this first section. What ideas stand out in their thinking?*
- Identify the implications of these examples:
  ✓ Diversity in entrepreneurship—these are three very different types of ventures started by very different individuals.
  ✓ Great potential—these ventures started small but grew rapidly (even if in a controlled fashion).
  ✓ Creative thinking—these people saw opportunities. (*What limits our ability to see opportunities?*)
  ✓ These entrepreneurs were very successful, but some more than

Video

All Lecture Support Materials come together under their appropriate objectives in the Instructor's Manual Lecture Notes, for thorough coverage of all objectives. Annotations tell you the appropriate times to integrate transparencies, transparency masters, and PowerPoint slides into your lectures. In addition, there is a video guide that provides possible questions and answers related to the "Small Business School" videos.

Transparencies

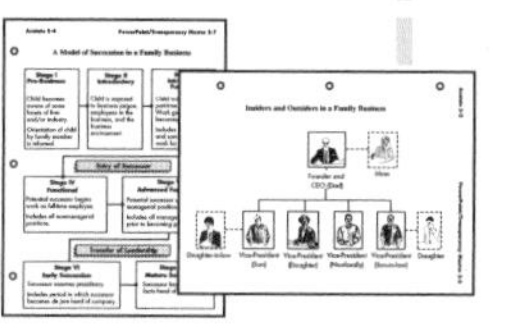
Transparency Masters

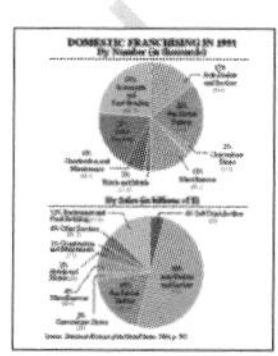
PowerPoint

SMALL BUSINESS MANAGEMENT

An Entrepreneurial Emphasis

13th Edition

JUSTIN G. LONGENECKER
Baylor University

CARLOS W. MOORE
Baylor University

J. WILLIAM PETTY
Baylor University

LESLIE E. PALICH
Baylor University

Australia · Canada · Mexico · Singapore · Spain · United Kingdom · United States

Small Business Management: An Entrepreneurial Emphasis, 13e

Justin G. Longenecker, Carlos W. Moore, J. William Petty, Leslie E. Palich

VP/Editorial Director:
Jack W. Calhoun

VP/Editor-in-Chief:
Dave Shaut

Sr. Publisher:
Melissa Acuña

Executive Editor:
John Szilagyi

Developmental Editor:
Ohlinger Publishing Services

Marketing Manager:
Jacquelyn Carillo

Production Editor:
Robert Dreas

Technology Project Manager:
Kristen Meere

Web Coordinator:
Karen Schaffer

Manufacturing Coordinator:
Doug Wilke

Production House:
Lifland et al., Bookmakers

Compositor:
Parkwood Composition Service, Inc.

Printer:
R. R. Donnelley
Willard, Ohio

Internal Designer:
Grannan Graphic Design/Brenda Grannan

Promotions Manager:
Jim Overly

Cover Designer:
Grannan Graphic Design/Brenda Grannan

Cover Images:
Guildhaus Photographics

Photography Manager:
Deanna Ettinger

Photo Researcher:
Charlotte Goldman

Printed in the United States of America
2 3 4 5 0 07 06 05

ISBN: 0-324-32342-5 book
0-324-22612-8 package
0-324-31719-0 Instructor Edition book
0-324-31400-0 Instructor Edition package

Library of Congress Control Number:
2004115360

For more information
contact South-Western,
5191 Natorp Boulevard,
Mason, Ohio 45040.
Or you can visit our Internet site at:
http://www.swlearning.com

Brief Contents

Contents

Starting from Scratch or Joining an Existing Business 47

Part 3

Developing the New Venture Business Plan 115

Part 4

Welcome to the 13th edition of *Small Business Management: An Entrepreneurial Emphasis*! As authors, we measure our success by the effectiveness of our presentation to you. And though you may not have selected this textbook personally, we consider you our customer nonetheless. We are sensitive to your learning needs. For this reason, we have taken your point of view into consideration in writing each chapter and have gone to great lengths to make the material informative, as well as easy and interesting to read. This edition continues to focus on that large segment of the economy represented by small businesses and on the entrepreneurial process that gives them life and vitality. In the paragraphs that follow, we summarize the special attributes of this book.

Follow Your Dreams

Entrepreneurs need to dream BIG dreams—to see opportunities where others see only failures. Did you know that Benjamin Franklin was admonished to stop experimenting with electricity? It's true! Trying to improve on the reliable and perfectly functional oil lamp was considered an absurd waste of time! And even Thomas Edison, a shrewd entrepreneur in his own right, tried to discourage his friend Henry Ford from working on his daring idea of building a motorcar. Convinced the idea was worthless, Edison advised Ford to give up this wild fancy and work for him. Ford, however, remained steadfast and tirelessly pursued his dream. Progress was slow. Although his first attempt produced a vehicle without a reverse gear, Ford knew he could make it happen—and, of course, he did. People like Franklin and Ford dreamed big dreams and dared to do great things, and now we all benefit from their achievements.

This book lays out, in a step-by-step fashion, the knowledge and insights needed to lead and manage a small business. Simultaneously, it focuses on a much broader concern—the pursuit of entrepreneurial dreams. Entrepreneurs build businesses to fulfill dreams—for themselves, for their families, for their employees, and for their communities. When we write about small business, therefore, we are writing about individuals whose business lives have an impact on a wide range of people.

The aim of the 13th edition of *Small Business Management: An Entrepreneurial Emphasis* is to provide instruction and guidance that will greatly improve your odds for success as you take your own entrepreneurial journey. It is our hope that what we present in this book—and in the tools and ancillaries that accompany it—will support the varied goals of those seeking independent business careers, either directly or indirectly, through the wise counsel of the instructor who has selected this book.

There has never been a more exciting time to be an entrepreneur! If you are committed strongly enough to your dream, in one creative way or another you will overcome the obstacles that lie ahead. New ventures can create tremendous personal value for both entrepreneurs and the investors who back them with time and money. New ventures can also protect and improve quality of life by creating jobs and providing new products and services.

Our best wishes to you for a challenging and successful learning experience!

Learn What's New

A central purpose of this revision of *Small Business Management* is to present current, relevant content in unique and interesting ways. When we started writing, we found many innovative ideas, trends, companies, and people to write *about*. We also found someone new to write *with*. Dr. Leslie Palich, the Ben H. Williams Professor of Entrepreneurship at Baylor University, has joined us as a co-author and has played a distinctive role in the development of this edition. A brief bio of Dr. Palich can be found on page xx. Each author brings a different discipline to the mix, but it is working together in the same environment that promotes the rich interchange of ideas you'll discover in this book.

With an abundance of real-world examples to keep both first-time readers and readers of earlier editions totally engaged, this edition of *Small Business Management* offers plenty that's new:

- "Living the Dream" boxes, featured in each chapter, capture entrepreneurs in action as they face the challenges of small business and entrepreneurship.
- Chapter 2, " Entrepreneurial Integrity: A Gateway to Small Business Opportunity," is new to this edition. How vital is integrity to managing a small business and building lasting relationships with stakeholder groups? We argue that sending a simple, clear, and consistent message about integrity gives small firms an advantage over their larger competitors and that taking actions that make such a message credible is essential.
- Chapter 13, "Customer Relationships: The Key Ingredient," brings a new focus to this edition by highlighting the importance of creating and managing customer relationships. Enriching the discussion is distinct, new content on customer relationship management (CRM) and on understanding consumer behavior in order to support a commitment to CRM.
- Chapter 17, "Global Marketing," has been substantially revised to focus on growth strategies. In assessing the implications for small businesses of an increasingly international competitive environment, we demonstrate that size need not limit an entrepreneur's global aspirations. Although the challenges of competing in a global economy are great, they are not insurmountable, as the many examples in the chapter convincingly prove.
- New video-enriched cases represent another first for *Small Business Management*. Seven new cases, which draw on the resources of the popular PBS television series "Small Business School," bring together high-interest video segments and in-text case material. Case instruction augmented by video filmed on location at

Auntie Anne's Pretzels, Boston Duck Tours, and other entrepreneurial businesses makes studying effective small business management all the more interesting.

Achieve Your Best

Small Business Management is organized so as to help students and future entrepreneurs achieve success in whatever field they choose. The wide spectrum of content, applications, cases, graphics, stories, and other details offered in *Small Business Management* has assisted many small business entrepreneurs in making their dreams come true. With a focus on learning, our features emphasize hands-on activities that capture student interest and guarantee practical knowledge.

- ***Unique Spotlight Features***. The chapter-opening "In the Spotlight" features profile an amazing collection of business owners, whose unique insights into how to start, run, and grow a business will help readers identify and explore the full range of issues facing today's business owners. More than half of the spotlights are video-enriched, because nothing helps students master the lessons of small business and entrepreneurship as much as seeing them put into practice.
- ***Simplified Financial Presentations***. Because concepts related to financial planning are not mastered easily, we have continued to simplify all financial presentations, striving to make them more intuitive. To students who have concerns about their ability to tackle the accounting and financial material, we say, "fear no more." For this new edition, we have developed a short animation designed to help students better understand the working-capital cycle; it can be found on this textbook's Web site at http://longenecker.swlearning.com.
- ***Multimedia Resources on CD-ROM***. We continue to offer multimedia resources on CD-ROM. The CD "Tools for Preparing a Simplified Business Plan," available with the purchase of a new textbook, provides templates in Microsoft Word and Excel to help students map out a take-it-to-the-bank plan.
- ***Unique Support for Building a Business Plan***. The material in Part 3, "Developing the New Venture Business Plan," is integral to learning how to develop workable plans and is closely aligned with the approaches to planning that we present in the textbook and on the accompanying CD.
- ***Integrated Learning System***. Our integrated learning system uses each chapter's learning objectives to give structure and coherence to the text content, study aids, and instructor's ancillaries, all of which are keyed to these objectives. The numbered objectives are introduced in the "Looking Ahead" section, and each is concisely addressed in the "Looking Back" section at the end of each chapter. These same objectives are tied to related exercises in the *Student Learning Guide*. Students who are having trouble with individual concepts can easily locate related materials in the text and in the *Student Learning Guide* simply by looking for the appropriate objective.

  The integrated learning system also simplifies lecture and test preparation. The lecture notes in the *Instructor's Manual* are grouped by learning objective and identify the acetates, masters, and PowerPoint slides that relate to each objective. Questions in the *Test Bank* are grouped by objective as well. A correlation table at the beginning of each *Test Bank* chapter permits selection of questions that cover all objectives or that emphasize objectives considered most important.
- ***Exploring the Web***. Structured Internet exercises appear at the end of every chapter. Designed to familiarize students with the best online resources for small businesses, "Exploring the Web" exercises direct students to specific Web sites, prompting them to perform targeted searches, analyze the effectiveness of what they find, and theorize about what could be done better. The future of technology in small businesses is wide open; these exercises go a long way toward ensuring that students are informed about the trends to watch. All exercises are new to this edition. An appendix of "Useful URLs" at the end of the book provides a helpful compilation of the most informative Web sites for small businesses and entrepreneurs.
- ***You Make the Call***. "You Make the Call" incidents at the end of each chapter are very popular with both students and instructors because they present realistic business situations that require examining key operating decisions. By having students take on the role of a small business owner, these exercises give them a leg up in addressing the concerns of small businesses.
- ***Cases***. Cases—many new to this edition, including seven new video cases—are available for each chapter, providing opportunities for students to apply chapter concepts to realistic entrepreneurial situations.
- ***Living the Dream***. Practical examples from the world of small business and entrepreneurship carry both instructional and inspirational value. "Living the Dream" boxes appear at critical junctures throughout the chapters, refueling and refreshing chapter concepts with documented experiences of practicing entrepreneurs.

Updated and Enhanced Supplements

All resources and ancillaries that accompany *Small Business Management: An Entrepreneurial Emphasis*, 13th edition, have been created to support a variety of teaching methods, learning styles, and classroom situations.

- ***Resource Integration Guide***. New to this edition, *Resource Integration Guide* is available to instructors when they receive their desk copies of *Small Business Management*. This four-color, laminated insert illustrates the full array of resources available for teaching the course, ensuring that instructors extract maximum value from this textbook's integrated resources.

- ***InfoTrac® College Edition.*** Packaged free with every new copy of *Small Business Management* is a four-month subscription to InfoTrac College Edition, an online research database that amasses more than five million full-text articles from nearly 5,000 scholarly and popular periodicals. With InfoTrac, students have anytime, anywhere access right from their desktops to journals like *Fortune*, *BusinessWeek*, *Entrepreneur*, *Fast Company*, *Newsweek*, and *Inc.*, to name a few. For instructors who routinely incorporate extra readings or research assignments into their course outline, directing students to log on to InfoTrac to access particular articles or to conduct their own searches provides a quick and convenient way to ensure that students gain a comprehensive view of the business environment from the most influential journals from around the world. For more information on InfoTrac, visit http://www.infotrac-college.com.
- ***Student Learning Guide.*** 0-324-22613-6. Prepared by Susan Peterson, of Scottsdale Community College, this valuable student supplement contains key points, brief definitions of chapter terms, and a variety of self-testing materials, including true/false, multiple-choice, fill-in-the-blank, and essay questions.
- ***Instructor's Manual.*** 0-324-22614-4. Written by Jim Roberts, of Baylor University, this manual contains annotated lecture outlines, with special discussion prompts related to the use of PowerPoint slides, transparency acetates, and transparency masters; answers to "Discussion Questions" and "Exploring the Web" exercises; comments on "You Make the Call" situations; and teaching notes for the cases. A guide to the use of the "Small Business School" video and a selection of transparency masters are also included.
- ***Instructor's Resource CD-ROM.*** 0-324-22615-2. Instructors: Get quick access to all instructor ancillaries from your desktop. This easy-to-use CD lets you electronically review, edit, and copy what you need.
- ***Test Bank.*** 0-324-22617-9. Thoroughly revised by Norm Bryan, of Georgia State University, the *Test Bank* includes true/false, multiple-choice, and essay questions. Also, for the first time, the *Test Bank* contains additional "You Make the Call" situations, beyond those in the text chapters. A correlation table at the beginning of each chapter enables the instructor to select those questions most appropriate for particular classes.
- ***ExamView® Testing Software.*** 0-324-22618-7. All questions from the printed *Test Bank* are available on the Instructor's Resource CD-ROM in South-Western's testing program, ExamView. This is an easy-to-use test-creation program, compatible with Windows and Macintosh operating systems.
- ***Microsoft® PowerPoint® for Instructors.*** 0-324-22616-0. Charlie Cook, of the University of West Alabama, has developed a set of over 500 full-color PowerPoint presentation slides to accompany *Small Business Management*, providing instructors with a complete set of notes and images for lectures. Slides are available for instructors to download from the textbook's Web site at http://longenecker.swlearning.com; they can also be found on the Instructor's Resource CD-ROM. A separate set of slides, tailored to help students with note-taking, is also available for download at http://longenecker.swlearning.com.
- ***"Small Business School" Video.*** Available in both VHS (0-324-32277-1) and DVD (0-324-32278-X) formats, selections from this popular television series on PBS stations let you in on some very big ideas at work in a variety of interesting and innovative small businesses. Curious about the franchising strategy of Auntie Anne's Pretzels? Interested in learning how the successful entrepreneurs at Specialty Cheese ensure quality and develop new products? Use these videos to bring the real world into your classroom, and let your students learn from the experts.
- ***Something Ventured Telecourse.*** This set of 26 video segments is available from INTELECOM, a not-for-profit producer of distance-learning courseware. The series covers a range of topics, from acquiring startup capital to franchising, risk management, marketing, and beyond. For more information, visit http://www.intelecom.org or call 626-796-7300.

  A *Telecourse Guide* (0-324-32303-4) to accompany this series, including learning objectives, assignments, video viewing questions, and self-tests, is available from Thomson South-Western.
- ***Transparency Acetates.*** 0-324-32304-2. A selection of must-have PowerPoint images in the form of overhead transparencies is available to instructors.
- ***Web Site.*** At this textbook's Web site, http://longenecker.swlearning.com, resources for both instructors and students can be located and utilized. You will also find links to additional case material, chapter quizzes, additional "Exploring the Web" exercises, downloadable ancillaries, and more.
- ***WebTutor™ Advantage on WebCT and on Blackboard.*** WebTutor™ Advantage on WebCT or WebTutor™ on Blackboard complements *Small Business Management* by providing interactive reinforcement that helps students grasp key concepts. WebTutor's online teaching and learning environment brings together content management, assessment, communication, and collaboration capabilities to enhance in-class instruction or deliver distance learning. For more information, including a demo, visit http://webtutor.thomsonlearning.com.

Optional Course Add-Ons

***BizPlan*Builder® *Express: A Guide to Creating a Business Plan with BizPlan*Builder.** 0-324-26144-6. BizPlan*Builder* Express—a workbook and CD package that includes the award-winning, best-selling software BizPlan*Builder* 2003 (version 8.1)—provides all the essentials for creating winning business plans, with step-by-step instructions for preparing each section of a plan, including ready-to-customize samples, prompts and advice, detailed marketing analysis, and straightforward financial tools. Full-featured and fully integrated with Microsoft Office's powerful word processor (Word 2000/2002) and spreadsheet (Excel 2000/2002) applications, BizPlan*Builder* also includes a template version for users of other operating systems and productivity software.

Profiles in Entrepreneurship: Leaving More Than Footprints. 0-324-26153-5. *Profiles in Entrepreneurship* is a two-hour video presentation on CD-ROM that showcases the firsthand experiences of 29 practicing entrepreneurs and will enhance any small business or entrepreneurship course. Opportunity recognition, risk assessment, leadership skills, and the ability to compensate for limited resources are just a few of the topics addressed in this CD-ROM collection. Along with the CD-ROM, students receive a text with brief descriptions of profiled entrepreneurs, including observations of their motivations, tactics, and strategies; highlights of their professional experience; and "I'm Glad You Asked Me That" question-and-answer sessions. Powerful anecdotes, personal tips, and shared interests and passions combine to provide students of entrepreneurship with (1) an up-close look at entrepreneurs in action and (2) a chance to consider how to develop their own edge in pursuing an entrepreneurial career.

Special Thanks and Acknowledgments

There are numerous individuals to whom we owe a debt of gratitude for their assistance in making this project a reality. In particular, we thank our friends at Thomson. We are especially indebted to John Szilagyi and Judy O'Neill, of Thomson, and Jeanne Yost, of Lifland et al., Bookmakers. They are true professionals! We also thank Elizabeth Vaughn and Karen Moore, whose excellent word-processing skills made our burden much easier to bear.

A talented team of writers contributed an outstanding set of ancillary materials. Special thanks go to Dr. Jim Roberts, holder of the Mrs. W. A. Mays Professorship in Entrepreneurship at Baylor University, for his preparation of the *Instructor's Manual*. We offer our thanks as well to Susan Peterson, of Scottsdale Community College, who prepared the *Student Learning Guide*; to Charlie Cook, of the University of West Alabama, who created the PowerPoint images; to Norm Bryan, of Georgia State University, who worked on the *Test Bank* materials; to Timothy J. Berry, president of Palo Alto Software, who provided the Sample Business Plan, used in Appendix A; and Kathy Bohley, of the University of Indianapolis, who helped generate the "Exploring the Web" exercises. We offer a special word of appreciation for the understanding and support of our wives—Frances, Karen, Donna, and Dianna—during this process.

For their helpful suggestions and thoughtful comments, which helped to shape this edition, we are grateful to the following reviewers and to many others who, for reasons of privacy, chose to remain anonymous:

David Ambrosini
Cabrillo College

Chandler Atkins
Adirondack Community College

Lee Baldwin
University of Mary/Hardin–Baylor

Francis B. Ballard
Florida Community College

Hilton Barrett
Elizabeth City State University

Bill Bauer
Carroll College—Waukesha, Wisconsin

Verona K. Beguin
Black Hills State University

Narendra C. Bhandari
Pace University, New York

Greg Bier
Stephens College

Karen Bishop
University of Louisville

Ross Blankenship
State Fair Community College

John Boos
Ohio Wesleyan University

Marvin Borgelt
University of Mary

Steven Bradley
Austin Community College

Don B. Bradley, III
University of Central Arkansas

Margaret Britt
Eastern Nazarene College

Mark Brosthoff
Indiana University

Penelope Stohn Brouwer
Mount Ida College

Rochelle R. Brunson
Alvin Community College

Kevin Chen
County College of Morris

Felipe Chia
Harrisburg Area Community College

Mike Cicero
Highline Community College

Michael D. Cook
Hocking College

Roy A. Cook
Fort Lewis College

George R. Corbett
St. Thomas Aquinas College

Karen Cranford
Catawba College

George W. Crawford
Clayton College & State University

Bruce Davis
Weber State University

Terri Davis
Howard College

Bill Demory
Central Arizona College

Michael Deneen
Baker College

Sharon Dexler
Southeast Community College

Warren Dorau
Nicolet College

Bonnie Ann Dowd
Palomar College

Michael Drafke
College of DuPage

Franklin J. Elliot
Dine College

Brian Fink
Danville Area Community College

Dennette Foy
Edison College

David W. Frantz
Purdue University

Darryl Goodman
Trident Technical College

William Grace
Missouri Valley College

William W. Graff
Maharishi University of Management

Mark Hagenbuch
University of North Carolina, Greensboro

James R. Hindman
Northeastern University/Dean College

Betty Hoge
Limestone College

Eddie Hufft
Alcorn State University

Sherrie Human
Xavier University

Larry K. Johansen
Park University

Michael Judge
Hudson Valley Community College

Mary Beth Klinger
College of Southern Maryland

Charles W. Kulmann
Columbia College of Missouri

Rosemary Lafragola
University of Texas at El Paso

William Laing
Anderson College

Ann Langlois
Palm Beach Atlantic University

Rob K. Larson
Mayville State University

David E. Laurel
South Texas Community College

Les Ledger
Central Texas College

Michael G. Levas
Carroll College

Richard M. Lewis
Lansing Community College

Thomas W. Lloyd
Westmoreland County Community College

Elaine Madden
Anne Arundel Community College

Kristina Mazurak
Albertson College

James J. Mazza
Middlesex Community College

Lisa McConnell
Oklahoma State University at Oklahoma City

Angela Mitchell
Wilmington College

Frank Mitchell
Limestone College

Douglas Moesel
University of Missouri—Columbia

Michael K. Mulford
Des Moines Area Community College

Bernice M. Murphy
University of Maine at Machias

Eugene Muscat
University of San Francisco

John J. Nader
Grand Valley State University

Charles "Randy" Nichols
Sullivan University

Donalus A. Okhomina, Sr.
Jackson State University

Rosa L. Okpara
Albany State University

Timothy O'Leary
Mount Wachusett Community College

Pamela Onedeck
University of Pittsburgh at Greensburg

Claire Phillips
North Harris College

Dean Pielstick
Northern Arizona University

Mark S. Poulos
St. Edward's University

Julia Truitt Poynter
Transylvania University

Fred Pragasam
University of North Florida

Mary Ellen Rosetti
Hudson Valley Community College

Jaclyn Rundle
Central College

John K. Sands
Western Washington University

Craig Sarine
Lee University

Duane Schecter
Muskegon Community College

Matthew Semadeni
Texas A&M University

Marjorie Shapiro
Myers University

Cindy Simerly
Lakeland Community College

James Sisk
Gaston College

Victoria L. Sitter
Milligan College

Bernard Skown
Stevens Institute of Technology

William E. Smith
Ferris State University

Bill Snider
Cuesta College

Roger Stanford
Chippewa Valley Technical College

Phil Stetz
Stephen F. Austin State University

James Swenson
Minnesota State University—Moorhead

Ruth Tarver
West Hills Community College

Darrell Thompson
Mountain View College

Melodie Toby
Kean University

Charles Torti
Schreiner University

Gerald Turner
Limestone College

Brian Wahl
North Shore Community College

Mike Wakefield
University of Southern California

Charles F. Warren
Salem State College

Janet Wayne
Baker College

Nat B. White, Jr.
South Piedmont Community College

Jim Whitlock
Brenau University

Ira Wilsker
Lamar Institute of Technology

Finally, we express our sincere thanks to the many instructors who use our text in both academic and professional settings. Ultimately, it is your evaluation that makes this project work. We want to know what you think. Please contact any of us as questions or needs arise; our telephone numbers, fax numbers, and e-mail addresses are provided below. We view ourselves as partners with you in this venture, and we want to be sensitive to your thoughts and needs whenever possible. Thank you for letting us serve you.

Justin G. Longenecker
Tel.: (254) 710-4258
Fax: (254) 710-1093
E-mail: Justin_Longenecker@baylor.edu

Carlos W. Moore
Tel.: (254) 710-6176
Fax: (254) 710-1068
E-mail: Carlos_Moore@baylor.edu

J. William Petty
Tel.: (254) 710-2260
Fax: (254) 710-1092
E-mail: Bill_Petty@baylor.edu

Leslie E. Palich
Tel.: (254) 710-6194
Fax: (254) 710-1093
E-mail: Les_Palich@baylor.edu

ABOUT THE AUTHORS

Justin G. Longenecker, *Baylor University* Justin G. Longenecker's authorship of *Small Business Management: An Entrepreneurial Emphasis* began with the first edition of this book and continues with extensive involvement in the preparation of the present edition. He has authored a number of books and numerous articles in such journals as the *Journal of Small Business Management*, the *Academy of Management Review*, *Business Horizons*, and the *Journal of Business Ethics*. Active in a number of professional organizations, he has served as president of the International Council for Small Business and is a Wilford White Fellow and a United States Association for Small Business and Entrepreneurship (USASBE) Fellow.

Dr. Longenecker grew up in a family business. After attending Central Christian College of Kansas for two years, he earned his bachelor's degree in political science from Seattle Pacific University, his M.B.A. from Ohio State University, and his Ph.D. from the University of Washington.

Carlos W. Moore, *Baylor University* Carlos W. Moore is the Edwin W. Streetman Professor of Marketing at Baylor University, where he has been a faculty member for more than 35 years. He has been honored as a Distinguished Professor by the Hankamer School of Business, where he teaches both graduate and undergraduate courses. Dr. Moore has authored articles in such journals as the *Journal of Small Business Management*, the *Journal of Business Ethics*, *Organizational Dynamics*, *Accounting Horizons*, and the *Journal of Accountancy*. His authorship of this textbook began with the sixth edition.

Dr. Moore received an Associate of Arts degree from Navarro Junior College in Corsicana, Texas, where he was later named Ex-Student of the Year. He earned a B.B.A. from The University of Texas at Austin, an M.B.A. from Baylor University, and a Ph.D. from Texas A&M University.

Besides his academic experience, Dr. Moore has business experience as the co-owner of a small ranch and as a partner in a small business consulting firm.

J. William Petty, *Baylor University* J. William Petty is Professor of Finance and the W. W. Caruth Chairholder in Entrepreneurship at Baylor University. In 2004, Dr. Petty was designated as a Master Teacher, the highest honor granted to Baylor University faculty members. He holds a Ph.D. and an M.B.A. from The University of Texas at Austin and a B.S. from Abilene Christian University. He has taught at Virginia Tech University and Texas Tech University. Before joining the Baylor faculty, Dr. Petty was Dean of the Business School at Abilene Christian University. His research interests include corporate restructuring, acquisitions of privately held companies, shareholder value–based management, the financing of small and entrepreneurial firms, and lender–borrower relationships. He has served as co-editor for the *Journal of Financial Research* and editor of the *Journal of Entrepreneurial and Small Business Finance*. He has published articles in a number of finance journals and is the co-author of two leading corporate finance textbooks—*Financial Management* and *Foundations of Finance*. Dr. Petty is also a co-author of *Value Based Management: The Corporate Response to the Shareholder Revolution*, published by Harvard Business School Press, and he is currently co-authoring a book on entrepreneurial finance, to be published by Oxford University Press. He was a subject matter expert for a best-practices study on shareholder value–based management funded by the American Productivity and Quality Center, and he was part of a research team for the Australian Department of Industry, studying the feasibility of establishing a public equity market for small- and medium-size enterprises in Australia. Dr. Petty currently serves on the board of an independent energy company.

Leslie E. Palich, *Baylor University* Leslie E. Palich is Associate Professor of Management and the Ben H. Williams Professor of Entrepreneurship at Baylor University, where he teaches graduate and undergraduate courses in strategic management and international management to entrepreneurship students and others in the Hankamer School of Business. He is also Associate Director of the Entrepreneurship Studies Program at Baylor. He holds a Ph.D. and an M.B.A. from Arizona State University and a B.A. from Manhattan Christian College. With more than three dozen publications to his credit, he has published his research in such journals as the *Journal of Management*, the *Academy of Management Review*, the *Journal of International Management*, the *Journal of Organizational Behavior*, and the *Strategic Management Journal*. He also is Director of the Baylor in Cuba Program and teaches a course in international entrepreneurship as part of the Baylor International Technology Entrepreneurship program at the University of Maastricht in the Netherlands. He often teaches in Cuba and in Europe.

Part One

ENTREPRENEURSHIP: A WORLD OF OPPORTUNITY

CHAPTERS

THE ENTREPRENEURIAL LIFE

In the Video Spotlight

Café Pilon **http://www.javacabana.com**

When the Souto brothers—Angel, Alberto, and Enrique—were forced to leave Cuba in the early 1960s, after the Cuban government appropriated their century-old family business, they arrived in the United States with the determination to rebuild. The video spotlight for this chapter takes you to Miami, Florida, where you will meet members of the Souto family. The Soutos began as door-to-door purveyors of fresh-ground, Cuban-roasted coffees, which they delivered directly to homes in their Miami neighborhood. Decades later, Café Pilon continues to thrive and grow, through both strategic acquisitions and smart business practices. Café Pilon, now doing business as Rowland Coffee Roasters, roasts and sells many of the very best Cuban espresso brands, including Café Pilon, Café Bustelo, and El Pico. Today, Rowland is one of the largest privately owned coffee producers in North America.

For the Soutos, the perfect business has always been the perfect blend of superior coffees, traditional Cuban roasting methods, and the slow cultivation of a very loyal group of customers. Indeed, one might say they've succeeded in capturing the high ground.

Video material provided by Hattie Bryant, Producer of Small Business School, the series on PBS Stations, Worldnet, and the Web at http://www.smallbusinessschool.org.

Chapter 1

Looking Ahead

After studying this chapter, you should be able to

1 *Discuss the availability of entrepreneurial opportunities and give examples of successful businesses started by entrepreneurs.*

2 *Explain the nature of entrepreneurship and how it is related to small business.*

3 *Identify some motivators or rewards of entrepreneurial careers.*

4 *Describe the various types of entrepreneurs and entrepreneurial ventures.*

5 *Identify five potential advantages of small entrepreneurial firms.*

6 *Discuss factors related to readiness for entrepreneurship and getting started in an entrepreneurial career.*

7 *Explain the concept of an entrepreneurial legacy and the challenges involved in crafting a worthy legacy.*

Would you like to become an entrepreneur, to start and operate a small business of your own? Perhaps you wonder whether such dreams can come true today. The good news is that thousands of individuals start such businesses every year. You are living in a world of entrepreneurial opportunity!

You are about to embark on a course of study that will prove invaluable if you elect to pursue a career in entrepreneurship or small business. An entrepreneurial career can provide an exciting life and substantial personal rewards, while also contributing to the welfare of society. This book is designed to give you an understanding of entrepreneurship and to help prepare you for the life of an entrepreneur.

ENTREPRENEURIAL OPPORTUNITIES

1 *Discuss the availability of entrepreneurial opportunities and give examples of successful businesses started by entrepreneurs.*

Entrepreneurial opportunities exist for those who can produce products or services desired by customers. A promising entrepreneurial opportunity is more than just an interesting idea. It involves a product or service that is so attractive to customers that they are willing to pay their hard-earned money for it. In other words, an entrepreneur must find a way to create value for customers.

Our working definition of **entrepreneurial opportunity**, as a desirable and timely innovation that creates value for interested buyers or end users, distinguishes between opportunities and ideas. It is important to note, however, that a given opportunity will not be equally attractive to everyone. Because of differences in experiences and perspectives, one person may see an opportunity where others do not. But, in any case, a true opportunity exists only for the entrepreneur who has the interest, resources, and capabilities required to succeed.

entrepreneurial opportunity
A value-creating innovation with market potential

Entrepreneurial opportunities exist today in a business world that differs markedly from the business world of yesterday. In this section, we will discuss the paths to successful entrepreneurial ventures taken by some present-day entrepreneurs.

Three Success Stories

We hope that you will receive inspiration from the three interesting stories of entrepreneurial success that follow. Perhaps you, too, will soon be part of a success story—one to be written in the days ahead! In addition, you will see that entrepreneurship takes many forms. These stories suggest a few of the numerous possibilities you can consider for your own career. Some of your own opportunities, of course, may be drastically different from those described.

Courtesy of SLR Contracting & Service Company, Inc.

Sundra Ryce

SLR CONTRACTING & SERVICE COMPANY (BUFFALO, NEW YORK) In 1996, 21-year-old Sundra Ryce launched SLR Contracting & Service Company (http://www.slrcontracting.com), a construction firm, in Buffalo, New York.[1] Construction is a traditionally male-dominated industry, but Ryce had grown up in it. Her father operated a construction company, and she had gained experience by helping in the business as a young girl. "I was in my father's business from about the age of 12," Ryce explains. "I would spend my summers organizing the company's accounts, filing papers, and doing other administrative tasks."

Starting a business calls for money. Ryce was fortunate in getting not only family business experience but also family business financing! Her parents provided $10,000 to enable her to get started. Even so, she had to use careful financial management. To save money, she rented two offices in her father's building. The startup funds were also used to open bank accounts and to cover the payroll for herself, a project manager, and two field employees. Of course, various administrative expenses also called for cash.

The business opened in September of 1996 and secured its first contract in October—a $20,000 job to repair the heating system of the local YWCA. In its first year, the company grossed $177,926. Work began to flow rapidly after that first contract was signed.

By 2003, the firm had 16 employees and was ranked No. 4 on the *Inc.* magazine list of fastest-growing inner-city companies in America. In 2002, its revenue was $1.8 million. Its clientele had grown to include such organizations as the U.S. Air Force; the VA Medical Center in Bath, New York; and the Buffalo Municipal Housing Authority.

This startup is unique in that it involves a very young woman who entered an industry in which the prevailing model is that of a male entrepreneur. Some would have expected Ryce to fail, but she succeeded in spite of her youth and gender. One of her great advantages was the experience in construction she had gained by working in the family business. Because of this experience, she possessed the necessary skills to begin to establish herself in the field and also knew the joys and unpleasantness such a life might involve. One might guess that she also had a successful contractor (her father) looking over her shoulder in the early days of the new venture!

Courtesy of FLAVORx

Kenny Kramm

FLAVORX (BETHESDA, MARYLAND) You've probably heard the phrase "Necessity is the mother of invention." Sometimes, necessity is also the mother of business startups. Kenny Kramm, a pharmacy technician, started FlavorX (http://www.flavorx.com) with his pharmacist father to help his infant daughter take her medicine.[2] The child, Hadley, had been diagnosed with cerebral palsy and was taking anti-seizure medications several times a day.

"She would throw it up, spit it out," Kramm recalls. "You knew every meal would turn into a nightmare." Kramm had known that children disliked swallowing medicine, but Hadley's condition made the problem a highly personal one. He urgently needed to overcome the "yuck" factor.

With his father, Kramm started experimenting in the family-owned Washington, D.C., Center Pharmacy with drops of food-grade flavorings to make medicines taste better. He had worked in his father's drugstore since childhood and had heard many parents groan over medicine a child would spit out. He also knew that many of them had tried to mix the medicine with foods like applesauce and ice cream.

As Kramm and his father experimented with various flavors, they found which flavors went best with different medicines. The flavors themselves are commercial products approved by the Food and Drug Administration and do not alter the stability or effectiveness of the drugs. Children typically have a choice of flavors, with the company's most requested flavors being bubble gum, grape, and watermelon.

In 1995, FlavorX became an independent company, selling its "systems"—consisting of recipes and refillable sets of flavorings—to other pharmacies. The practice of flavoring medicine had been applied unsystematically by various pharmacies. But FlavorX developed a large variety of flavors, adapting them to particular drugs and allowing children to have a choice. Today, customers can select from a menu of 42 flavors.

For the first few years, the new company sold only to independent pharmacies, reflecting the orientation of the father's pharmacy in which it began. In 1999, however, the firm started selling to chains, as the Kramms realized the great growth opportunities and also the potential for helping many thousands of children. The product is now in 10,000 chain pharmacies, 1,500 independent pharmacies, and 300 hospitals, and FlavorX has revenues exceeding $5 million and plans for rapid growth.

FlavorX represents an entrepreneurial venture that is unique in many ways. Kenny Kramm did not display the restless, driving urge of many entrepreneurs to create a business until the need to provide for his daughter's health and future security became a powerful motivator. The venture also grew out of another family business. Of even greater significance, perhaps, is the spotlight that this startup focuses on the social value of entrepreneurship—providing products that make life better for thousands of children and their parents. In the process, FlavorX became a successful business with great growth potential.

AUNTIE ANNE'S (GAP, PENNSYLVANIA) In the late 1980s, a Pennsylvania housewife started a pretzel business that grew so quickly it soon stretched across the United States.[3] The rapid growth was accomplished through franchising, another type of entrepreneurship.

Anne Beiler grew up in a Mennonite family in Lancaster County, Pennsylvania, and viewed the world from the back of a horse-drawn buggy for the first years of her life. She was married at 19 to a man who shared her commitment to faith and community service.

After living for several years in Texas, the Beilers and their two daughters moved back to Pennsylvania in 1987, with the dream of opening a free counseling center for couples and families. In order to help realize this dream, Beiler found a job paying $200 a week managing a concession stand at a Maryland farmers' market.

Courtesy of Auntie Anne's Pretzels

Anne Beiler

When a booth came up for sale at another farmers' market in Downingtown, Pennsylvania, Beiler borrowed $6,000 from her father-in-law and purchased it, sight unseen. She sold pizza, stromboli, ice cream, and hand-rolled soft pretzels. Eventually, the strong demand for pretzels eliminated other products. After an experience with a disappointing batch of pretzels, Beiler began experimenting with a recipe of her own. Her husband suggested a few additional ingredients, and soon the great-tasting Auntie Anne's pretzel was born.

In February of 1988, Beiler christened her fledgling company "Auntie Anne's" (http://www.auntieannes.com), a term of endearment used by her 30 nieces and nephews. The popularity of Auntie Anne's pretzels grew by word of mouth, and, before long, people began contacting Beiler with the request to start their own Auntie Anne's business. As a result, she began franchising in early 1989.

Today, with 800 store locations in 42 states and 13 international territories—including Indonesia, Singapore, Malaysia, Thailand, and the Philippines—Beiler's entrepreneurial talents have been recognized by *Inc.* magazine, which named her "Entrepreneur of the Year" twice. She has been featured on the "Oprah Winfrey Show" and on CNN's "Managing with Jane Hopkins." The firm has been ranked number 61 on *Entrepreneur* magazine's 2004 *Franchise 500* list and number 1 in the pretzel business category.

The Auntie Anne's success story features a young woman with limited resources who developed a better-tasting pretzel and built a successful, growing, and profitable business on that foundation. In addition, Auntie Anne's has created business opportunities for hundreds of others. Franchisees receive 6 to 11 days' training at the company's headquarters, store design assistance, and rights to use Auntie Anne's logos and trade names. This business relationship involves another type of entrepreneurship—owning a business as a franchisee and operating it in cooperation with the franchisor.

Evidence of Opportunities

In a private enterprise system, any individual is free to enter into business for himself or herself. In the previous three examples, we have described very different people who took that step—a young woman who grew up in a family business, a pharmacy employee who was suddenly confronted with the serious illness of his baby daughter, and a homemaker/farmers' market worker. In contrast to many others who have tried and failed, these individuals have achieved remarkable success.

At any given time, many potentially profitable business opportunities exist in the environment. But these opportunities must be recognized and grasped by individuals with abilities and desire strong enough to assure success. The startups just presented were quite successful; they were chosen to show the diverse, impressive opportunities that exist. In contrast to these examples, many individuals achieve success on a more modest level in business endeavors far different from those described here.

ENTREPRENEURSHIP AND SMALL BUSINESS

2 *Explain the nature of entrepreneurship and how it is related to small business.*

Thus far, we have discussed entrepreneurship and small business opportunities in a very general way. However, it is important to note that, despite many similarities, the terms *entrepreneur* and *small business manager* are not synonymous. Some entrepreneurial endeavors, for example, begin as small businesses but quickly grow into large businesses. They may still be entrepreneurial. We need, then, to clarify the meaning of these terms.

Who Are the Entrepreneurs?

entrepreneur
A person who starts and/or operates a business

Entrepreneurs are those individuals who discover market needs and launch new firms to meet those needs. They are risk takers who provide an impetus for change, innovation, and progress in economic life. (In contrast, salaried employees receive some specified compensation and do not assume ownership risks.)

In this book, we consider all active owner-managers to be entrepreneurs. We do not limit the term *entrepreneur* to only founders of business firms; we also apply the term to second-generation operators of family-owned firms, franchisees, and owner-managers who have bought out the founders of existing firms. Our definition, however, does exclude salaried managers of larger corporations, even those sometimes described as entrepreneurial because of their flair for innovation and their willingness to accept risk.

To comprehend the great contribution and tremendous potential of entrepreneurial ventures, think of the achievements of an entrepreneur such as Sam Walton. He launched the company we now recognize as a mammoth corporation: Wal-Mart. Started in 1962 in rural Arkansas, Wal-Mart reached a pinnacle—the top spot on the *Fortune 500* list—in 2002, being designated as the "mightiest corporation in America."[4]

What Is Small Business?

What does it mean to talk about "small business"? A neighborhood restaurant or bakery is clearly a small business, and General Motors is obviously not. But among small businesses, there is great diversity in size.

Being labeled a "small business" may convey the impression that such a business is unimportant. That impression, however, would be totally incorrect. The U.S. Small Business Administration reports that small firms[5]

- Represent more than 99.7 percent of all employers.
- Employ more than half of all private-sector employees.
- Pay 44.5 percent of total U.S. private payrolls.
- Generate 60 to 80 percent of net new jobs annually.
- Produce 13 to 14 times more patents per employee than do large patenting firms.

EXHIBIT 1-1 *The Independent Entrepreneur*

Source: By permission of John L. Hart FLP, and Creators Syndicate, Inc.

There have been many efforts to define the term *small business*, using such criteria as number of employees, sales volume, and value of assets. There is no generally accepted or universally agreed-on definition. Size standards are basically arbitrary, adopted to serve a particular purpose. For example, legislators sometimes exclude firms with fewer than 10 or 15 employees from certain regulations, so as to avoid imposing a financial burden on the owner of a very small business.

In this book, primary attention is given to businesses that meet the following criteria:

1. Financing for the business is supplied by one individual or only a few individuals.
2. Except for its marketing function, the business's operations are geographically localized.
3. Compared to the biggest firms in the industry, the business is small.
4. The number of employees in the business is usually fewer than 100.

Obviously, some small firms fail to meet all of the above standards. For example, a small executive search firm—a firm that helps corporate clients recruit managers from other organizations—may operate in many sections of the country and thereby fail to meet the second criterion. Nevertheless, the discussion of management concepts in this book is aimed primarily at the type of firm that fits the general pattern outlined by these criteria.

Thus, small businesses include tiny one-person firms—the kind you may decide to start. They also include small firms that have up to 100 employees. In most cases, however, they are drastically different in their structure and operations from the huge corporations that are generally featured in the business media.

THE PAYOFF OF ENTREPRENEURSHIP

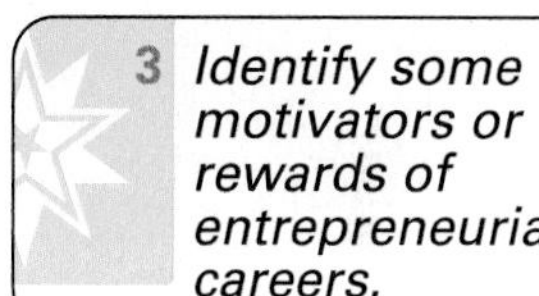
3 *Identify some motivators or rewards of entrepreneurial careers.*

What might cause you to consider running your own business? Clearly, different individuals seek different types of rewards or some combination of rewards. In some cases, the true nature of a person's motivations may not be recognized. The authors of one 2003 study reported that researchers had identified up to 38 different reasons for self-employment.[6] Consequently, our attempt to classify individuals' various motivations for embarking on an entrepreneurial career will, at best, identify only some of the more obvious reasons that people seek self-employment. Exhibit 1-2 summarizes the reasons discussed here.

EXHIBIT 1-2 *Entrepreneurial Incentives*

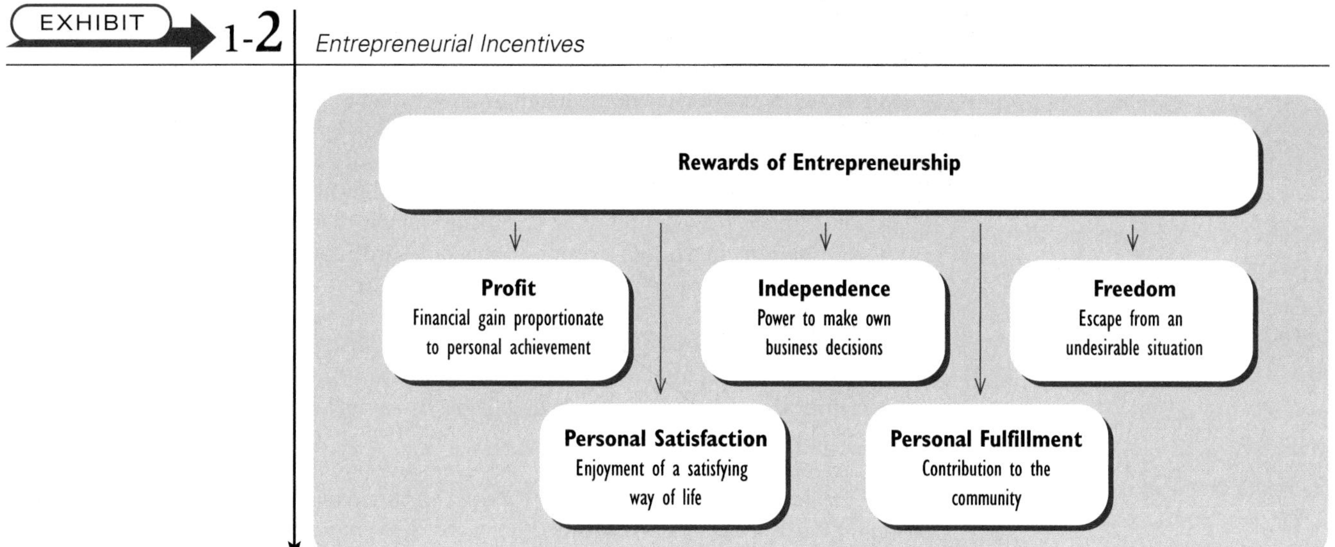
Rewards of Entrepreneurship
Profit
Financial gain proportionate to personal achievement
Independence
Power to make own business decisions
Freedom
Escape from an undesirable situation
Personal Satisfaction
Enjoyment of a satisfying way of life
Personal Fulfillment
Contribution to the community

Make Money (Profit)

Like any other job or career, entrepreneurship provides for one's financial needs. Starting one's own business is a way to earn money. Indeed, some entrepreneurs earn lots of money. In *The Millionaire Next Door*, Stanley and Danko conclude that self-employed people are four times more likely to be millionaires than are those who work for others.[7]

How much money should an entrepreneur expect in return for starting and running a business? Certainly, some profit is necessary for a firm's survival. Some entrepreneurs work just to have adequate profits to survive, while others receive a modest income for their time and investment. From an economic perspective, however, the financial return of a business should compensate its owner not only for his or her investment of personal time (in the form of a salary equivalent), but also for any personal money invested in the business (in the form of dividends and increased value of the firm). That is, entrepreneurs should seek a financial return that will compensate them for the time and money they invest and also reward them well for the risks and initiative they take in operating their own businesses.

A significant number of entrepreneurs are, no doubt, highly motivated by the prospect of profits. They have heard the stories about young people who launched dot-com companies and quickly became multimillionaires. While some entrepreneurs do become rich quickly, the majority do not. Instead, the goal should be to get rich *slowly*. Wealth will come, provided the business is economically viable and the owner has the patience and determination to make it happen.

Be Your Own Boss (Independence)

Freedom to operate independently is another reward of entrepreneurship. Its importance is evidenced by the results of a survey of small business owners.[8] Thirty-eight percent of those who had left jobs at other companies said that their main reason for leaving was that they wanted to be their own boss. Like these entrepreneurs, many people have a strong desire to make their own decisions, take risks, and reap the rewards. Being one's own boss can be an attractive ideal.

The smallest businesses (i.e., part-time businesses and one-person firms), of which there are millions in the United States, probably offer the greatest flexibility to entrepreneurs. Some of these businesses can even hang a "Gone Fishing" (or the equivalent) sign on the door when the entrepreneur feels the urge to engage in nonbusiness activities.

Obviously, most entrepreneurs don't carry their quest for flexibility to such lengths. But entrepreneurs in general appreciate the independence inherent in their chosen careers. They can do things their own way, reap their own profits, and set their own schedules.

Of course, independence does not guarantee an easy life. Most entrepreneurs work very hard for long hours. But they do have the satisfaction of making their own decisions within the constraints imposed by economic and other environmental factors, including undesirable working conditions. And they must remember that the customer is, ultimately, the boss.

Escape a Bad Situation (Freedom)

People sometimes use entrepreneurship as an escape hatch, to free themselves from an undesirable situation. Some may wish to leave an unpleasant job situation, while others may seek change out of necessity. After layoffs, for example, unemployed personnel with experience in professional, managerial, technical, and even relatively unskilled positions often contemplate the possibility of venturing out on their own. Individuals who have entered business ownership as a result of financial hardship or other severe negative conditions have been described as **reluctant entrepreneurs.**[9]

reluctant entrepreneur
A person who becomes an entrepreneur as a result of some severe hardship

Individuals may also flee a bureaucratic environment of a corporation that seems stifling or oppressive to them. "Dilbert," a cartoon strip that appears in many U.S. newspapers, highlights the worst features of such organizations. Entrepreneurship often provides an attractive alternative for individuals fleeing from such undesirable situations (sometimes called **refugees**).

refugee
A person who becomes an entrepreneur to escape an undesirable situation

Various other unpleasant circumstances can also serve as seedbeds for entrepreneurship. A professor may find that the processes of academia have become boring, or an immigrant may see entrepreneurship as a means of overcoming discrimination or limited employment opportunities.

Living the Dream *Entrepreneurial Challenges*

Engineers Become Entrepreneurs

A combination of motivations drives some entrepreneurial endeavors. Corporate constraints, for example, limited five Seattle engineers who worked for Physio-Control, a maker of defibrillators used by medical emergency workers to shock quivering hearts back to a normal rhythm. They wanted to make a defibrillator so small, inexpensive, and easy to use that an untrained person could use it in an emergency. One powerful motivator for these engineers was their desire to place this product in venues where it would save lives. Their employer recognized the potential value of the proposal but was facing other problems at the time and, therefore, rejected the idea. The engineers needed to escape the corporate environment in order to do good.

© Tim Boyle/Getty Images

As a result, Tom Lyster, Carl Morgan, Clint Cole, Brad Gliner, and John Harris left Physio-Control in 1992 and raised startup money for their business, Heartstream (http://www.heartstream.com), by using their own credit cards. Eventually, they secured $5 million in venture capital and developed the device. Their first big break came when American Airlines decided to put one on each of its planes; a few months later, the device saved its first passenger on a flight from Boston to Los Angeles.

Today, hundreds, and possibly thousands, of lives are saved annually by this device in airplanes, homes, and other places beyond hospital walls. These engineers escaped the limitations of their corporate environment and built a socially valuable enterprise by using their entrepreneurial skills. This business eventually became a part of the giant Philips Electronics.

http://www.heartstream.com

Sources: Robert Davis, "To Save Lives, Inventors Had to Change Minds," *USA Today*, July 30, 2003, pp. B1–B2; Rami Grunbourn, "Medical Device Firms Adjust to New Landscape," *Puget Sound Business Journal*, March 15, 1999; and "Just Hefting the Paperwork Could Give You a Coronary," *Puget Sound Business Journal*, November 25, 1996.

Enjoy a Satisfying Life (Personal Satisfaction)

Entrepreneurs frequently speak of the satisfaction they experience in their own businesses; some even refer to their work as fun. Part of their enjoyment may derive from their independence, but some of it reflects an owner's personal gratification from working with the firm's products and services—the pleasure, for example, that a ski shop operator gets from talking to other skiers about the sport and equipment related to it. An entrepreneur may also enjoy being the boss, attending Rotary Club, and serving as a civic leader in the community.

Most small business owners report satisfaction in their careers. In a poll conducted by the National Federation of Independent Business, small employers described the level of their personal satisfaction as "8" on a scale of "1" (extremely dissatisfied) to "10" (extremely satisfied).[10] A majority (51 percent) also indicated that they spend most of their time doing what they like to do best.

Even in a one-person business, the role of entrepreneur can sometimes bring an individual a sense of dignity or significance that makes life worth living. Lynn Cabral operates a hot dog stand along a bike trail in Arlington, Massachusetts. In 1993, a car accident left her permanently disabled and ended her career as producer for a cable channel in Boston. Even though she wears a leg brace from hip to toe and walks with a cane, she opened her snack cart business in 1998.

"Before this I spent about 90% of my mental energy trying to deal with chronic pain," says Cabral, whose disability once kept her from going out in public. "People used to point and say, 'There's the girl with the bad leg.' Now it's 'There's the hot dog lady.' That's a big change."[11]

The reward, then, may derive from a pleasurable activity, from enjoyable associations, from respect in the community, or from some other aspect of the business. For many entrepreneurs, the life satisfaction they receive is much more important than money or independence.

Contribute to the Community (Personal Fulfillment)

Some people are drawn to entrepreneurship by their desire to do good, to make some positive contribution to their communities. In many cases, this impulse is merely one element in a mix of motivations. In some endeavors, however, it is a particularly strong force behind the thinking of the entrepreneur.

The five engineers who created Heartstream (discussed earlier in this section) realized their proposed defibrillator would save many lives. They left their jobs with Physio-Control because that company was unable (or unwilling) to bankroll the development of the product at that time. Presumably, the engineers would have stayed and produced it at Physio-Control if adequate resources had been made available to them.

THE MANY VARIETIES OF ENTREPRENEURSHIP

4 Describe the various types of entrepreneurs and entrepreneurial ventures.

Entrepreneurship is marked by diversity—that is, there is great variety in the people and firms termed entrepreneurial. As a potential entrepreneur, you can be encouraged by this diversity. You do not need to fit some narrow stereotype.

Founder Entrepreneurs Versus Other Business Owners and Franchisees

founder
An entrepreneur who brings a new firm into existence

Generally considered to be "pure" entrepreneurs, **founders** may be inventors who initiate businesses on the basis of new or improved products or services. They may also be artisans who develop skills and then start their own firms. Or they may be enterprising individuals, often with marketing backgrounds, who draw on the ideas of others in starting new firms. Whether acting as individuals or as part of a group, founders bring firms into existence by surveying the market, raising funds, and arranging for the necessary facilities. The process of starting an entirely new business is discussed in detail in Chapter 3.

At some point after a new firm is established, it may be purchased or taken over by a second-generation family member or another entrepreneur who acts as administrator of the business. These "second-stage" entrepreneurs do not necessarily differ greatly from founding entrepreneurs in the way they manage their businesses. Sometimes, their well-established small firms grow rapidly, and their orientation may be more akin to that of a founder than to that of a manager. Nevertheless, it is helpful to distinguish between entrepreneurs who found or substantially change firms (the "movers and shakers") and those who direct the continuing operations of established firms.

franchisee
An entrepreneur whose power is limited by a contractual relationship with a franchising organization

Another category of entrepreneurs comprises franchisees. **Franchisees** differ from other business owners in the degree of their independence. Because of the constraints and guidance provided by contractual relationships with franchising organizations, franchisees function as limited entrepreneurs. Chapter 4 presents more information about franchisees.

High-Potential Ventures Versus Attractive Small Firms and Microbusinesses

Small businesses differ drastically in their growth potential. Amar V. Bhide, who studied the nature of entrepreneurial businesses, distinguished between promising startups and marginal startups.[12] According to Bhide, promising startups are those with the potential for attaining significant size and profitability, while marginal startups lack such prospects.

high-potential venture (gazelle)
A small firm that has great prospects for growth

A few businesses have such glowing prospects for growth that they are called **high-potential ventures**, or **gazelles**. Even within this group, there is variation in styles of operation and approaches to growth. Some are high-tech startups—the kind that once made Silicon Valley in California famous. The success stories have often featured a technology wizard with a bright idea, backed by venture capitalists eager to underwrite the next Microsoft. When such companies prosper, they usually grow at blinding speed and make their founders wealthy by being sold or going public.

attractive small firm
A small firm that provides substantial profits to its owner

In contrast to such high-potential ventures, **attractive small firms** offer substantial financial rewards for their owners. Entrepreneurial income from these ventures may easily range from $100,000 to $300,000 or more annually. They represent a strong segment of small businesses—solid, healthy firms that can provide rewarding careers.

microbusiness
A small firm that provides minimal profits to its owner

lifestyle business
A microbusiness that permits the owner to follow a desired pattern of living

The least profitable types of firms, including many service firms such as dry cleaners, beauty shops, and appliance repair shops, provide only very modest returns to their owners. They are called **microbusinesses**, and their distinguishing feature is their limited ability to generate significant profits. Entrepreneurs who devote personal effort to such ventures receive a profit that does little more than compensate them for their time. Many businesses of this type are called **lifestyle businesses** because they permit an owner to follow a desired pattern of living, even though they provide only modest returns. Businesses of this type do not attract investors.

Entrepreneurial Teams

Our discussion thus far has focused on entrepreneurs who function as individuals, each with his or her own firm. And this is usually the case. However, entrepreneurial teams are becoming increasingly common, particularly in ventures of substantial size. An **entrepreneurial team** consists of two or more individuals who combine their efforts to function in the capacity of entrepreneurs. In this way, the talents, skills, and resources of two or more entrepreneurs can be concentrated on one endeavor. This very important form of entrepreneurship is discussed at greater length in Chapter 8.

entrepreneurial team
Two or more people who work together as entrepreneurs on one endeavor

Artisan Versus Opportunistic Entrepreneurs

Because of their varied backgrounds, entrepreneurs display differences in the degrees of professionalism and in the management styles they bring to their businesses. The ways in which they analyze problems and approach decision making may differ radically. Norman R. Smith has suggested two basic entrepreneurial patterns, exemplified by artisan (or craftsman) entrepreneurs and opportunistic entrepreneurs.[13]

According to Smith, the education of the **artisan entrepreneur** is limited to technical training. Such entrepreneurs have technical job experience, but they typically lack good communication skills and managerial training. Artisan entrepreneurs' approach to business decision making is often characterized by the following features:

artisan entrepreneur
A person with primarily technical skills and little business knowledge who starts a business

- They are paternalistic—they guide their businesses much as they might guide their own families.
- They are reluctant to delegate authority.
- They use few (usually only one or two) capital sources to create their firms.
- They define marketing strategy in terms of the traditional components of price, quality, and company reputation.
- Their sales efforts are primarily personal.
- Their time orientation is short, with little planning for future growth or change.

Living the Dream

Entrepreneurial Challenges

The Guitar Man

Sherwood T. "Woody" Phifer, who builds handcrafted guitars, exemplifies the artisan entrepreneur. His business success rests on his extraordinary skill in building outstanding electric and acoustic guitars. His clientele includes such musicians as Ronnie Jordan, Mos Def, Will Lee, Ron Carter, Stanley Clark, Wyclef Jean, and George Benson. They obviously agree with Phifer's personally crafted slogan: "If you don't have a Woody, you just have a guitar."

Although Phifer began as a mathematics and physics major in college, his love of the guitar led him in a different direction—first to playing the guitar and then to working at repairing and restoring them. All of his instruments are made of wood and incorporate his own designs of bridge, tailpiece systems, and internal structures. According to Phifer, "Woodys" stand alone in the industry. As a talented artisan in a business of his own—Phifer Designs and Concepts—he is also a successful lifestyle entrepreneur.

http://www.woodyguitars.com

Source: Sonia Alleyne, "Guitar Man," *Black Enterprise*, Vol. 33, No. 9 (April 2003), p. 64.

A mechanic who starts an independent garage and a beautician who operates a beauty shop are examples of artisan entrepreneurs.

opportunistic entrepreneur A person with both sophisticated managerial skills and technical knowledge who starts a business

In contrast to the artisan entrepreneur, an **opportunistic entrepreneur** is one who has supplemented his or her technical education by studying such nontechnical subjects as economics, law, or history. Opportunistic entrepreneurs avoid paternalism, delegate authority as necessary for growth, employ various marketing strategies and types of sales efforts, obtain original capitalization from more than two sources, and plan for future growth. An example of an opportunistic entrepreneur is a small building contractor and developer who adopts a relatively sophisticated approach to management, including careful record keeping and budgeting, precise bidding, and systematic marketing research.

Smith's description of entrepreneurial styles illustrates two extremes: At one end is a craftsperson in an entrepreneurial position, and at the other end is a well-educated and experienced manager. The former "flies by the seat of the pants," and the latter uses systematic management procedures and something resembling a scientific approach. In practice, of course, the distribution of entrepreneurial styles is less polarized than that suggested by Smith's model, with entrepreneurs scattered along a continuum of managerial sophistication. This book is intended to help you move toward the opportunistic and away from the artisan end of the continuum.

Women Entrepreneurs

Although entrepreneurship and business in general have been male dominated for decades, the scene is rapidly changing. Between 1976 and 2000, women's share of total self-employment (entrepreneurship) grew from 22 percent to 38 percent.[14] During this same period, revenues of women-owned businesses increased by 33 percent, compared with a 24 percent increase for all firms. This represents substantial growth, even though women owners' total share of business revenue is still less than that of men owners.

Women are not only starting more businesses than they did previously; they are also establishing firms in nontraditional industries, with ambitious plans for growth and profit. Not too many years ago, female entrepreneurs confined themselves, for the most part, to operating beauty shops, small clothing stores, and other establishments catering especially to women. Though most startups by women are still focused on providing services, women's ownership of construction firms and similar businesses is growing rapidly.

Faced with losing the family farm, Elaine J. Martin started her Nampa, Idaho–based highway construction project company, MarCon Inc., in 1985.[15] To help Martin get started, her mother put up a $25,000 certificate of deposit as collateral so that she could borrow $25,000. At the time, Martin had no construction background. While looking for work in construction, she heard about the Idaho Department of Transportation highway fencing needs. Since she had been raised on a farm and knew how to build fence, she started bidding for highway work. To improve her chances, she went to the state library to study fencing and highway management. She eventually modified the business by getting into guardrail construction. Today, Martin runs a $6-million business in a male-dominated industry. In 2002, she was named the Idaho Small Business Person of the Year.

Female entrepreneurs obviously face problems common to all entrepreneurs. However, they must also contend with difficulties associated with their newness in entrepreneurial roles. Lack of access to credit has been a common problem for women who enter business. This is a troublesome area for most small business owners, but women often carry the added burden of discrimination.

Another barrier for some women is the limited opportunity they find for business relationships with others in similar positions. It takes time and effort to gain full acceptance and to develop informal relationships with others in local, mostly male, business and professional groups.

These conditions have improved in recent years, however, as women have assumed strong entrepreneurial roles. In a panel discussion of the issue, some women entrepreneurs emphasized the improved business climate:[16]

> *Cristi Cristich, founder of Cristek Interconnects, Inc.* (a maker of connectors and cabling for medical and military applications in Anaheim, California): "Access to capital and the acceptance of women in the workplace and as business owners has improved dramatically over the past 15 years."

Shari L. Parrack, president of Texas Motor Transportation Consultants (a professional registration, tax, and title service company in Houston, Texas): "In 2003, I find that being female does nothing but help me to grow my business. What was once a negative has become a positive."

Terrie Jones, CEO and owner of AGSI (a provider of Internet technology resource solutions in Atlanta, Georgia): "In 22 years, I've seen the business world evolve tremendously. . . . In the same way businessmen helped their 'fraternity brothers' in the past, they are more willing to help women today."

THE WINNING HAND OF ENTREPRENEURSHIP

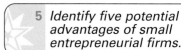

5 *Identify five potential advantages of small entrepreneurial firms.*

Small entrepreneurial firms need not be weaklings. Indeed, a look at the structure of the U.S. business community reveals small, entrepreneurial businesses to be a robust part of the total economy. The important role of small firms is documented by the research of David Birch, president of Cognetics Inc., an economics research firm in Cambridge, Massachusetts, who has argued persuasively that almost all new jobs in the United States are created in small businesses.[17]

How is it that small and entrepreneurial firms can hold their own and often gain an edge over successful, more powerful businesses? The answer lies in the ability of new and smaller firms to exploit opportunities.

In this overview, we'll take a look at some ways in which new firms can gain a competitive edge. In Chapter 3, we'll discuss specific strategies for exploiting these potential advantages and capturing the business opportunities they make possible.

Customer Focus

Business opportunities exist for those who can produce products and services desired by customers. If a business can make its product or service especially attractive, its prospects will brighten considerably.

Good customer service can be provided by a business of any size, of course. However, small firms have a greater potential than larger businesses do for achieving this goal. If properly managed, small entrepreneurial firms have the advantage of being able to serve customers directly and effectively, without struggling through layers of bureaucracy or breaking corporate policies that tend to stifle employee initiative. In many cases, customers are personally acquainted with the entrepreneur and other key people in the small business.

The first step toward creating customer satisfaction and getting customer loyalty is to earn it. One entrepreneur who has used his entrepreneurial aptitude in a number of business ventures has described the powerful potential of this process as follows: "Running your own business is easy, not hard! I don't mean the work itself is easy. You do need to work hard. But you can easily be successful. Just do for the customer what you say you are going to do, and do it every time."[18]

Not all small firms manage to excel in customer service, but many realize their potential for doing so. Having a smaller number of customers and a close relationship with those customers makes customer service a powerful tool for entrepreneurial businesses. For further discussion of this subject, see Chapter 13.

Quality Performance

There is no reason that a small business needs to take a back seat in achieving quality in operations. In service businesses, quality performance is closely linked to customer service. Think of your favorite restaurant, for example. What distinguishes it from other dining places? It may be the atmosphere, the freshness and taste of the food, or the attentiveness of servers who are quickly aware of your needs and who promptly refill your beverage glass or coffee cup. These elements of dining quality can be found in a very small restaurant. In fact, the owner of a small establishment can insist on high levels of quality without experiencing the frustration of a large-company CEO who may have to push a quality philosophy through many layers of bureaucracy.

Living the Dream

Focus on the Customer

A Customer-Oriented Body Shop

One small firm that excels in keeping a focus on the customer is Auto Body World of Phoenix, Arizona, the state's oldest and largest independent collision repair company. The business strives to make customers happy with its service. Its focus is epitomized in the slogan "Same Family, Same Quality, Same Integrity."

A recent customer reported her satisfaction with a simple bumper repair at Auto Body World: "After I had my bumper repaired, they detailed the car completely and called me on the phone later that night. They asked about my experience with the work, the workers, the rental car, the insurance company—in short, to see if I was a 'delighted customer'!"

A family business, Auto Body World was started by Warren Fait and is now run by his son, David. David Fait has taken top honors as the Greater Phoenix Chamber of Commerce's Small Business Person of the Year, and the company has won a Better Business Bureau ethics award and a national award as the "Collision Business of the Year." The trophy inscription attests to the firm's excellent customer service and quality performance: "The collision business that set a standard by which all others will be measured." Fait has said, "Our success has been, and will be, driven by our customers." Reflecting its success, the firm has expanded and now operates in seven locations in the Phoenix area.

http://www.autobodyworld.com

Sources: http://www.autobodyworld.com, April 21, 2004; Angela Gabriel, "Top Business Person: It Was Fait," *Business Journal of Phoenix*, June 28, 1999; and personal interview with Auto Body World customer Emily Kaufmann, August 19, 2003.

Many small firms excel in performing quality work, whether it is in auto repair, hair styling, financial audits, candy production, computer services, or clothing retailing. In quality management, entrepreneurial firms have a tool that enables them to compete effectively, not only with their peers but also with large corporations.

Integrity and Responsibility

The future is particularly bright for firms that add to excellent product quality and good customer service a solid reputation for honesty and dependability. Customers respond to evidence of integrity because they are aware of ethical issues. Experience has taught them that advertising claims are sometimes not accurate, that the fine print in contracts is sometimes detrimental to their best interests, and that businesses sometimes fail to stand behind their work.

Timmons and Stevenson conducted a study of 128 presidents/founders who were attending a management program at Harvard Business School. They were asked to identify the most critical concepts, skills and know-how for success at their companies.[19] Surprisingly, 72 percent of the respondents stated that the single most important factor in long-term success was high ethical standards. Consistently operating with integrity can set a small business apart as being trustworthy at a time when stories of corporate greed and corruption abound. Chapter 2 discusses the critical importance of integrity and its role in entrepreneurship.

Innovation

One might think that large companies would be the primary source of important inventions, but that isn't necessarily true. Many entrepreneurs are innovators, who see different and better ways of doing things. Between 1996 and 2000, for example, 1,071 United States firms were each awarded 15 or more patents.[20] Such firms are called *serial innovators*, and one-third of them were classified as small. This evidence makes clear the extensive innovation originating in small businesses.

Research departments of big businesses tend to emphasize the improvement of existing products. Creative ideas may be sidetracked because they are not related to existing products or because they are unusual. Unfortunately, preoccupation with an existing product can sometimes obscure the value of a new idea. Products like the computer and the pacemaker, for example, came from small firms.

Entrepreneurs can compete with firms of all sizes through the use of innovative methods. Such innovations include not only new products but also new ways of doing business.

Special Niche

If a small business can find a special niche of some type, it may compete with great strength in that area. The niche might consist of a uniquely specialized service or product, or it might be a focus on serving a particular geographical area.

By finding a special niche, a small business may avoid intense competition from big business. Lowe's Supermarkets of Littlefield, Texas, provides an example of a family business that followed this path to business success.[21] In 1964, Roger Lowe, Sr., and his father purchased a small supermarket in Olton, Texas. The family business shifted to the next generation in 1973, when Roger Lowe, Jr., joined the firm as vice president and CEO following the death of his grandfather. The business gradually expanded to 58 stores by adding supermarkets, mostly in small rural towns of west Texas and New Mexico. In many towns, Lowe's faces no local competitor. In the few locations where it competes head to head with large chains like Wal-Mart, Lowe's Supermarket distinguishes itself by offering product selections carefully tailored to the unique local and ethnic tastes of the neighborhood population.

GETTING STARTED

Starting any type of business career is exciting. Launching one's own business, however, can be absolutely breathtaking because of the extreme risk and great potential in such a venture. Let's think for a moment about some special concerns of individuals who are ready to get their feet wet in entrepreneurial waters.

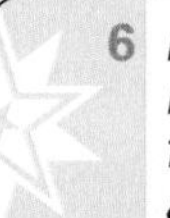

6 *Discuss factors related to readiness for entrepreneurship and getting started in an entrepreneurial career.*

Age and Entrepreneurial Opportunity

One practical question is, What is the right age to become an entrepreneur? As you might guess, there is no simple answer to this question. Most businesses require some background knowledge. In addition, most prospective entrepreneurs must first build their financial resources in order to make the necessary initial investments. A certain amount of time is usually required, therefore, to gain education, experience, and financial resources.

Though there are no hard-and-fast rules concerning the right age for starting a business, some age deterrents do exist. Young people are often discouraged from entering

Living the Dream — *Utilizing the Internet*

A Teenage Entrepreneur

Even teenagers can become entrepreneurs! There are no hard-and-fast rules that forbid teenagers, or even 90-year-olds, for that matter, from starting businesses of their own. Anyone can dream the dreams of entrepreneurship at any age!

One California teenager started a business for computer maintenance, upgrades, and Internet design.

> *While most of his 14-year-old friends were worrying about video games and girls, Jay Betancourt was thinking about his future. Betancourt decided to start a business that would not only earn him spending money but also help improve his computer skills. After completing copious amounts of paperwork and paying several licensing fees required by California state law, he opened Betancourt Industries, which he ran until his family moved to Bruceville-Eddy, Texas.*

By the time he left California, Betancourt had five employees and a long list of clients. In his new Texas location, the 17-year-old quickly relaunched the business and hired two friends who were in his high school business class. These young technicians help customers with installations, repairs, maintenance, upgrades, and general computer services. Even though they are not old enough to vote, they are becoming a productive unit in their local business community.

http://www.betancourtindustries.com

Source: Kendra Willeby, "17-Year-Old Launches His Own Business," *Waco Tribune-Herald Neighbor,* August 14, 2003, pp. 1, 9.

entrepreneurial careers by inadequacies in their preparation and resources. On the other hand, older people develop family, financial, and job commitments that make entrepreneurship seem too risky; they may have acquired interests in retirement programs or achieved promotions to positions of greater responsibility and higher salaries.

The ideal time for entrepreneurship, then, appears to lie somewhere between the mid-20s and the mid-30s, when there is a balance between preparatory experiences on the one hand and family obligations on the other. Research conducted by Paul Reynolds shows that the highest percentage of startups is in the 25- to 35-year age group.[22] Obviously, there are exceptions to this generalization: Some teenagers start their own firms, and some 50- and 60-year-olds walk away from successful careers in big business when they become excited by the prospects of entrepreneurship.

Characteristics of Successful Entrepreneurs

What kinds of people become successful entrepreneurs? It is not surprising that no well-defined entrepreneurial profile exists. Individual entrepreneurs differ greatly from each other. This should give you encouragement if you wish to start your own business; you do not need to fit some prescribed stereotype.

Some qualities are common, however, among entrepreneurs and probably contribute to their success. One of these characteristics is a strong commitment to or passion for the business. It is an attitude that results in tenacity in the face of difficulty and a willingness to work hard. Entrepreneurs do not give up easily.

internal locus of control
A belief that one's success depends on one's own efforts

external locus of control
A belief that one's life is controlled more by luck or fate than by one's own efforts

Such individuals are typically confident of their ability to meet the challenges confronting them. This factor of self-confidence was described by psychologist J. B. Rotter as an **internal locus of control**—a feeling that success depends on one's own efforts.[23] In contrast, an **external locus of control** reflects an attitude of dependence on luck or fate for success.

Entrepreneurs are also portrayed as risk takers. Certainly, they do assume risk. By investing their own money, they assume financial risk. If they leave secure jobs, they risk their careers. The stress and time required to start and run a business may place their families at risk. Even though entrepreneurs assume risk, they are what we might term moderate risk takers—accepting risks over which they have some control—rather than extreme risk takers, who accept outcomes depending purely on chance.

Timmons and Spinelli have summarized research on entrepreneurial characteristics.[24] They group what they describe as "desirable and acquirable attitudes and behaviors" into the following six categories:

1. *Commitment and determination.* Such entrepreneurs are tenacious, decisive, and persistent in problem solving.
2. *Leadership.* Such entrepreneurs are self-starters and team builders and focus on honesty in their business relationships.
3. *Opportunity obsession.* Such entrepreneurs are aware of market and customer needs.
4. *Tolerance of risk, ambiguity, and uncertainty.* Such entrepreneurs are risk takers, risk minimizers, and uncertainty tolerators.
5. *Creativity, self-reliance, and adaptability.* Such entrepreneurs are open-minded, flexible, uncomfortable with the status quo, and quick learners.
6. *Motivation to excel.* Such entrepreneurs are goal oriented and aware of their weaknesses and strengths.

Taking the Plunge

precipitating event
An event, such as losing a job, that moves an individual to become an entrepreneur

In starting a business, there comes a point at which the entrepreneur must "take the plunge." It may be scary because of the risks, but entrepreneurship is not for the faint of heart. For many people, the right time for beginning a business is hastened by some special circumstance, described as a **precipitating event**. The individual may be fired, for example, or discover an unusual opportunity with strong potential.

Criticizing management has the potential for creating change—especially in the life of the critic! Consequently, it can lead to a precipitating event. Dave and Annette King, a husband-and-wife team, were avid weekend players of slow-pitch softball.[25] While playing in a tournament in a small Colorado town, they made critical comments about the poor management of the event. The event manager asked them to leave and told them that if they thought they could do it better, they should try it. This was their precipitating event. The Kings' response was to do just that by creating Triple Crown Sports, and today they profitably run approximately 400 events a year in softball, baseball, soccer, and basketball.

It is difficult to say what proportion of new entrepreneurs make their move because of some particular event. Whether propelled by a precipitating event or not, those who decide on entrepreneurship must eventually summon their courage and take the plunge.

Growing and Managing the Business

An airplane pilot not only controls the plane during takeoff but also flies it and lands it. Similarly, entrepreneurs not only launch firms but also "fly" them; that is, they manage their firm's subsequent operation. In this book, you will find a discussion of the entire entrepreneurial process. It begins in the remainder of Part 1 (Chapter 2) with a discussion of the fundamental values of the firm. This discussion is followed in Parts 2 and 3 with a look at a firm's basic strategy, the various types of entrepreneurial ventures, and the initial planning that is required for business startups. Parts 4 through 6 deal with the management of a growing business, including its operations, marketing, and finances.

SUCCESS IN BUSINESS AND SUCCESS IN LIFE

7 Explain the concept of an entrepreneurial legacy and the challenges involved in crafting a worthy legacy.

In this chapter, we have discussed entrepreneurship and small business from a number of angles. As you contemplate such a career, we now urge you to broaden your perspective and to think about some of the values and intangibles that are part of the entrepreneurial life.

Looking Back at an Entrepreneurial Career

When an entrepreneur makes that final exit from the entrepreneurial stage, his or her business achievements become history. Reflecting on their lives and businesses at that point in their journeys, numerous entrepreneurs have come face to face with such questions as these: Was it a good trip? What kind of meaning does it hold for me now? Can I feel good about it? What are my disappointments? How did I make a difference? Such questions lead entrepreneurs to reassess their values, priorities, and commitments. By anticipating these questions, an entrepreneur can identify his or her most basic concerns early in the journey. Without such reflection, the entrepreneurial journey and its ending may prove disappointing.

Evaluating Accomplishments

Assessment of entrepreneurial performance requires establishing criteria. Obviously, no one standard can be applied. For example, a person who measures everything by the dollar sign would determine the degree of an entrepreneur's success by the size of his or her bank account.

The exiting entrepreneur will, at some point, think about achievements in terms of personal values and goals, rather than textbook criteria, popular culture, or financial rules of thumb. In all likelihood, a number of basic considerations will be relevant to the entrepreneur's sense of satisfaction.

In looking ahead to this time of looking back, one naturally thinks in terms of a legacy. A *legacy* consists of those things passed on or left behind. In a narrow sense, it describes material possessions bequeathed to one's heirs. In a broader sense, it refers to everything that one leaves behind—material items, good or bad family relationships, a record of integrity or avarice, a history of exploitation or contribution. An **entrepreneurial legacy** includes both tangible items and intangible qualities passed on not only to heirs but also to the broader society. One can appreciate, then, the seriousness with which the entrepreneur needs to consider the kind of legacy he or she is building.

entrepreneurial legacy
Material assets and intangible qualities passed on to both heirs and society

Winning the Wrong Game

It's easy for entrepreneurs to get caught up in an activity trap, working harder and harder to keep up with the busy pace of life. Ultimately, such entrepreneurs may find their business accomplishments overshadowed by the neglect or sacrifice of something more important to them. It's possible to score points in the wrong game or win battles in the wrong war.

This type of entrepreneurial error produces a defective legacy, a sense that one's professional achievements are to some extent faulty. Consider what happens, for example, when the legitimate goal of earning money becomes a consuming passion. The CEO of a former *Inc. 500* company has critiqued the entrepreneurial experience in this way:

> *I believe that when our companies fail to satisfy our fundamental need to contribute to the community and instead exist predominantly to fill a bank account, then we lose our souls. Life is short. No one's gravestone reads, "He made a lot of money." Making a difference in your own life, your employees' lives, and your customers' lives is the real payoff.*[26]

Ed Bonneau had revolutionized the distribution of sunglasses in the United States and eventually dominated that market with his highly successful business. While growing the firm, Bonneau had purchased Pennsylvania Optical (with its patents and contracts with Wal-Mart and Kmart) and industry giant Foster Grant (with its patents and manufacturing divisions).

Then, Bonneau sold the business and walked away from it all. Reflecting on the transaction, he said, "It was hard for me to figure out what to do with all this money." From a business standpoint, his was a huge entrepreneurial success story. However, in a comment on how he'd like to be remembered, Bonneau downplayed his financial wealth.

> *I would hope that they knew something else besides that I once ran the biggest sunglass company in the world. That's not the number one thing that I'd want to be known for. It's okay, but I'd much rather have that final assessment made by my kids and have them say, "He was a terrific dad." I never wanted to sacrifice my family or my church for my business.*[27]

And Bonneau's advice to younger entrepreneurs follows a similar theme:

> *Take God and your family with you when you go into business, and keep that balance in your life. Because when you get to be 60 years old and you look back over your life, if all you have is the biggest sunglass company in the world and a pot full of money in the bank . . . it won't be enough. Your life is going to be hollow, and you can't go back and redo it.*[28]

Entrepreneurs typically work—indeed, often must work—long hours, especially in the beginning. Sometimes, however, the obsession with work and the long hours become too extreme. Based on interviews with repeat entrepreneurs, Ilan Mochari summarized their reports of early mistakes: "If they had it to do all over again, most of the group would have spent more time away from their first companies, hanging with the family, schmoozing up other CEOs, and pondering the long-term picture."[29]

An excessive focus on money or work, then, can twist the entrepreneurial process. The outcome appears less satisfying and somehow less rewarding when the time for exit arrives.

Crafting a Worthy Legacy

In entrepreneurial terms, what constitutes a worthy legacy? One issue is the nature of the endeavor itself. A business that operates within the law, provides jobs, and serves the public provides a good foundation for a satisfying entrepreneurial experience. Although a business that peddles pornography on the Internet might make a lot of money for its owner, most Americans would dismiss it as an unworthy enterprise because of its harmful, destructive character.

Within many individuals is a streak of nobility that gives them a genuine concern for the well-being of others. Their positive attitudes propel them toward endeavors of practical service to society.

Bernard Rapaport, a highly successful, principled, and generous entrepreneur, has stressed the importance of the means one takes to achieve a given end. "Whatever it is you want to achieve," he said, "*how* you achieve it is more important than *if* you achieve it." At 84 years of age, reflecting on life and legacy, he said, "What do I want to do? I want to save the world."[30]

Such idealism can guide an entrepreneur into many endeavors that are useful to our economic system. A few entrepreneurial ventures are specifically designed to meet the particular needs of society. One entrepreneur known to the authors has in his later years launched a firm whose primary objective is to provide good, low-cost housing to families who cannot otherwise afford it. His motivation for this venture, after earlier successful businesses, is personal concern for the needs of low-income families.

For most entrepreneurs looking back on their careers, satisfaction requires that their businesses have been constructive or positive in their impact—at the least, their effect should have been benign, causing no harm to the social order. In most cases, entrepreneurial businesses make positive contributions by providing jobs and services. A few make even greater contributions by addressing special needs in society.

The criteria by which one evaluates entrepreneurship are necessarily personal. Stephen R. Covey suggests that the most effective way "to begin with the end in mind" is to develop a personal mission statement or philosophy or creed.[31] Though individuals will have different mission statements because their goals and values will differ, widely shared values will underlie many of their judgments.

Beginning with the End in Mind

An entrepreneur builds a business, a life, and a legacy day by day, starting with the initial launch and proceeding through the months and years of operation that follow. A person exiting an entrepreneurial venture has completed the business part of his or her legacy—it must be constructed during the life of the business itself.

Therefore, as Covey said, an entrepreneur needs to "begin with the end in mind" and to keep that end in mind while making the innumerable operating decisions that follow. By selecting the proper values and wisely balancing their application, an entrepreneur can make a satisfying exit, leaving a positive and substantial legacy to heirs, employees, the community, and the broader society.

It is the authors' deepest hope that your journey as an entrepreneur will be a richly rewarding experience, not only financially, but also, more importantly, in the things that matter most in life. Above all, we hope that your legacy will bring satisfaction to you and enhance the important relationships in your life. Go for it!

Looking Back

1 Discuss the availability of entrepreneurial opportunities and give examples of successful businesses started by entrepreneurs.

- An entrepreneurial opportunity is a desirable and timely innovation that creates value for interested buyers and end users.
- Exciting entrepreneurial opportunities exist for those who recognize them.
- However, a true opportunity exists only for those who have the interest, resources, and capabilities required to succeed.
- SLR Contracting and Service Company, FlavorX, and Auntie Anne's are examples of highly successful businesses started by entrepreneurs.

2 Explain the nature of entrepreneurship and how it is related to small business.

- Entrepreneurs are individuals who discover market needs and launch new firms to meet those needs.
- Owner-managers who buy out founders of existing firms, franchisees, and second-generation operators of family firms may also be considered entrepreneurs.
- Definitions of small business are arbitrary, but this book focuses on firms of fewer than 100 employees that have mostly localized operations and are financed by a small number of individuals.
- Most entrepreneurial firms are small when they begin, but a few grow (some very quickly) into large businesses.

3 Identify some motivators or rewards of entrepreneurial careers.

- Researchers have identified up to 38 different reasons for self-employment.
- Entrepreneurial motivators or rewards include profit, independence, freedom (escaping from a bad situation), personal satisfaction, and personal fulfillment (contributing to one's community).

4 Describe the various types of entrepreneurs and entrepreneurial ventures.

- Founders of firms are "pure" entrepreneurs, but those who acquire established businesses and franchisees may also be considered entrepreneurs.

- A few entrepreneurs start high-potential ventures (gazelles); other entrepreneurs operate attractive small firms and microbusinesses.
- Entrepreneurial teams consist of two or more individuals who combine their efforts to function as entrepreneurs.
- Based on their backgrounds and management styles, entrepreneurs may be characterized as artisan entrepreneurs or opportunistic entrepreneurs.
- The number of women entrepreneurs is growing rapidly, and they are entering many nontraditional fields.

5 Identify five potential advantages of small entrepreneurial firms.

- Entrepreneurial managers have an opportunity to know their customers well and to focus on meeting their needs.
- By emphasizing quality in products and services, small firms can build a competitive advantage.
- Independent business owners can build an internal culture based on integrity and responsibility in relationships both inside and outside the firm; such a culture helps strengthen the firm's position in a competitive environment.
- Many small firms and individual operators have demonstrated a superior talent for finding innovative products and developing better ways of doing business.
- Small firms that find a special niche of some type can gain an advantage in the marketplace.

6 Discuss factors related to readiness for entrepreneurship and getting started in an entrepreneurial career.

- The period between the mid-20s and mid-30s appears to be when a person's education, work experience, family situation, and financial resources are most likely to enable him or her to become an entrepreneur.
- There is no well-defined entrepreneurial profile, but many entrepreneurs have such helpful characteristics as a passion for their business, strong self-confidence, and a willingness to assume moderate risks.
- Successful entrepreneurs are also thought to possess leadership skills, a strong focus on opportunities, creativity and adaptability, and motivation to excel.
- Entry into entrepreneurial careers is often triggered by a precipitating event, such as losing a job.
- Once a business is launched, the entrepreneur must manage growth of the business and issues related to its ongoing operation.

7 Explain the concept of an entrepreneurial legacy and the challenges involved in crafting a worthy legacy.

- An entrepreneur's legacy includes not only money and material possessions but also nonmaterial things such as personal relationships and values.
- Part of the legacy is the contribution of the business to the community.
- A worthy legacy includes a good balance of values and principles important to the entrepreneur. Errors in choosing or applying goals and values can create a defective legacy.
- Building a legacy is an ongoing process that begins at the launch of the firm and continues throughout its operating life.

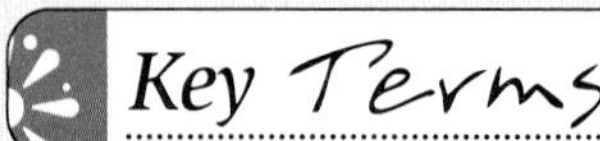

entrepreneurial opportunity, p. 3
entrepreneur, p. 6
reluctant entrepreneur, p. 8
refugee, p. 8
founder, p. 10
franchisee, p. 10
high-potential venture (gazelle), p. 10
attractive small firm, p. 10
microbusiness, p. 10
lifestyle business, p. 10
entrepreneurial team, p. 11
artisan entrepreneur, p. 11
opportunistic entrepreneur, p. 12
internal locus of control, p. 16
external locus of control, p. 16
precipitating event, p. 16
entrepreneurial legacy, p. 17

1. The outstanding success stories discussed at the beginning of the chapter are exceptions to the rule. What, then, is their significance in illustrating entrepreneurial opportunity? Are these stories misleading?
2. What is meant by the term *entrepreneur?*
3. Consider an entrepreneur you know personally. What was the most significant reason for his or her decid-

ing to follow an independent business career? If you don't already know the reason, discuss it with that person.

4. The motivators/rewards of profit, independence, and personal satisfaction are three reasons individuals enter entrepreneurial careers. What problems might be anticipated if an entrepreneur were to become obsessed with one of these rewards—for example, if she or he had an excessive desire to accumulate wealth, operate independently, or achieve a particular lifestyle?
5. What is the advantage of using an entrepreneurial team?
6. Distinguish between an artisan entrepreneur and an opportunistic entrepreneur.
7. Explain how customer focus and innovation can be special strengths of small businesses.
8. Why is the period from the mid-20s to the mid-30s considered to be the best time in life to become an entrepreneur?
9. Explain the concept of an entrepreneurial legacy.
10. Explain the following statement: "One can climb the ladder to success only to discover it is leaning against the wrong wall."

You Make the Call

SITUATION 1

In the following statement, a business owner attempts to explain and justify his preference for slow growth in his business.

> *I limit my growth pace and make every effort to service my present customers in the manner they deserve. I have some peer pressure to do otherwise by following the advice of experts—that is, to take on partners and debt to facilitate rapid growth in sales and market share. When tempted by such thoughts, I think about what I might gain. Perhaps I could make more money, but I would also expect a lot more problems. Also, I think it might interfere somewhat with my family relationships, which are very important to me.*

Question 1 Should this venture be regarded as entrepreneurial? Is the owner a true entrepreneur?

Question 2 Do you agree with the philosophy expressed here? Is the owner really doing what is best for his family?

Question 3 What kinds of problems is this owner trying to avoid?

SITUATION 2

Nineteen-year-old Kiersten Berger, now in her second year at a local community college, has begun to think about starting her own business. She has taken piano lessons since she was seven years old and is regarded as a very good pianist. The thought has occurred to her that she could establish a piano studio and offer lessons to children, young people, and even adults. The prospect sounds more attractive than looking for a salaried job when she graduates in a few months.

Question 1 If Kiersten Berger opens a piano studio, will she be an entrepreneur?

Question 2 Which type of reward(s) will be greatest in this venture?

Question 3 Even though she is an artisan, she will need to make decisions of a business nature. What decisions or evaluations may be especially difficult for her?

SITUATION 3

Dover Sporting Goods Store occupies an unimpressive retail location in a small city in northern Illinois. Started in 1935, it is now operated by Duane Dover—a third-generation member of the founding family. He works long hours trying to earn a reasonable profit in the old downtown area.

Dover's immediate concern is an announcement that Wal-Mart is considering opening a store at the southern edge of town. As Dover reacts to this announcement, he is overwhelmed by a sense of injustice. Why should a family business that has served the community honestly and well for 60 years have to fend off a large corporation that would take big profits out of the community and give very little in return? Surely, he reasoned, the law must offer some kind of protection against big business predators of this kind. Dover also wonders whether small stores such as his have ever been successful in competing against business giants like Wal-Mart.

Question 1 Is Dover's feeling of unfairness justified? Is his business entitled to some type of legal protection against moves of this type?

Question 2 How should Dover plan to compete against Wal-Mart, if and when this becomes necessary?

Experiential Exercises

1. Analyze your own education and experience as qualifications for entrepreneurship. Identify your greatest strengths and weaknesses.
2. Explain your own interest in each type of entrepreneurial reward. Point out which type of incentive is most significant for you personally and tell why.
3. Interview someone who has started a business, being sure to ask for information regarding the entrepreneur's background and age at the time the business was started. In your report of the interview, indicate whether the entrepreneur was in any sense a refugee, and show how the timing of her or his startup relates to the ideal time for startup explained in this chapter.
4. Interview a woman entrepreneur about what problems, if any, she has encountered in her business because she is a woman.

Exploring the Web

1. There's no time like the present. Go to the textbook Web site at **http://longenecker.swlearning.com**, if you haven't done so already, to learn what's there and how to navigate the site.
   a. Explore the links on the left-hand side of the Web site. List those links you might use throughout this course.
   b. Click on the interactive quiz link, read the instructions, take the quiz for Chapter 1, and e-mail the results to your instructor. (Note that you can also access an interactive quiz for each chapter by clicking on the interactive study center button and then on the interactive quiz link.)
   c. Click on the interactive study center, and then follow the link to learning aids. Take at least one of the self-assessments, which will help you learn more about the skills needed to be an entrepreneur. What did you discover about yourself?
2. In addition to the Small Business Administration Web site, which you can find at **http://www.sba.gov**, numerous other Web sites and online resources are available to assist entrepreneurs and small business owners. Using your favorite search engine, locate five sites that you think are particularly interesting and valuable. In your opinion, what makes them stand out?
3. This chapter highlights SLR Contracting and Service Company, FlavorX, and Auntie Anne's Pretzels as examples of entrepreneurial success. Using the Internet as a research tool, choose two or three other examples of businesses started by entrepreneurs, either thriving or struggling ones. Then explain why you chose these businesses, and identify what type of entrepreneurial venture each is.

Video Case 1

BOSTON DUCK TOURS (P. 526)

Tiring of work in investment banking, this entrepreneur left salaried employment, withstood the skepticism of others, and built an unusual but highly successful tourism business.

Alternative Cases for Chapter 1:

Case 4, Auntie Anne's, p. 531
Case 9, The Chocolate Farm, p. 540
Case 14, Lotus Chips' Recipe for Success, p. 552
Case 19, Gibson Mortuary, p. 561

ENTREPRENEURIAL INTEGRITY

A GATEWAY TO SMALL BUSINESS OPPORTUNITY

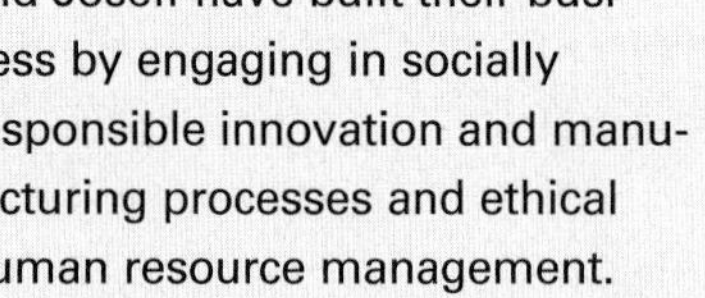

In the Video Spotlight

Diversified Chemical

When most people think of corporate social responsibility, large companies like Starbucks, Timberland, and Ben and Jerry's tend to come to mind. But small businesses are also in the forefront of community involvement and ethical business practices. The video spotlight for this chapter will take you to Diversified Chemical, located in Detroit, Michigan. Started in 1971 by George Hill (shown in photo) and Arnold Joseff, Diversified Chemical is now a holding company for four subsidiaries, which employ 200 people and generate $70 million in annual revenue. Hill and Joseff have built their business by engaging in socially responsible innovation and manufacturing processes and ethical human resource management.

Hill and Joseff do not limit their ethical practices to Diversified Chemical's processes and people, however. Rather, they leverage their moral values to be uplifting, positive forces in their community. Diversified Chemical is located in Detroit's inner city, and this proximity to the city's poverty-stricken communities is no accident. Instead of building new manufacturing locations in developing Detroit suburbs, Hill and Joseff reclaim abandoned buildings in economically struggling neighborhoods. The location of Diversified Chemical's facilities allows company employees to get involved in the community through mentoring and tutoring of underprivileged schoolchildren.

There is no doubt that running a socially responsible business has its challenges. But for Hill and Joseff, it has become a way to revive Detroit's economy and its spirits.

Video material provided by Hattie Bryant, Producer of Small Business School, the series on PBS Stations, Worldnet, and the Web at http://www.smallbusinessschool.org.

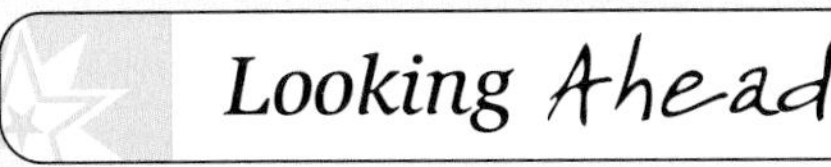

Chapter 2

Looking Ahead

After studying this chapter, you should be able to

1 *Define integrity and understand its importance to small businesses.*

2 *Explain how integrity applies to various stakeholder groups, including owners, customers, employees, and the community.*

3 *Identify challenges to integrity that arise in small businesses and explain the benefits of integrity to small firms.*

4 *Explain the impact of the Internet and globalization on the integrity of small businesses.*

5 *Describe practical approaches for building a business with integrity.*

6 *Describe the costs and opportunities of environmentalism to small businesses.*

Reports of corporate scandals continue to surface in the news. A quick look at the timeline in Exhibit 2-1 reveals just a few of those that have been reported in the past few years. This is certainly not a new phenomenon, but the number and intensity of these offenses seem to be on the rise. Corporations are run by people, after all, and it is reasonable to assume that some will give in to temptation as they make decisions for their companies. However, awareness of human frailties doesn't ease the shock of discovering that yet another corporation that enjoyed the public's trust has been compromised in a big way.

INTEGRITY AND ENTREPRENEURSHIP

1 *Define integrity and understand its importance to small businesses.*

Stories in the news media concerning insider trading, fraud, and bribery usually involve large corporations. However, in the less-publicized day-to-day activities of small businesses, decision makers regularly face ethical dilemmas and temptations to compromise principles for the sake of business or personal advantage. This strikes at the heart of integrity.

What Is Integrity?

integrity
An uncompromising adherence to doing what is right and proper

The seeds of corporate misdeeds are sown when individuals compromise their personal **integrity**—that is, they do not do what they believe to be right and proper, nor do they respond to what Max DePree, chairman emeritus of Herman Miller, Inc., calls "a fine sense of one's obligations."[1] The hallmarks of business integrity include such values as honesty, reliability, and fairness. Some acts, such as cheating on taxes, clearly violate this standard, while others are more subtle but just as inappropriate. For example, one entrepreneur who owned a flooring sales business often sold sheets of linoleum at first-quality prices, even though they were graded as "seconds" by the factory. To hide his deception, he developed an ink roller that changed the factory stamp from "SECONDS" to read "SECONDS TO NONE!" Those who caught the inaccuracy probably figured it was a typo and gave it no more thought, but unsuspecting customers were paying for first-quality flooring, only to receive imperfect goods. By anyone's measure, this shady business practice reveals a lack of integrity on the part of the entrepreneur.

As discussed in Chapter 1, the entrepreneurial experience is far more fulfilling when the entrepreneur understands that the core purpose of the business is to create value for interested customers. This perspective makes clear that relationships are critical and integrity is essential to success. Money is important, but it cannot be the only goal of interest. In fact, excessive focus on financial gain can quickly lead to distortions in business behavior; it certainly is the root cause of many ethical failings. In other words, integrity is as much about *what to do* as it is *who to be*.

EXHIBIT 2-1 *A Timeline of Selected Corporate Scandals*

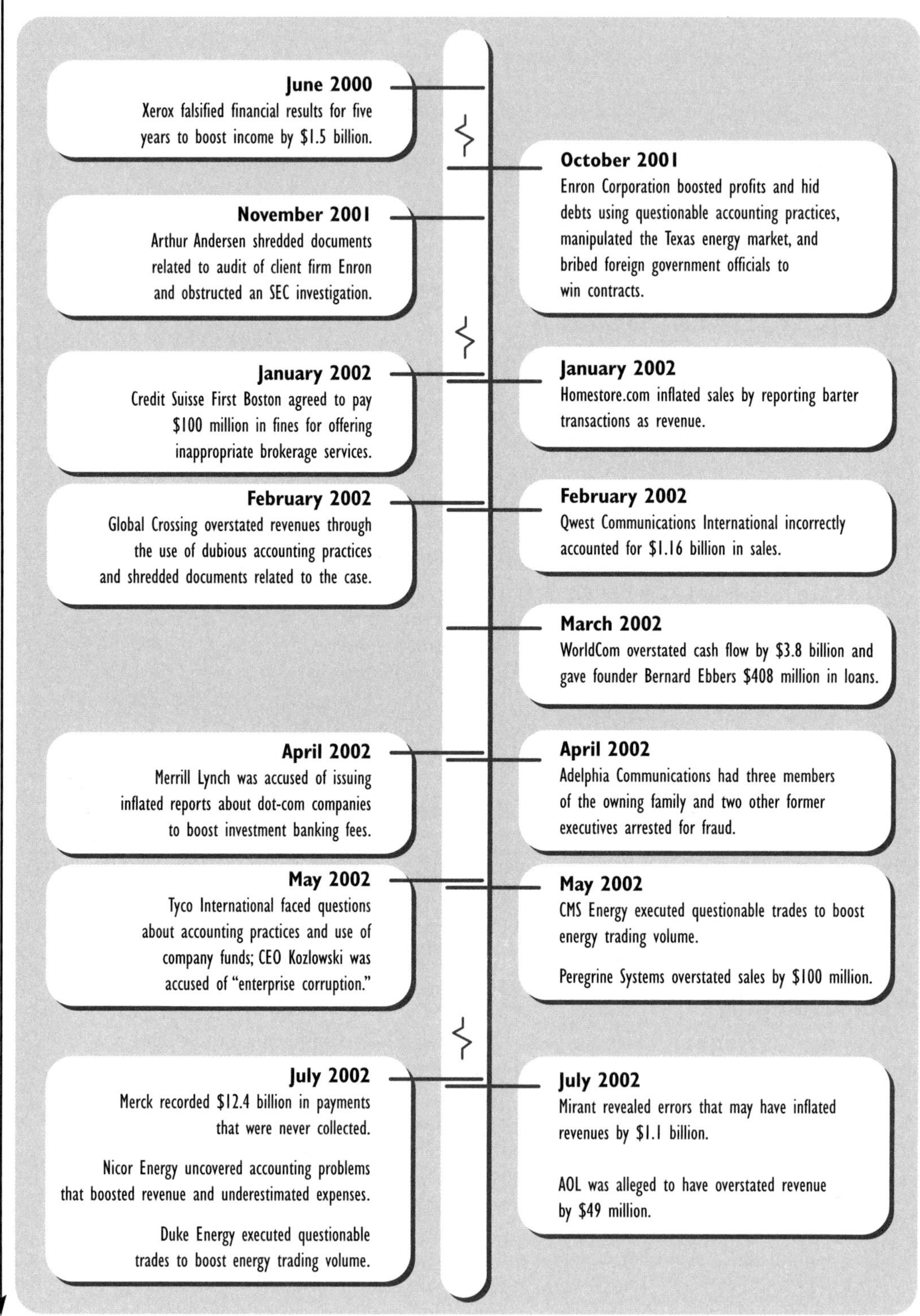

June 2000
Xerox falsified financial results for five years to boost income by $1.5 billion.
October 2001
Enron Corporation boosted profits and hid debts using questionable accounting practices, manipulated the Texas energy market, and bribed foreign government officials to win contracts.
November 2001
Arthur Andersen shredded documents related to audit of client firm Enron and obstructed an SEC investigation.
January 2002
Credit Suisse First Boston agreed to pay $100 million in fines for offering inappropriate brokerage services.
January 2002
Homestore.com inflated sales by reporting barter transactions as revenue.
February 2002
Global Crossing overstated revenues through the use of dubious accounting practices and shredded documents related to the case.
February 2002
Qwest Communications International incorrectly accounted for $1.16 billion in sales.
March 2002
WorldCom overstated cash flow by $3.8 billion and gave founder Bernard Ebbers $408 million in loans.
April 2002
Merrill Lynch was accused of issuing inflated reports about dot-com companies to boost investment banking fees.
April 2002
Adelphia Communications had three members of the owning family and two other former executives arrested for fraud.
May 2002
Tyco International faced questions about accounting practices and use of company funds; CEO Kozlowski was accused of "enterprise corruption."
May 2002
CMS Energy executed questionable trades to boost energy trading volume.
Peregrine Systems overstated sales by $100 million.
July 2002
Merck recorded $12.4 billion in payments that were never collected.
Nicor Energy uncovered accounting problems that boosted revenue and underestimated expenses.
Duke Energy executed questionable trades to boost energy trading volume.
July 2002
Mirant revealed errors that may have inflated revenues by $1.1 billion.
AOL was alleged to have overstated revenue by $49 million.

Note: Dates reflect when scandals became public knowledge.

Sources: John A. Byrne, Louis Lavalle, Nanette Byrnes, Marcia Vickers, and Amy Borrus, "How to Fix Corporate Governance," *BusinessWeek,* No. 3781 (May 6, 2002), pp. 68–75; Robert Frank, Cassel Bryan-Low, Mitch Pacelle, Rebecca Smith, Dennis Berman, Carrick Mollenkamp, Getta Anand, Ann Davis, Mark Maremount, Shawn Young, James Bandler, and Randall Smith, "Scandal Scorecard," *Wall Street Journal,* October 3, 2003, p. B1; John Waggoner and Thomas A. Fogarty, "Scandals Shred Investor's Faith," *USA Today,* May 2, 2002, pp. 1A, 2A; and http://www.forbes.com/2002/07/25/accountingtracker.html, September 26, 2003.

Lapses in integrity, once discovered, quickly make the headlines when they involve large, high-profile corporations, but the problem obviously does not end there. Small business owners and managers confront situations every day that require them to make ethical decisions. They must decide which course of action will preserve the integrity of the company and safeguard its reputation, a decision that can be especially difficult when doing the right thing runs counter to the immediate financial interests of the business.

Fortunately, many small firms strive to achieve the highest standards of truthfulness, fairness, and trustworthiness in their business relationships. Although unethical practices receive extensive attention in the news media, the majority of entrepreneurs and other business leaders are people of principle whose integrity regulates their quest for profits.

Doing the Right Thing

It is probably evident by now that the notion of integrity is closely tied to **ethical issues**, which involve questions of right and wrong. Such questions go far beyond what is legal or illegal. Entrepreneurs must often make decisions regarding what is honest, fair, and respectful.

ethical issues
Questions of right and wrong

Individuals who face ethical issues are sometimes tempted to place self-interest and personal financial gain ahead of the reasonable and legitimate interests of others. While self-interest is a legitimate force in human life, it can, when unchecked, lead to behavior that is unfair or harmful to others. And to act with integrity, an individual must consider the welfare of others.

In the short run, at least, honesty does not always pay—in fact, doing the right thing can be downright costly. In other situations, honesty may boost business profits. But most people who show integrity in their business lives do not weigh the economic benefits before deciding how honest and forthright they can afford to be. Instead, they live by the highest of standards simply because it's the right thing to do.

Rotary Club International, a worldwide organization of business and professional leaders, has set a high standard for business conduct. It calls on its members to ask the following four questions when they prepare to make a decision about the things they think, say, or do:[2]

- Is it the TRUTH?
- Is it FAIR to all concerned?
- Will it build GOODWILL and BETTER FRIENDSHIPS?
- Will it be BENEFICIAL to all concerned?

A similar approach has the individual asking herself or himself, "How would I feel if my decision were reported in the daily newspaper?" Or, the question can be even more personal: "How well could I explain this to my mother?" This exercise can help to keep the entrepreneur on the straight and narrow when it comes to guarding her or his integrity.

A FRAMEWORK FOR INTEGRITY

2 Explain how integrity applies to various stakeholder groups, including owners, customers, employees, and the community.

In order to pinpoint the types of ethical issues that are most troublesome for small companies, small business owners nationwide were asked the following question: "What is the most difficult ethical issue that you have faced in your work?" As might be expected, the question yielded a wide variety of responses, which have been grouped into the categories shown in Exhibit 2-2.

These responses provide a general idea of the kinds of issues that challenge the integrity of small business owners. As you can see in the exhibit, the issues mentioned most often are related to customers and competitors. However, the second most common category is concerned with the way a company treats its employees, including decisions about layoffs, workplace discrimination, fairness in promotions, and the like. The fact that this set of issues received almost as many responses as the first should not be surprising, given the challenges of the current economic climate. In fact, it is telling that this

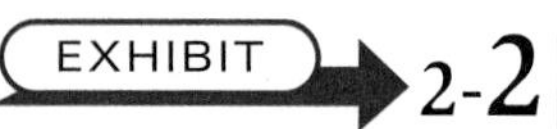

EXHIBIT 2-2 *Difficult Ethical Issues Facing Small Firms*

ETHICAL ISSUES	NUMBER OF RESPONDENTS	SAMPLE RESPONSES
Relationships with customers, clients, and competitors (relationships with outside parties in the marketplace)	111	"Avoiding conflicts of interest when representing clients in the same field" "Putting old parts in a new device and selling it as new" "Lying to customers about test results"
Human resource decisions (decisions relating to employment and promotion)	106	"Whether to lay off workers who [are] surplus to our needs and would have a problem finding work or to deeply cut executive pay and perks" "Sexual harassment" "Attempting to rate employees based on performance and not on personality"
Employee obligations to employer (employee responsibilities and actions that in some way conflict with the best interests of the employer)	90	"Receiving kickbacks by awarding overpriced contracts or taking gratuities to give a subcontractor the contract" "Theft of corporate assets" "Getting people to do a full day's work"
Management processes and relationships (superior–subordinate relationships)	63	"Reporting to an unethical person" "Having to back up the owner/CEO's lies about business capability in order to win over an account and then lie more to complete the job" "Being asked by my superiors to do something that I know is not good for the company or its employees"
Governmental obligations and relationships (compliance with governmental requirements and reporting to government agencies)	40	"Having to deal with so-called anti-discrimination laws which in fact force me to discriminate" "Bending state regulations" "Employing people who may not be legal [citizens] to work"
Relationships with suppliers (practices and deceptions that tend to defraud suppliers)	25	"Vendors want a second chance to bid if their bid is out of line" "Software copyright issues" "The ordering of supplies when cash flows are low and bankruptcy may be coming"
Environmental and social responsibilities (business obligations to the environment and society)	20	"Whether to pay to have chemicals disposed of or just throw them in a dumpster" "Environmental safety versus cost to prevent accidents" "Environmental aspects of manufacturing"

Source: Leslie E. Palich, Justin G. Longenecker, Carlos W. Moore, and J. William Petty, "Integrity and Small Business: A Framework and Empirical Analysis," Proceedings of the 49th World Conference of the International Council for Small Business, Johannesburg, South Africa, June 2004.

category was near the bottom of the list when entrepreneurs responded to the same survey six years earlier.[3] Times have changed.

The third category is related to the obligations of employees to their employers, focusing on the actions of personnel that may not align with the best interests of their companies. In fourth place are management processes and relationships. Management relationship issues can be especially disturbing because they reflect the moral fiber or culture of the firm, including weaknesses in managerial actions and commitments.

The results of this survey reveal that entrepreneurs must consider the interests of a number of groups when making decisions—owners (or stockholders), customers, employees, and the community. The individuals in these groups are sometimes referred to as stakeholders, indicating that they have a "stake" in the operation of the business. In essence, **stakeholders** are those who can affect or are affected by the performance of the company.

stakeholders
Individuals who can affect or are affected by the performance of the company

Because the interests of various stakeholder groups are different, they sometimes conflict; thus, decisions can be very difficult to make. And since there is often no obviously right or wrong position to take, managing the process can be extremely complicated.

One executive observed that running a business is sometimes like juggling (see Exhibit 2-3). In his words, "I am given four balls to balance: the customer's, the employees', the community's, and the stockholders', by which I mean profit. It's never made clear to me how I am to keep them all going, but I know for certain that there is one that I'd better not drop, and that's profit."[4]

As if the business juggler's job were not already difficult enough, we have added one more ball to the mix—government. Wandering beyond the limits of the law can quickly land a company in hot water, and there is no more certain way to compromise its integrity and its reputation. However, the concerns of all of these groups are fundamental to the management of the business. If neglected, any one group can use its influence to negatively affect the performance of the company.

Promoting the Owners' Interests

The Nobel Prize–winning economist Milton Friedman outlines the responsibilities of businesses to society in very focused terms: "There is only one social responsibility of business—to use its resources and engage in activities designed to increase its profits so long as it stays within the rules of the game, which is to say, engages in open and free competition without deception or fraud."[5]

Friedman is arguing that businesses should be expected simply to earn profits honestly; any other use of the firm's resources is justified only if it enhances the firm's value. Though we believe there is adequate room for entrepreneurs to adopt a broader view of their social

2-3 *Juggling the Interests of Stakeholder Groups and the Government*

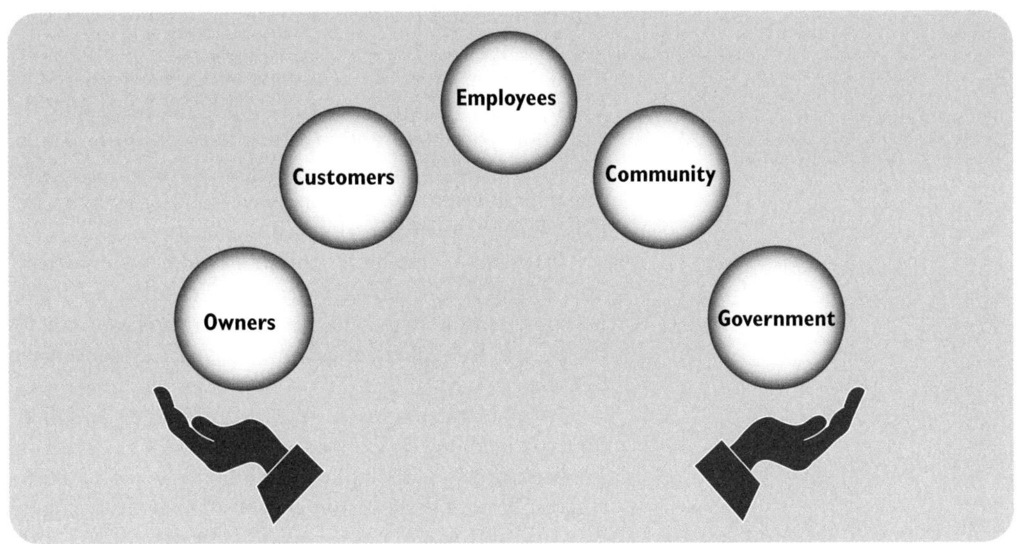

responsibilities, it is undeniable that an owner has a clear and legitimate right to benefit from the financial performance of the company.

Many businesses, even small ones, have more than one owner. When this is the case, high standards of integrity require an honest attempt to promote the interests of all the owners, which include a commitment to financial performance and protection of the firm's reputation. But this does not always happen, as Jeff Dennis found out the hard way. In 1989, he and three co-founders started a financial investment company called Ashton-Royce Capital Corporation. But when the venture started to take off, two of the partners decided to "check out" and spend a good part of their time in California in semiretirement. This left the two remaining co-founders with more of the day-to-day work of the business and a growing resentment about the unfairness of the situation. In time, the conflict led to the dissolution of what had been a very profitable business.[6] Though entrepreneurs should be able to make their own decisions about personal matters, such as where they live, they have an obligation to make decisions that protect the investment that others may have in the company. Integrity demands it!

In many small businesses, a number of people own a small part of the enterprise but have no direct involvement in its operation. When this is the case, questions concerning proper conduct can show up in a number of areas. For example, entrepreneurs sometimes face ethical issues when reporting financial information. They must decide the extent to which they will be honest and candid. Because a firm has considerable discretion in reporting performance results, financial reports can sometimes be misleading without technically being illegal. But providing misleading financial information could easily persuade the other owners to make poor decisions regarding their investment in the company. Furthermore, outsiders such as bankers, investors, and suppliers depend on a firm's financial reports to be accurate. It is always best to err on the side of honest disclosures that do not tend to mislead; this protects the reputation of the firm, and it is simply the right thing to do.

Respecting Customers

What do you call a business without customers? *Bankrupt!* Customers are obviously one of the most important stakeholder groups that a company must please. The fact that they are central to the purpose of any business has implications for integrity. Entrepreneurs who take customers seriously and care about them as individuals are apt to have more of them. And those they have are likely to return again and again because of that attitude.

Marc Katz sets an example as an entrepreneur with an appropriate view of customers. In 1978, after joining with a partner to buy a building where many other restaurants had failed, Katz began offering the first complete and authentic deli menu in Austin, Texas. Katz Deli thrives because customers love the high-quality food and Marc and his staff love the customers. Marc treats his guests as valued friends and family; in fact, he makes people feel as if they were visiting his home, where he had prepared a party for them. His driving motivation is not profit, though the deli is an undeniable success. Rather, it is his desire to provide a quality dining experience, marked by a genuine attitude of service.[7]

Katz Deli illustrates how a business can capitalize on integrity by treating customers with respect and building strong relationships with them. But entrepreneurs are often tempted to take advantage of customers or to be less than honest with them. When making marketing decisions, a business owner is confronted with a variety of ethical questions. For example, advertising content must sell the product or service but also tell "the truth, the whole truth, and nothing but the truth." Salespeople must walk a fine line between persuasion and deception. In some businesses, a salesperson might obtain contracts more easily by offering improper inducements to buyers or by joining with competitors to rig bids. This is clearly illegal, but it does happen.

Criticisms of unethical conduct in direct selling (that is, face-to-face selling) focus on such practices as pyramid schemes, bait-and-switch selling, and front-loading, in which new sales representatives are required to purchase large inventories, which they then must try to sell. In general, these practices are evidence of a simple lack of regard for the customer.

CyberRebates.com is an Internet company that failed to keep the interests of its customers front and center. The business closed its "cyberdoors" on May 16, 2001, and filed for bankruptcy, with millions of dollars owed to customers who had been promised rebates. Most of these customers had already received merchandise from the company, but they probably would never have bought these items at the obviously inflated prices were

Living the Dream

Focus on the Customer

The Best Leader Is a Great Servant

C. William Pollard is the former chairman of the board of ServiceMaster, one of the fastest-growing and most successful franchisors in American history. Pollard's story of his first formal encounter with the company highlights a paradox that drives the success of the firm: A great leader must first be a great servant.

> *My predecessors, Ken Hansen, who was then Chairman of the company, and Ken Wassner, who was then President and CEO of the company, were both involved in recruiting me to join the firm. They wanted me to come and initially head up the legal and financial affairs of the company, reporting directly to Ken Wassner. In the selling of the job, it was suggested to me that I, along with others, would be considered in the future for the CEO position of the company.*
>
> *The interviewing process took several months and as we were coming to what I thought was the final interview to confirm compensation and starting date, I decided that I needed to know more about what it would take to be CEO of ServiceMaster. As I pressed the point and tried to get some assurance of how I could become CEO, Ken Hansen stood up and told me that the interview was over. Ken Wassner ushered me to the front door. As I left ServiceMaster that morning, I concluded that it was over. I had blown the opportunity.*
>
> *A few days later, Ken Hansen called me on the phone and asked me if I wanted to have breakfast with him to discuss what had happened in his office. When we sat down for breakfast, he simply said: "Bill, if you want to come to ServiceMaster to contribute and serve, you will have a great future. But if your coming is dependent on a title, position or ultimately the CEO's position, then you will be disappointed. To be successful at ServiceMaster, you will have to learn to serve and to put the interest of others ahead of your own."*
>
> *His point was very simple. Never give a job or a title to a person who can't live without it. Determine at the front end whether the leader's self-interest or the interest of others will come first. Know whether he or she can define reality by being willing to do what [he or she asks] of others.*

Pollard was offered the job after all—and he accepted. But he spent the first six weeks of his career at ServiceMaster on the floor, cleaning up and performing the maintenance tasks that are part of the firm's business. Sometimes the shortest path to the top starts at the very bottom.

http://www.servicemaster.com

Source: C. William Pollard, "Leading in Turbulent Times," *Baylor Business Review*, Vol. 20, No. 1 (Spring 2003), pp. 22–29.

it not for the company's amazing rebate offers. One burned customer, a New York marketing executive, paid $120 for a hot-lather shaving machine just before the company went under. He received the product, which was probably worth about $25, but he will never see the 100 percent rebate. Another case involved a couple who said they were owed more than $86,000 by the company. These customers were drawn in by offers that were "too good to be true," and greed clearly played a role in this sad saga—but CyberRebates.com was the first to step over the line. The business made promises that were impossible to keep, and it was destined to collapse eventually. The only question left to answer is, Who will pay the price?[8]

Making a completely safe product and avoiding all errors in service are almost impossible goals to reach. But when a company delivers an excellent product with excellent service, customer satisfaction is sure to follow. Mike Jacobs, owner of two Wetzel's Pretzels franchises in California, believes his success has come from building employee teams that make things happen. With virtually no turnover in two years, Jacobs has communicated to his employees how important they are and how their performance impacts the business. In fact, their service orientation has generated sales of $1 million.[9] This suggests that a company's response to its customers will often be determined by its employees.

Valuing Employees

The level of integrity in a firm is reflected in the amount of respect given to employees. Through management decisions, an owner affects employees' personal and family lives. Issues of fairness, honesty, and impartiality are inherent in decisions and practices regarding hiring, promotions, salary increases, dismissals, layoffs, and work assignments. Employees are also concerned about privacy, safety, and health issues, and these should not be ignored.

In communicating with employees, an owner may be truthful and fair, vague, misleading, or totally dishonest. Some entrepreneurs treat outsiders with great courtesy but display demeaning behavior or attitudes toward subordinates, whom they regard as mere pawns in the game of business. Showing proper appreciation for subordinates as human beings and as valuable members of the team is an essential ingredient of managerial integrity. It is also wise, since employees are a firm's most important resource.

Jeanne Romano lost her job soon after being hired. As vice president of production at DeepCanyon.com, she was one of 32 employees laid off by the Seattle-based marketing research company when it closed its doors. However, Romano felt that the firm and its management had dealt honestly and fairly with employees regarding the closing. Two months earlier, they had let her know that it was "countdown time" for the enterprise. Job applicants received a realistic appraisal of bleak company prospects. Employees received two weeks' notice of closing and two weeks' severance pay. A career counselor came in to discuss the local job scene, and the company helped employees post their résumés on the Internet. Even while teetering on the brink of bankruptcy, DeepCanyon.com refused to compromise its integrity—and its former employees will never forget it.[10]

Small businesses do not always show the level of respect for employees that DeepCanyon.com expressed. And, unfortunately, lapses in integrity can sometimes be passed down from superiors to subordinates. Employees of small firms can face pressure from various sources to act in ways that conflict with their own sense of what is right and wrong. For example, a salesperson may feel pressured to compromise personal ethical standards in order to make a sale. Or an office employee may feel pressured by her or his boss to act unethically, perhaps by destroying documents. Such situations are guaranteed to produce an organizational culture that fails to promote integrity.

Fortunately, most employees of small firms do not face such pressures. In a nationwide survey of individuals holding managerial and professional positions in small firms, respondents reported feeling the following degrees of pressure to act unethically:[11]

No pressure	72.3%
Slight pressure	24.1%
Extreme pressure	3.6%

While it is encouraging to note that nearly three-fourths of the respondents reported an absence of pressure to compromise personal standards, the fact that more than one-fourth of the respondents experienced either slight or extreme pressure is disturbing. The strictness of a person's standards of integrity is, of course, related to that individual's perception of pressure to act unethically. That is, a person with low ethical standards would probably encounter few situations that violated his or her standards. However, a person with high ethical standards would find more situations that violated his or her personal norms. The ideal is to develop a business environment in which the best ethical practices are consistently and uniformly encouraged.

In some cases, employees may engage in unethical behavior at their employer's expense. They may fail in their ethical obligation to do "an honest day's work." Loafing on the job, working too slowly, and taking unjustified sick leave are all examples of such failure.

Other unethical behaviors are more flagrant. Some employees have feigned injuries and drawn fraudulent workers' compensation checks, thereby inflating their employer's insurance costs. Employee theft and embezzlement cost employers millions of dollars each year. Items stolen from employers include merchandise, tools, and equipment. In the case of embezzlement, of course, an employee steals money from the firm. This type of unethical behavior is extremely serious and clearly can cost the company a lot of money!

Social Responsibility and Small Business

To most people, an ethical business is one that not only treats customers and employees honestly but also acts as a good citizen in its community. These broader obligations of citizenship are called **social responsibilities**.

social responsibilities
Ethical obligations to customers, employees, and the community

Some regard social responsibility as a price of freedom to operate independently in a free economy. They believe that the public has certain social expectations regarding business behavior, not all of which are required by law. Accordingly, they regard some socially responsible expenditures as proper, even when they are costly.

To varying degrees, companies have increasingly been accepting responsibility to the communities where they do business. Their contribution starts with creating jobs and adding to local tax revenues, but many entrepreneurs feel a duty to give back even more to the community in return for the local support they enjoy—and they usually benefit from increased goodwill as a result. It is important to recognize that opinions differ as to the extent to which businesses are obligated to engage in socially desirable activities, and the response of small businesses to those obligations also varies. Some emphasize environmentalism, minority contracting, or regional economic development, while others focus their attention on volunteerism, philanthropy, or even day care for employees' dependents. Still others give only minimal attention to peripheral social issues.

EXAMPLES OF CITIZENSHIP IN THE COMMUNITY Craig Hall wrote a book called *The Responsible Entrepreneur* to encourage others to be more generous and appreciate how fulfilling this can be.[12] And it's more than just talk. His Dallas, Texas company—Hall Financial Group—donates 5 percent of its income to charity, and any employee can take off up to 40 hours a year to work with charitable organizations. But he firmly believes that his company gets a return on this investment. He observes, "In my experience, good things happen to good companies. Better employees and more customers gravitate toward you, and you establish loyalty."

PAR Educational Technologies, a computer firm in Scottsdale, Arizona, expresses its concern for the community by sponsoring a volunteer program for its 65 employees.[13] Employees are invited (but not coerced) to choose from a variety of volunteer projects. One of these projects is Habitat for Humanity, through which the employees help build houses for low-income families.

While volunteer efforts may be useful in building team spirit and making a company more attractive as an employer, volunteerism also draws on unselfish motivations. As Joel Barthelemy, president and CEO of PAR, said, "Both my parents have 'servant hearts,' and I may be influenced by that. . . . Volunteering also makes me feel good; it's more than just what's in it for Joel."[14]

Smaller businesses can demonstrate a sense of social responsibility in special ways. Fuller's Plumbing Service of Chula Vista, California, boasts a staff of five, including owner Steve Fuller. Particularly touched by an article that described the needs of the homebound elderly, Fuller decided to help out those in his community. The company's plumbers now repair toilets and faucets, unclog stoppages, and fix water system leaks for low-income seniors and disabled people. Fuller's attitude is illustrated by this comment: "I like to think I owe a little bit back to the community that has supported us for 40 years. . . . That's why I think we can contribute our services to people in need."[15]

VARYING VIEWS ON SOCIAL RESPONSIBILITY How do small business owners compare with big business CEOs in their view of social responsibility? The evidence is limited, but entrepreneurs who head small, growth-oriented companies seem to be more narrowly focused on profits and, therefore, less socially sensitive than are CEOs of large corporations. A study that compared small business entrepreneurs with large business CEOs concluded the following:

> *The entrepreneurial CEOs were found to be more economically driven and less socially oriented than their large-firm counterparts. Apparently, [corporate social responsibility] is a luxury many small growth firms believe they cannot afford. Survival may be the first priority.*[16]

In defense of small firm owners, we have to note that they are usually spending their own money rather than corporate funds. It is, of course, easier to be generous when spending someone else's money. Furthermore, small business philanthropy often takes the form of personal contributions by business owners.

Entrepreneurs must reconcile their social obligations with the need to earn profits. Meeting the expectations of society can be expensive. Small firms must sometimes purchase new equipment or make costly changes in operations in order to protect the environment. For example, auto repair shops incur additional costs when they dispose of hazardous waste, such as used oil and filters. It is evident that acting in the public interest often requires spending money, which reduces profits. There are limits to what particular businesses can afford.

Fortunately, many types of socially responsible action can be consistent with a firm's long-term profit objective. Some degree of goodwill is earned by socially responsible behavior. A firm that consistently fulfills its social obligations makes itself a desirable member of the community and may attract customers because of that image. Conversely, a firm that scorns its social responsibilities may find itself the target of restrictive legislation and discover that its customers and employees lack loyalty to the business. Researchers Melissa Baucus and David Baucus of Utah State University compared the long-term performance of 67 corporations convicted of corporate wrongdoing with the performance of 188 other firms.[17] They found that the law-abiding firms experienced significantly higher returns on assets and on sales. To some extent, therefore, socially responsible practices may have a positive impact on profits.

Recognizing a social obligation does not change a profit-seeking business into a charitable organization. Earning a profit is absolutely essential. Without profits, a firm will not long be in a position to recognize its social responsibilities.

Governmental Laws and Regulations

Government at all levels exists for a reason, though there is room to debate whether it has too much power or too little. It intervenes directly in the economy when it establishes laws to ensure healthy competition. But its reach extends into other business matters as well—workplace safety, equal employment opportunities, fair pay, clean air, and safe products, to name a few. Entrepreneurs must comply with governmental laws and regulations if they are to maintain integrity—and avoid spending time behind bars.

One glaring example of unethical behavior by small firm management is fraudulent reporting of income and expenses for income tax purposes. This conduct includes *skimming*—that is, concealing some income—as well as improperly claiming personal expenses as business expenses. We do not mean to imply that all or even most small firms engage in such practices. However, tax evasion does occur within small firms, and the practice is widespread enough to be recognized as a general problem.

The Internal Revenue Service regularly uncovers cases of income tax fraud. For example, the John E. Long family, the largest promoter of country folk art shows in the nation, was forced to pay millions in back taxes, and four members of the family were given prison terms for tax law violations.[18] The Longs did not record the cash they collected for admission to their shows. Instead, they deposited into corporate accounts only checks received from such sources as booth rentals and magazine sales. Unfortunately for the Longs, the IRS discovered 2,000 unreported deposits that members of the family made into 37 different accounts. The Longs had reported that their business was losing money when, in fact, it was doing very well.

THE CHALLENGES AND BENEFITS OF ACTING ETHICALLY

3 *Identify challenges to integrity that arise in small businesses and explain the benefits of integrity to small firms.*

When it comes to integrity and entrepreneurial ventures, it is important to recognize that the news is not all good: Small companies face unique challenges to integrity. At the same time, the news can be very positive: The benefits of integrity are real and can offer small businesses a distinct advantage in the marketplace.

The Vulnerability of Small Companies

Walking the straight and narrow may be more difficult and costly on Main Street than it is on Wall Street.[19] That is, small, privately held firms that are not part of the corporate world epitomized by Wall Street may face greater pressures than large businesses do to act unethically. For example, a lack of resources may make it difficult for owners of a small firm to resist extortion by public officials.

> *Professor William Baxter of the Stanford Law School notes that for such owners, delayed building permits or failed sanitation inspections can be "life-threatening events" that make them cave in to bribe demands. By contrast, he adds, "the local manager of Burger King is in a much better position" to tell these people to get lost.*[20]

Because a small firm is at a disadvantage relative to larger competitors that have superior resources, the firm's owner may be tempted to rationalize bribery as a way of offsetting what seems to be a competitive disadvantage and securing an even playing field.

Nick Molina, referring to the early days of his company, Let's Talk Cellular & Wireless, said, "Sometimes when you're backed up against the wall, your instincts take over, and you do what you have to do to survive."[21] When Molina sought to obtain space in the all-important Dadeland Mall in Miami, the leasing agent told him that his company needed to be "established" to be considered. So Molina manipulated financial reports to make his six-month-old firm look as though it had been in business for two years. Entrepreneurs in such difficult positions often try to rationalize their behavior by distinguishing between posturing (putting their "best foot forward") and lying.

The temptation for entrepreneurs to compromise ethical standards as they strive to earn profits is evident in the results of a study of entrepreneurial ethics.[22] In this research, entrepreneurs' views about various ethical issues were compared with those of other business managers and professionals. Participants were presented with 16 situations (or vignettes), each describing a business decision with ethical overtones. They were asked to rate the degree to which they found each action compatible with their personal ethical views. Here is one of the vignettes: "An owner of a small firm obtained a free copy of a copyrighted computer software program from a business friend rather than spending $500 to obtain his own program from the software dealer."

For the most part, the participants in this study, including entrepreneurs, expressed a moral stance; that is, they condemned decisions that were ethically questionable as well as those that were clearly illegal. For all situations, the average response of entrepreneurs and others indicated some degree of disapproval. For nine of the sixteen vignettes, the responses of entrepreneurs did not differ much from those of others. However, this was not the case with the remaining seven vignettes. In five cases, the entrepreneurs appeared significantly less moral (less disapproving of questionable conduct) than the other respondents.[23] Each of these situations involved an opportunity to gain financially by taking a profit from someone else's pocket. For example, entrepreneurs were less severe in their condemnation of collusive bidding and duplicating copyrighted computer software without paying the manufacturer for its use.

Obviously, a special temptation exists for entrepreneurs who are strongly driven to earn profits. However, this finding must be kept in perspective. Even though the entrepreneurs appeared less moral than the other business respondents in their reactions to five ethical issues, the majority of the entrepreneurs were actually *more* moral in their responses to two other issues that had no immediate impact on profit.[24] One of these issues involved an engineer's decision to keep quiet about a safety hazard that his employer had declined to correct.

Evidence shows, then, that most entrepreneurs exercise great integrity, but some are particularly vulnerable with regard to ethical issues that directly affect profits. While business pressures do not justify unethical behavior, they help explain the context in which the decisions are made. Decision making about ethical issues often calls for difficult choices on the part of the entrepreneur.

The Integrity Edge

The price of integrity is high, but the potential payoff is incalculable. For example, it is impossible to compute the value of a clear conscience. The entrepreneur who makes honorable decisions, even when it comes to the smallest of details, can take satisfaction in knowing that he or she did the right thing, even if things do not turn out as planned.

But integrity yields other important benefits as well. In their book *Becoming a Person of Influence*, John Maxwell and Jim Dornan conclude that integrity is crucial to business success. They cite notable research to make their point: A recent survey of 1,300 senior executives

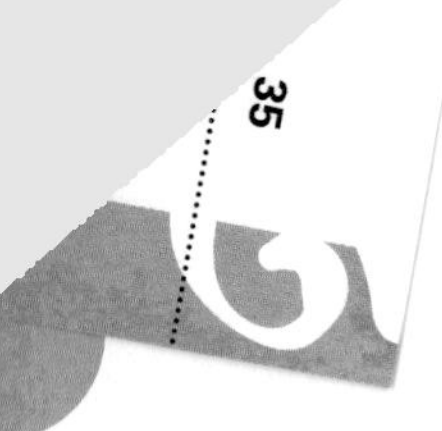

showed that 71 percent considered integrity to be the personal quality that is most necessary to success in business.[25] Though an entrepreneur may lack personal integrity and still achieve financial success, he or she must swim against a very swift current to do so.

In a study of 207 American firms, John Kotter and James Heskett, professors at the Harvard Business School, found that the more a company focuses on needs of shareholders alone, the lower its performance. Kotter and Heskett concluded that firms perform better when their cultures emphasize the interests of *all* stakeholders—customers, employees, stockholders, and the community. Over the 11-year period of the study, those companies that looked beyond the balance sheet "increased revenues by an average of 682 percent versus 166 percent for those companies that didn't, expanded their work forces by 282 percent versus 36 percent, grew their stock prices by 901 percent versus 74 percent, and improved their net incomes by 756 percent versus 1 percent."[26] While these results are highly impressive, they do not guarantee that doing the right thing will *always* lead to positive results for a company. However, these findings do suggest that exhibiting integrity in business does not rule out financial success—in fact, doing the right thing may actually boost the company's performance.

In a word, the greatest benefit of integrity is the *trust* it generates. Trust results only when the stated values of a company and its behavior in the marketplace match up. When a small business owner looks to the needs of others and follows through on her or his promises, stakeholders begin to take notice. Customers buy more of what a firm sells when they realize that the company is doing its best to make sure that the products it sells are of high quality and the customer service it offers is excellent. Employees are much more likely to "go the extra mile" for a small company when it is clear that they are more than simply replaceable parts in an impersonal machine.

And members of the community also respond positively to business integrity. When they are convinced that a firm is living up to its commitments to protect the environment and pay its fair share of taxes, their support can keep the company going even if it falls on hard times. But it all comes down to trust. If they conclude that the business is simply taking advantage of them, then all bets are off. There is no substitute for trust, and there is little hope for trust without integrity.

INTEGRITY IN AN EXPANDING ECONOMY

4 Explain the impact of the Internet and globalization on the integrity of small businesses.

For the entrepreneur with integrity, decisions are often complicated by emerging developments in the world economy. Businesses that operate across national boundaries, for example, must consider the ethical standards that exist in other cultures, which often differ from those of their own country. And firms using the Internet face a host of new ethical issues that have arisen in the e-marketplace. As small firms move toward international commerce and harness the power of the Internet to launch and sustain their enterprises, these issues become all the more important.

Integrity and the Internet

It is not surprising that issues of honesty, deception, and fraud are found on the Internet, just as they are in traditional commerce. Those who buy and sell on the Internet are some of the same people who populate malls and business firms. As in all business relationships, one quickly encounters questions of right and wrong.

One issue of great concern to Internet users is individual privacy. Businesses and consumers often disagree about how private the identity of visitors to Web sites should be. For example, businesses can use "cookies" to collect data on patterns of usage related to a particular Internet address. In this way, a business may create a detailed profile of customers, which it may then sell to other parties for profit. Businesses in the Internet industry—and even many of their customers—see the collection of personal information as helpful. A bookseller might, for example, welcome a customer back by name and tell him or her about a special book similar to those the customer ordered previously.

The extent to which an employer may monitor an employee's Internet activity is also being hotly debated. According to a survey conducted by the Society of Financial Service, 44 percent of workers surveyed considered it seriously unethical for employers to monitor employee e-mail.[27] In their opinion, such a practice constitutes snooping and an invasion of privacy. Employers, however, are concerned that employees may be wasting time dealing with personal e-mail, shopping online, and surfing the Internet. And it appears there is reason for concern. Websense Inc., a San Diego–based computer security company, found that 49 percent of employees in the small businesses it surveyed visited Web sites that were unrelated to their work. These workers spent an average of 11.1 hours a week on the Internet, and 31 percent of that time (3.4 hours) was spent on non-work-related sites.[28] Since this activity hinders productivity in the workplace, it is clearly problematic for the employer.

The privacy issue is receiving attention from both legislators and business leaders. The likely result will be voluntary action by businesses, as well as increased government regulation. Many businesses, including giants like IBM and AT&T, have created the position of chief privacy officer to deal with these issues.[29] And a number of firms have developed privacy policies—they either will not share personal data or will not share it if the customer requests privacy. These policies are usually spelled out on a firm's Web site.

Widespread use of the Internet has also focused attention on the issue of **intellectual property**. Traditionally, protection has been granted to original intellectual creations—whether inventions, literary works, or artistic products such as music—in the form of patents and copyrights. The law allows originators of such intellectual property to require compensation for its use. However, the Internet has made it easy for millions of users to copy intellectual property free of charge.

intellectual property
Original intellectual creations, including inventions, literary creations, and works of art, that are protected by patents or copyrights

> *In the virtual world, journalists, photographers, filmmakers, authors, and musicians are referred to as content providers, a phrase that neatly sums up two problems: first, the fungible nature of this "content," and second, the dicey question of who pays these artists if everything they create can be reproduced free on the Net a hundred million times.*[30]

Protection of intellectual property is a political as well as an ethical issue. Recent congressional hearings, lawsuits, and proposed legislation suggest that additions or changes to current laws are likely. This trend was highlighted on September 8, 2003, when the Recording Industry Association of America filed 261 lawsuits against individuals who had allegedly shared large libraries of music with others via the Internet.[31] And as use of the Internet continues to grow, it is safe to assume that property rights will become more difficult to protect; content providers are certain to take stronger and stronger measures to guard what is legally theirs.

International Issues of Integrity

Every country faces questionable business behavior within its borders, but some must deal with very serious forms of illegal business activity. In extreme cases, criminal gangs engage in business operations that might better be characterized as evil, rather than unethical. In the year 2000, for example, Italian authorities conducted raids in 28 cities, breaking up a criminal network of some 200 members in China, Russia, and Italy.[32] These gangs brought Chinese immigrants to Italy and forced them to work 12 to 16 hours a day in textile, apparel, shoe, and leather factories for little or no pay. Other raids have discovered children as young as 11 years old laboring under sweatshop conditions. It is likely that isolated instances of extreme criminal behavior also occur in the United States. In addition, some U.S. companies have exploited labor in countries with weak labor laws in order to procure products at low costs. Acts of this kind must be condemned and targeted by law enforcement agencies.

Of more widespread concern in the area of global business ethics is the following question: Does a payment to a customs employee or to a well-connected, helpful individual in another country constitute a tip, extortion, a consulting fee, or a bribe? The answer may depend on the size of the payment and also on the individual's country of origin. Cultures differ in what they condone as ethical and condemn as unethical.

In operating abroad, then, U.S. businesspeople encounter ethical issues that are clouded by cultural differences.[33] Frequently, they simply apply U.S. standards to the situation. In some cases, however, this approach has been criticized for resulting in **ethical imperialism**, an arrogant attempt to impose U.S. standards on other societies. Some guidance is provided by restrictions specified in the Foreign Corrupt Practices Act, which makes it illegal for U.S. businesses to use bribery in their dealings anywhere in the world. (Some allowance is made for small "grease payments," which are payments offered to speed up a legitimate process.) Regardless of local practices, U.S. firms must comply with these laws. Of course, "gray areas" exist, in which there are no obvious answers.

ethical imperialism
The belief that the ethical standards of one's own country can be applied universally

ethical relativism
The belief that ethical standards are subject to local interpretation

Another viewpoint is embodied in the saying "When in Rome, do as the Romans do." This philosophy, which might be termed **ethical relativism**, is troublesome, as it implies that anything goes if the local culture accepts it. Nicholas G. Moore, recently retired global chairman of PricewaterhouseCoopers, distinguished between business activities that reflect simple cultural differences and those, such as bribery, that are clearly unethical.

> *But the gray areas are tougher to deal with. Think about the issues we deal with here in the United States, and then transplant them to foreign soil. Issues like diversity, the environment, child labor. We are much more sensitive to these issues. Still, the answers are very, very gray. And if they're gray here, they are really murky overseas. They require clear thinking and organizational support.*[34]

To define its ethical landscape and work out its position on difficult issues, a small business must consider the nuances of its particular international environment. Training is also needed to ensure that each employee understands the firm's commitment to integrity.

BUILDING A BUSINESS WITH INTEGRITY

5 *Describe practical approaches for building a business with integrity.*

The goal of an entrepreneur with integrity is to have a business that operates honorably in all areas. This goal is not reached automatically, however. To build a business with integrity, management must provide the kinds of leadership, culture, and instruction that support appropriate patterns of thought and behavior.

A Strong Foundation

underlying values
Unarticulated ethical beliefs that provide a foundation for ethical behavior in a firm

The business practices that a firm's leaders or employees view as right or wrong reflect their **underlying values**. An individual's beliefs affect what that individual does on the job and how she or he acts toward customers and others. Of course, people sometimes engage in verbal posturing, speaking more ethically than they act. Thus, actual behavior provides the best clues to a person's underlying system of basic values. Behavior may reflect the level of a person's commitment (or lack thereof) to honesty, respect, and truthfulness—that is, to integrity in all of its dimensions.

Strongly held values sometimes require tough choices. The most ethical and the most economical actions may differ, since taking the "right" course of action can be expensive. In such cases, an entrepreneur who has strong, widely recognized moral values will still do the right thing simply because it is the right thing to do.

Values that serve as a foundation for integrity in business are based on personal views of the universe and the role of humankind in that universe. Such values, therefore, are part of basic philosophical and/or religious convictions. In the United States, Judeo-Christian values have traditionally served as the general body of beliefs underlying business behavior, although there are plenty of examples of honorable behavior based on principles derived from other religions. Since religious and/or philosophical values are reflected in the business practices of firms of all sizes, a leader's personal commitment to certain basic values is an important determinant of a small firm's commitment to business integrity.

A long-time observer of high-tech startups has commented on the significance of an entrepreneur's personal values:

> *I can tell you, even with the smallest high-technology companies, the product had to be good, the market had to be good, the people had to be good. But the one thing that was checked out most extensively by venture capitalists was the integrity of the management team. And if integrity wasn't there, it didn't matter how good the product was, how good the market was—they weren't funded.*[35]

Entrepreneurs who are deeply committed to underlying values of integrity operate their businesses in ways that reflect their personal interpretation of those values. After spending several years shuttling gamblers from Richmond, Virginia, to Atlantic City, New Jersey, bus driver Tom Winston became convinced that he should no longer take poor people to gamble away what little money they had. So he resigned and started his own company, Universal Tours, which avoids the lucrative casino runs.[36] Another business that places the entrepreneur's personal values above dollars is Ukrop's Super Markets, a

Living the Dream

Entrepreneurship and Integrity

A Healthy Diet of *VeggieTales*

Larry the Cucumber and Bob the Tomato may not be as famous as Lady and the Tramp, but they are tickling the fancy of kids who may not even like vegetables. Larry and Bob are the stars of *VeggieTales,* cartoons that stress positive messages for preschoolers, like doing good and sharing with others. Their videos have been so popular they have outsold some Disney productions at major retailers like Wal-Mart and Target.

VeggieTales is the brainchild of Philip Vischer (pictured in photo) and Michael Nawrocki, who decided that kids needed more exposure to entertaining programs that also teach biblical values. By 1993, they had raised $200,000 from friends and churchgoers to set up their company, Big Idea Productions. With plenty of faith and no shareholders, Vischer and Nawrocki (who also provide the voices for Bob and Larry, respectively) have been able to control the message of their productions and continue to stay on mission.

AP/Wide World Photos

By late 1995, Big Idea Productions had sold 150,000 copies of their two videos, "Where's God When I'm Scared?" and "God Wants Me to Forgive Them!?!" At more than $10 per copy, and with production costs running a reasonable $60,000 per video, this started to add up to serious money.

But it's not about the money. When major distributors refused to carry their videos unless the company toned down its religious message, the founders refused. They did, however, make some minor adjustments—for example, they eliminated references to God in the titles of later videos. The message of new projects, however, remains the same. And business continues to grow. The company has sold 30 million videos in its first decade of operations. And though Big Idea hit a serious bump in the road when it was acquired by Classic Media LLC in 2003, the product continues to sell. As Eric Ellenbogen, chairman of the new parent company, recognizes, "[Big Idea] has never let its audience down." It seems that Big Idea still has a big future.

http://www.bigidea.com

Sources: Jill Kipnis, "Big Idea Serves Up *VeggieTales,*" *Billboard,* Vol. 115, No. 7 (February 15, 2003), p. 37; Kemp Powers, "Gospel Truth," *Forbes,* Vol. 168, No. 4 (May 28, 2001), pp. 92–93; and Enrique Rivero, "Classic Media Acquires Big Idea and 'VeggieTales,'" *Video Store Magazine,* Vol. 25, No. 37 (September 7–13, 2003), p. 4.

Richmond, Virginia–area supermarket chain that does not sell alcohol, closes every Sunday, and donates 10 percent of its profits to charity. More than once, *Fortune* magazine has named Ukrop's to its list of the best 100 companies to work for. Ninety percent of its employees say they are proud of the company's involvement in the community.[37]

It seems apparent that a deep commitment to basic values affects behavior in the marketplace and gives rise to business principles that are widely appreciated and admired. Without a strong commitment to integrity on the part of small business leadership, ethical standards can easily be compromised.

Leading with Integrity

Entrepreneurs who care about ethical performance in their firms can use their influence as leaders and owners to urge and even insist that everyone in their firms display honesty and integrity in all operations. Ethical values are established by leaders in all organizations, and those at lower levels take their cues regarding proper behavior from the statements and conduct of top-level management.

In a small organization, the influence of a leader is more pronounced than it is in a large corporation, where leadership can become diffused. This fact is recognized by J. C. Huizenga, who in 1995 started a public school management company called Heritage Academies, which has been ranked as one of the fastest-growing U.S. companies by *Inc.* magazine.

> *The executive of a small company must often face moral challenges more directly, because he or she has more direct contact with customers, suppliers, and employees than an executive in a large corporation who may have a management team to deliberate with. The consequences of his or her choices often affect the business more significantly because of the size of the issue relative to the size of the company.*[38]

In a large corporation, the chief executive has to exercise great care to make sure that her or his precepts are shared by those in the many and varied divisions and subsidiaries. Some corporate CEOs have professed great shock on discovering behavior at lower levels that conflicted sharply with their own espoused principles.

Leaders of large corporations are also responsible to stockholders, most of whom focus a great deal of attention on corporate profits. The management team is under pressure to deliver an increase in earnings per share year after year. The position of an entrepreneur typically is much simpler.

The opportunity for establishing high standards of integrity is more apparent in small firms than in large ones. For example, an entrepreneur who believes strongly in honesty and truthfulness can insist that those principles be followed throughout the organization. In effect, the founder or head of a small business can say, "My personal integrity is on the line, and I want you to do it this way!" Such statements are easily understood. And such a leader becomes even more effective when he or she backs up such statements with appropriate behavior. In fact, a leader's behavior has much greater influence on employees than his or her stated philosophy does.

In summary, the personal integrity of the founder or owner is the key to a firm's ethical performance. The dominant role of this one person (or the leadership team) gives him or her (or the team) a powerful voice in the ethical performance of the small firm.

A Supportive Organizational Culture

Integrity in a business requires a supportive organizational culture. Ideally, every manager and employee should instinctively resolve every ethical issue by simply doing the "right" thing. An ethical culture requires an environment in which employees at every level are confident that the firm is fully committed to honorable conduct. To a considerable degree, strong leadership helps build this understanding. As a small business grows, however, personal interactions between the owner and employees occur less and less, creating a need to articulate and reinforce principles of integrity in ways that supplement the personal example of the entrepreneur.

The idealism and principles espoused by Rutledge & Company, a merchant bank in Greenwich, Connecticut, are reflected by a conference-room portrait that reminds employees "how to behave."[39] The portrait of an early business partner, V. P. "Bake" Baker (a "wonderfully principled man"), encourages today's employees to follow "Bake" principles such as these:

1. Do the right thing. Right and wrong are powerful concepts. A handshake with a person who tries to do the right thing is more comforting than a ton of legal documents signed by a bad guy.
2. Stick to your principles. Hire people who want to live by them, teach them thoroughly, and insist on total commitment.
3. Principles are not for sale.

code of ethics
Official standards of employee behavior formulated by a firm

At some point, the owner-manager of a small firm should formulate a **code of ethics** similar to that of most large corporations. (See Exhibit 2-4 for an example of such a code.) This code should express the principles to be followed by employees of the firm and give examples of these principles in action. A code of ethics might, for example, prohibit acceptance of gifts or favors from suppliers but point out standard business courtesies, such as free lunches, that might be accepted without violating the policy.[40]

If a code of ethics is to be effective, employees must be aware of its nature and convinced of its importance. At the very least, each employee should read and sign it. As a firm grows larger, employee training becomes necessary to ensure that the code is well understood and taken seriously. It is also imperative, of course, that management operate in a manner consistent with its own principles and deal decisively with any infractions.

At a minimum, a code of ethics should establish a foundation for business conduct. With training and consistent management, a firm can then develop the level of understanding employees need to act in the spirit of the code in situations not covered by specific rules.

2-4 | *The Ethical Code of The Dwyer Group*

CODE OF VALUES

We believe . . .

. . . in superior service to our customers, to our community, and to each other as members of The Dwyer Group family.

. . . in counting our blessings every day in every way.

. . . success is the result of clear, cooperative, positive thinking.

. . . that loyalty adds meaning to our lives.

. . . management should seek out and recognize what people are doing right, and treat every associate with respect.

. . . challenges should be used as learning experiences.

. . . our Creator put us on this earth to succeed. We will accept our daily successes humbly, knowing that a higher power is guiding us.

. . . in the untapped potential of every human being. Every person we help achieve their potential fulfills our mission.

. . . we must re-earn our positions every day in every way.

. . . in building our country through the free enterprise system. We demonstrate this belief by continually attracting strong people in The Dwyer Group.

We live our Code of Values by . . .

INTEGRITY

. . . making only agreements we are willing, able and intend to keep.

. . . communicating any potentially broken agreements at the first appropriate opportunity to all parties concerned.

. . . looking to the system for correction and proposing all possible solutions if something is not working.

. . . operating in a responsible manner: "above the line."

. . . communicating honestly and with purpose.

. . . asking clarifying questions if we disagree or do not understand.

. . . never saying anything about anyone that we would not say to him or her.

RESPECT

. . . treating others as we would like to be treated.

. . . listening with the intent to understand what is being said and acknowledging that what is said is important to the speaker.

. . . responding in a timely fashion.

. . . speaking calmly, and respectfully, without profanity or sarcasm.

. . . acknowledging everyone as right from their own perspective.

CUSTOMER FOCUS

. . . continuously striving to maximize internal and external customer loyalty.

. . . making our best effort to understand and appreciate the customer's needs in every situation.

HAVING FUN IN THE PROCESS!

Source: Reprinted with permission of The Dwyer Group, Waco, Texas.

Better Business Bureaus

In any sizable community, all types of business practices can be found. Some firms use highly questionable practices, such as bait advertising. In **bait advertising**, the seller lures customers in with a deceptive offer to sell a product at an attractive price, only to try to convince them to purchase more expensive products. Other firms are blatantly dishonest in the products or services they provide—for example, replacing auto parts that are perfectly good.

bait advertising
An insincere offer to sell a product or service at a very low price, used to lure customers in so that they can be switched later to a more expensive product or service

Because such practices reflect adversely on honest members of the business community, privately owned business firms in many cities have joined together to form Better

Business Bureaus. The purpose of these organizations is to promote integrity on the part of all business firms in the community.

Specifically, a Better Business Bureau's function is twofold: (1) It provides free buying guidelines and information a consumer should have about a company prior to completing a business transaction, and (2) it attempts to resolve questions or disputes concerning purchases. As a result, improper business practices often decline in a community served by a Better Business Bureau.

The creation of Better Business Bureaus reflects an initiative on the part of independent firms to encourage integrity within the business community. Although actions of this type and voluntary commitment to ethical performance within individual firms receive less press coverage than the lapses in integrity of some business leaders, such efforts to improve ethical performance contribute significantly to the effective functioning of the private enterprise system.

ENVIRONMENTALISM—COST OR OPPORTUNITY?

6 Describe the costs and opportunities of environmentalism to small businesses.

The social issues affecting businesses are numerous and diverse. Business firms are expected—at various times and by various groups—to help solve social problems in such areas as education, crime, ecology, and poverty. One movement of immediate concern to small businesses is environmentalism.

The Burden of Environmentalism

environmentalism
The effort to protect and preserve the environment

In recent decades, deterioration of the environment has become a matter of widespread concern. **Environmentalism**—the effort to preserve and redeem the environment—thus directly affects most business organizations. One source of pollution has been the industrial discharge of waste into streams, contaminants into the air, and noise into the areas surrounding the operations.

The interests of small business owners and environmentalists are not necessarily—or uniformly—in conflict. Some business leaders, including many in small business, have consistently worked and acted for the cause of conservation. For example, many small firms have modernized their equipment and changed their procedures to reduce air and water pollution. Others have taken steps to landscape and otherwise improve the appearance of plant facilities. Some small businesses have actually been in a position to benefit from the general emphasis on ecology. For example, those firms whose products are harmless to the environment are generally preferred by customers over competitors whose products pollute. Also, some small firms are involved in servicing pollution-control equipment. Auto repair shops, for example, service pollution-control devices on automobile engines.

Other small firms, however, are adversely affected by efforts to protect the environment. Livestock feeding lots, cement plants, pet-food processors, and iron foundries are representative of industries that are especially vulnerable to extensive environmental regulation. The cost impact of such regulation on businesses of these types is often severe. Indeed, requiring improvements has forced the closure of some firms. Many small foundries, for example, have been obliged to close because of costly environmental controls.

It is usually difficult for a small business to pass higher costs on to its customers; only in a very favorable market situation can a firm do this. The resulting economic hardships must, therefore, be recognized as a cost of environmental controls and evaluated accordingly. Requiring effective pollution control is especially hard on a small, marginal firm with obsolete equipment. In such a case, environmental regulation may simply hasten the inevitable closing of the firm.

The Potential of Environmentalism

While environmentalism represents a cost to some small businesses, it opens up great opportunities for others. In fact, startups have come to life precisely because of environmental concerns.

One current environmental challenge is disposing of used tires, and several startups have recognized that they can turn these cast-offs into cash through recycling. For example, GreenMan Technologies, Inc., recently reported more than $25 million in net sales by delivering tire-derived fuel to power plants, paper mills, and cement kilns. The company has been shredding several million tires a year into small "fuel chips," each of which contains the equiv-

Living the Dream

Entrepreneurial Challenges

Going Green Can Cost You Greenbacks

He may be the largest user of biodiesel in the United States, but he claims he is not an environmentalist—just a businessperson with ethical sensitivities. Grant Goodman is a 45-year-old entrepreneur who owns a ready-mix cement company called Rockland Materials. The company employs 230 people and operates a fleet of 120 trucks that used to add to the infamous brown cloud of smog that hovers over Phoenix, Arizona. Goodman's solution: Run the trucks on biodiesel, a biodegradable, nontoxic, sulfur-free fuel made from soybeans.

© David Harrison/Index Stock Imagery

Goodman first got the idea when he watched a news story about a school district that ran its vehicles on soybean-based fuel. He decided to try it himself—first with five of his trucks and then eventually with the entire fleet. Now he is looking for a way to do it better, by talking to fast-food chains in order to secure a steady supply of vegetable-oil waste that he can convert to biodiesel on his own. It turns out that French fries might be good for our (environmental) health after all!

However, the news is not all good. Large trucks burn a lot of fuel, and biodiesel costs at least 50 cents per gallon more than regular diesel fuel. Goodman estimates that he paid about $500,000 more to use biodiesel in just the first two years of his experiment in social responsibility. In an industry that runs on tight margins, this is no small cost. His efforts have earned him a prestigious award from the EPA and high praise from a number of high-profile publications, but no financial advantage. However, Goodman is not overly concerned about this; he believes the economics will improve over time. For now, he can take comfort from the fact that at least his plan allows his employees in Phoenix to breathe a little bit easier.

Sources: Paulette Thomas, "Owner Adapts to Keep His Trucks' Fuel Clean," *Wall Street Journal*, December 10, 2002, p. B6; Geoff Williams, "Green Machines," *Entrepreneur*, July 2003, p. 34; and http://www.biodiesel.org/resources/users/stories/rockland.shtm, September 15, 2003.

alent of around 2.5 gallons of petroleum. Another company, RB Rubber Products, Inc., recognized the same environmental development, but responded with a very different strategy. The company's 90 employees transform used tires into rubber mats that are sold as playground surfaces, liners for horse stables, commercial flooring, and other products. Finally, a company named Dodge-Regupol, Inc., turns old tires into "crumbs" and then converts these fragments into products such as playground tiles, sports venue surfaces, and automotive parts. Employing 150 workers, the company transforms more than two million tires each year.[41] Taking very different approaches, these three firms are responding to the opportunities created by environmentalism. And with more than 245 million tires being discarded in the United States every year, the opportunity is not likely to go away any time soon.

The emerging view of environmentalism goes well beyond recycling. Bill McDonough, former dean of the School of Architecture at the University of Virginia, started a small design firm called William McDonough+Partners. Featuring 30 architects, planners, designers, and support staff, the company focuses on the goal of launching what McDonough refers to as a "new industrial revolution," one that will lead to the safe manufacture of high-quality products without sacrificing business performance. As *Fortune* magazine reports, this movement could lead to some interesting products.

> *Fabrics you can eat. Buildings that can generate more energy than they consume. Factory with wastewater clean enough to drink. Even toxic-free products that, instead of ending up as poison in a landfill, decompose as nutrients into the soil. No more waste. No more recycling. And no more regulation.*[42]

McDonough has already captured the interest as well as the wallets of some very powerful corporations. For example, as part of a plan to transform the auto company that was founded by his great-grandfather, William Clay Ford, Jr., hired McDonough to lead the renovation of a huge Ford plant outside Detroit. Now, the glass roof of the plant floods the facility with natural light, which saves energy, and the reconstructed wetlands that surround the plant handle excess storm waters.[43]

McDonough's designs are not just environmentally friendly; they also save clients a lot of money and hassle. For example, it is projected that the wetlands at the Ford plant alone

will save the firm $35 million. And the inexpensive to construct, nearly transparent facility he built for Herman Miller, Inc., in Zeeland, Michigan, features a solar heating and cooling system that has cut energy costs by 30 percent. Productivity at the plant is up an amazing 24 percent! McDonough's product developments include soles for Nike shoes that safely biodegrade, a nylon that can be repeatedly recycled, and fabrics that can be eaten (but the firm makes no claims about taste).[44]

The ultimate goal is to save the planet, of course, but companies are unlikely to join the movement unless it actually generates value to shareholders. According to Stuart L. Hart, a professor of strategy at the University of North Carolina, this movement will provide huge opportunities for companies with "moxie" and creativity, as long as they can execute the plan.[45] This sounds like prime territory for small entrepreneurial companies, given their flexibility and innovative thinking. Entrepreneurs may be able to do well *and* do good—and guard the environment and their integrity at the same time.

Looking Back

1 Define integrity and understand its importance to small businesses.

- Integrity is an uncompromising adherence to doing what is right and proper.
- Integrity is as much about what the entrepreneur *should do* as it is about what he or she *should be.*
- Closely tied to integrity are ethical issues, which go beyond what is legal or illegal to include more general questions of right and wrong.

2 Explain how integrity applies to various stakeholder groups, including owners, customers, employees, and the community.

- The most troublesome ethical issues for small businesses involve relationships with customers, clients, and competitors; human resource decisions; and employees' obligations to their employers.
- When they make business decisions, entrepreneurs must consider the interests of all stakeholder groups.
- Research shows that about one-fourth of the employees in small businesses experience some degree of pressure to act unethically in their jobs.
- Most people consider an ethical business to be one that acts as a good citizen in its community.

3 Identify challenges to integrity that arise in small businesses and explain the benefits of integrity to small firms.

- The limited resources of small firms make them especially vulnerable to allowing or engaging in unethical practices.
- Research suggests that most entrepreneurs exercise great integrity, but some are likely to cut ethical corners when it comes to issues that directly affect profits.
- Exhibiting integrity in business may actually boost a firm's performance.
- The greatest benefit of integrity is the trust it generates.

4 Explain the impact of the Internet and globalization on the integrity of small businesses.

- Use of the Internet has highlighted ethical issues such as invasion of privacy and threats to intellectual property rights.
- Cultural differences complicate decision making for small firms operating in the global marketplace.

5 Describe practical approaches for building a business with integrity.

- The underlying values of business leaders and the behavioral examples of those leaders are powerful forces that affect ethical performance.
- An organizational culture that supports integrity is key to achieving appropriate behavior among a firm's employees.
- Small firms should develop codes of ethics to provide guidance for their employees.
- Many small businesses join Better Business Bureaus to promote integrity throughout the business community.

6 Describe the costs and opportunities of environmentalism to small businesses.

- Many small businesses help protect the environment, and some contribute positively by providing environmental services.
- Some small firms, such as pet-food processors, are adversely affected by costly environmental regulations.
- Small companies, such as those in the tire-recycling business, are sometimes launched precisely to take advantage of opportunities created by environmental concerns.
- Creating environmentally friendly products requires creativity and flexibility, areas in which small businesses tend to excel.

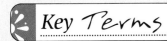

Key Terms

integrity, p. 25
ethical issues, p. 27
stakeholders, p. 29
social responsibilities, p. 33
intellectual property, p. 37
ethical imperialism, p. 37
ethical relativism, p. 38
underlying values, p. 38
code of ethics, p. 40
bait advertising, p. 41
environmentalism, p. 42

Discussion Questions

1. The owner of a small business felt an obligation to pay $15,000 to a subcontractor, even though, because of an oversight, the subcontractor had never submitted a bill. How can willingness to pay under these circumstances be reconciled with the profit goal of a business in a free enterprise system?
2. Give an example of an unethical business practice that you have personally encountered.
3. Based on your experience as an employee, customer, or observer of some particular small business, how would you rate its ethical performance? On what evidence or clues do you base your opinion?
4. Give some examples of the practical application of a firm's basic commitment to supporting the family life of its employees.
5. What is skimming? How do you think owners of small firms might attempt to rationalize such a practice?
6. What are some of the advantages of conducting business with integrity? Some people say they have no responsibility beyond maximizing the value of the firm in financial terms. Can this position be defended? If so, how?
7. Explain the connection between underlying values and integrity in business behavior.
8. Why might small business CEOs focus more attention on profit and less on social goals than large business CEOs do?
9. Give some examples of expenditures required on the part of small business firms to protect the environment.
10. Should all firms use biodegradable packaging? Would your answer be the same if you knew that using such packaging added 25 percent to the price of a product?

You Make the Call

SITUATION 1

Sally started her consulting business a year ago and has been doing very well. About a month ago, she decided she needed to hire someone to help her since she was getting busier and busier. After interviewing several candidates, she decided to hire the best one of the group, Mary. She called Mary on Monday to tell her she had gotten the job. They both agreed that she would start the following Monday and that Mary could come in and fill out all the hiring paperwork at that time.

On Tuesday of the same week, a friend of Sally's called her to say that she had found the perfect person for Sally. Sally explained that she had already hired someone, but the friend insisted. "Just meet this girl. Who knows, maybe you might want to hire her in the future!"

Rather reluctantly, Sally consented. "Alright, if she can come in tomorrow, I'll meet with her, but that's all."

"Oh, I'm so glad. I just know you're going to like her!" Sally's friend exclaimed.

And Sally did like her. She liked her a lot. Sally had met with Julie on Wednesday morning. She was everything that Sally had been looking for and more. In terms of experience, Julie far surpassed any of the candidates Sally had previously interviewed, including Mary. On top of that, she was willing to bring in clients of her own which would only increase business. All in all, Sally knew this was a win-win situation. But what about Mary? She had already given her word to Mary that she could start work on Monday.

Source: http://www.sba.gov/test/wbc/docs/manage/ethics.html, October 28, 2004.

Question 1 What decision on Sally's part would contribute most to the success of her business?

Question 2 What ethical reasoning would support hiring Mary?

Question 3 What ethical reasoning would support hiring Julie?

SITUATION 2

Software piracy is rampant in China. As a result, a bootleg copy of the latest release of Microsoft's Windows, which normally sells for more than $100 when purchased through a legitimate vendor, can be found on the streets of Shanghai for as little as $1. An assistant manager working for the Chinese subsidiary of an American educational services firm ponders the question of whether or not to buy 325 copies of pirated software through a local source for $1 each. Purchasing through an authorized vendor

would cost about 100 times more. He recognizes that he is up against extremely strong competitors that usually purchase pirated software to control costs, so paying the price for legitimate copies could make it difficult for the subsidiary to stay in business. Furthermore, social standards in China do not emphasize proprietary property rights.

Question 1 Is the assistant manager acting with integrity if he purchases unauthorized copies of the software on the street?

Question 2 What might be the long-term effects of deciding to buy the pirated software? Of insisting on buying only legitimate copies of the software?

Question 3 What course of action do you recommend? Why?

SITUATION 3

A self-employed commercial artist reports taxable income of $7,000. Actually, her income is considerably higher, but much of it takes the form of cash for small projects and thus is easy to conceal. She considers herself part of the "underground economy" and defends her behavior as a tactic that allows her small business to survive. If the business were to fail, she argues, the government would receive even less tax revenue.

Question 1 Is the need to survive a reasonable defense for the practice described here?

Question 2 If the practice of concealing income is widespread, as implied by the phrase "underground economy," is it really wrong?

Experiential Exercises

1. Examine a recent business periodical, and report briefly on some lapse in integrity that is in the news. (Log on to InfoTrac College Edition at http://www.infotrac-college.com to find articles on integrity in business.) Could this type of problem occur in a small business? Explain.
2. Employees sometimes take sick leave when they are merely tired, and students sometimes miss class for the same reason. Separate into groups of four or five, and prepare a statement on the nature of the ethical issue (if any) in these practices.
3. Visit or telephone the nearest Better Business Bureau office to research the types of inappropriate business practices it has uncovered in the community and the ways in which it is attempting to support practices that reflect integrity. Report briefly on your findings.
4. Interview an entrepreneur or a small business manager to discover how environmentalism affects her or his firm.

Exploring the Web

1. Go to **http://www.sba.gov/managing/leadership/ethics.html**, a site on business ethics and ethical leadership maintained by the Small Business Administration.
   a. After reading the short article on business ethics that you'll find there, take the accompanying quiz regarding your honesty and sincerity level.
   b. Write a short explanation about how you scored.
2. Many companies have codes of conduct or ethical business policies that stress the importance of ethical behavior in the workplace. Casual-dining operator Brinker International is an example of a large organization that has created a detailed ethics policy. Go to Brinker International's Web site at **http://www.brinker.com/corp_gov/ethical_business_policy.asp** and review its ethical business policy. What aspects of Brinker's policy would you implement in your small business?
3. *Business Ethics* magazine annually recognizes socially responsible companies with an award. Go to **http://www.business-ethics.com/annual.htm** and read about current and past winners. What ideas or lessons would you take from the winners to implement in your business?

Video Case 2

DIVERSIFIED CHEMICAL (P. 528)

This case describes a minority-owned holding company that has built its business by engaging in socially responsible innovation and manufacturing processes and ethical human resource management practices.

Alternative Cases for Chapter 2:

Case 13, Every Customer Counts, p. 550
Case 18, Douglas Electrical Supply, Inc., p. 559
Case 21, Fox Manufacturing, p. 565

STARTING FROM SCRATCH OR JOINING AN EXISTING BUSINESS

CHAPTERS

GETTING STARTED

In the Spotlight

Recycline, Inc. **http://www.recycline.com**

From trash to toothbrush—it just takes an opportunity and good strategy. Eric Hudson, founder and president of Recycline, Inc., confesses that his "Preserve" toothbrush (made of recycled plastic) has to overcome what he calls an "ick factor" if sales are to soar. Of course, consumers may find the idea of a recycled toothbrush easier to swallow if they know that only the handle is made of recycled plastic; the bristles themselves come from brand new nylon.

Surprisingly, Hudson's business idea did not originate from a concern for the environment and overcrowded landfills; rather, the entrepreneur formed his Somerville, Massachusetts, company in 1996 after finding it difficult to follow his dentist's instructions for brushing his teeth. Building on suggestions from dental-hygiene researchers, Hudson designed a toothbrush that cleans better than conventional designs, giving both patient and dentist something to smile about.

AP/Wide World Photos

Hudson's enterprise shows that personal experience can be a potent source of business ideas. For other entrepreneurs, the search for a business opportunity must be more deliberate, systematic, and far-ranging.

Once the business idea has been determined, a small business is much more likely to succeed if the underlying concept is guided by a carefully crafted strategy that can direct the enterprise and also allow it to adapt to the unexpected. This is certainly true of Recycline. For example, Hudson uses the theme of environmental concern to differentiate the Preserve toothbrush from dozens of competing products manufactured by established rivals. The Preserve handle is made from discarded items such as ketchup bottles and yogurt cups and then can itself later be recycled into such things as "plastic lumber," which is used on decks and park benches.

And recent marketing efforts have taken the business a step further. The company sells a single toothbrush for $3.75, but it also offers an annual "subscription" for $17.50 per year. With the subscription, the company reminds you when it is time to replace your toothbrush by sending you a new one every three months. This new twist in strategy should extend the appeal of the product and sustain the performance of the firm. In fact, the Preserve was recently declared the fastest growing toothbrush brand in America, and the product is now available online and in more than 1,000 stores in 49 states. Not bad for a strategy that redeems refuse.

Sources: http://www.enn.com, October 9, 2003; http://www.recycline.com, October 10, 2003; and Jay Lindsay, "Circle of Life Welcomes Plastic," *Waco Tribune-Herald,* November 12, 2000, p. 7B.

Chapter 3

Looking Ahead

After studying this chapter, you should be able to

1 *Identify several factors that determine whether an idea for a new venture is a good investment opportunity.*

2 *Give several reasons for starting a new business from scratch rather than buying a franchise or an existing business.*

3 *Distinguish among the different types and sources of startup ideas.*

4 *Describe external and internal analyses that might shape new venture opportunities.*

5 *Explain broad-based strategy options and focus strategies.*

Entrepreneurs are constantly starting up new and amazing businesses. In fact, it sometimes seems as though all of the best ideas have already been taken. But business ideas are like music—tomorrow's hit song may be just a tune rattling around in someone's head today. The best new businesses are yet to come . . . and yours may be one of them!

You might already have a business idea in mind that you would like to pursue. With good planning and the right strategy, you may soon be off and running as a successful entrepreneur. On the other hand, you may have a passionate desire to start your own company but are not sure you have come up with the right business idea to get you there. Or, perhaps you have an *idea* in mind but are not sure that it is a good business *opportunity*. No matter which group you fall into, this chapter will help to get you started on the right foot, with the right idea and the right strategy.

In Chapters 1 and 2, we talked about the mindset and lifestyle of the entrepreneur and the importance of integrity in the enterprise. Now, in Part 2, we will move forward a step or two and concentrate on topics that will assist the entrepreneur in deciding what kind of startup is best for him or her.

In this chapter, we will describe opportunity recognition and strategy setting for startups—businesses that did not exist before entrepreneurs created them. In later chapters, we will go beyond businesses "started from scratch" and consider business opportunities that already exist, including purchasing a franchise or buying out a business (Chapter 4) and joining a family business (Chapter 5).

IDENTIFYING STARTUP IDEAS

1 *Identify several factors that determine whether an idea for a new venture is a good investment opportunity.*

It is critical to determine whether an idea for a business actually represents a good opportunity. Many people have ideas about new products or services that seem like winners—but just because something is a good idea does not mean that it is a good opportunity, as you will see.

In fact, a person who becomes infatuated with an idea tends to underestimate the difficulty of developing market interest in that idea and building a company that can capture the opportunity. To qualify as a good investment opportunity, a product or service must meet a real market need with respect to its function, quality, durability, and price. Success ultimately depends on convincing consumers of the benefits of the product or service. According to Amar Bhide, a professor at Columbia University, "Startups with products that do not serve clear and important needs cannot expect to be 'discovered' by enough customers to make a difference."[1]

Many criteria exist for judging whether a new business idea is a good investment opportunity. Among the more fundamental requirements are the following:

- *Market factors.* The product or service must meet a clearly defined market need, and the timing must be right. Even when the concept is good, success requires a window of opportunity that remains open long enough for an entrepreneur to take advantage of it.

competitive advantage
A benefit that exists when a firm has a product or service that is seen by its target market as better than those of competitors

- *Competitive advantage.* In practical terms, a **competitive advantage** exists when a firm offers a product or service that customers perceive to be superior to those of its competitors. It follows that the business must be able to achieve an edge that can withstand challenges from rival businesses. Many startups fail because entrepreneurs do not understand the nature and importance of a competitive advantage.
- *Economics.* The venture needs to be financially rewarding, allowing for significant profit and growth potential. Its profit potential must be sufficient to allow for errors and mistakes and still provide acceptable economic benefits.
- *Management capability.* There must be a good fit between the entrepreneur and the opportunity. In other words, a business idea is an opportunity only for the entrepreneur who has the appropriate experience, skills, and access to the resources necessary for the venture's growth.
- *Fatal flaws.* There must be no fatal flaw in the venture—that is, no circumstance or development that could, in and of itself, make the business unsuccessful.

Exhibit 3-1 presents these five evaluation criteria more fully. Above all, beware of thinking that an idea is a "natural" and cannot miss. The market can deal harshly with those who have not done their homework. However, for those who succeed in identifying a meaningful opportunity, the rewards can be sizable. Thus, it is the *market* that ultimately determines whether an idea has potential as an investment opportunity.

CREATING A NEW BUSINESS FROM SCRATCH

2 Give several reasons for starting a new business from scratch rather than buying a franchise or an existing business.

Several motivations point to starting a business from scratch rather than pursuing other alternatives, such as buying a franchise or an existing business or joining a family business. They include the following:

1. Having a personal desire to develop the commercial market for a recently invented or newly developed product or service
2. Tapping into unique resources that are available, such as an ideal location, new equipment technologies, or exceptional employees, suppliers, and bankers
3. Avoiding undesirable features of existing companies, such as unfavorable precedents, policies, procedures, and legal commitments
4. Wanting the challenge of succeeding (or failing) on your own

Assuming that you have one or more of these reasons for considering a startup, you should still address several basic questions before making the commitment:

- What are some other types of startup ideas you might consider?
- What are some sources for additional new ideas?
- How can you identify a genuine opportunity that creates value, for both the customer *and* the company's owner(s)?
- How should you refine your idea?
- What might you do to increase your chances that the business will be successful?
- What competitive advantage could the business have over its rivals?

The entrepreneur's ability to carefully and honestly examine these questions will, in turn, determine the direction he or she will follow. We will examine the issues raised by these questions in the remainder of this chapter.

EXHIBIT 3-1 *Evaluation Criteria for a Startup*

	ATTRACTIVENESS	
Criterion	**Favorable**	**Unfavorable**
Market Factors		
Need for the product	Well identified	Unfocused
Customers	Reachable; receptive	Unreachable; strong loyalty to competitor's product
Value created by product or service for the customer	Significant	Not significant
Life of product	Longer than time required for customer to recover investment plus profit	Shorter than time required for customer to recover investment
Market structure	Emerging industry; not highly competitive	Mature or declining industry; highly concentrated competition
Market size	Sales of $100 million or more	Unknown or sales of less than $20 million
Market growth rate	Growing by at least 30% annually	Contracting or growing by less than 10% annually
Competitive Advantage		
Cost structure	Low-cost producer	No production cost advantage
Degree of control over		
Prices	Moderate to strong	Nonexistent
Costs	Moderate to strong	Nonexistent
Channels of supply	Moderate to strong	Nonexistent
Barriers to entry:		
Proprietary information or regulatory protection	Have or can develop	Not possible
Response/lead time advantage	Have or can develop	Nonexistent
Legal/contractual advantage	Proprietary or exclusive	Nonexistent
Contacts and networks	Well developed	Limited
Economics		
Return on investment	25% or more; durable	Less than 15%; fragile
Investment requirements	Small to moderate; easily financed	Large; financed with difficulty
Time required to break even or to reach positive cash flows	Under 2 years	More than 4 years
Management Capability	Management team with diverse skills and proven experience	Solo entrepreneur with no related experience
Fatal Flaws	None	One or more

Source: Jeffry A. Timmons and Stephen Spinelli, *New Venture Creation: Entrepreneurship for the 21st Century* (Boston: Irwin, 2004), pp. 92–93.

FINDING STARTUP IDEAS

3 *Distinguish among the different types and sources of startup ideas.*

Business ideas are not all equal, and they originate from many different sources. By recognizing the nature and origin of startup ideas, the entrepreneur can broaden the range of new ideas available for his or her consideration.

Types of Startup Ideas

Exhibit 3-2 shows the three basic types of ideas that develop into startups: ideas to enter new markets, ideas based on new technologies, and ideas to offer new benefits.

Type A ideas
Startup ideas centered around providing customers with an existing product not available in their market

Many startups develop from what we will call **Type A ideas**—those concerned with providing customers with a product or service that does not exist in a particular market but that exists somewhere else. Jeremy Kraus's firm, Jeremy's MicroBatch Ice Creams, is an example of a Type A idea. As a college student, Kraus applied the beer industry's microbrew strategy to ice cream, making small quantities and selling the product in limited editions. He went on to develop a relationship with the long-time distributor of Ben & Jerry's ice cream, Dreyer's, which agreed to market Jeremy's products in the New York area and, eventually, in other geographical markets as well.[2]

Type B ideas
Startup ideas, involving new technology, centered around providing customers with a new product

Some startups are based on **Type B ideas**, which involve new or relatively new technology. Malcolm Currie, for example, started Currie Technologies in Van Nuys, California, to produce electric bicycles and scooters in 1998. He now employs 40 people, and revenues reached $10 million in 2002.[3]

Type C ideas
Startup ideas centered around providing customers with an improved product

Type C ideas, those based on offering customers benefits from new and improved ways of performing old functions, probably account for the largest number of startups. In fact, most new ventures, especially in the service industry, are founded on "me, too" strategies—they set themselves apart through features such as superior service or lower prices. David Hartstein's effort to redefine the floral industry fits into the Type C category. His KaBloom, Ltd., outlets offer more than 200 varieties of fresh-cut flowers, compared with an average of 40 at large supermarket floral departments and 20 at most florists. KaBloom keeps its prices low—about half the industry norm—by buying directly from growers and distributors, as opposed to buying from wholesalers. Its online store charges less than half as much as 1-800-Flowers. KaBloom's physical stores are also better lighted and twice as large as many mom-and-pop shops. "A walk in our store is like a walk in a garden," says Hartstein. KaBloom began franchising in 2001.[4]

Sources of Startup Ideas

At this point, you may be saying, "I want to start a new business but haven't come up with a startup idea that sounds like a good investment opportunity." There are a number of sources you can turn to for inspiration. And if one source fails to lead you to the idea of your dreams, keep looking! Inspiration can come from many different places.

Several studies have revealed sources of ideas for small business startups. Exhibit 3-3 shows the results of one such study by the National Federation of Independent Business,

EXHIBIT 3-2 *Types of Ideas That Develop into Startups*

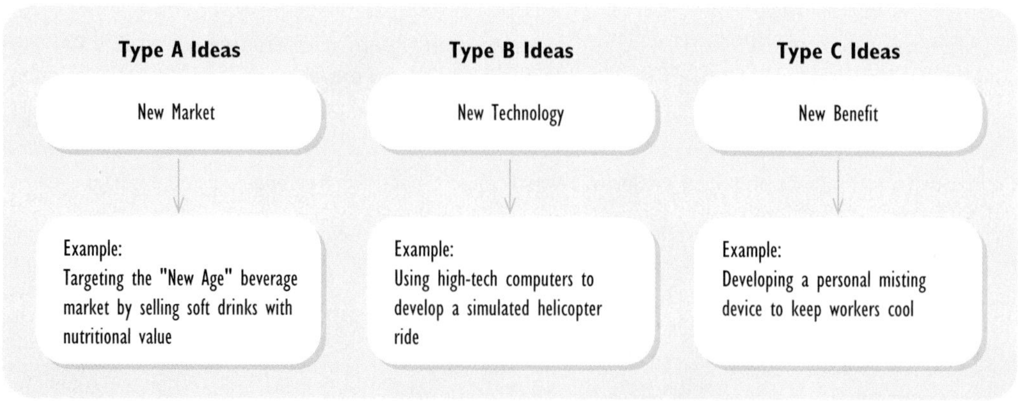

Living the Dream

Utilizing the Internet

Reflective Technology Saves Dog

Sometimes, an Internet startup develops when a new idea merges with new technology. Such was the case for Beth Marcus, of Bedford, Massachusetts. Marcus had an idea for a new product after a car almost struck her cockapoo, Luke, when they were on an evening stroll. The driver hadn't seen them and didn't even slow down. Marcus wanted to make it safer for her dog on these walks.

Marcus was aware of a new high-tech reflective fabric called IllumiNite.™ The technology embeds into the weave of a fabric millions of microscopic reflectors that reflect light back to its source. She decided to start her own firm, GlowDog® Inc., and use this technology to produce and sell light-reflective clothing for pets. Customers liked the dog jackets so much that they requested glow clothing for themselves!

GlowDog launched its first Web site in 1997. As the GlowDog product line continues to expand, Marcus is committed to providing quality products and a fun, interesting experience—as well as saving lives.

http://www.glowdog.com

Source: "Brief History of GlowDog," http://www.glowdog.com/history.htm, accessed August 2003.

which found that prior work experience accounted for 45 percent of new ideas. Personal interests and hobbies represented 16 percent of the total, and chance happenings accounted for 11 percent. Although an idea for a startup can come from virtually anywhere, we will focus on four possible sources: personal experience, hobbies, accidental discovery, and deliberate search.

PERSONAL EXPERIENCE The primary source of startup ideas is personal experience, either at work or at home. Knowledge gleaned from a present or former job often allows a person to see possibilities for modifying an existing product, improving a service, or duplicating a business concept in a different location.

Ken and Jennifer Miller started their outdoor-clothing company, Thousand Mile, based on Ken's personal experience as a lifeguard in Carlsbad, California. The faded

EXHIBIT 3-3 *Sources of Startup Ideas*

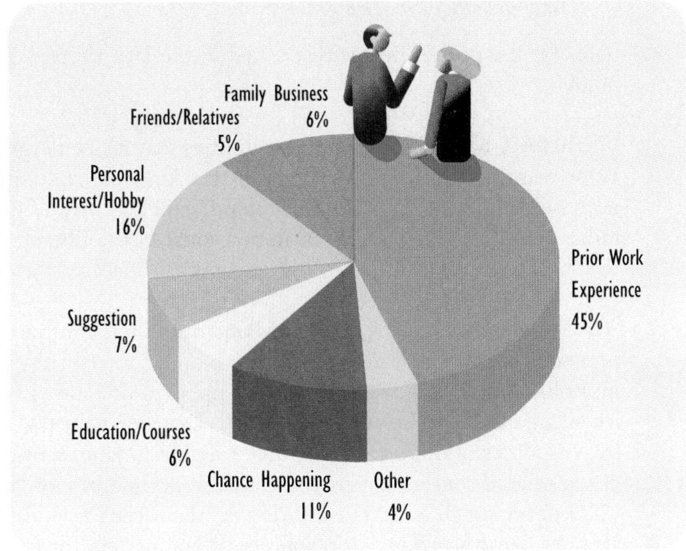

Source: Data developed and provided by the National Federation of Independent Business and sponsored by the American Express Travel Related Services Company, Inc.

trunks of fellow lifeguards inspired Ken and his wife-to-be, Jennifer, to buy $166 of material and make 30 pairs of swimming trunks. When the trunks quickly sold to Ken's co-workers, the couple knew their business idea was an attractive startup opportunity. After several years of development, they now have a complete line of mail-order outdoor wear.[5]

HOBBIES Sometimes hobbies grow beyond being leisure activities to become businesses. For instance, a person who loves skiing might start a ski equipment rental business as a way to make income from an activity that she enjoys.

Bill Martin and Greg Wright have a passion for the stock market and the Internet. As students at the University of Virginia and Rutgers University, respectively, they created a Web site called Raging Bull, with a message board where their friends could chat about stocks. The Web site received only a modest response until Martin and Wright conceived of an "ignored" button, which allows a user to block out messages she or he considers worthless or offensive. "We noticed that the biggest problem with message boards was spamming: people being vulgar or just dumb," says Wright. "We wanted people to enjoy what was valuable without worrying about the other stuff." The revised site attracted so many users that @Ventures, a venture capital firm, invested $2 million in the startup.[6]

serendipity
The faculty for making desirable discoveries by accident

ACCIDENTAL DISCOVERY Another source of new startup ideas—accidental discovery—involves something called **serendipity**, or the seeming ability to make desirable discoveries by accident. Anyone may stumble across a useful idea in the course of day-to-day living.

This is exactly what happened to Tia Wou, founder of Tote Le Monde, a handbag manufacturer in New York City. Wou had traveled to Bolivia for her friend's wedding in 1989 and loved the rich fabrics she saw in the marketplace.

> *Wou, who was working in fashion at the time, got a creative spark from that trip. A few years later, she traveled to Japan and was on the hunt for the perfect handbag. Not finding what she wanted, Wou recalled the beautiful fabrics in Bolivia. That's when it hit her: she could design handbags like the ones she was looking for in Japan, using the materials she'd seen in Bolivia, and sell them in America.*[7]

Today, her company produces lifestyle brands selling handbags, housewares, and travel pieces; sales are running about $1.5 million a year.

Consider also the invention of the pocket protector (called a "nerd pack" in some circles) by electrical engineer Gerson Strassberg in 1952. "It happened by accident," Strassberg says.

> *I was just starting up my company, and we were making the clear plastic covers that cover bankbooks. At that time, ballpoint pens were prone to leaking. One day I cut one side of the plastic longer than the other. The phone rang, so I stuck the plastic in my pocket and thought "Wow, this might make a great product."*[8]

Sales for the pocket protector peaked in the late 1960s, but Strassberg still sells close to 30,000 a year.

DELIBERATE SEARCH Startup possibilities may also emerge from an entrepreneur's deliberate search for new ideas. In fact, this kind of exploration may be especially useful because it stimulates a readiness of mind, which motivates prospective entrepreneurs to be more receptive to new ideas from any source. A deliberate search often involves looking for change-based opportunities, but it may take a number of other paths.

An Eye on Change Change is one of the most important sources of ideas for entrepreneurs. Whereas large firms prefer things to remain the same, entrepreneurs are much more likely to recognize change as an opportunity and to have the creativity and flexibility to adjust to it. Business guru Peter Drucker believes entrepreneurs should consider seven sources of opportunity as they prepare to launch or grow their enterprises.[9] These change-based sources of opportunity are outlined in Exhibit 3-4.

Drucker suggests that innovation is "the means by which the entrepreneur either creates new wealth-producing resources or endows existing resources with enhanced potential for creating wealth."[10] In other words, entrepreneurship harnesses the power of creativity to provide innovative products and services. Since change inspires innovation, recognizing shifts in the factors described in Exhibit 3-4 can expand the range of entrepreneurial opportunities.

Other Idea Leads If analyzing emerging changes does not reveal the specific entrepreneurial opportunity that is right for you, other sources of leads are available. The following have been useful to many entrepreneurs:

- Tapping personal contacts with potential customers and suppliers, professors, patent attorneys, former or current employees or coworkers, venture capitalists, and chambers of commerce
- Visiting trade shows, production facilities, universities, and research institutes
- Observing trends related to material limitations and energy shortages, emerging technologies, recreation, fads, pollution problems, personal security, and social movements
- Reading trade publications, bankruptcy announcements, Commerce Department publications, and business classifieds

Inc., *Entrepreneur*, and other periodicals are excellent sources of startup ideas, as they provide articles on the creativity of entrepreneurs and various business opportunities. Visiting the library and even looking through the Yellow Pages in other cities can spark new ideas as well. Traveling to other cities to visit entrepreneurs in your field of interest can also be extremely helpful. Of course, the Internet provides an unlimited amount of information regarding the startup process and even specific opportunities.

3-4 *Change-Based Sources of Entrepreneurial Opportunities*

Change Factor	Definition	Illustration
Industry Factors		
The unexpected	Unanticipated events lead to either enterprise success or failure.	Pet pharmaceuticals have been very successful, with more than 30% of dogs and cats now taking medication.
The incongruous	What is expected is out of line with what will work.	Low-fat ice cream was developed for those trying to lose weight.
Process needs	Current technology is insufficient to address an emerging challenge.	Carmakers offer gas-electric hybrid cars to deal with rising energy costs.
Structural change	Changes in technology, markets, etc., alter industry dynamics.	Growth in the use of the Internet for e-commerce has been dramatic.
Human and Economic Factors		
Demographics	Shifts in population size, age structure, ethnicity, and income distribution impact product demand.	Baby boomers are now in their prime income-earning years and are saving for retirement, promoting an increase in the need for financial planning.
Changes in perception	Perceptual variations determine product demand.	Perceived security threats have led to development of gated communities.
New knowledge	Learning opens the door to new product opportunities with commercial potential.	Increased knowledge of the Internet has fueled the growth of online investment firms.

A creative person can find useful ideas in many different places. If you follow the suggestions provided here, you just might hit new venture paydirt. However, these are only a few of the possibilities. We encourage you to seek and size up new venture ideas *in whatever circumstances you find yourself.* By considering a number of internal and external factors, you should be able to bring together the pieces of the opportunity puzzle.

USING INTERNAL AND EXTERNAL ANALYSES TO EVALUATE AN OPPORTUNITY

4 Describe external and internal analyses that might shape new venture opportunities.

In his book *Making Sense of Strategy*, Tony Manning points out that there are two general approaches for evaluating business opportunities: inside-out and outside-in. In other words, entrepreneurs can evaluate their own capabilities and then look at new products or services they might be able to offer to the market (inside-out), or they can first look for needs in the marketplace and then relate those opportunities to their own capabilities (outside-in).[11] Of course, there is yet another approach—both inside-out *and* outside-in. This is the approach that we recommend and will discuss further later in the chapter.

It is helpful to understand the finer points of the two basic methods, since they can reveal business ideas that may otherwise be overlooked. In addition, the perspective that an entrepreneur gains through these analyses can aid in identifying opportunities with potential among the many business ideas that are sure to surface.

Remember, an opportunity is not just an idea. A business opportunity must grow from an idea with the potential to develop into an enterprise that has a reasonable chance to succeed. This means that all of the pieces of the puzzle must come together, and in the right order. For example, the entrepreneur must have a serious interest in the new venture idea, as well as the resources and capabilities to start and operate it. The rest of this section contains suggestions for evaluating internal and external factors that may influence the potential of a startup opportunity.

Outside-In Analysis

According to recent research, entrepreneurs are more successful when they study the venture's context in order to identify business ideas and determine which of these ideas qualify as opportunities.[12] This outside-in analysis should consider both the general environment, or big picture, and the industry setting in which the venture might do business. The **general environment** is made up of very broad factors that influence all—or at least most—businesses in a society. In comparison, the **industry environment** is defined more narrowly as the factors that directly impact a given firm and all of its competitors.

general environment
The broad environment, encompassing factors that influence most businesses in a society

industry environment
The combined forces that directly impact a given firm and its competitors

THE GENERAL ENVIRONMENT The general environment has a number of important segments, as shown in Exhibit 3-5. Forces in the *macroeconomic segment* include changes in the rate of inflation, interest rates, and even currency exchange rates, all of which promote or

EXHIBIT 3-5 *Segments of the General Environment*

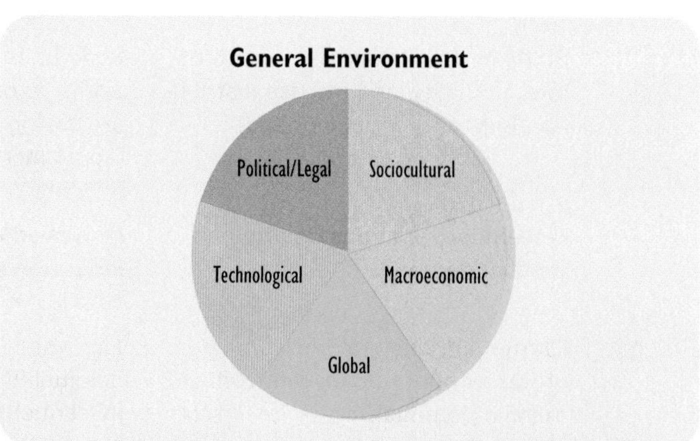

discourage business growth. The *sociocultural segment* represents societal trends that may affect consumer demand, opening up new markets and forcing others into decline. In the *political/legal segment*, changes in tax law and government regulation (such as safety rules) may pose a threat to businesses or devastate an inventive business concept.

The *technological segment* is perhaps most important to small businesses, since developments in this segment spawn—or wipe out—many new ventures. Professor H. J. Tsai learned firsthand that business opportunities can be found in the world of science. Tsai attached fluorescent proteins from jellyfish to DNA in fish; the result was a green fish that literally glows in the dark. Seeing the business potential of this breakthrough, Tsai partnered with Taikong Corporation, which is already selling the fish in foreign markets at a suggested retail price of $17.40. Deals with pet supply giants like Petsmart, which will allow the fish to be sold in the United States, are in the works. And to add variety, Tsai has extended the technology to come up with a fluorescent red fish and one that is half green and half red. With pets like these, who needs a nightlight?[13]

The *global segment* reflects international developments that create new opportunities to expand markets, outsource, and invest abroad. Sometimes, developments in the global segment actually lead to new business opportunities at home. For example, escalating fears of terrorism following the 9/11 attacks have created new possibilities for a variety of small businesses, such as Neoterik Health Technologies, a tiny gas-mask company that attracted the attention of Wall Street; ResQline Inc., a startup in Lakewood, New Jersey, offering a cable system that safely lowers people from tall buildings when they must be evacuated; and Colorado-based Stuffback, whose services include enabling "Good Samaritans" to return laptops, cell phones, PDAs, and other devices that are accidentally left behind at security checkpoints in airports.[14] As people and markets around the world become increasingly connected, the impact of the global segment on small business opportunities is sure to increase.

Some people believe that evaluation of the general environment is appropriate only for large firms that have a corporate staff to manage the process, but actually small businesses can also benefit from such analysis. For example, a recent report on technological developments in the general environment identified business opportunities, such as "space burials," that could emerge if the cost of launching payloads into space were greatly reduced. One small company has already moved in that direction. Houston-based Celestis markets burials in space at prices ranging from $995 to $12,500, using satellite launches to carry cremated remains into orbit. The company has already sent the remains of LSD advocate Timothy Leary and "Star Trek" creator Gene Roddenberry into deep space.[15]

THE INDUSTRY ENVIRONMENT An entrepreneur is even more directly affected by the startup's industry than by the general environment. In his book *Competitive Advantage*, Michael Porter lists five factors that determine the nature and degree of competition in an industry:[16]

- *New competitors.* How easy is it for new competitors to enter the industry?
- *Substitute products/services.* Can customers turn to other products or services to replace those that the industry offers?
- *Rivalry.* How intense is the rivalry among existing competitors in the industry?
- *Suppliers.* Are industry suppliers so powerful that they will demand high prices for inputs, thereby increasing the company's costs and reducing its profits?
- *Buyers.* Are industry customers so powerful that they will force companies to charge low prices, thereby reducing profits?

Exhibit 3-6 shows these five factors as weights that offset the potential attractiveness and profitability of a target industry. It illustrates how profits in an industry tend to be inversely related to the strength of these factors—that is, strong factors yield weak profits, whereas weak factors yield strong profits.

Entrepreneurs who understand industry influences can better assess market opportunities and guard against threats to their ventures. Obviously, the forces dominating an industry depend on its unique circumstances; the entrepreneur must recognize and understand these forces to position the venture in a way that makes the most of what the industry

EXHIBIT 3-6 *Major Factors Offsetting Market Attractiveness*

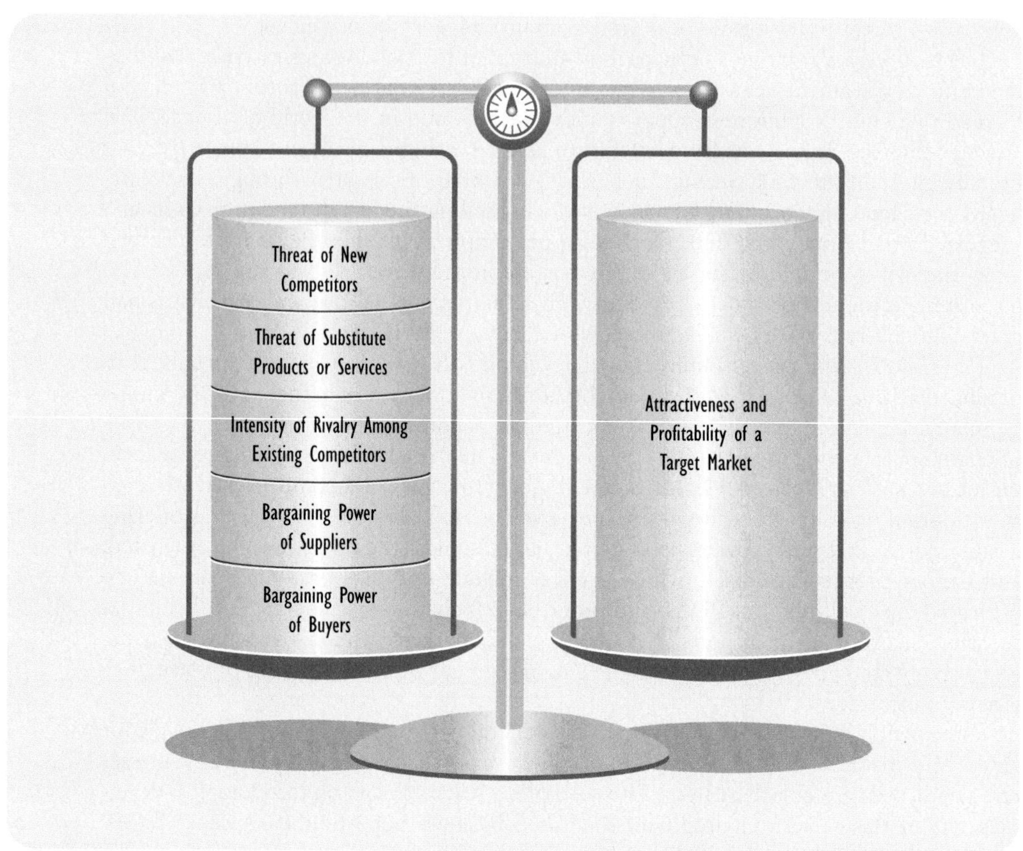

offers. In other words, analyzing Porter's five industry factors will provide a good overview of the competitive landscape.

Bill Waugh, founder of the restaurant chain Taco Bueno, helped develop the concept of Mexican fast-food restaurants in the 1960s, but only after he had extensively researched the fast-food industry in general and Mexican food in particular did he decide to launch his business. Based on what he learned, he wanted to acquire a franchise from El Chico, a national chain of Mexican restaurants, but he was turned down as a prospective franchisee. Not to be denied, Waugh decided that the research he had done provided a foundation for starting his own Mexican restaurant. Eighty-four restaurants later, he sold his business to Unigate, Ltd., a London-based company, for $32 million. Then, in the late 1980s, Waugh began the research process again, looking for his next venture. This time, he developed a concept for a new fast-food restaurant that sells hamburgers, which he named Burger Street. It is family owned and not franchised. By 2003, as a result of thorough research, he had 18 successful restaurants in operation in Texas and Oklahoma.[17]

Within the industry environment, it is important to determine the strength, position, and likely response of rival businesses. In fact, experts insist such analyses are critical to effective business plans. William A. Sahlman of Harvard University contends that every business plan should answer several questions about the competition:[18]

- Who are the new venture's current competitors?
- What resources do they control?
- What are their strengths and weaknesses?
- How will they respond to the new venture's decision to enter the industry?
- How can the new venture respond?

- Who else might be able to observe and exploit the same opportunity?
- Are there ways to co-opt potential or actual competitors by forming alliances?

This analysis helps an entrepreneur to evaluate the nature and extent of the competition and to fine-tune future plans. It can also help to identify business opportunities based on the competitive situation.

Big Dog Motorcycles knows the value of understanding the competition when crafting a strategy. In the heavyweight segment of motorcycle manufacturing, Harley-Davidson is the undisputed champion. However, there was a time when demand for its cruisers outstripped Harley's capacity to produce, leading to high dealer markups and two-year delays in the delivery of some models. That's when Big Dog Motorcycles entered the picture. Sheldon Coleman launched this startup in 1994 to respond to excess demand for Harleys, and it had more than $400,000 in sales the first year. Given untapped market potential, Big Dog focuses on providing highly customized cruisers at a premium price. As for the effectiveness of the strategy, the results speak for themselves. The company recently announced that it had posted nine straight years of record sales, exceeding $80 million in 2003 (an 82 percent increase over 2002).[19] The success of Big Dog Motorcycles proves the value of knowing the weaknesses of competitors and recognizing business opportunities.

Strategy expert Gary Hamel recommends that entrepreneurs take one more step when analyzing the industry—identifying the thinking that shapes behavior in the industry. For example, in the college textbook market, students assume they must buy a textbook rather than simply "rent" it for a semester. Such insights, when combined with awareness of changes in the general environment (including new technologies with market potential, lifestyle trends that call for new products or services, and political decisions that open foreign markets), can shed light on a path that leads to competitive advantage.[20]

Inside-Out Analysis

Identifying opportunities in the external environment is definitely worth the effort, but business concepts make sense only if they fit well with the internal potentials of the business. In other words, the entrepreneur's understanding of potential business opportunities should be combined with insights into what the entrepreneur and the startup are able to do. It should be noted that these concepts apply to existing businesses as well as startups.

RESOURCES AND CAPABILITIES In order to assess the internal potentials of a business, the entrepreneur must understand the difference between resources and capabilities. **Resources** are those basic inputs that a firm uses in its business, including capital, technology, equipment, and employees. Companies have both tangible and intangible resources. **Tangible resources** are visible and easy to measure. Plants and equipment, cash reserves, and trademarks are all tangible resources. These are very different from **intangible resources**, which are invisible and difficult to assess. Intangible assets include intellectual property rights such as patents and copyrights, as well as brand recognition and firm reputation.

resources
The basic inputs that a firm uses to conduct its business

tangible resources
Those organizational resources that are visible and easy to measure

intangible resources
Those organizational resources that are invisible and difficult to quantify

The terms are often used interchangeably, but resources technically are not the same as capabilities. Whereas resources are singular in nature, **capabilities** are best viewed as the integration of various resources in a way that boosts the firm's competitive advantage. Like a keyboard, which is of no practical value until it is integrated into a system of computer components, resources cannot provide competitive advantage until they are bundled into some useful configuration.

capabilities
The integration of various organizational resources that are deployed together to the firm's advantage

CORE COMPETENCIES Once entrepreneurs have an accurate view of the company's resources and capabilities, they are ready to identify its core competencies. **Core competencies** are those resources and capabilities that provide a firm with a competitive advantage over its rivals—such as the selection of gourmet coffees and the special "Starbucks experience" that have allowed the coffee icon to grow from a single store in the mid-1980s to more than 7,500 retail locations around the world today.[21] Core competencies emerge when a company learns over time to use its resources and capabilities in unique ways that reflect the "personality" of the enterprise. Entrepreneurs who can identify core competencies and apply them effectively can help their firms achieve a competitive advantage and superior performance.

core competencies
Those resources and capabilities that provide a firm with a competitive advantage over its rivals

Integrating Internal and External Analyses

SWOT analysis
A type of assessment that provides a concise overview of a firm's strategic situation

A solid foundation for competitive advantage requires a match between the strengths and weaknesses of a business and current opportunities and threats. This integration is best revealed through **SWOT analysis** (standing for *S*trengths, *W*eaknesses, *O*pportunities, and *T*hreats), which provides a simple overview of the firm's strategic situation. Exhibit 3-7 lists a number of factors that can be strengths, weaknesses, opportunities, and threats; however, these are merely representative of the countless possibilities that may exist.

In practice, a SWOT analysis provides a "snapshot view" of a firm's current situation. This is unfortunate, since firms perform better when they view their strategic setting as being in continuous motion. That is, firms with superior profitability are forward-thinking, using their current capabilities to position themselves for business opportunities to come. In short, the high-performance firms of the future will be those that improve on today's capabilities to meet the challenges of tomorrow.

Outside-in and inside-out analyses come together in the SWOT analysis to help an entrepreneur identify opportunities that match the venture. The entrepreneur can then determine the *best* opportunity by asking a few additional questions:

- Will the opportunity selected lead to others in the future?
- Will the opportunity help to build skills that open the door to new opportunities in the future?
- Will pursuit of the opportunity be likely to lead to competitive response by potential rivals?

Obviously, the most promising opportunities are those that lead to others (offering value and profitability over the long run), promote the development of additional skills that equip the firm to pursue new prospects, and yet do not provoke competitors to strike back.

Hugh Kenneth Holyoak has learned how one business can lead to another and how new skills can open the floodgates of opportunity. Holyoak, owner of Ken's Hatchery and Fish Farms, two commercial lakes, and a wild-pig hunting business, has introduced a number of fishy innovations over the years, including Ken's Floating Raceway Fish

EXHIBIT 3-7 | *Examples of SWOT Factors*

	POSITIVE FACTORS	NEGATIVE FACTORS
INTERNAL FACTORS	**Strengths** • Important core competencies • Financial strengths • Innovative capacity • Skilled or experienced management • Well-planned strategy • Effective entry wedge • Protection from competitive threats • Positive reputation in the marketplace • Proprietary technology	**Weaknesses** • Inadequate financial resources • Poorly planned strategy • Lack of management skills or experience • Inadequate innovation • Negative reputation in the marketplace • Inadequate facilities • Distribution problems • Inadequate marketing skills • Production inefficiencies
EXTERNAL FACTORS	**Opportunities** • Untapped market potential • New product or geographic market • Favorable shift in industry dynamics • Potential for market growth • Emerging technologies • Changes allowing foreign market entry • Deregulation • Increasing market fragmentation	**Threats** • New competitors • Rising demands of buyers or suppliers • Sales shifting to substitute products • Increased government regulation • Adverse shifts in the business cycle • Slowed market growth • Changing customer preferences • Adverse demographic shifts

Factory, the Scale-O-Matic Electric Fish Scaler, the E-Z Floating Fish Cage, and his own hybrid fish called the Georgia Giant. Noting that rising demand and disappearing wetlands have created a serious shortage of free-range frogs for dining and dissecting, he set his sights on the frog-farming business, offering an indoor frog-raising system that promises to generate substantial profits. Future prospects are bright indeed, given current demand. And because most frog farms are located in low-wage countries and use labor-intensive methods, competitive retaliation is unlikely.[22] By setting his sights on frog farming, Holyoak found a way to match external developments (rising demand for frogs) with internal capabilities (fish-raising know-how). With virtually no competition at the moment, related opportunities are sure to open up, and the skills Holyoak learns from frog farming are likely to benefit his fish-related operations as well.

Conducting outside-in and inside-out analyses and integrating their results builds a solid foundation for competitive advantage. With that foundation, the entrepreneur can begin to create a strategy for achieving superior financial performance, as illustrated in Exhibit 3-8.

SELECTING STRATEGIES THAT CAPTURE OPPORTUNITIES

5 *Explain broad-based strategy options and focus strategies.*

A **strategy** is, in essence, a plan of action for coordinating the resources and commitments of a business to boost its performance. Strategy selections should be guided by the firm's situation, rather than past choices, the latest industry fad, or whatever "feels" right at the moment. Choosing a strategy that makes sense for a particular entrepreneur and his or her startup is a critical first step toward superior performance. But keeping an eye on strategy options can also guide established companies toward success.

strategy
A plan of action that coordinates the resources and commitments of an organization to achieve superior performance

Broad-Based Strategy Options

Firms competing in the same industry can adopt very different strategies. Consider two lobster restaurants located on an island in the middle of Maine's Casco Bay, each competing directly with the other for nearly 50 years: Estes Lobster House and Cook's Lobster House. The two restaurants are close to each other and even share the same picture-perfect view, but they are miles apart in competitive approach.

Cook's is using marketing savvy and its notoriety from an appearance in a Visa credit-card commercial (because "they don't take American Express") to go upscale—expanding the menu, upgrading the décor, and raising prices to match. According to 42-year-old Curtis Parent, the current owner of Cook's, the goal is to attract a different crowd, a more sophisticated clientele from Boston and New York, who are willing to pay $20.95 for a 1¼-pound lobster with baked potato and salad. Business has increased more than 10 percent a year, so the strategy seems to be working.

EXHIBIT 3-8 *Setting a Direction for the Startup*

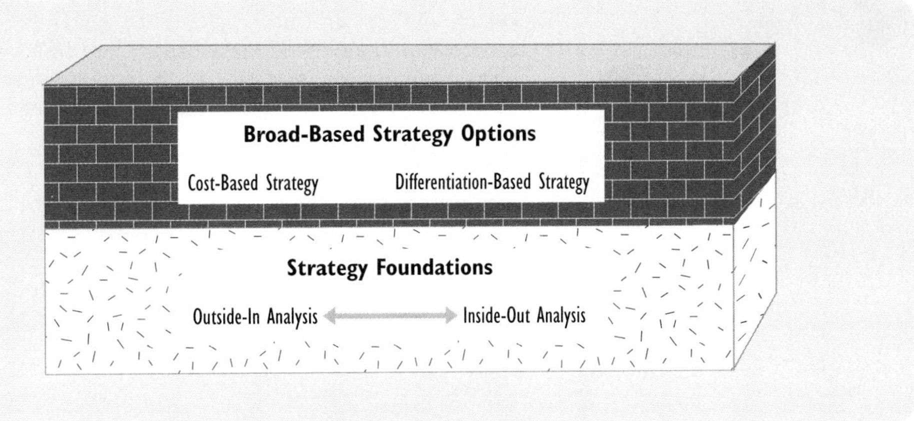

Estes's 58-year-old owner, Larry Croker, decided to take a different strategy, emphasizing low prices and paying close attention to costs. A one-pound boiled lobster in a paper tray costs $10.95, which Croker believes is about right. In his words, "People are looking for big portions and little prices." To hold the line on costs, Croker cut the menu in half and converted the operation to a counter-service system, which can function with only seven employees (down from 30 previously). He also takes competitive bids from suppliers for his paper needs, has set up a bulk deal for soft drinks, and relies on a local supplier for lobsters. The restaurant is popular, especially with local diners who think it offers better value for the money.

Though the restaurants differ in size, both strategies are working. During the summer months, Estes sells 4,000 pounds of lobster a week—about the same volume as Cook's. However, Estes is open less than half of the year, whereas Cook's is closed only from New Year's Day to Valentine's Day. Because of the shorter season and lower prices at Estes, this cost-based competitor grosses less than $1 million in revenue each year—well below the $2.5 million in annual revenue that Cook's takes in. But the lean cost structure at Estes makes it a successful business, while leaving room for the success of its upscale counterpart, Cook's.[23] The experiences of these two businesses illustrate how a competitive position can be guided by broad-based strategy options—creating an advantage related to cost or offering a differentiated product or service.

cost-based strategy
A plan of action that requires a firm to be the lowest-cost producer within its market

COST-BASED STRATEGY A **cost-based strategy**, like the one Estes Lobster House uses, requires a firm to be the lowest-cost producer within the market. The sources of cost advantages are varied, ranging from low-cost labor to efficiency in operations. Many people assume that cost-based strategies will not work for small companies, and this is often true. However, cost-advantage factors are so numerous and varied that, in some cases, small businesses may be able to use them with great success.

Kola Real is a fairly new startup, but today it is giving soft-drink giants like Coca-Cola and PepsiCo a real run for their money in Latin American markets. Kola Real was launched in 1988 by Eduardo and Mirtha Ananos when they realized that Coca-Cola was having a hard time getting its product to market in their home country, Peru. They took

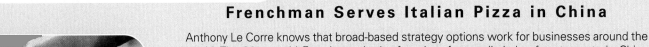

Living the Dream

Focus on the Customer

Frenchman Serves Italian Pizza in China

© Steve Mason/Photodisc Green/Getty Images

Anthony Le Corre knows that broad-based strategy options work for businesses around the world. The 32-year-old Frenchman is the founder of a small chain of restaurants in China called Hello Pizza, and business is good. However, the picture was not always so rosy; a change of strategy made all the difference.

In 1999, Le Corre started his first restaurant in Chongqing, a city in the heart of China, and sold pizzas for between $2.50 and $5 each. Unfortunately, it failed. But rather than give up, he chose to try again in 2001, this time in Shanghai. Based on lessons learned from his first attempt, Le Corre decided to focus his strategy on price this time around. He now offers single-serving pizzas for around $1.20, which is less than one-third of the price charged by his competitors. Le Corre claims Hello Pizza's prices are so low that the chain deserves a category of its own and really cannot be compared to market leader Pizza Hut and other rivals. The business is doing well. With four restaurants and three delivery centers in operation, Hello Pizza has already reached its break-even point.

But competing on price does not mean that a company can ignore quality and other features of differentiation. For example, Le Corre set up a central-processing facility, where all of the ingredients of his pizzas are prepared, weighed, and packaged before being shipped to the restaurants for "final assembly." This creates a more efficient, less costly process. But it also ensures consistent quality, which helps with marketing. According to Le Corre, "Our favorite way of marketing ourselves is through word of mouth from satisfied customers. So we market ourselves by providing the best value in all of the services we provide."

Sources: Leslie Chang, "Lessons from a $1.20 Pizza," *Wall Street Journal*, February 10, 2004, p. A14; EuroBiz, "Picolo Foodstuffs' Anthony Le Corre," www.sinomedia.net/eurobiz, November 2004; and http://www.chinatoday.com.cn/lachine/f2k2/f2k212/15.htm, March 5, 2004.

out a $30,000 mortgage on their home and moved to fill the gap, introducing their own backyard brew of a Coke-like beverage. Starting on a shoestring budget, they delivered their product in recycled beer bottles on which they had pasted their own labels by hand. Clearly, the company based its strategy on price right from the beginning.

> *To keep prices low, the Ananos family runs a lean operation. While Coke and Pepsi bottlers spend nearly 20% of their revenue on beverage concentrate from Atlanta-based Coke and PepsiCo [in] Purchase, N.Y., the Ananoses make their own. Instead of maintaining a fleet of trucks as most Coke and Pepsi bottlers do, Kola Real hires third parties for deliveries—even individuals with dented pick-up trucks. The company also does little advertising beyond an occasional radio spot, relying on word-of-mouth from penny-pinching housewives.*[24]

The strategy is paying off in a big way. Coke and Pepsi reign supreme in Mexico, whose amazing love for sweets has made it a $15 billion market for soft drinks—second in size only to the United States. However, Kola Real is making great gains there. After only two years in Mexico, the company has captured nearly 4 percent of the market with its product, which it sells under the "Big Cola" brand. In fact, the company has done so well that it really is no longer a small business. But the family is staying true to the strategy that has served it well. From its launch to the present, Kola Real has used price to establish its competitive advantage.

DIFFERENTIATION-BASED STRATEGY The second general option for building a competitive advantage is creating a **differentiation-based strategy**, an approach that emphasizes the uniqueness of a firm's product or service (in terms of some feature other than cost). A firm that can create and sustain an attractive differentiation strategy is likely to be a successful performer in the marketplace. For the strategy to be effective, the consumer must be convinced of the uniqueness and value of the product or service—whether real or perceived. A wide variety of operational and marketing tactics, ranging from promotion to design, can lead to product or service differentiation.

differentiation-based strategy
A plan of action designed to provide a product or service with unique attributes that are valued by consumers

Inventor Adam H. Oreck is convinced that his innovative footwear is the best in the world. Everyone has shoes, but Oreck believes that more people need to have "The World's Greatest Fitting Shoe"—the product he invented in 1984. His company, Tucson-based UFIT, Inc., offers shoes that combine stylish design with a patented lacing system that "interacts with the upper part of the shoe and the top of your foot." The result is a "closure system" that wraps the foot so as to provide the best support possible without putting pressure on the top of the foot. The design is certainly eye-catching. According to the company's Web site, several major footwear companies have attempted to copy the UFIT concept, but none has come close to duplicating its comfort-creating technology. It seems there is no substitute for Oreck's design; the product certainly stands apart from standard models of footwear.[25]

Focus Strategies

If one firm controlled the only known water supply in the world, its sales volume would be huge. This business would not be concerned about differences in personal preferences concerning taste, appearance, or temperature. It would consider its customers to be one market. As long as the water product was wet, it would satisfy everyone. However, if someone else discovered a second water supply, the first company's view of the market would change. The first business might discover that sales were drying up and take measures to modify its strategy. The level of rivalry would likely rise as competitors struggled for position in the industry.

If the potential for water sales were enormous, small businesses would eventually become interested in entering the market. However, given their limited resources and lack of experience, these companies would be more likely to succeed if they avoided head-to-head competition with industry giants and sought a protected market segment instead. In other words, they could be competitive if they implemented a **focus strategy**, adapting their efforts to concentrate on the needs of a specific niche within the market. To get started, these businesses might focus their resources on a fragment of the market that was small enough to escape the interest of major players (for example, filtered water delivered to individual homes) or perhaps take a completely new approach to permit access without immediate competitive response (for example, filling market gaps resulting from supply shortages).

focus strategy
A plan of action that isolates an enterprise from competitors and other market forces by targeting a restricted market segment

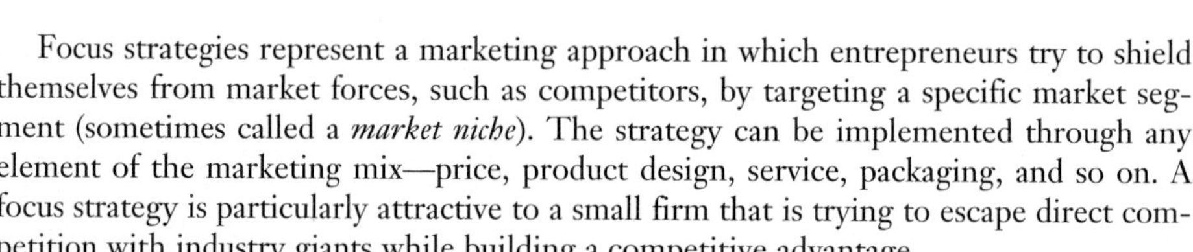

Focus strategies represent a marketing approach in which entrepreneurs try to shield themselves from market forces, such as competitors, by targeting a specific market segment (sometimes called a *market niche*). The strategy can be implemented through any element of the marketing mix—price, product design, service, packaging, and so on. A focus strategy is particularly attractive to a small firm that is trying to escape direct competition with industry giants while building a competitive advantage.

The two broad options discussed earlier—a cost-based strategy and a differentiation-based strategy—can also be used when focusing on a niche market. Although few entrepreneurs adopt a cost-based focus strategy, it certainly does happen. For example, Fredrick Bozin started the Watermarket Store in Fallbrook, California, with a cost-based focus strategy, using an efficient purification system to offer high-quality, good-tasting water to price-sensitive customers at a fraction of the price charged by competitors.[26]

Bozin's strategy varies greatly from the differentiation-based focus strategy that 32-year-old Chris Corso adopted. Following a brief, injury-plagued career as a minor-league baseball player, Corso has been trying to get back into the game—this time as the Chico, California–based maker and supplier of Sandlot Stiks, which he claims are the most durable wooden bats available. Though the three largest bat manufacturers control 90 percent of the market, niche firms like Corso's have developed a loyal following, especially among minor league players. Matt Ceriani is a catcher with one of the Arizona Diamondbacks' minor-league farm teams and a Sandlot Stiks customer. When asked about switching brands, Ceriani expresses his appreciation for the finer features of Corso's product: "It's like telling someone they have to switch from an IBM to a Mac." Corso makes around 2,500 bats a year, generating $70,000 in sales. And though new league rules may put him out of business, product quality and customer loyalty are keeping him in the game for now.[27]

Both Corso's bats and Bozin's water products serve limited market niches with a focus strategy. But the Watermarket Store competes on price, whereas Sandlot Stiks focuses on selling a unique, high-quality product to a narrow market segment.

ADVANTAGES AND DISADVANTAGES OF FOCUS STRATEGIES Focus strategies can be effective in both domestic and international markets. A decade ago, noted author John Naisbitt predicted that the future would see a huge global economy with smaller and smaller market niches. He further suggested that success in those niches would depend on speed to market and innovation, both of which typically are strengths of the small firm.[28] Recent evidence shows that Naisbitt's predictions are coming true, which suggests that small firms will likely see rich opportunities in the future, at home and abroad.

New ventures often fail because of poor market positioning or lack of a perceived advantage in the minds of customers in their target market. To minimize the chance of failure, an entrepreneur should consider the benefits of exploiting gaps in a market rather than going head to head with the competition. Focus strategies can be implemented in any of the following ways:

- Restricting focus to a single subset of customers
- Emphasizing a single product or service
- Limiting the market to a single geographical region
- Concentrating on superiority of the product or service

Many entrepreneurs have focused on market niches, and their creative efforts illustrate just how well these strategies can work. Historic Newspapers, Ltd., a British company, buys vintage newspapers from libraries as they convert their collections to digital and microfilm formats, and then the company sells them to individuals who want a souvenir to mark a specific date, such as a birthday or an anniversary. Business has been good. Historic Newspapers has more than 40 employees in the United States and Scotland and generates nearly $3 million a year from shipping old papers to interested customers in a vinyl portfolio with a certificate of authenticity. Their bestsellers usually cost around $40.

In 1976, Timothy Hughes founded a similar company in Williamsport, Pennsylvania, that follows a somewhat different strategy, focusing on newspapers that are collectible because they carry reports about historic events. The company had exceeded $680,000 in sales by early 2002.

Living the Dream

Focus on the Customer

A Bad Case of Puppy Love

Focus strategies usually emerge as creative answers to specific problems. At least that's the way it worked for Mitch Frankenberg and Jennifer Fredreck, a dog-loving husband-and-wife team from New York who moved to Vermont in search of a change. Having learned firsthand how difficult it is to travel with their dogs, they came up with the idea of starting a bed-and-breakfast for pet owners, which they call The Paw House Inn.

Courtesy of Mario D. Dogs Productions

They provide pet-friendly rooms that are easy to clean (in case of "accidents") and have even set up Mario's Playhouse, "a special inn just for dogs," where they can spend the night in a safe environment and mingle and play with other guests (dogs, that is). They even play special music to suit canine tastes. Dog owners love it! Because they know that their pets are being taken care of, Frankenberg says, the human guests "feel like they can relax when they are on vacation."

The place is getting rave reviews, and business is booming. In fact, the pet-sensitive couple is hoping to add a second location and to double their sales, which are already nearing $250,000 a year!

http://www.pawhouseinn.com

Sources: http://www.pawhouseinn.com, April 28, 2004, and Nichole L. Torres, "Good as Gold," *Entrepreneur,* October 2003, pp. 120, 123.

These companies and their competitors are trying to keep up with demand, but they all face the same problem—dwindling stocks of old newspapers. This is where creativity enters the picture. A number of these companies are adding reproductions to their offerings, even though customers prefer the real thing and the printing costs and royalties for reproductions cut into profits. Stephen A. Goldman Historic Newspapers in Parkton, Maryland, licenses images from old newspapers to television shows and co-publishes books that feature newspaper front pages on certain themes, such as baseball or the Civil War. The company reports rising revenues.[29] Yesterday's news is worth something after all, but it takes creativity to make the most of this market niche.

By selecting a particular focus strategy, an entrepreneur decides on the basic direction of the business. Such a choice affects the very nature of the business and is thus referred to as a **strategic decision**. A firm's overall strategy is formulated, therefore, as its leader decides how the firm will relate to its environment—particularly to the customers and competitors in that environment. One small business analyst expresses a word of caution about selecting a niche market:

strategic decision
A decision regarding the direction a firm will take in relating to its customers and competitors

> *Ventures that seek to capture a market niche, not transform or create an industry, don't need extraordinary ideas. Some ingenuity is necessary to design a product that will draw customers away from mainstream offerings and overcome the cost penalty of serving a small market. But features that are too novel can be a hindrance; a niche market will rarely justify the investment required to educate customers and distributors about the benefits of a radically new product.*[30]

Selection of a very specialized market is, of course, not the only possible strategy for a small firm. But focus strategies are very popular because they allow a small firm to operate in the gap that exists between larger competitors. If a small firm chooses to compete head to head with other companies, particularly large corporations, it must be prepared to distinguish itself in some way—for example, by attention to detail, highly personal service, or speed of service—in order to make itself a viable competitor.

Consider the extraordinary customer service of Zane's Cycles in Branford, Connecticut. Chris Zane has considered numerous modern business ideas to give his entrepreneurial venture the edge it needs to survive in the competitive world of bicycle dealerships. He has examined the merits of continuous learning, the benefits of surprise from guerrilla marketing, and the advantages of image branding. But the 39-year-old has determined that "doing anything to attract and keep customers" will continue to be the mainspring that drives the success of Zane's Cycles, one of the largest independent bicycle dealerships in the state. Zane gains and holds customers' loyalty by developing a relationship with them over time.

> *At Zane's Cycles, you never need a receipt to return merchandise. We know our customers, and we know them well. . . . A customer came into my store looking for a "Trail-a-bike," an accessory that would allow him to connect his daughter's bike to his. During our conversation, he explained that he had purchased a $350 trailer a couple of years earlier but had never used it because his daughter didn't like riding in it. I recalled his transaction, credited him the full amount of the purchase, and asked him to return the trailer when it was convenient. . . .*
>
> *Because I know my customers, I know that he has three daughters all under the age of seven. Since the initial trailer transaction, he has made four more purchases, and in three years as a customer, he has never asked for a discount, even during a multiple-bike transaction. Even if the trailer had been unsellable, the cost of the trailer was minimal compared to the profit we had already recognized from his previous purchases. To complete the story, we actually sold the trailer at a discount to a valuable customer within a week of having it returned.*[31]

Zane has been growing his business at 25 percent a year and now sells about 2,500 bikes a year from his 7,500-square-foot store. His advantage begins with a unique point of view. As Zane puts it, "The attitude [must change] from 'The customer is inconveniencing you and preventing you from doing your job' to 'The customer *is* your job.'"[32]

MAINTAINING THE POTENTIAL OF FOCUS STRATEGIES Firms that adopt a focus strategy tread a narrow line between maintaining a protected market and attracting competition. If their ventures are profitable, entrepreneurs must be prepared to face competition. In *Competitive Advantage*, Michael Porter cautions that a segmented market can erode under any of the following four conditions:[33]

1. The focus strategy is imitated.
2. The target segment becomes structurally unattractive because the structure erodes or because demand simply disappears.
3. The target segment's differences from other segments narrow.
4. New firms subsegment the industry.

The experience of Minnetonka, a small firm widely recognized as the first to introduce liquid hand soap, provides an example of how a focus strategy can be imitated. The huge success of its brand, Softsoap, quickly attracted the attention of several giants in the industry, including Procter & Gamble. Minnetonka's competitive advantage was soon washed away. Some analysts believe this happened because the company focused too much on the advantages of liquid soap in general and not enough on the particular benefits of Softsoap.

It should be clear that focus strategies do not guarantee a sustainable advantage. Small firms can boost their success, however, by developing and extending their competitive strengths. Good strategic planning can help point the way through these challenging situations.

PUTTING IT ALL TOGETHER

If you have come up with a business idea you are excited about, you have taken the first step toward an adventure into entrepreneurship. Performing an outside-in analysis will show you the really big picture (the general environment) and provide an overview of the industry and the competition. An inside-out analysis will help you match your resources and capabilities to the external environment. If a SWOT analysis suggests there is a fit between opportunities and threats in the external environment and the strengths and weaknesses of your planned enterprise, you can conclude that your *idea* is likely a promising business *opportunity*. Going one step further, you can use the strategy framework provided in this chapter to set a general direction for the venture—low cost or differentiation—and to learn how to find and maintain a market niche for your startup. You have come a long way!

But you may not be interested in starting a business from scratch. Is there room left in the entrepreneurial game for you? Absolutely! Chapters 4 and 5 will give you a closer look at franchise and buyout opportunities and help you figure out whether you want to join a family-owned business. These are all forms of entrepreneurship.

And what's the next step in moving toward the launch of the business of your dreams? A business plan! Chapters 6 through 12 will show you how to sort out the specifics of your business opportunity, from start to finish. After showing the importance of the business plan and providing a model to get you started (Chapter 6), the rest of Part 3 will help you plan for marketing (Chapter 7), human resources (Chapter 8), location and physical facilities (Chapter 9), and financial requirements (Chapters 10 and 11). Looking down the road a bit, Chapter 12 even shows you how to plan for the eventual harvest of your venture.

Looking Back

1 Identify several factors that determine whether an idea for a new venture is a good investment opportunity.

- To represent a good investment opportunity, a product or service must meet a real market need with respect to its function, quality, durability, and price.
- The fundamental requirements for a good business idea relate to market factors, competitive advantage, economics, management capability, and fatal flaws.

2 Give several reasons for starting a new business from scratch rather than buying a franchise or an existing business.

- Some entrepreneurs start businesses from scratch when they want to market a new product or service.
- Other entrepreneurs hope to tap into unique resources.
- Another reason that entrepreneurs start a new business from scratch is that they want to avoid undesirable features of existing companies.
- Still other entrepreneurs want the challenge of succeeding (or failing) on their own.

3 Distinguish among the different types and sources of startup ideas.

- Type A startup ideas are concerned with products or services that exist but are not present in all markets.
- Type B ideas involve new or relatively new technology.
- Type C ideas are based on new and improved ways of performing old functions.
- Sources of startup ideas include personal experience, hobbies, accidental discovery, and a deliberate search process.

4 Describe external and internal analyses that might shape new venture opportunities.

- Outside-in analysis considers the external environment, including the general environment and the industry environment.
- The major segments of the general environment are the macroeconomic, sociocultural, political/legal, technological, and global segments.
- The major forces that determine the level of competition within the industry environment are the threat of new competitors, the threat of substitute products or services, the intensity of rivalry among existing competitors, the bargaining power of suppliers, and the bargaining power of buyers.
- Opportunities arise for small businesses that are alert to changes in the general and industry environments.
- Inside-out analysis helps the entrepreneur to understand the internal potentials of the business.
- Tangible resources are visible and easy to measure, whereas intangible resources are invisible and difficult to quantify.
- Capabilities represent the integration of several resources in a way that boosts the firm's competitive advantage.
- Core competencies are those resources and capabilities that can be leveraged to enable a firm to do something that its rivals cannot do.
- A SWOT analysis provides an overview of a firm's strengths and weaknesses, as well as opportunities for and threats to the organization.

5 Explain broad-based strategy options and focus strategies.

- A competitive advantage can be created using broad-based strategy options—cost-based or differentiation-based strategies.
- A cost-based strategy requires the firm to become the lowest-cost producer within the market.
- Product differentiation is frequently used as a means of achieving superior performance.
- Focusing on a specific market segment is a strategy that small firms often use successfully.
- A focus strategy may involve restricting focus to a single subset of customers, emphasizing a single product or service, limiting the market to a single geographical region, or concentrating on product/service superiority.
- The basic direction of the business is chosen when the entrepreneur makes a strategic decision and selects a particular focus strategy.

Key Terms

competitive analysis, p. 50
Type A ideas, p. 52
Type B ideas, p. 52
Type C ideas, p. 52
serendipity, p. 54
general environment, p. 56
industry environment, p. 56
resources, p. 59
tangible resources, p. 59
intangible resources, p. 59
capabilities, p. 59
core competencies, p. 59
SWOT analysis, p. 60
strategy, p. 61
cost-based strategy, p. 62
differentiation-based strategy, p. 63
focus strategy, p. 63
strategic decision, p. 65

Discussion Questions

1. What is the difference between a good idea and a good opportunity?
2. Why might an entrepreneur prefer to launch an entirely new venture rather than buy an existing firm?
3. What are the three basic types of startup ideas? What are the most common sources of inspiration for startup ideas?
4. List the five segments of the general environment. Give a hypothetical example of a way in which each segment might affect a small business.
5. What are the primary factors shaping competition in an industry, according to Porter's model? In your opinion, which of these factors will have the greatest impact on industry prices and profits?
6. How are capabilities related to tangible and intangible resources?
7. What is SWOT analysis? How can SWOT analysis help the entrepreneur match opportunities in the external environment with organizational capabilities?
8. What are the two basic strategy options for creating a competitive advantage?
9. Explain what is meant by the term *focus strategy.*
10. What are the advantages and disadvantages of a focus strategy? What must an entrepreneur know and do to maintain the potential of a focus strategy?

You Make the Call

SITUATION 1

Marty Lane worked for a card company specializing in invitations and announcements. Every day for 25 years, he went to an office, sat at a desk, and took orders over the phone. He hated it. He was bored out of his mind. He didn't know what to do.

So he began skimming the business opportunities section of the Sunday *New York Times.* He wasn't sure what he was looking for. At almost 50 years of age, he had few business skills. Accounting was a foreign language to him. He figured that if he ever bought a business, it would have to be one that didn't require much specialized knowledge—something that would be relatively easy to manage. He considered a franchise, but he found that the good ones were very expensive. Then he came across an Italian-bread route for sale. He thought "How difficult could it be to run a delivery route?" He called the phone number in the ad and spoke with the business broker who was handling the sale.

It turned out that the route was in Queens, New York, not far from where Lane and his wife, Annabelle, lived. It was a one-person operation. The individual who owned it had had the route for 20 years and took home about $65,000 a year. He wanted $200,000 for the business, but he was willing to help finance the deal. If Lane would put $60,000 down, he could pay the balance over five years at 10 percent interest, or about $35,000 a year. That would leave Lane with an annual income of $30,000 until the debt was paid. Combined with Annabelle's salary, it would be enough to make ends meet. If he worked hard, moreover, he could expect his sales, and his income, to grow by 10 to 15 percent a year.

It seemed perfect. Lane went to meet with the owner and returned sounding even more enthusiastic. "This is a can't-miss deal," he told his wife. "The guy has signed contracts with all the places he delivers to, and none of them is more than 25 miles from here. I could do the entire route in seven hours."

However, Annabelle wasn't buying. "You're not quitting your job until you talk to an expert," she said. Lane agreed to meet with a broker.

On the date of the meeting, Lane brought all his paperwork along. He laid out the terms of the deal in great detail. "What do you think?" he asked.

The broker said, "Tell me something, Marty. Do you like this business?"

He shrugged. "I can't really say. I haven't tried it yet."

"What's involved in it besides picking up the bread and delivering it to the stores?"

"I'm not sure," he said. "Whatever it is, it can't be that complicated."

"What happens if the truck breaks down?"

"I don't know," he said. "I guess I'll just work it out."

After asking Lane a series of questions along those lines, the broker finally said, "Listen, Marty. You want to know if this deal makes sense from a financial standpoint. That's easy to check. The guy has an income tax return, and his sales are verifiable. This isn't a cash business, after all. He sells to delis and supermarkets. They pay by check. We can go over his expense figures and make sure they're realistic, but my guess is that the deal is OK. If you're asking me whether I could negotiate him down a little, the answer is probably yes."

Lane turned to his wife: "See, I told you he'd approve."

The broker said, "I didn't approve anything. Only you can do that, and you're not ready to."

"What do you mean?" he asked.

"You haven't done your homework," the broker said. "You don't know what you're actually going to do in this business, and you don't know if you'll be happy doing it."

"How am I going to find that out?" Lane asked.

Question 1 How would you suggest that Lane find out if he would be happy in this business?

Question 2 Would you recommend that Lane buy the business, given the asking price and terms of the deal?

Question 3 Is Lane relying too much on nonquantitative factors?

SITUATION 2

Amy Wright is the owner of Fit Wright Shoes, a manufacturer of footwear located in Alice, Texas. Her company has pledged that all customers will have a lifetime replacement guarantee on all footwear bought from the company. This guarantee applies to the entire shoe, even though another company makes parts of the product.

Question 1 Do you think a lifetime guarantee is too generous for this kind of product? Why or why not?

Question 2 What impact will this policy have on quality standards in the company? Be specific.

Question 3 What alternative customer service policies would you suggest?

SITUATION 3

Jay Sorenson of Portland, Oregon, created a product called the Java Jacket, which is a patented honeycombed insulating sleeve that slides over a paper cup containing a hot beverage to make it comfortable to hold. Having introduced the new product to the market, Sorenson already has cut deals with coffeehouses, specialty stores, and convenience stores nationwide. He started the business with $15,000 in 1993, but his 2003 sales were projected to be between $12 and 15 million. Sorenson is now in a position where he would like to continue expanding his business, but he is concerned that large and established competitors could introduce their own variations of the same product.

Source: Don Debelak, "Send in the Clones," *Entrepreneur,* September 2003, pp. 128–132.

Question 1 Will the market for Sorenson's product continue to grow in the years ahead?

Question 2 If he is successful, what sources of competition should he expect?

Question 3 What steps would you recommend that he take to protect his company from the onslaught of competition that is likely to come?

Experiential Exercises

1. Select a product that is manufactured by a small business, and look for the likely drivers of its attributes in the dynamics of the general and/or industry environments.
2. Examine a recent issue of a business publication, and describe the type of target market strategy you believe the magazine uses.
3. Visit a local small retailer, and ask the manager to describe the firm's customer service policies.
4. Working in small groups, write a brief but specific description of the best target market for a new product that is familiar to most of the class. A member of each group should read the group's market profile to the class.
5. Interview the owner of a local small business about the venture's performance outcomes. Find out what results were achieved, and then systematically explore how those performance outcomes have been reinvested in the business. For example, if the venture has yielded considerable customer loyalty, examine how that commitment has been leveraged for future results.
6. On the Web site of a small business, identify the factors in the external (general and industry) environment and the internal (organizational) environment around which the business seems to have been built. Does it appear to you that the firm is more sensitive to internal or external factors? Given your knowledge of the firm's business, is that good or bad?
7. The Electric Transportation Company sells electrically powered bicycles, like the ETC Express. Review the information found at http://store.nycewheels.com/etc.html. Using the terminology introduced in this chapter, identify the specific type of strategy the Electric Transportation Company is using as it expands its business.

Exploring the Web

1. Reread what this chapter has to say about the external and internal analyses that might help you evaluate a new venture opportunity. To assess the impact of these factors on your business idea, go to the Web site of Bplans.com (**http://www.bplans.com/st/#**), and click on the link to Success Potential Quiz. The quiz will appear in another window.
   a Take the quiz, and print out your score.
   b. What does your score imply for the future of your business?
2. It's never too early to start thinking about where you will get the funding to start your business. Go to **http://www.myownbusiness.org/s8**, and read the information about business financing on the Session 8 page.
   a. Take the quiz at the end of the article, and print the results.
   b. Where do you think you might find funding for your business idea?
   c. Name three other funding sources for a startup business not touched on by the My Own Business writers.
3. The editors of *Inc.* publish a series of "How-To" guides on the magazine's Web site at **http://www.inc.com** to help business owners start, run, and grow successful businesses. Go to the "How-To" guide on finance and capital at **http://www.inc.com/guides/finance/20797.html**.
   a. From among those listed on this Web site, read at least five articles on raising startup capital.
   b. Write a brief description of the information in the articles you selected, and summarize the best of the tips for raising startup capital.
4. Familiarize yourself with the resources provided by QuickMBA that can help a business owner "make sense of strategy." Go to **http://www.quickmba.com/strategy/**.
   a. Click on the PEST Analysis link and read about the PEST framework.
   b. Follow the SWOT Analysis link and use the information you find there to create a SWOT analysis for your small business or a small business that you're familiar with.

Case 3

BIOLIFE LLC (P. 530)

This case describes the experiences of two research scientists who discovered a new product and then launched a startup to take their innovative product to the market.

Alternative Cases for Chapter 3:

FRANCHISES AND BUYOUTS

In the Video Spotlight

Auntie Anne's http://www.auntieannes.com

Many small businesspeople begin by buying a franchise. Even though franchising may be seen as a silver bullet for beginning the entrepreneurial life, it is not without its challenges. In fact, the most desirable franchises can be hard to come by; an example is Auntie Anne's.

Company founder Anne Beiler started as the owner of a farmer's market stand in Downingtown, Pennsylvania, which she grew into a franchisor of 800 locations that generate $232 million in annual sales. Early on, Beiler figured out the way to grow her company was to offer franchise locations, so she sought out advice from business professionals and consulting organizations that specialized in franchising. Beiler developed a detailed operations system, and she only accepts franchisees who do things exactly by the book, the Auntie Anne way. Beiler also wants franchisees to be comfortable with the system and the product. Franchisees must have the money to buy a franchise, but they must also be successfully interviewed by Beiler and her management team. Once an agreement is signed, potential franchisees go to the training facility to learn the processes and culture, but that doesn't guarantee them a franchise: They can still be kicked out if they don't fit with the company's culture and goals. Because of Beiler's strict requirements, only 1 in 500 applicants becomes an Auntie Anne's franchisee.

Video material provided by Hattie Bryant, Producer of Small Business School, the series on PBS Stations, Worldnet, and the Web at http://www.smallbusinessschool.org.

Chapter 4

Looking Ahead

After studying this chapter, you should be able to

1 *Identify the major pros and cons of franchising.*

2 *Explain franchising options and the structure of the industry.*

3 *Describe the process for evaluating a franchise opportunity.*

4 *List four reasons for buying an existing business and describe the process of evaluating a business.*

Chapter 3 examined how entrepreneurs take their ideas, develop them into opportunities, and pursue their entrepreneurial dreams by starting a business from scratch. This chapter considers franchises and buyouts—startup options involving existing businesses.

THE PROS AND CONS OF FRANCHISING

1 *Identify the major pros and cons of franchising.*

"Look before you leap" is an old adage that should be heeded by entrepreneurs considering franchising. Entrepreneurs should not let their enthusiasm blind them to the realities—both good and bad—of franchising. Weighing the purchase of a franchise against alternative methods of starting a business is an important task, which requires careful consideration of many factors. Exhibit 4-1 illustrates the major advantages and disadvantages of franchising.

Given the different personal goals and circumstances of individuals, franchising will not be the ideal choice for all prospective entrepreneurs. However, many people find a franchise to be the best alternative. When you are evaluating future entrepreneurial opportunities, carefully weigh the pros and cons of franchising presented in this chapter.

In this book, we use a broad definition of franchising to encompass the term's diversity: **Franchising** is a marketing system revolving around a two-party legal agreement whereby one party (the **franchisee**) is granted the privilege to sell a product or service and conduct business as an individual owner but is required to operate according to methods and terms specified by the other party (the **franchisor**). For example, Subway (the franchisor) franchises quick-service, fast-food outlets to local owners (franchisees).

franchising
A marketing system involving a legal agreement, whereby the franchisee conducts business according to terms specified by the franchisor

franchisee
An entrepreneur whose power is limited by a contractual relationship with a franchisor

franchisor
The party in a franchise contract that specifies the methods to be followed and the terms to be met by the other party

Advantages of Franchising

Buying a franchise can be attractive for a variety of reasons. The greatest overall advantage by far is its probability of success. Business data on failures of franchises are difficult to find and evaluate. Nevertheless, the success rate for franchises seems to be much higher than that for nonfranchised businesses. One explanation for the lower failure rate is that most franchisors are highly selective when granting franchises. Many potential franchisees who qualify financially are still rejected.

There are three additional, and more specific, reasons why a franchise opportunity is appealing. A franchise is typically attractive because it offers (1) training, (2) financial assistance, and (3) operating benefits that are not easily available to the entrepreneur starting a business from scratch. Naturally, different franchises vary in strength in all these aspects. For example, McDonald's offers excellent training but no financing.

TRAINING The training received from franchisors is invaluable to many small entrepreneurs because it alleviates weaknesses in their managerial skills. Training by the franchisor often begins with an initial period of a few days or a few weeks at a central training school or another established location and then continues at a franchise site.

The training by Kwik Kopy Printing, a successful business services franchisor, is very extensive, covering the technical aspects of running a printing business as well as the standard topics of accounting, computer purchasing and use, and leadership. Its training

EXHIBIT 4-1 *Major Pluses and Minuses in the Franchising Calculation*

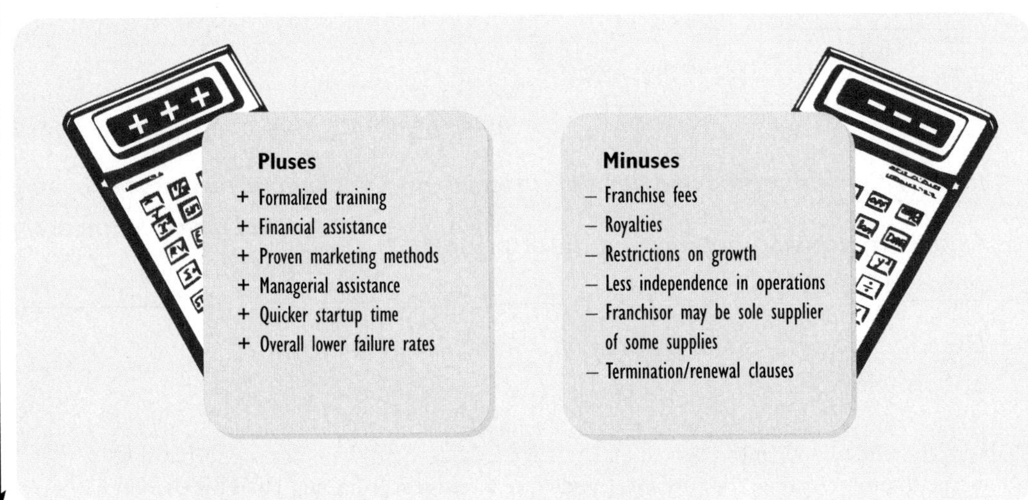

facility, located in the picturesque city of Northwest Forest, a few miles from Houston, Texas, looks like an amusement park, with a full-size replica of the Alamo. However, franchise trainees quickly realize that the three-week training program is very demanding. Classes start at 7:00 A.M. and conclude at 6:00 P.M., Monday through Friday, and they continue for a half-day on Saturday.

Pluses
+ Formalized training
+ Financial assistance
+ Proven marketing methods
+ Managerial assistance
+ Quicker startup time
+ Overall lower failure rates
Minuses
– Franchise fees
– Royalties
– Restrictions on growth
– Less independence in operations
– Franchisor may be sole supplier of some supplies
– Termination/renewal clauses

Another famous franchisor, McDonald's, is widely recognized for its off-site franchisee training effort at Hamburger University. Subway is also a strong believer in initial training for prospective franchisees. Consider this recent description of Subway's training philosophy:

Living the Dream — *Entrepreneurial Challenges*

Got Junk?

Courtesy of 1-800-Got-Junk?

The brightly painted truck reads "1-800-GOT-JUNK?" and serves as a rolling advertisement. Robert Burns, who formerly did fundraising and development for the Boy Scouts of America, purchased the Louisville territory of the relatively new franchise.

Burns had known for some time that he wanted to own a business, but he didn't know what business. After deciding that a franchise would be his best bet, he began looking into available franchise opportunities and discovered 1-800-GOT-JUNK? Burns carefully researched the company and its reputation before making the purchase. He also attended a seminar entitled "Owning Your Own Business," sponsored by the Louisville SCORE chapter. The seminar provided him with helpful information in the early phases of becoming a business owner.

The company hauls "junk" from both homes and businesses. Prices are based on volume: from one-eighth of the space in a truck to the whole truck. Anything that is still usable or can be recycled does not go to waste. All usable items are delivered to Goodwill or the Salvation Army; recyclables go to recycling centers; everything else goes to the landfill. The company does not pick up paints, chemicals, or hazardous materials.

Burns began the business with one truck and has since added a second. His entry costs into the business included a franchise fee, the price of a truck, and various other startup costs. Financing was done through Stock Yards Bank with an SBA-guaranteed loan.

1-800-GOT-JUNK? is growing, and Burns is working hard to develop a solid base of commercial customers. Even though it's hard work, Burns is enjoying himself. He says, "Since I left my job at the Boy Scouts, I don't feel like I have gone to work a single day. Building this business is like playing a game, and I am playing to win."

Sources: http://www.sba.gov/ky/kysuccess.html, August 2003; and personal communication with Robert Burns, April 2004.

People who see lunchmeat in their futures have to first prove they were paying attention in grade school. All would-be franchisees are given a test of basic math skills and English language ability, according to Subway's director of training, Alexander Dembski. "If you can't pass that test, you won't become a franchisee. We were getting in people who were sometimes very nice people, but did not have the ability to communicate with customers or employees, or did not have the basic math ability to understand how to analyze their business. We do them no favor letting them come in. We hurt ourselves, and we hurt them."

Once past that hurdle, the new franchisee gets into former high school history teacher Dembski's classroom at Subway headquarters in Milford, Conn. Dembski runs a two-week, 55-hour program and then sends students to Subway stores near headquarters for an additional 34 hours of on-the-job training.

The new franchisees spend an entire Saturday, usually the busiest lunch day of the week, helping out at a local store. "That full day in-store just made the loose ends come together for them," Dembski says. By the second week, the new sandwich makers run a shop by themselves.

There is a final exam at Subway, and about 10 percent of new franchisees flunk. They get to retake courses they may need or get one-on-one instruction if necessary. But until they pass, they can't own a Subway sandwich shop.[1]

Naturally, both the nature of a product and the type of business affect the amount and type of training needed by the franchisee. In most cases, training constitutes an important advantage of the franchising system, as it permits individuals who have had little training or education to start and succeed in businesses of their own.

Subsequent training and guidance may involve refresher courses and/or visits by a company representative to the franchisee's location from time to time. The franchisee may also receive manuals and other printed materials that provide guidance in operating the business. Although the franchisor normally places considerable emphasis on observing strict controls, much of the continuing training goes far beyond the application of controls. In particular cases, however, it may be difficult to distinguish between guidance and control.

Although many franchising systems have developed excellent training programs, be aware that this is by no means universal. Some unscrupulous promoters falsely promise extensive training and then leave the entrepreneur to run his or her own business with little or no guidance.

FINANCIAL ASSISTANCE The costs of starting an independent business are often high, and the typical entrepreneur's sources of capital are quite limited. The entrepreneur's standing as a prospective borrower is weakest at this time. By teaming up with a franchising organization, the aspiring franchisee may enhance her or his likelihood of obtaining financial assistance.

If the franchising organization considers the applicant to be a suitable prospect with a high probability of success, it frequently extends a helping hand financially. The franchisee is seldom required to pay upfront the complete cost of establishing the business. In addition, the beginning franchisee is normally given a payment schedule that can be met through successful operation. For example, in the early days of the Jiffy Lube franchise, the franchisor would loan the franchisee funds to purchase the real estate for a store. Also, the franchisor may permit the franchisee to delay payments for products or supplies obtained from the parent organization, thus increasing the franchisee's working capital.

Association with a well-established franchisor may also improve a new franchisee's credit standing with a bank. The reputation of the franchising organization and the managerial and financial controls that it provides serve to recommend the new franchisee to a banker. Also, the franchisor will frequently cosign a note with a local bank, thus guaranteeing the franchisee's loan.

The U.S. Small Business Administration (SBA) has introduced the Franchise Registry (http://www.franchiseregistry.com), which greatly expedites loan processing for small business franchisees. The Registry "enables lenders and SBA local offices to verify a franchise system's lending eligibility through the Internet. This reduces red tape, time, and cost for all concerned."[2] Listing on this registry means that the SBA has found that the particular franchise agreement does not impose unacceptable control provisions on the franchisee. Therefore, loan applications for registered franchises can be reviewed and processed more quickly.

Living the Dream

Focus on the Customer

Courtesy of Culver Franchising System, Inc.

Are You Ready to Work?

Craig and Lea Culver are particular about who buys their franchises and how their fast-food franchisees treat customers. When first developing the concept for Culver's back in 1984, the Culver family focused on treating customers right, and they still do. They now have 216 restaurants and revenue of $27 million annually.

The Culvers have been very careful in their selection of franchisees. Candidates must show a net worth of $500,000. "I won't even interview them if the right numbers aren't on the application," says Thomas Wakefield, who helps line up potential franchisees. And even if a franchisee can borrow the necessary capital, he or she must first complete a 60-hour evaluation. Once the paperwork for the chosen site has been submitted, the franchisee must attend a 16-week training program, including working in the classroom and on the job at a family-owned Culver's and assisting with two new restaurant openings. Ongoing training happens at the restaurant, off-site seminars, and an annual convention, as well as in Culver's Learning Support Center.

Most franchises are profitable in two years. "I want to create millionaires," says Craig Culver.

http://www.culvers.com

Sources: Erin Killian, "Butter 'Em Up," *Forbes*, Vol. 171, No. 12 (June 9, 2003), pp. 175–176; http://www.culvers.com/AboutCulvers/History.aspx, August 2003; and personal communication with Barbara Behling, director of Culver's public relations, May 2004.

OPERATING BENEFITS Most franchised products and services are widely known and accepted. For example, consumers will readily buy Baskin-Robbins ice cream or use PIP Printing services because they are aware of the reputation these businesses have. Travelers will recognize a restaurant or a motel because of its name or type of roof or some other feature such as the "Golden Arches" of McDonald's. They may turn into a Denny's restaurant or a Holiday Inn because of their previous experiences with the chain and their knowledge that they can depend on the food and service these outlets provide. Thus, franchising offers both a proven line of business and product/service identification.

An entrepreneur who enters into a franchising agreement acquires the right to use the franchisor's nationally advertised trademark or brand name. This serves to identify the local enterprise with the widely recognized product or service. Of course, the value of product identification depends on the type of product or service and the extent to which it has been promoted. In any case, the franchisor must maintain the value of its name by continued advertising and promotion.

In addition to a proven line of business and readily identifiable products or services, franchisors offer well-developed and thoroughly tested methods of marketing and management. The manuals and procedures supplied to franchisees enable them to function more efficiently from the start. This is one reason why franchisors insist on the observance of quality methods of operation and performance. If a franchise were allowed to operate at a substandard level, it could easily destroy customers' confidence in the entire system.

The existence of proven products and methods, however, does not guarantee that a franchise will succeed. For example, a location that the franchisor's marketing research shows to be satisfactory may turn out to be inferior. Or the franchisee may lack ambition or perseverance. But the fact that a franchisor has a record of successful operation proves that the system can work, because it has worked elsewhere.

Limitations of Franchising

Franchising is like a coin—it has two sides. We have presented the positive side of franchising, but it is important that you also learn about its negative side. Four shortcomings, in particular, permeate the franchise form of business: (1) the costs associated with the franchise, (2) the operating restrictions that can be a part of the franchise agreement, (3) the loss of entrepreneurial independence, and (4) a lack of franchisor support.

FRANCHISE COSTS Generally speaking, higher costs characterize the better known and more successful franchises. Franchise costs have several components, all of which need to be recognized and considered.

1. *Initial franchise fee.* The total cost of a franchise begins with an initial franchise fee, which may range from several hundred to many thousands of dollars. The initial fee for a Smoothie King is $25,000; McDonald's initial fee is $45,000.
2. *Investment costs.* Significant costs may be involved in renting or building an outlet and stocking it with inventory and other equipment. Also, certain insurance premiums, legal fees, and other startup expenses must be paid. It is often recommended that funds be available to cover personal expenses and emergencies for at least six months. A reputable franchisor will always provide a detailed estimate of investment costs; Exhibit 4-2 shows the information provided by Great Clips, a haircare salon franchise. Curves for Women, a women's workout facility, requires that a prospective franchisee have a minimum of $14,900 in startup cash. The total net worth requirement for a KFC restaurant exceeds $1,000,000—the prospective franchisee must have cash and other personal assets worth this amount.
3. *Royalty payments.* A common practice is for the franchisor to receive continuing royalty payments, based on a percentage of the franchisee's gross income. McAlister's Deli, for example, charges a 5 percent royalty fee. McDonald's currently charges a "service fee" of 4 percent of monthly sales plus the greater of (a) a monthly base rent or (b) a percentage rent that represents at least 8.5 percent of monthly sales.
4. *Advertising costs.* Many franchisors require that franchisees contribute to an advertising fund to promote the franchise. These fees are generally 1 to 2 percent of sales or even more.

If entrepreneurs could generate the same level of sales by setting up an independent business, they would save the franchise fee and some of the other costs. However, if the franchisor provides the benefits previously described, the money franchisees pay for their relationship with the franchisor may prove to be a very good investment.

EXHIBIT 4-2 | *Estimate of Investment Costs by Great Clips*

Description	Low	High
Initial Franchise Fee	$20,000	$ 20,000
Great Clips, Inc., Market Development Ad Fund Contribution	5,000	5,000
Total Initial Franchisee Fees	**$25,000**	**$ 25,000**
Travel and Living Expenses while Training	$1,500	$ 2,500
Architectural Fees	150	150
Leasehold Improvements	15,000	40,000
Rent and Security Deposits	1,000	8,000
Fixtures, Signage and Furnishings (including computer)	25,000	35,000
Freight	1,200	2,200
Local Sales Tax on Fixtures, Signage and Furnishings	0	1,500
Opening Inventory and Supplies	4,700	6,400
Grand Opening Advertising	10,000	10,000
Insurance	1,000	1,800
Lease Liability Fee	0	3,000
Lease Review Fee	0	1,500
Working Capital	12,000	45,000
Total Additional Fees	**$71,550**	**$157,050**
Total	**$96,550**	**$182,050**

Note: This is an estimate only of the capital needed to open and operate your salon during the initial 12 months after you open for business. Great Clips cannot guarantee that you will not have additional expenses starting the business.

Source: http://www.greatclipsfranchise.com/investment.htm; April 27, 2004.

RESTRICTIONS ON BUSINESS OPERATIONS Franchisors, understandably concerned about the image of their businesses, make every effort to control how franchisees conduct certain aspects of the franchise business. Thus, the franchisee is restricted in her or his ability to use personal business judgment. The following types of control are frequently exercised by a franchisor:

- Restricting sales territories
- Requiring site approval for the retail outlet and imposing requirements regarding outlet appearance
- Restricting goods and services offered for sale
- Restricting advertising and hours of operation

LOSS OF INDEPENDENCE Frequently, individuals leave salaried employment for entrepreneurship because they dislike working under the direct supervision and control of others. But when entering into a franchise relationship, such individuals may find that a different pattern of supervision has taken over. The franchisee surrenders a considerable amount of independence in signing a franchise agreement.

Even though the franchisor's influence on business operations may be helpful in ensuring success, the level of control exerted may be unpleasant to an entrepreneur who cherishes independence. In addition, some franchise contracts go to extremes, covering unimportant details or specifying practices that are more helpful to others in the chain than to the local operation. For example, a food franchise may be prevented from selling a nonapproved product in a local market.

Also, entrepreneurs should recognize that they can lose the right to a franchise if they do not abide by performance standards or fail to pay royalties. Additionally, there is no guarantee that a franchise will be renewed beyond the contracted time, which is typically 15 to 20 years.

LACK OF FRANCHISOR SUPPORT Just like a marriage, a franchisor/franchisee relationship can experience stress, which may lead to a breakup. Perceived lack of franchisor support sometimes creates disputes, especially when the franchisee believes the franchisor is not honoring its commitments.

Disputes may revolve around a lack of continued training, poor promotional support, or a number of other issues. Once a communication breakdown occurs between the two parties, the well-being of the franchise is in jeopardy. Entrepreneurs who are considering purchasing a franchise should recognize this inherent disadvantage of franchising.

FRANCHISING OPTIONS AND THE STRUCTURE OF THE FRANCHISING INDUSTRY

2 Explain franchising options and the structure of the industry.

The term *franchising* was derived from a French word meaning "freedom" or "exemption from duties." In business, franchising describes a unique type of business option that offers entrepreneurs the possibility of reducing the overall risk associated with buying an independent business or starting a business from scratch. The franchise arrangement allows new business operators to benefit from the accumulated business experience of all members of the franchise system.

Franchising Options

franchise contract
The legal agreement between franchisor and franchisee

franchise
The privileges conveyed in a franchise contract

product and trade name franchising
A franchise agreement granting the right to use a widely recognized product or name

The potential value of any franchising arrangement is defined by the rights contained in a legal agreement known as the **franchise contract**; the rights it conveys are called the **franchise.** The extent and importance of these rights may be quite varied. When the main benefit the franchisee receives is the privilege of using a widely recognized product name, the arrangement between the franchisor (supplier) and the franchisee (buyer) is called **product and trade name franchising**. Automobile tire outlets carrying the Goodyear brand name and soft drink bottlers distributing Dr Pepper are both engaged in this type of franchising.

Alternatively, entrepreneurs who receive an entire marketing and management system are participating in a broader type of arrangement referred to as **business format**

franchising. Fast-food outlets (e.g., Burger King), hotels and motels (e.g., Radisson), and business services (e.g., Mail Boxes Etc.) typically engage in this type of franchising. The volume of sales and the number of franchise units associated with business format franchising have increased steadily over the years.

business format franchising A franchise arrangement whereby the franchisee obtains an entire marketing system geared to entrepreneurs

A **master licensee** is a firm or individual having a continuing contractual relationship with a franchisor to sell its franchises. This independent company or businessperson is a type of middleman or sales agent. Master licensees are responsible for finding new franchisees within a specified territory. Sometimes, they even provide support services such as training and warehousing, which are more traditionally provided by the franchisor. Also gaining widespread usage is **multiple-unit ownership**, in which a single franchisee owns more than one unit of the franchised business. Some of these franchisees are **area developers**—individuals or firms that obtain the legal right to open several outlets in a given area.

master licensee An independent firm or individual acting as a sales agent with the responsibility for finding new franchisees within a specified territory

multiple-unit ownership Holding by a single franchisee of more than one franchise from the same company

area developers Individuals or firms that obtain the legal right to open several franchised outlets in a given area

Piggyback franchising refers to the operation of a retail franchise within the physical facilities of a host store. Examples of piggyback franchising include a cookie franchise doing business inside an Arby's fast-food outlet and a Krispy Kreme donut franchise operating within a Wal-Mart store. This form of franchising benefits both parties. The host store is able to add a new product line, and the franchisee obtains a location near prospective customers.

piggyback franchising The operation of a retail franchise within the physical facilities of a host store

The Structure of the Franchising Industry

Franchisors and franchisees are the two main parties in the franchise industry. A franchisor may be a manufacturer or another channel member (a wholesaler or retailer) that has an attractive business concept worthy of duplication. As shown in Exhibit 4-3, a franchise can be sold by the franchisor directly to individual franchisees or marketed through master licensees or area developers. Most franchisors also own one or more outlets that are not franchised. These outlets are referred to as company-owned stores.

In addition to these parties, the franchising industry contains other important groups. These groups, called *facilitators*, include industry associations, governmental agencies, and private businesses.

For example, International Franchise Association (http://www.franchise.org), or IFA, is an industry association that serves franchise members by attempting to safeguard and enhance the business and regulatory environment of the industry. It has over 30,000 members—franchisors, franchisees, and suppliers—that operate in more than 100 countries. Nevertheless, the IFA is highly selective, and not all companies applying for membership are accepted. Referring to itself as "The Voice of Franchising," the IFA sponsors legal and government affairs conferences, franchise management workshops, seminars on franchisor/franchisee relations, and trade shows. The IFA also champions the causes of minority

EXHIBIT 4-3 *The Structure of Franchising*

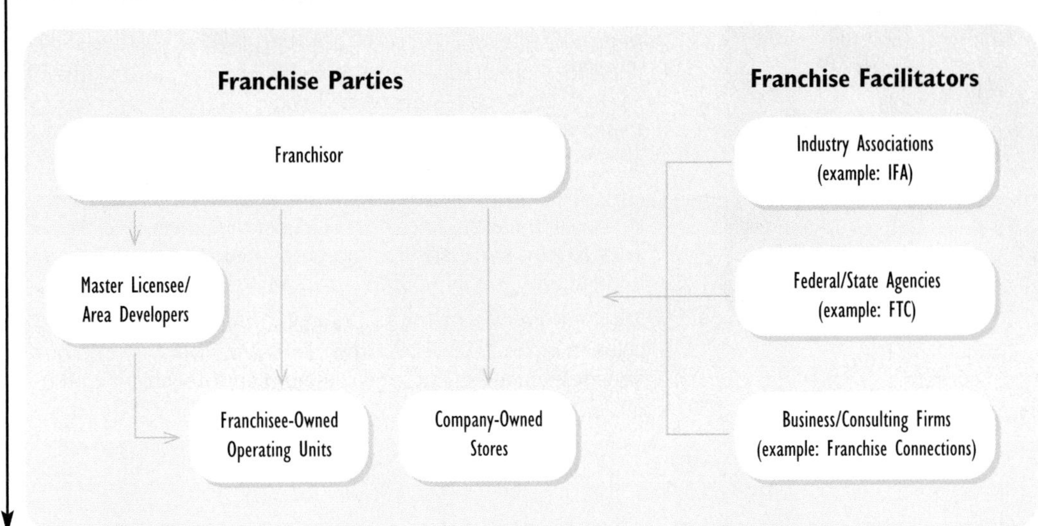

business groups. For example, the Women's Franchise Committee (WFC), formed in 1996, provides leadership conferences, mentoring programs, a network of professionals, and other services for women franchisees.

Numerous federal and state agencies are involved in the franchise industry. Agencies such as the Federal Trade Commission (http://www.ftc.gov), or FTC, provide information on franchise opportunities and enforce franchising laws and regulations. Presale franchise disclosure practices are subject to special scrutiny by these agencies.

A third category of facilitators includes private businesses providing franchise information and consulting services to franchisors and franchisees. For example, Franchise Connections (http://www.franchiseconnections.com) and The Franchise Company (http://www.thefranchisecompany.com) are two businesses that assist with franchising evaluation and offer development services.

EVALUATING FRANCHISE OPPORTUNITIES

3 *Describe the process for evaluating a franchise opportunity.*

After making a decision to pursue a franchising opportunity, the prospective franchisee must determine a franchise candidate and investigate it completely. As we discuss the investigation process, we will continue to use examples featuring Great Clips, a franchisor of haircare salons.

Selecting a Franchise

With the growth of franchising over the years, the task of selecting an appropriate franchise has become easier. Personal observation frequently sparks interest, or awareness may begin with exposure to an advertisement in a newspaper or magazine or on the Internet. The headlines of these advertisements usually highlight the financial and personal rewards sought by the entrepreneur. *Inc.*, *Entrepreneur*, and the *Wall Street Journal* are three examples of publications that include advertisements of franchisors.

Investigating the Potential Franchise

The nature of the commitment required in franchising justifies careful investigation. Launching a franchised business typically requires a substantial financial investment, usually many thousands of dollars. Furthermore, the business relationship generally continues over a period of years.

The evaluation process is a two-way effort. The franchisor wishes to investigate the franchisee, and the franchisee obviously wishes to evaluate the franchisor and the type of oppor-

Living the Dream

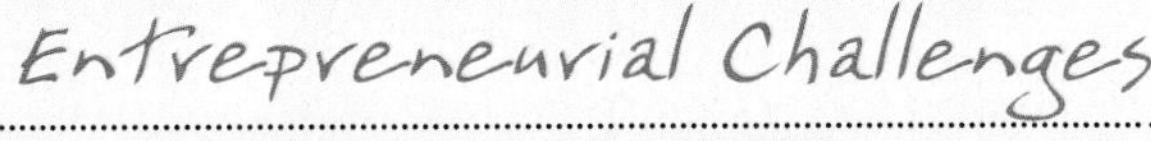

College Brothers Are Smoothies

© Frank Rogozienski

Right out of college, Jason and Jeff Jokerst took the entrepreneurial plunge. "I started thinking about graduation and what I was going to do after. I didn't want to go straight into a 9-to-5 job, because everyone I knew just hated it," says Jason. The brothers also thought that owning a franchise might be easier than starting from scratch.

Using a franchise referral network, the brothers discovered the Maui Wowi smoothie franchise. They purchased a kiosk franchise in March 2002, just as they were finishing college in San Diego. Financing was the most difficult part for the brothers. "I had to have my parents co-sign because I had no credit history. I have a couple of credit cards, but I haven't been around to buy houses . . . and prove I can pay that kind of stuff off," says Jeff.

The brothers opened the business in the summer of 2002 and are rapidly learning about accounting and managing employees and inventory. The business is doing well, and they're already expanding into other stadium cart franchises in the California area.

http://www.mauiwowi.com

Source: Devlin Smith, "You're the Boss," *Entrepreneur*, September 2003, p. 92. Reprinted with permission.

tunity being offered. Time is required for this kind of analysis. You should be skeptical of a franchisor who pressures you to sign a contract without time for proper investigation.

What should be the prospective entrepreneur's first step in evaluating a franchising opportunity? What sources of information are available? Do government agencies provide information on franchising? Basically, three sources of information should be tapped: (1) independent, third-party sources, (2) the franchisors themselves, and (3) existing and previous franchisees.

INDEPENDENT, THIRD-PARTY SOURCES OF INFORMATION State and federal agencies are valuable sources of franchising information. Since most states require registration of franchises, a prospective franchisee should not overlook state offices as a source of assistance. The Federal Trade Commission publishes the *Franchise Opportunities Handbook*, which is a useful directory of hundreds of franchisors. Also, a comprehensive listing of franchisors can be found in the *Franchise Opportunities Guide*, which is published by the International Franchise Association. Exhibit 4-4 displays selected listings from their online guide. Note the entry for Great Clips.

Business publications are also excellent sources of franchisor ratings. *Fortune*, *Entrepreneur*, and the *Wall Street Journal*, to name a few, can be found in most libraries, and all have Web sites with archives. In February 2004, *Entrepreneur* magazine contained a profile of the top 20 fastest-growing franchises in 2004 (see Exhibit 4-5 on page 83). A number of factors were considered in the rankings, the most important being financial strength and the franchising system's growth rate and size. Other considerations included litigation history and whether the company provides financing. Notice that Great Clips ranked number 18 in the listing!

A search of the Web uncovered several articles describing the Great Clips franchise. Frequently, such articles provide information not available from the franchisor or from government agencies. They often give an extensive profile of franchise problems and strategy changes within a company. Third-party coverage helps in evaluating the credibility of information provided directly by the franchisor. The Internet search also revealed that Great Clips is listed in the Small Business Administration's Franchise Registry, discussed earlier in this chapter.

In recent years, franchise consultants have appeared in the marketplace to assist individuals seeking franchise opportunities. Some consulting firms, such as FranCorp, present seminars on choosing the right franchise. Of course, the prospective franchisee needs to be careful to select a reputable consultant. Since franchise consultants are not necessarily attorneys, an experienced franchise attorney should evaluate all legal documents.

Living the Dream — *Entrepreneurial Challenges*

A "Diamond" of a Franchise

One afternoon on a shopping trip with her mother, entrepreneur Carrie McAbee saw a HairDiamond kiosk at a mall. Both the mother and the daughter thought it was a great concept—selling crystal hair accessories that attach easily to a client's hair. And the kiosk was located in the midst of customers in a buying environment. McAbee approached the kiosk owner and asked how to get into the business. She was referred to Specialty Retail Stores, Inc. (SRS), a franchise kiosk-concept developer.

SRS arranged the leasing and secured a prime location in a local mall in Bakersfield, California, and McAbee and her mother set up shop. Their location, next to Macy's and other women-targeted specialty stores, has been ideal. Their biggest problem has been managing employees. Nevertheless, the kiosk has done well, generating $400,000 in annual sales since opening in August 2002.

This franchise has helped McAbee, a 20-year-old mom, make a good living and still be able to spend time with her family.

http://specialtyretailstores.com/hairdiamond.htm

Source: Nichole L. Torres, "Cart Blanche," *Entrepreneur*, August 2003, p. 82. Reprinted with permission.

EXHIBIT 4-4 | *Profiles from the* Franchise Opportunities Guide

MAUI WOWI SMOOTHIES
COMPANY DETAILS
Description: Ranked in the Entrepreneur 500, we are the leading smoothie/espresso cart franchise in the world. With 24/7 support and extensive training, we offer a simple, profitable, and flexible business model.
Business Established: 1983
Franchised Since: 1997
# of Franchised Units: 250
Company Owned: 0
CONTACT INFO
Address: 5601 S. Broadway, Suite 200, Littleton, CO
Zip Code: 80121-8020
Country: USA
No-800: (888) 862-8555
Phone1: (303) 781-7800
Fax: (303) 781-2438
Primary Contact Name & Title: Rob Park—Director of Franchise Development
Secondary Contact Name & Title: Kera Vo & Sharon Hanson—Development Coordinators
Email: mauiifa@franchisehub.com
Website: http://www.mauiwowifranchise.com
FINANCIAL INFO
Startup Cash Required: $70,000–$200,000
Investment Required: $70,000–$300,000
Financial Comment: Third party
TRAINING: 4 days of training in Denver, CO
QUALIFICATIONS: Ability to follow a proven system. Ability to project a positive and constructive attitude. Desire to commit to accomplishing articulated goals. Liquidity of $70K and net worth of $250K.

SUBWAY WORLD HEADQUARTERS
COMPANY DETAILS
Description: At Subway we take pride in offering you an exceptional franchise opportunity. The investment is low, the operation is straightforward and easy to learn.
Business Established: 1965
Franchised Since: 1974
# of Franchised Units: 18,594
Company Owned: 0
CONTACT INFO
Address: 325 Bic Drive, Milford, CT
Zip Code: 06460-3072
Country: USA
No-800: (800) 888-4848
Phone1: (203) 877-4281
Fax: (203) 876-6688
Primary Contact Name & Title: Development Team
Secondary Contact Name & Title:
Email: franchise@subway.com
Website: http://www.subway.com
FINANCIAL INFO
Startup Cash Required: $30,000–$90,000
Investment Required: $69,300–$191,000
Financial Comment: Equipment leasing available. Prefer candidate with half toward investment available in cash; balance financeable.
TRAINING: Subway requires a mandatory two-week training session—50% hands-on and 50% in classroom.
QUALIFICATIONS: Operators with moderate business experience who are interested in building and successful in business. Goal-oriented people displaying a willingness to work within a proven structured system.

GREAT CLIPS, INC.
COMPANY DETAILS
Description: High-volume haircutting salon, specializing in haircuts and perms for the entire family.
Business Established: 1982
Franchised Since: 1983
# of Franchised Units: 1,877
Company Owned: 0
CONTACT INFO
Address: 7700 France Avenue South, Suite 425, Minneapolis, MN
Zip Code: 55435
Country: USA
No-800: (800) 947-1143
Phone1: (952) 893-9088
Fax: (952) 844-3443
Primary Contact Name & Title: Alan Majerko—Development Marketing Manager
Secondary Contact Name & Title: Sherry Overholser—Franchise Development Adm. Ass.
Email: franchise@greatclips.com
Website: http://www.greatclipsfranchise.com
FINANCIAL INFO
Startup Cash Required: $25,000
Investment Required: $94,550–$180,050
Financial Comment: 3rd party financing available
TRAINING: Comprehensive local market training and exceptional support in real estate, marketing, construction—both pre-opening and on a continuing basis.
QUALIFICATIONS: Maximum $250,000 net worth, $150,000 liquid net worth. No industry experience necessary.

CULVER'S
COMPANY DETAILS
Description: Culver's is famous for their cooked to order ButterBurgers and premium frozen custard. A quick service restaurant serving a great variety of sandwiches, salads, dinners, frozen custard desserts, beverages, and other menu items.
Business Established: 1984
Franchised Since: 1987
# of Franchised Units: 225
Company Owned: 5
CONTACT INFO
Address: 540 Water Street, Prairie du Sac, WI
Zip Code: 53578
Country: USA
Phone1: (608) 643-7980
Fax: (608) 643-7982
Primary Contact Name & Title: Development Department
Secondary Contact Name & Title: Apply on-line culvers.com
Email: franchise@culvers.com
Website: http://www.culvers.com
FINANCIAL INFO
Startup Cash Required: $250,000–$400,000
Investment Required: $354,250–$898,250
TRAINING: All operating franchisees complete an intense 16-week training program. The cost of this training is included in the initial franchise fee. Franchisees pay their own costs for transportation, lodging and meals. All training takes place in Wisconsin in one of our family-owned restaurants and at our Culver's Support Center in Prairie du Sac, Wisconsin.
QUALIFICATIONS: You will need $250,000 to $400,000 in liquid assets to qualify. Liquid assets do not include real estate (including home), automobile, personal effects, or borrowed funds. Applicant will be the owner/operator maintaining a minimum 50 percent ownership in the operating business entity and involved full-time in the day-to-day operations of the restaurant. Successfully completes a one week 60-hour evaluation program in Prairie du Sac, Wisconsin.

Source: http://gamma.franconnect.net/ifa/control/ifahome, April 27, 2004.

EXHIBIT 4-5 | *The 20 Fastest-Growing Franchises in 2004*

Franchise	Where Based	Contact Information	Description	Number of Franchises, 2003 (Growth, 2002–2003)
1. Subway	Milford, CT	(800)888-4848/(203)877-4281 www.subway.com	Submarine sandwiches & salads	19,238 (+2,473)
2. Curves	Waco, TX	(800)848-1096/(254)399-9285 www.buycurves.com	Women's fitness & weight-loss centers	5,833 (+2,387)
3. 7-Eleven Inc.	Dallas, TX	(800)255-0711 www.7-eleven.com	Convenience store	21,887 (+1,895)
4. Kumon Math & Reading Centers	Teaneck, NJ	(866)633-0740/(201)928-0444 www.kumon.com	Supplemental education	23,404 (+1,361)
5. Jan Pro Franchising Int'l., Inc.	Little River, SC	(800)668-1001/(704)945-7173 www.jan-pro.com	Commercial cleaning	2,226 (+960)
6. The Quizno's Franchise Co.	Denver, CO	(720)359-3300 www.quiznos.com	Submarine sandwiches, soups, salads	2,423 (+760)
7. Jani-King	Addison, TX	(800)552-5264 www.janiking.com	Commercial cleaning	10,349 (+755)
8. Coverall Cleaning Concepts	Ft. Lauderdale, FL	(800)537-3371/(954)351-1110 www.coverall.com	Commercial cleaning	7,480 (+750)
9. Liberty Tax Service	Virginia Beach, VA	(800)790-3863/(757)493-8855 www.libertytax.com	Income tax preparation services	984 (+410)
10. Jazzercise Inc.	Carlsbad, CA	(760/476-1750 www.jazzercise.com	Dance/exercise classes	5,826 (+370)
11. RE/MAX Int'l., Inc.	Englewood, CO	(800)525-7452/(303)770-5531 www.remax.com	Real estate	4,601 (+352)
12. Jackson Hewitt Tax Service	Parsippany, NJ	(800)475-2904 www.jacksonhewitt.com	Tax preparation services	3,709 (+323)
13. Choice Hotels Int'l	Silver Spring, MD	(800)547-0007 www.choicehotels.com	Hotels, inns, suites & resorts	4,740 (+314)
14. WSI Internet	Toronto, ON	(906)678-7588 www.wsicorporate.com	Internet services	1,236 (+312)
15. Dunkin' Donuts	Randolph, MA	(800)777-9983 www.dunkindonuts.com	Donuts & baked goods	5,835 (+298)
16. Action Int'l	Las Vegas, NV	(302)795-3188 www.action-international.com	Business coaching, consulting & training	555 (+247)
17. Baskin-Robbins USA Co.	Randolph, MA	(800)777-9983 www.baskinrobbins.com	Ice cream & yogurt	5,105 (+241)
18. Great Clips, Inc.	Minneapolis, MN	(800)947-1143/(952)893-9088 www.greatclipsfranchise.com	Family hair salons	1,935 (+215)
19. Rezcity.com	Englewood Cliffs, NJ	(800)669-9000/(201)567-8500 www.rezcity.biz	Online local city guides & travel store	215 (+215)
20. The UPS Store	San Diego, CA	(877)623-7253 www.theupsstore.com	Postal/business/ communications services	4,596 (+212)

Source: "The Race Goes to the Swift," *Entrepreneur*, February 2004, p. 80. Reprinted with permission of *Entrepreneur* Media, Inc. Fastest Growing Franchises for 2004, February 2004 issue of *Enterpreneur* Magazine, pg. 80, http://www.entrepreneur.com.

THE FRANCHISOR AS A SOURCE OF INFORMATION Obviously, the franchisor being evaluated is a primary source of information. However, information provided by a franchisor must be viewed in light of its purpose—to promote the franchise.

One way to obtain information about franchisors is to communicate directly with them. After finding the Internet address for Great Clips, we accessed its home page to learn more about the franchise. We made a request for information, and within a few days we received a packet containing an attractive brochure and a videotape. The brochure included such information as startup costs and franchisees' testimonials.

It is important for potential franchisees to remember that many of the financial figures provided in the franchisor's information packet are only estimates. While profit claims are becoming more common, reputable franchisors are careful not to misrepresent what a franchisee can expect to attain in terms of sales, gross income, and profits. The importance of earnings to a prospective franchisee makes the subject of profit claims a particularly sensitive one.

After an entrepreneur has expressed further interest in a franchise by completing the application form and the franchisor has tentatively qualified the potential franchisee, a meeting is usually arranged to discuss the disclosure document. A **disclosure document** is a detailed statement of such information as the franchisor's finances, experience, size, and involvement in litigation. The document must inform potential franchisees of any restrictions, costs, and provisions for renewal or cancellation of the franchise. Important considerations related to this document are examined more fully later in this chapter.

disclosure document
A detailed statement provided to a prospective franchisee, containing such information as the franchisor's finances, experience, size, and involvement in litigation

EXISTING AND PREVIOUS FRANCHISEES AS SOURCES OF INFORMATION There may be no better source of franchise facts than existing franchisees. Sometimes, however, the distant location of other franchisees precludes a visit to their business site. In that case, a simple telephone call can elicit that person's viewpoint. If possible, talk also with franchisees who have left the business; they can offer valuable input about their decision to give up the franchise.

Finding Global Franchising Opportunities

A great opportunity continues to exist for small business firms in the United States to franchise internationally. Traditionally, U.S. franchisors did most of their international franchising in Canada because of that country's proximity and language similarity. This, however, has changed. A combination of events, including the structuring of the European Union (EU) and the passage of the North American Free Trade Agreement (NAFTA), have opened other foreign markets to U.S. franchisors.[3]

Although the appeal of foreign markets is substantial, the task of franchising abroad is not easy. One franchisor's manager of international development expressed the challenge this way:

> *In order to successfully franchise overseas, the franchisor must have a sound and successful home base that is sufficiently profitable. The financial position of the franchisor must be secure and [the franchisor] must have resources which are surplus to—or can be exclusively diverted from—[its] domestic requirements. [The franchisor] must also have the personnel available to devote solely to international operations, and above all . . . must be patient. On the whole, the development of international markets will always take longer and make greater demands on the resources of the franchisor than first anticipated.*[4]

Several sources of international franchising information are available for entrepreneurs. Many U.S. government publications are helpful, as is the information on several Web sites, such as that of the *International Herald-Tribune*. Also, individual foreign countries may host Web sites that contain useful information about franchising opportunities in that country; the British Franchising Association's site at http://british-franchise.org is one example.

Considering Legal Issues in Franchising

THE FRANCHISE CONTRACT The basic features of the relationship between the franchisor and the franchisee are embodied in the franchise contract. This contract is typically a complex document, running to many pages. Because of its importance as the legal basis for the franchised business, the franchise contract should never be signed by the franchisee without legal counsel. In fact, reputable franchisors insist that the franchisee have legal counsel before signing the agreement. An attorney may anticipate trouble spots and note any objectionable features of the contract.

In addition to consulting an attorney, a prospective franchisee should use as many other sources of help as practical. In particular, he or she should discuss the franchise proposal with a banker, going over it in as much detail as possible. The prospective franchisee should also obtain the services of a professional accounting firm in examining the franchisor's statements of projected sales, operating expenses, and net income. An accountant can help in evaluating the quality of these estimates and in identifying projections that may be unlikely to be realized.

One of the most important features of the franchise contract is the provision relating to termination and transfer of the franchise. Some franchisors have been accused of devising agreements that permit arbitrary cancellation of the franchise relationship. Of course, it is reasonable for the franchisor to have legal protection in the event that a franchisee fails to obtain an appropriate level of operation or to maintain satisfactory quality standards. However, the prospective franchisee should be wary of contract provisions that contain overly strict cancellation policies. Similarly, the rights of the franchisee to sell the business to a third party should be clearly stipulated. A franchisor who can restrict the sale of the business to a third party could potentially assume ownership of the business at an unreasonably low price. The right of the franchisee to renew the contract after the business has been built up to a successful operating level should also be clearly stated in the contract.

FRANCHISE DISCLOSURE REQUIREMENTS The offer and sale of a franchise are regulated by both state and federal laws. At the federal level, the minimum disclosure standards are specified by Rule 436 of the Federal Trade Commission. The rule, formally entitled "Disclosure Requirements and Prohibitions Concerning Franchising and Business Opportunity Ventures," went into effect in October of 1979. A guide to the rule can be found on the Federal Trade Commission's Web site at http://www.ftc.gov/bcp/franchise/netrule.htm. Addresses of the state offices administering franchise disclosure laws can be found at http://www.ftc.gov/bcp/franchise/netdiscl.htm.

A document called the **Uniform Franchise Offering Circular (UFOC)** provides the accepted format for satisfying the franchise disclosure requirements of the FTC. The original UFOC format was amended in April 1993 by its creator, the North American Securities Administrators Association (NASAA). Effective January 1, 1996, all franchisors using the UFOC disclosure format were obliged to abide by the new amendments.

Uniform Franchise Offering Circular (UFOC)
A document accepted by the Federal Trade Commission as satisfying its franchise disclosure requirements

The UFOC disclosure must include information on a variety of items, including litigation and bankruptcy history, investment requirements, and conditions that would affect renewal, termination, or sale of the franchise. Most franchise experts recommend that a franchisee attorney and an accountant review the document.

Another option for the entrepreneur seeking to make his or her dream a reality is buying an existing business. In the next section, we discuss some of the issues facing the individual who chooses this alternative.

BUYING AN EXISTING BUSINESS

For would-be entrepreneurs, one alternative to starting from scratch or buying a franchise is to buy an established business. The decision to purchase an existing business should be made only after careful consideration of the advantages and disadvantages.

4 List four reasons for buying an existing business and describe the process of evaluating a business.

Reasons for Buying an Existing Business

The reasons for buying an existing business can be condensed into the following four general categories:

1. To reduce some of the uncertainties and unknowns that must be faced in starting a business from the ground up
2. To acquire a business with ongoing operations and established relationships with customers and suppliers

3. To obtain an established business at a price below what it would cost to start a new business or to buy a franchise
4. To begin a business more quickly than by starting from scratch

Let's examine each of these reasons in more detail.

REDUCTION OF UNCERTAINTIES A successful business has already demonstrated its ability to attract customers, control costs, and make a profit. Although future operations may be different, the firm's past record shows what it can do under actual market conditions. For example, just the fact that the location must be satisfactory eliminates one major uncertainty. Although traffic counts are useful in assessing the value of a potential location, the acid test comes when a business opens its doors at that location. This test has already been met in the case of an existing firm. The results are available in the form of sales and profit data. Noncompetition agreements are needed, however, to discourage the seller from starting a new company that will compete directly with the one being sold.

ACQUISITION OF ONGOING OPERATIONS AND RELATIONSHIPS The buyer of an existing business typically acquires its personnel, inventories, physical facilities, established banking connections, and ongoing relationships with trade suppliers and customers. Extensive time and effort would be required to build these elements from scratch. Of course, the advantage derived from buying an established firm's assets depends on the nature of the assets. For example, a firm's skilled, experienced employees constitute a valuable asset only if they will continue to work for the new owner. The physical facilities must not be obsolete, and the firm's relationships with banks, suppliers, and customers must be healthy. In any case, new agreements will probably have to be negotiated with current vendors and leaseholders.

A new business owner who fails to carefully consider the nature of the assets may face some unpleasant surprises. Consider the experience of Norman Savage. Shortly after buying a small mortgage company in Fort Wayne, Indiana, Savage learned that the seller had given some employees 20 percent pay increases after the deal was made, effectively buying for himself credit for being a generous boss and leaving the cost of that generosity for Savage to pay. In addition, some of the firm's business licenses were about to expire, and Savage had difficulty locating the necessary documents to renew them. To top it off, one of the office computers needed to be replaced.[5]

On the other hand, Thomas J. Cerri encountered no such problems when he bought Mill Valley Lumber Company in Mill Valley, California. He recalls, "When we took over, eight key employees stayed on with us, and it really made all the difference." The sales staff had nearly 100 years of experience among them and "seemed to be friends with everyone in the area." With a well-connected sales staff and other key employees staying on the job, Mill Valley Lumber continued to enjoy a close relationship with its customers, despite the invasion of giant competitors like Home Depot.[6]

A BARGAIN PRICE If the seller is more eager to sell than the buyer is to buy, an existing business may be available at what seems to be a low price. Whether it is actually a good buy, however, must be determined by the prospective new owner. Several factors could make a "bargain price" anything but a bargain. For example, the business may be losing money, the neighborhood location may be deteriorating, or the seller may intend to open another competing business nearby. On the other hand, if research indicates that the business indeed is a bargain, purchasing it is likely to turn out to be a wise investment.

A QUICK START Most entrepreneurs are eager to "get going" in their new business and may not be comfortable waiting the months and years sometimes required to launch a business from scratch. Buying an existing business may be an excellent way to begin operations much more quickly.

Finding a Business to Buy

Sometimes, in the course of day-to-day living and working, a would-be buyer comes across an opportunity to buy an existing business. For example, a sales representative for a manufacturer or a wholesaler may be offered an opportunity to buy a customer's retail business. In other cases, the prospective buyer needs to search for a business to buy.

Sources of leads about businesses available for purchase include suppliers, distributors, trade associations, and even bankers. Realtors—particularly those who specialize in the sale of business firms and business properties—can also provide leads. In addition, there are specialized brokers, called **matchmakers**, that handle all the arrangements for closing a buyout. A large number of matchmakers, such as Certified Business Brokers (http://www.certifiedbb.com) in Houston, Texas, deal with mergers and acquisitions of small and mid-sized companies in the United States.

matchmakers
Specialized brokers that bring together buyers and sellers of businesses

Entrepreneurs need to be wary of potential conflicts of interest with matchmakers. For example, if matchmakers are paid only if a buy–sell transaction occurs, they may be tempted to do whatever it takes to close the deal, even if doing so is detrimental to the buyer.

Investigating and Evaluating Available Businesses

Regardless of the source of the lead, a business opportunity requires careful evaluation—what some call **due diligence**. As a preliminary step, the buyer needs to acquire background information about the business, some of which can be obtained through personal observation or discussion with the seller. Talking with other informed parties, such as suppliers, bankers, employees, and customers of the business, is also important.

due diligence
The exercise of reasonable care in the evaluation of a business opportunity

RELYING ON PROFESSIONALS Although some aspects of due diligence require personal checking, a buyer can also seek the help of outside experts. The two most valuable sources of outside assistance are accountants and lawyers. It is also wise to seek out others who have acquired a business, in order to learn from their experience. Their perspective will be different from that of a consultant, and it will bring some balance to the counsel received.

The time and money spent on securing professional help in investigating a business can pay big dividends, especially when the buyer is inexperienced. However, the final consequences of a business purchase, good and bad, are borne by the buyer, and thus the prospective buyer should never leave the final decision to the experts. For one thing, it is a mistake to assume that professionals' help is either unbiased or infallible, particularly when their fees may be greater if the business is acquired. Prospective buyers should seek advice and counsel, but they must make the final decision themselves, as it is too important to entrust to someone else.

FINDING OUT WHY THE BUSINESS IS FOR SALE The seller's *real* reasons for selling may or may not be the *stated* ones. When a business is for sale, always question the owner's reasons for selling. There is a real possibility that the firm is not doing well or that underlying problems exist that will affect its future performance. The buyer must be wary, therefore, of taking the seller's explanations at face value. Here are some of the most common reasons that owners offer their businesses for sale:

- Old age or illness
- Desire to relocate in a different section of the country
- Decision to accept a position with another company
- Unprofitability of the business
- Loss of an exclusive sales franchise
- Maturing of the industry and lack of growth potential

A prospective buyer cannot be certain that the seller-owner will be honest in presenting all the facts about the business, especially concerning financial matters. Too frequently, sellers have "cooked the books" or taken unreported cash out of the business. The only way for the buyer to avoid an unpleasant surprise later is to do his or her best to determine whether the seller is an ethical person.

EXAMINING THE FINANCIAL DATA The first stage in evaluating the financial health of a firm is to review the financial statements and tax returns for the past five years or for as many years as they are available. *(If these statements are not available, think twice before buying the business.)* This first stage helps determine whether the buyer and seller are in the same ballpark. If so, the parties move on to the second stage (discussed in the next section)—valuing the firm.

To determine the history of the business and the direction in which it is moving, the buyer must examine financial data pertaining to the company's operation. If financial statements are available for the past five years, the buyer can use these to get some idea of trends for the business. As an ethical matter, the prospective buyer is obligated to show the financial statements to others—such as a potential lender or legal advisor—only on a need-to-know basis. To do otherwise is a violation of trust and confidentiality.

The buyer should recognize that financial statements can be misleading and may require normalizing to yield a realistic picture of the business. For example, business owners sometimes understate business income in an effort to minimize taxable income. On the other hand, expenses for such entries as employee training and advertising may be reduced to abnormally low levels in an effort to make the income look good in the hope of selling the business.

Other financial entries that may need adjustment include personal expenses and wage or salary payments. For example, costs related to personal use of business vehicles frequently appear as a business expense. Family members may receive excessive compensation or none at all. All entries must be examined to ensure that they relate to the business and are appropriate.

The buyer should also scrutinize the seller's balance sheet to see whether asset book values are realistic. Property often appreciates in value after it is recorded on the books. In contrast, physical facilities, inventory, and receivables may decline in value, so their actual worth is less than their accounting book value. Although these changes in value are generally not reflected in the accountant's records, they should be considered by the prospective buyer.

Valuing the Business

Once the initial investigation and evaluation have been completed, the buyer must arrive at a fair value for the firm. Valuing a business is not easy or exact, even in the best of circumstances. Despite the fact that buyers prefer audited financial statements, many firms operate without them. In valuing such firms, the buyer will have to rely on federal tax returns and state sales tax statements. It may also be helpful to scrutinize invoices and receipts—of both customers and suppliers—as well as the firm's bank statements.

Although numerous techniques are used for valuing a company, they are typically derivations of three basic approaches: (1) asset-based valuation, (2) market-comparable valuation, and (3) cash flow–based valuation. These techniques will be examined in detail in Appendix B.

Nonquantitative Factors in Valuing a Business

In addition to quantitative factors, there are a number of other factors to consider in evaluating an existing business. Although only indirectly related to a firm's future cash flows and financial position, some of these factors should be mentioned.

- *Competition.* The prospective buyer should look into the extent, intensity, and location of competing businesses. In particular, the buyer should check to see whether the business in question is gaining or losing in its race with competitors.
- *Market.* The ability of the market to support all competing business units, including the one to be purchased, should be determined. This requires marketing research, study of census data, and personal, on-the-spot observation at each competitor's place of business.
- *Future community development.* Examples of future developments in the community that could have an indirect impact on a business include a change in zoning ordinances already enacted but not yet in effect and a change from a two-way traffic flow to a one-way traffic flow.
- *Legal commitments.* Legal commitments may include contingent liabilities, unsettled lawsuits, delinquent tax payments, missed payrolls, overdue rent or installment payments, and mortgages of record against any of the real property acquired.

- *Union contracts.* The prospective buyer should determine what type of labor agreement, if any, is in force, as well as the quality of the firm's employee relations.
- *Buildings.* The quality of the buildings housing the business should be checked, with particular attention paid to any fire hazards. In addition, the buyer should determine whether there are any restrictions on access to the building.
- *Product prices.* The prospective owner should compare the prices of the seller's products with those listed in manufacturers' or wholesalers' catalogs and also with the prices of competing products in the locality. This is necessary to ensure full and fair pricing of goods whose sales are reported on the seller's financial statements.

Negotiating and Closing the Deal

The purchase price of a business is determined by negotiation between buyer and seller. Although the calculated value may not be the price eventually paid for the business, it gives the buyer an estimated value to use when negotiating price. Typically, the buyer tries to purchase the firm for something less than the full estimated value; of course, the seller tries to get more than that value.

In some cases, the buyer may have the option of purchasing the assets only, rather than the business as a whole. When a business is purchased as a total entity, the buyer takes control of the assets but also assumes any outstanding debt, including any hidden or unknown liabilities. Even if the financial records are audited, such debts may not surface. If the buyer instead purchases only the assets, then the seller is responsible for settling any outstanding debts previously incurred. An indemnification clause in the sales contract may serve a similar function, protecting the buyer from liability for unreported debt.

An important part of the negotiation process is the terms of purchase. In many cases, the buyer is unable to pay the full price in cash and must seek extended terms. At the same time, the seller may be concerned about taxes on the profit from the sale. Terms may become more attractive to the buyer and the seller as the amount of the down payment is reduced and/or the length of the repayment period is extended. Like a purchase of real estate, the purchase of a business is closed at a specific time. A title company or an attorney usually handles the closing. Preferably, the closing occurs under the direction of an independent third party. If the seller's attorney is the closing agent, the buyer should exercise caution—a buyer should never go through a closing without the aid of an experienced attorney who represents only the buyer.

A number of important documents are completed during the closing. These include a bill of sale, certifications as to taxing and other governmental regulations, and agreements pertaining to future payments and related guarantees to the seller. The buyer should apply for new federal and state tax identification numbers to avoid being held responsible for past obligations associated with the old numbers.

Looking Back

1 Identify the major pros and cons of franchising.

- Franchising is a formalized arrangement that describes a certain way of operating a small business.
- The overall advantage of franchising is its high rate of success.
- A franchise may be favored over other alternatives because it offers training, financial assistance, and operating benefits.
- The major limitations of franchising are its costs, restrictions on business operations, loss of entrepreneurial independence, and potential lack of franchisor support.

2 Explain franchising options and the structure of the industry.

- The main parties in the franchising system are the franchisor and the franchisee.
- The potential value of any franchising arrangement is determined by the rights contained in the franchise contract.
- In product and trade name franchising, the main benefit the franchisee receives is the privilege of using a widely recognized product name.
- In business format franchising, entrepreneurs receive an entire marketing and management system.

- A master licensee is a firm or individual having a continuing contractual relationship with a franchisor to sell its franchises.
- Multiple-unit ownership, in which a single franchisee owns more than one unit of a franchised business, is becoming widely used.
- Some of these single franchisees are area developers, individuals or firms that obtain the legal right to open several outlets in a given area.
- Piggyback franchising is the operation of a retail franchise within the physical facilities of a host store.
- Facilitating groups include industry associations, government agencies, and private businesses.

3 Describe the process for evaluating a franchise opportunity.

- The substantial investment required by most franchisors justifies careful investigation by a potential franchisee.
- Independent third parties, such as state and federal government agencies, the International Franchise Association, and business publications, can be valuable sources of franchise information.
- The most logical source of the greatest amount of information about a franchise is the franchisor.
- Existing and previous franchisees are good sources of information for evaluating a franchise.
- Sources of international franchising information include government publications and Web sites hosted by individual foreign countries.
- A franchise contract is a complex document and should be evaluated by a franchise attorney.
- An important feature of the franchise contract is the provision relating to termination and transfer of the franchise.
- Franchise disclosure requirements are specified by FTC Rule 436.
- The Uniform Franchise Offering Circular (UFOC) provides the accepted format for satisfying the franchise disclosure requirements of the FTC.

4 List four reasons for buying an existing business and describe the process of evaluating a business.

- Buying an existing firm can reduce uncertainties.
- In acquiring an existing firm, the entrepreneur can take advantage of the firm's ongoing operations and established relationships.
- An existing business may be available at a bargain price.
- The entrepreneur may be in a hurry to get the business going.
- Investigating a business requires due diligence.
- A buyer should seek the help of outside experts, the two most valuable sources of outside assistance being accountants and lawyers.
- The buyer needs to investigate why the seller is offering the business for sale.
- The financial data related to the business should always be examined.
- Nonquantitative information about the business for sale should also be used in determining its value.

Key Terms

franchising, p. 73
franchisee, p. 73
franchisor, p. 73
franchise contract, p. 78
franchise, p. 78
product and trade name franchising, p. 78
business format franchising, p. 79
master licensee, p. 79
multiple-unit ownership, p. 79
area developers, p. 79
piggyback franchising, p. 79
disclosure document, p. 84
Uniform Franchise Offering Circular (UFOC), p. 85
matchmakers, p. 87
due diligence, p. 87

Discussion Questions

1. What makes franchising different from other forms of business? Be specific.
2. What is the difference between product and trade name franchising and business format franchising? Which one accounts for the majority of franchising activity?
3. Identify and describe the parties in the franchising system.
4. Discuss the advantages and limitations of franchising from the viewpoints of the potential franchisee and the potential franchisor.
5. Should franchise information provided by a franchisor be discounted? Why or why not?
6. Do you believe that the Uniform Franchise Offering Circular is useful for franchise evaluation? Defend your position.

7. Evaluate loss of control as a disadvantage of franchising from the franchisor's perspective.
8. What are possible reasons for buying an existing company versus starting a new business from scratch?
9. What are some common reasons that owners offer their businesses for sale? Which of these reasons might a buyer consider to be negative?
10. What are some of the nonquantitative factors in valuing a business?

You Make the Call

SITUATION 1

Ethan Moore is a college student in Phoenix, Arizona, currently enrolled as an entrepreneurship major at a local university. Moore's home is in Chandler, Arizona, a nearby city, where he is considering purchasing a franchise. The franchise, which caught his interest while he was on a shopping trip to the Tucson Mall, is operated by an Idaho-based gumball company named Gumball Gourmet.

Moore talked to the owner of the franchise at the Tucson Mall while he was stocking the kiosk, which is set up in three tiers with 47 gumball machines and a money changer. The owner mentioned in their brief conversation that this particular kiosk had sold 12,000 gumballs in the last 30-day period.

From information he found at the Gumball Gourmet Web site, Moore determined that franchises are available with as little as a $25,000 investment.

Source: http://www.gumballgourmet.com, September 2003.

Question 1 What other Internet sites might provide helpful information to Moore as he tries to learn more about this franchise?

Question 2 What other questions should Moore have asked the Tucson franchisee?

Question 3 What information might a Uniform Franchise Offering Circular from Gumball Gourmet provide?

SITUATION 2

Scott Prewitt, 23, his brother Steven Prewitt, 29, and his brother-in-law Tony Mansoor, 21, have no experience in the restaurant business. But one of their goals is to start their own business and move their families from Jackson, Mississippi, to the mountains of western North Carolina. They are considering buying a Back Yard Burgers franchise.

As of March 4, 2003, the Back Yard Burgers, Inc., restaurant system comprised 122 units, including 80 franchised stores. The franchise, with headquarters in Memphis, Tennessee, specializes in charbroiled, freshly prepared food. The company began franchising in 1988 and currently has only U.S. franchises. The company uses a double drive-through concept for most of its restaurants, including the franchise that Prewitt and his family are considering.

The Prewitt family is concerned about their inexperience and the harsh weather in the snowy mountains of North Carolina.

Sources: http://www.backyardburger.com; and Tracy Stapp, "Never Say Die," *Entrepreneur,* December 2002, p. 130.

Question 1 How concerned do you think this family should be about their inexperience? Why?

Question 2 Will the proposed location in the mountains be a potential problem for this type of restaurant? Why or why not?

SITUATION 3

Judy Patterson, Connie Post, and Kriste Burnside were all friends, working together in the accounting department of a local manufacturing business in Waco, Texas. They enjoyed working out at a local exercise facility during their lunch hour.

One day, they learned that the owner of the gym was planning to move to Arizona and needed to sell the business. "We kind of hoped the owners of the company we worked for would buy it so we'd have free memberships," said Patterson. But that didn't happen, so the three friends formed a corporation to consider the purchase of the franchise.

Source: Mike Copeland, "Trio on Learning Curve," *Waco Tribune-Herald,* April 30, 2000, p. 4B.

Question 1 What sources of information about this franchise would you recommend that the friends consider?

Question 2 Is their work-out experience sufficient to prepare them for ownership of this franchise?

Question 3 Would the three friends be making a wise decision if they decided to buy this franchise? Why or why not?

SITUATION 4

Growth prospects have never been brighter for this 22-year-old manufacturer of custom-designed skylights, which has grown to more than $2 million in annual sales by letting light into homes, museums, symphony halls, upscale commercial buildings, and more. The California company ended last year with its strongest sales quarter since its current owners bought the business in 1995. Some 60 percent of its revenues come from jobs within California, where construction has remained steady throughout the economic downturn. Furthermore, the energy crisis has driven up demand for skylights, which pay for themselves in energy savings.

The manufacturer's state-of-the-art products also protect furniture and carpeting against fading from sunlight. The owners of the business are selling because they intend to move overseas. Their 22 staffers, including two installation crews and four sales and marketing professionals, appear willing to stay and help a new owner "illuminate" a variety of new growth opportunities.

The asking price is $675,000, with 60 percent down. The owners will consider financing a portion of the deal.

Source: Based on Jill Andresky Frazer, "A Blue-Sky Deal," *Inc.*, Vol. 24, No. 7 (July 2002), p. 40.

Question 1 Should a prospective buyer of this firm investigate other possible reasons why the owners might want to sell? Why or why not?

Question 2 What sales and revenue numbers are needed to evaluate the asking price?

Question 3 What nonquantitative factors might have an impact on the fairness of the asking price?

Experiential Exercises

1. Interview a local owner-manager of a widely recognized retail franchise, such as McDonald's. Ask him or her to explain the process of obtaining the franchise and what he or she considers to be the advantages of buying a franchise over starting a business from scratch.
2. Find a franchise advertisement in a recent issue of a business magazine. Research the franchise, and report back to the class with your findings.
3. As a class, consider the potential for locating a hypothetical new fast-food restaurant next to your campus. (Be as specific about the assumed location as you can.) Divide into two groups—one that supports buying a franchised operation and one that favors starting an independent, nonfranchised business. Plan a debate on the merits of each operation for the next class meeting.
4. Consult the Yellow Pages of your local telephone directory for the name of a business broker. Interview the broker and report to the class on how she or he values businesses.
5. In a business publication (e.g., *Inc.*), locate a listing or information about a business for sale. In class, discuss what information is needed to place a value on the business. Log on to InfoTrac College Edition at http://www.infotrac-college.com to find articles on valuing a business.

Exploring the Web

1. FranChoice's Web site is dedicated to helping people find best-fit franchise opportunities. Go to **http://www.franchoice.com/selftest.cfm** and take FranChoice's Franchise Aptitude self-test.
   a. Which of the listed characteristics stand out in your mind as most important for a successful franchise operator to have? Briefly explain your choice(s).
   b. Reread the chapter-opening Spotlight on Anne Beiler of Auntie Anne's. Of the characteristics listed on the self-test, which reflect Beiler's strongest aptitudes? Explain.
2. Everyone has heard about McDonald's Hamburger University, but many franchisors offer similar training and lifelong learning programs where franchisees come together to learn about quality, service, and value. Go to *Entrepreneur's* Web site at **http://www.entrepreneur.com** to learn more about the training programs of top franchisors.
   a. Follow the link to 2004 Franchise 500. Learn about the training programs of five different franchises by selecting the Training & Support tab. Write a short summary of the differences and similarities among the programs.
   b. This chapter points out that higher costs generally characterize the more successful franchises. These costs include the initial franchise fee, investment costs, royalty payments, and advertising costs. Compare and contrast the costs and fees of the same five franchises you used in part a, and briefly summarize why you think the costs and fees vary.

3. Return to *Entrepreneur's* Web site to examine the top global franchises indexed at the site. Go to **http://www.entrepreneur.com/franzone/listings/topglobal/0,5835,00.html** to link directly to the list of top global franchises.

a. Imagine that you were interested in opening a franchise outside of the United States. Decide in what country or region you would like to locate a business, and then find five franchises that are actively seeking franchisees in that country or region.

b. Select the one of those five franchises that you think represents the best opportunity, and explain why.

4. Buying an existing business is challenging and requires careful evaluation of potential opportunities. Online resources can be helpful in finding a business to buy and assessing its value.

a. Using the Web, find five online resources dedicated to helping people who want to buy a business.

b. Which of the five resources would you recommend to a friend who wanted to purchase a business? Why?

Video Case 4

AUNTIE ANNE'S (P. 531)

This case examines the franchise system created by entrepreneur Anne Beiler.

Alternative Cases for Chapter 4:

Case 9, The Chocolate Farm, p. 540
Case 14, Lotus Chips' Recipe for Success, p. 552

THE FAMILY BUSINESS

In the Spotlight

Aquascape Designs Inc. http://www.aquascapedesigns.com

A family business is like a double-edged sword—it cuts both ways, with unique advantages and disadvantages. Many of its advantages arise from the exceptional commitment of family employees to the enterprise because its performance has a profound effect on the family, financially and otherwise. On the downside, family businesses can face severe complications, including business conflicts that cross over to create problems in the entrepreneur's personal life, and vice versa. Greg Wittstock, the 33-year-old founder of Aquascape Designs Inc., has firsthand experience with the darker side of a family business.

Wittstock's company, based in Batavia, Illinois, designs and sells pond-building supplies both to do-it-yourselfers, who can install small backyard ponds for as little as $500 to $1,000, and to professionals, who charge from $5,000 to $250,000 to build ponds for owners of exotic Koi fish. Wittstock is willing to help contractors figure out how to deal with the challenges they face—from overcoming construction hurdles and employee management problems to finding ways to make money in the business—knowing that successful contractors will buy more supplies from Aquascape Designs.

© Ryan McVay/Photodisc Green/Getty Images

And the approach is working. Sales have grown dramatically, from $800,000 in 1995 to a projected $43 million or more in 2003.

But there have been a few serious bumps in the road along the way. Wittstock started his business in the summer of 1991. In September of that year, Greg's father, Gary, left his own engineering consulting firm to work with his son. But conflicts between father and son soon arose. Being polar opposites didn't help, nor did Greg's strong personality. Gary's attention to detail seriously cramped Greg's more creative entrepreneurial style, and soon the two were at each other's throats, battling for control of the company.

Over time, these problems took their toll on life beyond the business. In fact, Gary and his wife, Lauri (Greg's mother), divorced as a result of the conflict. As she describes it, "We really had a picture-perfect family, and it all came apart."

Distraught over the divorce, Gary withdrew from the day-to-day operations of the business and eventually sold his share of the company to Greg. In 1997, Gary started a new company called Pond Supplies of America, located only 20 miles from Aquascape Designs. The rivalry continues; father and son are now direct competitors in the marketplace. Both are successful, but at what cost?

Sources: http://www.aquascapedesigns.com/first_look.html, March 10, 2004; Bo Burlingham, "Building a Marketing Juggernaut," *Inc.*, November 2003, pp. 58–73; and Jim Ritter, "Rising Popularity of Backyard Ponds Ripples Through Suburbs," *Chicago Sun-Times*, July 21, 2003, p. 5.

Chapter 5

Looking Ahead

After studying this chapter, you should be able to

1. *Discuss the factors that make a family business unique.*
2. *Explain the cultural context of a family business.*
3. *Outline the complex roles and relationships involved in a family business.*
4. *Identify management practices that enable a family business to function effectively.*
5. *Describe the process of managerial succession in a family business.*

The word *entrepreneur* tends to conjure up an image of a hard-driving individual who comes up with a new product or service and defies the odds by launching a new business to bring it to market. This scenario was outlined in Chapter 3. In Chapter 4, we pointed out that many entrepreneurs do not start companies "from scratch," preferring instead to become their own boss through the purchase of either a franchise or an existing company. While these represent lower-risk opportunities, in many cases they still offer great financial potential.

A fourth type of opportunity—beyond startups, buyouts, and franchises—is to join a family business started by parents, grandparents, or other relatives. Startups catch more headlines and generate greater flash and excitement, but don't be deceived: *BusinessWeek* magazine recently noted that family business is alive and well in corporate America. Founders or members of their families were involved in the management of 177 of the 500 largest corporations in the United States (more than 35 percent of the total). Perhaps more astonishing, these family companies far outperformed their nonfamily counterparts. Over the last 10 years, family firms generated more annual income growth (21.1 percent) than did nonfamily firms (12.6 percent). And when the founder was still involved in the business, income growth averaged nearly 30 percent per year![1] These figures indicate that family businesses enjoy an edge in the marketplace.

For some people, joining the family business is a "no brainer," especially if they have been groomed for a position in the firm and look forward to its challenges. Others see a job in the family firm as merely one possibility among many career options to be considered during or after their college years. In any case, a family business offers another doorway to entrepreneurship for those whose families are involved in their own businesses. Ideally, the decision to join the family firm should be based on an understanding of the unique dynamics of such a business. This chapter examines the distinctive features that characterize the entrepreneurial alternative known as the family business.

THE FAMILY BUSINESS: A UNIQUE INSTITUTION

1 *Discuss the factors that make a family business unique.*

A family firm differs from other types of small businesses in many ways. For example, decision making is typically more complex since it involves a mixture of family and business values and interests. This section discusses some characteristics of this unique institution.

What Is a Family Business?

family business
A company that two or more members of the same family own or operate together or in succession

We define a **family business** as a company that two or more members of the same family own or operate together or in succession. The nature and extent of family members' involvement vary. In a number of firms, some family members work part-time. In a small restaurant, for example, one spouse may serve as host and manager, the other may keep the books, and the children may work in the kitchen or as servers. A recent National Federation of Independent Business study (NFIB) found that the family members most frequently involved in family businesses in the United States are spouses, siblings, children, and parents. In-laws participate in some cases, but this is far less common, and the involvement of other relatives, such as aunts, uncles, and cousins, is even more unusual.[2]

As our definition suggests, a firm is recognized as a family business if it passes from one generation to another. For example, people in the community think of Thompson's Plumbing Supply as a family business. The firm is now headed by Bill Thompson, Jr., son of the founder, who is deceased. Bill Thompson III has started to work on the sales floor, after serving in the stockroom during his high school years. He is the heir apparent, expected someday to replace his father.

In transferring firm leadership across generations, the Thompson family is beating the odds. The NFIB study reports that although 48 percent of American family business owners would like to see a family member eventually take over operation of their venture, only 13 percent of respondents believed this was "very likely" and another 22 percent thought it was "likely."[3] Research has shown that, in fact, around 30 percent of family businesses survive into the second generation, and less than 16 percent make it to the third.[4] We will discuss later the conflicts and challenges that often disrupt the transfer of the family business.

Now for the good news. As we have already noted, *BusinessWeek* found that family considerations may continue to be important even when these businesses become large corporations. In companies such as Wal-Mart, Levi Strauss, Ford Motor Company, and Marriott Corporation, the founding family is still involved to some extent in the ownership and operation of the business. In contrast to these extraordinary success stories, most family businesses are small. But small does not mean insignificant. Recent estimates suggest that family firms generate more than half of the business revenue in the United States and employ more than half of its workforce.[5] Clearly, these companies are vital to the U.S. economy.

Family and Business Overlap

Any family business is composed of both a family and a business. Although the family and the business are separate institutions—each with its own members, goals, and values—they overlap in the family firm. For many people, these two overlapping institutions represent the most important areas of their lives.

Families and businesses exist for fundamentally different reasons. The family's primary function is the care and nurturing of family members, while the business is concerned with the production and distribution of goods and/or services. The family's goals are the fullest possible development of each member, regardless of limitations in ability, and the provision of equal opportunities and rewards for each member; the business's goals are profitability and survival.

Individuals involved, directly or indirectly, in a family business have interests and perspectives that differ according to their particular situations. The model in Exhibit 5-1 shows the ways in which individuals may be involved—as members of the family, employees of the business, owners of the business, and various combinations of these. A family member working in the firm but having no ownership interest (sector 6) might favor more generous employment and advancement opportunities for family members than, say, a family member who owns part of the business but works elsewhere (sector 4) or an employee with neither family nor ownership interest (sector 3).

Differing interests can complicate the management process, creating tension and sometimes leading to conflict. Relationships among family members in a business are more sensitive than relationships among unrelated employees. For example, disciplining an employee who consistently arrives late is much more problematic if he or she is also a family member. Or, consider a performance review session between a parent-boss and a child-subordinate. Even with nonfamily employees, performance reviews can be potential minefields. The existence of a family relationship adds emotional overtones that vastly complicate the review process. As successful entrepreneur and author Lowell J. Spirer observes, no one wants his or her tombstone to read: "Here lies a parent or spouse who fired his own flesh and blood without just cause."[6]

Competition Between Business and Family

Which comes first, the family or the business? In theory, at least, most people opt for the family. Few business owners would knowingly allow the business to destroy their family. In practice, however, the resolution of such tensions becomes difficult. For example, despite

EXHIBIT 5-1 *The Three-Circle Model of Family Business*

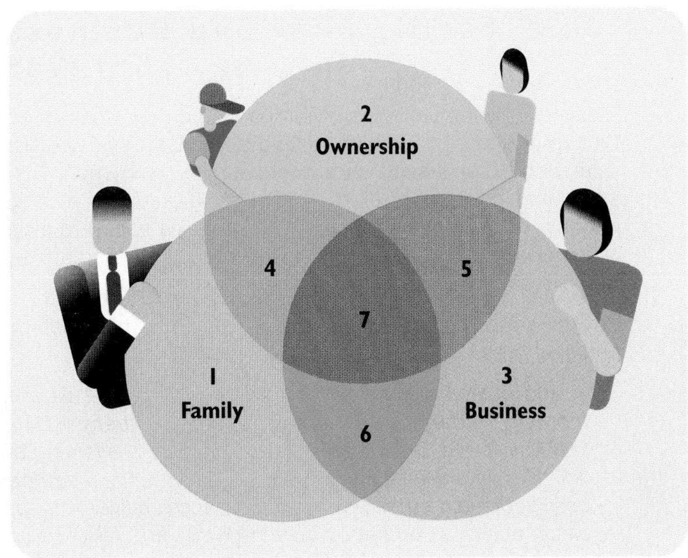

Source: Three-Circle Model developed by Renato Tagiuri and John A. Davis. Found in "Bivalent Attributes of the Family Firm." 1982. Working paper, Harvard Business School, Cambridge, MA. Reprinted 1996, *Family Business Review,* Vol. IX, No. 2, pp. 199–208.

being motivated by a sense of family responsibility, a parent may nevertheless become so absorbed in the business that he or she spends insufficient time with the children.

Many families are accustomed to making minor sacrifices for the good of the business. In many family businesses, for example, the long hours needed in the business sometimes mean missing dinner with the family or skipping a Little League baseball game. Families usually tolerate some inconveniences and disruptions to family life. Occasionally, however, the clash of business interests and family interests is so persistent or so severe that entrepreneurs must decide which comes first. Even when the stakes are high, some choose business over family. Others declare that their highest loyalty belongs to the family but deny it with their behavior.

When Heather Blease started Envisionet in Brunswick, Maine, to provide tech support and customer service for clients' Web sites, she still found time for her sons. She attended their sporting events and volunteered at kindergarten. But when the business grew to 1,000 employees and $12 million in revenues, it became more difficult for Blease to squeeze out family time. The business seemed to dominate every facet of her life. Blease tried to reserve evenings and weekends for her kids, but this was a struggle. She was asked a heart-breaking question by her seven-year-old son: "Mommy, do you love your company more than me?" Of course, Blease wished the question hadn't even needed to be asked. (Envisionet was later sold to Microdyne Outsourcing.)[7]

A magazine article, in which the author argued that trying to balance work and family was futile, drew sharply different reactions from two respondents:[8]

> *Favoring Work:* "I know many women who have had to make that tough choice more than once. It's not easy. But . . . given the choice, I realize I would still leap at the chance to build something great, namely, a business."
>
> *Favoring Family:* "I'm a man whose 'terra firma' is his faith and his family, not his business . . . ; whose concept of building something great includes the character of his kids and the strength of his marriage . . . ; and who, despite the pressures involved in starting a business, still considers work to be a means to an end, not an end in itself. . . . I could write more, but I've got to prepare for tonight's baseball practice: 13 sixth-grade boys are counting on their coach actually being there."

If a family business is to survive, its interests cannot be unduly compromised to satisfy family wishes. To grow, family firms must recognize that professional management is

Living the Dream

Entrepreneurship and Integrity

Family First and Business Second—In a Way That Works

Courtesy of Woodplay of Tampa Bay, Inc.

Nicole and Jason Gulledge of Tampa, Florida, were looking for a career change, something that would be new and interesting and could build on Nicole's background in real estate sales and Jason's skills as a do-it-yourself handyman. Thinking about their three-year-old son, Jake, led them to start a business in children's play equipment, which seemed like a good fit. They now sell and install high-quality backyard playsets as a franchisee of Raleigh, North Carolina–based Woodplay. The couple celebrated the grand opening of their new franchise, Woodplay of Tampa, on March 31, 2001.

But the couple has taken steps to ensure that business concerns do not crowd out their personal lives.

> *In and out of the store, family comes first. The Gulledges start business at 10 each morning so they can eat breakfast together before taking Jake to school. Nicole takes Fridays off and Jason has his Saturdays free, allowing each one-on-one time with their son. Sundays are family days. Jake's playset itself symbolizes the Gulledge family's success in blending their personal and franchise lives. "It has a picnic table underneath, and Jason and I had dinner by candlelight on [it]," Nicole says.*

http://www.woodplayusa.com

It is obvious that the Gulledges are serious about business, but they also place a priority on family—and on having a little fun along the way.

Sources: Devlin Smith, "All Work, All Play," *Entrepreneur,* March 2002, p. 106; http://www.woodplayusa.com, March 17, 2004; and http://www.entrepreneur.com/Magazines/copy_of_MA_SegArticle/0,4453,297193—-%OD-1-00.html, July 12, 2004.

needed and that family interests must sometimes be secondary. This fact is not lost on Ingvar Kamprad, founder of Ikea, a large family business based in Sweden.

Kamprad started Ikea to sell good furniture at reasonable prices to middle-class families. The business has since grown to be the world's biggest furniture retailer, with stores in 34 countries, but it is still a family business. Although Kamprad's personal fortune is estimated at an eyepopping $50 billion today, he retains a simple lifestyle, traveling tourist class, carrying his own bags, and wearing open-necked denim shirts. One of Kamprad's three sons—Peter, 40; Jonas, 37; and Matthias, 35—would seem the logical choice to succeed him, as each has worked for Ikea. But Kamprad is not one to de-emphasize the abilities needed to lead a business of this type, a business that has grown immensely during its brief existence. "I admire my three sons. They're very clever," says Kamprad, adding candidly, "but I don't think any of them is capable of running the company, at least not yet."[9]

The underlying idea is that family members can contribute to the success of a family business but that membership in the family does not automatically endow them with abilities needed in key positions. The health and survival of a family business require proper attention to both business and family interests, as well as a proper balancing of those interests. Otherwise, in the long run at least, results will be unsatisfactory for both. Decisions on the advancement of individual family members should be made carefully, based on leadership ability and in consultation with the firm's board of directors and/or other knowledgeable outside observers. Such decisions, furthermore, should be made in advance (and revised if necessary) rather than postponed until an emergency requires the hurried appointment of a new manager.

Advantages of a Family Business

Problems with family firms can easily blind young people to the unique advantages that come with participating in the business. The benefits associated with family involvement should be recognized and discussed when recruiting younger members to work in the family firm.

A primary benefit derives from the strength of family relationships. Family members have a unique motivation because the firm is a family firm. Business success is also family success. Studies have shown, for example, that family CEOs possess greater internal motivation than do nonfamily CEOs and have less need to receive additional incentives through compensation.[10] CEOs, and other family members as well, are drawn to the business because of family ties, and they tend to stick with the business through thick and thin. A downturn in business fortunes might cause nonfamily employees to seek greener pastures elsewhere, but a son or daughter may be reluctant to leave. The family name, the family welfare, and possibly the family fortune are at stake. In addition, a person's reputation in the family and in the business community may hinge on whether she or he can continue the business that Mom or Grandfather built.

Family members may also sacrifice income to keep a business going. Rather than draw large salaries or high dividends, they are likely to permit resources to remain in the business in order to meet current needs. Many families have postponed the purchase of a new car or new furniture long enough to let a business get started or to get through a period of financial stress, thereby greatly increasing the company's chances of survival.

Some family businesses use the family theme in promotions, to distinguish themselves from their competitors. Such promotional campaigns often attempt to convey the fact that family-owned firms have a strong commitment to the business, high ethical standards, and a personal commitment to serving their customers and the local community.

A Texas funeral home, founded in 1925, strongly emphasizes the family theme in its promotions. Here is a statement from its promotional letter:

> *Now, for the past 11 years the Funeral Home has been under the direction of Hatch Bailey, great-grandson and grandson of the founders. Yes, this absolutely is a family serving families.*
>
> *Does it matter that Wilkirson-Hatch-Bailey is Waco's Family-Owned Funeral Home? We think it makes all the difference in the world.*[11]

The letter then details the local roots, commitments, and longevity of the family and its business. It is signed, appropriately, by Hatch Bailey, Roberta Hatch Bailey, A. W. (Bill) Bailey, Jr., Wes Wilkirson Bailey, and Roy Bailey.

Other features of family involvement in a firm can also contribute to superior business performance. From their study of resource management in family businesses, business professors David Sirmon and Michael Hitt identified the following features of these firms that can offer unique advantages:[12]

1. *Firm-specific knowledge.* Family businesses often compete using firm-specific knowledge that is best shared and further developed by individuals who care deeply about the business and who trust one another.
2. *Shared social networks.* Family members bring valuable social capital to the business when they share their networks with younger members of the family and thus help to ensure the firm's future performance.
3. *A focus on the long run.* Family managers can take a long-range perspective more easily than can corporate managers who are being judged on year-to-year—or even quarterly—results.
4. *Preservation of the firm's reputation.* Because they have a stake in preserving the reputation of the family, family members are likely to maintain high standards when it comes to honesty in business dealings and other matters, such as offering quality and value to the consumer.
5. *Reduced cost of control.* Because key employees in a family business are related and trust one another, the firm can spend less on systems designed to reduce theft and to monitor employees' work habits.

The advantages just discussed are shown graphically in Exhibit 5-2.

THE CULTURE OF A FAMILY BUSINESS

Like other organizations, family firms develop certain ways of doing things and certain priorities that are unique to each firm. These special patterns of behaviors and beliefs comprise the firm's **organizational culture**. As new employees and family members enter the business, they pick up these special viewpoints and ways of operating.

2 Explain the cultural context of a family business.

EXHIBIT 5-2 *Advantages of a Family Business*

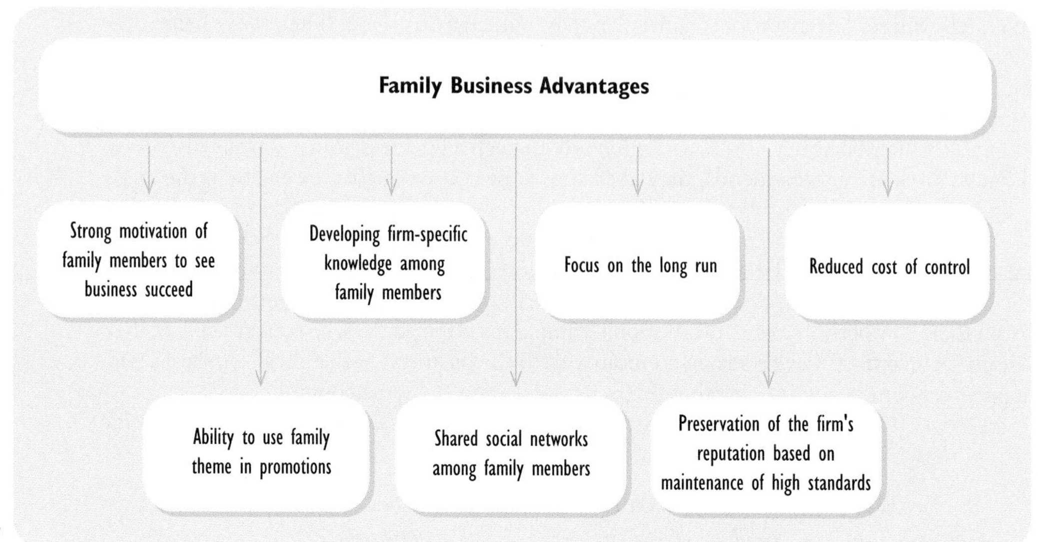

The Founder's Imprint on the Culture

organizational culture Patterns of behaviors and beliefs that characterize a particular firm

The distinctive values that motivate and guide an entrepreneur in the founding of a firm may help to create a competitive advantage for the new firm. For example, the founder may cater to customer needs in a special way and make customer service a guiding principle for the firm. The new firm may go far beyond normal industry practices in making sure customers are satisfied, even if it means working overtime or making a delivery on Saturday. Those who work in such an enterprise quickly learn that customers must always be handled with very special care.

In a family business, the founder's core values may become part of both the business culture and the family code—"the things we believe as a family." John Robben, the second-generation CEO of RobToy, Inc., describes the legacy of his father, who founded the firm:

> *But he left us much more than his confidence and his willingness to take a chance. My father never lied; nor did he ever cheat anyone or take a dollar he didn't honestly earn. He passed these values on, first to me and then, through me, to his grandchildren. It's funny how that worked. He never talked about these things, he just did them.*[13]

Robben's last sentence illustrates the way in which cultural values are transmitted. Family members and others in the firm learn what's important and absorb the traditions of the firm simply by functioning as part of the organization.

Ivan Lansberg has discussed a darker possibility—that of a founder's negative imprint on the organizational culture.[14] Successful business founders may develop an unhealthy *narcissism*, or exaggerated sense of self-importance. Such individuals occasionally develop a craving for attention, a fixation with success and public recognition, and a lack of empathy for others. Unfortunately, these attitudes can harm the business by creating a general feeling of superiority and a sense of complacency. While contributions of founders deserve proper acknowledgment, such extremes must be avoided.

Cultural Patterns

The culture of a particular firm includes numerous distinctive beliefs and behaviors. Close examination of those beliefs and behaviors will reveal various cultural patterns that help explain the way in which the firm functions.

The three-circle model pictured in Exhibit 5-1 is often used to illustrate the complexities of the family firm's interactive components: the business, the family, and the owners. Adapting this view, family business expert W. Gibb Dyer, Jr., has identified a set of cultural patterns that characterize family firms.[15] As illustrated in Exhibit 5-3, the business pattern,

EXHIBIT 5-3 *Cultural Configuration of a Family Firm*

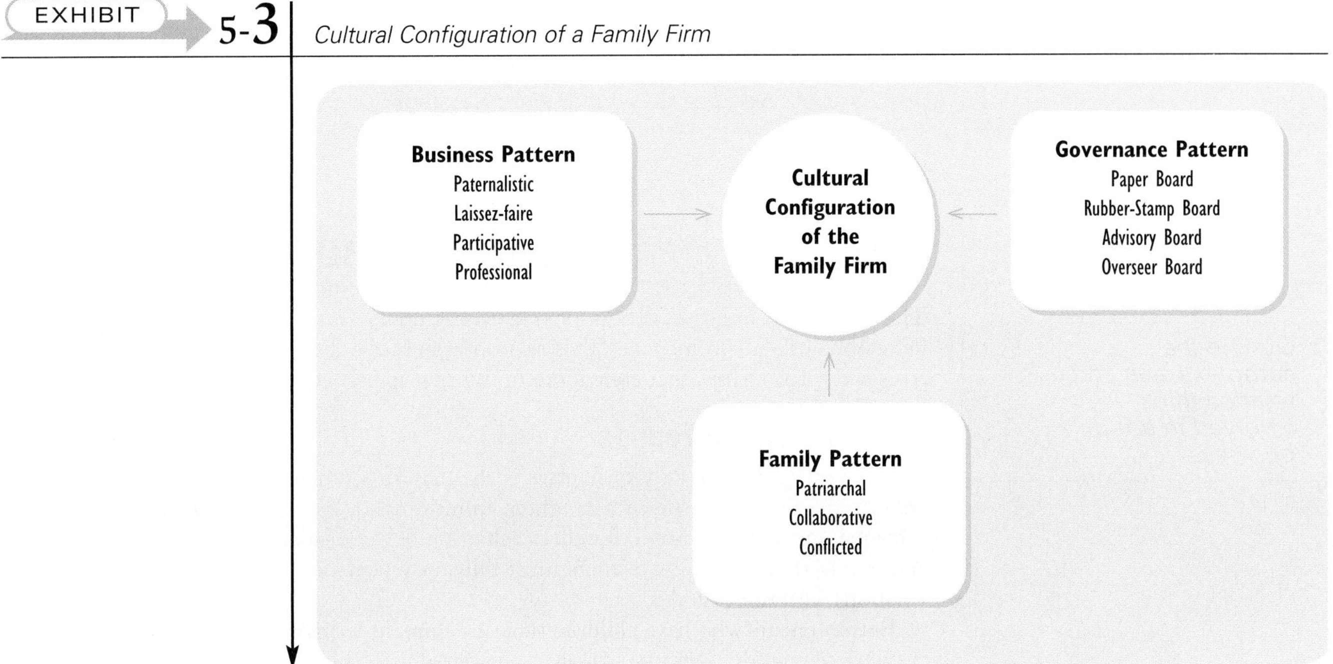

Source: W. Gibb Dyer, Jr., *Cultural Change in Family Firms* (San Francisco: Jossey-Bass, 1986), p. 22.

the family pattern, and the governance pattern form an overall **cultural configuration** that constitutes a family firm's total culture.

cultural configuration
The total culture of a family firm, consisting of the firm's business, family, and governance patterns

An example of a business pattern is a firm's system of beliefs and behaviors concerning the importance of quality. Members of an organization tend to adopt a common viewpoint concerning the extent to which effort, or even sacrifice, should be devoted to customer service and product quality. When the leader of a firm consistently demonstrates a commitment to serving customers, he or she encourages others to appreciate the same values. Through decisions and practices that place a high priority on customer service, therefore, the leader of a family business can build a business pattern based on a strong commitment to producing high-quality goods and services.

In the early stages of a family business, according to Dyer, a common cultural configuration consists of a paternalistic business pattern, a patriarchal family pattern, and a rubber-stamp board of directors (governance pattern). This simply means that family relationships are more important than professional skills, that the founder is the undisputed head of the clan, and that the board automatically supports the founder's decisions.

Culture and Leadership Succession

The process of passing the leadership of a family firm from one generation to another is complicated by, and interwoven with, changes in the family business pattern. To appreciate this point, think about the paternalistic/patriarchal cultural configuration, which is quite common in the early days of a family business. Changing conditions may render that cultural configuration ineffective. As a family business grows, it requires a greater measure of professional expertise. Thus, the firm may be pressured to break from the paternalistic mold, which gives first priority to family authority and less attention to professional abilities. Likewise, the aging of the founder and the maturation of the founder's children tend to weaken the patriarchal family culture with its one dominant source of authority—a parent who "always knows best."

Succession may occur, therefore, against the backdrop of a changing organizational culture. Or the change in leadership itself may play a role in introducing or bringing about a break with traditional methods of operation. To some extent, the successor may act as a change agent. For example, a son or daughter with a business degree may replace dated managerial practices with a more up-to-date professional approach.

As you can see, growth of the business and changes in leadership over time will make some cultural change necessary. However, certain values are timeless and should never be changed—the commitment to honesty, for example. While some traditions may embody inefficient business practices and require alteration, others are basic to the competitive strength and integrity of the firm. The topic of leadership succession will be considered in greater detail later in the chapter.

FAMILY ROLES AND RELATIONSHIPS

3 *Outline the complex roles and relationships involved in a family business.*

The overlapping of two institutions—a family and a business—makes the family firm incredibly difficult to manage. This section examines a few of the many possible family roles and relationships that contribute to this managerial complexity.

Mom or Dad, the Founder

A common figure in family businesses is the man or woman who founded the firm and plans to pass it on to a son or a daughter. In most cases, the business and the family have grown simultaneously. Some founders achieve a delicate balance between their business and family responsibilities. Others must diligently plan time for weekend activities and vacations with the children.

Entrepreneurs who have children typically think in terms of passing the business on to the next generation. Parental concerns associated with this process include the following:

- Does my child possess the temperament and ability necessary for business leadership?
- How can I, the founder, motivate my child to take an interest in the business?
- What type of education and experience will be most helpful in preparing my child for leadership?
- What timetable should I follow in employing and promoting my child?
- How can I avoid favoritism in managing and developing my child?
- How can I prevent the business relationship from damaging or destroying the parent–child relationship?

Of all the relationships in a family business, the parent–child relationship has been recognized for generations as the most troublesome. In recent years, the problems inherent in this relationship have been addressed by counselors, seminars, and numerous books. In spite of this extensive attention, however, the parent–child relationship continues to perplex numerous families involved in family businesses.

Husband–Wife Teams

Some family businesses are owned and managed by husband–wife teams. Their roles vary depending on their backgrounds and expertise. In some cases, the husband serves as general manager and the wife runs the office. In others, the wife functions as operations manager and the husband keeps the books. Whatever the arrangement, both individuals are an integral part of the business.

A potential advantage of the husband–wife team is the opportunity it affords a couple to share more of their lives. For some couples, however, the potential benefits become eclipsed by problems related to the business. Differences of opinion about business matters may carry over into family life. And the energy of both parties may be so dissipated by their work in a struggling company that little zest remains for a strong family life.

Many couples have developed coping patterns that involve both partners in raising the children. Doug and Kimberly Rath, for example, are an entrepreneurial couple who founded Talent Plus, a human resource firm in Lincoln, Nebraska.[16] When Kim was traveling on business, Doug faxed her their daughter's grades; after her son scored eight goals in one soccer game, Doug handed the boy his cellular phone as he walked off the field so that he could share the moment with Mom.

Sons and Daughters

Should sons and daughters be groomed for the family business, or should they pursue careers of their own choosing? In the entrepreneurial family, the natural tendency is to think in terms of a family business career and to push a child, either openly or subtly, in that direction. Little thought may be given to the basic issues involved, which include the child's talent, aptitude, and temperament. The child may be a chip off the old block but may also be an individual with different talents and aspirations. He or she may prefer music or medicine to the world of business and may fit the business mold very poorly. It is also possible that the abilities of the son or daughter may simply be insufficient for a leadership role. Or, a child's talents may be underestimated by parents simply because there has been little opportunity for the child to develop or demonstrate those talents.

Another issue is personal freedom. Today's society values the right of the individual to choose his or her own career and way of life. If this value is embraced by a son or daughter, that child must be granted the freedom to select a career of his or her own choosing.

A son or daughter may feel a need to go outside the family business, for a time at least, to prove that "I can make it on my own." To build self-esteem, he or she may wish to operate independently of the family. Entering the family business immediately after graduation from high school or college may seem stifling, as the child continues to "feel like a little kid with Dad telling me what to do."

If the family business is profitable, it does provide rewards. A son or daughter may be well advised to give serious consideration to accepting such an opportunity. If the business

Living the Dream — Entrepreneurial Challenges

Kids Will Be Kids . . . but Not Always Employees

To join or not to join? That is the question. And Sue Birley, professor of entrepreneurship and director of the Entrepreneurship Centre at Imperial College in London, wanted to know the answer. She surveyed 412 children of business owner-managers to see if they planned to enter the family business in the future and found that 80 percent of those who were not already working in the business did not intend to join it. And of those who intended to enter the business at some point, 70 percent planned to work somewhere else first. Respondents offered a variety of comments to explain their decisions.

- "I do not look to going into the family business straight away as I feel this is giving a commitment to work there for the rest of my life."
- "I would only want to join because I am genuinely qualified, not because I am the owner's daughter."
- "A large factor when working under a relative is the problem of self-worth. It is hard to feel like you are worth something when your father is the [managing director]."
- "I see the pressure my dad is under—this does put me off slightly—I want to enjoy my job as well as enjoying life outside work."
- "I have more choice over what I want to do as a career, and my personal interests would not be met by my father's company."
- "I haven't a clue what the family business does, although I am a part of it. I think my father presumes I am not interested because I don't want a business career."
- "Though I am sure it is not consciously done, it seems that the male grandchildren are being pushed toward the business while I, the eldest granddaughter, am positively discouraged."

These quotes reveal a wide range of reactions to the prospect of joining a family business, including disinterest, self-doubt, commitment worries, and even the perception of discrimination. They provide a small window on the concerns of sons and daughters of business owners as they ponder their futures. Clearly, this is a complex decision, which may explain why so few have firm plans to sign up with the family business anytime soon.

Source: Sue Birley, "Attitudes of Owner-Managers' Children Toward Family and Business Issues," *Entrepreneurship Theory and Practice*, Vol. 26, No. 3, (Summer 2002), pp. 5–19.

relationship is to be satisfactory, however, family pressure must be minimized. Both parties must recognize the choice as a business decision as well as a family decision—and as a decision that may be reversed.

Sibling Cooperation, Sibling Rivalry

In families with a number of children, two or more may become involved in the family business. This depends, of course, on the interests of the individual children. In some cases, parents feel fortunate if even one child elects to stay with the family firm. Nevertheless, it is not unusual for several siblings to take positions within the firm. Even those who do not work in the business may be more than casual observers on the sidelines because of their stake as heirs or partial owners.

At best, siblings work as a smoothly functioning team, each contributing services according to his or her respective abilities. Just as some families experience excellent cooperation and unity in their family relationships, some family businesses benefit from effective collaboration among brothers and sisters.

However, just as there are sometimes squabbles within a family, there can also be sibling rivalry within a family business. Business issues tend to generate competition, and this affects family, as well as nonfamily, members. Siblings, for example, may disagree about business policy or about their respective roles in the business. Rivalry quickly became a problem among the three siblings involved in Peter Pan Bus Lines in Springfield, Massachusetts.[17] As Paul and Mary tried to work with Peter Jr. at the bus line's corporate headquarters, the three third-generation family members began undercutting each other. The tension between Peter Jr. and Paul was particularly intense, and lower-level employees, when asked in employee surveys about company problems, put "company squabbles" at the top of the list. Eventually, the father split the ownership of the bus line and certain real estate holdings in such a way that the siblings could operate more independently of one another. The new arrangement did not bring the children closer but did eliminate a lot of friction.

In-Laws In and Out of the Business

As sons and daughters marry, daughters-in-law and sons-in-law become significant actors in the family business drama. Some in-laws become directly involved by accepting positions in the family firm. If a son or daughter is also employed in the firm, rivalry and conflict may develop. For example, family members may disagree about how rewards for performance should compare for an in-law and a son or daughter.

For a time, effective collaboration may be achieved by assigning family members to different branches or roles within the company. Eventually, competition for top leadership will force decisions that distinguish among children and in-laws employed in the business. Being fair and retaining family loyalty become more difficult as the number of family employees increases.

Sons, daughters, sons-in-law, and daughters-in-law who are on the sidelines are also participants with an important stake in the business. For example, if a daughter is married to someone on the family payroll, she will see a decision by a parent affecting her husband as both a family decision and a business decision. Giving the nod to a son-in-law thus becomes more than merely promoting another employee in a business.

In some family businesses, it's the family's attitude that ensures that in-laws are able to work directly and harmoniously with one another. Susan and David Hurst launched The Market at North Shore, a gourmet food and catering shop in Atlantic Beach, Florida. Later, they added Susan's mother, 64, who makes desserts, and David's mother, 62, who is the office manager. In some firms, such a mixture of family members could prove explosive and detrimental to the business. In this case, the combination works well and makes for a healthy business. "Customers are amazed I can work with my husband, my mother, and my mother-in-law and that we all still love each other," says Susan. "They took care of us for so many years, it's time to take care of them."[18]

The Entrepreneur's Spouse

One of the most critical roles in the family business drama is that of the entrepreneur's spouse. Traditionally, this role has been fulfilled by the male entrepreneur's wife and the mother of his children. However, more women are becoming entrepreneurs, and many husbands have now assumed the role of entrepreneur's spouse.

In order for the spouse to play a supporting role in the entrepreneur's career, there must be communication between the spouse and the entrepreneur and the spouse must be a good listener. The spouse needs to hear what's going on in the business; otherwise, she or he feels detached and must compete for attention. The spouse can offer understanding and act as a sounding board for the entrepreneur only if they communicate on matters of obvious importance to them both individually and as a family.

It is easy for the spouse to function as worrier for the family business. This is particularly true if there is insufficient communication about business matters. One spouse expressed her feelings in the following way: "I've told my husband that I have an active imagination—very active. If he doesn't tell me what's going on in the business, well, then I'm going to imagine what's going on and blow it all out of proportion. When things are looking dark, I'd rather know the worst than know nothing."[19]

As a parent, the spouse helps prepare the children for possible careers in the family business. The spouse may also serve as a mediator in business relationships between the entrepreneur and the children. One wife's comments to her husband, John, and son Terry illustrate the nature of this function:

- "John, don't you think that Terry may have worked long enough as a stockperson in the warehouse?"
- "Terry, your father is going to be very disappointed if you don't come back to the business after your graduation."
- "John, do you really think it is fair to move Stanley into that new office? After all, Terry is older and has been working a year longer."
- "Terry, what did you say to your father today that upset him?"

Ideally, the entrepreneur and his or her spouse form a team committed to the success of both the family and the family business. Such teamwork does not occur automatically—it requires a collaborative effort by both parties to the marriage.

PROFESSIONAL MANAGEMENT OF THE FAMILY FIRM

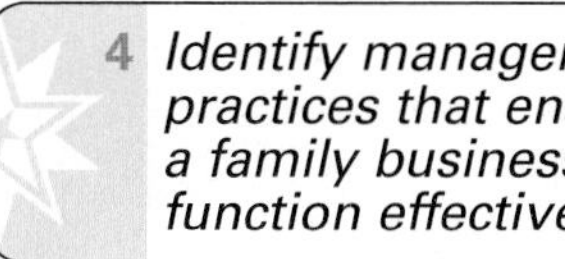
4 *Identify management practices that enable a family business to function effectively.*

The complexity of relationships in family firms requires enlightened management. To a considerable extent, this just means good professional management. However, certain techniques are particularly useful in dealing with the problems inherent in the family firm.

The Need for Good Management

Good management is necessary for the success of any business, and the family firm is no exception. Significant deviations for family reasons from what might be called good management practices, therefore, only serve to weaken the firm. Such a course of action runs counter to the interests of both the firm and the family.

A number of "best practices" have been proposed by John L. Ward, clinical professor and co-director of the Center for Family Enterprises at the Kellogg School of Management at Northwestern University.[20] Some of these practices are as follows:

1. Stimulate new thinking and fresh strategic insights.
2. Attract and retain excellent nonfamily managers.
3. Create a flexible, innovative organization.
4. Create and conserve capital.
5. Prepare successors for leadership.
6. Exploit the unique advantages of family ownership.

The family firm is a business—a competitive business. Observing these and other practices of good management will help the business thrive and permit the family to function as a family. Disregarding them will pose a threat to the business and impose strains on family relationships.

Nonfamily Employees in a Family Firm

Those employees who are not family members are still affected by family considerations. In some cases, their opportunities for promotion are lessened by the presence of family members who seem to have the inside track. Few parents will promote an outsider over a competent daughter or son who is being groomed for future leadership. The potential for advancement of nonfamily employees, therefore, may be limited, and they may experience a sense of unfairness and frustration.

Consider the case of a young business executive who worked for a family business that operated a chain of restaurants. When hired, he had negotiated a contract that gave him a specified percentage of the business based on performance. Under this arrangement, he was doing extremely well financially—until the owner called on him to say "I am here to buy you out." When the young man asked why, the owner replied, "You are doing too well, and your last name is not the same as mine!"

The extent of limitations on nonfamily employees depends on the number of family members active in the business and the number of managerial or professional positions in the business to which nonfamily employees might aspire. It also depends on the extent to which the owner demands competence in management and maintains an atmosphere of fairness in supervision. To avoid future problems, the owner should make clear, when hiring nonfamily employees, the extent of opportunities available and identify the positions, if any, that are reserved for family members.

Those outside the family may also be caught in the crossfire between family members who are competing with each other. It is difficult for outsiders to maintain strict neutrality in family feuds. If a nonfamily employee is perceived as siding with one of those involved in the feud, he or she may lose the support of other family members. Hard-working employees often feel that they deserve hazard pay for working in a firm plagued by family conflict.

Family Retreats

family retreat
A gathering of family members, usually at a remote location, to discuss family business matters

Some families hold retreats in order to review family business concerns. A **family retreat** is a meeting of family members, usually at a remote location, to discuss family business matters. An attempt is made to create an informal atmosphere. Nancy Upton, founder of the Institute for Family Business at Baylor University, has conducted many family retreats. She describes the general purpose and format of such retreats as follows:

> *The purpose of the retreat is to provide a forum for introspection, problem solving and policy making. For some participants this will be their first opportunity to talk about their concerns in a nonconfrontational atmosphere. It is also a time to celebrate the family and enhance its inner strength.*
>
> *A retreat usually lasts two days and is held far enough away so you won't be disturbed or tempted to go to the office. Every member of the family, including in-laws, should be invited.*[21]

The prospect of sitting down together to discuss family business matters may seem threatening to some family members. As a result, some families avoid extensive communication, fearing that it will stir up trouble. They assume that making decisions quietly or secretly will preserve harmony. Unfortunately, such an approach often conceals serious differences that become increasingly troublesome. Family retreats are designed to open lines of communication and to bring about understanding and agreement on family business issues.

Initiating discussion can be difficult, so family leaders often invite an outside expert or facilitator to lead early sessions. The facilitator can help develop an agenda and establish ground rules for discussion. While chairing early sessions, the moderator can establish a positive tone that emphasizes family achievements and encourages rational consideration of sensitive issues. If family members can develop an atmosphere of neutrality, however, they may be able to chair the sessions without using an outsider.

To ensure the success of a family business retreat, Steven White, CEO of S. D. White & Associates, suggests that these guidelines be followed:[22]

1. *Set a time and place.* The retreat should be held at a convenient time and in a central location so that everyone can be involved.

2. *Distribute an agenda prior to meeting.* An agenda helps participants organize their thoughts about the issues that are to be discussed.
3. *Plan a schedule in advance.* Details for sessions should be planned ahead of the retreat. Sufficient blocks of time should be provided to deal with important matters and room left in the schedule for refreshment breaks. It's a good idea to set aside one evening for the family to get together and do something fun as a group.
4. *Give everyone a chance to participate.* In sessions, family members should be honest, and they should not interrupt one another. The conversation may be allowed to wander a bit, if this is therapeutic, but the focus should stay on the business.
5. *Keep it professional.* The conversation may become emotional when sensitive topics are discussed, but it should never be allowed to become personal or to spiral out of control. Everyone should leave the retreat feeling good about what was accomplished.

But the talk at family retreats is not always about business. After a retreat, families often speak of the joy of sharing family values and stories of past family experiences. Thus, retreats can strengthen the family as well as the company.

Family Councils

A family retreat could pave the way for creation of a **family council**, in which family members meet to discuss values, policies, and direction for the future. A family council functions as the organizational and strategic planning arm of a family. It provides a forum for the ongoing process of listening to the ideas of all members and discovering what they believe in and want from the business. A family council formalizes the participation of the family in the business to a greater extent than does the family retreat. It can also be a focal point for planning the future of individual family members, the family as a whole, and the business, as well as how each relates to the other.

family council
An organized group of family members who gather periodically to discuss family-related business issues

A council should be a formal organization that holds regular meetings, keeps minutes, and makes suggestions to the firm's board of directors. Experts recommend that it be open to all interested family members and spouses of all generations. During the first several meetings, an acceptable mission statement is usually generated, as well as a family creed.

Family businesses that have such councils find them useful for developing family harmony. The meetings are often fun and informative and may include speakers who discuss items of interest. Time is often set aside for sharing achievements, milestones, and family history. The younger generation is encouraged to participate because much of the process is designed to increase their understanding of family traditions and business interests and to prepare them for working effectively in the business.

As with family retreats, an outside facilitator may be useful in getting a council organized and helping with initial meetings. Subsequently, the organization and leadership of meetings can rotate among family members.

Family Business Constitutions

Some experts suggest that families write a **family business constitution**, which is a statement of principles intended to guide a family firm through times of crisis and change, including the succession process. While this is not a legally binding document, it nonetheless helps to preserve the intentions of the founder(s) and ensure that the business survives periods of change largely intact. When a transfer between generations occurs and there is no guiding document, issues such as ownership, performance, and compensation can become flash points for conflict.[23]

family business constitution
A statement of principles intended to guide a family firm through times of crisis and change

When Randall Clifford's father died in 1994, the ownership and control of Ventura Transfer Co., the oldest trucking company in California, were suddenly called into question. Clifford's stepmother sued him and his three brothers for an interest in the business. Then, to make matters worse, the four Clifford brothers began to struggle among themselves for control of the company. After a drawn-out legal battle, the sons decided to enlist the help of a consultant to draft a family business constitution. The resulting document helped the family sort out many of the issues that had plagued the transition process.

A family business constitution cannot foresee every eventuality, but that is not a problem since a family business constitution is a "living, breathing document" that can be amended as needed.[24] The important point is that this document can smooth any transitions—such as a change in leadership, the subject of the next section.

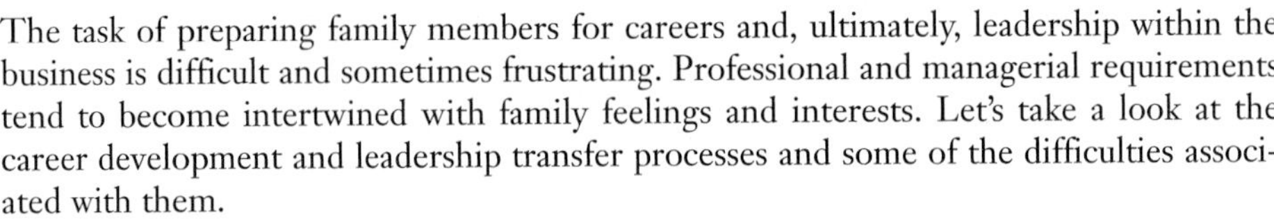

THE PROCESS OF LEADERSHIP SUCCESSION

5 Describe the process of managerial succession in a family business.

The task of preparing family members for careers and, ultimately, leadership within the business is difficult and sometimes frustrating. Professional and managerial requirements tend to become intertwined with family feelings and interests. Let's take a look at the career development and leadership transfer processes and some of the difficulties associated with them.

Available Family Talent

A stream can rise no higher than its source, and the family firm can be no more brilliant than its leader. The business is dependent, therefore, on the quality of leadership talent provided. If the available talent is not sufficient, the owner must bring in outside leadership or supplement family talent to avoid a decline under the leadership of second- or third-generation family members.

The question of competency is both a critical and a delicate issue. With experience, individuals can improve their abilities; younger people should not be judged too harshly early on. Furthermore, potential successors may be held back by the reluctance of a parent-owner to delegate realistically to them.

Living the Dream — *Entrepreneurial Challenges*

A Formal Wear Feud

© Mel Yates/Photodisc Red/Getty Images

Customers look great in tuxedos from Al's Formal Wear, but there is no way to dress up the company's history of conflict. Al Sankary launched his tux-rental venture in 1952 after he inherited a tailor shop in Fort Worth, Texas. The new thrust of the business led to early success, and Sankary was soon opening new stores in Dallas and in Tulsa, Oklahoma. In 1957, Sankary helped his sister and brother-in-law, Lillian and Alan Gaylor, open a shop in Houston. The Gaylor's shop quietly thrived, so they opened new stores and took steps to buy out Sankary's interest in the Houston operation.

At some point along the way, things turned contentious. The two families had different leadership styles and visions for the future, and this led to serious conflict. In the words of Jerry Sankary, Al's son, "We didn't see eye to eye on anything." The conflict escalated until it became clear that a "divorce" was necessary.

"It had to be done for the sake of the family," concluded Jack Sankary, Al's brother and the company's controller. "I could see the storm clouds ahead if this didn't happen."

In 1978, after a year-long legal battle, it was decided that the company would be divided. Al Sankary would get 34 stores, mostly in north Texas, and the Gaylors would get 26 stores in Houston. But there was still one unsettled issue: Who would get to use the name Al's Formal Wear? Neither side would give it up, so they both were allowed to keep it, but only within set geographic boundaries. The matter was settled.

But there is a family business story within this story, and it relates to succession planning. Alan and Lillian Gaylor developed a clear succession plan for their family's company, and their four children all played successful roles in the business at one time or another. The firm thrived on wise decisions regarding technology and management. In stark contrast, Al Sankary found it difficult to get his kids involved in the company, and those who did take positions there found it frustrating to work with their father. Things did not go well, which forced Sankary to make a number of difficult decisions, like closing some shops. But eventually, after undergoing triple-bypass surgery in 1998, the 75-year-old patriarch of Al's Formal Wear decided it was time to sell out—to the Gaylors. No more divided territories and no more bad blood in the family. The business that became two is now one again, and things are going well.

Today, the Gaylors have 115 stores in four states and a vision for further expansion. Having a plan for succession contributed to this happy ending.

Sources: http://www.alsformalwear.com, March 18, 2004; and Rodney Ho, "Family Feud in Formal Wear," *Wall Street Journal*, February 21, 2000, p. A16.

In some cases, a younger family member's skills may actually help to rescue the company, especially when a family business becomes mired in the past and fails to keep up with changing technology and emerging markets. In 1983, Tom Jennison opened Jennison Manufacturing Corporation, a gritty, small tool-and-die operation in Carnegie, Pennsylvania, a now-faded steel town. Its basic, simple products included parts for gas masks and injection molds for making toilet mechanisms. As Tom began to computerize the business in 1988, he ran into major problems and called on his son Mike, a junior at Penn State University. Mike came home to help his father get the system working smoothly and then joined the firm after graduation. He began developing a home-wiring control box—a device that would serve as a command center for things like home computer networks, stereo systems, telephone lines, and cable TV. Together, Tom and Mike are building a new facility and expect to employ 120 people in producing the new product. The rest of the business will continue to employ about 60 people. For Jennison Manufacturing, the process of transferring leadership to a second generation has involved not only training a potential successor but also moving into new areas of technology and new markets.[25]

In any case, a family firm need not accept the existing level of family talent as an unchangeable given. Instead, the business may offer various types of developmental programs to teach younger family members and thereby improve their skills. Some businesses, for example, include mentoring as a part of such programs.[26] **Mentoring** is the process by which a senior person in the firm guides and supports the work, progress, and professional relationships of a new or less-experienced employee.

mentoring
Guiding and supporting the work and development of a new or less-experienced organization member

Perhaps the fairest and most practical approach is to recognize the right of family members to prove themselves. A period of development and testing may occur either in the family business or, preferably, in another organization. If children show themselves to be capable, they earn the right to increased leadership responsibility. If potential successors are found, through a process of fair assessment, to have inadequate leadership abilities, preservation of the family business and the welfare of family members demand that they be passed over for promotion. The appointment of competent outsiders to these jobs, if necessary, increases the value of the firm for all family members who have an ownership interest in it.

Stages in the Process of Succession

Sons or daughters do not typically assume leadership of a family firm at a particular moment in time. Instead, a long, drawn-out process of preparation and transition is customary—a process that extends over years and often decades. Exhibit 5-4 portrays this process as a series of **stages in succession.**[27]

stages in succession
Phases in the process of transferring leadership of a family business from parent to child

PRE-BUSINESS STAGE In Stage I, a potential successor becomes acquainted with the business as a part of growing up. The young child accompanies a parent to the office, store, or warehouse or plays with equipment related to the business. This early stage does not entail any formal planning to prepare the child for entering the business. It simply forms a foundation for the more deliberate stages of the process that occur in later years.

INTRODUCTORY STAGE Like Stage I, Stage II includes experiences that occur before the successor is old enough to begin part-time work in the family business. It differs from Stage I in that family members deliberately introduce the child to certain people associated directly or indirectly with the firm and to other aspects of the business. In an industrial equipment dealership, for example, a parent might let the child ride on a bulldozer, explain the difference between a front loader and a backhoe, or introduce the child to the firm's banker.

INTRODUCTORY FUNCTIONAL STAGE In Stage III, the son or daughter begins to function as a part-time employee, often during vacations or after school. At this stage, the son or daughter develops an acquaintance with some of the key individuals employed in the firm. Such work often begins in the warehouse, office, or production department and may involve assignments in various functional areas as time goes on. The introductory functional stage includes the child's formal education as well as experience gained in other organizations.

FUNCTIONAL STAGE Stage IV begins when the potential successor enters full-time employment, typically following the completion of his or her formal education. Prior to moving into a management position, the son or daughter may work as an accountant, a

EXHIBIT 5-4 *A Model of Succession in a Family Business*

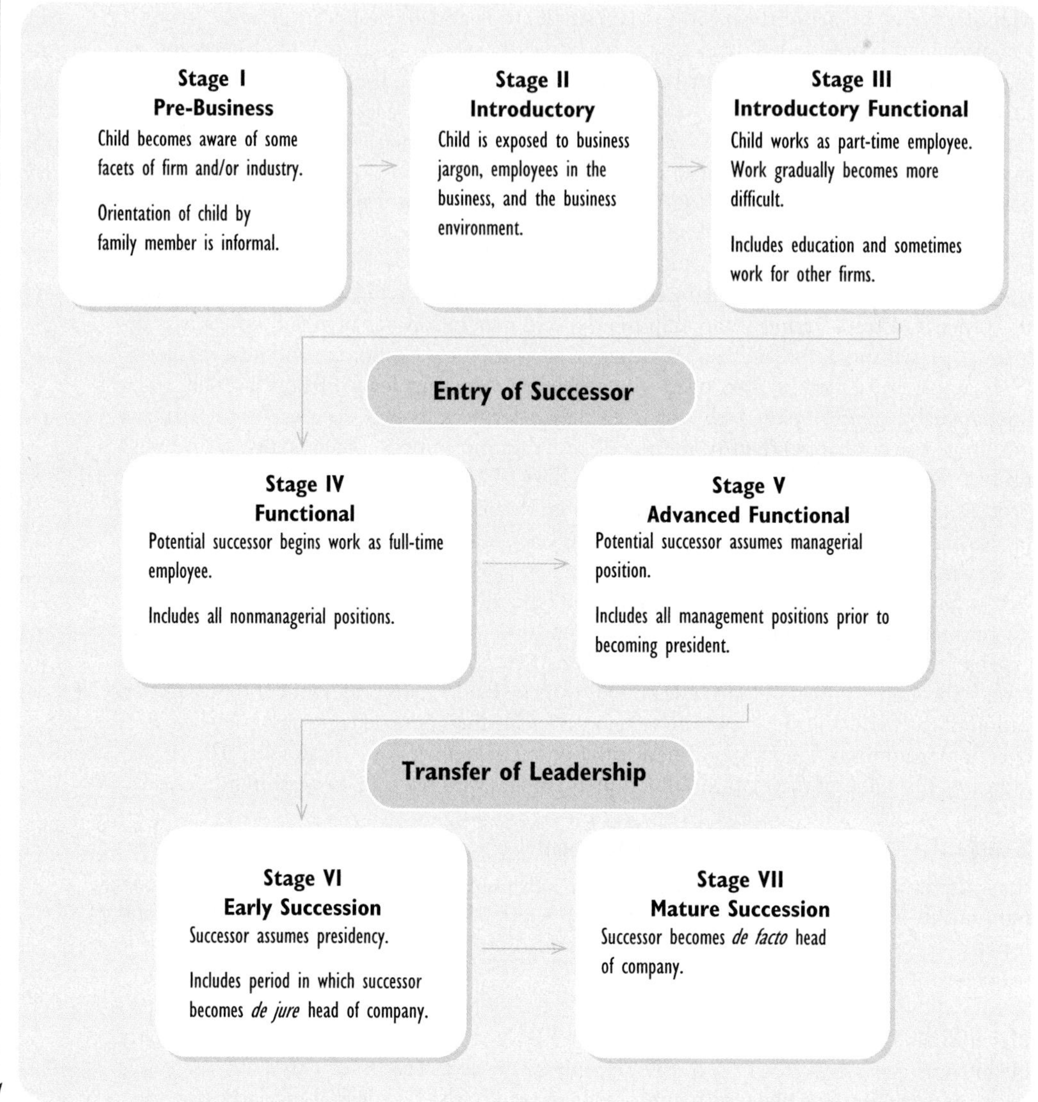

Source: Justin G. Longenecker and John E. Schoen, "Management Succession in the Family Business," *Journal of Small Business Management,* Vol. 16 (July 1978), pp. 1–6.

salesperson, or an inventory clerk, possibly gaining experience in a number of such positions.

ADVANCED FUNCTIONAL STAGE As the potential successor assumes supervisory duties, he or she enters the advanced functional stage, or Stage V. The management positions at this stage involve directing the work of others but not managing the entire firm.

EARLY SUCCESSION STAGE In Stage VI, the son or daughter is named president or general manager of the business. As *de jure* head of the business, he or she presumably exercises overall direction, but a parent is still in the background. The leadership role does not transfer as easily or absolutely as the leadership title does. The successor has not necessarily mastered the complexities of the role, and the predecessor may be reluctant to give up all decision making.

MATURE SUCCESSION STAGE Stage VII is reached when the transition process is complete. The successor is leader in fact as well as in name. In some cases, this does not occur until the predecessor dies. In the best-case scenario, Stage VII begins two or three years after the successor assumes the leadership title.

Reluctant Parents and Ambitious Children

When the founder of a business is preparing her or his child to take over the firm, the founder's attachment to the business must not be underestimated. Not only is a father, for example, tied to the firm financially—it is probably his primary, if not his only, major investment—but he is also tied to it emotionally. The business is his "baby," and he is understandably reluctant to entrust its future to one whom he sees as immature and unproven. Unfortunately, parents often have a way of seeing their children as immature long after their years of adolescence.

The child may be ambitious, well educated, and insightful regarding the business. His or her tendency to push ahead—to try something new—often conflicts with the father's caution. As a result, the child may see the father as excessively conservative, stubborn, and unwilling to change.

A study examined 18 family-owned businesses in which daughters worked as managers with their fathers. Interviews with family members produced this overall picture of the daughters' positions:

> *In 90 percent of the cases, the daughters reported having to contend with carryover, conflict, and ambiguity in their business roles in the firm and as daughters. While the majority of the women interviewed had previously worked in other organizations and had developed their identities as businesswomen, they discovered that when they joined the family business they were torn between their roles as daughter and their business roles. They found their relationships with the boss transformed, since the boss was not only the boss, but the father as well. These daughters reported that they often found themselves reduced to the role of "daddy's little girl" (and, in a few cases, "mommy's little girl"), in spite of their best intentions.*[28]

At the root of many such difficulties is a lack of understanding between parent and child. They work together without a map showing where they are going. Children in the business, and also their spouses, may have expectations about progress that, in terms of the founder's thinking, are totally unrealistic. The successor tends to sense such problems much more acutely than does his or her parent. But many of the problems could be avoided if a full discussion of the development process took place in advance.

Transfer of Ownership

A final and often complex step in the traditional succession process in the family firm is the **transfer of ownership**. Questions of inheritance affect not only the leadership successor but also other family members having no involvement in the business. In distributing their estate, parent-owners typically wish to treat all their children fairly, both those involved in the business and those on the outside.

transfer of ownership
Passing ownership of a family business to the next generation

One of the most difficult decisions is determining the future ownership of the business. If there are several children, for example, should they all receive equal shares? On the surface, this seems to be the fairest approach. However, such an arrangement may play havoc with the future functioning of the business. Suppose that each of five children receives a 20-percent ownership share, even though only one of them is active in the business. The child active in the business—the leadership successor—becomes a minority stockholder completely at the mercy of relatives on the outside.

A parent might attempt to resolve such a dilemma by changing the ownership structure of the firm. Those children active in the firm's management, for example, might be given common (voting) stock and others given preferred (nonvoting) stock. However, this is still troublesome because of the relative weaknesses of various ownership securities.

Tax considerations are relevant, of course, and they tend to favor gradual transfer of ownership to all heirs. As noted, however, transfer of equal ownership shares to all heirs may be inconsistent with the future efficient operation of the business. Tax advantages should not be allowed to blind one to possible adverse effects on management.

Ideally, the founder has been able to arrange his or her personal holdings to create wealth outside the business as well as within it. In that case, he or she may bequeath comparable shares to all heirs while allowing business control to remain with the child or children active in the business. Planning and discussing the transfer of ownership is not easy, but such action is recommended. Over a period of time, the owner must reflect seriously on family talents and interests as they relate to the future of the firm. The plan for transfer of ownership can then be firmed up and modified as necessary when it is discussed with the children or other potential heirs. In discussing exit strategies in Chapter 12, we explain a variety of possible financial arrangements for the transfer of ownership.

Looking Back

1 Discuss the factors that make a family business unique.

- Family members have a special involvement in a family business.
- Business interests (production and profitability) overlap family interests (care and nurturing) in a family business.
- Entrepreneurs face difficult choices in reconciling the competing demands of business and family.
- The advantages of a family business include the strong commitment of family members to the success of the firm, the ability to use a family theme in advertising, the development of firm-specific knowledge, the sharing of social networks among family members, a focus on long-term goals, an emphasis on the firm's reputation, and reduced cost of control.

2 Explain the cultural context of a family business.

- Special patterns of beliefs and behaviors constitute the organizational culture of a family business.
- The founder often leaves a deep imprint on the culture of a family firm.
- The cultural configuration is formed by the business pattern, family pattern, and governance pattern.
- Changes in culture often occur as leadership passes from one generation to the next.

3 Outline the complex family roles and relationships involved in a family business.

- A primary and sensitive relationship is that between founder and son or daughter.
- Some couples in business together find their marriage relationship strengthened, while others find it weakened.
- Sons, daughters, in-laws, and other relatives may either enjoy cooperation or engage in family quarrels as they work together in a family business.
- In-laws play a crucial role in the family business, either as direct participants or as sideline observers.
- The role of the founder's spouse is especially important, as he or she often serves as a mediator in family disputes and helps prepare the children for possible careers in the family business.

4 Identify management practices that enable a family business to function effectively.

- Good management practices are as important as good family relationships in the successful functioning of a family business.
- Family members should be treated fairly and consistently, in accordance with their abilities and performance.
- Motivation of nonfamily employees can be enhanced by open communication and fairness.
- Family retreats bring all family members together to discuss business and family matters.
- Family councils provide a formal framework for the family's ongoing discussion of family and business issues.
- Family business constitutions can guide a company through times of crisis or change.

5 Describe the process of managerial succession in a family business.

- The quality of leadership talent available in the family determines the extent to which outside managers are needed.
- Succession is a long-term process starting early in the successor's life.
- The succession process begins with the pre-business stage and includes part-time jobs and full-time managerial work.
- Tension often arises between the founder and the potential successor as the latter gains experience.
- Transfer of ownership involves issues of fairness, taxes, and managerial control.
- Discussing and planning the transfer of ownership is sometimes difficult but usually desirable.

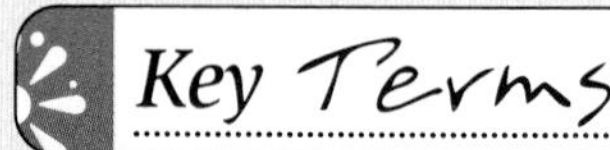

Key Terms

family business, p. 95
organizational culture, p. 99
cultural configuration, p. 101
family retreat, p. 106
family council, p. 107
family business constitution, p. 107
mentoring, p. 109
stages in succession, p. 109
transfer of ownership, p. 111

Discussion Questions

1. How are family businesses and other types of small businesses both similar and different? Explain what makes a business a family business.
2. Suppose that you, as founder of a business, have a sales manager position open. You realize that sales may suffer somewhat if you promote your son from sales representative to sales manager. However, you would like to see your son make some progress and earn a higher salary to support his wife and young daughter. How would you go about making this decision? Would you promote your son?
3. What benefits result from family involvement in a business?
4. Why does a first-generation family business tend to have a paternalistic/maternalistic business pattern and a patriarchal/matriarchal family pattern?
5. As a recent graduate in business administration, you are headed for a job in the family business. As a result of your education, you have become aware of some outdated business practices in the family firm. In spite of them, the business is showing a good return on investment. Should you rock the boat? How should you proceed in correcting what you see as obsolete traditions?
6. Describe a founder–son or founder–daughter relationship in a family business with which you are familiar. What strengths or weaknesses are evident in that business relationship?
7. Should a son or daughter feel an obligation to carry on a family business? What is the source of such a feeling?
8. Assume that you are an ambitious, nonfamily manager in a family firm and that one of your peers is the son or daughter of the founder. What, if anything, would keep you interested in pursuing a career with this company?
9. Identify and describe the stages outlined in the model of succession shown in Exhibit 5-4.
10. In making decisions about transferring ownership of a family business from one generation to another, how much emphasis should be placed on estate tax laws and other concerns that go beyond the family? Why?

You Make the Call

SITUATION 1

The three Dorsett brothers are barely speaking to each other. "Phone for you" is about all they have to say.

It hasn't always been like this. For more than 30 years, Tom, Harry, and Bob Dorsett have run the successful manufacturing business founded by their father. For most of that time, they have gotten along rather well. They've had their differences and arguments, but important decisions were thrashed out until a consensus was reached.

Each brother has two children in the business. Tom's oldest son manages the plant, Harry's oldest daughter keeps the books, and Bob's oldest son is an outside salesman. The younger children are learning the ropes in lower-level positions. The problem? Compensation. Each brother feels that his own children are underpaid and that some of his nieces and nephews are overpaid. After violent arguments, the Dorsett brothers just quit talking while each continues to smolder.

The six younger-generation cousins are still on speaking terms, however. Despite the differences that exist among them, they manage to get along with one another. They range in age from 41 down to 25.

The business is in a slump but not yet in danger. Because the brothers aren't talking, important business decisions are being postponed.

The family is stuck. What can be done?

Source: "Anger over Money Silences Brothers," *Nation's Business,* Vol. 78, No. 10 (October 1990), p. 62.

Question 1 Why do you think the cousins get along better than their fathers do?

Question 2 How might this conflict over compensation be resolved?

SITUATION 2

Harrison Stevens, second-generation president of a family-owned heating and air conditioning business, was concerned about his 19-year-old son, Barry, who worked as a full-time employee in the firm. Although Barry had made it through high school, he had not distinguished himself as a student or shown interest in further education. He was somewhat indifferent in his attitude toward his work, although he did reasonably—or at least minimally—satisfactory work. His father saw Barry as immature and more interested in riding motorcycles than in building a business.

Stevens wanted to provide his son with an opportunity for personal development. As he saw it, the process should begin with learning to work hard. If Barry liked the work and showed promise, he might eventually be groomed to take over the business. His father also held a faint hope that hard work might eventually inspire him to get a college education.

In trying to achieve these goals, Stevens sensed two problems. The first problem was that Barry obviously lacked proper motivation. The second problem related to his supervision. Supervisors seemed reluctant to be exacting in their demands on Barry. Possibly because they feared antagonizing the boss by being too hard on his son, they allowed Barry to get by with marginal performance.

Question 1 In view of Barry's shortcomings, should Harrison Stevens seriously consider him as a potential successor?

Question 2 How could Barry be motivated? Can Stevens do anything more to improve the situation, or does the responsibility lie with Barry?

Question 3 How could the quality of Barry's supervision be improved to make his work experience more productive?

SITUATION 3

Siblings Rob, 37, and Julie, 36, work in their family's $15 million medical products firm. Both are capable leaders and have experienced success in their respective areas of responsibility. Compared to Julie, Rob is more introverted, more thorough in his planning, and much better on detail and follow through. In contrast, Julie is more creative, more extroverted, and stronger in interpersonal skills. Since childhood, they have been rather competitive in their relationships. Their 62-year-old father is contemplating retirement and considering the possibility of co-leadership, with each child eventually holding a 50-percent ownership interest.

Question 1 If you were to choose one leader for the firm, based on the brief description above, which sibling would you recommend? Why?

Question 2 What are the strengths and/or weaknesses of the co-leadership idea? Would you favor it or reject it?

Question 3 How could the father secure practical advice to help with this decision?

Experiential Exercises

1. Interview a college student who has grown up in a family business about the ways he or she has been trained or educated, both formally and informally, for entry into the business. Prepare a brief report, relating your findings to the stages in succession shown in Exhibit 5-4.
2. Interview another college student who has grown up in a family business about parental attitudes toward his or her possible entry into the business. Submit a one-page report describing the extent of pressure on the student to enter the family business and the direct or indirect ways in which family expectations have been communicated.
3. Identify a family business and prepare a brief report on its history, including its founding, family involvement, and any leadership changes that have occurred.
4. Read and report on a biography or autobiography about a family in business or on a nonfictional book about a family business.

Exploring the Web

1. Search online for three interesting stories of family-owned businesses. Or, if you choose, log on to InfoTrac College Edition at **http://www.infotrac-college.com,** where articles on all aspects of family business can be researched and read online. It's worth taking a glance at InfoTrac, if you haven't done so already, just to get a sense of what you can find on the site and how its search functions work. To get started, take a look at the recent profile of HADCO from *BusinessWeek* magazine, which you can access by using the advanced search option to key in record number A118858479. The article examines the hiring and retention of nonfamily management talent by a successful real estate developer. Is a family-owned business in your future? Why or why not?
2. This chapter discusses the process of succession in a family business. Now go to **http://www.gofso.com/Premium/BS/fg/fg-succession.html** to find an online resource on planning for succession. What suggestions do you find on this Web site?
3. The cultural context of a family business is also discussed in this chapter. For an additional perspective on this topic, go to **http://www.familybizz.net**. Follow the link to the site's content on family culture. Discuss some of the differences outlined on this site between the "family system" and the "business system."

Case 5

THE BROWN FAMILY BUSINESS (P. 532)

This case presents the philosophy, criteria, and procedures adopted by one family to regulate work opportunities for family members in the family business.

Alternative Cases for Chapter 5:

Case 18, Douglas Electrical Supply, Inc., p. 559
Case 19, Gibson Mortuary, p. 561

Part Three

DEVELOPING THE NEW VENTURE BUSINESS PLAN

CHAPTERS

THE BUSINESS PLAN

VISUALIZING THE DREAM

In the Video Spotlight

Jagged Edge

Many small businesses are born from the desperation of the owner. Such was the case with Jagged Edge, designer and manufacturer of extreme sport outdoor wear. Sisters Margaret and Paula Quenemoen both enjoyed cold-weather extreme sports. Margaret enjoyed ice mountain climbing, and Paula did extreme solo long-distance trekking in the Himalayas. Both women were perpetually cold because they could not afford the proper gear. (Margaret trekked to the base camp of Mount Everest in a skirt and Tibetan yak jacket, and Paula did an ice-climbing photo shoot wearing pants held together with duct tape.)

When Margaret sold her first dozen headbands in an Aspen restaurant, Jagged Edge was born. The Quenemoens started with an as-you-go system, but it wasn't long before they realized they needed something more formal. The sisters developed a comprehensive business plan that provides any outside stakeholder with all the information it needs to know about Jagged Edge. Called "The Book," the plan helped the company secure financing at the prevailing low interest rates, thus freeing up resources previously earmarked for debt service. The plan is also used to educate new employees about the company, its mission, its goals, its finances, and its business foundation. For the Quenemoens, "The Book" might well be titled "All You Need to Know About Jagged Edge."

Video material provided by Hattie Bryant, Producer of Small Business School, the series on PBS Stations, Worldnet, and the Web at http://www.smallbusinessschool.org.

Chapter 6

Looking Ahead

After studying this chapter, you should be able to

1 *Explain what a business plan is, when it is needed, and what form it might take.*

2 *Explain how to tell a new venture's story to outsiders, especially investors.*

3 *List practical suggestions to follow in writing a business plan and outline the key sections of a business plan.*

4 *Identify available sources of assistance in preparing a business plan.*

5 *Maintain the proper perspective when writing a business plan.*

You're excited about an idea for a new business. But when you mention it to a business friend, she says, "You'll need to prepare a business plan." While the business idea sounds great, sitting down and writing some cold, formal document is not exactly your notion of fun and you wonder if it is really necessary. After all, you know an entrepreneur who started and successfully grew a company based on an idea developed on the back of an envelope over dinner at a local restaurant. And isn't it true that the founders of such notable companies as Pizza Hut, Mrs. Fields, and Crate & Barrel did not have business plans when they started?

AN OVERVIEW OF THE BUSINESS PLAN

We will return shortly to the question of whether you need a business plan. First, we will define the term *business plan.* Then we will explain why you may want to develop a business plan for your venture and the various forms the plan might take.

1 *Explain what a business plan is, when it is needed, and what form it might take.*

What Is a Business Plan?

There is no one correct definition of a business plan. After all, no one plan will work in all situations. But, in general, a **business plan** is a document that outlines the basic idea underlying a business and describes related startup considerations. A business plan is an entrepreneur's game plan; it crystallizes the dreams and hopes that motivate an entrepreneur to take the startup plunge. The business plan should lay out your basic idea for the venture and include descriptions of where you are now, where you want to go, and how you intend to get there.

business plan
A document that sets out the basic idea underlying a business and related startup considerations

A business plan is used primarily in two ways: (1) to provide a statement of goals and strategies for use by individuals within the firm and (2) to aid in the development of relationships with outsiders who could help the company achieve its goals. Exhibit 6-1 provides an overview of those who might have an interest in a business plan for a new venture. The insiders group consists of the internal users of the plan: the new firm's management and its employees. The second group consists of outsiders who are critical to the firm's success: its prospective customers, suppliers, and investors.

For the entrepreneur starting a new venture, a business plan has three basic objectives:

1. To identify the nature and the context of the business opportunity—that is, why does such an opportunity exist?
2. To present the approach the entrepreneur plans to take to exploit the opportunity
3. To recognize the factors that will determine whether the venture will be successful

David Gumpert offers a concise and practical definition of a business plan, focusing on how it should lead to action: "It's a document that convincingly demonstrates that your

EXHIBIT 6-1 *Users of Business Plans*

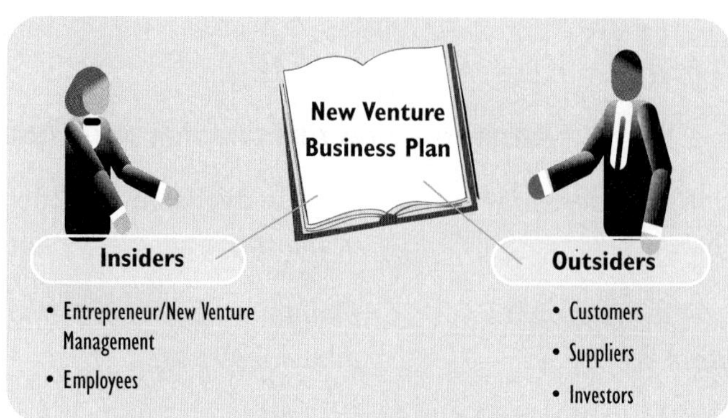

business can sell enough of its product or service to make a satisfactory profit and to be attractive to potential backers."[1] For Gumpert, the business plan is essentially a selling document used to convince key investors, both inside and outside the firm, that the venture has real potential. Equally important, it is an opportunity to convince yourself, the entrepreneur, that what appears to be a good idea is also a good investment opportunity, both economically and in terms of your personal goals.

The issue of your personal goals deserves careful thought: *If the business does not align with your personal goals, you are not likely to succeed and you certainly will not enjoy the trip.* So, be sure to think about your personal aspirations and the personal costs of starting a business before becoming immersed in the business opportunity itself.

Above all, in creating the business plan, you must identify the key variables for success or failure. By leading you to think about what could go right and what could go wrong, writing a business plan can help you to anticipate different situations that may occur. In fact, this is one of the more important functions of a business plan.

Do You Really Need a Plan?

To be quite honest, the answer to the question of whether you need a business plan is "It just depends." In some startup situations, the environment is just too turbulent for extensive planning to be beneficial. Entrepreneurs in new fields may find that there is not enough information to allow them to plan. In such situations, adaptability may be more important than a careful plan for the future. The last thing you want to do is hamper your ability to adapt when necessary if the adaptation doesn't fit the business plan. This does happen occasionally, especially when investors become so focused on "the plan" that they insist that the entrepreneur not vary from it.

Planning may also pose a problem when the timing of the opportunity is a critical factor. In some cases, becoming operational as quickly as possible may have to take priority over in-depth planning, but be careful not to use timing as an easy excuse not to plan. In his study of *Inc. 500* companies (firms identified by *Inc.* magazine as the fastest growing firms in the United States), Amar Bhide concludes that a lack of planning may even make sense with some companies: "Capital-constrained entrepreneurs cannot afford to do much prior analysis and research. The limited profit potential and high uncertainty of the opportunity they usually pursue also make the benefits low compared to the costs."[2]

Pizza Hut, Mrs. Fields, and Crate & Barrel are all examples of companies whose entrepreneurs did little planning, but succeeded beyond what most entrepreneurs could ever hope to do. These entrepreneurs were clearly more focused on capturing an opportunity than on taking the time to develop a business plan, and, after all, a "can do" attitude is essential when starting a new business.

Do these examples mean that as a general rule business plans are not important? To the contrary, most of us need the discipline that comes with writing a business plan. It may just be that a handful of entrepreneurs have the instincts and knowledge required to successfully start and grow a company, as did Gordon Segal and Frank Carney, founders of Crate & Barrel and Pizza Hut, respectively. Clearly, Segal and Carney are not the norm.

Most activity started without adequate preparation tends to be haphazard. In the words of Thomas Carlyle, the Scottish mathematician and writer, "Nothing is more terrible than activity without insight." This is particularly true of such a complex process as initiating a new business. Although planning is a mental process, it must go beyond the realm of speculation. Thinking about a proposed new business must become more thorough as rough ideas come together. Thus, a written plan helps to ensure systematic, complete coverage of the important factors to be considered in starting a new business. By identifying the variables that can affect the success or failure of the business, the business plan becomes a model that helps the entrepreneur and any employees focus on important issues and activities for the new venture.

A business plan is essential in order to gain additional capital from outside investors. Ask any investor for money today and the first thing she or he will ask is "Where is your business plan?" Furthermore, the business plan can be helpful in communicating the entrepreneur's vision to current—and prospective—employees of the firm. After all, entrepreneurs who are building good companies seldom, if ever, work alone.

Two Types of Business Plans

The solution is not to avoid planning, but to engage in *effective* planning, given the situation. As we have already discussed, different situations lead to different needs, which in turn lead to different types of business plans. The entrepreneur has two basic choices when it comes to writing a business plan: the summary plan or the comprehensive plan.[3]

Living the Dream

Entrepreneurial Challenges

A Lesson from the Internet: Under-Promise and Over-Deliver

During the dot-com boom of the late 1990s, putting money into a high-tech venture, especially if it dealt with the Internet, became the "in" thing for investors. For many aspiring small business owners, "it was depressing that people with a line of bull and a PowerPoint presentation were getting funded," says Kenneth Morse, managing director of the MIT Entrepreneurship Center, where students get guidance in how to start a business. Investors' return to more traditional investments was a relief to many entrepreneurs, including Christina Bauer, the founder of Mindful Technologies, a customer-service software company in Newton, Massachusetts.

Bauer got some hands-on tutoring in traditional business-building when, as a teenager, she worked for her father, a consultant to entrepreneurs. He would revise their business plans, then give them to her to type. She remembers that "he was very wary of anything other than customer revenue and then a bank loan" for financing a new company.

Dan Feshbach was skeptical as well. In 1983, Feshbach founded Mortgage Information Corp., which tracks the performance and risk of 30 million mortgages for the lending industry. In his words, he built the company "brick by brick." When he went looking for equity capital, Feshbach did the opposite of what many entrepreneurs did during the boom: He usually undersold what he thought his company could do, believing it better to err on the side of caution and to deliver more than originally promised.

"In the dot-com era, there was lots of pressure to oversell," says Feshbach, who was approached about partnership deals with some Net companies that are now out of business. But, reflecting on his many years of business experience, he says, "I never could buy into the short product cycles dot-coms were talking about—our predictive models took us six years to build." Feshbach continues, "Getting big companies to buy things from small companies that will change the way they do business does not happen overnight."

What's the lesson of the late-1990s Internet boom? Companies built on hype, rather than on sound business planning, don't last.

Source: Theresa Forsman, "Embracing the Brick-by-Brick Business Plan," *BusinessWeek Online*, August 27, 2001, http://www.businessweek.com/@@TI8@P4UQwxXwLgEA/magazine/content/01_35/b3746631.htm.

summary plan
A short form of a business plan that presents only the most important issues and projections for the business

THE SUMMARY PLAN The **summary plan** is a short form of a business plan, presenting only the most important issues and projections for the business. Focusing heavily on market issues, such as pricing, competition, and distribution channels, the summary plan provides little in the way of supporting information. This type of plan is adequate if you are seeking outside financing primarily from banks.

A short plan will satisfy most bankers, especially if it includes past and projected financial results. In fact, it is so rare for an entrepreneur to provide any form of a plan when requesting a loan that a brief summary plan may actually impress a banker. Furthermore, a summary plan may be helpful in trying to gauge investor interest, to see if writing a full-length plan would be worth the time and effort.

Finally, we noted earlier that extensive planning may be of limited value when there is a great amount of uncertainty in the environment or when timing is a critical factor in capturing an opportunity. But we suggest that a summary plan is usually better than no plan at all.

comprehensive plan
A full business plan that provides an in-depth analysis of the critical factors that will determine a firm's success or failure, along with all the underlying assumptions

THE COMPREHENSIVE PLAN When entrepreneurs and investors speak of a business plan, they are usually referring to a **comprehensive plan**, a full business plan that provides an in-depth analysis of the critical factors that will determine a firm's success or failure, along with all the underlying assumptions. Such a plan is beneficial when (1) describing a new opportunity (startup), (2) facing significant change in the business or the external environment (changing demographics, new legislation, or developing industry trends), or (3) explaining complex business situations.

Living the Dream *Entrepreneurial Challenges*

Business Planning on the College Campus

© Ann States

Ivory tower exercises? Not anymore. College business plan contests now offer competitors the chance to win significant amounts of cash and, sometimes, the opportunity to launch a business.

Every year, hundreds of undergraduate and M.B.A. students, in teams of three or four, begin working with professors to hone ideas for startups. By the end of the semester, they are groomed in the skills of presentation, armed with 20-page business plans, and ready to take on teams from other schools.

A team advised by Professor Charles Hofer of the University of Georgia at Athens, for example, wrote a business plan for a proposed venture called KidSmart. The plan was based on an idea for a fire alarm that replaces the usual ear-splitting warning with a digital recording of a parent's voice to wake children and direct them during an emergency. Judges were initially skeptical about the venture because it was essentially a one-product company in a market dominated by large players. And at Oregon's Venture Challenge, judge Tim Boyle, CEO of Columbia Sportswear, raised questions about KidSmart's sourcing in Asia.

The team took second place at the Venture Challenge, winning $10,000. They next competed at the MOOT CORP Competition, hosted at the University of Texas at Austin. By then, they had incorporated Boyle's feedback into their presentation. As part of their presentation, they played a dramatic video from *Dateline NBC,* which showed that their smoke detector was more likely to wake children than was a standard model. It was a classic Hofer moment; he drills into his teams the need to make their points dramatic. "There's got to be a story," he says.

KidSmart's story clicked with the judges. The plan won the $100,000 grand prize, and just in time. At a previous competition, a venture capitalist had seen KidSmart's plan and offered $750,000 of first-round funding. But the team felt they were better off waiting for strategic funding from an angel who knew the industry. "We labored over the decision and came very close," says KidSmart team member Bruce Black, "but a smart entrepreneur always has a contingency plan, and MOOT CORP gave us another option."

Source: Patrick J. Sauer, "How to Win Big and Get Ahead Fast," *Inc.*, Vol. 25, No. 11 (September 2003).

Christine and Denis Gagnon founded Christine & Denis Landscapes Limited, a lawn-care business, in Sherbrooke, Quebec. Four years later, they decided to expand their seasonal business into a year-round operation with the inclusion of a snow-removal service. Their strategy was to add different services for their clients, thereby allowing the firm to cover the fixed costs of the landscaping business in the winter months. To raise the capital needed for the expansion, the Gagnons wrote a business plan, raising $125,000 to finance the purchase of snow-removal equipment.[4]

Once convinced of the need for a business plan—either a summary plan or a comprehensive plan—the entrepreneur must decide the amount of effort to invest in preparing the plan. In making that decision, he or she has to make some tradeoffs, as preparing a plan requires time and money, two resources that are always in short supply. So, the issue goes beyond answering the question "Do I plan?" It includes deciding *how much* to plan.

It is important to emphasize again that *the attention given to planning will and should vary with the situation.* Before ruling out a business plan as unnecessary, an entrepreneur should give serious consideration to the nature and amount of planning that best fit the particular situation.

TELLING THE STORY TO OTHERS

2 Explain how to tell a new venture's story to outsiders, especially investors.

Although the entrepreneur is typically thought to be the primary risk taker in a startup, the entrepreneur and even the management team are by no means the only risk takers. To make the company successful, the entrepreneur must convince outsiders—prospective customers, suppliers, and investors—to become linked with the firm. As Amar Bhide explains: "Some entrepreneurs may have an innate capability to outperform their rivals, acquire managerial skills, and thus build a flourishing business. But it is difficult for customers (and others) to identify founders with these innate capabilities."[5]

By enhancing the firm's credibility, the business plan can serve as an effective selling tool with prospective customers and suppliers, as well as investors. A well-prepared business plan may be helpful in gaining a supplier's trust and securing favorable credit terms. Likewise, a plan can improve sales prospects by convincing prospective customers that the new firm is likely to be around for a long time to service a product or to continue as a procurement source.

Almost anyone starting a business faces the task of raising financial resources to supplement personal savings. This requires an effective presentation to bankers, individual investors, or venture capitalists. The business plan serves as the entrepreneur's calling card when he or she is approaching these sources of financing.

Attracting Investors

Many small firms do not seek outside capital, except in the form of small loans. But where there is a substantial need for outside capital, both investors and lenders use the business plan to understand the new venture, the type of product or service it will offer, the nature of the market, and the qualifications of the entrepreneur and the management team. Rarely today will a sophisticated investor consider investing in a new business before reviewing a properly prepared business plan.

The significance of the business plan in dealing with investors is aptly expressed by Mark Stevens, an advisor to small businesses:

> *If you are inclined to view the business plan as just another piece of useless paperwork, it's time for an attitude change. When you are starting out, investors will justifiably want to know a lot about you and your qualifications for running a business and will want to see a step-by-step plan for how you intend to make it a success.*[6]

The business plan is not, however, a legal document for actually raising the needed capital. When it comes time to solicit investment, a **prospectus**, or offering memorandum, must be used. This document contains all the information necessary to satisfy federal and state requirements for warning potential investors about the possible risks of the investment. But the prospectus alone is not an effective marketing document with which to sell a concept. An entrepreneur must first use the business plan to create interest in the startup and then follow up with a formal offering memorandum to those investors who seem genuinely interested.

prospectus
A marketing document used to solicit investors' monies

Living the Dream

Entrepreneurial Challenges

An Effective Presentation Makes the Difference

Courtesy of Springboard Enterprises

Welcome to Springboard Enterprises' grueling five-week boot camp, where 23 female entrepreneurs are being prepared to present their business plans at a venture capital forum. Springboard's success in helping women find financing is nothing less than phenomenal—about 40 percent of the presenters over the years have raised a total of $700 million! But the road to success is through a number of tough-minded "coaches" who have little mercy on presenters. For those who succeed, though, the rewards can be worth the effort. Read what Shoba Purushothaman, 39, the CEO of NewsMarket in New York City, wrote about the experience:

> *Best part of Springboard:* "At a practice session, a VC [venture capitalist] told me, 'Stop selling me your product and sell me the investment opportunity.' That was a turning point for me."
>
> *Worst part of Springboard:* "A number of VCs came to Springboard events only to meet other VCs."
>
> *How I think about my business now:* "Like a stock. Investors are like customers, but what they're buying is your stock. I also learned to value my company a lot more because of the things people latched on to at Springboard: the high margins that are possible, the no intuitive barriers to entry, and my low fixed costs."

Source: Susan Greco, "Finding the Perfect Pitch," *Inc.*, Vol. 24, No. 6 (June 2002), p. 95.

Understanding the Investor's Perspective

If you are preparing a business plan in order to seek significant outside capital, you must understand the investor's basic perspective. You must see the world as the investor sees it—that is, you must think as the investor thinks.

Most entrepreneurs perceive a new venture very differently than an investor perceives it. The entrepreneur characteristically focuses on the positive potential of the startup—what will happen if everything goes right. The prospective investor, on the other hand, plays the role of the skeptic, thinking more about what could go wrong. One investor in small firms, Daniel Lubin, admits, "The first thing I look for is a lie or bad information—a reason to throw it out."[7] An entrepreneur's failure to appreciate this difference in perspectives almost ensures rejection by investors. As noted by William Sahlman at the Harvard Business School,

> *What's wrong with most business plans? The answer is relatively straightforward. Most waste too much ink on numbers and devote too little to the information that really matters to intelligent investors. As every seasoned investor knows, financial projections for a new company—especially detailed, month-by-month projections that stretch out for more than a year—are an act of imagination.*
>
> *Don't misunderstand me: Business plans should include some numbers. But those numbers should appear mainly in the form of a business model that shows the entrepreneurial team has thought about failure. . . . The model should also address the break-even issue: At what level of sales does the business begin to make a profit? And even more important, when does cash flow turn positive? Without a doubt, these questions deserve a few pages in any business plan.*[8]

At the most basic level, a prospective investor has a single goal: to maximize potential return on an investment through cash flows that will be received, while minimizing risk exposure. Even venture capitalists, who are thought to be risk takers, want to minimize their risk. Like any informed investor, they look for ways to shift risk to others, usually to the entrepreneur.

Given the fundamental differences in perspective between the investor and the entrepreneur, the important question becomes "How do I write a business plan that will capture a prospective investor's interest?" There is no easy answer, but two facts are relevant: (1) Investors have a short attention span, and (2) certain features attract investors, while others repel them.

THE INVESTOR'S SHORT ATTENTION SPAN Kenneth Blanchard and Spencer Johnson wrote a popular book about being a one-minute manager—a manager who practices principles that can be applied quickly and produce great results.[9] Investors in startup and early-stage companies are, in a sense, one-minute investors. Because they receive many business plans, they cannot read them all in any detailed fashion. Tim Smith, a former officer of the Capital Southwest Corporation, a Dallas-based venture capital firm, observed, "We receive some 300 or more plans per year but invest only in three or four firms in any given year. Thus, we simply do not have the luxury to analyze each opportunity thoroughly."[10]

An example of an investor's short attention span was witnessed recently by one of the authors when he delivered an entrepreneur's business plan to a prospective investor with whom he had a personal relationship. The plan was well written, clearly identifying a need. While the investor was courteous and listened carefully, he made a decision not to consider the opportunity in a matter of five minutes. A quick read of the executive summary did not spark his interest, and the discussion quickly changed to other matters. We may be overstating the case when we refer to investors in startups and early-stage firms as one-minute investors, but even five minutes is not much time to work with.

BUSINESS PLAN FEATURES THAT ATTRACT OR REPEL INVESTORS In order to raise capital from outside investors, the business plan must speak the investors' language. The entrepreneur must know what is important and what is not important to investors and how to present the business idea or concept in a way that is meaningful to them. Otherwise, the entrepreneur will immediately lose credibility—and a potential source of financing.

Based on their experience with the MIT Enterprise Forum, Stanley R. Rich and David E. Gumpert identified characteristics of a business plan that enhance the probability of receiving funding from an investor. [The MIT Enterprise Forum (http://web.mit.edu/entforum) sponsors sessions across the United States in which aspiring entrepreneurs present business plans to panels of venture capitalists, bankers, marketing specialists, and other experts.] Exhibit 6-2 lists some of those features. For instance, to be effective, the plan cannot be extremely long or encyclopedic in detail. It should seldom exceed 40 pages in length, as investors generally will look at brief reports and avoid those that take too long to read. Also, the overall appearance of the report should be attractive, and the report should be well organized, with numbered pages and a table of contents.

Investors are more *market-oriented* than *product-oriented*, realizing that most patented inventions never earn a dime for the inventors. The essence of the entrepreneurial process is to identify new products or services that meet an identifiable customer need. Thus, it is essential for the entrepreneur to appreciate investors' concerns about market prospects.

On several occasions, the authors have had the opportunity to watch entrepreneurs present business plans to prospective investors. More than once, an entrepreneur has presented financial projections that were extremely optimistic—beyond being believable. The opportunity would still have been attractive with more conservative projections. But instead of being willing to adjust the forecasts to make them more credible to the investors, the entrepreneur continued to argue that the numbers were already "conservative." It's no surprise that investors declined to invest in these deals.

So, the importance of making a credible presentation—one that is believable to investors—is clear. With tongue only a little in cheek, Bill Sahlman at the Harvard Business School tells how investors interpret an entrepreneur's language in his "Glossary of Business Plan Terms" (see Exhibit 6-3). In writing and presenting a business plan, you may want to keep in mind how skeptical your audience is likely to be.

Finally, investors are quickly disillusioned by plans that contain page after page of detailed computer-generated financial projections, suggesting—intentionally or unintentionally—that the entrepreneur can predict with great accuracy what will happen. The experienced investor knows this isn't the case.

EXHIBIT 6-2 *Features of a Successful Business Plan*

- It must be arranged appropriately, with an executive summary, a table of contents, and chapters in the right order.
- It must be the right length and have the right appearance—not too long and not too short, not too fancy and not too plain.
- It must give a sense of what the founders and the company expect to accomplish three to seven years into the future.
- It must explain in quantitative and qualitative terms the benefit to the user of the company's products or services.
- It must present hard evidence of the marketability of the products or services.
- It must justify financially the means chosen to sell the products or services.
- It must explain and justify the level of product development which has been achieved and describe in appropriate detail the manufacturing process and associated costs.
- It must portray the partners as a team of experienced managers with complementary business skills.
- It must suggest as high an overall "rating" as possible of the venture's product development and team sophistication.
- It must contain believable financial projections, with the key data explained and documented.
- It must show how investors can cash out in three to seven years, with appropriate capital appreciation.
- It must be presented to the most potentially receptive financiers possible to avoid wasting precious time as company funds dwindle.
- It must be easily and concisely explainable in a well-orchestrated oral presentation.

Source: "Plans That Succeed," pp. 126–127 from *Business Plans That Win $$$: Lessons from the MIT Enterprise Forum* by Stanley R. Rich and David E. Gumpert. Reprinted by permission of Sterling Lord Literistic, Inc.

PREPARING A BUSINESS PLAN

3 *List practical suggestions to follow in writing a business plan and outline the key sections of a business plan.*

Two issues are of primary concern in preparing a business plan: (1) the basic format and effectiveness of the written presentation and (2) the content of the plan.

Formatting and Writing a Business Plan

The quality of a completed business plan ultimately depends on the quality of the underlying business concept. After all, the plan is not the business. A poorly conceived new venture idea cannot be rescued by good writing. A good concept may be destroyed, however, by writing that fails to communicate effectively.

Clear writing gives credibility to the ideas presented in a business plan. Factual support must be supplied for any claims or promises made. When promising to provide superior service or explaining the attractiveness of the market, for example, the entrepreneur must include strong supporting evidence. In short, the plan must be believable.

Written communication skills are necessary to present the business concept in an accurate, comprehensible, and enthusiastic way. Although it is beyond the scope of this book to discuss general writing principles, we offer the following practical suggestions for writing a business plan:

- Provide a table of contents and individual section tabs for easy reference.
- Place the plan in a loose-leaf binder to facilitate future revisions.
- To add interest and aid readers' comprehension, make liberal but effective use of visual aids, such as graphs, exhibits, and tabular summaries.
- Prominently indicate that all information in the plan is proprietary and confidential. Number every copy of the plan, and account for each outstanding copy by requiring a recipient of the plan to acknowledge receipt in writing.
- When a startup is based on proprietary technology, be cautious about divulging certain information—the details of a technological design, for example, or the

6-3 | *A Glossary of Business Plan Terms*

What They Say . . .	. . . and What They Really Mean
We conservatively project . . .	We read a book that said we had to be a $50 million company in five years, and we reverse-engineered the numbers.
We took our best guess and divided by 2.	We accidentally divided by 0.5.
We project a 10% margin.	We did not modify any of the assumptions in the business plan template that we downloaded from the Internet.
The project is 98% complete.	To complete the remaining 2% will take as long as it took to create the initial 98% but will cost twice as much.
Our business model is proven . . .	If you take the evidence from the past week for the best of our 50 locations and extrapolate it for all the others.
We have a six-month lead.	We tried not to find out how many other people have a six-month lead.
We only need a 10% market share.	So do the other 50 entrants getting funded.
Customers are clamoring for our product.	We have not yet asked them to pay for it. Also, all of our current customers are relatives.
We are the low-cost producer.	We have not produced anything yet, but we are confident that we will be able to.
We have no competition.	Only IBM, Microsoft, Netscape, and Sun have announced plans to enter the business.
Our management team has a great deal of experience . . .	Consuming the product or service.
A select group of investors is considering the plan.	We mailed a copy of the plan to everyone in Pratt's Guide.
We seek a value-added investor.	We are looking for a passive, dumb-as-rocks investor.
If you invest on our terms, you will earn a 68% rate of return.	If everything that could ever conceivably go right does go right, you might get your money back.

Source: Reprinted by permission of *Harvard Business Review.* From "How to Write a Great Business Plan" by William A. Sahlman, July-August 1997.

highly sensitive specifics of a marketing strategy—even to a prospective investor. You might want to develop an in-depth plan for internal purposes and then use appropriate extracts from it to put together a document that effectively supports your funding proposal. But, while you should be cautious about releasing proprietary information, you should not be overly worried about someone taking your idea and "beating you to the punch." If that can happen, you may be the wrong person for the business in the first place.

- Request that carefully chosen third parties who have themselves raised capital successfully—primarily other entrepreneurs—give their perspectives on the business concept and the effectiveness of the written plan.

Deciding on the Content of a Business Plan

In considering the content of a business plan, think first and foremost about the opportunity. Strategies and financial plans should come later. In the evaluation of an opportunity, give thorough consideration to the following basic and interdependent factors. Decisions about these factors will, in turn, help determine the rest of the content of a business plan for a startup.

- *The entrepreneurial team.* Nothing is more important than the people who are starting and managing the venture—their qualifications and the depth and breadth of experience they bring to the venture.

- *The opportunity.* A profile is needed of the business itself—what it will sell, to whom it will sell, and how rapidly it can grow. The industry and market outlook should include an assessment of everything that can go wrong or right, with a discussion of how the entrepreneurial team could respond to the various challenges.
- *The resources.* The critical resources for an entrepreneurial venture include not just money, but also the human assets (suppliers, accountants, lawyers, investors, etc.) and hard assets (accounts receivable, inventories, etc.). The entrepreneurial approach to resources is "doing the most with the least." The entrepreneur should think of ways to work with minimal resources and focus on "minimizing and controlling" rather than on "maximizing and owning."
- *The deal structure.* How a firm's financing is structured (debt versus equity) and how the ownership percentage is shared by the founders and investors have a significant impact on an entrepreneur's incentive to work hard. The goal is to find a win-win deal.
- *The big picture.* The *context* (or external factors) of an opportunity includes the regulatory environment, interest rates, demographic trends, inflation, and other factors that inevitably change but cannot be controlled by the entrepreneur.

While the issues listed above are important on their own as a foundation for an effective business plan, there must also be a good fit among all the factors. In other words, a good plan pulls together the right entrepreneurial team, the right opportunity, the right resources, the right deal structure, and the right context (see Exhibit 6-4). There will always be uncertainties and ambiguities; the unanticipated is bound to come up. But by addressing all these interdependent factors, you can be sure that you have made an attempt to deal with the important issues.

There is no single format or formula for writing a business plan, but there are guidelines a prospective entrepreneur can follow. Exhibit 6-5 summarizes the major sections common to most business plans, providing a bird's-eye view of the overall content. We will now briefly consider each of these sections. Chapters 7 through 12 take an in-depth look at each section of the business plan.

TITLE PAGE The title page is the first page of the business plan and should contain the following information:

- Company name, address, phone number, fax number, and Web address
- Company logo, if available

EXHIBIT 6-4 *Good Opportunities Have Good "Fit"*

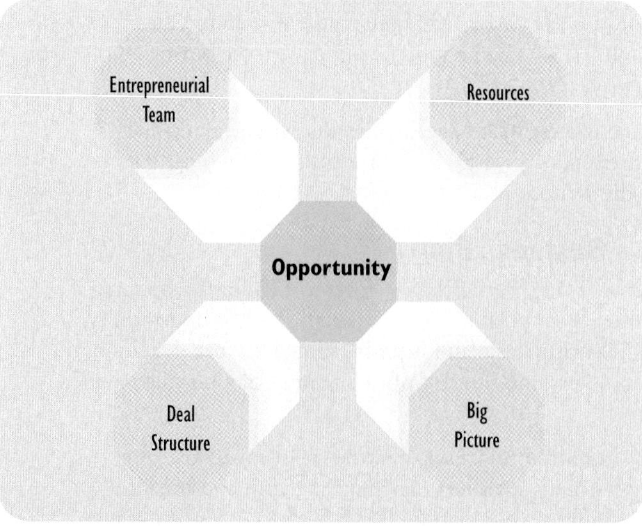

EXHIBIT 6-5 *Abbreviated Business Plan Outline*

Title Page: Provides names, addresses, and phone numbers of the venture and its owners and management personnel; date prepared; copy number; and contact person.

Table of Contents: Provides page numbers for the key sections of the business plan.

Executive Summary: Provides a one- to three-page overview of the total business plan. Written after the other sections are completed, it highlights their significant points and, ideally, creates enough excitement to motivate the reader to continue reading.

Vision and Mission Statement: Concisely describes the intended strategy and business philosophy for making the vision happen.

Company Overview: Explains the type of company, such as manufacturing, retail, or service; provides background information on the company if it already exists; describes the proposed form of organization—sole proprietorship, partnership, or corporation. This section should be organized as follows: company name and location, company objectives, nature and primary product or service of the business, current status (startup, buyout, or expansion) and history (if applicable), and legal form of organization.

Products and/or Services Plan: Describes the product and/or service and points out any unique features; explains why people will buy the product or service. This section should offer the following descriptions: products and/or services; features of the product or service providing a competitive advantage; available legal protection—patents, copyrights, trademarks; and dangers of technical or style obsolescence.

Marketing Plan: Shows who the firm's customers will be and what type of competition it will face; outlines the marketing strategy and specifies the firm's competitive edge. This section should offer the following descriptions: analysis of target market and profile of target customer; methods of identifying and attracting customers; selling approach, type of sales force, and distribution channels; types of sales promotions and advertising; and credit and pricing policies.

Management Plan: Identifies the key players—active investors, management team, and directors—citing the experience and competence they possess. This section should offer the following descriptions: management team, outside investors and/or directors and their qualifications, outside resource people and their qualifications, and plans for recruiting and training employees.

Operating Plan: Explains the type of manufacturing or operating system to be used; describes the facilities, labor, raw materials, and product processing requirements. This section should offer the following descriptions: operating or manufacturing methods, operating facilities (location, space, and equipment), quality-control methods, procedures to control inventory and operations, sources of supply, and purchasing procedures.

Financial Plan: Specifies financial needs and contemplated sources of financing; presents projections of revenues, costs, and profits. This section should offer the following descriptions: historical financial statements for the last three to five years or as available; pro forma financial statements for three to five years, including income statements, balance sheets, cash flow statements, and cash budgets (monthly for first year and quarterly for second year); break-even analysis of profits and cash flows; and planned sources of financing.

Note: Templates to assist you in preparing a simplified business plan are available on the CD-ROM that accompanies this textbook. For additional information on business plans, visit http://longenecker.swlearning.com.

- Names, titles, addresses, and phone numbers of the owners and key executives
- Date on which the business plan was issued
- Number of the copy (to help keep track of how many copies are outstanding)
- Name of the preparer, if other than the owners and key executives

TABLE OF CONTENTS The table of contents provides a sequential listing of the sections of the plan, with page numbers.

EXECUTIVE SUMMARY The **executive summary** is crucial for getting the attention of the one-minute investor. It must convey a clear and concise picture of the proposed venture and, at the same time, create a sense of excitement regarding its prospects. This means that it must be written—and, if necessary, rewritten—to achieve clarity and create

executive summary
A section of the business plan that conveys a clear and concise overall picture of the proposed venture

interest. Even though the executive summary comes at the beginning of the business plan, it provides an overview of the whole plan and should be written last. Depending on the situation and the preference of the entrepreneur, the executive summary may be in the form of a synopsis or a narrative.

Synopsis The synopsis is the more straightforward of the two summary formats. A synopsis briefly covers all aspects of the business plan, giving each topic relatively equal treatment. It relates, in abbreviated fashion, the conclusions of each section of the completed business plan. Although it is easy to prepare, the synopsis can be rather dry reading for the prospective investor.

Narrative Because the narrative tells a story, it can convey greater excitement than the synopsis. However, composing an effective narrative requires a gifted writer who can communicate the necessary information and engender enthusiasm without crossing the line into hyperbole. A narrative is more appropriate for businesses that are breaking new ground, with a new product, a new market, or new operational techniques. It is also a better format for ventures that have one dominant advantage, such as holding an important patent or being run by a well-known entrepreneur. Finally, the narrative works well for companies with interesting or impressive backgrounds or histories.[11]

mission statement
A concise written description of a firm's philosophy

MISSION STATEMENT The firm's **mission statement** concisely describes the intended strategy and business philosophy for making the entrepreneur's vision a reality. In a few sentences, it should convey how combined efforts in all areas of the business will move it toward its goal. In addition, it should distinguish the firm from all others. Mission statements can and do vary in length, content, format, and specificity. However, it is essential that a mission statement remain simple, believable, and achievable.

Exhibit 6-6 presents the executive summary and mission statement for FoodFun Lifeskills Instructional Software (FoodFun LIS). The founders of the firm plan to provide education/entertainment software for nonreading individuals with developmental disabilities.

COMPANY OVERVIEW The main body of the business plan begins with a brief description of the firm. If the firm is already in existence, its history is included. This section informs the reader of the type of business being proposed, the firm's objectives, where the firm is located, and whether it will serve a local or international market. In many cases, legal issues—especially those concerning the firm's form of organization—are addressed in this section of the plan. (Legal issues regarding the form of organization are discussed in Chapter 8.) In writing this section, the entrepreneur should answer the following questions:

- When and where was this business started?
- What changes have been made in structure and/or ownership?
- In what stage of development is the firm—for example, seed stage or full product line?
- What has been achieved to date?
- What is the firm's distinctive competence?
- What are the basic nature and activity of the business?
- What is its primary product or service?
- What customers will be served?
- What are the firm's objectives?
- What is the firm's form of organization—sole proprietorship, partnership, or corporation?
- What are the current and projected economic states of the industry?
- Does the firm intend to sell to another company or an investment group, does it plan to be a publicly traded company, or do the owners want to transfer ownership to the next generation of the family?

EXHIBIT 6-6 *FoodFun Lifeskills Instructional Software*

Executive Summary
FoodFun Lifeskills Instructional Software (FoodFun LIS) is a start-up organization whose vision is to create the finest education/entertainment software for non-reading individuals with developmental disabilities. The software product has been designed and created by a Ph.D. veteran of the special education industry, to meet the needs of this special customer segment. The software will be constructive by teaching certain lifeskills and will be fun to use, encouraging the student to use it as often as possible. FoodFun LIS was formed in January 2003 as an Illinois L.L.C. by founder and owner Sue Altamirankow, Ph.D., and will be based in Chicago.

The Market
FoodFun has identified four distinct market segments that will be interested in the software product. These segments are the most likely consumers of the software. The segments are as follows:

- **Centers for Independent Living**—These centers exist to help train individuals with developmental disabilities to live on their own. The curriculum is often based around four primary lifeskills that are necessary for the individual to have in order to successfully live independently.
- **School Districts**—All states are required to provide education for students of special needs until they reach the age of 21. The school districts are often the educational providers until the students are 18 and will be interested in FoodFun's software as they help the students gain fundamental lifeskills.
- **Proactive Parents**—Parents who are taking an active role in the education of their children will be looking for aids that they can use at home to help with their child's learning progress.
- **Agencies**—Many states have formed agencies that act as brokers to connect service providers with individuals. The agencies have generally been formed as a result of a settlement or payout from a lawsuit (including class action).

Parents are expected to purchase only one copy of the program, while the other segments will generally purchase multiple copies/site licenses and are likely to purchase upgrades to subsequent versions.

The Product
Grocery shopping and socialization/leisure are two of the main lifeskills which individuals with developmental disabilities are taught. FoodFun has developed a unique software product that is an effective teaching aid for these important skills.

Competitive Edge
There are several companies on the market selling educational products for this target segment. FoodFun LIS will leverage their competitive edge by incorporating entertainment into their software product, a means of creating interest and joy while using the software.

This interest and joy will increase the amount of time that the students use the software, thereby increasing the effectiveness of the program. FoodFun is convinced that when students enjoy what they are doing they are likely to use the product instead of having to be forced to use it.

Management
FoodFun has been founded and will be led by Dr. Sue Altamirankow. Sue has a Master's and Ph.D. in special education and has been teaching in the university setting for eight years. Her published thesis "Implications in Lifeskill Training for Individuals with Autism" was a ground-breaking paper that carefully studied all aspects of lifeskills. This was the foundation of her idea to start a software company. She realized that she could develop a study aid that would be fun and effective. It would be fun because the students would enjoy using it; it would be effective because it taught necessary lifeskills to individuals with developmental disabilities who begin to live more independently. FoodFun has forecasted revenues of $400,397 and $490,000 for years two and three. Net profit/sales has been forecasted to be 12.57% and 21.45% for those respective years.

Objectives

- Increase sales by triple for the first two years.
- Achieve 20% market penetration by year four.
- Assist more than 10,000 different individuals with developmental disabilities.

Mission
To develop fun-to-use educational software for non-readers with developmental disabilities. Our software will provide lifeskills training that empowers the individuals to make them more independent. We exist to make products that the market demands and have a positive impact on society.

Keys to Success

- Develop educational software that is constructive and fun. If it is not fun, it likely will not be used.
- Implement a strong marketing campaign to develop awareness of the software and its benefits within all of the training centers, school districts, brokerages, and among parents.
- Design strict financial controls for the organization.

Source: © 2003 PaloAlto Software, Inc. Reproduced with permission. Find more sample business plans at http://www.bplans.com.

products and/or services plan A section of the business plan that describes the product and/or service to be provided and explains its merits

PRODUCTS AND/OR SERVICES PLAN As its title reveals, the **products and/or services plan** discusses those products and/or services to be offered to the firm's customers. If a new or unique physical product is to be offered and a working model or prototype is available, a photograph of it should be included in this section of the business plan. Investors will naturally show the greatest interest in products that have been developed, tested, and found to be functional. Any innovative features should be identified and any patent protection explained. Although, in many instances, the product or service may be similar to those offered by competitors, any special features should be clearly identified. (Chapter 14 discusses this topic more fully.)

marketing plan A section of the business plan that describes the user benefits of the product or service and the type of market that exists

MARKETING PLAN As stated earlier, prospective investors and lenders attach a high priority to market considerations. They do not invest in products that are well engineered but unwanted by customers. The **marketing plan**, therefore, must identify user benefits and the type of market that exists. Depending on the type of product or service being offered, the marketing plan may be able not only to identify but also to quantify the financial benefit to the user—for example, by showing how quickly a user can recover the cost of the product or service through savings in operating costs. Of course, benefits may also take such forms as time savings or improvements in attractiveness, safety, or health.

The marketing plan should document customer interest by showing that a market exists and that customers are ready to buy the product or service. This market analysis must be detailed enough to provide a reasonable estimate of demand. An estimate of demand must be analytically sound and based on more than assumptions if it is to be accepted as credible by prospective investors. (Note that some business plans include a market analysis section as a precursor to the marketing plan section.)

The marketing plan must also examine the competition and describe elements of the proposed marketing strategy—for example, by specifying the type of sales force and the methods of promotion and advertising that will be used. (Chapter 7 provides in-depth coverage of the marketing plan.)

management plan A section of the business plan that describes a new firm's organizational structure and the backgrounds of its key players

MANAGEMENT PLAN Prospective investors look for well-managed companies. Of all the factors they consider, the quality of the management team is paramount; it is even more important than the nature of the product or service. Investors frequently say that they would rather have an "A" management team and a "B" product or service than a "B" team and an "A" product. Unfortunately, an entrepreneur's ability to conceive an idea for a new venture is no guarantee of her or his managerial ability. The **management plan**, therefore, must detail the proposed firm's organizational structure and the backgrounds of those who will fill its key positions.

Investors desire a well-balanced management team—one that includes financial and marketing expertise as well as production experience and innovative talent. Managerial experience in related enterprises and in other startup situations is particularly valuable in the eyes of prospective investors. (The factors involved in preparing the management plan are discussed in detail in Chapter 8.)

operating plan A section of the business plan that offers information on how a product will be produced or a service provided, including descriptions of the new firm's facilities, labor, raw materials, and processing requirements

OPERATING PLAN The **operating plan** offers information on how the product will be produced or the service provided; its importance varies from venture to venture. This plan discusses such items as location and facilities: how much space the business will need and what type of equipment it will require. (These aspects of the operating plan are discussed at length in Chapter 9.) The operating plan should also explain the firm's proposed approach to assuring quality, controlling inventory, and using subcontractors or obtaining raw materials. (These aspects are discussed in detail in Chapter 20.)

financial plan A section of the business plan that provides an account of the new firm's financial needs and sources of financing and a projection of its revenues, costs, and profits

pro forma statements Reports that project a firm's financial condition

FINANCIAL PLAN Financial analysis constitutes another crucial piece of the business plan; it is contained in the **financial plan**. **Pro forma statements**, which are projections of the company's financial statements, are presented for up to five years. The forecasts include balance sheets, income statements, and statements of cash flows on an annual basis for three to five years, as well as cash budgets on a monthly basis for the first year and on a quarterly basis for the second and third years. It is vital that the financial projections be supported by well-substantiated assumptions and explanations of how the figures have been determined.

While all the financial statements are important, statements of cash flows deserve special attention, because a business can be profitable but fail if it does not produce positive cash flows. A statement of cash flows identifies the sources of cash—how much will be generated from operations and how much will be raised from investors. It also shows how much money will be devoted to investments in such areas as inventories and equipment. The statement of cash flows should clearly indicate how much cash is needed from prospective investors and for what purpose.

Since experience tells them that the eventual return on their investment will depend largely on their ability to cash out, most investors want to invest in a privately held company for only a limited period and want to be told how and when they may expect to cash out of the investment. Therefore, the plan should outline the possible methods available to investors for exiting the firm. (The preparation of pro forma statements and the process of raising the needed capital are discussed in Chapters 10 and 11. Chapter 12 presents ways that an investor—and the entrepreneur—can cash out, or exit, the business investment.)

APPENDIX OF SUPPORTING DOCUMENTS The appendix should contain various supplementary materials and attachments to expand the reader's understanding of the plan. These supporting documents include any items referenced in the text of the business plan, such as the résumés of the key investors and owners/managers; photographs of products, facilities, and buildings; professional references; marketing research studies; pertinent published research; and signed contracts of sale.

The fact that it appears at the end of the plan does not mean that the appendix is of secondary importance. First, the reader needs to understand the assumptions underlying the premises set forth in the plan. Also, nothing is more important to a prospective investor than the qualifications of the management team. Thus, the presentation of the management team's résumés is no small matter, and each résumé should be carefully prepared.

What Not to Do

Entrepreneurs tend to fall prey to a number of mistakes when preparing a business plan. Below are some common mistakes that you will want to avoid.[12]

1. *Failing to provide solid data.* Too often, entrepreneurs make broad, unsubstantiated statements without good, solid data to support them. Investors want you to support every statement and every number in your projections. Vague ideas and confusing statements just won't work.
2. *Failing to describe the product in lay terms.* There may be a temptation to use too much industry jargon. Present your product or service in simple, understandable terms.
3. *Failing to thoroughly analyze the market.* Everyone has competitors. Saying "We have no competition" is almost a sure predictor of failure. You must show where your business will fit in your market and know the details of your competitors' strengths and weaknesses. If possible, include estimates of their market shares and profit levels.
4. *Including financial statements that are overly detailed or incomplete.* Entrepreneurs tend to err either by providing incomplete financial statements or by including page after page of monotonous financial data. Either extreme is unacceptable. Provide all of the following: pro forma income statements, balance sheets, and cash flow statements, with a complete list of the assumptions that underlie the financial information. Most importantly, make sure that the numbers make sense.
5. *Hiding weaknesses.* One difficult aspect of writing a business plan is effectively dealing with problems or weaknesses—and every business has them. An entrepreneur wants to make a good impression. However, ignoring or glossing over a negative issue when trying to raise capital can prove damaging or worse. If there are weaknesses in the plan, the investors will find them. At that point, an investor's question will be "What else haven't you told me?" The best way to properly handle weaknesses is to be open and straightforward and to have an action plan that effectively addresses the problem. To put it another way, *integrity matters.*
6. *Overlooking the fatal flaw.* Many opportunities have potential fatal flaws. The entrepreneur may become so infatuated with an opportunity that he or she cannot see such flaws. For instance, an entrepreneur might need to ask, "What is the possible

impact of new technology, e-commerce, or changes in consumer demand on the proposed venture?"

7. *Using bad grammar.* Nothing turns off a prospective investor faster than a poorly written business plan. Obtain a good editor, and then review, review, review.
8. *Making the overall plan too long.* The goal is not to write a long business plan, but to write a good business plan. People who read business plans appreciate brevity and view it as an indication of your ability to identify and describe in an organized way the important factors that will determine the success of your business.

The basic rule is to avoid features that are not acceptable to frequent readers of business plans. Otherwise, the plan will detract from the opportunity itself, and you may lose the chance to capture a good opportunity.

Each chapter in this part of the book (Chapters 6–12) ends with a special set of exercises to take you through the process of writing a business plan. These exercise sets consist of questions to be thoughtfully considered and answered. They are entitled "The Business Plan: Laying the Foundation," because they deal with issues that are important to starting a new venture and provide guidelines for preparing the different sections of a business plan.

RESOURCES FOR BUSINESS PLAN PREPARATION

4 *Identify available sources of assistance in preparing a business plan.*

When writing a business plan, it is important to know what works and what does not work. There are many books, Web sites, and computer software packages that you can use to guide you step by step through the preparation of a business plan. (A listing of some of these resources appears at the end of this chapter.)[13] Such resources can be invaluable. In general, however, you should resist the temptation to adapt an existing business plan for your own use. Changing the numbers and some of the verbiage of another firm's business plan is simply not effective.

Computer-Aided Business Planning

The use of a computer greatly facilitates preparation of a business plan. Its word-processing capabilities, for example, can speed up the writing of the narrative sections of the report. Computer spreadsheets are likewise helpful for preparing the financial statements needed in the plan.

A number of business plan software packages have been designed to help an entrepreneur think through the important issues in starting a new company and organize his or her thoughts to create an effective presentation. However, these software packages are not capable of producing a unique plan and thus may limit an entrepreneur's creativity and flexibility. Remember, there is no simple procedure for writing a business plan—no "formula for success"—despite what software advertisements may claim. If you recognize their limitations, however, you can use business plan software packages to facilitate the process.

Professional Assistance in Business Planning

As already discussed, company founders are most notably doers—and evidence suggests that they had better be, if the venture is to be successful. Furthermore, most entrepreneurs lack the breadth of experience and know-how, as well as the inclination, needed for planning.

An entrepreneur who is not able to answer the tough questions about the business may need a business planning advisor—someone accustomed to working with small companies, startups, and owners who lack financial management experience. Such advisors include accountants, marketing specialists, attorneys (preferably with an entrepreneurial mindset), incubator organizations, small business development corporations (SBDCs), and regional and local economic development offices.

An investment banker or financial intermediary can draw up a business plan as part of a firm's overall fundraising efforts. However, as explained by Jill Andresky Fraser,

> *His strategy will cost you—you may pay an hourly fee as well as a contingency percentage based on the amount raised or even an equity stake. However, a well-chosen intermediary will have contacts you lack, and may even help you reformulate your business plan entirely.*[14]

The Small Business Administration (SBA) and the Service Corps of Retired Executives (SCORE) can also be helpful. Both organizations have programs to introduce business owners to volunteer experts who will advise them.

Another source of assistance is the FastTrac Entrepreneurial Training Program sponsored by the Kauffman Center for Entrepreneurial Leadership in Kansas City. Located in universities, chambers of commerce, and SBDCs across the country, the FastTrac program teaches the basics of product development, concept recognition, financing strategies, and marketing research, while helping entrepreneurs create a written business plan in small, well-organized increments.

Securing help in business plan preparation does not relieve the entrepreneur of the responsibility for being the primary planner. Her or his ideas remain essential to producing a plan that is realistic and believable.

KEEPING THE RIGHT PERSPECTIVE

5 *Maintain the proper perspective when writing a business plan.*

To summarize, we contend that the business plan has an important place in starting and growing a business. As suggested in the chapter, writing an effective plan is important both for internal purposes and for telling the firm's story to outsiders who can contribute to the firm's success. But we also agree with Amar Bhide when he says that good judgment should be used in deciding if and how much to plan, given the circumstances. No single answer can be applied to all situations. Furthermore, it is important to avoid the misconception, held by too many entrepreneurs, that a good business plan will ensure success. The business plan, no matter how beneficial, is not the business. Building a good business involves much more. A good business plan leads to a successful company only when it is effectively executed by the entrepreneur and the management team.

Writing a business plan should be thought of as an ongoing process and not as the means to an end. In fact, when it comes to writing a plan, the process is just as important as the final outcome, which some entrepreneurs have difficulty accepting, given their orientation to "bottom line" results. But this point deserves to be repeated: *Writing a business plan is primarily an ongoing process and only secondarily the means to an outcome. The process is just as important as—if not more so than—the finished product.*

While your plan will represent your vision and goals for the firm, it will rarely reflect what actually happens. With a startup, too many unexpected events can affect the final outcome. Thus, a business plan is in large part an opportunity for an entrepreneur and management team to think about the potential key drivers of a venture's success or failure. Anticipating different scenarios and the ensuing consequences can significantly enhance an entrepreneur's adaptability—an essential quality for an entrepreneur, especially when so much is uncertain.

Now that you are aware of the role of the business plan in a new venture, you are ready for Chapters 7 through 12, which will closely examine each of the plan's components.

Looking Back

1 Explain what a business plan is, when it is needed, and what form it might take.

- A business plan is a document that sets out the basic idea underlying a business and describes related startup considerations. It should present the basic idea for a venture, describe where the entrepreneur is presently, indicate where she or he wants to go, and outline how she or he proposes to get there.
- A business plan has three basic objectives: to identify the nature and the context of a business opportunity, to present the approach the entrepreneur plans to take to exploit the opportunity, and to recognize factors that will determine whether the venture will be successful.
- A business plan may be of secondary importance if the environment is turbulent or if timing is such that the company needs to start operations as quickly as possible rather than slow down to write a business plan.
- The summary plan is a short form of a business plan that presents only the most important issues and projections for the business. This may be ideal if the

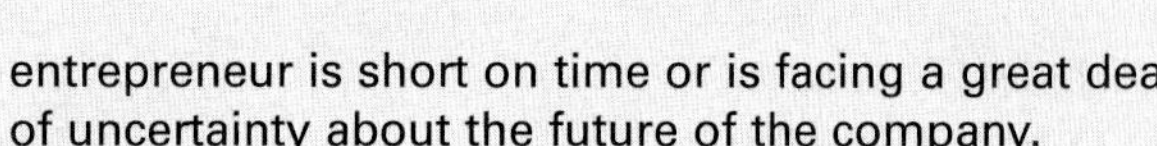

entrepreneur is short on time or is facing a great deal of uncertainty about the future of the company.

- A comprehensive plan is beneficial when (1) describing a new opportunity (startup), (2) facing significant change in the business or the external environment (changing demographics, new legislation, or developing industry trends), or (3) explaining complex business situations.

2 Explain how to tell a new venture's story to outsiders, especially investors.

- The business plan can serve as an effective selling tool with prospective customers, suppliers, and investors.
- In seeking financing, an entrepreneur must first use the business plan to create interest in the startup and then follow up with a formal offering memorandum to those investors who seem genuinely interested.
- When writing the business plan, remember that (1) investors have a short attention span and (2) certain features appeal to investors, while others are distinctly unappealing.

3 List practical suggestions to follow in writing a business plan and outline the key sections of a business plan.

- To maximize the effectiveness of a business plan, write clearly and provide factual support for any claims made.
- The entrepreneurial team, the opportunity, the resources, the deal structure, and the "big picture" are all interdependent factors that should be given consideration when thinking about the content of a business plan.
- Key sections of a business plan are the (1) title page, (2) table of contents, (3) executive summary, (4) vision and mission statement, (5) company overview, (6) products and/or services plan, (7) marketing plan, (8) management plan, (9) operating plan, (10) financial plan, and (11) appendix of supporting documents.
- Common mistakes often made by entrepreneurs when preparing a business plan include (1) failing to provide solid data, (2) failing to describe the product in lay terms, (3) failing to thoroughly analyze the market, (4) including financial statements that are overly detailed or incomplete, (5) hiding weaknesses, (6) overlooking the fatal flaw, (7) using bad grammar, and (8) making the plan overly long.

4 Identify available sources of assistance in preparing a business plan.

- A variety of books, Web sites, and computer software packages are available to assist in the preparation of a business plan.
- Professionals with planning expertise, such as attorneys, accountants, and marketing specialists, can provide useful suggestions and assistance in the preparation of a business plan.
- The Small Business Administration (SBA), the Service Corps of Retired Executives (SCORE), and the FastTrac Entrepreneurial Training Program can also be helpful.

5 Maintain the proper perspective when writing a business plan.

- Despite the potential benefits of a well-drafted plan, good judgment should be used in deciding how much to plan, in view of the specific circumstances.
- The business plan, no matter how beneficial, is not the business. A good business plan leads to a successful company only when it is effectively executed by the entrepreneur and the management team.
- A business plan can be viewed as an opportunity for the entrepreneur and the management team to think about the potential key drivers of a venture's success or failure.

Key Terms

business plan, p. 117
summary plan, p. 120
comprehensive plan, p. 120
prospectus, p. 121
executive summary, p. 127
mission statement, p. 128
products and/or services plan, p. 130
marketing plan, p. 130
management plan, p. 130
operating plan, p. 130
financial plan, p. 130
pro forma statements, p. 130

Discussion Questions

1. Describe what entrepreneurs mean when they talk about a business plan.
2. When should you write a business plan? When is it not necessary to write a plan?
3. Explain the two types of business plans. In what situation(s) would you use each type of plan?
4. How might a business plan be helpful in recruiting key management personnel?

5. How might an entrepreneur's perspective differ from that of an investor in terms of the business plan?
6. Discuss whether a sophisticated investor would really make a decision based on a five-minute review of a business plan.
7. Investors are said to be more market-oriented than product-oriented. What does this mean? What is the logic behind this orientation?
8. What advantages are realized by using a computer in preparing the narrative sections of a business plan? In preparing the financial plan?
9. Describe the mistakes that entrepreneurs sometimes make in writing a business plan.
10. If the income statement of a financial plan shows that the business will be profitable, why is there a need for a statement of cash flows?

You Make the Call

SITUATION 1

When they created RoundTable Group (RTG) Inc., Russ Rosenstein and Robert Hull envisioned a company offering one-stop shopping for intellectual expertise. They wanted to help businesspeople, management consultants, and litigation attorneys get answers to important questions from top-notch thinkers anywhere in the world through the Internet.

RTG's plan was to have a kind of SWAT team of professors who would answer questions based on their expertise. A team might consist of one or two professors, who would communicate with the client via e-mail, phone, or videoconferencing on projects that might involve a few hours or a few weeks of input. In the traditional management-consulting model, work on a project often lasts as long as a couple of years, and the team consists of a group of junior analysts, managers, and partners.

RTG assembled a database made up mainly of 3,000 university professors available to consult on an as-needed basis. The firm's fixed costs would be low because the professors would be paid only when they did billable work. But an unexpected wrinkle soon emerged. RTG's customers wanted RTG to start acting more like a traditional consulting firm. Business executives wanted face-to-face contact with the professors giving the information. They also wanted number crunching and follow-up analysis. And they wanted current, customized research.

That has left RTG at a crossroads. Should it try to become a more traditional management-consulting firm or continue to pursue its original mission of providing advice through Internet content and virtual links?

Taking the first path would mean providing support to clients, adding infrastructure and formalizing its operation by dividing it into distinct specialties. That would have the downside of making RTG's competitive point of differentiation murky. But the second path would risk putting off clients who say they want more.

Source: Elena De Lisser, "A Plan May Look Good, but Watch Out for the Real World," Startup Journal, *The Wall Street Journal Online,* http://www.startupjournal.com/howto/management/199908240948-lisser.html, January 15, 2004.

Question 1 What is the basic problem that Rosenstein and Hull need to resolve?

Question 2 What are the advantages and disadvantages of the proposed online consulting and the traditional approach to consulting?

Question 3 What do you think Rosenstein and Hull should do?

SITUATION 2

A young journalist is contemplating launching a new magazine that will feature wildlife, plant life, and nature around the world. The prospective entrepreneur intends for each issue to contain several feature articles—about the dangers and benefits of forest fires, the features of Rocky Mountain National Park, wildflowers found at high altitudes, and the danger of acid rain, for example. The magazine will make extensive use of color photographs, and its articles will be technically accurate and interestingly written. Unlike *National Geographic,* the proposed publication will avoid articles dealing with the general culture and confine itself to topics closely related to the natural world. Suppose you are a prospective investor examining a business plan prepared by this journalist.

Question 1 What are the most urgent questions you would want the marketing plan to answer?

Question 2 What details would you look for in the management plan?

Question 3 Do you think this entrepreneur would need to raise closer to $1 million or $10 million in startup capital? Why?

Question 4 At first glance, would you consider the opportunity potentially attractive? Why or why not?

SITUATION 3

John Martin and John Rose decided to start a new business to manufacture noncarbonated soft drinks. They believed that their location in East Texas, close to high-quality water, would give them a competitive edge. Although Martin and Rose had never worked together, Martin had 17 years of experience in the soft drink industry. Rose had recently sold his firm and had funds to help finance the venture; however, the partners needed to raise additional money from outside investors. Both men were excited about the opportunity and spent almost 18 months developing their business plan. The first paragraph of their executive summary reflected their excitement:

The "New Age" beverage market is the result of a spectacular boom in demand for drinks with nutritional value from environmentally safe ingredients and waters that come from deep, clear springs free of chemicals and pollutants. Argon Beverage Corporation will produce and market a full line of sparkling fruit drinks, flavored waters, and sports drinks that are of the highest quality and purity. These drinks have the same delicious taste appeal as soft drinks while using the most healthful fruit juices, natural sugars, and the purest spring water, the hallmark of the "New Age" drink market.

With the help of a well-developed plan, the two men were successful in raising the necessary capital to begin their business. They leased facilities and started production. However, after almost two years, the plan's goals were not being met. There were cost overruns, and profits were not nearly up to expectations.

Question 1 What problems might have contributed to the firm's poor performance?

Question 2 Although several problems were encountered in implementing the business plan, the primary reason for the low profits turned out to be embezzlement. Martin was diverting company resources for personal use, even using some of the construction materials purchased by the company to build his own house. What could Rose have done to avoid this situation? What are his options after the fact?

Experiential Exercises

1. Appendix A provides a business plan for an indoor soccer facility. Based on your reading of this chapter, write a one-page report on what you like about the plan and what you do not like.
2. A former chef wants to start a business to supply temporary kitchen help (such as chefs, sauce cooks, bakers, and meat cutters) to restaurants in need of staff during busy periods. Prepare a one-page report explaining which section or sections of the business plan would be most crucial to this new business and why.
3. Suppose that you wish to start a tutoring service for college students in elementary accounting courses. List the benefits you would realize from preparing a written business plan.
4. Interview a person who has started a business within the past five years. Prepare a report describing the extent to which the entrepreneur engaged in preliminary planning and his or her views about the value of business plans.

Exploring the Web

1. As you might imagine, the Web is full of resources that can help you develop a business plan. One such business plan site is the Entrepreneur's Center at The Beehive.
   a. Go to The Beehive Web site at **http://www.thebeehive.org/ecenter/start/** and click on the "Build a Business Plan" link. Before you can create a mini-plan, you'll need to register (it's free).
   b. Create a plan, print it out, and evaluate it.
2. This chapter highlights several organizations—SBDC, SBA, and SCORE—that can be extremely helpful during the planning phase of starting your own business.
   a. Go back to The Beehive's Entrepreneur's Center at **http://www.thebeehive.org/ecenter** and locate the offices of these organizations and others in your area that might be helpful to you.
   b. Many of these local organizations have their own Web sites that provide details on the services, workshops, and opportunities they sponsor. Check out several of these sites. Which interest you most? Briefly explain why.
3. Many software packages designed to assist in the writing of a business plan can be demo'd online. Use the Web to try out two different software applications. Which do you prefer? Why?

Case 6

ADGROVE.COM, INC. **(P. 534)**

This case presents the executive summary of a business plan.

Alternative Cases for Chapter 6:

Case 7, Specialty Cheese, p. 536
Case 8, Silver Zephyr Restaurant, p. 537

The Business Plan

LAYING THE FOUNDATION

Part 3 (Chapters 6 through 12) deals with issues that are important in starting a new venture. Chapter 6 has presented an overview of the business plan and its preparation. Chapters 7 through 12 focus on major segments of the business plan, such as the management plan, the marketing plan, and the financial plan. After you have carefully studied these chapters, you will have the knowledge you need to prepare a business plan.

Since applying what you study facilitates learning, we have included, at the end of each chapter in Part 3, a list of important questions that need to be addressed in preparing a particular segment of a business plan. In this chapter, we also include lists of books, Web sites, and software packages useful for preparing business plans.

Books on Preparing Business Plans

Abrams, Rhonda M. M., *Successful Business Plan: Secrets and Strategies* (Atlanta, GA: Rhonda, Inc., 1999). A step-by-step guide in loose-leaf-notebook format that includes business plan software to help you launch, finance, and run a profitable business.

Bangs, David H., *The Business Planning Guide: Creating a Winning Plan for Success*, 9th ed. (New York: Kaplan Professional Company, 2002). A guide for new venture capitalists that provides step-by-step strategies for compiling and completing a business plan and financial proposal.

Deloitte & Touche, LLP, *Writing an Effective Business Plan* (New York: Author, 2003).

Gevurtz, Franklin A., *Business Planning: Cases and Materials* (St. Paul, MN: West Group, 2000). A title in the University Casebook Series that takes a legal approach to business planning.

Hargrave, Lee E., *Plan for Profitability!: How to Write a Strategic Business Plan* (Titusville, FL: Four Seasons Publishers, 1999). Clearly and concisely teaches business plan writing based on the author's professional experience and strategic business plans that he has produced.

Harvard Business Review, *Harvard Business Review on Entrepreneurship* (Boston: Harvard Business Review Press, 1999). Offers basics of writing a business plan, obtaining venture capital funding, and strategies for successful marketplace realities.

Henricks, Mark, *Business Plans Made Easy* (Newburgh, NY: Entrepreneur Press, 1999).

Horan, James T., Jr., *The One Page Business Plan: Start with a Vision, Build a Company!* (Berkeley, CA: One Page Business Plan Company, 1998). Explains how to write concise, one-page business plans for startups, small- to mid-sized companies, corporate divisions, and nonprofits.

Kapron, Jill E., and JIAN Tools for Sale, Inc., *BizPlanBuilder Express: A Guide to Creating a Business Plan with BizPlanBuilder*, 2nd ed. (Mason, OH: South-Western, 2003). A workbook with CD-ROM package that includes BizPlanBuilder 8.1 software for Windows and Macintosh, providing all the essentials for creating business plans, with step-by-step instructions for preparing each section of a plan.

King, Jan B., *Business Plans to Game Plans: A Practical System for Turning Strategies into Action*, rev. ed. (Hoboken, NJ: John Wiley & Sons, 2004). An e-book that reveals five principles of business planning that guided the author to success and includes 60 charts, graphs, and worksheets for planning and assessment.

Patsula, Peter J., and Nowik, William (ed.), *Successful Business Planning in 30 Days: A Step-by-Step Guide for Writing a Business Plan and Starting Your Own Business*, 2nd ed. (Singapore: Patsula Media, 2002). Features fill-in worksheets, checklists, and forms, with business planning tips, profit tips, strategies, fact-filled quotes, and step-by-step instructions.

Peterson, Steven D., and Jaret, Peter E., *Business Plans Kit for Dummies* (Indianapolis, IN: For Dummies, 2001). A book and CD-ROM that cover business plans for every stage of planning and funding of different types of businesses—e-businesses, sole proprietorships, nonprofits—and for restructuring an existing company.

Pinson, Linda, and Jinnett, Jerry, *Anatomy of a Business Plan*, 5th ed. (Chicago: Enterprise/Dearborn, 2001).

Rich, Stanley R., and Gumpert, David E., *Business Plans That Win $$$: Lessons from the MIT Enterprise Forum* (New York: HarperCollins, 1987).

Rogoff, Edward, *Bankable Business Plans* (Mason, OH: South-Western, 2003). Reveals how to produce compelling and successful business plans for starting or expanding an enterprise.

Tiffany, Paul, and Peterson, Steven, *Business Plans for Dummies*, 2nd ed. (Indianapolis, IN: For Dummies, 2004).

Tooch, David, *Building a Business Plan*, 2nd ed. (Upper Saddle River, NJ: Prentice Hall, 2004). Provides step-by-step lessons with actual case studies—business plans can be authored with or without Palo Alto *Business Plan Pro* software.

Articles on Preparing Business Plans

Hormozi, Amir M., et al., "Business Plans for New or Small Businesses: Paving the Way to Success," *Management Decision*, Vol. 40, Nos. 7/8 (2002), pp. 755–763.

Rich, Stanley R., and Gumpert, David E., "How to Write a Winning Business Plan," *Harvard Business Review*, Vol. 63, No. 3 (May-June 1985), pp. 156–166.

Sahlman, William A., "How to Write a Great Business Plan," *Harvard Business Review*, Vol. 75, No. 4 (July-August 1997), pp. 114–121.

Schilit, W. K., "How to Write a Winning Business Plan," *Business Horizons*, Vol. 30, No. 5 (1987), pp. 13–22.

Online Resources for Preparing Business Plans

BPlans.com, Inc., *BPlans.com: The Business Planning Experts*, http://www.bplans.com. Online resource, provided by PaloAlto Software, designed for self-preparers, providing advice, sample plans, and links to many consultants.

Business Confidant, Inc., *Business Confidant: Your Business Planning Specialist*, http://www.businessconfidant.com. An online "one-stop resource" that provides strategic thinking, technical writing, and financial analytical skills needed to produce professional, investor-ready business plans.

Business PlanWare, *Business Plan Software . . .* , http://www.planware.org. Online resource, based in Ireland, that features financial projection and cash flow forecasting software, business plan freeware, white papers, and other tools and resources.

Dow Jones & Company, *Startup Journal: The Wall Street Journal Center for Entrepreneurs*, http://www.startupjournal.com/. An online resource that features a MiniPlan business assumptions test, sample business plans, and calculators for startup costs and cash flow, as well as articles on starting a business.

Entrepreneur.com, Inc., *Entrepreneur.com: Solutions for Growing Businesses*, http://www.entrepreneur.com. Use the site search engine to find articles and tips using keywords such as business plan writing.

Good-to-Go Business Plans Inc., *Good-to-Go Business Plans: Plans for Every Business*, http://www.goodtogobusinessplans.com. Provides a range of services, including business-specific templates in predrafted language and other tools and forms.

Small Business Administration, *Small Business Administration: Your Small Business Resource*, http://www.sba.gov. The federal government's online business planning and finance resource center classroom and library.

Software for Preparing Business Plans

JIAN, Inc., *BizPlan*Builder *2004*, http://www.jian.com. A suite of business planning software and other business tools.

PaloAlto Software, *Business Plan Pro 2005*, http://www.paloalto.com. Business plan–creating software featuring over 400 sample business plans.

Smart Online, Inc., *Smart Business Plan Deluxe*, http://www.smartonline.com. Software suite that features the "Smart Wizard," which guides users through the creation of a tailored business plan; includes a "Financial Advisor," which helps to find ways to fund businesses.

Company Description Questions

Now that you have learned the main concepts of business plan preparation, you can begin the process of creating a business plan by writing a general company description. In thinking about the key issues in starting a new business, respond to the following questions:

1. When and where is the business to start?
2. What is the history of the company?
3. What changes have been made in structure or ownership?
4. In what stage of development is the company?
5. What has been achieved to date?
6. What is the company's distinctive competence?
7. What are the basic nature and activity of the business?
8. What is its primary product or service?
9. What customers will be served?
10. What is the company's mission statement?
11. What are the company's objectives?
12. What is the company's form of organization?
13. What are the current and projected economic states of the industry?
14. Does the company intend to become a publicly traded company or an acquisition candidate?

THE MARKETING PLAN

In the Spotlight

Harvest Ventures **http://www.harvestventures.com**

Once a new venture idea is judged to be a true opportunity, the next step is to develop a marketing plan. The plan may be written, especially if financing is being pursued, or it may remain unwritten, in conceptual form, and be developed gradually over time.

Two brothers, Dan and Russell Schlueter of Waconia, Minnesota, began their planning at a Chicago pet trade show in 1977. They were exhibiting their existing product for dogs, Harvest Chews. "We walked [around] and saw a man everyone was ignoring . . . but he had a great demonstration. He put three or four cups of water in a bowl with just a small amount of [silica sand] pellets, and these pellets absorbed everything."

Both Dan and Russell had the same thought: The pellets could be used to make a superior cat litter product. Convinced they had a winning opportunity, the Schlueters struck a deal with a silica gel manufacturer in China to produce the pellets for them. Then, after some research, which involved handing out free samples to people with cats, they began developing a marketing plan for their new product.

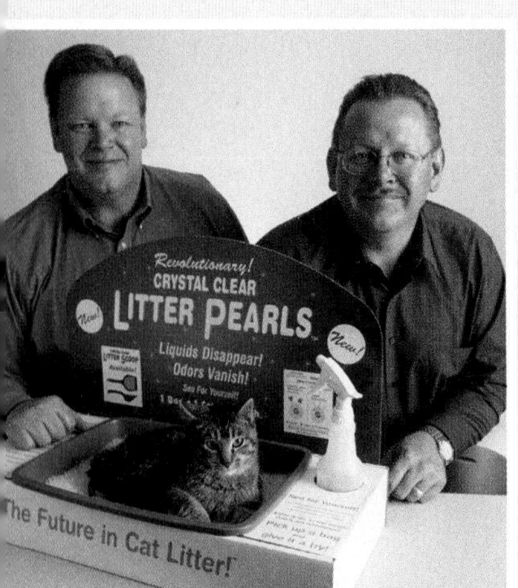

© Sal Skog

Price was a major concern. Would consumers pay $14 to $16 for a four-pound bag of the product, when a competitive product sold for $7 a bag? They needed a higher price to cover costs and believed customers would pay well for the convenience.

Next, they addressed the distribution issue. The Schlueters hit the pet trade show circuit and landed some distributors that served independent pet retailers. Later, the brothers introduced a variation of the product in grocery stores. A smaller bag was used because it required less shelf space and its higher per-pound price offered larger margins—two features always attractive to supermarket managers. Also, they decided on brand names—Ultra Pearl for the grocery store version and Crystal Clear Litter Pearls for the retail pet outlet product—and registered them as trademarks.

As you can see, these entrepreneurs developed their marketing plan over time, an option that worked well for them. In 1999, their product was voted Best New Cat Product at the 41st Annual American Pet Products Manufacturers Association Trade Show. And in November 2003, Harvest Ventures was bought by Ultra Pet Company, Inc.

Sources: http://www.harvestventures.com, April 15, 2004; Don Debelak, "Look What I Found," *Entrepreneur,* July 2002, p. 110, reprinted with permission; and "Acquisitions Pave Way for Ultra Pet Debut," http://www.petproductnews.com, March 29, 2004.

Chapter 7

Looking Ahead

After studying this chapter, you should be able to

1 *Describe small business marketing.*

2 *Identify the components of a formal marketing plan.*

3 *Discuss the nature of the marketing research process.*

4 *Define market segmentation and its related strategies.*

5 *Explain the different methods of forecasting sales.*

Unfortunately, some entrepreneurs ignore marketing in the early stages of planning new ventures. They concentrate on the cart and neglect the horse—emphasizing the idea behind the product or service while overlooking the marketing activities that will carry the idea to customers. Consider the following conversation between an aspiring entrepreneur and a marketing consultant:

> *Marketing Consultant:* May I see your marketing plan?
>
> *Entrepreneur:* You could if I had one, but I don't. It's a great concept, and I just know people will want to buy it.
>
> *Marketing Consultant:* How do you know that these people will be so eager to buy? Is this what your consumer research indicates?
>
> *Entrepreneur:* I don't have any research . . . but my friends tell me it's a fantastic idea that will sell like hotcakes.

Such optimism is commendable, but infatuation with an idea can have devastating consequences if the entrepreneur doesn't understand how to transfer the idea into a product or service that customers will purchase.

In Chapter 6, we discussed the importance of a new venture plan for both the entrepreneur and potential investors. In this chapter, we will look at the nature of marketing and the marketing plan. Then, in Chapters 8 through 12, we'll consider the major components of a business plan. Although our presentation will not cover the specific elements of all plans, the features we will discuss are important components of any well-written plan.

It is appropriate first to answer a few basic questions about marketing:

- How can marketing be defined?
- What are the components of an effective marketing philosophy?
- What does a consumer orientation imply about the business?

WHAT IS SMALL BUSINESS MARKETING?

1 *Describe small business marketing.*

Marketing means different things to different people. Some entrepreneurs view marketing as simply selling a product or service. Others see marketing as those activities directing the flow of goods and services from producer to consumer or user. In reality, small business marketing is much broader. It consists of many activities, some of which occur even before a product is produced and made ready for distribution and sale.

We begin with a comprehensive definition of small business marketing in order to convey its true scope to entrepreneurs. **Small business marketing** consists of those business activities that direct the creation, development, and delivery of a *bundle of satisfaction* from the creator to the targeted user and that satisfy the targeted user. Notice how this definition emphasizes the concept of a bundle of satisfaction—a core product or service

small business marketing
Business activities that direct the creation, development, and delivery of a bundle of satisfaction from the creator to the targeted user and that satisfy the targeted user

plus all its important extras. Ultimately, the business provides satisfaction to its customers, not merely the tangible product or intangible service that is the focus of the exchange. Consider Blue Nile Incorporated, which sells engagement rings and other jewelry on its Web site. Although jewelry is its core product, the bundle of satisfaction the firm provides includes more than jewelry. In keeping with the company's strong commitment to help customers make the right purchase, Blue Nile's Web site provides a great deal of extra information. This assistance, along with competitive prices and free shipping, is part of the bundle of satisfaction offered. And it appears to be working well. The average value of an order generated on Blue Nile's Web site is $1,000, which is very high for this type of business.[1]

Marketing Philosophies Make a Difference

Just as a person's personal philosophy influences the strategy that person uses to achieve personal goals, a firm's marketing philosophy determines how its marketing activities are developed, reflected in the marketing plan, and used to achieve business goals. Three different marketing perspectives that permeate small businesses are the production-oriented, sales-oriented, and consumer-oriented philosophies.

A *production-oriented philosophy* emphasizes the product as the single most important part of the business. The firm concentrates resources on developing the product or service in the most efficient manner, even if promotion, distribution, and other marketing activities are slighted. On the other hand, a *sales-oriented philosophy* deemphasizes production efficiencies and customer preferences in favor of a focus on sales. Achieving sales goals becomes the firm's highest priority. In contrast, a firm adopting a *consumer-oriented philosophy* believes that everything, including production and sales, centers around the consumer and his or her needs. The result: All marketing efforts begin and end with the consumer.

A Consumer Orientation—The Right Choice

Over the years, both large and small businesses have gradually shifted their marketing emphasis from production to sales and, more recently, to consumers. *We strongly recommend that all new businesses begin with a consumer orientation, as this philosophy is most consistent with long-term success.* Remember, customer satisfaction is not a means to achieving a goal—it *is* the goal!

Why have some small firms failed to adopt a consumer orientation when the benefits seem so obvious? The answer lies in three key factors. First, the state of competition always affects a firm's marketing orientation. If there is little or no competition and if demand exceeds supply, a firm is tempted to emphasize production. This is usually a short-term situation, however, and one that often leads to disaster.

Second, an entrepreneur may have strong production skills but be weak in marketing ability. Naturally, such owners will concentrate on production considerations.

Third, some entrepreneurs are simply too focused on the present. They expect the firm's marketing efforts to reap immediate dividends and, consequently, favor a sales-oriented philosophy. However, putting too much emphasis on selling merchandise often creates customer dissatisfaction, especially if high-pressure selling is used with little regard for customers' needs.

Both production- and sales-oriented philosophies may generate short-run success. However, a consumer orientation not only recognizes production efficiency goals and professional selling but also adds concern for customer satisfaction. In effect, a firm that adopts a consumer orientation incorporates the best of each marketing philosophy.

Once a small firm makes a commitment to customer orientation, it is ready to develop the marketing strategy to support this goal. Marketing activities include taking the steps necessary to locate and describe potential customers—a process called **market analysis**. Marketing activities also encompass the development of a marketing mix. Product, pricing, promotion, and distribution activities combine to form the **marketing mix**. Marketing research, market segmentation, and sales forecasting are additional key activities underlying market analysis and development of a marketing mix.

market analysis
The process of locating and describing potential customers

marketing mix
The combination of product, pricing, promotion, and distribution activities

Exhibit 7-1 depicts the major components of the marketing plan and the marketing activities required to generate the information needed for the plan—marketing research, market segmentation, and sales forecasting. In the remainder of the chapter, we will take a more in-depth look at these plan components and marketing activities.

EXHIBIT 7-1 *The Marketing Plan and Supporting Marketing Activities*

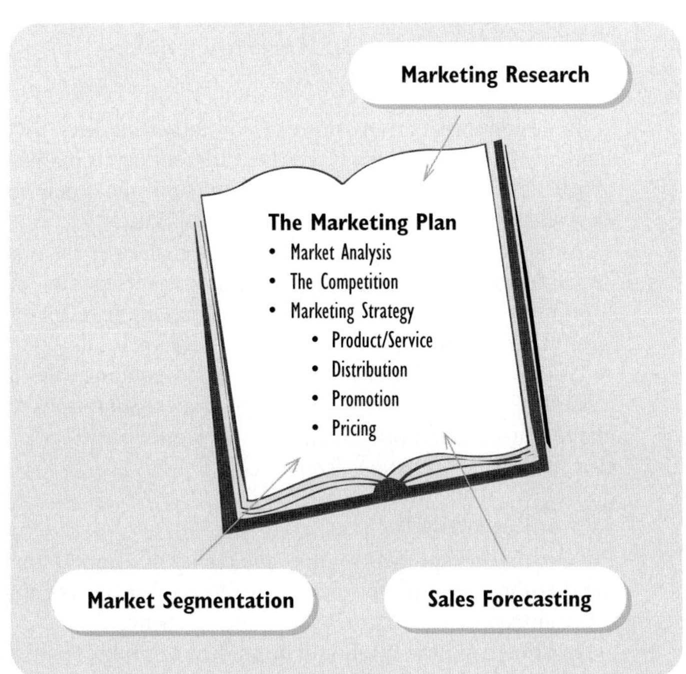

THE FORMAL MARKETING PLAN

2 *Identify the components of a formal marketing plan.*

After the entrepreneur's idea has been examined and judged to be a viable opportunity, he or she is ready to prepare the formal marketing plan. Each business venture is different; therefore, each marketing plan is unique. An entrepreneur should not feel it necessary to develop a cloned version of a plan created by someone else—even the one suggested by the authors of this textbook. Nevertheless, most marketing plans should cover market analysis, the competition, and marketing strategy.

We have provided several excerpts from actual marketing plans to show the "flavor" of certain sections. The following discussion is not intended to be complete or comprehensive. A more detailed treatment of marketing activities and strategies for both new and established small businesses is provided in Chapters 13 through 17. Much of this later material will also be helpful for writing the actual marketing plan.

Market Analysis

In the market analysis section of the marketing plan, the entrepreneur describes the target market. This description of potential customers is commonly called a **customer profile**. Marketing research information, compiled from both secondary and primary data, can be used to construct this profile. A detailed discussion of the major benefits to customers provided by the new product or service should also be included in this section of the plan. Obviously, these benefits must be reasonable and consistent with statements in the product and/or service section of the plan.

customer profile A description of potential customers in a target market

Review the following excerpt from the market analysis section of the marketing plan of Adorable Pet Photography, a home-based business located in Atlanta, Georgia.

Pets have always been an important part of the American family. However, as the American culture has changed in the last two decades, an even more prominent role for the pet has emerged. In today's mobile society, people often lose touch with their community, friends, and family, so they draw closer to their pets. As more people put off having children until later in life, pets are increasingly lapping up the luxuries that had once been reserved for human housemates. Making pets into family members is typical of an economy driven by middle-aged professionals with two-income households and fewer, if any, children. These "baby boomers" are now hitting the peak years of 35 to 65. In some cases, the pet alleviates the

Empty Nest Syndrome for older married couples. Their animals are not just pets but companions, and many consider their pets as their children. Society is getting better educated and more accepting of pets across the board, and there is existing research that proves pets are a benefit to one's health. . . . People are now treating their pets as children, a pampering not seen 20 years ago.[2]

If an entrepreneur envisions several target markets, each segment must have a corresponding customer profile. Likewise, different target markets may call for an equal number of related marketing strategies. Typically, however, a new venture will initially concentrate on a select few target markets—or even just one.

Another major component of market analysis is the actual sales forecast. It is usually desirable to include three sales forecasts covering the "most likely," "pessimistic," and "optimistic" scenarios. These scenarios provide investors and the entrepreneur with different numbers on which to base their decisions.

As we point out later in this chapter, forecasting sales for a new venture is extremely difficult. While it will be necessary to make assumptions during forecasting, they should be minimized. The forecasting method should be described and backed up by data wherever feasible.

The Competition

Frequently, entrepreneurs ignore the reality of competition for their new ventures, believing that the marketplace contains no close substitutes or that their success will not attract other entrepreneurs. This is simply not realistic.

Existing competitors should be studied carefully, and their key management personnel profiled. A brief discussion of competitors' overall strengths and weaknesses should be a part of the competition section of the plan. Also, related products currently being marketed or tested by competitors should be noted. An assessment should be made of the likelihood that any of these firms will enter the entrepreneur's target market.

Consider the following excerpt from the competition section of a marketing plan for the startup Yes, We Do Windows:

At this time there are 5 window cleaning services and 10 housecleaning services listed in my area Yellow Pages.

Taking the time to make phone calls to these competitors made me feel even better about my idea for a business. Many of these firms did not return calls, did not seem interested, and were unable to provide phone bids.

I can see two "musts" for the business: (a) my bids must be firm, and (b) my phone skills must be customer-oriented. If I can't answer the phone, I must find a phone person who fulfills these two musts. The image we're presenting here is "We aim to please. We're interested in servicing your home."[3]

Many competitors can be monitored by visiting their Web sites. Ann Blakeley, president of Orlando, Florida–based Earth Resources Corporation, a hazardous materials technology firm, uses search engines like AltaVista to check out her competitors. "I check every couple of months just to make sure nothing has changed," Blakeley says. "If any competitors have new products, odds are they'll put it on their Web pages."[4]

Marketing Strategy

A well-prepared market analysis and a discussion of the competition are important to the formal marketing plan. But the information on marketing strategy forms the most detailed section of the marketing plan and, in many respects, is subject to the closest scrutiny from potential investors. Such a strategy plots the course of the marketing actions that will make or break the entrepreneur's vision.

The following excerpt describes the marketing strategy of Fantastic Florals, a startup that imports handmade florals from Indonesia:

Fantastic Flowers, Inc. has a variety of silk flowers and products from which to choose. During the first two years, the product line will include tulips and roses; two kinds of flower arrangements; silk scarf and silk hair assessories; and seasonal bouquets. . . . FFI sets standard prices for each product line. These prices are not expected to experience significant *change over the next three years. Tulips and roses—$2.25; arranged flower 1—$18.99; arranged flower 2—$39.99; silk scarf—$15.99; other hair accessories—$9.99; and other/seasonal bouquet—$59.99. These prices exhibit quality products at reasonable costs to consumers. . . . The goal of FFI is to promote its products as fine collectibles for the collector or the gift-buyer. This will be done through promotions, direct-mail advertisements, appearances in related catalogs, and publicity events. . . . Products will be distributed through the retail store in Anytown Third Street Market or be pre-orders until FFI is able to further expand. Sales is one area that needs to be developed in order to better serve the consumer and meet objectives.*[5]

Four areas of marketing strategy should be addressed: (1) product decisions that will transform the basic product or service idea into a bundle of satisfaction, (2) distribution activities regarding the delivery of the product to customers, (3) pricing activities that will set an acceptable exchange value on the total product or service, and (4) promotion activities that will communicate the necessary information to target markets.

Obviously, the nature of a new venture has a direct bearing on the emphasis given to each of these areas. For example, a service business will not have the same distribution problems as a product business, and the promotional challenges facing a new retail store will be quite different from those faced by a new manufacturer. Despite these differences, we can offer a generalized format for presenting marketing strategy in a business plan.

THE PRODUCT AND/OR SERVICE SECTION Within the product and/or service section of the marketing plan, the entrepreneur includes the name of the product and/or service and the name of the business and why they were selected. Any legal protection that has been obtained for the names should be described. It is also important to explain the logic behind the name selection. An entrepreneur's family name, if used for certain products or services, may make a positive contribution to sales. In other situations, a descriptive name that suggests a benefit of the product may be more desirable. Whatever the logic behind the choice of names, the selection should be defended and the names registered with the appropriate agencies to provide protection.

Sometimes names selected for a business and a product or service may be challenged many years later, particularly if they haven't been registered. This is what Richard Hagelberg learned when he received a certified letter from the United States Olympic Committee in March 2000, saying Hagelberg had two years to change the name of his small playground equipment manufacturing business in Gary, Indiana, or else be sued. The company had been founded back in 1982 with the name Olympic Recreation. After much thought, Hagelberg decided to switch rather than fight. "We consulted our lawyer and were very careful to choose a name that wasn't trademarked," he said. He finally settled on Kidstuff Playsystems.[6]

Other components of the total product, such as the packaging, should be presented via drawings. Sometimes, it may be desirable to use professional packaging consultants to develop these drawings. Customer service plans such as warranties and repair policies need to be discussed here. These elements of the marketing strategy should be tied directly to customer satisfaction. (Chapter 13 further examines the importance of creating and maintaining good customer relationships.)

THE DISTRIBUTION SECTION Quite often, new ventures will use established intermediaries as their channels of distribution. This distribution strategy expedites the process and reduces the necessary investment. How those intermediaries will be persuaded to carry the new product should be explained in the distribution section of the marketing plan. Any intention the new business may have to license its product or service should also be covered in this section.

Some new retail ventures require fixed locations; others need mobile stores. The layouts and configurations of retail outlets should be explained here.

When a new firm's method of product delivery is exporting, the distribution section must discuss the relevant laws and regulations governing that activity. Knowledge of exchange rates between currencies and distribution options must be reflected in the material included in this section. (Distribution concepts are explained in detail in Chapter 14.)

THE PRICING SECTION At a minimum, the price of a product or service must cover the costs of bringing it to customers. Therefore, the pricing section must include a schedule

Living the Dream *Entrepreneurial Challenges*

Be Flexible

A good marketing plan includes a sound distribution strategy. Failure was narrowly avoided by entrepreneur Martha C. de la Torre when her *El Clasificado* venture adopted a poor approach to delivery of the Los Angeles–area Spanish language weekly newspaper. Here's her assessment of the situation:

> *When I started* El Clasificado, *I wanted to do a home-delivered weekly shopper for Spanish-speaking immigrants. I wrote an extensive business plan and projected the numbers to a T, but my weakness was that I stuck to it too closely for too long. I initially got a lot of clients, and they loved the unique home delivery, but sending it by mail and later distributing it door-to-door was just too costly.*

The costly distribution strategy of this business, founded in 1988, resulted in near bankruptcy, with the founder selling her home, refinancing her car, and maxing out her credit card to keep the business going. "The struggle finally began to end when I gave up on my original plans and we changed our distribution method," she says. Around 1994, the weekly newspaper shifted to a much cheaper bulk mail system. *El Clasificado* was also placed in major supermarkets and chains such as 7-Eleven. In addition, in 1996 de la Torre decided to place the paper in street racks to gain exposure to pedestrian traffic. From this time on, revenues began to grow.

http://www.elclasificado.com

"I've learned that you need to be flexible and creative and find the right formula that turns your great idea into a success," she says. The company now has 51 employees, with annual revenues of $3.5 million.

Source: Karen E. Klein, "Be Flexible or Fold," *My Business*, June/July 2002, pp. 13–14.

of both production and marketing costs. Break-even computations should be included for alternative prices. Naturally, forecasting methods used for analysis in this section should be consistent with those used in preparing the market analysis section. However, setting a price based exclusively on break-even analysis is not advisable, as it ignores other aspects of pricing. If the entrepreneur has found a truly unique niche, she or he may be able to charge a premium price—at least in the short run.

Competitors, if any, should be studied to learn what they are charging. To break into a market, an entrepreneur will usually have to price a new product or service within a reasonable range of the competition. (Chapter 15 examines break-even analysis and pricing strategy in more depth.)

THE PROMOTIONAL SECTION The promotional section of the marketing plan should describe the entrepreneur's approach to creating customer awareness of the product or service and motivating customers to buy. Among the many promotional options available to the entrepreneur are personal selling and advertising.

If personal selling is appropriate, the section should outline how many salespeople will be employed and how they will be compensated. The proposed system for training the sales force should be mentioned. If advertising is to be used, a list of the specific media should be included and advertising themes should be described. Often, it is advisable to seek the services of a small advertising agency. In this case, the name and credentials of the agency should be provided. A brief mention of successful campaigns supervised by the agency can add to the appeal of this section of the marketing plan. (Personal selling and advertising are discussed more extensively in Chapter 16.)

MARKETING RESEARCH FOR THE NEW VENTURE

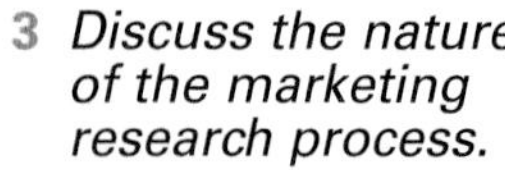
3 Discuss the nature of the marketing research process.

A marketing plan can be based on intuition alone, or intuition can be supplemented by sound market information. *In every case, it is advisable to write the marketing plan only after collecting and evaluating marketing research data.* A marketing plan based on research will undoubtedly be stronger than a plan without such a foundation.

The Nature of Marketing Research

Marketing research may be defined as the gathering, processing, reporting, and interpreting of marketing information. It is all about finding out what you want to know. A small business typically conducts less marketing research than does a big business, partly because of the expense involved but also because the entrepreneur often does not understand the basic research process. Our discussion of marketing research focuses on the more widely used practical techniques that entrepreneurs can employ as they analyze potential target markets and make preparations to develop their marketing plans.

marketing research
The gathering, processing, reporting, and interpreting of market information

Although a small business can conduct marketing research without the assistance of an expert, the cost of hiring such help is often money well spent, as the expert's advice may help increase revenues or cut costs. Marketing researchers are trained, experienced professionals, and prices for their research services typically reflect this. For example, focus groups run from $3,000 to $10,000 each, and a telephone survey may range anywhere from $5,000 to $25,000 or more, depending on the number of interviews and the length of the questionnaire. However, companies such as SurveySite, Inc. (http://www.surveysite.com), are now reducing overall research costs by taking advantage of the Internet to offer Web-based surveys and online focus groups.

Before committing to research, an entrepreneur should always estimate the projected costs of marketing research and compare them with the benefits expected. Although such analysis is never exact, it will help the entrepreneur decide what research should be conducted.

Living the Dream — Focus on the Customer

Launching Lashpro

An important step toward success for a new invention involves carefully researching the market to determine potential customer interest. The research conducted by Stephanie Kellar helped her successfully launch her innovative eyelash curler.

Her inspiration for the new design came after she pinched her face with the casing of a traditional curler model. Kellar set out to make improvements on the old design, but realized the need to find out what potential users thought.

> *She used a Usenet newsgroup called alt.fashion to gather information. According to Kellar, "I didn't want to tell people exactly what I was doing, so I would pose questions on the Usenet like, 'Has anyone had problems pinching their face with an eyelash curler?'" Over a few months, by continually posing questions on the Usenet, Kellar was able to get input from more than 100 people. The overall consensus was that the eyelash curlers currently on the market clearly had problems. Kellar was sure this was her great opportunity. Next, Kellar decided to make a pilot run of products so she could ensure the product was just right. "The biggest error people make is to put a product on the market before it's ready," she explains. So in 1996, Kellar produced a small run of eyelash curlers and gave test units to about 50 users she had met through the Usenet to see if they felt the product actually delivered the results Kellar promised. The product testers suggested a few adjustments, which she made.*

© Kathy Tarantola

Kellar also visited the patent depository section of the Boston Public Library to research past patents on eyelash curlers. After finding that other inventors hadn't really pursued her approach, Kellar decided to apply for a patent, which was eventually granted.

Kellar's research paid off, and she launched Lashpro in 2000 with a $19 retail price. Sales (primarily to high-end retailers) reached $100,000 in 2001. At this writing, sales have been suspended because of a temporary disruption in supply from the Chinese factory producing the Lashpro. Negotiations are in progress for a new supplier.

Sources: Don Debelak, "Want Some of This?" *Entrepreneur,* June 2002, pp. 124–127, reprinted with permission; and personal interview with Stephanie Kellar, October 23, 2003.

Steps in the Marketing Research Process

The typical steps in the marketing research process are (1) identifying the informational need, (2) searching for secondary data, (3) collecting primary data, and (4) interpreting the data gathered.

IDENTIFYING THE INFORMATIONAL NEED The first step in marketing research is to identify and define the informational need. Although this step seems almost too obvious to mention, the fact is that entrepreneurs sometimes commission surveys without pinpointing the specific information needed. Obviously, a broad statement such as "Our need is to know if the venture will be successful" will do little to guide the research process, but even a more specific goal can easily miss the mark. For example, an entrepreneur thinking about a location for a restaurant may decide to conduct a survey to ascertain customers' menu preferences and reasons for eating out when, in fact, what he or she needs to know most is how often residents of the target area eat out and how far they are willing to drive to eat in a restaurant.

Once a venture's informational needs have been defined correctly, research can be designed to concentrate on those specific needs. Later in this chapter, you will see a survey questionnaire developed for a car-wash owner who wanted to assess customer satisfaction. The informational need that the entrepreneur identified was clear: Determine the level of customers' satisfaction with the car-cleaning experience at his business.

secondary data
Market information that has been previously compiled

SEARCHING FOR SECONDARY DATA Information that has already been compiled is known as **secondary data**. Generally, gathering secondary data is less expensive than gathering new, or primary, data. Therefore, after defining informational needs, entrepreneurs should exhaust available sources of secondary data before going further into the research process. It may be possible to base much of the marketing plan for the new venture solely on secondary data. "It's a myth that only the big guys have the wherewithal to do market research," says Mary Beth Campau, assistant vice president for reference services at Dun & Bradstreet Information Services. "There is a wealth of timely information from a variety of sources available in public and university libraries throughout the United States. Just ask the librarians, and they'll be happy to point you in the right direction."[7]

Another helpful source of secondary data for the small firm is the Small Business Administration (http://www.sba.gov), or SBA. This agency publishes extensive bibliographies in many decision areas, including marketing research. Software programs and hundreds of Web sites (many offering free information) can also help an entrepreneur research customers.

Unfortunately, the use of secondary data has several drawbacks. One is that the data may be outdated. Another is that the units of measure in the secondary data may not fit the current problem. For example, a firm's market might consist of individuals with incomes between \$20,000 and \$25,000, while secondary data show the number of individuals with incomes between \$15,000 and \$50,000.

Finally, the question of credibility is always present. Some sources of secondary data are less trustworthy than others. Mere publication of data does not in itself make the data valid and reliable. It is advisable to compare several different sources to see whether they are reporting similar data. Professional research specialists can also help assess the credibility of secondary sources.

primary data
New market information that is gathered by the firm conducting the research

COLLECTING PRIMARY DATA If the secondary data are insufficient, a search for new information, or **primary data**, is the next step. Observational methods and questioning methods are two techniques used in accumulating primary data. Observational methods avoid interpersonal contact between respondents and the researcher, while questioning methods involve some type of interaction with respondents.

Observational Methods Observation is probably the oldest form of research in existence. Indeed, learning by observing is quite common. Thus, it is hardly surprising that observation can provide useful information for small businesses. An excellent method of observational research has been devised by Jean Sullivan, who experiments with new soup ideas for her Sudbury Soup Company, located in Concord, Massachusetts. She arranges tastings in most of the supermarkets where her soups are sold and closely observes shoppers' reactions to the samples she cooks for them.[8] Her method may not be very sophisticated, but it has proven to be extremely effective.

Observational methods can be inexpensive. Furthermore, they avoid the potential bias that can result from a respondent's contact with an interviewer during questioning. Observation—for example, counting customers going into a store—can be conducted by a person or by mechanical devices, such as hidden video cameras.

The cost of mechanical observation devices is rapidly declining, bringing them within the budget of many small businesses. When Scott Semel and Reed Chase wanted to learn more about their competitors and customers after buying a candy-importing company, Cody-Kramer Imports, in Blauvolt, New York, what did they do? They attended several major industry trade shows and checked out competitors' booths. They also wandered the aisles of candy retailers, observing whatever they could about candy-buying customers.[9]

Questioning Methods Surveys and experimentation are both questioning methods that involve contact with respondents. Surveys can be conducted by mail, telephone, or personal interview. Mail surveys are often used when target respondents are widely dispersed; however, they usually yield low response rates—only a small percentage of the surveys sent out are typically returned. Telephone surveys and personal interview surveys achieve higher response rates. However, personal interviews are very expensive, and individuals are often reluctant to grant personal interviews if they think a sales pitch is coming. Some marketing researchers, such as i.think inc., offer firms a new way to survey customers—through an online questionnaire. Although some Web sites claim that online surveys have better response rates than do paper surveys, Internet surveying is still very new and data on response rates are questionable.

A questionnaire is the basic instrument guiding the researcher and the respondent when a survey is taken. A questionnaire should be developed carefully and pre-tested before it is used in the market. Several considerations should be kept in mind when designing and testing a questionnaire:

- Ask questions that relate to the issue under consideration. An interesting question may not be relevant. A good test of relevance is to assume an answer to each question and then ask yourself how you would use that information.
- Select the form of question that is most appropriate for the subject and the conditions of the survey. Open-ended and multiple-choice questions are two popular forms.
- Carefully consider the order of the questions. Asking questions in the wrong sequence can produce biased answers to later questions.
- Ask the more sensitive questions near the end of the questionnaire. Age and income, for example, are usually sensitive topics.
- Carefully select the words in each question. They should be as simple, clear, and objective as possible.
- Pre-test the questionnaire by administering it to a small sample of respondents who are representative of the group to be surveyed.

Exhibit 7-2 shows a questionnaire developed for a car-wash owner. This survey illustrates how the considerations above can be incorporated into a questionnaire. Note the use of both multiple-choice and open-ended questions. As it turned out, responses to the open-ended questions were particularly useful to this firm.

INTERPRETING THE DATA GATHERED After the necessary data have been gathered, they must be transformed into usable information. Without interpretation, large quantities of data are only isolated facts. Methods of summarizing and simplifying information for users include tables, charts, and other graphics. Descriptive statistics (for example, the average response) are most helpful during this step in the research procedure. Inexpensive personal computer software is now available to perform statistical calculations and generate report-quality graphics.

It is important to remember that formal marketing research is not always necessary in launching a new venture. Bill Madway, founder and president of Madway Business Research, Inc., in Malvern, Pennsylvania, says, "Sometimes, you cannot answer a question with research . . . you just have to test it. Then the question is whether you can afford to

EXHIBIT 7-2 *Small Business Survey Questionnaire*

PLEASE—WE NEED YOUR HELP!

You're The Boss.* All of us here at Genie Car Wash have just one purpose . . . *TO PLEASE YOU!

Date ______________________ Time of Visit ______________________

How are we doing?

	Yes	No		
1. Personnel–courteous and helpful?				
Service writer	☐	☐		
Vacuum attendants	☐	☐		
Cashier	☐	☐		
Final finish & inspection	☐	☐		
Management	☐	☐		
2. Do you feel the time it took to wash your car was . . .				
Right amount of time	☐			
Too much time	☐			
Not enough time	☐			
	Excel	**Good**	**Avg**	**Poor**
3. How do you judge the appearance of the personnel?	☐	☐	☐	☐
4. Please rate the quality of workmanship of the interior of your car.				
Inside vacuum	☐	☐	☐	☐
Dashboard	☐	☐	☐	☐
Doorjambs	☐	☐	☐	☐
Ash trays	☐	☐	☐	☐
Windows	☐	☐	☐	☐
Console	☐	☐	☐	☐
5. Please rate the quality of workmanship of the exterior of your car.				
Tires and wheels	☐	☐	☐	☐
Bumpers and chrome	☐	☐	☐	☐
Body of car	☐	☐	☐	☐
Grill	☐	☐	☐	☐
6. Please rate the overall appearance of our facility.				
Outside building & grounds	☐	☐	☐	☐
Inside building	☐	☐	☐	☐
Rest rooms	☐	☐	☐	☐
7. Please rate your overall impression of the experience you had while at Genie Car Wash.	☐	☐	☐	☐

It is important that we clean your car to your satisfaction. Additional comments will be appreciated.

____

____

____

OPTIONAL

Your Name ______________________

Address ______________________

City ______________________ State ____________ Zip ____________

Thank you!

test something that might not work. If there's very little risk involved or you can test it on a very small scale, you might decide to jump in. But the bigger the risk, the more valuable advance information becomes."[10]

As important as marketing research is, it should never be allowed to suppress entrepreneurial enthusiasm or be used as a substitute for a hands-on feel for the target market. It should be viewed as a supplement to, not a replacement for, intuitive judgment and cautious experimentation in launching new products and services. Ultimately, the marketing plan should reflect the entrepreneur's belief about what is the best marketing strategy for her or his firm.

UNDERSTANDING POTENTIAL TARGET MARKETS

4 *Define market segmentation and its related strategies.*

To prepare the market analysis section of the marketing plan, an entrepreneur needs a proper understanding of the term *market*, which means different things to different people. It may refer to a physical location where buying and selling take place ("They went to the market"), or it may be used to describe selling efforts ("We must market this product aggressively"). Still another meaning is the one we emphasize in this chapter: A **market** is a group of customers or potential customers who have purchasing power and unsatisfied needs. Note carefully the three ingredients in this definition of a market.

market
A group of customers or potential customers who have purchasing power and unsatisfied needs

1. A market must have buying units, or *customers*. These units may be individuals or business entities. Thus, a market is more than a geographic area; it must contain potential customers.
2. A market must contain buying units with *unsatisfied needs*. Consumers, for instance, will not buy unless they are motivated to do so—and motivation can occur only when a customer recognizes his or her unsatisfied needs. It would be extremely difficult, for example, to sell luxury urban apartments to desert nomads!
3. Customers in a market must have *purchasing power*. Assessing the level of purchasing power in a potential market is very important. Customers who have unsatisfied needs but who lack money and/or credit do not constitute a viable market because they have nothing to offer in exchange for a product or service. In such a situation, no transactions can occur.

In light of our definition of a market, determining market potential is the process of locating and investigating buying units that have both purchasing power and needs that can be satisfied with the product or service that is being offered.

Market Segmentation and Its Variables

In Chapter 3, cost-advantage and marketing-advantage strategies were applied to marketplaces that were relatively homogeneous, or uniform, in nature. These strategies can also be used to focus on a limited market within an industry. In his book *Competitive Advantage*, Michael Porter refers to this type of competitive strategy—in which cost and marketing advantages are achieved within narrow market segments—as a *focus strategy*.[11]

A focus strategy depends on market segmentation and becomes a consideration in competitive markets. Formally defined, **market segmentation** is the process of dividing the total market for a product or service into groups with similar needs, such that each group is likely to respond favorably to a specific marketing strategy. Developments in the cell phone industry provide a good example of real-world market segmentation. Initially, cell phone service providers aimed at a broad market and practiced very little market segmentation. But as competition developed, they began to focus on market segments, such as small businesses, families, younger customers, and customers who want to transfer text materials and photographs.

market segmentation
The division of a market into several smaller groups with similar needs

In order to divide the total market into appropriate segments, an entrepreneur must consider **segmentation variables**, which are parameters that identify the particular dimensions that distinguish one form of market behavior from another. Two broad sets of segmentation variables that represent major dimensions of a market are benefit variables and demographic variables.

segmentation variables
The parameters used to distinguish one form of market behavior from another

benefit variables
Specific characteristics that distinguish market segments according to the benefits sought by customers

BENEFIT VARIABLES The definition of a market highlights the unsatisfied needs of customers. **Benefit variables** are related to customer needs since they are used to identify segments of a market based on the benefits sought by customers. For example, the toothpaste market has several benefit segments. The principal benefit to parents might be cavity prevention for their young children, while the principal benefit to teenagers might be fresh breath. Toothpaste is the product in both cases, but it has two different market segments.

DEMOGRAPHIC VARIABLES Benefit variables alone are insufficient for market analysis; it is impossible to implement forecasting and marketing strategy without defining the market further. Therefore, small businesses commonly use demographic variables as part of market segmentation. Recall the definition of a market—customers with purchasing power and unsatisfied needs. **Demographic variables** refer to certain characteristics that describe customers and their purchasing power. Typical demographic variables are age, marital status, gender, occupation, and income.

demographic variables
Specific characteristics that describe customers and their purchasing power

Marketing Strategies Based on Segmentation Considerations

There are several types of strategies based on market segmentation efforts. The three types discussed here are the unsegmented approach, the multisegment approach, and the single-segment approach. These strategies can best be illustrated by using an example—a hypothetical small firm called the Community Writing Company.

THE UNSEGMENTED STRATEGY When a business defines the total market as its target, it is following an **unsegmented strategy** (also known as **mass marketing**). This strategy can sometimes be successful, but it assumes that all customers desire the same basic benefit from the product or service. This may hold true for water but certainly does not hold true for shoes, which satisfy numerous needs through a wide range of styles, prices, colors, and sizes. With an unsegmented strategy, a firm develops a single marketing mix—one combination of product, price, promotion, and distribution. Its competitive advantage must be derived from either a cost or a marketing advantage. The unsegmented strategy of the Community Writing Company is shown in Exhibit 7-3. The Community Writing Company's product is a lead pencil that is sold at the single unit price of $0.79 and is

unsegmented strategy (mass marketing)
A strategy that defines the total market as the target market

EXHIBIT 7-3 *An Unsegmented Market Strategy*

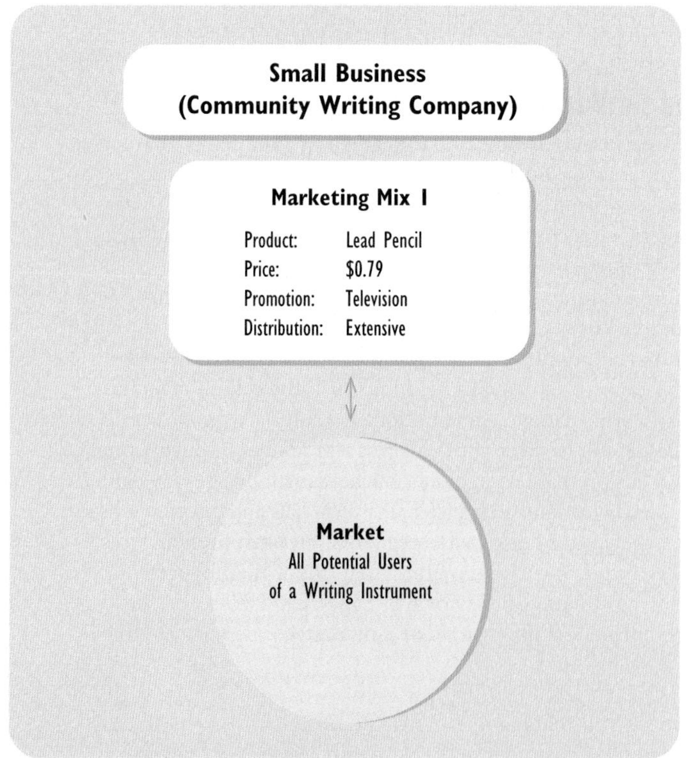

promoted through one medium and an extensive distribution plan. Even with an unsegmented strategy, some segmenting must occur. Note in Exhibit 7-3 that the market does not include everyone in the universe—just those who might use writing instruments.

THE MULTISEGMENT STRATEGY With a view of the market that recognizes individual segments with different preferences, a firm is in a better position to tailor marketing mixes to various segments. If a firm determines that two or more market segments have the potential to be profitable and then develops a unique marketing mix for each segment, it is following a **multisegment strategy**.

multisegment strategy A strategy that recognizes different preferences of individual market segments and develops a unique marketing mix for each

Let's assume that the Community Writing Company has recognized three separate market segments: students, professors, and executives. Following the multisegment approach, the company develops a competitive advantage with three marketing mixes, based on differences in pricing, promotion, distribution, or the product itself, as shown in Exhibit 7-4. Marketing Mix 1 consists of selling felt-tip pens to students through college bookstores at the lower-than-normal price of $0.49 and supporting this effort with a promotional campaign in campus newspapers. With Marketing Mix 2, the company markets the same pen to universities for use by professors. Professional magazines are the promotional medium used in this mix, distribution is direct from the factory, and the product price is $1.00. Finally, Marketing Mix 3, which is aimed at corporate executives, consists of selling a gold fountain pen, priced at $50.00, only in exclusive department stores and promoting it by personal selling. Note the distinct differences in these three marketing mixes. Obviously, many other segments exist for a simple product such as a pen. Entrepreneur Patrick H. Pinkston, for example, serves a very unique target segment with limited-edition pens of diamond, gold, and platinum for an average price of $45,000.[12] Small businesses tend to resist early on the use of the multisegment strategy because of the risk of spreading resources too thinly among several marketing efforts.

EXHIBIT 7-4 *A Multisegment Market Strategy*

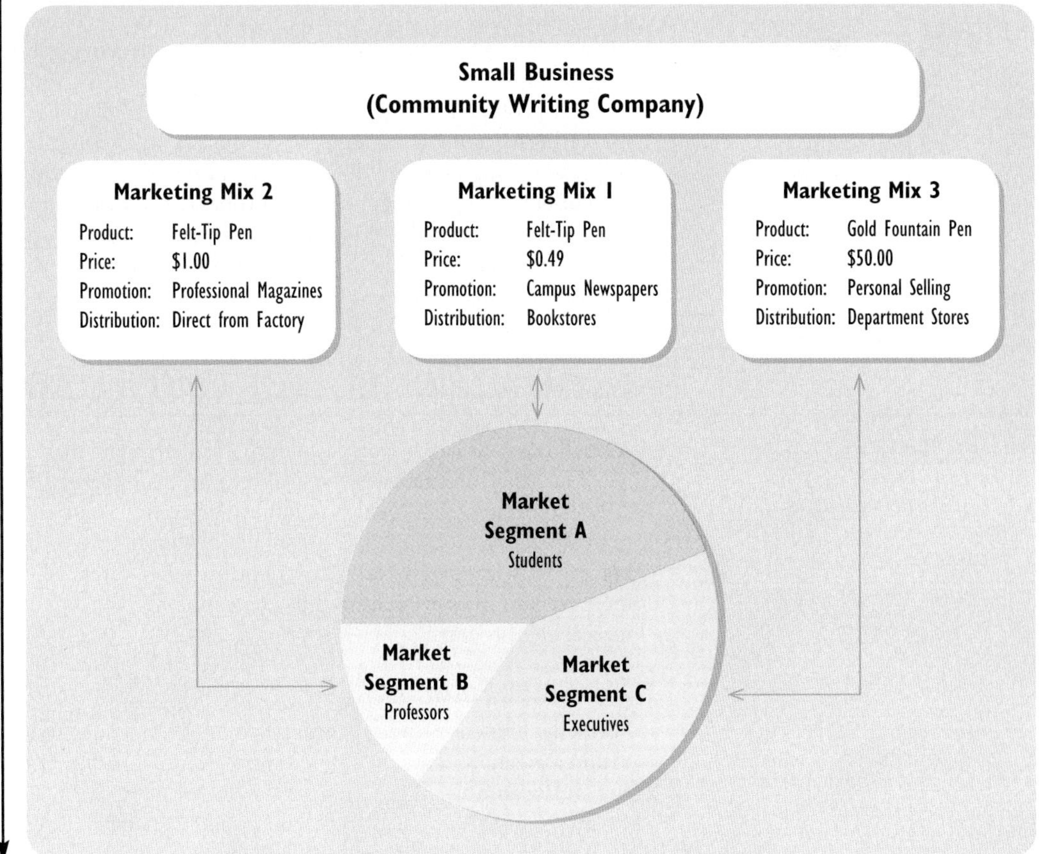

Living the Dream

Entrepreneurial Challenges

Courtesy of Buffalo Drummer, Buffalo, Minnesota

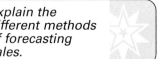

http://www.questproductsinc.com

Solving the Puzzle

Many entrepreneurs select a single-segment approach and implement the strategy with a licensing agreement. This is the route that entrepreneur Marlene Carlson chose.

Carlson, of Cokato, Minnesota, invented a special shoe targeted to parents with young children who have trouble putting their shoes on the correct feet. Her shoes feature a picture of a dinosaur, with the dinosaur's back half on the left shoe and its front half on the right shoe—put the shoes on correctly and the dinosaur appears.

She originally believed her new product could be manufactured in the United States and sold through traditional channels. After obtaining a patent, which was "based on the position of the design [on the shoe] and covers the overlay of the image on the adjacent toe sections," she contacted L.A. Gear and a few other major shoe manufacturers, about the product, but these negotiations failed. Carlson explored the possibility of having the shoes made by a small U.S. manufacturing concern or buying shoes from overseas and having the dinosaur image silk-screened on the toes. She even considered personally selling the shoes directly to stores or at fairs.

Eventually, an employee at L.A. Gear, who worked in product development, suggested she contact Quest Products, an Illinois corporation that develops and markets consumer products through clubs, drugstores, and mass retail chains across the United States. She did, and in July 2002 Carlson decided to license the product to Quest. Quest now sells the white leather shoes, named Puzzle Toes, with two Velcro straps and a blue or purple dinosaur in Wal-Mart stores for a suggested retail price of $12.97. Quest also "changed the packaging, changed the colors, and came up with the packaging slogan 'Got it left and got it right.'"

Carlson's choice of a single-segment strategy seems appropriate for her situation.

Sources: Don Debelak, "The Big Picture," *Entrepreneur,* November 2003, pp. 144–146, reprinted with permission; and http://www.questproductsinc.com, November 28, 2003.

single-segment strategy
A strategy that recognizes the existence of several distinct market segments but focuses on only the most profitable segment

THE SINGLE-SEGMENT STRATEGY When a firm recognizes that several distinct market segments exist but chooses to concentrate on reaching only one segment, it is following a **single-segment strategy**. The segment selected is the one that promises to offer the greatest profitability. Once again, a competitive advantage is achieved through a cost- or marketing-advantage strategy. In Exhibit 7-5, the Community Writing Company decides to pursue a single-segment approach and selects the student market segment.

The single-segment approach is probably the wisest strategy for small businesses to use during initial marketing efforts. It allows a small firm to specialize and make better use of its limited resources. Then, once its reputation has been built, the firm will find it easier to enter new markets.

ESTIMATING MARKET POTENTIAL

5 *Explain the different methods of forecasting sales.*

A small business can be successful only if an adequate market exists for its product or service. The sales forecast is the typical indicator of market adequacy. Forecasting is particularly important prior to writing the marketing plan. An entrepreneur who enters the marketplace without a forecast is much like an enthusiastic swimmer who leaves the diving board without checking the depth of the water. Many types of information from numerous sources are required to determine market potential. This section examines the forecasting process.

The Sales Forecast

sales forecast
A prediction of how much of a product or service will be purchased within a market during a specified time period

Formally defined, a **sales forecast** estimates how much of a product or service can be sold within a given market in a defined time period. The forecast can be stated in terms of dollars and/or units.

Because a sales forecast revolves around a specific target market, the market should be defined as precisely as possible. The market description forms the forecasting boundary. If

EXHIBIT 7-5 *A Single-Segment Market Strategy*

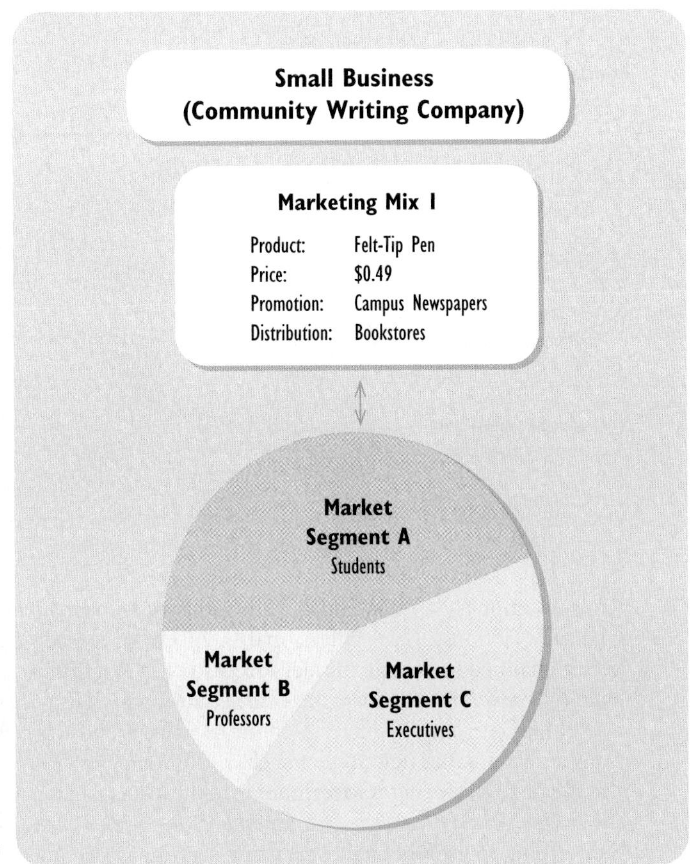

the market for electric razors is described as "men," the sales forecast will be extremely large. A more precise definition, such as "men between the ages of 15 and 25 who are dissatisfied with nonelectric shavers," will result in a smaller but possibly more useful forecast.

It is also important to note that a sales forecast implies a specified time period. One sales forecast may cover a year or less, while another may extend over several years. Both short-term and long-term forecasts are needed for a well-constructed business plan.

A sales forecast is an essential component of the business plan because it is critical to assessing the feasibility of a new venture. If the market is insufficient, the business is destined for failure. A sales forecast is also useful in other areas of business planning. Production schedules, inventory policies, and personnel decisions all start with a sales forecast. Obviously, a forecast can never be perfect; entrepreneurs should remember that a forecast can be wrong in either direction—underestimating potential sales or overestimating potential sales.

Limitations to Forecasting

For a number of practical reasons, forecasting is used less frequently by small firms than by large firms. First, for any new business, forecasting circumstances are unique. Entrepreneurial inexperience, coupled with a new idea, represents the most difficult forecasting situation, as illustrated in Exhibit 7-6. An ongoing business that requires only an updated forecast for its existing product is in the most favorable forecasting position.

Second, a small business manager may be unfamiliar with methods of quantitative analysis. While not all forecasting must be quantitatively oriented—qualitative forecasting is helpful and may be sufficient—quantitative methods have repeatedly proven their value in forecasting.

Third, the typical small business entrepreneur lacks familiarity with the forecasting process and/or personnel with such skills. To overcome these deficiencies, some small

EXHIBIT 7-6 *Dimensions of Forecasting Difficulty*

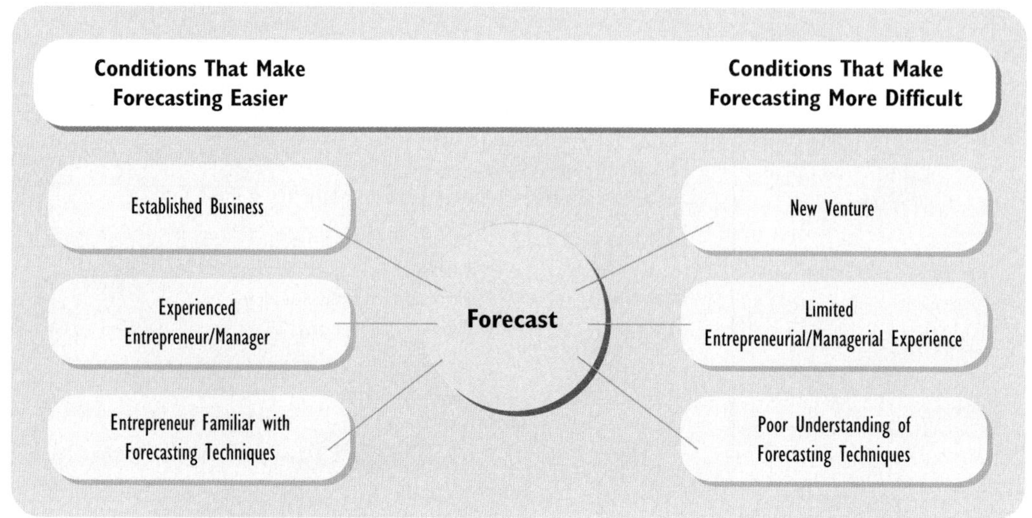

firms attempt to keep in touch with industry trends through contacts with appropriate trade associations. The professional members of a trade association staff are frequently better qualified to engage in sales forecasting. Most libraries have a copy of *National Trade and Professional Associations of the United States*, which lists these groups. Entrepreneurs can also obtain current information about business trends by regularly reading trade publications and economic newsletters such as the *Kiplinger Washington Letter*, *BusinessWeek*, and the *Wall Street Journal*. Government publications, such as the *Survey of Current Business*, the *Federal Reserve Bulletin*, and *Monthly Labor Review*, are also of interest in a general way. Subscribing to professional forecasting services is also a way to obtain forecasts of general business conditions or specific forecasts for given industries.

Despite the difficulties, a small business entrepreneur should not neglect the forecasting task. Instead, he or she should remember how important the sales outlook in the business plan is to obtaining financing. The statement "We can sell as many as we can produce" does not satisfy the information requirements of potential investors.

The Forecasting Process

Estimating market demand with a sales forecast is a multistep process. Typically, the sales forecast is a composite of several individual forecasts, so the process involves merging these individual forecasts properly.

The forecasting process can be characterized by two important dimensions: (1) the point at which the process is started and (2) the nature of the predicting variable. Depending on the starting point, the process may be designated as a *breakdown process* or a *buildup process.* The nature of the predicting variable determines whether the forecasting is direct or indirect.

breakdown process (chain-ratio method)
A forecasting method that begins with a larger-scope variable and works down to the sales forecast

THE STARTING POINT In the **breakdown process**, sometimes called the **chain-ratio method**, the forecaster begins with a variable that has a very large scope and systematically works down to the sales forecast. This method is frequently used for consumer products forecasting. The initial variable might be a population figure for the target market. Through the use of percentages, an appropriate link is built to generate the sales forecast. For example, consider the market segment identified by the hypothetical Community Writing Company. Assume that the target market is older students (25 years of age or over), seeking convenience and erasability in their writing instrument. Assume further that the initial geographic target is the state of Idaho. Exhibit 7-7 outlines the breakdown process. The more links in the forecasting chain, the greater the potential for error.

buildup process
A forecasting method in which all potential buyers in the various submarkets are identified and then the estimated demand is added up

In contrast to the breakdown process, the **buildup process** calls for identifying all potential buyers in a target market's submarkets and then adding up the estimated demand. For example, a local dry-cleaning firm forecasting demand for cleaning high

7-7 *Sales Forecasting with the Breakdown Method*

Linking Variable	Source	Estimating Value	Market Potential*
1. Idaho state population	U.S. census of population		1,366,000
2. State population in target age category	*Sales & Marketing Management Survey of Buying Power*	12%	163,920
3. Target age enrolled in colleges and universities	Idaho Department of Education	30%	49,176
4. Target age college students preferring convenience over price	Student survey in a marketing research class	50%	24,588
5. Convenience-oriented students likely to purchase new felt-tip pen within next month	Personal telephone interview by entrepreneur	75%	18,441
6. People who say they are likely to purchase who actually buy	Article in *Journal of Consumer Research*	35%	6,454
7. Average number of pens bought per year	Personal experience of entrepreneur	4	25,818
			↑ SALES FORECAST FOR IDAHO

*Figures in this column, for variables 2–7, are derived by multiplying the percentage or number in the Estimating Value column by the amount on the previous line of the Market Potential column.

school letter jackets might estimate its market share within each area school as 20 percent. Then, by determining the number of high school students obtaining a letter jacket at each school—perhaps from school yearbooks—an analyst could estimate the total demand.

The buildup process is especially helpful for industrial goods forecasting. To estimate potential, forecasters often use data from the census of manufacturers by the U.S. Department of Commerce. The information can be broken down according to the North American Industry Classification System (NAICS), which classifies businesses by type of industry. Once the code for a group of potential industrial customers has been identified, the forecaster can obtain information on the number of establishments and their geographic location, number of employees, and annual sales. A sales forecast can be constructed by summing this information for several relevant codes.

THE PREDICTING VARIABLE In **direct forecasting**, which is the simplest form of forecasting, sales is the forecasted variable. Many times, however, sales cannot be predicted directly and other variables must be used. **Indirect forecasting** takes place when surrogate variables are used to project the sales forecast. For example, if a firm lacks information about industry sales of baby cribs but has data on births, the strong correlation between the two variables allows planners to use the figures for births to help forecast industry sales for baby cribs.

We hope that the marketing research, market segmentation, and forecasting tools presented here will help you create an excellent marketing plan, one that is well tailored to meet the needs of your business.

direct forecasting
A forecasting method in which sales is the estimated variable

indirect forecasting
A forecasting method in which variables related to sales are used to project future sales

Looking Back

1 Describe small business marketing.

- Three distinct marketing philosophies are the production-, sales-, and consumer-oriented philosophies.
- A small business should adopt a consumer orientation to marketing, as that philosophy is most consistent with long-term success.
- Small business marketing consists of numerous activities, including market analysis and determining the marketing mix.

2 Identify the components of a formal marketing plan.

- The marketing plan should include sections on market analysis, the competition, and marketing strategy.
- The market analysis should include a customer profile.
- Four areas of marketing strategy that should be discussed in the marketing plan are decisions affecting the total product and/or service, distribution decisions, pricing decisions, and promotional decisions.

3 Discuss the nature of the marketing research process.

- Marketing research involves the gathering, processing, reporting, and interpreting of marketing information.
- The cost of marketing research should be evaluated against its benefits.
- The steps in marketing research are identifying the informational need, searching for secondary data, collecting primary data, and interpreting the data gathered.

4 Define market segmentation and its related strategies.

- A focus strategy relies on market segmentation, which is the process of dividing the total market for a product or service into groups, each of which is likely to respond favorably to a specific marketing strategy.
- Three types of market segmentation strategies are (1) the unsegmented approach, (2) the multisegment approach, and (3) the single-segment approach.
- The unsegmented strategy—when a business defines the total market as its target—is also known as mass marketing.
- A firm that determines that two or more market segments have the potential to be profitable and then develops a unique marketing mix for each segment is following a multisegment strategy.
- A firm that follows a single-segment strategy recognizes that several distinct market segments exist but chooses to concentrate on reaching only one segment.

5 Explain the different methods of forecasting sales.

- A sales forecast is an estimation of how much of a product or service will be purchased within a market during a defined time period.
- The forecasting process may be either a breakdown or a buildup process and may be either direct or indirect, depending on the predicting variable.

Key Terms

small business marketing, p. 141
market analysis, p. 142
marketing mix, p. 142
customer profile, p. 143
marketing research, p. 147
secondary data, p. 148
primary data, p. 148
market, p. 151
market segmentation, p. 151
segmentation variables, p. 151
benefit variables, p. 151
demographic variables, p. 152
unsegmented strategy (mass marketing), p. 152
multisegment strategy, p. 153
single-segment strategy, p. 154
sales forecast, p. 154
breakdown process (chain-ratio method), p. 156
buildup process, p. 156
direct forecasting, p. 157
indirect forecasting, p. 157

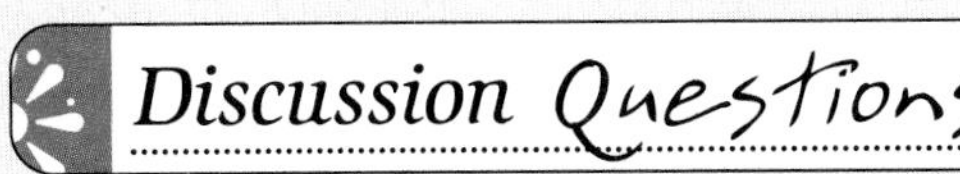

Discussion Questions

1. What is the scope of small business marketing? Has it always been as broad as it is now? Why or why not?
2. How do the three marketing philosophies differ? Select a product and discuss marketing tactics that could be used to implement each philosophy.
3. What are the obstacles to adopting a consumer orientation in a small firm?
4. Briefly describe each of the components of a formal marketing plan.
5. What are the steps in the marketing research process?
6. What are the major considerations in designing a questionnaire?
7. Briefly explain the three components of the definition of a market, as presented in this chapter.
8. What types of variables are used for market segmentation? Would a small firm use the same variables as a large business? Why or why not?
9. Explain the difference between a multisegment strategy and a single-segment strategy. Which one is more likely to be appealing to a small firm? Why?
10. Explain why forecasting is used more widely by large firms than by small ones.

You Make the Call

SITUATION 1

In 1991, brothers Josh and Seth Frey were driving an ice cream truck. After buying a former postal vehicle and converting it into a dessert-mobile, they operated it between semesters at the University of Wisconsin at Madison. Seth, a senior, planned to join the corporate world after graduating, but Josh was enjoying being his own boss. Josh felt he had finally figured out his future, but he didn't want to be the neighborhood ice cream guy for the rest of his life.

What else could he sell? Care packages. Josh was impressed that a few dorms at his university offered care packages for parents to send to their kids. How could Josh improve on the product? The care packages should be offered campus-wide, he thought.

Source: Geoff Williams, "Staying Power," *Entrepreneur,* Vol. 26, No. 6 (June 1998), p. 154.

Question 1 What type of research could Josh use to estimate demand for the care packages?

Question 2 How could he develop a sales forecast for his product?

Question 3 Would the Internet be helpful to his marketing plan?

SITUATION 2

Alibek Iskakov has opened a small café named Oasis in Kokshetau, a city in Kazakhstan. In order to get primary data on the market for his café, he conducted a survey of 100 people—45 men and 55 women. Forty-eight respondents were between 18 and 24 years old, 38 were between 25 and 50 years old, and 14 were over 50 years old. The survey asked the following questions:

1. How often do you visit restaurants?
2. What is your favorite restaurant in Kokshetau? Why?
3. What is the most important factor for you in choosing a restaurant?
4. Would a small, neat café with traditional food appeal to you?
    a. (If no) Why not?
    b. (If yes) When would you patronize it?
5. How much are you willing to pay for dinner?

Question 1 What are the strengths and weaknesses of the sample used in this survey?

Question 2 Evaluate the questions used in the survey.

SITUATION 3

Mary Wilson is a 31-year-old wife and mother who wants to start her own company. She has no previous business experience but has an idea for marketing an animal-grooming service, with an approach similar to that used for pizza delivery. When a customer calls, she will arrive in a van in less than 30 minutes and will provide the grooming service. Many of her friends think the idea has promise but dismiss her efforts to seriously discuss the venture. However, Wilson is not discouraged; she plans to purchase the van and the necessary grooming equipment.

Question 1 What target market or markets can you identify for Wilson? How could she forecast sales for her service in each market?

Question 2 What advantage does her business have over existing grooming businesses?

Question 3 What business name and promotional strategy would you suggest that Wilson use?

Experiential Exercises

1. Interview a local small business manager about what he or she believes is the marketing philosophy followed by the business.
2. Assume you are planning to market a new facial tissue. Write a detailed customer profile, and explain how you would develop the sales forecast for this product. Log on to InfoTrac College Edition at http://www.infotrac-college.com to find articles on forecasting sales.
3. Interview a local small business owner to determine the type of marketing research, if any, he or she has used.
4. Visit a local small retailer and observe its marketing efforts—for example, salesperson style, store atmosphere, and warranty policies. Report your observations to the class, and make recommendations for improving these efforts to increase customer satisfaction.

Exploring the Web

1. About.com is a large and complex site offering advice and information on a wide range of topics. Its marketing advice and information pages are viewable at **http://marketing.about.com/**. Click on "Topic Index on Marketing," and then follow the additional links to "Small Business Marketing." Compare and contrast the sources listed. Then identify the best tips for using market segmentation strategies.
2. Go to the Small Business Administration's Web site at **http://www.sba.gov**. Select "Starting" from among the site's "Custom Views."
   a. Click on the "Marketing Research" link. What sources of secondary information are listed on this Web page?
   b. Next click on "Competitive Analysis." Based on your business idea, answer the six questions provided on the site, and begin the process of benchmarking your competition.
   c. You can find the site's information on target markets at **http://www.sba.gov/starting_business/marketing/target.html**. Define the target segment or segments for your business idea. Which of the market segments discussed on the site—demographic, psychographic, use-based, benefit, or geographic—make the most sense for your business?

Video Case 7

SPECIALTY CHEESE (P. 536)
The well-conceived marketing plan of this cheese producer is discussed by its corporate-refugee founder.

Alternative Cases for Chapter 7:

Case 1, Boston Duck Tours, p. 526
Case 14, Lotus Chips' Recipe for Success, p. 552

The Business Plan

LAYING THE FOUNDATION

As part of laying the foundation for your own business plan, respond to the following questions regarding the marketing plan, marketing research, market segmentation, and sales forecasting.

Marketing Plan Questions

1. What is the customer profile for your product or service?
2. How will you identify prospective customers?
3. What geographic area will you serve?
4. What are the distinguishing characteristics of your product or service?
5. What steps have already been taken to develop your product or service?
6. What do you plan to name your product or service?
7. Will there be a warranty?
8. How will you set the price for your product or service?
9. What type of distribution plan will you use?
10. Will you export to other countries?
11. What type of selling effort will you use?
12. What special selling skills will be required?
13. What types of advertising and sales promotion will you use?

Marketing Research Questions

1. What types of research should be conducted to collect the information you need?
2. How much will this research cost?
3. What sources of secondary data will address your informational needs?
4. What sources of relevant data are available in your local library?
5. What sources of outside professional assistance would you consider using to help with marketing research?

Market Segmentation Questions

1. Will you focus on a limited market within the industry?
2. What segmentation variables will you use to define your target market?
3. If you determine that several distinct market segments exist, will you concentrate on just one segment?

Forecasting Questions

1. How do you plan to forecast sales for your product or service?
2. What sources of forecasting assistance have you consulted?
3. What sales forecasting techniques are most appropriate to your needs?
4. What is the sales forecast for your product or service?

THE HUMAN RESOURCE PLAN

MANAGERS, OWNERS, ALLIES, AND DIRECTORS

In the Video Spotlight

Tires Plus

This video spotlight will take you to Tires Plus, a company started from a partnership between two Shell Oil executives. It is not uncommon to hear of small business partnerships starting out with 50-50 ownership. As those companies grow and mature, however, the downside to this type of ownership arrangement becomes apparent. When a business is owned in equal shares, difficult decisions can paralyze the company because no one person can have the last word.

To avoid this serious pitfall, Tom Gegax (shown in photo) and Don Gullet, founders of Tires Plus, used a majority/minority partnership arrangement. Gegax was the majority partner with 55 percent ownership, and Gullet was the minority partner with 45 percent. Both partners had complementary skills that helped the company thrive. Under this ownership structure, Tires Plus grew from three converted gas stations to 150 stores employing 2,000 people who generated $200 million in annual sales.

This kind of growth did not go unnoticed in the business community, and Gegax and Gullet were approached about taking the company public. But in their mind, public ownership was not the best solution for Tires Plus. When Gegax and Gullet ultimately decided to sell their business, they looked for a single buyer to whom they could transfer ownership.

Video material provided by Hattie Bryant, Producer of Small Business School, the series on PBS Stations, Worldnet, and the Web at http://www.smallbusinessschool.org.

Chapter 8

Looking Ahead

After studying this chapter, you should be able to

1 *Describe the characteristics and value of a strong management team.*

2 *Explain the common legal forms of organization used by small businesses.*

3 *Identify factors to consider in choosing among the primary legal forms of organization, including tax consequences.*

4 *Describe the unique features and restrictions of three specialized organizational forms: limited partnerships, S corporations, and limited liability companies.*

5 *Explain the nature of strategic alliances and their uses in small businesses.*

6 *Describe the effective use of boards of directors and advisory councils.*

Popular notions aside, most successful entrepreneurs do not operate as "Lone Rangers" in the business world. In fact, research suggests that enterprises that thrive are usually led by talented and effective *teams* of entrepreneurs, among whom are individuals who have prior experience in developing new ventures.[1] Entrepreneurship experts Jeffrey Timmons and Stephen Spinelli emphasize this point: "*Owning and running the whole show effectively puts a ceiling on growth. . . . It is extremely difficult to grow a higher potential venture by working single-handedly. Higher potential entrepreneurs build a team, an organization, and a company.*"[2]

In all but the simplest businesses, the entrepreneur's personal talents must be supplemented with the experience and abilities of other individuals. The prospects for any venture are most promising when a firm's leadership is composed of competent, resourceful, and tenacious individuals. It is important, therefore, that an entrepreneur identify and attract a strong management team. A business plan that provides for strong leadership is appealing to both potential investors and prospective managerial personnel.

Whether potential investors and prospective managerial personnel have the opportunity to also become partial owners of the company depends on the ownership structure selected by the entrepreneur—that is, the legal form of organization. The direction of the business will be strongly affected by whether the entrepreneur chooses to go with a sole proprietorship, a partnership, a corporation, or one of various other forms. The selection should take into account the needs of the business, including tax implications.

A new business rarely has the financial resources to incorporate within the organization all the human resources desired. One solution is to acquire allies; another is to profit from the expertise of outside directors. Strategic alliances are becoming increasingly important to small businesses, as are active, objective boards of directors.

The quality of an entrepreneur's decisions with regard to the management team, the form of organization, strategic alliances, and the board of directors can greatly enhance the performance of the company. On the other hand, even *brilliant* ideas can be doomed if human resources are not properly deployed.

BUILDING A MANAGEMENT TEAM

1 *Describe the characteristics and value of a strong management team.*

If a firm is extremely small, the founder will probably be the key manager and perhaps the only manager. In most firms, however, others share leadership roles with the owner or owners. The concept of a management team, therefore, is relevant to small business. In general, the **management team** consists of individuals with supervisory responsibilities, as well as nonsupervisory personnel who play key roles in the business. For example, members of the management team might include a financial manager who supervises a small office staff and an individual who directs the marketing effort.

management team
Managers and other key persons who give a company its general direction

Strong management can make the best of a good business idea by securing the resources needed to make it work. Of course, even a highly competent management team cannot rescue a firm that is based on a weak business concept or that lacks adequate resources. The importance of strong management to startups is evident in the attitudes of prospective investors, who consider the quality of a new venture's management to be the single most important factor in decisions to invest or not to invest. One entrepreneurship expert sums up popular opinion this way: "If there is one issue on which the majority of theorists and practitioners agree, it is that a high-quality management team is a key ingredient in the success of many high-growth ventures . . . and most of the reasons for failure may be traced to specific flaws in the venture team."[3]

A management team brings greater strength to a venture than does an individual entrepreneur. One reason is that a team can provide a diversity of talent to meet various managerial needs. This is particularly important for high-tech startups. In addition, a team can provide greater assurance of continuity, since the departure of one member of a team is less devastating to a business than the departure of a sole entrepreneur.

The competence required in a management team depends on the type of business and the nature of its operations. For example, a software development firm and a restaurant call for drastically different types of business experience. Whatever the business, a small firm needs managers with an appropriate combination of educational background and experience. In evaluating the qualifications of an applicant for a key position, an entrepreneur needs to know whether she or he has experience in a related type of business, as a manager, or as an entrepreneur.

Living the Dream *Entrepreneurial Challenges*

Two Heads Are Better Than One

© Ted's Montana Grill, Inc.

Ted Turner is an entrepreneur of unquestionable success—in fact, many would say he is nothing short of a visionary. Developing Turner Broadcasting System into a television powerhouse was just the beginning. It wasn't long before he launched or bought out a number of other amazing enterprises, including what is perhaps the crown jewel of Turner's entrepreneurial accomplishments—CNN, the 24-hour all-news cable channel. But there have been a few bumps along the way, too—about $7 billion worth! After losing most of his personal wealth because of troubled mergers with Time Warner and America Online, Turner vowed to return to his entrepreneurial roots.

Still worth more than $1 billion, Turner set his sights on the restaurant business. He joined efforts with George McKerrow, a kindred entrepreneurial spirit, and the dynamic duo launched Ted's Montana Grill, a chain of relatively upscale restaurants specializing in buffalo meat–based dishes (mostly burgers, steaks, and stews). Turner had been raising buffalo for decades and felt that using buffalo meat would lend a mystique to the restaurant concept they had planned.

Although Turner is funding about 80 percent of the venture, McKerrow offers indispensable insights from his many years of experience in the steakhouse business. "What we've got," says Turner, "is synergy. We're two old guys who think alike—and trust one another." In other words, the strength of the company comes from this dynamic entrepreneurial team.

"Ted doesn't get into the day-to-day operations of the company," says McKerrow. "That's my job. [Turner's job] is to be the creative genius in this firm—and the public face of Ted's Montana Grill."

The combination must be working. By mid-2004, the company had more than 20 restaurants, with plans to open another 30 to 36 the following year. The busiest location (in Denver, Colorado) does more than $2.5 million in business a year, exceeding the target of $2 million. Not bad, considering that the average McDonald's restaurant does only $1.6 million annually. Of course, Ted Turner is no average entrepreneur, and neither is McKerrow. But despite their past individual successes, they recognized that two heads can be better than one when it comes to launching a new venture.

Sources: John Anderson, "The Mouth Will Rise Again," *Inc.*, Vol. 26, No. 2 (February 2004), pp. 49–56; http://www.tedsmontanagrill.com, April 8, 2004; http://www.pbs.org/newshour/updates/aoltw_01-30-03.html, April 9, 2004; and Peter Thal Larsen, "A Maverick Entrepreneur Prepares for His Final Act," *Financial Times*, February 8, 2003, p. 11.

Achieving Balance

Not all members of a management team need competence in all areas—the key is balance. If one member has expertise in finance, another should have an adequate marketing background. And there should be someone who can supervise employees effectively.

Even when entrepreneurs recognize the need for team members with varying expertise, they frequently seek to replicate their own personalities and management styles. While personal compatibility and the cooperation of team members are necessary for effective collaboration, a healthy situation exists when the qualifications of team members are diverse.

Planning the company's leadership, then, should produce a management team that will be able to give competent direction to the new firm. The team should be balanced in terms of covering the various functional areas and offering the right combination of education and experience. It may comprise both insiders and outside specialists. For example, a small firm may benefit by developing working relationships with such external organizations as a commercial bank, a law firm, and a certified public accounting firm. A number of outside sources of managerial assistance are identified and discussed in Chapter 18. (The role of an active board of directors in providing counsel and guidance to the management team is discussed later in this chapter.)

Specifying Structure

In addition to selecting members of the management team, an entrepreneur must design an internal management structure that defines relationships among all members of the organization. Relationships among the various positions—such as advertising manager, marketing director, financial officer, and human resource manager—should be determined. Although these relationships need not be worked out in great detail, planning should be sufficient to ensure orderly operations and avoid an overlapping of responsibilities that invites conflict.

The management plan should be drawn up in a way that provides for business growth. Any unfilled positions should be specified, and job descriptions should spell out the duties of and necessary qualifications for such positions. Methods for selecting key employees should also be explained. Compensation arrangements, including bonus or other incentive plans for key organization members, should be carefully considered and specified in the plan.

CHOOSING A LEGAL FORM OF ORGANIZATION

2 Explain the common legal forms of organization used by small businesses.

In launching a new business, an entrepreneur must choose a form of legal organization, which will determine who the actual owners of the business are. The most basic options are the sole proprietorship, partnership, and C corporation. More specialized forms of organization exist, but many small businesses find one of the common forms suitable for their needs. After outlining the primary options, we will look first at some criteria for choosing among them and then at three specialized forms that derive from the basic options. Exhibit 8-1 shows the various basic forms of organization.

The Sole Proprietorship Option

sole proprietorship
A business owned by one person

A **sole proprietorship**, the most rudimentary business form, is a company owned by one person. An individual proprietor has title to all business assets and is subject to the claims of creditors. He or she receives all of the firm's profits but must also assume all losses, bear all risks, and pay all debts. Although it is usually appropriate only for a new small business, forming a sole proprietorship is the simplest and cheapest way to start operation. The vast majority of small businesses (some 70 percent) adopt this legal structure.[4]

In a sole proprietorship, an owner is free from interference by partners, shareholders, and directors. However, a sole proprietorship lacks some of the advantages of other legal forms. For example, there are no limits on the owner's personal liability—that is, the owner of the business has **unlimited liability**, and thus his or her personal assets can be taken by business creditors if the enterprise fails. For this reason, the sole proprietorship form is a practical choice for only very small businesses. In addition, sole proprietors are not employees of the business and cannot receive the advantage of many tax-free fringe benefits such as insurance and hospitalization plans, which are customarily provided by corporations for their employees.

unlimited liability
Liability on the part of an owner that extends beyond the owner's investment in the business

EXHIBIT 8-1 *Basic Forms of Legal Organization for Small Businesses*

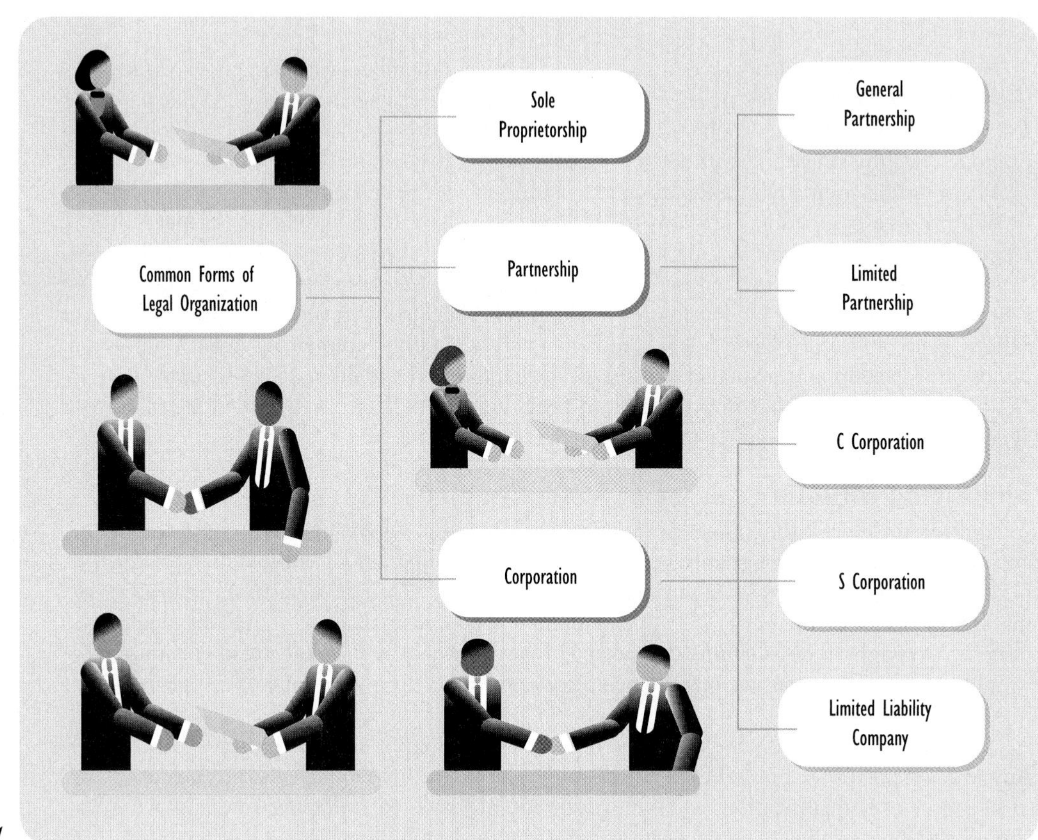

The death of the owner terminates the legal existence of a sole proprietorship. Thus, the possibility of the owner's death may cloud relationships between a business and its creditors and employees. It is important that the owner have a will, because the assets of the business minus its liabilities will belong to her or his heirs. In a will, a sole proprietor can give an executor the power to run the business for the heirs until they can take it over or it can be sold.

Another contingency that must be provided for is the possible incapacity of the sole proprietor. For example, if she or he were badly hurt in an accident and hospitalized for an extended period, the business could be ruined. A sole proprietor can guard against this contingency by giving a competent person legal power of attorney to carry on in such circumstances.

In some cases, circumstances argue against employing the sole proprietorship option. If the nature of a business involves exposure to legal liability—for example, the manufacture of a potentially hazardous product or the operation of a child care facility—a legal form that provides greater protection against personal liability is likely to be a better choice. For most companies, however, various forms of insurance are available to deal with the risks of a sole proprietorship, as well as those related to partnerships.[5] The partnership option will be considered next.

The Partnership Option

partnership
A legal entity formed by two or more co-owners to carry on a business for profit

A **partnership** is a legal entity formed by two or more co-owners to operate a business for profit. Because of a partnership's voluntary nature, owners can set it up quickly, avoiding many of the legal requirements involved in creating a corporation. A partnership pools the managerial talents and capital of those joining together as business partners. As in a sole proprietorship, however, the owners share unlimited liability.

QUALIFICATIONS OF PARTNERS Any person capable of contracting may legally become a business partner. Individuals may become partners without contributing capital or having a claim to assets at the time of dissolution; such persons are partners only in regard to management and profits. The formation of a partnership involves consideration not only of legal issues but also of personal and managerial factors. A strong partnership requires partners who are honest, healthy, capable, and compatible.

Operating a business as a partnership has benefits, but it is also fraught with potential problems. Most experts discourage partnerships as a way to run a business, even though there are good and bad qualities associated with this form of organization (see Exhibit 8-2). The benefits of partnerships include the ability to share the workload as well as the emotional and financial burdens of the enterprise and to buy management talent that might otherwise break the budget. And it should not be overlooked that partners can add companionship to life in a small business.

However, many believe the personal conflicts common in partnerships more than offset the benefits, and partners often fall short of one another's expectations. Of course, decision making is more complicated in partnerships because leadership is shared, and the dilution of equity must be considered. While some of the difficulties of partnerships are financial in nature, most are relational—for example, coping with a partner's dishonesty or dealing with differing priorities. Partnerships clearly have both disturbing and redeeming qualities, so the issue is not black and white. The important point is that *a partnership should be formed only if it appears to be the best option when all features of the enterprise are taken into consideration.*

Many entrepreneurs have learned about partnerships the hard way—from "the school of hard knocks." Based on the experiences of those who have seen firsthand the extraordinary ups and debilitating downs of partnerships, the following insights may help entrepreneurs make the most of this form of organization.

- *Capitalize on the unique advantages of a partnership.* It is important to recognize the advantages of partnerships and to build on the synergies that can result from

EXHIBIT 8-2 *The Advantages and Disadvantages of Partnerships*

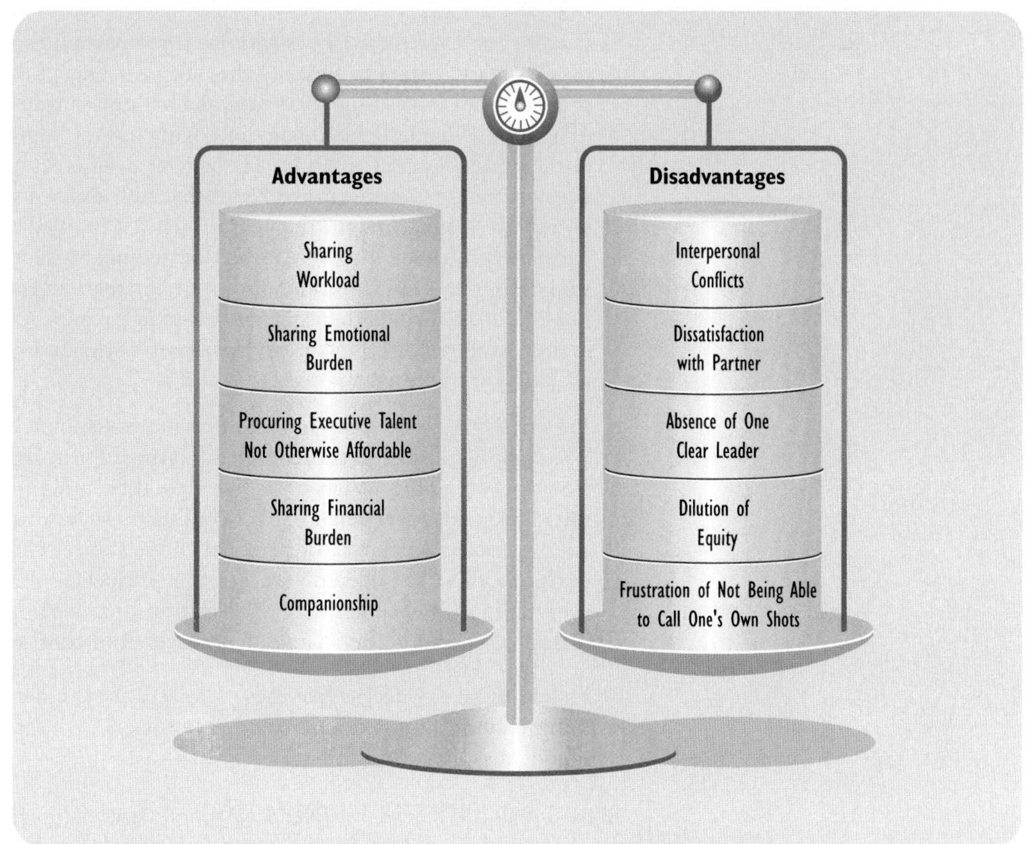

them. For example, Brian Miller, co-owner of the marketing firm MillerWhite in Terre Haute, Indiana, was grateful that his partner could "keep the ship sailing" while he was out of work for seven months having treatments for leukemia.[6] Even when partners are devoting full time to the business, working together can increase the quality and efficiency of decision making by focusing more energy and thought on the challenges being faced at any given time.

- *Choose your partner carefully.* In their book *Lessons from the Edge*, entrepreneurship experts Jana Matthews and Jeff Dennis observe,"Partnerships are just like marriages; some of them work, some don't. But the long-term success of a partnership depends first on picking the right partner."[7] Many sources are available to help you find that perfect someone—for example, trade magazines, client contacts, professional associations, even online matching services like BusinessPartner.com. But identifying a promising partner is just a start—you also need to be sure that your goals, values, and work habits are compatible with and your skills complementary to those of your prospective partner before committing to the deal. Above all, team up with a person you can trust, since the actions of your partner can legally bind you, even if a decision is made without your knowledge or consent.[8]
- *Be open, but cautious, about partnerships with friends.* If trust is critical to the success of a partnership, then wouldn't it be best to look first to friends as potential partners? Not necessarily. Valued relationships can take a quick turn for the worse when a business deal gets rocky, and a Dr. Jekyl friend can sometimes transform into a Mr. Hyde business associate when money enters the picture. And remember, the stakes are high: a minor business deal can quickly ruin a very important friendship.[9]
- *Test-drive the relationship, if possible.* Of course, the best way to determine if you can work well with another person is to actually give the partnership a try before finalizing the deal. Karen Cheney, author of the book *How to Start a Successful Home Business*, recommends trying more limited forms of business collaboration before jumping in with both feet. For example, you could share a booth at a trade show and observe the behavior, style, and work habits of the person you hope to team up with. This allows you to assess his or her strengths and weaknesses before committing to a long-term relationship.[10]
- *Create a combined vision for the business.* It's important that partners be "on the same page" when it comes to forming the business concept they hope to develop together. This takes time, patience, and a lot of conversation. Hal Scogin, owner of a multimedia design company in Olympia, Washington, discovered just how challenging the process can be. He had hopes of creating a company with two partners, but it soon became obvious that they did not see the business in the same way. Scogin thought the venture was a multimedia design company, but his partners considered it to be a technology company. Needless to say, the partnership did not last long.[11] Some of the specific matters you should discuss before joining forces include the expectations of all partners (contributions of time, money, expertise, etc.), planned division of work, anticipated vacation time, and the division of profits and losses.
- *Prepare for the worst.* Keep in mind that more than half of all partnerships fail. That is why most experts recommend having an exit strategy for the partnership from the beginning. What looks like a good business arrangement at the outset can quickly fall apart when market conditions shift, a partner becomes involved in another business venture, or personal circumstances change. For example, the birth of a child, a sudden divorce, or the unexpected death of a spouse can alter everything. If it becomes necessary, exiting a partnership is far more difficult when plans for such an unfortunate outcome were not considered early on.

Failure to take concerns like these into account can derail efforts to build an effective working relationship or doom an otherwise workable partnership to an unnecessary or painful demise.

RIGHTS AND DUTIES OF PARTNERS An oral partnership agreement is legal and binding, but memory is always less than perfect. In his book *Legal Guide for Starting and Running a*

Small Business, author and practicing business attorney Fred Steingold strongly recommends that partners sign a written **partnership agreement** to avoid problems later on.[12] This document, which explicitly delineates the partners' rights and duties, should be drawn up before the venture is launched. Though the partners may choose to have an attorney draw up the agreement in order to ensure that all important features are included, many other sources of assistance (such as online resources) also are available to guide you through this process. For example, a recent Google search on partnership agreements pulled up a number of helpful resources.

partnership agreement
A document that states explicitly the rights and duties of partners

Unless the articles of the partnership agreement specify otherwise, a partner is generally recognized as having certain implicit rights. For example, partners share profits or losses equally, unless they have agreed to a different ratio.

In a partnership, each party has **agency power**, which means that a business decision by one partner binds all members of the firm, even if the other partners were not consulted in advance or didn't approve the agreement or contract. And as with a sole proprietorship, the scale of personal liability of the partners can be terrifying. The assets of the business are at risk, of course, but so are the personal assets of the partners, including their homes, cars, and bank accounts. Good faith, together with reasonable care in the exercise of managerial duties, is required of all partners in the business. Since the partnership relationship is fiduciary in character, a partner cannot compete in another business and remain a partner. Nor can a partner use business information solely for personal gain.

agency power
The ability of any one partner to legally bind the other partners

HELP FOR AILING PARTNERSHIPS All partnerships experience stress, and many do not survive the challenge. According to Dr. David Gage, a psychologist who runs Business Mediation Associates in Washington, D.C., the "divorce" rate of business partnerships is higher than that of marriages. Typically, the problems stem from turf battles over control.[13]

Complications can arise even if partners have been careful to match their expectations at the start of the partnership and the business arrangement has been formalized through a partnership agreement. When problems emerge and trust begins to break down, partners should move quickly to try to resolve underlying issues. If they cannot do so, they should consider hiring a business mediator. Working with a business mediator can be expensive (sometimes $500 an hour or more), but the dissolution of the partnership is likely to be far more costly.[14]

TERMINATION OF A PARTNERSHIP Death, incapacity, or withdrawal of a partner ends a partnership and requires liquidation or reorganization of the business. While liquidation

Living the Dream — *Entrepreneurship and Integrity*

When Doing Less Is Worth More

When Andy Morris launched his public relations firm in 2001, he offered his long-time colleague, Judith King, a 20-percent stake in the new company. But while King worked only one day a week, Morris was putting in about six. It soon became clear that the division of ownership wasn't fair—to King, that is.

"I brought in a heck of a lot of business," she says. Morris agreed, crediting his "brilliant strategist" of a partner for helping the company grow 400 percent in two years. So in 2002, King was made a 50-percent owner, even though she still only shows up a couple of days a week.

"It's not a matter of the hours we put in," Morris says. "It's the results we produce."

Morris's experience shows just how difficult it can be to determine up front what constitute reasonable financial shares in a partnership. In the name of fairness, adjustments sometimes need to be made over time.

© Ryan McVay/Photodisc Green/Getty Images

Source: "Dividing the Corporate Pie," *Inc.*, Vol. 25, No. 7 (July 2003), p. 46. By Staff, © 2004 Gruner + Jahr USA Publishing. First published in *Inc.* Magazine. Reprinted with permission.

often results in substantial losses to all partners, it may be legally necessary, because a partnership represents a close personal relationship of the parties that cannot be maintained against the desire of any one of them.

This disadvantage may be partially overcome at the time a partnership is formed by stipulating in the articles that surviving partners can continue the business after buying the decedent's interest. This option can be facilitated by having each partner carry life insurance that names the other partners as beneficiaries.

The C Corporation Option

corporation
A business organization that exists as a legal entity and provides limited liability to its owners

legal entity
A business organization that is recognized by the law as having a separate legal existence

C corporation
An ordinary corporation, taxed by the federal government as a separate legal entity

In 1819, Chief Justice John Marshall of the United States Supreme Court defined a **corporation** as "an artificial being, invisible, intangible, and existing only in contemplation of the law." With these words, the Supreme Court recognized the corporation as a **legal entity**, meaning that it can file suit and be sued, hold and sell property, and engage in business operations that are stipulated in the corporate charter. In other words, a corporation is a separate entity from the individuals who own it. The ordinary corporation—often called a **C corporation** to distinguish it from more specialized forms—is discussed in this section.

A corporation is chartered under state laws. The length of its life is independent of its owners' (stockholders') lives. The corporation, *not* its owners, is liable for the debts of the business. Directors and officers represent the corporation as its agents and can enter into agreements on its behalf.

corporate charter
A document that establishes a corporation's existence

THE CORPORATE CHARTER To form a corporation, one or more persons must apply to the secretary of state (at the state level) for permission to incorporate. After preliminary steps—including payment of an incorporation fee—have been completed, the written application (which should be prepared by an attorney) is approved by the secretary of state and becomes the **corporate charter**. This document—sometimes called *articles of incorporation* or *certificate of incorporation*—shows that the corporation exists.

A corporation's charter should be brief, in accord with state law, and broad in its statement of the firm's powers. Details should be left to the *corporate bylaws*, which outline the basic rules for ongoing formalities and decisions of corporate life, including the scheduling of regular meetings of the directors and shareholders, the means of calling for a special meeting of these groups, and the number of votes required to approve corporate decisions.

stock certificate
A document specifying the number of shares owned by a stockholder

pre-emptive right
The right of stockholders to buy new shares of stock before they are offered to the public

RIGHTS AND STATUS OF STOCKHOLDERS Ownership in a corporation is evidenced by **stock certificates**, each of which stipulates the number of shares owned by a stockholder. An ownership interest does not confer a legal right to act for the firm or to share in its management. It does, however, provide the stockholder with the right to receive dividends in proportion to stockholdings—but only when the dividends are properly declared by the firm. Ownership of stock typically carries a **pre-emptive right**, or the right to buy new shares, in proportion to the number of shares already owned, before new stock is offered for public sale.

The legal status of stockholders is fundamental, of course, but it may be overemphasized. In many small corporations, the owners typically serve both as directors and as managing officers. The person who owns most or all of the stock can control a business as effectively as if it were a sole proprietorship. Thus, this form of organization works well for individual- and family-owned businesses, where maintaining control of the firm is important.

LIMITED LIABILITY OF STOCKHOLDERS For most stockholders, their limited liability is a major advantage of the corporate form of organization. Their financial liability is limited to the amount of money they invest in the business. Creditors cannot require them to sell personal assets to pay corporation debts. However, small corporations are often in a somewhat shaky financial condition during their early years of operation. As a result, a bank that makes a loan to a small firm may insist that the owners assume personal liability for the firm's debts by signing the promissory notes not only as representatives of the firm but personally as well. If the corporation is unable to repay the loan, the banker can then look to the owners' personal assets to recover the amount of the loan. In this case, the corporate advantage of limited liability is lost.

Why would owners agree to personally guarantee a firm's debt? Simply put, they may have no choice if they want the money. Most bankers are not willing to loan money to an entrepreneur who is not prepared to put his or her own personal assets at risk.

DEATH OR WITHDRAWAL OF STOCKHOLDERS Unlike a partnership interest, ownership in a corporation is readily transferable. Exchange of shares of stock is sufficient to convey an ownership interest to a different individual.

Stock of large corporations is exchanged constantly without noticeable effect on the operation of the business. For a small firm, however, a change of owners, though legally similar, can involve numerous complications. For example, finding a buyer for the stock of a small firm may prove difficult. Also, a minority stockholder in a small firm is vulnerable. If two of three equal shareholders in a small business sold their stock to an outsider, the remaining shareholder would then be at the mercy of that outsider.

The death of a majority stockholder can have unfortunate repercussions in a small firm. An heir, the executor, or a purchaser of the stock might well insist on direct control, with possible adverse effects for other stockholders. To prevent problems of this nature, legal arrangements should be made at the outset to provide for management continuity by surviving stockholders and fair treatment of a stockholder's heirs. As in the case of a partnership, mutual insurance can ensure the ability to buy out a deceased stockholder's interest.

MAINTAINING CORPORATE STATUS Establishing a corporation is one thing; keeping that status is another. Certain steps must be taken if the corporation is to retain its status as a separate entity. For example, the corporation must hold annual meetings of both the shareholders and the board of directors, keep minutes to document the major decisions of shareholders and directors, maintain bank accounts that are separate from owners' bank accounts, and file a separate income tax return for the business.

Criteria for Choosing an Organizational Form

3 *Identify factors to consider in choosing among the primary legal forms of organization, including tax consequences.*

Choosing a legal form for a new business deserves careful attention because of the various, sometimes conflicting features of each organizational option. Depending on the particular circumstances of a specific business, the tax advantages of one form, for example, may offset the limited-liability advantages of another form. Some tradeoffs may be necessary. Ideally, an experienced attorney should be consulted for aid in selecting the most appropriate form of organization.

Some entrepreneurship experts insist that the two most basic forms of business—sole proprietorship and partnership—should *never* be adopted. While these forms clearly have drawbacks, they are workable. A recent report by the IRS shows that nearly three-fourths of all new businesses are formed as sole proprietorships; 8 percent are set up as partnerships, and 21 percent are established as corporations.[15]

Exhibit 8-3 summarizes the main considerations in selecting one of the three primary forms of ownership. A description of each factor follows.

INITIAL ORGANIZATIONAL REQUIREMENTS AND COSTS Organizational requirements and costs increase as the formality of the organization increases. That is, a sole proprietorship is typically less complex and less expensive to form than a partnership, and a partnership is less complex and less expensive to form than a corporation. In view of the relatively modest costs, however, this consideration is of minimal importance in the long term.

LIABILITY OF OWNERS A sole proprietorship and a partnership have the inherent disadvantage of unlimited liability for the owners. With these forms of organization, there is no distinction between the firm's assets and the owners' personal assets. In contrast, the corporate form limits the owners' liability to their investment in the business. If a corporation is small, however, its owners are often required to guarantee a loan personally.

CONTINUITY OF BUSINESS A sole proprietorship is immediately dissolved on the owner's death. Likewise, a partnership is terminated on the death or withdrawal of a partner, unless the partnership agreement states otherwise. A corporation, on the other hand, offers continuity. The status of an individual investor does not affect the corporation's existence.

TRANSFERABILITY OF OWNERSHIP Ownership is transferred most easily in the corporation. The ability to transfer ownership, however, is intrinsically neither good nor bad. Its desirability depends largely on the owners' preferences. In certain businesses, owners may want the option of evaluating any prospective new investors. In other circumstances, unrestricted transferability may be preferred.

Living the Dream

Entrepreneurial Challenges

Simplicity Can Be Costly

Choosing a form of organization merely for the sake of simplicity can sometimes cost an entrepreneur dearly—and in more than just money! Max Baer ran a production studio in Memphis, Tennessee. Against the advice of his attorney, he decided to operate the business as a sole proprietorship to make startup easier. Things were going well, but the simple life came to an abrupt end when he was sued by a former employee. That's when the folly of Baer's decision became evident. The litigation went on for nearly a year; during that agonizing period, Baer was tormented by the possibility of losing all of his personal assets, including his house, his boat, and his savings account. Fortunately, the suit was settled for a modest sum, and Baer learned his lesson. He decided to convert his business to a corporation and enjoy the peace of mind that comes with limited liability.

The sole proprietorship may be the easiest way to get started, but it is far from the safest. According to Jerome Katz, professor of management at Saint Louis University, the sole proprietorship "is the scariest of all [organizational forms] because everything you have is on the line." Some attorneys advise entrepreneurs to use the sole proprietorship form during the early startup phase. But once the business plan is developed and the entrepreneur starts to negotiate financing, they usually recommend a shift to a form that offers shelter against personal liability.

Sources: Chris Harrison, "Form Is Everything," *E-Merging Business*, Fall-Winter 2000, pp. 196–199; Bridget McCrea, "Incorporating Facts," *Black Enterprise*, Vol. 33, No. 7 (February 2003), p. 40; and Matthew Swibel, "Corporate Cover," *Forbes*, Vol. 170, No. 12 (December 9, 2002), pp. 164–166.

MANAGEMENT CONTROL A sole proprietor has absolute control of the firm. Control within a partnership is normally based on the majority vote—an increase in the number of partners reduces each partner's voice in management. Within a corporation, control has two dimensions: (1) the formal control vested in the stockholders who own the majority of the voting common shares and (2) the functional control exercised by the corporate officers in conducting daily operations. In a small corporation, these two forms of control usually rest in the same individuals.

EXHIBIT 8-3 *Comparison of Basic Legal Forms of Organization*

Form of Organization	Initial Organizational Requirements and Costs	Liability of Owners	Continuity of Business
Sole proprietorship	Minimum requirements; generally no registration or filing fee	Unlimited liability	Dissolved upon proprietor's death
General partnership	Minimum requirements; generally no registration or filing fee; written partnership agreement not legally required but strongly suggested	Unlimited liability	Unless partnership agreement specifies differently, dissolved upon withdrawal or death of partner
C corporation	Most expensive and greatest requirements; filing fees; compliance with state regulations for corporations	Liability limited to investment in company	Continuity of business unaffected by shareholder withdrawal or death
Form of organization preferred	Proprietorship or partnership	C corporation	C corporation

ATTRACTIVENESS FOR RAISING CAPITAL A corporation has a distinct advantage when raising new equity capital, due to the ease of transferring ownership through the sale of common shares and the flexibility in distributing the shares. In contrast, the unlimited liability of a sole proprietorship and a partnership discourages new investors.

INCOME TAXES Income taxes frequently have a major effect on an owner's selection of a form of organization. To understand the federal income tax system, you must consider the following twofold question: "Who is responsible for paying taxes, and how is tax liability ascertained?" The three major forms of organization are taxed in different ways.

Sole Proprietorship Self-employed individuals who operate a business as a sole proprietorship report income from the business on their individual federal income tax returns. They are then taxed at the rates set by law for individuals. For tax year 2004, the tax rates for a married couple reporting their income jointly were as follows:

Range of Taxable Income	Tax Rate
$0–$14,300	10%
$14,301–$58,100	15%
$58,101–$117,250	25%
$117,251–$178,650	28%
$178,651–$319,100	33%
Over $319,100	35%

As an example, assume that a sole proprietor, who is married and files a joint return with her spouse, has taxable income of $150,000 from a business. The taxes owed on this income would be $31,957.50, computed as follows:

Income		× Tax Rate	=	Taxes
First	$ 14,300	10%		$ 1,430.00
Next	$ 43,800	15%		$ 6,570.00
Next	$ 59,150	25%		$14,787.50
Next	$ 32,750	28%		$ 9,170.00
Total	$150,000			$31,957.50

Transferability of Ownership	Management Control	Attractiveness for Raising Capital	Income Taxes
May transfer ownership in company name and assets	Absolute management freedom	Limited to proprietor's personal capital	Income from the business is taxed as personal income to the proprietor
Requires the consent of all partners	Majority vote of partners required for control	Limited to partners' ability and desire to contribute capital	Income from the business is taxed as personal income to the partners
Easily transferred by transferring shares of stock	Shareholders have final control, but usually board of directors controls company policies	Usually the most attractive form for raising capital	The C corporation is taxed on its income and the stockholder is taxed if and when dividends are received
Depends on the circumstances	Depends on the circumstances	C corporation	Depends on the circumstances

Partnership A partnership reports the income it earns to the Internal Revenue Service, but the partnership itself does not pay any taxes. The income is allocated to the partners according to their agreement. The partners each report their own shares of the partnership income on their personal tax returns and pay any taxes owed.

C Corporation The C corporation, as a separate legal entity, reports its income and pays any taxes related to these profits. The owners (stockholders) of the corporation need only report on their personal tax returns any amounts paid to them by the corporation in the form of dividends. For tax year 2004, the corporate tax rates were as follows:

Range of Taxable Income	Tax Rate
$0–$50,000	15%
$50,001–$75,000	25%
$75,001–$100,000	34%
$100,001–$335,000	39%
$335,001–$10,000,000	34%
$10,000,001–$15,000,000	35%
$15,000,001–$18,333,333	38%
Over $18,333,333	35%

Thus, the tax liability of the K&C Corporation, with $150,000 in taxable income, would be $41,750, calculated as follows:

Income		×	Tax Rate	=	Taxes
First	$ 50,000		15%		$ 7,500
Next	$ 25,000		25%		$ 6,250
Next	$ 25,000		34%		$ 8,500
Next	$ 50,000		39%		$19,500
Total	$150,000				$41,750

If the K&C Corporation paid a dividend to its owners in the amount of $40,000, the owners would need to report this dividend income when computing their personal income taxes. Thus, the $40,000 would be taxed twice, first as part of the corporation's income and then as part of the owners' personal income. However, taxes on qualifying dividends have recently been reduced to 5 percent for taxpayers in the 10- or 15-percent tax bracket and to 15 percent for taxpayers in higher tax brackets. (All double taxation could be avoided if the firm were set up as an S corporation, a specialized organization form discussed in the next section.)

ordinary income
Income earned in the ordinary course of business, including any salary

capital gains and losses
Gains and losses incurred from sales of property that are not a part of the firm's regular business operations

Section 1244 stock
Stock that offers some tax benefit to the stockholder in the case of corporate failure

An owner who decides to organize a C corporation would do well to consider issuing Section 1244 stock. Then, in the case of business failure, the owner could realize a tax savings that would not be allowed with regular stock. For tax purposes, **ordinary income** is income earned in the everyday course of business. Salary is considered ordinary income. **Capital gains and losses** are financial gains and losses incurred from the sale of property that is not a part of a firm's regular business operations, such as gains or losses from the sale of common stock. Typically, capital losses may be deducted only from capital gains, not from ordinary income. However, holding stock issued pursuant to Section 1244 of the Internal Revenue Code—**Section 1244 stock**—somewhat protects the stockholder in case of corporate failure. If such stock becomes worthless, the loss (up to $100,000 on a joint tax return) may be treated as an *ordinary* tax-deductible loss.

4 Describe the unique features and restrictions of three specialized organizational forms: limited partnerships, S corporations, and limited liability companies.

Specialized Forms of Organization

The majority of new and small businesses use one of the three major organizational forms just described—the sole proprietorship, partnership, or C corporation. However, other specialized types of organizations are also used by small firms. Three of these specialized forms deserve consideration: the limited partnership, the S corporation, and the limited liability company.

THE LIMITED PARTNERSHIP The **limited partnership** is a special form of partnership involving at least one general partner and one or more limited partners. The **general partner** remains personally liable for the debts of the business; **limited partners** have limited personal liability as long as they do not take an active role in the management of the partnership. In other words, limited partners risk only the capital they invest in the business. An individual with substantial personal wealth can, therefore, invest money in a limited partnership without exposing his or her personal assets to liability claims that might arise through activities of the business. If a limited partner becomes active in management, however, his or her limited liability is lost. To form a limited partnership, partners must file a certificate of limited partnership with the proper state office, as state law governs this form of organization.

limited partnership
A partnership with at least one general partner and one or more limited partners

general partner
A partner in a limited partnership who has unlimited personal liability

limited partner
A partner in a limited partnership who is not active in its management and has limited personal liability

S corporation (Subchapter S corporation)
A type of corporation that is taxed by the federal government as a partnership

THE S CORPORATION The designation **S corporation**, or **Subchapter S corporation**, is derived from Subchapter S of the Internal Revenue Code, which permits a business to retain the limited-liability feature of a C corporation while being taxed as a partnership. To obtain S corporation status, a corporation must meet certain requirements, including the following:

- No more than 75 stockholders are allowed. (Husband and wife count as one stockholder.)
- All stockholders must be individuals or certain qualifying estates and trusts. (The rules have been modified in recent years to allow more types of trusts to hold Subchapter S stock.)
- Only one class of stock can be outstanding.
- Fiscally, the corporation must operate on a calendar year basis.
- Nonresident alien stockholders are not permitted.

A restriction preventing S corporations from owning other corporations, including C corporations, has recently been removed, resulting in tax advantages for some small firms. Whereas in the past different businesses had to be legally separate, the new rules permit individual subsidiaries to consolidate under one S corporation and submit one tax return.[16]

An S corporation does not pay corporate income taxes and instead passes taxable income or losses on to the stockholders. This allows stockholders to receive dividends from the corporation without double taxation on the corporation's profit (once through a corporate tax and again through a personal tax). A competent tax attorney should be consulted before S status is elected, as tax law changes have considerable effect on the S corporation arrangement.

limited liability company
A corporation in which stockholders have limited liability but pay personal income taxes on business profits

THE LIMITED LIABILITY COMPANY The **limited liability company** is the newest form of organization. It can have just one owner in every state except Massachusetts (which requires two or more owners). This form differs from the C corporation in that it avoids double taxation. Limited liability companies do not pay tax on corporate income but simply pass that income on to their owners, who pay taxes on it as part of their personal income taxes.

The major advantage of the limited liability company over the partnership form is the limited liability that it affords. While general partners are exposed to personal liability, owners in a limited liability company are, as the name implies, protected with respect to their personal assets.

According to Peter Faber, a New York tax attorney, the limited liability company is usually the best choice for new businesses. It has the same ability as the S corporation to pass taxable income on to shareholders, and compared to an S corporation, the limited liability company is easier to set up, is more flexible, and offers some significant tax advantages.[17] But a limited liability company isn't always the best way to go. For example, under the following conditions, it would be better to use a C corporation:

- You want to provide extensive fringe benefits to owners or employees. The C corporation can deduct these benefits, and they are not treated as taxable income to the employees.
- You want to offer stock options to employees. Since limited liability companies do not have stock, they cannot offer such incentives.
- You hope to go public or sell out at some time in the future. A C corporation can go public or sell out to another corporation in a tax-free, stock-for-stock exchange.

- You plan to convert to a C corporation eventually. You cannot change from a passthrough entity like a limited liability company without paying additional taxes.

FORMING STRATEGIC ALLIANCES

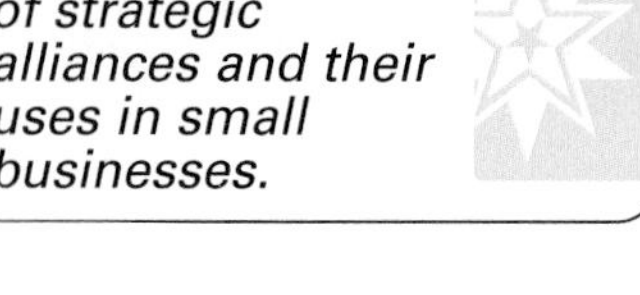
5 *Explain the nature of strategic alliances and their uses in small businesses.*

strategic alliance
An organizational relationship that links two or more independent business entities in a common endeavor

A **strategic alliance** is an organizational relationship that links two or more independent business entities in some common endeavor. Without affecting the independent legal status of the participating business partners, it provides a way for firms to improve their individual effectiveness by sharing certain resources.

According to Gene Slowinski, a strategic alliance expert, "Strategic alliances are definitely becoming crucial in building businesses of all kinds and at an earlier stage than ever before. . . . They can significantly decrease [time to launch] for startups by allowing them to access someone else's worldclass resources."[18] Since a competitive advantage often goes to the entrepreneur who is quick to exploit it, many small business owners see strategic alliances as an essential part of their plan for growth. Such alliances represent one way to cope with the rapid pace of change in today's business environment. (See Chapter 17 for a discussion of strategic alliances as a strategy option for global enterprises.)

Strategic Alliances with Large Companies

Large corporations create strategic alliances not only with other large corporations but also with small businesses. Typically, these alliances are formed to join the complementary skills and expertise of the partnered firms, in order to promote the competitive edge of both (or all) parties. Large manufacturers, for example, sometimes team up with innovative small manufacturers in product development efforts. The financial resources of the large firm and the creativity of the small company can be combined to the benefit of both businesses. Also, giant retailers form alliances with smaller suppliers so as to work hand in hand to achieve specific quality requirements and meet demanding delivery schedules.

Combining the speed, flexibility, and creative energy of a small business with the infrastructure of a large corporation can be a winning strategy. Consider the case of A.L.I. Technologies, Inc. (ALI), a Canadian digital-imaging firm. In 1997, with potent technology but only 40 employees, ALI formed a strategic alliance with IBM to develop large-scale medical image storage systems for regional hospital networks. On its own, ALI did not have the financial strength, expertise, and reputation to achieve its global ambitions; it needed IBM's deep pockets and connections to reach new markets. As the ALI/IBM alliance shows, a well-designed strategic alliance can create synergies that generate new business opportunities for both partners.[19] Today, A.L.I. Technologies is called McKesson Imaging Group, having been purchased by McKesson Corporation in July 2002.

Alliances with large firms can give a tremendous boost to the business of a small company, but some small businesses are discovering that bigger isn't always better. The advantages offered by the financial depth and expansive market reach of large firms must be weighed against potentially serious bureaucratic complications. Janice Bryant Howroyd, chairman and CEO of ACT-1 Group, a small staffing and human resource management company based in Torrance, California, jumped at the chance to work with a multinational staffing firm. In the rush to tie up an important deal, she did not examine the contract closely enough, and her company ended up paying a hefty price. One year after the contract ended, the multinational firm still owed ACT-1 Group $1.2 million. And one invoice discrepancy held up payments to ACT-1, choking its cash flow and forcing the company to close a regional office. The company still has not recovered $300,000 that it is owed.[20] Clearly, partnerships with large firms offer great advantages, but there is a potential downside to being so dependent on a single relationship.

Strategic Alliances with Small Companies

Small businesses can also form strategic alliances with other small firms in ways that enhance mutual competitive strength. Consider the case of Alan Wolan. A postcard entrepreneur in New York City, Wolan sold advertising on postcards that were given away in bars, restaurants, health clubs, and retail stores.[21] Restaurateurs and others were happy to carry the free cards, which helped create goodwill that could turn into repeat business. Wolan believed the business held great promise, but he lacked money and found that competitors in other areas were in a similar position. All of them shared a sense of urgency as they watched the progress of a large and better financed competitor, Max Racks, which seemed poised to conquer the market in metropolitan areas.

In the summer of 1995, Wolan's Five Fingers Inc. and two other firms in Los Angeles and Chicago started a network, later named GoCard, designed to enable them to sell national distribution to big accounts such as the Gap, Tanqueray, and Hanes. The group soon expanded to include 7 firms in 14 cities. They buy supplies together and share knowledge but otherwise remain autonomous. Although the future strength of this strategic alliance is uncertain, its benefits have been sufficient to bond the alliance members.

Strategic alliances hold great promise for small entrepreneurial businesses. By combining resources with carefully selected partners, small firms can increase their competitive strength and reach goals that would otherwise be too costly or too difficult for them to accomplish on their own.

Setting Up and Maintaining Successful Strategic Alliances

Although an appropriate strategic alliance may be essential to business growth, finding a suitable partner can be challenging. Many small business owners have given up in frustration after months—even years—of trying to establish such connections.

Launched in 1999, Staffcentrix is an Internet outsourcing company based in Woodstock, Connecticut. Despite having only $10,000 in first-year sales, the company was able to form alliances with Microsoft, the United Nations, and Waterside Productions. How did co-founders Christine Durst and Michael Haaren pull it off? First, they identified potential e-mail contacts by scouring the Web sites of prospective partners and taking note of anyone associated with any projects parallel to Staffcentrix's interests. Using this information, they created a "contact profile," which detailed each contact's personal involvement with these projects. Then Durst and Haaren sent personal e-mail messages

Living the Dream *Entrepreneurial Challenges*

Monks Close to Death

Forming a strategic alliance with a nonprofit organization can give an entrepreneur some added marketing muscle. Just ask Sam Mulgrew, a casket maker in Iowa. Knowing that profit margins on caskets average 15–20 percent for the big manufacturers, Mulgrew designed and built a line of simple wooden caskets. But he ran into a problem: Without an established position in the market, he was never able to sell more than 40 caskets in a year. He figured that joining with a trusted partner could only help.

Courtesy of Trappist Caskets

Rescue came from a most unlikely source—the Trappist monks of the 150-year-old New Melleray Abbey near Dubuque, Iowa. Mulgrew had heard that the monks were finding it hard to support themselves from sales of the corn and soybeans they grew on the monastery's 3,400-acre property, so he approached them with the idea of combining his business with their good name and labor. An agreement was reached and in January of 2000, Trappist Caskets was born. Today, the monks produce caskets using trees harvested from the monastery's own woods and sell them at prices ranging from $695 for a simple pine casket to as much as $1,795 for a premium black walnut version.

"Making caskets is a fitting occupation for these monks," says Mulgrew, now general manager of the business. "These are spiritual men who value the integrity of fine workmanship and the economy of living by their hands."

The monks use no nails in making the high-quality, solid wood caskets. And with a dozen monks and about as many laymen doing the work, Trappist Caskets produced and sold enough caskets to reach $1 million in sales in 2003 (doubling 2002 sales). The firm markets its products through Catholic newspapers, parish newletters, and the Internet.

"The phone never stops ringing," say Mulgrew. "We've found there's a huge demand for simple, handmade caskets. We'll produce about 600 caskets this year, triple what we did in year one." For these Trappist monks in Iowa, life is good.

http://www.trappistcaskets.com

Sources: Jeff Bailey, "Nonprofit Can Provide a Brand Name That Sells," *Wall Street Journal*, September 9, 2003, p. B11; http://www.trappistcaskets.com, April 22, 2004; http://www.agjournal.com/story.cfm?story_id=2234, September 23, 2003; and http://www.motherearthnews.com/187/diy187_funeral.html, September 23, 2003.

to these contacts, promoting an alliance with Staffcentrix. Within months, the company was up and running with big-name partners.[22]

For help in making essential linkages, especially with large corporations, many entrepreneurs consult strategic alliance matchmakers. These brokers provide two basic services. First, they maintain a wealth of contacts with decision makers at corporations that have the resources small companies need to fill in the gaps in their operations. Second, they help entrepreneurs fine-tune their alliance proposals to ensure that corporate insiders take them seriously.

Mick Dusche, a product manager at Microsoft, estimates that he gets hundreds of partnership requests a month. "To get my time or my developers' time," Dusche explains, "they need to show us an articulate, crisp business plan about why we should be willing to invest our resources."[23]

Strategic alliances are not any simpler to maintain than they are to set up. Many alliances encounter trouble along the way, and a number of them fail altogether. In fact, recent research indicates that two-thirds of all alliances run into serious problems within two years of their creation, and 70 percent of them do not survive.[24] Fortunately, when setting up alliances, entrepreneurs can take steps to improve their chances of success:

- Establish a healthy network of contacts. These people can lead you to still other contacts, and eventually to the one you need. Industry analysts, executive recruiters, public relations agencies, business reporters, and even the government can provide important leads.
- Identify and contact individuals within a firm who are likely to return your call. "Dialing high" (calling contacts at the vice presidential level or higher) works in small- or medium-sized firms, but in large firms you may need to call managers or other mid-level employees to get a response.
- Outline the partner's potential financial benefits from the alliance. If possible, show that your firm can deliver value to the alliance across several fronts.
- Learn to speak and understand the "language" of your partner. You will not pick up on subtle messages in conversations with partners unless you know how they communicate, and this can eventually make or break the alliance.

The goal is to form strategic alliances that are beneficial to all partners and to manage these alliances effectively. In their book *Everyone Is a Customer*, Jeffrey Shuman, Janice Twombly, and David Rottenberg point out that a key to successful strategic alliances is understanding the true nature of the relationship: Relationships are advertised as being between companies, whereas in reality relationships are built between people. And that's a very important distinction."[25]

MAKING THE MOST OF A BOARD OF DIRECTORS

6 Describe the effective use of boards of directors and advisory councils.

board of directors
The governing body of a corporation, elected by the stockholders

In entrepreneurial firms, the **board of directors** tends to be small (usually five or six members) and serves as the governing body for corporate activity. Elected by the stockholders, it in turn elects the firm's officers, who manage the enterprise with the help of management specialists. The directors also set or approve management policies, consider reports on operating results from the officers, and declare dividends (if any).

All too often, the majority stockholder in a small corporation (the entrepreneur) appoints a board of directors only to fulfill a legal requirement or as mere window dressing for investors. Such owners make little or no use of directors in managing their companies. In fact, the entrepreneur may actively resist efforts of these directors to provide managerial assistance. When appointing a board of directors, such an entrepreneur tends to select personal friends, relatives, or businesspersons who are too busy to analyze the firm's circumstances and are not inclined to argue. Entrepreneurs who take a more constructive approach find an active board to be both practical and beneficial, especially when the members are informed, skeptical, and independent.

Making use of boards of directors is becoming increasingly attractive for a number of reasons. The growing complexity of small businesses, arising in part from globalization and technological developments, makes the expertise of well-chosen directors especially valuable. In a family business, outsiders can play a unique role in helping evaluate family talent and mediate differences among family members.

Contributions of Directors

Small businesses stand to gain significantly from a strong board of directors, especially when its members help the entrepreneur look beyond the next few months to make important, long-term strategic decisions. According to Pat Gross, a director at three public companies, "The ultimate value of a director is [in his or her ability] to step back and see the forest for the trees."[26]

A well-selected board of directors can also bring supplementary knowledge and broad experience to corporate management. By virtue of their backgrounds, directors can fill gaps in the experience of a management team. The board should meet regularly to provide maximum assistance to the chief executive. In board meetings, ideas should be debated, strategies determined, and the pros and cons of policies explored. In this way, the chief executive is assisted by the experience of all the board members. Their combined knowledge makes possible more intelligent decisions on issues crucial to the firm.

By utilizing the experience of a board of directors, the chief executive of a small corporation is in no way giving up active control of its operations. Instead, by consulting with and seeking the advice of the board's members, he or she is simply drawing on a larger pool of business knowledge. A group will typically make better decisions than will a single individual working in isolation.

An active board of directors serves management in several important ways: by reviewing major policy decisions, by advising on external business conditions and on proper reaction to the business cycle, by providing informal advice from time to time on specific problems that arise, and by offering access to important personal contacts. With a strong board, a small firm may gain greater credibility with the public, as well as with the business and financial communities.

Selection of Directors

Many resources are available to an entrepreneur who is attempting to assemble a cooperative and experienced group of directors. The firm's attorney, banker, accountant, other business executives, and local management consultants might all be considered as potential directors, but such individuals lack the independence needed to critically review an entrepreneur's plans. Also, the owner is already paying for their expertise. For this reason, the owner needs to consider the value of an outside board—one with members whose income does not depend on the firm. The National Association of Corporate Directors recently surveyed the directors of nearly 100 boards of entrepreneurial firms and found that, on average, 28 percent were independent outside directors. This number is increasing—which is good—but the study also reports that private company boards tend to have only half as many independent members as their public counterparts.[27]

Objectivity is a particularly valuable contribution of outside directors. They can look at issues more dispassionately than can insiders who are involved in daily decision making. Outside directors, for example, are freer to evaluate and to question a firm's ethical standards. Some operating executives, without the scrutiny of outside directors, may rationalize unethical or illegal behavior as being in the best interest of the company.

In a family business, an outside board can help mediate and resolve issues related to leadership succession, in addition to providing more general direction. As outsiders, they bring to the business a measure of detachment from potentially explosive emotional differences.

Working with outside board members is not always easy. Dennis Gertmenian is the founder, chairman, and CEO of Ready Pac Produce Inc., an Irwindale, California–based produce-packaging company. The business has about 2,500 employees, but it is a private entity and thus is not required by law to have a corporate board. Nonetheless, Gertmenian decided long ago to establish a board of directors. Board members have had a profound impact on Gertmenian's decision making, most notably by persuading him to back out of a plan to provide jobs in an economically depressed area and by encouraging him to take a hit on his personal real-estate portfolio. But the tough decisions the board has advised him to make have ultimately improved the business. Gertmenian reflects, "I wasn't taking the time to formally structure some of the areas of my company that needed attention from a long-term point of view, such as: What are we doing with our banking relationship a year from now? What is our strategic plan? I had a plan, but it was in my mind, not written down."[28] CEOs can spend as much as 20 percent of their time on board-related activities, but the time commitment is worth the cost if the directors are doing their jobs well.

The nature and needs of a business will help determine the qualifications required in its directors. For example, a firm that faces a marketing problem may benefit greatly from the counsel of a board member with a marketing background. Business prominence in the community is not essential, although it may help give the company credibility and enable it to attract other well-qualified directors. Having a "fat" Rolodex can only be helpful, as directors with influential business contacts can contribute greatly to the company's performance.[29]

After deciding on the qualifications to look for, a business owner must seek suitable candidates as board members. Effective directors will be honest and accountable, offer valuable insights based on business experience, and enhance the company's credibility with its stakeholders (especially customers and suppliers). Suggestions for such candidates may be obtained from the firm's accountant, attorney, banker, and other associates in the business community. Owners or managers of other, noncompeting small companies, as well as second- and third-level executives in large companies, are often willing to accept such positions. Before offering candidates positions on the board, however, a business owner would be wise to do some discreet background checking.

Compensation of Directors

The compensation paid to board members varies greatly, and some small firms pay no fees at all. Compensation is usually offered in the form of an annual retainer, board meeting fees, and pay for committee work. (Directors may serve on committees that oversee executive compensation, audit the company's financial reports, and perform other critical functions.) A recent study found that entrepreneurial firms pay, on average, over $12,500 in total annual compensation for directors of private companies and almost $26,000 for public firm directors.[30] Obviously, board membership is less likely to be limited to local talent if the company is willing to pay directors' travel expenses when they attend meetings. Some small businesses also offer board members stock-option packages, depending on industry practice and plans for growth.[31]

The relatively modest compensation offered for the services of well-qualified directors suggests that financial compensation is not their primary motivation for serving on a board. Reasonable compensation is appropriate, however, if directors are making important contributions to the firm's operations.

An Alternative: An Advisory Council

advisory council
A group that functions like a board of directors but acts only in an advisory capacity

In recent years, increased attention has been directed to the legal responsibilities of directors. Because outside directors may be held responsible for illegal company actions, even though they are not directly involved in wrongdoing, some individuals are reluctant to accept directorships. Thus, some small companies use an **advisory council** as an alternative to a board of directors. Qualified outsiders are asked to serve on a council as advisors to the company. This group then functions in much the same way as a board of directors does, except that its actions are only advisory in nature.

The legal liability of members of an advisory council is not completely clear. However, limiting their compensation and power is thought to lighten, if not eliminate, the personal liability of members.[32] Since it is advisory in nature, the council also may pose less of a threat to the owner and possibly work more cooperatively than a conventional board.

Looking Back

1 Describe the characteristics and value of a strong management team.

- A strong management team nurtures a good business idea and helps provide the necessary resources to make it succeed.
- The skills of management team members should complement each other, forming an optimal combination of education and experience.
- A small firm can enhance its management by drawing on the expertise of outside professional groups.
- An entrepreneur should create a management structure that defines relationships among all members of the organization.

2 Explain the common legal forms of organization used by small businesses.

- The most basic legal forms of organization used by small businesses are the sole proprietorship, partnership, and C corporation.
- In a sole proprietorship, the owner receives all profits and bears all losses. The principal disadvantage of this form is the owner's unlimited liability.
- In a partnership, which should be established on the basis of a written partnership agreement, success depends on the partners' ability to build an effective working relationship.
- Corporations are particularly attractive because of their limited-liability feature. The fact that ownership is easily transferable makes them well suited for combining the capital of numerous owners.

3 Identify factors to consider in choosing among the primary legal forms of organization, including tax consequences.

- Nearly three-fourths of all new businesses are organized as sole proprietorships, 8 percent are set up as partnerships, and 21 percent are formed as corporations.
- The key factors in the choice among different legal forms of organization are organizational requirements and costs, liability of the owners, continuity of the business, transferability of ownership, management control, attractiveness for raising capital, and income taxes.
- Self-employed individuals who operate businesses as sole proprietorships report income from the businesses on their individual tax returns.
- A partnership reports the income it earns to the Internal Revenue Service, but the partnership itself does not pay income taxes. The income is allocated to the owners according to their partnership agreement.
- A C corporation reports its income and pays any taxes due on this corporate income. Individual stockholders must also pay personal income taxes on dividends paid to them by a corporation.
- Holding Section 1244 stock helps to protect the stockholder in case of corporate failure. If such stock becomes worthless, the loss (up to $100,000) may be treated as an ordinary tax-deductible loss.

4 Describe the unique features and restrictions of three specialized organizational forms: limited partnerships, S corporations, and limited liability companies.

- In a limited partnership, general partners have unlimited liability, while limited partners have only limited liability as long as they are not active in the firm's management.
- S corporations, also called Subchapter S corporations, enjoy a special tax status that permits them to avoid the corporate tax but requires individual stockholders to pay personal taxes on their proportionate shares of the business profits.
- In limited liability companies, individual owners have the advantage of limited liability but pay only personal income taxes on the firm's earnings.

5 Explain the nature of strategic alliances and their uses in small business.

- Strategic alliances allow business firms to combine their resources without compromising their independent legal status.
- Strategic alliances may be formed by two or more independent businesses to achieve some common purpose. For example, a large corporation and a small business or two or more small businesses may collaborate on a joint project.
- Strategic alliance matchmakers can help small businesses find suitable alliance partners.
- Entrepreneurs can improve their chances of creating and maintaining a successful alliance by establishing productive connections, identifying the best person to contact, confirming the long-term benefits of the alliance, and learning to speak the partner's "language."

6 Describe the effective use of boards of directors and advisory councils.

- Boards of directors can assist small corporations by offering counsel and assistance to their chief executives.
- To be most effective, members of the board should include properly qualified, independent outsiders.
- One alternative to an active board of directors is an advisory council, whose members are not personally liable for the company's actions.

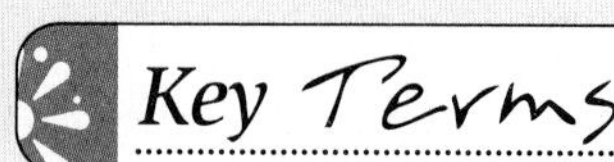

Key Terms

management team, p. 163
sole proprietorship, p. 165
unlimited liability, p. 165
partnership, p. 166
partnership agreement, p. 169
agency power, p. 169
corporation, p. 170
legal entity, p. 170
C corporation, p. 170
corporate charter, p. 170
stock certificate, p. 170
pre-emptive right, p. 170
ordinary income, p. 174
capital gains and losses, p. 174
Section 1244 stock, p. 174
limited partnership, p. 174
general partner, p. 174
limited partner, p. 174
S corporation (Subchapter S corporation), p. 175
limited liability company, p. 175
strategic alliance, p. 176
board of directors, p. 178
advisory council, p. 180

Discussion Questions

1. Why would investors tend to favor a new business led by a management team over one headed by a lone entrepreneur? Is this preference justified?
2. Discuss the merits of the three major legal forms of organization.
3. Does the concept of limited liability apply to a sole proprietorship? Why or why not?
4. Suppose a partnership is set up and operated without a formal partnership agreement. What problems might arise? Explain.
5. Evaluate the three major forms of organization in terms of management control by the owner and sharing of the firm's profits.
6. What is an S corporation, and what is its principal advantage?
7. Why are strategic alliances important for many small businesses? What steps can an entrepreneur take to create strategic alliances and to prevent their failure?
8. How might a board of directors be of value to management in a small corporation? What qualifications are essential for a director? Is ownership of stock in the firm a prerequisite for being a director?
9. What may account for the failure of most small corporations to use boards of directors as more than rubber stamps?
10. How do advisory councils differ from boards of directors? Which would you recommend to a small company owner? Why?

You Make the Call

SITUATION 1

Ted Green and Mark Stroder became close friends as 16-year-olds when both worked part-time for Green's dad in his automotive parts store. After high school, Green went to college, while Stroder joined the National Guard Reserve and devoted his weekends to auto racing. Green continued his association with the automotive parts store by buying and managing two of his father's stores.

In 1995, Green conceived the idea of starting a new business that would rebuild automobile starters, and he asked Stroder to be his partner in the venture. Originally, Stroder was somewhat concerned about working with Green because their personalities are so different. Green has been described as outgoing and enthusiastic, while Stroder is reserved and skeptical. However, Stroder is now out of work, and so he has agreed to the offer. They will set up a small shop behind one of Green's automotive parts stores. Stroder will do all the work; Green will supply the cash.

The "partners" have agreed to name the business STARTOVER, and now they need to decide on a legal form of organization.

Question 1 How relevant are the individual personalities to the success of this entrepreneurial team? Do you think Green and Stroder have a chance to survive their "partnership"? Why or why not?

Question 2 Do you consider it an advantage or a disadvantage that the members of this team are the same age?

Question 3 Which legal form of organization would you propose for STARTOVER? Why?

Question 4 If Stroder and Green decided to incorporate, would STARTOVER qualify as an S corporation? If so, would you recommend this option? Why or why not?

SITUATION 2

Matthew Freeman started a business in 1993 to provide corporate training in project management. He initially organized his business as a sole proprietorship. Until 1999, he did most of his work on a contract basis for Corporation Education Services (CES). Under the terms of his contract, Freeman was responsible for teaching 3- to 5-day courses to corporate clients—primarily *Fortune 1000* companies. He was compensated according to a negotiated daily rate, and expenses incurred during a course (hotels, meals, transportation, etc.) were reimbursed by CES. Although some expenses were not reimbursed by CES (such as those for computers and office supplies), Freeman's expenses usually amounted to less than 1 percent of his revenues.

In 1999, Freeman increasingly found himself working directly with corporate clients rather than contracting with CES. Over the years, he had considered incorporating but had assumed the costs and inconveniences of this option would outweigh the benefits. However, some of his new clients said that they would prefer to contract with a corporation rather than with an individual. And Freeman sometimes wondered about potential liability problems. On the one hand, he didn't have the same liability issues as some other businesses—he worked out of his home, clients never visited his home office, all courses were conducted in hotels or corporate facilities, and his business involved only services. But he wasn't sure what would happen if a client were dissatisfied with the content and outcomes of his instruction. Finally, he wondered whether there would be tax advantages to incorporating.

Question 1 What are the advantages and disadvantages of running the business as a sole proprietorship? As a C corporation?

Question 2 If Freeman decided to incorporate his business, which types of corporations could he form? Which type would you recommend? Why?

SITUATION 3

For years, a small distributor of welding materials had followed the practice of most small firms, treating the board of directors as merely a legal necessity. Composed of two co-owners and a retired steel company executive, the board was not a working board. But the company, run informally with traditional management methods, was profitable.

After attending a seminar, the majority owner decided that a board might be useful for more than legal or cosmetic purposes. Thus, he invited two outsiders—both division heads of larger corporations—to join the board. This brought the membership of the board to five. The majority owner believed the new members would be helpful in opening up the business to new ideas.

Question 1 Can two outside members on a board of five make any real difference in the way the board operates?

Question 2 Evaluate the owner's choices for board members.

Question 3 What will determine the usefulness or effectiveness of this board? Do you predict that it will be useful? Why or why not?

Experiential Exercises

1. Prepare a one-page résumé of your personal qualifications to launch a term-paper-typing business at your college or university. Then write a critique that might be prepared by an investor, evaluating your strengths and weaknesses as shown on the résumé.
2. Interview an attorney whose clients include small businesses. Inquire about the legal considerations involved in choosing the form of organization for a new business. Report your findings to the class.
3. Interview the partners of a local business. Inquire about the factors they considered when drawing up their partnership agreement. Report your findings to the class.
4. Discuss with a corporate director, attorney, banker, or business owner the contributions of directors to small firms. Prepare a brief report on your findings. If you discover a particularly well-informed individual, suggest that person to your instructor as a possible speaker.

Exploring the Web

1. Go to the Small Business Administration's Web site at **http://www.sba.gov**. Select "Starting" from among the site's "Custom Views." Then find the link for "Forms of Ownership" and read about legal forms of organization. Think about how you plan to structure your business. What are the long-term implications of the business form you have under consideration?
2. The SBA's Choosing a Business Structure Wizard, which you can access at **http://app1.sba.gov/exsysweb/client/bizform/bizformmenu.html**, can help you determine what form of business ownership is right for you. Follow the Wizard's instructions and provide a summary of your quiz results.
3. Log on to InfoTrac College Edition at **http://www.infotrac-college.com**, and locate "10 Tips for Creating Strong Ties," an article by Ed Rigsbee. Ed Rigsbee is the president of Rigsbee Research and maintains a Web site at **http://www.rigsbee.com** on the topics of partnering and alliances. Compare Rigsbee's 10 tips with the recommendations given in this chapter to help entrepreneurs improve their chances of success when setting up and maintaining strategic alliances. How are they similar? Different?
4. Visit the Women's Business Center at **http://www.onlinewbc.gov**. Choose "Business Basics" and then follow the "Management" link. Browse the content provided under the heading "Developing Your Boardroom Skills." What suggestions might you take from this Web site with respect to selecting a board member with the marketing expertise you may lack?

Case 8

SILVER ZEPHYR RESTAURANT (P. 537)

This case presents issues that relate to choosing a legal form of organization.

Alternative Cases for Chapter 8:

Case 1, Boston Duck Tours, p. 526
Case 18, Douglas Electrical Supply, Inc., p. 559

The Business Plan

LAYING THE FOUNDATION

As part of laying the foundation to prepare your own business plan, respond to the following questions regarding your management team, legal form of organization, strategic alliances, and board of directors.

1. Who are the members of your management team? What skills, education, and experience do they bring to the team?
2. What other key managers do you plan to recruit?
3. Do you plan to use consultants? If so, describe their qualifications.
4. What are your plans for future employee recruitment?
5. What will be the compensation and benefit plans for managers and other employees?
6. What style of management will be used? What will be the decision-making process in the company? What mechanisms are in place for effective communication between managers and employees? If possible, present a simple organization chart.
7. How will personnel be motivated? How will creativity be encouraged? How will commitment and loyalty be developed?
8. What employee retention and training programs will be adopted? Who will be responsible for job descriptions and employee evaluations?
9. Who will have an ownership interest in the business?
10. Will the business function as a sole proprietorship, partnership, or corporation? If a corporation, will it be a C corporation, an S corporation, or a limited liability company?
11. What are the liability implications of this form of organization?
12. What are the tax advantages and disadvantages of this form of organization?
13. If a corporation, where will the corporation be chartered and when will it be incorporated?
14. What attorney or legal firm has been selected to represent the firm? What type of relationship exists with the firm's attorney or law firm?
15. What legal issues are presently or potentially significant?
16. What licenses and/or permits may be required?
17. What strategic alliances are in place, and what others do you plan to establish in the future? Describe the forms and nature of these alliances. What are the responsibilities of and benefits to the parties involved? What are the exit strategies?
18. Who are the directors of the company? What are their qualifications? How will they be compensated?

THE LOCATION PLAN

In the Video Spotlight

Nicole Miller Company

As this video spotlight illustrates, the proper location for a business depends on the type of business as well as a host of other factors. For example, do you need a technically skilled workforce? Do you need to be close to your raw material supply? How important is it for you to be located near your customers?

Fashion designer Nicole Miller has multiple needs, so her company has multiple locations. Garments are designed, fitted, and manufactured in the garment district in New York City. Over 100,000 people work in the garment district, giving Miller access to a great deal of tailoring talent. Finished garments are warehoused in another New York location before being sold in department stores, in boutiques, and over the Internet.

Initially, Miller and Bud Konheim (CEO of Nicole Miller Company) sold primarily to department stores, but buyers would never purchase an entire season's line. Since Miller wanted to see her whole line hang together, she and Konheim decided to open Nicole Miller boutiques. This added a different type of location to their distribution channel, as well as a more selective one—there are only 30 Nicole Miller boutiques.

Konheim has also been aggressive in using technology in the business, so he moved quickly to the Internet. From the beginning of the Internet explosion, Nicole Miller has used the Internet as an operations tool as well as an additional selling site.

Video material provided by Hattie Bryant, Producer of Small Business School, the series on PBS Stations, Worldnet, and the Web at http://www.smallbusinessschool.org.

Chapter 9

Looking Ahead

After studying this chapter, you should be able to

1 *Describe the five key factors in locating the brick-and-mortar startup.*

2 *Discuss the challenges of designing and equipping a physical facility.*

3 *Understand both the attraction and the challenges of creating a home-based startup.*

4 *Understand the potential benefits of locating a startup on the Internet.*

The entrepreneur who decides to purchase a franchise or an existing business usually receives considerable location guidance from the franchisor or members of the existing firm. But for the entrepreneur who chooses to start a venture from scratch, the location decision is very time consuming. Regardless of how the decision is made, all location intentions should be described in the business plan.

LOCATING THE BRICK-AND-MORTAR STARTUP

1 *Describe the five key factors in locating the brick-and-mortar startup.*

In many cases, the choice of a location is a one-time decision. However, an entrepreneur may later consider relocating the business to reduce operating costs or gain other advantages. For example, a California entrepreneur, Mitchell Greif, CEO of Coast Converters, is relocating his plastic bag manufacturing plant to Las Vegas, Nevada, because of the high taxes and pricey real estate in Los Angeles.[1] Also, as a business grows, it is sometimes desirable to expand operations to other locations to be closer to customers.[2]

In this chapter, we will discuss three primary options for the initial location decision—a traditional physical building, the entrepreneur's home, and a Web site on the Internet. Although we recognize that the Internet can be an integral part of operations for both a traditional and a home-based business, we treat dot-com ventures as a separate location category because of their significance as a sole sales outlet for small businesses. Exhibit 9-1 depicts the three location options.

The Importance of the Location Decision

The importance of the initial decision as to where to locate a traditional physical building—a **brick-and-mortar store**—is underscored by both the high cost of such a store and the hassle of pulling up stakes and moving an established business. Also, if the site is particularly poor, the business may never be successful, even with adequate financing and superior managerial ability. The importance of location is so clearly recognized by national chains that they spend thousands of dollars investigating sites before establishing new stores.

brick-and-mortar store
The traditional physical store from which businesses have historically operated

The choice of a good location is much more vital to some businesses than to others. For example, the site chosen for a dress shop can make or break the business because it must be convenient for customers. In contrast, the physical location of the office of a painting contractor is of less importance, since customers do not need frequent access to the facility. Even painting contractors, however, may suffer if their business site is poorly chosen. For example, some communities are more willing or able than others to invest resources to keep property in good condition, thereby providing greater opportunities for painting jobs.

Key Factors in Selecting a Good Location

Five key factors, shown in Exhibit 9-2, guide the location selection process: customer accessibility, business environment conditions, availability of resources, the entrepreneur's personal preference, and site availability and costs. Other factors relevant to location include neighbor mix (who's next door?), security and safety (how safe is the neighborhood?), services (is there municipal trash pickup?), past tenants' fate (what happened to them?), and the life-cycle stage of the area (is the site in the embryonic, mature, or declining stage?).[3]

EXHIBIT 9-1 *Location Options for the Startup*

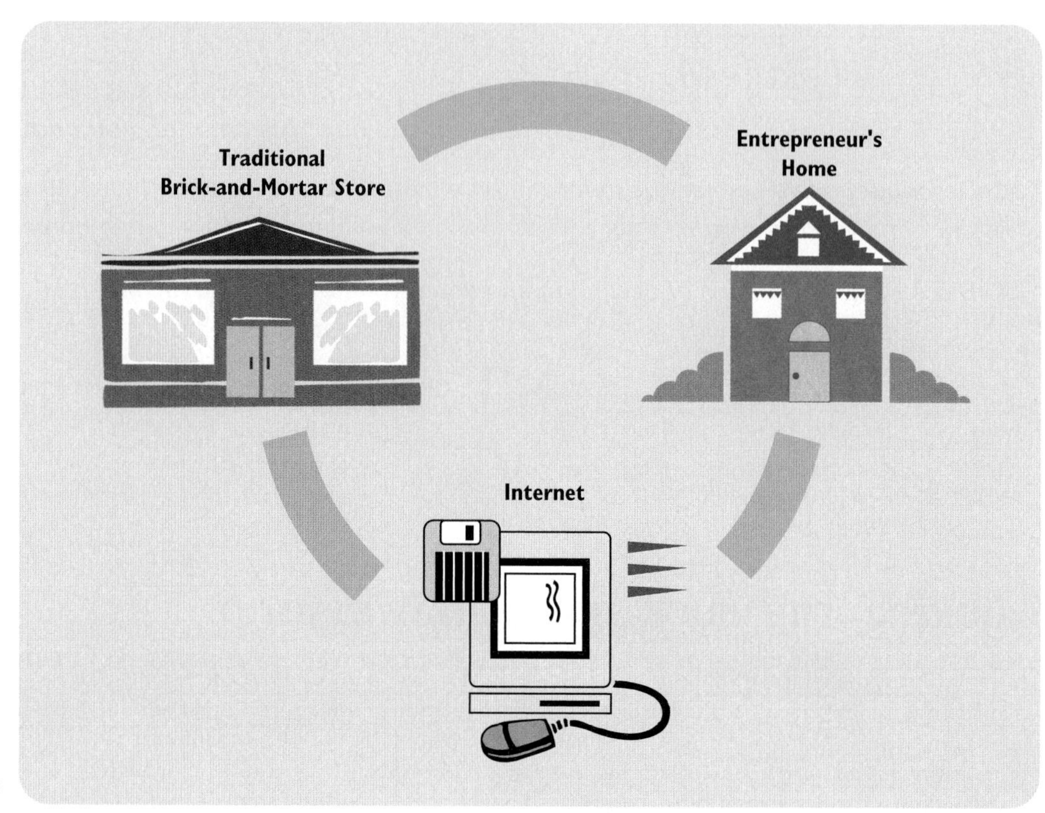

In a particular situation, one factor may carry more weight than others. However, each of the five key factors should always have some influence on the final location decision.

CUSTOMER ACCESSIBILITY Customer accessibility is generally an important consideration in selecting a location. Retail outlets and service firms are typical examples of businesses that must be located so as to make access convenient for target customers. Rarely will customers be willing to regularly travel long distances to shop. That's why Glenn Campbell and Scott Molander decided to sell hats in high-traffic areas. Each store, located in a shopping mall or airport, offers a vast assortment of officially licensed baseball-style hats. The first store was opened in 1995, and in five years the company, Hat World Corp.,

EXHIBIT 9-2 *Five Key Factors in Determining a Good Business Location*

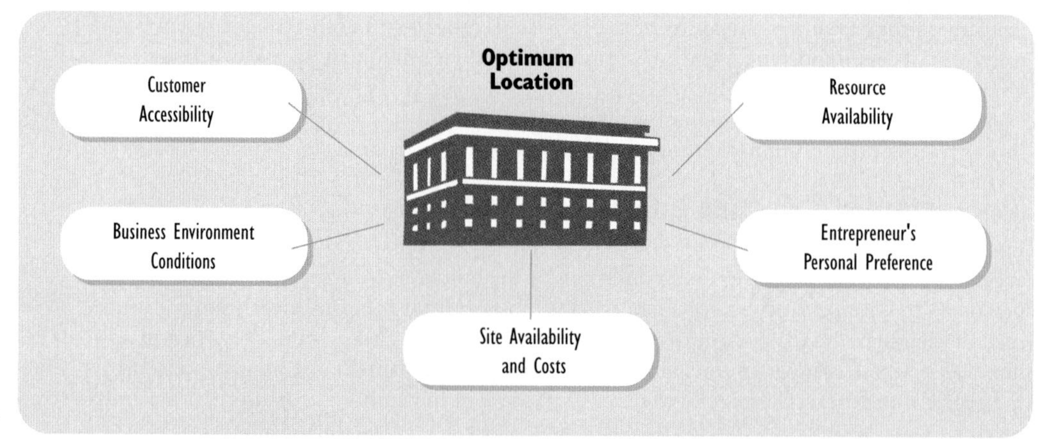

had grown to 157 stores. By 2003, it had purchased several competitors and was operating more than 483 stores in 45 states.[4]

Many products, such as snack foods and gasoline, are convenience goods, which require a retail location close to target customers; otherwise, consumers will substitute competitive brands when a need arises. Services such as tire repair and hair styling also require a location readily accessible to customers.

Customer accessibility is vital in industries in which the cost of shipping the finished product is high relative to the product's value. For example, packaged ice and soft drinks must be produced near consuming markets, because transporting these products can be an expensive process.

Convenient access for customers is one reason small businesses have successfully created such a strong presence on the Internet. With the appropriate computer connection, customers can access a small business's home page from anywhere in the world. (Locating a startup on the Internet is discussed later in this chapter.)

The need to locate close to niche market customers often dictates a site that otherwise would be less than desirable. For example, a small apparel retail store, Transfer Clothing Inc., is located underground in a subway station in New York City. It's one of 165 merchants peddling magazines, food, clothing, and haircuts in New York's subway stations. The Cavern Supply Company, a cafeteria, is located 750 feet straight down in Carlsbad Caverns National Park. Cavern Supply contends daily with 80 percent humidity and bats.[5] Neither business occupies an attractive site. However, they both recognize the need to be accessible to potential customers.

BUSINESS ENVIRONMENT CONDITIONS A startup business is affected in a number of ways by the environment in which it operates. Environmental conditions can hinder or promote success. Weather is one important environmental factor influencing the location as well as the demand for products such as air conditioners and outdoor swimming pools. For example, consider entrepreneur Tsering Gyalzen, who is planning to build a cybercafé, containing eight laptop computers and solar-powered generators, at the 17,400-foot-high base camp of Mount Everest. He will be forced to construct a temporary structure because the base camp sits on a glacier that moves several inches each day.[6]

Competition, legal requirements, and tax structure are a few of the many other critical environmental factors. Every entrepreneur seeks profits; therefore, all factors affecting the financial picture are of great concern. State and local governments can help or hinder a new business by forgiving or levying taxes. Considerable variation exists across the United States in state corporate income taxes, with only a few states having no such tax. One state with an advantageous tax policy is Wyoming. Its Web site proudly states, "The state of Wyoming does not levy a personal or corporate income tax. There is no current legislation in the works to create an income tax."[7] Obviously, the best time to evaluate environmental conditions is prior to making a location commitment.

Many states offer location incentives. One strategy is to establish **enterprise zones** in order to bring jobs to economically deprived areas. Sponsored by local city/county governments, these zones lure businesses by offering regulatory and tax relief. In exchange for locating or expanding in these areas, eligible business firms receive total exemption from the property taxes normally assessed on a new plant and equipment for three to five years. Oregon had 49 enterprise zones as of January 2003.[8] Enterprise zones are not a cure-all. Locating in an enterprise zone will not solve problems created by poor management or make up for an ill-conceived idea. However, enterprise zones can be used as a catalyst to help jump-start a small firm.

enterprise zones
State-designated areas that are established to bring jobs to economically deprived regions through regulatory and tax incentives

While most efforts of state and city governments are designed to support startups, some cities have regulations that restrict new business operations under certain circumstances. For example, Detroit, Michigan, doesn't permit vendors to sell any hot food except hot dogs and sausages. And in San Diego, California, shoeshiners are banned from public areas.[9]

AVAILABILITY OF RESOURCES The availability of resources associated with producing a product and operating a business should also be considered in selecting a location. Raw materials, labor supply, and transportation are some of the factors that have a bearing on location. Nearness to raw materials and suitability of labor supply are particularly critical considerations in the location of a manufacturing business. (Recall Nicole Miller's strategy.)

Nearness to Raw Materials If required raw materials are not abundantly available in all areas, a region in which these materials abound offers special location advantages. For a business dependent on bulky or heavy raw materials that lose much of their bulk or weight in the manufacturing process, proximity to these materials is a powerful force driving the location decision. A sawmill is an example of a business that must stay close to its raw materials in order to operate economically.

Suitability of Labor Supply A manufacturer's labor requirements depend on the nature of its production process. Availability of workers, wage rates, labor productivity, and a history of peaceful relations with employees are all particularly important considerations for labor-intensive firms. In some cases, the need for semiskilled or unskilled labor justifies locating in an area with surplus labor. In other cases, firms find it desirable to seek a pool of highly skilled labor.

Availability of Transportation Access to good transportation is important to almost all firms. For example, good highways and bus systems provide customers with convenient access to retail stores. For small manufacturers, quality transportation is especially vital. They must carefully evaluate all the trucking routes that support their transportation needs, considering the costs of both transporting supplies to the manufacturing location and shipping the finished product to customers. It is critical that they know whether these costs will allow their product to be competitively priced.

PERSONAL PREFERENCE OF THE ENTREPRENEUR As a practical matter, many entrepreneurs tend to discount customer accessibility, business environment conditions, and resource availability and consider only their personal preference in locating a business. Often, their personal preference is their home community; the possibility of locating elsewhere never enters their mind. Just because an individual has always lived in a particular town, however, does not automatically make the town a satisfactory business location!

On the other hand, locating a business in one's home community is not necessarily illogical. In fact, this offers certain advantages. From a personal standpoint, the entrepre-

Living the Dream — *Entrepreneurial Challenges*

Staying Home

Courtesy of Dyson

http://www.dyson.com

James Dyson's experience provides a good example of the kind of dilemma that may confront entrepreneurs when circumstances—such as profit—conflict with a decision to locate their business in their home community.

Dyson, 55, smiles when he talks about bringing his neon-colored, warhead-shaped, English-made vacuum cleaners to America. His upright, bagless vacuum cleaner is the result of 15 years of innovation and failed prototypes. By creating a technology of spinning air in a plastic cone to achieve a superior cleaning action, Dyson has dominated his niche in the European market and more recently carved a big slice out of the U.S. market.

From the start, Dyson's production facilities have been located in his home community of Malmesbury, England. For years, his firm has been the town's largest employer at the Tetbury Hill site. "I live here, this is my home, and it is the home of everybody here at Dyson," he said. "We love being here; we're a big employer and, I hope, a big contributor to the community."

Nevertheless, Dyson recently decided to move the manufacture of his upright vacuum to the Far East—Malaysia—where labor costs are much cheaper. This has resulted in a loss of 800 jobs in a town with only 4,500 residents. Even Prime Minister Tony Blair has said he is "deeply disappointed" by the decision.

The jobs remaining in Malmesbury are primarily in research and development. So, according to Dyson, his products are still "British-engineered."

Sources: Joshua Levine, "Carpet Diem," *Forbes*, Vol. 170, No. 8 (October 14, 2002), pp. 206–207; "Dyson Plant Shuts Up Shop," http://news.bbc.co.uk/1/hi/england/2282809.stm, April 8, 2004; and "Blair 'Disappointed' over Dyson's Jobs," http://news.bbc.co.uk/1/hi/england/1805050.stm, April 8, 2004.

neur generally appreciates and feels comfortable with the atmosphere of the home community, whether it is a small town or a large city. From a practical business standpoint, the entrepreneur can more easily establish credit. Hometown bankers can be dealt with more confidently, and other businesspersons may be of great service in helping evaluate a given opportunity. If potential customers are local residents, the prospective entrepreneur probably has a better idea of their tastes and preferences than an outsider would have. Relatives and friends may be the entrepreneur's first customers and may help advertise his or her products or services.

Sometimes the choice is a location offering unique lifestyle advantages. Entrepreneur Pete Nelson has a home office 10 feet off the ground, in a stand of 70-year-old Douglas fir trees in Fall City, Washington, where he operates TreeHouse Workshop, a general contracting business. Nelson and his wife, Judy, enjoy the outdoor location of their home-based business, where they are "face-to-beak with woodpeckers and wrens" on the other side of their office window.[10] Personal preference, however, should not be allowed to take priority over obvious location weaknesses.

SITE AVAILABILITY AND COSTS Once an entrepreneur has settled on a certain area of the country, a specific site must still be chosen. The availability of potential sites and the costs associated with obtaining them must be investigated.

Site Availability After evaluating a site for his new business, one entrepreneur is said to have exclaimed, "It must be a good site—I know of four businesses that have been there in the last two years!" Fortunately, such a misguided approach to site evaluation is not typical of entrepreneurs, many of whom recognize the value of seeking professional assistance in determining site availability and appropriateness. Local realtors can serve as a good source of insight.

If an entrepreneur's top choices are unavailable, other options must be considered. One choice is shared facilities. In recent years, business incubators have sprung up in all areas of the country. A **business incubator** is a facility that rents space to new businesses or to people wishing to start businesses. Incubators are often located in recycled buildings, such as abandoned warehouses or schools. They serve fledgling businesses by making space available, offering management advice, and providing clerical assistance, all of which help lower operating costs. An incubator tenant can be fully operational the day after moving in, without buying phones, renting a copier, or hiring office employees.

business incubator
A facility that provides shared space, services, and management assistance to new businesses

The purpose of business incubators is to see new businesses hatch, grow, and leave the incubator. Most incubators—though not all—have some type of government or university sponsorship and are motivated by a desire to stimulate economic development. Although the building space provided by incubators is significant, their greatest contribution is the business expertise and management assistance they provide.

Site Costs Ultimately, the site selection process must depend on evaluation of relevant costs. Unfortunately, an entrepreneur is frequently unable to afford the "best" site. The costs involved in building on a new site may be prohibitive, or the purchase price of an existing structure may exceed the entrepreneur's budget.

Assuming that a suitable building is available, the entrepreneur must decide whether to lease or buy. Although ownership confers greater freedom in the modification and use of a building, the advantages of leasing usually outweigh these benefits. We recommend that most new firms lease for two reasons:

1. A large cash outlay is avoided. This is important for a new small firm, which typically lacks adequate financial resources.
2. Risk is reduced by avoiding substantial investment and by postponing commitments for space until the success of the business is assured and the nature of building requirements is better known.

When entering into a leasing agreement, the entrepreneur should check the landlord's insurance policies to be sure there is proper coverage for various types of risks. If not, the lessee should seek coverage under his or her own policy. It is important to have the terms of the leasing agreement reviewed by an attorney. Sometimes, an attorney can arrange for special clauses to be added to a lease, such as an escape clause that allows the lessee to exit

Living the Dream

Entrepreneurial Challenges

From High Tech to Low Tech

© Larry Ford

A growing number of ex-"dot-comers" are starting businesses from scratch in low-tech fields and locating in low-tech areas of cities. One such entrepreneur is Brian Benavidez, laid-off director of business development for an online marketer. In October 2002, he used funds from personal savings, credit cards, and friends to open Sparky's American Food in Brooklyn, New York.

Benavidez spent months tasting hot dogs before selecting a variety made from dry-aged beef. When combined with custom-baked buns from a local bakery, it makes for a great-tasting hot dog. Currently, he employs five people to prepare and serve these hormone- and antibiotic-free hot dogs.

Benavidez was inspired to start his business after watching a video documentary about hot dog vendors. "Everybody seemed so happy when they talked about hot dogs," he recalls. "I said, 'That's the type of excitement I want in my next job.'"

Sparky's is located in a former fish warehouse, with cracked concrete walls, rough wooden beams, bare light bulbs, and varnished pine tables. A picture of Benavidez's dog, Sparky, marks the entrance, which was once a loading dock—about as low-tech a business location as there is.

Sources: http://www.newyorkmetro.com/pages/details/9183.htm, April 8, 2004; and Mark Henricks, "Back to Basics," *Entrepreneur,* September 2003, pp. 19–20, reprinted with permission.

the agreement under certain conditions. And an attorney can ensure that an entrepreneur will not be unduly exposed to liability for damages caused by the gross negligence of others. Consider the experience of one firm that wished to rent 300 square feet of storage space in a large complex of offices and shops. On the sixth page of the landlord's standard lease, the firm's lawyer found language that could have made the firm responsible for the entire 30,000-square-foot complex if it burned down, regardless of blame!

DESIGNING AND EQUIPPING THE PHYSICAL FACILITIES

2 *Discuss the challenges of designing and equipping a physical facility.*

A location plan should describe the physical space in which the business will be housed and include an explanation of equipment needs. Although the plan may call for a new building or an existing structure, ordinarily a new business occupies an existing building, with minor or major remodeling.

Challenges in Designing the Physical Facilities

When specifying building requirements, the entrepreneur must avoid committing to a space that is too large or too luxurious. At the same time, the space should not be too small or too austere for efficient operation. Buildings do not produce profits directly; they merely house the operations and personnel that do so. Therefore, the ideal building is practical, not pretentious.

The general suitability of a building for a given type of business operation depends on the functional requirements of the business. For example, a restaurant should ideally be on one level. Other important factors are the age and condition of the building, fire hazards, heating and air conditioning, lighting and restroom facilities, and entrances and exits. Obviously, these factors are weighted differently for a factory operation than for a wholesale or retail operation. But in any case, the comfort, convenience, and safety of the business's employees and customers must not be overlooked.

Challenges in Equipping the Physical Facilities

The final step in arranging for physical facilities is the purchase or lease of equipment and tools. The types of equipment and tools required obviously depend on the nature of the business. Even within the three areas discussed here—manufacturing, retailing, and office equipment—there is great variation in the need for tools and equipment.

MANUFACTURING EQUIPMENT Machines used in a factory may be either general purpose or special purpose.

General-Purpose Equipment **General-purpose equipment** requires a minimal investment and is easily adapted to varied types of operations. Small machine shops and cabinet shops, for example, utilize this type of equipment. General-purpose equipment for metalworking includes lathes, drill presses, and milling machines. In a woodworking plant, general-purpose machines include ripsaws, planing mills, and lathes. In each case, jigs, fixtures, and other tooling items set up on the basic machinery can be changed so that two or more shop operations can be accomplished using the same piece of equipment. General-purpose equipment contributes important flexibility in industries in which products are so new that the technology is not yet well developed or there are frequent design changes.

general-purpose equipment
Machines that serve many functions in the production process

Special-Purpose Equipment **Special-purpose equipment** can reduce costs in industries in which the technology is fully established and capacity operation is more or less ensured by high sales volume. Bottling machines and automobile assembly-line machinery are examples of special-purpose equipment used in factories. A milking machine in a dairy is an example of special-purpose equipment used by small firms. A small firm cannot, however, use special-purpose equipment economically unless it makes a standardized product on a fairly large scale. Using special-purpose machines with specialized tooling results in greater output per machine-hour of operation. The labor cost per unit of product is, therefore, lower. However, the initial cost of such equipment is much higher, and it has little or no resale value because of its highly specialized function.

special-purpose equipment
Machines designed to serve specialized functions in the production process

RETAIL STORE EQUIPMENT Small retailers need merchandise display racks or counters, storage racks, shelving, mirrors, seats for customers, customer pushcarts, cash registers, and other items to facilitate selling. Such equipment may be costly, but it is usually less expensive than that necessary for a factory operation.

If a store is intended to serve a high-income market, its fixtures should display the elegance and style expected by such customers. For example, polished mahogany showcases with bronze fittings lend a richness to the atmosphere. Indirect lighting, thick rugs, and big easy chairs also contribute to an air of luxury. In contrast, a store that caters to lower-income customers should concentrate on simplicity, as luxurious fixtures create an atmosphere inconsistent with low prices.

OFFICE EQUIPMENT Obviously, every business office needs furniture, storage cabinets, and other such items. The more challenging task is selecting office equipment—computers, fax machines, copiers, printers, and telephone systems—that reflects the latest advances in technology applicable to a particular business.

The location plan should list the major pieces of equipment needed to furnish a business office. Careful selection of equipment helps a business operate efficiently. Also, by identifying major equipment needs in this section of the business plan, the entrepreneur can ensure that the financial section of the plan includes funds for their purchase.

Building Image

All new ventures, whether they are retailers, wholesalers, manufacturers, or service businesses, should be concerned with projecting the appropriate image to customers and the public at large. The appearance of the workplace should create a favorable impression about the quality of a firm's product or service and, generally, about the way the business is operated. For a small firm, it is important to use the physical facilities to convey the image of a stable, professional company.

LOCATING THE STARTUP IN THE ENTREPRENEUR'S HOME

Rather than lease or buy a commercial site, many entrepreneurs elect to use their basement, garage, or spare room for their business operation, creating a **home-based business**. In the past, a home location for a business was regarded as second-rate. "Ten years ago, if you were working out of your home, it was like you had some sort of disease," says Don Vlaek, a former employee at a pizza business who now works from his home as a consultant. But times have changed, and home-based entrepreneurs no longer feel

3 Understand both the attraction and the challenges of creating a home-based startup.

home-based business
A business that maintains its primary facility in the residence of its owner

embarrassed about their location. The home office, once simply a stage in the growth of many businesses, is a viable permanent option for some. At present, many entrepreneurs have no plans to ever move out of the home.

The Attraction of Home-Based Businesses

Why do many entrepreneurs find operating a business at home so attractive? Although motivations vary (see Exhibit 9-3), the main attractions of a home-based business relate to financial and family lifestyle consideration.

FINANCIAL CONSIDERATIONS Like most business ventures, a home-based business has an important goal—earning money—and locating at home helps increase profits by reducing costs. This was the motivation of Bianca Wright, who does freelance writing for magazines. She needed a computer, office supplies, and an Internet connection for her home-based business venture. Since she already owned a computer, her startup costs were only about $150.[11]

The cost of a "real office" prompted Mike Ball to operate his ad agency from a former boathouse/garage that overlooks Whitmore Lake, near Ann Arbor, Michigan. Ball started working at home in 1991, intending to relocate to a commercial site.

> *But when the time came, he asked himself, why assume the monthly overhead of rent on a 2,000-square-foot office, which he would have to fill with a secretary/office manager, a production assistant, an art director, and perhaps an account executive—employees he'd have to pink-slip should business fluctuate? . . . Ball decided to stay the course, sailing on with his virtual company and sub-contracting work out to other home-based entrepreneurs. He communicates with them, and with his clients by fax, E-mail, and a corporate Web site.*[12]

Receiving full compensation for her work was Rose Anne Raphael's motivation for starting a home-based business. Her boyfriend noticed her employer was billing clients seven times as much as Raphael was earning. "I was getting paid $17 an hour and the company was billing clients at $125 an hour for my work. . . . That's when I thought I had the opportunity to become self-employed," says Raphael. She's been running a public-relations firm out of a one-bedroom apartment in Berkeley, California, ever since.[13]

FAMILY LIFESTYLE CONSIDERATIONS Many young entrepreneurs remain in a family business because of close family ties. Similarly, entrepreneurs who locate business operations in the home are frequently motivated by the desire to spend more time with family members. Consider the following examples:

> *Nine years of hard work at two Chicago ad agencies had earned Barbara Casey an account executive title and a comfortable $50,000 salary. But after giving birth to her first child five years ago, Casey decided to cut back to a four-day week. Her boss objected, so Casey walked out and started a small ad shop in her Naperville, Illinois home. When her business outgrew the guest bedroom, she and her husband bought a bigger house.*[14]

> *Eighteen months ago, Daniel A. Shlifer parlayed a job as a professional speaker's "go-fer" into a home-based business offering support services for speakers and others. Now his Longboat Key, Florida–based business has so much work he subcontracts out some of it so he can still jet ski and watch dolphins frolic in the Gulf of Mexico. "I tried to design a business where I would be at home and in a beautiful area where I can [fish], ride my jet skis and enjoy what this place has to offer," said Mr. Shlifer, who has the Gulf of Mexico as a backyard.*[15]

> *Back in 1996, . . . Joe Roetheli was working in Kansas City for the U.S. Department of Agriculture. Asked to move back to Washington, D.C., where he had worked for six years previously, he demurred. He had had enough of the traffic, crime and high costs of an urban environment. . . . Furthermore, [his] sons, then in high school, were very outspoken about not wanting to return to the D.C. area. Joe spent about six weeks in the basement, mixing lotions and potions, and came up with a formula that turned Ivan's breath (the family dog) into Tupelo honey. [The] company's incorporation followed quickly, in August 1996, and that's when the home adventure really began.*[16]

EXHIBIT 9-3 *Entrepreneurs' Reasons for Operating a Home-Based Business*

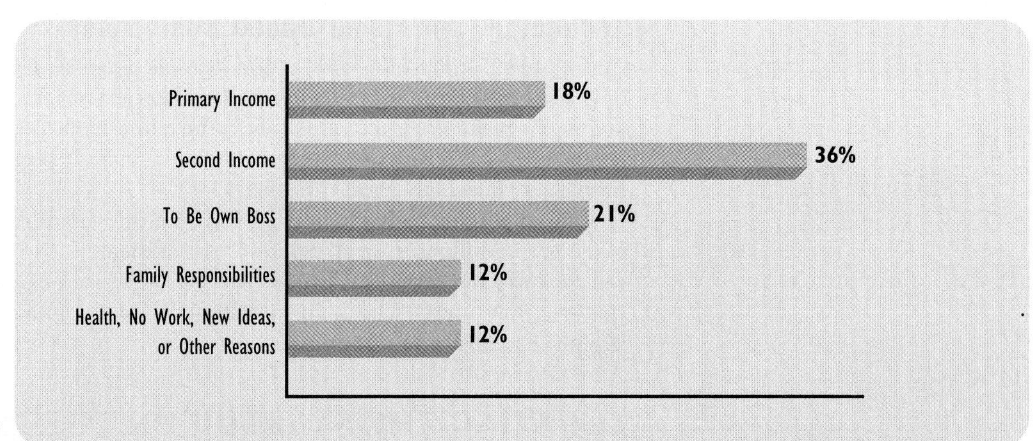

Source: "Home-Based Business: The Hidden Economy," *The Small Business Advocate*, Vol. 19, No. 2 (Spring 2000), p. 6.

The Challenges of Home-Based Businesses

Just as most businesses located at commercial sites have their problems, home-based businesses face special challenges attributable to their location. We will briefly examine two of these challenges—business image and legal considerations. Another major challenge—family and business conflicts—was discussed in Chapter 5.

BUSINESS IMAGE Maintaining an image of professionalism when working at home is a major challenge for home-based entrepreneurs. Allowing young children to answer the telephone, for example, may undermine a professional image. Likewise, a baby crying or a dog barking in the background during a phone call can be distracting to a client.

If clients or salespeople visit the home-based business, it is critical that a professional office area be maintained. Space limitations sometimes make this difficult. Such was the experience of Scott Walker, owner of a family-owned firm, IceBreaker Enterprises of Atlanta, which manufactures the novelty party game Walla Balla. His office is located in the basement of his home. Walker recalls the day a salesperson came to the office: "She came into the house and down the dark stairs to our dimly lit basement office. Throughout the entire meeting, I could tell she was uncomfortable about her surroundings."[17]

LEGAL CONSIDERATIONS Some local laws pose a problem for home-based businesses. **Zoning ordinances**, for example, regulate the types of enterprises permitted in various geographical areas. Some cities outlaw any type of home-based business within city limits.

zoning ordinances
Local laws regulating land use

Many zoning laws, dating as far back as the 1930s, have never been updated. The intent of such laws is to protect a neighborhood's residential quality by preventing commercial signs and parking problems. Unfortunately, some entrepreneurs first become aware of these zoning laws when neighbors initiate zoning enforcement action. Consider "good neighbor" Lauren Januz of Libertyville Township, Illinois.

> *One of Januz's neighbors was running a landscaping and tree-service business out of his home. He erected a large fence to obscure the view of his heavy equipment which was fine with the subdivision's other residents, but he had 10 to 15 workers parking their cars on the street every day. "This is an area of $300,000 homes, and a lot of the cars were really wrecks," explains Januz. Although several neighbors approached the offending property owner, he made no attempt to correct the problem, and a complaint was finally filed with the Lake County Building and Zoning Department. He ended up selling the property and relocating the business.*[18]

There are also tax issues related to a home-based business. Generally, a separate space must be clearly devoted to business activities in order for the entrepreneur to claim a tax deduction. A certified public accountant can be helpful in explaining these tax regulations.

Insurance considerations may also affect a home-based business. An entrepreneur's homeowner's policy is not likely to cover business activities, liabilities, and equipment.

Technology and Home-Based Businesses

Advancements in business-application technology are a major catalyst in the rapid growth of home-based businesses. Personal computers, fax machines, voice mail, and e-mail are among the technological tools that help the home-based business compete effectively with commercial-site businesses. Such technology makes it possible to operate many types of businesses almost anywhere.

One important technological tool available to home-based businesses is the World Wide Web. Millions of small firms—many of them based at home—are using the Web to sell products and services. Virtually every product sold in traditional retail outlets is now sold over the Internet. In the next section, we will examine the potential of the Internet as a place to host a new business.

LOCATING THE STARTUP ON THE INTERNET

4 *Understand the potential benefits of locating a startup on the Internet.*

We currently live in a digital economy fueled by the tremendous growth of the Internet. Access to the Internet continues to transform the way we live and the way business is conducted. It is important for aspiring entrepreneurs to learn as much as they can about cyberspace because *there's opportunity online*—despite the bursting of the dot-com bubble in 2002.

What is the Internet, and how does it support e-commerce? What benefits does e-commerce offer the startup? What business models reflect an e-commerce strategy? These are the primary questions we address in this section of the chapter. We hope that our discussions will help you understand both the opportunities and the limitations associated with today's digital economy. Additional e-commerce topics are discussed in other chapters.

What Is E-Commerce?

e-commerce
The paperless exchange of business information via the Internet

What does the term *e-commerce* really describe? **E-commerce** means electronic commerce, or the paperless exchange of business information via the Internet. It is an alternative means of conducting business transactions that traditionally have been carried out by telephone, by mail, or face to face in brick-and-mortar stores. Internet businesses continue to grow in numbers, despite a crash in Web-based stocks in 2000 and 2002.

Although the Internet, like the telephone, is basically a tool that parties use to communicate with each other, it is a communication medium unlike any previously available to companies. A Web location reshapes the way small firms conduct business, while also providing an alternative to the brick-and-mortar store.

Benefits of E-Commerce to Startups

Electronic commerce benefits a startup in a number of ways. Basically, it offers the new firm the opportunity to compete with bigger businesses on a more level playing field. Limited resources frequently restrict the ability of small firms to reach beyond local markets. Confined to their brick-and-mortar world, small firms typically serve a restricted geographic area. But the Internet blurs geographic boundaries. E-commerce allows any business access to customers almost anywhere. The Internet is proving to be a great equalizer, giving small firms a presence comparable to that of the giants in the marketplace. For example, Jill-Anne Partain operates her handbag manufacturing business in Lexington, Virginia—a favorable production site—and then uses the Web to sell her upscale products for as much as $550 each. Partain employs no sales or marketing staff, relying on the one-to-one relationships created with her customers through the Internet. Her company, Pilgrim Designs, was named one of the top 30 "style-packed" Web sites by *Harper's Bazaar* magazine.[19]

An e-commerce operation can help the startup with early cash flow problems by compressing the sales cycle—that is, reducing the time between receiving an order and converting the sale to cash. E-commerce systems can be designed to generate an order, authorize a credit card purchase, and contact a supplier and shipper in a matter of minutes, all without human assistance. The shorter cycle translates into quicker payments from customers and improved cash flows to the business.

E-commerce also enables small firms to build on one of their greatest strengths—customer relationships. The Internet has brought new life and technology to bear on the old-fashioned notion of customer service. **Electronic Customer Relationship Marketing (eCRM)** is an electronically based system that emphasizes customer relationships. At the heart of eCRM is a customer-centric data warehouse. A typical eCRM system allows an e-commerce firm to integrate data from Web sites, call centers, sales force reports, and other customer contact points, with the goal of building customer loyalty.

Electronic Customer Relationship Marketing (eCRM)
An electronically based system that emphasizes customer relationships

There are, of course, innumerable other benefits that small firms can reap from e-commerce; space does not allow us to discuss them all here. And as e-commerce continues to evolve, additional benefits will emerge.

E-Commerce Business Models

The dictionary defines an opportunity as a "combination of circumstances favorable for a chance to advance oneself." Thus, it is logical to study the circumstances surrounding e-commerce in order to uncover the potential of the Internet as a startup location. Let's begin by examining some existing e-commerce business models.

The term **business model** describes a group of shared characteristics, behaviors, and goals that a firm follows in a particular business situation. Online business firms differ in their decisions concerning which customers to serve, how best to become profitable, and what to include on their Web sites. Exhibit 9-4 shows some possible alternatives for business models. None of these models can currently be considered dominant, and some Internet businesses cannot be described by any single model. The real world of e-commerce contains endless combinations of business models. However, it is important to keep in mind that a poorly devised business model can be a major factor in business failure.

business model
A group of shared characteristics, behaviors, and goals that a firm follows in a particular business situation

TYPE OF CUSTOMERS SERVED Marketing theory classifies traditional brick-and-mortar firms as manufacturers, wholesalers, or retailers, depending on the customers they serve. E-commerce businesses also are commonly distinguished according to customer focus. There are three major categories of e-commerce business models: business-to-business (B2B), business-to-consumer (B2C), and auction sites. In this section, we examine some strategies used by e-commerce firms within these three categories.

Business-to-Business Models The dollar amounts generated by firms using a **business-to-business (B2B) model** (selling to business customers) are significantly greater than those listed for firms with a business-to-consumer (B2C) model (selling to final consumers). Because B2B success stories generally receive less publicity than B2C ventures do, the potential of a B2B opportunity may be overlooked. Aspiring entrepreneurs should be sure to consider the B2B model.

business-to-business (B2B) model
A business model based on selling to business customers electronically

All B2B firms do not look alike. One form of B2B strategy emphasizes sales transactions. By using online capabilities, a B2B firm can achieve greater efficiency in its selling

9-4 *E-Commerce Business Models*

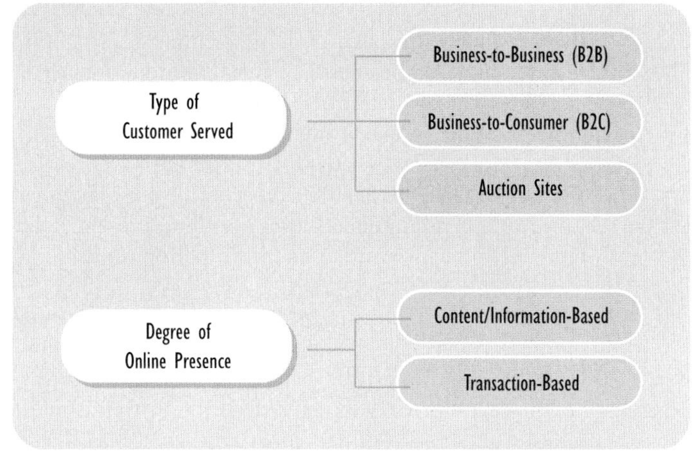

and buying. Dell Computer Corporation is a good example. By dealing directly with its corporate customers online, it is able to build computers to specifications *after* an order is placed. Inventory storage and carrying costs are reduced, and dealing directly with Dell allows the buyer to pay less. Through online connections with hundreds of suppliers, Dell also is able to implement more efficient delivery of parts for its factories.

As B2B e-commerce models continue to develop and evolve, new versions will emerge. The wise entrepreneur will continue to monitor these changes to learn where opportunities lie.

business-to-consumer (B2C) model
A business model based on selling to final customers electronically

Business-to-Consumer Models In contrast to a B2B model, a **business-to-consumer (B2C) model** has final consumers as customers. In the traditional retail setting, customers generally approach a business location (a brick-and-mortar store) with the intent of shopping or purchasing. Alternatively, customers might purchase via telephone or mail order, using a printed catalog. The B2C model introduces another alternative for consumers—buying online.

Amazon.com represents the classic B2C firm, which is directly focused on individual final consumers. B2C ventures are extremely diverse in the products they sell, with offerings ranging from clothing to pet items, computer software, toys, and groceries. The B2C model offers three main advantages over brick-and-mortar retailing: speed of access, speed of transaction, and round-the-clock access to products and services, often referred to as **24/7 e-tailing**.

24/7 e-tailing
Electronic retailing providing round-the-clock access to products and services

It is true that many final consumers avoid online shopping for several reasons, the primary ones being reluctance to send credit card data electronically and to purchase a product without first seeing it. However, B2C dot-com businesses have the ability to quickly change merchandise mixes and prices, as well as the appearance of their "store" (their Web site). Traditional merchants located in brick-and-mortar stores find such changes very costly and time-consuming.

Auction Site Models Some entrepreneurs sell their wares over the Internet without either a Web site or a storefront, by means of e-commerce sites based on the auction site model. Internet **auction sites** are Web-based businesses offering participants—primarily final consumers, but also businesses—the ability to list products for bidding by potential buyers. Revenues to the auction site are derived from listing fees and commissions on sales.

auction sites
Web-based businesses offering participants the ability to list products for bidding

The earliest e-commerce auction sites dealt with collectibles. For example, consider entrepreneur Geri Loendorf's business.

> *Unplanned but undeniably successful is an accurate description of Geri Loendorf's Fullerton, California, jewelry business, dubbed GEMdesign. While working full time in a graphic arts job, Loendorf had to take more and more time off due to family obligations. But fewer work hours meant smaller paychecks, so to supplement her income, Loendorf turned to eBay in hopes of auctioning off some of her old jewelry creations that were languishing in storage. To her surprise, her bejeweled stickpins and hat pins quickly sold out, with customers asking for more. "It surprised the heck out of me that the pins took off the way they did," laughs Loendorf.*[20]

But now such sites are conduits for almost any kind of product. EBay is one of the largest e-commerce businesses using this model. The search engine Yahoo! also has an auction site, which offers free postings and no commissions (http://auctions.yahoo.com). And there are many, many others.

DEGREE OF ONLINE PRESENCE A second broad way of categorizing e-commerce models relates to the firm's intended level of online presence. The role of a Web site can range from merely offering content and information to enabling complex business transactions.

content/information-based model
A business model in which the Web site provides information but not the ability to buy or sell products and services

Content/Information-Based Model In a **content/information-based model** of e-commerce, a Web site provides access but not the ability to buy or sell products and services. During the early days of e-commerce, the *content model* was the model of choice. For example, America Online (AOL) began with this model. Originally, revenue for AOL

Living the Dream

Utilizing the Internet

Student Entrepreneur Turns to "Blogging"

One of the newest Internet crazes is "blogging," or Web logging—creating an online venue to chronicle a person's thoughts. Bloggers produce online journals to trade comments with friends and readers. Small firms have found blogs easy to use and thus an attractive platform from which to promote a sale on an overstocked item or to give an employee special recognition.

Adam Weinroth used his winter break from the University of Texas in 2001 to build his initial version of the Easyjournal Web site, designed to attract novice bloggers. Now, Easyjournal has over 70,000 registered members. The site offers both a free account and a paid account with additional features. These features include a public comment board and journal templates, as well as other services. The site also brings in revenue from advertising.

Weinroth has built his site on a shoestring budget of less than $10,000. He is, however, working on a business plan that would enable him to continue with site upgrades.

Blogging is growing rapidly, and Weinroth is riding the wave of its popularity.

© John C. Livas/Austin American-Statesman

http://www.easyjournal.com

Sources: http://www.easyjournal.com/about.html, April 8, 2004; and Kirk Ladendorf, "Blogging It Through," *Waco Tribune-Herald*, August 14, 2003, p. 4B; and "Ease into Business Blogging," *MyBusiness*, October-November 2004, p. 24.

came from fees paid by users for the privilege of connecting and gaining access to its content. Today, many content models are still found, mostly in countries where Internet usage by small firms is less developed.

A slight variation of the content model is the *information-based model*. A Web site built on this model contains information about the business, its products, and other related matters but doesn't charge for its use. It is typically just a complement to an existing brick-and-mortar store. An example of an information-based model is provided by WeMailSmiles.com. Betty Jo Houck, of Cuyahoga Falls, Ohio, operates this Web site, which displays lawn ornaments. Information regarding the products is available on the site, but online orders can be placed only by linking to another site.[21]

Transaction-Based Model In a **transaction-based model** of e-commerce, a Web site provides a mechanism for buying or selling products or services. The transaction-based model, which is at the very heart of e-commerce, calls for Web sites to be online stores where visitors go to shop, click, and buy.

transaction-based model
A business model in which the Web site provides a mechanism for buying or selling products or services

Many Internet ventures sell a single product or service. For example, Huber and Jane Wilkinson, based in Waco, Texas, market their reading comprehension program, Ideachain, through their MindPrime, Inc., Web site. Similarly, Phil Rockell and his wife, Stephanie, of Helotes, Texas, sell hillbilly teeth pacifiers only from their Web site. Other ventures are direct extensions of a brick-and-mortar store, creating a click-and-mortar strategy. For example, if you were interested in purchasing a new printer, you might research options on Office Depot's Web site and then choose to either buy your selection online or drive to the neighborhood Office Depot store and pick up the printer there. Gradually, a small firm can add to and improve its Web site store until all of its products are available online.

Clearly, the location decision is complicated but vital to a successful venture. Take your time, and make a wise choice.

Looking Back

1 Describe the five key factors in locating the brick-and-mortar startup.

- Customer accessibility is a key factor in the location decision of retail and service businesses.
- Climate, competition, legal requirements, and the tax structure are types of environmental factors affecting the location decision.
- Availability of resources such as raw materials, labor supply, and transportation is important to location decisions.
- The entrepreneur's personal preference is a practical consideration in selecting a location.
- An appropriate site must be available and priced within the entrepreneur's budget.

2 Discuss the challenges of designing and equipping a physical facility.

- The ideal building is practical, not pretentious.
- The general suitability of a building depends on the functional requirements of the business.
- The comfort, convenience, and safety of the business's employees and customers must not be overlooked.
- Most small manufacturing firms must use general-purpose equipment, although some can use special-purpose equipment for standardized operations.
- The cost of special-purpose equipment is high, and it has little or no resale value because of its highly specialized function.
- Small retailers must have merchandise display racks and counters, mirrors, and other equipment that facilitates selling.
- Display counters and other retailing equipment should create an atmosphere appropriate for customers in the retailer's target market.
- Entrepreneurs must select office equipment that reflects the latest advances in technology applicable to a particular business.

3 Understand both the attraction and the challenges of creating a home-based startup.

- Home-based businesses are started to both make money and incorporate family lifestyle considerations.
- Operating a business at home can pose challenges, particularly in the areas of business image and legal considerations.
- Technology, especially the Web, has helped entrepreneurs start home-based businesses.

4 Understand the potential benefits of locating a startup on the Internet.

- E-commerce offers small firms the opportunity to compete with bigger companies on a more level playing field.
- Internet operations can help small firms with cash flow problems by compressing sales cycles.
- E-commerce enables small firms to build stronger customer relationships.
- New versions of the business-to-business (B2B) model continue to develop and evolve.
- The three main advantages of online business-to-consumer (B2C) firms are speed of access, speed of transaction, and continuous access to products and services, often referred to as 24/7 e-tailing.
- Auction sites are online firms that bring buyers and sellers together.
- The role of a Web site can range from merely offering content and information to permitting the buying and selling of products and services online.

Key Terms

brick-and-mortar store, p. 187
enterprise zones, p. 189
business incubator, p. 191
general-purpose equipment, p. 193
special-purpose equipment, p. 193
home-based business, p. 193
zoning ordinances, p. 195
e-commerce, p. 196
Electronic Customer Relationship Marketing (eCRM), p. 197
business model, p. 197
business-to-business (B2B) model, p. 197
business-to-consumer (B2C) model, p. 198
24/7 e-tailing, p. 198
auction sites, p. 198
content/information-based model, p. 198
transaction-based model, p. 199

Discussion Questions

1. What are the key attributes of a good business location? Which of these would probably be most important for a retail location? Why?
2. What is the special appeal of an enterprise zone to an entrepreneur seeking the best site for his or her business?
3. Which resource factors might be most vital to a new manufacturing venture that produces residential home furniture? Why?
4. Is the hometown of the business owner likely to be a good location? Is it logical for an owner to allow personal preferences to influence a decision about business location? Explain your answers.
5. Discuss the conditions under which a new small manufacturer should buy (a) general-purpose equipment and (b) special-purpose equipment.
6. Under what conditions would it be most appropriate for a new firm to buy rather than lease a building for the business?
7. What factors should an entrepreneur evaluate when considering a home-based business? Be specific.
8. Discuss how zoning and tax laws might impact the decision to start a home-based business.
9. Discuss the two different ways of categorizing business models used for e-commerce.
10. Contrast B2B and B2C businesses. Identify some of the reasons final consumers give for not using online shopping.

You Make the Call

SITUATION 1

Gary Fuller and his wife, Kelly Kimberly, have a dream of owning a successful restaurant. Three and a half years ago, Fuller was vice president of operations for a Cincinnati Bell affiliate; Kimberly was a public relations consultant. Now, they are considering a startup venture in Houston, Texas.

Early in their research, they uncovered some discouraging statistics about the restaurant industry: Profit margins run about 1 to 5 percent; one in three new restaurants don't last a year; and, because of the current economy, plans for new restaurants have been shelved by many existing companies. One industry consultant they contacted said the cost of setting up an average restaurant, like a diner, is around $300 per square foot—excluding property costs.

Source: Emily Lambert, "No Free Lunch," *Forbes,* Vol. 171, No. 12 (June 9, 2003), p. 154.

Question 1 How important will the location decision be to these two entrepreneurs? Why?

Question 2 What types of permits and zoning ordinances might they need to consider if they decide to pursue their dream?

Question 3 How could a presence on the Internet help with the success of this venture?

SITUATION 2

Estate Administrators and Liquidators is based in Sacramento, California, and is owned and operated by entrepreneur Sally Wheeler-Valine. Since 1990, the firm has served people seeking to sell the household goods of deceased friends or relatives.

The business auctions items at the deceased person's home, splitting the proceeds with the family. Any unsold items are taken back to the firm's store and sold, generating a commission based on the selling price.

To accommodate the large volume of merchandise she sells, Wheeler-Valine operates out of a new 13,000-square-foot store. Business revenues climbed for several years, peaking in 1997. However, in 1999, revenues slumped drastically.

Source: Based on a story by Susan Hanson, "Store's Demise Blamed on Web Auctions," *Inc.,* July 2000, p. 41.

Question 1 What impact, if any, do you think that Internet-based businesses have had on Wheeler-Valine's business?

Question 2 In what way(s) could she use e-commerce to grow her business?

Question 3 How much presence on the Web, if any, do you think she should consider?

Question 4 What do you think will happen to this firm if it ignores the Internet?

SITUATION 3

A business incubator rents space to a number of small firms that are just beginning operations or are fairly new. In addition to supplying space, the incubator provides a receptionist, computer, conference room, fax machine, and copy machine. It also offers management counseling and assists new businesses in getting reduced advertising rates and reduced legal fees. One client of the incubator is a jewelry repair, cleaning, and remounting service that does work on a contract basis for pawn shops and jewelry stores. Another is a home health-care company that employs a staff of nurses to visit the homes of elderly people who need daily care but who cannot afford or are not yet ready to go to a nursing home.

Question 1 Evaluate each of the services offered by the incubator in terms of its usefulness to these two businesses. Which of the two businesses seems to be a better fit for the incubator? Why?

Question 2 If rental costs for incubator space were similar to rental costs for space outside the incubator, would the benefits of the services offered seem to favor location in the incubator? Why or why not?

SITUATION 4

Entrepreneur Karen Moore wants to start a catering and decorating business to bring in money to help support her two young children. Moore is a single parent; she works in the banking industry but has always had the desire to start a business. She enjoys decorating for friends' parties and is frequently told, "You should do this professionally. You have such good taste, and you are so nice to people."

Moore has decided to take this advice but is unsure whether she should locate in a commercial site or in her home, which is in rural central Texas. She is leaning toward locating at home because she wants more time with her children. However, she is concerned that the home-based location is too far away from the city, where most of her potential customers live.

Initially, her services would include planning for wedding receptions and other special events, designing flower arrangements, decorating the sites, and even cooking and serving meals.

Question 1 What do you see as potential problems with locating Moore's new business at home?

Question 2 What do you see as the major benefits for Moore of a home-based business?

Question 3 How could Moore use technology to help her operate a home-based business?

Experiential Exercises

1. Search for articles in business periodicals that provide rankings of states or cities as business sites. Log on to InfoTrac College Edition at http://www.infotrac-college.com to find articles on site rankings. Report on your findings.
2. Identify and evaluate a local site that is now vacant because of a business closure. Point out the strengths and weaknesses of that location for the former business, and comment on the part location may have played in the closure.
3. Interview a small business owner concerning the strengths and weaknesses of his or her business's location. Prepare a brief report summarizing your findings.
4. Interview a local small business that you believe might benefit from e-commerce. Prepare a report on the e-commerce strategy being pursued or the reasons this particular business is not involved in e-commerce.
5. Contact the Chamber of Commerce office in your local area and ask what e-commerce assistance it provides to small firms. Report on your findings.

Exploring the Web

1. Go to the Women's Business Center at **http://www.onlinewbc.gov** and search for information on choosing a business location. Choose the "Business Basics" tab on the site's main page and follow the "Starting Your Business" link to "Choosing a Location for Your Business," where you will find a lengthy list of questions developed to help you zero in on locations appropriate to your business.
   a. Answer several of the location questions in terms of your business plan.
   b. Are there questions on the list that you had not yet considered? What are they and why are they important to your location decision?
2. The mission of the Nolo Web site is to "make the legal system work for everyone—not just lawyers." Test the veracity of this claim. Visit the site at **http://www.nolo.com**, click on the "Plain-English Law Centers" tab, and then drill down one more level to Nolo's Small Business Law Center.
   a. Read the information related to home-based businesses and generate a list of five points that you would consider before starting a home-based business.
   b. List several ways that you could document use of a home office for tax deduction purposes.

3. The Nolo Web site's Law Center at **http://www.nolo.com/lawcenter/** also includes coverage of Internet law.
   a. Link to at least three online resources on this topic provided by Nolo.
   b. Evaluate the potential of the Internet to host a fashion-accessory business similar to Pilgrim Designs, mentioned in the text on page 196. Summarize your thoughts in a one-page document. Be sure to consider obstacles concerning domain name and dispute resolution related to online purchases.

Case 9

THE CHOCOLATE FARM (P. 540)
The experience of two young entrepreneurs demonstrates how the Web can be a good location for a business startup.

Alternative Case for Chapter 9:
Case 16, Solid Gold Health Products for Pets, p. 555

The Business Plan

LAYING THE FOUNDATION

As part of laying the foundation for preparing your own business plan, respond to the following questions regarding location.

Brick-and-Mortar Startup Location Questions

1. How important are your personal reasons for choosing a location?
2. What business environment factors will influence your location decision?
3. What resources are most critical to your location decision?
4. How important is customer accessibility to your location decision?
5. What special resources do you need?
6. How will the formal site evaluation be conducted?
7. What laws and tax policies of state and local governments have been considered?
8. What is the cost of the proposed site?
9. Is an enterprise zone available in the area where you want to locate?

Physical Facility Questions

1. What are the major considerations in choosing between a new and an existing building?
2. What is the possibility of leasing a building or equipment?
3. How feasible is it to locate in a business incubator?
4. What is the major objective of your building design?
5. What types of equipment do you need for your business?

Home-Based Startup Location Questions

1. Will a home-based business be a possibility for you?
2. What are the advantages and disadvantages of a home-based business?
3. Have you given consideration to family lifestyle issues?
4. Will your home project the appropriate image for the business?
5. What zoning ordinances, if any, regulate the type of home-based business you want to start?

Internet Startup Questions

1. What type of customers will be served by the Internet startup?
2. What degree of online presence will you strive for?

THE FINANCIAL PLAN: PART 1

PROJECTING FINANCIAL REQUIREMENTS

In the Spotlight

DailyCandy

In this day and age, even dot-com firms have to think about how to become profitable sooner, rather than later. Having a great concept, but no profits for the foreseeable future, is no longer acceptable. Entrepreneur Dany Levy understands the importance of becoming profitable as soon as possible.

Levy, a journalist turned entrepreneur, runs a profitable, popular Internet company called DailyCandy. Every morning, this ad revenue–based firm feeds its reported 90,000 e-mail subscribers their regimen of what's hip at that very moment.

To get the word out, I sent e-mails to all of my journalist and nonjournalist friends, asking them to forward them to all of their friends. The e-mail gave them a taste of what DailyCandy was going to be, and it said something like, "Sign up now. Be first. Be in the know." Before I launched, I had 700 subscribers. Knowing people in the magazine industry helped, not really in generating press, but in growing my subscriber list and giving me credibility. Any time you branch out in an industry, it helps to have already made a name for yourself.

In the beginning, I made it my primary goal to spend as little as possible and to work hard on growing my subscriber base, developing a brand, and building a product people could trust. In my head I set the goal of one year to become profitable. It ended up being a year and a half. We sold our first ad in the fall of 2000, and by the third quarter of 2001 we became profitable.

One reason my company is still here and growing is that I didn't go along with the cash-shredding of that time. I didn't take venture capital, hire 200 people, and spend money like crazy. I had the mentality of, "I don't care if I'm running a lemonade stand or a dot-com, it's the same thing. How much do the lemons cost and how much are people buying? Maybe I'd better find some cheaper lemons or make less lemonade. Maybe I need to improve the quality of my lemonade."

Courtesy of www.DailyCandy.com

Source: Bobbie Gossage, "How I Did It," *Inc.*, Vol. 26, No. 2 (February 2004), p. 60.

Chapter 10

Looking Ahead

After studying this chapter, you should be able to

1 *Describe the purpose and content of the income statement, the balance sheet, and the cash flow statement.*

2 *Forecast a new venture's profitability.*

3 *Determine asset requirements, evaluate financial sources, and estimate cash flows for a new venture.*

4 *Explain the importance of using good judgment when making projections.*

A good idea may or may not be a good investment opportunity. As we discussed in Chapter 3, a good investment opportunity requires a product or service that meets a definite customer need and creates a sustainable competitive advantage. To be attractive, an opportunity must generate strong profits relative to the required amount of investment.

Therefore, projections of a venture's profits, its asset and financing requirements, and its cash flows are essential in determining whether a venture is economically feasible. In order to make such financial projections, an entrepreneur must have a good understanding of financial statements.

UNDERSTANDING FINANCIAL STATEMENTS

The goal in this chapter is not to make you an accountant, but to help you understand the consequences of your decisions; otherwise, you can get into big trouble!

1 *Describe the purpose and content of the income statement, the balance sheet, and the cash flow statement.*

In the sections that follow, you will learn how to construct **financial statements**, also called **accounting statements.** Three basic financial statements provide important information about a firm's performance and resources: the income statement, the balance sheet, and the cash flow statement. Only with this essential information can you assess a firm's potential. Let's begin with a discussion of the income statement.

The Income Statement

An **income statement**, or **profit and loss statement**, indicates the amount of profits generated by a firm over a given time period, usually monthly or yearly. In its most basic form, the income statement may be represented by the following equation:

$$\text{Sales (revenue)} - \text{Expenses} = \text{Profits}$$

As Exhibit 10-1 (on page 207) shows, an income statement begins with sales, or revenue, from which is subtracted the **cost of goods sold** (that is, the cost of producing or acquiring the product or service) to yield the firm's **gross profit**. Next, **operating expenses**, consisting of marketing and selling expenses, general and administrative expenses, and depreciation expense, are deducted to determine **operating income** (also called *earnings before interest and taxes*).

The first section of the income statement shows the consequences of management's decisions about the *operations* of the business, which involve the processes of buying and selling the firm's products or services. More specifically, the operating income of a firm includes the results of the following activities:

1. The pricing decisions for the product or service and the number of units sold (*selling price* × *units sold* = *total sales*)
2. The cost of producing or acquiring the goods or service to be sold (*cost of goods sold*)
3. The expenses incurred in selling and marketing the firm's product or service
4. The firm's overhead expenses (*general and administrative expenses and depreciation expenses*)

financial statements (accounting statements)
Reports of a firm's financial performance and resources, including an income statement, a balance sheet, and a cash flow statement

income statement (profit and loss statement)
A financial report showing the profit or loss from a firm's operations over a given period of time

cost of goods sold
The cost of producing or acquiring goods or services to be sold by a firm

gross profit
Sales less the cost of goods sold

operating expenses
Costs related to marketing and selling a firm's product or service, general and administrative expenses, and depreciation

operating income
Earnings or profits after operating expenses but before interest and taxes are paid

What Should You Do?

Your brother-in-law has asked you to help him finance what he considers to be a "great opportunity." He plans to sell a new brand of European clothing that is becoming popular in the United States. He thinks that a location close to the nearby university, from which you both graduated, would be ideal. He estimates that the financing could come mostly from a bank loan and credit from suppliers. However, together you would need to put in $5,000; he'd invest $3,000, leaving you to invest the remaining $2,000.

It's not that you don't trust him, but you have decided to undertake your own investigation into the opportunity. After considerable effort, you have developed what you think are realistic estimates of the potential profitability for the venture. You have also estimated how much money it would take to start the business.

There's a slight problem, however: Your six-month-old puppy tore up your worksheets. After putting the dog in the backyard, you pick up the pieces and begin reconstructing your work. The remnants of your hard work are as follows:

Advertising expense $16,000
Inventories $14,000
Interest expense $1,000
Cash needed in the business $6,000
Equipment $10,000
Sales $75,000
Cost of goods sold $40,000
Rent $4,000
Accounts payable $6,000
Office overhead $14,000
Depreciation expense $10,000
90-day bank loan $10,000

As you let the dog back into the house, you try to remember how all the pieces fit together. Once you have organized the information, what will you conclude about your brother-in-law's "great opportunity"?

What you will study in this chapter will help you decide if your sister married an entrepreneur in the rough or if he should keep his day job and forget about becoming a business owner. So, read on to see if you should join him as a partner in the business.

Operating activities do not include *financing* expenses. That is, no interest expense (the cost of using debt financing) has been subtracted to this point. **Earnings before taxes** are found by deducting the firm's **financing costs**—the firm's interest expense on its debt—from the firm's operating income.

Next, the firm's income taxes are calculated, based on its earnings before taxes and the applicable tax rate. For instance, if a firm had earnings before taxes of $100,000 and its tax rate was 28 percent, then it would owe $28,000 in taxes (0.28 × $100,000 = $28,000). *A word about taxes:* When entrepreneurs sell their products or services on a cash-only basis, some may be tempted *not* to report all income for tax purposes. Besides being stupid, such a decision is neither legal nor ethical. Our advice: *Don't even think about not reporting taxable income.*

The number resulting when taxes are subtracted from earnings is the **net income available to owners** (usually called **net income**), which represents income that may be reinvested in the firm or distributed to its owners—provided, of course, the cash is available to do so. As you will come to understand, *a positive net income on an income statement does not necessarily mean that a firm has generated positive cash flows.*

Exhibit 10-2 (on page 208) shows the 2005 income statement for Petri & Associates Leasing, Inc., an equipment leasing company. The company had sales of $850,000 for the 12-month period ending December 31, 2005. The cost of goods sold was $550,000, resulting in a gross profit of $300,000. The company had $200,000 in operating expenses, which included marketing expenses, general and administrative expenses, and **depreciation expense** (the costs related to fixed assets, allocated over their useful life). After total operating expenses were subtracted, the company's operating income (earnings before interest and taxes) amounted to $100,000. To this point, we have calculated profits based only on expenses related to the firm's operating activities. We have thus far excluded interest expense, which is a result of the firm's financing decisions—something we will consider shortly. Therefore, the figure for operating income represents the income that Petri & Associates would generate if it had no debt.

The figure for operating income is important to the owners because it best measures a company's profitability on its asset investment, before any money is distributed to investors and creditors. As a result, it is a good measure of the economic attractiveness of a business opportunity. For example, assume that a firm's total assets are $100,000 (financed with $40,000 in debt and $60,000 in equity) and that operating income and net income are $15,000 and $10,000, respectively. Thus, the firm's management used a total $100,000 investment (from both debt and ownership equity) to generate $15,000 in profits, for a 15 percent return on the asset investment ($15,000 ÷ $100,000 = 0.15). The net income, on the other hand, is the income that remains for the owners after payment of interest and taxes and does not measure the return on the firm's total assets.

Petri & Associates' interest expense of $20,000 (the expense it incurred by using debt financing) is then deducted to arrive at the company's earnings (profits) before taxes of $80,000. If we assume a 25 percent tax rate, the company will have to pay $20,000 in

financing costs
The amount of interest owed to lenders on borrowed money

earnings before taxes
Earnings or profits after operating expenses and interest expenses but before taxes

net income available to owners (net income)
Income that may be distributed to the owners or reinvested in the company

depreciation expense
Costs related to a fixed asset, such as a building or equipment, allocated over its useful life

EXHIBIT 10-1 *The Income Statement: An Overview*

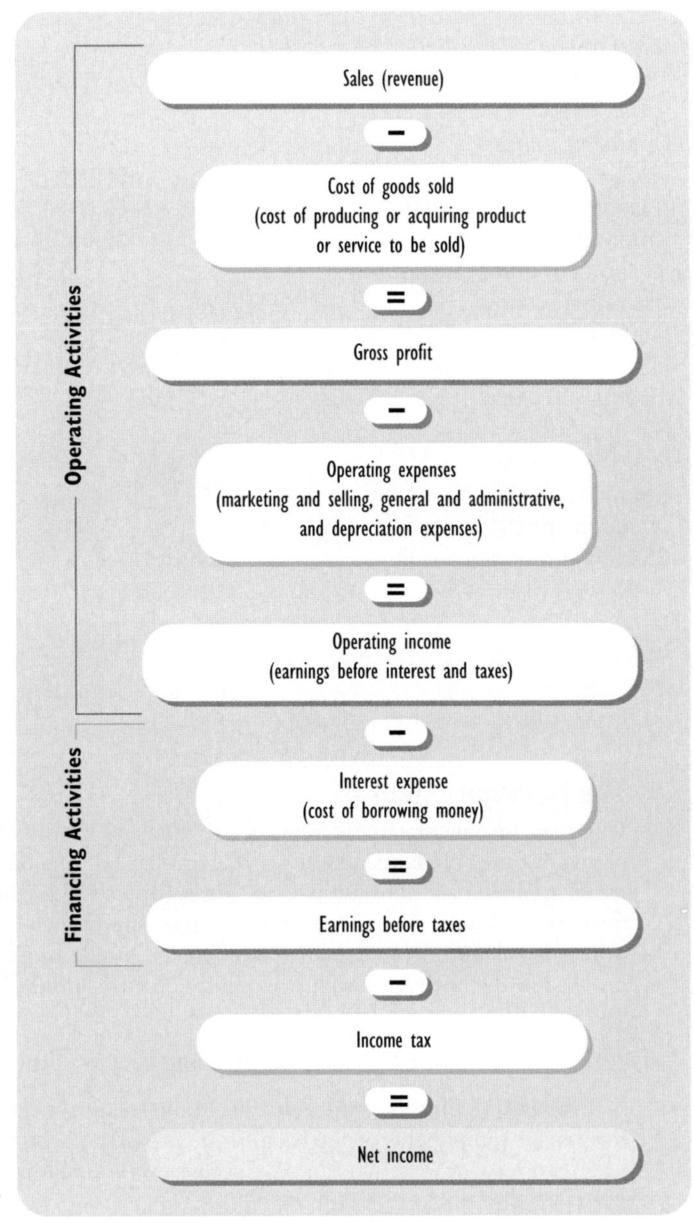

income taxes, leaving a net income of $60,000. The net income of $60,000 represents the "bottom line" of the income statement. This amount is the profit that was earned for the firm's owners on their investment. However, as shown at the bottom of Exhibit 10-2, dividends in the amount of $15,000 were paid to Petri's stockholders (owners); the remaining $45,000 ($60,000 net income less $15,000 in dividends) was retained by the firm and will appear as an increase in retained earnings on the balance sheet. *Dividends to a firm's owners, unlike interest expense, are not considered an expense in the income statement.* Instead, they are viewed as a distribution to the owners.

In summary, the income statement answers the question "How profitable is the business?" In providing the answer, the income statement reports financial information related to five broad areas of business activity:

1. Sales (revenue)
2. Cost of producing or acquiring the goods or services
3. Operating expenses
4. Financing costs
5. Tax payments

EXHIBIT 10-2 *Income Statement for Petri & Associates Leasing, Inc., for the Year Ending December 31, 2005*

Sales revenue		$850,000
Cost of goods sold		550,000
Gross profit on sales		$300,000
Operating expenses:		
Marketing expenses	$90,000	
General and administrative expenses	80,000	
Depreciation expense	30,000	
Total operating expenses		$200,000
Operating income		$100,000
Interest expense		20,000
Earnings before taxes		$ 80,000
Income tax (25%)		20,000
Net income		$ 60,000
Net income		$ 60,000
Dividends paid		15,000
Change in retained earnings		$ 45,000

The Balance Sheet

balance sheet A financial report showing a firm's assets, liabilities, and ownership equity at a specific point in time

current assets (gross working capital) Assets that can be converted into cash within a company's operating cycle

While an income statement reports the financial results of business operations over a period of time, a **balance sheet** provides a snapshot of a business's financial position at a *specific point in time.* Thus, a balance sheet captures the cumulative effects of all earlier financial decisions. At a given point in time, the balance sheet shows the assets a firm owns, the liabilities (or debt) outstanding or owed, and the amount the owners have invested in the business (ownership equity). In its simplest form, a balance sheet follows this formula:

$$\text{Total assets} = \text{Outstanding debt} + \text{Ownership equity}$$

Exhibit 10-3 illustrates the elements in the balance sheet of a typical firm. Each of the three main components of the balance sheet—assets, debt, and ownership equity—is discussed in the following sections.

Test Your Understanding

The Income Statement

Construct an income statement, using the following information. What are the firm's gross profit, operating income, and net income? Which expense is a *noncash* expense? (Check your solution to this problem with the answer shown on page 215.)

Interest expense	$10,000
Cost of goods sold	160,000
Marketing expenses	70,000
Administrative expenses	50,000
Sales	400,000
Stock dividends	5,000
Income tax	20,000
Depreciation expense	20,000

ASSETS A company's assets, shown on the left side of Exhibit 10-3, fall into three categories: (1) current assets, (2) fixed assets, and (3) other assets.

Current assets, or **gross working capital**, comprise those assets that are relatively liquid—that is, assets that can be converted into cash within the firm's normal operating cycle. Current assets primarily include cash, accounts receivable, and inventories. Ineffective management of current assets is a prime cause of financial problems in small companies. (We will discuss this issue more thoroughly in Chapter 22.)

- *Cash.* Every firm must have cash for current business operations. A reservoir of cash is needed to compensate for the uncertainty of the cash flows into a

EXHIBIT 10-3 *The Balance Sheet: An Overview*

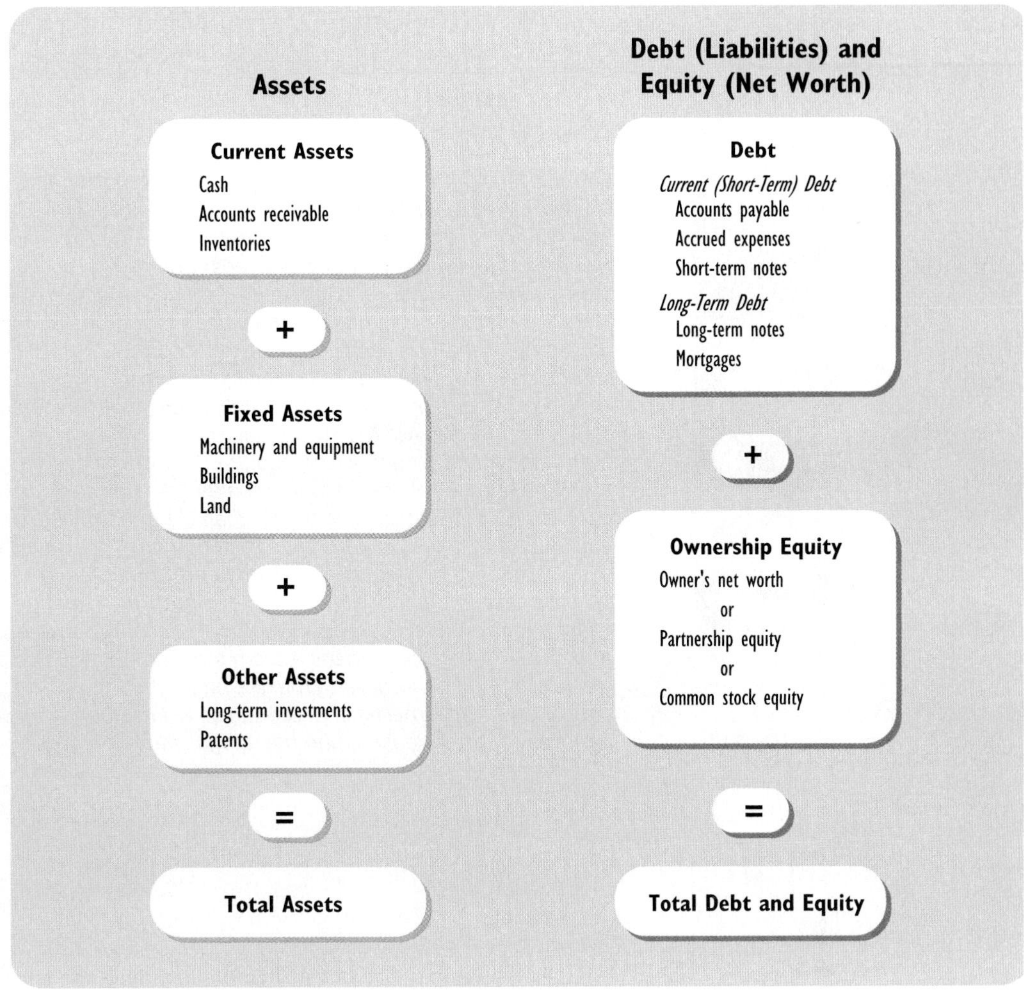

business (cash receipts) and out of a business (cash expenditures). Thus, the size of a firm's cash reservoir is determined not only by the volume of sales, but also by the predictability of cash receipts and cash payments.

- *Accounts receivable.* The firm's **accounts receivable** consist of payments due from its customers from previous credit sales. Accounts receivable can become a significant asset for firms that sell on a credit basis.

accounts receivable
The amount of credit extended to customers that is currently outstanding

- *Inventories.* The raw materials and products held by the firm for eventual sale constitute **inventory**. Although their relative importance differs from one type of business to another, inventories often account for a major part of a firm's working capital. Seasonality of sales and production levels affect the size of inventories. Retail stores, for example, may find it desirable to carry a larger-than-normal inventory during the pre-Christmas season.

inventory
A firm's raw materials and products held in anticipation of eventual sale

Fixed assets are the more permanent assets in a business. They may include machinery and equipment, buildings, and land. Some businesses are more capital-intensive than others—for example, a motel is more capital-intensive than a gift store—and, therefore, have more fixed assets.

fixed assets
Relatively permanent assets intended for use in the business, such as plant and equipment

Most fixed assets are also **depreciable assets**, as their value declines, or depreciates, over time. Although the depreciation expense for a given year is shown as an expense in the income statement, the balance sheet reports the cumulative depreciation, taken over the life of the asset. For instance, assume that a truck purchased for $20,000 is being depreciated over four years. The depreciation expense for each year would be $5,000

depreciable assets
Assets whose value declines, or depreciates, over time

Living the Dream

Entrepreneurial Challenges

Are Your Employee Meetings Like This One?

Some firms have adopted a policy of sharing information about their financial performance with their employees. Atlas Container Corp. is one such business.

Courtesy of Atlas Container

It's 2 in the afternoon, and about 150 people, most of Atlas Container Corp.'s Maryland employees, are filing noisily into the big room off the shop floor known as the Learning Center. As the room fills up, there's a scramble for seats: Pretty soon a five-line financial statement for the month is on the screen at the front, and CEO Paul Centenari is deep into a discussion of Atlas's recent performance.

"Look at this number," he yells, his tone carrying that elusive mix of "Isn't this cool?" and "Pay attention!" found in the voices of the best teachers. "Look at this! Is this high or low?" The audience members whoop. They know the answer to this one: Several people shout out, "High!" Grinning, Centenari chucks a pack of M&Ms in the direction of the first person to answer. "High? How high? Where should it be?" More shouted answers, more M&Ms sailing across the room. People know that their monthly bonuses, not to mention the health of their employer, depend on these financials.

The number of the moment is sales, general, and administrative expenses, or SG&A, which at 14.2% of sales is higher than Centenari wants it to be. ("We're gonna cut two points off that. We've got a team working on it," he says.) But it could be operating profits, monthly shipments, or indeed pretty much anything that will determine whether Atlas makes its financial goals. The point of the meeting isn't to solve problems, rather just to make sure everybody knows the score. Some employees will be asked to join that SG&A team or perhaps a team working on reducing paper waste. Others might be asked to work Saturdays to make a production goal or to postpone some elective maintenance on the machinery. Centenari wants them to know the reasons for all those moves. And the reasons, he has taught them, lie in the financials.

Source: John Case, "The Power of Listening," *Inc.*, Vol. 25, No. 3 (March 2003), p. 70.

($20,000 ÷ 4 years = $5,000). When the firm buys the truck, the original cost of $20,000 is shown in the balance sheet as a **gross fixed asset**. Each year, the cumulative depreciation expense, or what is called **accumulated depreciation**, is subtracted from the original cost to yield the **net fixed asset**. For this example, the balance sheet at the end of each year would appear as follows:

gross fixed assets
Original cost of depreciable assets before any depreciation expense has been taken

accumulated depreciation
Total depreciation expense taken over the assets' life

net fixed assets
Gross fixed assets less accumulated depreciation

	Year 1	Year 2	Year 3	Year 4
Gross fixed asset	$20,000	$20,000	$20,000	$20,000
Accumulated depreciation	5,000	10,000	15,000	20,000
Net fixed asset	$15,000	$10,000	$ 5,000	$ 0

The third category, **other assets**, includes such intangible assets as patents, copyrights, and goodwill. For a startup company, organizational costs—costs incurred in organizing and promoting the business—may also be included in this category.

other assets
Assets other than current assets and fixed assets, such as patents, copyrights, and goodwill

DEBT AND EQUITY The right side of the balance sheet in Exhibit 10-3, showing debt and equity, indicates how a firm is financing its assets. Financing comes from two main sources: debt (liabilities) and ownership equity. Debt is money that has been borrowed and must be repaid by some predetermined date. Ownership equity, on the other hand, represents the owners' investment in the company—money they have personally put into the firm without any specific date for repayment. Owners recover their investment by withdrawing money from the firm in the form of dividends or by selling their interest in the firm.

debt
Business financing provided by creditors

Debt is financing provided by a creditor. As shown in Exhibit 10-3, it is divided into (1) current, or short-term, debt and (2) long-term debt. **Current debt**, or **short-term liabilities**, includes borrowed money that must be repaid within the next 12 months. Sources of current debt may be classified as follows:

current debt (short-term liabilities)
Borrowed money that must be repaid within 12 months

- **Accounts payable** represent the credit extended by suppliers to a firm when it purchases inventories. The purchasing firm usually is given 30 or 60 days to pay for the inventory. This form of credit is also called **trade credit**.

accounts payable (trade credit)
Outstanding credit payable to suppliers

- **Accrued expenses** are expenses that have been incurred but not yet paid. For example, employees may have performed work for which they will not be paid until the following week or month. Accrued taxes are taxes that are owed but have not been paid.

accrued expenses
Short-term liabilities that have been incurred but not paid

- **Short-term notes** represent cash amounts borrowed from a bank or other lending source for a short period of time, such as 90 days. Short-term notes are a primary source of financing for most small businesses, as these businesses have access to fewer sources of long-term capital than do their larger counterparts.

short-term notes
Cash amounts borrowed from a bank or other lending sources that must be repaid within a short period of time

Long-term debt includes loans from banks or other sources that lend money for longer than 12 months. When a firm borrows money for 5 years to buy equipment, it signs an agreement—a long-term note—promising to repay the money in 5 years. When a firm borrows money for 30 years to purchase real estate, such as a warehouse or office building, the real estate usually stands as collateral for the long-term loan, which is called a **mortgage**. If the borrower is unable to repay the loan, the lender can take the real estate in settlement.

long-term debt
Loans from banks or other sources with repayment terms of more than 12 months

mortgage
A long-term loan from a creditor for which real estate is pledged as collateral

Ownership equity is money that the owners invest in a business. Note that they are *residual owners* of the business; that is, if the company is liquidated, creditors are always paid before the owners are paid.

ownership equity
Owners' investments in a company, plus profits retained in the firm

The amount of ownership equity in a business is equal to (1) the total amount of the owners' investments in the business plus (2) the cumulative profits (net of any losses) since the firm's beginning less any dividends paid to the owners. The second item (profits less dividends) is frequently called **retained earnings**—because these earnings have been reinvested in the business instead of being distributed to the owners. Thus, the basic formula for ownership equity is as follows:

retained earnings
Profits less withdrawals (dividends) over the life of the business

$$\text{Ownership equity} = \text{Owners' investment} + \overbrace{\text{Cumulative profits} - \text{Cumulative dividends paid to owners}}^{\textbf{Earnings retained within the business}}$$

Exhibit 10-4 (on page 212) presents balance sheets for Petri & Associates for December 31, 2004, and December 31, 2005, along with the dollar changes in the balance sheet from 2004 to 2005. By referring to the columns representing the two balance sheets, we can see the financial position of the firm at the beginning *and* at the end of 2005.

The 2004 and 2005 balance sheets for Petri & Associates show that the firm began 2005 (ended 2004) with $800,000 in total assets and ended 2005 with total assets of $920,000. We can also see how much has been invested in current assets (cash, accounts receivable, and inventories) and in fixed assets.

We next observe how much debt and equity were used to finance the assets. Debt represents approximately one-third of the total financing and equity about two-thirds. In 2005, total debt was $300,000, relative to $920,000 in total debt and equity, or 33 percent. Stated differently, the firm's assets were financed 33 percent by debt and 67 percent by equity. Also, about half of the equity came from investments made by the owners (common stock), and the other half came from reinvesting profits in the business (retained

Test Your Understanding

The Balance Sheet

Construct a balance sheet, using the following information. What are the firm's current assets, net fixed assets, total assets, current liabilities, long-term debt, total ownership equity, and total debt and equity? (Check your solution to this problem with the answer shown on page 217.)

Gross fixed assets	$75,000
Cash	10,000
Other assets	15,000
Accounts payable	40,000
Retained earnings	15,000
Accumulated depreciation	20,000
Accounts receivable	$50,000
Long-term note	5,000
Mortgage	20,000
Common stock	100,000
Inventories	70,000
Short-term notes	20,000

EXHIBIT 10-4 | *Balance Sheets for Petri & Associates Leasing, Inc., for December 31, 2004 and 2005*

	2004	2005	Changes
Assets			
Current assets:			
Cash	$ 45,000	$ 50,000	$ 5,000
Accounts receivable	75,000	80,000	5,000
Inventories	180,000	220,000	40,000
Total current assets	$300,000	$350,000	$ 50,000
Fixed assets:			
Gross fixed assets	$860,000	$960,000	$100,000
Accumulated depreciation	(360,000)	(390,000)	(30,000)
Net fixed assets	$500,000	$570,000	$ 70,000
TOTAL ASSETS	$800,000	$920,000	$120,000
Debt (Liabilities) and Equity			
Current liabilities:			
Accounts payable	$ 15,000	$ 20,000	$ 5,000
Short-term notes	60,000	80,000	20,000
Total current liabilities (debt)	$ 75,000	$100,000	$ 25,000
Long-term debt	150,000	200,000	50,000
Total debt	$225,000	$300,000	$ 75,000
Ownership equity:			
Common stock	$300,000	$300,000	$ 0
Retained earnings	275,000	320,000	45,000
Total ownership equity	$575,000	$620,000	$ 45,000
TOTAL DEBT AND EQUITY	$800,000	$920,000	$120,000

earnings). Referring back to the income statement in Exhibit 10-2, note that the $45,000 increase in retained earnings, shown in the Changes column in Exhibit 10-4, is the firm's net income for the year less the dividends paid to the owners.

In summary, financing for a new business derives from two sources: debt and ownership equity. Debt is money borrowed from financial institutions, suppliers, and other lenders. Ownership equity represents the owners' investment in the company, either through cash invested in the firm or through profits retained in the business (shown as retained earnings on the balance sheet).

Thus far, we have discussed the income statement and the balance sheet as separate reports. But they actually complement each other to give an overall picture of the firm's financial situation. Because the balance sheet is a snapshot of a firm's financial condition at a point in time and the income statement reports results over a given period, both are required to determine a firm's financial position.

Exhibit 10-5 (on page 216) shows how the income statement and the balance sheet fit together. To understand how a firm performed during 2005, you must know the firm's financial position at the beginning of 2005 (balance sheet on December 31, 2004), its financial performance during the year (income statement for 2005), and its financial position at the end of the year (balance sheet on December 31, 2005). As you will soon see, all three statements are needed to measure Petri & Associates' cash flows for 2005.

The Cash Flow Statement

If you spend time with an entrepreneur, eventually you are likely to hear the phrase "CASH IS KING!" (We capitalize the saying because it is always said with passion.) Cash flow problems are a constant concern of small business owners. Even a "successful" company may encounter problems with cash flows. For this reason, the ability to understand a cash flow statement is *extremely* important. A **cash flow statement** shows the sources of a firm's cash and its uses of the cash. In other words, it answers the questions "Where did the cash come from?" and "Where did the cash go?"

cash flow statement
A financial report showing a firm's sources and uses of cash

An entrepreneur recently told us how intimidated she felt when her accountant presented the firm's monthly financial reports and how difficult she found it to understand cash flows. Our advice was to get a new accountant—one who would explain the statements carefully—and also to spend the time necessary to gain a solid understanding of the financial statements and the firm's cash flows.

It's important to understand that the profits shown on a company's income statement are not the same as its cash flows, although both are measures of a firm's performance. Many entrepreneurs have been deceived by a good-looking income statement, only to discover that their companies were running out of cash. Effectively managing cash flows is essential. To do so, the small business owner must understand the sources and uses of the firm's cash. In the words of author Jan Norman, "Even profitable companies can go broke. That's a difficult truth for start-up business owners to swallow. But the sooner you learn that when you're out of cash, you're out of business, the better your chances for survival will be."[1]

PROFITS VERSUS CASH FLOWS An income statement is not a measure of cash flows because it is calculated on an *accrual* basis rather than a *cash* basis. This is an important point to understand. In **accrual-basis accounting**, income is recorded when it is earned—whether or not the income has been received in cash—and expenses are recorded when they are incurred—even if money has not actually been paid out. In **cash-basis accounting**, income is reported when cash is received, and expenses are recorded when they are paid.

For a number of reasons, profits based on an accrual accounting system will differ from those based on a cash flow accounting system:

1. Sales reported in an income statement include both *cash* sales and *credit* sales. Thus, total sales do not correspond to the actual cash collected.
2. Some inventory purchases are financed by credit, so inventory purchases do not exactly equal cash spent for inventories.
3. The depreciation expense shown in the income statement is a noncash expense. It reflects the costs associated with using an asset that benefits the firm's operations over a period of more than one year, such as a piece of equipment used over five years.
4. Frequently, not all of the income tax shown in the income statement is paid in the period reported. Instead, some tax expense may be accrued as tax payable and paid in later periods.

. . . and What About Your Brother-in-Law?

With an understanding of the income statement and balance sheet, let's return to your brother-in-law's proposition that you join him as a partner in the clothing business. You have reconstructed the following income statement and balance sheet from the fragments of your dog-chewed papers.

Projected Income Statement	
Sales	$75,000
Cost of goods sold	40,000
Gross profit	$35,000
Operating expenses:	
Office overhead	$14,000
Advertising expense	16,000
Rent	4,000
Depreciation expense	10,000
Total operating expenses	$44,000
Operating income	($ 9,000)
Interest expense	1,000
Earnings before taxes	($10,000)
Income tax	0
Net income	($10,000)

Projected Balance Sheet	
Cash	$ 6,000
Inventories	14,000
Current assets	20,000
Equipment	10,000
Total assets needed	$30,000
Accounts payable	$ 6,000
90-day bank loan	10,000
Total current debt	$16,000
Brother-in-law's investment	$ 3,000
Your investment	2,000
Total ownership equity	$ 5,000
Debt and equity	$21,000
Additional financing needed	$ 9,000
Total debt and equity needed	$30,000

So, based on your estimates, the venture can be expected to incur a loss of $10,000. Furthermore, the balance sheet suggests that the business will need $30,000 for investments in assets. Adding debt financing of $16,000, $3,000 from your brother-in-law, and $2,000 from you gives $21,000—not the needed $30,000. The business will need an additional $9,000 (that is, $9,000 will be required for total debt and equity to equal total assets). Maybe, just maybe, this is not quite the opportunity your brother-in-law perceives it to be. At the very least, he needs to do a better job of understanding what will be required.

MEASURING A FIRM'S CASH FLOWS As discussed earlier, the cash flow statement measures a firm's cash inflows and outflows. Exhibit 10-6 (on page 214) presents this statement for Petri & Associates for the year ending December 31, 2005. It shows that the data required for computing a firm's cash flows come from both the income statement and the balance sheets. Also, we can see that there are three main sections of the statement:[2]

accrual-basis accounting
A method of accounting that matches revenues when they are earned against the expenses associated with those revenues, no matter when they are paid

cash-basis accounting
A method of accounting that reports transactions only when cash is received or a payment is made

EXHIBIT 10-5 *The Fit of the Income Statement and Balance Sheet*

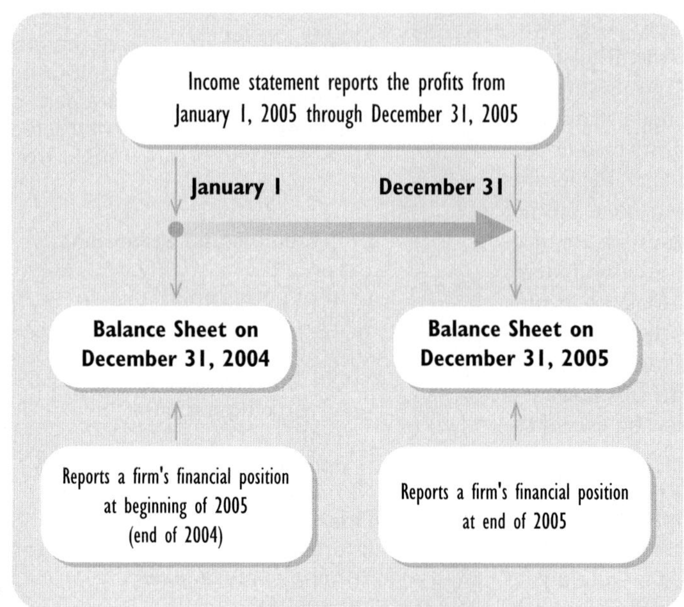

1. Cash flows from normal operations (operating activities)
2. Cash flows related to the investment in or sale of assets (investment activities)
3. Cash flows related to financing the firm (financing activities)

cash flows from operations Net cash flows generated from operating a business, calculated by adding back to operating income depreciation, deducting income taxes, and factoring in any changes in net working capital

We will now consider each of the three parts of the cash flow statement.

Operating Activities The first part of a cash flow statement reflects cash flows from operations. **Cash flows from operations** are the net cash flows generated from a firm's

EXHIBIT 10-6 *Cash Flow Statement for Petri & Associates Leasing, Inc., for the Year Ending December 31, 2005*

			Source of information:
Operating activities:			
Operating income	$100,000		Income statement
Depreciation	30,000		Income statement
Income tax	(20,000)		Income statement
Adjusted income		$110,000	
Increase in accounts receivable	($ 5,000)		Balance sheets
Increase in inventories	(40,000)		Balance sheets
Increase in accounts payable	5,000		Balance sheets
Change in net working capital		($ 40,000)	
CASH FLOWS FROM OPERATIONS		$ 70,000	
Investment activities:			
Gross fixed assets		($100,000)	Balance sheets
Financing activities:			
Interest expense	($ 20,000)		Income statement
Dividends	(15,000)		Income statement
Short-term notes	20,000		Balance sheet
Long-term debt	50,000		Balance sheet
TOTAL FINANCING ACTIVITIES		$ 35,000	
Increase in cash		$ 5,000	

Living the Dream

Entrepreneurial Challenges

Want to Succeed? Then Understand Your Financial Statements

When Eddie Cerda took over Atlas Radiator in 1990 after working at the company for 12 years, he quickly discovered that radiators weren't all he needed to understand. He found that financial details, like a pinhole leak, could devastate his business.

"To run a successful business, it's important to have a solid grasp of finances," says Cerda, whose Santa Fe Springs, California–based company earns $2 million in sales annually. Cerda started meeting regularly with his accountant to understand more about his company's finances.

"Anyone can learn how to put a product together. The bottom line is what it costs to make it, and you can only know that by understanding the financial aspects of your business," says Cerda, who has 28 employees. "Financial statements give an accurate picture of overall expenses. If you're paying too much for labor or utilities, it will show up on your financials and you can make adjustments."

Financial statements are more valuable than many business owners realize, says CPA Dave Stevens. "All too often, small business owners only look at the bank balance, which is just one indicator of how well a business is doing," he says. "Financial statements may be historical in nature, but they're immensely helpful, because a study of history can help us avoid the mistakes of the past. They can be used to spot trends, strengths, weaknesses, and opportunities for additional business."

Source: Julie Bawden Davis, "What You Need to Know About Your Financials," *MyBusiness*, August-September 2003, p. 42.

normal day-to-day business activities—purchasing inventories on credit, selling on credit, paying for the inventories, and finally collecting on the sales made on credit.

As shown in Exhibit 10-6, Petri & Associates' cash flows from operations are computed as follows:

adjusted income
After-tax cash flow

net working capital
Money invested in current assets other than cash less accounts payable and accruals

Step 1: Begin with Petri's operating income (earnings before interest and taxes) of $100,000; add back $30,000 in depreciation expense, since it is not a cash expense; and subtract $20,000 in income tax to get the after-tax cash flow, or what we call **adjusted income**, which in this case is a cash inflow of $110,000.

Step 2: Subtract Petri & Associates' $40,000 increase in **net working capital**—money invested in current assets other than cash less accounts payable and accruals. Looking at Petri's balance sheets in Exhibit 10-4, we see that accounts receivable and inventories increased by $45,000 (a use of cash) and that accounts payable increased by $5,000 (a source of cash).

The $110,000 in cash inflow (step 1) less the $40,000 addition to net working capital (step 2) results in cash flows from operations of $70,000.

Investment Activities When equipment or some other depreciable asset is purchased or sold, cash flows occur that are not shown in the income statement. Petri & Associates spent $100,000 on new plant and equipment, based on the change in gross fixed assets (see Exhibit 10-4) from $860,000 to $960,000. This $100,000 expenditure is shown in the second section of the cash flow statement.

How Did You Do?

Understanding the Income Statement

On page 208, you were asked to develop an income statement based on the information provided. Your results should be as follows:

Sales	$400,000
Cost of goods sold	160,000
Gross profit	$240,000
Operating expenses:	
Marketing expenses	$ 70,000
Administrative expenses	50,000
Depreciation expense	20,000
Total operating expenses	$140,000
Operating income	$100,000
Interest expense	10,000
Earnings before taxes	$ 90,000
Income tax	20,000
Net income	$ 70,000

Note: The stock dividends are not shown as an expense in the income statement but will appear as a reduction in retained earnings in the balance sheet.

Living the Dream

Entrepreneurial Challenges

Profits Are Good, but Cash Is Essential

OnRamp Access, founded in 1994 in Austin, Texas, is a company that provides Internet access, custom Web design, and co-location services. In the beginning, Chad and Elisa Kissinger introduced the Internet to weekend shoppers at a kiosk in Barton Creek Mall. Selling dial-up access and books on how the Internet works, OnRamp Access was born over a four-weekend period that resulted in 14 new customers.

Chad says his biggest advantage as a small business owner is "the ability to move quickly on an idea without company bureaucracy getting in the way. There is no greater selling advantage than to have the president of the company look a customer in the eye and say, 'You have my word that you'll be happy.'"

Since its beginning, OnRamp Access has survived ups and downs, including a devastating fire. But like many small business owners, the Kissingers have shown resilience over time. As Chad says, "We've been in business for [over a decade] while maintaining profitability and treating all of our employees and customers right. Although we aren't wealthy (yet!), we've derived a great deal of satisfaction out of making our work life rewarding."

So what has Chad Kissinger learned as a small business owner? "Sell high, buy low, collect fast and pay slow. Whether you are profitable or not, if you run out of available cash, you are dead."

Source: "A Texas Small Business Talks to OSBA Staff About Their Struggles, Victories and Plans for the Future," *Small Business Advocate*, a bi-monthly newsletter by the Office of Small Business Assistance (OSBA), Vol. 5, No. 3 (May-June 2003).

Financing Activities The third section of the cash flow statement presents the cash inflows and outflows resulting from financing activities. These activities include (1) paying dividends and interest expense, (2) increasing or decreasing short-term and long-term debt, which means borrowing more money (an increase in debt) or paying off debt (a decrease in debt), and (3) issuing stock (source of cash) or repurchasing stock (use of cash). Petri paid $35,000 in interest and dividends, but borrowed an additional $70,000, resulting in a net cash inflow of $35,000 from financing activities.

To summarize, Petri & Associates generated $70,000 in cash flows from operations, invested $100,000 in plant and equipment, and received $35,000 net from financing activities, for a net increase in cash of $5,000. This can be verified from the balance sheets (see Exhibit 10-4), which show that Petri's cash increased $5,000 during 2005 (from $45,000 to $50,000).

Interpreting the Cash Flow Statement

As already noted, the three basic categories of activities related to a firm's cash flows are operating activities, investment activities, and financing activities. When thinking about the basic nature of a firm's cash flows, consider the following four cash flow patterns, which vary with respect to the three categories of activities. As Exhibit 10-7 illustrates, each of these patterns provides information about the firm.

Pattern 1. A firm with cash flow pattern 1 has positive cash flows from operations, negative investment cash flows, and positive cash flows from financing. This company (like Petri & Associates) is using its cash flows from operations and new financing to expand the firm's operations.

Pattern 2. Cash flow pattern 2 depicts a firm that is using cash flows from operations to expand the business, pay down debt, and/or pay its owners.

Pattern 3. Cash flow pattern 3 describes a company that is encountering negative cash flows from operations, which are being covered by selling assets and by borrowing or acquiring more equity financing.

Pattern 4. A firm with cash flow pattern 4 has negative cash flows from operations and is growing the company's fixed assets through increased financing. This pattern would

EXHIBIT 10-7 *Cash Flow Patterns*

	CASH FLOW RELATED TO		
Cash Flow Pattern	**Operation**	**Investments**	**Financing**
1	+	–	+
2	+	–	–
3	–	+	+
4	–	–	+

describe a startup business that has yet to break even, is investing in assets to produce future cash flows, and is having to raise capital to make that happen.

Other cash flow patterns exist, but the four patterns just described are sufficient to illustrate how to interpret a company's cash flow statement. Now that you have an understanding of a firm's financial statements, we'll discuss how to develop pro forma financial statements, an important part of any business plan.

FINANCIAL FORECASTING

2 *Forecast a new venture's profitability.*

Using the basic financial information discussed so far in this chapter, an owner-manager can develop **pro forma financial statements**, or projected financial statements. The necessity of financial forecasting is described quite aptly by small business consultant Paul A. Broni:

> *It doesn't matter whether you're applying for your first bank loan or your fifth, or whether you're seeking venture capital or debt financing. Sooner or later, you'll have to prepare a set of financial projections. Lenders will look for a strong likelihood of repayment; investors will calculate what they think is the value of your company.*[3]

The purpose of pro forma financial statements is to answer three questions:

1. How profitable can the firm be expected to be, given the projected sales levels and the expected sales–expense relationships?
2. How much and what type of financing (debt or equity) will be used?
3. Will the firm have adequate cash flows? If so, how will they be used; if not, where will the additional cash come from?

Preparing historical financial statements, such as income statements, balance sheets, and cash flow statements, is not a difficult task; accountants have perfected that process. Projecting the financials for a new company is another matter, however, and presents a real challenge. However, it is not hopeless, as explained by Rhonda Abrams, a business plan consultant:

How Did You Do?

Understanding the Balance Sheet?
On page 211, you were asked to develop a balance sheet based on the financial data provided. Your results should be as follows:

Assets	
Cash	$ 10,000
Accounts receivable	50,000
Inventories	70,000
Total current assets	$130,000
Gross fixed assets	$75,000
Accumulated depreciation	(20,000)
Net fixed assets	$55,000
Other assets	15,000
TOTAL ASSETS	$200,000
Debt and Equity	
Accounts payable	$ 40,000
Short-term notes	20,000
Total current debt	$ 60,000
Long-term note	5,000
Mortgage	20,000
Total long-term debt	$ 25,000
Total debt	$ 85,000
Common stock	100,000
Retained earnings	15,000
Total ownership equity	$115,000
TOTAL DEBT AND EQUITY	$200,000

pro forma financial statements
Statements that project a firm's financial performance and condition

One of the biggest challenges for a new company doing a business plan is figuring out the financial statements. If you have an existing business, you have a pretty good sense of how much things will cost, how much staff you'll need, and the sales you're likely to make. But when you're just starting out, these things seem a complete mystery.

They're not. At least not entirely. Every decision you make when planning your business has a number attached: If you choose to exhibit at a trade show, there's a cost associated with that; if you choose to locate your business in one town versus another, there's a cost associated with that.

How do you do this homework? The best place to start is by speaking with others in your industry, attending trade shows, and contacting your industry association. Another excellent source is the RMA Annual Statement Studies, which look at actual financial statements of companies in certain industries.[4]

Let's take a look at the process for projecting a firm's profitability, financing requirements, and cash flows.

Forecasting Profitability

Profits reward an owner for investing in a company and constitute a primary source of financing for future growth. Therefore, it is critical for an entrepreneur to understand the factors that drive profits. A firm's net income is dependent on four variables:

1. *Amount of sales.* The dollar amount of sales equals the price of the product or service times the number of units sold or the amount of service rendered.
2. *Cost of goods sold and operating expenses.* This variable includes (a) the cost of producing the firm's products or services, (b) expenses related to marketing and distributing the product, (c) general and administrative expenses, and (d) depreciation expenses. These expenses should be classified as either *fixed* operating expenses (those that do

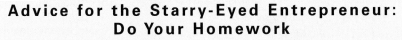

Living the Dream — *Entrepreneurial Challenges*

Advice for the Starry-Eyed Entrepreneur: Do Your Homework

Photo by Bruce Richardson

A lot of planning and hard work are required to have a successful company. Kay Snipes, co-owner of the Magnolia & Ivy Tearoom, knows all about that from personal experience.

Kay Snipes was winding down from a 12-hour shift at the resort-based tearoom she owns with her sister, but still had the energy of an early morning television newscaster. "It's fun and it's a lot of hard work," says the co-owner of Magnolia & Ivy Tearoom at Sandestin Golf & Beach Resort on Florida's northwest coast. "You love your children and you will do for them like you wouldn't do for anybody else. You'll go without pay, you'll stay up late." You nurture your business the same way, she says.

A former pharmacy technician, Snipes and her pharmacist husband decided in 1995 to close up their combination drugstore and gift shop to follow the dream of creating something more original. The Snipeses, along with Kay's sister, Terri Eager, opened their first Magnolia & Ivy Tearoom off a main highway in Parrott, Georgia (population: 83), in August of 1995. A month later, they opened a second parlor in their hometown of Cuthbert, Georgia. As the concept caught on, they continued to expand, with as many as five locations, including two co-located in bed and breakfast inns.

Because many people inquired about franchising their concept, Snipes and Eager created a spin-off business—a four-day conference called "Open a Tearoom for Profit." To date, they've held more than 22 conferences and trained 700 women from 45 states.

Snipes tells others, "Follow your dream, but have a plan and do your homework." She explains, "We have a lot of starry-eyed people come to our conferences, and we tell them 'This is not a hobby, this is a business.' It's not about buying the beautiful china, it's about making the rent."

Source: Julie S. Bettinger, "Take It Seriously and Test Your Market," *Florida Trend*, February 12, 2004, p. 17.

not vary with a change in sales volume) or *variable* operating expenses (those that change proportionally with sales).

3. *Interest expense*. An entrepreneur who borrows money agrees to pay interest on the loan principal. For example, a loan of $25,000 for a full year at a 12 percent interest rate results in an interest expense of $3,000 for the year (0.12 × $25,000).
4. *Taxes*. A firm's income taxes are figured as a percentage of taxable income (earnings before taxes).

Let's consider a hypothetical example that demonstrates how to estimate a new venture's profits. Assume that Kate Lynn is planning to start a new business called Cameron Products, Inc., which will make crown molding for luxury homes. A newly developed lathe will allow the firm to be responsive to varying design specifications in a very economical manner. Based on a study of potential market demand and expected costs-to-sales relationships, Lynn has made the following estimates for the first two years of operations:

1. *Amount of sales*. Lynn expects to sell the firm's product for $125 per unit, with total sales for the first year projected at 2,000 units, or $125 × 2,000 = $250,000, and total sales for the second year projected at 3,200 units, or $125 × 3,200 = $400,000.
2. *Cost of goods sold and operating expenses*. The fixed cost of goods sold (including production costs and employee salaries) is expected to amount to $100,000 per year, while fixed operating expenses (marketing expenses, general and administrative expenses) are estimated at $46,000 per year. In addition, depreciation will be $4,000 annually. The variable costs of producing the crown molding will be around 20 percent of dollar sales, and the variable operating expenses will be approximately 30 percent of dollar sales. In other words, at a selling price of $125 per unit, the combined variable costs per unit, both for producing the crown molding and for marketing it, will be 50 percent of the sales price (0.20 + 0.30) × $125 = $62.50.
3. *Interest expense*. Based on the anticipated amount of money to be borrowed and the corresponding interest rate, Lynn expects interest expense to be $8,000 in the first year, increasing to $12,000 in the second year.
4. *Taxes*. Income taxes will be 25 percent of earnings before taxes (taxable income).

Given the above estimates, we can forecast Cameron Product's net income as shown in the pro forma statement in Exhibit 10-8. We first enter our assumptions on an Excel spreadsheet (rows 1–10). Then in rows 13–28, we see the two years of pro forma income statements (columns B and C) and the equations used to compute the numbers (columns D and E).

The computations in Exhibit 10-8 indicate that Cameron Products, Inc., will have a $33,000 loss in its first year, followed by a positive net income of $28,500 in its second year. A startup typically experiences losses for a period of time, frequently as long as two or three years.[5] In a real-world situation, an entrepreneur should project the profits of a new company three to five years into the future, as opposed to the two-year projection shown for Cameron Products, Inc.

Let's now shift our attention from forecasting profits to estimating asset and financing requirements.

Forecasting Asset and Financing Requirements and Cash Flows

3 *Determine asset requirements, evaluate financial sources, and estimate cash flows for a new venture.*

The amount and types of assets required for a new venture will vary, depending on the nature of the business. High-technology businesses—such as computer manufacturers, designers of semiconductor chips, and gene-splicing companies—often require millions of dollars in investments. Most service businesses, on the other hand, require minimal initial capital.

Most firms of any size need both working capital (cash, accounts receivable, inventories, etc.) and fixed assets. For instance, a food store requires operating cash, inventories, and possibly limited accounts receivable. In addition, the owner will have to acquire cash registers, shopping carts, shelving, office equipment, and a building. The need to invest in assets results in a corresponding need for financing.

In many small firms, owners have a tendency to underestimate the amount of capital the business requires. Consequently, the financing they get may be inadequate. Without

EXHIBIT 10-8 *Pro Forma Income Statements for Cameron Products, Inc.*

	A	B	C	D	E
1	ASSUMPTIONS				
2	Year 1 projected units of sales	2,000			
3	Year 2 projected units of sales	3,200			
4	Selling price	$ 125			
5	Fixed cost of goods sold	$100,000			
6	Fixed operating expenses	$ 46,000		Equations based on assumptions	
7	Depreciation expense	$ 4,000			
8	Variable cost of goods sold	20%			
9	Variable operating expenses	30%			
10	Income tax rate	25%			
11				Equations for	
12		Year 1	Year 2	Year 1	Year 2
13	Sales	$250,000	$400,000	=B2*B4	=B3*B4
14	Cost of goods sold				
15	Fixed cost of goods sold	$100,000	$100,000	=B5	=B5
16	Variable cost of goods sold (20% of sales)	$ 50,000	$ 80,000	=B8*B13	=B8*C13
17	Total cost of goods sold	$150,000	$180,000	=B15+B16	=C15+C16
18	Gross profits	$100,000	$220,000	=B13–B17	=C13–C17
19	Operating expenses				
20	Fixed operating expenses	$ 46,000	$ 46,000	=B6	=B6
21	Depreciation expense	$ 4,000	$ 4,000	=B7	=B7
22	Variable operating expenses (30% of sales)	$ 75,000	$120,000	=B13*B9	=C13*B9
23	Total operating expenses	$125,000	$170,000	=B20+B21+B22	=C20+C21+C22
24	Operating income	($ 25,000)	$ 50,000	=B18–B23	=C18–C23
25	Interest expense	$ 8,000	$ 12,000	Given	Given
26	Earnings before taxes	($ 33,000)	$ 38,000	=B24–B25	=C24–C25
27	Taxes (25% of earnings before tax)	0	$ 9,500	0	=C26*B10
28	Net income	($ 33,000)	$ 28,500	=B26–B27	=C26–C27

the money to invest in assets, they try to do without anything that is not absolutely essential and try to spend less money on those essential items.

Trying to minimize the firm's investments is actually the best way to proceed—if not carried to an extreme. However, small problems can become large ones when inadequate resources are available to support the business. Clearly, the goal of the entrepreneur is to "minimize and control," rather than "maximize and own," resources. To the extent possible, the entrepreneur should use other people's resources—for instance, lease rather than buy, negotiate with suppliers to provide inventory "just in time" to minimize the investment, and arrange to collect money owed the firm before having to pay the firm's bills. This is called **bootstrapping**, and it's the most common way that entrepreneurs accomplish more with less. When Cecilia Levine, the owner of MFI, a manufacturing firm, had the opportunity to get a contract to make clothing for a *Fortune 500* company, she became a master of bootstrapping.

bootstrapping
Minimizing a firm's investments

> *I never expected the fast growth and demand that my services would have. To finance the growth, debt financing would have been helpful, but it was not an option. The definition of*

credit in the dictionary reads, "The ability of a customer to obtain goods or services before payment, based on the trust that payment is going to be made in the future." What it does not say is that for a banker, trust means having collateral, and without collateral you don't get credit. But I still had children to feed and the desire to succeed so I looked for another form of financing—BOOTSTRAPPING.

I had a major customer who believed in me, and who had the equipment I needed. He sold me the equipment and then would reduce his weekly payment of my invoices by an amount to cover the cost of the equipment. Also, the customer paid me each Friday for what we produced and shipped that week. Everyone who worked for me understood that if we didn't perform and finish the needed production for the week, we didn't get paid by our customer. When I received the payment from the customer, I was then able to pay my employees. We were a team, and we understood the meaning of cash flow. Therefore, we performed.[6]

A limited amount of working capital makes forecasting all the more important, as there is much less slack in the system when surprises occur. Moreover, the uncertainties surrounding an entirely new venture make estimating asset and financing requirements difficult. Even for an established business, forecasts are never exact. Therefore, when seeking financing, an entrepreneur must be able to give informed answers about the firm's needs. His or her ability to answer questions regarding the amount of money needed, the purposes for which it will be used, and when and how the lender or creditor will be paid back is vital. Only careful analysis can provide answers to these questions.

To gather needed information, an entrepreneur may use a double-barreled approach to project asset requirements by (1) using industry standard ratios to estimate dollar amounts and (2) cross-checking those dollar amounts by applying break-even analysis and searching for relevant information from a variety of sources. Robert Morris Associates, Dun & Bradstreet, banks, trade associations, and similar organizations compile industry standard ratios for numerous types of businesses. If standard ratios cannot be found, then common sense and educated guesswork must be used to estimate asset requirements.

The analysis of capital requirements should also take into consideration the owner's personal financial situation, especially if no other income is available to make ends meet. Whether or not the owner's personal living expenses during the initial period of operation are part of the business's capitalization, they must be considered in the financial plan. Inadequate provision for personal expenses will inevitably lead to a diversion of business assets and a departure from the plan. Therefore, failing to incorporate these expenses into the financial plan as a cash outflow raises a red flag to any prospective investor.

In fact, a real danger exists that an entrepreneur will neglect personal finances later as well. As a firm grows, an increasing percentage of the owner's net worth is tied up in the firm. One survey of entrepreneurs found that, on average, 53 percent of business owners' wealth was invested in their businesses. Another survey by Financial Services Inc., of Columbus, Ohio, discovered that 63 percent of small business owners did not think they had planned adequately for their company's future or for their personal financial health.[7] SBA director Hector Barreto explains it well:

Small-business people don't know that they don't know when it comes to financial planning. They're busy building the business, and they don't start asking questions until a need or problem comes up. Entrepreneurs are doing a disservice to their businesses when they ignore even the most basic financial planning. The process isn't as time-consuming or as expensive as you might think."[8]

The key to effectively forecasting financing requirements is first understanding the relationship between a firm's projected sales and its assets. A firm's sales are the primary force driving future asset needs. Exhibit 10-9 depicts this relationship, which can be expressed as follows: *The greater a firm's sales, the greater the asset requirements will be and, in turn, the greater the need for financing.*

DETERMINING ASSET REQUIREMENTS Since asset needs tend to increase as sales increase, a firm's asset requirements are often estimated as a percentage of sales. Therefore, if future sales have been projected, a ratio of assets to sales can be used to estimate asset requirements. Suppose, for example, that a firm's sales are expected to be $1 million.

EXHIBIT 10-9 *Assets-to-Sales Financing Relationships*

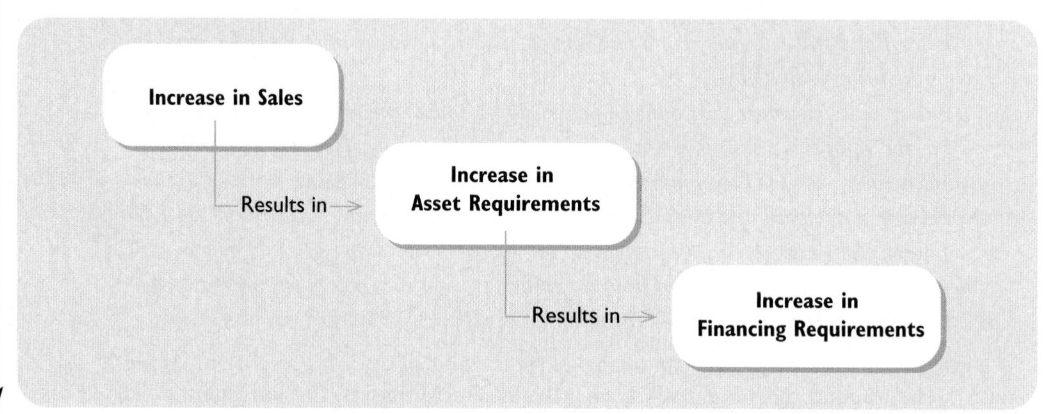

If assets in the firm's particular industry tend to run about 50 percent of sales, the firm's asset requirements would be estimated to be $0.50 \times \$1,000,000 = \$500,000$.

Although the assets-to-sales relationship varies over time and with individual firms, it tends to be relatively constant within an industry. For example, assets as a percentage of sales average 20 percent for grocery stores, compared to 65 percent for oil and gas companies. This method of estimating asset requirements is called the **percentage-of-sales technique**. It can also be used to project figures for individual assets, such as accounts receivable and inventories.

percentage-of-sales technique
A method of forecasting asset investments and financing requirements

To illustrate the percentage-of-sales technique, let's return to Exhibit 10-8, which shows the pro forma income statements developed for Cameron Products, Inc. We'll now consider what Kate Lynn needs in terms of assets to support the firm's activities.

In financial forecasting, it is best to begin with projected sales, which Lynn expects to be \$250,000 and \$400,000 in years 1 and 2, respectively (see Exhibit 10-8). After consid-

Living the Dream *Entrepreneurial Challenges*

Think About Personal Finances, Too

The great irony for many entrepreneurs is that building value in their companies requires such sacrifices that their personal finances suffer. Loren Comitor's story illustrates the dilemma experienced by many entrepreneurs.

Before starting his own business 22 years ago, Comitor was earning the kind of salary and benefits most people only dream about. He says, "Overnight, I went from a very comfortable corporate blanket to a parachute jump of survival. And the question was, would I manage to get the chute open in time?" Today, Comitor's advertising business, CCM&A, in Northbrook, Illinois, supports a comfortable life for his family of four. But the sacrifices Comitor made while launching his company took their toll on his personal finances: "I haven't even begun saving for my kids' college education. I'm living well, but sometimes it doesn't seem like much to show for all those years of work building my own business."

Roy Ballentine, a financial advisor, offers this advice: "It's in an entrepreneur's best interest to diversify personal assets outside the company when possible. Every year, I've watched one or two business owners go from having an enormous personal net worth—all tied up in their companies—to losing almost everything, because their businesses hit a glitch and creditors were able to seize almost everything."

Ballentine's advice is sound, but difficult—if not impossible—to follow when trying to get a new company up and running. But, at some point, an entrepreneur must take the time to consider his or her personal financial situation.

Source: "Are You Financially Fit?" Inc. Online, 1998.

erable investigation into the opportunity, Lynn estimated the firm's current asset requirements (cash, accounts receivable, and inventories) as a percentage of sales:

Assets	Percentage of Sales
Cash	5%
Accounts receivable	10%
Inventories	25%

Lynn will need equipment, at a cost of $10,000. She has found a building suitable for a manufacturing facility for $40,000. Combined, these items total gross fixed assets of $50,000. Given the anticipated sales and the assets-to-sales relationships, she was able to forecast the asset requirements for her venture as follows. If

	Year 1	Year 2
Sales	$250,000	$400,000

then

Assets	Assumptions	Year 1	Year 2
Cash	5% of sales	$ 12,500	$ 20,000
Accounts receivable	10% of sales	25,000	40,000
Inventories	25% of sales	62,500	100,000
Total current assets		$100,000	$160,000
Gross fixed assets	Equipment and building costs	$ 50,000	$ 50,000
Accumulated depreciation	$4,000 annually	(4,000)	(8,000)
Net fixed assets		$ 46,000	$ 42,000
TOTAL ASSETS		$146,000	$202,000

Thus, Lynn expects to need $146,000 in assets by the end of the first year and $202,000 by the conclusion of the second year. Although the figures used to obtain these estimates are only rough approximations, the estimates should be relatively close if Lynn has identified the assets-to-sales relationships correctly and if sales materialize as expected. Let's now consider the corresponding financing requirements.

DETERMINING FINANCING REQUIREMENTS There must be a corresponding dollar of financing for every dollar of assets. To effectively forecast a company's financing needs, an entrepreneur must understand certain basic principles that govern the financing of firms, which can be stated as follows:

1. The more assets a firm needs, the greater the firm's financial requirements. Thus, a firm experiencing rapid sales growth has greater asset requirements and, consequently, greater pressure to find financing—and that pressure can be intolerable if not managed carefully.
2. A firm should finance its growth in such a way as to maintain proper liquidity. **Liquidity** measures the degree to which a firm has current assets available to meet maturing short-term debt. The need for adequate liquidity in small firms deserves special emphasis. A common weakness in small business financing is a disproportionately small investment in liquid assets. Too much money is tied up in assets that are difficult to convert to cash. A conventional measurement of liquidity is the **current ratio**, which compares a firm's current assets to its current liabilities.

$$\text{Current ratio} = \frac{\text{Current assets}}{\text{Current liabilities}}$$

To ensure payment of short-term debts as they come due, an entrepreneur should, as a general rule, maintain a current ratio of at least 2—that is, have current assets equal to twice current liabilities.

3. The amount of total debt that can be used in financing a business is limited by the amount of funds provided by the owners. A bank will not provide all the financing for a firm; owners must put some of their own money into the venture. Thus, a business plan should specify that at least half of the firm's financing will come from the

liquidity
The degree to which a firm has working capital available to meet maturing debt obligations

current ratio
A measure of a company's relative liquidity, determined by dividing current assets by current liabilities

debt ratio
A measure of the fraction of a firm's assets that are financed by debt, determined by dividing total debt by total assets

spontaneous financing
Short-term debts, such as accounts payable, that automatically increase in proportion to a firm's sales

external equity
Capital that comes from the owners' investment in a firm

profit retention
The reinvestment of profits in a firm

internal equity
Capital that comes from retaining profits within a firm

owners and the rest will come from debt. In other words, management should limit the firm's **debt ratio**, which expresses debt as a percentage of total assets.[9]

$$\text{Debt ratio} = \frac{\text{Total debt}}{\text{Total assets}}$$

4. Some types of short-term debt—specifically, accounts payable and accrued operating expenses—maintain a relatively constant relationship with sales; that is, they rise or fall spontaneously as a firm's sales increase or decrease. Such **spontaneous financing** grows as a natural consequence of increases in the firm's sales. For instance, a rise in sales requires more inventories, causing accounts payable to increase when a firm purchases inventory on credit. If sales increase by $1, accounts payable might increase by $.15 or, in other words, 15 percent of sales. This type of financing is significant for most smaller companies. The rest of debt financing must come from loans by banks and other lending sources.
5. There are two sources of equity: external and internal. Initially, the equity in a company comes from the investment the owners make in the firm. These funds represent **external equity**. Once the company is in operation, additional equity may come from **profit retention**, as profits are retained within the company rather than being distributed to the owners. These funds are called **internal equity**. For the typical small firm, internal equity is the primary source of capital for financing growth. (Be careful not to think of retained profits as a big cash resource. As already noted, a firm may have significant earnings but no cash to reinvest. This problem will be discussed further in Chapters 22 and 23.)

In summary,

$$\begin{matrix}\text{Total asset} \\ \text{requirements}\end{matrix} = \begin{matrix}\text{Total sources} \\ \text{of financing}\end{matrix} = \begin{matrix}\text{Spontaneous} \\ \text{financing}\end{matrix} + \begin{matrix}\text{Profits} \\ \text{retained} \\ \text{within the} \\ \text{business}\end{matrix} + \begin{matrix}\text{External} \\ \text{sources of} \\ \text{debt}\end{matrix} + \begin{matrix}\text{External} \\ \text{sources of} \\ \text{equity}\end{matrix}$$

This equation captures the essence of forecasting financial requirements. The entrepreneur who thoroughly understands these relationships should be able to accurately forecast his or her firm's financial requirements.

Recall that for Cameron Products, Inc., Kate Lynn projected asset requirements of $146,000 and $202,000 for years 1 and 2, respectively. Lynn next made estimates of the financing requirements based on the following facts and assumptions:

1. Lynn negotiated with a supplier to receive 30 days' credit on inventory purchases, which means that accounts payable will average about 8 percent of sales.[10]
2. Accrued expenses, such as wages owed but not yet paid, are expected to run approximately 4 percent of annual sales.
3. Lynn plans to invest $110,000 of her personal savings to provide the needed equity for the business. She will receive common stock for her investment.
4. The bank has agreed to provide a short-term line of credit of $25,000 to Cameron Products, which means that the firm can borrow up to $25,000 as the need arises.
5. The bank has also agreed to help finance the purchase of a building for manufacturing and warehousing the firm's product. Of the $40,000 needed, the bank will lend the firm $35,000, with the building serving as collateral for the loan. The loan will be repaid in equal principal payments of $3,500 plus interest on the remaining note balance each year.
6. As part of the loan agreement, the bank has imposed two restrictions: (1) The firm's current ratio (current assets ÷ current liabilities) must stay at 2.0 or above, and (2) no more than 50 percent of the firm's financing may come from debt, either short term or long term (that is, total debt should be no more than 50 percent of total assets). Failure to comply with either of these conditions will cause the bank loans to come due immediately.

With this information, we can estimate the initial sources of financing for Cameron Products as follows. If

	Year 1	Year 2
Sales	$250,000	$400,000

then

Sources of Financing	Assumptions	Year 1	Year 2
Accounts payable	8% of sales	$ 20,000	$ 32,000
Accrued expenses	4% of sales	$ 10,000	16,000
Mortgage	$35,000 – $3,500 annual payments	$ 31,500	$ 28,000
Common stock	Founder's investment	$110,000	$110,000

Any remaining financing up to $25,000 can come from the bank line of credit. If the line of credit is inadequate to meet the firm's needs, Lynn will have to put more equity into the business.

Based on the information above, Lynn can now develop the complete pro forma balance sheets for Cameron Products, Inc. Exhibit 10-10 shows the assumptions made, the equations underlying the numbers, and the actual balance sheets, as developed in an Excel spreadsheet.

Several points about the projected balance sheets presented in Exhibit 10-10 need to be clarified:

1. Assets and sources of financing (debt and equity) must always balance. Note that Cameron Products' asset requirements of $146,000 for the first year and $202,000 for the second year are the same as the firm's debt and equity totals.
2. To bring sources of financing into balance with total assets, Cameron Products will need to borrow on the company's $25,000 short-term line of credit. However, only $7,500 of the $25,000 line of credit is needed to bring the total debt and equity to $146,000 in the first year, but this increases to $20,500 to complete the $202,000 total financing at the end of the second year.
3. Based on Lynn's projections, the firm should be able to satisfy the bank's loan restrictions, maintaining both a current ratio of 2.0 or more and a debt ratio of less than 50 percent. The computations are as follows:

Ratio	Computation	Year 1	Year 2
Current ratio =	$\frac{\text{Current assets}}{\text{Current liabilities}}$	$\frac{\$100{,}000}{\$37.500} = 2.67$	$\frac{\$160{,}000}{\$68{,}500} = 2.34$

and

Debt ratio =	$\frac{\text{Total debt}}{\text{Total assets}}$	$\frac{\$69{,}000}{\$146{,}000} = 0.4, \text{ or } 47\%$	$\frac{\$96{,}500}{\$202{,}000} = 0.48, \text{ or } 48\%$

DETERMINING CASH FLOWS Given the pro forma income statements and balance sheets for Cameron Products, Inc., we can now develop cash flow statements as well. The complete cash flow statements are presented in Appendix 10B. The following summary shows the primary sources and uses of the firm's cash flows:

Cash Flows	Year 1	Year 2
Operating activities	($ 78,500)	$10,000
Investment activities	($ 50,000)	0
Financing activities	$141,000	($ 2,500)
Increase (decrease) in cash	$ 12,500	$ 7,500

Clearly, the first year will be critical for Cameron Products, given the negative cash flows from operating and investment activities. The large financing requirements will most likely present a serious challenge to the new venture. In the second year, however, cash flows should not be as great a problem—not unless Lynn has been overly optimistic about being able to turn the cash flows from operations around and about not needing to make any significant capital investments.

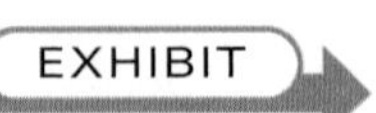

EXHIBIT 10-10 | *Projected Balance Sheets for Cameron Products, Inc.*

	A	B	C	D	E
1	ASSUMPTIONS				
2	Year 1 projected sales	$250,000			
3	Year 2 projected sales	$400,000			
4	Cash/sales	5%			
5	Accounts receivable/sales	10%			
6	Inventories/sales	25%		Equations based on assumptions	
7	Accounts payable/sales	8%			
8	Accrued expenses/sales	4%			
9	Cost of equipment	$ 10,000			
10	Building cost	$ 40,000			
11		**Year 1**	**Year 2**	Equations for	
12	**ASSETS**			**Year 1**	**Year 2**
13	Cash	$ 12,500	$ 20,000	=B2*B4	=B3*B4
14	Accounts receivable	25,000	40,000	=B2*B5	=B3*B5
15	Inventories	62,500	100,000	=B2*B6	=B3*B6
16	Total current assets	$100,000	$160,000	=B13+B14+B15	=C13+C14+C15
17	Gross fixed assets	$ 50,000	$ 50,000	Given	Given
18	Accumulated depreciation	($ 4,000)	($ 8,000)	Given	Given
19	Net fixed assets	46,000	42,000	=B17+B18	=C17+C18
20	Total assets	$146,000	$202,000	=B16+B19	=C16+C19
21					
22	**DEBT AND EQUITY**				
23	Accounts payable	$ 20,000	$ 32,000	=B2*B7	=B3*B7
24	Accrued expenses	10,000	16,000	=B2*B8	=B3*B8
25	Short-term line of credit	7,500	20,500	Required financing	Required financing
26	Total current liabilities	$ 37,500	$ 68,500	=B23+B24+B25	=C23+C24+C25
27	Mortgage	31,500	28,000	Original loan of $35,000 – annual payment of $3,500	Year 1 balance of $31,500 – annual payment of $3,500
28	Total debt	$ 69,000	$ 96,500	=B26+B27	=C26+C27
29	Equity				
30	Owner's investment	$110,000	$110,000	Given	Given
31	Retained earnings	(33,000)	(4,500)	Year 1 loss	Year 1 loss + Year 2 profit
32	Total equity	$ 77,000	$105,500	=B30+B31	C30+C31
33	Total debt and equity	$146,000	$202,000	=B28+B32	=C28+C32
34					
35	Current ratio (current assets ÷ current liabilities)	2.67	2.34	=B16/B26	=C16/C26
36	Debt ratio (total debt ÷ total assets)	47%	48%	=B28/B20	=C28/C20

The importance of carefully monitoring a new company's cash flows cannot be overemphasized. The calculation of the cash flows for Cameron Products, Inc., demonstrates that income statements and balance sheets do not provide the entrepreneur with adequate information about a firm's cash flows. Taking your eye off your firm's cash flows could be a fatal mistake and is certainly one to be avoided.

GOOD FORECASTING REQUIRES GOOD JUDGMENT

4 Explain the importance of using good judgment when making projections.

The forecasting process requires an entrepreneur to exercise good judgment in planning, particularly when the planning is providing the basis for raising capital. The overall approach to forecasting is straightforward—entrepreneurs make assumptions and, based on these assumptions, determine financing requirements. But entrepreneurs may be tempted to overstate their expectations in order to acquire much needed financing. Here are some practical suggestions about making financial forecasts:[11]

1. *Develop realistic sales projections.* Entrepreneurs often think they can accomplish more than they actually are able to, especially when it comes to forecasting future sales. When graphed, their sales projections for a new venture often resemble a hockey stick—the sales numbers are flat or rise slightly at first (like the blade of a hockey stick) and then soar upward like a hockey stick's handle. Such projections are always suspect—only the most astonishing changes in a business or market can justify such a sudden, rocket-like performance.
2. *Build projections from clear assumptions about marketing and pricing plans.* Don't be vague, and don't guess. Spell out the kinds of marketing you plan to do—for example, state specifically how many customers you expect to attract. Paul A. Broni offers this advice:

   When putting together your income statement, revenues should show more than just the projected sales figure for each year. You should also show how many units you plan to sell, as well as the mix of revenue (assuming that you have more than one product or service). If you have a service business, you may also want to show how many customers or clients you will have each year. Investors will look at that number to determine whether it's realistic for you to sell to that many customers. For example, if your plan is to go from 12 customers in the first year to 36 customers in the second, can the sales team you've built accomplish that goal? What about marketing and advertising? Does your budget account for the money you'll need to spend to support such an effort?[12]

3. *Do not use unrealistic profit margins.* Projections are immediately suspect if profit margins (profits ÷ sales) or expenses are significantly higher or lower than the average figures reported by firms in the industry with similar revenues and numbers of employees. In general, a new business should not expect to exceed the industry average in profit margins. Frequently, entrepreneurs assume that as their company grows it will achieve economies of scale, and gross and operating profit margins will improve. In fact, as the business grows and increases its fixed costs, its operating profit margins are likely to suffer in the short run. If you insist in your projections that the economies can be achieved quickly, you will need to explain your position.
4. *Don't limit your projections to an income statement.* Entrepreneurs frequently resist providing a balance sheet and cash flow statement. They feel comfortable projecting sales and profits but do not like having to commit to assumptions about the sources and uses of capital needed to grow the business. Investors, however, want to see those assumptions in print, and they are particularly interested in the firm's cash flows—and you should be as well.
5. *Provide monthly data for the upcoming year and annual data for succeeding years.* Many entrepreneurs prepare projections using only monthly data or only annual data for an entire three- or five-year period. Given the difficulty in forecasting accurately beyond a year, monthly data for the later years are not particularly believable. From year two on, annual projections are adequate.
6. *Avoid providing too much financial information.* Computer spreadsheets are extremely valuable in making projections and showing how different assumptions affect the

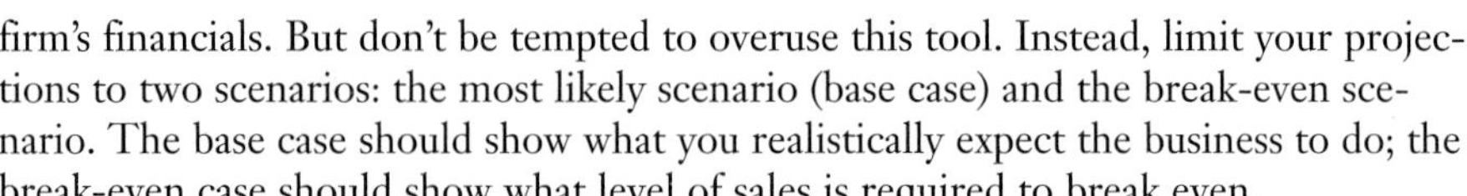

firm's financials. But don't be tempted to overuse this tool. Instead, limit your projections to two scenarios: the most likely scenario (base case) and the break-even scenario. The base case should show what you realistically expect the business to do; the break-even case should show what level of sales is required to break even.

7. *Be certain that the numbers reconcile—and not by simply plugging in a figure.* All too often, entrepreneurs plug a figure into equity to make things work out. While everyone makes mistakes, that's one you want to avoid because it can result in a loss of credibility.
8. *Follow the plan.* After you have prepared the pro forma financial statements, check them against actual results at least once a month, and modify your projections as needed.

These suggestions, if followed, will help avoid the old problem of overpromising and underdelivering. Given the nature of starting a business, entrepreneurs at times simply have to have faith that they will be able to deliver on what they promise, even though it may not be clear exactly how this will be accomplished. Risk is part of the equation, and often things will not go as planned. But integrity requires you to honor your commitments, and that cannot be done if you have made unrealistic projections about what you can accomplish.

The information provided in this chapter on financial planning for a new company will serve as a foundation for the examination of an entrepreneur's search for specific sources of financing in Chapter 11.

Looking Back

1 Describe the purpose and content of the income statement, the balance sheet, and the cash flow statement.

- An income statement presents the financial results of a firm's operations over a given time period in selling the product or service, in producing or acquiring the goods or services, in running the firm, in financing the firm, and in paying taxes.
- A balance sheet provides a snapshot of a firm's financial position at a specific point in time, showing the amount of assets the firm owns, the amount of outstanding debt, and the amount of ownership equity.
- The income statement cannot measure a firm's cash flows, as it is calculated on an accrual basis rather than on a cash basis.
- Measuring cash flows involves calculating a firm's after-tax cash flows from operations and then subtracting any investments and adding any additional financing received.

2 Forecast a new venture's profitability.

- The purpose of pro forma financial statements is to determine (1) future profitability based on projected sales levels, (2) how much and what type of financing will be used, and (3) whether the firm will have adequate cash flows.
- A firm's net income is dependent on (1) amount of sales, (2) cost of goods sold and operating expenses, (3) interest expense, and (4) taxes.
- Estimates of fixed operating expenses and variable operating expenses, based on the projected level of sales, are deducted from gross sales profits to obtain a forecasted operating profit.

3 Determine asset requirements, evaluate financial sources, and estimate cash flows for a new venture.

- Funding for a new venture should cover its asset requirements and also the personal living expenses of the owner.
- A direct relationship exists between sales growth and asset needs; as sales increase, more assets are required. And, for every dollar of assets needed, there must be a corresponding dollar of financing.
- The two basic types of capital used in financing a company are debt financing and ownership equity.
- A firm's cash flows involve three activities: operations, investments, and financing.

4 Explain the importance of using good judgment when making projections.

- It is important to develop realistic sales projections and profit margins to establish your credibility with investors.
- Be clear about the assumptions on which you are making your projections, and provide data to support those assumptions.
- Although risk is always involved in starting a new business, integrity requires that you honor your commitments.

Key Terms

financial statements (accounting statements), p. 205
income statement (profit and loss statement), p. 205
cost of goods sold, p. 205
gross profit, p. 205
operating expenses, p. 205
operating income, p. 205
financing costs, p. 206
earnings before taxes, p. 206
net income available to owners (net income), p. 206
depreciation expense, p. 206
balance sheet, p. 208
current assets (gross working capital), p. 208
accounts receivable, p. 209
inventory, p. 209
fixed assets, p. 209
depreciable assets, p. 209
gross fixed assets, p. 210
accumulated depreciation, p. 210
net fixed assets, p. 210
other assets, p. 210
debt, p. 210
current debt (short-term liabilities), p. 210
accounts payable (trade credit), p. 211
accrued expenses, p. 211
short-term notes, p. 211
long-term debt, p. 211
mortgage, p. 211
ownership equity, p. 211
retained earnings, p. 211
cash flow statement, p. 212
accrual-basis accounting, p. 213
cash-basis accounting, p. 213
cash flows from operations, p. 214
adjusted income, p. 215
net working capital, p. 215
pro forma financial statements, p. 217
bootstrapping, p. 220
percentage-of-sales technique, p. 222
liquidity, p. 223
current ratio, p. 223
debt ratio, p. 224
spontaneous financing, p. 224
external equity, p. 224
profit retention, p. 224
internal equity, p. 224

Discussion Questions

1. What is the relationship between an income statement and a balance sheet?
2. Explain the purposes of the income statement and balance sheet.
3. Distinguish among (a) gross profit, (b) operating income (earnings before interest and taxes), and (c) net income available to owners.
4. Why aren't a firm's cash flows equal to its profit?
5. Describe the three major components of a cash flow statement.
6. Interpret a firm's cash flow statement that shows negative cash flows from operations, negative cash flows from investments, and positive cash flows from financing.
7. What determines a company's profitability?
8. Describe the process for estimating the amount of assets required for a new venture.
9. Distinguish between ownership equity and debt.
10. How are a startup's financial requirements estimated?

You Make the Call

SITUATION 1

The Donahoo Furniture Sales Company was formed on December 31, 2004, with $1,000,000 in equity plus $500,000 in long-term debt. On January 1, 2005, all of the firm's capital was held in cash. The following transactions occurred during January 2005.

- January 2: Donahoo purchased $1,000,000 worth of furniture for resale. It paid $500,000 in cash and financed the balance using trade credit that required payment in 60 days.
- January 3: Donahoo sold $250,000 worth of furniture that it had paid $200,000 to acquire. The entire sale was on credit terms of net 90 days.
- January 15: Donahoo purchased more furniture for $200,000. This time, it used trade credit for the entire amount of the purchase, with credit terms of net 60 days.
- January 31: Donahoo sold $500,000 worth of furniture, for which it had paid $400,000. The furniture was sold for 10 percent cash down, with the remainder payable in 90 days. In addition, the firm paid a cash dividend of $100,000 to its stockholders and paid off $250,000 of its long-term debt.

Question 1 What did Donahoo's balance sheet look like at the outset of the firm's life?

Question 2 What did the firm's balance sheet look like after each transaction?

Question 3 Ignoring taxes, determine how much income Donahoo earned during January. Prepare an income statement for the month. Recognize an interest expense of 1 percent for the month (12 percent annually)

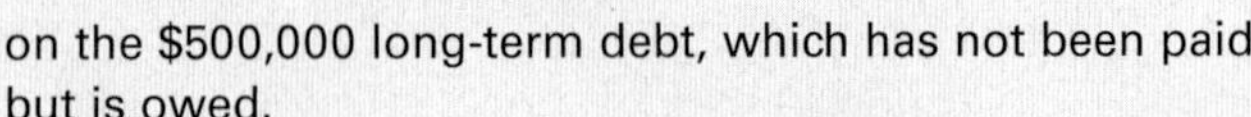

on the $500,000 long-term debt, which has not been paid but is owed.

Question 4 What was Donahoo's cash flow for the month of January?

SITUATION 2

At the beginning of 2005, Mary Abrahams purchased a small business, the Turpen Company, whose income statement and balance sheets are shown below.

Income Statement for the Turpen Company for 2005

Sales revenue		$175,000
Cost of goods sold		105,000
Gross profit		$ 70,000
Operating expenses:		
Depreciation	$ 5,000	
Administrative expenses	20,000	
Selling expenses	26,000	
Total operating expenses		$ 51,000
Operating income		$ 19,000
Interest expense		3,000
Earnings before taxes		$ 16,000
Taxes		8,000
Net income		$ 8,000

Balance Sheets for the Turpen Company for 2004 and 2005

	2004	**2005**
Assets		
Current assets:		
Cash	$ 8,000	$ 10,000
Accounts receivable	15,000	20,000
Inventories	22,000	25,000
Total current assets	$45,000	$ 55,000
Fixed assets:		
Gross fixed assets	$50,000	$ 55,000
Accumulated depreciation	15,000	20,000
Total fixed assets	$35,000	$ 35,000
Other assets	12,000	10,000
TOTAL ASSETS	$92,000	$100,000
Debt (Liabilities) and Equity		
Current debt:		
Accounts payable	$10,000	$ 12,000
Accruals	7,000	8,000
Short-term notes	5,000	5,000
Total current debt	$22,000	$ 25,000
Long-term debt	15,000	15,000
Total debt	$37,000	$ 40,000
Equity	$55,000	$60,000
TOTAL DEBT AND EQUITY	$92,000	$100,000

The firm has been profitable, but Abrahams has been disappointed by the lack of cash flows. She had hoped to have about $10,000 a year available for personal living expenses. However, there never seems to be much cash available for purposes other than business needs. Abrahams has asked you to examine the financial statements and explain why, although they show profits, she does not have any discretionary cash for personal needs. She observed, "I thought that I could take the profits and add depreciation to find out how much cash I was generating. However, that doesn't seem to be the case. What's happening?"

Question 1 Given the information provided by the financial statements, what would you tell Abrahams? (As part of your answer, calculate the firm's cash flows.)

Question 2 How would you describe the cash flow pattern for the Turpen Company?

SITUATION 3

Cameron Products, Inc., used as an example in this chapter, is an actual firm (although some of the facts were changed to maintain confidentiality). Kate Lynn bought the firm from its founding owners and moved its operations to her hometown. Although she estimated the firm's asset needs and financing requirements, she cannot be certain that these projections will be realized. The figures merely represent the most likely case. Lynn also made some projections that she considers to be the worst-case and best-case sales and profit figures. If things do not go well, the firm might have sales of only $200,000 in its first year. However, if the potential of the business is realized, Lynn believes that sales could be as high as $325,000. If she needs any additional financing beyond the existing line of credit, she could conceivably borrow another $5,000 in short-term debt from the bank by pledging some personal investments. Any additional financing would need to come from Lynn herself, thereby increasing her equity stake in the business.

Source: Personal conversation with Kate Lynn. (Numbers are hypothetical.)

Question If all of Cameron Products' other relationships hold, how will Lynn's worst-case and best-case projections affect the income statement and balance sheet in the first year?

Experiential Exercises

1. Interview an owner of a small firm about the financial statements she or he uses. Ask the owner how important financial data are to her or his decision making.
2. Acquire a small firm's financial statements. Review the statements and describe the firm's financial position. Find out if the owner agrees with your conclusions.
3. Dun & Bradstreet and Robert Morris Associates compile financial information about many companies. They provide, among other information, income statements and balance sheets for an

average firm in an industry. Go to a library, look up financial information on two industries of your choice, and compute the following data for each industry:

a. The percentages of assets in (1) current assets and (2) fixed assets (plant and equipment)
b. The percentages of financing from (1) spontaneous financing and (2) internal equity
c. The cost of goods sold and the operating expenses as percentages of sales
d. The total assets as a percentage of sales

Given your findings, how would you summarize the differences between the two industries?

4. Obtain the business plan of a firm that is 3 to 5 years old. Compare the techniques used in the plan to forecast the firm's profits and financing requirements with those presented in this chapter. If actual data are available, compare the financial forecasts with the eventual outcome. What accounts for the differences?

Exploring the Web

1. Bplans.com is owned and maintained by PaloAlto Software, Inc., as a free resource for entrepreneurs. Find the Planning Solutions portion of the Bplans.com site by going to **http://bplans.com/contentkit**. Choose the "Interactive Calculators" link.

a. Link to the "Starting Costs Calculator" and run through the exercise to determine the startup costs for your new business. Once you have computed your starting costs, print the page. To print, right click and then choose Print from the popup menu.
b. Return to the Interactive Calculators page and click on "Cash Flow Calculator." What happens when you change the calculator's variables?

2. For some first-hand experience with debt ratios, go to **http://www.anz.com**, the site of the Australian and New Zealand Banking Group. Choose the "Business" tab, then "Business Toolkit," "Benchmark Your Business," and "Debt Ratio." Read the site's content about debt ratios and, if possible, use the simple calculator to determine your business's debt ratio.

a. What are the advantages and disadvantages of a high debt ratio (greater than 0.50)?
b. Why is the debt ratio useful as a business benchmark?

3. Visit the CCH Business Owner's Toolkit at **http://www.toolkit.cch.com** to get an overview of what the site offers. CCH is a leading provider of business and tax information. Read more about financing basics at **http://toolkit.cch.com/text/P10_2000.asp**. What figures are needed to calculate the debt-to-equity ratio?

Case 10

STEGMART (P. 541)

This case provides the data necessary to prepare pro forma financial statements for a small startup company.

Alternative Cases for Chapter 10:

Case 3, Biolife LLC, p. 530
Case 6, AdGrove.com, Inc., p. 534
Case 23, Artho, Inc., p. 570

The Business Plan

LAYING THE FOUNDATION

As part of laying the foundation to prepare your own business plan, you will need to develop the following:

1. Historical financial statements (if applicable) and five years of pro forma financial statements, including balance sheets, income statements, and statements of cash flows.
2. Monthly cash budgets for the first year and quarterly cash budgets for the second year. (See Chapter 22 for an explanation of cash budgets.)
3. Profit and cash flow break-even analysis. (See Chapter 15 for an explanation of break-even analysis.)
4. Financial resources required now and in the future, with details on the intended use of funds being requested.
5. Underlying assumptions for all pro forma statements.
6. Current and planned investments by the owners and other investors.

Appendix 10A

COMPUTING CASH FLOWS FOR PETRI & ASSOCIATES, INC.

In Chapter 10, we presented the cash flow statement, giving the highlights and describing how it can be interpreted. We refrained from showing the details of the computations, realizing that for most people, these details are not essential to understanding the statement. But cash flows are such a critical issue for entrepreneurs that we have provided this appendix to ensure a greater understanding for anyone with the desire to know more.

THE PROCESS AND DATA

We must re-emphasize that *the profits shown on a company's income statement are not the same as its cash flows.* To compute a firm's cash flows, we begin with selected information from the income statement and then make adjustments based on changes in the balance sheets from the end of the prior year to the end of the current year. We will illustrate this process by returning to our example of Petri & Associates, Inc., used in Chapter 10.

Exhibit A10-1 incorporates Petri & Associates' 2005 income statement (from Exhibit 10-2) and the changes in the balance sheets from December 31, 2004 to December 31, 2005 (from Exhibit 10-4). The information from the income statement needed for computing cash flows is in bold print. Also, to simplify the data from the balance sheets, we have done the following:

1. Eliminated all the totals (for example, *total current assets*).
2. Shown only the change in *gross fixed assets* and not in *accumulated depreciation* or *net fixed assets*, because these are affected by the firm's depreciation expense, a noncash expense.
3. Disregarded the change in *retained earnings*, which is already recognized through the inclusion of the firm's income and dividend payments in the cash flow statement.

All remaining changes directly affect a firm's cash flows and must be considered.

COMPONENTS OF THE CASH FLOW STATEMENT

As explained in Chapter 10, there are three components of a cash flow statement:

1. *Cash flows from operations*, consisting of the cash generated from the firm's normal day-to-day business activities
2. *Investment in long-term assets*, such as purchasing or selling fixed assets
3. *Financing activities*, including paying dividends and interest expense, increasing or decreasing short-term or long-term debt, and issuing or repurchasing stock

Let's examine the computation of each of the above components in turn.

Operating Activities

A firm's *cash flows* from operations consist of two elements: (1) after-tax profits adjusted for any noncash expenses, such as depreciation, and (2) changes in the company's working capital.

We start with operating income (earnings before interest and taxes). Then we (1) add back depreciation expense, since it is not a cash expense even though it is shown as an

EXHIBIT A10-1 *Income Statement and Balance Sheet Changes for Petri & Associates, Inc., for the Year Ending December 31, 2005*

Income Statement		
Sales		$850,000
Cost of goods sold		550,000
Gross profit on sales		$300,000
Operating expenses:		
Marketing expenses	$90,000	
General and administrative expenses	80,000	
Depreciation expense	**30,000**	
Total operating expenses		$200,000
Operating income		**$100,000**
Interest expense		20,000
Earnings before taxes		$ 80,000
Income tax (25%)		**20,000**
Net income		$ 60,000
Net income		$ 60,000
Dividends paid		**15,000**
Change in retained earnings		$ 45,000

Balance Sheet Changes: Dec. 31, 2004 to Dec. 31, 2005	
Cash	$ 5,000
Accounts receivable	5,000
Inventories	40,000
Gross plant and equipment	100,000
Accounts payable	$ 5,000
Short-term notes	20,000
Long-term debt	50,000
Common stock	0

expense in the income statement, and (2) subtract income taxes to get the cash flow on an after-tax basis, or adjusted income. For Petri & Associates, we have

Operating income	$100,000
Depreciation	30,000
Income taxes	(20,000)
Adjusted income	$110,000

Next, we factor in the change in net working capital, which is not reported in the income statement. Net working capital is the current assets (accounts receivable and inventories) less short-term debt (accounts payable and accruals) that are part of the firm's operating cycle. An increase in net working capital is subtracted because it is a *cash outflow*, and a decrease in net working capital is added because it is a *cash inflow*. For Petri & Associates, the changes in net working capital are as follows:

	Changes
Increase in accounts receivable (cash outflow)	($ 5,000)
Increase in inventories (cash outflow)	(40,000)
Increase in accounts payable (cash inflow)	5,000
Net cash flow for working capital	($40,000)

So, cash flows from operations may be calculated as follows:

Operating activities:		
Operating income	$100,000	
Depreciation	30,000	
Income taxes	(20,000)	
Adjusted income		$110,000
Increase in accounts receivable (cash outflow)	($ 5,000)	
Increase in inventories (cash outflow)	(40,000)	
Increase in accounts payable (cash inflow)	5,000	
Change in net working capital		($ 40,000)
Cash flows from operations		$ 70,000

Investment Activities

As already noted, *depreciation expense is not a cash flow*. This entry in the income statement is the accountant's effort to allocate the cost of an asset over its useful life. However, when equipment or some other depreciable asset is purchased or sold, cash flows occur that are not shown in the income statement. Petri & Associates spent $100,000 on new plant and equipment, as reflected in the change in gross fixed assets.

Financing Activities

The third section of the cash flow statement presents the cash inflows and outflows resulting from financing activities, including (1) paying dividends and interest expense, (2) increasing or decreasing short-term or long-term debt, and (3) issuing stock or repurchasing stock.

Petri & Associates paid $35,000 in interest and dividends, but borrowed an additional $70,000 in debt, resulting in a net cash inflow of $35,000 from financing activities. Exhibit A10-2 shows Petri & Associates' cash flow statement for the year ending 2005.

EXHIBIT A10-2 *Cash Flow Statement for Petri & Associates, Inc., for the Year Ending December 31, 2005*

Operating activities:		
Operating income	$100,000	
Depreciation	30,000	
Income taxes	(20,000)	
Adjusted income		$110,000
Increase in accounts receivable (cash outflow)	($ 5,000)	
Increase in inventories (cash outflow)	(40,000)	
Increase in accounts payable (cash inflow)	5,000	
Change in net cash flow for working capital		($ 40,000)
CASH FLOWS FROM OPERATIONS		$ 70,000
Investment activities:		
Increase in gross fixed assets (cash outflow)		($100,000)
Financing activities:		
Interest expense	($ 20,000)	
Dividends	(15,000)	
Increase in short-term notes	20,000	
Increase in long-term debt	50,000	
TOTAL FINANCING ACTIVITIES		$ 35,000
Increase in cash		$ 5,000

Appendix 10B

CASH FLOW STATEMENTS FOR CAMERON PRODUCTS, INC.

	Year 1	Year 2
Operating activities:		
Operating income	($ 25,000)	$ 50,000
Depreciation expenses	4,000	4,000
Taxes	0	(9,500)
Adjusted income	($ 21,000)	$ 44,500
Increase in accounts receivable (cash outflow)	($ 25,000)	($ 15,000)
Increase in inventories (cash outflow)	(62,500)	(37,500)
Increase in accounts payable (cash inflow)	20,000	12,000
Increase in accruals (cash inflow)	10,000	6,000
Net cash flow for working capital	($ 57,500)	($ 34,500)
Cash flows from operations	**($ 78,500)**	**$ 10,000**
Investment activities:		
Increase in gross fixed assets (cash outflow)	($ 50,000)	$ 0
Cash flows from investments	**($ 50,000)**	**$ 0**
Financing activities:		
Interest expense	($ 8,000)	($ 12,000)
Increase in short-term notes	11,000	11,500
Increase in long-term debt	28,000	(2,000)
Increase in stock	110,000	$ 0
Cash flows from financing	**$141,000**	**($ 2,500)**
Increase (decrease) in cash	$ 12,500	$ 7,500

THE FINANCIAL PLAN, PART 2

FINDING SOURCES OF FUNDS

In the Video Spotlight

We'll Show You the Money

One of the most difficult aspects of starting your own business can be finding financing. Tom Gegax and Don Gullet, founders of Tires Plus, discovered that even though they had $30,000 in cash, they couldn't find a bank to loan them the other $60,000 they needed to start their business. (See the Spotlight for Chapter 8.) These two former executives of Shell Oil Company were told they didn't have enough experience! With seasoned businessmen being turned down for loans based on those numbers, where can entrepreneurs go when they need to finance most, if not all, of their new venture?

Sohrab Vossoughi started Ziba Design, the renowned industrial design firm, with the $400 that he and his wife had left after they sold their house and paid all their outstanding debts. José Navarro runs the most efficient drugstore chain in the United States, Navarro Pharmacy, a business his father started by cashing in a life insurance policy. Frank Jao, a real estate developer (shown in the photo), was turned down for so many loans that he finally asked the bank for an exact list of requirements he needed to fulfill. And Tim Hennessey's frustration with venture capital companies led him to structure a series of notes that enabled him to start his freshwater tropical fish company with very limited financing.

Video material provided by Hattie Bryant, Producer of Small Business School, the series on PBS Stations, Worldnet, and the Web at http://www.smallbusinessschool.org.

Chapter 11

Looking Ahead

After studying this chapter, you should be able to

1 Describe how the nature of a firm affects its financing sources.

2 Evaluate the choice between debt financing and equity financing.

3 Identify the typical sources of financing used at the outset of a new venture.

4 Discuss the basic process for acquiring and structuring a bank loan.

5 Explain how business relationships can be used to finance a small firm.

6 Describe the two types of private equity investors that offer financing to small firms.

7 Distinguish among the different government loan programs available to small companies.

8 Explain when large companies and public stock offerings can be sources of financing.

Chapter 10 addressed two questions: (1) *How much* financing is needed? and (2) *What types* of financing are available? Three basic types of financing were identified:

1. *Profit retention*, where the firm finances its growth through cash flows from operations, rather than distributing the cash to the owners in the form of dividends.
2. *Spontaneous financing*, such as accounts payable, which increases automatically with increases in sales. For instance, as a firm's sales grow, it purchases more inventories and suppliers extend the firm more credit, which increases accounts payable.
3. *External financing*, which comes from outside lenders and investors. Lenders (such as bankers) and investors (such as common stockholders, partners, or sole proprietors) provide equity financing.

This chapter discusses sources of spontaneous and external financing for small firms. But first we consider *how* a company should be financed. An understanding of this core issue is critical to identifying appropriate sources of financing.

THE NATURE OF A FIRM AND ITS FINANCING SOURCES

1 Describe how the nature of a firm affects its financing sources.

Four basic factors determine how a firm is financed: (1) the firm's economic potential, (2) the size and maturity of the company, (3) the nature of its assets, and (4) the personal preferences of the owners with respect to the tradeoffs between debt and equity.

A Firm's Economic Potential

A firm with potential for high growth and large profits has many more possible sources of financing than does a firm that provides a good lifestyle for the owner but little in the way of attractive returns to investors. Only those firms providing rates of returns that exceed the investor's required rate of return create value for the investor. In fact, most investors in startup companies limit their investment to firms that offer potentially high returns within a 5- to 10-year period. Clearly, a company that provides a comfortable lifestyle for its owner but insufficient profits to attract outside investors will be more limited in finding alternative sources of financing.

Company Size and Maturity

The size and maturity of a company have a direct bearing on the types of available financing. In its most recent survey of small business finance, the Small Business Administration found a positive relationship between the use of bank debt and firm size. Larger and older firms have access to bank credit that simply is not available to younger and smaller companies. The survey also found that smaller firms rely more on personal loans and credit cards for financing.[1] In the early years of a business, most entrepreneurs bootstrap their financing—that is, they depend on their own initiative to come up with the necessary capital. Only after the business has an established track record will most bankers and other financial institutions be interested in providing financing.

Even venture capitalists limit how much they will invest in startup companies. Many equity investors believe that the additional risk associated with startups is too great relative to the returns they can expect to receive. On average, about three-fourths of a venture capitalist's investments are in later-stage businesses; only a few venture capitalists focus heavily on startups. Similarly, bankers demand evidence that the business will be able to repay a loan—and that evidence usually must be based on what the firm has done in the past and not what the owner says it will achieve in the future. So, a firm's life cycle position is a critical factor in raising capital.

Types of Assets

There are two kinds of assets a bank looks at when it considers financing a company: tangible and intangible. Tangible assets, which can be seen and touched, include inventories, equipment, and buildings. The cost of these assets appears on the firm's balance sheet, which the banker receives as part of the firm's financial statements. Tangible assets serve as great collateral when a firm is requesting a bank loan. On the other hand, intangible assets, such as goodwill or past investments in research and development, have little value as collateral. As a result, companies with substantial tangible assets have a much easier time borrowing money than do companies with intangible assets.

Living the Dream *Entrepreneurial Challenges*

Can't Get It Done the Traditional Way? Try Bootstrapping

In 1997, just two years after launching her company, Sheryl McCaleb needed more elbowroom. Hair Prosthesis Institute (HPI), which makes custom hair prosthetics for women and children, was growing faster than McCaleb had anticipated. She had already increased her physical space from 800 to 1,200 square feet but needed to expand again.

Unfortunately, rents near HPI's location in Nashville, Tennessee, were more than McCaleb was willing to pay. Shifting her strategy, she began to look for property to buy and found a 9,000-square-foot office building a mile from her original office. The building, however, needed considerable TLC. Not only would McCaleb need to raise more than $700,000 to buy the building, but she would also need a sizeable amount for repairs and renovation.

McCaleb didn't have that kind of capital—or enough collateral for a jumbo mortgage. Her solution: Find a partner with financial wherewithal.

She joined forces with a friend in the building-supply business, and the two formed a company to make the purchase. "He asked for controlling interest, but I didn't mind because he brought so much to the table," McCaleb says. Besides financial liquidity, the partner had a long track record of business success and could mentor McCaleb.

What's more, the partner's building-supply connections helped the duo to get discounts on materials needed for the renovation. McCaleb also bartered as much as possible, exchanging HPI's services for lower rates on everything from cleaning to new carpeting. The lower renovation costs enabled McCaleb to keep rents down, which benefited HPI as one of the building's new tenants.

In this win-win scenario, McCaleb's partner made a healthy profit on his investment, while McCaleb acquired commercial property, established strong credit, and gleaned more financial savvy.

"This has been one of the best business moves I've ever made," she says.

Source: "Partner Power," *FastTrac Connections Newsletter*, http://www.Fasttrac.org, April 2004.

Owner Preferences for Debt or Equity

The owner of a company faces the question "Should I finance with debt or equity or some mix of the two?" The answer depends, in part, on his or her personal preference. The ultimate choice between debt and equity involves certain tradeoffs, which will be explained in the following section.

DEBT OR EQUITY FINANCING?

2 *Evaluate the choice between debt financing and equity financing.*

Most providers of financial capital specialize in *either* debt or equity financing. Furthermore, the choice between debt and equity financing must be made early in a firm's life cycle and may have long-term financial consequences. To make an informed decision, a small business owner needs to recognize and understand the tradeoffs between debt and equity with regard to (1) potential profitability, (2) financial risk, and (3) voting control. The tradeoffs are presented graphically in Exhibit 11-1. Let's consider each of these tradeoffs in turn.

Potential Profitability

Anyone who owns a business wants it to be profitable. Of course, profits can be measured as a dollar amount, such as $500,000. However, the really important question is how much profit the business makes relative to the size of the investment. In other words, the owner is primarily interested in the rate of return on the investment. Making $500,000 in profits may sound great, but not if the owner must invest $50 million to earn it. It would be better to purchase a certificate of deposit that earned, say, 3 percent or even 2 percent; any rate over 1 percent would provide income greater than $500,000.

To see how the choice between debt and equity affects potential profitability, consider the Levine Company, a new firm that's still in the process of raising needed capital.

EXHIBIT 11-1 *Tradeoffs Between Debt and Equity*

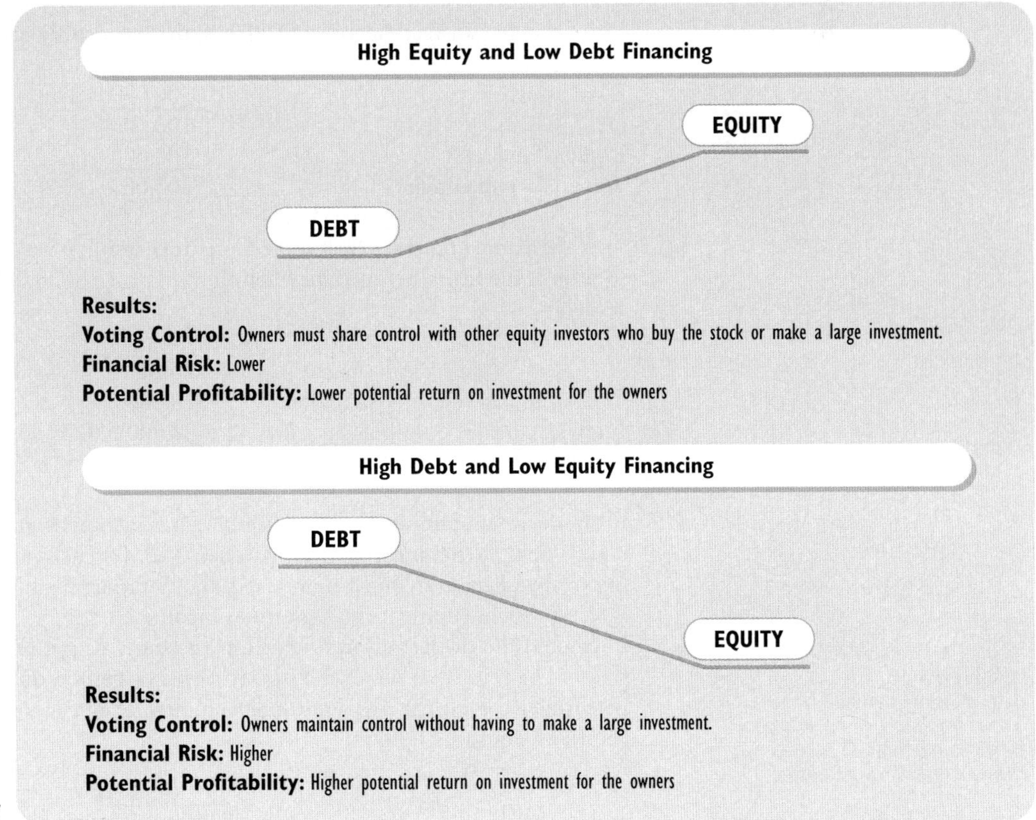

High Equity and Low Debt Financing
EQUITY
DEBT
Results:
Voting Control: Owners must share control with other equity investors who buy the stock or make a large investment.
Financial Risk: Lower
Potential Profitability: Lower potential return on investment for the owners
High Debt and Low Equity Financing
DEBT
EQUITY
Results:
Voting Control: Owners maintain control without having to make a large investment.
Financial Risk: Higher
Potential Profitability: Higher potential return on investment for the owners

- The owners have already invested $100,000 of their own money in the new business. To complete the financing, they need another $100,000.
- Levine is considering one of two options for raising the additional $100,000: (1) investors who would provide $100,000 for a 30 percent share of the firm's outstanding stock or (2) a bank that would lend the money at an interest rate of 8 percent, so the interest expense each year would be $8,000 (0.08 × $100,000).
- The firm's operating income (earnings before interest and taxes) is expected to be $28,000, determined as follows:

Sales	$150,000
Cost of goods sold	80,000
Gross profit	$ 70,000
Operating expenses	42,000
Operating income (earnings before interest and taxes)	$ 28,000

- With the additional $100,000 financing, the firm's total assets would be $200,000 ($100,000 original equity plus $100,000 in additional financing).
- Based on the projected operating income of $28,000 and assets of $200,000, the firm expects to earn $0.14 for each $1 of assets invested ($28,000 income ÷ $200,000 assets). In other words, there will be a 14 percent **return on assets**, which is the rate of return earned on a firm's total assets invested.

return on assets
Rate of return earned on a firm's total assets invested, computed as operating income divided by total assets

$$\text{Return on assets} = \frac{\text{Operating income}}{\text{Total assets}}$$

If the firm raises the additional $100,000 in equity, its balance sheet will appear as follows:

Total assets	$200,000
Debt	$ 0
Equity (founders and new investors)	200,000
Total debt and equity	$200,000

But if the firm instead borrows $100,000, the balance sheet will look like this:

Total assets	$200,000
Debt (8% interest rate)	$100,000
Equity (founders)	100,000
Total debt and equity	$200,000

If we assume no taxes (just to keep matters simple), we can use the above information to project the firm's net income when the additional $100,000 is financed by either equity or debt:

	Equity	**Debt**	
Operating income	$28,000	$28,000	
Interest expense	0	(8,000)	(0.08 × $100,000)
Net income	$28,000	$20,000	

From these computations, we can see that net income is greater if the firm finances with equity ($28,000 net income) than with debt ($20,000 net income). But the owners are having to invest *twice* as much money ($200,000 rather than $100,000) to avoid the $8,000 interest expense and get the higher net income.

Should the owners always finance with equity to get higher net income? Not necessarily. The return on the owner's investment, or **return on equity**, is a better measure of performance than the absolute dollar amount of net income. We measure the owners' return on equity as follows:

return on equity
Rate of return earned on the owner's equity investment, computed as net income divided by owner's equity investment

$$\text{Return on equity} = \frac{\text{Net income}}{\text{Owners' equity investment}}$$

So when the firm uses *only* equity financing, the return on equity is 14 percent, computed as follows:

$$\text{Return on equity} = \frac{\text{Net income}}{\text{Owners' equity investment}}$$

$$= \frac{\$28,000}{\$200,000} = 0.14, \text{ or } 14\%$$

Return on equity if the firm finances with all equity (common stock)

But if the additional financing comes from debt, with interest expense of $8,000 and equity investment of only $100,000, the rate of return on equity is 20 percent, calculated as follows:

$$\text{Return on equity} = \frac{\text{Net income}}{\text{Owners' equity investment}}$$

$$= \frac{\$20,000}{\$100,000} = 0.20, \text{ or } 20\%$$

Return on equity if the firm finances with half debt and half equity

Thus, Levine's return on equity is higher if half the firm's financing comes from equity and half from debt. By using only equity, Levine's owners will earn $0.14 for every $1 of equity invested; but by also using debt, they will earn $0.20 for every $1 of equity invested. So, in terms of a rate of return on their investment, Levine's owners get a better return by borrowing money at 8 percent interest than by using equity financing. That makes sense, because the firm is earning 14 percent on its assets but only paying creditors at an 8 percent rate. Levine's owners benefit from the difference. These relationships are shown in Exhibit 11-2.

As a general rule, *as long as a firm's rate of return on its assets (operating income ÷ total assets) is greater than the cost of the debt (interest rate), the owners' rate of return on equity will increase as the firm uses more debt.*

EXHIBIT 11-2 *Debt Versus Equity at the Levine Company*

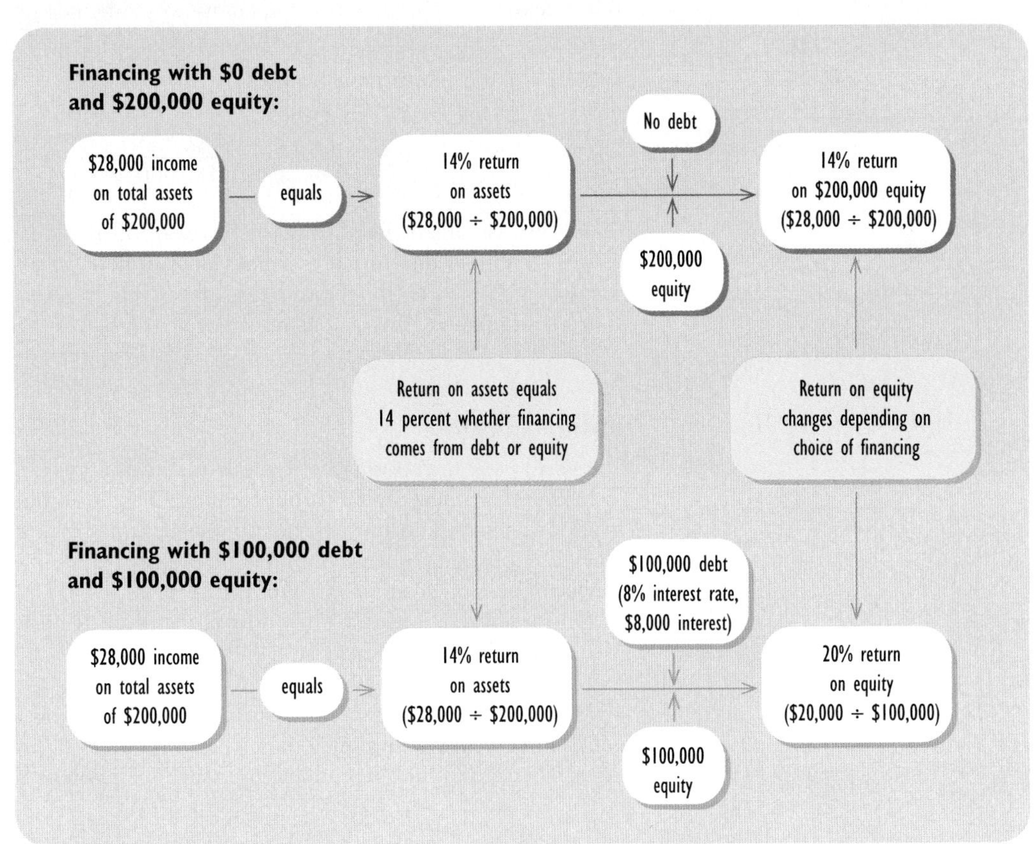

Financial Risk

If debt is so beneficial in terms of producing a higher rate of return for the owners, why shouldn't Levine's owners use as much debt as possible—even 100 percent debt—if they can? Then the rate of return on the owners' equity investment would even be higher—unlimited, in fact, if the owners did not have to invest any money.

That's the good news. The bad news: *Debt is risky*. If the firm fails to earn profits, creditors will still insist on their interest payments. Debt demands its pound of flesh from the owners regardless of the firm's performance. In an extreme case, creditors can force a firm into bankruptcy if it fails to honor its financial obligations.

Equity, on the other hand, is less demanding. If a firm does not reach its goal for profits, an equity investor must accept the disappointing results and hope for better results next year. Equity investors cannot demand more than what is earned.

Another way to view the negative side of debt is to contemplate what happens to the return on equity if a business has a bad year. Suppose, instead of earning 14 percent on its assets, or $28,000 in operating profits, the Levine Company earns a mere $2,000, or only 1 percent on its assets of $200,000. The return on equity would again depend on whether the firm used debt or equity to finance the second $100,000 investment in the company. The results would be as follows:

	Equity	Debt	
Operating income	$2,000	$2,000	
Interest expense	0	(8,000)	(0.08 × $100,000)
Net income	$2,000	($6,000)	

If the added financing came in the form of equity, the return on equity would be 1 percent:

$$\text{Return on equity} = \frac{\text{Net income}}{\text{Owners' equity investment}}$$

$$= \frac{\$2{,}000}{\$200{,}000} = 0.01, \text{ or } 1\%$$

But if debt was used, the return on equity would be negative 6 percent:

$$\text{Return on equity} = \frac{\text{Net income}}{\text{Owners' equity investment}}$$

$$= \frac{-\$6{,}000}{\$100{,}000} = -0.06, \text{ or } -6\%$$

In this case, the owners would be better off if they financed solely with equity. Thus, debt is a two-edged sword; it cuts both ways. If debt financing is used and things go well, they will go *very* well for the owners—but if things go badly, they will go *very* badly. In short, debt financing makes business more risky.

Voting Control

The third issue in choosing between debt and equity is the degree of control retained by owners. Raising new capital through equity financing would mean giving up a part of the firm's ownership, and most owners of small firms resist giving up control to outsiders. They do not want to be accountable in any way to minority owners, much less take the chance of possibly losing control of the business.

Out of an aversion to losing control, many small business owners choose to finance with debt rather than with equity. They realize that debt increases risk, but it also permits them to retain full ownership of the firm.

With an understanding of the basic tradeoffs to be considered when choosing between debt and equity, we can now look at specific sources of financing. Where do small business owners go to find the money to finance their companies?

Living the Dream

Entrepreneurial Challenges

Debt or Equity? You Have to Choose

Before asking for money, an entrepreneur needs to decide whether she or he is willing to give up ownership in the business (that is, use equity financing) or would prefer to pay interest on a loan (that is, use debt financing). The answer can have serious implications for both the business and the entrepreneur's personal relationships, as Jill Crawley learned.

When Crawley and her husband began making plans to open Coriander, a 50-seat restaurant in Sharon, Massachusetts, two friends expressed interest in investing. But as the discussions progressed, it became clear that the parties' motivations differed. The Crawleys wanted a loan, while their friends wanted an ownership stake in the restaurant—something the Crawleys realized, when push came to shove, that they had no interest in giving up. They ultimately raised $75,000—including low-interest loans—from their parents, other family members, and a couple of other close friends. "These are people who sincerely want to see us realize our dreams," Crawley says. "They're not going to be hanging over our shoulders and looking at our books."

Although the Crawleys did not want, and maybe did not need, investors who expected a say in how Coriander was to be run, they should have understood that equity investors usually bring more to an investment opportunity than their wallets. For this reason, an entrepreneur needs to be very careful when seeking investors. David Deeds, a professor at Case Western, warns, "You want to get the right people on board. The wrong investor can suck up an amazing amount of your time and force you to divert resources away from building the business."

In short, a good investor can bring more to the table than just cash. Entrepreneurs just need to be sure that they can cope with whatever that "more" may be.

Source: Alison Stein Wellner, "Blood Money," *Inc.*, January 2004, p. 52.

SOURCES OF FINANCING

3 *Identify the typical sources of financing used at the outset of a new venture.*

When initially financing a small business, an entrepreneur will typically rely on personal savings and then attempt to gain access to the savings of family and friends. Only if these sources are inadequate will the entrepreneur turn to more formal channels of financing, such as banks and outside investors.

Exhibit 11-3 gives an overview of the sources of financing of smaller companies. As indicated, some sources of financing—such as banks, business suppliers, asset-based lenders, and the government—are essentially limited to providing debt financing. Equity financing for most entrepreneurs comes from personal savings and, in rare instances, from selling stock to the public. Other sources—including friends and family, venture capitalists, other individual investors, and large corporations—may provide either debt or equity financing, depending on the situation. Keep in mind that the use of these and other sources of funds is not limited to a startup's initial financing. Such sources may also be used to finance a firm's day-to-day operations and business expansions.

To gain insight into how startups are financed, consider the responses given by owners of *Inc. 500* firms—the 500 fastest growing privately held firms in the United States—when they were asked in 2003 about the financing sources they used to start their firms; the results are shown in Exhibit 11-4. Even for these high-growth firms, 70 percent of the startup financing came from the founders' personal savings, with another 10 percent coming from friends and family and 8 percent from bank loans. The remaining sources of financing were relatively insignificant in starting the firms. However, within five years, the *Inc. 500* entrepreneurs had, on average, raised 17 percent of their financing from private investors and 12 percent from venture capitalists.[2]

In presenting the different sources of financing for smaller companies, we will look at (1) sources "close to home"—personal savings, friends and family, and credit cards; (2) bank financing, which becomes a primary financing source as the firm grows; (3) business

EXHIBIT 11-3 *Sources of Funds*

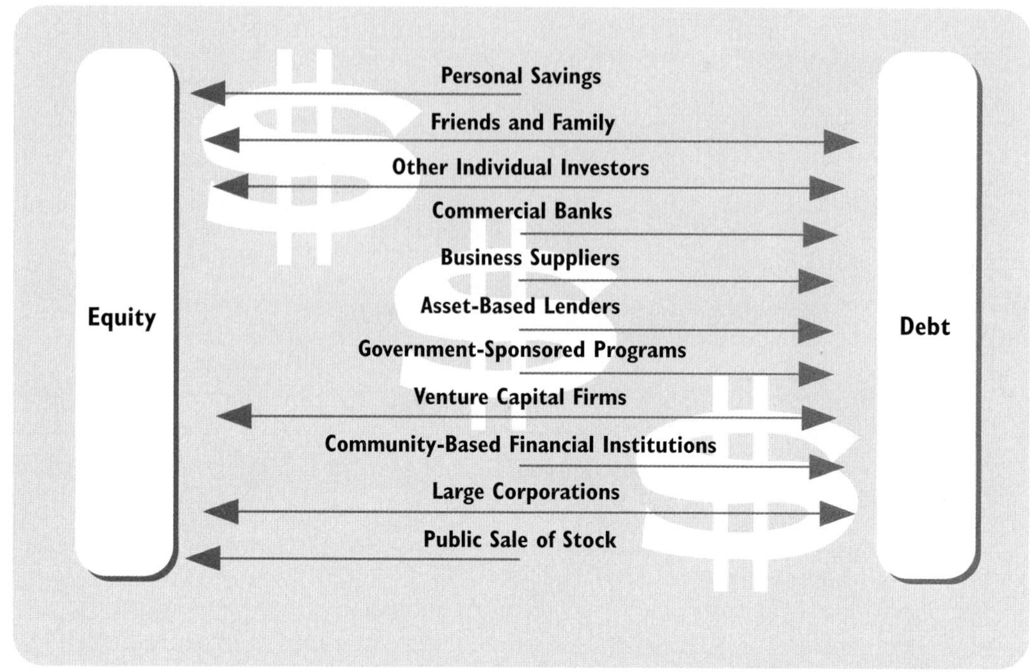

suppliers and asset-based lenders; (4) private equity investors; (5) the government; and (6) large companies and stock sales.

Sources Close to Home

The search for financial support usually begins close to home. The aspiring entrepreneur basically has three sources of early financing: (1) personal savings, (2) friends and family, and (3) credit cards.

PERSONAL SAVINGS It is imperative for an entrepreneur to have some personal investment in the business, which typically comes from personal savings. Indeed, personal savings is by far the primary source of equity financing used in starting a new business. With few exceptions, the entrepreneur must provide an equity base. A new business needs

11-4 *Startup Financing for* Inc. 500 *Companies in 2003*

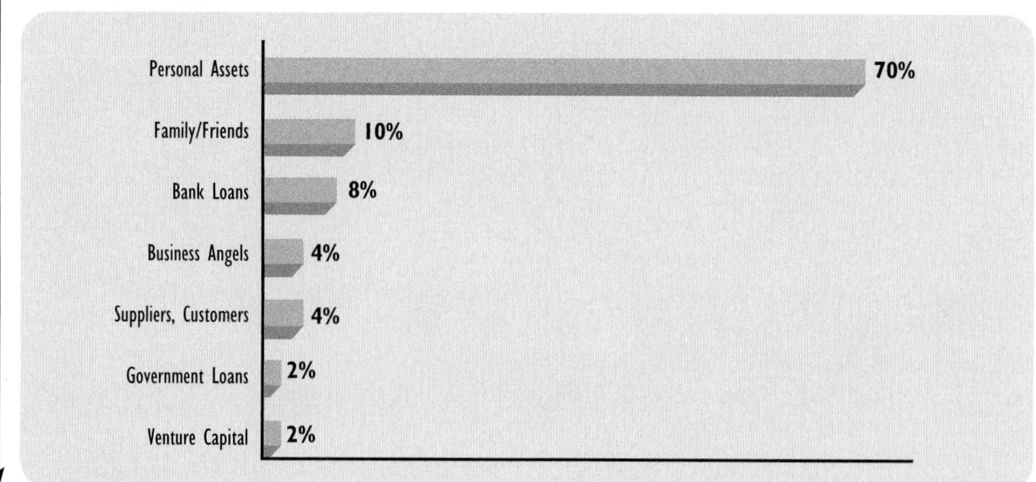

Source: Mike Hofman, "The Big Picture," *Inc.*, Vol. 25, No. 12 (October 2003), p. 87.

equity to allow for a margin of error. In its first few years, a firm can ill afford large fixed outlays for debt repayment. Also, a banker—or anyone else for that matter—is unlikely to loan a venture money if the entrepreneur does not have his or her own money at risk.

A problem for many people who want to start a business is a lack of sufficient personal savings for this purpose. It can be very discouraging when the banker asks, "How much will you be investing in the business?" or "What do you have for collateral to secure the bank loan you want?" There is no easy solution to this problem, which is faced by an untold number of entrepreneurs. Nonetheless, many individuals who lacked personal savings for a startup have found a way to accomplish their goal of owning their own company. In most cases, it required creativity and some risk taking—as well as sometimes finding a partner who could provide the financing or friends and relatives who were willing to help.

FRIENDS AND FAMILY Personal savings is *the* primary source of financing for most small business startups, with friends and family following in a distant second place. Exhibit 11-5 shows that friends, close family, and other relatives provide almost 80 percent of startup capital from personal sources beyond personal savings.

Entrepreneurs who acquire financing from friends and family are putting more than just their financial futures on the line—they're putting important personal relationships in jeopardy, too. "It's the highest risk money you'll ever get," says David Deeds, professor of entrepreneurship at Case Western Reserve University in Cleveland. "The venture may succeed or fail, but either way, you still have to go to Thanksgiving dinner."

At times, loans from friends or relatives may be the only available source of new financing. Such loans can often be obtained quickly, as this type of financing is based more on personal relationships than on financial analyses. However, friends and relatives who provide business loans sometimes feel that they have the right to offer suggestions concerning the management of the business. Also, hard business times may strain the relationship. But if relatives and friends are the only available source of financing, the entrepreneur has no alternative. To minimize the chance of damaging important personal relationships, the entrepreneur should plan to repay such loans as soon as possible. In addition, any agreements made should be put in writing, as memories tend to become fuzzy over time. It's best to clarify expectations up front, rather than be disappointed or angry later.

The best advice comes from James Hutcheson, president of Regeneration Partners, a Dallas-based consulting group that specializes in family-owned businesses:

Living the Dream *Entrepreneurial Challenges*

To Raise Money, Invest Money—and Time

Before approaching investors about financing, entrepreneurs typically invest their own money and time in order to prove that the opportunity is a good one. Cal Simmons, co-author of *Every Business Needs an Angel*, advises, "I would much rather talk to an entrepreneur who has already put his money and his effort into proving the concept. And I think most angels feel the same way right now."

Courtesy of Zoe Foods

Tori Stuart anticipated this before she looked for angels to fund Zoe Foods, her Needham, Massachusetts, natural foods company. She networked with everyone, getting the buzz out on the street about Zoe's Flax & Soy Granola Cereals and Bars, which naturally provide fiber, omega-3s, phytoestrogens, and iron—keys to healthy living. It also helped to have a product that already had enthusiastic customers supporting it. "The challenge in raising money is communicating [about our company and product] because we're in the natural foods sector," says Stuart, 36. "[Not all] investors are natural foods consumers." Getting investors to believe in a product they weren't familiar with presented its own set of unique challenges.

But starting to network early—and forging connections long before she even needed capital—is ultimately what helped Stuart and her management team raise $1.2 million, even at the height of economic difficulties that marked 2001. "Start months before you need to," says Stuart. "And to some extent, you have to put the economy out of your mind."

Source: Nicole L. Torres, "Playing an Angel," *Entrepreneur*, May 2002, pp. 130, 138.

EXHIBIT 11-5 *Sources of Personal Capital for Small Firms*

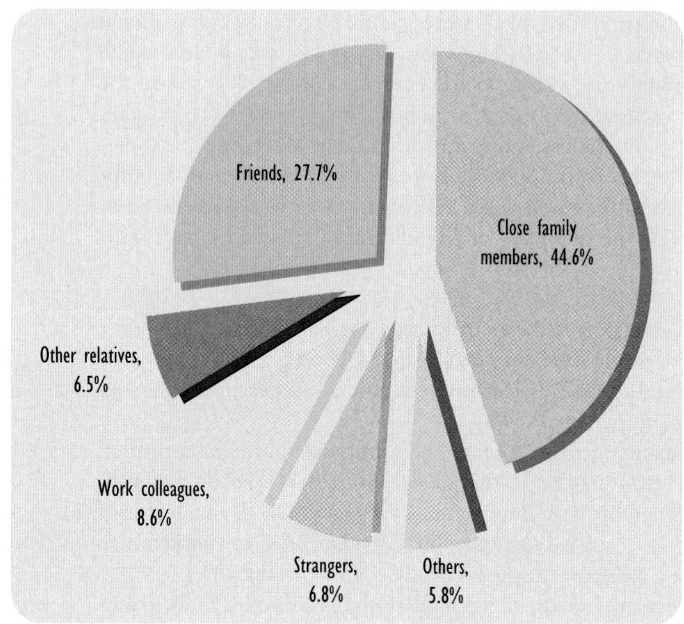

Source: "Entrepreneurship Monitor 2002," *Wall Street Journal*, August 26, 2003, p. B8.

> *Entrepreneurs [should] approach their relatives only after they have secured investments or loans from unbiased outside sources. "Go and get matching funds," he says. "If you need $25,000, then first get $12,500 from others before asking your family for the rest. If you can't do it that way—and if you don't have your own skin in the game—then you need to think twice about why you're asking someone you love to give you money. I believe you should get others to back the idea as well, so a parent or relative doesn't feel as though the money is a gift but rather a worthwhile investment. It puts a higher level of accountability into the entire process."*[3]

So, use friends and family only as a last resort. But do it if necessary—and carefully and meticulously clarify expectations.

CREDIT CARDS With unsolicited offers of a "free" card arriving in the mail all the time, credit cards have become readily available to almost anyone who is willing to apply. Using credit cards to help finance a small business has become increasingly common among entrepreneurs. It has been estimated that approximately half of all entrepreneurs use credit cards at one time or another to finance a startup or business expansion.

For someone who cannot acquire more traditional financing, such as a bank loan, credit card financing may be an option—not a great option, but a necessary one. The interest costs can become overwhelming over time, especially because of the tendency to borrow beyond the ability to repay. So it is essential that an entrepreneur using credit card financing impose strict self-discipline to avoid becoming over-extended.

Why use credit cards? Along with being perhaps the only option open to the entrepreneur, credit cards have the advantage of speed. A lender at a bank has to be convinced of the merits of the business opportunity, and that involves extensive preparation. Credit-card financing, on the other hand, requires no justification of the use of the money.

Speed was certainly the main appeal of credit-card financing for Kelli Greene, who used 10 credit cards plus her savings to launch Pacific Data Designs in 1994. Greene had a day job and spent all of her downtime developing the software that would eventually become the company's hallmark product. "I had no time to talk to a bank, and I didn't want to make the effort of writing a plan," she says. The credit cards, which together accounted for about $50,000 in cash advances, funded Pacific's first 20 months. After that the company generated enough cash flow from its operations to avoid further financing.[4]

Living the Dream *Entrepreneurial Challenges*

A Risky Source of Financing, but Sometimes Necessary

Sitting behind his desk at a marketing firm, Chris Baggott often daydreamed of owning his own business. In 1992, he finally took the plunge. At the age of 31, he quit his job and bought Sanders Dry Cleaning, a local store that he eventually built into a chain with seven outlets. To make it happen, Baggott borrowed $45,000 from his physician father-in-law, James Twiford Anderson, who also agreed to co-sign a $600,000 bank loan.

© Tyagan Miller

With the financing in place and 10 years of marketing experience, Baggott thought he was set. And then the whole "business casual" trend caught fire. "People stopped wearing suits," Baggott recalls. Revenue fell to just $60,000 a month, far short of Baggott's original projections of $110,000. What's more, he owed $14,000 in monthly payments to the bank. Propping up the business with credit cards, he began missing loan payments—and the loan officer's phone calls went straight to his father-in-law. Says Baggott, "He'd call us and say, 'What the heck is going on here?' And then he'd have to write a check to cover it from his own funds."

Eventually, Baggott felt he had no choice but to sell the business, pay his debts, and move on. But there was one investor he couldn't repay—his father-in-law, who ultimately lost tens of thousands of dollars on the venture. "It was painful," Baggott says, though his father-in-law was "great" about it.

"You win some, lose some; it's trite to say, but it's true," says Anderson, who knows from running his own practice and from some real estate ventures that things don't always go as planned. "I know whatever project Chris goes into, he puts his heart and soul into it." Still, Baggott felt the business losses put a strain on their relationship.

In October 2000, Baggott launched another business: ExactTarget, an e-mail marketing firm. Baggott again turned to friends and family—but this time, he went out of his way to emphasize the risk involved: "I said, 'Here's our business plan, but this is just a plan, and the chances are good that you'll never see this money again.' "

Ultimately, he raised more than $1 million, and this time, it's going better. ExactTarget has grown from 2 to almost 70 employees over the past three years, and while Baggott won't share exact figures, he says sales grew 1,000 percent last year and more than 400 percent this year. Among his new investors: his father-in-law. How did he muster the courage to turn to him? "You've got to have supreme confidence that you're doing the right thing," Baggott says. "I knew I had a great idea, and I felt an obligation to let him in. Had I not let him in, and then I made money in this business, how much would that have strained our relationship?"

Source: Alison Stein Wellner, "Blood Money," *Inc.*, December 2003, p. 48.

Clearly, credit cards provide a primary source of financing for many entrepreneurs, particularly early in the game. But the eventual goal is to use credit cards as a method of payment and not as a source of credit. In other words, the sooner you can pay your credit card balance in full each month, the sooner you will be growing a viable business.

Bank Financing

4 *Discuss the basic process for acquiring and structuring a bank loan.*

Commercial banks are the primary providers of debt capital to small companies. However, banks tend to limit their lending to providing for the working-capital needs of *established* firms. Quite simply, they want firms with proven track records and preferably plenty of collateral in the form of hard assets. Bankers are especially reluctant to loan money to finance losses, R&D expenses, marketing campaigns, and other "soft" assets. Such expenditures should be financed by equity sources. Nevertheless, it is wise to cultivate a relationship with a banker earlier rather than later, and well in advance of making a loan request.

TYPES OF LOANS Bankers primarily make business loans in one of three forms: lines of credit, term loans, and mortgages.

Living the Dream

Plastic Can Be Very Expensive

© Photodisc/Getty Images

Americans are often said to be addicted to plastic, and that's especially true for entrepreneurs. But convenience aside, financing with credit cards can be risky. It's easy to get in over your head—just ask Matt Jung and Chip George.

In 1995, as undergraduates at Michigan's Hope College, the pair founded Comfort Research, a Grand Rapids manufacturer of funky, beanbag-like chairs. "We had no assets," says Jung. "We were taking anything we could get." For the most part, that meant credit cards. Demand for their products soared, and with little cash on hand, the pair used credit for everything from buying equipment and raw materials to travel expenses and daily operating costs. "We tried not to look at the rates," says Jung.

Despite their efforts to make the minimum monthly payments, after six years of operation they found they owed about $17,000 at an excruciating 23 percent interest rate. "You can play the balance transfer game, and we were able to do it a couple of times," Jung says. "But it got to the point that a lot of credit card companies wouldn't let us take advantage of those lower rates anymore." Comfort Research grew rapidly, with $2 million in annual revenue by 2002. But it still took Jung three years to pay off his debts, which included several thousand dollars in interest.

These days, Jung—who now taps a line of bank credit when he needs funding—pays off his credit cards at the end of each month. "It's a very expensive way to borrow money," he says of credit cards. "I think they should be a last resort."

Source: Bobbie Gossage, "Charging Ahead," *Inc.*, January 2004, p. 42.

line of credit
An informal agreement between a borrower and a bank as to the maximum amount of funds the bank will provide at any one time

revolving credit agreement
A legal commitment by a bank to lend up to a maximum amount

Lines of Credit A **line of credit** is an informal agreement or understanding between the borrower and the bank as to the maximum amount of credit the bank will provide the borrower at any one time. Under this type of agreement, the bank has no legal obligation to provide the stated capital. (A similar arrangement that does legally commit the bank is a **revolving credit agreement**.) The entrepreneur should arrange for a line of credit in advance of an actual need because banks extend credit only in situations about which they are well informed. Attempts to obtain a loan on a spur-of-the-moment basis are generally ineffective.

term loan
Money loaned for a 5- to 10-year term, corresponding to the length of time the investment will bring in profits

Term Loans Under certain circumstances, banks will loan money on a 5- to 10-year term. Such **term loans** are generally used to finance equipment with a useful life corresponding to the loan's term. Since the economic benefits of investing in such equipment extend beyond a single year, banks can be persuaded to lend on terms that more closely match the cash flows to be received from the investment. For example, if equipment has a useful life of seven years, it might be possible to repay the money needed to purchase the equipment over, say, five years. It would be a mistake for a firm to borrow money for a short term, such as six months, when the money is to be used to buy equipment that is expected to last for seven years. *Failure to match the loan's payment terms with the expected cash inflows from the investment is a frequent cause of financial problems for small firms.* The importance of synchronizing cash inflows with cash outflows when structuring the terms of a loan cannot be overemphasized.

chattel mortgage
A loan for which items of inventory or other moveable property serve as collateral

real estate mortgage
A long-term loan with real property held as collateral

Mortgages Mortgages, which represent a long-term source of debt capital, are of two types: chattel mortgages and real estate mortgages. A **chattel mortgage** is a loan for which certain items of inventory or other movable property serve as collateral. The borrower retains title to the inventory but cannot sell it without the banker's consent. A **real estate mortgage** is a loan for which real property, such as land or a building, provides the collateral. Typically, these mortgages extend over 25 or 30 years.

UNDERSTANDING A BANKER'S PERSPECTIVE To be effective in acquiring a loan, an entrepreneur needs to understand a banker's perspective about making loans. All bankers have two fundamental concerns when they make a loan: (1) how much income the loan will provide the bank, either in interest income or in other forms of income such as fees, and (2) the likelihood that the borrower will default on the loan. A banker is not rewarded adequately to assume large amounts of risk and will, therefore, design loan agreements so as to reduce the risk to the bank.

In making a loan decision, a banker always considers the "five C's of credit": (1) the borrower's character, (2) the borrower's *capacity* to repay the loan, (3) the *capital* being invested in the venture by the borrower, (4) the *conditions* of the industry and economy, and (5) the *collateral* available to secure the loan. These issues are readily apparent in the six questions that Jack Griggs, a banker and long-time lender to small businesses, wants answered before he will make a loan:[5]

1. Do the purpose and amount of the loan make sense, both for the bank and for the borrower?
2. Does the borrower have strong character and reasonable ability?
3. Does the loan have a certain primary source of repayment?
4. Does the loan have a certain secondary source of repayment?
5. Can the loan be priced profitably to the customer and to the bank, and are this loan and the relationship good for both the customer and the bank?
6. Can the loan be properly structured and documented?

Obtaining a bank loan requires cultivation of a banker and personal selling. Although a banker's review of a loan request certainly includes analysis of economic and financial considerations, this analysis is best complemented by a personal relationship between the banker and the entrepreneur. This is not to say that a banker would allow personal feelings to override the facts provided by a careful loan analysis. But, after all, a banker's decision as to whether to make a loan is driven in part by the banker's confidence in the entrepreneur as a person and a professional. Intuition and subjective opinion based on past experience often play a role here.

When seeking a loan, an entrepreneur will be required to provide certain information in support of the loan request. Failure to provide such information in an effective manner will almost certainly result in rejection by the banker. Thus, the goal is not merely to present the needed information, but to make an *effective* presentation. Providing inaccurate information or not being able to justify assumptions made in forecasting financial results is sure to make the banker question the entrepreneur's business acumen.

A well-prepared written presentation—something like a shortened version of a business plan—is helpful, if not necessary. Capturing the firm's history and future in writing suggests that the entrepreneur has given thought to where the firm has been and is going. As part of the presentation, the banker will want to know early on answers to the following questions:

- How much money is needed?
- What is the venture going to do with the money?
- When is the money needed?
- When and how will the money be paid back?

Furthermore, a banker will want, if at all possible, to see the following detailed financial information:

- Three years of the firm's historical financial statements, if available, including balance sheets, income statements, and cash flow statements
- The firm's pro forma financial statements (balance sheets, income statements, and cash flow statements), in which the timing and amounts of the debt repayment are included as part of the forecasts
- Personal financial statements showing the borrower's net worth (net worth = assets − debt) and estimated annual income. A banker simply will not make a loan

without knowing the personal financial strength of the borrower. After all, in the world of small business, the owner *is* the business.

SELECTING A BANKER The wide variety of services provided by banks makes choosing a bank a critical decision. For a typical small firm, the provision of checking-account facilities and the extension of short-term (and possibly long-term) loans are the two most important services of a bank. Normally, loans are negotiated with the same bank in which the firm maintains its checking account. In addition, the firm may use the bank's safety deposit vault or its services in collecting notes or securing credit information. An experienced banker can also provide management advice, particularly in financial matters, to a new entrepreneur.

The location factor limits the range of possible choices of banks. For convenience in making deposits and conferring about loans and other matters, a bank should be located in the same general vicinity as the firm. All banks are interested in their home communities and, therefore, tend to be sympathetic to the needs of local business firms. Except in very small communities, two or more local banks are usually available, thus permitting some freedom of choice.

Banks' lending policies are not uniform. Some bankers are extremely conservative, while others are more willing to accept some risks. If a small firm's loan application is neither obviously strong nor patently weak, its prospects for approval depend heavily on the

Living the Dream

Entrepreneurial Challenges

Buy or Build?

Three words sum up Karin Mills's business philosophy: refurbish, recycle, reuse. "If I can spruce up a room or equipment, I've saved thousands for something else," says the Carrboro, North Carolina, restaurateur. "I don't know what I'd do if I had a slab of land and had to decide what kind of building to put there. But it would probably be square." That's because Mills and business partner Linda Bourne have encountered some unusual structures. When launching their first venture in 1998, Spotted Dog Restaurant & Bar, they had to contend with a V-shaped building with narrow walkways. Then they set their sights on establishing a restaurant in a train car, which they fashioned into an old-fashioned soda shop.

Both times, they made the most of unique opportunities, absent major commercial funding. Growth was swift, particularly after they added catering to the business mix, but their facilities were ill-equipped to handle the increased output. Then came their big break—a thriving dessert café for sale in an eclectic Durham, North Carolina, neighborhood. Not only would it provide more elbowroom, but it was also an opportunity to expand their ice cream business.

For this transaction, the women needed more than a little help from family and friends, who had been the main source of outside funding for their business collaboration up to that point. And despite their early successes, they had to work hard to get a bank on board for such a major expansion. That they were buying an operating business with an established clientele undoubtedly helped, but the bankers needed assurance. "We fielded questions about whether we were biting off more than we could chew," Mills recollects. "We knew it sounded ridiculous that adding another business would make it easier, but in the long run, we knew it would meet all these other needs."

A local bank eventually agreed to provide funding for the acquisition in early 2003. Had the women wanted to build their own facility, though, the outcome might have been different. "We probably wouldn't have gotten the loan," Mills admits. "But if I go back in a year, either to buy a business or to expand, they would look at me in a different light."

The truth is, Mills's credit prospects are probably better if she continues to buy rather than build. Lenders tend to view buyouts more favorably, because the acquired business has a credit history, existing assets, and a customer base, while organic growth may take the entrepreneur into untested territory. Another advantage is the potential for seller financing, which often provides more favorable terms than would otherwise be available.

Source: Crystal Detamore-Rodman, "New or Used?" *Entrepreneur*, December 2003, pp. 74–76.

bank's approach to small business accounts. Differences in willingness to lend have been clearly established by research studies, as well as by the practical experience of many business borrowers.

NEGOTIATING THE LOAN In negotiating a bank loan, the owner must consider the terms that will accompany the loan. Four key terms are included in all loan agreements: (1) the interest rate, (2) the loan maturity date, (3) the repayment schedule, and (4) the loan covenants.

Interest Rate The interest rate charged by banks is usually stated in terms of either the prime rate or the LIBOR. The **prime rate** is the rate of interest charged by banks on loans to their most creditworthy customers. The **LIBOR (London InterBank Offered Rate)** is the interest rate that London-based banks charge other banks in London, which is considerably lower than the prime rate. This rate is published each day in the *Wall Street Journal.*

prime rate
The interest rate charged by a commercial bank on loans to its most creditworthy customers

LIBOR (London InterBank Offered Rate)
The interest rate charged by London banks on loans to other London banks

If a banker quotes a rate of "prime plus three" and the prime rate is 5 percent, the interest rate for the loan will be 8 percent. If, alternatively, the bank is willing to loan at "LIBOR plus four" when the LIBOR is at 3 percent, then the loan rate will be 7 percent. Typically, the interest will be lower if the loan rate is tied to the LIBOR than if it is based on the prime rate. The use of the LIBOR as a base rate for determining the interest rate for a business loan developed in the late 1990s, as banks began competing more aggressively for loans.

The interest rate can be a floating rate that varies over the loan's life—that is, as the prime rate or LIBOR changes, the interest rate on the loan changes—or it can be fixed for the duration of the loan. An entrepreneur known to the authors was recently given an option to pay interest on a new loan at (1) LIBOR plus 2, in which case the interest rate would change (float) each month as the LIBOR changed, or (2) a fixed rate of 6 percent. At the time, the LIBOR was 3 percent. So the entrepreneur had the option of paying an interest rate of 5 percent, which could increase if the LIBOR increased, or a constant rate of 6 percent for the duration of the loan.

Although a small firm should always seek a competitive interest rate, concern about the interest rate should not override consideration of the loan's maturity date, its repayment schedule, and any loan covenants.

Loan Maturity Date As already noted, a loan's term should coincide with the use of the money—short-term needs require short-term financing, while long-term needs demand long-term financing. For example, since a line of credit is intended only to help a firm with its short-term needs, it is generally limited to one year. Some banks require that a firm "clean up" a line of credit one month each year. Because such a loan can be outstanding for only 11 months, the borrower can use the money to finance seasonal needs but cannot use it to provide permanent increases in working capital, such as accounts receivable and inventories.

Repayment Schedule With a term loan, the loan is set to be repaid over 5 to 10 years, depending on the type of assets used for collateral. However, the banker may impose a **balloon payment**—a very large payment that the borrower is required to make at a specified point about halfway through the term over which the payments were calculated, repaying the rest of the loan in full. For instance, assume that you borrow $50,000 at an interest rate of 6 percent. If the loan were to be repaid in equal monthly payments over seven years, the amount of each payment would be $730.[6] However, if the lender imposes a balloon payment whereby the rest of the loan comes due in full in three years rather than seven years, the lender can then reassess the quality of the loan and decide whether to collect the balance or to renew the loan.

balloon payment
A very large payment that the borrower is required to make at a specified point about halfway through the term over which the payments were calculated, repaying the rest of the loan in full

Loan Covenants In addition to setting the interest rate and specifying when and how the loan is to be repaid, a bank normally imposes other restrictions, such as loan covenants, on the borrower. **Loan covenants** require certain activities (positive covenants) and limit other activities (negative covenants) of the borrower to increase the chance that the borrower will be able to repay the loan. Some types of loan covenants a borrower might encounter include the following:

loan covenants
Bank-imposed restrictions on a borrower that enhance the chances of timely repayment

1. A bank will usually require that the business provide financial statements on a monthly basis or, at the very least, quarterly.

2. As a way to restrict a firm's management from siphoning cash out of the business, the bank may limit managers' salaries. It also may prohibit any personal loans from the business to the owners.
3. A bank may put limits on various financial ratios to make certain that a firm can handle its loan payments. For example, to ensure sufficient liquidity, the bank may require that the firm's current assets be at least twice its current liabilities (that is, current assets ÷ current liabilities must be equal to or greater than 2). Or the bank might limit the amount of debt the firm can borrow in the future, as measured by the ratio of total debt to the firm's total assets (total debt ÷ total assets).[7]
4. The borrower will normally be required to personally guarantee the firm's loan. A banker wants the right to look at both the firm's assets and the owner's personal assets before making a loan. If a business is structured as a corporation, the owner and the corporation are separate legal entities and the owner can escape personal liability for the firm's debts—that is, the owner has **limited liability**. However, most banks are not willing to lend money to any small business without the owner's personal guarantee as well. That's what Stephen Satterwhite, founder of Entelligence, a provider of e-business solutions, discovered when he sought financing for the firm. A banker offered to extend a $150,000 line of credit but required that the loan be secured not only by the company's assets, but also by the personal assets of Satterwhite and those of an Entelligence investor and board member.[8]

limited liability
The restriction of an owner's legal financial responsibilities to the amount invested in the business

When Bill Bailey, owner of Cherokee Communications, a pay-phone company located in Jacksonville, Texas, borrowed money, the loan was made on certain conditions—conditions that were intended to protect the banker. If Cherokee violated these loan covenants, the loan would become due immediately—or Bailey would have to get the banker's blessing to continue operations without repaying the loan at the time. Some of the loan covenants were as follows:[9]

- Bailey, as the owner, was required to personally guarantee the loan.
- The firm had to provide monthly financial statements to the bank within 30 days of the month's end.
- There were to be no dividend payments to the owners.
- Bailey could not change the fundamental nature of the business.
- Without prior agreement, there could be no additional liens on equipment by other lenders.
- Debt could not exceed a specified amount, nor could it be greater than a specified percentage of the firm's total assets.
- Without prior approval, no assets could be sold and no acquisitions or mergers with other firms could take place.
- The proceeds of the loan could not be used for any other purpose than that designated by the bank.
- There was a limit on the amount of capital expenditures the firm could make.
- Executive compensation could not exceed a specified amount.
- The firm's net worth could not fall below a specified amount.

Often, the indirect costs of borrowing, such as burdensome loan restrictions or covenants, have more impact on a growing business than the loan itself. A bank may require the borrower to keep a certain percentage of the outstanding loan balance in an account, for example, or it may charge a penalty if any of the loan principal is prepaid.

Even firms with straightforward financing needs should bear in mind that a variety of factors determine the cost of a loan, not just the interest rates and fees a lender charges for reviewing and preparing documents.

Some practical advice on loan covenants comes from Jill Andresky Fraser, finance editor for *Inc.* magazine:[10]

Living the Dream — Entrepreneurial Challenges

Beware of Loan Covenants

Like many growing companies, Safe Handling Inc., a transportation and warehouse services business in Auburn, Maine, has relied on a range of financing during its 12-year history: funding for equipment purchases, working capital loans, and term debt, often from multiple lenders.

While meeting each creditor's reporting obligations is time-consuming, the $5 million-plus company is more concerned about how loan covenants could jeopardize future funding. It has even paid off loan balances rather than allow a lender's requirements to stifle growth.

"We are mindful of the alternative of paying off a lender to maintain simplicity for growth," says CFO Bill Howell. "We need to be positioned for future borrowings to fund growth, and we can't do that with onerous collateralization requirements."

Source: Crystal Detamore-Rodman, "The Burden of Borrowing," *Entrepreneur*, April 2003, p. 53.

1. Ask to see a sample list of the covenants before the closing date so that you can avoid a situation in which desperation for funds—or a lack of careful analysis—persuades you to simply sign anything. Make certain that you can live with the bank's terms about the consequences of being out of compliance.
2. To see if you could have complied with all loan covenants, especially key ratios, if your loan had been in place during the most recent one-, two-, and three-year period, analyze your company's past performance over these periods.
3. If results indicate possible future problems, schedule a visit with your banker and suggest more realistic covenants.

Business Suppliers and Asset-Based Lenders

5 *Explain how business relationships can be used to finance a small firm.*

Companies that have business dealings with a new firm are possible sources of funds for financing inventories and equipment. Both wholesalers and equipment manufacturers/suppliers can provide trade credit (accounts payable) or equipment loans and leases.

ACCOUNTS PAYABLE (TRADE CREDIT) Credit extended by suppliers is very important to a startup. In fact, trade (or mercantile) credit is the source of short-term funds most widely used by small firms. **Accounts payable (trade credit)** are of short duration—30 days is the customary credit period. Most commonly, this type of credit involves an unsecured, open-book account. The supplier (seller) sends merchandise to the purchasing firm; the buyer then sets up an account payable for the amount of the purchase.

accounts payable (trade credit) Financing provided by a supplier of inventory to a given company

The amount of trade credit available to a new company depends on the type of business and the supplier's confidence in the firm. For example, wholesale distributors of sunglasses—a very seasonal product line—often provide trade credit to retailers by granting extended payment terms on sales made at the start of a season. The sunglass retailers, in turn, sell to their customers during the season and make the bulk of their payments to the wholesalers after they have sold and collected the cash for the sunglasses. Thus, the retailer obtains cash from sales before paying the supplier. More often, however, a firm has to pay its suppliers prior to receiving cash from its customers. In fact, this can be a serious problem for many small firms, particularly those that sell to large companies. (This issue will be addressed in a discussion of asset management in Chapter 22.)

EQUIPMENT LOANS AND LEASES Some small businesses, such as restaurants, use equipment that is purchased on an installment basis through an **equipment loan**. A down payment of 25 to 35 percent is usually required, and the contract period normally runs from three to five years. The equipment manufacturer or supplier typically extends credit on the basis of a conditional sales contract (or mortgage) on the equipment. During the loan period, the equipment cannot serve as collateral for another loan.

equipment loan An installment loan from a seller of machinery used by a business

Instead of borrowing money from suppliers to purchase equipment, an increasing number of small businesses are beginning to lease equipment, especially computers, photocopiers, and fax machines. Leases typically run for 36 to 60 months and cover 100 percent of the cost of the asset being leased, with a fixed rate of interest included in the lease payments. However, manufacturers of computers and industrial machinery, working hand in hand with banks or financing companies, are generally receptive to tailoring lease packages to the particular needs of customers.

It has been estimated that 80 percent of all firms lease some or all of their business equipment. Three reasons are commonly given for the increasing popularity of leasing: (1) the firm's cash remains free for other purposes, (2) lines of credit (a form of bank loan discussed later in this chapter) can be used for other purposes, and (3) leasing provides a hedge against equipment obsolescence.

While leasing is certainly an option to be considered for financing the acquisition of needed equipment, an entrepreneur should not simply assume that leasing is always the right decision. Only by carefully comparing the interest charged on a loan to the implied interest cost of a lease, calculating the tax consequences of leasing versus borrowing, and examining the significance of the obsolescence factor can an owner make a good choice. Also, the owner must be careful about contracting for so much equipment that it becomes difficult to meet installment or lease payments.

asset-based loan
A line of credit secured by working-capital assets

ASSET-BASED LENDING As its name implies, an **asset-based loan** is a line of credit secured primarily by assets such as receivables, inventory, or both. The lender cushions its risk by advancing only a percentage of the value of a firm's assets—generally, 65 to 85 percent against receivables and up to 55 percent against inventory. Also, assets such as equipment (if not leased) and real estate can be used as collateral for an asset-based loan. Asset-based lending is a viable option for young, growing businesses caught in a cash flow bind.

factoring
Obtaining cash by selling accounts receivable to another firm

Of the several categories of asset-based lending, the most frequently used is factoring. **Factoring** is an option that makes cash available to a business before accounts receivable payments are received from customers. Under this option, a factor (often owned by a bank holding company) purchases the accounts receivable, advancing to the business from 70 to 90 percent of the amount of an invoice. The factor, however, has the option of refusing to advance cash on any invoice considered questionable. The factor charges a servicing fee, usually 2 percent of the value of the receivables, and an interest charge on the money advanced prior to collection of the receivables. The interest charge may range from 2 to 3 percent above the prime rate.

6 Describe the two types of private equity investors that offer financing to small firms.

Private Equity Investors

Over the past decade, private equity markets have been the fastest growing source of financing for entrepreneurial ventures that have potential for becoming significant businesses.[11] For an entrepreneur, these sources fall into two categories: business angels and venture capitalists.

informal venture capital
Funds provided by wealthy private individuals (business angels) to high-risk ventures

business angels
Private individuals who invest in others' entrepreneurial ventures

BUSINESS ANGELS A large number of private individuals invest in others' entrepreneurial ventures. They are primarily people with moderate to significant business experience and may on rare occasions be affluent professionals, such as lawyers and physicians. This type of financing has come to be known as **informal venture capital** because no established marketplace exists in which these individuals regularly invest. These investors have also acquired the label **business angels**. Interestingly, when the term *angel* originated in the early 1900s, it referred to investors on Broadway who made risky investments to support theatrical productions.[12] John Garcia's story is a relatively typical example of the progression from entrepreneur to business angel:

> *It was 1982 when he sold his surgical supply company to Baxter Healthcare and started looking for investment opportunities. It wasn't long before he found several small, private companies looking for financial help—including a little-known retail concept called Mail Boxes Etc. Garcia's investments eventually returned several times his money, catapulting him into angel investing. Now, at 45, he makes a full-time job of connecting businesses with angel capital.*[13]

Business angels represent the oldest and largest segment of the U.S. venture capital industry, which consists of more than three million individuals, typically with an average net worth in excess of $1 million (excluding personal residences). The majority of these individuals are self-made millionaires, who have substantial business and entrepreneurial experience.[14] A few of the better recognized business angels are Ken Oshman, founder of Rolm Corporation; Paul Allen, co-founder of Microsoft Corporation; and Warren Musser, founder of Safeguard Scientifics. These three individuals alone have helped finance a large group of new companies. But even more important are the untold numbers of private investors across the country who, without fanfare, invest millions in new companies each year.

Business angels generally make investments that are relatively small—over 80 percent of business angels invest in startup firms with fewer than 20 employees. They invest locally, usually no more than 50 miles from their homes. Some limit their investments to industries in which they have had experience, while others invest in a wide variety of business sectors.[15] For instance, Terry Stevens, a successful entrepreneur turned business angel, has invested in restaurants, a sporting goods firm, a title company, and an advertising specialty firm.

The traditional way to find informal investors is through contacts with business associates, accountants, and lawyers. Other entrepreneurs are also a primary source of help in identifying prospective investors. In addition, there are now over 150 formal angel networks and angel alliances. Among them are the Dallas Angels, who describe themselves in this way:

> *The Dallas Angels are a group of private investors who invest in and assist early-stage, North Texas companies. We are made up of high net worth individuals from a wide range of backgrounds, including CEO's, senior executives, and entrepreneurs. Our members act on their own behalves and make individual investment decisions. We meet every one to two months to review opportunities.*[16]

Such groups are not limited to major cities, but can also be found in most other cities of any reasonable size.

Along with providing needed money, private investors frequently contribute know-how to new businesses. Because many of these individuals invest only in the types of business in which they have had experience, they can be very demanding. Thus, the entrepreneur must be careful in structuring the terms of any such investors' involvement.

VENTURE CAPITAL FIRMS In addition to business angels who provide *informal* venture capital, small businesses also may seek out **formal venture capitalists**, groups of individuals who form limited partnerships for the purpose of raising capital from large institutional investors, such as pension plans and university endowments. Within the group, a venture capitalist serves as the general partner, with other investors constituting the limited partners. As limited partners, such investors have the benefit of limited liability.

formal venture capitalist
Individuals who form limited partnerships for the purpose of raising venture capital from large institutional investors

The venture capitalist raises a predetermined amount of money, called a "fund." Once the money has been committed by the investors, the venture capitalist screens and evaluates investment opportunities in high-potential startups and existing firms. For example, the Sevin Rosen Funds in Dallas, Texas, raised $600 million for the Sevin Rosen Fund VIII. The money was then used to invest in a portfolio of companies.

For the investment, the venture capitalist receives the right to own a percentage of the entrepreneur's business. Reaching agreement on the exact percentage of ownership often involves considerable negotiation. The primary issues are (1) the firm's expected profits in future years and (2) the venture capitalist's required rate of return. Once an investment has been made, the venture capitalist carefully monitors each of the companies, usually through a representative who serves on the firm's board.

Most often, investments by venture capitalists take the form of convertible debt or convertible preferred stock. In this way, venture capitalists ensure themselves senior claim over the owners and other equity investors in the event the firm is liquidated, but they can convert to stock and participate in the increased value of the business if it is successful. These investors generally try to limit the length of their investment to between 5 and 7 years, though it is frequently closer to 10 years before they are able to cash out.

Although venture capital as a source of financing receives significant coverage in the business media, few small companies, especially startups, ever receive this kind of funding. No more than 1 or 2 percent of the business plans received by any venture capitalist are eventually funded—not exactly an encouraging statistic. Failure to receive funding from a venture capitalist, however, does not indicate that the venture lacks potential. Often, the venture is simply not a good fit for the investor. So, before trying to compete for venture capital financing, an entrepreneur should assess whether the firm and the management team are a good fit for such financing and for which venture capitalists in particular.

7 *Distinguish among the different government loan programs available to small companies.*

The Government

Several government programs provide financing to small businesses. Over the past decade, federal and state governments have allocated increasing, but still limited, amounts of money to financing new businesses. Local governments have likewise increased their involvement in providing financial support to startups in their areas. Though funds are available, they are not always easy to acquire. Time and patience on the part of the entrepreneur are required. Let's take a look at some of the more familiar government loan programs offered by various agencies.

THE SMALL BUSINESS ADMINISTRATION The federal government has a long history of helping new businesses get started, primarily through the programs and agencies of the

Mezzanine Financing

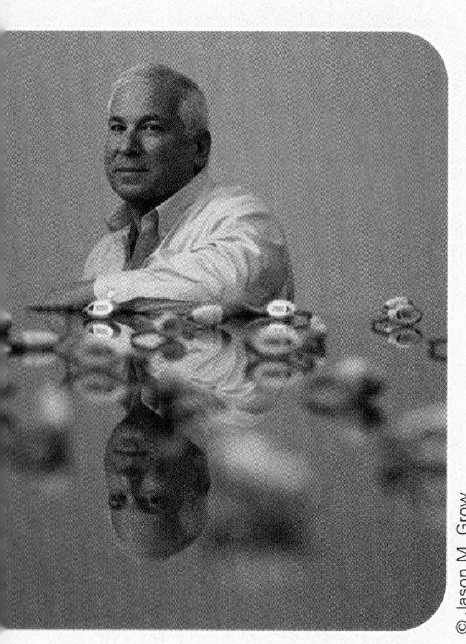

© Jason M. Grow

Medport LLC was poised to take its biggest step ever. The Providence, Rhode Island, manufacturer of medical devices had just signed a licensing agreement with watch manufacturer Timex to design and market digital thermometers carrying the Timex brand. Now, CEO Jeff Jacober, who had founded the company in 1996 with bank loans and his own savings and nurtured it into a $15 million business, needed cash to build up enough inventory to service the big pharmacy chains. "We needed money to make the leap forward," Jacober says. "We really wanted external capital."

What Jacober didn't want was a new investor second-guessing his decisions. That ruled out venture capitalists, as well as most other equity investors. Taking on more bank debt wasn't an option either, as bankers would have balked at the amount of debt already on Medport's balance sheet. So Jacober turned to a so-called mezzanine lender—Ironwood Capital Advisors LLC, based in Avon, Connecticut. Within weeks, Medport had an agreement in principle for $1.5 million.

As the name implies, mezzanine funds sit roughly at the center of the corporate financing scale, between the least risky (senior bank debt) and the most risky (equity) financing—just as the mezzanine section of a theater is sandwiched between the orchestra seats and the balcony. Investments by mezzanine lenders are typically hybrids, involving subordinated debt with an equity component. In most cases, the debt is repayable in a single "bullet" payment in five years' time and carries an annual interest rate of 12 to 14 percent.

Few entrepreneurs think about mezzanine financing—and it's little wonder why. Such funds came of age in the 1980s, when they played an integral role in financing that era's multibillion-dollar leveraged buyouts. Given the limited number of LBOs in recent years, mezzanine funds have been searching for alternative investments. Increasingly, that means privately held, small- and medium-size businesses that exhibit promise but have trouble obtaining adequate bank credit or venture capital. According to Dan Gardenswartz, principal of Sage Group LLC, a Los Angeles–based investment bank, "The goal is to find an established business with a good growth plan," such as a proposed acquisition or new product.

For Jacober, Ironwood was a perfect partner. Not only does Ironwood believe in his plan, the fund has experience investing in companies in the wholesale distribution business. "If we get some kind of unexpected hiccup in the business plan, they won't panic," Jacober says. He used the $1.5 million to finance the Timex expansion and pay down bank debt, which will allow him to use bank debt again for any future financings. In exchange, he will pay 12 percent a year in interest for the next five years and has given Ironwood warrants to acquire about 5 percent of the company's stock.

Source: Suzanne McGee, "From Buyouts to Small Biz," *Inc.*, August 2003, p. 40.

Small Business Administration (SBA). For the most part, the SBA does not loan money, but rather serves as a guarantor of loans made by financial institutions. The five primary SBA programs are the 7(a) Loan Guaranty Program, the Certified Development Company (CDC) 504 Loan Program, the 7(m) Microloan Program, small business investment companies (SBICs), and the Small Business Innovative Research (SBIR) Program.

The 7(a) Loan Guaranty Program The **7(a) Loan Guaranty Program** serves as the SBA's primary business loan program to help qualified small businesses obtain financing when they might not be eligible for business loans through normal lending channels. Guaranty loans are made by private lenders, usually commercial banks, and may be for as much as $750,000. The SBA guarantees 90 percent of loans not exceeding $155,000. For loans exceeding $155,000, the guaranty percentage is 85 percent. To obtain a guaranty loan, a small business must submit a loan application to a lender, such as a bank. After an initial review, the lender forwards the application to the SBA. Once the loan has been approved by the SBA, the lender disburses the funds. The loan proceeds can be used for working capital, machinery and equipment, furniture and fixtures, land and building, leasehold improvements, and debt refinancing (under special conditions). Loan maturity is up to 10 years for working capital and generally up to 25 years for fixed assets.

7(a) Loan Guaranty Program
Loan program that helps small companies obtain financing through a guaranty provided by the SBA

The Certified Development Company (CDC) 504 Loan Program The **Certified Development Company (CDC) 504 Loan Program** provides long-term, fixed-rate financing to small businesses to acquire real estate or machinery and equipment for expansion or modernization. The lender in this instance is a certified development company, which is financed by the SBA. The borrower must provide 10 percent of the cost of the property, with the remaining amount coming from a bank and a certified development company funded by the SBA.

Certified Development Company (CDC) 504 Loan Program
SBA loan program that provides long-term financing for small businesses to acquire real estate or machinery and equipment

The 7(m) Microloan Program The **7(m) Microloan Program** grants short-term loans of up to $35,000 to small businesses and not-for-profit child-care centers for working capital or the purchase of inventory, supplies, furniture, fixtures, and machinery and equipment. The SBA makes or guarantees a loan to an intermediary, which in turn makes the microloan to the applicant. As an added benefit, the lender provides business training and support programs to its microloan borrowers.

7(m) Microloan Program
SBA loan program that provides short-term loans of up to $35,000 to small businesses and not-for-profit child-care centers

Small Business Investment Companies **Small business investment companies (SBICs)** are privately owned banks that provide long-term loans and/or equity capital to small businesses. SBICs are licensed and regulated by the SBA, from which they frequently obtain a substantial part of their capital at attractive rates of interest. SBICs invest in businesses with (1) fewer than 500 employees, (2) a net worth of no more than $18 million, and (3) after-tax income not exceeding $6 million during the two most recent years.

small business investment companies (SBICs)
Privately owned banks, regulated by the Small Business Administration, that provide long-term loans and/or equity capital to small businesses

The Small Business Innovative Research (SBIR) Program The **Small Business Innovative Research (SBIR) Program** helps finance small firms that plan to transform laboratory research into marketable products. Eligibility for the program is based less on the potential profitability of a venture than on the likelihood that the firm will provide a product of interest to a particular federal agency.

Small Business Innovative Research (SBIR) program
A government program that helps to finance companies that plan to transform laboratory research into marketable products

STATE AND LOCAL GOVERNMENT ASSISTANCE State and local governments have become more active in financing new businesses. The nature of the financing varies, but each program is generally geared to augment other sources of funding. For instance, the city government of Des Moines, Iowa, established the Golden Circle Loan Guarantee Fund to guarantee bank loans of up to $250,000 to small companies.

COMMUNITY-BASED FINANCIAL INSTITUTIONS **Community-based financial institutions** are lenders that serve low-income communities and receive funds from federal, state, and private sources. They are increasingly becoming a source of financing for small companies that otherwise would have little or no access to startup funding. Typically, community-based lenders provide capital to businesses that don't have the potential for the spectacular growth demanded by venture capitalists, but do have the potential to make modest profits, serve the community, and create jobs. An example of a community-based financial institution is the

community-based financial institution
A lender that uses funds from federal, state, and private sources to provide financing to small businesses in low-income communities

Delaware Valley Reinvestment Fund, which provides financing for small companies in Philadelphia's inner-city area.

8 *Explain when large companies and public stock offerings can be sources of financing.*

Where Else to Look

The sources of financing that have been described thus far represent the primary avenues for obtaining money for small firms. The remaining sources are generally of less importance but should not be ignored by an entrepreneur in search of financing.

LARGE CORPORATIONS Large corporations at times make funds available for investment in smaller firms when it is in their self-interest to maintain a close relationship with such a firm. Larger firms are now becoming even more involved in providing financing and technical assistance to smaller businesses. For instance, some large high-tech firms prefer to invest in smaller firms that are conducting research of interest, rather than conduct the research themselves.

An example of a large corporation investing in smaller firms is Coca-Cola, which in early 2001 invested $250,000 in eight startups. The purpose of the investments was to develop technologies that would benefit operations, such as bottling and distribution. Coca-Cola also hopes to profit when the companies go public. The program—involving a wholly owned subsidiary called Fizzion—is part of a push to make Coca-Cola more innovative. By involving employees in startups, the company can give managers "a real sense for what it's like to move against deadlines of time and money," says Fizzion CEO Chris Lowe. Although large companies also face those issues, they're "not of the same character or ilk" as in a startup, Lowe says.[17]

STOCK SALES Another way to obtain capital is by selling stock to outside individual investors through either private placement or public sale. Finding outside stockholders can be difficult when a new firm is not known and has no ready market for its securities, however. In most cases, a business must have a history of profitability before its stock can be sold successfully.

Whether it is best to raise outside equity financing depends on the firm's long-range prospects. If there is opportunity for substantial expansion on a continuing basis and if other sources are inadequate, the owner may logically decide to bring in other owners. Owning part of a larger business may be more profitable than owning all of a smaller business.

private placement
The sale of a firm's capital stock to selected individuals

Private Placement One way to sell common stock is through **private placement**, in which the firm's stock is sold to selected individuals—usually the firm's employees, the owner's acquaintances, members of the local community, customers, and suppliers. When a stock sale is restricted to private placement, an entrepreneur can avoid many requirements of the securities laws.

initial public offering (IPO)
The issuance of stock that is to be traded in public financial markets

Public Sale When small firms—typically, *larger* small firms—make their stock available to the general public, this is called going public, or making an **initial public offering (IPO)**. The reason often cited for a public sale is the need for additional working capital.

In undertaking a public sale of its stock, a small firm subjects itself to greater governmental regulation, particularly following the rash of corporate scandals in publicly owned companies such as Enron, Tyco, and WorldCom. In response to corporate malfeasance in recent years, the U.S. Congress passed legislation, including the Sarbanes-Oxley Act, to monitor public companies more carefully. This has resulted in a significant increase in the cost of being a publicly traded company—especially for small firms. Also, publicly traded firms are required to report their financial results quarterly in 10Q reports and annually in 10K reports to the Securities and Exchange Commission (SEC). The SEC carefully scrutinizes these reports before they can be made available to the public. At times, the SEC requirements can be very burdensome.

Common stock may also be sold to underwriters, which guarantee the sale of securities. Compensation and fees paid to underwriters typically make the sale of securities in this manner expensive. Fees frequently range from 20 to 26 percent of the value of the total stock issue. Options and other fees may cause the actual costs to run even higher. The reason for the high costs is, of course, the elements of uncertainty and risk associated with public offerings of the stock of small, relatively unknown firms.

Looking Back

1 Describe how the nature of a firm affects its financing sources.

- There are four basic factors that determine how a firm is financed: (1) the firm's economic potential, (2) the size and maturity of the company, (3) the nature of the firm's assets, and (4) the personal preference of the owners as they consider the tradeoffs between debt and equity.
- An entrepreneurial firm that has high growth potential has many more possible sources of financing than does a firm that provides a good lifestyle for the owner but nothing in the way of attractive returns to investors.
- The size and maturity of a company have a direct bearing on the types of financing that are available.
- Tangible assets serve as great collateral when a business is requesting a bank loan; intangible assets have little value as collateral.

2 Evaluate the choice between debt financing and equity financing.

- Choosing between debt and equity financing involves tradeoffs with regard to potential profitability, financial risk, and voting control.
- Borrowing money rather than issuing common stock (ownership equity) creates the potential for higher rates of return to the owners and allows the owners to retain voting control of the company, but it also exposes the owners to greater financial risk.
- Issuing common stock rather than borrowing money results in lower potential rates of return to the owners and the loss of some voting control, but it does reduce their financial risk.

3 Identify the typical sources of financing used at the outset of a new venture.

- The aspiring entrepreneur basically has three sources of early financing: (1) personal savings, (2) friends and family, and (3) credit cards.
- Personal savings is the primary source of equity financing used in starting a new business; a banker or other lender is unlikely to loan a venture money if the entrepreneur does not have his or her own money at risk.
- Loans from friends and family may be the only available source of financing and are often easy and fast to obtain, though such borrowing can place the entrepreneur's most important personal relationships in jeopardy.
- Credit card financing provides easily accessible financing, but with high interest costs that may become overwhelming at times.
- Only if these sources are inadequate will the entrepreneur turn to more formal channels of financing, such as banks and outside investors.

4 Discuss the basic process for acquiring and structuring a bank loan.

- Bankers primarily make business loans in one of three forms: lines of credit, term loans, and mortgages.
- In making a loan decision, a banker always considers the "five C's of credit": (1) the borrower's *character*, (2) the borrower's *capacity* to repay the loan, (3) the *capital* being invested in the venture by the borrower, (4) the *conditions* of the industry and economy, and (5) the *collateral* available to secure the loan.
- Obtaining a bank loan requires cultivation of a banker and personal selling, including a presentation that addresses (1) how much money is needed, (2) what the venture is going to do with the money, (3) when the money is needed, and (4) when and how the money will be paid back.
- Other detailed financial information might be requested, including three years of the firm's historical financial statements, the firm's pro forma financial statements, and personal financial statements showing the borrower's net worth and estimated annual income.
- An entrepreneur should carefully evaluate available banks before choosing one, basing the decision on factors such as the bank's location, the extent of services provided, and the bank's lending policies.
- In negotiating a bank loan, the owner must consider the accompanying terms, which typically include the interest rate, the loan maturity date, the repayment schedule, and the loan covenants.

5 Explain how business relationships can be used to finance a small firm.

- Business suppliers can offer trade credit (accounts payable), which is the source of short-term funds most widely used by small firms.
- Suppliers also offer equipment loans and leases, which allow small businesses to use equipment purchased on an installment basis.
- Asset-based lending is financing secured by working-capital assets, such as accounts receivable and inventory.

6 Describe the two types of private equity investors that offer financing to small firms.

- Business angels are private individuals, generally having moderate to significant business experience, who invest in others' entrepreneurial ventures.
- Formal venture capitalists are groups of individuals who form limited partnerships for the purpose of raising capital from large institutional investors, such as pension plans and university endowments.

7 **Distinguish among the different government loan programs available to small companies.**

- The federal government helps new businesses get started through the programs and agencies of the Small Business Administration (SBA), which include the 7(a) Loan Guaranty Program, the Certified Development Company (CDC) 504 Loan Program, the 7(m) Microloan Program, small business investment companies (SBICs), and the Small Business Innovative Research (SBIR) Program.
- State and local governments finance new businesses in varying manners, though programs are generally geared to augmenting other sources of funding.
- Community-based financial institutions are lenders that use funds from federal, state, and private sources to serve low-income communities and small companies that otherwise would have little or no access to startup funding.

8 **Explain when large companies and public stock offerings can be sources of financing.**

- Large companies may finance smaller businesses when it is in their self-interest to have a close relationship with the smaller company.
- Stock sales, in the form of either private placements or public sales, may provide a few high-potential ventures with equity capital.

Key Terms

return on assets, p. 240
return on equity, p. 240
line of credit, p. 248
revolving credit agreement, p. 248
term loan, p. 248
chattel mortgage, p. 248
real estate mortgage, p. 248
prime rate, p. 251
LIBOR (London InterBank Offered Rate), p. 251
balloon payment, p. 251
loan covenants, p. 251
limited liability, p. 252
accounts payable (trade credit), p. 253
equipment loan, p. 253
asset-based loan, p. 254
factoring, p. 254
informal venture capital, p. 254
business angels, p. 254
formal venture capitalists, p. 255
7(a) Loan Guaranty Program, p. 257
Certified Development Company (CDC) 504 Loan Program, p. 257
7(m) Microloan Program, p. 257
small business investment companies (SBICs), p. 257
Small Business Innovative Research (SBIR) Program, p. 257
community-based financial institution, p. 257
private placement, p. 258
initial public offering (IPO), p. 258

Discussion Questions

1. How does the nature of a business affect its sources of financing?
2. How is debt different from equity?
3. Explain the three tradeoffs that guide the choice between debt financing and equity financing.
4. Assume that you are starting a business for the first time. What do you believe are the greatest personal obstacles to obtaining funds for the new venture? Why?
5. If you were starting a new business, where would you start looking for capital?
6. Explain how trade credit and equipment loans can provide initial capital funding.
7. a. Describe the different types of loans made by a commercial bank.
   b. What does a banker need to know in order to decide whether to make a loan?
8. Distinguish between informal venture capital and formal venture capital.
9. In what ways does the federal government help with initial financing for small businesses?
10. What advice would you give an entrepreneur who was trying to finance a startup?

You Make the Call

SITUATION 1

David Bernstein needs help financing his Lodi, New Jersey–based Access Direct Inc., a six-year-old $3.5 million company. "We're ready to get to the next level," says Bernstein. "But we're not sure which way to go." Access Direct spruces up and then sells used computer equipment for corporations; it is looking for up to $2 million in order to expand. "Venture capitalists, individual investors, or banks," says Bernstein, who owns the company with four partners, "we've thought about them all."

Question 1 What is your impression of Bernstein's perspective on raising capital to "get to the next level"?

Question 2 What advice would you offer Bernstein as to both appropriate and inappropriate sources of financing in his situation?

SITUATION 2

Carter Dalton is well on his way to starting a new venture—Max, Inc. He has projected a need for $350,000 in initial capital. He plans to invest $150,000 himself and either borrow the additional $200,000 or find a partner who will buy stock in the company. If Dalton borrows the money, the interest rate will be 6 percent. If, on the other hand, another equity investor is found, he expects to have to give up 60 percent of the company's stock. Dalton has forecasted earnings of about 16 percent in operating income on the firm's total assets.

Question 1 Compare the two financing options in terms of projected return on the owner's equity investment. Ignore any effect from income taxes.

Question 2 What if Dalton is wrong and the company earns only 4 percent in operating income on total assets?

Question 3 What should Dalton consider in choosing a source of financing?

SITUATION 3

Steve Peplin is the president of Talan Products, a metal stamper based in Cleveland. Peplin has a long-term relationship with his banker. But recently his firm ran into financial difficulty, and the bank is demanding that Peplin personally guarantee 100 percent of the company's loans. Peplin would prefer not to do so, but isn't sure that he has a choice.

Source: "Hands On," *Inc.*, Vol. 25, No. 8 (August 2003), p. 50.

Question 1 Should Peplin be surprised by the bank's demand for a personal guarantee? Why or why not?

Question 2 What would you advise Peplin to do?

Experiential Exercises

1. Interview a local small business owner to determine how funds were obtained to start the business. Be sure you phrase questions so that they are not overly personal, and do not ask for specific dollar amounts. Write a brief report on your findings.
2. Interview a local banker about lending policies for small business loans. Ask the banker to comment on the importance of a business plan to the bank's decision to loan money to a small business. Write a brief report on your findings.
3. Review recent issues of *Entrepreneur* or *Inc.*, and report to the class on the financing arrangements of firms featured in these magazines.
4. Interview a stockbroker or investment analyst on his or her views regarding the sale of common stock by a small business. Write a brief report on your findings.

Exploring the Web

1. As noted in this chapter, several government loan programs provide financing to small businesses. To find out more about the loan programs of the Small Business Administration, one of the more familiar sources of government loans, go to the SBA Web site at **http://www.sba.gov**. Choose "Financing Your Business," then "Snap Shot."
   a. What standard loan programs does the SBA offer?
   b. Search the SBA site further to determine what special-purpose loans the SBA offers and what each loan's purpose is.
2. Return to the CCH's Business Owner's Toolkit at **http://www.toolkit.cch.com/text/P10_2000.asp** and find content related to the basics of debt versus equity financing. What are the most common options for small business equity financing?
3. Although initial public offerings (IPOs) may not be in the cards for many small businesses, some larger small businesses may make their stock available to the general public. To learn what *Entrepreneur* magazine has to say on this subject, visit **http://www.entrepreneur.com/article/0,4621,300892,00.html** and read the article on initial public offerings. Explain the basic steps in a typical timetable for an initial public offering.

Case 11

CALVERT TOYOTA (P. 543)

This case illustrates the use of bank financing for a new venture.

Alternative Case for Chapter 11:

Case 4, Auntie Anne's, p. 531

The Business Plan

LAYING THE FOUNDATION

As part of laying the foundation for your own business plan, respond to the following questions regarding the financing of your venture:

1. What is the total financing required to start the business?
2. How much money do you plan to invest in the venture? What is the source of this money?
3. Will you need financing beyond what you personally plan to invest?
4. If additional financing is needed for the startup, how will you raise it? How will the financing be structured—debt or equity? What will the terms be for the investors?
5. According to your pro forma financial statements, will there be a need for additional financing within the first five years of the firm's life? If so, where will it come from?
6. How and when will you arrange for investors to cash out of their investment?

THE HARVEST PLAN

In the Spotlight

Type A Multimedia Network http://www.typea.net

Anna Belyaev hates messes. The 35-year-old CEO wants everything perfect at her aptly named e-learning company Type A. That's why she and her business partner, Arlo Leach, recently spent a day away from their Chicago office, to plan what will happen when they're ready to leave their five-year-old company.

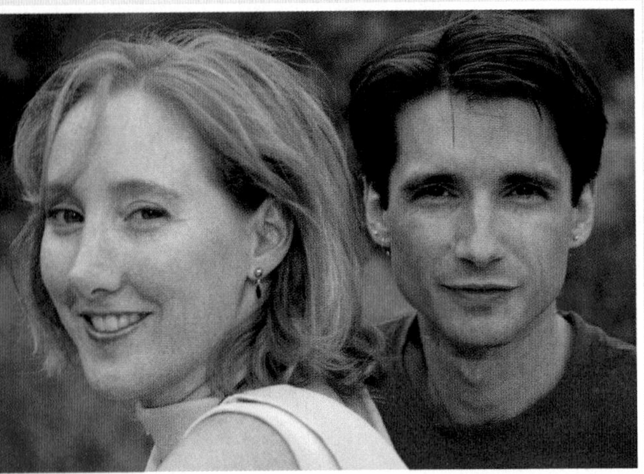

Steve Mearek/arloandanna.com

"A lot of business owners don't want to think about their exit strategies," says Belyaev. "But like it or not, somehow or other, you're going to exit at some point."

Business owners who don't have children or other family interested in the business will likely end up selling to strangers, employees, or partners. Regardless of the buyer, there are several things owners can do in the years leading up to the sale to ensure the highest selling price for the business and the smoothest transition.

Planning for the future ended up helping Belyaev and Leach's business right away. Belyaev says they changed their hiring and promotion strategies when they realized they needed to groom a successor. Looking at Type A's business plan as a work-in-progress rather than a document collecting dust revitalized their outlook on the business.

The foresight of this young CEO proves that harvest plans aren't only for those with graying hair.

Source: Shannon Scully, "Planning Your Exit Strategy," *MyBusiness*, October-November 2003, p. 33.

Chapter 12

Looking Ahead

After studying this chapter, you should be able to

1 *Explain the importance of having a harvest, or exit, plan.*

2 *Describe the options available for harvesting.*

3 *Explain the issues in valuing a firm that is being harvested and deciding on the method of payment.*

4 *Provide advice on developing an effective harvest plan.*

In previous chapters, we have talked about recognizing business opportunities and developing strategies for capturing these opportunities. Such activities represent the cornerstone for everything a company does. But that's not the end of the story. Experience suggests that an entrepreneur developing a company strategy should think about more than just starting (founding or acquiring) and growing a business; the entrepreneurial process is not complete until the owners and any other investors have exited the venture and captured the value created by the business. This final—but extremely important—phase can be enhanced through an effective harvest, or exit, plan.

THE IMPORTANCE OF THE HARVEST

1 *Explain the importance of having a harvest, or exit, plan.*

In recent times, there have been an unprecedented number of opportunities for entrepreneurs to sell their firms. In the last few years, investors have been actively buying firms in the same industry and then consolidating them into a single, larger company. Many entrepreneurs who founded companies in the 1970s and 1980s are—or soon will be—engaged in harvesting their businesses. They are transferring ownership either to the next generation of family members or to other investors and individuals who have an interest in the business.

Most entrepreneurs do not like to think about the harvest, even though few events in the life of an entrepreneur, and of the firm itself, are more significant. Consequently, the decision to harvest is frequently the result of an unexpected event, possibly a crisis, rather than a well-conceived strategy.

harvesting (exiting)
The process used by entrepreneurs and investors to reap the value of a business when they leave it

Harvesting—or **exiting**, as it frequently called—is the method entrepreneurs and investors use to get out of a business and, ideally, reap the value of their investment in the firm. Many entrepreneurs successfully grow their businesses but fail to develop effective harvest plans. As a result, they are unable to capture the full value of the business that they have worked so hard to create.

Joe Maskrey, former CEO of InfoGraphic Systems in Garden Grove, California, is a great example of an entrepreneur who did capture the value of his investment by anticipating the harvest. Twenty-two months before he sold his company to General Electric, Maskrey hired a valuation firm. The valuation came in at $18 million and set off a process that led to the eventual sale. "It gave an idea of what would be a really good scenario for us to go for as an exit strategy," says Maskrey, now president of the new company, GE Interlogix InfoGraphics. Under its earlier business model, Maskrey's company would have been valued at a multiple of earnings. But by adopting a somewhat different business strategy geared more toward growth, Maskrey put InfoGraphics in a category of companies valued at a multiple of sales. Armed with a plan, Maskrey sold InfoGraphics for a price he characterizes as "a lot more" than its $18 million appraised value.[1]

An entrepreneur needs to understand that harvesting encompasses more than merely selling and leaving a business; it involves capturing value (cash flows), reducing risk, and creating future options—the reason we prefer the term *harvest* over *exit*. In addition, there are personal, nonfinancial considerations for the entrepreneur. An owner may receive a lot of money for the firm but still be disappointed with the harvest if he or she is not prepared for a change in lifestyle. Thus, carefully designing an intentional exit strategy is as essential to an entrepreneur's personal success as it is to his or her financial success.

The word *success* has different meanings for different people. In this chapter, we offer suggestions for achieving a "successful" harvest, whatever your definition may be. But it is a mistake to define success only in terms of the harvest; there should also be success in the entrepreneurial journey. So, throughout the chapter, we provide examples of different entrepreneurs' definitions of success and encourage you to think about what *success* means to you. Arriving at the end of the journey only to discover that your ladder was leaning against the wrong wall is one of life's tragedies.

The harvest is vitally important to a firm's investors as well as its founder. Investors who provide high-risk capital—particularly angels and venture capitalists—generally insist on a well-thought-out harvest strategy. They realize that it is easy to put money into a business, but difficult to get it out. As a result, a firm's appeal to investors is driven by the availability of harvest options. If investors are not convinced that opportunities will exist for harvesting their investment, there will be no investment.

METHODS OF HARVESTING A BUSINESS

2 *Describe the options available for harvesting.*

The four basic ways to harvest an investment in a privately owned company are (1) selling the firm, (2) releasing the firm's cash flows to its owners, (3) offering stock to the public through an initial public offering (IPO), and (4) issuing a private placement of the stock. These options are shown graphically in Exhibit 12-1.

Selling the Firm

In any harvest strategy, the financial questions associated with the sale of a firm include how to value the firm and how to structure the sale. Most frequently, an entrepreneur's motivation for selling a company relates to retirement and estate planning and a desire to diversify her or his portfolio of investments.

Living the Dream *Entrepreneurial Challenges*

Success Means Making a Difference

Courtesy of Tennessee Bun Company

Cordia Harrington wants to make more money—but not so that she can buy a Mercedes or a bigger house. The owner of Tennessee Bun Company in Nashville, Tennessee, wants to grow her resources to help others.

"The bigger my business gets and the more money I make, the more people I can affect every week," says Harrington, whose facility bakes 60,000 buns an hour for distribution to regional and overseas McDonald's and Pepperidge Farms outlets.

Harrington gives thanks daily for her bread company and what it allows her to do. As a single mother of three boys, she lived a difficult life for many years before she became a business owner. Now that she is a success, Harrington feels obligated to help others.

"My passion is to help other people discover the incredible potential in themselves," says Harrington, who has guided 11 families out of debt and into business as McDonald's franchise owners. Prior to entering the baking business, Harrington owned several McDonald's franchises herself.

Harrington doesn't deny the thrill of acquiring nice stuff. "I really enjoy material things," she admits. "But getting something is usually more exciting in the time leading up to the purchase than after you've actually bought it." To her, buying more things no longer brings the same satisfaction as helping employees or acquaintances change their financial futures.

http://www.buncompany.com

Source: Rex Hammock and Shannon Scully, "Success: What's Your Definition?" *MyBusiness*, December-January 2004, p. 55.

EXHIBIT 12-1 *Methods for Harvesting a Business*

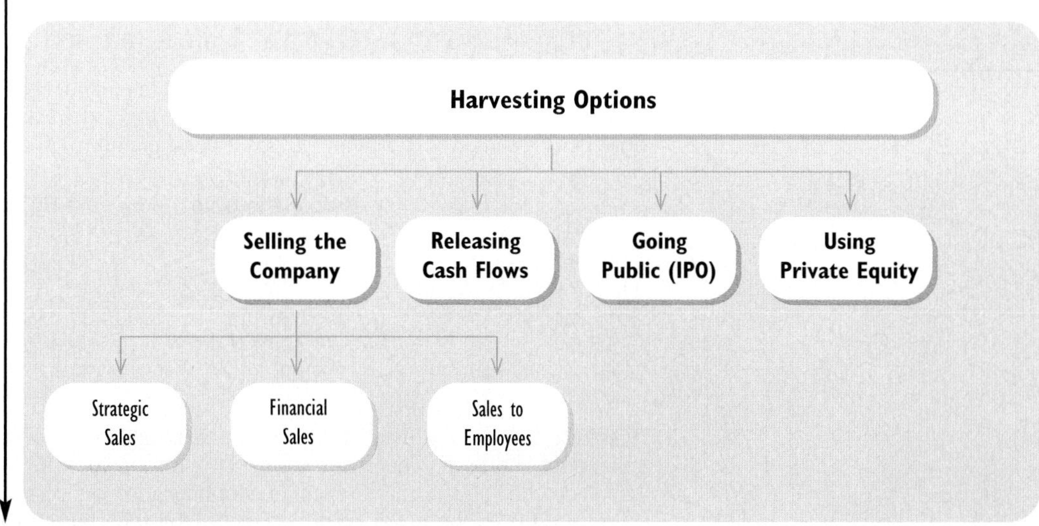

Sale transactions can, for all practical purposes, be reduced to three types, based on the motives of the buyers: sales to strategic buyers, sales to financial buyers, and sales to employees. A strategic buyer is interested in synergies that can be gained from the acquisition, a financial buyer is more often interested in the firm as a stand-alone business, and an employee buyer is primarily interested in preserving employment and participating in the success of the business. Let's consider each type of transaction in more detail.

SALES TO STRATEGIC BUYERS From a seller's perspective, the key point to remember about a sale to a strategic buyer is that the value such buyers place on a business depends on the synergies they think they can create by combining the acquired firm with complementary businesses. Since the value of a business to a buyer is derived from both its stand-alone characteristics and its synergies, strategic buyers often will pay a higher price than will financial buyers, who value the business only as a stand-alone entity. Thus, in strategic acquisitions, the critical issue is the degree of strategic fit between the firm to be harvested and the potential buyer. If the potential buyer is a current rival and if the acquisition would provide long-term, sustainable competitive advantages (such as lower cost of production or superior product quality), the buyer may be willing to pay a premium for the firm.

SALES TO FINANCIAL BUYERS Unlike strategic buyers, buyers in financial acquisitions look primarily to a firm's stand-alone, cash-generating potential as its source of value. Often, the value a financial buyer hopes to tap depends on stimulating future sales growth, reducing costs, or both. This fact has an important implication for the owner of the firm being purchased. The buyer often will make changes in the firm's operations that translate into greater pressures on the firm's personnel, resulting in layoffs that the current owner might find objectionable. As a result, financial acquisitions are not popular among many small business owners.

In earlier years, the **leveraged buyout (LBO)**, a financial acquisition involving a very high level of debt financing, became synonymous with the **bust-up LBO**, in which the new owners pay the debt down rapidly by selling off the acquired firm's assets. Frequently, acquisitions were financed with $9 in debt for every $1 in equity—thus the name *leveraged* buyout.

More recently, however, the bust-up LBO has been replaced by the build-up LBO. As the name suggests, the **build-up LBO** involves constructing, out of a group of smaller firms, a larger enterprise that might eventually be taken public via an initial public offering (IPO). Large private investors have successfully refined the build-up LBO and tapped public capital markets at unprecedented levels.

The process begins with the acquisition of a company, which then acquires a number of smaller businesses that in some way complement it. These subsequent acquisitions may

leveraged buyout (LBO)
A purchase heavily financed with debt, where the future cash flow of the target company is expected to be sufficient to meet debt repayments

bust-up LBO
A leveraged buyout involving the purchase of a company with the intent of selling off its assets

build-up LBO
A leveraged buyout involving the purchase of a group of similar companies with the intent of making the firms into one larger company

Living the Dream — Entrepreneurial Challenges

A Close Look at an LBO

Robert Hall, the former owner of Visador Corporation, sold his firm to a financial buyer, who financed the purchase as a leveraged buyout (LBO). A look at the company's financial structure before and after the sale provides a good picture of an LBO.

	Before the Sale	After the Sale
Current liabilities	$ 3,433,532	$11,018,041
Long-term liabilities	1,350,000	47,720,878
Deferred income taxes	569,736	1,742,165
Total liabilities	$ 5,353,268	$60,481,084
Equity	12,948,456	6,789,340
Total liabilities and equity	$18,301,724	$67,270,424

Visador's before-sale and after-sale numbers differ in two important respects. First, the total debt and equity increased from $18.3 million to $67.3 million. This increase was the result of changing from historical accounting numbers to numbers that reflect the firm's current value to the buyer. In other words, the founders of Visador had invested just over $18 million in the firm during their years of ownership, up to the point of the acquisition. However, the buyer believed the business was worth over $67 million.

Second, there was $0.41 in debt per $1 in equity prior to the sale; after the sale, there was $8.91 in debt for every $1 in equity. This large increase in debt required the new management to change the way in which the firm operated. The goal was no longer to make a profit; instead, the focus was on generating sufficient cash flows to service the debt. This goal was accomplished through significant reduction in the number of employees and elimination of any activities that did not contribute to the cash flow objectives. These changes were very disappointing to Hall, who had many close friends among those who eventually lost their jobs.

Source: Personal interview with Robert Hall, former CEO of Visador Corporation, 1998.

expand capacity in related or new businesses. The newly formed combination is operated privately for five to seven years in order to establish a successful track record, and then it is taken public. These acquisitions continue to rely heavily on debt financing, but to a lesser extent than bust-up LBOs.

Build-up LBOs have occurred in a number of industries where smaller companies frequently operate, such as funeral services and automobile dealerships. Such LBOs frequently include the firm's top management as significant shareholders in the acquired firm—in which case the arrangement is referred to as a **management buyout (MBO)**. An MBO can contribute significantly to a firm's operating performance by increasing management's focus and intensity. Thus, an MBO is a potentially viable means of transferring ownership of both large and small businesses. In many entrepreneurial businesses, managers have a strong incentive to become owners, but lack the financial capacity to acquire the firm. An MBO can solve this problem through the use of debt financing, which is often underwritten in part by the firm's owner.

management buyout (MBO) A leveraged buyout in which the firm's top managers become significant shareholders in the acquired firm

SALES TO EMPLOYEES Established by Congress in 1974, **employee stock ownership plans (ESOPs)** have gradually been embraced by more than 10,000 companies. Once established, an ESOP uses employees' retirement contributions to buy company stock from the owner and holds it in trust; over time, the stock is distributed to employees' retirement plans. In a leveraged ESOP, the stock is purchased with borrowed money. Most businesses with ESOPs are small, and only a handful of them have ever been publicly traded.

employee stock ownership plan (ESOP) A method by which a firm is sold either in part or in total to its employees

"It's common for an owner to start by selling a portion of the company and maintaining ownership of the rest," observes Martin Staubus, a consultant with the Beyster Institute. "Owners love that they can sell their stock for full value and with large and unique tax advantages; and as shareholders, employees work harder because they gain a piece of the benefit. While an ESOP can be a great exit strategy, it's also a good way to run the business while you're still there."[2]

Employee ownership is not a panacea. Although advocates maintain that employee ownership improves motivation, leading to greater effort and reduced waste, the value of increased employee effort resulting from improved motivation varies significantly from firm to firm. Selling all or part of a firm to employees works only if the company's employees have an owner mentality—that is, they do not think in "9-to-5" terms. An ESOP may provide a way for the owner to sell the business, but if the employees lack the required mind-set, it will not serve the business well in the future. Daniel Brogan, CEO of Earl Walls Associates, an employee-owned design and engineering firm in San Diego, explains, "You have to implement [an ESOP] early enough. . . . The staff has to be mentally prepared to take over and run a company. And you have to continue hiring people who share an ownership mindset."[3]

Releasing the Firm's Cash Flows

The second harvest strategy involves the orderly withdrawal of the owners' investment in the form of the firm's cash flows. The withdrawal process could be immediate if the owners simply sold off the assets of the firm and ceased business operations. However, for a value-creating firm—one that earns attractive rates of return for its investors—this does not make economic sense. The mere fact that a firm is earning high rates of return on its assets indicates that the business is worth more as a going concern than a dead one. Thus, shutting down the company is not an economically rational option. Instead, the owners might simply stop growing the business; by doing so, they increase the cash flows that can be returned to the investors.

In a firm's early years, all its cash is usually devoted to growing the business. Thus, the firm's cash flow during this period is zero—or, more likely, negative—requiring its owners to seek outside cash to finance future growth. As the firm matures and opportunities to grow the business decline, sizable cash flows frequently become available to its owners. Rather than reinvest all the cash in the firm, the owners can begin to withdraw the cash, thus harvesting their investment. If they decide to do so, only the amount of cash necessary to maintain current markets is retained and reinvested; there is little, if any, effort to grow the present markets or expand into new markets.

Harvesting by withdrawing a firm's cash from the business has two important advantages: The owners can retain control of the firm while they harvest their investment, and

Living the Dream *Entrepreneurial Challenges*

The Employee Learning Curve in an ESOP

When the managers of Foldcraft Company, a seating manufacturer in rural Kenyon, Minnesota, first introduced the ESOP concept in 1984, their employees were more familiar with the term *stock* in reference to cattle and pigs than dollars and cents, says CEO Steve Sheppard: "That's how little our employees knew about running a company when this began. But now our employees can access hourly data about profitability and sales volume. We are an information-fed organization that understands our actions and how they feed the bottom line."

It didn't happen overnight. Management was dedicated to making the ESOP work by educating employees. Today, quarterly creative education sessions are used to share information and keep learning exciting. Employees attend annual seminars about employee ownership, and incentives keep them motivated to learn more and continue to cross-train.

"Many companies have the idea that employees will work harder and smarter just because they're offered ownership, but the ESOP by itself will not make anything different," Sheppard says. "It just gives you the opportunity to rally around a common cause, to provide broad training and business development. That can bring about dramatic changes in the way people behave, but the teaching and training has to be continuous."

Source: Nancy Mann Jackson, "The ABCs of ESOPs," *MyBusiness*, February-March 2003.

they do not have to seek out a buyer or incur the expenses associated with consummating a sale. There are disadvantages, however. Reducing reinvestment, when the firm faces valuable growth opportunities, results in lost value creation and could leave a firm unable to sustain its competitive advantage. The end result may be an unintended reduction in harvestable value below the potential value of the firm as a long-term going concern. Also, there may be tax disadvantages to an orderly liquidation, compared with other harvest methods. For example, if a firm simply distributes the cash as dividends, the income may be taxed both as corporate income and as personal dividend income to the stockholders. (Of course, this would not be a problem for a sole proprietorship, partnership, limited liability company, or S corporation.)

Finally, for the entrepreneur who is simply tired of day-to-day operations, siphoning off the cash flows over time may require too much patience. Unless other people in the firm are qualified to manage it, this strategy may be destined to fail.

Going Public

The third method of harvesting a firm is going public. Many entrepreneurs consider the prospect of an initial public offering (IPO) as the "holy grail" of their career, as firms involved in an IPO are generally star performers. However, most entrepreneurs do not really understand the IPO process, especially when it comes to (1) how going public relates to the harvest and (2) the actual process by which a firm goes public.

initial public offering (IPO)
The first sale of shares of a company's stock to the public

THE IPO AS A HARVEST STRATEGY An **initial public offering (IPO)** is used primarily as a way to raise additional equity capital to finance company growth, and only secondarily as a way to harvest the owner's investment. Lisa D. Stein, vice president of Salomon Smith Barney, offered the following reasons for going public:[4]

- To raise capital to repay outstanding debt
- To support future growth
- To fund future acquisitions

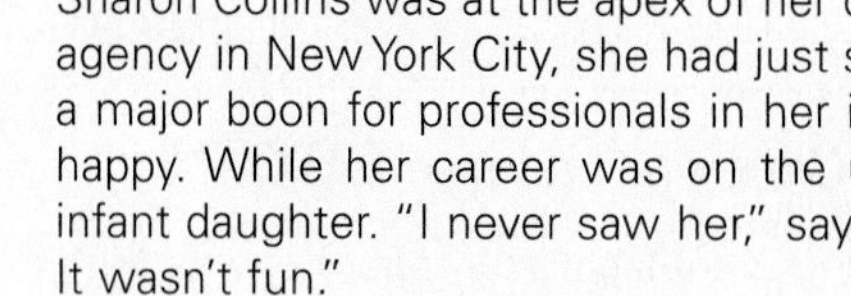

Living the Dream Entrepreneurial Challenges

Success Means Balancing Work and Family

© Chuck St. John Photography

http://www.secondsitestudio.com

Sharon Collins was at the apex of her career. A graphic designer for a large, corporate ad agency in New York City, she had just seen her work featured at the Art Directors Club—a major boon for professionals in her industry. But something was missing. She wasn't happy. While her career was on the upswing, Collins missed spending time with her infant daughter. "I never saw her," says Collins. "I decided I just couldn't do it anymore. It wasn't fun."

So 11 years ago, she left her corporate job and started Second Site Studio, a design firm that she runs out of her home in Tallahassee, Florida. "When I was a kid, I had no idea what my father did," she says. "It's so different for my daughter. The business is woven into our lives."

Collins doesn't have a set work schedule. Her clients dictate her daily routine. "When I don't have a lot to do, we may go play after she is home from school," says Collins, who helps out with a Girl Scout troop and takes her daughter to afternoon ballet classes. "But the opposite is true when I'm busy. I may work into the night."

Collins hopes the erratic schedule teaches her daughter discipline. "She understands that when you have work to do, you do it. It's such a valuable lesson for a child."

And though she makes more money now than she ever would have climbing the corporate ladder, the money isn't her greatest reward. "My daughter and I have a totally different relationship than if I'd been a 9-to-5 mom."

Source: Rex Hammock and Shannon Scully, "Success: What's Your Definition?" *MyBusiness*, December-January 2004, http://www.mybusinessmag.com/fullstory.php3?sid=903, May 2004.

- To create a liquid market for the company's stock
- To broaden the company's shareholder base
- To create ongoing interest in the company and its continued development

For entrepreneurs, however, having publicly traded stock can be beneficial in that a public market provides a ready means of selling stock and thus may facilitate the eventual harvest of their investment. In fact, there is evidence that IPOs eventually lead to an exit. Specifically, it has been shown that the median percentage of ownership by a firm's officers and directors declines from 68 percent to 18 percent in the 10 years following an IPO.[5] Thus, while an IPO is not primarily a harvest mechanism, going public does provide the owners with increased liquidity—which facilitates their eventual exit.

THE IPO PROCESS The basic steps in the IPO process are as follows:[6]

Step 1. The firm's owners decide to go public.

Step 2. If not already completed, an audit of the last three years' financial statements is conducted.

Step 3. An investment banker is selected to guide management in the IPO process.

Step 4. An S-1 Registration Statement is filed with the SEC. (The Registration Statement is subject to an SEC review period of approximately 30 to 35 days.)

Step 5. Management responds to comments by the SEC and issues a Red Herring/ Prospectus, describing the firm and the offering.

Step 6. Management spends the next 10 to 15 days "on the road," explaining the firm's attributes to potential investors.

Step 7. On the day before the offering is released to the public, the actual offering price is decided upon. Based on the demand for the offering, the shares will be priced to create active trading of the stock.

Step 8. Months of work come to fruition in a single event—offering the stock to the public and seeing how it is received.

The IPO process may be one of the most exhilarating—but frustrating and exhausting—experiences of an entrepreneur's life. Owner-managers frequently discover that they do not like being exposed to the variability of public capital markets and to the prying questions of public-market investors. In a survey of the *Inc. 100* companies, CEOs who had participated in public offerings indicated that they had spent, on average, 33 hours per week for four and a half months on the offering.[7] To many, the cost of the IPO process seemed exorbitant. They found themselves being misunderstood and having little influence on the decisions being made, and they were frequently disillusioned with investment bankers and the entire process. At some point, they wondered where they had lost control of the process—a feeling shared by many entrepreneurs involved in a public offering.

To understand an IPO, you must consider the shift in power that occurs during the process. When the chain of events begins, the firm's managers are in control. They dictate whether or not to go public and who the investment banker will be. After the prospectus has been prepared and the road show is under way, however, the firm's managers, including the entrepreneur, are no longer the primary decision makers. The investment banker is now in control. Finally, the marketplace, in concert with the investment banker, begins to take over. Ultimately, it is the market that dictates the final outcome.

In addition to being prepared for the shift in control, it is important that the entrepreneur understand the investment banker's motivations in the IPO process. Who is the investment banker's primary customer? Clearly, the issuing firm is compensating the underwriter for its services through the fees paid and participation in the offering. But helping a firm with an IPO is usually not as profitable for the investment banker as are other activities, such as involvement in corporate acquisitions. And the investment banker is also selling the securities to the customers on the other side of the trade. These are the people who will continue to do business with the investment banker in the future. Thus, the investment banker is somewhat conflicted as to who is the "customer."

Although many entrepreneurs seek to take their firms public through an IPO, this strategy is appropriate only for a limited number of firms. And even for this small group, an IPO is more a means of raising growth capital than a harvest strategy.

Using Private Equity

private equity
Money provided by venture capitalists or private investors

The fourth method of harvesting is the use of private equity. With an IPO, a portion of the firm's equity is sold in *public* equity markets. There is, however, an alternative in which *private* equity is infused to help a family-controlled firm transfer ownership from one generation to the next and eventually to outside investors, while at the same time providing capital for growth. **Private equity** is money provided by venture capitalists or private investors. The private investors may be individuals or small groups of individuals who act together to invest in companies.

Trying to meet the owners' need for cash and the firm's need for growth capital while retaining control is perhaps the most difficult task facing family firms. The difficulty is compounded when the family is attempting to transfer ownership and leadership to the next generation. The situation can be further complicated by the retiring owner's need to diversify, for estate planning purposes, assets held within the business.

In the transfer of ownership within a family-owned firm, tradeoffs among three factors are of primary importance: (1) liquidity for exiting family members, (2) continued financing for company growth, and (3) maintenance of family control of the firm. In a survey of entrepreneurs who had transferred or were planning to transfer ownership of their busi-

Living the Dream — *Entrepreneurial Challenges*

The Harvest: Easier Said Than Done

Harvesting a business requires entrepreneurs to do something that most find very difficult: let go of their personal vision for the company's future. Also, if harvesting involves selling the company, the entrepreneur's best prospect may be one of the firm's competitors—perhaps a long-time adversary.

For Linda Bush, co-founder of SafeRent Inc., a Denver company that performs credit and background checks on prospective tenants for apartment-house owners, the big competitor was First American Corporation, a huge Santa Ana, California, title-insurance concern that also does tenant screening.

With big real-estate investment trusts and other institutions taking over the ownership and management of rental units from mom-and-pop landlords, faster and more accurate credit and background checks were in demand. Founded in 1998, SafeRent was the first company to assign tenants a numerical score so as to aid property rental firms in evaluating prospective renters.

Bush, 43, wanted to broaden SafeRent's product line to help apartment firms manage their overall business—analyzing tenant turnover, vacancy times, and rental pricing to maximize profits. But broadening SafeRent's line meant "an additional round of investment," which became tougher to obtain as the Internet bubble burst.

At the same time, the basic tenant-scoring business became hotly competitive, with First American using its lower costs and sales-force muscle to win market share and squeeze SafeRent. "We've woken up the sleeping giant, First American, and they're coming after us," Bush recalls thinking.

She was enjoying the fight, but could see that SafeRent might lose. A board member helped clarify the situation, telling her, "SafeRent's a product, not a company."

It was time to sell. "We thought First American was the natural," Bush says. "We did talk to some others and thereby got a better price from First American."

And what of her vision for her business? "First American is investing in the screening division," Bush says, but adds, "I am concerned that the cultures are very different. Innovating new products was more important—transforming the industry—to us than profit. They're very profit-driven."

Source: Jeff Bailey, "Selling the Firm—and Letting Go of the Dream," *Wall Street Journal*, December 10, 2002, p. B6.

nesses, 85 percent of the respondents stated that maintaining control of the firm was "very important." About 45 percent also considered providing capital for the firm's future growth and meeting the personal liquidity needs of family members "very important." When asked how the transfer had been or would be financed, the entrepreneurs responded as follows:[8]

Gift	38%
Seller financing	24%
Acquirer's personal financing	14%
Third-party financing	12%
Other	12%

This sample indicates that family-owned firms use a limited number of alternatives to finance transitions. In many cases, the owners exiting the firm apparently had sufficient personal liquidity that they did not require external financing. Others financed the transition from the firm's operating cash flows, but only by limiting the firm's growth opportunities. The primary source for those who sought third-party financing was a banker.

Recognizing the need for creativity, some investment groups have developed financing approaches that more fully recognize the needs of exiting family owners whose firms have significant growth potential. One such approach is the Private IPO, a trademarked process designed for mature, successful family businesses that are not "in play."[9]

To understand the Private IPO, consider the following example. Assume that a company could be sold for $50 million through a leveraged buyout (LBO), where the sale would most likely be financed through 80 percent debt, consisting of about $28 million in senior debt and $12 million in subordinated debt, and 20 percent equity. Many entrepreneurs would find such an arrangement intolerable, even though they would have cashed out. They simply would not want their company subjected to such a high-leverage transaction. As an alternative to an LBO, the sellers might consider the Private IPO, which provides less cash but allows the family to retain control. The firm just described would be sold for $45 million—10 percent less than the LBO price. The sellers would receive $38 million in cash, not the full $45 million. Instead of relinquishing all or most of their ownership, however, the family owners would receive 51 percent of the equity in exchange for the $7 million retained in the company. The remaining $38 million of the purchase price would be financed from two sources: $24 million in senior debt and $14 million provided by a private investor, consisting of $7 million in common equity for 49 percent of the firm's ownership and $7 million in preferred stock. The preferred stock would have an annual dividend (to be paid in additional shares of stock in the first years of the transaction), as well as warrants for additional common stock to bring the private investor's economic (but not voting) ownership up to 65 percent—but only if management did not make its projections. For instance, management might predict that current earnings would increase 60 percent over the next five years. If this goal was realized, then management would keep the 51 percent economic share of the firm when the eventual harvest occurred. If the goal was not realized, management's economic ownership would be scaled down, depending on how far off-target earnings were. However, ownership would not fall below 35 percent. This deal structure is represented in Exhibit 12-2.

The differences between the two capital structures are clear. The debt ratio is much lower in the Private IPO than in the LBO, allowing for a lower interest rate on the debt and permitting the firm's cash flows to be used to grow the firm, rather than pay down debt. This arrangement allows the senior generation of owners to cash out, while the next generation retains control and the cash to grow the firm—a win-win situation. The younger generation also has the potential to realize significant economic gains if the firm performs well.

FIRM VALUATION AND THE HARVEST

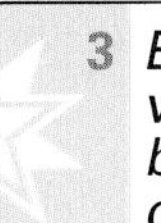
3 *Explain the issues in valuing a firm that is being harvested and deciding on the method of payment.*

As a firm moves toward the harvest, two questions regarding value are of primary importance: the harvest value (what the firm is worth) and the method of payment.

The Harvest Value

Valuing a company may be necessary on numerous occasions during the life of the business—but it is never more important than at the time of the exit. Owners can harvest only

EXHIBIT 12-2 *Private Equity Financing*

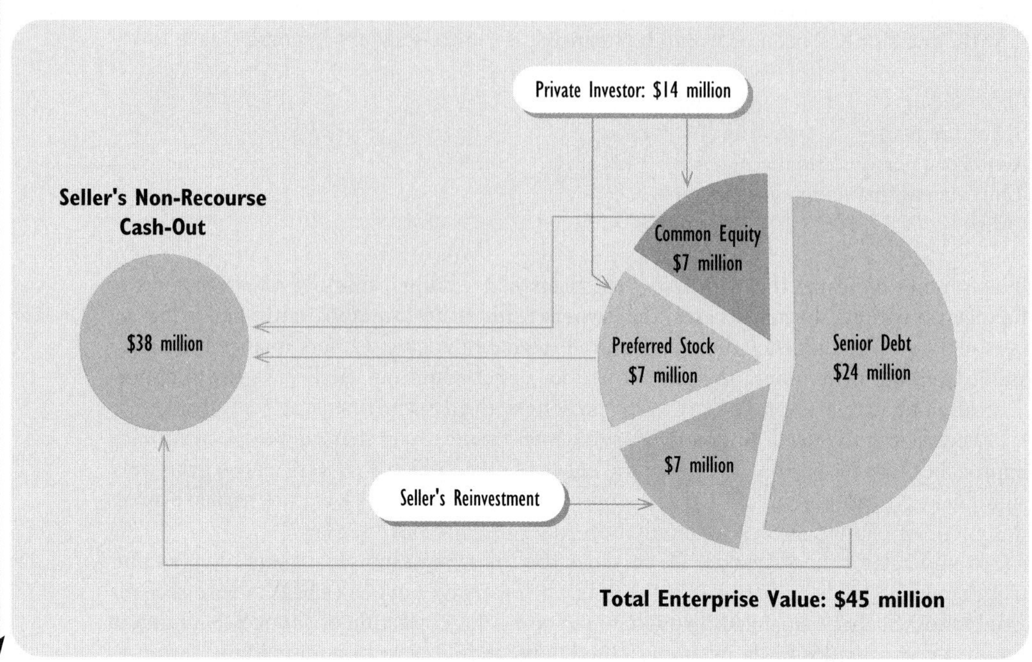

opportunity cost of funds The rate of return that could be earned on another investment of similar risk

what they have created. Value is created when a firm's return on invested capital is greater than the investors' **opportunity cost of funds**, which is the rate of return that could be earned on an investment of similar risk.

Growing a venture to the point of diminishing returns and then selling it to others who can carry it to the next level is a proven way to create value. How this incremental value

Living the Dream — Entrepreneurial Challenges

Success Means Independence

Lurita Doan wasn't considered successful at her old job. A computer programmer for a large federal contractor, Doan couldn't help thinking outside the box—and that wasn't a good thing. When she went to her managers 13 years ago with an idea to customize software for their clients, they basically told her to go back to her cubicle and be quiet.

Devastated and a little angry, Doan quit her job a few weeks later and started her own company, New Technology Management, Inc., an IT company that specializes in border security and systems integration.

"Success is being my own boss and having it done my way," says Doan. "I'm really hard-headed. I know what is right. I have a way of doing things that adheres to excellence."

Though her hard work produces a comfortable salary, Doan says she is happy driving a Saturn—because independence is what drives her to work each morning. "The most amazing part of owning a business is that it's up to me to make it work. I can do what I want, and I don't have to check with anyone," Doan says.

http://www.ntmi.com

Source: Rex Hammock and Shannon Scully, "Success: What's Your Definition?" *MyBusiness*, December-January 2004, http://www.mybusinessmag.com/fullstory.php3?sid=903, May 2004.

is shared between the old and the new owners depends largely on the relative strengths of each party in the negotiations—that is, who wants the deal the most or who has the best negotiating skills.

Business valuation is part science and part art, so there is no precise formula for determining the price of a private company. Rather, the price is determined by a sometimes intricate process of negotiation between buyer and seller. Much is left to the negotiating skills of the respective parties. But one thing is certain: There must be a willing buyer. It doesn't matter what a firm's owner believes the business is worth; it is worth only what someone who has the cash is prepared to pay.

The specific approaches to and methods for valuing a company are described in Appendix B at the end of the book. As described in the appendix, buyers and sellers frequently base the harvest value of a firm on a multiple of earnings. For instance, a company might be valued at five times its earnings. (Entrepreneur Robert Hall sold one of his firms for a multiple of earnings; his experience provides the basis for the example used in Appendix B.)

The Method of Payment

The actual value of the firm is only one issue; another is the method of payment. Harvesting owners can be paid in cash or in stock of the acquiring firm, with cash generally being preferred over stock. Entrepreneurs who accept stock in payment are frequently disappointed, as they are unable to affect the value of the stock once they have sold the firm. Only an entrepreneur who has great faith in the firm's stock should accept it in payment, and even then he or she is taking a big chance by not being well diversified. Having such a large investment in only one stock is risky, to say the least.

Living the Dream *Entrepreneurial Challenges*

Accepting Stock for Payment Can Be Risky

In 1969, J. O. Stewart, Jr., of El Paso, Texas, joined with four other local businessmen and professionals to start a new company, El Paso Disposal, Inc. After a number of years, the name of the firm was changed to International Environmental Industries, Inc. (IEII).

In the latter half of the 1990s, the waste industry began consolidating, as several publicly traded companies purchased smaller, privately held companies. Stewart and his partners had several opportunities to sell their firm, but were never quite ready to do so. Finally, in June 1999, Stewart agreed to meet with the chief financial officer of Waste Connections Inc. (WCI) at the Waste Expo in Dallas to discuss the possibility of selling IEII. Shortly thereafter, Stewart met with Ron Mittelstaedt, chief executive officer of WCI, in Phoenix to discuss WCI, the industry, and Stewart's thoughts on selling his company. Then, on July 13, 1999, WCI executives came to El Paso and met with Stewart to begin preliminary discussions about the value of IEII. At that meeting, they made a tentative verbal offer based on the financial information (in legal terminology, "subject to due diligence"). Mittelstaedt and Stewart then began serious, detailed negotiations over the telephone. Mittelstaedt returned to El Paso to meet with Stewart and made a final written offer that was virtually everything Stewart wanted.

Stewart accepted WCI's offer, which called for Stewart to be paid mostly in WCI stock, which had a market price of about $25 at the time. The deal was consummated, and Stewart received the WCI shares for his company. Everything was great, but not for long. As fate would have it, the president of one of the major publicly traded companies in the industry had committed fraud. The fallout caused the stock prices of all the publicly traded firms in the industry to decline sharply. Within six months, the value of WCI shares had decreased from $25 to $12, which meant that the value of Stewart's shares fell by half—a tremendous loss in value for the entrepreneur.

The moral of the story: Unless you get cash for your company, you can't be sure of its actual selling price.

Source: Interview with J. O. Stewart, March 2000.

From an investor's viewpoint, cash is best—except for the tax consequences. As one investor advised, "Start with cash and work down from there." However, venture capitalists may not have a preference between stocks and cash if their limited partners—frequently pension funds—have no preference, as long as the sale of the stock is not restricted in any way.

DEVELOPING AN EFFECTIVE HARVEST PLAN

4 *Provide advice on developing an effective harvest plan.*

We have discussed why planning for the harvest is important, despite the tendency of many entrepreneurs to ignore it until some crisis or unanticipated event comes along. We have also described the methods for exiting. However, there is still a lot that can be said about developing a harvest plan. In the sections that follow, we provide suggestions on crafting an effective exit strategy.[10]

Manage for the Harvest

Entrepreneurs frequently do not appreciate the difficulty of harvesting a company. One investor commented that exiting a business is "like brain surgery—it's done a lot, but there are a lot of things that can go wrong." Harvesting, whether through a sale or a stock offering, takes a lot of time and energy on the part of the firm's management team and can be very distracting from day-to-day affairs. The result is often a loss of managerial focus and momentum, leading to poor performance.

Uncertainties accompanying an impending sale often lower employee morale. The stress can affect the whole organization, as employees become anxious about the prospect of a new owner. Lynn Baker, at Sutter Hill Ventures, offers this advice: "Don't start running the company for the liquidity event. Run the business for the long haul." Jim Porter, at CCI Triad, describes the situation in Silicon Valley in the 1990s, where some owners carried the practice to an extreme:

> *Some people don't think in terms of long-term value as much as short-term returns. This carries over into developing an IPO exit strategy. I see a growing number of people who are already planning their next company before they are finished with the first company. They are looking to exit the first one, get the money out and start the second one, get the money out, and pyramid their return. In a hot market, you can do that and get away with it. There are professional company starters.*

So, while an entrepreneur should not be caught unaware, there is also the risk of becoming so attentive to "playing the harvest game" that one forgets to keep first things first.

Investors are always concerned about how to exit, and entrepreneurs need to have a similar mind-set. Peter Hermann, general partner at Heritage Partners, a private equity investment group, notes, "People generally stumble into the exit and don't plan for it." However, for Hermann, "The exit strategy begins when the money goes in." Similarly, Gordon Baty, at Zero Stage Capital, Inc., enters each investment with a clear understanding of its investment horizon and harvest plan. In his words, "We plan for an acquisition and hope for an IPO." Jack Kearney, at Dain Rauscher Inc., indicates that an exit strategy should be anticipated in advance, unless "the entrepreneur expects to die in the CEO chair. . . . The worst of all worlds is to realize, for health or other reasons, that you have to sell the company right now." Jim Knister, at the Donnelly Corporation, advises entrepreneurs to start thinking two or three years ahead about how they are going to exit so that they can correctly position their companies.

This type of advice is particularly important when the entrepreneur is planning an IPO. Running a public company requires information disclosures to stockholders that are not required of a privately held firm. Specifically, this means (1) maintaining an accounting process that cleanly separates the business from the entrepreneur's personal life, (2) selecting a strong board of directors that can and will offer valuable business advice, and (3) managing the firm so as to produce a successful track record of performance.

Having a harvest plan in place is also very important, because the window of opportunity can open and close quickly. Remember that the opportunity to exit is triggered by the arrival of a willing and able buyer, not just an interested seller. For an IPO, a hot market may offer a very attractive opportunity, and a seller must be ready to move when the opportunity arises.

Living the Dream

Entrepreneurial Challenges

Good Accounting Contributes to a Good Harvest

Good accounting records are important when it comes to selling your business, regardless of the size of the firm.

Marc Moore and his partners planned for their exit before they even started their former business, Payroll Transfers Inc. "From the very beginning we ran it as if it were a public company because we wanted the option to sell privately or do an IPO," says Moore, who now owns DTNet Group, a conglomerate of companies in Tampa. The discipline of running a private company like a public one forced the partners to keep perfect books, a major plus when it was time to sell.

Donna Touchette's bookkeeping for her small family-owned business, Dana Market, was so precise that bank officials complimented her the day she closed on the sale of her convenience store. "The bank said the sale went smoothly because of our books," says Touchette, who sold the Kingman, Arizona, business earlier this year. "When you own a business, it's easy to walk up to the register and take a draw, but then you can't prove your sales later." Touchette thanks her father for lessons in bookkeeping precision. "If there was a quarter missing at the end of the month, he wanted to know where it was."

Using these kinds of checks and balances in your accounting pays off when you're putting a price tag on your business. Organizing your books can't be done at the eleventh hour, says Garrett Sutton, author of *How to Buy and Sell a Business*: "First impressions are lasting. And in the rush of commerce, you don't have time to make sure everything is up-to-date. Your books need to be in great shape upfront."

Source: Shannon Scully, "Planning Your Exit Strategy, *MyBusiness*, October-November 2003, pp. 43–44.

In summary, an entrepreneur should be sure to anticipate the harvest. In the words of Ed Cherney, an entrepreneur who has sold two companies, "Don't wait to put your package together until something dramatic happens. Begin thinking about the exit strategy and start going through the motions, so that if something major happens, you will have time to think through your options."

Expect Conflict—Emotional and Cultural

Having bought other companies does not prepare entrepreneurs for the sale of their own company. Entrepreneurs who have been involved in the acquisition of other firms are still ill-prepared for the strains and stress associated with selling their own businesses. Jim Porter, who has been involved in a number of acquisitions, says, "It's definitely a lot more fun to buy something than it is to be bought." One very real difference between selling and buying comes from the entrepreneur's personal ties to the business that he or she helped create. A buyer can be quite unemotional and detached, while a seller is likely to be much more concerned about nonfinancial considerations.

For this reason and many others, entrepreneurs frequently do not make good employees. The very qualities that made them successful entrepreneurs can make it difficult for them to work under a new owner. In fact, an entrepreneur who plans to stay with the firm after a sale can become disillusioned quickly and end up leaving prematurely.

Lynn Baker observes, "There is a danger of culture conflict between the acquiring versus the acquired firm's management. The odds are overwhelming that somebody who's been an entrepreneur is not going to be happy in a corporate culture." When Ed Bonneau sold his wholesale sunglass distribution firm, he was retained as a consultant, but the buyer never sought his advice. Bonneau recalled that he "could not imagine that someone could or would buy a company and not operate it. The people who bought the firm had no operations expertise or experience whatsoever and, in fact, didn't care that much about it."

These conflicts occur to varying degrees whenever an entrepreneur remains with the company after the sale. Although the nature of the conflict varies, the intensity of the feelings does not. An entrepreneur who stays with the company should expect culture conflict and be pleasantly surprised if it does not occur.

Living the Dream

Entrepreneurial Challenges

Success Means Making Money

Chicago business owner Joe King never minces words. He's not ashamed to say profits equal success at Le Passage, a 10,000-square-foot restaurant that King opened with three partners in 2000. "The ultimate goal of doing business is to make money," says King, who started his career in the food industry in New York City 28 years ago. "No one opens a business to break even."

Being successful in the tumultuous restaurant industry is an accomplishment. As King points out, "Success in business has nothing to do with a full dining room. It's the bottom line you bring in from the fruits of your labor."

http://www.lepassage.tv

Though not prone to acquiring material possessions, King dreams of a life with more time for travel, a luxury the restaurant industry rarely allows. He hopes that one day his meticulous budgets will pay off in the form of a sailboat. "I just want to get on it and go," says King, who met his wife of 12 years on a sailboat in the Caribbean.

Source: Rex Hammock and Shannon Scully, "Success: What's Your Definition?" *MyBusiness*, December-January 2004, http://www.mybusinessmag.com/fullstory.php3?sid=903, May 2004.

Get Good Advice

Entrepreneurs learn to operate their businesses through experience gained in repeated day-to-day activities. However, they may engage in a harvest transaction only once in a lifetime. "It's an emotional roller-coaster ride," says Ben Buettell, who frequently represents sellers of small and mid-size companies.[11] Thus, entrepreneurs have a real need for good advice, both from experienced professionals and from those who have personally been through a harvest. In seeking advice, be aware that the experts who helped you build and grow your business may not be the best ones to use when it's time to sell the company, as they may not have the experience needed in that area. So, choose your advisors carefully.

Bill Dedmon, at Southwest Securities, advises, "Don't try to do it alone, because it's a demanding process that can distract you from your business." Jack Furst, at Hicks, Muse, Tate, & Furst, believes that advisors can give entrepreneurs a reality check. He contends that, without independent advice, entrepreneurs frequently fall prey to thinking they want to sell unconditionally, when in fact they really want to sell only if an unrealistically high price is offered.

Professional advice is vital, but entrepreneurs stress the importance of talking to other entrepreneurs who have sold a firm or taken it public. No one can better describe what to expect—both in events and in emotions—than someone who has had the experience. This perspective nicely complements that of the professional advisor.

Perhaps the greatest misconception among entrepreneurs is that an IPO is the end of the line. They often feel that taking their firm public through an IPO means they have "made it." The fact is that going public is but one transition in the life of a firm. Many entrepreneurs are surprised to learn that a public offering is just the beginning, not an end.

An entrepreneur will not be able to cash out for some time after the completion of the IPO. In a sense, investors in the new stock offering have chosen to back the entrepreneur as the driving force behind the company—that is, they have invested in the entrepreneur, not the firm. While the daily stock price quotes will let the management team keep score, the business will have to reach another plateau before the founder can think about placing it in the hands of a new team and going fishing. Ed Bonneau talks of being surprised in this matter:

> *The question of an IPO was put to me a number of times over the years. I had some investment bankers come and look at our company to talk about going public; they said, "Yeah, you can go public." Then they asked me why I wanted to go public. I said, "For one thing, I want*

some money out of the company. I have every dime I've got stuck in here." They responded that I couldn't do that. I asked what they meant. They responded, "Getting money out [is] not the purpose of going public."

Lynn Baker describes the typical entrepreneur's thinking about an IPO as "the *Bride Magazine* syndrome in which the entrepreneur is like the bride-to-be who becomes fixated on the events of the wedding day without thinking clearly about the years of being married that will follow. Life as head of a public corporation is very different from life at the helm of a private firm. Major investors will be calling every day expecting answers—sometimes with off-the-wall questions." Under these circumstances, getting good advice is a must.

Understand What You Want

For an entrepreneur, harvesting a business that has been an integral part of life for a long period of time can be a very emotional experience. When an entrepreneur has invested a substantial part of his or her working life in growing a business, a real sense of loss may accompany the harvest. Walking away from employees, clients, and one's identity as a small business owner may not be the wonderful ride into the sunset that was expected.

Thus, entrepreneurs should think very carefully about their motives for exiting and what they plan to do after the harvest. Frequently, entrepreneurs have great expectations about what life is going to be like with a lot of liquidity, something many of them have never known. The harvest does provide the long-sought liquidity, but some entrepreneurs find managing money—in contrast to operating their own company—less rewarding than they had expected.

Entrepreneurs may also become disillusioned when they come to understand more fully how their sense of personal identity was intertwined with their business. While Jim Porter understands that a primary purpose of exiting is to make money, watching a number of owners cash out has led him to conclude that the money is not a very satisfying aspect of the event:

The bottom line is that you need more than money to sustain life and feel worthwhile. I see people who broke everything to make their money. They were willing to sacrifice their wives,

---

Living the Dream — *Entrepreneurship and Integrity*

Harvesting Is About More Than Money

When Ed Avis bought the trade magazine *Modern Reprographics* at the age of 29, he knew he wouldn't want to publish a magazine about blueprints for the rest of his life. So, in 1998, five years after he bought the magazine, he turned around and sold it to competitors for a substantial profit.

Though it might sound like the perfect plan, Avis learned plenty of lessons during his first harvest that he'll remember when he's ready to leave his current book publishing company, Oak Park, Illinois–based Marion Street Press.

"I learned that money is not what makes a good life," says Avis, who plans to stay at his current company until he retires. "When I'm 65 and I sell this company, I'm not just going to go with the highest bidder. At first, everyone's end result is to sell their business and make a lot of money," he says. "But having a company you can look back on and be proud of is worth more than a pot of gold."

Courtesy of Marion Street Press/www.marionstreetpress.com

http://www.marionstreetpress.com

Source: Shannon Scully, "Planning Your Exit Strategy," *MyBusiness*, October-November 2003, p. 35.

their family, and their own sense of values to make money. I remember one person who was flying high, did his IPO, and went straight out and bought a flaming red Ferrari. He raced it down the street, hit a telephone pole, and died the day his IPO money came down. You see these guys, including a few of the people involved in the first Triad IPO, go crazy. They went out and bought houses in Hawaii, houses in Tahoe, new cars, and got things they didn't need.

Peter Hermann believes that "seller's remorse" is definitely a major issue for a number of entrepreneurs. His advice is "Search your soul and make a list of what you want to achieve with the exit. Is it dollars, health of the company, your management team or an heir apparent taking over?" The answers to these and similar questions determine to a significant extent whether the exit will prove successful in all dimensions of an entrepreneur's life. There can be conflicting emotions, such as those expressed by Bill Bailey, founder of the Cherokee Corporation:

There is a period in your life when you get up in age and you begin thinking more about your family. For me, it became important for the first time in my life to have money available to do some long-range personal planning for myself, and for my family. But if there is any one thing to be understood when you are selling a business or anything else, it is the excitement of the journey and the enjoyment for doing what you're doing that matters.

Entrepreneurs are also well advised to be aware of potential problems that may arise after the exit. There are stories about people selling a firm or going public and then losing everything. Ed Cherney says, "It is more difficult to handle success than it is to handle struggling. People forget what got them the success—the work ethic, the commitment to family, whatever characteristics work for an entrepreneur. Once the money starts rolling in, . . . people forget and begin having problems."

And for the entrepreneur who believes that it will be easy to adapt to change after the harvest, even possibly to start another company, William Unger, at the Mayfield Fund, quotes from Machiavelli's *The Prince*: "It should be remembered that nothing is more difficult than to establish a new order of things."

Living the Dream — Entrepreneurial Challenges

Courtesy of GroundFloor Media, Inc.

http://www.groundfloormedia.com

Success Means Loving Your Work

Laura Love doesn't have a job. In the three years since she opened her public relations firm in Boulder, Colorado, Love has created an environment that no longer feels like work.

"About six months after I opened the business, it hit me: I don't have a job—I have a life that I've built," says Love, who worked for a startup technology firm before opening GroundFloor Media.

For many small business owners, success is being able to look forward to the beginning of each day. It's genuinely enjoying what they do and building a legacy, instead of living for Fridays. Love refers to her holistic approach to success: She is happy, her family is happy, and her seven employees are happy.

For Love, running a business is about more than working toward a single goal; it's about celebrating the small steps along the way. Love says, "If your entire focus is on buying a yacht, you miss out on all the things that give you the self-confidence to run a business."

Source: Rex Hammock and Shannon Scully, "Success: What's Your Definition?" *MyBusiness*, December-January 2004, http://www.mybusinessmag.com/fullstory.php3?sid=903, May 2004.

WHAT'S NEXT?

Entrepreneurs by their very nature are purpose-driven people. So, after the exit, an entrepreneur who has been driven to build a profitable business will need something larger than the individual to bring meaning to his or her life.

Many entrepreneurs have a sense of gratitude for the benefits they have received from living in a capitalist system. As a result, they want to give back, both with their time and with their money. The good news is that there is no limit to the number of worthy charitable causes, including universities, churches, and civic organizations. And, it may be that when all is said and done, the call to help others with a new venture may be too strong for an individual with an entrepreneurial mind-set to resist. But whatever you decide to do, do it with passion and let your life benefit others in the process.

Looking Back

1 Explain the importance of having a harvest, or exit, plan.

- Harvesting, or exiting, is the means entrepreneurs and investors use to get out of a business and, ideally, reap the value of their investment in the firm.
- Harvesting is about more than merely selling and leaving a business. It involves capturing value (cash flows), reducing risk, and creating future options.
- A firm's accessibility to investors is driven by the availability of harvest options.

2 Describe the options available for harvesting.

- There are four basic ways to harvest an investment in a privately owned company: (1) selling the firm, (2) releasing the firm's cash flows to its owners, (3) offering stock to the public through an IPO, and (4) issuing a private placement of the stock.
- In a sale to a strategic buyer, the value placed on a business depends on the synergies that the buyer believes can be created.
- Financial buyers look primarily to a firm's stand-alone, cash-generating potential as the source of its value.
- In leveraged buyouts (LBOs), high levels of debt financing are used to acquire firms.
- With bust-up LBOs, the assets are then sold to repay the debt.
- With build-up LBOs, a number of related businesses are acquired, which may eventually be taken public via an initial public offering (IPO).
- A management buyout (MBO) is an LBO in which management is part of the group buying the company.
- In an employee stock ownership plan (ESOP), employees' retirement contributions are used to purchase shares in the company.
- The orderly withdrawal of an owner's investment in the form of the firm's cash flows is one method of harvesting a firm.
- An initial public offering (IPO) is used primarily as a way to raise additional equity capital to finance company growth, and only secondarily as a way to harvest the owner's investment.
- Private equity is a form of outside financing that can allow the original owners to cash out.
- Trying to finance liquidity and growth while retaining control is perhaps the most difficult task facing family firms.

3 Explain the issues in valuing a firm that is being harvested and deciding on the method of payment.

- Value is created when a firm's return on invested capital is greater than the investors' opportunity cost of funds.
- A firm will have greater value in the hands of new owners if the new owners can create more value than the current owners can.
- Often, buyers and sellers base the harvest value of a firm on a multiple of its earnings.

- Cash is generally preferred over stock and other forms of payment by those selling a firm.

4 Provide advice on developing an effective harvest plan.

- Investors are always concerned about exit strategy.
- Entrepreneurs who plan to stay with a business after a sale can became disillusioned quickly and end up leaving prematurely.
- Entrepreneurs frequently do not appreciate the difficulty of selling or exiting a company. Having bought other companies does not prepare entrepreneurs for the sale of their own firm.
- Entrepreneurs have a real need for good advice, both from experienced professionals and from those who have personally been through a harvest.
- Going public is not the end, but only a transition in the life of a firm.

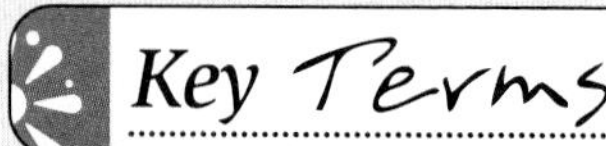

Key Terms

harvesting (exiting), p. 265
leveraged buyout (LBO), p. 267
bust-up LBO, p. 267
build-up LBO, p. 267
management buyout (MBO), p. 268
employee stock ownership plan (ESOP), p. 268
initial public offering (IPO), p. 270
private equity, p. 272
opportunity cost of funds, p. 274

Discussion Questions

1. Explain what is meant by the term *harvesting*. What is involved in harvesting an investment in a privately held firm?
2. Why should an owner of a company plan for eventually harvesting his or her company?
3. Contrast a sale to a strategic buyer with one to a financial buyer.
4. Explain the term *leveraged buyout*. How is a leveraged buyout different from a management buyout?
5. Distinguish between bust-up LBOs and build-up LBOs.
6. What is the primary purpose of an initial public offering (IPO)? How does an IPO relate to a harvest?
7. Why might an entrepreneur find going public a frustrating process?
8. What determines whether a firm has value to a prospective purchaser?
9. What problems can occur when an entrepreneur sells a firm but continues in the management of the company?
10. How may harvesting a firm affect an entrepreneur's personal identity?

You Make the Call

SITUATION 1

Bill and Francis Waugh founded Casa Bonita. They started with a single fast-food Mexican restaurant in Abilene, Texas. At the time, they both worked seven days a week. From that small beginning, they expanded to 84 profitable restaurants located in Texas, Oklahoma, Arkansas, and Colorado. Over the years, other restaurant owners expressed an interest in buying the firm; however, the Waughs were not interested in selling. Then an English firm, Unigate Limited, offered them $32 million for the business and said Bill could remain the firm's CEO. The Waughs were attracted by the idea of having $32 million in liquid assets. They flew to London to close the deal. On the flight home, however, Bill began having doubts about their decision to sell the business. He thought, "We spent 15 years of our lives getting the business where we wanted it, and we've lost it." After their plane landed in New York, they spent the night and then flew back to London the next day. They offered the buyers $1 million to cancel the contract, but Unigate's management declined the offer. The Waughs flew home disappointed.

Question 1 How could the Waughs be disappointed with $32 million?

Question 2 What should the Waughs have done to avoid this situation?

Question 3 What advice would you offer Bill about continuing to work for the business under the new owners?

SITUATION 2

Ed and Barbara Bonneau started their wholesale sunglass distribution firm 30 years ago with $1,000 of their own money and $5,000 borrowed from a country banker in Ed's hometown. The firm grew quickly, selling sunglasses and reading glasses to such companies as Wal-Mart, Eckerd Drugs, and Phar-Mor. In addition, the Bonneaus enjoyed using the company to do good things. For example, they had a company chaplain, who was available when employees were having family problems, such as a death in the family. Although the company had done well, the market had matured recently and profit margins narrowed significantly. Wal-Mart, for example, was insisting on better terms, which meant significantly lower profits for the Bonneaus. Previously, Ed had set the prices that he needed to make a good return on his investment. Now, the buyers had consolidated, and they had the power. Ed didn't enjoy running the company as much as he had in the past, and he was finding greater pleasure in other activities; for instance, he served on a local hospital board and was actively involved in church activities.

Just as Ed and Barbara began to think about selling the company, they were contacted by a financial buyer, who wanted to use their firm as a platform and then buy up several sunglass companies. After negotiations, the Bonneaus sold their firm for about $20 million. In addition, Ed received a retainer fee for serving as a consultant to the buyer. Also, the Bonneaus' son-in-law, who was part of the company's management team, was named the new chief operating officer.

Question 1 Do you agree with the Bonneaus' decision to sell? Why or why not?

Question 2 Why did the buyers retain Ed as a consultant? (In answering this question, you might consider the quote by Bonneau in the chapter.)

Question 3 Do you see any problem with having the Bonneaus' son-in-law become the new chief operating officer?

SITUATION 3

At age 63, Michael Lipper sold his firm to Reuters. His assessment of the sale follows:

> *One of the reasons we sold our business to Reuters was because we knew we probably couldn't manage the technology of the future by ourselves. Any entrepreneur who builds a business for as long as I have would be dishonest if he did not suffer a certain sadness [from selling]. If [Reuters] make a wonderful success out of this, there may be some ego pain. If they muck it up, they've damaged our name and hurt our people.*

Lois Silverman co-founded CRA Managed Care (now known as Concentra Managed Care). When the firm went public in 1995, Silverman's stake was over $10 million. After taking Concentra public, Silverman gave up all involvement in day-to-day operations. Along with 12 other successful businesswomen, she formed the not-for-profit Commonwealth Institute, to help women entrepreneurs set up boards and secure capital. She also became involved with a newspaper called *Women's Business*. She later told this story:

> *The other day a man said to me on a golf course, "I hope I hit this ball, because since I've left my business, I don't know what to do with myself." And I said to myself, "I'm so lucky."*

Question 1 Compare the people in the above true stories in terms of their feelings about exiting their firms.

Question 2 What might explain the difference between those who have positive feelings about cashing out and those who do not?

Experiential Exercises

1. Check your local newspaper for a week or so to find a privately held company that has been sold recently. Try to determine the motivation for the sale. Did it have anything to do with the prior owners' desire to cash out of the business? If so, try to find out what happened.
2. Ask a local family business owner about future plans to harvest the business. Has the owner ever been involved in a harvest? If so, ask the owner to describe what happened and how it all worked out, as well as what he or she learned from the experience. If not, ask whether the owner is aware of any company whose owners cashed out. Visit that company owner to inquire about the exit event.
3. Visit a local CPA to learn about his or her involvement in helping entrepreneurs cash out of companies.
4. Search a business magazine to identify a firm that has successfully completed an initial public offering (IPO). See what you can find out about the event on the Internet. Then log on to InfoTrac College Edition at http://www.infotrac-college.com to find articles on recent IPOs.

Exploring the Web

1. To find out more about harvest and exit strategies of small firms, go to the U.S. Chamber of Commerce Web site at **http://www.uschamber.com/sb**. Choose "Learn" and then "Getting Out of Your Business." What are the exit routes to consider, according to the Chamber, when you own a small business?
2. Valuing a business is a topic covered extensively at the CCH's Business Owner Toolkit Web site, which you may have visited before (see the Exploring the Web exercises for Chapters 10 and 11). Drill a bit deeper into the site by keying in this URL on firm valuation: **http://www.toolkit.cch.com/text/P11_2200.asp**.
   a. Explain the role of a business appraiser.
   b. When setting a price for a small business, what must one consider?
3. Go to BizPlanIt's Web site at **http://www.bizplanit.com**. Choose "BizPlan Resources," "Virtual BizPlan," "Exit Strategy," and then "Business Plan Basics."
   a. What are some common mistakes related to exit strategy and how might they be avoided?
   b. What are the most common exit strategies and what are the advantages and disadvantages of each?
   c. Which exit strategy is the most likely option for your proposed small business?

Video Case 12

TIRES PLUS (P. 548)

This case discusses the process and options to be considered by an entrepreneur who is exiting a business.

Alternative Case for Chapter 12:

Case 2, Diversified Chemical, p. 528

Part Four

FOCUSING ON THE CUSTOMER: MARKETING GROWTH STRATEGIES

CHAPTERS

CUSTOMER RELATIONSHIPS

THE KEY INGREDIENT

In the Video Spotlight

Texas Jet

Many small businesses are competing directly with large companies that are able to reach great economies of scale and offer rock-bottom prices. What can a small business do when it just can't match the prices of its larger (or same-sized) competitors? At Texas Jet, owner Reed Pigman decided to compete on service.

On a trip to Meacham Field in Fort Worth, Texas, Pigman asked pilots about their experience with the Meacham operators. When the pilots told him they weren't wild about the service they were getting, he saw a great opportunity and invested heavily in building an aircraft sales and service business. When Pigman finally received his permit to sell fuel, his fixed costs were so high that he had to charge a premium. He had to rethink how he was competing in his industry.

Faced with going out of business, Pigman turned his attention to creating an executive terminal, selling fuel, taking care of pilots, and hangaring airplanes. Reed Pigman has proved that generally people will pay more for higher quality. Although Texas Jet's fuel prices are higher, Pigman offers amenities like the use of company cars, recreation rooms, shower facilities, and air conditioners to keep planes cool while they're on the ground. Pilots can get fuel any number of places, but Texas Jet provides unique services that the competition has not yet matched.

Video material provided by Hattie Bryant, Producer of Small Business School, the series on PBS Stations, Worldnet, and the Web at http://www.smallbusinessschool.org.

Chapter 13

Looking Ahead

After studying this chapter, you should be able to

1 *Define customer relationship management (CRM) and explain its importance to a small firm.*

2 *Discuss the significance of providing extraordinary customer service.*

3 *Illustrate how technology, such as the Internet, can improve customer relationships.*

4 *Describe the techniques for creating a customer profile.*

5 *Explain how consumers are decision makers and why this is important to understanding customer relationships.*

6 *Describe certain psychological influences on consumer behavior.*

7 *Describe certain sociological influences on consumer behavior.*

Always remember that the customer (consumer) is at the heart of every marketing effort. Therefore, a better understanding of consumers and the transactional relationships a firm has with them will lead to more effective marketing strategies.

Chapter 13 is the first in a sequence of chapters comprising Part 4, Focusing on the Customer: Marketing Growth Strategies. It examines customer relationship management (CRM) and argues that CRM is a key factor in small business survival and growth. Chapters 14 through 17 discuss numerous marketing topics reflecting the all-important customer focus developed in this chapter.

WHAT IS CUSTOMER RELATIONSHIP MANAGEMENT?

1 *Define customer relationship management (CRM) and explain its importance to a small firm.*

Customer relationship management means different things to different people. To some, it is symbolized by simple smiles or comments such as "thank you" and "come again" communicated to customers who have just made a purchase. For others, CRM embodies a much broader marketing effort, culminating in nothing short of complete customization of products and/or services to fit individual customer needs. The goals of a CRM program for most small firms fall somewhere between these two views.

Regardless of the level of a firm's commitment to customer relationship management, the central message of every CRM program is "Court customers for more than a one-time sale." A firm that strongly commits to this idea will appreciate the many benefits a CRM program can offer.

customer relationship management (CRM)
A marketing strategy of maximizing shareholder value through winning, growing, and keeping the right customers

Formally defined, **customer relationship management (CRM)** is a marketing strategy of maximizing shareholder value through winning, growing, and keeping the right customers.[1] In a way, CRM is a mind-set—the implementation of customer-centric strategies, which put customers first so that the firm can succeed. CRM involves treating customers the way the entrepreneur would want to be treated if he or she were a customer.

The central idea of CRM isn't new. For decades, entrepreneurs have recognized the importance of treating customers well; "the customer is king" is an old adage. What is new is giving this tradition a name and using technology to implement many of its techniques. Modern CRM focuses on (1) customers rather than products; (2) changes in processes, systems, and culture; and (3) all channels and media involved in the marketing effort, from the Internet to field sales.

The forerunners of many modern CRM techniques were developed in the 1960s by marketers like Sears and various book clubs. They simply stored information about their customers in computers for reasons other than invoicing. Their goals were to learn who their customers were, what they wanted, and what sort of interests they had. Then along came marketers with ideas about the potential benefits of adopting a customer orientation, followed by the rise of the Internet.

It should be noted that CRM, in its pure form, has nothing to do with technology, although Internet technology has definitely been a major force in CRM's development. Just as putting on the latest $200 pair of technologically designed basketball shoes doesn't make the wearer an NBA player, buying or developing CRM computer software does not, in itself, lead to higher customer retention. But it can help if it is used properly. (The role of technology in CRM is discussed later in this chapter.) Most importantly, there must be company-wide commitment to the concept if CRM is to be productive.

The Importance of CRM to the Small Firm

As depicted in Exhibit 13-1, a small firm's next sale comes from one of two sources—current customers or new customers. Both current and potential customers are valued by a small firm, but sometimes current customers are taken for granted and ignored. While marketing efforts devoted to bringing new customers into the fold are obviously important, keeping existing customers is an even higher priority. A CRM program addresses this priority. Brian Vellmure of Initium Technology, a provider of CRM solutions to small firms, identified five economic benefits of maintaining relationships with current customers:[2]

- Acquisition costs for new customers are huge.
- Long-time customers spend more money than new ones.
- Happy customers refer their friends and colleagues.
- Order-processing costs are higher for new customers.
- Old customers will pay more for products.

Essential Materials for a CRM Program

When you build something—a house, for example—you have a plan (usually called a blueprint) that lists appropriate materials or component parts. Likewise, assembling a CRM program requires a plan so that the entrepreneur will know what people, processes, and so on (parts) she or he needs—and there are many parts in a successful CRM program. In the remainder of this chapter, we discuss two vital building blocks of any CRM program: (1) outstanding transactional relationships with customers and (2) knowledge of consumer behavior. These blocks may be constructed with a variety of "materials," as depicted in Exhibit 13-2. In the sections that follow, we examine those materials we believe to be tremendously important in constructing these two building blocks.

EXHIBIT 13-1 *Sources of the Next Sale*

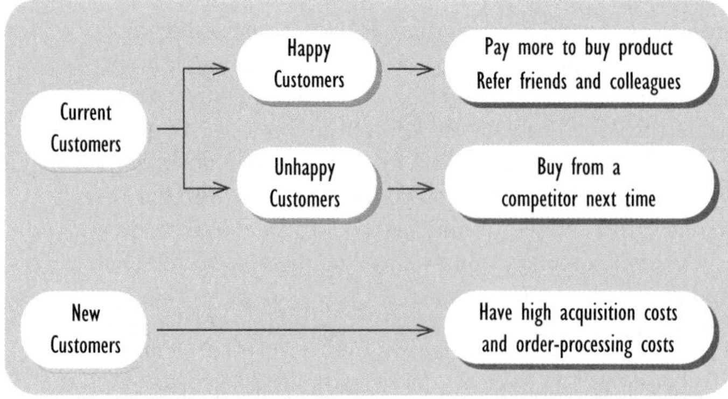

13-2 *Essential Materials of a Successful CRM Program*

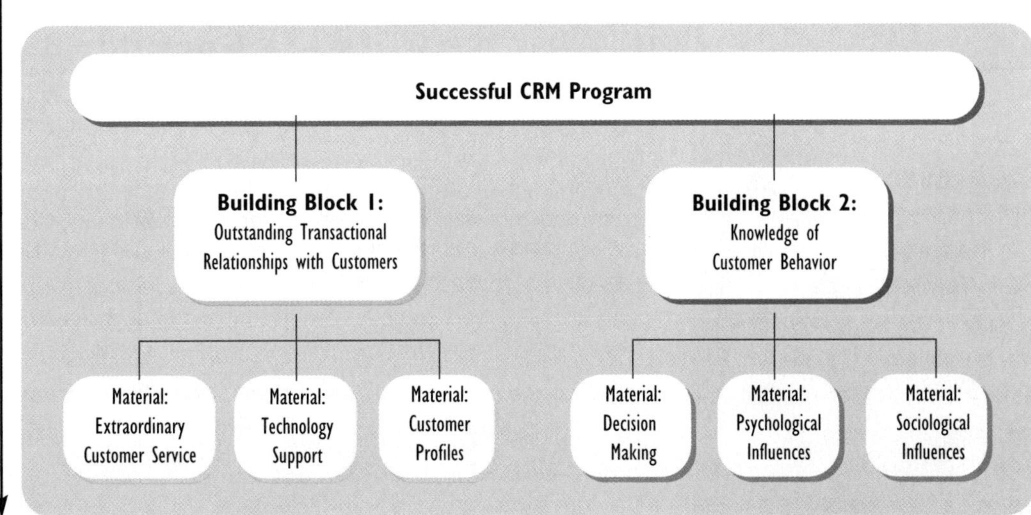

CREATING TRANSACTIONAL RELATIONSHIPS THROUGH EXTRAORDINARY SERVICE

2 *Discuss the significance of providing extraordinary customer service.*

To be successful in the long run, small firms need to concentrate on creating positive transactional relationships with customers. A **transactional relationship** is an association between a business and a customer that relates to a purchase or a business deal. Consumers who have positive interactions with a business usually become loyal customers. Three basic beliefs underlie our emphasis on providing exceptional customer service:

transactional relationship
An association between a business and a customer that relates to a purchase or a business deal

1. Superior customer service creates customer satisfaction.
2. Customer satisfaction produces customer loyalty.
3. Small firms possess greater potential for providing superior customer service than do large firms.

As these beliefs suggest, failure to emphasize customer service jeopardizes the attainment of customer satisfaction and customer loyalty.

Components of Customer Satisfaction

A number of factors under a firm's control contribute to customer satisfaction. One classic article discussing satisfied customers identifies the following four key elements:[3]

1. The most basic benefits of the product or service—the elements that customers expect all competitors to deliver
2. General support services, such as customer assistance
3. A recovery process for counteracting customers' bad experiences
4. Extraordinary services that excel in meeting customers' preferences and make the product or service seem customized

Extraordinary service is the factor that small firms are in a unique position to offer. Relationship marketing proponent Patrick Daly, who oversees a customer relations program for a company in Redwood City, California, suggests the following ways to provide extraordinary service:[4]

- *Naming names.* In today's detached, "just give me your account number" world, nothing is more well received than individual, personalized attention. Even

Living the Dream

Focus on the Customer

Gifts Are Good for Business

Courtesy of GiftTree.com

http://www.gifttree.com

Customer relationship management extends beyond contacts with final consumers. It also applies to a small firm's relationships with corporate buyers.

Consider Craig Bowen's Vancouver, Washington–based GiftTree, which helps corporate customers outsource their gift giving. The site "handles all of a firm's gift giving, from baby announcements to holiday perks, sending out anything from fruit baskets and flowers to desk clocks and stationery sets." The key to success in this type of business, according to Bowen, is customer service.

At GiftTree, profits do not supersede customer satisfaction, but rather follow it. To that end, Bowen has developed in-house CRM software with several capabilities.

> *Features such as an online address book allow users to save time by storing important dates and addresses. A live chat feature allows visitors to chat online with a gift specialist. The company's computer system also alerts operators when a customer inserts a potentially erroneous zip code. Perhaps most importantly, GiftTree personally confirms the delivery of each order. "The costs and complexities of delivery notification are enormous," says Bowen. "But steps like that are what allow us to excel in this industry. We always try to increase value. That's how any company makes it."*

In a society where time is at a premium, clicking a mouse to "send an elegant birthday or graduation gift is appealing, when the alternative is skipping dinner to fight crowds at the mall and waiting in line at the post office." Creating satisfied customers helped GiftTree to attain $8.5 million in sales revenue in 2002.

Sources: "Home-Grown Firm Climbs Corporate Ladder," http://www.ecrmguide.com/print.php/3311631, February 11, 2004; http://www.gifttree.com, May 26, 2004; and "Successful Dot-Com Offers Strategies for Success," http://www.articlecity.com, May 26, 2004.

though you may already be courteous and friendly to customers, greeting them by name is valued 10 times more on the "worthy of loyalty" scale.

- *Custom care*. Customers pretty much know what they do and don't want from your company. If you remember what they want on an individual basis—even if it's something as simple as knowing a dry cleaning customer likes light starch in his collars—then you have mastered one of the key elements of a strong loyalty program.
- *Keeping in touch*. You can't communicate enough on a me-to-you basis with your customers. And don't just connect to make a pitch. Clip out a newspaper or magazine article that pertains to a customer's business and send it to him or her with a note saying "FYI—thought you'd be interested." When customers know that you're taking time to think about them, they don't forget it.
- *"Boo-boo research."* Part of any customer loyalty program is taking the time to reach out to lost customers to learn why they went elsewhere. In many cases, just contacting them and showing them that you really care about getting their business will win them back—along with their contribution to your profits.

Providing exceptional customer service can give small firms a competitive edge, regardless of the nature of the business. Small firms must realize that it costs far more to replace a customer than to keep one. Offering top-notch customer service is something they can do better than can large firms.

Evaluating a Firm's Customer Service Health

Establishing an effective customer service program begins with determining the firm's "customer service quotient," which indicates how well the firm is currently providing service to its customers. Exhibit 13-3 shows an example of a self-assessment questionnaire, to be completed by an entrepreneur or a firm's managers.

13-3 *Evaluating Your Firm's Customer Service Quotient*

For each statement, rate your business based on the following scale:

1 Are you kidding?
2 Hardly ever
3 Sometimes
4 Usually
5 It's our way of life!

Our culture

1. We're committed to do whatever it takes to create satisfied customers. ____
2. We try to do things right the first time. ____
3. As the owner, I show by example that customer service is important. ____
4. Serving our customers' needs takes priority over meeting our internal needs. ____

Total score divided by 4 = ____

Customer alignment

1. When we sell, we aim for a partnership approach. ____
2. In our marketing materials, we don't promise what we can't deliver. ____
3. We know the features and benefits that matter most to our customers. ____
4. We design new products/services based on information provided by our customers. ____

Total score divided by 4 = ____

Problem solving

1. We review customer complaints. ____
2. We constantly ask our customers for feedback. ____
3. We regularly look for ways to eliminate errors, based on customer input. ____

Total score divided by 3 = ____

Using customer information

1. We've determined what our customers expect from us. ____
2. We frequently interact with our customers. ____
3. All employees know what's important to our customers. ____

Total score divided by 3 = ____

Customer outreach

1. We make it easy for our customers to deal with us. ____
2. We aim to resolve all customer complaints. ____
3. We encourage "wowing the customer." ____

Total score divided by 3 = ____

Qualified and empowered staff

1. I respect my employees. ____
2. All employees firmly understand our product/service. ____
3. All employees possess the right tools and skills to perform their jobs well. ____
4. All employees are encouraged to resolve customer issues. ____
5. All employees feel that customer satisfaction is part of their job. ____

Total score divided by 5 = ____

Now evaluate how well your organization focuses on customer satisfaction. Low scores suggest opportunities for improvement.

Source: Adapted from Forum Corporation's Self-Test for a Customer-Driven Company, in "How to Create a Customer Service Plan," an Edward Lowe In-Depth Business Builder, http://peerspectives.org, June 3, 2004.

How good or bad is the quality of customer service among both large and small firms? One recent survey of consumers, reported in *USAToday*, described the situation this way:[5]

> ***On the phone***. *Some 80% of the nation's companies still haven't figured out how to do a decent job getting customers the assistance they need, says Jon Anaton, who oversees Purdue University's Center for Customer-Driven Quality and is research director at the consulting firm BenchmarkPortal.*
>
> ***Online***. *Some 35% of all email inquiries to companies don't get a response within seven days, according to industry estimates. And about 25% never get a response at all, Forrester estimates.*

In "IVR" hell. *To save on labor costs, many of America's largest companies have installed software that the industry calls Interactive Voice Response (IVR) systems. Yet more than 90% of financial service consumers say they don't like these systems, Forrester reports.*

In a rage. *Nearly one in three customers say they have raised their voices at customer service reps and nearly one in 10 say they have cursed at them over the past year, according to a national phone survey by Customer Care Measurement & Consulting.*

In response. *Two-thirds of the estimated 800,000 consumer complaints that have been passed along over the past three years to PlanetFeedback.com's trouble shooting Web site share the same theme: not getting a response from a company, says Sue MacDonald, marketing director.*

Handling Customer Complaints

The way customer service issues are most commonly recognized is through customer complaints. Every firm strives to eliminate customer complaints. When they occur, however, they should be analyzed carefully to uncover possible weaknesses in customer service.

What is the special significance of customer complaints to small businesses? It is that small firms are *potentially* in a much better position than are big businesses to respond to such complaints and, thereby, to achieve customer satisfaction. Why? Because most problems are solvable by simply dealing with issues as they arise, thus giving customers more attention and respect. And showing respect is often easier for a small firm, because it has fewer employees and can vest in each employee the authority to act in customers' best interests. In contrast, a large business often assigns that responsibility to a single manager, who does not have daily contact with customers.

What do consumers do when they are displeased? As Exhibit 13-4 shows, consumers have several options for dealing with their dissatisfaction, and most of these options threaten repeat sales. Only one—a private complaint to the offending business—is desirable to the business. Customers' multiple complaint options emphasize the importance of quality customer service—both before and after a sale.

Managers can also learn about customer service concerns through personal observation and other research techniques. By talking directly to customers or by playing the customer's role anonymously—for example, by making a telephone call to one's own busi-

EXHIBIT 13-4 *Consumer Options for Dealing with Product or Service Dissatisfaction*

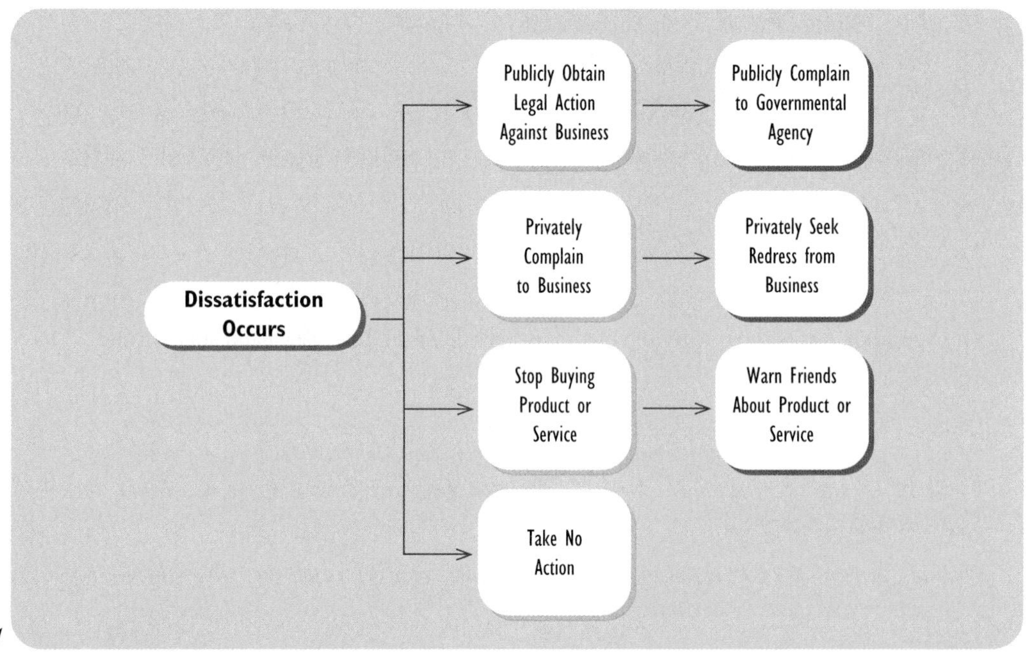

ness—a manager can evaluate service. Some restaurants and motels invite feedback on customer service by providing comment cards to customers.

Consider the efforts of Mike Faith, CEO and founder of Headsets.com, which sells telephone headsets, headphones, and audio conferencing equipment online. Based in San Francisco, California, his firm takes customer service seriously. It rewards its customer service representatives based on customer satisfaction, which is partially gauged by a survey questionnaire included in every invoice sent to customers. As a way to encourage responses, those who return a completed survey receive $10 off their next purchase.[6]

Whatever method is used, evaluating customer service is essential for any business. Reflect on the success that one firm had after developing customer service tactics. Sewell Village Cadillac, a car dealership in Dallas, Texas, is famous for customer service. Its owner, Carl Sewell, began the service journey in 1967 when Sewell Village was in third place among three Dallas Cadillac dealers. He realized that most people didn't like doing business with car dealers. Therefore, he simply began asking customers what they didn't like about car dealers. Three major areas of dissatisfaction were identified—service hours, being without a car during service, and poor or incorrect repairs. By responding to these concerns—for example, by scheduling more service hours—Sewell Village Cadillac improved its customer satisfaction image.

Although many types of customer service cost very little, there are definite costs associated with superior customer service before, during, and after a sale. These costs can be reflected in the price of a product or service, or they can sometimes be recouped

Living the Dream

Focus on the Customer

Outsourcing the Help Desk—Help!

Expectations for the proverbial bottom line may tempt a business to disregard vital customer service practices—at least in the short run. Cost-cutting methods help improve the bottom line, but they can be counterproductive if they also reduce levels of customer service. As president and CEO, Gary Griffiths manages a small firm named Everdream. Headquartered in Fremont, California, the company offers "a comprehensive and integrated suite of hosted desktop services that protect, manage, and support" an enterprise's information technology. In 2002, after much deliberation and analysis, Griffiths shifted a portion of Everdream's work overseas to cut costs and also to free up resources for growth. By outsourcing, Griffiths expected to trim 25 percent off operating expenses related to the firm's Help Desk, which provides 24/7 live support to resolve both hardware and software problems of customers. Its primary function is to support Everdream's slogan: "Any problem. Any time. No excuses."

But shortly after hiring 40 customer service representatives in San José, Costa Rica, Griffiths began to hear customer complaints. "Right away, the customers knew something had changed," says Griffiths.

Language was a problem, and about 10 percent of callers reported "unacceptable levels" of static. Even when the calls were crystal clear, the advice Everdream clients were receiving was not the friendly cure-all they had come to expect. For example, resetting a system password, typically a 5-minute job, was taking more than 10 minutes. Seemingly overnight, the company's trademark customer service, one of its key advantages in the marketplace, was starting to erode. Griffiths began to wonder if the outsourcing decision had been the wrong one to make.

Finally, just seven months after setting up the Help Desk in Costa Rica, Everdream began a gradual phaseout of the new customer service reps. Then Everdream turned its efforts to mending fences with unhappy customers.

Today, despite the lingering consequences, Griffiths believes that Everdream is a stronger company because of the experience. There is always an unfavorable impact on the bottom line when customer satisfaction is not a firm's major concern.

http:www.everdream.com

Sources: Michelle Prather, "Oh Brother Profile of Everdream Corp.," *Business Start-Ups*, July 2000; "Help Desk," http://www.everdream.com June 1, 2004; Rod Kurtz, "Case Study: The Problem," *Inc.*, July 2004, pp. 48–49; and Beth Ellyn Rosenthal, "Why a Silicon Valley Supplier Brought Its Offshore Call Center Home," http://www.outsourcing-offshore.com/silicon.html, June 1, 2004.

separately, based on the amount of service requested—through extended product warranties, for example. Most customers are willing to pay a premium for good service.

USING TECHNOLOGY TO SUPPORT CUSTOMER RELATIONSHIP MANAGEMENT

3 Illustrate how technology, such as the Internet, can improve customer relationships.

Long-term transactional relationships with customers are fostered by good information. A logical time to gather these data is during direct customer contacts, such as when a product is being sold. Customers may be contacted in many ways, including phone calls, letters, faxes, personal interactions, and e-mail. The ability to enjoy one-on-one contact with customers has always been a competitive advantage for small firms. Numerous software packages containing word-processing, spreadsheet, and database tools are also available to assist in supporting customer contacts.

Recently, CRM software has become available. These computer programs help companies gather all customer contact information into a single data management program. Web-based marketers, in particular, are attracted to CRM technology. Online shoppers expect excellent customer service. According to Paula Rosenblum, retail research director at AMR Research in Boston, Massachusetts, computer-based customer service tools do not always need to be elaborate. For high-end products, such as furniture, CRM tools like live chat are popular. However, for inexpensive retail products and niche products, customer service simply means having an easy-to-use site.[7]

Deciding which marketing activity should get initial CRM support is not always easy. However, the sales department is a popular place to start, because sales endeavors generate the greatest amount of customer contact. CRM focuses on such sales activities as accurate and prompt order filling, follow-up contacts to ensure customer satisfaction, and the use of a user-friendly call center to handle all inquiries, including complaints.

Chris McCann, president of 1-800-flowers.com, seems to be ahead of the competition when it comes to incorporating technology into his business. By 1992, in the early days of the Internet, 1-800-flowers.com already had an online presence; by the late 1990s, it had

Living the Dream *Entrepreneurial Challenges*

A Bare-Bones CRM Strategy

© Larry Ford

Understandably, many small firms view computer-based customer relationship management technology as a little overwhelming. CRM software's promises of streamlined customer service and simplified sales efforts do seem unrealistic at times.

Nevertheless, entrepreneur David Bolotsky—who uses some CRM ideas in his Web-based company, Uncommon Goods—is a believer. Although he's "waiting a bit" before jumping into big-time CRM, Bolotsky is currently focusing on logistics issues dealing with expansion of his catalog business, which sells unique, high-quality home accessories and gift items.

He has added to the firm's Web site a function that gives customer service employees quick access to customers' accounts, allowing them to view a customer's shopping or service history. The company has also created an e-mail notification function that allows customers who request products that aren't in stock to sign up for e-mail notification when the company re-stocks the product. And Bolotsky plans to expand his use of CRM software soon.

http://www.uncommongoods.com

Sources: Melissa Campanelli, "Relationship Issues," *Entrepreneur*, July 2002, pp. 42–43; and http://www.uncommongoods.com, May 27, 2004.

a full-fledged e-commerce operation. Now McCann is using SAS CRM software to build close relationships with customers. He notes, "Everybody's available 24/7. The foundations of our early success have become a commodity. In order to retain our competitive advantage, we have to migrate toward becoming a customer-intimate company."[8]

Using a product called Enterprise Miner, his business can sift through data looking for patterns that can, in turn, be used to increase response rates of site visitors and tag the most profitable customers. For example, one customer might shop only once a year to purchase, say, roses on Valentine's Day. Chances are such a customer will not be making additional buys and probably wouldn't appreciate repetitive marketing contacts. But another customer whose history shows purchases for occasions throughout the year might be responsive to more frequent contact and special offers. The SAS CRM software makes it possible to e-mail selected customers once a month to remind them of upcoming dates that the customers have pre-registered, thereby increasing the chance that they will make a purchase.

Having ample support resources for CRM information technology can be a concern for a small firm. This concern has led some entrepreneurs to outsource certain applications. For example, hosted call centers, which handle e-mail and Web communications for clients, may be more cost effective than comparable in-house centers, a crucial consideration for many cash-strapped small firms. In addition to cost, lack of in-house expertise is a major justification for using these outside services. According to Forrester Research, almost 60 percent of small to mid-sized businesses with fewer than 1,000 employees are interested in outsourcing some type of application.[9]

Small firms aren't always happy, however, with the hosted-service option. Consider the situation facing the investment firm Tiedemann Trusts, whose vice president of operations, Kathy Beers, has been looking for a CRM application for the firm's 20 employees to use. Since Tiedemann handles financial data, the firm is unwilling to risk using a hosted service. "I can't have any data off-site," Beers says.[10]

BUILDING CUSTOMER PROFILES FOR A CRM PROGRAM

4 *Describe the techniques for creating a customer profile.*

Most entrepreneurs say that the best way to stay in touch with customers and to identify their needs is to talk to them. Such conversations lead to a detailed understanding of who that customer really is and thus permit creation of a **customer profile**, a collection of information about a customer including demographic data, attitudes, preferences, and other behavioral characteristics, as defined by CRM goals. In a very small business, the customer profiles maintained in the entrepreneur's head often constitute the firm's CRM "database." At some point in a firm's growth, however, it becomes impossible for the entrepreneur to continue to develop profiles solely in this manner. It is then time to turn to formal, computer-based databases.

customer profile
A collection of information about a customer including demographic data, attitudes, preferences, and other behavioral characteristics, as defined by CRM goals

Customer profiles are essential to a successful CRM program, as they represent building material for the required knowledge of customers. Customer contact data, from sources such as warranty cards and accounting records, can be used to develop a profile. For Web-based ventures, current information can be collected at the point of contact, as customers order online.

What types of information should be included in a customer profile? Four major categories of information have been identified:[11]

- *Transactions*. A complete purchase history with accompanying details (price paid, SKU, delivery date).
- *Customer contacts*. Sales calls and service requests, including all customer- and company-initiated contacts.
- *Descriptive information*. Background information used for segmentation and other data analysis purposes.
- *Responses to marketing stimuli*. Information on whether or not the customer responded to a direct marketing initiative, a sales contact, and/or any other direct contact.

13-5 *Simplified Model of Consumer Behavior*

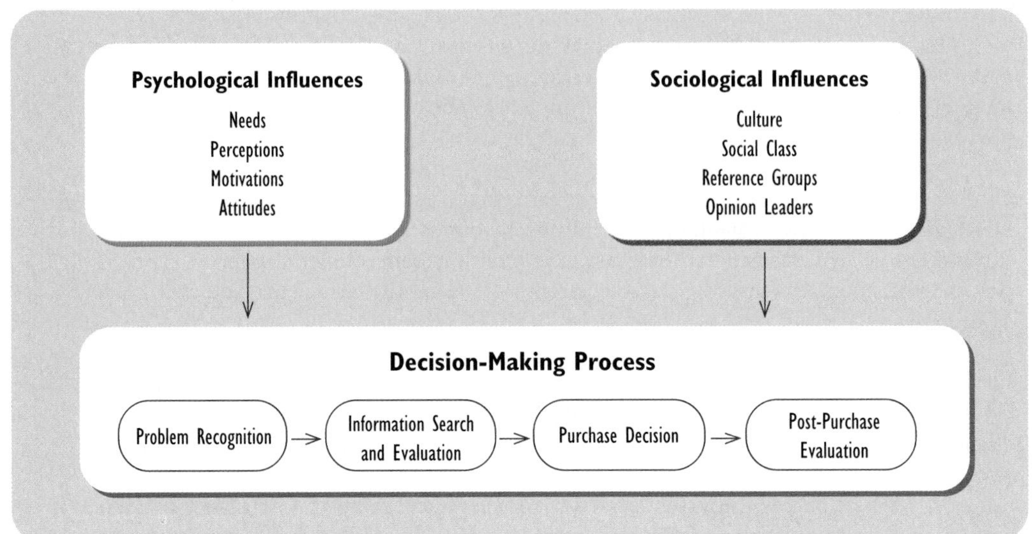

Formal interviews with customers provide another way to gather profile information. These interviews can be oral or they can take the form of a questionnaire. Consider, for example, Rejuvenation Lamp and Fixtures, in Portland, Oregon, which sells reproduction light fixtures mainly through catalogs and its Web site. Its system for understanding its customers includes a questionnaire:

> *In every box of lights that is shipped, the company includes a questionnaire with a return stamp. The questionnaire is humorous and fun to fill out. It not only collects information about the purchases, it asks [customers] what products they might want that Rejuvenation doesn't carry. The "how can we help you?" message, combined with the prepaid return and humorous presentation, earns Rejuvenation thousands of responses each month.*[12]

Entrepreneur Mac McConnell conducts surveys of walk-in customers at his Artful Framer Gallery in Plantation, Florida. Based on the results of one recent survey, which consisted of a simple one-page questionnaire, he reworked his business to better satisfy customers' desires. The survey showed that quality was top priority and price was last. He dropped the low-end line and made higher-priced museum framing his specialty.[13]

Customer profiles primarily reflect demographic variables such as age, gender, and marital status, but they can also include behavioral, psychological, and sociological information. Understanding the aspects of consumer behavior presented in the following sections can help entrepreneurs create customer profiles that go beyond demographics. Some entrepreneurs might even want to consider taking a course to broaden their knowledge of consumer behavior concepts; such courses are commonly offered at local colleges. Exhibit 13-5 presents a simple model of consumer behavior structured around three interrelated aspects: the decision-making process, psychological influences, and sociological influences.

CUSTOMERS AS DECISION MAKERS

5 *Explain how consumers are decision makers and why this is important to understanding customer relationships.*

According to the model of consumer behavior shown in Exhibit 13-5, consumer decision making comprises four stages:

Stage 1: Problem recognition

Stage 2: Information search and evaluation

Stage 3: The purchase decision

Stage 4: Post-purchase evaluation

We'll use this widely accepted model to examine decision making among small business customers.

Problem Recognition

Problem recognition (stage 1) occurs when a consumer realizes that her or his current state of affairs differs significantly from some ideal state. Some problems are routine conditions of depletion, such as a lack of food when lunchtime arrives. Other problems arise less frequently and may evolve slowly. Recognition of the need to replace the family dining table, for example, may take years to develop.

A consumer must recognize a problem before purchase behavior can begin. Thus, the problem-recognition stage cannot be overlooked. Many small firms develop their product strategy as if consumers were in the later stages of the decision-making process, when in reality they have not yet recognized a problem!

Many factors influence consumers' recognition of a problem—either by changing the actual state of affairs or by affecting the desired state. Here are a few examples:

- A change in financial status (a job promotion with a salary increase)
- A change in household characteristics (the birth of a baby)
- Normal depletion (using up the last tube of toothpaste)
- Product or service performance (breakdown of the DVD player)
- Past decisions (poor repair service on a car)
- The availability of products (introduction of a new product)

An entrepreneur must understand the problem-recognition stage in order to decide on the appropriate marketing strategy to use. In some situations, a small business owner needs to *influence* problem recognition. In other situations, she or he may simply be able to *react* to problem recognition by consumers.

Information Search and Evaluation

The second stage in consumer decision making involves consumers' collection and evaluation of appropriate information from both internal and external sources. The consumer's principal objective is to establish **evaluative criteria**—the features or characteristics of the product or service that the consumer will use to compare brands.

Small business owners should understand which evaluative criteria consumers use to formulate their evoked set. An **evoked set** is a group of brands that a consumer is both aware of and willing to consider as a solution to a purchase problem. Thus, the initial challenge for a new firm is to gain *market awareness* for its product or service. Only then will the brand have the opportunity to become part of consumers' evoked sets.

evaluative criteria
The features or characteristics of a product or service that customers use to compare brands

evoked set
A group of brands that a consumer is both aware of and willing to consider as a solution to a purchase problem

Purchase Decision

Once consumers have evaluated brands in their evoked set and made their choice, they must still decide how and where to make the purchase (stage 3). A substantial volume of retail sales now comes from non-store settings such as catalogs, TV shopping channels, and the Internet. These outlets have created a complex and challenging environment in which to develop marketing strategy. Consumers attribute many different advantages and disadvantages to various shopping outlets, making it difficult for the small firm to devise a single correct strategy. Sometimes, however, simple recognition of the factors can be helpful.

Of course, not every purchase decision is planned prior to entering a store or looking at a mail-order catalog. Studies show that most types of purchases from traditional retail outlets are not intended prior to the customers' entering the store.[14] This fact places tremendous importance on such features as store layout, sales personnel, and point-of-purchase displays.

Post-Purchase Evaluation

The consumer decision-making process does not end with a purchase. Small firms that desire repeat purchases from customers (and they all should) need to understand post-purchase behavior (stage 4). Exhibit 13-6 illustrates several consumer activities that occur

EXHIBIT 13-6 | *Post-Purchase Activities of Consumers*

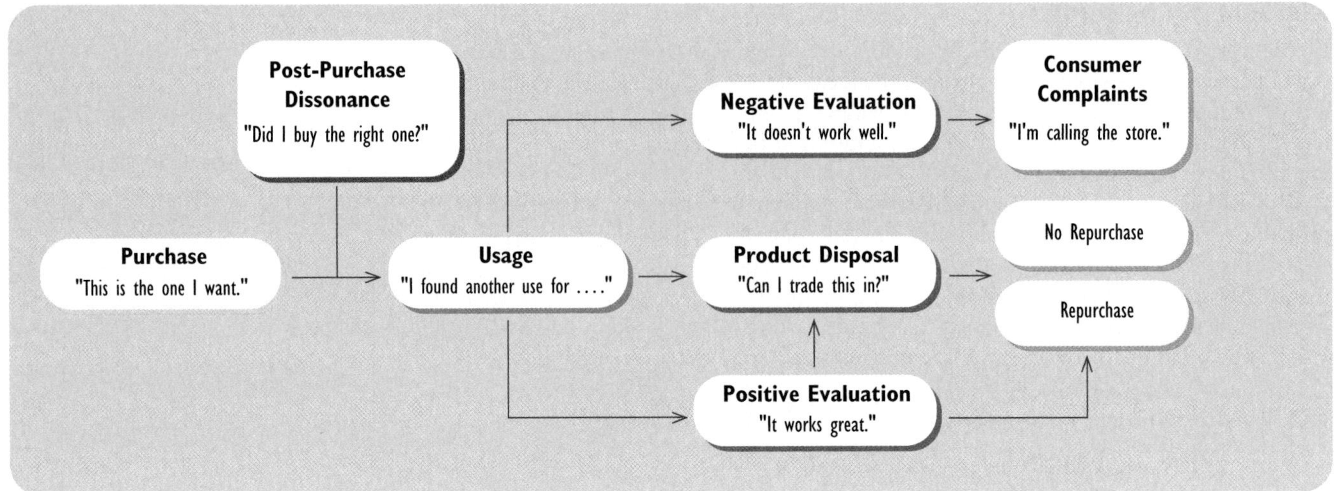

during post-purchase evaluation. Two of these activities—post-purchase dissonance and consumer complaints—are directly related to customer satisfaction.

cognitive dissonance
The anxiety that occurs when a customer has second thoughts immediately following a purchase

Post-purchase dissonance is a type of **cognitive dissonance**, a tension that occurs immediately following a purchase decision when consumers have second thoughts as to the wisdom of their purchase. This anxiety is obviously uncomfortable for consumers and can negatively influence product evaluation and customer satisfaction. Small firms need to find effective ways to manage cognitive dissonance among their customers.

UNDERSTANDING PSYCHOLOGICAL INFLUENCES ON CUSTOMERS

6 Describe certain psychological influences on consumer behavior.

The next major component of the consumer behavior model, as presented in Exhibit 13-5, is psychological influences. The four psychological influences that have the greatest relevance to small businesses are needs, perceptions, motivations, and attitudes.

Needs

needs
The starting point for all behavior

Needs are often described as the starting point for all behavior. Without needs, there would be no behavior. Although consumer needs are innumerable, they can be identified as falling into four categories—physiological, social, psychological, and spiritual.

Consumers' needs are never completely satisfied, thereby ensuring the continued existence of business. One of the more complex characteristics of needs is the way in which they function together in generating behavior. In other words, various needs operate simultaneously, making it difficult to determine which need is being satisfied by a specific product or service. Nevertheless, careful assessment of the needs–behavior connection can be very helpful in developing marketing strategy. Different purchases of the same product satisfy different needs. For example, consumers purchase food products in supermarkets to satisfy physiological needs. But they also purchase food in status restaurants to satisfy their social and/or psychological needs. Also, certain foods are demanded by specific market segments to satisfy those consumers' religious, or spiritual, needs. A needs-based strategy would result in a different marketing approach in each of these situations.

Perceptions

perception
The individual processes that give meaning to the stimuli confronting consumers

A second psychological factor, **perception**, encompasses those individual processes that ultimately give meaning to the stimuli confronting consumers. When this meaning is severely distorted or entirely blocked, consumer perception can cloud a small firm's mar-

Focus on the Customer

A Recipe for Service

Focusing on customer needs is not always easy, particularly in relation to a person's eating-out experience. Because people seldom patronize a restaurant merely to satisfy a hunger need, other needs must also be recognized. This makes the development of an overall bundle of satisfaction challenging. But America's "poshest inn" has a recipe for success.

The Inn at Little Washington in Virginia, founded in 1978 by chef Patrick O'Connell and partner Reinhardt Lynch, uses a five-course system to deliver the perfect dining experience. One component requires the restaurant captain to assign a "mood rating" to an arriving party—an assessment of the guests' apparent state of mind. This rating is entered into a computer and placed on a spool in the kitchen in view of the entire staff. The lower the number, the more effort targeted at the guests—perhaps a tableside visit from the owner or maybe even a kitchen tour. O'Connell believes that people aren't impressed by what you know or what you can offer until they see that you care—and caring in any meaningful way requires insight into what people are feeling and why.

In O'Connell's system, staffers must convey an extraordinary degree of competence and also have a positive attitude toward their job. Employees are also forbidden to ever say "no" to a guest.

> *If a guest asks if an appetizer is sweet, a waiter won't answer no—even if it's incredibly spicy. Instead, the waiter describes the ingredients that make up the dish so diners can understand exactly what they're ordering and make their own informed decision. The phrase "I don't know" is also discouraged. Following several months of apprenticeship and training, all new waiters undergo a rigorous test, in which veteran staffers ask every imaginable question, from when the inn was built to peculiarities of the menu. Only after passing the test are waiters considered "full cut," meaning worthy of a portion of the significant tip pool.*

This wonderful food and extraordinary service understandably come at a high price. A weekday meal costs customers an average of $78. O'Connell's inn has earned several awards for outstanding service, including one that named the restaurant America's "best" for 2003.

Sources: Tahl Raz, "A Recipe for Perfection," *Inc.*, Vol. 25, No. 7 (July 2003), pp. 36–37; and Laura Werlin, "The Inn at Little Washington," http://www.sallys-place.com, May 27, 2004. By Tahl Raz, © 2004 Gruner + Jahr USA Publishing. First published in *Inc.* Magazine. Reprinted with permission.

keting effort and make it ineffective. For example, a retailer may mark its fashion clothing "on sale" to communicate a price reduction from usual levels, but customers' perceptions may be that "these clothes are out of style."

Perception is a two-sided coin. It depends on the characteristics of both the stimulus and the perceiver. Consumers attempt to manage huge quantities of incoming stimuli through **perceptual categorization**, a process by which things that are similar are perceived as belonging together. Therefore, if a small business wishes to position its product alongside an existing brand and have it accepted as comparable, the marketing mix should reflect an awareness of perceptual categorization. Similar quality can be communicated through similar prices or through a package design with a color scheme similar to that of an existing brand. These techniques will help a consumer fit the new product into the desired product category.

perceptual categorization
The process of grouping similar things so as to manage huge quantities of incoming stimuli

Small firms that use an existing brand name for a new product are relying on perceptual categorization to pre-sell the new product. If, on the other hand, the new product is generically different or of a different quality, a unique brand name should be selected to create a unique perceptual categorization by the consumer.

If a consumer has strong brand loyalty to a product, it is difficult for other brands to penetrate his or her perceptual barriers. That individual is likely to have distorted images of competing brands because of a pre-existing attitude. Consumers' perceptions thus present a unique communication challenge.

Motivations

Unsatisfied needs create tension within an individual. When this tension reaches a certain level, the individual becomes uncomfortable and is motivated to reduce the tension.

Everyone is familiar with hunger pains, which are manifestations of the tension created by an unsatisfied physiological need. What directs a person to obtain food so that the hunger pains can be relieved? The answer is motivation. **Motivations** are goal-directed forces that organize and give direction to tension caused by unsatisfied needs. Marketers cannot create needs, but they can offer unique motivations to consumers. If an acceptable reason for purchasing a product or service is provided, it will probably be internalized by the consumer as a motivating force. The key for the marketer is to determine which motivations the consumer will perceive as acceptable in a given situation. The answer is found through an analysis of other consumer behavior variables.

motivations
Forces that organize and give direction to the tension caused by unsatisfied needs

Like physiological needs, the other three classes of needs—social, psychological, and spiritual—can be similarly connected to behavior through motivations. For example, when incomplete satisfaction of a person's social needs is creating tension, a firm may show how its product can fulfill those social needs by providing acceptable motivations to that person. A campus clothing store might promote styles that communicate that the college student wearing those clothes has obtained membership in a group such as a fraternity or sorority.

Understanding motivations is not easy. Several motivations may be present in any situation, and they are often subconscious. However, they must be investigated in order for the marketing effort to be successful.

Attitudes

Like the other psychological variables, attitudes cannot be observed, but everyone has them. Do attitudes imply knowledge? Do they imply feelings of good or bad, favorable or unfavorable? Does an attitude have a direct impact on behavior? The answer to each of these questions is a resounding yes. An **attitude** is an enduring opinion, based on a combination of knowledge, feeling, and behavioral tendency.

attitude
An enduring opinion based on knowledge, feeling, and behavioral tendency

An attitude may act as an obstacle or a catalyst in bringing a customer to a product. For example, consumers with the belief that a local, family-run grocery store has higher prices than a national supermarket chain may avoid the local store. Armed with an understanding of the structure of a particular attitude, a marketer can approach the consumer more intelligently.

UNDERSTANDING SOCIOLOGICAL INFLUENCES ON CUSTOMERS

7 Describe certain sociological influences on consumer behavior.

Sociological influences, as shown in Exhibit 13-5, comprise the last component of the consumer behavior model. Among these influences are culture, social class, reference groups, and opinion leaders. Note that each of these sociological influences represents a different degree of group aggregation: Culture involves large masses of people, social classes and reference groups are smaller groups of people, and opinion leaders are single individuals who exert influence.

Culture

In marketing, **culture** refers to the behavioral patterns and values that characterize a group of customers in a target market. These patterns and beliefs have a tremendous impact on the purchase and use of products. Marketing managers often overlook the cultural variable because its influences are so neatly embedded within the society. Culture is somewhat like air; you do not think about its function until you are in water over your head! International marketers who have experienced more than one culture can readily attest to the reality of cultural influence.

culture
Behavioral patterns and values that characterize a group of consumers in a target market

The prescriptive nature of culture should concern the entrepreneur. Cultural norms create a range of product-related acceptable behaviors that influence what consumers buy. However, because culture does change by adapting slowly to new situations, what works well as a marketing strategy today may not work a few years from now.

An investigation of culture within a narrower boundary—defined by age, religious preference, ethnic orientation, or geographical location—is called *subcultural analysis*.

Living the Dream

Utilizing the Internet

Customers Love Taco Talk

Courtesy of California Tortilla

The Internet provides small firms with the ability to distribute information about their products and services and sell them online. It can also be an effective tool for maintaining ongoing communications with customers, thereby cultivating positive customer motivations for the next purchase—reasons to buy again.

Pam Felix, who started her quick-service Mexican restaurant California Tortilla in Bethesda, Maryland, in 1995, wanted an effective way to increase contacts with customers. As a result, she launched a company Web site in 2000, with the primary goal of building an e-mail list to improve communication with customers.

The Web site focuses on promotional ideas that make customers feel good, with the overriding theme of "having fun." Consider some of the statements on the site:

"We've got over 75 different hot sauces that'll blow your head off!"

"We've got spunky cashiers!"

"We've got the Monday Night Mystery Price Burrito Wheel!"

"We've got Pop Tart Day!"

"We've got Freeze Pop Day! (Which is just like Pop Tart Day without the toasting option.)"

"We've got Yappy Hour for dogs! (Again, no toasting option.)"

"We've got *Taco Talk*—the burrito newsletter read by tens of people nationwide!"

"I'm not sure I had any expectations [for the Internet]," says Felix. "But since I put out a goofy, monthly newsletter that most people seem to like, I thought at the very least I could keep conveying that goofy mom-and-pop feel via the Internet." And it has all worked well to help her build favorable relationships with customers. "People feel like they have a personal connection with us—and that's something the big chains are never going to have with their customers," Felix believes.

The Internet also provides feedback, identifying the restaurant's strengths and weaknesses. Plus, Felix says, "I get a lot of funny/strange e-mails that I get to use in the newsletter. . . . I ran out of things to say about burritos about 6 years ago."

http://www.californiatortilla.com

Sources: Sharon Fling, "California Tortilla Customers Love Taco Talk," http://www.geolocal.com/public, May 27, 2004; and http://www.californiatortilla.com, May 27, 2004.

Here, too, unique patterns of behavior and social relationships must concern the marketing manager. For example, the needs and motivations of the youth subculture are far different from those of the senior citizen subculture, and certain food preferences are unique to particular ethnic cultures. Small business managers who familiarize themselves with cultures and subcultures are able to create better marketing mixes.

Social Class

Another sociological factor affecting consumer behavior is social class. **Social classes** are divisions within a society having different levels of social prestige. The social class system has important implications for marketing. Different lifestyles correlate with different levels of social prestige, and certain products often become symbols of a type of lifestyle.

social classes
Divisions within a society having different levels of social prestige

For some products such as grocery staples, social class analysis will probably not be very useful. For others such as home furnishings, such analysis may help explain variations in shopping and communication patterns.

Unlike a caste system, a social class system provides for upward mobility. The social status of parents does not permanently fix the social class of their child. Occupation is probably the single most important determinant of social class. Other determinants used in social class research include possessions, source of income, and education.

Reference Groups

reference groups
Groups that an individual allows to influence his or her behavior

Technically, social class could be considered a reference group. However, marketers are generally more concerned with small groups such as families, work groups, neighborhood groups, or recreational groups. **Reference groups** are those smaller groups that an individual allows to influence his or her behavior.

The existence of group influence is well established. The challenge to the marketer is to understand why this influence occurs and how it can be used to promote the sale of a product. Individuals tend to accept group influence because of the benefits they perceive as resulting from it. These perceived benefits give the influencers various kinds of power. Five widely recognized forms of power, all of which are available to the marketer, are reward, coercive, referent, expert, and legitimate power.

Reward power and coercive power relate to a group's ability to give and to withhold rewards. Rewards may be material or psychological. Recognition and praise are typical psychological rewards. A Pampered Chef party is a good example of a marketing technique that takes advantage of reward power and coercive power. The ever-present possibility of pleasing or displeasing the hostess-friend tends to encourage the guests to buy.

Referent power and expert power involve neither rewards nor punishments. They exist because an individual attaches great importance to being like the group or perceives the group as being knowledgeable. Referent power influences consumers to conform to a group's behavior and to choose products selected by the group's members. Children will often be affected by referent power, so marketers can create a desire for products by using cleverly designed advertisements or packages.

Legitimate power involves the sanctioning of what an individual ought to do. We are most familiar with legitimate power at the cultural level, where it is evident in the prescriptive nature of culture, but it can also be used in smaller groups.

Opinion Leaders

opinion leader
A group leader who plays a key communications role

According to widely accepted communication principles, consumers receive a significant amount of information through individuals called **opinion leaders**, who are group members playing a key communications role.

Generally speaking, opinion leaders are knowledgeable, visible, and exposed to the mass media. A small business firm can enhance its own image by identifying with such leaders. For example, a farm-supply dealer may promote its products in an agricultural community by holding demonstrations of these products on the farms of outstanding local farmers, who are the community's opinion leaders. Similarly, department stores may use attractive students as models when showing campus fashions.

Looking Back

1 Define customer relationship management (CRM) and explain its importance to a small firm.

- Customer relationship management (CRM) is a marketing strategy of maximizing shareholder value through winning, growing, and keeping the right customers.
- The central message of every CRM program is "Court customers for more than a one-time sale."
- CRM is primarily a mind-set—the implementation of customer-centric strategies, which put customers first so that the firm can increase profits.
- A CRM program recognizes the importance of keeping current customers satisfied to ensure their loyalty, given the costs associated with attracting a new customer.
- Constructing a CRM program requires a plan so that the entrepreneur will know what people, processes, and so on he or she needs.
- Two vital building blocks of any CRM program are outstanding transactional relationships with customers and knowledge of consumer behavior.

2 Discuss the significance of providing extraordinary customer service.

- To be successful in the long run, small firms must provide outstanding service in order to develop and maintain loyal customers, as it costs far more to replace a customer than to keep one.
- Extraordinary service is the factor that small firms are in a unique position to offer.

- Providing exceptional customer service can give small firms a competitive edge, regardless of the nature of the business.
- Establishing an effective customer service program begins with determining the firm's "customer service quotient," which indicates how well the firm is currently providing service to its customers.
- The way customer service problems are most commonly recognized is through customer complaints.
- Managers can also learn about customer service problems through personal observation and other research techniques.
- Although many types of customer service cost very little, there are definite costs associated with superior levels of customer service.

3 Illustrate how technology, such as the Internet, can improve customer relationships.

- Long-term transactional relationships are built with information gathered from positive customer contacts.
- CRM technology helps companies gather all customer contact information into a single data management program.
- Web-based marketers, in particular, are attracted to CRM technology.
- CRM focuses on such sales functions as accurate and prompt order filling, follow-up contacts to ensure customer satisfaction, and the use of a user-friendly call center to handle all inquiries, including complaints.
- Having ample support resources for CRM information technology can be a concern for a small firm, and this concern has led some entrepreneurs to outsource certain applications.
- Hosted call centers require lower deployment costs than do comparable in-house centers, a crucial consideration for many cash-strapped small firms.

4 Describe the techniques for creating a customer profile.

- In a very small business, customer profiles are developed in the entrepreneur's head during conversations with customers.
- Customer profiles are essential to a successful CRM program, as they represent building material for the required knowledge of customers.
- Four categories of customer profile information are transactions, customer contacts, descriptive information, and responses to marketing stimuli.
- Formal interviews with customers provide another way to gather customer profile information.

5 Explain how consumers are decision makers and why this is important to understanding customer relationships.

- Consumer decision making involves four stages that are closely tied to ultimate customer satisfaction.
- Problem recognition (stage 1) occurs when a consumer realizes that her or his current state of affairs differs significantly from some ideal state.
- The second stage in consumer decision making involves consumers' collection and evaluation of appropriate information from both internal and external sources.
- Once consumers have evaluated brands in their evoked set and made their choice, they must still decide how and where to make the purchase (stage 3).
- Post-purchase evaluation (stage 4) may lead to cognitive dissonance, negatively influencing customer satisfaction with the product or service.

6 Describe certain psychological influences on consumer behavior.

- The four psychological influences that have the greatest relevance to small businesses are needs, perceptions, motivations, and attitudes.
- Needs are often described as the starting point for all behavior.
- Perception encompasses those individual processes that ultimately give meaning to the stimuli confronting consumers.
- Motivations are goal-directed forces that organize and give direction to tension caused by unsatisfied needs.
- An attitude is an enduring opinion, based on a combination of knowledge, feeling, and behavioral tendency.

7 Describe certain sociological influences on consumer behavior.

- Among the sociological influences are culture, social class, reference groups, and opinion leaders.
- In marketing, *culture* refers to the behavioral patterns and values that characterize a group of customers in a target market.
- Social classes are divisions within a society having different levels of social prestige.
- Reference groups are those smaller groups that an individual allows to influence his or her behavior.
- According to widely accepted communication principles, consumers receive a significant amount of information through opinion leaders, who are group members playing a key communications role.

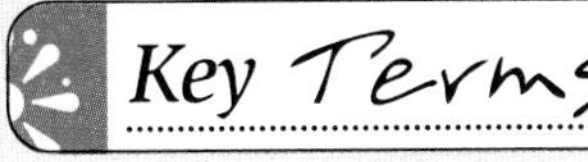

customer relationship management (CRM), p. 287
transactional relationship, p. 289
customer profile, p. 295
evaluative criteria, p. 297
evoked set, p. 297
cognitive dissonance, 298
needs, p. 298
perception, p. 298

perceptual categorization, p. 299
motivations, p. 300
attitude, p. 300
culture, p. 300
social classes, p. 301
reference groups, p. 301
opinion leader, p. 301

Discussion Questions

1. Define customer relationship management. What is meant by the statement "CRM is primarily a mindset"?
2. Does CRM put more emphasis on current or potential customers? Why?
3. What are the two essential building blocks of a successful CRM program? What "materials" are used to construct these building blocks?
4. Why is a small firm potentially in a better position to achieve customer satisfaction than is a big business?
5. Discuss how technology supports customer relationship management.
6. What types of information should be part of a customer profile?
7. What techniques or sources of information can be used to develop a customer profile?
8. Briefly describe the four stages of the consumer decision-making process. Why is the first stage so vital to consumer behavior?
9. List the four psychological influences on consumers that were discussed in this chapter. What is their relevance to consumer behavior?
10. List the four sociological influences on consumers that were discussed in this chapter. What is their relevance to consumer behavior?

You Make the Call

SITUATION 1

Jeremy Shepherd is the founder of PearlParadise.com, in Santa Monica, California. His jewelry business recognizes the importance of ensuring that customers keep coming back.

However, Shepherd is uncertain as to which customer retention techniques he should use to develop a strong foundation of repeat customers. PearlParadise.com's Web site has the software capabilities to support customer interaction.

Source: Melissa Campanelli, "Happy Returns," www.entrepreneur.com/mag/article/0,1539,312420,00.htm, January 2004.

Question 1 What customer loyalty techniques would you recommend to Shepherd?

Question 2 What information would be appropriate to collect about customers in a database?

Question 3 What specific computer-based communication could be used to achieve Shepherd's goal?

SITUATION 2

Paul Layer is the owner of Aspen Funeral Alternatives in Albuquerque, New Mexico. Aspen is located in a converted restaurant with fluorescent lights, and its chapel has chairs, not pews. "It looks more like your insurance company or local business office, rather than a funeral home," Layer says.

Aspen has adopted a strategy of discounted prices for funeral products and services. Its Web site (http://www.aspenfuneral.com) promotes low-cost alternatives with no fancy facilities, no limousines, and no hearses. A general price list, covering Aspen's professional services, use of its facilities, and caskets, is posted on the site.

Sources: Lorrie Grant, "Funeral Stores Sell Inevitable in Style," *USAToday*, May 30, 2001, p. 3B; and http://www.aspenfuneral.com, June 8, 2004.

Question 1 What psychological concepts of consumer behavior are relevant to marketing this service? Be specific.

Question 2 How can the stages of consumer decision making be applied to a person's decision to use a particular funeral home?

Question 3 What types of CRM could be used by this type of business?

SITUATION 3

In the late 1990s, entrepreneur Neil Peterson was traveling in Europe when he observed what to him was a new way to own a car. It was called car sharing. Under this concept, the customer doesn't buy a car outright but uses the vehicle as a person would a timeshare property. The concept isn't totally new to the United States but hasn't yet caught on.

Peterson has big plans. He wants to bring the car-sharing concept to large U.S. cities. His research, based on American Automobile Association data, showed that the average cost of owning or leasing a new car, including insurance, is around $625 a month. He believes the average car-sharing member will pay only $100 a month.

Source: Kortney Stringer, "How Do You Change Consumer Behavior?" http://www.entrepreneur.com/Your_Business/YB_PrintArticle/0,2361,310457,00.html, June 7, 2004.

Question 1 What sociological issues may have an impact on the success of this venture?

Question 2 In which consumer decision-making stage do you believe Peterson's potential customers will be located? Why?

Experiential Exercises

1. For several days, make notes on your own shopping experiences. Summarize what you consider to be the best customer service you receive.
2. Interview a local entrepreneur about her or his company's consumer service efforts. Summarize your findings.
3. Interview a local entrepreneur about what types of customer complaints the business receives. Also ask how he or she deals with different complaints. Report your findings to the class.
4. Consider your most recent meaningful purchase. Compare the decision-making process you used to the four stages of decision making presented in this chapter. Report your conclusions.

Exploring the Web

1. Go to the SBA's Online Business Center at **http://www.onlinewbc.gov/docs/market/KeepingCustomers.html** and read the article entitled "Strategies for Keeping Customers." According to the text, what are the four strategies one can use to improve customer satisfaction? Briefly explain each strategy.
2. Visit the SBA Web site at **http://www.sba.gov/**. Click on "Managing" and then follow the link under "Marketing Topics" to "Customer Service." What are the "Five Rules of Customer Care" that one can follow to help keep customers happy?
3. Go to the tutor2u Web site at **http://www.tutor2u.net/**. Under "Quizzes," click on "Marketing" and take the quiz on "Buying Behaviour." How did you score?

Case 13

EVERY CUSTOMER COUNTS (P. 550)

A stressful relationship with a customer raises questions about customer relationship management practices in this business.

Alternative Cases for Chapter 13:

Case 15, Waco Composites I, Ltd., p. 554
Case 20, Texas Nameplate Company, p. 563

PRODUCT AND SUPPLY CHAIN MANAGEMENT

In the Video Spotlight

Fluker Cricket Farms

This chapter's video spotlight features Fluker Cricket Farms, located across the Mississippi River from Baton Rouge, Louisiana. Founder Richard Fluker turned the company over to his children after the death of his wife, even though the son he tapped to be president was only 19. Soon thereafter, David, Howard, and Diane Fluker began to enhance the company's marketing efforts by focusing on direct mailing, new product development, and expanded distribution channels. From crickets, the firm, under David's leadership, branched out to another type of feeder insect—mealworms, which turned out to be a great success. When David (shown in photo) approached Howard about selling something else, Howard suggested breeding iguanas, and he now oversees the iguana farm that the company developed in El Salvador.

Not all product development has been an instant success, however. David thought that the company was well positioned to market mice to the pet and zoo industries. Although the company had a customer list well suited to sales of mice, it encountered great difficulty in breeding mice. Undeterred, David created a chocolate-covered cricket as a trade show giveaway, which became an important new product.

New products have enabled David, Howard, and Diane Fluker to ship over 2.5 million live crickets and hundreds of thousands of live mealworms per week, not to mention iguanas and chocolate-covered crickets, to customers around the world.

Video material provided by Hattie Bryant, Producer of Small Business School, the series on PBS Stations, Worldnet, and the Web at http://www.smallbusinessschool.org.

Chapter 14

Looking Ahead

After studying this chapter, you should be able to

1. *Explain the challenges associated with growth in a small firm.*
2. *Explain the role of innovation in a firm's growth.*
3. *Identify stages in the product life cycle and the new product development process.*
4. *Describe the building of a firm's total product.*
5. *Explain product strategy and the alternatives available to small businesses.*
6. *Describe the legal environment affecting product decisions.*
7. *Explain the importance of supply chain management.*
8. *Specify the major considerations in structuring a distribution channel.*

In Chapter 13, you learned that entrepreneurs need to make a strong commitment to customer relationship management (CRM). Furthermore, you learned that marketing programs must reflect consumer behavior concepts if CRM efforts are to sustain the firm's competitive advantage. In this chapter we address product decisions and supply chain management, which together have a significant impact on the total bundle of satisfaction targeted to customers.

TO GROW OR NOT TO GROW

1 *Explain the challenges associated with growth in a small firm.*

Once a new venture is launched, the newly created firm settles into day-to-day operations. Its marketing plans reflect current goals as well as any thoughts of expansion or growth, which will impact marketing activities.

Entrepreneurs differ in their desires for growth. Some want to grow rapidly, while others prefer a modest growth rate. Many prefer not to grow at all—just maintaining the status quo is challenge enough, and this becomes the driving force behind their marketing decisions.

Despite this attitude, growth sometimes happens unexpectedly. The entrepreneur is then forced to concentrate all efforts on meeting demand. Consider the case of an entrepreneur named Jerry. After he showed a new line of flannel nightgowns to a large chain-store buyer, the buyer immediately ordered 500 of the gowns, with delivery expected in five days! Jerry agreed to the order even though he had material on hand for only 50 gowns. He emptied his bank account to purchase the necessary material and frantically begged former college classmates to join him in cutting and sewing the gowns. After several sleepless nights, he fulfilled the order.[1] The lesson: Growing quickly can be a stressful proposition.

For many small firms, however, growth is an expected and achievable goal. In some cases, fast growth is part of the initial business plan. For example, Karen McMasters launched her first online baby products business in February 2000. Just three years later, she started AllCola.com, a Web site where Coca-Cola memorabilia is sold. Then, in January 2004, she started a third online company to sell different lines of baby items. She is excited about all three ventures because she always wanted to grow. McMasters recommends planning to start multiple companies because that way, "you know what steps need to be taken and in what order."[2]

Successful growth seldom occurs on its own. Many factors—including financing—must be considered and managed carefully. When a firm experiences rapid growth in sales volume, the firm's income statements will generally reflect growing profits. However, rapid growth in sales and profits may be hazardous to the firm's cash flows. A "growth trap" can occur, because growth tends to demand additional cash more rapidly than such cash is generated in the form of additional profits.

Inventory, for example, must be expanded as sales volume increases; additional dollars must be expended for merchandise or raw materials to accommodate the higher level of sales. Similarly, accounts receivable must be expanded proportionally to meet the increased sales volume. Obviously, a growing, profitable business can quickly find itself in a financial bind—growing profitably while its bank accounts dwindle.

The growth problem is particularly acute for small firms. Quite simply, increasing a small firm's sales by 100 percent is easier than achieving the same percentage growth for a *Fortune 500* firm. And doubling sales volume in a small firm makes it a much different business. This fact, combined with difficulty in obtaining external funding, may have potential detrimental effects if cash is not managed carefully. In short, a high-growth firm's need for additional financing may exceed its available resources, even though the firm is profitable. Without additional resources, the firm's cash balances may decline sharply, leaving it in a precarious financial position.

Growth also places huge demands on a small firm's personnel and the management style of its owners. For example, entrepreneurs Scott Semel and Reid Chase, owners of Cody-Kramer Imports, a Blauvelt, New York, candy distributor, experienced a tripling of private-label orders from the same period the year before. Their six-person staff was too small to handle the growth. They quickly hired a production supervisor to coordinate shipments, but it "was hard for us to let go for a long, long time—probably to the detriment of the company," explains Semel.[3] High demand for products can stretch a firm's staff too thin and result in burnout, apathy, and poor overall performance.

Despite these and other challenges, the entrepreneurial spirit continues to carry small firms forward in pursuit of growth. Business expansion can occur in many ways. One path to growth is paved with innovation.

INNOVATION: A PATH TO GROWTH

2 *Explain the role of innovation in a firm's growth.*

From a menu of growth options, enterpreneurs generally choose the one they believe will lead to the best outcomes. But any such option must be designed to lead to outcomes like superior profitability, increased market share, and improved customer satisfaction. These are some "fruits" of competitive advantage, and they all contribute to the value of the firm.

Competitive Advantage and Innovation

Well-known economist Joseph Schumpeter viewed entrepreneurship as "creative destruction"—that is, making improvements to existing products, manufacturing methods, organizational processes, and other such factors to create new business opportunities. In his view, the spirit of innovation permeates any entrepreneurial enterprise.

As indicated in Chapter 1, entrepreneurs often simply see a different and better way of doing things. Studies have shown that small entrepreneurial firms produce twice as many innovations per employee as large firms, and these innovations account for half of all those created and an amazing 95 percent of all *radical* innovations.[4] It could be said that innovation provides the soil in which startups' competitive advantage can take root and grow, taking on a life of its own. Some of the most widely recognized examples of small firm innovation are soft contact lenses, the Zipper, safety razors, overnight national delivery, and air conditioning.

There is a certain glamour associated with innovation, but coming up with and perfecting new products or services is often difficult. Consider a new technology designed to scan a person's body and determine his or her exact dimensions. Developed and marketed by Image Twin Inc., of Cary, North Carolina, it has been used by big-name players like Levi Strauss to provide jeans with a custom fit and footwear giant Nike to offer perfect-fitting shoes. The technology offers conveniences for both stores and customers—it makes dressing rooms obsolete, it ensures a better fit and thus fewer returns, and it even stores scanned measurements for future use. But when Rebecca Quick, a reporter for the *Wall Street Journal*, used an Image Twin scanner (a virtual dressing room) to try on clothes, she found that the software misread her dimensions and fashioned an exaggerated "pear shaped" figure for the reporter. This produced a shocking image that did not exactly promote a sale and certainly provided a less-than-perfect fit.[5] That's one way to eliminate repeat business!

Needless to say, the risk of failure increases when innovation is the goal. With this in mind, we offer a few "rules of thumb" that may help to reduce that risk somewhat.

- *Base innovative efforts on your experience.* Innovative efforts are more likely to succeed when you know something about the product or service technology. Entrepreneur Donna Boone, who swam competitively for her Ashburn, Virginia, high school, used her swimming experience to successfully open four indoor-swim schools throughout the Washington, D.C., area, all within five years.[6]
- *Focus on products or services that have been largely overlooked.* You are more likely to strike "pay dirt" in a vein that has not already been fully mined and one in which competitors are few. Inventors and entrepreneurs Ron L. Wilson II and Brian LeGette didn't think their product category had been fully mined. These co-founders of the firm 180s LLC in Baltimore, Maryland, put a new twist on the familiar earmuff. Their ear warmers fit around the back of the neck and don't mess up the hair. So far, 4.5 million have been sold in 42 countries.[7]
- *Be sure there is a market for the product or service you are hoping to create.* This business fundamental is as applicable to innovation in startups as it is to innovation in existing businesses. For example, people who want help losing weight are everywhere. So if William Longley, founder of Scientific Intake in Atlanta, Georgia, can reach the target market for his invention, he should do well. Longley's firm produces a retainer-like device, called the DDS System, that specially trained dentists fit into the top of a person's mouth. The $500 device slows down eating, which translates into less food consumption and, theoretically, weight loss.[8]
- *Pursue innovation that customers will perceive as adding value to their lives.* It is not enough to create a product or service that you believe in; people become customers when *they* conclude that it will provide value they cannot find elsewhere. Entrepreneur Sharon Bennett followed this risk-reduction recommendation. Her creation is based on her concern for the welfare of pets. Wanting owners to have more humane control of their dogs when tugging on the leash, she developed a head collar, which she markets with the EasyWalker name.[9]
- *Focus on new ideas that will lead to more than one product or service.* Success with an initial product or service is critical, of course, but investment in innovation packs even more of a punch when it also leads to other innovative products or services. The experience of scientist James A. Patterson provides a good example of this strategy. His discovery, a topical brown powder that stops bleeding when sprinkled on minor cuts and scrapes, is named "QR," short for "quick relief." His Sarasota, Florida, company Biolife, which he began with a partner, is already adding products such as SportsQR, NosebleedQR, and Kid'sQR, as well as products for the hospital market.[10] (See Case 3 for more information about Biolife.)
- *Raise sufficient capital to launch the new product or service.* It is easy to underestimate the cost of bringing an innovation successfully to market. Many small firms run short of cash before they are able to do so. Be prepared to look for new sources of capital along the way. Steve Dunn recognized the importance of obtaining sufficient capital to extend his new line of baby products in a competitive market, especially after previous successes resulted in outside venture capitalists knocking at his door. Founded in 1991, Munchkin, Inc., has created products that "transform the ordinary to a new level of innovation and creativity." Located in Van Nuys, California, the company is the top seller of baby utensils at Wal-Mart.[11]

Small companies that are "one-hit wonders" may find that the ride comes to an abrupt and unpleasant ending. While some innovation can provide a launch pad for a new and interesting business, continued innovation is critical to sustaining competitive advantage in the years to come.

Sustainability and Innovation

How can a company sustain its competitive advantage? Various strategies can help. For example, some entrepreneurs with sophisticated technology obtain patents, and this is often a wise thing to do. Others try to operate "below the radar screen" of competitors to avoid attracting attention, but this limits their growth. Some businesses find protection through contracts. In 1970, Doyle Owens started a company called Unclaimed Baggage, which sells luggage that is left at airports. In 1996, Owens sold the business to his son, Bryan, who has since expanded it by an amazing 400 percent. The business concept is simple—so how has Unclaimed Baggage been able to dominate the niche without contest? The answer is that the company has long-term contracts with major airports around the world, thereby blocking other companies from getting into the game.[12]

sustainable competitive advantage A value-creating position that is likely to endure over time

A business can take steps to slow down threats from competitors, but no competitive advantage lasts forever.[13] Research has emphasized the importance of **sustainable competitive advantage**, a value-creating position that is likely to endure over time.[14] To incorporate sustainability into strategy, the entrepreneur should use the unique capabilities of the firm in a way that competitors will find difficult to imitate. Sooner or later, however, rivals will discover a way to copy any value-creating strategy.[15] Therefore, it is also important to think of new ways to reinvest performance outcomes (financial returns, customer goodwill, etc.) so that the basis of competitive advantage can be renewed over the long run.

Competitive advantage tends to follow a fairly consistent pattern. Building a competitive advantage requires resource commitments that lead to a performance payoff. However, returns from that competitive advantage will always diminish over time.

Exhibit 14-1 illustrates the competitive advantage life cycle, which has three stages: develop, deploy, and decline. Simply put, a firm must invest resources to *develop* a competitive advantage, which it can later *deploy* to boost its performance. But that position will eventually *decline* as rival firms build these advantages into their own strategies.[16]

In order to maintain performance over time, firms must produce a continuous stream of competitive advantages so as to keep performance from falling off. However, tomorrow's

Living the Dream

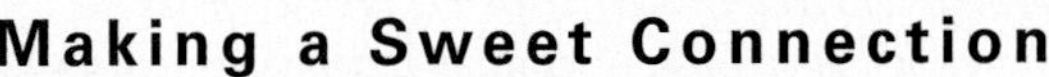

Making a Sweet Connection

Courtesy of Dylan's Candy Bar

http://www.dylanscandybar.com

A small firm can try to extend the unique capabilities that constitute its competitive advantage to other value-creating ventures. One New York City–based retailer of candies and related items is giving it a try.

In October 2001, Dylan Lauren—daughter of well-known designer Ralph Lauren—founded Dylan's Candy Bar, which claims to offer the widest assortment of novelty candy in the world. The flagship store on the Upper East Side of Manhattan offers a "traditional 'sweets' store by creating a unique and completely unmatched shopping experience in a visually awe-inspiring environment." Store fixtures resemble candy, and the store stocks more than 5,000 varieties of candy.

Recently, she took the business online, offering 85-plus products, including apparel, candy baskets, and candy spa items like candles and soap. The online approach is to use an "mmm-commerce" wireless campaign, which allows site visitors to send wireless phone users coupons redeemable for candy and merchandise in her brick-and-mortar stores now located in Texas and Florida.

Music is one of the attractions of the Web site. Visitors, for a small fee, can download ring tones to their cell phones, including such songs as "Lollipop, Lollipop" and "I Want Candy." Users can also contact friends using the site's free text-messaging service. "The ring tones and SMS messages are a very effective, vital marketing tool as they drive traffic, not only back to the Web site, but directly into the stores," according to Shane Igoe, president of Youie, the wireless marketing solutions company supporting the Web site.

Sources: Beth Cox, "mmm-commerce—How Sweet Can It Be?" http://ecommerce.internet.com/news, April 25, 2004; http://www.dylanscandybar.com, April 25, 2004; and April Y. Pennington, "Eye Candy," *Entrepreneur*, April 2004, p. 168.

EXHIBIT 14-1 *The Competitive Advantage Life Cycle*

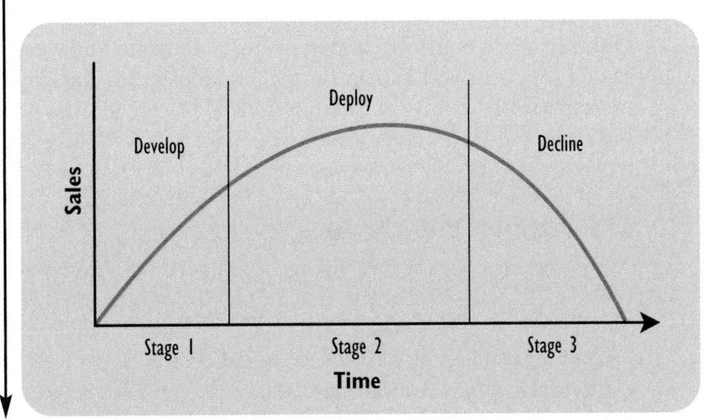

performance can be maintained only if it is supported by today's surplus resources. In other words, a firm must launch a new competitive advantage *before* the current strategy has run its course (see Exhibit 14-2). And that is what many small companies are doing. A 2003 study of 751 small business owners, funded by the National Federation of Independent Business, found that about 35 percent reported having invested in a technology or process that was new to their business during the previous 12 months.[17] Entrepreneurs are more likely to maintain venture performance if they keep an eye on the future.

Etrema is a high-technology startup in Ames, Iowa, that is acutely aware of the need to continually refresh its competitive advantage. The company found a way to use Terfenol-D, a rare earth alloy, to create a product called Whispering Windows, which is a pair of chrome disks that can turn any window, wall, or conference table into an audio speaker. Though they cost a pricey $1,500 a pair, market interest is significant—and growing. The 40-employee company has a lock on the market for now, since no one else in the United States knows how to manufacture the product affordably. However, Etrema executives predict that they have about seven years before competitors find a way to make Terfenol-D more cheaply (three Chinese companies already make pirated versions) or to replace it with something that works even better. Thinking ahead, Etrema scientists are scrambling to discover new applications (for example, would Terfenol-D work in hearing aids?) and to develop a successor to the alloy. And employees of the company often make what they call "missionary calls" to find partners who would be willing to work with Etrema in creating new applications for the product, such as the dry razor they hope to develop with Remington.[18] The moral of the story is clear: Competitive advantage is sustainable only for those companies that are already planning for the future.

EXHIBIT 14-2 *Sustaining Competitive Advantage*

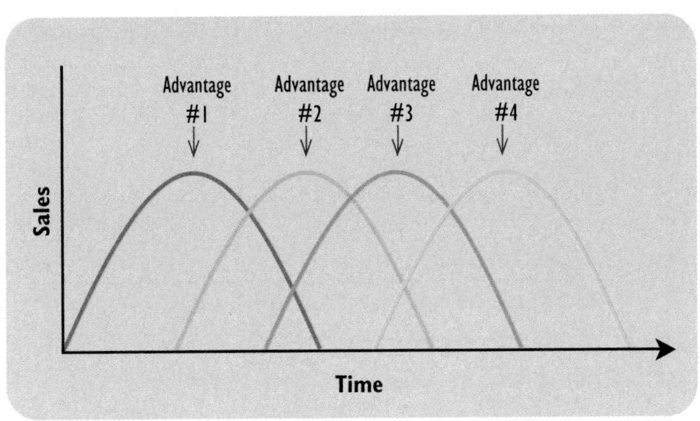

THE PRODUCT LIFE CYCLE AND NEW PRODUCT DEVELOPMENT

3 *Identify stages in the product life cycle and the new product development process.*

Our discussion of growth and innovation illustrated how entrepreneurial firms can be part of new product development for the marketplace. At this point, we will focus our discussion more narrowly to answer the questions What creates the need for innovation in a specific business? and How can innovation be managed? We will examine these challenges by looking at the product life cycle concept and a four-stage approach to new product development.

The Product Life Cycle

product life cycle
A detailed picture of what happens to a specific product's sales and profits over time

An important concept underlying sound product strategy is the product life cycle, which visualizes the sales and profits of a product from the time it is introduced until it is no longer on the market. The **product life cycle** provides a detailed picture of what happens to an *individual* product's or service's sales and profits; it has a shape similar to that of the competitive advantage life cycle, depicted in Exhibit 14-1 on page 311. Progressing through the product life cycle in Exhibit 14-3 takes on the characteristics of a roller-coaster ride, which is the way many entrepreneurs describe their experiences with the life cycles of their products. The initial stages are characterized by a slow and, ideally, upward movement. The stay at the top is exciting but relatively brief. Then, suddenly, the decline begins, and downward movement is rapid. Also, note the typical shape of the profit curve in Exhibit 14-3. The introductory stage is dominated by losses, with profits peaking in the growth stage.

The product life cycle concept is important to the small business manager for three reasons. First, it helps the entrepreneur to understand that promotion, pricing, and distribution policies should all be adjusted to reflect a product's position on the curve. Second, it highlights the importance of rejuvenating product lines, whenever possible, before they die. Third, it is a continuing reminder that the natural life cycle of a product follows the classic sigmoid curve—a tilted S-shaped curve describing the time line of life itself—and, therefore, that innovation is necessary for a firm's survival. According to Charles Handy, author of *The Age of Paradox*, the best time to begin a new curve is before the existing curve of the product life cycle peaks.

The New Product Development Process

A major responsibility of the entrepreneur is to find, evaluate, and introduce new products. This responsibility requires that the entrepreneur establish a process for developing new products. In big businesses, committees or entire departments are created for that purpose. Even in small firms, however, new product development needs to be a formalized process.

EXHIBIT 14-3 *The Product Life Cycle*

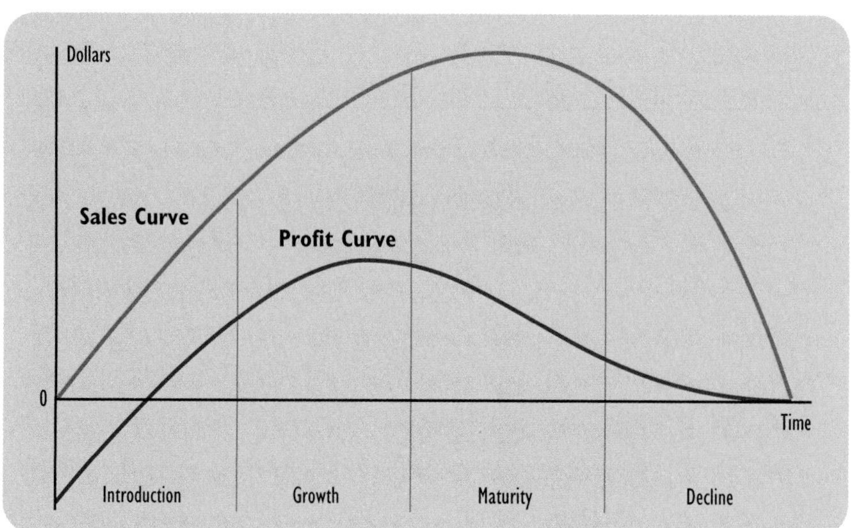

Entrepreneurs tend to treat new product development as a mountainous task—and it usually is. Many find that the following four-stage, structured approach is the best way to tackle product development.

IDEA ACCUMULATION The first stage of the new product development process—idea accumulation—involves increasing the pool of ideas under consideration. New products start with ideas, and these ideas have varied origins. The many possible sources include the following:

- Sales, engineering, or other personnel within the firm
- Government-owned patents, which are generally available on a royalty-free basis
- Privately owned patents listed by the U.S. Patent Office
- Other small companies that may be available for acquisition or merger
- Competitors' products and advertising
- Requests and suggestions from customers

BUSINESS ANALYSIS Business analysis is the second stage in new product development. Every new product idea must be carefully studied in relation to several financial considerations. Costs and revenues are estimated and analyzed with techniques such as break-even analysis. Any idea failing to show that it can be profitable is discarded during the business analysis stage. Four key factors need to be considered in conducting a business analysis:

1. *The product's relationship to the existing product line*. Some firms intentionally add very different products to their product mix. However, in most cases, any product item or product line added should be consistent with—or somehow related to—the existing product mix. For example, a new product may be designed to fill a gap in a firm's product line or in the range of prices of the products it currently sells. If the product is completely new, it should have at least a family relationship to existing products. Otherwise, the new product may call for drastic and costly changes in manufacturing methods, distribution channels, type of promotion, and/or manner of personal selling.
2. *Cost of development and introduction*. One problem in adding new products is the cost of their development and introduction. Considerable capital outlays may be necessary, including expenditures for design and development, marketing research to establish sales potential and volume potential, advertising and sales promotion, patents, and additional equipment. One to three years may pass before profits are realized on the sale of a new product.
3. *Available personnel and facilities*. Obviously, having adequate skilled personnel and production equipment is preferable to having to add employees and buy equipment. Thus, introducing new products is typically more appealing if the personnel and the required equipment are already available.
4. *Competition and market acceptance*. Still another factor to be considered in a business analysis is the potential competition facing a proposed product in its target market. Competition must not be too severe. Some studies, for example, suggest that new products can be introduced successfully only if 5 percent of the total market can be secured. The ideal solution, of course, is to offer a product that is sufficiently different from existing products or that is in a cost and price bracket where it avoids direct competition.

DEVELOPMENT OF THE PRODUCT The next stage of new product development entails sketching out the plan for branding, packaging, and other supporting efforts such as pricing and promotion. An actual prototype may be needed at this stage. After these components have been evaluated, the new product idea may be judged a misfit and discarded or passed on to the next stage for further consideration.

PRODUCT TESTING The last step in the product development process is product testing. Through testing, the physical product should be proven acceptable. While the product can be evaluated in a laboratory setting, a limited test of market reaction to it should also

be conducted. Consider the modest test marketing done by Millie Thomas, president of RGT Enterprises, Inc., in Fort Collins, Colorado, who wanted to develop a new children's toothbrush but had little money for market testing. She took a clay prototype of her triangular-stemmed toothbrush to pediatric dentists and day-care centers to get parents' reactions to the new design. There was a very positive response, so after a few design refinements, she began production. Her products are now sold in stores nationwide.[19]

BUILDING THE TOTAL PRODUCT

4 *Describe the building of a firm's total product.*

A major responsibility of marketing is to transform a basic product concept into a total product. Even when an idea for a unique new pen has been developed into physical reality in the form of the basic product, it is still not ready for the marketplace. The total product offering must be more than the materials molded into the shape of the new pen. To be marketable, the basic product must be named, have a package, perhaps have a warranty, and be supported by other product components. Let's examine a few of the components of a total product offering.

Branding

brand
A verbal and/or symbolic means of identifying a product

brand image
People's overall perception of a brand

brand name
A brand that can be spoken

brand mark
A brand that cannot be spoken

An essential element of a total product offering is a brand. A **brand** is a means of identifying the product—verbally and/or symbolically. Small firms are involved in "branding," whether they realize it or not. A small firm may neither know nor care, but it has a brand identity. Exhibit 14-4 depicts the components of a firm's brand identity. The intangible **brand image** component—people's overall perception of a brand—may even be more important to acceptance of a firm's bundle of satisfaction than the tangible brand mark and brand name elements. For example, prior to 2003, Martha Stewart had arguably one of the strongest brand images in the marketplace. However, her personal legal troubles tarnished the Martha Stewart brand and even resulted in suspension of her popular home design/cooking show on national television.

The tangible components of brand identity are brand names and brand marks. A **brand name** is a brand that can be spoken—like the name Dell. A **brand mark** is a brand that cannot be verbalized—like the golden arches of McDonald's.

Since a product's brand name is so important to the image of the business and its products, careful attention should be given to the selection of a name. In general, five rules apply in naming a product:

1. *Select a name that is easy to pronounce and remember*. You want customers to remember your product. Help them do so with a name that can be spoken easily—for example, TWO MEN & A TRUCK (a moving service) or Water Water Everywhere (a lawn irrigation business). Before choosing to use your own family name to identify a product, evaluate it carefully to ensure its acceptability.

EXHIBIT 14-4 *Components of a Brand Identity*

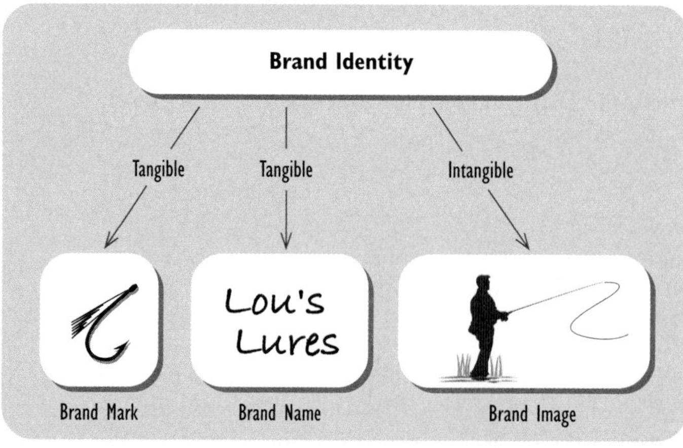

2. *Choose a descriptive name*. A name that is suggestive of the major benefit of the product can be extremely helpful. As a name for a sign shop, Sign Language correctly suggests a desirable benefit. Blind Doctor is a creative name for a window blind repair business. The Happy Company is a great name for a small firm producing bath toys for young children. However, Rocky Road would be a poor name for a business selling mattresses!
3. *Use a name that can have legal protection*. Be careful to select a name that can be defended successfully. Do not risk litigation by copying someone else's brand name. A new soft drink named Doc Pepper would likely be contested by the Dr Pepper company.
4. *Select a name with promotional possibilities*. Exceedingly long names are not, for example, compatible with good copy design on billboards, where space is at a premium. A competitor of the McDonald's hamburger chain is called Bob's, a name that will easily fit on any billboard. Radar Ball is a good name for a golf ball implanted with a homing chip that sends a signal to a hand-held device, allowing the ball to be found when it is lost.
5. *Select a name that can be used on several product lines of a similar nature*. Customer goodwill is often lost when a name doesn't fit a new line. The name Just Brakes is excellent for an auto service shop that repairs brakes—unless the shop later plans to expand into muffler repair and other car repair services.

A brand mark also has tremendous value. The Nike swish and the Chevy badge are marks widely associated with their owners. A small firm's special "signature," or logo, should symbolize positive images of the firm and its products. And if you don't get it right initially, consider a new design. This is what Penny Pritzker did a few years after launching the Parking Spot, an off-airport parking service, in 1998. The original logo on the company's shuttle buses and other sites reflected a "ho-hum image." In 2000, the Parking Spot unveiled a new design sporting "black spots of different sizes dancing against a vibrant yellow background."[20] She now operates 11 sites in 6 cities.

Another example of a successful logo change is provided by the privately held shoe manufacturer White Mountain Footwear, based in Lisbon, New Hampshire. Its black and white logo in block lettering was judged to be dated and unrepresentative of the fashion-forward image it was marketing. A new logo was designed—a stylized W that reflects the letter M, "like a mountain's mirror image in a lake."[21] (Take a look at the logo on the company's Web site at http://www.whitemt.com.) According to Elinor Selame, president of BrandEquity, who designed the logo, "The logo can be your company's hardest-working employee."[22]

Michael Bierut, a partner at the design firm Pentagram, offers the following tips about logo design:

1. *Be simple*. Some of the best logos are the simplest. Target has made a red circle with a red dot in the middle seem the very essence of affordable, hip practicality. H&R Block uses a green square in association with its name. Simple things are easy to remember and tend not to become outdated quickly.
2. *Leave it open to interpretation*. Don't try to design a logo that will explain at a glance the complete nature of your company. A logo that raises a question and is open to interpretation is better than one that attempts to offer all the answers.
3. *Be relentlessly consistent*. Companies with strong graphic identities have built those identities through years of use. Pick a typeface. Pick a color. Use them over and over again, on everything. Before long, you'll find yourself with an identifiable look and feel. That's more valuable than a logo, and anyone can afford it.
4. *Don't be embarrassed about design*. Things like logos and colors are considered "cosmetic," and businesspeople sometimes avoid focusing on them. But most design-driven companies got to be that way thanks to a highly placed advocate, such as Thomas Watson at IBM or Steve Jobs at Apple. For a design program to work, it needs to be seen to be championed by important people.
5. *Get good advice*. You can go pretty far with common sense. But sooner or later, you'll need to hire a professional graphic designer. The Web site of the American Institute of Graphic Arts (http://www.aiga.org), the largest professional organization for

Living the Dream

Focus on the Customer

Developing a Clean Brand

Small firms frequently question the value of branding, possibly because they assume it relates only to identifying a physical product or intangible service. In reality, branding is a broader concept, encompassing the total image of the small firm.

But entrepreneur Shelly Mars is a believer! In 1999, she left a career in high-tech research to launch Ecoluxe, an organic dry-cleaning company in the Boston, Massachusetts, area. She replaced chemical cleaning solvents that are linked to cancer and birth defects with an organic, 100 percent biodegradable cleaner invented by her and a team of chemists. Mars realized that her business name, and her brand, should bring to customers' minds an image different from that of the typical dry cleaner.

Her target customers live in upscale neighborhoods, so Mars decided to do the cleaning off-site so the stores could stay "brighter, cleaner and friendlier." She also avoided the use of coupons, which she felt would focus customers on price, thereby diluting the brand. Instead, Ecoluxe aligned itself with events like Earth Day to build a strong brand image. "Once you're very clear about your message, [branding] is important," she says. Mars estimates that she spent over $50,000 on branding in her first year of operation.

http://www.ecoluxe.net

Ecoluxe is doing well, with sales of more than $1 million in 2003. The company was voted "Best Dry Cleaner" in *Boston Magazine*'s "Best of Boston" readers' poll in both 2002 and 2003.

Sources: Emily Rosenblum, "Why I Do What I Do: Shelly Mars, Founder, Ecoluxe Dry Cleaner," http://www.healthwell.com, April 23, 2004; http://www.ecoluxe.net, April 25, 2004; and Chris Penttila, "Battle of the Brand," *Entrepreneur*, March 2004, p. 54.

graphic designers, offers information about how to find and work with experienced professionals.

6. *Don't expect miracles*. Your company's image is the sum total of many factors. Make sure that your company looks, sounds, and feels smart in every way, every time it goes out in public. That is actually much better than a logo.[23]

trademark
A legal term identifying a firm's exclusive right to use a brand

service mark
A brand that a company has the exclusive right to use to identify a service

Trademark and **service mark** are legal terms indicating the exclusive right to use a brand. Once an entrepreneur has found a name or symbol that is unique, easy to remember, and related to the product or service, an attorney who specializes in trademarks and service marks should be hired to run a name or symbol search and then to register the trade name or symbol. The protection of trademarks is discussed later in this chapter.

Packaging

Packaging is another important part of the total product offering. In addition to protecting the basic product, packaging is a significant tool for increasing the value of the total product.

Consider for a moment some of the products you purchase. How many do you buy mainly because of a preference for package design and/or color? Innovative packaging is frequently the deciding factor for consumers. If products are otherwise similar to competitive products, their packaging may create the distinctive impression that makes the sale. For example, biodegradable packaging materials may distinguish a product from its competition. The original L'eggs packaging design—the shape of an egg containing ladies' stockings—is an example of creative packaging that sells well.

Labeling

Another part of the total product is its label. Labeling serves several important purposes for manufacturers, which apply most labels. One purpose is to display the brand, particularly when branding the basic product would be undesirable. For example, a furniture brand is typically shown on a label and not on the basic product. On some products, brand

Living the Dream — *Entrepreneurial Challenges*

Packaging the Right Look

Business growth may be stunted even when a firm's marketing strategy is otherwise strong. One problem may be poor packaging.

As president of a family business begun more than 89 years ago in Milwaukee, Wisconsin, Margaret Gile represents the third generation in her family to make candy. Through internal growth and mergers, the business has expanded into what is now called Quality Candy Shoppes/Buddy Squirrel of Wisconsin, Inc. The company owns and operates 13 retail locations.

Recent attempts to move into the gift marketplace required Gile to take a closer look at the firm's packaging of its product. She found that "our packaging didn't reflect an upscale, finished look. The company's dated red, black, and white boxes were fine for the wholesale candy industry years ago. But now, more retail candy sellers want the option of selling chocolate directly to the public without having to repackage it."

To be successful in the upscale candy industry, Gile's candy had to look as fancy as it tasted. Top-notch ingredients made for quality candy, but the company's outdated packaging was a hindrance. Therefore, the signature boxes were redesigned internally and externally to represent the upscale image.

"Biting the bullet and updating our packaging was very important to sustaining growth," says Gile.

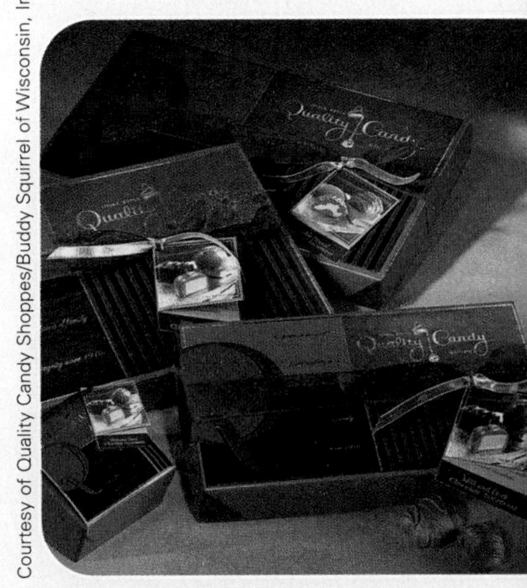

Courtesy of Quality Candy Shoppes/Buddy Squirrel of Wisconsin, Inc.

http://www.qcbs.com

Sources: http://www.qcbs.com/AboutUs/AboutUs.html, April 25, 2004; and Shannon Scully, "Why Image Matters," *MyBusiness*, December-January 2003, p. 31, reprinted with permission.

visibility is highly desirable; Louis Vuitton handbags would probably not sell as well with the name label only inside the purse.

A label is also an important informative tool for consumers. It often includes information on product care and use and may even provide information on how to dispose of the product.

Laws concerning labeling requirements should be reviewed carefully. Be innovative in your labeling information, and consider including information that goes beyond the specified minimum legal requirements.

Making Warranties

A **warranty** is simply a promise, written or unwritten, that a product will do certain things or meet certain standards. All sellers make an implied warranty that the seller's title to the product is good. A merchant seller, who deals in goods of a particular kind, makes the additional implied warranty that those goods are fit for the ordinary purposes for which they are sold. A written warranty on a product is not always necessary. In fact, many firms operate without written warranties, believing that a written warranty will serve only to confuse customers or make them suspicious.

warranty
A promise that a product will perform at a certain level or meet certain standards

Warranties are important for products that are innovative, relatively expensive, purchased infrequently, relatively complex to repair, and positioned as high-quality goods. A business should consider the following factors in rating the merits of a proposed warranty policy:

- Cost
- Service capability
- Competitive practices
- Customer perceptions
- Legal implications

PRODUCT STRATEGY

5 *Explain product strategy and the alternatives available to small businesses.*

product strategy
The way the product component of the marketing mix is used to achieve a firm's objectives

product item
The lowest common denominator in the product mix—the individual item

product line
The sum of related individual product items

product mix
The collection of a firm's total product lines

product mix consistency
The similarity of product lines in a product mix

product
A total bundle of satisfaction—including a service, a good, or both—offered to consumers in an exchange transaction

Product strategy includes decisions related to the product mix. It covers choices involving branding, packaging, labeling, and other elements comprising the core component of the bundle of satisfaction, whether product and/or service.

Specifically, **product strategy** describes the manner in which the product component of the marketing mix is used to achieve the objectives of a firm. A **product item** is the lowest common denominator in a product mix. It is the individual item, such as one brand of bar soap. A **product line** is the sum of the related individual product items. The relationship is usually defined generically. Two brands of bar soap are two product items in one product line. A **product mix** is the collection of product lines within a firm's ownership and control. A firm's product mix might consist of a line of bar soaps and a line of shoe polishes. **Product mix consistency** refers to the closeness, or similarity, of the product lines. The more items in a product line, the more depth it has. The more product lines in a product mix, the greater the breadth of the product mix. Exhibit 14-5 shows the product lines and product mix of the firm 180s LLC, mentioned on page 309.

Product Marketing Versus Service Marketing

Traditionally, marketers have used the word *product* as a generic term describing both goods and services. However, whether goods marketing and services marketing strategies are the same is questionable. As shown in Exhibit 14-6, certain characteristics—tangibility, amount of time separating production and consumption, standardization, and perishability—lead to a number of differences between the two strategies. Based on these characteristics, for example, a pencil fits the pure goods end of the scale and a haircut fits the pure services end. The major implication of this distinction is that marketing services presents unique challenges that are not faced in product strategy development.

Although we recognize the benefit of examining the marketing of services as a unique form, space limitations require that it be subsumed under the umbrella category of product marketing. Therefore, from this point on, a **product** will be considered to include the total bundle of satisfaction offered to customers in an exchange transaction—whether it be a service, a good, or a combination of the two. In addition to the physical product or core service, a product also includes complementary components, such as packaging or a warranty. Of course, the physical product or core service is usually the most important element in the total bundle of satisfaction. But sometimes that main element is perceived by customers to be similar for all products. In that case, complementary components become the most important features of the product. For example, a particular brand of cake mix

EXHIBIT 14-5 *Product Lines and Product Mix for 180s LLC*

DEPTH OF THE PRODUCT LINES		Ear Warmers	Gloves	Sunglasses
	Performance	• Dynamic	5 styles	• Tangle • Dovetail • Mortise • Integral • Festo
	Sport	• 4-way • Fleece	7 styles	
	Kids' Sport	• Fleece	3 styles	
	Casual	• Suede • Heathered Knit	6 styles	
	Activewear	• Cord • Knit • Fleece	6 styles	

Source: http://www.180s.com, May 25, 2004.

EXHIBIT 14-6 *Services Marketing Versus Goods Marketing*

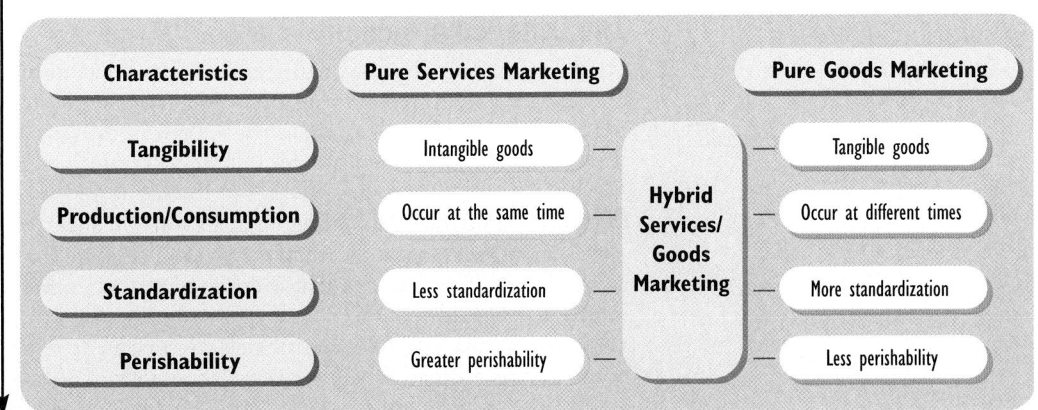

may be preferred by consumers not because it is a better mix, but because of the unique toll-free telephone number on the package that can be called for baking hints. Or a certain dry cleaner may be chosen over others because it treats customers with respect, not because it cleans clothes exceptionally well.

Product Strategy Options

Failure to clearly understand product strategy options will lead to ineffectiveness and conflict in the marketing effort. The major product strategy alternatives of a small business can be condensed into six categories, based on the nature of the firm's product offering and the number of target markets:

1. One product/one market
2. One product/multiple markets
3. Modified product/one market
4. Modified product/multiple markets
5. Multiple products/one market
6. Multiple products/multiple markets

Each alternative represents a distinct strategy, although two or more of these strategies can be pursued concurrently. A small firm, however, will usually pursue the alternatives in the order listed. Also, keep in mind that once any product strategy has been implemented, sales can be increased through certain additional growth tactics. For example, within any market, a small firm can try to increase sales of an existing product by doing any or all of the following:

- Convincing nonusers in the targeted market to become customers
- Persuading current customers to use more of the product
- Alerting current customers to new uses for the product

When small firms add products to their product mix, they generally select related products. But there are, of course, strategies that involve unrelated products. For example, a local dealer selling Italian sewing machines might add a line of microwave ovens, a generically unrelated product. A product strategy that includes a new product quite different from existing products can be very risky. However, this strategy is occasionally used by small businesses, especially when the new product fits existing distribution and sales systems or requires similar marketing knowledge.

Adding a new, unrelated product to the product mix to target a new market is an even higher-risk strategy, as a business is attempting to market an unfamiliar product in an unfamiliar market. One electrical equipment service business recently added a private employment agency. If successful, this product strategy could provide a hedge against volatile shifts in market demand. A business that sells both snowshoes and suntan lotion expects that demand will be high in one market or the other at all times.

6 Describe the legal environment affecting product decisions.

The Legal Environment

Strategic decisions about growth, innovation, product development, and the total product offering are always made within the guidelines and constraints of the legal environment of the marketplace. Let's examine a select few of the laws by which the government protects both the rights of consumers and the marketing assets of firms.

CONSUMER PROTECTION Federal regulations on such subjects as labeling and product safety have important implications for product strategy. The Nutrition Labeling and Education Act of 1990 requires that every food product covered by the law have a standard nutrition label, listing the amounts of calories, fat, salt, and nutrients. The law also addresses the accuracy of advertising claims such as "low salt" and "fiber prevents cancer." Some experts estimate labeling costs at thousands of dollars per product.

To protect the public against unreasonable risk of injury, the federal government enacted the Consumer Product Safety Act of 1972. This act created the Consumer Product Safety Commission to set safety standards for toys and other consumer products and to ban goods that are exceptionally hazardous.

PROTECTION OF MARKETING ASSETS Exhibit 14-7 shows the four primary means firms can use to protect certain marketing assets. The examples shown are representative of trademarks, patents, copyrights, and trade dress.

EXHIBIT 14-7 *Protecting Marketing Assets*

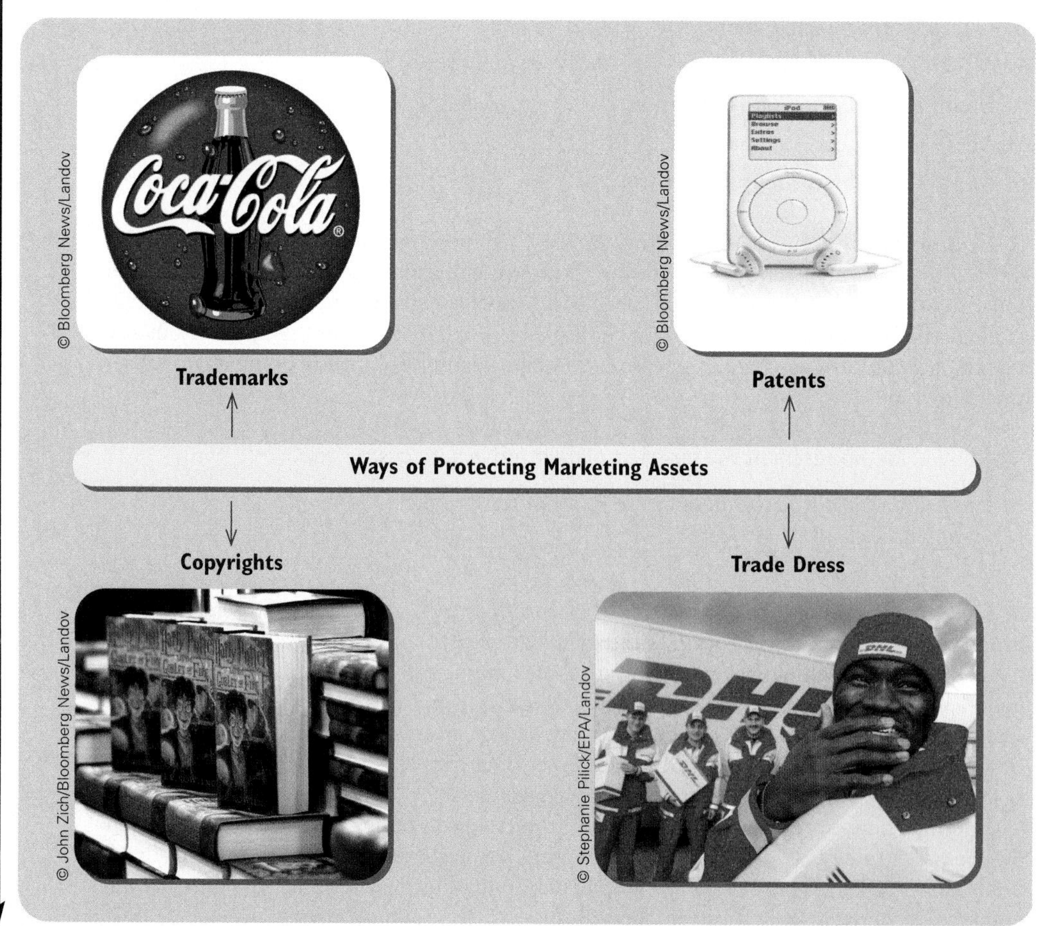

Trademark Protection Protecting a trademark is important to a manufacturer or merchant. In some cases, a color or scent can be part of a trademark. Small manufacturers, in particular, often find it desirable to feature an identifying trademark in advertising.

Since names that refer to products are often registered trademarks, potential names should be investigated carefully to ensure that they are not already in use. Given the complexity of this task, many entrepreneurs seek the advice of attorneys experienced in trademark search and registration.

An entrepreneur may conduct a trademark search personally, however, by using the Trademark Search Library of the U.S. Patent and Trademark Office (PTO) in Arlington, Virginia. A trademark search can also be made on the Internet by going to http://www.uspto.gov.

Common law recognizes a property right in the ownership of trademarks. However, reliance on common-law rights is not always adequate. For example, Microsoft Corporation, the major supplier of personal computer software, claimed it had common-law rights to the trademark *Windows* because of the enormous industry recognition of the product. Nevertheless, when Microsoft filed a trademark application in 1990 seeking to gain exclusive rights to the name *Windows*, the U.S. Patent and Trademark Office rejected the bid, claiming that the word was a generic term and, therefore, in the public domain.

Registration of trademarks is permitted under the federal Lanham Trademark Act, making protection easier if infringement is encountered. The act was revised in 1989 and now allows trademark rights to begin with merely an "intent to use," along with the filing of an application and payment of fees. Prior to this revision, a firm had to have already used the mark on goods shipped or sold. A trademark registered after November 16, 1989, remains effective for 10 years and may be renewed for additional 10-year periods. Application for such registration can be made online to the U.S. Patent and Trademark Office.

A small business must use a trademark properly in order to protect it. Two rules can help. The first rule is to make every effort to see that the trade name is not carelessly used as a generic name. For example, the Xerox company never wants people to say that they are "xeroxing" something when they are using one of its competitors' copiers. The second rule is to inform the public that the trademark is a trademark by labeling it with the symbol ™. If the trademark is registered, the symbol ® or the phrase "Registered in the U.S. Patent and Trademark Office" should be used.

Patent Protection A **patent** is the registered, exclusive right of an inventor to make, use, or sell an invention. The two primary types of patents are utility patents and design patents. A **utility patent** covers a new process or protects the function of a product. A **design patent** covers the appearance of a product and everything that is an inseparable part of the product. Utility patents are granted for a period of 20 years, while design patents are effective for 14 years. Patent law also provides for **plant patents**, which cover any distinct and new variety of living plants.

patent
The registered, exclusive right of an inventor to make, use, or sell an invention

utility patent
Registered protection for a new process or a product's function

design patent
Registered protection for the appearance of a product and its inseparable parts

plant patent
Registered protection for any distinct and new variety of living plant

Items that may be patented include machines and products, improvements on machines and products, and original designs. Some small manufacturers have patented items that constitute the major part of their product line. Indeed, some businesses such as Polaroid and IBM can trace their origins to a patented invention. Small business owners preparing a patent application often retain a patent attorney to act for them. A patent search can be conducted on the Internet.

Lawsuits concerning patent infringements are costly and should be avoided, if possible. Coming up with the money and legal talent to enforce this legal right is one of the major problems associated with patent protection in small businesses. Monetary damages and injunctions are available, however, if an infringement can be proved.

Copyrights A **copyright** is the exclusive right of a creator (author, composer, designer, or artist) to reproduce, publish, perform, display, or sell work that is the product of that person's intelligence and skill. Works created on or after January 1, 1978, receive copyright protection for the duration of the creator's life plus 70 years. A "work made for hire" is protected for 95 years from its publication or 120 years from its creation, whichever is shorter. Copyrights are registered in the Copyright Office of the Library of Congress, whose Web site (http://www.copyright.gov) provides a huge amount of useful material about copyrights.

copyright
The exclusive right of a creator to reproduce, publish, perform, display, or sell his or her own works

Under the Copyright Act of 1976, copyrightable works are automatically protected from the moment of their creation. However, any work distributed to the public should contain a copyright notice. This notice consists of three elements (which can be found on the copyright page in the front of this textbook):

1. The symbol ©
2. The year the work was published
3. The copyright owner's name

The law provides that copyrighted work cannot be reproduced by another person or persons without authorization. Even photocopying of such work is prohibited, although an individual may copy a limited amount of material for such purposes as research, criticism, comment, and scholarship. A copyright holder can sue a violator for damages.

trade dress
Elements of a firm's distinctive image not protected by a trademark, patent, or copyright

Trade Dress A small business may also possess a valuable intangible asset called trade dress. **Trade dress** describes those elements of a firm's distinctive operating image not specifically protected under a trademark, patent, or copyright. Trade dress is the "look" that a firm creates to establish its marketing advantage. For example, if the employees of a pizza retailer dress as prison guards and prisoners, a "jailhouse" image could become uniquely associated with this business and, over time, become its trade dress. One court has defined trade dress as "the total image of a product, including features such as size, shape, color or color combinations, texture, graphics, or even particular sales techniques."[24] Although there are currently no statutes covering trade dress, the courts are beginning to recognize the value of this asset.

SUPPLY CHAIN MANAGEMENT

7 Explain the importance of supply chain management.

supply chain management
A system of management that integrates and coordinates the means by which a firm creates or develops a product or service and delivers it to customers

Supply chain management is a system of management that integrates and coordinates the ways in which a firm finds the raw materials and necessary components to produce a product or service, builds the actual product or service, and then delivers it to customers. Recent attention directed toward supply chain management has motivated attempts by both small and large firms to create a more competitive, customer-driven supply system. In other words, effective supply chain management can potentially lower the costs of inventory, transportation, warehousing, and packaging while increasing customer satisfaction.

The Internet and available software are major stimulants of current developments in supply chain management. Pre-Internet, communication between parties in the supply chain was slow or nonexistent. But the Internet, along with its simple, universally accepted communication standards, has brought suppliers and customers together in a way never before thought possible.

A comprehensive discussion of supply chain management is beyond the scope of this book. However, in this part of the chapter, we will concentrate on the function of intermediaries, the various distribution channels that comprise a supply chain, and the basics of logistics. Entrepreneurs often regard distribution as the least glamorous marketing activity. Nevertheless, an effective distribution system is just as important as a unique package, a clever name, or a creative promotional campaign. Thus, a small business manager should understand the basic principles of distribution, which apply to both domestic and international distribution activities.

distribution
Physically moving products and establishing intermediary relationships to support such movement

physical distribution (logistics)
The activities of distribution involved in the physical relocation of products

channel of distribution
The system of relationships established to guide the movement of a product

In marketing, **distribution** encompasses both the physical movement of products and the establishment of intermediary (middleman) relationships to achieve product movement. The activities involved in physically moving a product are called **physical distribution (logistics)**; the system of relationships established to guide the movement of a product is called the **channel of distribution**.

Distribution is essential for both tangible and intangible goods. Since distribution activities are more visible for tangible goods (products), our discussion will focus on products. Most intangible goods (services) are delivered directly to the user. An income tax preparer and a barber, for example, serve clients directly. However, marketing a person's labor can involve channel intermediaries. An employment agency, for example, provides an employer with temporary personnel.

Intermediaries

Intermediaries can often perform marketing functions better than the producer of a product can. A producer can perform its own distribution functions—including delivery—if the geographic area of the market is small, customers' needs are specialized, and risk levels are low, as they might be for a producer of doughnuts. However, intermediaries generally provide more efficient means of distribution if customers are widely dispersed or if special packaging and storage are needed. Many types of small firms, such as retail stores, function as intermediaries.

Some intermediaries, called **merchant middlemen**, take title to the goods they distribute, thereby helping a firm to share or totally shift business risk. Other intermediaries, such as **agents** and **brokers**, do not take title to goods and, therefore, assume less market risk than do merchant middlemen.

merchant middlemen
Intermediaries that take title to the goods they distribute

agents/brokers
Intermediaries that do not take title to the goods they distribute

Channels of Distribution

8 Specify the major considerations in structuring a distribution channel.

A channel of distribution can be either direct or indirect. In a **direct channel**, there are no intermediaries—the product goes directly from producer to user. An **indirect channel** of distribution has one or more intermediaries between producer and user.

Exhibit 14-8 depicts the various options available for structuring a channel of distribution. E-commerce (online merchandising) and mail-order marketing are direct channel systems for distributing consumer goods. Amazon.com is an example of an online merchandiser that uses a direct channel to final consumers. The systems shown on the right-hand side of Exhibit 14-8 are indirect channels involving one, two, or three levels of intermediaries. As a final consumer, you are naturally familiar with retailers. Industrial purchasers are equally familiar with industrial distributors. Channels with two or three

direct channel
A distribution system without intermediaries

indirect channel
A distribution system with one or more intermediaries

EXHIBIT 14-8 *Alternative Channels of Distribution*

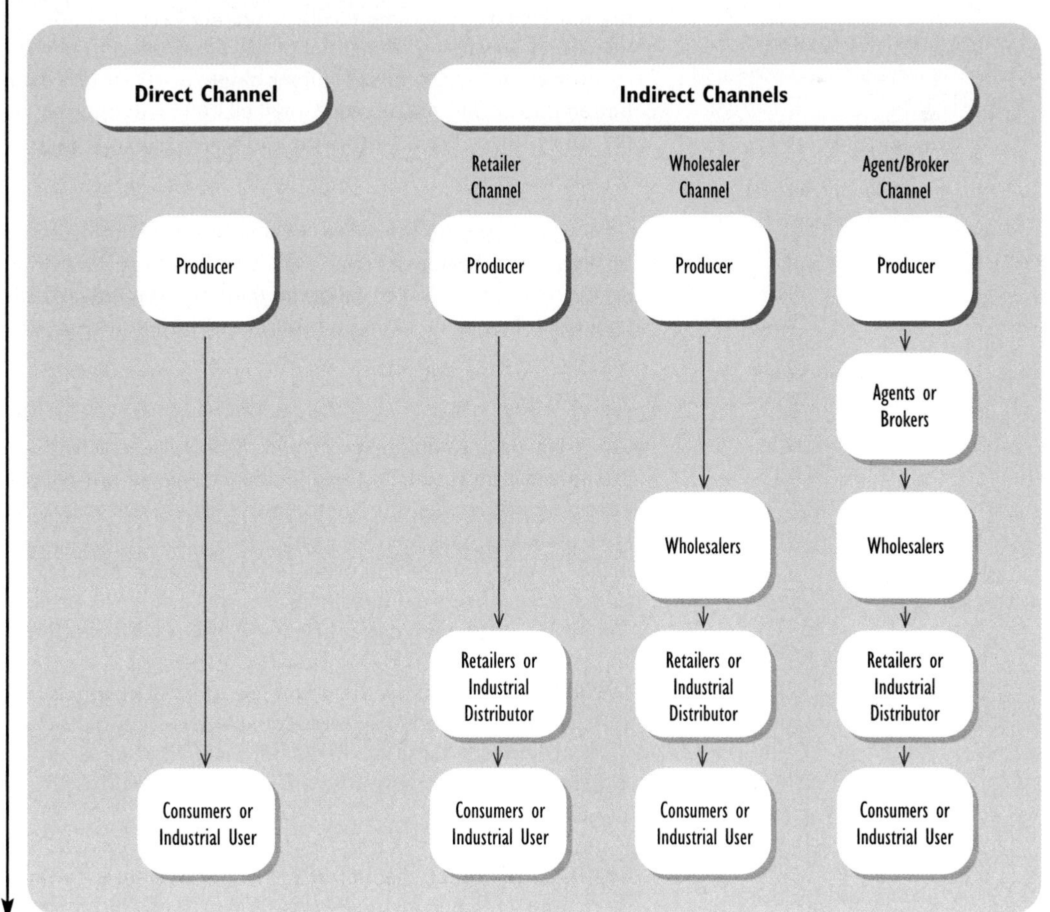

Living the Dream

Entrepreneurial Challenges

Boosting a Small Player's Sales with Big Player Distribution

Courtesy of ClearPlay

Entrepreneur Matt Jarman is a small player in a large field. But partnering with RCA has landed his parental control software in DVD players that are on the shelves of Wal-Mart! This channel of distribution will most certainly boost ClearPlay sales dramatically.

Founded by Jarman and his brother Lee, the 11-employee Utah-based company produces filtering software on a programmable chip that allows the DVD user to choose content options via an on-screen menu. The filters—for violence, sex, nudity, and language—give instructions to the DVD player to skip over or mute objectionable content previously identified and labeled by ClearPlay movie professionals. The DVD player comes preloaded with ClearPlay filters for 100 movies. Additional filters can be downloaded by subscribers to a personal computer and then burned onto a blank CD for transfer to the DVD player's memory.

The RCA DVD player is also available for purchase online at Wal-Mart's Web site. Wal-Mart spokeswoman Karen Burke says the store's strategy is "based on what we think our customers want." Reflecting a similar stance, Wal-Mart stores currently do not carry any music CDs that have parental advisory labels.

Jarman says ClearPlay doesn't have a religious agenda. But it "feels good knowing that you can watch great Hollywood movies without having to worry about the profanity, nudity and gory violence," says the ClearPlay Web site.

Sources: http://www.clearplay.com, May 5, 2004; "ClearPlay to Clean Up Hollywood," http://www.cbsnews.com/stories, May 5, 2004; Mike Snider, "Hollywood Riled Up over ClearPlay," *USAToday*, May 6, 2004, p. 12D; and http://www.Wal-Mart.com/catalog/product, May 5, 2004.

stages of intermediaries are probably the ones most typically used by small firms producing products with geographically large markets. It is important to note that a small firm may use more than one channel of distribution—a practice called **dual distribution**.

dual distribution
A distribution system that involves more than one channel

Firms that successfully employ a single distribution channel may switch to dual distribution if they find that an additional channel will improve overall profitability. For example, the Boston Book Company, in business since 1979, occupies a shop in downtown Boston, Massachusetts, but also maintains a Web site where books can be purchased online.

A logical starting point in structuring a distribution system is to observe systems used by competing businesses. Such analysis should reveal some practical alternatives. However, a small firm must attend to certain important factors when building a channel of distribution. The three main considerations in building a channel of distribution are costs, coverage, and control.

COSTS The absence of intermediaries does not make a direct channel inherently less expensive than an indirect channel. The least expensive channel may be indirect. For example, a firm producing handmade dolls need not purchase trucks and warehouses to distribute its product directly to customers but can instead rely on established intermediaries that own such facilities. Small firms should look at distribution costs as an investment—spending money in order to make money. They should ask themselves whether the money they "invest" in intermediaries (by selling the product to them at a reduced price) would still get the job done if they used direct distribution.

COVERAGE Small firms can often use indirect channels of distribution to increase market coverage. Suppose a small manufacturer's internal sales force can make 10 contacts a week with final users of the firm's product. Creating an indirect channel with 10 industrial distributors, each making 10 contacts a week, could expose the product to 100 final users a week.

CONTROL A direct channel of distribution is sometimes preferable because it provides more control. Intermediaries may not market a product as desired. An entrepreneurial firm must carefully select intermediaries that provide the desired support.

Control is the main reason Robin Rose, of Robin Rose Ice Cream in Venice, California, distributes her products directly to customers. The reputation of Robin Rose ice cream depends on its freshness and quality; therefore, she has purposely remained small in order to control both the production and the distribution of her ice cream.[25]

The Scope of Physical Distribution

In addition to the intermediary relationships that make up a channel, there must also be a system of physical distribution. The main component of physical distribution is transportation. Additional components are storage, materials handling, delivery terms, and inventory management. The following sections briefly examine all of these topics except inventory management, which is discussed in Chapter 20.

TRANSPORTATION The major decision regarding physical transportation of a product is which method to use. Available modes of transportation are traditionally classified as airplanes, trucks, railroads, pipelines, and waterways. Each mode has unique advantages and disadvantages. The choice of a specific mode of transportation is based on several criteria: relative cost, transit time, reliability, capability, accessibility, and traceability.

Transportation intermediaries are legally classified as common carriers, contract carriers, and private carriers. **Common carriers**, which are available for hire to the general public, and **contract carriers**, which engage in individual contracts with shippers, are subject to regulation by federal and/or state agencies. Lines of transport owned by the shippers are called **private carriers**.

common carriers
Transportation intermediaries available for hire to the general public

contract carriers
Transportation intermediaries that contract with individual shippers

private carriers
Lines of transport owned by the shippers

STORAGE Lack of space is a common problem for small businesses. When a channel system uses merchant middlemen or wholesalers, title to the goods is transferred, as is responsibility for the storage function. On other occasions, the small business must plan

Living the Dream — *Entrepreneurship and Integrity*

Keeping a Promise

"Do you promise to tell the truth, the whole truth, and nothing but the truth . . . ?" is part of the widely recognized pledge required by the American judicial system. A lesser known requirement in business is the Federal Trade Commission rule on keeping promises made about delivery dates. The Mail or Telephone Order Merchandise Rule, adopted in 1975, spells out the ground rules for promises about shipments. The rule applies to goods ordered via phone, mail, fax, and the Internet and requires that advertisers must have a reasonable basis for stating that they can ship within a certain time period.

© Larry Ford

Eric Lituchy, co-founder and CEO of Delightful Deliveries, Inc., in Syosset, New York, knows that honoring delivery promises is the law but also believes it is just good business practice. The company's virtual gourmet store, started in 1998, offers gift baskets of food items and fresh flower bouquets. Delightful Deliveries partners with 25 manufacturers, such as Mrs. Field's Original Cookies, which receive the orders from Lituchy's Web site and, in turn, ship directly to the customer. Customers select an "Arrives By" date from a menu on the Web site. Lituchy says, "Every vendor has to give us a set time that they will take an order and guarantee [when] it will ship out, so we can put that on our site." Delightful Deliveries then promises this delivery date to the customer.

Lituchy was aware of the FTC rule when he first developed his Web site. However, customers' needs were the driving force for developing the software supporting timely delivery and continuing efforts to spot any problems with the delivery system and get them fixed quickly.

http://www.delightfuldeliveries.com

Lituchy keeps his delivery promises well. Sales are projected to reach several million dollars in 2004.

Source: Melissa Campanelli, "Stand and Deliver," *Entrepreneur*, November 2003, p. 57. Reprinted with permission.

for its own warehousing. If a firm is too small to own a private warehouse, it can rent space in public warehouses. If storage requirements are simple and do not involve much special handling equipment, a public warehouse can provide economical storage.

MATERIALS HANDLING A damaged product in the right place at the right time is worth little. Therefore, a physical distribution system must arrange for suitable materials-handling methods and equipment. Forklifts, as well as special containers and packaging, are part of a materials-handling system.

DELIVERY TERMS A small but important part of a physical distribution system is the delivery terms, specifying which party is responsible for several aspects of the distribution:

- Paying the freight costs
- Selecting the carriers
- Bearing the risk of damage in transit
- Selecting the modes of transport

The simplest delivery term and the one most advantageous to a small business as seller is F.O.B. (free on board) origin, freight collect. This shifts all the responsibility for freight costs to the buyer. Title to the goods and risk of loss also pass to the buyer at the time the goods are shipped.

Logistics companies specialize in transportation and distribution services, providing trucking, packaging, and warehousing services for small- and medium-sized companies with limited in-house staffing. Many small businesses believe that using these third-party logistics firms is more cost-effective than carrying out the same functions in-house. For example, Premier Inc., of Greenwich, Connecticut, uses a firm named APL Logistics to handle packaging and shipping of its health and beauty-aid products. Products produced in plants around the country go to the APL warehouse in Dallas, Texas, and are then shipped to distribution outlets nationwide.

Looking Back

1 Explain the challenges associated with growth in a small firm.

- Growth sufficient to maintain the status quo is a goal of some entrepreneurs.
- Growing a business too quickly can be stressful for the small firm.
- A growth trap may occur when a firm's growth soaks up cash faster than it can be generated.
- Growth also puts pressure on a small firm's personnel.

2 Explain the role of innovation in a firm's growth.

- Coming up with and perfecting new products or services is often not easy.
- The risk of failure increases when innovation is the goal.
- Innovation is a means by which a firm can sustain its competitive advantage.

3 Identify stages in the product life cycle and the new product development process.

- The product life cycle portrays a product from introduction through growth and maturity to sales decline.
- The new product development process is a four-stage approach: idea accumulation, business analysis, development of the product, and product testing.

4 Describe the building of a firm's total product.

- The brand identity of a firm and/or product has an important intangible image component.
- The name is a critical component of a product; it should be easy to pronounce and remember, descriptive, eligible for legal protection, full of promotional possibilities, and suitable for use on several product lines.
- Packaging is a significant tool for increasing total product value.

- A label is an important informative tool, providing instructions on product use, care, and disposal.
- A warranty can be valuable for achieving customer satisfaction.

5 Explain product strategy and the alternatives available to small businesses.

- Product strategy describes how a product is used to achieve a firm's goals.
- There are six major product strategy alternatives which are based on the nature of the firm's product offering and the number of target markets.

6 Describe the legal environment affecting product decisions.

- Federal legislation regarding labeling and product safety was designed to protect consumers.
- The legal system provides protection for a firm's marketing assets through trademarks, patents, copyrights, and trade dress.

7 Explain the importance of supply chain management.

- Effective supply chain management can potentially lower the costs of inventory, transportation, warehousing, and packaging.
- Distribution encompasses both the physical movement of products and the establishment of relationships to guide the movement of products from producer to user.
- Intermediaries provide an efficient means of distribution if customers are widely dispersed or if special packaging and storage are needed.

8 Specify the major considerations in structuring a distribution channel.

- A distribution channel can be either direct or indirect; some firms successfully employ more than one channel of distribution.
- Costs, coverage, and control are the three main considerations in building a channel of distribution.
- Transportation, storage, materials handling, delivery terms, and inventory management are the main components of a physical distribution system.

Key Terms

sustainable competitive advantage, p. 310
product life cycle, p. 312
brand, p. 314
brand image, p. 314
brand name, p. 314
brand mark, p. 314
trademark, p. 316
service mark, p. 316
warranty, p. 317
product strategy, p. 318
product item, p. 318
product line, p. 318
product mix, p. 318
product mix consistency, p. 318
product, p. 318
patent, p. 321
utility patent, p. 321
design patent, p. 321
plant patent, p. 321
copyright, p. 321
trade dress, p. 322
supply chain management, p. 322
distribution, p. 322
physical distribution (logistics), p. 322
channel of distribution, p. 322
merchant middlemen, p. 323
agents/brokers, p. 323
direct channel, p. 323
indirect channel, p. 323
dual distribution, p. 324
common carriers, p. 325
contract carriers, p. 325
private carriers, p. 325

Discussion Questions

1. Discuss some of the limitations on growth in a small firm.
2. Describe the recommendations for reducing risk associated with innovation in a small business.
3. How does an understanding of the product life cycle concept help with product strategy?
4. Discuss briefly each stage of the product development process.
5. What are some of the product strategy options available to a small firm? Which ones are most likely to be used?
6. Identify and briefly describe the three ways to increase sales of an existing product once a product strategy has been implemented.
7. Select two product names, and then evaluate each with respect to the five rules for naming a product.

8. Explain how registration of a small firm's trademark would be helpful in protecting its brand.
9. Why do small firms need to consider indirect channels of distribution for their products? Why involve intermediaries in distribution at all?
10. Discuss the major considerations in structuring a channel of distribution.

You Make The Call

SITUATION 1

Linda McMahan was getting numerous compliments on a handbag she carried to The University of Texas events. She had purchased the handbag, which carried the UT name, at a local store but felt the quality of the bag was poor. She and her sister-in-law, Sue Craft McMahan, decided to become partners and produce and sell high-end handbags emblazoned with the college logo.

The pair designed four different types of bags—a large totebag, a smaller bag, a crescent-shaped handbag, and a "bolder" game-day bag—all marked with The University of Texas emblem. Early responses to the product line were overwhelming. They've now set their sights on other big-name schools.

Source: Nichole L. Torros, "Smells Like School Spirit," *Entrepreneur*, December 2003, p. 132.

Question 1 What problems, if any, do you see with the use of the university's brand?

Question 2 What strategy should they pursue to obtain cooperation from the university?

Question 3 What distribution options are likely to be used?

SITUATION 2

John Kowalski, of Aliquippa, Pennsylvania, is the man behind the Load Hog, a device that enables pickup truck beds to function like dump trucks. The Load Hog evolved from a product originally introduced by an Australian importer back in 1992. After years of product development by Kowalski, the Load Hog, with a price tag of $350,000, exhibits virtually no trace of the Australian product.

Kowalski and his wife, Carol, have promoted the Load Hog to truck dealers as an after-market product. They have exhibited at outdoor-vehicle and specialty-equipment shows and have sold around 400 of the units by mail order. More recently, they have launched a Web site (http://www.loadhog.com).

Source: Leigh Buchanan, "Pickup Artist," *Inc.*, Vol. 23, No. 8 (June 2001), pp. 68–73.

Question 1 Do you think there may be other channels of distribution that Kowalski might use? If so, what are they?

Question 2 What other related products might be added to the product mix?

Question 3 What do you think about the choice of the name for the device?

SITUATION 3

Kim Hodges operates a 3-year-old furniture company named Metallika in Waco, Texas. Does the name sound familiar? According to a lawyer for the heavy-metal rock band Metallica, it sounds too familiar. In a letter to Hodges, the lawyer wrote, "Specifically, we need you to change the name of your business to a name that does not include the terms Metallika, Metalika, Metallica, Metalica, or any name, term, logo, domain name or vanity telephone number similar thereto."

The lawyer said if Hodges chooses not to change the name of his company, they might sue for damages, company profits, and attorneys' fees.

Source: Mike Copeland, "Metallika Rocked by Metallica," *Waco Tribune Herald*, December 9, 2000, p. 1A.

Question 1 What course of action would you recommend to Hodges?

Question 2 What can Hodges say in defense of the name he chose for his furniture business?

Experiential Exercises

1. Interview the owner or owners of a local manufacturing business to find out how they view innovation in their market. Summarize your findings.
2. Ask some owners of small firms in your area to describe their new product development processes. Report your findings to the class.
3. Visit a local retail store and observe brand names, package designs, labels, and warranties. Choose good and bad examples of each of these product components, and report back to the class.
4. Consider your most recent meaningful purchase. Compare the decision-making process you used to

the four stages of the new product development process. Report your conclusions to the class.

5. Interview two different types of local retail merchants (for example, a boutique owner and a manager of a franchise) to determine how the merchandise in their stores was distributed to them. Contrast the channels of distribution used, and write a brief report on your findings.

Exploring the Web

1. Visit the Web site of tutor2u, an online learning resource, at **http://www.tutor2u.net**. Click on "Quizzes," then "Branding," and take the "Marketing—Introduction to Brands" quiz. How did you score?
2. Go to **http://www.wsu.edu:8080/~brians/errors/brand_names.html**, a page on Washington State University's Web site, and read the text on brand names. What examples are provided there of brand names that have been converted into generic ones? What other examples can you think of?

Case 14

LOTUS CHIPS' RECIPE FOR SUCCESS (P. 552)

Two women entrepreneurs experience many marketing challenges as they operate their new business.

Alternative Cases for Chapter 14:

Case 7, Specialty Cheese, p. 536
Case 9, The Chocolate Farm, p. 540

PRICING AND CREDIT DECISIONS

In the Video Spotlight

Calise & Sons Bakery

Calise & Sons Bakery has been baking and serving bread in New England for nearly a century, and during that time, the industry has changed in many important ways. For much of the time, business was done on a handshake, and prices rose to keep up with inflation. Today, however, bread is nearly a commodity, and the Calises have seen market prices for the same product decline by nearly 20 percent.

In order to maintain acceptable profitability levels, the Calise brothers have been selective about what kind of business they take. For example, they shy away from state contracts, which pay over 40 percent less than commercial contracts do. And they try not to be the lowest-priced producer because, in the long run, deeply discounted pricing has negative consequences. The brothers also make sure that the company gets paid weekly, according to its credit terms. New accounts are watched closely to ensure that they start out on the right track.

Like Reed Pigman at Texas Jet, the Calise brothers have decided to operate their business using a premium pricing strategy, and it's working. Despite extreme pricing pressure and stringent credit standards, Calise & Sons Bakery employs 170 people and generates over $13 million in annual sales.

Video material provided by Hattie Bryant, Producer of Small Business School, the series on PBS Stations, Worldnet, and the Web at http://www.smallbusinessschool.org.

Chapter 15

Looking Ahead

After studying this chapter, you should be able to

1 *Discuss the role of cost and demand factors in setting a price.*

2 *Apply break-even analysis and markup pricing.*

3 *Identify specific pricing strategies.*

4 *Explain the benefits of credit, factors that affect credit extension, and types of credit.*

5 *Describe the activities involved in managing credit.*

Because a value must be placed on a product or service by the provider before it can be sold, pricing decisions are a critical issue in small business marketing. The **price** of a product or service specifies what the seller requires for giving up ownership or use of that product or service. Often, the seller must extend credit to the buyer in order to make the exchange happen. **Credit** is simply an agreement between buyer and seller that payment for a product or service will be received at some later date.

price
A specification of what a seller requires in exchange for transferring ownership or use of a product or service

credit
An agreement between a buyer and a seller that provides for delayed payment for a product or service

Pricing and credit decisions are vital because they influence the relationship between the business and its customers. Also, these decisions directly affect both revenue and cash flow. Of course, customers dislike price increases and restrictive credit policies; therefore, the entrepreneur needs to set prices and design credit policies as wisely as possible, to avoid the need for frequent changes. This chapter examines both the pricing decisions and the credit decisions of small firms.

SETTING A PRICE

1 *Discuss the role of cost and demand factors in setting a price.*

In setting a price, the entrepreneur decides on the most appropriate value for the product or service being offered for sale. This task might seem easy, but it isn't. The first pricing lesson is to remember that total sales revenue depends on just two components—sales volume and price—and even a small change in price can drastically influence revenue. Consider the following situations, *assuming no change in demand*:

Situation A

Quantity sold	×	Price per unit	=	Gross revenue
250,000	×	$3.00	=	$750,000

Situation B

Quantity sold	×	Price per unit	=	Gross revenue
250,000	×	$2.80	=	$700,000

The price per unit is only $0.20 lower in Situation B than in Situation A. However, the total difference in revenue is $50,000! Clearly, a small business can lose significant revenues if a price is set too low.

Pricing is also important because it indirectly affects sales quantity. Setting a price too high may result in lower quantities sold, reducing total revenue. In the above example, quantity sold was assumed to be independent of price—and it very well may be for such a small change in price. However, a larger increase or decrease might substantially affect the quantity sold. Pricing, therefore, has a dual influence on total sales revenue. It is important *directly* as part of the gross revenue equation and *indirectly* through its impact on demand.

Before beginning a more detailed analysis of pricing, we should note that services are generally more difficult to price than products because of their intangible nature. However, the impact of price on revenue and profits is the same. Because estimating the cost of providing a service and the demand for that service is a more complex process, the following discussions will focus on product pricing.

Living the Dream — *Focus on the Customer*

Let's Talk

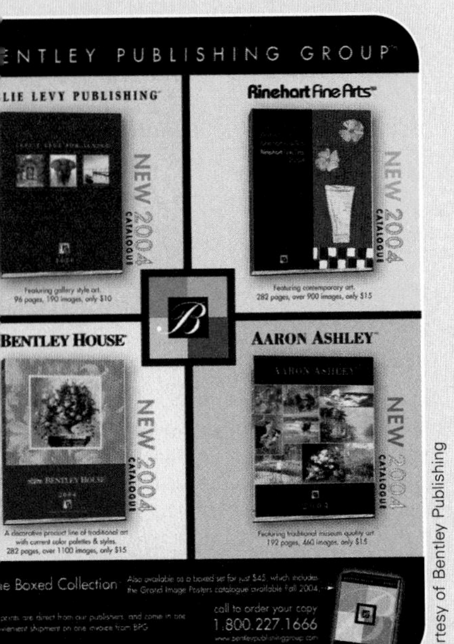

Courtesy of Bentley Publishing

Raising prices charged to customers is never a comfortable thing to do, but it has to happen sometimes. Keeping a clear focus on individual customer needs as you increase prices can minimize negative customer reaction.

Consider the price increases of Bentley Publishing Group, a 60-employee business based in Walnut Creek, California, that sells art prints and posters. In 2001, president and founder Robert Sher was faced with sharp increases in labor and rent costs. It had been almost three years since the last price increase, but that was about to change.

Sher worried that higher prices would drive away customers. But with shrinking margins, he had no choice but to make some price adjustments. "There is only so much you can do to reduce costs," he says.

For starters, Sher didn't raise prices on all items. And he kept communication open with customers, letting them know that he was even more willing than before to give volume discounts. "We trained our sales force to be very sensitive to the needs of key customers," he said. "We presented it as, 'Yes, prices are going up, and here's why. But there's some flexibility.' "

Sher also examined his inventory database, which provided detailed information on the color, size, subject matter, and style of nearly 8,000 prints. So if a large customer balked at paying $6.50—the new, higher price—for a particular print, Sher could quickly offer a similar one for $5.

Although price increases are tough, in Sher's case the discounting strategies kept most customers from jumping ship.

Source: Emily Barker, "Let's Make a Deal," *Inc.*, Vol. 24, No. 1 (January 2002), p. 95. By Emily Barker, © 2004 Gruner + Jahr USA Publishing. First published in *Inc.* Magazine. Reprinted with permission.

Cost Determination for Pricing

total cost
The sum of cost of goods sold, selling expenses, and overhead costs

For a business to be successful, its pricing must cover total cost plus some profit margin. Pricing, therefore, must be based on an understanding of the basic behavior of costs. As illustrated in Exhibit 15-1, **total cost** includes three components. The first is the cost of goods offered for sale. An appliance retailer, for example, must include in the selling price the cost of the appliance and related freight charges. The second component is the selling cost, which includes the direct cost of the salesperson's time (salary plus commissions), as well as the cost of other selling activities such as advertising and sales promotion. The third component is the overhead cost applicable to the given product. Included in this cost

EXHIBIT 15-1 *The Three Components of Total Cost in Determining Price*

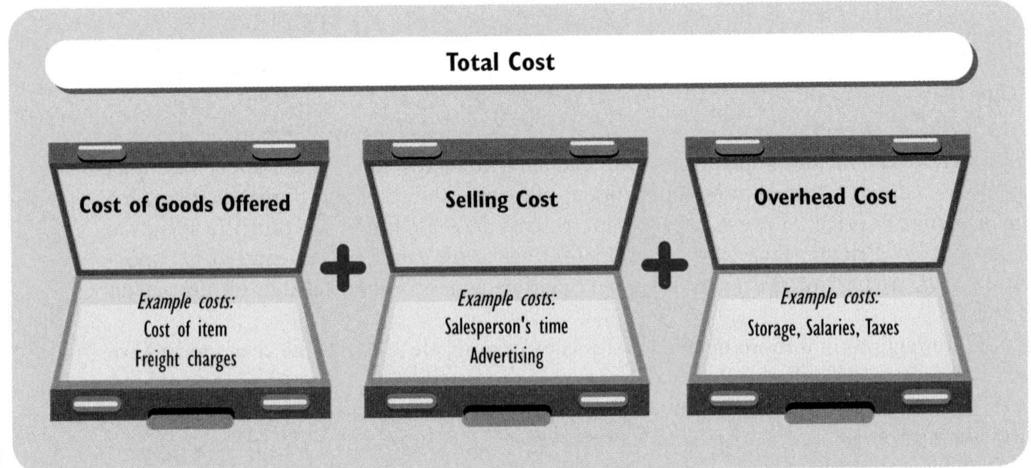

are warehouse storage, office supplies, utilities, taxes, and employee salaries and wages. *All* of these cost classifications must be incorporated into the pricing process.

Costs behave differently as the quantity produced or sold increases or decreases. **Total variable costs** are those that increase in total as the quantity of product increases. Material costs and sales commissions are typical variable costs incurred as a product is made and sold. **Total fixed costs** are those that remain constant at different levels of quantity sold. For example, advertising campaign expenditures, factory equipment costs, and salaries of office personnel are fixed costs.

total variable costs
Costs that vary with the quantity produced or sold

total fixed costs
Costs that remain constant as the quantity produced or sold varies

An understanding of the behavior of different kinds of costs can help a seller minimize pricing mistakes. Although fixed and variable costs do not behave in the same way, small businesses often treat them identically. An approach called average pricing exemplifies this high-risk practice. With **average pricing**, you divide the total cost (fixed costs plus variable costs) over a previous period by the quantity sold in that period to arrive at an average cost, which is then used to set the current price. For example, consider the cost structure of a firm selling 25,000 units of a product in 2004 at a sales price of $8.00 each (see Exhibit 15-2). The average unit cost at the 2004 sales volume of 25,000 units is $5.00 (that is, $125,000 ÷ 25,000). The $3.00 markup provides a profit at this sales volume (25,000 × $3 = $75,000).

average pricing
An approach in which total cost for a given period is divided by quantity sold in that period to set a price

However, the impact on profit will be great if sales in 2005 reach only 10,000 units and the selling price has been set at the same $3.00 markup, based on the average cost in 2004 (see Exhibit 15-3). At the lower sales volume (10,000 units), the average unit cost increases to $9.50 (that is, $95,000 ÷ 10,000). This increase is, of course, attributable to the need to spread the constant fixed cost over fewer units. *Average pricing overlooks the reality of higher average costs at lower sales levels.*

On rare occasions, pricing at less than total cost can be used as a special short-term strategy. Suppose some fixed costs are ongoing even if part of the production facility is temporarily idle. In this situation, pricing should cover all marginal or incremental costs—that is, those costs incurred specifically to get additional business. In the long run, however, all costs must be covered.

How Customer Demand Affects Pricing

Cost analysis can identify a level below which a price should not be set for normal purposes: a minimum price. However, it does not show how much the final price might exceed that minimum figure and still be acceptable to customers. Demand factors must be considered before this determination can be made.

elasticity of demand
The degree to which a change in price affects the quantity demanded

elastic demand
Demand that changes significantly when there is a change in the price of the product

inelastic demand
Demand that does not change significantly when there is a change in the price of the product

ELASTICITY OF DEMAND Customer demand for a product is often sensitive to the price level. *Elasticity* is the term used to describe this sensitivity, and the effect of a change in price on the quantity demanded is called **elasticity of demand.** A product is said to have **elastic demand** if an increase in its price *lowers* total revenue or a decrease in its price *raises* total revenue. A product is said to have **inelastic demand** if an increase in its price *raises* total revenue or a decrease in its price *lowers* total revenue.

In some markets, the demand for products is very elastic. With a lower price, the amount purchased increases sharply, thus providing higher revenue. For example, in the personal computer industry, a decrease in price will frequently produce a more than

15-2 *Cost Structure of a Hypothetical Firm, 2004*

Sales revenue (25,000 units @ $8)		$200,000
Total costs:		
Fixed costs	$75,000	
Variable costs ($2 per unit)	50,000	
		125,000
Gross margin		$ 75,000

$$\text{Average cost} = \frac{\$125{,}000}{25{,}000} = \$5$$

15-3 *Cost Structure of a Hypothetical Firm, 2005*

Sales revenue (10,000 units @ $8)		$80,000
Total costs:		
Fixed costs	$75,000	
Variable costs ($2 per unit)	20,000	
		95,000
Gross margin		($15,000)

$$\text{Average cost} = \frac{\$95{,}000}{10{,}000} = \$9.50$$

proportionate increase in quantity sold, resulting in higher total revenues. For products such as salt, however, the demand is highly inelastic. Regardless of price, the quantity purchased will not change significantly, because consumers use a fixed amount of salt.

The concept of elasticity of demand is important because the degree of elasticity sets limits on or provides opportunities for higher pricing. A small firm should seek to distinguish its product or service in such a way that small price increases will incur little resistance from customers and thereby yield increasing total revenue.

PRICING AND A FIRM'S COMPETITIVE ADVANTAGE Several factors affect the attractiveness of a product or service to customers. One factor is the firm's competitive advantage—a concept discussed in Chapter 3. If consumers perceive the product or service as an important solution to their unsatisfied needs, they will demand more.

Only rarely will competing firms offer identical products and services. In most cases, products differ in some way. Even if products are physically similar, the accompanying services typically differ. Speed of service, credit terms offered, delivery arrangements, personal attention from a salesperson, and warranties are but a few of the factors that distinguish one product from another. A unique and attractive combination of goods and services may well justify a higher price.

prestige pricing
Setting a high price to convey an image of high quality or uniqueness

A pricing tactic that reflects competitive advantage is **prestige pricing**—setting a high price to convey an image of high quality or uniqueness. Its influence varies from market to market and product to product. Because higher income markets are less sensitive to price variations than lower income ones, prestige pricing typically works better in high-income markets.

Products sold in markets with low levels of product knowledge are also good candidates for prestige pricing. When customers have low product knowledge, they often use price as a surrogate indicator of quality. For example, a company selling windshield-washer fluid found that the product cost pennies to manufacture and, therefore, was profitable even when sold at a very low price. However, the firm recognized an opportunity and raised its price repeatedly, making prestige pricing extremely profitable. Another example is found in the testimony of Chris J. Ketron, owner of Gallery House Furniture in Bristol, Virginia:

> *We . . . were bringing in around $30,000 monthly in revenues—a tiny amount next to the megadollars in my area. I thought that lowering my prices would enable me to compete better. What I found out was that my price cutting provoked a "must be something wrong with it" attitude among my customers. I ditched the lower prices and started to display higher-end merchandise. . . . I'm now doing . . . more in sales . . . and I'm selling fewer pieces to get it.*[1]

APPLYING A PRICING SYSTEM

2 Apply break-even analysis and markup pricing.

A typical entrepreneur is unprepared to evaluate a pricing system until he or she understands potential costs, revenue, and product demand for the venture. To better comprehend these factors and to determine the acceptability of various prices, the entrepreneur can use break-even analysis. An understanding of markup pricing is also valuable, as it provides the entrepreneur with an awareness of the pricing practices of intermediaries—wholesalers and retailers.

Break-Even Analysis

Break-even analysis enables the entrepreneur to compare alternative cost and revenue estimates in order to determine the acceptability of each price. A comprehensive break-even analysis has two phases: (1) examining revenue–cost relationships and (2) incorporating sales forecasts into the analysis. Break-even analysis is typically presented by means of formulas or graphs; this discussion uses a graphic presentation.

EXAMINING COST AND REVENUE RELATIONSHIPS The objective of the first phase of break-even analysis is to determine the sales volume level at which the product, at an assumed price, will generate enough revenue to start earning a profit. Exhibit 15-4(a) presents a simple break-even chart reflecting this comparison. Total fixed costs are represented by a horizontal section at the bottom of the graph, indicating that they do not change with the volume of production. The section for total variable costs is a triangle that slants upward, depicting the direct relationship of total variable costs to output. The entire area below the upward-slanting total cost line represents the combination of fixed and variable costs. The distance between the sales and total cost lines gives the profit or loss position of the company at any level of sales. The point of intersection of these two lines is called the **break-even point**, because sales revenue equals total cost at this sales volume.

break-even point
Sales volume at which total sales revenue equals total costs

To evaluate other break-even points, the entrepreneur can plot additional sales lines for other prices on the chart. On the flexible break-even chart shown in Exhibit 15-4(b), the higher price of $18 yields a more steeply sloped sales line, resulting in an earlier break-even point. Similarly, the lower price of $7 produces a flatter revenue line, delaying the break-even point. Additional sales lines could be plotted to evaluate other proposed prices.

Because it shows the profit area growing larger and larger to the right, the break-even chart implies that quantity sold can increase continually. Obviously, *this assumption is unrealistic* and should be clarified by modifying the break-even analysis with information about the way in which demand is expected to change at different price levels.

15-4 | *Break-Even Graphs for Pricing*

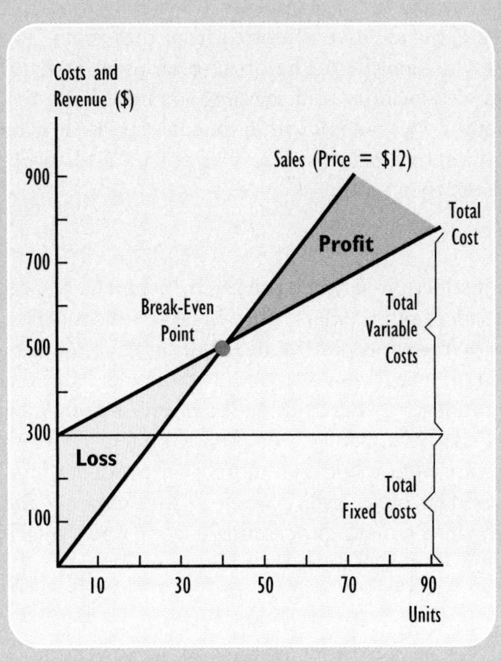

(a)

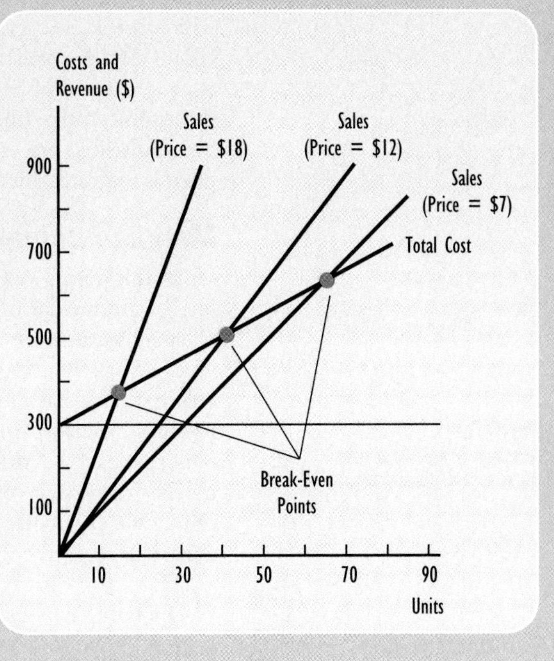

(b)

Living the Dream — *Entrepreneurial Challenges*

Pricing by Software

Small firms have used computer software to perform accounting tasks efficiently for many years. But there is a new twist in small business software: It can now assist small firms with pricing.

One entrepreneur using this new pricing software is Bob Olsen, president of Peregrine Outfitters, a Vermont-based sporting goods wholesaler. His 15-year-old company serves as the intermediary between 600 manufacturers and 1,800 retail stores. As Olsen says, "We have the thinnest margins on the food chain."

With only 38 employees, Olsen lacked the resources to properly analyze factors such as shipping charges and order sizes—factors affecting Peregrine's operating costs and, ultimately, pricing. He decided he needed more information. After purchasing and installing pricing software by Houston-based Acorn Systems in March 2002, he learned that some customers were placing only very small orders that failed to cover Peregrine's costs. By the time salespeople took the calls and located the products, the company was already losing money. Based on this information, Olsen began offering customers a price break for ordering more products in each order. He also learned from the data that by switching from two-day to three-day delivery he could save enough money to cut some prices while maintaining overall margins.

Olsen is convinced the $80,000 software is worth the investment. "What the software's taught us about our business is invaluable," he says.

Source: Madine Heintz, "The Price Is Right," *Inc.*, Vol. 25, No. 7 (July 2003), p. 40. By Madine Heintz, © 2004 Gruner + Jahr USA Publishing. First published in *Inc.* Magazine. Reprinted with permission.

INCORPORATING SALES FORECASTS The indirect impact of price on the quantity that can be sold complicates pricing decisions. Demand for a product typically decreases as price increases. However, in certain cases, price may influence demand in the opposite direction, resulting in increased demand for a product at higher prices. Therefore, estimated demand for a product at various prices, as determined through marketing research (even if it is only an informed guess), should be incorporated into the break-even analysis.

An adjusted break-even chart that incorporates estimated demand is developed by using the initial break-even data and adding a demand curve. A schedule showing the estimated number of units demanded and total revenue at three prices is shown in Exhibit 15-5, along with a break-even graph on which a demand curve is plotted from these data. This graph allows a more realistic profit area to be identified. The break-even point in Exhibit 15-5 for a unit price of $18 corresponds to a quantity sold that appears impossible to reach at the assumed price (the break-even point does not fall within the sales curve), leaving $7 and $12 as feasible prices. Clearly, the preferred price is $12. The potential for profit at this price is indicated by the shaded area in the graph.

Markup Pricing

Up to this point, we have made no distinction between pricing by manufacturers and pricing by intermediaries such as wholesalers and retailers, since break-even concepts apply to all small businesses, regardless of their position in the distribution channel. Now, however, we briefly present some of the pricing formulas used by wholesalers and retailers in setting their prices. In the retailing industry, where businesses often carry many different products, **markup pricing** has emerged as a manageable pricing system. With this cost-plus approach to pricing, retailers are able to price hundreds of products much more quickly than they could using individual break-even analyses. In calculating the selling price for a particular item, a retailer adds a markup percentage (sometimes referred to as a markup rate) to cover the following:

markup pricing
Applying a percentage to a product's cost to obtain its selling price

- Operating expenses
- Subsequent price reductions—for example, markdowns and employee discounts
- Desired profit

15-5 A Break-Even Graph Adjusted for Estimated Demand

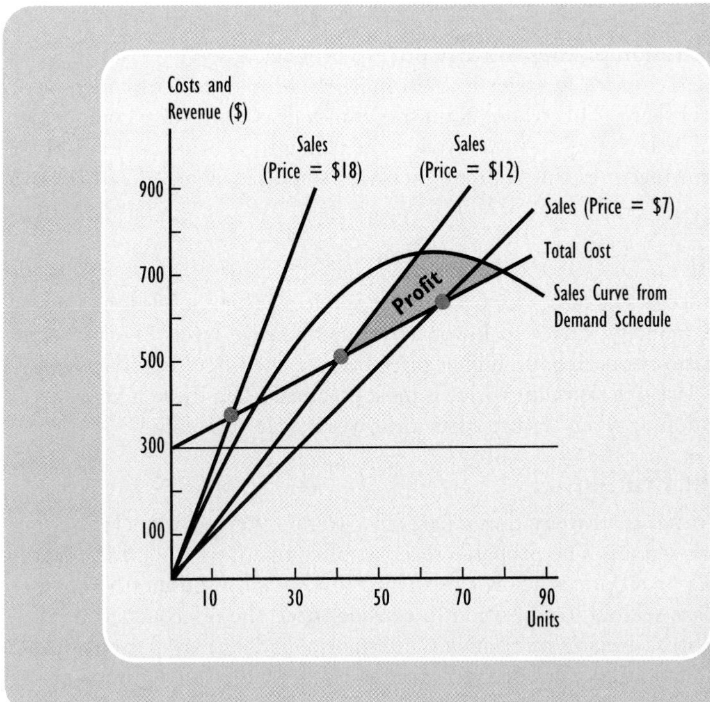

Price ($)	Demand (Units)	Revenue ($)
7	90	630
12	60	720
18	15	270

It is important to have a clear understanding of markup pricing computations. Markups may be expressed as a percentage of either the *selling price* or the *cost*. For example, if an item costs $6 and sells for $10, the markup of $4 represents a 40 percent markup of the selling price [($4 markup ÷ $10 selling price) × 100] or a 66⅔ percent markup of the cost [($4 markup ÷ $6 cost) × 100]. Two simple formulas are commonly used for markup calculations:

$$\frac{\text{Markup}}{\text{Selling price}} \times 100 = \text{Markup expressed as a percentage of selling price}$$

or

$$\frac{\text{Markup}}{\text{Cost}} \times 100 = \text{Markup expressed as a percentage of cost}$$

To convert markup as a percentage of selling price to markup as a percentage of cost, use the following formula:

$$\frac{\text{Markup as a percentage of selling price}}{100\% - \text{Markup as a percentage of selling price}} \times 100 = \text{Markup expressed as a percentage of cost}$$

To convert the other way, use this formula:

$$\frac{\text{Markup as a percentage of cost}}{100\% + \text{Markups as a percentage of cost}} \times 100 = \text{Markup expressed as a percentage of selling price}$$

SELECTING A PRICING STRATEGY

3 *Identify specific pricing strategies.*

Although techniques such as break-even analysis yield a good idea of a feasible price for a specific product, their seemingly precise nature is potentially misleading. Such analyses are only one kind of tool for pricing and should not by themselves determine the final price. *Price determination must also consider market characteristics and the firm's current marketing strategy.*[2] Pricing strategies that reflect these additional considerations include penetration pricing, skimming pricing, follow-the-leader pricing, variable pricing, price lining, and what the market will bear.

Penetration Pricing

penetration pricing strategy
Setting lower than normal prices to hasten market acceptance of a product or service or to increase market share

A firm that uses a **penetration pricing strategy** prices a product or service at less than its normal, long-range market price in order to gain more rapid market acceptance or to increase existing market share. This strategy can sometimes discourage new competitors from entering a market niche if they mistakenly view the penetration price as a long-range price. Obviously, a firm that uses this strategy sacrifices some profit margin to achieve market penetration.

Skimming Pricing

skimming price strategy
Setting very high prices for a limited period before reducing them to more competitive levels

A **skimming price strategy** sets prices for products or services at high levels for a limited period of time before reducing prices to lower, more competitive levels. This strategy assumes that certain customers will pay a higher price because they view a product or service as a prestige item. Use of a skimming price is most practical when there is little threat of short-term competition or when startup costs must be recovered rapidly.

Follow-the-Leader Pricing

follow-the-leader pricing strategy
Using a particular competitor as a model in setting prices

A **follow-the-leader pricing strategy** uses a particular competitor as a model in setting a price for a product or service. The probable reaction of competitors is a critical factor in determining whether to cut prices below a prevailing level. A small business in competition with larger firms is seldom in a position to consider itself the price leader. If competitors view a small firm's pricing as relatively unimportant, they may permit a price differential to exist. On the other hand, some competitors may view a smaller price-cutter as a direct threat and counter with reductions of their own. In such a case, the use of a follow-the-leader pricing strategy accomplishes very little.

Variable Pricing

variable pricing strategy
Setting more than one price for a good or service in order to offer price concessions to certain customers

Some businesses use a **variable pricing strategy** to offer price concessions to certain customers, even though they may advertise a uniform price. Lower prices are offered for various reasons, including a customer's knowledge and bargaining strength. In some fields of business, therefore, firms make two-part pricing decisions: They set a standard list price but offer a range of price concessions to particular buyers—for example, those that purchase large quantities of their product.

dynamic pricing strategy
Charging more than the standard price when the customer's profile suggests that the higher price will be accepted

Sellers using a type of variable pricing strategy called a **dynamic pricing strategy** charge *more* than the standard price after gauging a customer's financial means and desire for the product. The information-gathering capability of the Internet has allowed such retailers as Amazon.com to use dynamic pricing. Consider this account of Amazon.com's pricing strategy:

> *The Internet was supposed to empower consumers, letting them compare deals with the click of a mouse. But it is also supplying retailers with information about their customers that they never had before, along with the technology to use all this accumulated data. While prices have always varied by geography, local competition and whim, retailers were never able to effectively target individuals until the Web.*
>
> *"Dynamic pricing is the new reality, and it's going to be used by more and more retailers," said Vernon Keenan, a San Francisco Internet consultant. "In the future, what you pay will be determined by where you live and who you are. It's unfair, but that doesn't mean it's not going to happen."*
>
> *With its detailed records on the buying habits of 23 million consumers, Amazon is perfectly situated to employ dynamic pricing on a massive scale. But its trial ran into a snag . . . when the regulars discussing DVDs at the Web site DVDTalk.com noticed something odd.*
>
> *One man recounted how he ordered the DVD of Julie Taymor's "Titus," paying $24.49. The next week he went back to Amazon and saw that the price had jumped to $26.24. As an experiment, he stripped his computer of the electronic tags that identified him to Amazon as a regular customer. Then the price fell to $22.74.*[3]

Price Lining

A **price lining strategy** establishes distinct price categories at which similar items of retail merchandise are offered for sale. For example, men's suits (of differing quality) might be sold at $250, $450, and $800. The amount of inventory stocked at different quality levels would depend on the income levels and buying desires of a store's customers. A price lining strategy has the advantage of simplifying the selection process for the customer and reducing the necessary minimum inventory.

price lining strategy
Setting a range of several distinct merchandise price levels

What the Market Will Bear

The strategy of pricing on the basis of what the market will bear can be used only when the seller has little or no competition. Obviously, this strategy will work only for nonstandardized products. For example, a food store might offer egg roll wrappers that its competitors do not carry. Busy consumers who want to fix egg rolls but have neither the time nor the knowledge to prepare the wrappers themselves will buy them at any reasonable price.

A Final Note on Price Strategies

In some situations, local, state, and federal laws must be considered in setting prices. For example, the Sherman Antitrust Act generally prohibits price fixing. Most federal pricing legislation is intended to benefit small firms as well as consumers by keeping large businesses from conspiring to set prices that stifle competition.

When a small business markets a line of products, some of which may compete with each other, pricing decisions must take into account the effects of a single product price on the rest of the line. For example, the introduction of a cheese-flavored chip will likely affect sales of an existing naturally flavored chip. Pricing can become extremely complex in these situations.

Continually adjusting a price to meet changing marketing conditions can be both costly to the seller and confusing to buyers. An alternative approach is to use a system of discounting designed to reflect a variety of needs. For example, a seller may offer a trade discount to a particular buyer (such as a wholesaler) because that buyer performs a certain

Living the Dream — *Focus on the Customer*

Value Pricing

Entrepreneurs sometimes price their products and services too low, creating customer expectations that are difficult to escape later on. Synergy Investment, now headquartered in Westborough, Massachusetts, encountered this problem. The firm, founded in 1994 by Daniel Gould, age 25, provides turnkey implementation of personalized energy-efficient solutions for lighting and building systems.

This startup created a niche in which there were few competitors. However, a low pricing strategy kept Gould hustling, offering his customers what he calls "the Wal-Mart attitude—give them rock-bottom prices all the time." Using this strategy, Gould found that he didn't have much to show for all his work. "Basically, I was giving it away," he says. With more experience came recognition of the true value of his service. Gould realized, "I could've charged more, and people wouldn't have blinked."

Gould, now 33, has continually raised his prices over the past few years but remains a low-cost provider. "When I started the business, I was happy just to draw a salary," he says. "It's been a slow awakening to what is necessary to charge to be slightly profitable by the end of the year." The company, with a team of 24 people, generated close to $12 million in sales in 2003.

Synergy has performed lighting service for clients such as Macy's; Verizon; Bed, Bath and Beyond; and the Pepsi Bottling Group. The firm was ranked number 219 on the *Inc. 2000* list of the 500 fastest growing companies in America.

http://www.synergyinv.com

Sources: http://www.synergyinv.com, October 11, 2003; and Rifka Rasenwein, "If Only . . . ," *Inc. 2000*, Vol. 22, No. 15 (October 17, 2000), p. 104. By Rifka Rasenwein, © 2004 Gruner + Jahr USA Publishing. First published in *Inc.* Magazine. Reprinted with permission.

marketing function for the seller (such as distribution). The stated, or list, price is unchanged, but the seller offers a lower actual price by means of a discount.

Small firms should not treat bad pricing decisions as uncorrectable mistakes. Remember, pricing is not an exact science. *If the initial price appears to be off target, make any necessary adjustments and keep on selling!*

OFFERING CREDIT

4 *Explain the benefits of credit, factors that affect credit extension, and types of credit.*

In a credit sale, the seller provides goods or services to the buyer in return for the buyer's promise to pay later. The major reason for granting credit is to make sales; credit encourages decisions to buy by providing an incentive for customers to buy now and pay later. Most firms offering credit actively promote this option to potential customers. An added bonus to the seller is credit records containing customer information that can be used for sales promotion, such as direct-mail appeals to customers.

Benefits of Credit

If credit buying and selling did not benefit both parties in a transaction, their use would cease. Borrowers obviously enjoy the availability of credit, and small firms, in particular, benefit from the extension of credit by their suppliers. Credit provides small firms with working capital, often allowing marginal businesses to continue operations. Additional benefits of credit to borrowers are as follows:

- The ability to satisfy immediate needs and pay for them later
- Better records of purchases on credit billing statements
- Better service and greater convenience when exchanging purchased items
- Establishment of a credit history

Traditional short-term creditors include suppliers and local banks. These lenders extend credit to small businesses in order to facilitate increased sales volume and also to earn money on unpaid balances. They expect the increased revenue to more than offset the costs of extending credit, so profits will increase. Other benefits of credit to sellers are as follows:

- Closer association with customers because of implied trust
- Easier selling through telephone- and mail-order systems and over the Internet
- Smoother sales peaks and valleys, since purchasing power is always available
- Easy access to a tool with which to stay competitive

Factors That Affect Selling on Credit

An entrepreneur must decide whether to sell on credit or for cash only. In many cases, credit selling cannot be avoided, as it is standard trade practice in many types of business. It is important to note that in today's marketplace credit-selling competitors will almost always outsell a cash-only firm.

Although a seller always hopes to increase profits by allowing credit sales, it is not a risk-free practice. Small firms frequently shift or at least share credit risk by accepting credit cards carried by customers rather than offering their own credit. For example, the operator of a Texaco gasoline station may accept Texaco credit cards and other major credit cards, thereby avoiding credit management. The business will pay a fee to the credit card company, but that cost may be less than the expense of managing its own independent credit system, especially when losses from bad debts are factored in. A retailer following this strategy must obtain merchant status with individual credit card companies. This is not an automatic process and can be problematic, particularly for home-based businesses.

Unfortunately, the cost of accepting major credit cards for payment over the Internet has increased. To deal with Internet fraud, small e-retailers turn to third-party firms that specialize in handling Internet credit card payments. These firms provide a degree of fraud protection for the small business. First-time entrepreneur Margaret Cobbs, founder

Living the Dream

Entrepreneurial Challenges

Give Me Credit

Courtesy of Tommy Wald/NetForce Technologies

Riata Technologies, formerly NetForce Technologies, was founded in 1993 in Austin, Texas, by Tommy Wald. The firm was one of the first independent computer network consulting firms in the area. Seven years later, Riata was number 290 on the *Inc. 2000* list of the 500 fastest growing firms. Its growth was partially subsidized by credit received from various lenders.

In its startup days, obtaining a line of credit was not always easy. Some banks rejected Wald's credit applications because they thought the firm was too small (Riata now has 27 employees). Later, banks spurned credit requests from Riata because they thought that the firm was saddled with too many asset restrictions required by existing Small Business Administration loans.

In 1998, the company once again sought help from banks, as the firm was in desperate need of a larger line of credit. The negotiations shocked Riata's comptroller, Sherri Holland. At one bank, where the salesperson had promised no hidden fees, she discovered that "receivables financing involved cash-management fees: $85 a month for a lock box, 40 cents per check deposited in the lock box, $15 a month for account processing, and $75 a month for the ability to check postings online." The requirement of a lock box meant that all of Riata's accounts receivable payments would automatically go toward paying off the credit line, effectively transferring all control to the bank.

Understandably, Holland was unhappy with these conditions and turned down all offers. Finally, she sought out an investment bank, which eventually extended a $300,000 line of credit. This investment bank doesn't require a lock box, nor do its fees fluctuate based on a monthly accounts receivable review.

Revenue in 2002 was $5.8 million. Wald is proud that his business has finally passed the point of relying on federal and bank loans. "It makes you feel good," he says, "that you can finally graduate to that level of respect."

http://www.riata-tech.com

Sources: Ilan Machari, "Who Needs a Bank Anyway?" *Inc.*, Vol. 22, No. 2 (February 2000), pp. 129–130; http://www.riata-tech.com, October 11, 2003; and "Netforce Changes to Riata," http://austin.bizjournals.com, August 31, 2001.

of Velma Handbags in Redwood City, California, recently had a brush with Internet fraud when someone in Romania attempted to purchase several handbags from the Web site using a stolen credit card. Fortunately, the theft was stopped by CCNow, a Delaware-based Internet credit card service employed by Velma Handbags. This service, however, carries a relatively high price: CCNow collects 9 percent of every sale that Velma Handbags makes online. "That kind of makes you ache," says Cobbs.[4] Examples of other credit card–processing companies include Charge.com, eCommerce Exchange, Merchant Accounts Express, and the Canadian corporation InternetSecure, Inc.

Also, if a small firm makes credit sales online, it is subject to "chargebacks" whenever buyers dispute a transaction. Some credit card companies assess fines and threaten account termination if the number of chargebacks is excessive.

Four factors related to the entrepreneur's decision to extend credit are the type of business, credit policies of competitors, customers' income levels, and the availability of working capital.

TYPE OF BUSINESS Retailers of durable goods typically grant credit more freely than do small grocers that sell perishables or small restaurants that serve primarily local customers. Indeed, most consumers find it necessary to buy big-ticket items on an installment basis, and such a product's life span makes installment selling feasible.

CREDIT POLICIES OF COMPETITORS Unless a firm offers some compensating advantage, it is expected to be as generous as its competitors in extending credit. Wholesale hardware companies and retail furniture stores are examples of businesses that face stiff competition from credit sellers.

INCOME LEVEL OF CUSTOMERS The age and income level of a retailer's customers are significant factors in determining its credit policy. For example, a drugstore adjacent to a high school might not extend credit to high school students, who are typically undesirable credit customers because of their lack of maturity and income.

AVAILABILITY OF WORKING CAPITAL There is no denying that credit sales increase the amount of working capital needed by the business doing the selling. Open-credit and installment accounts tie up money that may be needed to pay business expenses.

Types of Credit

consumer credit
Financing granted by retailers to individuals who purchase for personal or family use

trade credit
Financing provided by a supplier of inventory to a given company

There are two broad classes of credit: consumer credit and trade credit. **Consumer credit** is granted by retailers to final consumers who purchase for personal or family use. A small business owner can sometimes use his or her personal consumer credit to purchase supplies and equipment for use in the business. **Trade credit** is extended by nonfinancial firms, such as manufacturers and wholesalers, to business firms that are customers. Consumer credit and trade credit differ with respect to types of credit instruments, the paperwork, sources for financing receivables, and terms of sale. Another important distinction is that credit insurance is available only for trade credit.

A recent study of credit and small business, sponsored by the National Federation of Independent Business, reports extensively on credit use by small firms.[5] For example, the survey found that 45 percent of small business owners feel that their most significant problem in getting paid is slow or late payment.

CONSUMER CREDIT The three major kinds of consumer credit accounts are open charge accounts, installment accounts, and revolving charge accounts. Many variations of these credit accounts are also used.

open charge account
A line of credit that allows the customer to obtain a product at the time of purchase, with payment due when billed

Open Charge Accounts When using an **open charge account**, a customer obtains possession of goods (or services) at the time of purchase, with payment due when billed. Stated terms typically call for payment at the end of the month, but it is customary to allow a longer period than that stated. There is no finance charge for this kind of credit if the balance on the account is paid in full at the end of the billing period. Customers are not generally required to make a down payment or to pledge collateral. Small accounts at department stores are good examples of open charge accounts.

installment account
A line of credit that requires a down payment, with the balance paid over a specified period of time

Installment Accounts An **installment account** is a vehicle for long-term consumer credit. A down payment is normally required, and annual finance charges can be 20 percent or more of the purchase price. Payment periods are commonly from 12 to 36 months, although automobile dealers often offer an extended payment period of 60 months or even longer. An installment account is useful for large purchases such as cars, washing machines, and televisions.

revolving charge account
A line of credit on which the customer may charge purchases at any time, up to a preestablished limit

Revolving Charge Accounts A **revolving charge account** is a variation of the installment account. A seller grants a customer a line of credit, and charged purchases may not exceed the credit limit. A specified percentage of the outstanding balance must be paid monthly, forcing the customer to budget and limiting the amount of debt that can be carried. Finance charges are computed on the unpaid balance at the end of the month. Although credit cards offer this type of account, they are discussed separately in the next section because of their significance.

CREDIT CARDS Credit cards, frequently referred to as plastic money, have become a major source of retail credit. As just mentioned, credit cards are usually based on a revolving charge account system. Based on the sponsor, we can distinguish three basic types of credit cards: bank credit cards, entertainment credit cards, and retailer credit cards.

Bank Credit Cards The best known bank credit cards are MasterCard and VISA. Bank credit cards are widely accepted by retailers that want to offer credit but don't provide their own credit cards. Most small business retailers fit into this category. In return for a set fee (usually 2 to 5 percent of the purchase price) paid by the retailer, the bank takes the responsibility for making collections. Some banks charge annual membership fees to their cardholders. Also, cardholders are frequently able to obtain cash up to the credit limit of their card.

Entertainment Credit Cards Well-known examples of entertainment credit cards are American Express and Diner's Club cards. While these cards have traditionally charged an annual fee, American Express recently started offering the Blue Card, which has no fee for use. Originally used for services, these cards are now widely accepted for sales of merchandise. As with bank credit cards, the collection of charges on an entertainment credit card is the responsibility of the sponsoring agency.

Retailer Credit Cards Many companies—for example, department stores, oil companies, and telephone companies—issue their own credit cards for specific use in their outlets or for purchasing their products or services from other outlets. Customers are usually not charged annual fees or finance charges if their balance is paid each month.

TRADE CREDIT Firms selling to other businesses may specify terms of sale, such as 2/10, net 30. This means that a 2 percent discount is given by the seller if the buyer pays within 10 days of the invoice date. Failure to take this discount makes the full amount of the invoice due in 30 days. For example, with these terms, a buyer paying for a $100,000 purchase within 10 days of the invoice date would save 2 percent, or $2,000.

Sales terms for trade credit depend on the product sold and the buyer's and the seller's circumstances. The credit period often varies directly with the length of the buyer's turnover period, which obviously depends on the type of product sold. The larger the order and the higher the credit rating of the buyer, the better the sales terms will be, assuming that individual terms are fixed for each buyer. The greater the financial strength and the more adequate and liquid the working capital of the seller, the more generous the seller's sales terms can be. Of course, no business can afford to allow competitors to outdo it in reasonable generosity of sales terms. In many types of business, terms are so firmly set by tradition that a unique policy is difficult, if not impossible, for a small firm to implement.

MANAGING THE CREDIT PROCESS

5 *Describe the activities involved in managing credit.*

Unfortunately, many small firms pay little attention to their credit management systems until bad debts become a problem. Often, this is too late. Credit management should precede the first credit sale (in the form of a thorough screening process) and then continue throughout the credit cycle.

As mentioned previously, many small firms transfer all or part of the credit function to another party. For example, a small repair shop or retail clothing store that accepts VISA or MasterCard is transferring much of the credit risk; in effect, the fee that the business pays the credit card company covers the credit management process. Nevertheless, a number of small firms want to offer their own credit to their customers and, therefore, need to understand the credit function. Let's take a look at some of the major considerations in developing and operating a comprehensive credit management program for a small business.

Evaluation of Credit Applicants

In most retail stores, the first step in credit investigation is having the customer complete an application form. The information obtained on this form is used as the basis for examining an applicant's creditworthiness. Since the most important factor in determining a customer's credit limit is her or his ability to pay the obligation when it becomes due, it is crucial to evaluate the customer's financial resources, debt position, and income level. The amount of credit requested also requires careful consideration. Drugstore customers usually need only small amounts of credit. On the other hand, business customers of wholesalers and manufacturers typically expect large credit lines. In the special case of installment selling, the amount of credit should not exceed the repossession value of the goods sold. Automobile dealers follow this rule as a general practice.

Living the Dream

Entrepreneurial Challenges

It's Collection Time

Courtesy of Parker LePla

Entrepreneurs who operate firms offering customer credit must anticipate a time when they may feel the pinch of reduced cash flow as they wait for payment.

Back in 2001, when the Internet bubble burst, accounts receivable started to accrue at Lynn Parker's public relations and branding firm. "We had several hundred thousand dollars in overdue accounts . . . our chances of ever seeing the money they owed us [went belly up]," says Parker, 45, cofounder of the Seattle-based Parker LePla. "We knew we were going to have to make collecting accounts receivable a priority."

Parker created an efficient collection plan, ranging from simple e-mails from the account executive to the stronger tactic of giving the matter to an attorney. "We instituted a flow-chart process indicating what steps each employee should take for every day the account was overdue 30 days," said Parker. The results? Accounts over 90 days old shrank from $450,000 to $45,000 in six months.

An effective plan should become an indispensable and permanent part of every business. "It's good, common-sense business," says Parker.

Source: Sean P. Melvin, "It's Payback Time," *Entrepreneur*, April 2002, pp. 67–68. Reprinted with permission.

THE FOUR CREDIT QUESTIONS In evaluating the credit status of applicants, a seller must answer the following questions:

1. Can the buyer pay as promised?
2. Will the buyer pay?
3. If so, when will the buyer pay?
4. If not, can the buyer be forced to pay?

The answers to these questions have to be based in part on the seller's estimate of the buyer's ability and willingness to pay. Such an estimate constitutes a judgment of the buyer's inherent creditworthiness. For credit to be approved, the answers to questions 1, 2, and 4 should be "yes" and the answer to question 3 should be "on schedule."

Every applicant is creditworthy to some degree; a decision to grant credit merely recognizes the buyer's credit standing. But the seller must consider the possibility that the buyer will be unable or unwilling to pay. When evaluating an applicant's credit status, therefore, the seller must decide how much risk of nonpayment to assume.

THE TRADITIONAL FIVE C'S OF CREDIT Ability to pay is evaluated in terms of the five C's of credit: character, capital, capacity, conditions, and collateral.

- *Character* refers to the fundamental integrity and honesty that should underlie all human and business relationships. For business customers, character is embodied in the business policies and ethical practices of the firm. Individual customers who are granted credit must be known to be morally responsible persons.
- *Capital* consists of the cash and other liquid assets owned by the customer. A prospective business customer should have sufficient capital to underwrite planned operations, including an appropriate amount invested by the owner.
- *Capacity* refers to the customer's ability to conserve assets and faithfully and efficiently follow a financial plan. A business customer should utilize its invested capital wisely and capitalize to the fullest extent on business opportunities.
- *Conditions* refer to such factors as business cycles and changes in price levels, which may be either favorable or unfavorable to the payment of debts. For example,

economic recession places a burden on both businesses' and consumers' abilities to pay their debts. Other adverse factors that might limit a customer's ability to pay include fires and other natural disasters, strong new competition, and labor problems.

- *Collateral* consists of designated security given as a pledge for fulfillment of an obligation. It is a secondary source for loan repayment in case the borrower's cash flows are insufficient for repaying a loan.

Sources of Credit Information

One of the most important, and most frequently neglected, sources of credit information is a customer's previous credit history. Properly analyzed, credit records show whether a business customer regularly takes cash discounts and, if not, whether the customer's account is typically slow. One small clothing retailer has every applicant reviewed by a Dun & Bradstreet–trained credit manager, who maintains a complete file of D&B credit reports on thousands of customers. Recent financial statements of customers are also on file. These reports, together with the retailer's own credit information, are the basis for decisions on credit sales, with heavy emphasis on the D&B credit reports. Nonretailing firms should similarly investigate credit applicants.

Manufacturers and wholesalers can frequently use a firm's financial statements as an additional source of information. Obtaining maximum value from financial statements requires a careful ratio analysis, which will reveal a firm's working-capital position, profit-making potential, and general financial health (as discussed in Chapter 23).

Pertinent data may also be obtained from outsiders. For example, arrangements may be made with other sellers to exchange credit data. Such credit information exchanges are quite useful for learning about the sales and payment experiences others have had with the seller's own customers or credit applicants.

Another source of credit information for the small firm, particularly about commercial accounts, is the customer's banker. Some bankers willingly supply credit information about their depositors, considering this to be a service that helps those firms or individuals obtain credit in amounts they can successfully handle. Other bankers believe that credit information is confidential and should not be disclosed.

Organizations that may be consulted with reference to credit standings are trade-credit agencies and credit bureaus. **Trade-credit agencies** are privately owned and operated organizations that collect credit information on businesses only, not individual consumers. After analyzing and evaluating the data, trade-credit agencies make credit ratings available to client companies for a fee. Manufacturers and wholesalers are especially interested in Dun & Bradstreet's reference book and credit reports. Dun & Bradstreet, Inc. (http://www.dnb.com), a nationwide, general trade-credit agency, offers a wide array of credit reports, with costs ranging from less than $60 for a Credit Scoring Report to over $120 for a detailed Comprehensive Report. Available to subscribers only, its reference book covers most U.S. businesses and provides a credit rating, an evaluation of financial strength, and other key credit information on each firm.

trade-credit agencies
Privately owned organizations that collect credit information on businesses

Credit bureaus are the most common type of consumer reporting agency. These private companies maintain credit histories on individuals, based on reports from banks, mortgage companies, department stores, and other creditors. These companies make possible the exchange of credit information on persons with previous credit activity. Some credit bureaus do not require a business firm to be a member in order to get a credit report. The fee charged to nonmembers, however, is considerably higher than that charged to members. Most credit bureaus operate on one of the three online data-processing networks: Experian (formerly TRW Credit Data); Equifax, Inc.; or TransUnion Corporation.[6]

credit bureaus
Privately owned organizations that summarize a number of firms' credit experiences with particular individuals

Aging of Accounts Receivable

Many small businesses can benefit from an **aging schedule**, which divides accounts receivable into categories based on the length of time they have been outstanding. Typically, some accounts are current and others are past due. Regular use of an aging schedule allows troublesome collection trends to be spotted so that appropriate actions can be taken. With experience, a small firm can estimate the probabilities of collecting accounts of various ages and use them to forecast cash conversion rates.

aging schedule
A categorization of accounts receivable based on the length of time they have been outstanding

Exhibit 15-6 presents a hypothetical aging schedule for accounts receivable. According to the schedule, four customers have overdue credit, totaling $200,000. Only customer

EXHIBIT 15-6 *Hypothetical Aging Schedule for Accounts Receivable*

	CUSTOMER ACCOUNT NUMBER					
Account Status (Days past due)	**001**	**002**	**003**	**004**	**005**	**Total**
120 days	—	—	$50,000	—	—	$ 50,000
90 days	—	$ 10,000	—	—	—	10,000
60 days	—	—	—	$40,000	—	40,000
30 days	—	20,000	20,000	—	—	40,000
15 days	$50,000	—	10,000	—	—	60,000
Total overdue	$50,000	$ 30,000	$80,000	$40,000	$ 0	$200,000
Not due (beyond discount period)	$30,000	$ 10,000	$ 0	$10,000	$130,000	$180,000
Not due (still in discount period)	$20,000	$100,000	$ 0	$90,000	$220,000	$430,000
Credit rating	A	B	C	A	A	—

005 is current. Customer 003 has the largest amount overdue ($80,000). In fact, the schedule shows that customer 003 is overdue on all charges and has a past record of slow payment (indicated by a credit rating of C). Immediate attention must be given to collecting from this customer. Customer 002 should also be contacted, because, among overdue accounts, this customer has the largest amount ($110,000) in the "Not due" classification. Customer 002 could quickly have the largest amount overdue.

Customers 001 and 004 require a special kind of analysis. Customer 001 has $10,000 more overdue than customer 004. However, customer 004's overdue credit of $40,000, which is 60 days past due, may well have a serious impact on the $100,000 not yet due ($10,000 in the beyond-discount period plus $90,000 still in the discount period). On the other hand, even though customer 001 has $50,000 of overdue credit, this customer's payment is overdue by only 15 days. Also, customer 001 has only $50,000 not yet due ($30,000 in the beyond-discount period plus $20,000 still in the discount period), compared to the $100,000 not yet due from customer 004. Both customers have an A credit rating. In conclusion, customer 001 is a better potential source of cash. Therefore, collection efforts should be focused on customer 004 rather than on customer 001, who may simply need a reminder of the overdue amount of $50,000.

Billing and Collection Procedures

Timely notification of customers regarding the status of their accounts is one of the most effective methods of keeping credit accounts current. Most credit customers pay their bills on time if the creditor provides them with information verifying their credit balance. Failure on the seller's part to send invoices delays payments.

Overdue credit accounts tie up a seller's working capital, prevent further sales to the slow-paying customer, and lead to losses from bad debts. Even if a slow-paying customer is not lost, relations with this customer are strained for a time at least.

A firm extending credit must have adequate billing records and collection procedures if it expects prompt payments. Also, a personal acquaintance between seller and customer must not be allowed to tempt the seller into being less than businesslike in extending further credit and collecting overdue amounts. Given the seriousness of the problem, a small firm must decide whether to undertake collecting past-due accounts directly or turn the task over to an attorney or a collection agency.

Perhaps the most effective weapon in collecting past-due accounts is reminding the debtors that their credit standing may be impaired. Impairment is certain if the account is turned over to a collection agency. Delinquent customers will typically attempt to avoid damage to their credit standing, particularly when it would be known to the business community. This concern underlies and strengthens the various collection efforts of the seller.

A small firm should deal compassionately with delinquent customers. A collection technique that is too threatening not only may fail to work but also could cause the firm to lose the customer or become subject to legal action.

Many business firms have found that the most effective collection procedure consists of a series of steps, each somewhat more forceful than the preceding one. Although the procedure typically begins with a gentle written reminder, subsequent steps may include additional letters, telephone calls, registered letters, personal contacts, and referral to a collection agency or attorney. The timing of these steps may be carefully standardized so that each one automatically follows the preceding one in a specified number of days.

Various ratios can be used to monitor expenses associated with credit sales. The best known and most widely used expense ratio is the **bad-debt ratio**, which is computed by dividing the amount of bad debts by the total amount of credit sales. The bad-debt ratio reflects the efficiency of credit policies and procedures. A small firm may thus compare the effectiveness of its credit management with that of other firms. A relationship exists among bad-debt ratio, profitability, and size of the firm. Small profitable retailers have a much higher bad-debt ratio than large profitable retailers do. In general, the bad-debt losses of small firms range from a fraction of 1 percent of net sales to percentages large enough to put them out of business!

bad-debt ratio
The ratio of bad debts to credit sales

Credit Regulation

The use of credit is regulated by a variety of federal laws, as well as state laws that vary considerably from state to state. Prior to the passage of such legislation, consumers were often confused by credit agreements and were sometimes victims of credit abuse.

By far the most significant piece of credit legislation is the federal Consumer Credit Protection Act, which includes the 1968 Truth-in-Lending Act. Its two primary purposes are to ensure that consumers are informed about the terms of a credit agreement and to require creditors to specify how finance charges are computed. The act requires that a finance charge be stated as an annual percentage rate and that creditors specify their procedures for correcting billing mistakes.

Other federal legislation related to credit management includes the following:

- *The Fair Credit Billing Act* provides protection to credit customers in cases involving incorrect billing. A reasonable time period is allowed for billing errors to be corrected. The act does not cover installment credit.

Living the Dream *Focus on the Customer*

Stick to a Friendly Reminder

Using a customer-friendly approach to collecting accounts can help a small firm build strong client relationships. A friendly, relaxed appeal for payment is frequently better than the old "talk-tough" approach.

An early practitioner of this softer approach to collecting overdue accounts is Jack Renton, who was a credit manager for a construction firm in Australia. There, he learned about "these little stickers that helped speed payments." Renton and his wife, Patience, with help from their three children, began a part-time business printing and selling these stickers in 1965. The stickers, which they sold out of the family garage, feature animal characters and have slogans like "friendly reminder," "we value your business," and "don't like to put the bite on you. . . ." In 1989, barely out of college, the Rentons' son Peter joined the family business, with plans for expansion to the United States.

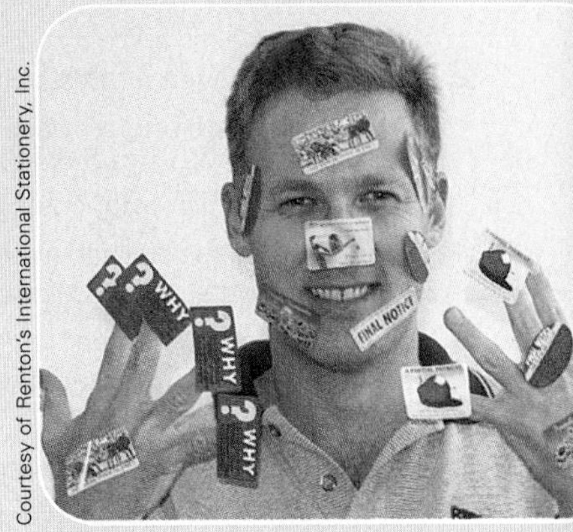

Courtesy of Renton's International Stationery, Inc.

Today, Peter Renton is president of Rentons' International Stationery, Inc., in Denver, Colorado. The company claims to have the largest selection of collection, thank you, and holiday stickers available anywhere. "We believe that business is about people and, in particular, about relationships between people," says Renton.

Beginning with a gentle reminder is a good way to avoid sending customers running in the opposite direction. And the colorful messages of sticker manufacturer Peter Renton help small businesses do just that.

http://www.rentons.com

Source: http://www.rentons.com, October 10, 2003.

- *The Fair Credit Reporting Act* gives certain rights to credit applicants regarding reports prepared by credit bureaus. Amendments such as the FACT Act, signed into law in December 2003, have strengthened privacy provisions and defined more clearly the responsibilities and liabilities of businesses that provide information to credit reporting agencies.
- *The Equal Credit Opportunity Act* ensures that all consumers are given an equal chance to obtain credit. For example, a person is not required to reveal his or her sex, race, national origin, or religion to obtain credit.
- *The Fair Debt Collection Practices Act* bans the use of intimidation and deception in collection, requiring debt collectors to treat debtors fairly.

Pricing and credit decisions are of prime importance to a small firm because of their direct impact on its financial health. *Ultimately, experience will be the entrepreneur's best teacher*, but we hope that the concepts presented in this chapter will help smooth the trip.

Looking Back

1 Discuss the role of cost and demand factors in setting a price.

- The revenue of a firm is a direct reflection of two components: sales volume and price.
- Price must be sufficient to cover total cost plus some margin of profit.
- A firm should examine elasticity of demand—the relationship of price and quantity demanded—when setting a price.
- A product's competitive advantage is a demand factor in setting price.

2 Apply break-even analysis and markup pricing.

- Analyzing costs and revenue under different price assumptions identifies the break-even point, the quantity sold at which total costs equal total revenue.
- The usefulness of break-even analysis is enhanced by incorporating sales forecasts.
- Markup pricing is a generalized cost-plus system of pricing used by intermediaries with many products.

3 Identify specific pricing strategies.

- Penetration pricing and skimming pricing are short-term strategies used when new products are first introduced into the market.
- Follow-the-leader and variable pricing are special strategies that reflect the nature of the competition's pricing and concessions to customers.
- A price lining strategy simplifies choices for customers by offering a range of several distinct prices.
- State and federal laws must be considered in setting prices, as well as any impact that a price may have on other product line items.

4 Explain the benefits of credit, factors that affect credit extension, and types of credit.

- Credit offers potential benefits to both buyers and sellers.
- Type of business, credit policies of competitors, income level of customers, and availability of adequate working capital affect the decision to extend credit.
- The two broad classes of credit are consumer credit and trade credit.

5 Describe the activities involved in managing credit.

- Evaluating the credit status of applicants begins with the completion of an application form.
- A customer's willingness to pay is evaluated through the five C's of credit: character, capital, capacity, conditions, and collateral.
- Pertinent credit data can be obtained from several outside sources, including formal trade-credit agencies such as Dun & Bradstreet.
- An accounts receivable aging schedule can be used to improve the credit collection process.
- A small firm should establish a formal procedure for billing and collecting from charge customers.
- It is important that a small firm follow all relevant credit regulations.

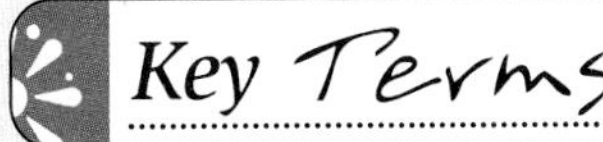

Key Terms

price, p. 331
credit, p. 331
total cost, p. 332
total variable costs, p. 333
total fixed costs, p. 333
average pricing, p. 333
elasticity of demand, p. 333
elastic demand, p. 333
inelastic demand, p. 333
prestige pricing, p. 334
break-even point, p. 335
markup pricing, p. 336
penetration pricing strategy, p. 338
skimming price strategy, p. 338
follow-the-leader pricing strategy, p. 338
variable pricing strategy, p. 338
dynamic pricing strategy, p. 338
price lining strategy, p. 339
consumer credit, p. 342
trade credit, p. 342
open charge account, p. 342
installment account, p. 342
revolving charge account, p. 342
trade-credit agencies, p. 345
credit bureaus, p. 345
aging schedule, p. 345
bad-debt ratio, p. 347

Discussion Questions

1. Why does average pricing sometimes result in a pricing mistake?
2. Explain the importance of total fixed and variable costs to the pricing decision.
3. How does the concept of elasticity of demand relate to prestige pricing? Give an example.
4. If a firm has fixed costs of $100,000 and variable costs per unit of $1, what is the break-even point in units, assuming a selling price of $5 per unit?
5. What is the difference between a penetration pricing strategy and a skimming price strategy? Under what circumstances would each be used?
6. If a small business conducts its break-even analysis properly and finds the break-even volume at a price of $10 to be 10,000 units, should it price its product at $10? Why or why not?
7. What are the major benefits of credit to buyers? What are its major benefits to sellers?
8. How does an open charge account differ from a revolving charge account?
9. What is meant by the terms 2/10, net 30? Does it pay to take discounts when they are offered?
10. What is the major purpose of aging accounts receivable? At what point in credit management should this activity be performed? Why?

You Make the Call

SITUATION 1

Steve Jones is the 35-year-old owner of a highly competitive small business, which supplies temporary office help. Like most businesspeople, he is always looking for ways to increase profit. However, the nature of his competition makes it very difficult to raise prices for the temps' services, while reducing their wages makes recruiting difficult. Jones has, nevertheless, found an area—bad debts—in which improvement should increase profits. A friend and business consultant met with Jones to advise him on credit management policies. Jones was pleased to get this friend's advice, as bad debts were costing him about 2 percent of sales. Currently, Jones has no system for managing credit.

Question 1 What advice would you give Jones regarding the screening of new credit customers?

Question 2 What action should Jones take to encourage current credit customers to pay their debts? Be specific.

Question 3 Jones has considered eliminating credit sales. What are the possible consequences of this decision?

SITUATION 2

Tom Anderson started his records storage business in the New York metropolitan area in 1991. His differentiation strategy was to offer competitive prices while providing state-of-the-art technology, easy access to his warehouse, and, of course, great service.

After opening the business, Anderson learned that most potential customers had already signed long-term storage contracts with competitors. These contracts included a removal fee for each box permanently removed from the storage company's warehouse, making it difficult for customers to consider switching.

Anderson believes that the survival of his company hinges on his view of what the essence of his business is. In other words, is he operating a storage company or a real estate business? He is convinced that he must answer this question before making any decision regarding pricing strategy.

Question 1 What do you think Anderson means when he asks, "Is my business storage or real estate?" Why do you think he feels a need to ask this question prior to developing a pricing strategy?

Question 2 What pricing strategy would be effective in combatting the existing contractual relationships between potential customers and competitors?

Question 3 Assuming that business costs would allow Anderson to lower prices, what problems do you see with this approach?

Question 4 Do you believe his business could benefit from offering credit to customers? Why or why not?

SITUATION 3

Paul Bowlin owns and operates a tree removal, pruning, and spraying business in a large metropolitan area with a population of approximately 200,000. The business started in 1975 and has grown to the point where Bowlin uses one and sometimes two crews, with four or five employees on each crew. Pricing has always been an important tool in gaining business, but Bowlin realizes that there are ways to entice customers other than quoting the lowest price. For example, he provides careful cleanup of branches and leaves, takes out stumps below ground level, and waits until a customer is completely satisfied before taking payment. At the same time, he realizes his bids for tree removal jobs must cover his costs. In this industry, Bowlin faces intense price competition from operators with more sophisticated wood-processing equipment, such as chip grinders. Therefore, he is always open to suggestions about pricing strategy.

Question 1 What would the nature of this industry suggest about the elasticity of demand affecting Bowlin's pricing?

Question 2 What types of costs should Bowlin evaluate when he is determining his break-even point?

Question 3 What pricing strategies could Bowlin adopt to further his long-term success in this market?

Question 4 How can the high quality of Bowlin's work be used to justify somewhat higher price quotes?

Experiential Exercises

1. Interview a small business owner regarding his or her pricing strategy. Try to ascertain whether the strategy being used reflects the total fixed and variable costs of the business. Prepare a report on your findings.
2. Interview a small business owner regarding his or her policies for evaluating credit applicants. Summarize your findings in a report.
3. Interview the credit manager of a retail store about the benefits and drawbacks of extending credit to customers. Report your findings to the class.
4. Ask several small business owners in your community who extend credit to describe the credit management procedures they use to collect bad debts. Report your findings to the class.

Exploring the Web

1. The Marketing Teacher Web site maintains lessons on topics related to marketing. Go to **http://www.marketingteacher.com/Lessons/lesson_pricing.htm** and read the pricing strategies lesson.
   a. After reading the lesson, draw the pricing strategies matrix on a piece of paper.
   b. Click on the "Exercise" link and complete the companion exercise on pricing, placing the six examples in the correct matrix quadrant.
   c. Click on the "Quiz" link and take the 10-question quiz on pricing. Print your quiz results and, if so instructed, turn in your quiz and completed pricing matrix diagram to your instructor.

2. Go to Cleveland-based KeyCorp's Web site at **http://www.key.com**. Key is the largest bank-based financial services firm in the United States. Follow the links from KeyCorp's homepage to "Small Business," then "Solutions Center," "Tools and Resources," "Offering Credit to Your Customers," and "Accepting Credit Cards." Read the short article on boosting sales through achieving merchant status with credit card companies.
   a. What kinds of fees should you expect to be assessed when accepting payment from your customers by credit card?
   b. How might you attempt to lower these fees?

Case 15

WACO COMPOSITES I, LTD. (P. 554)

In this case, a competitor's action motivates a price change by a small manufacturer.

Alternative Case for Chapter 15:

Case 13, Every Customer Counts, p. 550

PROMOTIONAL PLANNING

In the Spotlight

Highland Park Curves

A new business seldom has enough money to fund its promotional needs. While an entrepreneur's creative thinking and hard work can partially compensate for this limitation, one simple alternative is to rely on an assortment of inexpensive media.

Entrepreneurs Joseph and Flora DeRose of Highwood, Illinois, chose this option after purchasing a Curves for Women franchise from the Waco, Texas–based company. Badly in need of name recognition within the community, they felt they couldn't wait to reap the benefits of an upcoming national advertising campaign sponsored by the franchisor. So they purchased ads locally—in print publications, on movie screens, on restaurant placemats, and even in church bulletins.

Courtesy of Curves, Highland Park

These relatively inexpensive media seemed to work well, but Joseph felt, "If you're going to spend money to make people aware of your business, you might as well do something worthwhile at the same time." Therefore, the DeRoses switched some of their promotional focus to sponsoring events like "Food for Friends," which benefits local food pantries, and the American Cancer Society Walk.

The couple also used sales promotional tools to spread the word to potential customers about their fitness business. During the franchise's first year of operation, it distributed over $5,000 worth of shirts, hats, socks, and other promotional items! "We'll continue to find worthwhile ways to benefit others and spread our name at the same time," says Joseph DeRose.

At the end of 2003, the Highland Park Curves franchise had more than 800 members, and the entrepreneurs had purchased a second Curves franchise in nearby Kenosha, Wisconsin.

Source: Cathy Cain-Blank, "Extra! Extra!" *Imprint*, Spring 2004, p. 34.

Chapter 16

After studying this chapter, you should be able to

1 Describe the communication process and the factors determining a promotional mix.

2 Explain methods of determining the appropriate level of promotional expenditure.

3 Describe personal selling activities.

4 Identify advertising options for a small business.

5 Discuss the use of sales promotional tools.

The old adage "Build a better mousetrap and the world will beat a path to your door" suggests that innovation is the foundation of a successful marketing strategy. Unfortunately, the narrow focus of the saying minimizes the roles of other vital marketing activities, such as promotion. Promotion informs customers about any new, improved "mousetrap" and how interested buyers can find the "door." Customers also must be persuaded that the new mousetrap is actually better than their old one. Clearly, entrepreneurs cannot rely on product innovation alone; they need to understand the promotional process in order to develop an effective marketing strategy for their particular "mousetrap."

Let's begin with a simple definition of *promotion.* **Promotion** consists of marketing communications that inform potential consumers about a firm or its product or service and try to persuade them to buy it. Small businesses use promotion in varying degrees; a given firm seldom uses all of the many promotional tools available. In order to simplify our discussion of the promotional process, we group the techniques discussed in this chapter into three traditional categories—personal selling, advertising, and sales promotional tools.

promotion
Marketing communications that inform and persuade consumers

Before examining the categories in the promotional process, let's first look at the basic process of communication that characterizes promotion. If an entrepreneur understands that promotion is just a special form of communication, she or he will be better able to grasp the entire process.

THE COMMUNICATION PROCESS IN PROMOTION

1 Describe the communication process and the factors determining a promotional mix.

Promotion is based on communication. In fact, promotion is wasted unless it effectively communicates a firm's message.

Communication is a process with identifiable components. As shown in Exhibit 16-1, every communication involves a source, a message, a channel, and a receiver. Each of us communicates in many ways each day, and these exchanges parallel small business communications. Part (a) in Exhibit 16-1 depicts a personal communication—parents communicating with their daughter, who is away at college. Part (b) depicts a small business communication—a firm communicating with a customer.

As you can see, many similarities exist between the two. The receiver of the parents' message is their daughter. The parents, the source in this example, use three different channels for their message: e-mail, a personal visit, and a special gift. The receiver of the message from the XYZ Company is the customer. The XYZ Company uses three message channels: a newspaper, a sales call, and a business gift. The parents' e-mail and the company's newspaper advertising both represent nonpersonal forms of communication—there is no face-to-face contact. The parents' visit to their daughter and the sales call made by the company's representative are personal forms of communication. Finally, the flowers and care package and the business gift are both special methods of communication. Thus, the promotional efforts of the small firm, like the communication between parents and

EXHIBIT 16-1 *Similarity of Personal and Small Business Communication Processes*

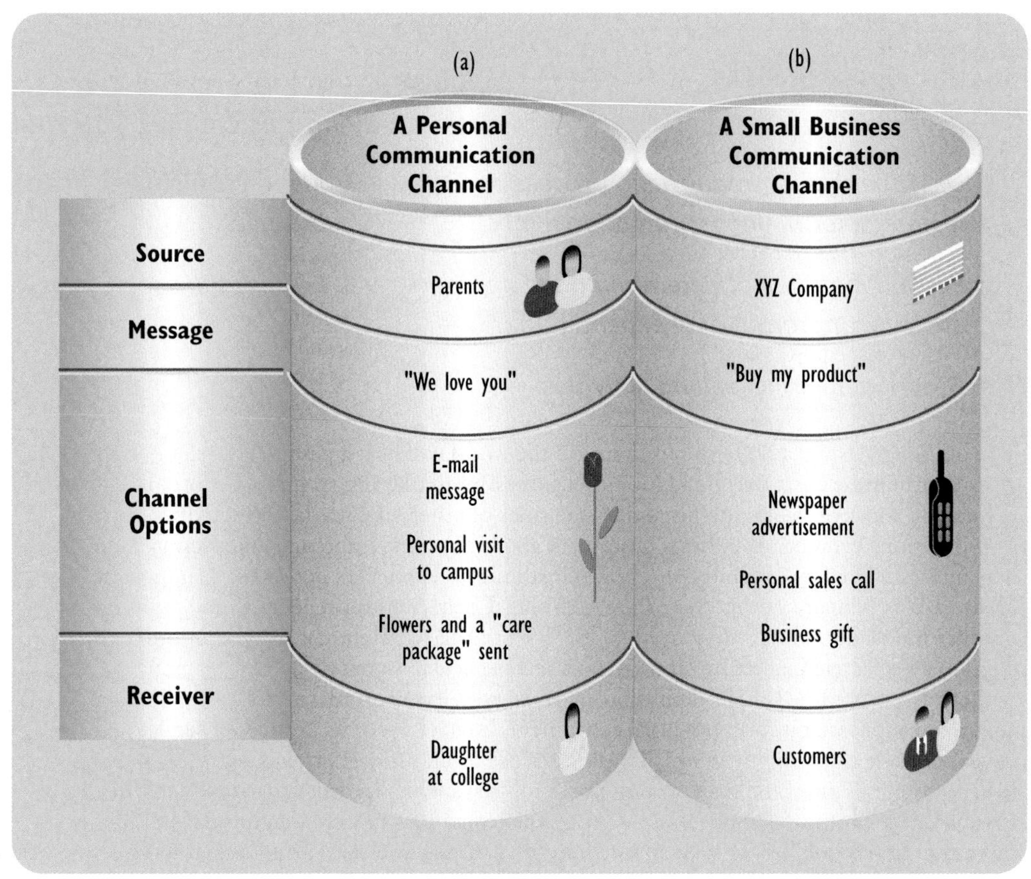

daughter, can be viewed as encompassing nonpersonal (advertising), personal (personal selling), and special (sales promotion) forms of communication.

promotional mix
A blend of nonpersonal, personal, and special forms of communication aimed at a target market

A term commonly used to denote a particular combination of promotional methods is *promotional mix*. A **promotional mix** describes the blend of nonpersonal, personal, and special forms of communication techniques used in a promotional campaign. The particular combination of the various promotional methods—advertising, personal selling, and sales promotional tools—is determined by many factors. One important factor is the geographical nature of the market to be reached. A widely dispersed market generally requires mass coverage through advertising, in contrast to the more costly individual contacts of personal selling. On the other hand, if the market is local or if the number of customers is relatively small, personal selling may be more feasible.

Another factor is the size of the promotional budget. Small firms may not select certain forms of promotion because the costs are just too high. Television advertising, for example, is generally more expensive than radio advertising.

A third factor that heavily influences the promotional mix is the product's characteristics. If a product is of high unit value, such as a mobile home, personal selling will be a vital ingredient in the mix. Personal selling is also an effective method for promoting highly technical products, such as automobiles or street-sweeping machinery, because a customer normally has limited knowledge about such products. On the other hand, nonpersonal advertising is more effective for a relatively inexpensive item, like razor blades.

There are, of course, many other considerations to be evaluated when developing a unique promotional mix. Nevertheless, promotional planning should always strive to begin with the optimum mix of techniques. The entrepreneur can then make any necessary adjustments—for example, by cutting back on the effort or seeking more funds to support the promotional plan.

DETERMINING THE PROMOTIONAL BUDGET

Unfortunately, no mathematical formula can answer the question "How much should a small business spend on promotion?" There are, however, four common sense approaches to budgeting funds for small business promotion:

2 *Explain methods of determining the appropriate level of promotional expenditure.*

1. Allocating a percentage of sales
2. Deciding how much can be spared
3. Spending as much as the competition does
4. Determining what it will take to do the job

Allocating a Percentage of Sales

Often, the simplest method of determining how much to budget for promotion is to earmark promotional dollars based on a percentage of sales. A firm's own past experiences should be evaluated to establish a promotion-to-sales ratio. If 2 percent of sales, for example, has historically been spent on promotion with good results, the firm should budget 2 percent of forecasted sales for future promotion. Secondary data on industry averages can be used for comparison. *Advertising Age* magazine is one of several sources that report what firms are doing with their advertising dollars.

A major shortcoming of this method is an inherent tendency to spend more on promotion when sales are increasing and less when they are declining. If promotion stimulates sales, then reducing promotional spending when sales are down is illogical. Unfortunately, new firms have no historical sales figures on which to base their promotional budgets.

Deciding How Much Can Be Spared

Another piecemeal approach to promotional budgeting widely used by small firms is to spend whatever is left over when all other activities have been funded. The decision about promotional spending might be made only when a media representative sells an owner on a special deal that the business can afford. Such an approach to promotional spending should be avoided because it ignores promotional goals.

Spending as Much as the Competition Does

Sometimes, a small firm builds a promotional budget based on an analysis of competitors' budgets. By duplicating the promotional efforts of close competitors, the business hopes to reach the same customers and will at least be spending as much as the competition. Obviously, if the competitor is a large business, this method is not feasible. However, it can be used to react to short-run promotional tactics by small competitors. Unfortunately, this approach may result in the copying of competitors' mistakes as well as their successes.

Determining What It Will Take to Do the Job

The preferred approach to estimating promotional expenditures is to decide what it will take to do the job. This method requires a comprehensive analysis of the market and the firm's goals. If these estimates are reasonably accurate, the entrepreneur can determine the total amount that needs to be spent.

In many cases, the best way for a small business to set promotional expenditures incorporates all four approaches. In other words, compare the four estimated amounts and set the promotional budget at a level that is somewhere between the maximum and minimum amounts (see Exhibit 16-2). After the budget has been determined, the entrepreneur must then decide how dollars will be spent on the various promotional methods. Which methods are chosen depends on a number of factors. We will now examine personal selling, a frequent choice for small firms.

PERSONAL SELLING IN THE SMALL FIRM

Many products require **personal selling**—promotion delivered in a one-on-one environment. Personal selling includes the activities of both the inside salespeople of retail, wholesale, and service establishments and the outside sales representatives who call on

3 *Describe personal selling activities.*

16-2 *Four-Step Method for Determining a Promotional Budget*

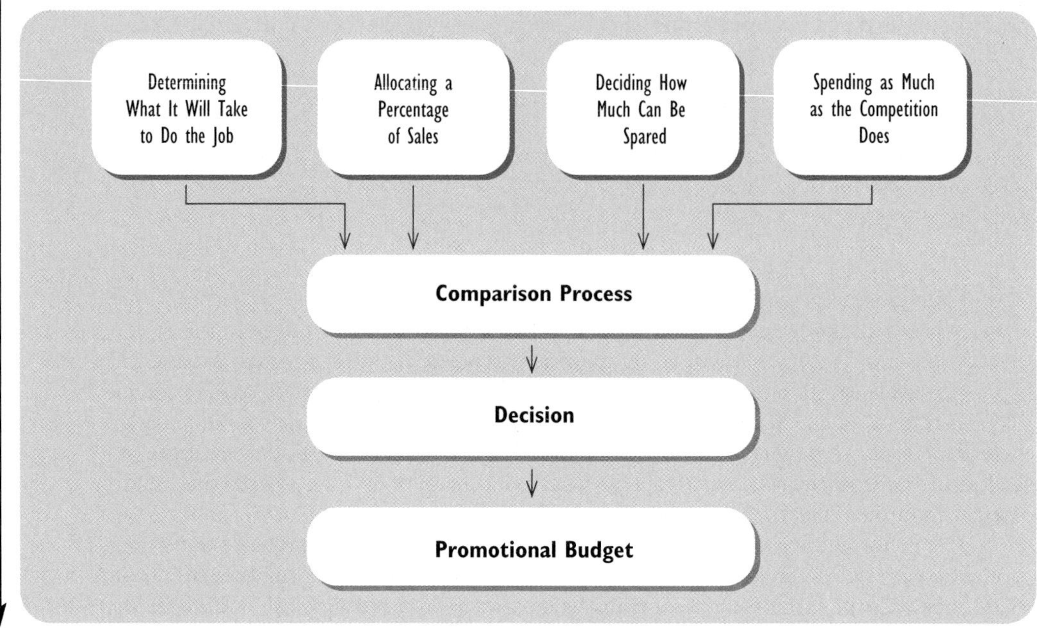

personal selling
A sales presentation delivered in a one-on-one manner

business customers and final consumers. Frequently, the entrepreneur is the primary salesperson for a venture.

The Importance of Product Knowledge

Effective selling is built on a foundation of product knowledge. If a salesperson is well acquainted with a product's advantages, uses, and limitations, she or he can educate customers by successfully answering their questions and countering their objections. Most customers expect a salesperson to provide knowledgeable answers—whether the product is a camera, a coat, an automobile, paint, a machine tool, or office equipment. Customers are seldom experts on the products they buy; however, they can immediately sense a salesperson's knowledge or ignorance. Personal selling degenerates into mere order-taking when a salesperson lacks product knowledge.

The Sales Presentation

The heart of personal selling is the sales presentation to a prospective customer. At this crucial point, an order is either secured or lost. A preliminary step leading to an effective sales presentation is **prospecting**, a systematic process of continually looking for new customers. Prospecting also includes consideration of whether a potential customer can be served by the company.

prospecting
A systematic process of continually looking for new customers

USING PROSPECTING TECHNIQUES One of the most efficient prospecting techniques is obtaining *personal referrals*. Such referrals come from friends, customers, and other businesses. Initial contact with a potential customer is greatly facilitated when the salesperson is able to say, "You were referred to me by . . . ."

Another source of prospects is *impersonal referrals* from media publications, public records, and directories. Newspapers and magazines, particularly trade magazines, often identify prospects by reporting on new companies and new products. Wedding announcements in a newspaper can serve as impersonal referrals for a local bridal shop. Public records of property transactions and building permits can be impersonal referrals for, say, a garbage pick-up service, which might find prospective customers among those planning to build houses or apartment buildings.

Prospects can also be identified without referrals through *marketer-initiated contacts.* Telephone calls or mail surveys, for example, help locate prospects. In a market survey conducted to identify prospects for a small business, an author of this book used a mail

Living the Dream

Entrepreneurial Challenges

Owner Ties Sales Force to Product

Many small firms select personal selling as their means of promotion, because it offers both flexibility and control. Henry Jacobson, for example, uses personal selling to meet the needs of Mulberry Neckwear, of which he is co-founder and CEO.

Jacobson started Mulberry Neckwear in the late 80s with a friend, entrepreneur Katie Smith. Jacobson is the necktie designer, and Smith is the marketing person. They started operations in a room in Jacobson's house, choosing the name Mulberry because silkworms love to eat the leaves of the mulberry shrub.

Mulberry shuns conventional advertising and in-store promotions and instead relies on its own sales force to "work" department store floors. Jacobson believes few department store personnel know "a printed silk tie from a hand-woven one" and for that reason his neckwear needs the retail attention only his sales pros can provide. "Even though you might look at us and say we're a manufacturer, ask anyone who works for us and they'll tell you we're in retail," he says. Tracking sales on a daily basis is important at Mulberry and gives salespeople extra incentives to sell slow-moving brands.

Headquartered in San Rafael, California, the company has more than 100 employees and distributes ties to 1,500 stores nationwide, including almost every major department store in America. Jacobson's use of his salespeople appears to be working well.

http://www.mulberryneckwear.com

Sources: http://www.mulberryneckwear.com/about.html, April 10, 2004; and Michael Fitzgerald, "When Your Neck Is on the Line," *Inc.*, December 2003, pp. 45–46.

questionnaire. The questionnaire, which asked technical questions about a service, concluded with the following statement: "If you would be interested in a service of this nature, please check the appropriate space below and your name will be added to the mailing list."

Finally, prospects can be identified by recording *customer-initiated contacts*. Inquiries by a potential customer that do not lead to a sale can still create a "hot prospect." Small furniture stores often require their salespeople to fill out a card for each person visiting the store. These prospects are then systematically contacted over the telephone or by e-mail, and contact information is updated periodically. Firms with Web sites can similarly follow up on visitors who have made inquiries.

PRACTICING THE SALES PRESENTATION Practicing always improves a salesperson's success rate; after all, "practice makes perfect." Prior to making a sales presentation, a salesperson should give his or her presentation in front of a spouse, a mirror, or a cassette recorder. Even better, he or she may want to use a camcorder to make a practice video.

The salesperson should be aware of possible customer objections to the product and be prepared to handle them. Most objections can be categorized as relating to (1) price, (2) product, (3) timing, (4) source, (5) service, or (6) need. Although there is no substitute for actual selling experience, salespeople find training helpful in learning how to deal with customers' objections. One sales textbook suggests the following techniques for responding to customers' objections.[1] The first two responses are appropriate when a potential buyer states an objection that is factually untrue; the remaining suggestions can be used when a buyer raises a valid objection.

- *Direct denial*: Follow denial by giving facts to back up the denial.
- *Indirect denial*: Follow an expression of concern about the prospect's objection with a denial.
- *Boomerang technique*: Turn the valid objection into a valid reason to buy.
- *Compensation method*: Admit to agreeing with the objection and then proceed to show compensating advantages.
- *Pass-up method*: Acknowledge the concern expressed by the prospect and then move on.

MAKING THE SALES PRESENTATION Salespeople must adapt their sales approach to customers' needs. A "canned" sales talk will not succeed with most buyers. For example, an individual selling personal computers must demonstrate the capacity of the equipment to fill a customer's particular needs. Similarly, a boat salesperson must understand the special interests of particular customers and speak their language. Every sales objection must be answered explicitly and adequately.

Successful selling involves a number of psychological elements. Personal enthusiasm, friendliness, and persistence are required. Approximately 20 percent of all salespeople secure as much as 80 percent of all sales made because they bring these elements to the task of selling.

Some salespeople have special sales techniques that they use with success. One automobile salesperson, for example, offered free driving lessons to people who had never taken a driver's training course or who needed a few more lessons before they felt confident enough to take the required driving test. When such customers were ready to take the driving test, this salesperson would accompany them to the examination to provide moral support. Needless to say, these special efforts were greatly appreciated by new drivers who were in the market for cars.

Customer Goodwill and Relationship Selling

A salesperson must look beyond the immediate sale to building customer goodwill and creating satisfied customers who will continue buying from the company in the future. Selling effectiveness is enhanced when a salesperson displays a good appearance, has a pleasant personality, and uses professional etiquette in all contacts with customers. A salesperson can also build goodwill by listening carefully to the customer's point of view. Courtesy, attention to details, and genuine friendliness will help gain the customer's acceptance.

Of course, high ethical standards are of primary importance in creating customer goodwill. Such standards rule out any misrepresentation of the product and require confidential treatment of a customer's plans.

Cost Control in Personal Selling

Both efficient and wasteful methods exist for achieving a given volume of sales. For example, routing traveling salespeople economically and making appointments prior to arrival can save time and transportation expenses. The cost of an outside sales call on a customer is likely to be considerable—perhaps hundreds of dollars—so efficient scheduling is crucial. Moreover, a salesperson for a manufacturing firm, say, can contribute to cost economy by pushing certain products, thereby giving the factory a more balanced production run. Similarly, a salesperson can increase profits by emphasizing high-margin products.

The Compensation Program for Salespeople

Salespeople are compensated in two ways for their efforts—financially and nonfinancially. A good compensation program allows its participants to work for both forms of reward, while recognizing that a salesperson's goals may be different from the entrepreneur's goals. For example, an entrepreneur may seek nonfinancial rewards that are of less importance to salespeople.

NONFINANCIAL REWARDS Personal recognition and the satisfaction of reaching a sales quota are examples of nonfinancial rewards recognized by salespeople. Small retail businesses sometimes post the photograph of the top salesperson of the week or the month for all to see. Engraved plaques are also given as a more permanent record of sales achievements.

FINANCIAL REWARDS Typically, financial compensation is the more critical factor for salespeople. Two basic plans used for financial compensation are commissions and straight salary. Each plan has specific advantages and limitations for the small firm.

Most small businesses would prefer to use commissions as compensation, because such an approach is simple and directly related to productivity. Usually, a certain percentage of the sales generated by the salesperson represents his or her commission. A commission plan thereby incorporates a strong incentive for sales effort—no sale, no commission! Also, with this type of plan, there is less drain on the firm's cash flow until a sale is made.

The straight salary form of compensation provides salespeople with more security because their level of compensation is ensured, regardless of sales made. However, working for a straight salary can potentially reduce a salesperson's motivation, by providing income despite low or no sales performance.

Combining the two forms of compensation creates the most attractive plan for a small business. It is common practice to structure combination plans so that salary represents the larger part of compensation for a new salesperson. As the salesperson gains experience, the ratio is adjusted to provide more money from commissions and less from salary.

ADVERTISING PRACTICES FOR SMALL FIRMS

4 *Identify advertising options for a small business.*

Another significant promotional expenditure for the small firm is advertising. **Advertising** is the impersonal presentation of an idea that is identified with a business sponsor. Ideas in advertising are communicated to consumers through media such as television, radio, magazines, newspapers, billboards, and the Internet.

advertising
The impersonal presentation of a business idea through mass media

Advertising Objectives

As its primary goal, advertising seeks to sell by informing, persuading, and reminding customers of the existence or superiority of a firm's product or service. To be successful, it must rest on a foundation of product quality and efficient service. It is important to remember that advertising can bring no more than temporary success to an otherwise inferior product. Advertising must always be viewed as a complement to a good product and never as a replacement for a bad product.

The entrepreneur must avoid creating false expectations with advertising, as such expectations can effectively reduce customer satisfaction. Advertising can accentuate a trend in the sale of an item or product line, but it seldom has the power to reverse a trend. It must, consequently, be able to reflect changes in customer needs and preferences.

At times, advertising may seem to be a waste of money. It is expensive and adds little value to the product. But the primary alternative to advertising is personal selling, which is often more expensive and time-consuming.

Types of Advertising

The two basic types of advertising are product advertising and institutional advertising. **Product advertising** is designed to make potential customers aware of a particular product or service and create a desire for it. **Institutional advertising**, on the other hand, conveys information about the business itself. It is intended to make the public aware of the company and enhance its image so that its product advertising will be more credible and effective. For example, Bill Weber is continually concerned with his company's image in the community as he attempts to sell garage door products from his Dayton, Ohio, location. In his advertising, Weber stresses that the company is locally owned, and he participates in local community events as part of his image-building efforts. "It's more than buying radio ads," says Weber, who frequently serves as the local high school football broadcaster. "Our company is connected to the town, because people feel like they know our family. Promoting the family-owned image has been good business."[2]

product advertising
The presentation of a business idea designed to make potential customers aware of a specific product or service and create a desire for it

institutional advertising
The presentation of information about a particular firm, designed to enhance the firm's image

Most small business advertising is of the product type. Small retailers' ads stress products almost exclusively—weekend specials at a supermarket, for example, or sportswear sold exclusively in a women's shop. It is important to note, however, that the same advertisement can convey both product and institutional themes. Furthermore, a firm may stress its product in newspaper advertisements, while using institutional advertising in the Yellow Pages. Decisions regarding the type of advertising to be used should be based on the nature of the business, industry practice, available media, and the objectives of the firm.

Obtaining Assistance with Advertising

Most small businesses rely on others' expertise to create their promotional messages. Fortunately, there are several sources for this specialized assistance: advertising agencies, suppliers, trade associations, and advertising media.

Advertising agencies can provide the following services:

- Furnish design, artwork, and copy for specific advertisements and/or commercials
- Evaluate and recommend the advertising media with the greatest "pulling power"
- Evaluate the effectiveness of different advertising appeals
- Advise on sales promotions and merchandise displays
- Conduct market-sampling studies to evaluate product acceptance or determine the sales potential of a specific geographic area
- Furnish mailing lists

Since advertising agencies charge fees for their services, an entrepreneur must make sure that the return from those services will be greater than the fees paid. Quality advertising assistance can best be provided by a competent agency. For example, Flowers & Partners, an agency specializing in small business clients, offers a program called Underdog Advertising to assist small firms with package design, media planning, new product development, and public relations.[3] Of course, with the high level of computer technology currently available, creating print advertising in-house is becoming increasingly common among small firms.

Other outside sources may assist in formulating and carrying out promotional programs. Suppliers often furnish display aids and even entire advertising programs to their dealers. Trade associations also provide helpful assistance. In addition, the advertising media can provide some of the same services offered by an ad agency.

Frequency of Advertising

Determining how often to advertise is an important and highly complex issue for a small business. Obviously, advertising should be done regularly, and attempts to stimulate interest in a firm's products or services should be part of an ongoing promotional program. One-shot advertisements that are not part of a well-planned promotional effort lose much of their effectiveness in a short period. Deciding on the frequency of advertising involves a host of factors, both objective and subjective, and a wise entrepreneur will seek professional advice.

Of course, some non-continuous advertising may be justified, such as advertising to prepare consumers for acceptance of a new product. Such advertising may also be used to suggest to customers new uses for established products or to promote special sales.

Where to Advertise

Most small firms restrict their advertising, either geographically or by customer type. Advertising media should reach—but not overreach—a firm's present or desired target market. From among the many media available, a small business entrepreneur must choose those that will provide the greatest return for the advertising dollar.

The most appropriate combination of advertising media depends on the type of business and its current circumstances. A real estate sales firm, for example, may rely almost exclusively on classified advertisements in the local newspaper, supplemented by institutional advertising in the Yellow Pages of the telephone directory. A transfer-and-storage firm may use a combination of radio, billboard, and Yellow Pages advertising to reach individuals planning to move household furniture. A small toy manufacturer may emphasize television advertisements and participation in trade fairs. A local retail store may concentrate on display advertisements in the local newspaper. The selection of media should be based not only on tradition but also on a careful evaluation of the various methods that are available to cover a firm's particular market.

A good way to build a media mix is to talk with representatives from each medium. A small firm will usually find these representatives willing to recommend an assortment of media, not just the ones they represent. Before meeting with these representatives, the entrepreneur should learn about the strengths and weaknesses of each medium. Exhibit 16-3 summarizes important facts about several traditional advertising media. Study this information carefully, noting the particular advantages and disadvantages of each medium.

Web advertising
Advertising appearing on the World Wide Web

A new type of promotion not covered in Exhibit 16-3 is **Web advertising**, or advertising appearing on the World Wide Web. Advertisers of all types have flocked to the Internet, hoping that the information superhighway will be the next great mass medium. The nature of Web advertising is examined in the next section.

16-3 | *Advantages and Disadvantages of Traditional Advertising Media*

Medium	Advantages	Disadvantages
Newspapers	Geographic selectivity and flexibility; short-term advertiser commitments; news value and immediacy; year-round readership; high individual market coverage; co-op and local tie-in availability; short lead time	Little demographic selectivity; limited color capabilities; low pass-along rate; may be expensive
Magazines	Good reproduction, especially for color; demographic selectivity; regional selectivity; local market selectivity; relatively long advertising life; high pass-along rate	Long-term advertiser commitments; slow audience buildup; limited demonstration capabilities; lack of urgency; long lead time
Radio	Low cost; immediacy of message; can be scheduled on short notice; relatively no seasonal change in audience; highly portable; short-term advertiser commitments; entertainment carryover	No visual treatment; short advertising life of message; high frequency required to generate comprehension and retention; distractions from background sound; commercial clutter
Television	Ability to reach a wide, diverse audience; low cost per thousand; creative opportunities for demonstration; immediacy of messages; entertainment carryover; demographic selectivity with cable stations	Short life of messages; some consumer skepticism about claims; high campaign cost; little demographic selectivity with network stations; long-term advertiser commitments; long lead times required for production; commercial clutter
Outdoor media	Repetition; moderate cost; flexibility; geographic selectivity	Short message; lack of demographic selectivity; high "noise" level distracting audience

Source: Charles W. Lamb, Jr., Joseph F. Hair, Jr., and Carl McDaniel, *Marketing* (Cincinnati: South-Western, 2004), p. 505.

Web Advertising

The Internet has provided an entirely new way for small firms to advertise. With color graphics, two-way information exchanges, streaming video, and 24-hour availability, online advertising is challenging traditional media for promotional dollars. Web advertising allows advertisers to reach large numbers of global buyers in a timely manner, at less expense, and with more impact than many alternative forms of advertising.

Most large businesses have a presence on the Web, and more and more small firms are using Internet technology. The basic methods of Web promotion are (1) banner ads and pop-ups, (2) e-mail, (3) sponsorships and linkages, and (4) a corporate Web site.

BANNER ADS AND POP-UPS **Banner ads** are advertisements that appear across a Web page, most often as moving rectangular strips. In contrast, **pop-up ads** burst open on Web pages, but do not have movement. When viewers respond by clicking on an ad, they are automatically linked to the site providing the product or sales activity. Both banner and pop-up ads can be placed on search engine sites or on related Web pages. The effectiveness of this form of advertising has not been documented, but these ads may work well with a targeted campaign.

banner ads
Advertisements that appear across a Web page, most often as moving rectangular strips

pop-up ads
Advertisements that burst open on computer screens

Unfortunately, online audiences often greet banner ads with little excitement. "A lot of Internet banner ads are like billboards on the side of the highway," says Martha Deevy, of Charles Schwab & Co. "People drive right past them and don't bother to look."[4]

DIRECT E-MAIL PROMOTION **E-mail promotion**, in which electronic mail is used to deliver a firm's message, provides a low-cost way to pinpoint customers and achieve response rates higher than those for banner ads. However, as more and more businesses use e-mail for this purpose, customer inboxes are becoming cluttered. And users are reluctant to open some e-mail messages, fearing computer viruses.

e-mail promotion
Advertising delivered by means of electronic mail

Living the Dream

Entrepreneurial Challenges

Audience Can Bear to Listen

Courtesy of The Vermont Teddy Bear Company®

http://www.vermontteddybear.com

In 1981, playing with his son Graham and his collection of teddy bears prompted John Sortino to have an entrepreneurial idea. Sortino noticed that the tags on all of his son's bears identified them as being foreign made. He decided to bring the American teddy bear tradition back home by selling bears handcrafted in his wife's sewing room. When a customer suggested packaging the teddy bears and adding a delivery service and other extras like gourmet candy to create mail-order gifts, the Bear-Gram concept was born.

The Vermont Teddy Bear Company, based in Shelbourne, Vermont, was launched in 1990, using well-known radio personalities on radio station Z-100 in New York City. A decade and a half later, the company continues to concentrate on radio advertising. The majority of its advertising budget of $9.1 million a year is devoted to radio commercials, which are heard in all 50 states and on more than 500 stations. "We do some stuff in other media, but 95 percent of our advertising has been with radio," says Gerry Howatt, the company's media-buying manager.

Even in today's era of cheap mass e-mail advertising, the traditional medium of radio can still offer a small firm a relatively inexpensive and extremely dependable option.

Sources: http://www.store.yahoo.com/vtbear/ourstory.html, April 10, 2004; Elizabeth J. Goodgold, "Bear Market," *Entrepreneur*, September 2002, http://www.entrepreneur.com/mag/article/0,1539,30227,00.html, April 20, 2004; and "Living Up and Down the Dial," *Inc.*, Vol. 25, No. 3 (March 2003), p. 46.

Larry and Charlene Woodward operate their book business, Dogwise, from Yakima, Washington. When new books are published, Dogwise sends personalized e-mails to people who have previously purchased books on similar subjects. "Customers love it, and we sell lots of books every time we send a batch of e-mails," says Larry. Before using e-mail to promote new books, the company sent postcards to its customers.[5]

Obstacles to e-mail promotion do exist. For example, receiving unsolicited e-mails, better known as *spam*, has turned many customers against this type of promotion. Consequently, Congress passed the Can-Spam Act of 2003, which took effect January 1, 2004.[6] However, legitimate e-mails are now being blocked by anti-spamming software. In 2003, Bill Broadbent, co-founder and CEO of T-ShirtKing.com of Mountainair, New Mexico, was sending a weekly e-mail newsletter to more than 300,000 people on a list that contained only e-mail addresses of people who had requested the newsletter on the firm's Web site. Despite the customers' desire to receive the newsletters, anti-spamming software caused the newsletters to go into spam boxes and never be read by many recipients.[7]

Web sponsorship
A type of advertising in which a firm pays another organization for the right to be part of that organization's Web page

linkage
A type of advertising agreement in which one firm pays another to include a click-on link on its site

SPONSORSHIPS AND LINKAGES In **Web sponsorship**, a firm pays to be part of another organization's Web page. When the Web page includes a click-on link to the paying firm's site, there is said to be a **linkage**. Research shows that a significant number of online purchases originate from online links. Unfortunately for many firms that choose to advertise through Web sponsorship, blocking software from such companies as WebWasher prevents ads from appearing on a viewer's Web page.[8]

CORPORATE WEB SITES The fourth form of Web advertising involves a more serious commitment by a small firm—launching a corporate Web site. Numerous decisions must be made prior to launching a site. Three critical startup tasks are related to the promotional success of a corporate Web site: (1) creating and registering a site name, (2) building a user-friendly site, and (3) promoting the site.

Creating and Registering a Site Name The Domain Names System (DNS) allows users to find their way around the Internet. Selecting the best domain name for a corporate Web site is an important promotional decision. Contrary to general opinion, plenty of Web site names remain available. Domain names can have up to 63 characters preceding the domain designation. The three most popular domain designations are .com, .net, and .org.[9]

Since a domain name gives a small business its online identity, it's desirable to select a descriptive and appealing name. "It's no harder to make up names for dot-coms than for colas," says Ira Bachrack of San Francisco's NameLab.[10]

Obviously, some of the shorter, more creative names have already been taken. But, like real estate, Web site names can be bought and sold. Marc Ostrofsky, former CEO of Information Publishing, owns more than 100 domain names. He purchased the name "business.com" in 1997 from a British Internet service provider for $150,000 and later sold it for $7.5 million.[11]

Once a desired name has been selected, it should be checked for availability and then registered. The Internet Corporation for Assigned Names and Numbers (ICANN) is a nonprofit corporation currently overseeing the global Internet. ICANN, however, does not register names; this must be done through a domain registration firm. InterNic, a registered service mark of the U.S. Department of Commerce, provides an Accredited Registrar Directory that lists ICANN-accredited domain registrars, such as Namesecure. Several domain registrars allow a search of the Internet to see if a proposed name is already taken.

Building a User-Friendly Web Site First impressions are important, and high-quality Web design gives a small e-commerce business the opportunity to make a good first impression on each visitor. The technical aspects of developing a Web site are beyond the scope of this chapter. Fortunately, there are many technical specialists available to help design and build a site. Our purpose here is simply to provide some useful tips about Web site design.

Exhibit 16-4 (on page 364) shows 10 design tips for e-commerce Web sites. The home page of The Gorilla Glue Company, which promotes its glue online, is shown in Exhibit 16-5 (on page 365). Although the glue cannot be ordered directly from the company's

Living the Dream

Utilizing the Internet

You Can't Eat Technology

Cheesecake first appeared on the menu at Eli's the Place for Steak restaurant in 1977. The restaurant's version of the rich and creamy dessert soon became Chicago's favorite. In 1980, entrepreneur Marc Schulman (Eli's son) decided to spin off Eli's Cheesecake and focus solely on the line of sweets. When the Internet emerged, Eli's went online with AOL. In 1998, the company launched its own Web site, offering both purchasing options and interactive content.

Courtesy of The Eli's Cheesecake Company

However, Schulman recognized that although technology can help improve personal service—a key to Eli's business philosophy—it's important to continue to work at it. "The system won't do everything," he says. "In our case, you can't eat technology."

Schulman insisted that customers have the opportunity to e-mail him directly, through a link on the homepage of Eli's Cheesecake. He enjoys getting feedback from customers and never wants a customer to have to sift through layers of people to get an answer. To him, it's the same sort of personal service his father provided for 70 years. "My dad is the ultimate one-on-one marketer," he says. "I use the same personal touch; I've just adapted it with technology."

Schulman updates the site's content regularly, including features about the latest events at Eli's Cheesecake World—the factory where the desserts are made. "You've got to have ways to make changes easily," he says. "If a customer goes online and finds information about an event that it turns out happened last year, they get frustrated and leave."

The company bakes more than 10,000 cheesecakes a day for customers in all 50 states and parts of Europe and Asia.

http://www.elischeesecake.com

Sources: Shannon Scully, "Sink or Swim," *MyBusiness*, February-March 2004, pp. 22–23; http://www.cityofchicago.org/dpd/MadeInChicago/Elis.html, April 10, 2004; and http://www.elischeesecake.com/history/legend.htm, April 10, 2004.

EXHIBIT 16-4 Web Site Design Tips

Tip 1: Make It Easy to Buy
This tip may seem vague and ambiguous, but it truly is the most important recommendation. Put yourself in your customer's shoes and test your designs. Isolate issues that might block users from making a successful purchase. Ask questions, such as

- How many pages and clicks does it take to make a purchase?
- How much information do users have to fill out initially, versus when they make a second-time purchase?
- Can a quick purchase be made directly from the home page?
- Does the site provide clear instructions on how to store selected items before completing a transaction?
- How well does the site communicate with a user?
- Does the site acknowledge users' actions and provide clear, concise feedback as users progress through the purchasing process?
- Can users collect multiple items before checking out?

Tip 2: Make a Strong First Impression
The e-commerce home page must make a strong first impression. This is where users are grounded to your company and persuaded to start shopping. It is first and foremost important to provide branding for your store. Next, it is important to provide a clear visual definition of your store's categories or departments. This can be accomplished with tabs or within the navigation bar.

Tip 3: Minimize Distractions: Advertising Isn't Always Necessary
You may consider not providing any advertisements on the home page or in other places throughout the purchase process. Remember that the goal of your home page is to encourage shopping and purchasing. You don't want to deter or lose users by having them click on another company's advertisement.

Tip 4: Make It Personal
Looking for a way to build a strong rapport with your shoppers? Provide personalization for the user, after the user registers as a shopper or member. Use this information to provide a personalized greeting to the home page or various department pages. *Welcome, Najia, enjoy your shopping experience.* Provide a private place that requires a password, where each user can check past orders, order status, wish lists, gift certificates, and so forth.

Tip 5: Avoid Long Instructions
If you need to include long instructions on how to use the site or make a purchase, it is time to redesign! To complete a quick purchase, a user needs minimal-to-no instructions. Most users will not read long instructions, and may turn away in confusion.

Tip 6: Provide Visual Clues to Location
For stores that have multiple departments, it is important to create a sense of varying location. This can be accomplished by changing colors on the navigation bar or the background page, and by providing different titles with text or graphics.

Tip 7: Show Off Products
If at all possible, provide photographs of individual products. Process the photos in three sizes: thumbnail, medium, and large. A thumbnail photo is best used in a list of several products. At the individual product level, provide a medium size image, and the ability to click to view the enlarged version of the product. The larger view is not necessary, but worth considering if your product has details that are not reflected in the medium or thumbnail photograph.

The more details you can provide about the product the better. If you have a long page about the product, be sure to provide the option to purchase or add to your basket or cart from both the top and the bottom of the informational text.

Tip 8: Encourage Spontaneous Purchases
This can be accomplished in various ways. If a product is mentioned on the home page, place product images and details, the sale price, and a direct link to purchase the item. In a news or feature article, include direct links to purchase products discussed within the article. Or on the side column, where advertisements for other companies traditionally would go, create intimate, focused advertisements for your products, with a direct link to purchase the items from the advertisements.

Tip 9: Alternate Background Colors in Long Lists
One good visual trick to make a long table of items easier to read is to alternate a light color background for each row or item. You can see an example of this if you search on an author's name at barnesandnoble.com. The search results return in alternate item background colors of gray and white.

Tip 10: Allow Users to Collect Items
Provide a shopping basket or a place for users to collect items before checking out. Never make the user fill out the lengthy payment, shipping, and other forms more than once in a transaction! At the product level, provide a link to check out and a link to add that product to the shopping cart while continuing to shop.

One item-storage feature that is currently becoming popular is called a wish list. This feature is similar to a shopping cart, but it does not provide purchasing features. Think of it as a place to store items as you are shopping. Perhaps when items in your wish list go on sale, the site can notify you.

Source: Nadja Vol Ochs, "Easy-to-Buy E-Commerce Site Design Tips," http://www.microsoft.com/technet/prodtechnol/sscomm/reskit/sitedes.mspx, August 3, 2004.

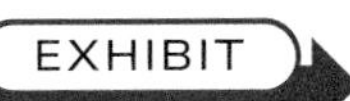

16-5 *Home Page for the Gorilla Glue Product*

Source: http://www.gorillaglue.com. Reprinted by permission of The Gorilla Glue Company.

Web site, links are provided to other sites where the product can be purchased. Customer testimonials can also be viewed on the company's site.

There are many reasons why Web sites fail to retain customers. One of the most frequent problems is slow downloading. Online shoppers are a fickle bunch, and the slightest inconvenience sends them away. If a page takes more than 20 to 30 seconds to load, there's a high chance of abandonment, as Rick Edler discovered. Edler launched a low-tech Web site for his real estate business, Edler Group, at a cost of $285 in 1997. When he later decided he needed something fancier, he hired a Web developer who built a site filled with color graphics and motion—at a cost of $7,000. But it took too long to download. Traffic was below expectations. "So much was happening," Edler says. "You just stared at it like you were watching a commercial. We were scaring people away."[12] The site was finally scrapped and replaced by a new, simpler version.

Web sites also will fail if they do not satisfy visitors' information needs. Frequently, this is because designers look inward to the business for Web design ideas, rather than outward to customer needs.

Promoting the Web Site How do customers learn about a Web site? You have to tell them—and there are many ways to do this. A Web address can be promoted both to existing customers and to prospects by including the URL on print promotions, business cards, letterhead, and packaging. Special direct mail and radio campaigns can also be designed for this purpose. Additionally, a Web site can be promoted by placing banner advertisements on other Web sites, where a quick click will send users to the advertised site. The advantage of banner advertisements is that they are placed in front of thousands of visitors to other Web sites. Payment for banner advertising is usually based on the number of people who actually click on the banner.

Probably the most direct approach to Web site promotion is making sure that the site is listed in Internet search engines. Search engines are databases, available on the Internet, that allow users to find Web sites based on keywords included in the site's pages. If a popular search engine does not list a firm's Web site, many potential visitors will undoubtedly miss it. Registering a site with a search engine is free. However, to get a position at or near the top of a search listing, you may have to pay. For example, Mark Kini, of Boston

16-6 *Options for Getting Your Web Site Listed in Search Engines*

1. Use a Free Submission Service
Basically, free submission services offer to submit your Web site to as many as 500 of the top search engines for free. And while that may sound like a great deal to the inexperienced site owner, the truth is that using a free submission service will cost you traffic and sales. Every search engine has a different "rule book" that it uses to decide where your Web site will rank. Because they submit the same information to every single engine, free submission services are useless in achieving top-ranking positions for your firm.

2. Use a Low-Cost, Automated Submission Service
Low-cost, automated submission services offer to submit your Web site to as many as 900+ search engines for a minimal fee (usually between $40 and $80). Much like the free submission services, automated submission services automatically submit the same set of information to ALL of the search engines. Once again, your Web site is being submitted to multiple search engines without being optimized to meet their individual requirements.

3. Do It Yourself by Manually Submitting Your Web Site to Individual Search Engines
This is one of the best ways to submit your Web site to the search engines. Visit each search engine separately, and manually submit the information for each Web page you wish to have listed. On the downside, submitting your Web site this way can be very time consuming and labor intensive. Also, there are no professionals to help you.

4. Use a Professional Search Engine Consultant
Search engine consultants will educate you and work with you to maximize your site's exposure in each search engine. They know all of the latest tricks and techniques for securing a top spot and will show you exactly what you need to do to optimize your Web site for the best possible ranking.

5. Use Submission Software
Most of the software out there does exactly what the free and low-cost automated submission services do—it submits the same set of information to all of the search engines. So, your site is never optimized, and you never secure the top ranking you need.

Final Thoughts: However you decide to submit your Web site to the search engines, take your time. Don't rush in and make mistakes that could destroy your chances of securing a top ranking. Remember that search engines receive thousands of requests every day from people who want to make changes to their listing!

Source: Adapted from http://www.marketingtips.com/newsletter/issue50/page1.html, July 27, 2004.

Chauffeur, spent about $60,000 in 2002 purchasing keywords and placement for his limousine service site in search engines. This seemed to be a great deal of money to promote the 18-person firm, but it has been effective. Anyone typing a phrase like "Boston limo service" into the search field would get a clickable ad for Kini's business.[13]

Obviously, your Web site should include keywords that someone looking for that particular subject might use. Many businesses try to get to the top of a search engine's results by designing their Web sites to match a particular search engine's ranking index. If they don't, business can be hurt. For example, after Google adjusted how it ranked sites in its index, the Unforgettable Honeymoon Web site of Renee Duane, of Portland, Oregon, literally disappeared from searches. Her business, which packages honeymoon tours, felt the impact. "We used to get e-mails and calls every day from people who found us on Google. That's come to a complete stop," she says.[14] Specific content is also important; for example, including brands with descriptions can improve your placement.

There are several ways of submitting a Web site to search engines. A description of submission options, adapted from the Internet Marketing Center's Web site, is shown in Exhibit 16-6.

SALES PROMOTIONAL TOOLS

5 *Discuss the use of sales promotional tools.*

Sales promotion serves as an inducement to buy a certain product while typically offering value to prospective customers. Generally, **sales promotion** includes any promotional technique, other than personal selling or advertising, that stimulates the purchase of a particular good or service.

Sales promotion should seldom comprise all the promotional efforts of a small business. Typically, it should be used in combination with personal selling and advertising. Popular sales promotional tools include specialties, contests, premiums, trade show exhibits, point-of-purchase displays, free merchandise, publicity, sampling, and coupons. For example, Dan Banfe, CEO of Banfe Products in Westville, New Jersey, a provider of soil and mulch to nurseries, uses an incentive program to promote his company's products. Banfe treats his sales staff and loyal customers to free week-long getaways in exotic locales, such as Cancun and Curacao, when they earn a certain level of points based on quantities ordered. For smaller customers, who have no hope of reaching the necessary points, Banfe holds a yearly raffle for a free trip.[15]

sales promotion
An inclusive term for any promotional techniques other than personal selling and advertising

The scope of this textbook does not allow discussion of all of these promotional tools. However, we will briefly examine specialties, trade show exhibits, and publicity.

Specialties

The most widely used specialty item is a calendar. Other popular specialty items are pens, key chains, coffee mugs, and shirts. Almost anything can be used as a specialty promotion, as long as each item is imprinted with the firm's name or other identifying slogan.

The distinguishing characteristics of specialties are their enduring nature and tangible value. Specialties are referred to as the "lasting medium." As functional products, they are worth something to recipients. Specialties can be used to promote a product directly or to create goodwill for a firm; they are excellent reminders of a firm's existence.

Finally, specialties are personal. They are distributed directly to the customer in a personal way; they can be used personally; and they have a personal message. A small business needs to retain its unique image, and entrepreneurs often use specialties to achieve this objective. More information on specialties is available on the Web site of the Promotional Products Association International at http://www.ppa.org.

Trade Show Exhibits

Advertising often cannot substitute for trial experiences with a product, and a customer's place of business is not always the best environment for product demonstrations. Trade show exhibits allow potential customers to get hands-on experience with a product.

Living the Dream — *Utilizing the Internet*

If the Shoe Fits, Wear It

Sometimes, entrepreneurs decide to copy marketing tactics used by big businesses, if they think the ideas will work well for their small firm. Scott Savitz did just this when he launched the Boston-based online footwear venture Shoebuy.com in 2000.

Amazon.com and other online marketers have experimented with offering free shipping ever since the Internet's earliest days, and it seems to work. Several major Internet research firms concur that free shipping offers by Web-based companies encourage customers to fill their shopping carts more than they would otherwise.

Courtesy of Shoebuy.com, Inc.

Savitz, the 34-year-old president, CEO, and founder of Shoebuy.com, says, "We decided we didn't want to even enter this business if we couldn't sell a product that offered free shipping, because we thought it was part of the whole value proposition." Free shipping encourages buyers to take a little more risk; in the case of Shoebuy.com, they end up buying multiple pairs of shoes since they know the merchandise will be shipped at no charge to them.

Shoebuy.com is able to make this promotional offer because it doesn't have salespeople to pay or warehouse space to maintain. It works one on one with manufacturers, which send out products directly to the customer. Other benefits promoted to shoppers by Shoebuy.com are no sales tax, free returns and exchanges, a 110-percent price guarantee, and a 100-percent sales purchase guarantee.

Shoebuy.com employs 13 full-time employees and has enjoyed five straight quarters of profitability. The site offers over 200 brands and one billion dollars in "accessible" inventory.

http://www.shoebuy.com

Source: Melissa Campanelli, "Shipping Out," *Entrepreneur*, June 2003, pp. 42–44; and http://www.shoebuy.com/sb/contact/press.jsp, April 10, 2004. Reprinted with permission.

Trade show exhibits are of particular value to manufacturers. The greatest benefit of these exhibits is the potential cost savings over personal selling. Trade show groups claim that the cost of an exhibit is less than one-fourth the cost of sales calls. Many small manufacturers agree that exhibits are more cost-effective than advertising. One Web site devoted to marketing tactics lists some helpful tips regarding trade shows:[16]

- *Check out the trade show's history*. Does the show regularly attract large crowds? Will the show be adequately promoted to your potential customers?
- *Prepare a professional-looking display*. You do not need to have the biggest, flashiest booth on the trade show floor to attract attendees. But signs, photographs of your products, and other business-related elements used in the display should appear to be professionally prepared.
- *Have a sufficient quantity of literature on hand*. Have plenty of professionally prepared brochures or other handouts to distribute, and have them prepared well in advance of the show.
- *Make sure you have a good product*. If your product doesn't work or doesn't work properly, you'll lose more customers than you'll ever gain.
- *Do pre-show promotion*. To get the most traffic at your booth, send out mailings prior to the show inviting your customers and prospects to stop by your booth. Insert announcements in bills you send out, on your Web page, and in ads you run near the show date.
- *Have a giveaway or gimmick*. The giveaway or gimmick doesn't have to be big or elaborate. Samples of your product given away at intervals during the show are ideal. Novelty items such as keychains, pencils, and pads of paper with your company name and product name are good, too.
- *Train booth personnel*. Choose your booth staff carefully, and be sure they know how to deal with the public, especially prospective customers.
- *Follow up*! Have a plan in place for following up on leads as soon as you get home from the show.

Publicity

publicity Information about a firm and its products or services that appears as a news item, usually free of charge

Of particular importance to small firms is **publicity**, which provides visibility for a business at little or no cost. Publicity can be used to promote both a product and a firm's image; it is a vital part of public relations for the small business. A good publicity program requires regular contacts with the news media.

Although publicity is not always free, the return on a relatively small investment can be substantial. For example, Cypriana Porter, owner of the educational toy store The Gingerbread House, in Wolcott, New York, wanted to get the attention of the news media. To this end, she came up with the idea of Puzzleman, Defender of Creativity—a man in a superhero costume. Puzzleman visits her store to encourage creative play among its young customers. When she first introduced Puzzleman, Porter invited a local television station to the superhero's debut. The station later invited Puzzleman to be a guest on one of its shows. The local newspaper even dubbed the character "Wolcott's Own Superhero." Puzzleman has participated in programs at the local library and fire department and has appeared in town parades. The total cost of this publicity was less than $500.[17] Other examples of publicity efforts that entail some expense include involvement with school yearbooks and youth athletic programs. While the benefits are difficult to measure, publicity is nevertheless important to a small business and should be used at every opportunity.

When to Use Sales Promotion

A small firm can use sales promotion to accomplish various objectives. For example, small manufacturers can use it to stimulate channel members—retailers and wholesalers—to market their product. Wholesalers can use sales promotion to induce retailers to buy inventories earlier than they normally would, and retailers, with similar promotional tools, may be able to persuade customers to make a purchase.

Consider Scott Androff and Bruce Hilsen, co-founders of TwinStar Industries in Bloomington, Minnesota. After introducing Atmos-Klear Odor Eliminator, a non-toxic biodegradable spray that gets rid of odors, they needed a low-cost promotional tactic. Androff decided to use publicity. His strategy was to send a news release to magazines and newspapers, followed up by a phone call to the editors. The company also demonstrated the product at trade shows. Prior to using these two promotional tactics, sales had been slow, but they've now picked up considerably.[18]

Strategic Alliances and Sales Promotion

Joining with another firm to promote products is a form of strategic alliance. For example, if a local dry cleaner and a nearby independent tailor had similar customers, they might share the cost of a coupon program, increasing the visibility of both firms without taking away each other's business. Small firms, however, are traditionally very independent and only recently have begun to recognize the benefits of cross-promotion.

Ideally, the discussions in this chapter have helped you understand the role that promotion plays in the marketing process. It is a complex activity, and entrepreneurs need to recognize their limitations in this area and seek professional advice when necessary.

Looking Back

1 Describe the communication process and the factors determining a promotional mix.

- Every communication involves a source, a message, a channel, and a receiver.
- A promotional mix is a blend of nonpersonal, personal, and special forms of communication techniques.
- A promotional mix is influenced primarily by three important factors: the geographical nature of the market, the size of the promotional budget, and the product's characteristics.

2 Explain methods of determining the appropriate level of promotional expenditure.

- Earmarking promotional dollars based on a percentage of sales is a simple method for determining expenditures.
- Spending only what can be spared is a widely used approach to promotional budgeting.
- Spending as much as the competition does is a way to react to short-run promotional tactics of competitors.
- The preferred approach to determining promotional expenditures is to decide what it will take to do the job, while factoring in elements used in the other methods.

3 Describe personal selling activities.

- A sales presentation is a process involving prospecting, practicing the presentation, and then making the presentation.
- Salespeople are compensated for their efforts in two ways—financially and nonfinancially.
- The two basic plans for financial compensation are commissions and straight salary, but the most attractive plan for a small firm combines the two.

4 Identify advertising options for a small business.

- Common advertising media include television, radio, magazines, newspapers, billboards, and the Internet.
- Product advertising is designed to promote a product or service, while institutional advertising conveys an idea regarding the business itself.
- A small firm must decide how often to advertise, where to advertise, and what the message will be.
- A firm's Web advertising generally takes the form of banner ads and pop-ups, e-mail, sponsorships and linkages, and a corporate Web site.

5 Discuss the use of sales promotional tools.

- Sales promotion includes all promotional techniques other than personal selling and advertising.
- Typically, sales promotional tools should be used along with advertising and personal selling.
- Three widely used sales promotional tools are specialties, trade show exhibits, and publicity.
- Cross-promotion between firms is a form of strategic alliance.

Key Terms

promotion, p. 353
promotional mix, p. 354
personal selling, p. 355
prospecting, p. 356
advertising, p. 359
product advertising, p. 359
institutional advertising, p. 359
Web advertising, p. 360
banner ads, p. 361
pop-up ads, p. 361
e-mail promotion, p. 361
Web sponsorship, p. 362
linkage, p. 362
sales promotion, p. 366
publicity, p. 368

Discussion Questions

1. Describe the parallel relationship that exists between a small business communication and a personal communication.
2. Discuss the advantages and disadvantages of each approach to budgeting funds for promotion.
3. Outline a system of prospecting that could be used by a small camera store. Incorporate all the techniques presented in this chapter.
4. Why are a salesperson's techniques for handling objections so important to a successful sales presentation?
5. Assume you have the opportunity to "sell" your course instructor on the idea of eliminating final examinations. Make a list of the objections you expect to hear from your instructor, and describe how you will handle each objection, using some of the techniques listed on page 357.
6. What are some nonfinancial rewards that could be offered to salespeople?
7. What are the advantages and disadvantages of compensating salespeople by salary? By commissions? What do you think is an acceptable compromise?
8. What are some approaches to advertising on the Web?
9. Discuss some recommendations for designing an effective Web site.
10. How do specialties differ from trade show exhibits and publicity? Be specific.

You Make the Call

SITUATION 1

The driving force behind Cannon Arp's new business was several bad experiences with his car—two speeding tickets and four minor fender-benders. Consequently, his insurance rates more than doubled, which resulted in Arp's idea to design and sell a bumper sticker that read "To Report Bad Driving, Call My Parents at . . . ." With a $200 investment, Arp printed 15,000 of the stickers, which contain space to write in the appropriate telephone number. He is now planning a promotion to support his strategy of distribution through auto parts stores.

Question 1 What role, if any, should personal selling have in Arp's total promotional plan?

Question 2 Arp is considering advertising in magazines. What do you think about this medium for promoting his product?

Question 3 Of what value might publicity be for selling Arp's stickers? Be specific.

SITUATION 2

Cheree Moore owns and operates a small business that supplies delicatessens with bulk containers of ready-made salads. When served in salad bars, the salads appear to have been freshly prepared from scratch at the delicatessen. Moore wants additional promotional exposure for her products and is considering using her fleet of trucks as rolling billboards. If the strategy is successful, she may even attempt to lease space on other trucks. Moore is concerned about the cost-effectiveness of the idea and whether the public will even notice the advertisements. She also wonders whether the image of her salad products might be hurt by this advertising medium.

Question 1 What suggestions can you offer that would help Moore make this decision?

Question 2 How could Moore go about determining the cost-effectiveness of this strategy?

Question 3 What additional factors should Moore evaluate before advertising on trucks?

SITUATION 3

Corinna Lathan is co-founder and CEO of AnthroTronix, which is currently located in the business incubator at the University of Maryland. Founded in July 1999, the company is a human factors engineering firm committed to optimizing interactions between people and technology.

With co-founder Jack M. Vice, Lathan is developing a Muppet-like robot for use as a therapeutic tool with children with speech, learning, and physical disabilities. The robot has been tested at a Maryland hospital, where the medical director says the kids using the device have shown measurable improvement. Here's how the robot, named JesterBot, works:

> *A child puts on leg- or armbands and a hat embedded with radio transceivers and sensors. By waving a hand, say, or nodding her head, she sends out radio signals that are interpreted by a central processing unit in the JesterBot. . . . During exercises, the JesterBot can gauge a child's range of motion, while electronically reporting the results of the session to a therapist via a data port hooked up to a PC.*

To launch the product, the company needs additional funding, which it hopes to get soon.

Source: Nicole Ridgway, "Robo-Therapy," *Forbes*, Vol. 167, No. 11 (March 14, 2001), p. 216.

Question 1 When the product is ready to launch, what kinds of promotion should the company use? Why?

Question 2 What techniques might this firm use to set the promotional budget?

Question 3 In what way, if any, could Internet promotion help this business?

Experiential Exercises

1. Interview the owners of one or more small businesses to determine how they develop their promotional budget. Classify the owners' methods into one or more of the four approaches described in this chapter. Report your findings to the class.
2. Plan a sales presentation. With a classmate role-playing a potential buyer, make the presentation in class. Ask the other students to critique your technique.
3. Locate a small business Web site and evaluate the promotional effectiveness of the site.
4. Interview a media representative about advertising options for small businesses. Summarize your findings for the class.

Exploring the Web

1. Go to the Bank of America's Web site at **http://www.bankofamerica.com**. Click on "Small Business," and then follow the link under "Resource Center" to "Growing Your Business." Click on the workshop called "Advertising Your Business." How might an average figure for advertising and promotion costs be calculated?
2. Return to the Bank of America's Web site (**http://www.bankofamerica.com**). Now click on the workshop entitled "Promoting Your Business."
   a. How many trade shows are held in the United States each year?
   b. What are the pros and cons of trade shows?
3. Visit *Entrepreneur* magazine's Web site at **http://www.entrepreneur.com/article/0,4621,306484,00.html**. Read the article entitled "Nail Your Sales Presentation," in which business coach Tony Parinello offers advice on turning prospects into clients. What are some of the do's and don'ts Parinello suggests for sales presentations?

Video Case 16

SOLID GOLD HEALTH PRODUCTS FOR PETS (P. 555)

In this case, promotional issues are addressed by a dog food entrepreneur.

Alternative Cases for Chapter 16:

Case 1, Boston Duck Tours, p. 526
Case 9, The Chocolate Farm, p. 540

GLOBAL MARKETING

In the Spotlight

Ice Age Ice **http://www.iceageice.de**

There's nothing like an ice-cold drink on a hot summer day, right? Well . . . not if you are European, it seems. One 23-year-old German remarks that people order a Coke and "what you get consists of 30 to 40 percent frozen water." Other Europeans believe that ice is bad for the teeth and stomach.

For these reasons and others, many Europeans give ice the cold shoulder. But Matthew Meredith, a 29-year-old native of Baltimore, Maryland, had a gut feeling that demand for ice in Europe was about to heat up as a result of rising summer temperatures. Willing to gamble on his hunch, Meredith turned down a job in investment banking in 2003 to move to Germany and launch Ice Age Ice, a company that offers "attractive, inexpensive, high-quality and reliable [ice products] for external cooling and for use in beverages."

© David Chasey/Getty Images

But starting an ice company in Europe made for some tough sledding. Meredith could not get credit from German banks, and finding an ice machine in Europe that was capable of producing hundreds of bags of ice per hour was even more of a challenge. Furthermore, he had to teach customers how to use the product.

One called asking how long the ice would last. Wouldn't it melt in the car on the way home? Another wondered if Mr. Meredith could add lemon flavoring, so she wouldn't have to drink plain ice water.

Working 12 hours a day at the plant and the company's headquarters (nothing fancy, just an area that is walled off from the production floor) and staying in a cheap apartment in Frankfurt's red-light district do not make for easy living, but Meredith is intent on building a niche industry in Europe. Heat waves during the last few summers have greatly boosted consumer demand. In fact, Ice Age Ice is now "maxed out" on production—that is, the company has only about enough manufacturing and freezer capacity to serve its current customers. Though the company continues to struggle, Meredith is determined to hang in there.

As Meredith's experience with Ice Age Ice illustrates, starting an international business that taps overseas customers is no easy task. However, it is always an adventure, and there is much to learn from the experience.

Sources: http://www.iceageice.de, July 16, 2004; http://serve.com/shea/eis.htm, June 2, 2004; and Neale E. Boudette, "An American Pushes Europe to Embrace a Modern Ice Age," *Wall Street Journal*, August 19, 2003, pp. A1–A2.

Chapter 17

Looking Ahead

After studying this chapter, you should be able to

1. *Describe the potential of small firms as global enterprises.*
2. *Identify the basic forces prompting small firms to engage in global expansion.*
3. *Identify and compare strategy options for global businesses.*
4. *Explain the challenges that global enterprises face.*
5. *Recognize the sources of assistance available to support international business efforts.*

For many small businesses, going global is no longer just an interesting thing to do—it is essential to the long-term health and performance of the company. There was a time when national economies were isolated by trade and investment barriers, differences in language and culture, distinctive business practices, and various government regulations. However, these dissimilarities are fading over time as market preferences converge, trade barriers fall, and national economies integrate to form a global economic system. This process is the essence of **globalization**. Though the trend toward convergence has been developing for some time now, the pace is quickening, creating global opportunities that did not exist even a few years ago. And with the astounding rate of economic growth in countries such as China and India, it would be unwise to ignore overseas opportunities.

globalization
The expansion of international business, encouraged by converging market preferences, falling trade barriers, and the integration of national economies

As hindrances to globalization diminish, the commercial potential of markets abroad continues to grow. To track this trend, the Heritage Foundation and the *Wall Street Journal* publish the *Index of Economic Freedom*, an analysis of trade policy, wages and prices, government intervention, and other similar variables in 161 nations. According to the 2004 report, economic freedom continues to advance throughout the world, with 75 countries posting better scores than for the previous year. And the benefits of economic liberty speak for themselves: Countries with high levels of economic freedom also enjoy higher rates of long-term economic growth and substantially greater prosperity than do those with less economic freedom. For example, Hong Kong and Singapore have the most economic freedom, and each country has a per capita GDP exceeding $24,000, whereas Zimbabwe ranks 153rd and has a per capita GDP of only $559.[1] This positive impact on prosperity translates into increased demand for products and services in international markets, fueling interest in global enterprises.

SMALL BUSINESSES AS GLOBAL ENTERPRISES

1 *Describe the potential of small firms as global enterprises.*

The potential of a global business is clear, but does that potential extend to small companies? Research has shown that recent startups and even the smallest of businesses are internationalizing at an increasing rate. In fact, small companies in virtually all major trading countries are increasingly being launched with cross-border business activities in mind. These are sometimes called **born-global firms.**[2] As global communication systems become more efficient and trade agreements pry open national markets to foreign competition, entrepreneurs are focusing more on international business. Today's sophisticated technologies are expensive to develop and quickly replaced; therefore, it is important to recover R&D costs over a larger market and in less time by taking advantage of international sales. Small firms may decide to go global to expand their opportunities, or they may be forced to enter foreign markets in order to compete with those firms in their industry that have already done so. In any case, the research is clear: *Size does not necessarily limit a firm's international activity, and small companies often become global competitors to take advantage of their unique resources.*[3]

born-global firms
Small companies launched with cross-border business activities in mind

In 1995 Bob Williams and Dave Ogborne launched Air Excellence International near Pittsburgh, Pennsylvania, as a born-global business, to renovate commercial jetliner interiors. Its first customer was a Venezuelan company that contracted for restoration work on a single jetliner. Business has gradually expanded as larger airlines have contracted for the company's services. Early on, the firm nearly doubled its workforce each year, and that pace of growth continues as more renovation work is scheduled. Demonstrating its commitment to international business, the company opened a second facility in Shannon, Ireland, and acquired UK–based Aircraft Interiors International to serve European airlines.[4] Air Excellence International has shown that the global marketplace is not limited to large multinational firms.

The fact that many firms are going global does not mean that it is *easy* for small firms; the challenges small businesses face in international markets are considerable. First, a small business owner must decide whether the company is up to the task. To help entrepreneurs assess the impact of going global on a small business, the U.S. Department of Commerce publishes *A Basic Guide to Exporting*. This handbook outlines important questions entrepreneurs should consider when assessing readiness for the challenges of global business (see Exhibit 17-1).

Once small business owners decide to expand internationally, they should study the cultural, political, and economic forces in foreign markets to figure out how best to adapt the product or service to local demand or make other adjustments necessary to ensure smooth entry. A practice that is acceptable in one culture may be considered unethical or morally wrong in another. When cultural lines are crossed, even gestures as simple as a "good morning" and a handshake may be misunderstood. The entrepreneur must evalu-

17-1 *Questions to Consider Before Going Global*

Management Objectives	• What are the company's reasons for going global? • How committed is top management to going global? • How quickly does management expect its international operations to pay off?
Management Experience and Resources	• What in-house international expertise does the firm have (international sales experience, language skills, etc.)? • Who will be responsible for the company's international operations? • How much senior management time should be allocated to the company's global efforts? • What organizational structure is required to ensure success abroad?
Production Capacity	• How is the present capacity being used? • Will international sales hurt domestic sales? • What will be the cost of additional production at home and abroad? • What product designs and packaging options are required for international markets?
Financial Capacity	• How much capital can be committed to international production and marketing? • How are the initial expenses of going global to be covered? • What other financial demands might compete with plans to internationalize? • By what date must the global effort pay for itself?

Source: U.S. Department of Commerce, *A Basic Guide to Exporting*, cited in John B. Cullen, *Multinational Management: A Strategic Approach* (Cincinnati, OH: South-Western College Publishing, 2002), p. 396.

ate the proper use of names and titles and be aware of different cultural styles and business practices. The cultural challenges of doing business abroad are great.

Entrepreneurs are likely to make costly mistakes if they fail to study a foreign market carefully. For example, a U.S. mail-order concern offering products to the Japanese didn't realize that the American custom of asking for a credit card number before taking an order would be seen as an insult by customers. This misstep was corrected when a consultant explained that in Japan, where business deals may be secured with a handshake rather than a contract, such an approach is interpreted as indicating a lack of trust. Such insights can go a long way in preventing blunders before they occur.

Differences in types of trading systems and import requirements can also make international trade challenging. A small manufacturer of diagnostic and surgical eye care equipment discovered that a global company must regularly modify its products to meet rigid design specifications, which vary from country to country. For example, before the firm could sell its testing device in Germany, it had to remove an on/off switch on the product's alarm. Such adjustments are an unavoidable part of conducting global business.

Trade barriers are falling in some regions of the world, as countries agree to eliminate **tariffs** (taxes charged on imported goods) and trade restrictions. In 1989, Canada and the United States signed the Free Trade Agreement (FTA), which gradually eliminated most tariffs and other trade restrictions between the two countries. This free trade area was extended in 1993, when the United States, Canada, and Mexico established the **North American Free Trade Agreement (NAFTA)**, which phases out tariffs over 15 years. These agreements have promoted commerce within North America, just as the formation of the **European Union (EU)** in 1993 facilitated trade among its member countries. Plans for expansion of the EU are already coming together. These agreements and others have eased formal barriers to trade among nations, but cultural, political, and economic differences (discussed later in the chapter) still pose a formidable challenge for small companies.

tariffs
Taxes charged on imported goods

North American Free Trade Agreement (NAFTA)
An agreement that encourages free trade between the United States, Canada, and Mexico by removing trade restrictions

European Union (EU)
An organization whose purpose is to facilitate free trade among member countries in Europe

THE FORCES DRIVING GLOBAL BUSINESSES

2 *Identify the basic forces prompting small firms to engage in global expansion.*

At one time, most entrepreneurs in the United States were content to position their startups for the home market and look forward to the day when international sales *might* materialize. With untapped market potential at home and few overseas competitors, many small business owners used this strategy successfully. Today, however, more small businesses are planning from the start to penetrate all available markets, both domestic and foreign.

Given the difficulty of international business, why would any entrepreneur want to get involved? Among the reasons small firms have for going global are some that have motivated international trade for centuries. Marco Polo traveled to China in 1271 to explore the trading of western goods for exotic Oriental silk and spices, which would then be sold in Europe. Clearly, the motivation to take domestic goods to foreign markets and bring foreign goods to domestic markets is as relevant today as it was in 1271. Consider the clothing designer who sells western wear in Tokyo or the independent Oriental rug dealer who scours the markets of Morocco to locate low-cost sources of high-quality Persian rugs.

Complementing these traditional reasons for going global are advantages that once were of little interest to small companies. One small business international trade expert describes the motivations to go global as follows:

> *Certainly the overall motivation is increased sales, but that is the simple answer. A more complex analysis opens the door to the real fun—the larger game. Ultimately the goal of global trade is to expand the scope and reach of your company so that the tools and resources available to fight your competition give your company an unbeatable edge—an edge that renews and transforms itself faster than the competition can keep up.*[5]

In other words, many small firms are looking to do more than simply expand a profitable market when they get involved in international business. No longer insulated from global challengers, they must consider the dynamics of the new competitive environment. The rival on the other side of the street may be a minor threat compared to an online competitor on the other side of the globe!

One way to adjust to these emerging realities is by innovating. In many industries, innovation is essential to competitiveness, and this can give a small company an advantage over its large firm counterparts. Small businesses that invest heavily in research and development often outperform large competitors. But as R&D costs rise, they often cannot be recovered from domestic sales alone. Increasing sales in international markets may be the only viable way to recover the firm's investment. In some cases, this may require identifying dynamic markets that are beginning to open around the world and locating in or near those markets.[6]

The basic forces behind global expansion can be divided into four general categories (see Exhibit 17-2): expanding markets, gaining access to resources, cutting costs, and capitalizing on special features of location. Within each category fall some tried and true motivations, as well as some new angles that have emerged with the global economy. We discuss each of these four categories in the sections that follow.

Expanding the Market

More than 95 percent of the world's population lives outside the United States. Thus, globalization greatly increases the size of an American firm's potential market.

COUNTRIES TARGETED Because the primary motivation for going global is to develop market opportunities outside the home country, the focus of globalization strategies tends to be on those countries with the greatest commercial potential. In the past, these were the developed countries (those with high levels of widely distributed wealth). Today, however, companies are paying greater attention to emerging markets, where income and buying power are growing rapidly. The U.S. Department of Commerce has labeled the largest of these countries as Big Emerging Markets (see Exhibit 17-3).

Because of their immense populations and potential market demand, countries such as China and India have attracted the greatest attention from international firms. Combined, these two nations account for nearly 40 percent of the world's six billion inhabitants, thus providing fertile ground for international expansion. Small companies are among the competitors battling for position in these emerging markets.

Dahlgren & Co. is a 170-employee firm based in Crookston, Minnesota, that specializes in the custom processing, roasting, flavoring, and packaging of sunflower seed products. Of the firm's $50 million in sales, 50 percent comes from exports to more than 30

EXHIBIT 17-2 *Basic Forces Driving Global Enterprises*

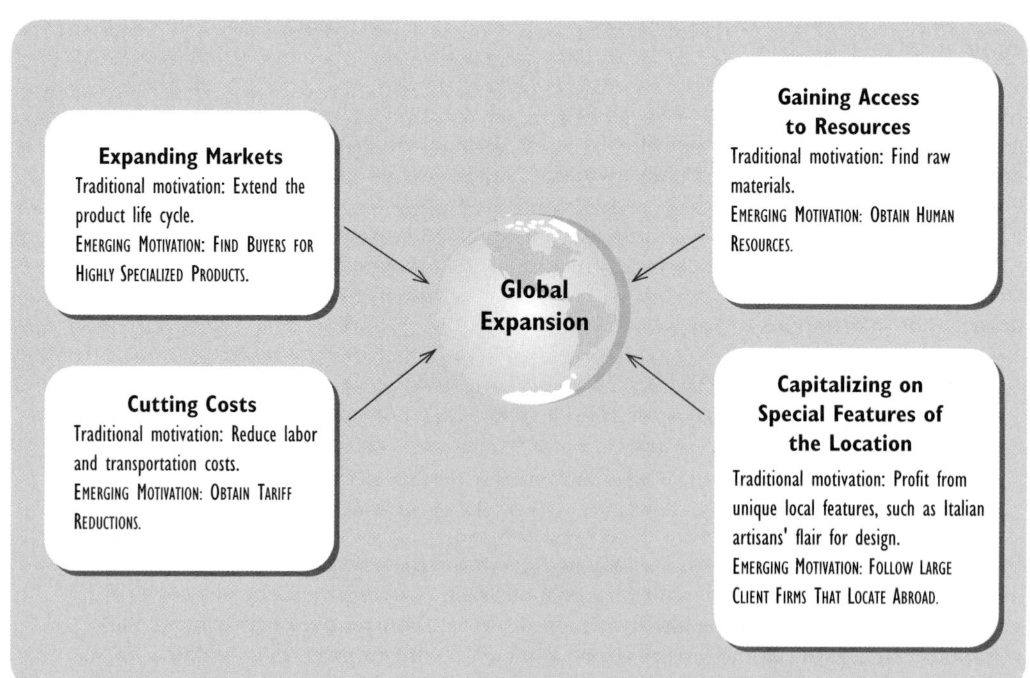

17-3 | *Big Emerging Markets*

Country	2002 Population (in millions)	2002 Wealth (GNI per capita)	2001–2002 Economic Growth (GDP growth, %)
Argentina	36.5	4,220	−10.9
Brazil	174.5	2,830	1.5
China	1,300.0	960	8.0
India	1,000.0	470	4.6
Indonesia	211.7	710	3.7
Mexico	100.8	5,920	0.9
Poland	38.6	4,570	3.0
South Africa	45.3	2,500	3.0
South Korea	47.6	9,930	6.3
Turkey	69.6	2,400	7.8
World	**6,200.0**	**5,120**	**1.9**

Source: Adapted from The World Bank Group, "World Development Indicators, 2003," http://www.worldbank.org/data/countrydata/glossary.html, June 4, 2004.

countries around the world. In an effort to boost Dahlgren's business overseas, Tom Miller, vice president of international sales, recently visited China to meet with the president of a snack-food company there. The effort paid off with a $1 million contract. This is a huge deal for a small business, but it only scratches the surface of the potential of a market with a population of well over one billion people. Dahlgren & Co. recognizes the potential of the Chinese market, which is why its Web site features pages in Chinese as well as in English.[7]

In 1991, Hong Lu formed Unitech Telecom to sell telecommunications access equipment and services to government-owned phone companies. In its first full year of production, the company had $4 million in equipment sales, almost all of them in China. But Lu was not the first to recognize the country's vast business potential. He quickly learned that telecom giants such as Lucent, Motorola, and Siemens already had a dominant position in the nation's capital, Beijing. "We were nobody—too small for people to pay attention to us," he recalls. Convinced that China had plenty of business potential to tap, Lu turned his attention to the coastal city of Hangzhou. With a population of one million, this urban area offered a sizable customer base, an educated workforce, and less bureaucratic red tape to slow down the fast-moving venture. Since that shift, Lu's firm (now called UTStarcom, Inc.) has done well in China, and the future of the telecommunications industry there looks very bright indeed.[8]

PRODUCTS PROMOTED In the mid-1960s, international business authority Raymond Vernon observed that firms tended to introduce new products in the United States first and then sell them in less-advanced countries later, as demand in the home market declined.[9] In other words, they used international expansion to extend a product's life cycle.

Although this approach is still effective under some circumstances, it has become less viable as customer preferences, income levels, and delivery systems have become more similar and product life cycles have contracted. Consider the following observations that are based on the experience of two small business practitioners:

> *The time lags between U.S. and foreign adoption have . . . disappeared. Today it is essential to roll out new products in several countries almost simultaneously. . . . No longer does the small company have the luxury of using cash flow from domestic sales to support the building of international marketing a few years later. The ever-shortening product cycle virtually dooms such a strategy. Terrific. Now, in addition to getting the product to work, setting up your new team, getting some U.S. customers, and finding money, you now have to worry about selling in six or eight additional countries, most of whom don't even speak English!*[10]

Living the Dream

Focus on the Customer

Brightstar Shines in the Cell Phone Universe

© Andy Shaw/Bloomberg News/Landov

http://www.brightstarcorp.com

Demand for cell phones is surging in Latin America—especially in Argentina, where consumers purchased 5 million handsets in 2004, more than three times the 1.5 million sold in 2003 and more than 10 times the number sold in 2002. Driving a good part of this expansion is a company called Brightstar Corporation, which buys cell phones and sells them to wireless carriers across Latin America.

Miami, Florida–based Brightstar was founded in 1997 by 33-year-old R. Marcelo Claure (now CEO of the company) and has grown to be the second-largest Hispanic-owned business in the United States. The company has posted double-digit growth every year since its founding. Today, the company employs 700 people and operates 21 facilities in 16 countries, and its 2003 revenue exceeded $1.2 billion. How did this startup expand so quickly? A big part of the answer is Claure's emphasis on innovation.

Innovation can go far beyond lab work and research and development efforts. It can also involve creative leadership approaches, cutting-edge incentive programs, and unique marketing strategies, among other things.

In 1998, Ericsson made Brightstar the main distributor of its cell phones in Latin America—a low-risk decision, given the manufacturer's limited role in the region. This presented Claure with a number of problems as well as a chance to demonstrate his bent toward innovation. Customers complained that Ericsson's phones were the ugliest and most expensive in the market, but Brightstar had no control over design features or price. However, it did control shipping, so it made shipping terms irresistible. Claure announced to his customers, "You'll have no minimum order, no projection requirements, you can pay in longer than 30 days, and we'll deliver direct." Most manufacturers would ship phones only as far as Florida or Texas, to avoid the confusing maze of customs requirements and import duties associated with shipping to Latin American customers. Brightstar was offering to take many of the hassles out of delivery, and this was new. Customers quickly signed up, and Brightstar doubled its market share in the region within a year.

Sometimes, reaching international markets just requires a little more innovation, which is the strong suit of most entrepreneurial firms.

Sources: http://www.brightstarcorp.com, July 16, 2004; Cara Cannella, "Telecom," *Inc.*, Vol. 25, No. 11, Fall 2003, pp. 125–130; Chris McDougall, "Closing the Deal," *Inc.*, Vol. 26, No. 3, March 2004, pp. 70–84; and "Hot Hands," *Latin Trade*, Vol. 12, No. 6, June 2004, p. 40.

Products that sell at home are now more likely to be introduced very quickly abroad, with little or no adaptation in many cases. The role of television programs, movies, and print media in shaping cultural tastes throughout the world has eased the entry of small businesses into international markets. American interests have long held a starring role in the cultural arena, inspiring widespread purchases of products such as blue jeans and fast food and generating international interest in U.S. sports and celebrities. By informing consumers about the lifestyles of others, globalization is leading the world toward common consumer preferences.

In addition to the trendy products associated with popular culture, another type of product well suited to international markets is the very specialized product. As technology makes possible increasingly sophisticated products, markets are demanding more differentiated products that satisfy their unique needs and interests. Fewer consumers in the home market are likely to be interested in a highly differentiated (and often more expensive) product, so it may become necessary to search for international markets with the same unique demand in order to increase sales enough to recover product development costs. Because small companies often follow focused business strategies (with limited domestic market potential) and aspire to grow rapidly, efforts to exploit the competitive advantage of specialized products across international markets may be even more important to them than to their larger counterparts.[11]

Martin Goodwin and Bob Henry work with a very specialized product in international markets. MSS Global, their Riverside, California, company, has progressed from a basement venture to a global enterprise in just a few years. It all started in 1993, when Goodwin ran a supermarket and a few general stores owned by his family. To monitor inventories, price products, and issue purchase orders, he used a dozen separate software programs. In an effort to streamline the process, Goodwin teamed up with Henry, a computer systems specialist, to develop an integrated software package that would handle all of these functions. Goodwin and Henry created Retail, the first Windows-compatible software program for retailers. The product tracks inventory, calculates pricing, gathers customer data, and tracks cashier productivity, so sales trends can be determined with only a few computer keystrokes.

The market interest in the United States for this focused product was healthy but limited, leaving MSS Global with scant opportunity to recover development costs. To overcome this constraint, Goodwin and Henry decided to go global. Using strategic partnerships (including an alliance with Microsoft), MSS Global managed to sell nearly 25,000 licenses in 20 countries before the close of the year 2000—amazing growth for a company with only 10 employees! And the expansion continues. To date, the company has sold more than 40,000 licenses and has set up international offices in Europe, Asia, South America, and Central America. With so much of its revenue coming from international markets, MSS Global can attest to the importance of going global to exploit a competitive advantage.[12]

MAKING THE MOST OF EXPERIENCE No matter which countries are targeted or products promoted, market expansion has the potential to provide benefits beyond the standard per-unit profits on additional items sold. As volume expands, a firm usually can find ways to work smarter or to generate efficiencies. Analysts first observed these **experience curve efficiencies** in the aircraft manufacturing industry. They noticed that each time a manufacturer doubled its total output, the production cost per aircraft dropped by 20 percent. In other words, per-unit costs declined by 20 percent when the firm manufactured four units instead of two, declined again by 20 percent when the firm made eight units instead of four, and so on.

experience curve efficiencies
Per-unit savings gained from the repeated production of the same good

What can explain this gain in efficiency? Most credit the outcome to learning effects and economies of scale. **Learning effects** occur when the insight an employee gains from experience leads to improved work performance. Learning effects can also take place at the level of the firm if the experiences of individual employees are shared, leading to improved practices and production routines across the organization. These gains from learning are greatest during the startup period and gradually decline over time. Efficiencies from **economies of scale**, on the other hand, continue to rise as the business grows and volume increases, because these savings arise from spreading investment across more units of output and acquiring more specialized (and thus more efficient) plants, equipment, and employees.

learning effects
Insights, gained from experience, that lead to improved work performance

economies of scale
Efficiencies that result from expansion of production

Small firms can accelerate the gains from experience curve efficiencies by emphasizing international expansion, assuming that they can manage the growth. Prior to the 1990s, startups were encouraged to consider international expansion only after they had established a solid position in their domestic market. Times have changed. Recent studies have shown that starting with a global presence or globalizing early in a company's life leads to increased performance, especially sales growth. And for high-potential ventures, sales growth is usually considered one of the most important dimensions of performance. The benefits of learning effects and economies of scale are especially apparent in startups based on complex technologies. The possibility of achieving experience curve efficiencies through accelerated globalization of emerging technologies is likely to stimulate the interest of startups and small companies in international business.[13]

Gaining Access to Resources

Just as fortune seekers abandoned their comfortable lives in the eastern United States to flock to California following the discovery of gold at Sutter's Mill in 1848, small firms today leave the United States to gain access to essential raw materials and other factors of production. For example, the oil fields of Kuwait are tended not just by employees of the global oil giants, but also by hundreds of support personnel who work for small companies that have contracted to assist their large clients. These small players choose to locate operations in Kuwait (or Mexico, Saudi Arabia, Venezuela, etc.) for one simple reason: That's where the oil is! The same principle holds for manufacturers that require scarce inputs. For example, stainless steel makers have set up production in the Dominican

Republic to obtain the ore deposits they need, and aluminum producers have relocated to Iceland to tap the country's abundant hydroelectric and geothermal energy.[14]

Though small firms have traditionally pursued international ventures to obtain raw materials, increasingly the focus of their search is skilled labor. For example, David Birch, a well-known entrepreneurship expert, relates the story of a personal friend who owns a small software development company in Chicago. To hire people to do routine computer programming, he found it necessary to locate his programming operation in Russia.[15] Despite the fact that installation of a telephone can take several months and gangsters sometimes pay visits to demand protection money, the entrepreneur was lured to Russia by its talented but low-priced human capital, a necessary resource that he found to be in short supply in the United States. Of course, American businesses of all sizes have been accessing foreign labor increasingly through contracts with independent providers, an

Living the Dream *Entrepreneurial Challenges*

Opportunity Knocks, but Not Necessarily at Home

© Sondeep Shankar/Bloomberg News/Landov

International outsourcing has become a hot issue in the last few years, in part because of sluggish job growth in the United States. And this form of outsourcing is clearly growing in popularity. According to a recent survey by Forrester Research Inc., 15 percent of the large firms surveyed employ outsourcing as a permanent part of their strategy. Results such as these have caused some to speculate that outsourcing is solely a large-firm practice; however, the evidence does not support this conclusion. For example, an informal survey of venture capitalists by *BusinessWeek* magazine suggests that 20 to 25 percent of the enterprises they invest in employ similar practices. In many cases, offshoring is a matter of survival for small businesses.

Wayne Youngers, CEO of Youngers & Sons Manufacturing Company, Inc., in Viola, Kansas, was shocked to learn from one of his customers that the shaft that his company makes for use in hydraulic equipment and sells for $6 can be bought for $2 or less in China, without sacrificing quality. This led Youngers to review his entire product line to see which parts could be manufactured overseas, and he concluded that eventually 50 percent of his production could be outsourced. For Youngers, offshoring isn't a matter of choice; it's a matter of survival.

In 1999, 38-year-old Swain Porter led a group of former Microsoft executives to launch a startup called Catalytic Software. The grand vision of the investors was to create a low-cost, high-quality, just-in-time software development firm—located close to Hyderabad, India. While some of the challenges Porter has faced are unique (having to keep a water buffalo from stepping on the company's fiber-optic lines comes quickly to mind), most are normal needs such as obtaining funding for expansion, finding new clients, and securing talented programmers. As it turns out, software development is an industry that has moved quickly toward offshore operations.

In 2002, Michael Calderone started an online coffee business called Smiles Coffee. As with most small companies, cash was always an issue. Therefore, investing in an in-house customer service department was out of the question for the Henderson, Nevada–based venture. The only reasonable option was to outsource the operation. Calderone worked through a call center in the Philippines, where nine dedicated and friendly customer service representatives patiently answered his customers' questions, and they did so very inexpensively. On average, his reps earned about $3,600 per year—a fraction of the cost of call center staff in the United States. The 43-year-old Calderone admits that using offshore labor was an uncomfortable option, but concluded that this strategy was essential, since it allowed him to free up the investment needed to grow the rest of his business.

In the end, small firms that choose to outsource internationally are seeking two things: reduced costs and superior talent. These two factors are always important to the success of small companies.

Sources: Spencer E. Ante and Robert D. Hof, "Look Who's Going Offshore," *BusinessWeek*, May 17, 2004, p. 79; Timothy Appel, "Small Firms Outsource Abroad by Tapping Offshore Producers," *Wall Street Journal*, January 7, 2004, p. A2; Eric Wahlgren, "The Outsourcing Dilemma," *Inc.*, April 2004, pp. 41–42; and Kara Swisher, "U.S. Tech Town Rises in India," *Wall Street Journal*, January 7, 2002, p. A1.

arrangement known as **international outsourcing**, or **offshoring**. This has been especially popular in countries such as India and China, where relatively high-skilled labor is low in cost.[16]

international outsourcing (offshoring)
A strategy that involves accessing foreign labor through contracts with independent providers

Cutting Costs

Sometimes firms go global to reduce the cost of doing business. Among the costs that firms have traditionally reduced by venturing abroad are those for raw materials, labor, and manufacturing overhead.

Kirkham Motorsports is headquartered in Provo, Utah, where 10 employees complete the final assembly of the company's high-performance Cobra automobiles. To be cost-competitive, however, the firm relocated the labor-intensive production of aluminum car bodies and frames to a MiG (Russian fighter jet) factory in Mielec, Poland, where 40 workers apply their advanced metal-fabrication skills to turn out these automotive works of art.[17] Perhaps Cobra buyers will savor the notion that their lightning-fast cars were constructed in a facility that once produced the jet aircraft that continue to command respect the world over.

Although Kirkham went global to control labor costs, the critical factor is not always labor. For example, transportation costs would likely be the controlling factor for a small business that sells cement products used in construction (concrete columns, bridge girders, decorative statues)—goods that are extremely heavy but do not command a premium price. Since the cost of overseas transportation could exceed the price of the product, international sales would make sense only if the firm were to locate production in-country and near customers.

The advantages of globalization in reducing labor and transportation costs have long been recognized. However, the emerging global economy has brought a new means of lowering costs through relocation. In recent years, a number of countries have formed regional free trade areas, within which commerce is facilitated by reducing tariffs, simplifying commercial regulations, or even—in the case of the EU—adopting a common currency. These cost-cutting measures can be a powerful inducement to small firms to move into the prescribed area. For example, after the enactment of NAFTA, a number of Japanese firms located manufacturing facilities in Mexico to reap the advantage of reduced tariffs on trade within that region.

Capitalizing on Special Features of Location

Some of the benefits of location are simply the result of unique features of a local environment. For example, Italian artisans have long been well known for their flair for design, and Japanese technicians have shown an ability to harness optical technologies for application in both cameras and copiers. Small companies that depend on a particular strength may find that it makes sense to locate in a region that provides fertile ground for that type of innovation.

Other special benefits of location derive from deliberate government policy. To attract high-tech companies, the government of Dubai, a tiny Arab sheikdom of 800,000 citizens with a land mass about the size of Rhode Island, has stepped up enforcement of copyright laws, causing software piracy to fall from 99 percent to 40 percent. Coupled with generous tax breaks and favorable treatment of firms locating in this Persian Gulf city-state, this initiative has been an undeniable success. It has attracted hundreds of companies from the United States and elsewhere, including computer hardware manufacturers, software development firms, and other technology providers.[18] And despite the instability in the Middle East, Dubai Internet City continues to attract more and more companies of all sizes.[19]

Even the appeal of regional free trade areas lies partly in locational features unrelated to cost. As the European countries talked about coming together in the EU, many non-European executives worried that a "Fortress Europe" mentality would arise. That is, they assumed that increased trade among European countries would discourage trade with other nations. In response, many businesses—large and small—located physical facilities in Europe to guarantee future access to that market. In hindsight, they have concluded that the EU has not seriously hindered trade with firms outside of Europe; nonetheless, firms have taken similar measures to ensure market access in other trade areas.

Finally, a recent trend among small businesses is to follow large client firms to their new locations. As major corporations locate their operations abroad, their small suppliers may find it necessary to go global along with the client firms to ensure the continuation of important sourcing contracts. The small business owner may have no personal desire to expand internationally, but dependence on a major customer relocating abroad might leave the owner with no alternative. Ford Motor Corporation is convinced that taking its suppliers overseas ensures quality, reduces startup costs, and helps meet local-content restrictions. So when the auto giant decided to open a new plant in Europe, it offered a multi-year contract to Loranger Manufacturing Corporation, a small automobile parts manufacturer based in Warren, Pennsylvania. But there was a catch: The contract required Loranger to locate near the new plant. Since Ford was its primary customer, the small supplier accepted the offer and in 1993 opened its Hungarian facility to manufacture plastic parts for Ford. Within a decade, Loranger had 150 employees and was generating nearly $10 million a year in sales.[20]

Traditional and emerging motivations for small businesses to go global are numerous, but the ultimate incentive is this: If you fail to seize an international market opportunity, someone else will. Under these conditions, the best defense is a good offense. Establishing a position outside of the domestic setting may preempt rivals from exploiting those opportunities and using them against you in the future.

STRATEGY OPTIONS FOR GLOBAL FIRMS

3 *Identify and compare strategy options for global businesses.*

Once an entrepreneur has decided to go global, the next step is to plan a strategy that matches the potential of the firm. Throughout most of the 20th century, many small companies were hesitant to step into the world of global trade. Today, such firms are showing signs of "accelerated internationalization." In some industries, even the smallest and newest of companies must globalize just to survive.[21] For most small businesses, the first step toward globalization is a decision to export a product to other countries or to import goods from abroad to sell in the domestic market. These initial efforts are often followed by more sophisticated non-export strategies, such as licensing, franchising, forming strategic alliances with international partners, or even locating facilities abroad (see Exhibit 17-4).

Exporting

exporting
Selling products produced in the home country to customers in another country

Exporting involves the sale of products produced in the home country to customers in another country. The U.S. Small Business Administration recently announced that small firms represent approximately 97 percent of American exporters, contributing more than 29 percent of the value of exported goods.[22] Exporting is popular among small businesses because it provides a manageable way of expanding into the international arena:

17-4 *Strategy Options for Global Enterprises*

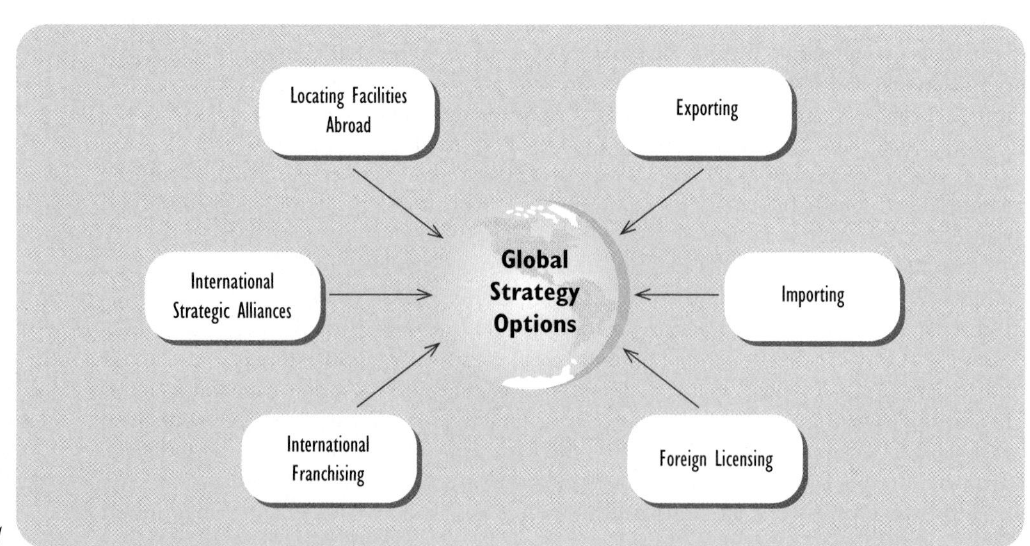

With increasing global competition, falling barriers to international trade, and improved international communication and information networks, many firms are pressed to compete in international markets. . . . Exporting may offer an effective means for firms to achieve an international position . . . without overextending their capabilities or resources.[23]

Put another way, small export companies can market and distribute their products in other countries without incurring the expense of supporting costly operations in those markets. If the financial benefits from international sales more than offset shipping costs and tariffs, exporting is a favorable option.

One way small companies can look into an export program is to join a **trade mission**—a trip organized to help small business owners meet potential buyers abroad and navigate cultural and regulatory obstacles in foreign markets. Mary Ellen Mooney took this approach when she joined a trade mission organized by a consortium of California state trade groups to explore potential markets along Mexico's Baja Peninsula. Mooney is co-owner of Mooney Farms, a 50-employee family business located in Chico, California, that produces sun-dried tomato products. Her three-day visit to Mexico led to a contract to sell $1,200 of product each month to a restaurant in Ensenada—a limited success, but a start nonetheless. She hopes to sell more product south of the border, targeting larger urban centers like Guadalajara, Mexico City, and perhaps even Acapulco. After her trip to Mexico, Mooney planned to visit other potential markets, including Venezuela and Canada. Given the advantages of organized tours, other entrepreneurs are dusting off their passports and signing up to participate. As one spokesperson for a trade mission observed, "There are more trade missions than ever before, and a growing perception that access to world markets is easier than ever."[24]

trade mission
A trip organized to help small business owners meet with potential buyers abroad and learn about cultural and regulatory obstacles in foreign markets

In some cases, exporting to international markets may actually promote business in the domestic market, especially when seasonal demand in the home market offsets that from abroad. Very Special Chocolats, a small Canadian producer of specialty chocolates, has turned to global opportunities in Asia so as to use its factory in Azusa, California, more efficiently. The firm has $15 million invested in its four production lines in California and employs 100 full-time workers to operate the facility. To manage the spike in demand for chocolates around Christmas, the firm would hire as many as 350 temporary employees for just a few months. Allowing much of its facility to remain idle during the off-season left Very Special Chocolats with a permanent investment that generated product for only part of the year. The excess capacity was becoming a serious financial burden for the small confectioner. To deal with this challenge, the company decided to move into Asian markets, such as Japan, Taiwan, South Korea, and China, where the cycle of holidays is different. Thanks to exports to these countries (representing 15 percent of the firm's total sales), the company is now able to operate its plant full time for nine months out of the year.[25]

The rise of the Internet has fueled vigorous growth in export activity. Small firms see the Internet as a powerful tool for increasing their international visibility, allowing them to connect with customers who were previously beyond their reach. Entertainment Earth is an Internet toy retailer, based in North Hollywood, California, that specializes in collectible action figures. Founders Aaron and Jason Labowitz have earned profit margins as great as 20 percent, and recent projections show the company's annual sales exceeding $7 million. The typical customer is 32 years old, has income above $65,000 per year, and would prefer not to be seen in a toy store. Because the business is Internet-based, it has customers around the world. Jochen Till, 29, lives in Munich, Germany, and loves doing business with the company. This owner of around 300 action figures has decided that Entertainment Earth's "service is so good that [he won't] even shop the Web for alternatives." Clearly, Entertainment Earth knows its globe-spanning market well, which is consistent with the high marks the company gets from e-commerce rating services.[26]

Importing

The flip side of exporting is **importing**, which involves selling goods from abroad in the firm's home market. When a small company finds a product abroad that has market potential at home or identifies a product that would sell at home but cannot find a domestic producer, an import strategy may be the only solution. Rich Birnbaum is the founder of ProWorth, a bare-bones operation in Englewood Cliffs, New Jersey, that also employs his brother, as well as several high school students and retirees part-time. Birnbaum sells exquisite Swiss brand-name watches and diamond jewelry through eBay, other online

importing
Selling goods produced in another country to buyers in the home country

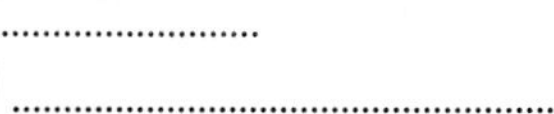

Living the Dream

The Internet Can Make a World of Difference

barewalls.com
Covering the world with great art, one bare wall at a time.

Courtesy of Barewalls Interactive Art, Inc.

The Internet remains a popular means for small businesses to reach customers, especially when marketing goods and services internationally. Barewalls was created in 1996 to sell art prints and posters online, reaching out to clients who want a fast, easy, and affordable way to decorate their home or office. Using the power of the Internet, Barewalls offers customers access to more than 150,000 art items, all at the click of a mouse.

Has the strategy helped the company reach an international market? Lorne Lieberman, 32-year-old CEO and co-founder of the Sharon, Massachusetts–based company, says that it has. He observes, "Relationships and word-of-mouth [were] built, allowing us to have a presence [overseas]." Indeed, through its global strategy, the company increased sales by 20 percent between 2002 and 2003, and the Internet stands at the center of that strategy. Most of its global sales come from Australia, Canada, Japan, South Korea, and the United Kingdom.

Appropriate Web site development can help to spur international sales—for example, offering a second- or third-language version of the site or using universally understood symbols to identify important features, such as the shopping cart. To connect culturally with an overseas market, small business owners may hire or partner with someone with local insights who can help them reach their target market. However, the greatest challenges usually involve routine matters, like providing fast and affordable shipping and distribution. And, of course, there is always the problem of fraud, so it's important to pay attention to any red flags that signal potentially false orders.

Internet-based commerce is not without its challenges. But it deserves serious consideration because of the awesome potential it holds for small companies with international aspirations.

http://www.barewalls.com

Sources: http://www.barewalls.com, July 16, 2004; and Melissa Campanelli, "A World of Goods," *Entrepreneur*, December 2003, pp. 60–61.

auction services, and the firm's Web site. Birnbaum decided to use eBay because the customer acquisition costs are limited to the cost of a listing, which allows him to keep prices low. The venture has been very successful. Launched in January 1999, the company racked up $1 million in sales by that year's end, allowing Birnbaum to pay himself a salary of about $100,000 and still break even. And what about the future? The optimistic founder expects sales to increase thirty-fold within a few years—as long as Americans continue to want the fine imports that ProWorth has to offer, that is.[27]

Yalanda Lang has an import story with an interesting twist. While shopping in Milan, Italy, Lang watched two women coddling an overpriced bag and decided on the spot that she could design and produce a better product. A new business was born. Lang, an American with European design training, borrowed $50,000 of her parents' personal savings to start a company called INDE (for "independent"). Her plan was to produce high-end women's handbags, positioned to compete with prestige brands like Gucci and Fendi. However, she learned early on that American retail buyers would purchase only low-end handbags from U.S. manufacturers; they look to European producers for prestige products. Lang therefore had no choice but to start her company as an international business. "Strangely enough," she concluded, "to compete, I need to be in Europe to sell in America." Lang's goal today is the same as it was at the start: import more of the firm's European-made products into the American market.[28] It's a simple strategy, but it seems to be working.

Foreign Licensing

Exporting is the most popular international strategy among small firms, but there are also other options. Because of limited resources, many small firms are hesitant to go global. One way to deal with this constraint is to follow a licensing strategy. **Foreign licensing** allows a company in another country to purchase the rights to manufacture and sell a firm's products in overseas markets. The firm buying these rights is called the **licensee**. The licensee makes payments to the **licensor**, or the firm selling those rights, normally in the form of **royalties**—a fee paid for each unit produced.

foreign licensing
Allowing a company in another country to purchase the rights to manufacture and sell a company's products in international markets

licensee
The company buying licensing rights

licensor
The company selling licensing rights

royalties
Fees paid by the licensee to the licensor for each unit produced under a licensing contract

International licensing has its drawbacks. For example, the licensee makes all the production and marketing decisions, and the licensor must share returns from sales with the licensee. However, foreign licensing is the least expensive way to go global, since the licensee bears all the cost and risk of setting up a foreign operation.[29]

Recall that MSS Global (described on pages 378–379) uses a foreign licensing strategy; the company has sold more than 40,000 licenses around the globe. Co-founder Martin Goodwin admits that his small company could never have achieved such rapid expansion on its own: "For us to set up an office and learn that culture and all the tax rules and then to advertise—it's a tremendous headache." Licensing agreements with major computer hardware manufacturers covering the South and Central American markets have paid off. MSS Global may not have a marketing team, a direct sales staff, or even venture capital, but the company makes money every time IBM or NCR sells its product to a foreign retailer. This is the beauty of foreign licensing.[30]

Small companies tend to think of products when they explore international licensing options, but licensing intangible assets such as proprietary technologies, copyrights, and trademarks may offer even greater potential returns. Just as Disney licenses its famous Mickey Mouse character to manufacturers around the world, a small retailer called Peace Frogs is using licensing to introduce its copyrighted designs in Spain. As Peace Frogs' founder and president, Catesby Jones, explains, "We export our Peace Frogs T-shirts directly to Japan, but in Spain per capita income is lower, competition from domestic producers is stronger, and tariffs are high, so we licensed a Barcelona–based company the rights to manufacture our product."[31] From this agreement, Peace Frogs generates additional revenue with almost no added expense.

Foreign licensing can also be used to protect against **counterfeit activity**, or the unauthorized use of intellectual property. Licensing rights to a firm in a foreign market provides a local champion to ensure that other firms do not use protected assets in an inappropriate way.

counterfeit activity
The unauthorized use of intellectual property

International Franchising

International franchising is a variation on the licensing theme. The franchisor offers a standard package of products, systems, and management services to the franchisee, which provides capital, market insight, and hands-on management. Though international franchising was not widely used before the 1970s, today it is the fastest-growing market entry strategy of U.S. firms, with Canada as the dominant market (followed by Japan and the United Kingdom, in that order). This approach is especially popular with U.S. restaurant chains that want to establish a global presence. McDonald's, for example, has raised its famous golden arches in 119 countries around the world. But international franchising is useful to small companies as well. Danny Benususan is the owner of Blue Note, a jazz club in Manhattan that is now in its second decade of operation. Considered one of the top venues in the world for jazz and other forms of music, this club has attracted the attention of international businesspeople who have established franchises in Milan, Tokyo, Osaka, Fukuoka, Nagoya, and Seoul. Now under the management of Blue Note International, the club has successfully established itself as the world's only franchised jazz club network.[32] Blue Note has proved that there is more than one way for a small business to globalize.

international franchising
Selling a standard package of products, systems, and management services to a company in another country

International Strategic Alliances

Moving beyond licensing, some small businesses have expanded globally by joining forces with large corporations in cooperative efforts. An **international strategic alliance** allows firms to share risks and pool resources as they enter a new market, matching the local partner's understanding of the target market (culture, legal system, competitive conditions, etc.) with the technology or product knowledge of its alliance counterpart. One of the advantages of this strategy is that both partners take comfort in knowing that neither is "going it alone."

international strategic alliance
A combination of efforts and/or assets of companies in different countries for the sake of pooling resources and sharing the risks of an enterprise

Business Marketing Group (BMG), Inc., is a small firm that specializes in forging strategic alliances between startups and large technology firms. When BMG paired Microsoft with a small information technology company called FullArmor, the startup gained help in designing its software to run on Microsoft Windows, as well as access to Microsoft-faithful customers at home and abroad. This alliance enabled FullArmor to form a second (but separate) alliance with Entex Information Services to provide services and solutions for Windows. Entex is owned by Siemens AG, the German engineering powerhouse. Entex/Siemens is one of the top 10 global service providers, so the strategic alliance with Entex has provided FullArmor with indirect access to many international customers—access that FullArmor would not have been able to achieve as an independent enterprise.

Locating Facilities Abroad

A small business with advanced global aspirations may choose to establish a foreign presence of its own in strategic markets, especially if the firm has already developed an international customer base. Most small companies start by locating a production facility or sales office overseas. As discussed earlier, one avenue pursued by Mary Ellen Mooney in her quest to expand her farming and sun-dried tomatoes business to Mexico and other points south was to join a trade mission. But Mooney Farms also opened a processing facility in Caborca, Mexico, a region known for high-quality fruits and vegetables. By locating its state-of-the-art facility in Caborca, Mooney Farms was able to take advantage of a favorable local climate that allows the company to process tomatoes 10 months out of the year and supply customers with products year round.[33]

Opening an overseas sales office can be a very effective strategy, but small business owners should wait until sales in the local market are great enough to justify the move. An overseas office is costly to establish, staff, manage, and finance; thus, this alternative is beyond the reach of most small companies. Furthermore, the anticipated advantages of overseas offices are sometimes difficult to achieve. Often U.S. firms locate their first international sales office in Canada, but some small companies are finding it profitable to open an office that provides access to the European region (the English-speaking United Kingdom and Ireland are popular locations).

Some small firms have grand ambitions that go beyond locating a production facility or sales office overseas. Firms in this category are likely to plan independent operations, such as purchasing a foreign business from another firm through what is known as a **cross-border acquisition** or starting a **greenfield venture** by forming from scratch a new wholly owned subsidiary in another country. In either case, go-it-alone strategies are complex and costly. These options give firms maximum control over their foreign operations and eliminate the need to share any revenues generated; however, they force companies to bear the entire risk of these expensive undertakings. If the subsidiary is a greenfield venture, the firm may have much to learn about running an enterprise in a foreign country, managing host-country nationals, and developing an effective marketing strategy. The commercial potential of a wholly owned international subsidiary may be great, but the challenges of managing it can be even greater. This option is not for the faint of heart.

cross-border acquisition
The purchase by a business in one country of a company located in another country

greenfield venture
A wholly owned subsidiary formed from scratch in another country

CHALLENGES TO GLOBAL BUSINESSES

4 Explain the challenges that global enterprises face.

Small businesses face challenges; small *global* businesses face far greater challenges. How well can a small firm do in the global marketplace? The success of enterprising entrepreneurs in international markets proves that small firms can do better than survive—they can thrive! However, success is unlikely without careful preparation. Small business owners must recognize the unique challenges facing global firms and adjust their plans accordingly. Specifically, they need to pay attention to political risks, economic risks, and managerial limitations.

Political Risk

The potential for a country's political forces to negatively affect the performance of business enterprises operating within its borders is referred to as **political risk**. Often, this risk is related to the instability of a nation's government, which can create difficulties for outside companies. Potential problems range from threats as trivial as new regulations restricting the content of television advertising to challenges as catastrophic as a government takeover of private assets. Political developments can threaten access to an export market, require a firm to reveal trade secrets, or even demand that work be completed in-country. Exhibit 17-5 highlights variations in political risk across nations, based on the "Country Risk Rankings" published in *Euromoney* magazine. Countries are color-coded to indicate their riskiness—green represents "go," or safe, countries; yellow, "proceed with caution" countries; and red, "stop and think very carefully" countries. Firms hoping to do business in "red" countries should make appropriate adjustments.

political risk
The potential for political forces in a country to negatively affect the performance of businesses operating within its borders

EXHIBIT 17-5 "Country Risk Rankings" Map

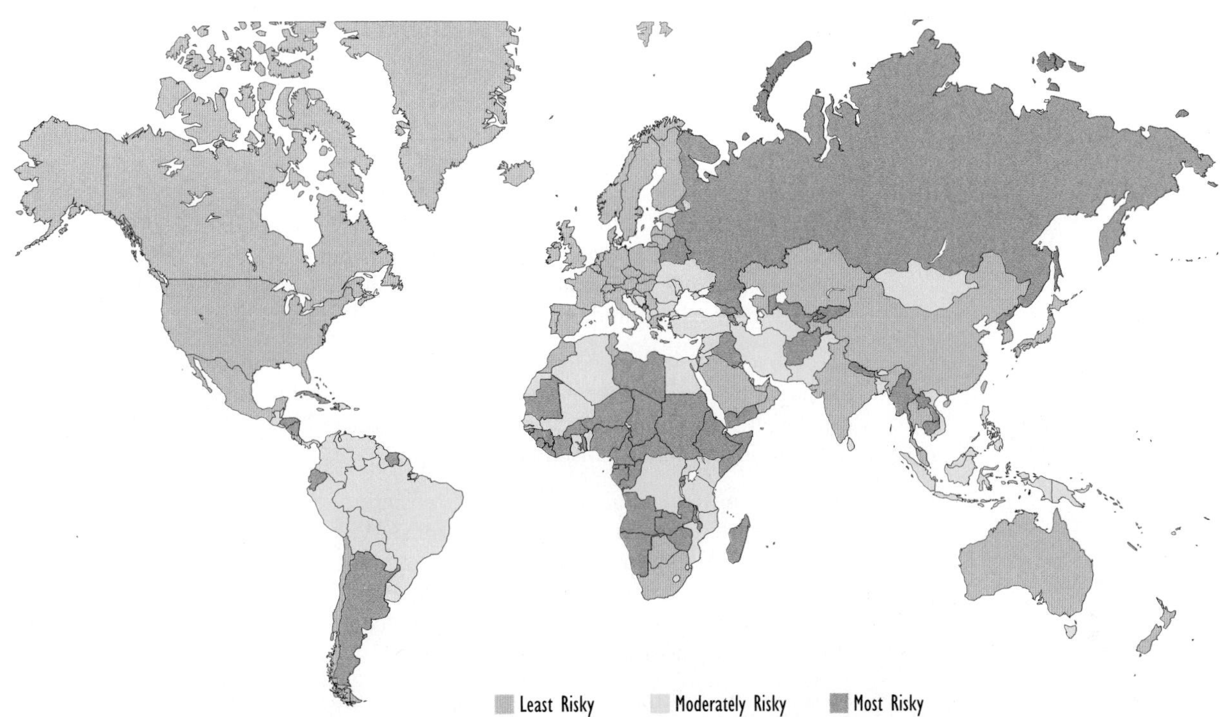

Source: Paul Pedzinksi and Andrew Newby, "Risk Improvement Defies Politics," *Euromoney*, Vol. 35, No. 419, March 2004, pp. 128–134.

Economic Risk

Economic risk is the probability that a government will mismanage its economy and change the business environment in ways that hinder the performance of firms operating there. Economic risk and political risk are therefore related. Two of the most serious problems resulting from economic mismanagement are inflation and fluctuations in exchange rates. While a discussion of these factors is beyond the scope of this textbook, it is important to recognize that inflation reduces the value of a country's currency on the foreign exchange market, thereby decreasing the value of cash flows the foreign firm receives from its operations in the local market.

economic risk
The probability that a government will mismanage its economy and thereby change the business environment in ways that hinder the performance of firms operating there

Exchange rates represent the value of one country's currency relative to that of another country—for example, the number of Mexican pesos that can be purchased with one U.S. dollar. Sudden or unexpected changes in these rates can be a serious problem for small international firms, whether the firm exports to that market or has a local presence there.

exchange rate
The value of one country's currency relative to that of another country

Mary Ellen Mooney of Mooney Farms has kept an eye on the European market, as well as that of Mexico. She recognized the potential of exporting her sun-dried tomato products to France and came close to striking a deal with a local distributor a few years ago, but the negotiations fell through when the dollar rose sharply against European currencies.[34] To understand her dilemma, suppose the French distributor was willing to pay 5 euros for a package of sun-dried tomatoes. If the dollar and the euro were exchanged one-to-one, Mooney could convert the 5 euros to $5.00. If $4.50 covered her costs of production, transportation, insurance, and so on, then Mooney would earn a $.50 profit ($5.00 – 4.50) per unit. But, in reality, Mooney's deal fell through because the dollar *rose* in value relative to the local currency. For the sake of illustration, let's assume the exchange rate dropped to .80 euro per dollar. This would mean that units selling for 5 euros would be worth only $4.00 each, which would result in a $.50 loss on every sale.

Mooney's experience illustrates how a good deal can quickly fall apart if exchange rates take a turn for the worse. This risk is especially serious for small companies that are just

getting established in international markets. Such firms must take measures to protect against currency-related risks, such as stating contracts in U.S. dollars and using currency-hedging strategies.

Managerial Limitations

Conducting business internationally will never be as easy as doing business at home—it is likely to stretch managerial skills and resources to the limit. Global commerce complicates every task and raises difficult questions related to every function of the firm.

- *Product Planning*. Will the product/service satisfy customer tastes? Does the foreign location have the employees we need to manufacture the products we plan to offer? Do available workers have the skills required for our operations? Will government restrictions hinder our planned product introductions?
- *Marketing*. How will we conduct marketing research? Who should be included in the target market? What sales projections are reasonable in the international market? What price should we charge for our product? How can we deal with counterfeit products manufactured locally?
- *Finance*. Can we maintain cash flow for our international operations? How will we manage currency exchange rate fluctuations? Will government policy impact capital transfers? Will local law allow us to send home profits from the foreign market? Does the host country government maintain sufficient foreign currency reserves to allow us to take profits out of the country? Will barter or other forms of countertrade be necessary to do business?
- *Management*. Will the management approaches we use at home work in the international setting? How can we identify the people best suited for overseas positions

Living the Dream — *Entrepreneurial Challenges*

Currencies Can Cut Both Ways

A solid international contract can fall through when currency exchange rates shift unfavorably. On the other hand, an advantageous shift might increase global sales.

Bob Pattison, 47, and Tim Yourieff, 49, own Neil Pryde Sails International, a boat sail manufacturer headquartered in Milford, Connecticut. They have found that shifts in currency exchange rates can provide a nice boost to business. At one time, 90 percent of the company's revenue was derived from the U.S. market. But terrorism fears and economic woes cut deeply into domestic boat sales (down 22 percent since 2000), and this sent the company's revenues into "the perfect storm."

What saved Neil Pryde was a weakening U.S. dollar, which made its product more affordable to European boat owners, a very lucrative market. The company launched a strong push into Europe, starting in late 2002, and the results have been very good. After the dollar fell 25 percent against the euro, Pattison and Yourieff were able to absorb the 14 percent tariff charged by the European Union and still price their product about 10 percent below local competitors.

For Neil Pryde Sails, the news has been good in recent years, but the risk of fluctuations may not bode well for small companies. For example, if the euro weakens against the dollar in the future, American companies with outstanding contracts in Europe will find that the value of that business will fall proportionately. In an attempt to eliminate this risk, some small firms price all contracts in U.S. dollars. More than likely, however, a shift in exchange rates would still leave these firms "holding the bag," ramping up for sales that inevitably fall through. It is a tremendous gamble. However, other options such as locating production abroad or using financial contracts to hedge currency exchange risks are available, and these can take some of the "guesswork" out of international business.

http://www.neilprydesails.com

Sources: Eric Wahlgren, "Trade Winds," *Inc.*, November 2003, pp. 36–38; Knowledge@Wharton, "Does the Blowback from Dollar-Denominated Contracts Do More Harm Than Good?" April 7–20, 2004, http://knowledge.wharton.upenn.edu/weblink/61.cfm, July 16, 2004.

with our company? How much should we pay our local employees? How should we work with labor unions in foreign locations? How can we overcome language, culture, and communication barriers? Can we develop a trusting relationship with foreign employees? What should we do when ethical standards are different in the host nation? Given that the Foreign Corrupt Practices Act prohibits U.S. firms from engaging in certain behaviors, how can we compete when our foreign rivals offer bribes to obtain preferential treatment?

- *Accounting*. What will it take to integrate accounting systems across global operations? How do we account for currency conversions that are constantly changing? Can we harmonize accounting rules that vary from country to country? Does our accounting system capture the information necessary for international trading?
- *Legal Issues*. What are the IRS reporting requirements for international firms? How can we be sure that we are paying appropriate taxes in the home and host environments? What is required to comply with local government regulations? Will host country trade restrictions, including tariffs and nontariff barriers, hinder our export program? Do we have patent protections to shield our key technologies?

As you can see, international business decisions are complicated, which explains why many small firm owners choose to focus solely on their home market. However, the motivations to go global are sound, and others have already proved that it can be done. You can do it, too, if you plan carefully and take advantage of the resources available to help you achieve your global aspirations.

ASSISTANCE FOR GLOBAL ENTERPRISES

5 *Recognize the sources of assistance available to support international business efforts.*

Help is available to small companies with international interests—you need only open your eyes to find it. Once you decide to enter the global marketplace, you will be amazed at how many resources there are to help you.

Analyzing Markets and Planning Strategy

Among the many activities required to prepare a small firm for the challenges of going global, two are especially fundamental to success abroad: finding international markets that fit the company's unique potentials and putting together a game plan for entry into the markets targeted.

A small business should begin its research of foreign markets and entry strategy options by exhausting secondary sources of information. The U.S. government offers a number of publications on how to locate and exploit global market opportunities. The Small Business Administration's Office of International Trade is responsible for helping small companies expand abroad. The international programs and services of the SBA are delivered through U.S. Export Assistance Centers (USEACs).

One excellent source of information about global marketing is *Opportunities in Exporting*, which is available on the Web site of the SBA's Office of International Trade (http://www.sba.gov/oit). Also available from the same source is the *SBA Guide to Exporting*, which provides an overview of export strategy that is useful for new and experienced exporters. This nuts-and-bolts handbook is designed to guide small firms through the complexities of going global, with chapters focused specifically on identifying markets, choosing an entry strategy, managing transactions, financing trade, arranging transportation, and forming strategic alliances.

Though not focused on small businesses alone, the International Trade Administration of the U.S. Department of Commerce maintains a Web site (http://www.ita.doc.gov) that supplies helpful insights about international expansion. Publications such as *World Trade* magazine (http://www.worldtrademag.com) can also be useful, providing timely, in-depth analyses of world trade markets and business issues. Beyond these resources, state and private organizations are excellent sources of trade information, trade leads, and company databases. One such source, TradePort (http://www.tradeport.org), offers information online to promote international trade with California-based companies.

Talking with someone who has lived in or even just visited a potential foreign market can be a valuable way to learn about it. For example, conversations with international students at a local university can be very helpful. However, the best way to study a foreign market is to visit the country personally. A representative of a small firm can do this either as an individual or as a member of an organized group.

Connecting with International Customers

A small company cannot sell abroad unless it connects with customers in targeted international markets. But, have no fear—numerous resources are available to help you connect.

TRADE LEADS Trade leads are essential in identifying potential customers in target markets. Exhibit 17-6 lists several sources of trade leads. Accessed via the Internet, they provide an inexpensive way to establish vital links with buyers in target markets.

TRADE MISSIONS Joining a trade mission is another excellent way to evaluate a foreign market and link up with overseas customers. As mentioned earlier, a trade mission is a planned visit to a potential foreign market, designed to introduce U.S. firms to prospec-

17-6 *A Sample of International Trade Leads on the Web*

Bidmix.com	Bidmix.com provides an electronic marketplace for buying and selling worldwide. No membership is required to use the site to search for leads or post new leads. Users can also receive e-mail about new trade leads.
Meetbuyer.com	This site is designed for users all over the world. It features a company directory of members and a product search option. Membership is free.
TradeLeads.com	Use of TradeLeads.com requires a membership. Nonmembers can post leads, but they are unable to read or search for leads.
World Bank FundLine	The World Bank's Private Sector Development Department operates this site to connect potential equity investors with enterprises. Coverage includes countries in Central and Eastern Europe and the former Soviet Union.
World Trade Markets	World Trade Markets allows firms to capture, disseminate, and search Trade Point Trade Leads throughout the world. This database is updated daily by the United Nations, Trade Points, World Trade Markets agents and research staff, and the Internet public.
World Trade Zone	This site fosters international trade. It features a categorized company directory and a searchable listing of trade leads and hosts a mailing list for trade leads.
ASIA: Asian Sources On-Line	Designed for sourcing operations (volume buyers) in Asia, this site can be searched by country, product, or supplier. It also features other services, such as e-mail alerts, forums, product news, and libraries.
EUROPE: ECeurope.com	This site offers a business-to-business trading bulletin board that helps small- to medium-sized companies access trade leads. Membership is required, but it is free.
Australia: Australia on Display	This site provides trade leads to thousands of Australian companies and their products or services. Users can browse by industry category or keyword.
India: India Trade Board	India Trade Board posts business-to-business messages. Search, buy, and sell options are available.
Ireland: ITW, Business to Business	The Irish Trade Web is a very helpful site for those interested in entering the European market through an agency in Ireland or for companies looking for Irish products to import.

Source: The Michigan State University CIBER Web site, http://www.ciber.msu.edu/busres/static/trade%2Dleadsold.htm, May 7, 2004.

tive foreign buyers and to establish strategic alliances. These missions usually involve groups of 5 to 10 business executives and are designed to maximize international sales. Members of the group typically pay their own expenses and share in the operating costs of the mission. Foreign governments sometimes sponsor trade missions in order to promote business links with U.S. firms.

TRADE INTERMEDIARIES Perhaps the easiest way to break into international markets is to use a **trade intermediary**, which is an agency that distributes products to international customers on a contract basis. These agencies tap their established web of contacts, as well as their local cultural and market expertise. In short, an intermediary can manage the entire export end of a business, taking care of everything except filling the orders—and the results can be outstanding. American Cedar, Inc., located in Hot Springs, Arkansas, is a producer of cedar products. With the assistance of a trade intermediary, American Cedar gets 30 percent of its sales from exporting. Company president Julian McKinney reports, "We displayed our products at a trade show, and an export management company found us. They helped alleviate the hassles of exporting directly. Our products are now being distributed throughout the European Community from a distribution point in France."[35] An export management company is only one of the many types of trade intermediaries. Exhibit 17-7 describes the trade intermediaries that can best provide the assistance small businesses need.

trade intermediary
An agency that distributes a company's products on a contract basis to customers in another country

EXHIBIT 17-7 *Trade Intermediaries Most Suited for Small Businesses*

Export Management Companies	An export management company (EMC) acts as the export department for one or several producers of goods or services. It solicits and transacts business in the names of the producers it represents or in its own name, in exchange for a commission, salary, or retainer plus commission. Some EMCs provide immediate payment for the producer's products by either arranging financing or directly purchasing products for resale. The best EMCs know their products and the markets they serve very well and usually have well-established networks of foreign distributors already in place. This immediate access to foreign markets is one of the principal reasons for using an EMC.
Export Trading Companies	An export trading company (ETC) facilitates the export of U.S. goods and services. Like an EMC, this type of intermediary can either act as the export department for producers or take title to the product and export for its own account. Some ETCs are set up and operated by producers. These can be organized along multiple- or single-industry lines and can also represent producers of competing products.
Export Agents, Merchants, or Remarketers	Export agents, merchants, or remarketers purchase products directly from the manufacturer, packing and marking the products according to their own specifications. They then sell these products overseas in their own names through their contacts and assume all risks for accounts. In transactions with these intermediaries, a firm gives up control over the marketing and promotion of its product. This can hinder future sales abroad if the product is underpriced or incorrectly positioned in the market or if after-sales service is neglected.
Piggyback Marketers	Piggyback marketers are manufacturers or service firms that distribute a second firm's product or service. This is commonly seen when a U.S. company has a contract with an overseas buyer to provide a wide range of products or services.

Source: U.S. Department of Commerce, *A Basic Guide to Exporting* (Washington: Department of Commerce and Unz & Co., Inc.), http://www.unzco.com/basicguide/c4.html, July 13, 2004.

Financing

Arranging financing is perhaps the biggest barrier to international expansion. The more information small firms have about direct and indirect sources of financing, the more favorably they tend to view foreign markets. Sources of this information include private banks and the Small Business Association.

PRIVATE BANKS Commercial banks typically have a loan officer who is responsible for handling foreign transactions. Large banks may have an entire international department. Exporters use banks to issue commercial letters of credit and to perform other financial activities associated with exporting.

letter of credit
An agreement issued by a bank to honor a draft or other demand for payment when specified conditions are met

A **letter of credit** is an agreement to honor a draft or other demand for payment when specified conditions are met. It helps to assure a seller of prompt payment. A letter of credit may be revocable or irrevocable. An irrevocable letter of credit cannot be changed unless both the buyer and the seller agree to the change. The following steps outline the procedure typically followed when payment is made by an irrevocable letter of credit confirmed by a U.S. bank:

1. After the exporter and the buyer agree on the terms of sale, the buyer arranges for its bank to open a letter of credit. (Delays may be encountered if, for example, the buyer has insufficient funds.)
2. The buyer's bank prepares an irrevocable letter of credit, including all instructions to the seller concerning the shipment.
3. The buyer's bank sends the irrevocable letter of credit to a U.S. bank, requesting confirmation. The exporter may request that a particular U.S. bank be the confirming bank, or the buyer's bank will select one of its U.S. correspondent banks.
4. The U.S. bank prepares a letter of confirmation to forward to the exporter along with the irrevocable letter of credit.
5. The exporter carefully reviews all conditions in the letter of credit. The exporter's freight forwarder is generally contacted to make sure that the shipping date can be met. If the exporter cannot comply with one or more of the conditions, the buyer should be alerted at once.
6. The exporter arranges with the freight forwarder to deliver the goods to the appropriate port or airport.
7. When the goods are loaded, the freight forwarder completes the necessary documents.
8. The exporter (or the freight forwarder) presents to the U.S. bank documents indicating full compliance.
9. The bank reviews the documents. If they are in order, the documents are forwarded to the buyer's bank for review and then transmitted to the buyer.
10. The buyer (or agent) obtains the documents that may be needed to claim the goods.
11. A draft, which may accompany the letter of credit, is paid by the exporter's bank at the time specified; if paid earlier, it may be discounted.

A guarantee from a reputable bank that the exporter will indeed be paid is critical to a small business that has stretched its resources to the limit just to enter the global game and thus cannot afford an uncollected payment. But what if the small business is on the import end of the exchange? How will its interests be protected? The letter of credit provides security for the receiving firm as well, because the exporter does not receive payment from the bank until it has released the title, or proof of ownership, of the delivered goods. Once the product has been shipped and the title transferred, the exporter receives a document called a **bill of lading**, which the bank requires before it will pay on the letter of credit. In brief, the letter of credit ensures that the exporter will receive payment only when the goods are delivered in-country, and it also guarantees that the exporter will be paid.

bill of lading
A document indicating that a product has been shipped and the title to that product has been transferred

SMALL BUSINESS ADMINISTRATION The Small Business Administration (SBA) serves small U.S. firms primarily through its regional, district, and branch offices. Small businesses that are either already exporting or interested in doing so can receive valuable information from the SBA through conferences and seminars, instructional publications, and export counseling. An extended list of the financial assistance programs offered by the SBA to small firms is posted on the agency's Web site at http://www.sba.gov/financing/index.html.

It is clear that a growing number of small firms are choosing to participate in international business. The reasons for this expansion include both time-honored motivations and those emerging in the new competitive landscape. To achieve their global aspirations, most small businesses follow an export strategy; however, this is not the only alternative. Small companies can also implement international strategies that involve licensing, franchising, developing strategic alliances, or establishing a presence in foreign markets. In any case, firms that enter the global arena are certain to run up against serious challenges that purely domestic firms do not have to face. This is the nature of the terrain, but assistance is available in abundance from a number of private and public agencies. With a little help and a lot of hard work, your company can succeed in the global marketplace.

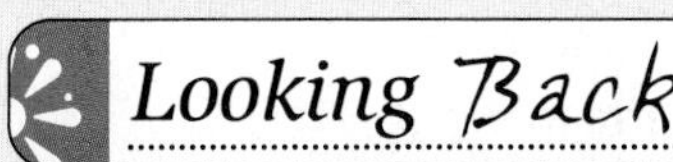

Looking Back

1 Describe the potential of small firms as global enterprises.

- Recent startups and even the smallest of businesses are internationalizing at an increasing rate.
- Small companies called born-global firms are increasingly being launched with cross-border business activities in mind.
- Small business owners who decide to go global must study the cultural, political, and economic forces in the foreign markets to figure out how best to adapt products and ensure smooth entry.
- Trade barriers are falling in some regions of the world, making it easier for small businesses to go global.

2 Identify the basic forces prompting small firms to engage in global expansion.

- Since more than 95 percent of the world's population lives outside the United States, globalization greatly expands the size of a firm's potential market.
- The 10 Big Emerging Markets are attracting small firms that wish to tap their enormous market potential.
- Small businesses with a highly differentiated product may need an international market in order to increase sales enough to recover product development costs.
- Going global can accelerate gains from experience curve efficiencies (resulting from learning effects and economies of scale), especially for startups based on complex technologies.
- Sometimes small businesses go global to gain access to resources, including raw materials and skilled labor.
- Another reason small firms enter foreign markets is to cut their costs in such areas as labor, transportation, or tariffs.
- Small businesses may want to capitalize on special features of an international location: exploiting the unique features of a local environment, taking advantage of favorable government policies, establishing a presence within an emerging trade area, or following a large client firm.

3 Identify and compare strategy options for global businesses.

- Exporting is the international strategy most commonly used by small firms. It can be facilitated by using the Internet to increase their international visibility and joining trade missions that help them make contacts abroad.
- Importing involves selling goods from abroad in the home market. It is a strategy that should be used when products manufactured abroad have market potential at home.
- Non-export strategies include foreign licensing, international franchising, international strategic alliances, and locating facilities abroad. They can be more complex than export strategies, but some (especially licensing) are actually the safest options for the small global business.

4 Explain the challenges that global enterprises face.

- Political risk is the potential for a country's political forces to negatively affect the performance of small businesses operating there. Political risk varies greatly across nations.
- Economic risk is the probability that a government will mismanage its economy and change the business environment in ways that hinder the performance of firms operating there (most notably through inflation and fluctuations in exchange rates).

- Globalization raises numerous concerns related to every function of the firm, thus stretching managerial skills and resources to the limit.

5 Recognize the sources of assistance available to support international business efforts.

- Numerous public and private organizations provide assistance to small businesses in analyzing markets and planning a strategy.
- Small businesses can connect with international customers by reviewing sources of trade leads, joining trade missions, or using the services of trade intermediaries.
- For assistance in financing its entry into a foreign market, a small firm can turn to private banks (which can issue letters of credit) and programs initiated by the Small Business Administration.

Key Terms

globalization, p. 373
born-global firms, p. 373
tariffs, p. 375
North American Free Trade Agreement (NAFTA), p. 375
European Union (EU), p. 375
experience curve efficiencies, p. 379
learning effects, p. 379
economies of scale, p. 379
international outsourcing (offshoring), p. 381
exporting, p. 382
trade mission, p. 383
importing, p. 383
foreign licensing, p. 384
licensee, p. 384
licensor, p. 384
royalties, p. 384
counterfeit activity, p. 385
international franchising, p. 385
international strategic alliance, p. 385
cross-border acquisition, p. 386
greenfield venture, p. 386
political risk, p. 386
economic risk, p. 387
exchange rate, p. 387
trade intermediary, p. 391
letter of credit, p. 392
bill of lading, p. 392

Discussion Questions

1. Discuss the importance of a careful cultural analysis to a small firm that wishes to enter an international market.
2. How have trade agreements helped reduce trade barriers? Do you believe these efforts will continue?
3. Do you believe that small companies should engage in international business? Why or why not?
4. Identify the four basic forces driving small businesses to enter the global business arena. Which do you think is the most influential in the globalization of small firms?
5. Give examples of some emerging motivations persuading small business owners to go global. Are any of these motivations likely to remain powerful forces ten years from now? Twenty years from now?
6. Why is exporting the most popular global strategy among small businesses? Do you think this should be the case?
7. What impact has the Internet had on the globalization of small firms? How do you think small companies will use the Internet for business in the future?
8. What non-export strategies can small businesses adopt? In view of the unique needs and capabilities of small firms, what are the advantages and disadvantages of each of these strategies?
9. What are the three main challenges small businesses face when they go global? What strategies can a small company use to deal with each of these challenges?
10. What forms of assistance are available to small global firms? Which is likely to be of greatest benefit to small companies? Why?

You Make the Call

SITUATION 1

Bill Moss and several other small business owners joined a trade mission to China to explore market opportunities there. The group learned that China has a population of 1.3 billion and is the third-fastest-growing export market for small- and medium-sized U.S. firms. Average annual income for farmers in China is approximately $285 per person; typical urban income is about $827, with an average of $1,557 a year in more prosperous cities like Shanghai. In any given year, the Chinese software market grows by 30 percent and the number of Internet users quadruples. Furthermore, the demand for management consulting services is increasing, especially information technology consulting. Members of the group were surprised by the number of people who had cell phones and regularly surfed the Internet, especially in large urban centers such as Beijing, Shanghai, and Guangzhou. On the downside, they found that counterfeit goods (from clothing and leather goods to software and CDs) were readily available at a fraction of the cost of legitimate merchandise and that local merchants expressed an interest in doing business only with vendors with whom they had established relationships.

Sources: Data from http://www.china.org.cn/english/2002/Feb/26975.htm and http://www.china.org.cn/BAT/28231.htm.

Question 1 What types of businesses would prosper in China? Why?

Question 2 What are the challenges and risks associated with doing business in China?

Question 3 What steps should Moss take to address these challenges and risks in order to increase his chance of success in the market?

SITUATION 2

Lynn Cooper owns and operates BFW, Inc., in Lexington, Kentucky, where she produces fiber-optic lights and headgear-mounted video cameras used for medical exams and surgery. She sees exporting as a means of increasing sales, but with just one employee, she wonders how best to handle the additional marketing and distribution exporting would require.

Question 1 What sources of information would be helpful to Cooper?

Question 2 Would you recommend that she consider using an international distributor? If so, what characteristics should she look for in a distributor?

Question 3 Do you think exporting is a feasible alternative for Cooper at this time? Why or why not?

SITUATION 3

Dr. Juldiz Afgazar, a native of the Republic of Kazakhstan, had been invited to spend a semester in the United States as a visiting scholar in entrepreneurial finance. Kazakhstan gained its independence from the former Soviet Union in 1991, and only after that were laws passed allowing citizens to own private businesses. Dr. Afgazar wanted to learn more about the free market economy of the United States to determine whether such a system could be implemented in Kazakhstan.

Prior to this visit to the United States, Dr. Afgazar had not traveled extensively outside her country. Although she enjoyed many aspects of U.S. culture, she was particularly impressed by the seemingly unlimited quantity and variety of goods and foods that were readily available. After a visit to a local restaurant's pizza buffet, she became an avid fan of American-style pizza! Dr. Afgazar found the crisp yeast crust, spicy tomato sauce, melted mozzarella cheese, and assortment of toppings to be a delicious combination. Pizza was an entirely new type of food for her, since it was not available in Kazakhstan. A true entrepreneur, Dr. Afgazar began to wonder if a pizza restaurant could be successful in her country.

Source: Developed by Elisabeth J. Teal of Northern Georgia College and State University, Dahlonega, Georgia, and Aigul N. Toxanova of Kokshetau Higher College of Management and Business, Kazakhstan.

Question 1 What obstacles would an entrepreneur have to overcome to establish a pizza restaurant in a country with a developing market-based economy, such as Kazakhstan?

Question 2 Is Dr. Afgazar's idea of developing a pizza restaurant in Kazakhstan ahead of its time? That is, do you think the economy of Kazakhstan is sufficiently developed to support a pizza restaurant?

Question 3 What methods could an entrepreneur use to evaluate the likelihood of success of a pizza restaurant in Kazakhstan?

Experiential Exercises

1. Conduct phone interviews with 10 local small business owners to see if they engage in international business. Discuss their reasons for going global or for choosing to do business only domestically.
2. Contact a local banker to discuss the bank's involvement with small firms participating in international business. Report your findings to the class.
3. Review recent issues of *Entrepreneur, Inc.*, or other small business publications, and be prepared to discuss articles related to international business. You can also log onto InfoTrac College Edition at http://www.infotrac-college.com to find articles on international business.
4. Log onto InfoTrac College Edition at http://www.infotrac-college.com to find an article about a small business that first expanded internationally using an entry strategy other than exporting. From what you understand of the company's situation, suggest guidelines that could lead a firm to go global with non-export strategies.
5. Consult secondary sources to develop a political/economic risk profile for a given country. Select a small company and explain what it would have to do to manage these risks if it were to enter the market of the country profiled.
6. Speak with the owner of a small international company. Which sources of assistance did that entrepreneur use when launching the global initiative? Which sources did the entrepreneur find most helpful? Which did the entrepreneur find least helpful?

Exploring the Web

1. Go to the Small Business Administration's Office of International Trade Web site (**http://www.sba.gov/oit/**). Click on the various tabs to learn about what programs and services the SBA offers. Summarize a particular program or service described here that interests you.
2. At the BuyUSA.com Web site, maintained by the U.S. Department of Commerce (**http://www.buyusa.com**), business owners can purchase a subscription that will allow them to connect with "thousands of international buyers, distributors and agents." Explain how your business could use this Web site.
3. Return to the SBA's Office of International Trade Web site (**http://www.sba.gov/oit**). This time, click on "Exporting Guide" and read Chapter 3 of the "SBA Guide to Exporting." What methods of foreign market entry are discussed there?

Case 17

SUNNY DESIGNS, INC. (P. 557)

This case describes the experiences of an entrepreneur as he attempts to expand his furniture business by establishing a production facility in China.

Alternative Case for Chapter 17:

Case 7, Specialty Cheese, p. 536

Part Five

MANAGING GROWTH IN THE SMALL BUSINESS

CHAPTERS

PROFESSIONAL MANAGEMENT IN THE ENTREPRENEURIAL FIRM

In the Spotlight

Online Business Services, Inc.

Entrepreneurs who start a new business must exhibit strong leadership skills if their firm is to survive and grow. Joshua Schechter started Online Business Services, Inc., with his brother Jeff in 1993 to provide payroll services for San Antonio businesses. The brothers soon faced a leadership challenge. Employee problems were jeopardizing client relationships and the business itself.

According to Schechter, he and Jeff realized that they needed to turn over more work responsibilities to their employees. These employees, moreover, needed to be people who "share the same vision and values, and they're not easy to find." After delegating some of the work that he personally had been doing, Schechter found that some employees were not as careful as he was in meeting tax deposit deadlines for clients. This was one of several signs that the business was experiencing a leadership vacuum, as the entrepreneurs had failed to train and motivate their employees adequately. They had not conveyed their own vision for the company to their employees.

© Javier Pierini/Photodisc Red/Getty Images

"The number one challenge in a growing business," Schechter said, "is transferring your spirit—that entrepreneurial spirit that enables you to get it all done, get it done right, and go above and beyond the requirements. . . . Our values include things like honesty, integrity, doing your job with a smile, doing it right the first time." Recognizing the leadership problem, the Schechter brothers worked hard to weed out employees who didn't share their values and to hire and train new ones until they had just the crew they required.

The business has prospered, growing to 13 employees and $1.1 million in annual revenue. The Schechters discovered that certain milestones require reengineering of the business. "There's one at 400 clients, and there's another at 1,000 clients. . . . Every time we hit a milestone, we have to reinvent the business." As they discovered, the leadership in a growing business must change and grow as the business itself grows.

Source: Jana Matthews and Jeff Dennis, *Lessons from the Edge* (New York: Oxford University Press, 2003), pp. 44–48.

Chapter 18

Looking Ahead

After studying this chapter, you should be able to

1 *Discuss the entrepreneur's leadership role.*

2 *Explain the distinctive features of small firm management.*

3 *Identify the managerial tasks of entrepreneurs.*

4 *Describe the problem of time pressure and suggest solutions.*

5 *Explain the various types of outside management assistance.*

Only tiny one-person businesses can avoid leadership and management problems. And even in those cases, individual entrepreneurs must engage in what might be called self-management. In all other firms, however, the entrepreneur must find a way to integrate the efforts of employees and to give direction to the business. This is absolutely necessary in order for production employees, salespeople, and support service personnel to work together effectively. Even long-established businesses need vigorous leadership if they are to avoid stagnation or failure. This chapter examines the leadership challenges facing entrepreneurs and the managerial activities required as firms mature and grow.

ENTREPRENEURIAL LEADERSHIP

1 *Discuss the entrepreneur's leadership role.*

Leadership roles differ greatly depending on the size of the business and its stage of business growth. A business that is just beginning, for example, faces problems and uncertainties unlike those of a family firm that has been functioning well over several generations. We must begin, therefore, with the recognition that leadership cannot be reduced to simple rules or processes that fit all situations.

What Is Leadership?

The question is simple, but the answer is not. Here is the response of a contemporary business leader, Richard Barton, former president and CEO of Expedia, Inc., to the question "How do you define leadership?"

> *I'll tell you what it's not. It's not management.*
>
> *I think a lot of people—especially at large companies—get confused. You have all these people with titles that have some kind of "manager" in it, and people talking about "management." I hate the word* management. *Management is passive. Management is minding the store. Management is something that you have to do, that you don't necessarily enjoy doing. Leadership to me means leaning forward, looking ahead, trying to improve, being fired up about what you're doing and being able to communicate that, verbally and nonverbally, to those around you.*
>
> *Leaders don't lean back, leaders lean forward.*[1]

Clearly, leadership is concerned with pointing the way. It is far more focused on the destination than on the details of getting there. Entrepreneurs must convey their vision of the firm's future to other participants in the business so that everyone involved can contribute most effectively to the accomplishment of the mission.

Although leaders must also engage in some of the more mundane processes of management, particularly as the business grows, the first task of the entrepreneur is to create and communicate the vision.

Leadership Qualities of Founders

The entrepreneur is the trailblazer who enlists others, both team members and outsiders, to work with him or her in a creative endeavor. Others may then buy into this vision for the venture as they join their efforts with those of the entrepreneur.

In a totally new venture, the leader faces major uncertainties and unknowns. Amar V. Bhide has discussed the qualities needed by individuals who are launching "promising startups," or startups having the prospect of attaining significant size or profitability.[2] One quality that Bhide identifies is a tolerance for ambiguity—a condition almost always present in launching a new business. Because of the inherent uncertainty, another necessary quality is a capacity for adaptation, the ability to adjust to unforeseen problems and opportunities. These qualities are useful in most settings but are particularly important in business startups.

What Makes an Effective Leader?

A quality that is apparently *not* necessary in a business leader is a flashy, highly charismatic, take-charge personality; it is not the norm and is not required. In a classic study of companies that went from "good" to "great" over a period of several years, Jim Collins and his research team discovered that the great leaders were not egocentric stars but, rather, were often described as "quiet, humble, modest, reserved, shy, gracious, mild-mannered, self-effacing."[3] Even so, these leaders exhibited a resolve and a determination to do whatever was needed to make their companies great. It seems clear, therefore, that effective leadership is based not on a larger-than-life personality but, instead, on a focus on the attainment of business goals.

In most small firms, leadership of the business is personalized. The owner-manager is not a faceless unknown, but an individual whom employees see and relate to in the course of their normal work schedules. This situation is entirely different from that of large corporations, where most employees never see the chief executive. If the employer–employee relationship is good, employees in small firms develop strong feelings of personal loyalty to their employer.

In a large corporation, the values of top-level executives must be filtered through many layers of management before they reach those who produce and sell the products. As a result, the influence of those at the top tends to be diluted by the process. In contrast, personnel in a small firm receive the leader's messages directly. This face-to-face contact facilitates their understanding of the leader's vision as well as her or his stand on integrity, customer service, and other important issues.

Leadership Styles

Leaders use many different styles of leadership, and the styles may be described in various ways. Certain leadership styles may be better suited to certain situations, and most leaders choose from a variety of approaches as they deal with different issues. Daniel Goleman has described the following six distinct leadership styles:[4]

1. *Coercive leaders* demand immediate compliance.
2. *Authoritative leaders* mobilize people toward a vision.
3. *Affiliative leaders* create emotional bonds.
4. *Democratic leaders* build consensus.
5. *Pacesetting leaders* set high standards and expect excellence.
6. *Coaching leaders* develop people.

An entrepreneur may use different styles at different times as she or he attempts to get the best out of the organization and its employees. Even coercive leadership might be necessary and expected, for example, in a genuine emergency, although it would not be appropriate in most settings.

For the large majority of entrepreneurial firms, leadership that recognizes and values individual worth is strongly recommended. Several decades ago, many managers were hard-nosed autocrats, giving orders and showing little concern for those who worked under them. Over the years, this style of leadership has given way to a gentler and more effective variety that emphasizes respect for all members of the organization and shows an appreciation both for their work and for their potential.

empowerment
Giving employees authority to make decisions or take actions on their own

Progressive managers frequently seek some degree of employee participation in decisions that affect personnel and work processes. In many cases, managers carry this leadership approach to a level called **empowerment**. The manager who uses empowerment goes beyond solicitation of employees' opinions and ideas by increasing their authority to act on their own and to make decisions about the processes they're involved with. Here is a description of worker empowerment at a small auto body shop called European Collision Center in Cambridge, Massachusetts:

> *Bodymen take "ownership" of a car while it's in the shop, staying with it start to finish. No one looks over their shoulders: "There are a set of parameters, then they have to be responsible," says owner Wayne Stevenson. Workers are cross-trained to take on new tasks and sent back to school yearly to keep skills up to date. Customers love what they get, and Stevenson's [business volume] has doubled every year for five years.*[5]

Some companies carry employee participation a step further by creating self-managed **work teams.** Each work team is assigned a given task or operation; its members manage the task or operation without direct supervision and assume responsibility for the results. When work teams function properly, the number of supervisors needed decreases sharply.

work teams
Groups of employees with freedom to function without close supervision

Management practices that include a high level of involvement by employees contribute to productivity and profits, according to research studies. Pfeffer and Veiga have explained the reasons for improved performance as follows:

> *Simply put, people work harder because of the increased involvement and commitment that comes from having more control and say in their work; people work smarter because they are encouraged to build skills and competence; and people work more responsibly because more responsibility is placed in hands of employees farther down in the organization. These practices work not because of some mystical process, but because they are grounded in sound social science principles that have been shown to be effective by a great deal of evidence. And, they make sense.*[6]

DISTINCTIVE CHARACTERISTICS OF SMALL FIRM MANAGEMENT

2 *Explain the distinctive features of small firm management.*

As one entrepreneur commented, "Unless you thrive on chaos, a small company can be tough." Small firm operations are not always chaotic, of course, but small business owners face challenges that differ greatly from those of corporate executives. Furthermore, small companies experience change in their leadership and management processes as they move from point zero—their launching—to the point where they employ a full staff of **professional managers**, trained in the use of systematic, analytical methods.

professional manager
A manager who uses systematic, analytical methods of management

Professional-Level Management

There is, of course, much variation in the way business firms, as well as other organizations, are managed. Between the extremes of very unskilled and highly professional types of management lies a continuum. At the less professional end of this continuum are entrepreneurs and other managers who rely largely on past experience, rules of thumb, and personal whims in giving direction to their businesses. In most cases, their ideas of motivation are based on the way they were treated in earlier business or family relationships.

Other entrepreneurs and managers display much more professionalism. They are analytical and systematic in dealing with management problems and issues. Because they emphasize getting the facts and working out logical solutions, their approach is sometimes described as scientific in nature. The challenge for small firm leaders is to develop as much professionalism as possible, while still retaining the entrepreneurial spirit in the enterprise.

Limitations of Founders as Managers

Founders of new firms are not always good organization members. As discussed in Chapter 1, they are creative, innovative, risk-taking individuals who have the courage to strike out on their own. Indeed, they are often propelled into entrepreneurship by precipitating events, sometimes involving their difficulty in fitting into conventional organizational roles. Even charismatic leaders may fail to appreciate the need for good management practices as the business grows. Understandably, their orientation frequently differs from that of professional managers.

Some entrepreneurs are professional in their approach to management, and some corporate managers are entrepreneurial in the sense of being innovative and willing to take risks. Nevertheless, a founder's less-than-professional management style has been known to act as a drag on business growth. Ideally, the founder is able to add a measure of professional management without sacrificing the entrepreneurial spirit and basic values that have given the business a successful start.

Managerial Weakness in Small Firms

Although some large corporations experience poor management, small businesses seem particularly vulnerable to this weakness. Many small firms are marginal or unprofitable businesses, struggling to survive from day to day. At best, they earn only a bare living for their owners. They operate, but to say that they are managed would be an exaggeration.

Consider American Dixie Group, Inc., founded by Lay Cooper in 1989 in Albany, New York, to build the industrial machines used in food processing, packaging, and plastics making.[7] The business became successful, was praised for its problem-solving wizardry, and served customers like Nestlé and Campbell Soup. As long as the business remained small, with no more than two dozen employees in the shop and a half dozen or so projects in the pipeline, it apparently performed quite well. As it expanded, however, it ran into problems. Suppliers began griping about late payments, and customers became unhappy because of delayed deliveries and shoddy workmanship. In September 1998, American Dixie Group filed for bankruptcy; it had failed because it lacked professional management.

Managerial weakness of the type just described is all too typical of small firms. The good news, however, is that poor management is neither universal nor inevitable.

Constraints That Hamper Management

Managers of small firms, particularly new and growing companies, are constrained by conditions that do not trouble the average corporate executive—they must face the grim reality of small bank accounts and limited staff. A small firm often lacks the money for slick sales brochures, and it cannot afford much in the way of marketing research. The shortage of cash even makes it difficult to employ an adequate number of clerical employees. Such limitations are painfully apparent to large-firm managers who move into management positions in small firms.

A financial analyst at General Motors who became CEO of a smaller, entrepreneurial company described the drastic changes he faced:

> *You have to get used to moving the decimal points over a few places. At GM I was involved in billion-dollar analyses of new plants. Now I have to sign off on things like a trade show booth. For us it's a big deal.*
>
> *Every thousand dollars means something. I had to make a decision whether I should lease a copier the other day. Can we afford to do it? Should we do it right now?*[8]

Small firms typically lack adequate specialized professional staff. Most small business managers are generalists. Lacking the support of experienced specialists in such areas as marketing research, financial analysis, advertising, and human resource management, the manager of a small firm must make decisions in these areas without the expertise that is available in a larger business. This limitation may be partially overcome by using outside management assistance. But coping with a shortage of internal professional talent is part of the reality of managing entrepreneurial firms.

Firm Growth and Managerial Practices

As a newly formed business becomes established and grows, its organizational structure and pattern of management change. To some extent, management in any organization must adapt to growth and change. However, the changes involved in the early growth stages of a new business are much more extensive than those that occur with the growth of a relatively mature business.

A number of experts have proposed models related to the growth stages of business firms.[9] These models typically describe four or five stages of growth and identify various management issues related to each stage. Exhibit 18-1 shows four stages of organizational growth characteristic of many small businesses. As firms progress from Stage 1 to Stage 4,

EXHIBIT 18-1 *Organizational Stages of Small Business Growth*

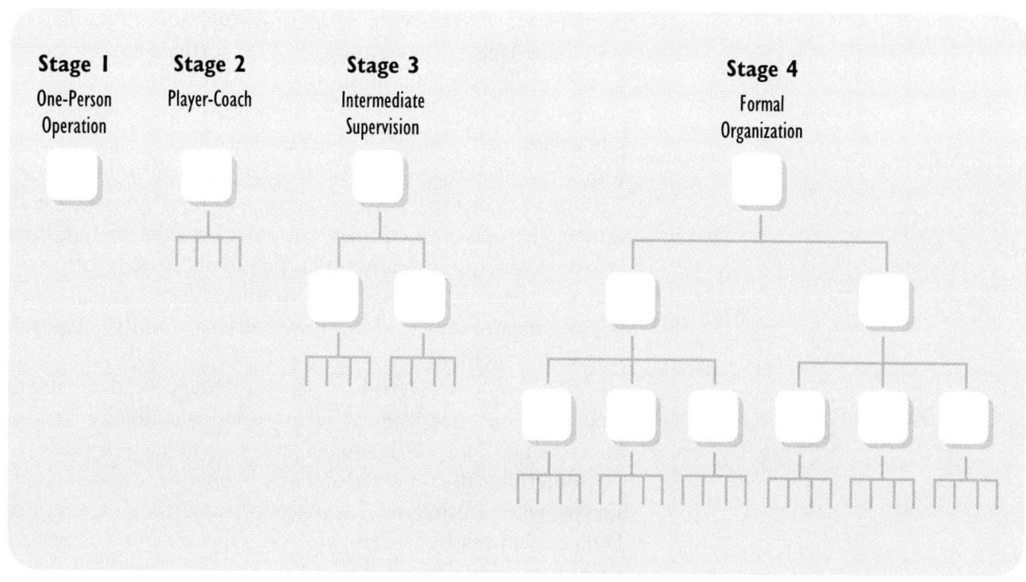

they add layers of management and increase the formality of operations. Though some firms skip the first one or two stages by starting as larger businesses, thousands of small firms make their way through each of the stages pictured in Exhibit 18-1.

In Stage 1, the firm is simply a one-person operation. Some firms begin with a larger organization, but the one-person startup is by no means rare. Many businesses remain one-person operations indefinitely. In Stage 2, the entrepreneur becomes a player-coach, which implies continuing active participation in the operations of the business. In addition to performing the basic work—whether making the product, selling it, writing checks, or keeping records—the entrepreneur must also coordinate the efforts of others.

Living the Dream — Entrepreneurial Challenges

Finding People Who Can Manage

As a firm grows, the entrepreneur needs to fill key positions with individuals who have the capacity to perform well as managers. Can the best salesperson or most skilled technician be advanced to a higher level? Sometimes, but not always.

Courtesy of Iatria Day Spas

Erika Mangrum was a year into her business and was feeling pressured to promote a star employee to general manager. "She wanted more responsibility and more pay," says Mangrum, co-founder and president of Iatria Day Spas and Health Center, a 40-employee company in Raleigh, North Carolina. Mangrum felt a deep sense of loyalty to this employee, who had been with the company from the start, so she went ahead with the promotion. However, it wasn't long before Mangrum realized she was promoting doom and gloom.

The new manager's rudeness and inability to manage conflict created customer complaints and tension among employees. The manager left 14 months after the promotion. Unfortunately, the business also lost key employees in the turmoil.

To avoid such situations, entrepreneurs must sometimes resist pressure to promote star employees. Today, Mangrum assigns employees to big projects to assess their ability to work with others before she promotes them.

Source: Chris Penttila, "Can You Manage?" *Entrepreneur*, July 2003, pp. 74–75.

A major milestone is reached in Stage 3, when an intermediate level of supervision is added. In many ways, this is a turning point for the small firm, because the entrepreneur must rise above direct, hands-on management and work through an intervening layer of management. Stage 4, the stage of formal organization, involves more than increased size and multi-layered organization. The formalization of management entails adoption of written policies, preparation of plans and budgets, standardization of personnel practices, computerization of records, preparation of organizational charts and job descriptions, scheduling of training conferences, institution of control procedures, and so on. While some formal managerial practices may be adopted prior to Stage 4, the steps shown in Exhibit 18-1 outline a typical pattern of development for successful firms. Flexibility and informality may be helpful when a firm is first started, but the firm's growth necessitates greater formality in planning and control. Tension often develops as the traditional easy-going patterns of management become dysfunctional. Great managerial skill is required of the entrepreneur in order to preserve a "family" atmosphere while introducing professional management.

As a firm moves from Stage 1 to Stage 4, the pattern of entrepreneurial activities changes. The entrepreneur becomes less of a doer and more of a manager. Managers who have strong doing skills often have weak managing skills.

Sometimes the personal skills or brilliance of the entrepreneur can enable a business to survive while business skills are being acquired. This was the case with Ronald and Rony Delice, twin Haitian-born brothers, who are igniting fashion runways and men's clothing with their edgy designs.[10]

Their father worked as a tailor in Haiti, and their mother was a seamstress in New York City. After earning degrees in fashion merchandising from New York City's acclaimed Fashion Institute of Technology, Ronald and Rony began work as custom tailors and designers. They soon started their own business and quickly won awards for their designs. In 2003, their company, with revenues projected at $475,000, listed such celebrities as actor Will Smith and basketball star Latrell Sprewell among its clients.

The business side of their venture, however, presented the biggest challenge. The twins found that keeping the books, paying bills, and preparing a business plan were much harder than designing clothing. As Ronald explained it, "We're more artists than business people." Overcoming that challenge meant bringing in qualified people.

Small firms that hesitate to move through the various organizational stages and acquire the necessary professional management limit their rate of growth. On the other hand, a small business may attempt to grow too quickly. If an entrepreneur's primary strength lies in product development or selling, for example, a quick move into Stage 4 may saddle the entrepreneur with managerial duties and deprive the organization of her or his valuable talents.

In his study of the origin and evolution of new businesses, Amar V. Bhide found that entrepreneurs play different roles in starting businesses than they play in building what he calls long-lived firms.[11] Likewise, the personal qualities involved in starting businesses differ from the qualities required to develop long-lived firms. This helps explain why so few ventures actually become established businesses with staying power. Growing a business requires maturation and adaptation on the part of the entrepreneur.

MANAGERIAL TASKS OF ENTREPRENEURS

3 Identify the managerial tasks of entrepreneurs.

Thus far, our discussion of the management process has been very general. Now it is time to look more closely at how entrepreneurs implement their leadership in organizing and directing the firm's operations.

Planning Activities

Most small business managers plan to some degree. However, the amount of planning they do is typically less than ideal. Also, what little planning there is tends to be haphazard and focused on specific, immediate issues—for example, how much inventory to purchase, whether to buy a new piece of equipment, and other questions of this type. Circumstances affect the degree to which formal planning is needed, but most businesses could function more profitably by increasing the amount of planning done by managers and making it more systematic.

The payoff from planning comes in several ways. First, the process of thinking through the issues confronting a firm and developing a plan to deal with those issues can improve productivity. Second, planning provides a focus for a firm: Managerial decisions over the course of the year can be guided by the annual plan, and employees can work consistently toward the same goal. Third, evidence of planning increases credibility with bankers, suppliers, and other outsiders.

TYPES OF PLANS A firm's basic path to the future is spelled out in a document called a **long-range plan**, or **strategic plan**. As noted in Chapter 3, strategy decisions concern such issues as niche markets and features that differentiate a firm from its competitors. Such planning is essential even in established businesses, in order to ensure that changes in the business environment can be addressed as they occur.

long-range plan (strategic plan)
A firm's overall plan for the future

Short-range plans are action plans designed to deal with activities in production, marketing, and other areas over a period of one year or less. An important part of a short-range operating plan is the **budget**—a document that expresses future plans in monetary terms. A budget is usually prepared one year in advance, with a breakdown by quarters or months. (Budgeting is explained more fully in Chapter 23.)

short-range plan
A plan that governs a firm's operations for one year or less

budget
A document that expresses future plans in monetary terms

PLANNING TIME Small business managers all too often succumb to the "tyranny of the urgent." Because they are busy putting out fires, they never get around to planning. Planning is easy to postpone and, therefore, easy for managers to ignore while concentrating on more urgent issues in such areas as production and sales. And, just as quarterbacks focusing on a receiver may be blindsided by blitzing linebackers, managers who have neglected to plan may be bowled over by competitors.

Creating an Organizational Structure

While an entrepreneur may give direction through personal leadership, she or he must also define the relationships among the firm's activities and among the individuals on the firm's payroll. Without some kind of organizational structure, operations eventually become chaotic and morale suffers.

THE UNPLANNED STRUCTURE In small companies, the organizational structure tends to evolve with little conscious planning. Certain employees begin performing particular functions when the company is new and retain those functions as it matures.

This natural evolution is not all bad. Generally, a strong element of practicality characterizes these types of organizational arrangements. The structure is forged through the experience of working and growing, rather than being derived from a textbook or another firm's organizational chart. Unplanned structures are seldom perfect, however, and growth typically creates a need for organizational change. Periodically, therefore, the entrepreneur should examine structural relationships and make adjustments as needed for effective teamwork.

THE CHAIN OF COMMAND A **chain of command** implies superior–subordinate relationships with a downward flow of instructions, but it involves much more. It is also a channel for two-way communication. As a practical matter, strict adherence to the chain of command is not advisable. An organization in which the primary channel of communication was rigid would be bureaucratic and inefficient. Nevertheless, frequent and flagrant disregard of the chain of command quickly undermines the position of the bypassed manager.

chain of command
The official, vertical channel of communication in an organization

In a **line organization**, each person has one supervisor to whom he or she reports and looks for instructions. All employees are directly engaged in the firm's work, producing, selling, or performing office or financial duties. Most very small firms—for example, those with fewer than 10 employees—use this form of organization.

line organization
A simple organizational structure in which each person reports to one supervisor

A **line-and-staff organization** is similar to a line organization in that each person reports to a single supervisor. However, a line-and-staff structure also has staff specialists who perform specialized services or act as management advisors in specific areas (see Exhibit 18-2). Staff specialists may include a human resource manager, a production control technician, a quality control specialist, and an assistant to the president. The line-and-staff organization is widely used in small businesses.

line-and-staff organization
An organizational structure that includes staff specialists who assist management

SPAN OF CONTROL The **span of control** is the number of employees who are supervised by a manager. Although some authorities have stated that six to eight people are all that

span of control
The number of subordinates supervised by one manager

EXHIBIT 18-2 *Line-and-Staff Organization*

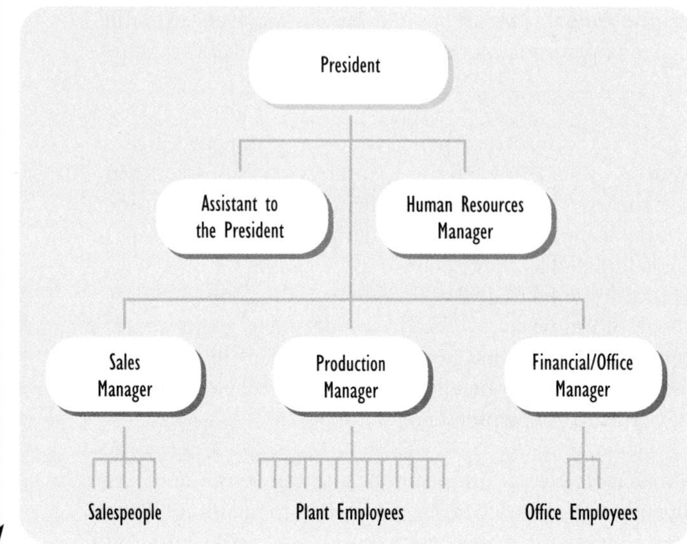

one individual can supervise effectively, the optimal span of control is actually a variable that depends on a number of factors. Among these factors are the nature of the work and the manager's knowledge, energy, personality, and abilities. In addition, if the abilities of subordinates are better than average, the span of control may be broadened accordingly.

As a very small firm grows and adds employees, the entrepreneur's span of control is extended. The entrepreneur often has a tendency to stretch the span too far—to supervise not only the first five or six employees hired, but also all the employees added as time goes on. Eventually, a point is reached at which the attempted span of control exceeds the entrepreneur's reach, demanding more time and effort than he or she can devote to the business. It is at this point that the entrepreneur must establish intermediate levels of supervision and dedicate more time to management, moving beyond the role of player-coach.

Understanding Informal Groups

The types of organizational structures just discussed address the formal relationships among members of an organization. All organizations, however, also have informal groups composed of people with something in common, such as jobs, hobbies, carpools, or affiliations with civic associations.

Although informal groups are not created by management, managers should observe them and evaluate their effect on the functioning of the total organization. An informal group, for example, may foster an attitude of working hard until the very end of the working day or doing the opposite—easing up and coasting for the last half-hour. Ordinarily, no serious conflict arises between informal groups and the formal organization. Informal leaders often emerge who influence employee behavior. The wise manager understands the potentially positive contribution of informal groups and the inevitability of informal leadership.

Informal interaction among subordinates and managers can facilitate work performance and can also make life in the workplace more enjoyable for everyone. The value of compatible work groups to the individual became painfully clear to one college student working on a summer job:

> *I was employed as a forklift driver for one long, frustrating summer. Soon after being introduced to my work group, I knew I was in trouble. A clique had formed and, for some reason, resented college students. During lunch breaks and work breaks, I spent the whole time by myself. Each morning, I dreaded going to work. The job paid well, but I was miserable.*[12]

Delegating Authority

Through **delegation of authority**, a manager grants to subordinates the right to act or to make decisions. Turning over some functions to subordinates by delegating authority frees the superior to perform more important tasks.

delegation of authority
Granting to subordinates the right to act or make decisions

Although failure to delegate may be found in any organization, it is often a special problem for entrepreneurs, given their backgrounds and personalities. Because they frequently must pay for mistakes made by subordinates, owners are inclined to keep a firm hold on the reins of leadership in order to protect the business.

Inability or unwillingness to delegate authority is manifested in numerous ways. For example, employees may find it necessary to clear even the most minor decisions with the boss. At any given time, a number of subordinates may be trying to get the attention of the owner to resolve some issue that they lack the authority to settle. This keeps the owner exceptionally busy—rushing from assisting a salesperson to helping iron out a production bottleneck to setting up a new filing system. Entrepreneurs often work long hours, and those who have difficulty delegating compound the problem, imposing on themselves even longer work hours.

Stephen R. Covey has distinguished between what he calls "gofer" delegation and "stewardship" delegation.[13] Gofer delegation refers to work assignments in which the supervisor-delegator controls the details, telling subordinates to "go for this" or "go for that." This is not true delegation. Stewardship delegation, on the other hand, focuses on results and allows the individual receiving an assignment some latitude in carrying it out. Only stewardship delegation provides the benefits of delegation to both parties.

Controlling Operations

Despite good planning, organizations seldom function perfectly. As a result, managers must monitor operations to discover deviations from plans and to ensure that the firm is functioning as intended. Managerial activities that check on performance and correct it when necessary are part of managerial control; they serve to keep the business on course.

Living the Dream — *Entrepreneurial Challenges*

Delegating Difficulty

Many entrepreneurs have problems in turning their own duties over to others. Russ Lewis, who operates a small bakery in Vermont with his wife, Linda, faces this problem at a very basic level. He personally bakes between 2,000 to 3,500 loaves of bread each day and finds it extremely tiring. As Linda puts it, "I don't think he loves it anymore."

© Kindra Clineff/Index Stock Imagery

The five-year-old bakery, which supplies restaurants and cafés, produces great bread and provides the owners with the highest income they've ever had, but it also dominates their lives.

> *They employ three other people—more in summer months when Vermont swells with tourists—but limit the workers' duties to things other than baking. So, six days a week Mr. Lewis wakes at 12:30 A.M., is in the bakery by 1 A.M., first doing croissants and then loaves of artisan bread, heading home around 2 P.M.*
>
> *When they're especially busy, "I'll just start two or three hours earlier," Mr. Lewis says. "I haven't seen prime-time television in five years. It's not natural. Your body never gets used to it."*
>
> *Ms. Lewis starts a little later and finishes a little later, handling deliveries and paperwork. [She says,] "Russ always says, 'I'm so tired of being so tired.'" Indeed, they're too tired to change the habits that make them so tired.*

The business could be taken to a different level, but Russ is finding it difficult to give up his duties or control. As he puts it, "I enjoy baking, but I like to handle everything myself." Until he can learn to delegate, Russ Lewis will be a victim of his own success.

Source: Jeff Bailey, "Enterprise: The Long-Term Perils of Being a Control Freak," *Wall Street Journal*, March 25, 2003, p. B-6.

The control process begins with the establishment of standards. This is evidence of the connection between planning and control, for it is through planning and goal setting that control standards are established. Planners translate goals into norms (standards) by making them measurable. A goal to increase market share, for example, may be expressed as a projected dollar increase in sales volume for the coming year. Such an annual target may, in turn, be broken down into quarterly target standards so that corrective action can be taken early if performance begins to fall below the projected amount.

As Exhibit 18-3 shows, performance measurement occurs at various stages of the control process. Performance may be measured at the input stage (perhaps to determine the quality of materials purchased), during the process stage (perhaps to determine if the product being manufactured meets quality standards), and/or at the output stage (perhaps to check the quality of a completed product).

Corrective action is required when performance deviates significantly from the standard in an unfavorable direction. To prevent the deviation from recurring, such action must be accompanied by an analysis of the cause of the deviation. If the percentage of defective products increases, for example, a manager must determine whether the problem is caused by faulty raw materials, untrained workers, or some other factor. For a problem to be effectively controlled, corrective action must identify and deal with the real cause.

Communicating

Another key to a healthy organization is effective communication—that is, getting managers and employees to talk with each other and openly share problems and ideas. To some extent, the management hierarchy must be set aside so that personnel at all levels can speak freely with those higher up. The result is two-way communication—a far cry from the old-fashioned idea that managers give orders and employees simply carry them out. The need for good communication has been eloquently expressed as follows: "It's a no-brainer—you've got to talk, email, and kibitz with employees. The speed with which information moves through a company is critical to how well the mechanism works. Information is the oil that turns the gears."[14]

To communicate effectively, managers must tell employees where they stand, how the business is doing, and what the firm's plans are for the future. While negative feedback may be necessary at times, giving positive feedback to employees is the primary tool for establishing good human relations. Perhaps the most fundamental concept managers need to keep in mind is that employees are people, not machines. As people, they quickly detect insincerity but respond to honest efforts to treat them as mature, responsible individuals. In short, an atmosphere of trust and respect contributes greatly to good communication.

EXHIBIT 18-3 *Stages of the Control Process*

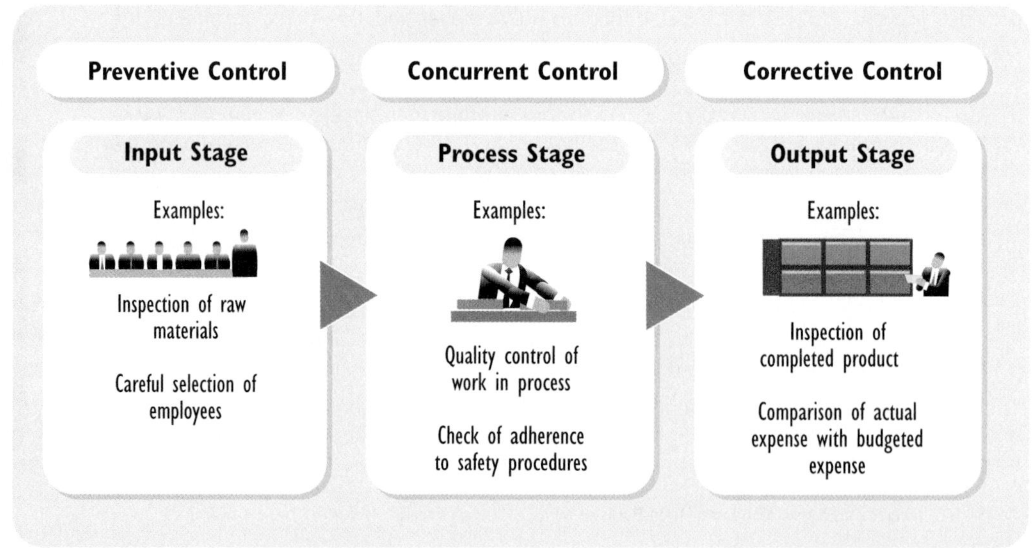

Any of the following practical techniques can be used to stimulate two-way communication:

- Periodic performance review sessions to discuss employees' ideas, questions, complaints, and job expectations
- Bulletin boards to keep employees informed about developments affecting them and/or the company
- Suggestion boxes to solicit employees' ideas
- Formal staff meetings to discuss problems and matters of general concern
- Breakfast or lunch with employees to socialize and just talk

These methods and others can be used to supplement the most basic of all channels for communication—the day-to-day interaction between each employee and his or her supervisor.

Negotiating

In operating a business, entrepreneurs and managers must personally interact with other individuals much of the time. Some contacts involve outsiders, such as suppliers, customers, bankers, realtors, and providers of business services. Typically, the interests of the parties are in conflict, to some degree at least. A supplier, for example, wants to sell a product or service for the highest possible price, and the buyer wants to purchase it for the lowest possible price. To have a successful business, a manager must reach agreements that both meet the firm's requirements and contribute to good relationships over time.

Even within the business, personal relationships pit different perspectives and personal interests against one another. Subordinates, for example, frequently desire changes in their work assignments or feel that they are worth more to the company than their salary level indicates. Managers in different departments may compete for services offered by a maintenance department or a computer services unit.

The process of developing workable solutions through discussions or interactions is termed **negotiation**. All of us are negotiators in our daily lives, both inside and outside our family relationships. Conflicting interests, desires, and demands require that we reconcile, or negotiate, the differences in order to live together peacefully.

negotiation
A two-way communication process used to resolve differences in needs, goals, or ideas

Many people consider negotiation to be a win–lose game; that is, one party must win, and the other must lose. There is a problem, however, with this concept of negotiation. If both parties do not feel that they have won, the loser will go away with thoughts of getting even in subsequent negotiations. Such feelings do not contribute to good long-term relationships. In contrast, other negotiators advocate a win–win strategy. A win–win negotiator tries to find a solution that will satisfy at least the basic interests of both parties.

Implementing a win–win strategy in relationships involves thinking about one's own interests and also exploring the interests of the other party. After clarifying the interests of the various parties and their needs, the negotiator can explore various alternatives to identify their overall fit, looking for a solution that will produce a workable plan for all. There are situations, of course, in which a win–win solution is impossible, but this type of solution should be pursued as frequently as possible.

A foundation for successful negotiating is created by developing strong relationships between the negotiating parties. In Exhibit 18-4, Frank L. Acuff provides examples of comments that contribute to cooperative relationships.

PERSONAL TIME MANAGEMENT

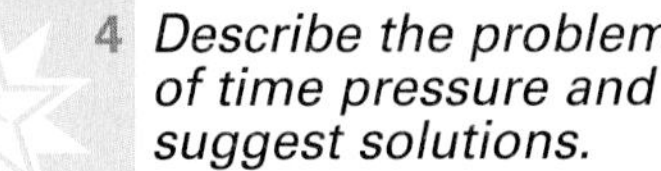
4 *Describe the problem of time pressure and suggest solutions.*

A typical entrepreneur spends much of the working day on the front line—meeting customers, solving problems, listening to employee complaints, talking with suppliers, and the like. She or he tackles such problems with the assistance of only a small staff. As a result, the owner-manager's energies and activities are diffused, and time becomes a scarce resource.

The Problem of Time Pressure

The hours worked by most new business owners are particularly long. Many owner-managers in small firms work from 60 to 80 hours per week. A frequent and unfortunate result

EXHIBIT 18-4 | *World-Class Tips for Building Relationships*

Fifteen Statements That Will Help Build Solid Relationships (or at Least Keep You Out of Deep Soup)

1. "I'm very pleased to meet you."
2. "Could you tell me more about your proposal?"
3. "I have a few more questions I'd like to ask you."
4. "We might be able to consider X if you could consider Y."
5. "Let me try to summarize where we stand now in our discussion."
6. "I'm very happy to see you again."
7. "Could you tell me more about your concerns?"
8. "Let me tell you where I have a concern."
9. "I feel disappointed that we haven't made more progress."
10. "I really appreciate the progress that we've made."
11. "Thank you."
12. "Can I answer any more questions about our organization or proposal?"
13. "What would it take for us to close this deal?"
14. "I've enjoyed doing business with you."
15. "I haven't talked to you since we signed the contract. I just wanted to follow up with you to see how things are working out."

Source: Reprinted from *How to Negotiate Anything with Anyone, Anywhere Around the World.* Copyright © 1997 Frank Acuff. Used with the permission of the publisher, AMACOM, a division of American Management Association, New York, NY. All rights reserved. http://www.amacombooks.org.

of such a schedule is inefficient work performance. Owner-managers may be too busy to see sales representatives who could supply market information on new products and processes, too busy to read technical or trade literature that would tell them what others are doing and what improvements might be adapted to their own use, too busy to listen carefully to employees' opinions and grievances, and too busy to give employees the instructions they need to do their jobs correctly.

Getting away for a vacation seems impossible for some small business owners. In extremely small firms, owners may find it necessary to close the business during their absence. Even in somewhat larger businesses, owners may fear that the firm will not function properly if they are not there. Unfortunately, keeping one's nose to the grindstone in this way may cost an entrepreneur dearly in terms of personal health, family relationships, and effectiveness in business leadership.

Time Savers for Busy Managers

Part of the solution to the problem of time pressure is application of the managerial activities discussed in the preceding section. For example, when possible, the manager should assign duties to subordinates who can work without close supervision. For such delegation to work, of course, a manager must first select and train qualified employees.

The greatest time saver is the effective use of time. Little will be accomplished if an individual flits from one task to another and back again. Use of modern technology, including cell phones, e-mail, the Internet, and similar aids, can be very helpful in allowing a manager to make the most of his or her time.

The first step in time management should be to analyze how much time is normally spent on various activities. Relying on general impressions is not only unprofessional but also unscientific and likely to involve error. For a period of several days or (preferably) several weeks, the manager should record the amounts of time spent on various activities during the day. An analysis of these figures will reveal a pattern, indicating which projects and tasks consume the most time and which activities are responsible for wasted time. It will also reveal chronic time wasting due to excessive socializing, work on trivial matters, coffee breaks, and so on.

After eliminating practices that waste time, a manager can carefully plan his or her use of available time. A planned approach to a day's or week's work is much more effective than a haphazard do-whatever-comes-up-first approach. This is true even for small firm managers whose schedules are continually interrupted in unanticipated ways.

Many time management specialists recommend the use of a daily written plan of work activities. This plan may be a list of activities scribbled on a note pad or a formal computerized schedule, but it should reflect priorities. By classifying duties as first-, second-, or third-level priorities, a manager can identify and focus attention on the most crucial tasks.

Effective time management requires self-discipline. An individual may begin with good intentions but lapse into habitually attending to whatever he or she finds to do at the moment. Procrastination is a frequent thief of time. Many managers delay unpleasant and difficult tasks, retreating to trivial and less threatening activities and rationalizing that they are getting those duties out of the way in order to be able to concentrate better on the more important tasks.

OUTSIDE MANAGEMENT ASSISTANCE

5 *Explain the various types of outside management assistance.*

Because entrepreneurs tend to be better doers than they are managers, they should consider the use of outside management assistance. Such outside assistance can supplement the manager's personal knowledge and the expertise of the few staff specialists on the company's payroll.

The Need for Outside Assistance

Entrepreneurs are often deficient in managerial skills and lack opportunities to share ideas with peers. Consequently, they may experience a sense of loneliness, a sense that is magnified by the small staff in most new enterprises. Some entrepreneurs reduce their feelings of isolation by joining such groups as the Young Entrepreneurs' Organization (http://www.yeo.org) and the Young Presidents' Organization (http://www.ypo.org), which allow them to meet with peers from other firms and share problems and experiences.[15] In addition to peer groups, there is a variety of other forms of outside managerial assistance available to entrepreneurs.

By obtaining help from outsiders, entrepreneurs can overcome some of their managerial deficiencies and also reduce their sense of loneliness. Outsiders can bring a detached, often objective point of view and new ideas. They may also possess knowledge of methods, approaches, and solutions beyond the experience of a particular entrepreneur.

Sources of Management Assistance

Entrepreneurs seeking management assistance can turn to any number of sources, including business incubators, SBA programs, and management consultants. Other approaches the entrepreneur can take to obtain management help include consulting public and university libraries, attending evening classes at local colleges, and considering the suggestions of friends and customers.

BUSINESS INCUBATORS As discussed in Chapter 9, a business incubator is an organization that offers both space and managerial and clerical services to new businesses. There are now hundreds of incubators in the United States, and the number is growing rapidly. Most of them involve the participation of government agencies and/or universities, although some have been launched as purely private endeavors. The primary motivation in establishing incubators has been a desire to encourage entrepreneurship and thereby contribute to economic development.

Often, individuals who wish to start businesses are deficient in pertinent knowledge and lacking in appropriate experience. In many cases, they need practical guidance in marketing, record keeping, management, and preparation of business plans. Business incubators offer new entrepreneurs on-site business expertise; the services available in an incubator are shown in Exhibit 18-5.

An incubator provides a supportive atmosphere for a business during the early months of its existence, when it is most fragile and vulnerable to external dangers and internal errors. If the incubator works as it should, the fledgling business gains strength quickly and, within a year or so, leaves the incubator setting.

EXHIBIT 18-5 *Services Provided by Business Incubators to New Firms*

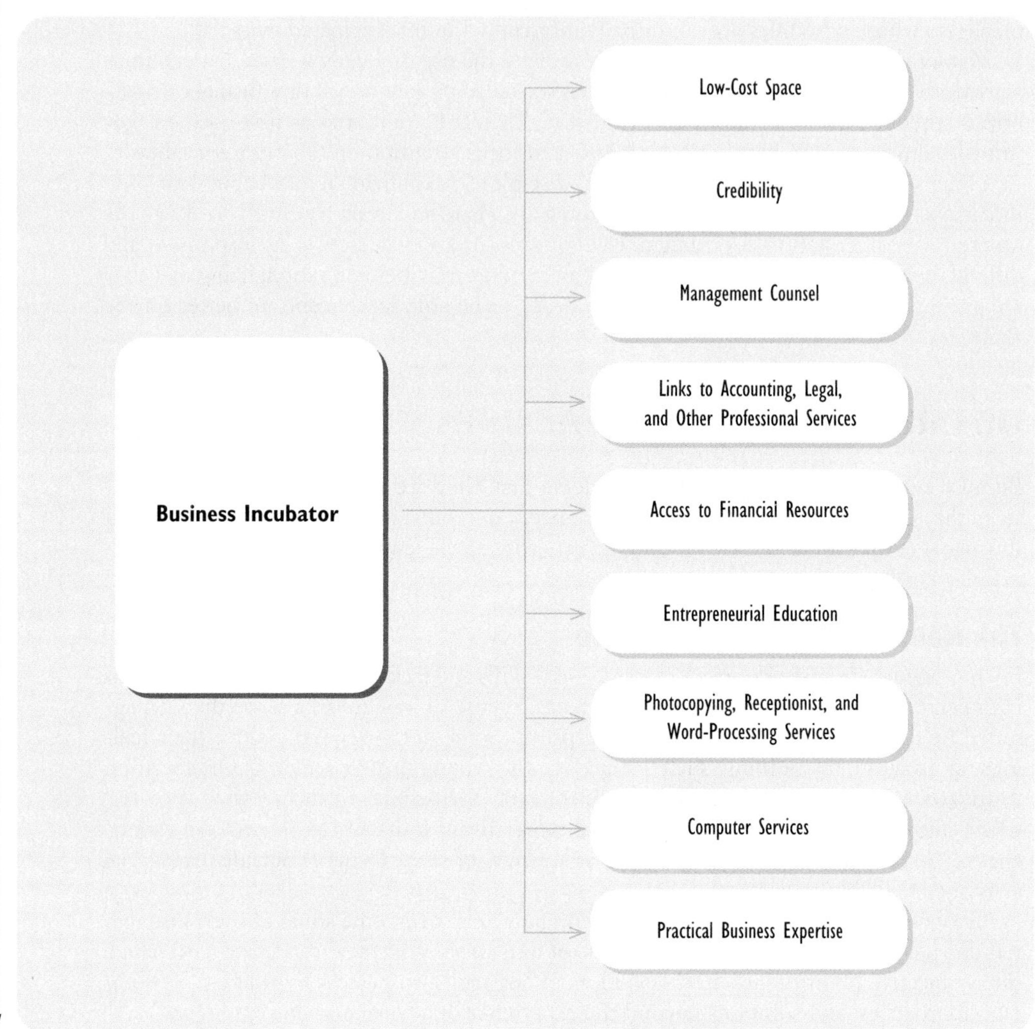

Yvette Berke started Adapt Consulting, a firm that does environmental consulting, in an incubator in Thousand Oaks, California.[16] Locating in the incubator gave her access to conference rooms, a fax, a copier, the Internet, a kitchen, and teleconferencing equipment. Her firm advises businesses in the area of nonhazardous waste and helps them establish recycling and other programs. In addition to serving clients in the United States, Berke is now conducting business in Singapore, Malaysia, Sri Lanka, and other Pacific Rim countries.

Internet incubators, which provide beginning services to dot-com startups that are little more than an idea, are rapidly growing in number.[17] Like other incubators, they provide business advice, office services, and connections to financing. Most of them also provide seed capital in exchange for an equity stake in the business.

STUDENT CONSULTING TEAMS Many colleges and universities have student consulting teams willing to assist small businesses. These teams of upper-class and graduate students, under the direction of a faculty member, work with owners of small firms in analyzing and devising solutions to their business problems.

The program has mutual benefits: It provides students with a practical view of business management and supplies small firms with answers to their problems. The students who participate are typically combined in teams that provide a diversity of academic background. Individual teams, for example, may include students specializing in management, marketing, accounting, and finance.

SERVICE CORPS OF RETIRED EXECUTIVES (SCORE) By appealing to any SBA field office, small business managers can obtain free management advice from a group called the **Service Corps of Retired Executives,** or **SCORE** (http://www.score.org). SCORE is an organization of retired business executives who serve as consultants to small business managers on current problems. Functioning under the sponsorship of the SBA, SCORE provides an opportunity for retired executives to contribute to the business community and, in the process, help small business managers solve their problems. The relationship is thus mutually beneficial. By demonstrating the worth of consulting services, experiences with SCORE may encourage entrepreneurs to utilize paid consultants as their firms grow.

Service Corps of Retired Executives (SCORE)
An SBA-sponsored group of retired executives who give free advice to small businesses

Stories abound of SCORE's successfully assisting small firms. Judson Lovering, an entrepreneur who operated a specialty bakery in New England, wished to improve the business.[18] A SCORE business counselor, a former small business owner, helped him capitalize on the bakery's most popular products and eliminate low-profit offerings. This required Lovering to decline some specialty orders that had made the business a "personal bakery" without adequate profit margins. As a result of the advice Lovering received from SCORE, the bakery has consistently shown business growth.

SMALL BUSINESS DEVELOPMENT CENTERS (SBDCs) Small business development centers (SBDCs), which are patterned after the Agricultural Extension Service, are affiliated with colleges or universities as a part of the SBA's overall program of assistance to small business. SBDCs provide direct consultation, continuing education, research assistance, and export services. One of their special priorities is to lend support to minority-owned firms. The staff typically includes faculty members, SCORE counselors, professional staff, and graduate student assistants.

small business development centers (SBDCs)
University-affiliated centers offering consulting, education, and other support to small businesses

MANAGEMENT CONSULTANTS Management consultants serve small businesses as well as large corporations. Types of consultants range from large global firms to one- and two-person operations. Small firm managers, however, are often reluctant to use outside advisors. Some of their reasons are reflected in the comments in Exhibit 18-6.

Some small businesses need analysis by consultants—especially businesses that have paid very little attention to their productivity. When Mario Arcari and Gregory Goldfarb started Hi-Tech Manufacturing in Schiller Park, Illinois, they were "just two guys and a shop making machine parts," as Arcari put it.[19] The business grew, but there were problems.

> *Orders were processed on the fly. About 1% of all product material was left over as "scrap" and dumped or paid for out of Hi-Tech's pocket, costing thousands every year. There were no procedures to handle customer complaints. Machines went for months without maintenance checks. Imperfect parts—too long or short by fractions of an inch—were often shipped. Companies like Lockheed-Martin refused to talk to Hi-Tech until it had a quality-control program.*[20]

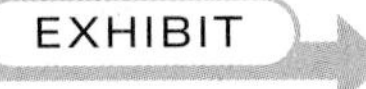

18-6 *Reasons Small Firm Managers Shun Outside Advice*

1. "I can solve the problem myself."
2. "I don't want anyone throwing up roadblocks to my plans."
3. "Professional advisors should be used only as a last resort."
4. "An outsider could never understand my business."
5. "High-powered experts wouldn't be interested in my business."
6. "An advisor will raise a lot of issues I don't have time to bother with right now."
7. "I don't want to share any information with an outsider."
8. "Professional advisors cost too much."
9. "Our longtime attorney (or accountant or banker) is a friend and knows us best. We don't need anyone else."
10. "I'm unsure of how relationships with professional advisors work."

Source: Craig E. Aronoff and John L. Ward, "Why So Few Business Owners Get and Accept Good Advice," *Small Business Forum,* Vol. 14, No. 2 (Fall 1996), pp. 26–37.

By obtaining consulting help from the nonprofit Chicago Manufacturing Center, these entrepreneurs were able to eliminate many wasteful practices, reduce scrap, and increase customer satisfaction. The $15,000 consulting fee was easily recovered in the revenue resulting from the firm's improved performance.

To ensure client–provider satisfaction, the owner and the consultant should reach a mutual understanding on the nature of the assistance to be provided before it begins. Any consulting fees should be specified, and the particulars of the agreement should be put in writing. Fees are often quoted on a per diem basis and might easily range from $500 to $5,000 or more. Although the cost may seem high, it must be evaluated in terms of the expertise that it buys.

Directories are available to help entrepreneurs find the right management consultant. One such directory is published by the Institute of Management Consultants USA, 521 Fifth Avenue, New York, NY 10175 (http://www.imcusa.org). The code of ethics to which institute members subscribe is an indication of their desire to foster professionalism in their work.

networking
The process of developing and engaging in mutually beneficial relationships

ENTREPRENEURIAL NETWORKS Entrepreneurs can also gain management assistance from peers through **networking**—the process of developing and engaging in mutually beneficial informal relationships. As business owners meet other business owners, they discover a commonality of interests that leads to an exchange of ideas and experiences. The settings for such meetings may be trade associations, civic clubs, fraternal organizations, or any other situation that brings businesspeople into contact with one another. Of course, the personal network of an entrepreneur is not limited to other entrepreneurs, but those individuals may be the most significant part of his or her network.

Entrepreneurs are linked by several kinds of ties: instrumental, affective, and moral. An *instrumental tie* is one formed when the parties engage in mutually rewarding activities—for example, exchanging useful ideas about certain business problems. An *affective tie* relates to emotional sentiments—for example, a shared vision about actions small businesses must take when faced with giant competitors or with the government. A *moral tie* involves some type of obligation—for example, a mutual commitment to the principle of private enterprise or to the importance of integrity in business transactions. In personal networks of entrepreneurs, affective and moral ties are believed to be stronger than instrumental ties.[21] This suggests that a sense of identity and self-respect may be a significant product of entrepreneurial networks.

Living the Dream *Entrepreneurial Challenges*

Networking and Incubators

© Bayete Ross-Smith

http://www.onthemovestaffing.com

Networking and incubators are two routes entrepreneurial firms can take to obtain outside management help. In 1998, Vaneese Johnson used $10,000 of personal savings to establish On the Move Staffing Service, a San Francisco–based full-service staffing firm, in her home. Johnson networked with city officials and local business leaders, and within months she landed her first deal with a major client—a $60,000 contract with major league baseball's San Francisco Giants for employees to run concession stands, clean the facilities, and so on.

As the business grew, Johnson needed additional and more professional space in which to interview people and conduct business. Through networking, she found the Renaissance Entrepreneurship Center, a nonprofit organization that provides support services for microbusinesses. For $150 per month, she obtained use of 100 square feet of space, fax and copy machines, a mailbox, a receptionist who served all of the businesses in the building, and consulting services as needed.

By growing through networking and using an incubator location, the firm increased revenues from $35,000 in the first year to $1.2 million in 2002.

Source: Nicole Lewis, "The Power of Networking," *Black Enterprise*, Vol. 33, No. 11 (June 2003), p. 51.

OTHER BUSINESS AND PROFESSIONAL SERVICES A variety of business and professional groups provide management assistance. In many cases, such assistance is part of the business relationship. Sources of management advice include bankers, certified public accountants, attorneys, insurance agents, suppliers, trade associations, and chambers of commerce.

It takes initiative to draw on the management assistance available from such groups. For example, rather than confining his or her business relationship with a certified public accountant (CPA) to audits and financial statements, the owner-manager must think to ask the CPA to advise on a much broader range of subjects.

> *Besides offering advice on tax matters, a good accountant can help in a variety of situations. When you hire or fire, what benefits or severance package should you offer? When you're planning to open a new branch, will your cash flow support it? When you embark on a new sideline, will the margins be adequate? When you reduce insurance, what's the risk? When you factor receivables, how will it affect the balance sheet? When you take on a big account, what's the downside if you lose the account? Or when you cut expenses, how will the cuts affect the bottom line?*[22]

As you can see from these examples, potential management assistance often comes disguised as service from professionals and firms encountered in the normal course of business activity. By staying alert for and taking advantage of such opportunities, an entrepreneur can strengthen a small firm's management and improve its operations with little, if any, additional cost.

Looking Back

1 Discuss the entrepreneur's leadership role.

- Entrepreneurs must establish and communicate a vision of the firm's future.
- Founding entrepreneurs need a tolerance for ambiguity and a capacity for adaptation.
- Entrepreneurs need a resolve to make the business succeed more than they need a flashy personality.
- An entrepreneur exerts strong, personal influence in a small firm.
- Progressive managers use various leadership styles, including participative management, empowerment, and work teams.

2 Explain the distinctive features of small firm management.

- A founder's less-than-professional management style can adversely affect business growth.
- Founders tend to be more action-oriented and less analytical than professional managers.
- Small firms are particularly vulnerable to managerial inefficiency.
- Small firm managers face special financial and personnel constraints.
- As a new firm grows, it adds layers of supervision and increases formality of management.
- A firm's growth necessitates that the entrepreneur become more of a manager and less of a doer.

3 Identify the managerial tasks of entrepreneurs.

- Both long-range planning and short-range planning are required but often postponed or neglected.
- Managers must create an organizational structure to provide for orderly direction of operations.
- Informal groups within the organization can be encouraged to make a beneficial contribution to the firm.
- Managers who delegate authority successfully can devote more time to more important duties.
- Managers exercise control by monitoring operations in order to detect and correct deviations from plans.
- Effective two-way communication is important in building a healthy organization.
- Managers must be able to negotiate with both insiders and outsiders.

4 Describe the problem of time pressure and suggest solutions.

- Time pressure creates inefficiencies in the management of a small firm because the entrepreneur's energies are diffused.
- The greatest time saver is the effective use of time, which requires self-discipline.
- A manager can reduce time pressure through such practices as eliminating wasteful activities and planning work carefully.

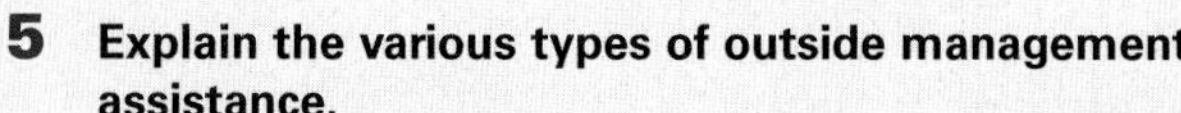

5 Explain the various types of outside management assistance.

- Outside management assistance can be used to remedy staff limitations and reduce entrepreneurs' sense of isolation, among other things.
- Business incubators provide guidance as well as space for beginning businesses.
- Three government- and/or university-sponsored sources of assistance are student consulting teams, the Service Corps of Retired Executives (SCORE), and Small Business Development Centers (SBDCs).
- Management assistance may be obtained by engaging management consultants and by networking with other entrepreneurs.
- Professionals such as bankers and CPAs also provide management assistance.

Key Terms

empowerment, p. 400
work teams, p. 401
professional manager, p. 401
long-range plan (strategic plan), p. 405
short-range plan, p. 405
budget, p. 405
chain of command, p. 405
line organization, p. 405
line-and-staff organization, p. 405
span of control, p. 405
delegation of authority, p. 407
negotiation, p. 409
Service Corps of Retired Executives (SCORE), p. 413
small business development centers (SBDCs), p. 413
networking, p. 414

Discussion Questions

1. Would most employees of small firms welcome or resist a leadership approach that sought their ideas and involved them in meetings to let them know what was going on? Why might some employees resist such an approach?
2. Is the quality of management likely to be relatively uniform in all types of small businesses? If not, what might account for differences?
3. What are the four stages of small business growth outlined in this chapter? How do management requirements change as the firm moves through these stages?
4. Some professional football coaches have written game plans that they consult from time to time during games. If coaches need formal plans, does it follow that small business owners also need them as they engage in their particular type of competition? Why?
5. What type of small firm might effectively use a line organization? When might it be necessary to change the firm's structure? To what type of structure? Why?
6. Explain the relationship between planning and control in a small business. Give an example.
7. There is a saying that goes "What you do speaks so loudly I can't hear what you say." What does this mean, and how does it apply to communication in small firms?
8. What practices can a small business manager use to conserve time?
9. What are some advantages and possible drawbacks for a startup retail firm of locating in a business incubator?
10. Are student consulting teams of greater benefit to the client firm or to the students involved?

You Make the Call

SITUATION 1

In one small firm, the owner-manager and his management team use various methods to delegate decision making to employees at the operating level. New employees are trained thoroughly when they begin, but no supervisor monitors their work closely once they have learned their duties. Of course, help is available as needed, but no one is there on an hour-to-hour basis to make sure employees are functioning as needed and that they are avoiding mistakes.

Occasionally, all managers and supervisors leave for a day-long meeting and allow the operating employees to run the business by themselves. Job assignments are defined rather loosely. Management expects employees to assume responsibility and to take necessary action whenever they see that something needs to be done. When employees ask for direction, they are sometimes simply told to solve the problem in whatever way they think best.

Question 1 Is such a loosely organized firm likely to be as effective as a firm that defines jobs more precisely and monitors performance more closely? What are the advantages and the limitations of the managerial style described above?

Question 2 How might such managerial methods affect morale?

Question 3 Would you like to work for this company? Why or why not?

SITUATION 2

A few years after successfully launching a new business, an entrepreneur found himself spending 16-hour days running from one appointment to another, negotiating with customers, drumming up new business, signing checks, and checking up as much as possible on his six employees. The founder realized that his own strength was in selling, but general managerial responsibilities were very time consuming and interfered with his sales efforts. He even slept in the office two nights a week.

Despite his hard work, however, he knew that employees weren't organized and that many problems existed. He lacked the time to set personnel policies or to draw up job descriptions for his six employees. One employee even took advantage of the laxity in supervision to skip work sometimes. Invoices were sent to customers late, and delivery schedules were sometimes missed. Fortunately, the business was profitable in spite of the numerous problems.

Question 1 Is this founder's problem one of time management or general managerial ability? Would it be feasible to engage a management consultant to help solve the firm's problems?

Question 2 If this founder asked you to recommend some type of outside management assistance, would you recommend a SCORE counselor, a student consulting team, a CPA firm, a management consultant, or some other type of assistance? Why?

Question 3 If you were asked to improve this firm's management system, what would be the first steps you would take? What would be your initial goal?

SITUATION 3

After an inauspicious start in a spare bedroom in his home, an entrepreneur's business had flourished. He wondered if he had the necessary talent to ensure its continued success. The business had grown to 100 employees and then to 200 employees. When the business was small, the entrepreneur could figure out the solutions to problems on a case-by-case basis, but the problems were becoming increasingly complicated.

Question 1 What kinds of practices or procedures will this entrepreneur need to adopt to enable the business to continue to operate successfully?

Question 2 What resources might this entrepreneur use to get good feedback to help him assess his competence and understand the issues his growing business is facing?

Experiential Exercises

1. Interview a management consultant, SCORE member, university director of student consulting teams, or representative of a CPA firm to discuss small business management weaknesses and the willingness or reluctance of small firms to use consultants. Prepare a report on your findings.
2. Diagram the organizational relationships in a small business of your choice. Report on any organizational problems that are apparent to you or that are recognized by the manager or others in the firm.
3. Prepare a report on your personal observations of leadership and delegation of authority by a supervisor in an organization where you have been an employee or volunteer. Include references to the type of leadership exercised and the adequacy of delegation of authority, if any; clarity of instructions; and any problems involved.
4. Select an unstructured time block of one to four hours in your schedule—that is, hours that are not regularly devoted to class attendance, sleeping, and so on. Carefully record your use of that time period for several days. Prepare a report summarizing your use of the time and outlining a plan to use it more effectively.

Exploring the Web

1. Go to *Inc.* magazine's Web site at **http://www.inc.com** and follow these links— "How To," then "Leadership and Strategy"—until you arrive at the How-To Guide.
   a. Read three articles, and make note of their titles and authors.
   b. What suggestions from these articles would you implement in your small business and why?
2. Take a time-management quiz. Go to the Small Business Network, a Web site maintained by American Express, at **http://home3.americanexpress.com/smallbusiness**. Follow the link to "Articles & Discussions," choose "Day to Day Management," and then take the Managing Time and Resources quiz.
   a. Print out your quiz results.
   b. What is your opinion of the advice you received at this site on better managing your time?
3. Two influential and informative online resources for small businesses and entrepreneurs are provided by SCORE ("Counselors to America's Small Business") and the SBDC. Explore the SCORE (**http://www.score.org/**) and SBDC (**http://www.sba.gov/sbdc/**) Web sites.
   a. What resources on the SCORE Web site do you like the most, and how would you utilize them?
   b. What SBDC resources do you like the most, and how would you utilize them?

Case 18

DOUGLAS ELECTRICAL SUPPLY, INC. (P. 559)

An outside trainer-consultant encounters quality issues that touch on leadership and integrity.

Alternative Cases for Chapter 18:

Case 4, Auntie Anne's, p. 531
Case 19, Gibson Mortuary, p. 561
Case 20, Texas Nameplate Company, p. 563

MANAGING HUMAN RESOURCES

In the Video Spotlight

Orange Tree Imports

When she was just out of college, Carol Schroeder, better known as Orange, opened a specialty retail store in the historic district of Madison, Wisconsin. She has nurtured Orange Tree Imports ever since, and she wants to inspire the same kind of commitment in her employees.

Orange does this by providing meaningful work. To her, this means encouraging employee input on all major decisions. Even though she has ultimate veto power, Orange calls her organizational structure a participative democracy. Staff members conduct group interviews and have a say in whether job candidates are hired. Employees organize their work tasks, make their own work schedules, and receive reward vouchers when they fill in for a coworker. Orange also trains employees on new products and conducts tasting sessions for the food products sold at the store. That way, employees are better able to describe to customers the differences between brands and flavors.

The involved approach to human resources has created a tightly knit community of employees at Orange Tree Imports. In over 20 years, Orange has employed more than 120 people, and she's still in touch with almost all of them. In fact, she has staff reunions about every five years.

Video material provided by Hattie Bryant, Producer of Small Business School, the series on PBS Stations, Worldnet, and the Web at http://www.smallbusinessschool.org.

Chapter 19

Looking Ahead

After studying this chapter, you should be able to

1 *Explain the importance of employee recruitment and list some sources that can be useful in finding suitable applicants.*

2 *Identify the steps to take in evaluating job applicants.*

3 *Describe the role of training for both managerial and nonmanagerial employees in a small firm.*

4 *Explain the various types of compensation plans, including the use of incentive plans.*

5 *Discuss the human resource issues of employee leasing, legal protection, labor unions, and the formalizing of employer–employee relationships.*

Honest, competent, motivated employees are a valuable resource for any business. Therefore, it is vitally important that entrepreneurs manage employees well.

Small businesses cannot and should not try to duplicate the personnel practices of giant corporations such as Wal-Mart and General Motors, but they can use personnel management methods that are more suitable for smaller firms. This chapter deals with human resource management practices that work best for entrepreneurial firms.

RECRUITING PERSONNEL

1 *Explain the importance of employee recruitment and list some sources that can be useful in finding suitable applicants.*

Recruitment brings applicants to a business; the goal is to obtain a pool of applicants large enough to contain a number of talented prospects. In a subsequent stage of the selection process, management decides which applicants are "keepers."

The Need for Quality Employees

In his classic study of good-to-great companies (companies that advanced from being really good to become truly great), Jim Collins found that the great companies first "got the right people on the bus."

> *The executives who ignited the transformations from good to great did not first figure out where to drive the bus and then get people to take it there. No, they* first *got the right people on the bus (and the wrong people off the bus) and* then *figured out where to drive it. They said, in essence, "Look, I don't really know where we should take this bus. But I know this much: If we get the right people on the bus, the right people in the right seats, and the wrong people off the bus, then we'll figure out how to take it someplace great."*[1]

This reasoning is particularly relevant to personnel in key positions, as the right people in the right places provide a strong foundation for any business. In a broad sense, this concept is applicable to all employees, in view of their direct or indirect impact on business accomplishments.

Employees affect profitability in many ways. In most small firms, salespeople's attitudes and their ability to serve customer needs directly affect sales revenue. Also, payroll is one of the largest expense categories for most businesses, having a direct impact on the bottom line. By recruiting the best possible personnel, a firm can improve its returns on each payroll dollar.

Recruitment and selection of employees establish a foundation for a firm's ongoing human relationships. In a sense, the quality of a firm's employees determines its potential. A solid, effective organization can be built only with a talented, ambitious workforce.

The Lure of Entrepreneurial Firms

Competing for well-qualified business talent requires small firms to identify their distinctive advantages, especially when recruiting outstanding prospects for managerial and professional positions. Fortunately, there are some very good reasons to work for an entrepreneurial business. This is especially true of growing enterprises led by individuals or teams with a compelling vision of a desirable and attainable future. It is exciting to work for a company that is going somewhere!

The work itself can also attract talented prospects. The opportunity to make decisions and to obtain general management or professional experience at a significant level is appealing to many individuals. Rather than toiling in obscure, low-level, specialized positions during their early years, capable newcomers can quickly move into positions of responsibility in a well-managed small business. In such positions, they can see the "fruits of their labor" and how it makes a difference in the success of the company.

Small firms can structure the work environment to offer professional, managerial, and technical personnel greater freedom than they would normally have in a larger business. In this type of environment, individual contributions can be recognized rather than hidden under the numerous layers of a bureaucratic organization. In addition, compensation packages can be designed to create powerful incentives. Flexibility in work scheduling and job-sharing arrangements are other potential advantages.

Sources of Employees

To recruit effectively, the small business manager must know where and how to find qualified applicants. Sources are numerous, and it is impossible to generalize about the best source in view of differences in companies' personnel needs and the quality of the sources from one locality to another. The following discussion describes some sources of employees most popular among small firms.

HELP-WANTED ADVERTISING Hanging a "Help Wanted" sign in the window is one traditional form of recruiting used by some small firms. A similar but more aggressive form of recruiting consists of advertising in the classifieds sections of local newspapers. For some technical, professional, and managerial positions, firms may advertise in trade and professional journals. Although the effectiveness of help-wanted advertising has been questioned by some, many small businesses recruit in this way.

Living the Dream *Entrepreneurial Challenges*

Luring Employees to an Entrepreneurial Firm

THQ Inc. competes with deep-pocketed giant corporations in the video game market. It started in 1990 with several dozen employees and has proven itself a tough competitor. As a startup, THQ used its smaller size as a selling point. According to CEO Brian Farrell, "We let people know, 'You'll be a big fish in a somewhat smaller pond here at THQ.'"

One of the firm's secret weapons is its ability to attract brilliant game developers. These game developers are lured with a combination of creative freedom and financial incentives. They get to share in the firm's successes, because anyone who designs a great game at THQ is noticed and given greater responsibility. And their jobs are structured in such a way that they can avoid the drudgery of bureaucratic or otherwise unpleasant tasks they might have to endure at other businesses.

Even though THQ is still much smaller than the industry's major competitors, it has achieved great success and now has more than 700 employees.

Source: Donna Fuscaldo, "Special Report: Small Business, The Key Employees," *Wall Street Journal*, October 28, 2002, pp. R-1, R-10.

WALK-INS A firm may receive unsolicited applications from individuals who walk into the place of business to seek employment. Walk-ins are an inexpensive source of personnel, particularly for hourly work, but the quality of applicants varies. If qualified applicants cannot be hired immediately, their applications should be kept on file for future reference. In the interest of good community relations, all applicants should be treated courteously, whether or not they are offered jobs.

SCHOOLS Secondary schools, trade schools, colleges, and universities are desirable sources of personnel for certain positions, particularly those requiring no specific work experience. Some secondary schools and colleges have internship programs that enable students to gain practical experience in business firms. Applicants from secondary and trade schools have a limited but useful educational background to offer a small business. Colleges and universities can supply candidates for positions in management and in various technical and professional fields. In addition, many colleges are excellent sources of part-time employees.

PUBLIC EMPLOYMENT OFFICES At no cost to small businesses, employment offices in each state offer information on applicants who are actively seeking employment and administer the state's unemployment insurance program. These offices, located in all major cities, are for the most part a useful source of clerical workers, unskilled laborers, production workers, and technicians. They do not actively recruit but only counsel and assist those who come in. Although public employment offices can be a source of good employees, the individuals they work with are, for the most part, untrained or only marginally qualified.

PRIVATE EMPLOYMENT AGENCIES Numerous private firms offer their services as employment agencies. In some cases, employers receive these services without cost because the applicants pay a fee to the agency; however, more often, the hiring firms are responsible for the agency fee. Private employment agencies tend to specialize in people with specific skills, such as accountants, computer operators, and managers.

EXECUTIVE SEARCH FIRMS When filling key positions, small firms sometimes turn to executive search firms, often called **headhunters**, to locate qualified candidates. The key positions for which such firms seek applicants are those paying a minimum of $50,000 to $70,000 per year. The cost to the employer may run from 30 to 40 percent of the first year's salary. Because of the high cost, use of headhunters may seem unreasonable for small, entrepreneurial firms. At times, however, the need for a manager who can help a firm "move to the next level" justifies the use of an executive search firm. A headhunter is usually better able than the small firm to conduct a wide-ranging search for individuals who possess the right combination of talents for the available position.

headhunter
A search firm that locates qualified candidates for executive positions

EMPLOYEE REFERRALS If current employees are good employees, their recommendations of suitable candidates may provide excellent prospects. Ordinarily, employees will hesitate to recommend applicants unless they believe in their ability to do the job. Many small business owners say that this source accounts for more new hires than any other. A few employers go so far as to offer financial rewards for employee referrals that result in the hiring of new employees.

John Boyce of Janitron, a small cleaning-service company in St. Louis, found it difficult to recruit relatively unskilled workers.[2] When he offered a $100 referral bonus to his building managers and supervisors, however, he soon found 47 entry-level employees for his 225-employee company. (The bonus is not paid unless the new employee stays for at least 90 days.)

INTERNET RECRUITING Recruiters are increasingly seeking applicants on the Internet. A variety of Web sites, such as http://www.careerbuilder.com, http://www.monster.com, and http://www.hotjobs.com, allow applicants to submit their résumés and permit potential employers to search those résumés for qualified applicants. And as the Internet is becoming more and more popular as a source of applicants, many firms are posting job openings on their own Web sites.

TEMPORARY HELP AGENCIES The temporary help industry, which is also growing rapidly, supplies employees (or temps)—such as word processors, clerks, accountants, engineers, nurses, and sales clerks—for short periods of time. By using an agency such as Kelly

Living the Dream *Entrepreneurial Challenges*

Searching for Seasonal Applicants

For some businesses, finding suitable applicants is a major problem, with none of the traditional sources working well. Randy Plumley operates a Dallas-area landscaping business, Dyna-Mist Inc., with very seasonal labor demands. The jobs require low skills and outdoor physical labor in temperatures that often soar above 100 degrees. The business's winter lull, moreover, means that most of its employees lack year-round employment.

Plumley depends largely on immigrant workers, all of whom must have legal documentation. But finding good applicants is a problem. His foreman even cruises other work sites and hands out business cards. A few years ago, Plumley paid $1,000 per employee to hire 10 workers through an employment program operated by the Mexican consulate.

Since good workers are so hard to find, the firm strives to retain competent employees by giving pay raises quickly, helping with personal needs, and allowing time for visits home. Better retention helps, but recruiting is always difficult for this type of business.

Source: Susan Warren, "The Transient Workers," *Wall Street Journal*, October 28, 2002, p. R-4.

Services or Manpower, small firms can deal with seasonal fluctuations and absences caused by vacation or illness. For example, a temporary replacement might be obtained to fill the position of an employee who is taking leave following the birth of a child—a type of family leave now mandated by law for some employees. In addition, the use of temporary employees provides management with an introduction to individuals whose performance may justify an offer of permanent employment. Staffing with temporary employees is less practical when extensive training is required or continuity is important.

Diversity in the Workforce

Over time, the composition of the workforce has changed with respect to race, ethnicity, gender, and age. In 1980, for example, 76 percent of the workforce was White; by 2000, only 69 percent was White.[3] Much of this change can be attributed to the growing proportion of Hispanic workers. The balance is shifting rapidly toward greater **workforce diversity**, not only because of increased participation of racial minorities but also because of higher proportions of women and older workers.

workforce diversity
Differences among employees in terms of such dimensions as gender, age, ethnicity, and race

The challenge for human resource management is to adapt to the fact that the pool of potential employees is now much more diverse. To remain fully competitive, business owners need to step up recruitment of women and minorities and be open to innovative ways to access the available pool of applicants. When Dick Snow found it difficult to recruit American teenagers for summer work at his six East Coast Ben and Jerry's ice cream stores, his solution was to hire 12 British ice cream scoopers through the British Universities North American Club.[4] By developing an awareness of the potential in various parts of the talent pool, small firms can improve the effectiveness of their recruitment methods.

Job Descriptions

A small business manager should analyze the activities or work to be performed and determine the number and kinds of jobs to be filled. Knowing the job requirements permits more intelligent selection of applicants for specific jobs, based on their individual capacities and characteristics.

Certainly, an owner-manager should not select personnel simply to fit rigid specifications of education, experience, or personal background. Rather, he or she must concentrate on the overall ability of an individual to fill a particular position in the business. Making this determination requires an outline, or summary, of the work to be performed.

Duties listed in such job descriptions should not be defined too narrowly. It is important that job descriptions minimize unnecessary overlap but also avoid creating a "that's not my job" mentality. Technical competence is as necessary in small firms as it is in large businesses, but versatility and flexibility may be even more important. Engineers may occasionally need to make sales calls, and marketing people may need to pinch-hit in production.

In the process of examining a job, an analyst should list the knowledge, skills, abilities, and other characteristics that an individual must have to perform the job. This statement of requirements is called a **job specification** and may be a part of the job description. A job specification for the position of stock clerk, for example, might state that the individual must be able to lift 50 pounds and must have completed 10 to 12 years of schooling.

job specification
A list of skills and abilities needed to perform a specific job

Job descriptions are mainly an aid in personnel recruitment, but they also have other uses. For example, they can give employees a focus in their work, provide direction in training, and supply a framework for performance review.

EVALUATING PROSPECTS AND SELECTING EMPLOYEES

Recruitment activities identify prospects for employment. Subsequent steps are needed to evaluate these candidates and to extend job offers. To reduce the risk of taking an uninformed gamble on applicants of unknown quality, an employer can take the following steps.

2 Identify the steps to take in evaluating job applicants.

Step 1: Using Application Forms

By using an application form, an employer can collect enough information to determine whether a prospect is minimally qualified and to provide a basis for further evaluation. Typically, an application asks for the applicant's name, address, Social Security number, educational history, employment history, and references.

Although an application form need not be elaborate or lengthy, it must be carefully written to avoid legal complications. In general, a prospective employer cannot seek information about sex, race, religion, color, national origin, age, or disabilities. The information requested should be focused on helping the employer make a better job-related assessment. For example, an employer is permitted to ask whether an applicant has graduated from high school. However, a question regarding the year the applicant graduated would be considered inappropriate, because the answer would reveal the applicant's age.

Step 2: Interviewing the Applicant

An interview permits the employer to get some idea of the applicant's appearance, job knowledge, intelligence, and personality. Any of these factors may be significant to the job to be filled. Although the interview is an important step in the selection process, it should not be the only step. Some managers have the mistaken idea that they are infallible judges of human nature and can choose good employees on the basis of interviews alone. Care must be taken in the interview process, as in the design of application forms, to avoid asking questions that conflict with the law. If possible, applicants should be interviewed by two or more individuals in order to minimize errors in judgment.

Time spent in interviewing, as well as in other phases of the selection process, can save time and money later on. In today's litigious society, firing an employee can be quite difficult and expensive. A dismissed employee can bring suit even when an employer had justifiable reasons for the dismissal.

The value of the interview depends on the interviewer's skill and methods. Any interviewer can improve his or her interviewing by following these generally accepted guidelines:

- Before beginning the interview, determine the job-related questions you want to ask the applicant.
- Conduct the interview in a quiet setting.
- Give your entire attention to the applicant.
- Put the applicant at ease.
- Never argue.
- Keep the conversation at a level appropriate for the applicant.
- Listen attentively.

- Observe closely the applicant's speech, mannerisms, and attire if these characteristics are important to the job.
- Try to avoid being unduly influenced by the applicant's trivial mannerisms or superficial resemblance to other people you know.

Employment interviewing should be seen as a two-way process. The applicant is evaluating the employer while the employer is evaluating the applicant. In order for the applicant to make an informed decision, he or she needs a clear idea of what the job entails and an opportunity to ask questions.

Step 3: Checking References and Other Background Information

Careful checking with former employers, school authorities, and other references can help an employer avoid the serious consequences of hiring mistakes. Suppose, for example, that you hired an appliance technician who later burglarized a customer's home. Had you checked the applicant's background for a criminal record, you might have been able to prevent this unfortunate occurrence. In some cases, checking of references occurs prior to an interview with the applicant.

It is becoming increasingly difficult to obtain more than the basic facts concerning a person's background because of the potential for lawsuits brought against employers by disappointed applicants. Although reference checks on a prior employment record do not constitute infringements on privacy, the fact that third parties are often reluctant to divulge negative information limits the practical usefulness of reference checking.

For a fee, private investigation agencies or credit bureaus will supply an applicant's history (financial, criminal, employment, and so on). If a prospective employer requests a credit report to establish an applicant's eligibility for employment, the Fair Credit Reporting Act requires that the applicant be notified in writing that such a report is being requested.

Step 4: Testing the Applicant

Many kinds of jobs lend themselves to performance testing. For example, an applicant for a secretarial or clerical position may be given a standardized keyboarding or word-processing test. With a little ingenuity, employers can improvise practical tests that are clearly related to the job in question.

Psychological examinations may also be used by small businesses, but the results can be misleading because of difficulty in interpreting the tests or in adapting them to a particular business. In addition, the U.S. Supreme Court has upheld the Equal Employment Opportunity Commission's requirement that any test used in making employment decisions must be job-related.

Living the Dream *Entrepreneurial Challenges*

Testing a Promising Candidate

In 2001, Marvis Nichols took over Computer Friends, a Pittsburgh business that provides information-technology services for small companies. When the recession made it difficult to find new business, she decided to hire a sales representative. She was impressed with one prospect, a woman experienced in selling technical services. But to be sure the candidate was right for the job, Nichols retained her for a one-time project—a networking event that was intended to produce sales leads.

Nichols then took the prospective sales manager with her to follow-up meetings. This trial period showed Nichols that her initial impression of the prospective hire was totally wrong. Nichols was aghast at the prospect's bizarre combination of aggression and confusion. "At the end of the day, I felt it was a disaster," she says.

If Nichols had hired the sales representative before that meeting, she would never have known about her jarring meeting demeanor. A practical test averted a hiring disaster!

Source: Paulette Thomas, "Case Study: Not Sure of a New Hire? Put Her to a Road Test," *Wall Street Journal*, January 7, 2003, p. B-7.

Useful tests of any kind must meet the criteria of **validity** and **reliability**. For a test to be valid, its results must correspond well with job performance; that is, the applicants with the best test scores must generally be the best employees. For a test to be reliable, it must provide consistent results when used at different times or by various individuals.

validity
The extent to which a test assesses true job performance ability

reliability
The consistency of a test in measuring job performance ability

Step 5: Requiring Physical Examinations

A primary purpose of physical examinations is to evaluate the ability of applicants to meet the physical demands of specific jobs. By law, a conditional offer of employment must precede such an exam. Also, care must be taken to avoid discriminating against those who are physically disabled. The Americans with Disabilities Act requires employers to make "reasonable" adaptations to facilitate the employment of such individuals.

The law permits drug screening of applicants, and this can be included as part of the physical examination process. Since few small firms have staff physicians, most of them make arrangements with a local doctor or clinic to perform physical examinations.

TRAINING AND DEVELOPING EMPLOYEES

Once an employee has been recruited and added to the payroll, the process of training and development must begin. The purpose of this process is to transform a new recruit into a well-trained technician, salesperson, manager, or other employee.

3 *Describe the role of training for both managerial and nonmanagerial employees in a small firm.*

Purposes of Training and Development

One obvious purpose of training is to prepare a new recruit to perform the duties for which he or she has been hired. There are very few positions for which no training is required. If an employer fails to provide training, the new employee must learn by trial and error, which frequently wastes time, materials, and money and may sometimes alienate customers.

Training to improve skills and knowledge should not be limited to new hires; the performance of current employees can often be improved through additional training. In view of the constant change in products, technology, policies, and procedures in the world of business, continual training is necessary to update knowledge and skills—in firms of all sizes. Only with such training can employees meet the changing demands being placed on them.

Both employers and employees have a stake in the advancement of qualified personnel to higher-level positions. Preparation for advancement usually involves developmental efforts—possibly of a different type than those needed to sharpen skills for current duties. Because personal development and advancement are prime concerns of able employees, a small business can profit from careful attention to this phase of the personnel program. Opportunities to grow and move up in an organization not only improve the morale of current employees but also serve as an inducement for potential applicants.

Orientation for New Personnel

The development process begins with an individual's first two or three days on the job. It is at this point that the new employee tends to feel lost and confused, confronted with a new physical layout, a different job title, unknown fellow employees, a different type of supervision, changed hours or work schedule, and/or a unique set of personnel policies and procedures. Any events that conflict with the newcomer's expectations are interpreted in light of his or her previous work experience, and these interpretations can either foster a strong commitment to the new employer or lead to feelings of alienation.

Recognizing the new employee's sensitivity at this point, the employer can contribute to a positive outcome through proper orientation. Taking steps to help the newcomer adjust will minimize her or his uneasiness in the new setting.

Some phases of the orientation can be accomplished by informal methods. Persistence Software, a 110-person company in San Mateo, California, uses bagels and muffins as a means of introducing newcomers to the rest of the staff.[5] On the first morning of work for a new employee, a tray of breakfast food is strategically placed near her or his desk. An e-mail invites everyone to come by and get acquainted.

Other phases of the orientation must be structured or formalized. In addition to explaining specific job duties, supervisors should outline the firm's policies and procedures in as much detail as possible. A clear explanation of performance criteria and the way in which an employee's work will be evaluated should be included in the discussion. The new employee should be encouraged to ask questions, and time should be taken to provide careful answers. The firm may facilitate the orientation process by providing a written list of company practices and procedures in the form of an employee handbook. The handbook may include information about work hours, paydays, breaks, lunch hours, absences, holidays, names of supervisors, employee benefits, and so on. Since new employees are faced with an information overload at first, a follow-up orientation after a week or two is advisable.

Training to Improve Quality

Employee training is an integral part of comprehensive quality management programs. Although quality management is concerned with machines, materials, and measurements, it also focuses on human performance.

Training programs can be designed to promote higher quality workmanship. The connection between effective quality management programs and employee training has been supported by a study of small manufacturing firms.[6]

Christian Kar, operator of Espresso Connection, an 11-store chain of drive-through coffee bars in Everett, Washington, found he was losing customers at the same time he was advertising for new ones. In an effort to keep the customers he already had, he beefed up employee training. New hires now spend a week learning how to use the equipment and prepare drinks. Later, they undergo another 40 hours of on-the-job training at a store. By improving customer service, the business almost doubled daily store revenues and increased per-store profits by 50 percent.[7]

To a considerable extent, training for quality performance is part of the ongoing supervisory role of all managers. In addition, special classes and seminars can be used to teach employees about the importance of quality control and ways in which to produce high-quality work.

Training of Nonmanagerial Employees

If a company has job descriptions or job specifications, these may be used to identify abilities or skills required for particular jobs. To a large extent, such requirements determine the appropriate type of training.

Phenix and Phenix, a small literary publicity firm based in Austin, Texas, encourages sharing of learning among its employees.[8] Anyone attending a "learning situation"—which might be anything from a breakfast meeting to a several-day seminar—is expected to write up a summary and present it at a staff meeting or distribute it.

For all classes of employees, more training is accomplished on the job than through any other method. However, on-the-job training may be haphazard unless it uses effective methods of teaching. One program designed to make on-the-job training effective is known as **Job Instruction Training**. The steps in this program, shown in Exhibit 19-1, are intended to help supervisors become more effective in training employees.

Job Instruction Training
A systematic step-by-step method for on-the-job training of nonmanagerial employees

Development of Managerial and Professional Employees

A small business has a particularly strong need to develop managerial and professional employees. Whether the firm has only a few key positions or many, it must ensure that the individuals who hold these positions function effectively. Incumbents should be developed to the point that they can adequately carry out the responsibilities assigned to them. Ideally, other staff members should be trained as potential replacements in case key individuals retire or leave for other reasons. Although an entrepreneur often postpones grooming a personal replacement, this step is crucial in ensuring a smooth transition in the firm's management.

Establishing a management training program requires serious consideration of the following factors:

- *The need for training.* What vacancies are expected? Who needs to be trained? What type of training and how much training are needed to meet the demands of the job description?
- *A plan for training.* How can the individuals be trained? Do they currently have enough responsibility to permit them to learn? Can they be assigned additional

EXHIBIT 19-1 *Steps in Job Instruction Training*

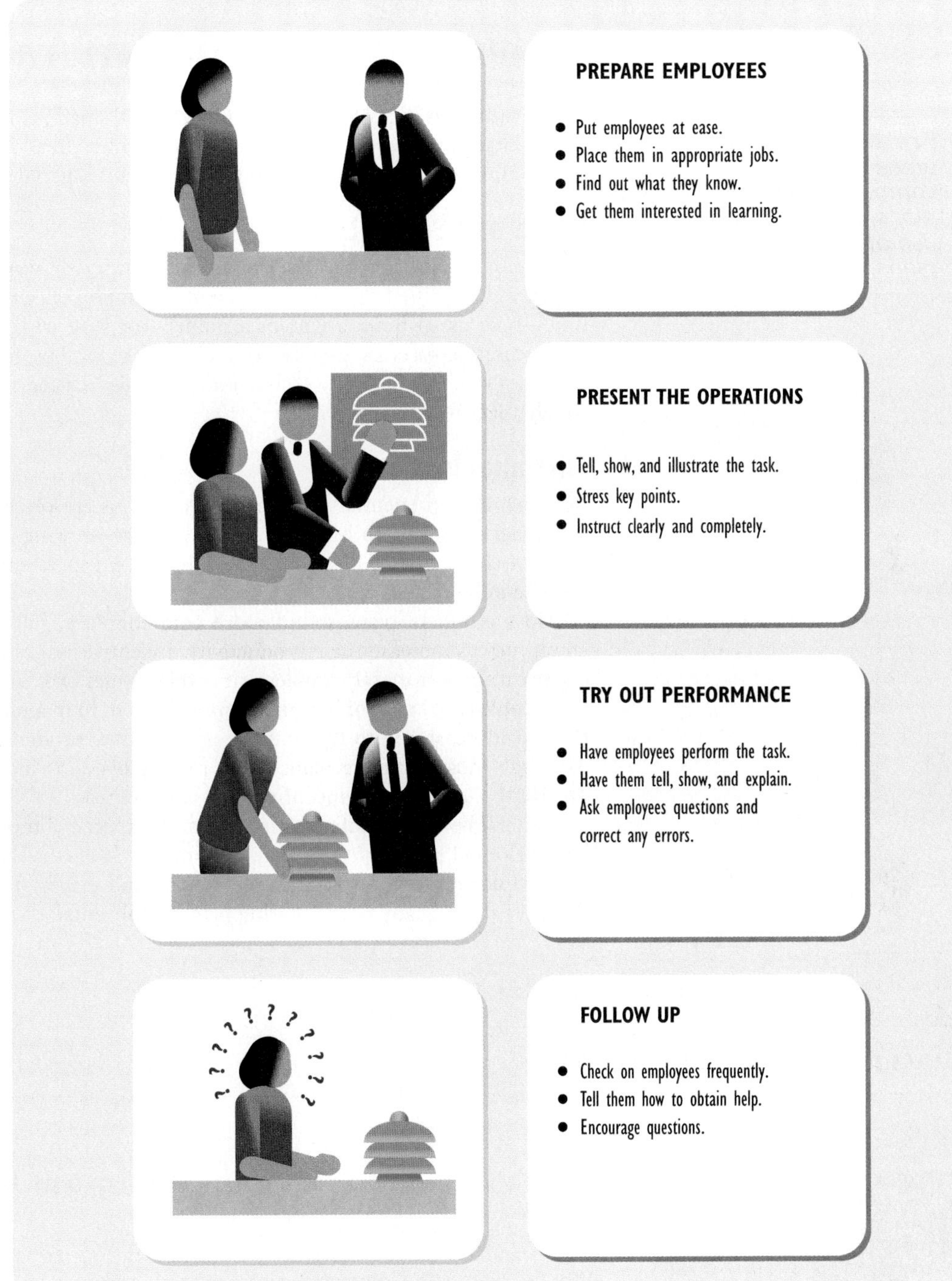
PREPARE EMPLOYEES
• Put employees at ease.
• Place them in appropriate jobs.
• Find out what they know.
• Get them interested in learning.
PRESENT THE OPERATIONS
• Tell, show, and illustrate the task.
• Stress key points.
• Instruct clearly and completely.
TRY OUT PERFORMANCE
• Have employees perform the task.
• Have them tell, show, and explain.
• Ask employees questions and correct any errors.
FOLLOW UP
• Check on employees frequently.
• Tell them how to obtain help.
• Encourage questions.

duties? Should they be given temporary assignments in other areas—for example, should they be shifted from production to sales? Would additional schooling be beneficial?

- *A timetable for training*. When should training begin? How much can be accomplished in the next six months or one year?
- *Employee counseling*. Do the individuals understand their need for training? Are they aware of their prospects within the firm? Has an understanding been reached as to the nature of training? Have the employees been consulted regularly about progress in their work and the problems confronting them? Have they been given

the benefit of the owner's experience and insights without having decisions made for them?

COMPENSATION AND INCENTIVES FOR EMPLOYEES

4 Explain the various types of compensation plans, including the use of incentive plans.

Compensation is important to all employees, and small firms must acknowledge the role of the paycheck in attracting and motivating personnel. In addition, small firms can offer several nonfinancial incentives that appeal to both managerial and nonmanagerial employees.

Wage and Salary Levels

In general, small firms must be roughly competitive in wage and salary levels in order to attract well-qualified personnel. Payments to employees either are based on increments of time—such as an hour, a day, or a month—or vary with the output of the employees. Compensation based on time is most appropriate for jobs in which performance is not easily measured. Time-based compensation is also easier to understand and used more widely than incentive systems.

Financial Incentives

In young entrepreneurial ventures, stock options are often used to attract and hold key personnel. The option holders can share in the growing—perhaps even skyrocketing—value of the company's stock. If the business prospers sufficiently, such personnel can become millionaires.

Most incentive plans sound more commonplace, but all are designed to motivate employees to increase their productivity. Incentive wages may constitute an employee's entire earnings or merely supplement regular wages or salary. The commission system for salespeople is one type of incentive compensation. In manufacturing, employees are sometimes paid according to the number of units they produce, a practice called piecework. Although most incentive plans apply to employees as individuals, such plans may also involve the use of group incentives and team awards.

General bonus or profit-sharing plans are especially important for managers and other key personnel, although they may also include lower-level employees. These plans provide employees with a "piece of the action" and may or may not involve assignment of shares of stock. Many profit-sharing plans simply entail distribution of a specified share of

Living the Dream — *Entrepreneurship and Integrity*

www.kucinephoto.com. Copyright C. Kucine photography 2004

More Than Minimum Wages

Small businesses often struggle to pay their lowest-level employees even the minimum wage required by law. However, some employers, such as Borealis Breads, located in Wells, Maine, try to improve the lives of their employees by paying a so-called living wage.

Jim Amaral, owner of Borealis Breads, started bumping up the wages of his 60 employees until, in 2001, they reached $8 an hour. The business has benefited along with the employees. Amaral sees improvement in recruiting and retention, particularly in the baking and early-morning delivery positions. He believes that the business has also gained in terms of its public image with customers and the community.

Source: Chris Penttila, "Who's Paying?" *Entrepreneur*, December 2001, pp. 88–90.

all profits or profits in excess of a target amount. Profit sharing serves more directly as a work-related incentive in small firms than in large firms, because the connection between individual performance and success can be more easily appreciated in a small firm.

Performance-based compensation plans must be designed carefully if they are to work successfully. Such plans should be devised with the aid of a consultant and/or public accounting firm. Some keys to developing effective bonus plans are the following:

- *Set attainable goals*. Performance-based compensation plans work best when workers believe that they can meet the targets. Tying pay to broad, companywide results leaves workers feeling frustrated and helpless. Complex financial measures or jargon-heavy benchmarks should be avoided, because they mean little to most people.
- *Include employees in planning*. Employees should have a voice in developing performance measures and changes to work systems. Incentive plans should be phased in gradually so that employees have a chance to get used to them.
- *Keep updating goals*. Performance-based plans must be continually adjusted to meet the changing needs of workers and customers. The life expectancy of such a plan may be no more than three or four years.

Fringe Benefits

fringe benefits
Supplements to compensation, designed to be attractive and beneficial to employees

Fringe benefits, which include payments by the employer for such items as Social Security, vacation time, holidays, health insurance, and retirement compensation, are expensive. The cost to many firms is equal to 40 percent or more of salary and wage payments. Furthermore, the cost of some benefits, such as health care, has been increasing at a double-digit rate annually. In general, small firms are somewhat less generous than large firms in providing fringe benefits for their employees. Even so, the cost of such benefits is a substantial part of total labor costs for most small businesses.

Though fringe benefits are expensive, a small firm cannot ignore them if it is to compete effectively for good employees. A small but growing number of small businesses now use flexible benefit programs (or cafeteria plans), which allow employees to select the types of fringe benefits they wish to receive.[9] All employees receive a core level of coverage, such as basic health insurance, and then are allowed to choose how an employer-specified amount is to be divided among additional options—for example, child care reimbursement, dental care, pension fund contributions, and additional health insurance.

For small companies that wish to avoid the detailed paperwork associated with administering cafeteria plans, outside help is available. Many small firms—including some with fewer than 25 employees—turn over the administration of their flexible benefit plans to outside consulting, payroll accounting, or insurance companies that provide such services for a monthly fee.

The costs of fringe benefits have made some of them prohibitively expensive. A number of firms, however, have devised relatively inexpensive fringe benefits, tailored to their particular situation—benefits that make employment more attractive for their employees. Some of the more affordable benefits are shown in Exhibit 19-2.

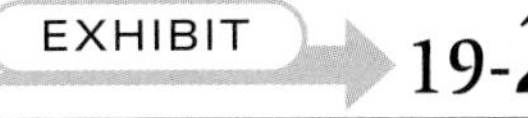

19-2 | *Some Affordable Perks*

1. Recognize major life events for employees, such as marriage or the birth or adoption of a child, with a small financial gift.
2. Give employees a paid day off on their birthday.
3. Offer employees $100 a year to use for personal enrichment, such as taking an art class, getting a massage, or attending a play—anything that makes them happy makes them more productive.
4. Bring bagels or donuts to work one Friday a month.
5. Offer recruitment bonuses to those who refer potential employees who stay with your company at least six months or more—one good employee leads to another.

Source: Kathleen Landis, "Blue Sky Thinking," *MyBusiness,* June-July 2003, p. 39.

Employee Stock Ownership Plans

employee stock ownership plans (ESOPs)
Plans through which a firm is sold either in part or in total to its employees

Some small firms have created **employee stock ownership plans (ESOPs)**, by which they give employees a share of ownership in the business.[10] These plans may be structured in a variety of ways. For example, a share of annual profits may be designated for the purchase of company stock, which is then placed in a trust for employees. When coupled with a commitment to employee participation in business operations, ESOPs can motivate employees, resulting in improvements in productivity.

ESOPs also provide a way for owners to cash out and withdraw from a business without selling the firm to outsiders. (See Chapter 12 for a discussion of this topic.)

SPECIAL ISSUES IN HUMAN RESOURCE MANAGEMENT

5 *Discuss the human resource issues of employee leasing, legal protection, labor unions, and the formalizing of employer–employee relationships.*

So far, this chapter has dealt with the recruitment, selection, training, and compensation of employees. In addition to these primary activities, human resource management can encompass a number of other, more general issues. Several of these—employee leasing, legal protection, labor unions, the formalizing of employer–employee relationships, and the need for a human resource manager—are the focus of this section.

Employee Leasing

employee leasing
The "renting" of personnel from an organization that handles paperwork and administers benefits for those employees

professional employment organization (PEO)
A personnel-leasing company that places employees on its own payroll and then "rents" them to employers on a permanent basis

Leasing equipment and property has long been an accepted alternative to buying them. **Employee leasing**, as surprising as it may seem, has become a common alternative to direct hiring. An estimated 2,500 or more employee-leasing companies, also known as **professional employment organizations (PEOs)**, have emerged in recent years with the specific purpose of "renting" personnel to small businesses. For a fee of 1 to 5 percent of payroll, a PEO writes paychecks, pays payroll taxes, and files the necessary reports with government agencies. Although small firms using this service avoid a certain amount of paperwork, they do not usually escape the tasks of recruitment and selection. Typically, the employees of a small firm are simply shifted to the leasing company's payroll at some specified date. In most cases, the firm still determines who works, who gets promoted, and who gets time off.

Many employees like the leasing arrangement. It may allow small employers to provide better benefit packages, since leasing companies generally cover hundreds or thousands of employees and thus qualify for better rates. Of course, the small business must bear the cost of insurance and other benefits obtained through a leasing company, in addition to a basic service fee.

A note of caution about selecting a leasing company: As leasing companies have proliferated in recent years, a number of them have run into financial trouble and left employers liable for unpaid claims. Some states have enacted legislation to protect employer-clients, and more regulation is likely.

Another note of caution pertains to the application of government regulations to small businesses. Very small firms are often excluded from specific regulations. For example, firms with fewer than 15 employees are exempt from the Americans with Disabilities Act. When these employees officially become part of a large leasing organization, however, the small firm using the leased employees becomes subject to the law.

Legal Protection of Employees

Civil Rights Act
Legislation prohibiting discrimination based on race, color, religion, sex, or national origin

Employees are afforded protection by a number of federal and state laws.[11] One of the most far-reaching statutes is the **Civil Rights Act**, originally enacted in 1964, and its amendments. This law, which applies to any employer of more than 15 people, prohibits discrimination on the basis of race, color, religion, sex, or national origin. Other laws extend similar protection to the aged and handicapped. Any employment condition is covered, including hiring, firing, promotion, transfer, and compensation.

The Civil Rights Act includes protection against sexual harassment. Given the growing attention to sexual harassment in our society, this issue must be addressed by small firms as well as large corporations. Education and prompt response to complaints are the best tools for avoiding the damage of sexual harassment and the possibility of liability claims. The following practical action steps have been expressly recommended for small businesses:

1. Establish clear and meaningful policies and procedures regarding sexual harassment in the workplace.
2. Meet with employees and supervisory personnel to discuss the policies.
3. Investigate any and all complaints of sexual harassment fairly and thoroughly.
4. Take timely and appropriate action against all violators.[12]

The health and safety of employees are protected by the **Occupational Safety and Health Act** of 1970. This law, which applies to business firms of any size involved in interstate commerce, created the Occupational Safety and Health Administration (OSHA) to establish and enforce necessary safety and health standards.

Occupational Safety and Health Act
Legislation that regulates the safety of workplaces and work practices

Compensation of employees is regulated by the minimum wage and overtime provisions of the **Fair Labor Standards Act (FLSA)**, as well as by other federal and state laws. The FLSA applies to employers involved in interstate commerce and having two or more employees; it sets the minimum wage (which is periodically updated by Congress) and specifies time-and-a-half pay for more than 40 hours per week.

Fair Labor Standards Act (FLSA)
Federal law that establishes a minimum wage and provides for overtime pay

The **Family and Medical Leave Act** of 1993 was passed and signed into law by President Clinton in February 1993. The law requires firms with 50 or more employees to allow workers as much as 12 weeks of unpaid leave for childbirth, the adoption of a child, or other specified family needs. The worker must have been employed by the firm for 12 months and have worked at least 1,250 hours. Furthermore, the employer must continue health-care coverage during the leave and guarantee that the employee can return to the same or a comparable job.

Family and Medical Leave Act
Legislation that assures employees of unpaid leave for childbirth or other family needs

Labor Unions

Most entrepreneurs prefer to operate independently and to avoid unionization. Indeed, most small businesses are not unionized. To some extent, this results from the predominance of small business in services, where unionization is less common than in manufacturing. Also, unions typically focus their attention on large companies.

However, labor unions are not unknown in small firms. Many types of small business—building and electrical contractors, for example—negotiate labor contracts and employ unionized personnel. The need to work with a union formalizes and, to some extent, complicates the relationship between a small firm and its employees.

If employees wish to bargain collectively—that is, to be represented in negotiations by a union—the law requires the employer to participate in such bargaining. The demand for labor union representation may arise from employees' dissatisfaction with the work environment and employment relationships. By following constructive human resource policies, a small firm can minimize the likelihood of labor organization or improve the relationship between management and union.

Formalizing of Employer–Employee Relationships

As explained earlier in this chapter, the management system of small firms is typically less formal than that of larger ones. A degree of informality can, in fact, be a virtue in small organizations. As personnel are added, however, the benefits of informality decline and its costs increase. Large numbers of employees cannot be managed effectively without some system for regulating employer–employee relationships. This situation can be best understood in terms of a family relationship. House rules are generally unnecessary when only two people are living in the home. But when several children are added to the mix, Mom and Dad soon start sounding like a government regulatory agency.

Growth, then, produces pressure to formalize personnel policies and procedures. Determining how much formality to introduce and how soon involves judgment. Some employee issues should be formalized from the very beginning; on the other hand, excessive regulation can become paralyzing.

One way to formalize employer–employee relationships is to prepare a personnel policy manual or employee handbook, which meets a communication need by letting employees know the firm's basic ground rules. It can also provide a basis for fairness and consistency in management decisions affecting employees. The content of an employee handbook may be as broad or as narrow as desired. It may include an expression of company philosophy—an overall view of what the company considers important, such as standards of excellence or quality considerations. More specifically, personnel policies usually cover such topics as recruitment, selection, training, compensation, vacations, grievances, and discipline. Such policies should be written carefully, however, to avoid misunderstandings. In some states, an employee handbook is considered part of the employment contract.

Procedures relating to management of personnel may also be standardized. For example, a performance review system may be established and a timetable set up for reviews—perhaps an initial review after six months and subsequent reviews on an annual basis.

The Need for a Human Resource Manager

A firm with only a few employees cannot afford a full-time specialist to deal with personnel problems. Some of the more involved human resource techniques used in large businesses may be far too complicated for small businesses. As a small firm grows in size, however, its personnel problems will increase in both number and complexity.

The point at which it becomes logical to hire a human resource manager cannot be specified precisely. In view of the increased overhead cost, the owner-manager of a growing business must decide whether circumstances would make it profitable to employ a personnel specialist. Hiring a part-time human resource manager—a retired personnel manager, for example—is a possible first step in some instances.

Conditions such as the following favor the appointment of a human resource manager in a small business:

- There are a substantial number of employees (100 or more is suggested as a guide).
- Employees are represented by a union.
- The labor turnover rate is high.
- The need for skilled or professional personnel creates problems in recruitment or selection.
- Supervisors or operative employees require considerable training.
- Employee morale is unsatisfactory.
- Competition for personnel is keen.

Living the Dream | *Entrepreneurial Challenges*

Using Employee Committees

As a small firm grows, it must decide how much formality to introduce into managing its human resources and when to introduce it. More rules and regulations are inevitable as size increases, but some firms try to preserve a less formal, more personal touch as long as possible.

Avoidance of bureaucracy is evident in the management of Spectrum Signal Processing, Inc., a hardware and software designer in Burnaby, British Columbia. The firm has grown to 180 employees, but it still does not have a human resource department. Instead, it utilizes an employee committee, originally created to deal with specific employee dissatisfactions, to address such issues as performance appraisals, company training, mentoring, orientation, and the employee handbook. The committee, with a rotating membership of 12 employees, appears to be serving a transitional function for Spectrum, as it moves from less to more formality as it grows.

Spectrum's positive focus on managing its human resources is evident in the following statement: "Our individual team members' personalities, capabilities and can-do attitudes make Spectrum what it is—a place where quality work is acknowledged and emphasized, and where all team members are empowered decision-makers!"

http://www.spectrumsignal.com

This statement seems to say, "We are trying to avoid the bureaucracy that afflicts big business by empowering our employees through use of an employee committee."

Sources: http://www.spectrumsignal.com, December 8, 2000; and Christopher Caggiano, "Worker, Rule Thyself," *Inc.*, Vol. 21, No. 2 (February 1999), pp. 89–90.

Until a human resource manager is hired, however, the owner-manager typically functions in that capacity. His or her decisions regarding employee selection and compensation, as well as other personnel issues, will have a direct impact on the operating success of the firm.

Looking Back

1 Explain the importance of employee recruitment and list some sources that can be useful in finding suitable applicants.

- Recruitment of good employees contributes to customer satisfaction and to profitability.
- Small firms can attract applicants by stressing unique work features and opportunities.
- Recruitment sources include help-wanted advertising, walk-ins, schools, public and private employment agencies, executive search firms, employee referrals, the Internet, and temporary help agencies.
- The increasing diversity of the workforce requires a broadening of the scope of recruitment.
- Job descriptions outline the duties of the job; job specifications identify the skills needed by applicants.

2 Identify the steps to take in evaluating job applicants.

- In the first step, application forms help the employer obtain preliminary information from applicants. (Employers must avoid questions about sex, race, religion, color, national origin, age, and disabilities.)
- Additional evaluation steps are interviewing the applicant, checking references and other background information, and testing the applicant.
- The final evaluation step is often a physical examination, which may include drug screening.

3 Describe the role of training for both managerial and nonmanagerial employees in a small firm.

- Training enables employees to perform their jobs effectively and also prepares them for advancement.
- An orientation program helps introduce new employees to the firm and its work environment.
- Training is one component of a firm's quality management program.
- Training and development programs are appropriate for both managerial and nonmanagerial employees.

4 Explain the various types of compensation plans, including the use of incentive plans.

- Small firms must be competitive in salary and wage levels.
- Payments to employees either are based on increments of time or vary with employee output.
- Incentive systems relate compensation to various measures of performance.
- Fringe benefit costs are often equal to 40 percent or more of payroll costs.
- Employee stock ownership plans enable employees to own a share of the business.

5 Discuss the human resource issues of employee leasing, legal protection, labor unions, and the formalizing of employer–employee relationships.

- Small firms can reduce paperwork by transferring personnel to the payroll of a leasing company.
- All small businesses with more than 15 employees must observe laws prohibiting discrimination and protecting employee health and safety.
- Some small businesses must work with labor unions.
- As small firms grow, they must adopt more formal methods of human resource management.
- Employment of a human resource manager becomes necessary at some point as a firm continues to add employees.

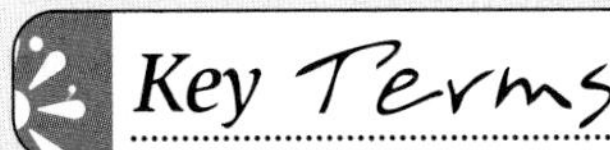

Key Terms

headhunter, p. 423
workforce diversity, p. 424
job specification, p. 425
validity, p. 427
reliability, p. 427
Job Instruction Training, p. 428
fringe benefits, p. 431
employee stock ownership plans (ESOPs), p. 432
employee leasing, p. 432
professional employment organization (PEO), p. 432
Civil Rights Act, p. 432
Occupational Safety and Health Act, p. 433
Fair Labor Standards Act (FLSA), p. 433
Family and Medical Leave Act, p. 433

Discussion Questions

1. As a customer of small businesses, you can appreciate the importance of employees to their success. Describe one experience you had in which an employee's contribution to his or her employer's success was positive and one in which it was negative.
2. What factor or factors would make you cautious about going to work for a small business? Could these reasons for hesitation be overcome? How?
3. In what ways is the workforce becoming more diverse, and how do these changes affect recruitment by small firms?
4. Based on your own experience as an interviewee, what do you think is the most serious weakness in the interviewing process? How could it be remedied?
5. What steps and/or topics would you recommend for inclusion in the orientation program of a printing firm with 65 employees?
6. Choose a small business with which you are well acquainted. Determine whether adequate provisions have been made for replacement of key management personnel when it becomes necessary. Is the firm using any form of executive development?
7. What problems are involved in using incentive plans in a small firm? How would the nature of the work affect management's decision concerning the use of such a plan?
8. Is the use of a profit-sharing plan desirable in a small business? What might lessen such a plan's effectiveness in motivating employees?
9. How does employee leasing differ from using a temporary help agency? What are the greatest benefits of employee leasing?
10. Explain the impact of the Civil Rights Act and the Fair Labor Standards Act on human resource management.

You Make the Call

SITUATION 1

The following is an account of one employee's introduction to a new job:

> *It was my first job out of high school. After receiving a physical exam and a pamphlet on benefits, I was told by the manager about the dangers involved in the job. But it was the old-timers who explained what was really expected of me.*
>
> *The company management never told me about the work environment or the unspoken rules. The old-timers let me know where to sleep and which supervisors to avoid. They told me how much work I was supposed to do and which shop steward to see if I had a problem.*

Question 1 To what extent should a small firm use "old-timers" to help introduce new employees to the workplace? Is it inevitable that newcomers will look to old-timers to find out how things really work?

Question 2 How would you rate this firm's orientation effort? What are its strengths and weaknesses?

Question 3 Assume that this firm has fewer than 75 employees and no human resource manager. Could it possibly provide more extensive orientation than that described here? How? What low-cost improvements, if any, would you recommend?

SITUATION 2

Technical Products, Inc., distributes 15 percent of its profits quarterly to its eight employees. This money is invested for their benefit in a retirement plan and is fully vested after five years. An employee, therefore, has a claim to the retirement fund even if he or she leaves the company after five years of service.

The employees range in age from 25 to 59 and have worked for the company from 3 to 27 years. They seem to have recognized the value of the program. However, younger employees sometimes express a preference for cash over retirement benefits.

Question 1 What are the most important reasons for structuring the profit-sharing plan as a retirement program?

Question 2 What is the probable motivational impact of this compensation system?

Question 3 How will an employee's age affect the appeal of this plan? What other factors are likely to strengthen or lessen its motivational value? Should it be changed in any way?

SITUATION 3

Alibek Iskakov recently opened a small café, called Oasis, in Kokshetau, a city in Kazakhstan. The café, which is quite small, has seating for 20 customers and employs 7 people.

Iskakov, the owner, has no experience in the restaurant business but has three years' experience in retailing and managing. He believes this experience will help him make intelligent decisions concerning management of the café. Iskakov oversees operations and assists wherever needed.

Zhanna Suleymenova was hired by Iskakov as an accountant and assistant manager. He hired her to be sure someone would always be at the café. He expects her to do the accounting and to make suggestions that will help him operate the café efficiently. She is the key person in the operation, with sound accounting experience and a little food service experience. The other employees are two cooks, two waitresses (who double as hostesses and bartenders), and a dishwasher.

Thus far, the café's operations have not run smoothly.

Source: This case was prepared by Dr. Aigul N. Toxanova and Yuliya L. Tkacheva, Kokshetau Institute of Economics and Management, Kokshetau, Kazakhstan.

Question 1 What is the most obvious weakness in the human resource management of this small café?

Question 2 Given that the restaurant has just opened, is it overstaffed or understaffed?

Experiential Exercises

1. Interview the director of the placement office for your college or university. Ask about the extent to which small firms use the office's services, and obtain the director's recommendations for improving college recruiting by small firms. Prepare a one-page summary of your findings.
2. Examine and evaluate the help-wanted section of a local newspaper. Summarize your conclusions and formulate some generalizations about small business advertising for personnel. Log on to InfoTrac College Edition at http://www.infotrac-college.com to find articles on advertising for employees.
3. With another student, form an interviewer–interviewee team. Take turns posing as job applicants for a selected type of job vacancy. Critique each other's performance, using the interviewing principles outlined in this chapter.
4. With another student, take turns role-playing trainer and trainee. The student-trainer should select a simple task and teach it to the student-trainee, using the Job Instruction Training method outlined in Exhibit 19-1. Jointly critique the teaching performance after each episode.

Exploring the Web

1. As the text clearly demonstrates, finding the right employees for a small business can be extremely challenging. The Employers Organisation offers a range of human resource services to local governments in the United Kingdom. Go to **http://www.lg-employers.gov.uk**, and follow the links for "Recruitment and Retention," "Recruitment Guide," and "Attracting the Right Candidate."
   a. Read about whether to recruit internally or externally. What is your assessment of the advice given and the methods discussed?
   b. Now follow the link to "Sources of Recruitment." Which of the recruitment sources would you employ? Why?
2. Go to the Online Women's Business Center, a site maintained by the Small Business Administration, at **http://www.onlinewbc.gov**. Drill into the site, following these links: "Business Basics," "Starting Your Business," and "The Value of Cultural Diversity."
   a. How does the site explain and use the term *margin(s) of society*?
   b. Give some of the reasons people from the "margins of society" might favor working for a small entrepreneurial firm.
3. Carter McNamara, a contributor to the Free Management Library, wrote an article entitled "Employee Training and Development: Reasons and Benefits." Go to the Free Management Library Web site at **http://www.managementhelp.org** and follow the links to "Training and Development" and "Reasons and Benefits for Training and Development."
   a. Read McNamara's article, and then list some common reasons for employee training and development.
   b. What are some typical topics of employee training?
4. The U.S. Equal Employment Opportunity Commission (EEOC) publishes on its Web site advice and information of interest to small businesses. To learn about employment laws that the EEOC enforces, go to **http://www.eeoc.gov**, choose "Employers & EEOC—Small Business" and "An Overview of EEOC and Small Businesses." What EEOC laws apply to small businesses?

Case 19

GIBSON MORTUARY (P. 561)

This case explores the human resource problems encountered by one small family business.

Alternative Cases for Chapter 19:

Case 2, Diversified Chemical, p. 528
Case 15, Every Customer Counts, p. 550
Case 18, Douglas Electrical Supply, Inc., p. 559
Case 20, Texas Nameplate Company, p. 563

MANAGING OPERATIONS

In the Video Spotlight

Wahoo's Fish Taco

Wing Lee-Lam, Mingo Lee, and Ed Lee grew up in Brazil over a restaurant owned by their parents. When they decided to go into the restaurant business in California, they had a tremendous amount of experience. For a while, the three brothers operated Wahoo's Fish Taco on an informal, old-school basis, keeping everything "between the ears." But once their chain of surfer restaurants grew beyond three stores, they realized that they couldn't be everywhere at once.

The brothers brought in a fourth partner, Steve Kafaridis (shown in the photo), to implement the necessary operational systems to help Wahoo's grow. Kafaridis standardized everything that happens in the restaurants. He created inventory sheets for each restaurant to follow when ordering food and supplies; developed metrics for food appearance, taste, temperature, and texture; and established the 10-second rule for service.

Kafaridis has enhanced his detail-oriented focus on operations with a passionate focus on customers. Rather than insist on meeting sales quotas, Kafaridis wants Wahoo's managers to learn customers' names. Wing Lee-Lam recognizes the contributions that Kafaridis has made to the company's success: "An efficient store makes you a lot more money than just a bunch of guys working." Indeed, Wahoo's Fish Taco now boasts 22 locations, employs over 300 people, and generates over $22 million in annual sales.

Video material provided by Hattie Bryant, Producer of Small Business School, the series on PBS Stations, Worldnet, and the Web at http://www.smallbusinessschool.org.

Chapter 20

Looking Ahead

After studying this chapter, you should be able to

1. *Explain the key elements of total quality management (TQM) programs.*
2. *Discuss the nature of the operations process for both products and services.*
3. *Explain how reengineering and other methods of work improvement can increase productivity and make a firm more competitive.*
4. *Discuss the importance of purchasing and the nature of key purchasing policies.*
5. *Describe ways to control inventory and minimize inventory costs.*

Every business uses some type of **operations process** to create products or services for its customers. This process consists of the activities involved in creating value for customers and earning their dollars. A bakery, for example, purchases ingredients, combines and bakes them, and makes bakery products available to customers at some appropriate location. For a hair salon, a service business, the operations process includes the purchase of supplies and the shampooing, haircutting, and other procedures involved in serving its clients.

operations process
The activities that create value for customers through production of a firm's goods and services

Such operations are at the heart of any business; indeed, they are the reasons for its very existence. It should come as no surprise, then, that their design and effectiveness can lead to great success or doom the business to failure.

In this chapter, we examine the ways in which a business can function economically and profitably, providing the quality level of product or service that is desired by customers. Attention to the operations process is an important means of building the firm's competitive strength in the marketplace.

QUALITY GOALS OF OPERATIONS MANAGEMENT

Quality must be more than a slogan. Owners of successful small firms realize that quality management is serious business and that a strong commitment is essential for the realization of quality goals.

1 *Explain the key elements of total quality management (TQM) programs.*

Quality as a Competitive Tool

Quality may be defined as the characteristics of a product or service that determine its ability to satisfy stated and implied needs. Quality obviously has many dimensions. For example, a restaurant's customers base their perceptions of its quality on the taste of the food, the attractiveness of the décor, the friendliness and promptness of servers, the cleanliness of silverware, the type of background music, and numerous other factors. The operations process establishes a level of quality as a product is being produced or as a service is being provided. Although costs and other considerations cannot be ignored, quality must remain a primary focus of a firm's operations.

quality
The features of a product or service that enable it to satisfy customers' needs

International competition is increasingly turning on quality differences. Automobile manufacturers in the United States, for example, now place greater emphasis on quality in their attempts to compete effectively with foreign producers. However, it is not solely big business that needs to make quality a major concern; the operations process of a small firm also deserves careful scrutiny. Many small firms have been slow to give adequate attention to producing high-quality goods and services. In examining the operations process, therefore, small business managers must direct special attention to achieving superior product or service quality.

The American Society for Quality (ASQ) has been the leading quality improvement organization in the United States for more than 50 years and has introduced many quality

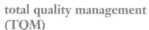

total quality management (TQM) An all-encompassing management approach to providing high-quality products and services

improvement methods throughout the world. Among these is an approach known as **total quality management (TQM)**, an aggressive effort by a firm to achieve superior quality. Total quality management is an all-encompassing, quality-focused management approach to providing products and services that satisfy customer requirements. Firms that implement TQM programs are making quality a major goal.

Many businesses merely give lip service to achieving high quality standards; others have introduced quality programs that have failed. As Exhibit 20-1 shows, the most successful quality management efforts incorporate three elements—a focus on customers, a supportive organizational culture, and the use of appropriate tools and techniques.

The Customer Focus of Quality Management

A firm's quality management efforts should begin with a focus on the customers who purchase its products or services. Without such a focus, the quest for quality easily degenerates into an aimless search for some abstract, elusive ideal.

CUSTOMER EXPECTATIONS Quality is ultimately determined by the extent to which a product or service satisfies customers' needs and expectations. Customers have expectations regarding the quality of both products (durability and attractiveness, for example) and services (speed and accuracy, for example). A customer is concerned with *product quality* when purchasing a camera or a loaf of bread; the customer's primary concern is *service quality* when having an automobile repaired or a suit tailor made. Frequently, a customer expects some combination of product *and* service quality—when buying a lawnmower, a customer may be concerned with the performance of the lawnmower, knowledge and courtesy of the salesperson, credit terms offered, and terms of the warranty.

Customers often have in mind specific standards that are relevant to a product or service. In the following comments, customers reveal their expectations regarding three types of service businesses:[1]

Automobile Repair Customers:

- Be competent. ("Fix it right the first time.")
- Explain things. ("Explain why I need the suggested repairs—provide an itemized list.")
- Be respectful. ("Don't treat me like I'm stupid.")

Hotel Customers:

- Provide a clean room. ("Don't have a deep-pile carpet that can't be completely cleaned. . . . You can literally see germs down there.")

EXHIBIT 20-1 *Essential Elements of Successful Quality Management*

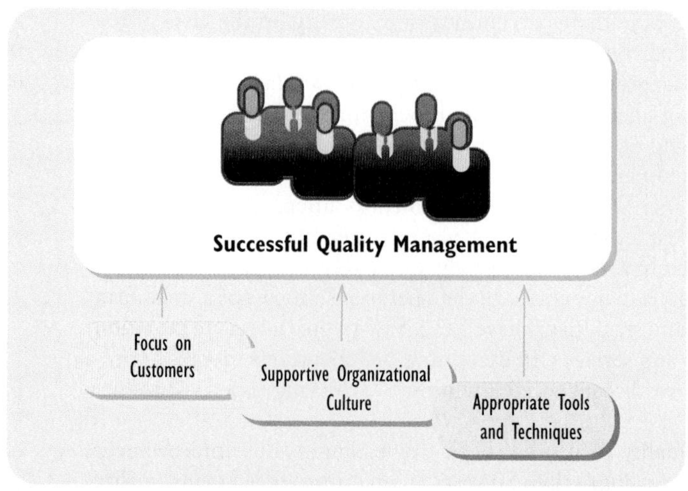

- Provide a secure room. ("Have good bolts and a peephole on the door.")
- Treat me like a guest. ("It is almost like they're looking me over to decide whether they're going to let me have a room.")
- Keep your promises. ("They said the room would be ready, but it wasn't at the promised time.")

Equipment Repair Customers:

- Share my sense of urgency. ("Speed of response is important. One time I had to buy a second piece of equipment because of the huge down time with the first piece.")
- Be competent. ("Sometimes I'm quoting stuff from their instruction manuals to their own people, and they don't even know what it means.")
- Be prepared. ("Have all the parts ready.")

A genuine concern for customer needs and customer satisfaction is a powerful force that energizes the total quality management effort of a business. When customer satisfaction is seen merely as a means of increasing profits, its effect on quality is negligible. When the customer becomes the focal point of quality efforts, however, real quality improvement occurs, and profits tend to grow as a result.

CUSTOMER FEEDBACK Attentive listening to customers' opinions can provide information about their level of satisfaction. Employees having direct contact with customers can serve as the eyes and ears of the business in evaluating existing quality levels and customer needs. Unfortunately, many managers are oblivious to the often subtle feedback from customers. Preoccupied with operating details, managers may not listen carefully to, let alone solicit, customers' opinions. Employees having direct contact with customers—servers in a restaurant, for example—are seldom trained or encouraged to obtain information about customers' quality expectations. Careful management and training of servers could make them more alert to consumers' tastes and attitudes and provide a mechanism for reporting these reactions to management.

Experts now recommend that firms work hard to involve and empower customers in efforts to improve quality.[2] The marketing research methods of observation, interviews,

Living the Dream *Focus on the Customer*

Great Quality Leads to Cult Status

When California's In-N-Out Burger chain opened an outlet in Phoenix, cars stacked up for blocks and lines of hamburger lovers spilled into the streets. When it debuted in San Francisco, lines of customers snaked out the doors for weeks. Why? Some people believe that In-N-Out simply makes the best burger in the world!

© Marianna Day Massey/ZUMA/Corbis

It's no ordinary burger. Made of freshly ground beef and served on buns baked that day, with sides of hand-cut potatoes, the burgers have won culinary praise from the likes of Julia Child. Founded in 1948 as a single tiny drive-through in a Los Angeles suburb, the business has stuck with the original menu of burgers, fries, sodas, and ice cream shakes—no chicken, no salads, no desserts, and no toys for the kids, just great quality! For fours years in a row, In-N-Out has topped all burger chains in customer satisfaction surveys.

In-N-Out is a family business, with 83-year-old Esther Snyder, who prepared the first burgers in 1948, still serving as its president. Even though In-N-Out has grown to 175 outlets, it has maintained its superb quality standards by sticking to its family control and refusing to franchise or go public. Its customers have clearly responded to the high quality of its food and service.

Sources: Mike Steere, "A Timeless Recipe for Success," *Business 2.0*, September 2003, pp. 47–49; and http://www.in-n-out.com, April 23, 2004.

and customer surveys, as described in Chapter 7, can be used to investigate customers' views regarding quality. Some businesses, for example, provide comment cards for their customers to use in evaluating service or product quality.

Organizational Culture and Total Quality Management

A crucial element of effective quality management is a supportive company culture. The values, beliefs, and traditional practices followed by members of a business firm may be described as the firm's **organizational culture**. Some firms are so concerned with quality levels that they will refund money if a service or product is unsatisfactory or will schedule overtime work to avoid disappointing a customer. Quality is a primary value in such a business's organizational culture. Quality management experts believe that a quality-oriented culture is necessary if a firm is to achieve outstanding success.

organizational culture
The behaviors, beliefs, and values that characterize a particular firm

Time and training are required to build a TQM program that elicits the best efforts of everyone in the organization in producing a superior-quality product or service. A small business that adopts a total quality management philosophy commits itself to the pursuit of excellence in all aspects of its operations. Dedication to quality on an organization-wide basis is sometimes described as a *cultural phenomenon*.

Total quality management goes beyond merely ensuring that existing standards are met. Its objective is **continuous quality improvement**, an ongoing effort to improve quality. For example, if a production process has been improved to a level where there is only 1 defect in 100 products, the process must then be shifted to the next level and a new goal set of no more than 1 defect in 200 or even 500 products. The ultimate goal is zero defects—a goal that has been popularized by many quality improvement programs.

continuous quality improvement
A constant and dedicated effort to improve quality

Continuous quality improvement efforts may include **benchmarking**, which is the process of identifying the best products, services, and practices of other businesses; carefully studying those examples; and using any insights gained to improve one's own operations. A simple type of benchmarking occurs when owner-managers eat in competitors' restaurants or shop in competitors' stores and then use what they learn to make improvements in their own businesses.

benchmarking
The process of studying the products, services, and practices of other firms and using the insights gained to improve quality internally

Tools and Techniques of Total Quality Management

Another element in effective quality management consists of the various tools, techniques, and procedures needed to ensure high-quality products and services. Once the focus is on the customer and the entire organization is committed to providing top-quality products and services, operating methods become important. Implementing a quality management program requires developing practical procedures for training employees, inspecting products, and measuring progress toward quality goals. We will discuss three important areas—employee participation, the inspection process, and the use of statistical methods of quality management.

EMPLOYEE PARTICIPATION In most organizations, employee performance is a critical quality variable. Obviously, employees who work carefully produce better-quality products than those who work carelessly. The admonition "Never buy a car that was produced on a Friday or a Monday!" conveys the popular notion that workers lack commitment to their work and are especially careless prior to and immediately after a weekend away from the assembly line. The vital role of personnel in producing a high-quality product or service has led managers to seek ways to involve employees in quality management efforts.

Chapter 18 discussed the implementation of work teams and empowerment of employees as approaches to building employee involvement in the workplace. Many businesses have adopted these approaches as part of their TQM programs. Japanese firms are particularly noted for their use of work teams. Many self-managed work teams, both in Japan and in the United States, monitor the quality level of their work and take any steps necessary to continue operating at the proper quality level.

The quality circle is another technique that solicits the contributions of employees in improving the quality of products and services. Originated by the Japanese, it is widely used by small firms in the United States and other parts of the world. A **quality circle** consists of a group of employees, usually a dozen or fewer. Such groups meet on company time, typically about once a week, to identify, analyze, and solve work-related problems, particularly those involving product or service quality. Quality circles can tap employees' potential to make enthusiastic and valuable contributions.

quality circle
A group of employees who meet regularly to discuss quality-related problems

THE INSPECTION PROCESS Management's traditional method of maintaining product quality has been **inspection**, which consists of examining a part or a product to determine whether or not it is acceptable. An inspector often uses gauges to evaluate important quality variables. For effective quality control, the inspector must be honest, objective, and capable of resisting pressure from shop personnel to pass borderline cases.

inspection
The examination of a product to determine whether it meets quality standards

Although the inspection process is usually discussed with reference to *product* quality, comparable steps can be used to evaluate *service* quality. Follow-up calls to customers of an auto repair shop, for example, might be used to measure the quality of the firm's repair services. Customers can be asked whether recent repairs were performed in a timely and satisfactory manner.

In manufacturing, **inspection standards** consist of design tolerances that are set for every important quality variable. These tolerances indicate, in discrete terms, the variation allowable above and below the desired level of quality. Inspection standards must satisfy customer requirements for quality in finished products. Traditionally, inspection begins in the receiving room, where the condition and quantity of materials received from suppliers are checked. Inspection is also customary at critical processing points—for example, *before* any operation that might conceal existing defects and *after* any operation that might produce an excessive amount of defects. Of course, final inspection of finished products is of utmost importance.

inspection standard
A specification of a desired quality level and allowable tolerances

Inspecting each item in every lot processed, called *100 percent inspection*, might seem to ensure the elimination of all bad materials and all defective products prior to shipment to customers. However, such inspection goals are seldom reached, and this method of inspection is both time-consuming and costly. Furthermore, inspectors often make honest errors in judgment, both in rejecting good items and in accepting defective items. Also, some types of inspection, such as opening a can of vegetables, destroy the product, making 100 percent inspection impractical.

In an inspection, either attributes or variables may be measured. **Attribute inspection** determines quality acceptability based on attributes that can be evaluated as being either present or absent. For example, a light bulb either lights or doesn't light; similarly, a water hose either leaks or doesn't leak.

attribute inspection
The determination of product acceptability based on whether it will or will not work

Variable inspection, in contrast, determines quality acceptability based on where variables (such as weight) fall on a scale or continuum. For example, if a box of candy is to be sold as containing a minimum of one pound of candy, an inspector may judge the product acceptable if its weight falls within the range of 16 ounces to 16.5 ounces.

variable inspection
The determination of product acceptability based on a variable such as weight or length

STATISTICAL METHODS OF QUALITY CONTROL The use of statistical methods can often make controlling product and service quality easier, less expensive, and more effective. As some knowledge of quantitative methods is necessary to develop a quality control method using statistical analysis, a properly qualified employee or outside consultant must be available. The savings made possible by use of an efficient statistical method can often justify the consulting fees required to devise a sound plan.

Acceptance sampling involves taking random samples of products and measuring them against predetermined standards. Suppose, for example, that a small firm receives a shipment of 10,000 parts from a supplier. Rather than evaluate all 10,000 parts, the purchasing firm might check the acceptability of a small sample of parts and then accept or reject the entire order. The smaller the sample, the greater the risk of either accepting a defective lot or rejecting a good lot due to sampling error. A larger sample reduces this risk but increases the cost of inspection. A well-designed plan strikes a balance, simultaneously avoiding excessive inspection costs and minimizing the risk of accepting a bad lot or rejecting a good lot.

acceptance sampling
The use of a random, representative portion to determine the acceptability of an entire lot

Statistical process control involves applying statistical techniques to control work processes. Items produced in a manufacturing process are not completely identical, although the variations are sometimes so small that the items seem to be exactly alike. Careful measurement, however, can pinpoint differences. Usually, these differences can be plotted in the form of a normal curve, which aids in the application of statistical control techniques.

statistical process control
The use of statistical methods to assess quality during the operations process

The use of statistical analysis makes it possible to establish tolerance limits that allow for inherent variation due to chance. When measurements fall outside these tolerance limits, however, the quality controller knows that a problem exists and must search for the cause. The problem might be caused by variations in raw materials, machine wear, or changes in employees' work practices. Consider, for example, a candy maker that is producing one-pound boxes of chocolates. Though the weight may vary slightly, each box must weigh at least 16 ounces. A study of the operations process has determined that the actual target weight must be 16.5 ounces, to allow for the normal variation between 16 and 17 ounces. During the production process, a box is weighed every 15 or 20 minutes. If the weight of a box falls outside the tolerance limits—below 16 or above 17 ounces—the quality controller must immediately try to find the problem and correct it.

control chart
A graphic illustration of the limits used in statistical process control

A **control chart** graphically shows the limits for the process being controlled. As current data are entered, it is possible to tell whether a process is under control or out of control. Control charts may be used for either variable or attribute inspections. Continuing improvements in computer-based technology have advanced the use of statistical control processes in small firms.

International Certification for Quality Management

ISO 9000
The standards governing international certification of a firm's quality management procedures

A firm can obtain international recognition of its quality management program by meeting a series of standards, known as **ISO 9000**, developed by the International Organization for Standardization in Geneva, Switzerland. The certification process requires full documentation of a firm's quality management procedures, as well as an audit to ensure that the firm is operating in accordance with those procedures. In other words, the firm must show that it does what it says it does. ISO 9000 certification can give a business credibility with purchasers in other countries and thereby ease its entry into export markets. However, substantial costs are involved in obtaining certification.

ISO 9000 certification is particularly valuable for small firms, because they usually lack a global image as producers of high-quality products. Buyers in other countries, especially in Europe, view this certification as an indicator of supplier reliability. Some large U.S. corporations, such as the Big Three automobile makers, require their domestic suppliers to con-

Living the Dream *Entrepreneurship and Integrity*

Quality and Social Responsibility

Total quality management looks at operations processes not only as they affect product quality but also as they affect the quality of the environment. The same organization that established ISO 9000 certification has also created ISO 14001 certification to specify how companies should set up and improve their operations processes in order to control the impact of vehicle and smokestack emissions, noise, and other fallout on air, water, and soil.

SWD Inc., a small metal-finishing company located in Addison, Illinois, opened for business in 1980 with just three employees in a 9,000-square-foot leased facility. Because customers, especially auto manufacturers, seek product quality certification, SWD decided to apply for environmental certification at the same time that it sought ISO 9000 certification. In 1998, it received the ISO 14001 environmental certification, and it has become a flourishing business with 95 employees.

One phrase in SWD's mission statement reads, "Be a leader in environment conservation." Tim Delawder, son of the founder and the firm's vice president of operations, cites some practical benefits from good environmental management: "At this point, it's more of a tool to make your organization stronger. If I produce more product with less water, energy and chemistry, I've just saved money."

This viewpoint suggests that quality management, even as it affects the environment, can—sometimes at least—be good for customers, the community, and the stockholders.

Prompt Service... at Competitive Prices
SWD INC.
FASTENER SORTING CORPORATION
• Black Oxide • Passivating • Phosphating • Sorting • Assembling
QS 9000
ISO 9002
ISO 14001
910 S. Stiles Drive
Addison, IL 60101-4913
Phone: (630) 543-3003
Fax: (630) 543-3028
www.swdinc.com

Courtesy of SWD Inc.

http://www.swdinc.com

Sources: Mark Henricks, "A New Standard," *Entrepreneur*, October 2002, pp. 83–84; Lee Strouse, "Metal Finisher Forges Quality Alliance," *Finishers' Management*, February 1999; and "Company History," http://www.swdinc.com, November 13, 2003.

form to these standards. Small firms, therefore, may need ISO 9000 certification either to sell more easily in international markets or to meet the demands of their domestic customers.

Quality Management in Service Businesses

As discussed earlier, maintaining and improving quality are no less important for service businesses—such as motels, dry cleaners, accounting firms, and automobile repair shops—than for manufacturers. In fact, many firms offer a combination of tangible products and intangible services and effectively manage quality in both areas.

In recent years, the public has expressed growing dissatisfaction with the general quality of customer service. Studies by such groups as the Council of Better Business Bureaus and the University of Michigan reveal that consumers find good service to be increasingly rare.[3] Part of this dissatisfaction may be explained by the practice among many large corporations of gearing the quality of service they provide to the profitability of the customer. Better customers get better service. Increasing customer dissatisfaction with poor service—exemplified by automated telephone answering systems that do not allow callers to speak to a live representative, long lines, and reluctance to respond to customer problems—opens the door for small service-oriented firms. Although some services are too costly to be used as powerful competitive weapons, much high-quality service simply requires attention to detail.

Measurement problems are always an issue in assessing the quality of a service. It is easier to measure the length of a piece of wood than the quality of motel accommodations. As noted earlier, however, methods can be devised for measuring the quality of services. For example, a motel manager might maintain a record of the number of problems with travelers' reservations, complaints about the cleanliness of rooms, and so on.

For many types of service firms, quality control constitutes management's most important responsibility. All that such firms sell is service, and their success depends on customers' perceptions of the quality of that service.

THE OPERATIONS PROCESS

2 *Discuss the nature of the operations process for both products and services.*

The operations process is necessary to get the job done—that is, to perform the work and create the quality expected by customers. Thus far, this chapter has discussed the way quality concerns drive operations management. Let's now turn to other important aspects of business operations.

The Nature of the Operations Process

operations management Planning and controlling the process of converting inputs to outputs

Operations management involves the planning and control of a conversion process. It includes acquiring inputs and then overseeing their transformation into products and services desired by customers. An operations process is required whether a firm produces a tangible product, such as clothing or bread, or an intangible service, such as dry cleaning or entertainment. The production process in clothing manufacturing, the baking process in a bakery, the cleaning process in dry cleaning, and the performance process in entertainment are all examples of operations processes.

Despite their differences, all operations processes are similar in that they change inputs into outputs. Inputs include money, raw materials, labor, equipment, information, and energy—all of which are combined in varying proportions, depending on the nature of the finished product or service. Outputs are the products and/or services that a business provides to its customers. Thus, the operations process may be described as a conversion process. As Exhibit 20-2 shows, the operations process converts inputs of various kinds into products, such as baked goods, or services, such as dry cleaning. A printing plant, for example, uses inputs such as paper, ink, the work of employees, printing presses, and electric power to produce printed material. Car wash facilities and motor freight firms, which are service businesses, also use operating systems to transform inputs into car-cleaning and freight-transporting services.

Managing Operations in a Service Business

The operations of firms providing services differ from those of firms producing products in a number of ways. One of the most obvious is the intangible nature of services. As pointed out earlier, managers of businesses such as auto repair shops and hotels face

EXHIBIT 20-2 *The Operations Process*

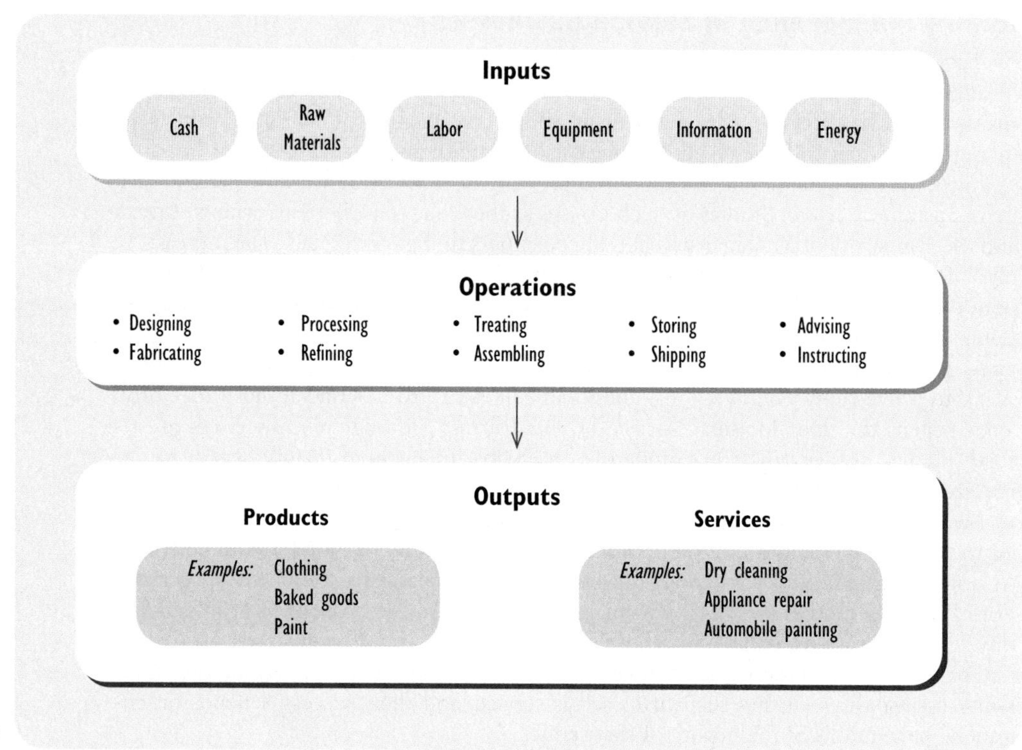

special challenges in assuring and controlling the quality of their services, given the difficulty inherent in measuring and controlling intangibles.

Another distinctive feature of most service businesses is the extensive personal interaction of employees with customers. In a physical fitness facility, for example, the customer is directly involved in the process and relates personally to trainers and other service personnel. In a beauty salon, the customer is a participant in the various processes of hair styling. The more extensive the relationship between customer and service provider, the more important the relationship is in achieving customer satisfaction and the more likely employees and customers are to develop social bonds and share information.

Some service businesses have taken unique steps to understand the service provider–customer connection. Herb Kelleher, founder of Southwest Airlines, wanted top management to get close enough to customers to see what they had to say about various facets of the company.[4] To this end, each officer of the company was sent into the field each quarter to fill a customer contact position. Research into employee–customer relations had shown that greater closeness with customers enabled employees to understand and report customer sentiment more accurately.

For a service business, the critical importance of its relationship with customers carries implications for managing personnel. For example, those making hiring decisions must consider the employee's role in relating to the firm's clientele and select individuals capable of relating well. Employee training must also emphasize the skills needed to serve customers well and encourage employees to find ways to improve customer satisfaction. Employee relationships with customers can create unique problems in scheduling work, as we will discuss later in this chapter.

The adoption of various technologies has enabled customers of many businesses to provide more of their own services. Self-service gasoline stations permit customers to pay at the pump, and many telephone systems allow customers to obtain information without speaking to a salesperson or other personnel. The extent to which such systems are satisfactory from a customer point of view depends on whether they are more convenient than traditional systems and whether they function efficiently and accurately in meeting customers' needs.[5]

Living the Dream

Focus on the Customer

Getting the Details Right Makes for Happy Customers

Operating details can make or break a business, especially in an industry such as food service. In 1971, Richard Melman, a highly successful restaurateur, started his first restaurant in Chicago—R. J. Grunt's, a low-priced burger joint. Based on its success, Melman moved on to open other kinds of restaurants, and R. J. Grunt's languished. Cost-conscious managers cut back on some of the best ingredients and became less meticulous in food preparation. Eventually, the eatery began to lose money.

There were discussions about closing the restaurant, but in 2002, Melman brought his son, R. J. (named in honor of that first restaurant), over to R. J. Grunt's from another of his highly successful restaurants. And a special assistant showed up regularly to help him—Richard Melman himself. They found problems—the milk shakes weren't as good as they used to be, and neither were the hamburgers and fries.

> *The Melmans began tinkering with the shakes and malts, increasing the amount of ice cream used, buying better malt powder, adding flavors and better displaying them on the menu. Sales doubled to about 100 a day on weekends.*
>
> *The burger was deconstructed. "How does it* not *fall apart?" Mr. Melman asked. Placed on top of the meat, the tomato slides off, so they tucked it underneath. Grilling instructions—"only flip once, no smashing, light salt and pepper"—were posted and enforced. They bought a new toaster for the buns.*
>
> *Mr. Melman's son, R. J., accustomed to a regular mob willing to wait a half-hour or more for a table at Wildfire [a high-class restaurant], came to appreciate those waiting a few minutes at Grunt's.*
>
> *"I've learned here to talk to guests and to recognize our regulars," he says.*
>
> *January 2003 was Grunt's best month in nine years.*

The business was rescued by carefully attending to the details of its basic operations and correcting the weaknesses that were afflicting the system.

Source: Jeff Bailey, "A Restaurant's Turnaround Is All in the Details," *Wall Street Journal*, May 20, 2003, p. B-3.

Types of Manufacturing Operations

Manufacturing operations differ in the degree to which they are repetitive. Some factories produce the same product day after day and week after week. Other production facilities have great flexibility and often change the products they produce. There are three types of manufacturing operations—job shops, repetitive manufacturing, and batch manufacturing.

Job shops are characterized by short production runs. Only one or a few products are produced before the general-purpose machines are shifted to a different production setup. Each job may be unique, requiring a special set of production steps to complete the finished item. Machine shops exemplify this type of operation.

job shops
A type of manufacturing operation in which short production runs are used to produce small quantities of unique items

Firms that produce one or relatively few standardized products use **repetitive manufacturing**, which is considered mass production as it involves long production runs. Repetitive manufacturing is associated with the assembly-line production of automobiles and other high-volume products. Highly specialized equipment can be employed, because it is used over and over again in manufacturing the same item. Few small business firms engage in repetitive manufacturing.

repetitive manufacturing
A type of manufacturing operation in which long production runs are used to produce a large quantity of a standardized product

An intermediate type of production is called **batch manufacturing**. Batch manufacturing involves more variety (and less volume) than repetitive manufacturing but less variety (and more volume) than job shops. In batch manufacturing, one production run of 100 standardized units may be followed by a second production run of 100 units of another type of standardized product. A bottling plant that fills bottles with several varieties of soft drinks is engaging in batch manufacturing.

batch manufacturing
A type of manufacturing operation that is intermediate (between job shops and repetitive manufacturing) in volume and variety of products

Operations Planning and Scheduling

In manufacturing, production planning and scheduling procedures are designed to achieve the orderly, sequential flow of products through a plant at a rate commensurate with scheduled deliveries to customers. In order for this objective to be reached, it is essential to avoid production bottlenecks and to utilize machines and personnel efficiently. Simple, informal control procedures are often used in small plants. If a procedure is simple and the output small, a manager can keep things moving smoothly with a minimum of paperwork. Eventually, however, any manufacturing organization experiencing growth will have to establish formal procedures to ensure production efficiency.

Because service firms are so closely tied to their customers, they are limited in their ability to produce services and hold them in inventory for customers. An automobile repair shop must wait until a car arrives, and a beauty shop cannot function until a customer is available. A retail store can perform some of its services, such as transportation and storage, but it, too, must wait until the customer arrives to perform other services.

Part of the scheduling task for service firms relates to planning employees' working hours. Restaurants, for example, schedule the work of servers to coincide with variations in customer traffic. In a similar way, stores and medical clinics increase their staff to meet times of peak demand. Other strategies of service firms focus on scheduling customers. Appointment systems are used by many automobile repair shops and beauty shops, for example. Service firms such as dry cleaners and plumbers take requests for service and delay delivery until the work can be scheduled. Still other firms, such as banks and movie theaters, maintain a fixed schedule of services and tolerate some idle capacity. Some businesses attempt to spread out customer demand by offering incentives to use services at off-peak hours—examples include early-bird dinner specials at a restaurant and lower-price tickets for afternoon movies.

Plant Maintenance

Murphy's Law states that if anything can go wrong, it will. In operating systems that use tools and equipment, there is indeed much that can go wrong. The maintenance function is intended to correct malfunctions of equipment and, as far as possible, to prevent breakdowns from occurring.

THE ROLE OF MAINTENANCE Effective maintenance contributes directly to product and service quality and thus to customer satisfaction. Poor maintenance often creates problems for customers. A faulty shower or a reading lamp that doesn't work, for example, makes a motel stay less enjoyable for a traveler.

Equipment malfunctions and breakdowns not only cause problems for customers but also increase costs for the producing firm. Employees may be unproductive while repairs are being made, and expensive manufacturing equipment may stand idle when it should be producing. Furthermore, improperly maintained equipment wears out more rapidly and requires early replacement, thus adding to the overall costs of operation.

The nature of maintenance work obviously depends on the type of operations process and the type of equipment being used. In an office, for example, machines that require maintenance include computers, fax machines, copiers, and related office equipment. Maintenance services are usually obtained on a contract basis—either by calling for repair personnel when a breakdown occurs and/or by scheduling periodic servicing. In manufacturing firms that use more complex and specialized equipment, plant maintenance is much more difficult and clearly requires the close attention of management. In small plants, maintenance work is often performed by regular production employees. As a firm expands its facilities, it may add specialized maintenance personnel and eventually create a maintenance department.

preventive maintenance
Activities intended to prevent machine breakdowns, injuries to people, and damage to facilities

corrective maintenance
Repairs necessary to restore equipment or a facility to good condition

TYPES OF MAINTENANCE Plant maintenance activities fall into two categories. **Preventive maintenance** consists of inspections and other activities intended to prevent machine breakdowns and damage to people and buildings. **Corrective maintenance** includes both the major and the minor repairs necessary to restore equipment or a facility to good condition.

A small firm can ill afford to neglect preventive maintenance. A machine that is highly critical to the overall operation must be inspected and serviced regularly to avoid costly breakdowns.

Major repairs, which are a part of corrective maintenance, are unpredictable as to time of occurrence, repair time required, loss of output, and cost of downtime. Because of this unpredictability, some small manufacturers contract with outside service firms for major repair work.

COMPETITIVE STRENGTH THROUGH IMPROVED PRODUCTIVITY

3 *Explain how reengineering and other methods of work improvement can increase productivity and make a firm more competitive.*

A society's standard of living depends, to some extent, on its **productivity**—the efficiency with which inputs are transformed into outputs. Similarly, the competitive strength of a particular business depends on its productivity. This section discusses approaches that can be used by small businesses to become more competitive through improved productivity.

productivity
The efficiency with which inputs are transformed into outputs

The Importance of Improving Productivity

To remain competitive, a firm should continually try to improve its productivity. Improvement efforts vary greatly. Some involve major reorganizations or changes in technology, while others merely upgrade existing operations.

A business firm's productivity may be expressed as follows:

$$\text{Productivity} = \frac{\text{Outputs}}{\text{Inputs}} = \frac{\text{Products and/or services}}{\left(\begin{array}{c}\text{Labor + Energy + Cash + Raw materials}\\ \text{+ Equipment + Information}\end{array}\right)}$$

A firm improves its productivity by doing more with less—increasing outputs and/or decreasing inputs. This can be accomplished in many different ways. For example, a small restaurant may improve its pastry making by sending the chef to cooking school, buying better ingredients, getting a more efficient oven, or redesigning the kitchen.

Michael Hammer argues that companies that are doing well today rely primarily not on a clever plan or hot concept but on innovation. Here's his formula for achieving a solid advantage in the marketplace:

> *It depends on how regular, mundane, basic work is carried out. If you can consistently do your work faster, cheaper, and better than the other guy, then you get to wipe the floor with him—without any accounting tricks. Relentless operational innovation is the only way to establish a lasting advantage.*[6]

At one time, productivity and quality were viewed as potentially conflicting. However, production at a high quality level reduces scrap and rework. Therefore, quality enhancement, automation, and other improvements in operations methods can also boost productivity.

Improving productivity in the labor-intensive service sector is especially difficult, since managers have less opportunity to take advantage of automation. Nevertheless, small service firms can find ways to become more efficient. At one time, for example, customers in barber shops wasted time waiting for barbers who took them on a first-come, first-served basis. To improve the system, many shops now use an appointment schedule. A drop-in customer can still get service immediately if a barber isn't busy or else sign up for the first convenient appointment. Such a system provides continuity in the barber's work schedule and reduces delays and frustration for customers.

Reengineering for Improved Productivity

In the early 1990s, Michael Hammer and James Champy described a method for restructuring companies to provide better service for customers. In their best-selling book *Reengineering the Corporation*, Hammer and Champy defined **reengineering** as "the fundamental rethinking and radical redesign of business processes to achieve dramatic improvements in critical, contemporary measures of performance, such as cost, quality, service, and speed."[7]

reengineering
A fundamental restructuring to improve the operations process

Reengineering is concerned with improving the way in which a business operates, whether that business is large or small. Hammer and Champy concentrated their early analysis on large corporations such as Wal-Mart, Taco Bell, and Bell Atlantic, which redesigned their rigid bureaucratic structures to become more efficient. Firms that engage in reengineering seek fundamental improvements by asking questions about why they perform certain functions the way they do. They expect to make dramatic, radical changes rather than minimal adjustments to traditional operating methods. Reengineering involves careful analysis of the basic processes followed by a firm in creating goods and services for customers.

Reengineering's emphasis on basic processes is crucial and holds the potential for substantial improvements in operations. Like effective quality control efforts, it directs attention to activities that create value for the customer. Essentially, reengineering asks how the operations process can be better managed, even if it means eliminating traditional departmental lines and specialized job descriptions.

Upgrading Information Systems

In recent years, small firms have made extensive improvements in productivity by using computers, new software, and Internet links with suppliers and customers. Earlier tedious, paper-based processes for tracking orders, work in progress, and inventory have been simplified and accelerated.

Consider Dee Electronics, a 62-employee company that operates an electronics distribution center in Cedar Rapids, Iowa.[8] By 1999, it was selling 50,000 items such as switches, fuses, and circuit breakers, with all sales documented by a huge amount of paper. By shifting to a paperless, wireless computer network, the business greatly increased its efficiency of operation and recouped its $65,000 investment in just five months.

Management information systems are in a continuous stage of reinvention and improvement. Microsoft, for example, is spending billions of dollars to offer software that will automate practically every aspect of a company's business (such as order processing and inventory management) and create a base layer of technology upon which smaller software makers can build applications.[9]

Operations Analysis

Improving productivity for an overall operation involves analyses of work flow, equipment, tooling, layout, working conditions, and individual jobs. For a specific manufacturing process, it means finding answers to questions such as these:

- Are the right machines being used?
- Can one employee operate two or more machines?

Living the Dream *Utilizing the Internet*

Improved Productivity in Trucking

A small company can improve its bottom line by finding ways to operate more efficiently. In many cases, modern technology can give a helping hand.

Murray Kennedy and his wife, Linda, haul everything from computers to aircraft parts in their self-owned 18-wheel tractor-trailer. They can gross some $6,600 for a 3,000-mile one-way trip, but the key to better profitability lies in finding freight for the return drive.

For a number of years, the Kennedys have relied on Landstar, a logistics company, to find a return load. Eventually, they obtained a laptop computer with which to search Landstar's online network for available freight. But because they still had to pull over at truck stops in order to log on, they often missed the best deals.

> *Now, without leaving the truck, he [Murray] or Linda uses a cell phone equipped with customized software that lets them dial directly into Landstar's Web site. Kennedy bought the phone himself for $149, and pays only $15 a month to dial in. Using the number pad and a small screen, he recently used the system to locate a shipment of automotive parts in Charlotte, N.C., that needed to go to a Chrysler plant near his home. The search took him five minutes. Kennedy estimates that he could save a full day each trip because he no longer must wait for freight. The time savings could boost his revenues 20%.*

Source: Rachel Harrison, "The Hands-On, Logged-On Worker," *Forbes*, Vol. 166, No. 12 (October 30, 2000), p. 138.

- Can automatic feeders or ejectors be used?
- Can power tools replace hand tools?
- Can the jigs and fixtures be improved?
- Is the workplace properly arranged?
- Is each operator's motion sequence effective?

Work methods can be analyzed for service or merchandising firms as well as for manufacturers. For example, a small plumbing company serving residential customers might examine its service vehicles to make sure they are equipped with the best possible assortment and arrangement of parts, tools, and supplies. In addition, the company might analyze the planning and routing of repair assignments to minimize backtracking and wasting of time.

Relatively simple changes can sometimes improve productivity. Julie Northcutt founded Chicagoland Caregivers LLC in 2002 to provide in-home care for seniors who would otherwise have to move into assisted living or nursing homes.[10] Northcutt found that the hiring of nurse's aides and others took so much of her time that she was missing important calls from clients. She solved the problem by adding a phone line specifically for job seekers, requiring them to supply certain information. Now Northcutt can check the information when free of client work and call prospects who sound promising.

Sometimes, in their efforts to improve highly repetitive operations, analysts examine detailed motions of individual employees. By applying the **laws of motion economy**, which concern work arrangement, the use of the human hands and body, and the design and use of tools, they can often make work easier and more efficient.

laws of motion economy
Guidelines for increasing the efficiency of human movement and tool design

PURCHASING POLICIES AND PRACTICES

4 Discuss the importance of purchasing and the nature of key purchasing policies.

Although its importance varies with the type of business, **purchasing** constitutes a key part of operations management for most small businesses. Through purchasing, firms obtain materials, merchandise, equipment, and services to meet production and marketing goals. For example, manufacturing firms buy raw materials, merchandising firms purchase goods to be sold, and all types of firms obtain supplies.

purchasing
The process of obtaining materials, equipment, and services from outside suppliers

The Importance of Purchasing

The quality of a finished product depends on the quality of the raw materials used. If a product must be made with great precision and close tolerances, the manufacturer must acquire high-quality materials and component parts. Then, if the manufacturer uses a well-managed production process, excellent products will result. Similarly, the acquisition of high-quality merchandise makes a retailer's sales to customers easier and reduces the number of necessary markdowns and merchandise returns.

Purchasing also contributes to profitable operations by ensuring that goods are delivered when they are needed. Failure to receive materials, parts, or equipment on schedule can cause costly interruptions in production operations. In a retail business, failure to receive merchandise on schedule may mean a loss of sales and, possibly, a permanent loss of customers who were disappointed.

Another aspect of effective purchasing is securing the best possible price. Cost savings go directly to the bottom line, and purchasing practices that seek out the best prices can have a major impact on the financial health of a business.

Note, however, that the importance of the purchasing function varies according to the type of business. In a small, labor-intensive service business—such as an accounting firm—purchases of supplies are responsible for a very small part of the total operating costs. Such businesses are more concerned with labor costs than with the cost of supplies or other materials they may require in their operations process.

Purchasing Practices and Profitability

A small firm can increase the cost effectiveness of its purchasing activities by adopting appropriate purchasing practices. Through decisions related to making or buying, outsourcing, and other procurement issues, the firm's management can optimize both present and future earnings.

make-or-buy decision
A firm's choice between producing and purchasing component parts for its products

MAKING OR BUYING Many firms face **make-or-buy decisions**. Such decisions are especially important for small manufacturing firms that have the option of making or buying component parts for products they produce. A less obvious make-or-buy choice exists with respect to certain services—for example, purchasing janitorial or car rental services versus providing for those needs internally. Some reasons for making component parts, rather than buying them, follow:

- More complete utilization of plant capacity permits more economical production.
- Supplies are assured, with fewer delays caused by design changes or difficulties with outside suppliers.
- A secret design may be protected.
- Expenses are reduced by an amount equivalent to transportation costs and the outside supplier's selling expense and profit.
- Closer coordination and control of the total production process may facilitate operations scheduling and control.
- Products produced may be of higher quality than those available from outside suppliers.

Some reasons for buying component parts, rather than making them, follow:

- An outside supplier's part may be cheaper because of the supplier's concentration on production of the part.
- Additional space, equipment, personnel skills, and working capital are not needed.
- Less diversified managerial experience and skills are required.
- Greater flexibility is provided, especially in the manufacture of a seasonal item.
- In-plant operations can concentrate on the firm's specialty—finished products and services.
- The risk of equipment obsolescence is transferred to outsiders.

The decision to make or buy should be based on long-run cost and profit optimization, as it may be expensive to reverse. Underlying cost differences need to be analyzed carefully, since small savings from either buying or making may greatly affect profit margins.

outsourcing
Purchasing products or services that are outside the firm's area of competitive advantage

OUTSOURCING Buying products or services from other business firms is known as **outsourcing**. As mentioned earlier, firms can sometimes save money by buying from outside suppliers specializing in a particular type of work, especially services such as accounting, payroll, janitorial, and equipment repair services. The expertise of these outside suppliers may enable them to provide better-quality services by virtue of their specialization.

Rob Exline, owner of a Salina, Kansas, machine shop, rebuilds and repairs equipment used on natural-gas pipelines.[11] When his shop became extremely busy, Exline outsourced work to machine-shop competitors who were looking for work, rather than expand his own facility. Believing that the heavier schedule was only temporary, he wanted to postpone the purchase of additional equipment.

Chapter 19 explained the practice of employee leasing, through which a small firm transfers its employees to a leasing company, which then leases them back to the small firm. In effect, the small firm is outsourcing the payroll preparation process.

BUYING ON THE INTERNET In increasing numbers, small firms are buying on the Internet as an alternative method of purchasing. Many tasks that once required telephone calls or out-of-office time can now be accomplished simply and quickly on the Web. The changing purchasing environment has been described as follows:

> *In years past, small-business owners had scant buying power, little access to resources and information, and a dearth of applications to help them manage their businesses. The Internet has changed all that. Today's connected small-business owners can find themselves sitting*

Living the Dream — *Entrepreneurial Challenges*

Outsourcing the Production Process

When fashion stylist Natalie Chanin designed and hand-sewed a one-of-a-kind garment from a recycled T-shirt, she realized she had a product that would sell. Lacking experience in finance and marketing, she joined a business partner, Enrico Marone-Cinzano, to form Project Alabama.

Chanin was unable to find a manufacturer in New York to do the extensive handwork required. The shirts are adorned and embroidered with everything from flowers to roosters, requiring a labor-intensive process. The work's resemblance to quilting inspired her to think of the quilting circles back in her native Alabama. After locating a group of women in Alabama who could provide the skilled handwork necessary to produce the uniquely decorated shirts, she outsourced the basic production process.

Even though it's made from recycled T-shirts, Chanin's unique, high-fashion product is sold at prices as high as $2,000, in stores in the United States, Europe, and Asia. The shirts are featured in such stores as Barney's in New York, Brown's in London, and Maxfield's in Los Angeles. Thanks to outsourcing, the product is created by a contemporary version of the old-fashioned quilting circle.

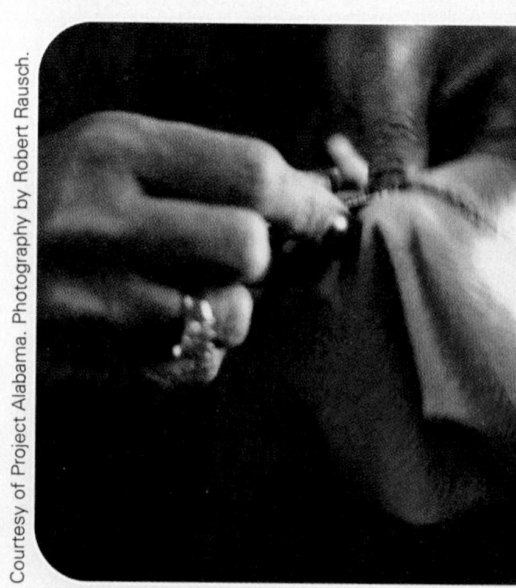
Courtesy of Project Alabama. Photography by Robert Rausch.

http://www.projectalabama.com

Sources: April Y. Pennington, "Snapshot: Natalie Chanin and Enrico Marone-Cinzano," *Entrepreneur*, February 2003, p. 20; Julia Reed, "Art of the Craft: Sweet Home Alabama," *Vogue*, March 2002, pp. 280ff; and http://www.projectalabama.com, November 19, 2003.

happily as hundreds of suppliers, large and small, bid for their business. Instead of buying costly software packages, they can rent only the applications they need, and add more as the company grows. And they can outsource nearly any function—from business planning and human resources management to the purchase of office supplies.[12]

Even small farmers are beginning to investigate purchasing on the Internet as a way of reducing costs. Jerry Brightbill, who farms 4,200 acres near Cotton Center, Texas, with his father and brother, visited a Web site called XSAg.com, looking for deals on farm supplies.[13] He found that he could buy herbicides at 20 percent or more off the list price and eventually spent $40,000 during the year at this one site. XSAg is only one of many Internet companies targeting the farm market. It seems probable that many of the nation's more than 2 million farmers, as well as millions of other small firms, will continue to increase their buying on the Internet.

DIVERSIFYING SOURCES OF SUPPLY Small firms often must decide whether it is desirable to use more than one supplier when purchasing a given item. The somewhat frustrating answer is "It all depends." For example, a business would rarely need more than one supplier when buying a few rolls of tape. However, several suppliers might be involved when a firm is buying a component part to be used in hundreds of products.

A small firm might prefer to concentrate purchases with one supplier for any of the following reasons:

- A particular supplier may be superior in its product quality.
- Larger orders may qualify for quantity discounts.
- Orders may be so small that it is impractical to divide them among several suppliers.
- The purchasing firm may, as a good customer, qualify for prompt treatment of rush orders and receive management advice, market information, and financial leniency in times of crisis.

Also, a small firm may be linked to a specific supplier by the very nature of its business—if it is a franchisee, for example. Typically, the franchise contract requires purchasing from the franchisor.

The following reasons favor diversifying rather than concentrating sources of supply:

- Shopping among suppliers allows a firm to locate the best source in terms of price, quality, and service.
- A supplier, knowing that competitors are getting some of its business, may provide better prices and service.
- Diversifying supply sources provides insurance against interruptions caused by strikes, fires, or similar problems with sole suppliers.

Some firms compromise by following a purchasing policy of concentrating enough purchases with a single supplier to justify special treatment and, at the same time, diversifying purchases sufficiently to maintain alternative sources of supply.

Relationships with Suppliers

Before choosing a supplier, a purchaser should be thoroughly familiar with the characteristics of the materials or merchandise to be purchased, including details of construction, quality and grade desired, intended use, maintenance or care required, and the importance of style features. In manufacturing, the purchaser must especially focus on how different grades and qualities of raw materials affect various manufacturing processes.

SELECTING SUPPLIERS A number of factors are relevant in deciding which suppliers to use on a continuing basis. Perhaps the most significant are price and quality. Price differences are clearly important to a firm's bottom line, if not offset by quality issues or other factors.

Quality differences are sometimes difficult to detect. For some types of materials, statistical controls can be applied to evaluate vendors' shipments. In this way, the purchaser can obtain overall quality ratings for various suppliers. The purchaser can often work with a supplier to upgrade quality. If satisfactory quality cannot be achieved, the purchaser clearly has a reason for dropping the supplier.

Supplier location becomes especially important if a firm tries to keep inventory levels low, depending instead on rapid delivery of purchased items when they are needed. A supplier's overall reliability in providing goods and services is also significant. The purchaser must be able to depend on the supplier to meet delivery schedules and to respond promptly to emergency situations.

The services offered by a supplier must also be considered. The extension of credit by suppliers provides a major portion of the working capital of many small firms. Some suppliers plan sales promotions, provide merchandising aids, and offer management advice.

BUILDING GOOD RELATIONSHIPS WITH SUPPLIERS Good relationships with suppliers are essential for firms of any size, but they are particularly important for small businesses. The small firm is only one among dozens, hundreds, or perhaps thousands buying from that supplier. And the small firm's purchases are often small in volume and, therefore, of little concern to the supplier.

To implement a policy of fair play and to cultivate good relations with suppliers, a small firm should try to observe the following purchasing practices:

- Pay bills promptly.
- Give sales representatives a prompt, courteous hearing.
- Avoid abrupt cancellation of orders merely to gain a temporary advantage.
- Avoid attempts to browbeat a supplier into special concessions and/or unusual discounts.
- Cooperate with the supplier by making suggestions for product improvement and/or cost reduction, whenever possible.
- Provide courteous, reasonable explanations when rejecting bids, and make fair adjustments in the case of disputes.

Some large corporations, such as UPS, Dell, FedEx, and Office Depot, have made special efforts to reach out to small business purchasers.[14] By offering various kinds of assistance, such suppliers can strengthen small firms, which then continue as customers. Of course, it still makes sense to shop around, although low prices can sometimes be misleading. The low bid for an air conditioning system sought by one small firm was one-half the next lowest bid. It looked too good to be true, and it was. When examined closely, the low bid was found to have left out crucial items.

Managerial help provided by Hallmark Cards to some 4,000 independently owned small shops called Hallmark Gold Crown Stores has been described as follows:

> *Hallmark helped hundreds of the independents renegotiate leases last year, providing local real-estate market data and other help to keep rents lower.*
>
> *Hallmark also provides employee hiring and training programs, customer-satisfaction surveys, theft-prevention plans and a newsletter that spotlights best selling products and slow sellers, helping the retailers better plan their buying.*
>
> *An inventory management system installed in about 1,000 of the Gold Crown stores—mostly in ones whose owners operate multiple stores—has helped increase inventory turns, which lifts cash flow.*
>
> *And it helps merchants, with precise numbers, to make difficult decisions to get rid of product lines that move slowly, including collectibles, which were so hot in the 1990s but now have cooled off.*[15]

Building strong relationships with larger suppliers can clearly help small firms become more competitive.

DEVELOPING STRATEGIC ALLIANCES As mentioned in Chapter 8, some small firms have found it advantageous to develop **strategic alliances** with suppliers. This form of partnering enables the buying and selling firms to work much more closely together than is customary in a simple contractual arrangement.

strategic alliance
An organizational relationship that links two or more independent business entities in a common endeavor

New Pig Corporation, a 300-employee company in Tipton, Pennsylvania, sought to improve its competitive strength by developing better working relationships with suppliers. This company produces sock-like materials used to soak up industrial spills and buys some element of each of the 3,000 different products it sells. New Pig's goals for partnering with its suppliers were to reduce the time needed to introduce products, improve product quality, engage in joint problem solving, make joint adjustments to market conditions, and involve suppliers early in product development. One of the early benefits of the firm's collaboration with its suppliers was a change in a shipping method that resulted in savings of hundreds of thousands of dollars.[16]

INVENTORY MANAGEMENT AND OPERATIONS

5 *Describe ways to control inventory and minimize inventory costs.*

Inventory management is not glamorous, but it can make the difference between success and failure for a small firm. The larger the inventory investment, the more vital proper inventory management is. Inventory management is particularly important in small retail or wholesale firms, as inventory typically represents a major financial investment by these firms.

Objectives of Inventory Management

Both purchasing and inventory management share the same objective: to have the right goods in the right quantities at the right time and place. As shown in Exhibit 20-3, achieving this general objective requires pursuing more specific subgoals of inventory control—ensuring continuous operations, maximizing sales, protecting assets, and minimizing inventory costs.

Ensuring continuous operations is particularly important in manufacturing, as delays caused by lack of materials or parts can be costly. Furthermore, sales can be maximized by completing production in a timely manner and by stocking an appropriate assortment of merchandise in retail stores and wholesale establishments. Protecting inventory against theft, shrinkage, and deterioration and optimizing investment costs likewise contribute to operational efficiency and business profits.

EXHIBIT 20-3 *Objectives of Inventory Management*

Inventory Cost Control

economic order quantity (EOQ) The quantity to purchase in order to minimize total inventory costs

Maintaining inventory at an optimal level—the level that minimizes stockouts and eliminates excess inventory—saves money and contributes to operating profits. To determine the optimal level, managers must pay close attention to purchase quantities, because those quantities affect inventory levels. The ideal quantity of an item to purchase (at least some of which will be carried in inventory) is the number of items that minimizes total inventory costs. This number is called the **economic order quantity (EOQ)**.

If a firm could order merchandise or raw materials and carry inventory with no expenses other than the cost of the items, there would be no need to be concerned about what quantity to order at any given time. However, inventory costs are affected by both the costs of purchasing and the costs of carrying inventory—that is,

$$\text{Total inventory costs} = \text{Total carrying costs} + \text{Total ordering costs}$$

As noted earlier, carrying costs include storage costs, insurance premiums, the cost of money tied up in inventory, and losses due to spoilage or obsolescence. Carrying costs go up as inventories increase in size. Ordering costs, on the other hand, include expenses associated with preparing and processing purchase orders and expenses related to receiving and inspecting the purchased items. The cost of placing an order is a fixed cost; therefore, total ordering costs increase as a firm purchases smaller quantities more frequently. Quantity discounts, if available, favor the placement of larger orders.

The point labeled EOQ in Exhibit 20-4 is the lowest point on the total costs curve; it coincides with the intersection of the carrying costs and ordering costs curves. In cases in which sufficient information on costs is available, this point can be calculated with some precision.[17] Even when the economic order quantity cannot be calculated with precision, a firm's goal must be to minimize both ordering costs and carrying costs.

ABC INVENTORY ANALYSIS Some inventory items are more valuable or more critical to a firm's operations than others. Therefore, those items have a greater effect on costs and profits. As a general rule, managers should attend most carefully to those inventory items entailing the largest investment.

ABC method A system of classifying items in inventory by relative value

One approach to inventory analysis, the **ABC method**, classifies inventory items into three categories based on value. The purpose of the ABC method is to focus managerial attention on the most important items. The number of categories could easily be expanded to four or more, if that seemed more appropriate for a particular firm.

In the A category are a few high-value inventory items that account for the largest percentage of total dollars or are otherwise critical in the production process and, therefore, deserve close control. They might be monitored, for example, by an inventory system that keeps a running record of receipts, withdrawals, and balances of each such item. In this way, a firm can avoid an unnecessarily heavy investment in costly inventory items. Category B items are less costly but deserve moderate managerial attention because they still make up a significant share of the firm's total inventory investment. Category C contains low-cost

EXHIBIT 20-4 *Graphic Portrayal of the Economic Order Quantity*

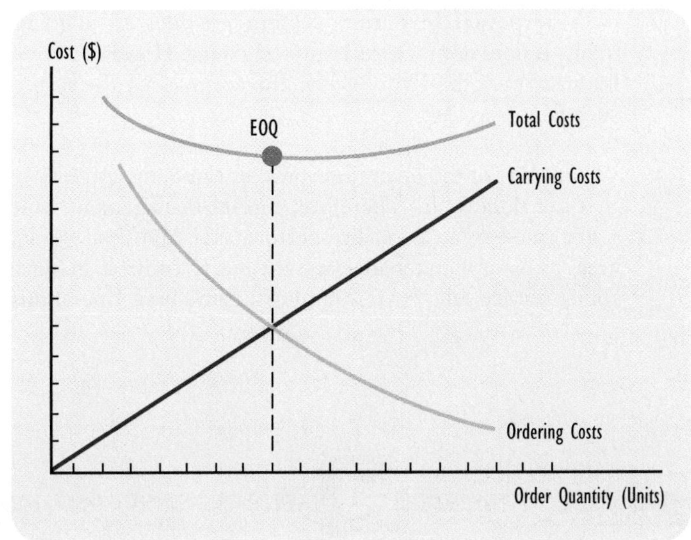

or noncritical items, such as paperclips in an office or nuts and bolts in a repair shop. The carrying costs of such items are not large enough to justify close control. These items might simply be checked periodically to ensure that a sufficient supply is available.

JUST-IN-TIME INVENTORY SYSTEM Optimizing inventory levels remains a goal of all operations managers. The **just-in-time inventory system** attempts to cut inventory carrying costs by reducing inventory to an absolute minimum. Popularized in Japan as *kanban*, the just-in-time system has led to cost reductions there and in other countries. New items are received, presumably, just as the last item of that type from existing inventory is placed into service. Many large U.S. firms have adopted some form of the just-in-time system for inventory management, and small businesses can also benefit from its use.

just-in-time inventory system
A method of reducing inventory levels to an absolute minimum

Adoption of a just-in-time system necessitates close cooperation with suppliers. Supplier locations, production schedules, and transportation schedules must be carefully considered, as they all affect a firm's ability to obtain materials quickly and in a predictable manner—a necessary condition for using a just-in-time inventory system.

The potential for failure is high in the just-in-time system. Out-of-stock situations, which arise when delays or mistakes occur, may result in interrupted production or unhappy customers. Most firms using the just-in-time inventory system maintain some safety stock (a reserve amount for use in emergency) to minimize difficulties of this type. Although safety stock represents a compromise of the just-in-time philosophy, it protects a firm against large or unexpected withdrawals from inventory and delays in receiving replacement items.

Inventory Record-Keeping Systems

The larger the business is, the greater the need for record keeping, but even a very small business needs a system for keeping tabs on its inventory. Because manufacturers are concerned with three broad categories of inventory (raw materials and supplies, work in process, and finished goods), their inventory records are more complex than those of wholesalers and retailers. Small firms should emphasize simplicity in their control methods. Too much control is as wasteful as it is unnecessary.

In most small businesses, inventory records are computerized. A large variety of software programs are available for this purpose; the manager, in consultation with the firm's accounting advisors, can select the software best suited for the particular business.

A **physical inventory system** depends on an actual count of items on hand. The counting is done in physical units such as pieces, gallons, and boxes. By using this method, a firm presumably gains an accurate record of its inventory level at a given point in time. Some businesses have an annual shutdown to count everything—a complete physical

physical inventory system
A method that provides for periodic counting of items in inventory

cycle counting
A system of counting different segments of the physical inventory at different times during the year

perpetual inventory system
A method for keeping a running record of inventory

inventory. Others use **cycle counting**, scheduling different segments of the inventory for counting at different times during the year. This simplifies the inventorying process and makes it less of an ordeal for the business as a whole.

A **perpetual inventory system** provides an ongoing, current record of inventory items. It does not require a physical count. However, a physical count of inventory should be made periodically to ensure the accuracy of the system and to make adjustments for such factors as theft.

Any part of the operations process can damage a firm's sales and profit performance if it is not done well. Therefore, careful management is needed, not only in such often-highlighted areas as quality performance and cost efficiency but also in such mundane areas as plant maintenance and inventory control. Achieving the goal of satisfactory customer service calls for fine-tuning a firm's basic operations.

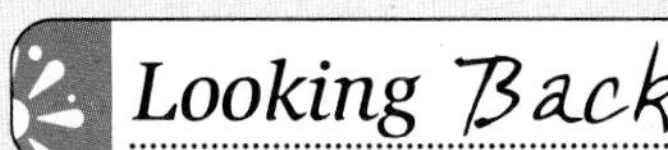

Looking Back

1 Explain the key elements of total quality management (TQM) programs.

- Quality of products or services is a primary goal of the operations process.
- Quality management efforts are focused on meeting customer needs.
- Effective quality management requires an organizational culture that places a high value on quality.
- Quality management tools and techniques include employee involvement, quality circles, inspections, and statistical analysis.
- Small firms can obtain international certification of quality performance by meeting ISO 9000 standards.
- Service businesses can benefit from use of quality management programs.

2 Discuss the nature of the operations process for both products and services.

- Operations processes vary from one industry to another, but they all change inputs into outputs.
- Service and manufacturing operations typically differ in the extent of their contact with customers and the level of difficulty of establishing quality standards.
- The three types of manufacturing operations are job shops, repetitive manufacturing, and batch manufacturing.
- Operations management involves planning and scheduling activities that transform inputs into products or services.
- Proper plant maintenance is necessary for efficient operation and achievement of quality performance.
- Preventive maintenance is needed to minimize breakdowns in machinery; corrective maintenance is used to restore equipment to good condition.

3 Explain how reengineering and other methods of work improvement can increase productivity and make a firm more competitive.

- The competitive strength of a business depends on its level of productivity.
- Reengineering involves restructuring firms by redesigning their basic work processes.
- Many small firms have improved productivity by using computers, new software, and Internet links with suppliers and customers.
- Laws of motion economy can be applied to make work easier and more efficient.

4 Discuss the importance of purchasing and the nature of key purchasing policies.

- Purchasing is important because it affects quality and profitability.
- A key decision for manufacturers is whether to make or buy components.
- In outsourcing, a small firm contracts with outside suppliers for accounting, repair, or other services and products.
- Small firms are doing more purchasing on the Internet, and many are finding bargains online.
- Decisions concerning diversifying sources of supply must take into account both the advantages and the disadvantages of having multiple suppliers.
- Careful selection of suppliers will identify those offering the best price, quality, and services.
- Paying bills promptly and dealing professionally with suppliers will help build good relationships, which in turn can bring benefits, such as training provided by a supplier.
- Strategic alliances enable small firms to work closely with their suppliers.

5 Describe ways to control inventory and minimize inventory costs.

- The calculation of economic order quantities, ABC inventory analysis, and the just-in-time inventory system can all help minimize inventory costs.
- Inventory record-keeping systems include the physical inventory method and the perpetual inventory method.

Key Terms

operations process, p. 439
quality, p. 439
total quality management (TQM), p. 440
organizational culture, p. 442
continuous quality improvement, p. 442
benchmarking, p. 442
quality circle, p. 442
inspection, p. 443
inspection standard, p. 443
attribute inspection, p. 443
variable inspection, p. 443
acceptance sampling, p. 443
statistical process control, p. 443
control chart, p. 444
ISO 9000, p. 444
operations management, p. 445
job shops, p. 447
repetitive manufacturing, p. 447
batch manufacturing, p. 447
preventive maintenance, p. 448
corrective maintenance, p. 448
productivity, p. 449
reengineering, p. 449
laws of motion economy, p. 451
purchasing, p. 451
make-or-buy decision, p. 452
outsourcing, p. 452
strategic alliance, p. 455
economic order quantity (EOQ), p. 456
ABC method, p. 456
just-in-time inventory system, p. 457
physical inventory system, p. 457
cycle counting, p. 458
perpetual inventory system, p. 458

Discussion Questions

1. Defend the customer focus of quality management.
2. Explain what is meant by total quality management.
3. A small manufacturer does not believe that statistical quality control charts and sampling plans are useful. Can traditional methods suffice? Can 100 percent inspection by final inspectors eliminate all defective products? Why or why not?
4. What are some distinctive features of operations processes in service firms?
5. Customer demand for services is generally not uniform during a day, week, or other period of time. What strategies can be used by service firms to better match a firm's capacity to perform services to customer demand for services?
6. Explain the purpose and nature of reengineering.
7. Doing something rapidly and doing it well are often incompatible. How can quality improvement possibly contribute to productivity improvement?
8. What conditions make purchasing a particularly vital function in a small business? Can the owner-manager of a small firm safely delegate purchasing authority to a subordinate? Explain.
9. Under what conditions should a small manufacturer either make component parts or buy them from others?
10. Explain the basic concept underlying the calculation of an economic order quantity.

You Make the Call

SITUATION 1

The owner of two pizza restaurants in a city with a population of 150,000 is studying her firm's operations to be sure the firm is functioning as efficiently as possible. About 70 percent of the firm's sales represent dine-in business, and 30 percent come from deliveries. The owner has always attempted to produce a good-quality product and minimize the waiting time of customers both on- and off-premises.

A recent magazine article suggested that quality is now generally abundant and that quality differences in businesses are narrowing. The writer advocated placing emphasis on saving time for customers rather than producing a high-quality product. The owner is contemplating the implications of this article for the pizza business.

Realizing that her attention should be focused, she wonders whether to concentrate primary managerial emphasis on delivery time.

Question 1 Is the writer of the article correct in believing that quality levels now are generally higher and that quality differences among businesses are minimal?

Question 2 What are the benefits and drawbacks of placing the firm's primary emphasis on minimizing customer waiting time?

Question 3 If you were advising the owner, what would you recommend?

SITUATION 2

Derek Dilworth, owner of a small manufacturing firm, is trying to rectify the firm's thin working capital situation by carefully managing payments to major suppliers. These suppliers extend credit for 30 days, and customers are expected to pay within that time period. However, the suppliers do not automatically refuse subsequent orders when a payment is a few days late. Dilworth's strategy is to delay payment of most invoices for 10 to 15 days beyond the due date. Although he is not meeting the "letter of the law," he believes that the suppliers will go along with him rather than lose future sales. This practice enables Dilworth's firm to operate with sufficient inventory, avoid costly interruptions in production, and reduce the likelihood of an overdraft at the bank.

Question 1 What are the ethical implications of Dilworth's payment practices?

Question 2 What impact, if any, might these practices have on the firm's supplier relationships? How serious would this impact be?

SITUATION 3

The owner of a small food products company was confronted with an inventory control problem involving differences of opinion among his subordinates. His accountant, with the concurrence of his general manager, had decided to "put some teeth" into the inventory control system by deducting inventory shortages from the pay of route drivers who distributed the firm's products to stores in their respective territories. Each driver was considered responsible for the inventory on his or her truck.

When the first "short" paychecks arrived, drivers were angry. Sharing their concern, their immediate supervisor, the regional manager, first went to the general manager and then, getting no satisfaction there, appealed to the owner. The regional manager argued that there was no question about the honesty of the drivers. He said that he personally had created the inventory control system the company was using, and he admitted that the system was complicated and susceptible to clerical mistakes by the driver and by the office. He pointed out that the system had never been studied by the general manager or the accountant, and he maintained that it was ethically wrong to make deductions from the small salaries of honest drivers for simple record-keeping errors.

Question 1 What is wrong, if anything, with the general manager's approach to making sure that drivers do not steal or act carelessly? Is some method of enforcement necessary to ensure careful adherence to the inventory control system?

Question 2 Is it wrong to deduct from drivers' paychecks shortages documented by inventory records?

Question 3 How should the owner resolve this dispute?

Experiential Exercises

1. Outline the operations process involved in your present educational program. Be sure to identify inputs, operations, and outputs.
2. Outline, in as much detail as possible, your customary practices in studying for a specific course. Evaluate the methods you use, and specify changes that might improve your productivity.
3. Using the ABC inventory analysis method, classify some of your personal possessions into the three categories. Include at least two items in each category.
4. Interview the manager of a bookstore about the type of inventory control system used in the store. Write a report in which you explain the methods used to avoid buildup of excessive inventory and any use made of inventory turnover ratios (ratios that relate the dollar value of inventory to the volume of sales).

Exploring the Web

1. For an additional perspective on quality and the managerial and organizational commitment necessary to achieve the highest quality standards, find the Total Quality Management (TQM) tutorial Web site at **http://home.att.net/~iso9k1/tqm/tqm.html**. Then choose the "Introduction" link and read the content provided there.
   a. According to the site's content provider, TQM is the foundation for what activities? What are the principles of TQM, as discussed on this site?
   b. Of these TQM activities and principles, which seem to focus most on the customer?
2. The Automotive Service Association is a leading organization for owners and managers of automotive services businesses. Go to the association's Web site and read the article on improving inventory control by Rick Lavely. It can be found at **http://asashop.org/autoinc/march/invntctr.htm**. Lavely discusses different ways an auto shop can determine inventory profitability.
   a. According to the article, how can an owner/manager determine the cost to order? What does cost to order imply for selling parts from inventory?
   b. At the end of the article, the author gives five basic rules for inventory control. List these rules. Do you agree that they are rules to live by?
3. This chapter discusses how a firm can obtain international recognition of its quality improvement programs through the International Organization for Standardization. Go to the ISO Web site at **http://www.iso.org** and then answer the following questions based on information you find there.
   a. What is the ISO? You can find the answer to this question by choosing "Introduction" on the main page.
   b. Now use the site to learn more about ISO 9000 and ISO 14001. What additional information did you learn about these particular forms of certification?

Video Case 20

TEXAS NAMEPLATE COMPANY (P. 563)

A manufacturer receives a national award for increasing product quality while simultaneously decreasing turnover, improving morale, raising productivity, and doubling sales.

Alternative Cases for Chapter 20:

Case 18, Douglas Electrical Supply, p. 559
Case 21, Fox Manufacturing, p. 565

MANAGING RISK

In the Spotlight

RD Systems

To look at its offices, you would not expect RD Systems, Inc., to be the site of one of the most far-reaching social and economic experiments in the country. Housed in a featureless metal box in an industrial office park about 20 miles north of Rockford, Illinois, the 30-year-old manufacturing company is the very picture of an old-fashioned, traditional business. It has also been the picture of stability: Half of its 40 employees have worked there for more than five years.

© Jeff Sciortino

So it came as a shock to president Jo Ribordy-Christofferson, 41, when four years ago Blue Cross & Blue Shield of Illinois, her insurer of 10 years, announced that the premium for the plan she offered employees was going to shoot up 60 percent. RD Systems had always paid 100 percent of its employees' premiums, and Ribordy-Christofferson knew that she risked losing her highly sought-after engineers if she offered less. To cut costs, she switched from her preferred-provider organization (PPO) to a high-deductible plan from another insurer, but found that its customer service was unacceptable. Something else had to be done.

That's how old-economy RD Systems came to offer an innovative type of coverage known as "consumer-driven" health insurance. It gives employees more responsibility for managing their medical spending and will save the company $49,000 this year, a reduction of about 30 percent from what Ribordy-Christofferson estimates it would have paid under the old arrangement.

And while Ribordy-Christofferson no longer pays all of her employees' costs, the new plan offers perks to keep her workers happy and healthy. "There just isn't a downside," Ribordy-Christofferson says. "This is health insurance pushing in the right direction."

Source: Michelle Andrews, "Affordable Health Care: How Smart Small Businesses Are Keeping Their Insurance Bills Down and Their Employees Smiling," *Fortune Small Business*, May 2004, p. 44.

Chapter 21

Looking Ahead

After studying this chapter, you should be able to

1 *Define risk and explain the nature of risk.*

2 *Explain how risk management can be used in coping with business risks.*

3 *Describe the different types of business risk.*

4 *Explain the basic principles used in evaluating an insurance program.*

5 *Identify the different types of business insurance coverage.*

Because we live in a world of uncertainty, how we see risk is vitally important in almost all dimensions of our life. Risk must certainly be considered in making any business decisions. As sixth-century Greek poet and statesman Solon wrote,

> *There is risk in everything that one does, and no one knows where he will make his landfall when his enterprise is at its beginning. One man, trying to act effectively, fails to foresee something and falls into great and grim ruination, but to another man, one who is acting ineffectively, a god gives good fortune in everything and escapes from his folly.*[1]

While Solon gave more credit than we would to Zeus for the outcomes of ventures, his insight reminds us that little is new in this world, including the need to acknowledge and compensate as best we can for the risks we encounter. Peter Bernstein describes the importance of understanding the concept of risk as follows:

> *The revolutionary idea that defines the boundary between modern times and the past is the mastery of risk: the notion that the future is more than a whim of the gods and that men and women are not passive before nature. Until human beings discovered a way across that boundary, the future was a mirror of the past or the murky domain of oracles and soothsayers who held a monopoly over knowledge of anticipated events.*[2]

Risk means different things to different people, depending on the context and on how they feel about taking chances. For a student, risk might be represented by the possibility of failing an exam. For a coal miner, risk might be represented by the chance of an explosion in the mine. For a retired person, risk could mean the likelihood of not being able to live comfortably on his or her limited income. An entrepreneur's risk takes the form of the chance that a new venture will fail.

It is often said, "Nothing is certain except death and taxes." Entrepreneurs might extend this adage to say, "Nothing is certain except death, taxes, and small business risks." Chapter 1 noted the moderate risk-taking propensities of entrepreneurs and their desire to exert some control over the risky situations in which they find themselves. In keeping with this desire, they seek to minimize business risks as much as possible. Our study of this important topic begins with a definition of risk.

WHAT IS RISK?

1 *Define risk and explain the nature of risk.*

Simply stated, **risk** is "a condition in which there is a possibility of an adverse deviation from a desired outcome that is expected or hoped for."[3] Applied to a business, risk translates into the possibility of losses associated with the assets and the earnings potential of the firm. Here, the term *assets* includes not only inventory and equipment but also such factors as the firm's employees and its reputation.

Note: We express our appreciation to William R. Feldhaus, associate professor of risk management and insurance at Georgia State University, for serving as the contributing author to this chapter.

risk
A condition in which there is a possibility of an adverse deviation from a desired outcome that is expected or hoped for

market risk
The uncertainty associated with an investment decision

pure risk
The uncertainty associated with a situation where only loss or no loss can occur

Business risks can be classified into two broad categories: market risk and pure risk. **Market risk** is the uncertainty associated with an investment decision. An entrepreneur who invests in a new business hopes for a gain but realizes that the eventual outcome may be a loss. Only after identifying the investment opportunity, developing strategies, and committing resources will she or he find out whether the final result is a gain or a loss.

Pure risk is used to describe a situation where only loss or no loss can occur—there is no potential gain. Owning property, for instance, creates the possibility of loss due to fire or severe weather; the only outcomes are loss or no loss. As a general rule, only pure risk is insurable. That is, insurance is not intended to protect investors from market risks, where the chances of both gain and loss exist. Later in the chapter, different categories of pure risk will be described, but for now, let's focus on risk management.

RISK MANAGEMENT

2 Explain how risk management can be used in coping with business risks.

risk management
Ways of coping with risk that are designed to preserve the assets and earning power of a firm

Risk management consists of all efforts to preserve the assets and earning power of a business. Since risk management has grown out of insurance management, the two terms are often used interchangeably. However, risk management has a much broader meaning, covering both insurable and uninsurable risks and including non-insurance approaches to reducing all types of risk. Risk management involves more than trying to obtain the most insurance for each dollar spent; it is concerned with finding the best way possible to reduce the cost of handling risk. Insurance is only one of several approaches to minimizing the pure risks a firm encounters.

The Process of Risk Management

Five steps are required to implement risk management and its goal of preserving a firm's assets and earning power.[4]

Step 1: Identify risks. It is essential that a business owner be aware of the risks the firm faces. To reduce the chance of overlooking important risks, a business should adopt a systematic approach to identifying pure risks. Useful identification methods include insurance policy checklists, questionnaires, analysis of financial statements, and careful analysis of a firm's operations.

Step 2: Evaluate risks. Once the various risks have been identified, they must be evaluated in terms of the potential size of each loss and the probability that it will occur. At a minimum, risks should be classified into three groups: critical (loss could result in bankruptcy), important (loss would require investment of additional capital to continue operations), and unimportant (loss could easily be covered with current income or existing assets).

risk control
Minimizing potential losses by preventing, avoiding, or reducing risk

loss prevention
Stopping loss from happening

loss avoidance
Avoiding loss by choosing not to engage in hazardous activities

loss reduction
Lessening the frequency, severity, or unpredictability of losses

risk financing
Making funds available to cover losses that could not be eliminated by risk control

risk transfer
Buying insurance or making contractual arrangements with others in order to transfer risk

Step 3: Select methods to manage risk. The two approaches used in dealing with risk are risk control and risk financing.

Risk control is designed to minimize loss through prevention, avoidance, and/or reduction. **Loss prevention**, as its name implies, focuses on stopping loss from happening. For example, if a mail-order business finds that goods are being damaged in the delivery process, it may switch to a more secure and reliable delivery service, thus eliminating property damage and customer dissatisfaction. **Loss avoidance** is achieved by choosing not to engage in a hazardous activity. For instance, the risk of losing critical computer records can be avoided by storing backup files at a different physical location. Keeping backup disks in the desk drawer in the same office as the computer will do little good if the desk is damaged by fire or water. **Loss reduction** addresses the potential frequency, severity, or unpredictability of loss by lessening the impact of the loss on the business. Crisis planning is a form of loss reduction in that it provides a template to follow in the case of a catastrophic loss. Installing automatic sprinkler systems in a building is another good example of loss reduction. If a fire occurs in a building with an automatic sprinkler system, the sprinklers will be activated, minimizing the amount of fire damage to the building.

Risk financing, on the other hand, focuses on making funds available for losses that cannot be eliminated by risk control; it involves transferring the risk or retaining the risk. **Risk transfer** is accomplished largely through buying insurance but can also be achieved by making contractual arrangements that transfer the risk to others. Contractual arrangements, for example, can include subcontracting an activity or purchasing a fidelity bond to protect against employee fraud. **Risk retention** entails financing loss through operating revenues or retained earnings. One common form of risk retention is **self-insurance**, in which part of a firm's earnings is designated as a cushion against possible future losses. Self-insurance can take a general or a specific form. In its general form, a part of the firm's earnings is earmarked for a contingency fund against possible future losses, regardless of the source. In its specific form, a self-insurance program designates funds to individual loss categories such as property, healthcare, or workers' compensation. Some firms have begun to rely heavily on self-insurance, particularly in the area of medical coverage for employees. For several years now, the cost of health insurance has increased 10–15 percent annually—and much more in some instances. For instance, in 2002, Flat Rock Furniture, a manufacturing firm in Waldron, Indiana, paid $326,000 in health insurance premiums for the firm's 80 employees. The firm's owner, Van McQueen, was sadly surprised when the insurance company increased the firm's premiums for 2003 to $480,000—a 47 percent increase in a single year! McQueen decided to self-fund employee health benefits—and saved $325,000 on what the firm would have paid the insurance company.[5]

risk retention
Financing loss intentionally, through operating revenues or retained earnings

self-insurance
Designating part of a firm's earnings as a cushion against possible future losses

It should be understood, however, that self-insurance is not suitable for every small firm. As a rule of thumb, a firm should have a net worth of at least $250,000 and at least 25 employees to be self-funded. Moreover, very few firms can practice unlimited self-insurance, especially when it comes to liability claims. Unless a small company has insurance to cover losses above a certain level, any large loss could put it out of business. Finally, self-insurance plans need to be approved and monitored to protect the interests of those covered.

In choosing the appropriate method for managing risk, the small business owner should consider the size of each potential loss, its probability of occurrence, and what resources would be available to cover the loss if it did occur. Exhibit 21-1 shows the appropriate risk management techniques for potential losses of different probabilities (low frequency and high frequency) and loss amounts (low severity and high severity).

Step 4: Implement the decision. Once the decision has been made to use a particular technique or techniques to manage a firm's risks, this decision must be followed by action, such as purchasing insurance and/or setting aside dedicated funds to cope with any risks that have been retained. Failure to act—or even procrastination—could be a fatal error.

Step 5: Evaluate and review. Evaluation and review of the chosen risk management technique are essential because conditions change—new risks arise, and old ones disappear. Also, reviewing earlier decisions to use specific methods may identify mistakes made previously.

Risk Management and the Small Firm

Regardless of the nature of a business, risk management is a serious issue for small firms, as well as large companies. Too often in the past, small businesses paid insufficient attention to analyzing potential risk. "Small companies often spend more time planning their company picnics than for an event that could put them out of business," explains Katherine Heaviside, a partner in Epoch 5, a Huntington, New York, public relations firm that specializes in crisis communication.[6] Today, such a practice is unthinkable. The small business owner must take an active role in managing the risks of her or his firm.

Risk management in a small firm differs from that in a large firm in several ways. First, insurance companies are not always eager to insure small firms and may even turn them down in some cases. Also, in a large firm, the responsibilities of risk management are frequently assigned to a specialized staff manager. It is more difficult for a small company to cope with risk management since its risk manager is usually the owner and the owner wears so many hats. Furthermore, risk management is not something that requires immediate attention—until something happens. Although small businesses have been slow to focus on managing risk, a prudent small business owner will take the time to identify the different types of risks faced by the firm and find ways to cope with them.

EXHIBIT 21-1 *Tools for Managing Risk*

	High Frequency	Low Frequency
High Severity	• Loss prevention • Loss avoidance • Loss reduction	• Self-insurance • Contractual agreements
Low Severity	• Loss reduction • Risk retention	• Risk retention

Note: To find a listing of the risk management tools appropriate for dealing with a potential loss, see the box corresponding to the severity and frequency of the potential loss.

CLASSIFYING BUSINESS RISKS

3 *Describe the different types of business risk.*

The pure risks that face any business can be put into the following categories: property risks, liability risks, and personnel risks. Let's take a look at these risks, related to the physical, legal, and human aspects of a business.

Property Risks

In the course of establishing a business, an owner acquires property that will be necessary to provide the goods and services of the business. If this property is damaged or destroyed, the business sustains a loss. In addition, the temporary loss of use of the property can add to the negative financial impact on the business. Several characteristics of business property and the risks associated with it are worthy of attention.

real property
Land and anything physically attached to the land, such as buildings

personal property
Any property other than real property, including machinery, equipment, furniture, fixtures, stock, and vehicles

replacement value of property
The cost to replace or replicate property at today's prices

actual cash value (ACV)
An insurance term that refers to the depreciated value of a property

There are two general types of property—real property and personal property. **Real property** consists of land and anything physically attached to land, such as buildings. Some business owners purchase land and buildings, while others choose to lease needed real property. It is interesting to note, however, that some leases make the lessee responsible for any damage or loss to the leased premise. **Personal property** can simply be defined as any property other than real property. Personal property includes such items as machinery, equipment, furniture, fixtures, stock, and vehicles. While the location of real property is static, personal property can be moved from place to place.

Property can be valued in a number of ways. The **replacement value of property** is the cost to replace or replicate the property at today's prices. For example, a building that was constructed 10 years ago at a cost of $200,000 may have a current replacement value of $250,000 because of the rising costs of materials and labor. The term **actual cash value (ACV)** is an insurance term that refers to the depreciated value of a property. Assuming a rate of depreciation of 3 percent per year for the 10-year-old building in the previous example, we would find the building to have an estimated actual cash value of $175,000 [that is, $250,000 − (0.03 × 10 × $250,000)]. Traditionally, commercial property insurance has valued all property loss at the actual cash value of the damaged or lost property.

peril
A cause of loss, either through natural events or through the acts of people

PERILS A **peril** is defined as a cause of loss. Some perils are naturally occurring events, such as windstorms, floods, earthquakes, and lightning. The location of property may increase the likelihood of its loss from certain perils—for example, coastal properties are more susceptible to wind damage and flooding, and properties near fault lines are more prone to damage from earthquakes.

Not all perils, however, are natural events; some are related to the actions of people. Perils such as robbery and employee dishonesty involve criminal acts performed by people against business owners. The advent of electronic commerce (e-commerce) has led to new forms of dishonest acts, such as hacking, denial of access, and improper use of confidential information.

direct loss
A loss in which physical damage to property reduces its value to the property owner

LOSSES Usually, when you think of property loss, you envision a **direct loss**, in which physical damage to property reduces its value to the property owner. The direct loss of property as a result of windstorm, fire, or explosion is obvious to everyone and has the potential to significantly hamper any business.

A less obvious type of property loss is an **indirect loss**, which arises from inability to carry on normal operations due to a direct loss. For example, if a delivery truck is damaged in an accident, the resulting loss of use can impair the ability of a business to get its goods to customers. The indirect loss component of this event may cause a reduction in revenue or an increase in expense (from outsourcing the delivery function), either of which will have an adverse impact on business income.

indirect loss
A loss arising from inability to carry on normal operations due to a direct loss to property

It should be pointed out that business income can also be reduced by events or conditions that are not related to direct losses. For example, a strike by UPS employees a few years ago created serious logistical problems for many of its business customers, which were unable to receive goods from suppliers or deliver goods to customers. The financial impact of such a labor action may be just as real to a business as physical damage to property, but the insurance protection available for indirect losses applies only when *direct* damage events trigger the loss of use. More will be said on this issue later in the chapter.

Liability Risks

A growing business risk today is the legal liability that may arise from various business activities. A society creates laws to govern interactions among its members. Individual rights and freedoms are protected by these laws. If a business or any of its agents violates these protected rights, the business can be held accountable for any resulting loss or damage to the affected party. Legal liability may arise from statutory liability, contractual liability, or tort liability.

STATUTORY LIABILITY Some laws impose a statutory obligation on a business. For example, each state has enacted **workers' compensation legislation** that creates an absolute liability on the employer to provide certain benefits to employees when they are injured in a work-related event. This means that fault is not an issue; an employer is responsible for work-related injuries without regard to fault. While the benefits differ slightly from state to state, most workers' compensation statutes require employers to provide the

workers' compensation legislation
Laws that obligate the employer to pay employees for injury or illness related to employment, regardless of fault

Living the Dream *Entrepreneurial Challenges*

A Quick Reaction to a Catastrophic Event

Lonnie Lehrer thought he was prepared for anything. The CEO of Leros Point to Point, a New York City limousine service, had redundant computer systems for his dispatch software, a battery backup for each computer, off-site copies of his customer data, even a spare generator. If New York were nailed by a bad winter storm or another big blackout, Leros would still be in business.

© John Lawrence/Getty Images

Then the first plane hit the World Trade Center on September 11, 2001, and all Lehrer's plans went down with it. "Ninety percent of our business is tied to the airports," says Lehrer, 55. "We went from being a $7 million company to a $700,000 company overnight."

Lehrer knew if he didn't move fast, he'd be out of business in a week. Within two days, he'd slashed his own salary by 50 percent, negotiated a moratorium on loan payments with Ford Motor Co., and told his drivers they'd be facing a few lean months of partial salaries until business picked up. He also had to drop drivers who were independent contractors, lay off two staffers, and reassign others temporarily.

But Lehrer's quick reaction paid off. Business slowly returned and is now better than ever. Leros Point to Point acquired two smaller companies and expanded operations, bringing annual revenues to nearly $9 million in 2002.

Another reason for Leros's rebound: "Some of our competition disappeared after 9/11," Lehrer said. "The ones who were already on shaky ground just faded away." The fact that Leros had any disaster plan at all puts it ahead of most companies.

Source: Daniel Tynan, "In Case of Emergency," *Entrepreneur*, April 2003, pp. 59–60.

following benefits to employees injured at work: coverage of medical expenses, compensation for lost wages, payment of rehabilitation expenses, and death benefits for employees' families.

This statutory liability is potentially significant for any business. The attacks on the World Trade Center provided a stark example of the magnitude of this liability, especially for employers with a large concentration of employees. Marsh, Inc., the leading insurance broker in the world, lost over 300 employees in the 9/11 disaster, creating an enormous financial obligation on the part of the employer to the families of the victims. Most businesses protect themselves from this financial loss through the purchase of workers' compensation insurance. Some large employers choose to self-insure, although most purchase extra insurance protection to guard against catastrophic events such as the 9/11 tragedy.

CONTRACTUAL LIABILITY Businesses often enter into contracts with other parties. These contracts could involve a lease of premises, a sales contract with a customer, or an agreement with an outsourcing firm. Nobody enjoys reading pages of contracts, but it is important to closely examine all contracts to determine the risks assumed. For example, some lease agreements require the lessee to be responsible for any loss or damage to the leased premises. This usually requires the lessee to purchase some form of property insurance or lessee liability coverage to deal with this loss potential.

Insurance agents and brokers can be helpful in assessing the risk presented by contractual agreements. Be sure to include all contracts in the initial risk assessment process.

torts
Wrongful acts or omissions for which an injured party can take legal action against the wrongdoer for monetary damages

TORT LIABILITY Civil wrongs include breach of contract and torts. **Torts** are wrongful acts or omissions for which an injured party can take legal action against the wrongdoer for monetary damages. Tort actions commonly include an allegation of negligence. Four elements must be present for someone to be found guilty of a negligent act.

First, there must exist a legal duty between the parties. For example, a restaurant owner has a legal duty to provide patrons with food and drink that are fit for consumption. Likewise, an employee making a delivery for an employer has a duty to operate a vehicle safely on public roads.

reasonable (prudent person) standard
The typical standard of care, based on what a reasonable or prudent person would have done under similar circumstances

The second element is the failure to provide the appropriate standard of care. The standard of care normally used is the **reasonable (prudent person) standard**, based on what a reasonable or prudent person would have done under similar circumstances. This standard of care may be elevated, however, if a "professional" is involved. In professional liability actions, the standard of care is determined by the established standards of the profession. For example, a negligence action against a CPA would use the standards of the accounting profession as the benchmark. Expert witnesses are often used to help establish the standard and what clients can reasonably expect.

The third element in establishing negligence is the presence of injury or damages. Negligence may exist, but if no injury or damage is sustained by the claimant, tort liability does not exist. Two types of damages may be awarded in a tort action:

compensatory damages
Economic or noneconomic damages intended to make the claimant whole, by indemnifying the claimant for any injuries or damage arising from the negligent action

economic damages
Compensatory damages that relate to economic loss, such as medical expense, loss of income, or the cost of property replacement/restoration

noneconomic damages
Compensatory damages for such losses as pain and suffering, mental anguish, and loss of consortium

punitive damages
A form of punishment that goes beyond compensatory damages, intending to punish wrongdoers for gross negligence or a callous disregard for the interests of others and to have a deterrent effect

- *Compensatory Damages.* **Compensatory damages** are intended to make the claimant whole—that is, to indemnify the claimant for any injuries or damage arising from the negligent action. Compensatory damages can be economic or noneconomic in nature. **Economic damages** relate to economic loss, such as medical expenses, loss of income, or the cost of property replacement/restoration. Economic damages are relatively easy to quantify. **Noneconomic damages** include such losses as pain and suffering, mental anguish, and loss of consortium. In comparison to economic damages, noneconomic damages are difficult to express in financial terms. Civil courts usually have a hard time setting these awards, and many of today's substantial awards include a large amount of noneconomic damages.
- *Punitive Damages.* **Punitive damages** are a form of punishment that goes beyond any compensatory damages. Punitive damages have a dual purpose. First, they punish wrongdoers in instances where there is gross negligence or a callous disregard for the interests of others. Second, punitive damages are intended to have a deterrent effect, sending a message to society that such conduct will not be tolerated.

The final element in a successful tort liability claim is demonstrating that the negligent act is the **proximate cause** of the loss—that is, there is a causal link between the negligence and the damages sustained. There may be negligence and there may be damages, but if no link can be established between the two, there is no tort liability.

proximate cause
In the area of tort liability, a negligent act with a causal link to the damages sustained

Tort liability can arise from a number of business activities. Some of the more significant sources of tort liability follow.

- *Premises Liability*. People can sustain injuries while on a business's premises. Retailers have significant premises liability exposure, with many customers entering stores to purchase goods. Some other businesses, however, have little in the way of premises liability. A consulting firm or a Web-design business would not typically have clients visit its business location; therefore, its premises liability exposure would be minimal.
- *Professional Liability*. Any business providing professional services to the public is potentially subject to professional liability claims. Recognizing this exposure is important, since separate liability insurance is necessary to properly protect a business from professional liability claims.
- *Employee Liability*. As mentioned previously, employers have a statutory obligation to pay certain benefits to employees injured in the course of employment. Negligence on the part of the employer is not an issue; this is a statutory obligation of the employer to its employees.
- *Vehicular Liability*. If a business uses vehicles for various purposes, the business has vehicular liability exposure. Even a business that does not own or lease vehicles has potential liability if employees use their own personal vehicles for business purposes.
- *Product Liability*. The products or services provided by a business can be a source of legal liability. In addition, any directions or advice given by the business regarding the utilization of products can become a source of liability as well. For example, if a retailer assembles a product for a customer, any mistakes made in the assembly process could result in a tort claim against the seller.
- *Directors and Officers Liability*. An increasing concern among businesses today is the threat of suits against the directors and officers of an organization. This exposure is greatest for publicly held firms, but it exists also for private firms and nonprofit organizations. For example, a business owner who accepts membership on the board of a YMCA or other nonprofit organization may possibly be sued by someone who has a claim against that organization.

Personnel Risks

Personnel risks are risks that directly affect individual employees, but may have an indirect impact on a business as well. The primary risks in this category include premature death, poor health, and insufficient retirement income.

personnel risks
Risks that directly affect individual employees, but may have an indirect impact on a business as well

PREMATURE DEATH The risk associated with death is not if but when. We all expect to die; however, there is a risk that we may die early in life. This risk poses a potential financial problem for both the family of the person and his or her employer. Individuals deal with this risk by maintaining a healthy lifestyle and purchasing life insurance to protect family members who rely on their income.

Employers can be quite adversely impacted by the untimely death of an employee if that employee cannot be easily replaced. And what if a partner or owner of the business dies? Normally, such an event triggers a buyout of the interest of the deceased owner. Life insurance is often used to fund these buyout provisions. A more lengthy discussion of this issue is beyond the scope of this book, but it is an important consideration in preserving the continuity of a successful business venture.

POOR HEALTH A more likely occurrence than death of an employee is poor health. The severity of poor health varies, ranging from a mild disorder to a more serious, disabling malady. And as with premature death, the consequences of this event may affect an employer as well as family members.

The financial consequences of poor health have two dimensions. First are medical expenses, which can range from the cost of a doctor's visit to catastrophic expenses related to needed surgeries and hospitalization. Second are consequences of the inability to work. Disability most often is a temporary condition, but it can be lengthy or permanent. A worker's permanent disability can have the same financial impact on her or his family as death.

Employers often provide some form of health insurance as a benefit of employment. In some instances, the cost of health insurance is shared by the employer and the employee; in most instances, however, the bulk of the cost is absorbed by the employer. In addition to the health insurance costs, the fact that the employer is without the services of the employee for some time period may add to the adverse financial impact on the business.

INSUFFICIENT RETIREMENT INCOME The final category of personnel risk involves the possibility of outliving one's wealth. The goal here is to defer income and accumulate sufficient wealth to provide a satisfactory level of income during the nonworking years.

There are three primary sources of retirement income. Social Security provides a retirement income benefit, although for most retirees this benefit is not sufficient to meet expected consumption during retirement. To supplement this income, most workers have a retirement program associated with their employment. In the past, these programs were primarily funded by employers as a form of deferred compensation. While employer-focused pension plans still exist, it is more common today to encounter an employee-focused retirement plan, where the employee can elect to defer current income for retirement. Usually, these plans are partially funded by employers as an incentive for employees to participate. Finally, individual saving can be utilized to accumulate wealth for retirement. All of these sources should be carefully considered in the retirement income planning process.

INSURANCE FOR THE SMALL BUSINESS

Insurance provides one of the most important means for small firms to transfer business risks. The cost and availability of insurance are primary concerns of owners of small firms. In a survey conducted by the National Federation of Independent Business, 28 percent of the companies responding cited insurance as their largest problem, far exceeding any other issue.[7] This concern is on the minds of most—if not all—small company owners.

In the past, purchasing business insurance was a matter of filling out an application and sending in a check for the first month's premium. Today, insurance of many kinds is harder to find, is less affordable, and offers less protection than at any time in recent years. As a result, entrepreneurs are shopping around, changing insurance companies more often, negotiating harder, and, in some cases, changing their operations or even reducing or eliminating their insurance coverage.[8] Based on a recent survey, the National Federation of Independent Business concluded:

> *Insurance has become a serious small-business concern over the last several years. Its cost has risen inexorably. Though premium increases have been associated most often with employee health and product and professional liability insurance, complaints have been registered about other lines of insurance as well. The complaints have recently become louder and more frequent. In addition, the complaints have not been confined to premium increases. They have moved to availability, exclusions, fits, and even claims.*[9]

The difficulties being experienced by small business owners with respect to insurance are evident in the following statistics:[10]

- Fifteen percent of small businesses do not even purchase business insurance to protect their enterprises; and more than 17 percent have reduced coverage.
- Thirty percent have increased their deductibles.
- Eighteen percent of small businesses have changed their operations to reduce the risk of incurring a claim.
- Thirty-five percent of firms with 3 to 199 employees offer no health benefits to employees.

Living the Dream

Entrepreneurial Challenges

Working Without Coverage

Patricia Daughrity has had to forgo health insurance—for her company and her family. As the owner of the wholesale bakery Farm & Garden Foods in Ripley, New York, Daughrity, 32, saw her HMO premiums double in two years, to $600 a month per employee. She had already chosen the highest deductible ($1,000), switched plans, and shopped around, but still couldn't come up with an affordable alternative. So, in 2002, she canceled her health insurance plan—for herself, her family, and her business.

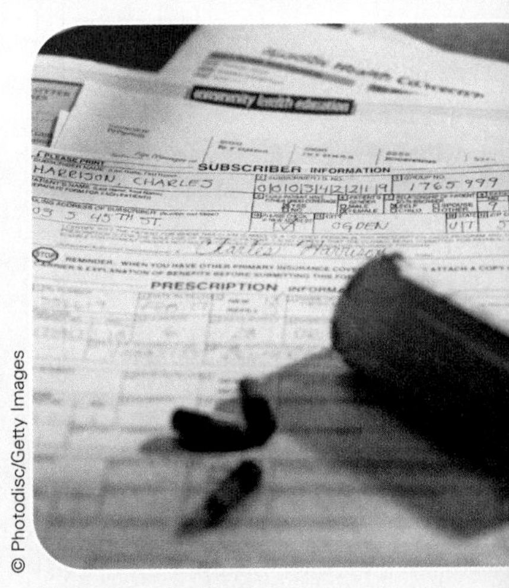
© Photodisc/Getty Images

Daughrity, along with her husband and 4-year-old daughter, is feeling the loss. She's expecting a baby this year and is paying all of the medical costs out of her own pocket. "We're budgeting $20,000. We just hope we're way over the mark," she says. "With the monthly premiums and co-pays and other expenses, I don't see what the allure is for insurance. We're learning to live without it." (She recently checked prices; her old insurer now charges $900 a month. What's more, the insurance company considered her pregnancy a preexisting condition and so wouldn't cover the bills.)

But she didn't want to leave her employees with nothing. She gives her four employees medical discount cards, bought through a small business advocacy group. The cards can be used to help pay for prescriptions and chiropractic, dental, and optometric bills. Her cost is $200 a year, plus $140 per card. "It's not insurance," she says, "but it is something."

Source: Lisa Kalis, "Working Without a Net," *Fortune Small Business*, May 2004, p. 46.

But, despite the problems, a sound insurance program is imperative for the proper protection of a small business. Small business owners are learning that, in order to keep insurance costs down, they must take an active role and become their own risk managers. (See Exhibit 21-2.) They can no longer afford to sit back and wait for suggestions from insurance agents. Instead, they need to formulate and offer their own ideas, based on an understanding of the basic principles of a sound insurance program.

Basic Principles of a Sound Insurance Program

4 *Explain the basic principles used in evaluating an insurance program.*

What kinds of risks can be covered by insurance? What types of coverage should be purchased? How much coverage is adequate? Unfortunately, there are no clear-cut answers to these questions. A reputable insurance agent can provide valuable assistance to a small firm in evaluating risks and designing proper protection plans, but an entrepreneur should become as knowledgeable as possible about what insurance is available. Basic principles in evaluating an insurance program include identifying business risks to be insured, limiting coverage to major potential losses, and relating premium costs to probability of loss.

IDENTIFYING INSURABLE BUSINESS RISKS Although the most common insurable risks were pointed out earlier, other less obvious risks may be revealed only by careful investigation. A small firm must first obtain risk coverages required by law or by contract, such as workers' compensation insurance and automobile liability insurance. As part of the risk-identification process, plant and equipment should be reevaluated periodically by competent appraisers in order to ensure that adequate insurance coverage is maintained.

LIMITING COVERAGE TO MAJOR POTENTIAL LOSSES A small firm must determine the magnitude of loss that it could bear without serious financial difficulty. If the firm is sufficiently strong, it may decide to avoid purchasing unnecessary insurance by covering only those losses exceeding a specified minimum amount. It is important, of course, to guard against underestimating the severity of potential losses.

RELATING PREMIUM COSTS TO PROBABILITY OF LOSS Because insurance companies must collect enough premiums to pay the actual losses of insured parties, the cost of insurance is proportional to the probability of occurrence of the insured event. As the loss becomes more certain, premium costs become so high that a firm may find that insurance

EXHIBIT 21-2 *Risk-Taking Begins Early*

"WE'RE STARTING FIRST-AID TRAINING, DAD. I NEED $150,000 FOR MALPRACTICE INSURANCE."
SCHWADRON

Source: © Harley L. Schwadron

is simply not worth the cost. Thus, insurance is most applicable and practical for *improbable* losses—that is, situations where the probability that the loss will occur is low, but the overall cost of the loss would be high. Larry Joiner, owner of West Coast Roofing and Waterproofing Company in Naples, Florida, reduced his insurance coverage by raising damage deductibles on his building and cutting back on vehicle-damage insurance. Because his roofing company could be swept away by a hurricane coming off the Gulf of Mexico, Joiner modified his coverage to use premium dollars where losses were likely to be most costly. "You've got to be alert," says Joiner, "and you've got to care about these insurance details yourself."[11]

5 *Identify the different types of business insurance coverage.*

Common Types of Business Insurance

It is beyond the scope of this chapter to describe all forms of business insurance. But we'll look at a few common types: business owner's policies, key-person insurance, and disability insurance.

BUSINESS OWNER'S POLICIES Some business insurance policies are generic contracts that contain numerous options to fit the coverage needs of individual insurance buyers. These types of policies could conceivably address the needs of a wide range of potential buyers, from small commercial enterprises to large and complex business organizations.

An alternative approach to insurance policy design is to create a policy appropriate for a certain class of insured. For example, a homeowner's policy is designed to meet the property and liability insurance needs of individuals who own their residences. A version of homeowner's insurance has been adapted to meet the needs of those individuals who live in leased houses or apartments.

business owner's policy (BOP)
A business version of a homeowner's policy, designed to meet the property and liability insurance needs of small business owners

The **business owner's policy (BOP)** is a business version of the homeowner's policy, designed to meet the property and liability insurance needs of small business owners. Fortunately, the eligibility criterion for a BOP is fairly broad, with the only excluded classes being manufacturers, financial institutions, and auto repair facilities. A BOP is intended to be a comprehensive contract that needs few enhancements. A brief description of the coverage provided by a BOP follows.

Property Covered. A BOP can be used to cover both real property and personal property. For businesses that own buildings or other structures or are required to be responsible for property damage to non-owned real property, real property coverage can be provided. Businesses that do not have the responsibility for real property damage can elect to insure personal property only, including furniture and fixtures, equipment, stock, and supplies.

Perils Covered. Insurers use two approaches to define the perils covered by property insurance. With the **named-peril approach**, the specific perils covered are identified. Any loss caused by a peril not named in the policy is not covered. In contrast, with the **all-risk approach**, all direct damages to property are covered except those caused by perils specifically excluded. In other words, if a particular peril is not excluded in an all-risk policy, any loss caused by that peril is covered.

BOPs offer both named-peril and all-risk options; the choice is up to the insured. The named-peril option covers damage done by fire, lightning, explosion, windstorm and hail, smoke, aircraft and vehicles, riot and civil commotion, vandalism, sprinkler leakage, sinkhole collapse, and volcanic action, as well as certain transportation perils. The all-risk option covers all direct physical damage and loss, except that caused by such perils as earth movement, flood, war, nuclear explosions, and intentional damage caused by the insured. The all-risk option is generally preferable for the insured, but the benefit of an enhanced scope of coverage must be evaluated in terms of the additional cost.

named-peril approach
An approach to defining the perils covered in an insurance policy by identifying the specific perils covered

all-risk approach
An approach to defining the perils covered in an insurance policy by stating that all direct damages to property are covered except those caused by perils specifically excluded

Valuation. A unique, attractive feature of a BOP is that both real and personal property are valued on a replacement-cost basis. This means that all property damage and loss will be reimbursed at the rate required to rebuild or replace the property. For example, if the roof of a building is damaged, the cost of repairing the damage will be covered. Likewise, damage and loss to equipment will be evaluated based on the cost of repairing or replacing the equipment.

Insurance to Value. Most property insurance policies contain a provision called **insurance to value**, which requires the insured to carry a minimum policy limit relative to the actual value of the property. A BOP is unique in that it contains no insurance to value feature, but the prevalence of insurance to value in property insurance policies requires that we include it in our discussion. The most common version of this feature is a **coinsurance provision** that requires the property be insured for at least 80 percent of its value. If that minimum is not carried, a penalty is applied to any covered loss. For example, if an insured building had a replacement value of \$500,000, the 80 percent policy limit would require that the property be insured for at least \$400,000 (\$500,000 × 0.80). If the building was insured for only \$300,000 and an insured loss of \$100,000 occurred, the recovery would be limited to \$75,000, calculated as follows:

insurance to value
A common provision in property insurance policies that requires the insured to carry a minimum policy limit relative to the actual value of the property

coinsurance provision
The most common version of the insurance to value feature, requiring that property be insured for at least 80 percent of its value or a penalty will be applied to any covered loss

$$\begin{aligned}\text{Coinsurance provision} &= \frac{\text{Insured value}}{\text{Policy limit \%} \times \text{Replacement value}} \times \text{Property loss}\\ &= \frac{\$300{,}000}{0.80 \times \$500{,}000} \times \$100{,}000\\ &= 0.75 \times \$100{,}000\\ &= \$75{,}000\end{aligned}$$

Thus, insuring for less than the actual property value can be expensive, costing much more than what an entrepreneur might save in premiums. "A far better approach," explains Jerry Milton, an insurance industry consultant, "is to insure for full value with a larger deductible." Milton advises a business owner to increase coverage if the property value increases for any reason."[12]

Business Interruption. As mentioned previously, the financial loss associated with a property loss is not limited to direct damage to the property. There may be an indirect loss as well, usually associated with the loss of use of the affected property. **Business interruption coverage** provides a business with reimbursement for the loss of anticipated income plus continuing expenses that cannot be met because of the negative impact on

business interruption coverage
Coverage that reimburses a business for the loss of anticipated income plus continuing expenses that cannot be met because of the negative impact of a direct loss on business revenues

business revenues. Recognizing the potential impact of an indirect loss is particularly important for small businesses, as they may not be able to survive financially without business interruption insurance protection.

Business interruption coverage is an integral part of a BOP. Two limits are applicable to this coverage. First, the time period is limited to 12 months. This is generally not a problem, since most small businesses can be fully restarted within that period, even after sustaining substantial direct damage. Second, the dollar limit for business interruption losses is a shared limit with direct damage coverage. Thus, when setting property damage limits in a BOP, the insured must consider the potential loss due to both direct damage and business interruption.

commercial general liability (CGL) coverage
Coverage providing payment for bodily injury and property damage for which the insured business is liable

General Liability Coverage. A BOP integrates business property coverage with the liability coverage needed by most small businesses. It contains **commercial general liability (CGL) coverage**, which provides payment for bodily injury and property damage for which the insured business is liable. The CGL coverage takes care of premises liability exposure, product liability exposure, and other potential liabilities of the business. It does not cover vehicle liability, professional liability, or employee liability, which all require a separate policy for adequate protection.

medical payments coverage
Coverage providing payment for injuries sustained by customers and the general public, with no fault required on the part of the insured

Medical Payments Coverage. BOP **medical payments coverage** provides payment for injuries sustained by customers and the general public. The unique feature of medical payments coverage is that it does not require any fault on the part of the insured. This "no fault" coverage pays the medical expenses of others up to a per-person limit described in the policy.

LIFE AND DISABILITY INSURANCE Two types of insurance provide coverage for key individuals within a business: key-person insurance and disability insurance.

key-person insurance
Coverage that provides benefits upon the death of a firm's key personnel

KEY-PERSON INSURANCE By carrying **key-person insurance**, a small business can protect itself against the death of key personnel. Such insurance may be written on an individual or group basis. It is purchased by a firm, with the firm as the sole beneficiary.

Most small business advisors suggest term insurance for key-person insurance policies, primarily because of lower premiums. How much key-person insurance to buy is more difficult to decide. Face values of such policies usually begin around $50,000 and may go as high as several million dollars.

DISABILITY INSURANCE One risk that small businesses do not normally consider is loss due to disability of a partner or other key employee of the company. Statistics, however, show that there is a 75 percent chance that one of two partners in their mid-30s will become disabled for at least three months before age 65. Although the risk of disability is much greater than the risk of death, partnerships are much more likely to purchase life insurance than disability insurance. In fact, 98 percent of partnerships and closely held corporations have a life insurance buyout agreement, but only 17 percent have disability insurance on partners or other key employees.[13]

disability insurance
Coverage that provides benefits upon the disability of a firm's partner or other key employee

The most common type of **disability insurance** provides for the payment of a portion (typically two-thirds) of the disabled person's normal monthly income for a period of time after the disability occurs. However, it protects only the disabled person and not the business. Alternatively, partners can purchase disability buyout insurance. This type of disability insurance protects both partners by guaranteeing that the healthy partner will have enough cash for a buyout of the disabled partner without draining capital from the business.

Another option is key-person disability insurance, which replaces revenue lost because of the disability of a key employee. For example, if a firm's top salesperson, who brings in $5,000 a month, becomes disabled, this coverage will provide up to 125 percent replacement income for a year or more to give the firm time to recruit and train someone else.

Another type of disability insurance is designed to cover fixed overhead expenses, such as rent, utilities, employee salaries, and general office expenses, while an owner or other key employee recuperates. This type of insurance is especially well suited for a sole proprietorship, since the firm would have no income if the owner were unable to work.

Looking Back

1 Define risk and explain the nature of risk.

- Risk is a condition in which there is a possibility of an adverse deviation from a desired outcome.
- Business risks can be classified into two broad categories: market risk and pure risk.
- Market risk is the uncertainty associated with an investment decision.
- Pure risk exists in a situation where only loss or no loss can occur—there is no potential gain.
- In general, only pure risk is insurable.

2 Explain how risk management can be used in coping with business risks.

- Risk management is concerned with protection of the assets and the earning power of a business against loss.
- Risk management involves identifying and evaluating the severity of risks, selecting methods for managing risk, implementing the decision, and evaluating and reviewing prior decisions.
- The two ways to manage business risks are risk control and risk financing. Risk control is designed to prevent, avoid, or reduce risk, while risk financing involves transferring the risk to someone else or retaining the risk within the firm.

3 Describe the different types of business risk.

- Pure risks that face any business fall into three groups: property risks, liability risks, and personnel risks.
- Property risks involve potential damage to or loss of real property (e.g., land and buildings) and personal property (e.g., equipment).
- For insurance purposes, property may be valued based on its replacement value or its actual cash value (ACV).
- A peril is defined as a cause of loss, either from naturally occurring events or from the actions of people.
- Property losses are categorized as direct losses, arising from obvious physical damage, or indirect losses, which result from inability to carry on normal operations because of a direct loss to property.
- Liability risks arise from statutory liabilities, contractual liabilities, or tort liabilities.
- Personnel risks, such as premature death, poor health, and insufficient retirement income, directly affect individuals, but may indirectly impact the business as well.

4 Explain the basic principles used in evaluating an insurance program.

- Basic principles of a sound insurance program include (1) identifying the business risks to be insured, (2) limiting coverage to major potential losses, and (3) relating the cost of premiums to the probability of loss.
- A firm must first secure risk coverage required by law or by contract.
- Property should be revalued periodically to be certain that adequate insurance is being maintained.
- A company should determine the magnitude of loss it can sustain without serious financial difficulty.
- The cost of insurance is proportional to the probability of occurrence of the insured event.

5 Identify the different types of business insurance coverage.

- A business owner's policy (BOP) is a business version of a homeowner's policy, designed to meet the property and liability insurance needs of small business owners.
- A BOP can cover both real property and personal property; offers named-peril and all-risk options; values property on a replacement-cost basis; and includes business interruption coverage, commercial general liability (CGL) coverage, and medical payments coverage.
- Insurers use two approaches to define the perils covered by property insurance: with the named-peril approach, the specific perils covered are identified; with the all-risk approach, all direct damages to property are covered except those caused by perils specifically excluded.
- Most property insurance policies contain an insurance to value provision that requires the insured to carry a minimum policy limit relative to the actual value of the property. The most common version of this feature is a coinsurance provision that requires the property be insured for at least 80 percent of its value.
- Two types of insurance provide coverage for key individuals within a business: key-person insurance and disability insurance.

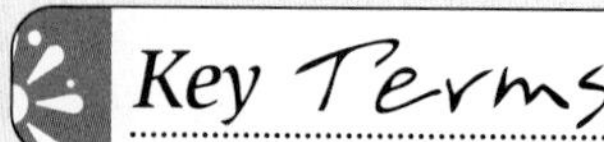

Key Terms

risk, p. 464
market risk, p. 464
pure risk, p. 464
risk management, p. 464
risk control, p. 464
loss prevention, p. 464
loss avoidance, p. 464
loss reduction, p. 464
risk financing, p. 464
risk transfer, p. 464
risk retention, p. 465
self-insurance, p. 465
real property, p. 466
personal property, p. 466
replacement value of property, p. 466
actual cash value (ACV), p. 466
peril, p. 466
direct loss, p. 466
indirect loss, p. 467
workers' compensation legislation, p. 467
torts, p. 468
reasonable (prudent person) standard, p. 468
compensatory damages, p. 468
economic damages, p. 468
noneconomic damages, p. 468
punitive damages, p. 468
proximate cause, p. 469
personnel risks, p. 469
business owner's policy (BOP), p. 472
named-peril approach, p. 473
all-risk approach, p. 473
insurance to value, p. 473
coinsurance provision, p. 473
business interruption coverage, p. 473
commercial general liability (CGL) coverage, p. 474
medical payments coverage, p. 474
key-person insurance, p. 474
disability insurance, p. 474

Discussion Questions

1. Define risk and then distinguish between pure risk and market risk.
2. What are the different types of risk that a business may encounter? What are the basic ways to manage risk in a business?
3. Describe the different sources of legal liability.
4. If you were shopping in a small retail store and somehow sustained an injury such as a broken arm, under what circumstances would you sue the store? Explain.
5. Can a small firm ever safely assume that business risks will never turn into losses sufficient to bankrupt it? Why or why not?
6. When is it logical for a small business to utilize self-insurance?
7. Why might a small business owner decide not to purchase business insurance?
8. Under what conditions would purchasing life insurance on a business executive constitute little protection for a business? When is such life insurance helpful?
9. Describe a business owner's policy. List the advantages of this type of policy, and tell what types of insurance coverage are available with a BOP.
10. What is the purpose of a coinsurance provision and how does it work?

You Make the Call

SITUATION 1

The Amigo Company manufactures motorized wheelchairs in its Bridgeport, Michigan, plant, under the supervision of Alden Thieme. Alden is the brother of the firm's founder, Allen Thieme. The company has 100 employees and does $10 million in sales a year. Like many other firms, Amigo is faced with increased liability insurance costs. Although Alden is contemplating dropping all coverage, he realizes that the users of the firm's product are individuals who have already suffered physical and emotional pain. Therefore, if an accident occurred and resulted in a liability suit, a jury might be strongly tempted to favor the plaintiff. In fact, the company is currently facing litigation. A woman in an Amigo wheelchair was killed by a car on the street. Because the driver of the car had no insurance, Amigo was sued.

Question 1 Do you agree that the type of customer to whom the Amigo Company sells should influence its decision regarding insurance?

Question 2 In what way, if any, should the outcome of the current litigation affect Amigo's decision about renewing its insurance coverage?

Question 3 What options does Amigo have if it drops all insurance coverage? What is your recommendation?

SITUATION 2

Pansy Ellen Essman is a 42-year-old grandmother who is chairperson of a company that does $5 million in sales each year. Her company, Pansy Ellen Products, Inc., based in Atlanta, Georgia, grew out of a product idea that Essman had as she was bathing her squealing, squirming granddaughter in the bathroom tub. Her idea was to produce a sponge pillow that would cradle a child in the tub, thus freeing the caretaker's hands to clean the baby. From this initial product, the company expanded its product line to include nursery lamps, baby food organizers, strollers, and hook-on baby seats. Essman has seemingly managed her product mix risk well. However, she is concerned that other sources of business risk may have been ignored or slighted.

Question 1 What types of business risk do you think Essman might have overlooked? Be specific.

Question 2 Would a risk-retention insurance program be a good possibility for this company? Why or why not?

Question 3 What kinds of insurance coverage should this type of company carry?

SITUATION 3

H. Abbe International, owned by Herb Abbe, is a travel agency and freight forwarder located in downtown Minneapolis. When the building that housed the firm's offices suffered damage as a result of arson, the firm was forced to relocate its 2 computers and 11 employees. Moving into the offices of a client, Abbe worked from this temporary location for a month before returning to his regular offices. The disruption cost him about $70,000 in lost business and moving expenses. In addition, he had to lay off four employees.

Question 1 What are the major types of risk faced by a firm such as H. Abbe International? What kind of insurance will cover these risks?

Question 2 What kind of insurance would have helped Abbe cope with the loss resulting from arson? In purchasing this kind of insurance, what questions must be answered about the amount and terms?

Question 3 Would you have recommended that Abbe purchase insurance that would have covered the losses in this case?

Experiential Exercises

1. Log on to InfoTrac College Edition at http://www.infotrac-college.com to find articles on new small business startups. Select one new firm that is marketing a product and another that is selling a service. Compare their situations relative to business risks. Report on your analysis to the class.
2. Contact a local small business owner and obtain his or her permission to conduct a risk analysis of the business. Report to the class on the business's situation in regard to risk and what preventive or protective actions you would suggest.
3. Arrange to interview the owner or one of the agents of a local insurance company. Determine in the interview the various types of coverage the company offers for small businesses. Write a report on your findings.

Exploring the Web

Go to the Small Business Administration's Web site at **http://www.sba.gov**. Click on "Library," then "E-books and Publications." Read the "Small Business Risk Management Guide" (MP-28).

1. What are the major categories of loss that a business owner must address to be sure that she or he has adequate insurance coverage for the business?
2. What employee benefits are required by law? What optional benefits might you provide to employees to attract the most qualified individuals?
3. List the ways you can limit your exposure to loss. Explain at least two of these methods.
4. What services do insurance companies provide to policyholders?
5. Print and complete "Appendix A: Checklist for Insurance Needs." If you don't already have a business of your own, base your answers on a business you hope to start.

Case 21

FOX MANUFACTURING INC. (P. 565)

This case reviews the events and the owner's actions following the loss of a firm's manufacturing plant from a fire.

Part Six

UNDERSTANDING THE NUMBERS

CHAPTERS

MANAGING ASSETS

In the Spotlight

Home and Garden Party, Ltd.

Home and Garden Party, Ltd., is a home-based party planning business featuring home decor items such as hand-turned stoneware pottery, framed prints, and brass accessories. The firm was started by Steve and Penny Carlile in 1996. Their story is very similar to those told by other entrepreneurs about the potential opportunity and the risk resulting from unexpected growth in the early years. Penny Carlile describes the firm's first three years in these words:

> *Our first year in business was very slow. We held events in several cities, and we ran ads in newspapers explaining our business and the opportunity for individuals to be part of an independent sales force, or what we called "designers." During 1996 and the first half of 1997, we developed a strong home office staff. . . . The next 18 months were exciting, but frightening to say the least.*
>
> *1998 was a very difficult year because our growth outpaced our production and fulfillment abilities. Our sales in 1997 were $1,200,000. In 1998, our sales jumped to $15,400,000 and we were overwhelmed. Our problem was compounded by the fact that we manufactured approximately 65 percent of all the products we sold. We not only had to invest in shipping and warehousing infrastructure, we also had to completely re-engineer our production facilities to keep pace with the growth. We ran out of product, refunded money, and sent gift certificates. For several months, it appeared as if we would implode. The solution to our dilemmas was based on three things:*
>
> - *We knew we had to deal directly and honestly with the problem. We needed to let our designers know that we understood we had failed them and that we were committed to fixing the problem.*
> - *We determined what areas were causing us the most pain and dealt with them immediately. System changes were implemented in every department.*
> - *We made large capital contributions to the company through equity injections, personal loans, and bank loans.*
>
> *Our company has continued to grow, but the stress of 1998 is a constant reminder that we need to constantly work to get ahead of potential problems. Continuing to improve the process and to develop exceptional employees is the key to preparing for the challenges we face ahead.*

Courtesy of Home & Garden Party, Ltd.

Source: Personal description by Penny and Steve Carlile of the first three years of operations in their business, May 19, 2004.

Chapter 22

Looking Ahead

After studying this chapter, you should be able to

1 *Describe the working-capital cycle of a small business.*

2 *Identify the important issues in managing a firm's cash flows, including the preparation of a cash budget.*

3 *Explain the key issues in managing accounts receivable, inventory, and accounts payable.*

4 *Discuss the techniques commonly used in making capital budgeting decisions.*

5 *Describe the capital budgeting practices of small firms.*

This chapter considers some of the issues that the Carliles had to face when the need arose—an urgent need, in their case—to invest in the firm, in terms of both working capital and long-term investments, such as those for computer systems, equipment, and buildings.

THE WORKING-CAPITAL CYCLE

1 *Describe the working-capital cycle of a small business.*

Ask the owner of a small business about financial management and you will hear about the joys and tribulations of managing cash, accounts receivable, inventories, and accounts payable. **Working-capital management**—managing short-term assets (current assets) and short-term sources of financing (current liabilities)—is extremely important to most small firms. In fact, there may be no financial discipline that is more important, and yet more misunderstood. Good business opportunities can be irreparably damaged by ineffective management of a firm's short-term assets and liabilities.

working-capital management
The management of current assets and current liabilities

The key issue in working-capital management is to avoid running out of cash. And understanding how to manage cash effectively requires knowledge of the working-capital cycle. "Business owners should be thinking about this issue from day one," says Stephen King, president of Virtual Growth, a New York City–based financial-consulting firm. Many entrepreneurs overlook effective cash management because they have other issues on their minds. "So long as more money seems to be coming into the business than going out, many company owners don't give cash management a second thought. And that leaves them vulnerable to all kinds of cash flow dangers."[1]

Net operating working capital consists primarily of three assets—cash, accounts receivable, and inventories—less two sources of short-term debt—accounts payable and accruals.[2] A firm's **working-capital cycle** is the flow of resources through these accounts as part of the firm's day-to-day operations. As shown in Exhibit 22-1, the steps in a firm's working-capital cycle are as follows:

net operating working capital
The sum of a firm's current assets (cash, accounts receivable, and inventories) less accounts payable and accruals

working-capital cycle
The daily flow of resources through a firm's working-capital accounts

Step 1. Purchase or produce inventory for sale, which increases accounts payable—assuming the purchase is a credit purchase—and increases inventories on hand.

Step 2. a. Sell the inventory for cash, which increases cash, or
b. Sell the inventory on credit, which increases accounts receivable.

Step 3. a. Pay the accounts payable, which decreases accounts payable and decreases cash.
b. Pay operating expenses and taxes, which decreases cash.

Step 4. Collect the accounts receivable when due, which decreases accounts receivable and increases cash.

Step 5. Begin the cycle again.

EXHIBIT 22-1 *Working-Capital Cycle*

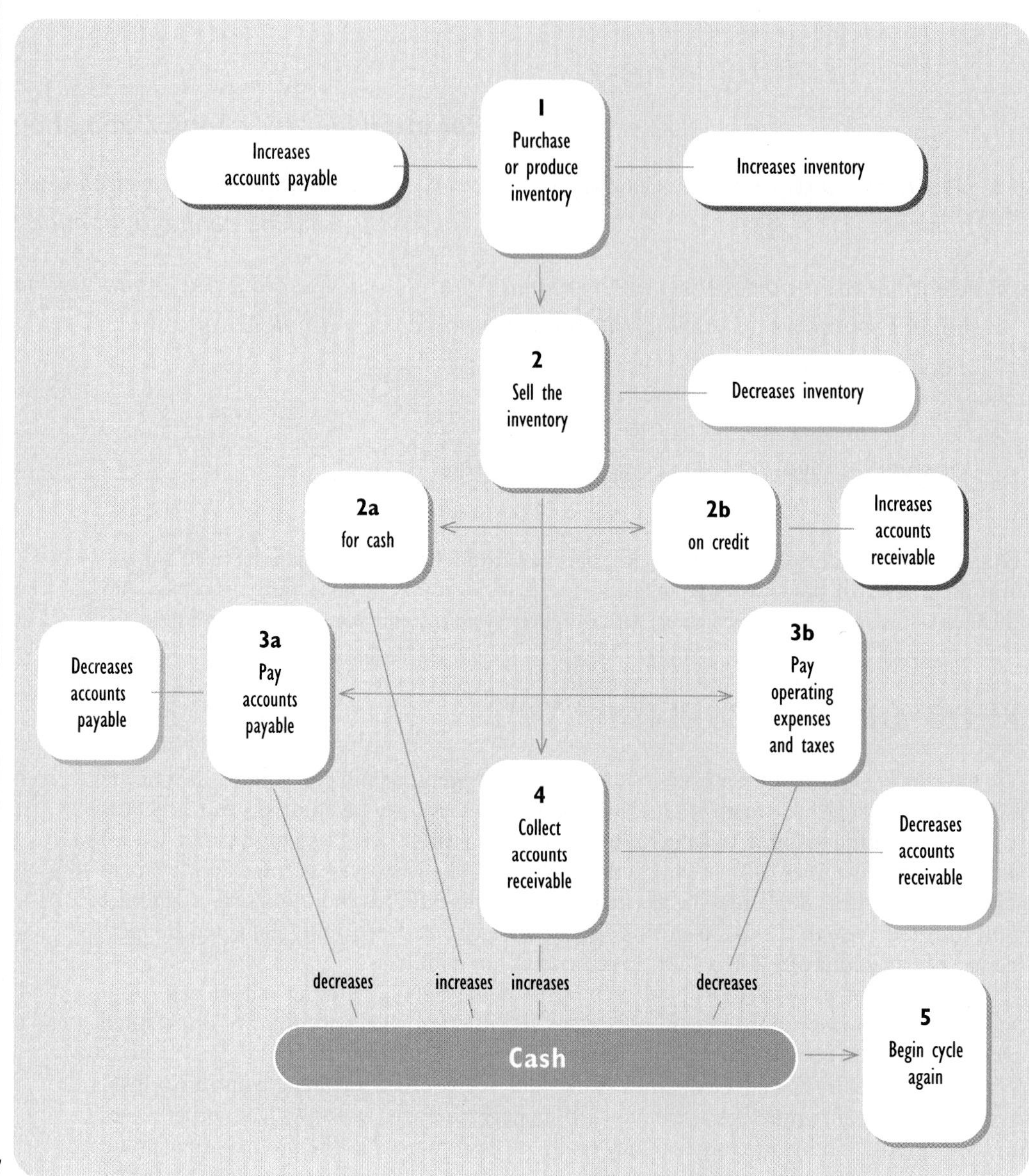

Depending on the industry, the working-capital cycle may be long or short. For example, it is short and repeated quickly in the grocery business; it is longer and repeated more slowly in an automobile dealership. Whatever the industry, however, management should be working continuously to shorten the cycle.

The Timing and Size of Working-Capital Investments

It is imperative that owners of small companies understand the working-capital cycle, in terms of both the timing of investments and the size of the investment required (for example, the amounts necessary to maintain inventories and accounts receivable). The owner's failure to understand these relationships underlies many of the financial problems of small companies.

Exhibit 22-2 shows the chronological sequence of a hypothetical working-capital cycle. The time line reflects the order in which events unfold, beginning with an investment in inventory and ending with collection of accounts receivable. The key dates in the figure are as follows:

Day a. Inventory is ordered in anticipation of future sales.

Day b. Inventory is received.

Day c. Inventory is sold on credit.

Day d. Accounts payable come due and are paid.

Day e. Accounts receivable are collected.

The investing and financing implications of the working-capital cycle reflected in Exhibit 22-2 are as follows:

- Money is invested in inventory from day *b* to day *c*.
- The supplier provides financing for the inventories from day *b* to day *d*.
- Money is invested in accounts receivable from day *c* to day *e*.
- Financing of the firm's investment in accounts receivable must be provided from day *d* to day *e*. This time span, called the **cash conversion period**, represents the number of days required to complete the working-capital cycle, which ends with the conversion of accounts receivable into cash. During this period, the firm no longer has the benefit of supplier financing (accounts payable). The longer this period lasts, the greater the potential cash flow problems for the firm.

cash conversion period
The time required to convert paid-for inventories and accounts receivable into cash

Examples of Working-Capital Management

Exhibit 22-3 offers two examples of working-capital management by firms with contrasting working-capital cycles: Pokey, Inc., and Quick Turn Company. On August 15, both firms buy inventory that they receive on August 31, but the similarity ends there.

Pokey, Inc., must pay its supplier for the inventory on September 30, before eventually reselling it on October 15. It collects from its customers on November 30. As you can see, Pokey, Inc., must pay for the inventory two months prior to collecting from its customers. Its cash conversion period—the time required to convert the paid-for inventories and accounts receivable into cash—is 60 days. The firm's managers must find a way to finance this investment in inventories and accounts receivable, or else they will experience cash flow problems. Furthermore, although increased sales should produce higher profits, they will compound the cash flow problem.

Now consider Quick Turn Company's working-capital cycle, shown in the bottom portion of Exhibit 22-3. Compared to Pokey, Quick Turn Company has an enviable working-capital position. By the time Quick Turn must pay for its inventory purchases (October 31), it has sold its product (September 30) and collected from its customers (October 31).

EXHIBIT 22-2 *Working-Capital Time Line*

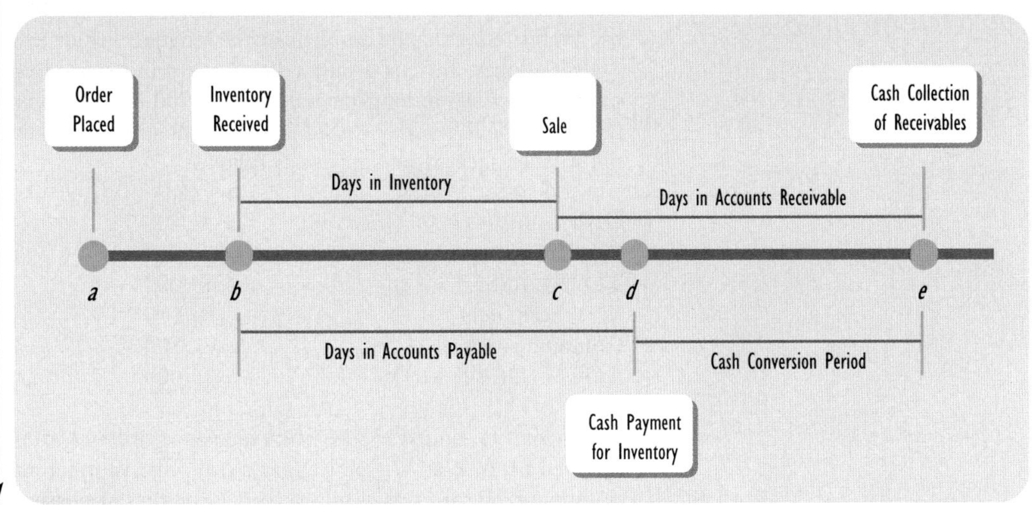

EXHIBIT 22-3 *Working-Capital Time Lines for Pokey, Inc., and Quick Turn Company*

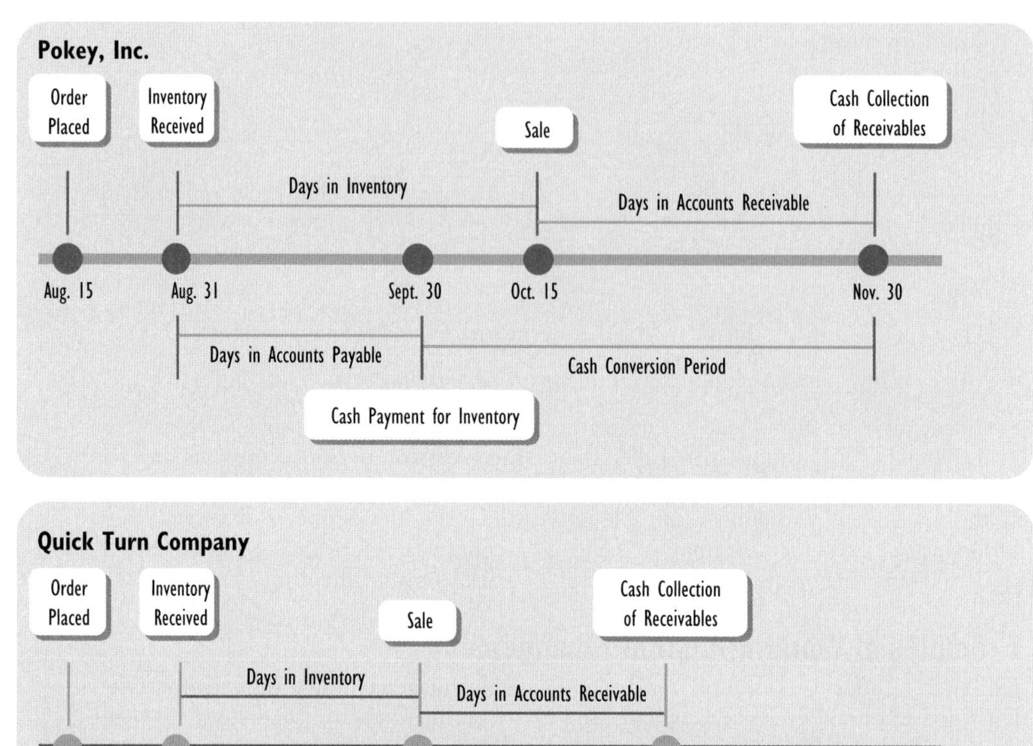

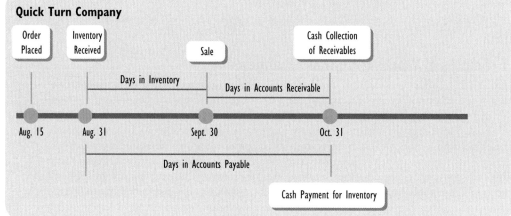

Thus, there is no cash conversion period because the supplier is essentially financing Quick Turn's working-capital needs.

To gain an even better understanding of the working-capital cycle, let's see what happens to Pokey's balance sheet and income statement. To do so, we will need more information about the firm's activities. A month-by-month listing of its activities and their effects on its balance sheet follow. Pay close attention to the firm's working capital, especially its cash balances. (You can learn more about the working-capital cycle by going to the Web site for this textbook at http://longenecker.swlearning.com.)

July: Pokey, Inc., is a new company, having started operations in July with $1,000, financed by $300 in long-term debt and $700 in common stock. At the outset, the owner purchased $600 worth of fixed assets, leaving the remaining $400 in cash. At this point, the balance sheet would appear as follows:

Cash	$ 400
Fixed assets	600
TOTAL ASSETS	$1,000
Long-term debt	300
Common stock	700
TOTAL DEBT AND EQUITY	$1,000

August: On August 15, the firm's managers ordered $500 worth of inventory, which was received on August 31 (see Exhibit 22-3). The supplier allowed Pokey 30 days from the time the inventory was received to pay for the purchase; thus, inventories and accounts payable both increased by $500 when the inventory was received. As a result of these transactions, the balance sheet would appear as follows:

	July	August	Changes: July to August
Cash	$ 400	$ 400	
Inventory	0	500	+$500
Fixed assets	600	600	
TOTAL ASSETS	$1,000	$1,500	
Accounts payable	$ 0	$ 500	+$500
Long-term debt	300	300	
Common stock	700	700	
TOTAL DEBT AND EQUITY	$1,000	$1,500	

So far, so good—no cash problems yet.

September: On September 30, the firm paid for the inventory; both cash and accounts payable decreased by $500.

	July	August	September	Changes: August to September
Cash	$ 400	$ 400	($ 100)	−$500
Inventory	0	500	500	
Fixed assets	600	600	600	
TOTAL ASSETS	$1,000	$1,500	$1,000	
Accounts payable	$ 0	$ 500	$ 0	−$500
Long-term debt	300	300	300	
Common stock	700	700	700	
TOTAL DEBT AND EQUITY	$1,000	$1,500	$1,000	

Now Pokey, Inc., has a cash flow problem in the form of a cash deficit of $100.

October: October was a busy month for Pokey. On October 15, merchandise was sold on credit for $900; sales (in the income statement) and accounts receivable increased by that amount. The firm incurred operating expenses (selling and administrative expenses) in the amount of $250, to be paid in early November; thus, operating expenses (in the income statement) and accrued expenses (current liabilities in the balance sheet) increased by $250. (An additional $25 in accrued expenses resulted from accruing taxes that will be owed on the firm's earnings.) Finally, in October, the firm's accountants recorded $50 in depreciation expense (to be reported in the income statement), resulting in accumulated depreciation on the balance sheet of $50. The results are as follows:

	July	August	September	October	Changes: September to October
Cash	$ 400	$ 400	($ 100)	($ 100)	
Accounts receivable	0	0	0	900	+$900
Inventory	0	500	500	0	−500
Fixed assets	600	600	600	600	
Accumulated depreciation	0	0	0	(50)	−50
TOTAL ASSETS	$1,000	$1,500	$1,000	$1,350	
Accounts payable	$ 0	$ 500	$ 0	$ 0	
Accrued operating expenses	0	0	0	250	+$250
Income tax payable	0	0	0	25	+25
Long-term debt	300	300	300	300	
Common stock	700	700	700	700	
Retained earnings	0	0	0	75	+75
TOTAL DEBT AND EQUITY	$1,000	$1,500	$1,000	$1,350	

The October balance sheet shows all the activities just described, but there is one more change in the balance sheet: It now shows $75 in retained earnings, which had been $0 in

the prior balance sheets. As you will see shortly, this amount represents the firm's income. Note also that Pokey, Inc., continues to be overdrawn by $100 on its cash. None of the events in October affected the firm's cash balance. All the transactions were the result of accruals recorded by the firm's accountant, offsetting entries to the income statement. The relationship between the balance sheet and the income statement is as follows:

Change in the Balance Sheet		**Effect on the Income Statement**	
Increase in accounts receivable of $900	→	Sales	$900
Decrease in inventories of $500	→	Cost of goods sold	$500
Increase in accrued operating expenses of $250	→	Operating expenses	$250
Increase in accumulated depreciation of $50	→	Depreciation expense	$50
Increase in accrued taxes of $25	→	Tax expense	$25

November: In November, the accrued expenses were paid, which resulted in a $250 decrease in cash along with an equal decrease in accrued expenses. At the end of November, the accounts receivable were collected, yielding a $900 increase in cash and a $900 decrease in accounts receivable. Thus, net cash increased by $650. The final series of balance sheets is as follows:

	July	**August**	**September**	**October**	**November**	**Changes: October to November**
Cash	$ 400	$ 400	($ 100)	($ 100)	$ 550	+$650
Accounts receivable	0	0	0	900	0	−900
Inventory	0	500	500	0	0	
Fixed assets	600	600	600	600	600	
Accumulated depreciation	0	0	0	(50)	(50)	
TOTAL ASSETS	$1,000	$1,500	$1,000	$1,350	$1,100	
Accounts payable	$ 0	$ 500	$ 0	$ 0	$ 0	
Accrued operating expenses	0	0	0	250	0	−$250
Income tax payable	0	0	0	25	25	
Long-term debt	300	300	300	300	300	
Common stock	700	700	700	700	700	
Retained earnings	0	0	0	75	75	
TOTAL DEBT AND EQUITY	$1,000	$1,500	$1,000	$1,350	$1,100	

As a result of the firm's activities, Pokey, Inc., reported $75 in profits for the period. The income statement for the period ending November 30 is as follows:

Sales revenue		$900
Cost of goods sold		500
Gross profit		$400
Operating expenses:		
Cash expense	$250	
Depreciation expense	50	
Total operating expenses		$300
Operating income		$100
Income tax (25%)		25
Net income		$ 75

The $75 in profits is reflected as retained earnings on the balance sheet to make the numbers match.

The somewhat contrived example of Pokey, Inc., illustrates an important point that deserves repeating: An owner of a small firm must understand the working-capital cycle of his or her firm. Although the business was profitable, Pokey ran out of cash in September and October (–$100) and didn't recover until November, when the accounts receivable were collected. This 60-day cash conversion period represents a critical time when the firm must find another source of financing if it is to survive. Moreover, when sales are ongoing throughout the year, the problem can be an unending one, unless financing is found to support the firm's sales. Also, as much as possible, a firm should arrange for earlier payment by customers (preferably in advance) and negotiate longer payment schedules with suppliers (preferably over several months).

An understanding of the working-capital cycle provides a basis for examining the primary components of working-capital management: cash flows, accounts receivable, inventory, and accounts payable.

MANAGING CASH FLOWS

2 *Identify the important issues in managing a firm's cash flows, including the preparation of a cash budget.*

It should be clear by now that the core of working-capital management is monitoring cash flows. Cash is continually moving through a business. It flows in as customers pay for products or services, and it flows out as payments are made to other businesses and individuals who provide products and services to the firm, such as employees and suppliers. The typically uneven nature of cash inflows and outflows makes it imperative that they be properly understood and managed. Keith Lowe, an experienced entrepreneur and co-founder of the Alabama Information Technology Association, expresses it this way:

> *If there's one thing that will make or break your company, especially when it's small, it's cash flow. A banker once told me that of the many companies he saw go out of business, the majority of them were profitable—they just got in a cash crunch, and that forced them to close. If you pay close attention to your cash flow and think about it every single day, you'll have an edge over almost all your competitors, and you will keep growing while other companies fall by the wayside. The amount of attention you pay to cash flow can literally mean the difference between life and death for your company.*[3]

The Nature of Cash Flows Revisited

A firm's net cash flow may be determined quite simply by examining its bank account. Monthly cash deposits less checks written during the same period equal a firm's net cash flow. If deposits for a month add up to $100,000 and checks total $80,000, the firm has a net positive cash flow of $20,000. The cash balance at the end of the month is $20,000 higher than it was at the beginning of the month.

Exhibit 22-4 graphically represents the flow of cash through a business; it includes not only the cash flows that arise as part of the firm's working-capital cycle (shown in Exhibit 22-1) but other cash flows as well, such as those from purchasing fixed assets and issuing stock. More specifically, cash sales, collection of accounts receivable, payment of expenses, and payment for inventory reflect the inflows and outflows of cash that relate to the working-capital cycle, while the other items in Exhibit 22-4 represent other, longer-term cash flows.

As has been emphasized on several occasions, calculating net cash flow requires that we distinguish between sales revenue and cash receipts—they are seldom the same. Revenue is recorded at the time a sale is made but does not affect cash flow at that time unless the sale is a cash sale. Cash receipts, on the other hand, are recorded when money actually flows into the firm, often a month or two after the sale. Similarly, it is necessary to distinguish between expenses and disbursements. Expenses occur when materials, labor, or other items are used. Payments (disbursements) for these expense items may be made later when checks are issued. Depreciation, while shown as an expense, is not a cash outflow.

Given the difference between cash flows and profits, it is absolutely essential that the entrepreneur develop a cash budget to anticipate when cash will enter and leave the business. In the next section, we will describe and illustrate the cash budgeting process.

The Cash Budget

The **cash budget** is a primary tool for managing cash flows. The budget is concerned specifically with dollars received and paid out. In contrast, the income statement takes items into consideration before they affect cash—for example, expenses that have been incurred but not yet paid and income earned but not yet received.

cash budget
A planning document strictly concerned with the receipt and payment of dollars

By using a cash budget, an entrepreneur can predict and plan the cash flows of a business. *No single planning document is more important in the life of a small company, either for*

EXHIBIT 22-4 *Flow of Cash Through a Business*

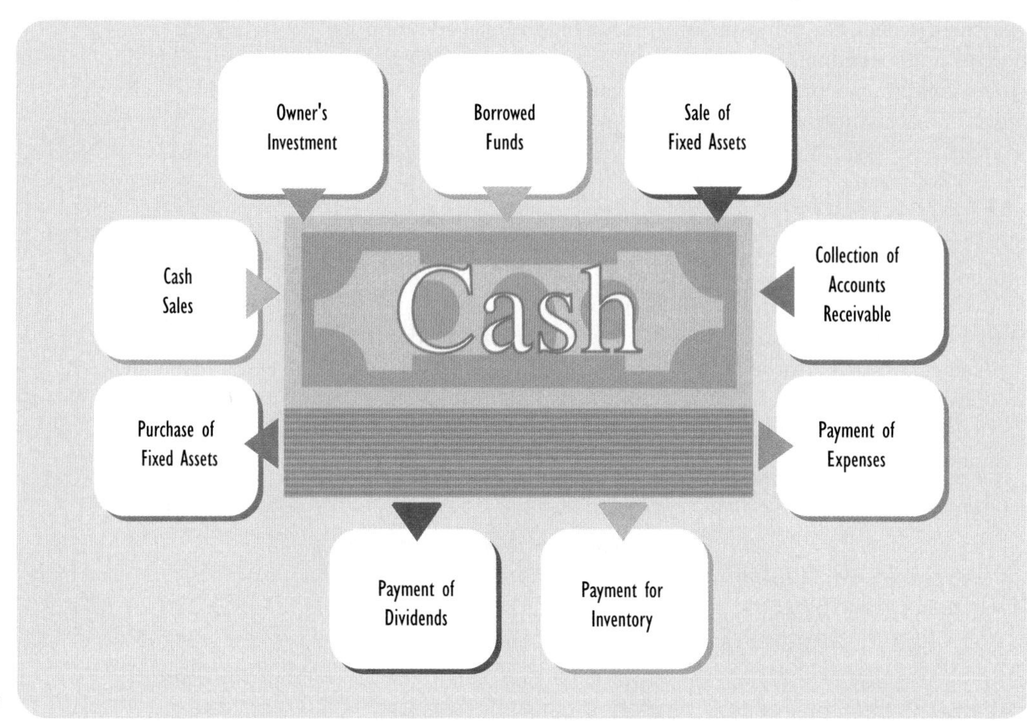

avoiding cash flow problems when cash runs short or for anticipating short-term investment opportunities if excess cash becomes available. The importance of cash planning is emphasized by accountant Steve Mayer: "As difficult as it is for a business owner to prepare projections, it's one of the most important things one can do. Projections rank next to business plans and mission statements among things a business must do to plan for the future."[4]

To better understand the process of preparing a cash budget, consider the example of the Davies Corporation, a manufacturer of containers. Its owner, Peggy Davies, wishes to

Living the Dream *Entrepreneurial Challenges*

Batten Down the Hatches

Katie B. Tyler is no stranger to financial difficulties. Sixteen years ago, her interior construction company, Tyler II, in Charlotte, North Carolina, was hit by an economic slowdown. Business just stopped. She panicked, cut her salary in half, and drained the company's cash reserves to keep the business going. Her tactics worked, and the business has grown through the years.

Because the forecasts for 2001 were not positive, Tyler did not want to take any chances—she took steps to prepare for hard times. She made an agreement with her bank to double the company's credit line to $1 million. Internally, she increased the business development budget by 50 percent and promoted the office manager to client relations manager to ensure that current customers continued to be satisfied. Although the economic projections caused plans for a new $1 million headquarters to be delayed, Tyler is confident: "I plan to stay on a steady course and not panic."

Tyler's cool demeanor may not be characteristic of small business owners during an economic downturn. In fact, economists say that entrepreneurs are especially hard hit because they have fewer cash reserves than large companies, less access to credit markets, and less geographic diversity in global and domestic markets. To combat these added obstacles, entrepreneurs should thoroughly examine cash flows, operating costs, and overhead.

Source: Janin Friend, "Batten Down the Hatches," *BusinessWeek Online*, http://www.businessweek.com, February 5, 2001.

develop a monthly cash budget for the next quarter (July through September) and has made the following forecasts.

- Historical and predicted sales:

Historical Sales		Predicted Sales	
April	$ 80,000	July	$130,000
May	100,000	August	130,000
June	120,000	September	120,000
		October	100,000

- Of the firm's sales dollars, 40 percent are collected the month of the sale, 30 percent one month after the sale, and the remaining 30 percent two months after the sale.
- Inventory is purchased one month before the sales month and is paid for in the month in which it is sold. Purchases equal 80 percent of projected sales for the next month.
- Cash expenses have been estimated for wages and salaries, rent, utilities, and tax payments, all of which are reflected in the cash budget.
- Interest on a $40,000 bank note (with the principal due in December) is payable at an 8 percent annual rate for the three-month period ending in September.
- The firm has a $20,000 line of credit with its bank at an interest rate of 12 percent annually (1 percent monthly). The interest owed is to be paid monthly.
- The firm's beginning cash balance for the budget period is $5,000. This amount should be maintained as a minimum cash balance.

Based on this information, Davies has prepared a monthly cash budget for the three-month period ending September 30. Exhibit 22-5 shows the results of her computations, which involved the following steps:

Step 1. Determine the amount of collections each month, based on the projected collection patterns.

Step 2. Estimate the amount and timing of the following cash disbursements:
 a. Inventory purchases and payments. The amount of the purchases is shown in the boxed area of the table, with payments made one month later.
 b. Rent, wages, tax payments, utilities, and interest on the long-term note
 c. Quarterly interest on a $40,000 bank note is $800 ($40,000 times 8 percent times ¼ year).
 d. Interest to be paid on any outstanding short-term borrowing. For example, the table shows that for the month of July the Davies Corporation will need to borrow $10,600 to prevent the firm's cash balance from falling below the $5,000 acceptable minimum. Assume that the money will be borrowed at the end of July and that the interest will be payable at the end of August. The amount of the interest in August is $106, or 1 percent of the $10,600 cumulative short-term debt outstanding at the end of July.

Step 3. Calculate the net change in cash (cash receipts less cash disbursements).

Step 4. Determine the beginning cash balance (ending cash balance from the prior month).

Step 5. Compute the cash balance before short-term borrowing (net change in cash for the month plus the cash balance at the beginning of the month).

Step 6. Calculate the short-term borrowing or repayment—the amount borrowed if there is a cash shortfall for the month or the amount repaid on any short-term debt outstanding.

Step 7. Compute the cumulative amount of short-term debt outstanding, which also determines the amount of interest to be paid in the following month.

EXHIBIT 22-5 *Three-Month Cash Budget for the Davies Corporation for July–September*

		May	June	July	August	September
	Monthly sales	$100,000	$120,000	$130,000	$130,000	$120,000
	Cash receipts:					
	Cash sales for month			$ 52,000	$ 52,000	$ 48,000
	1 month after sale			36,000	39,000	39,000
	2 months after sale			30,000	36,000	39,000
Step 1	Total collections			$118,000	$127,000	$126,000
	Purchases (80% of sales)		$104,000	$104,000	$ 96,000	$ 80,000
	Cash disbursements					
Step 2a	Payments on purchases			$104,000	$104,000	$ 96,000
Step 2b	Rent			3,000	3,000	3,000
	Wages and salaries			18,000	18,000	16,000
	Tax payment			1,000		
	Utilities (2% of sales)			2,600	2,600	2,400
Step 2c	Interest on long-term note					800
Step 2d	Short-term interest (1% of short-term debt)				106	113
	Total cash disbursements			$128,600	$127,706	$118,313
Step 3	Net change in cash			−$ 10,600	−$ 706	$ 7,687
Step 4	Beginning cash balance			5,000	5,000	5,000
Step 5	Cash balance before borrowing			−$ 5,600	$ 4,294	$ 12,687
Step 6	Short-term borrowing (payments)			10,600	706	−7,687
	Ending cash balance			$ 5,000	$ 5,000	$ 5,000
Step 7	Cumulative short-term debt outstanding			$ 10,600	$ 11,306	$ 3,619

As you can see in Exhibit 22-5, the firm does not achieve a positive cash flow until September. Short-term borrowing must be arranged, therefore, in both July and August. By preparing a cash budget, the Davies Corporation can anticipate these needs and avoid the nasty surprises that might otherwise occur.

A cash budget should anticipate occasions when a small business has idle funds or has generated unexpected excess funds. Taking advantage of the many short-term investment opportunities that are available, including certificates of deposit and money market certificates, can put excess cash to work for a firm.

MANAGING ACCOUNTS RECEIVABLE

3 *Explain the key issues in managing accounts receivable, inventory, and accounts payable.*

Chapter 15 discussed the extension of credit by small firms and the managing and collecting of accounts receivable. This section considers the impact of credit decisions on working capital and particularly on cash flows. The most important factor in managing cash well within a small firm is the ability to collect accounts receivable quickly.

How Accounts Receivable Affect Cash

Granting credit to customers, although primarily a marketing decision, directly affects a firm's cash account. By selling on credit and thus allowing customers to delay payment, the selling firm delays the inflow of cash.

The total amount of customers' credit balances is carried on the balance sheet as accounts receivable—one of the firm's current assets. Of all noncash assets, accounts receivable are closest to becoming cash. Sometimes called *near cash*, or *receivables*, accounts receivable typically are collected and become cash within 30 to 60 days following a sale.

The Life Cycle of Accounts Receivable

The receivables cycle begins with a credit sale. In most businesses, an invoice is then prepared and mailed to the purchaser. When the invoice is received, the purchaser processes it, prepares a check, and mails the check in payment to the seller.

Under ideal circumstances, each of these steps is taken in a timely manner. Obviously, delays can occur at any stage of this process. For example, a shipping clerk may batch invoices before sending them to the office for processing, thus delaying the preparation and mailing of invoices to customers. Such a practice will also delay the receipt of customers' money and its deposit in the bank—money which is then used to pay bills. In other words, receivables may be past due because of problems in a company's organization, where information is not getting transferred on a timely basis among salespeople, operations departments, and accounting staff. The result: delayed payments from customers and larger investments in accounts receivable.

Credit management policies, practices, and procedures affect the life cycle of receivables and the flow of cash from them. It is important for small business owners, when establishing credit policies, to consider cash flow requirements as well as the need to stimulate sales. A key goal of every business should be to minimize the average time it takes customers to pay their bills. By streamlining administrative procedures, a firm can facilitate the task of sending out bills, thereby generating cash more quickly.

If a firm is encountering a cash flow problem, it may well have something to do with poor management of accounts receivable. For example, an evaluation of receivables may indicate that you are being too shy about collecting, says Ira Davidson, director of the Small Business Development Center at Pace University in New York City. Davidson counseled one business owner who showed him nine months' worth of uncollected receivables. "He was afraid to collect because they might not pay and he'd lose customers," says Davidson. Maintaining effective credit policies and collecting on a timely basis are fundamental to good cash management in a small business.[5]

Here are some examples of credit management practices that can have a positive effect on a firm's cash flows:

- Minimize the time between shipping, invoicing, and sending notices on billings.
- Review previous credit experiences to determine impediments to cash flows, such as continued extension of credit to slow-paying or delinquent customers.

Living the Dream — *Entrepreneurial Challenges*

How to Collect from Anyone (Even Enron)

Not a day goes by that Bob Fisher doesn't thank his lucky stars for Nettie Morrison. But on March 21, 2002, he was particularly grateful that she worked for him.

That was the day that Foresight, Fisher's 50-employee software company in Dublin, Ohio, received a $1,635 check from Enron. The same Enron that, 109 days earlier, had filed for bankruptcy. Yet the check, which fully covered Enron's renewal of a one-year licensing contract with Foresight, was sent to Morrison, the company's accounts receivable specialist, as though Enron were doing business as usual.

How did she manage to wrest payment from Enron when so many others couldn't? Preventive diligence. Enron had been a Foresight customer since 1997. Almost a year earlier, when the news of Enron's accounting irregularities first broke, Morrison started calling her Houston contacts almost weekly—even though the contract didn't expire until February 2002. Using her internal connections, she worked her way to the Enron employee with the power to pay up.

By starting early, maintaining good relationships, and remaining persistent, Morrison got her payment.

Source: Ilan Mochari, "Thirty Ways to Get Paid Within 30 Days," *Inc.*, Vol. 24, No. 9 (September 2002), pp. 67–68.

- Provide incentives for prompt payment by granting cash discounts or charging interest on delinquent accounts.
- Age accounts receivable on a monthly or even a weekly basis to identify quickly any delinquent accounts.
- Use the most effective methods for collecting overdue accounts. For example, prompt phone calls to overdue accounts can improve collections considerably.
- Use a **lock box**—a post office box for receiving remittances. If the firm's bank maintains the lock box to which customers send their payments, it can empty the box frequently and immediately deposit any checks received into the firm's account.

lock box
A post office box for receiving remittances from customers

Accounts Receivable Financing

Some small businesses speed up the cash flow from accounts receivable by borrowing against them. By financing receivables, these firms can often secure the use of their money 30 to 60 days earlier than would be possible otherwise. Although this practice was once concentrated largely in the garment business, it has expanded to many other types of small businesses, such as manufacturers, food processors, distributors, home building suppliers, and temporary employment agencies. Such financing is provided by commercial finance companies and by some banks.

Two types of accounts receivable financing are available. The first type uses a firm's **pledged accounts receivable** as collateral for a loan. Payments received from customers are forwarded to the lending institution to pay off the loan. In the second type of financing, a business sells its accounts receivable to a finance company, a practice known as *factoring* (discussed earlier in Chapter 11). The finance company thereby assumes the bad-debt risk associated with receivables it buys.

pledged accounts receivable
Accounts receivable used as collateral for a loan

The obvious advantage of accounts receivable financing is the immediate cash flow it provides for firms that have limited working capital. As a secondary benefit, the volume of borrowing can be quickly expanded proportionally in order to match a firm's growth in sales and accounts receivable.

A drawback to this type of financing is its high cost. Rates typically run several points above the prime interest rate, and factors charge a fee to compensate them for their credit

Living the Dream | *Entrepreneurial Challenges*

Factoring Can Make the Difference

A reputable factor can prove invaluable to a small firm at a critical time in its life. Consider James Choung's $6 million laundry and dry-cleaning business, Newtex.

The business was started with the help of a Korean American bank, as are many Korean enterprises. Choung had come to the United States to train as a nuclear engineer and had worked on nuclear submarines in Newport News, Virginia, until the Navy stopped building them. With a wife and four children (in private schools), he needed income, and he decided to buy a tony dry cleaner in Manhattan. He soon expanded his South Bronx plant, selling laundry services to restaurants and hotels and doing laundry for hotel guests.

His books told him he was making a lot of money, but as he hired people and leased machines, he found that his cash flow out was higher than his cash flow in. The mailing of monthly bills to his customers was preceded by several weeks of expenses. (And "the monthly bill," he says, "just starts the clock.") He found that few restaurants and hotels paid in less than 30 days after the receipt of his bills—and many took more than 60 days.

Choung's primary Korean bank was unwilling to study the credit ratings of New York City restaurants and hotels or to take on faith that receivables would eventually be paid. Factoring was what kept Newtex alive. "For me," he says, "factoring is cash flow."

Choung now employs 60 people, and nearly all his $6 million in annual revenue passes through the hands of his factor. Without it, the business couldn't have survived.

Source: Martin Mayer, "Taking the Fear Out of Factoring," *Inc.*, Vol. 25, No. 14 (December 2003), p. 92.

investigation activities and for the risk that customers may default in payment. Another weakness of accounts receivable financing is that pledging receivables may limit a firm's ability to borrow from a bank by removing a prime asset from its available collateral.

MANAGING INVENTORIES

Inventory is a "necessary evil" in the financial management system. It is "necessary" because supply and demand cannot be managed to coincide precisely with day-to-day operations; it is an "evil" because it ties up funds that are not actively productive.

Reducing Inventory to Free Cash

Inventory is a bigger problem for some small businesses than for others. The inventory of many service firms, for example, consists of only a few supplies. A manufacturer, on the other hand, has several inventories—raw materials, work in process, and finished goods. Also, retailers and wholesalers, especially those with high inventory turnover rates such as firms in grocery distribution, are continually involved in solving inventory management problems.

Chapter 20 discussed several ideas related to purchasing and inventory management that are designed to minimize inventory-carrying costs and processing costs. The emphasis in this section is on practices that will minimize average inventory levels, thereby releasing funds for other applications. The correct minimum level of inventory is the level needed to maintain desired production schedules and/or a certain level of customer service. A concerted effort to manage inventory can trim inventory excess and pay handsome dividends.

Monitoring Inventory

One of the first steps in managing inventory is to discover what's in inventory and how long it's been there. Too often, items are purchased, warehoused, and essentially forgotten. A yearly inventory for accounting purposes is inadequate for proper inventory control. Items that are slow movers may sit in a retailer's inventory beyond the time when markdowns should have been applied.

Computers can provide assistance in inventory identification and control. Although physical inventories may still be required, their use will only serve to supplement the computerized system.

Controlling Stockpiles

Small business managers tend to overbuy inventory for several reasons. First, an entrepreneur's enthusiasm may lead him or her to forecast greater demand than is realistic. Second, the personalization of the business-customer relationship may motivate a manager to stock everything customers want. Third, a price-conscious manager may be overly susceptible to a vendor's appeal to "buy now, because prices are going up."

Managers must exercise restraint when stockpiling. Improperly managed and uncontrolled stockpiling may greatly increase inventory-carrying costs and place a heavy drain on the funds of a small business.

MANAGING ACCOUNTS PAYABLE

Cash flow management and accounts payable management are intertwined. As long as a payable is outstanding, the buying firm can keep cash equal to that amount in its own checking account. When payment is made, however, that firm's cash account is reduced accordingly.

Although payables are legal obligations, they can be paid at various times or even renegotiated in some cases. Therefore, financial management of accounts payable hinges on negotiation and timing.

Negotiation

Any business is subject to emergency situations and may find it necessary to ask creditors to postpone its payable obligations. Usually, creditors will cooperate in working out a solution because it's in their best interest for a client firm to succeed.

Living the Dream — *Entrepreneurial Challenges*

Just-in-Time Inventory: Good for Small Firms, Too

© L.E. Baskow/Portland Tribune

The same principles that have increased efficiency in large-scale production are being applied effectively in smaller firms as well. Gamblin Artist's Oil Colors is one example of a small company that is benefiting from the concept of just-in-time manufacturing.

Gamblin, an oil paint manufacturer in Portland, Oregon, is owned and operated by Martha and Robert Gamblin. Twenty years ago, Robert, a painter, decided that someone should make paints with the artist in mind—and so he did. He started slowly, selling only three different colors of paint. Today, Gamblin Artist's Oil Colors sells 87 colors of oil paint worldwide.

With increased selection and production have come new questions about how to manage the inventory. The Gamblins hired Charlie Martin, a manufacturing consultant for the Oregon Manufacturing Extension Partnership, to introduce a more efficient inventory handling system.

The Gamblins had been making colors in batches of 1,200 tubes, which would remain in inventory for three to six months. With Martin's help, the Gamblins reduced their batch size to 500 tubes, while producing a single color at a time. The new manufacturing system also allowed the company to decrease the amount of time inventory is held to approximately six weeks. Thus, less cash is tied up in inventory at any one time.

Since implementing the new system, the Gamblins have freed up about $200,000 in cash to grow the business and launch an advertising campaign.

Source: Jane Applegate, "Just-in-Time Manufacturing," http://www.entrepreneur.com, February 2000.

Timing

"Buy now, pay later" is the motto of many entrepreneurs. By buying on credit, a small business is using creditors' funds to supply short-term cash needs. The longer creditors' funds can be borrowed, the better. Payment, therefore, should be delayed as long as acceptable under the agreement.

Typically, accounts payable (trade credit) involve payment terms that include a cash discount. With trade-discount terms, paying later may be inappropriate. For example, terms of 3/10, net 30 offer a 3 percent potential discount. Exhibit 22-6 shows the possible settlement costs over the credit period of 30 days. Note that for a $20,000 purchase, a settlement of only $19,400 is required if payment is made within the first 10 days ($20,000 less the 3 percent discount of $600). Between day 11 and day 30, the full settlement of $20,000 is required. After 30 days, the settlement cost may exceed the original amount, as late-payment fees are added.

The timing question then becomes "Should the account be paid on day 10 or day 30?" There is little reason to pay $19,400 on days 1 through 9, when the same amount will settle the account on day 10. Likewise, if payment is to be made after day 10, it makes sense to wait until day 30 to pay the $20,000.

By paying on the last day of the discount period, the buyer saves the amount of the discount offered. The other alternative of paying on day 30 allows the buyer to use the

EXHIBIT 22-6 *An Accounts Payable Timetable for Terms of 3/10, Net 30*

Timetable (days after invoice date)	Settlement Costs for a $20,000 Purchase
Day 1 through 10	$19,400
Day 11 through 30	$20,000
Day 31 through and thereafter	$20,000 + possible late penalty + deterioration in credit rating

seller's money for an additional 20 days by forgoing the discount. As Exhibit 22-6 shows, the buyer can use the seller's $19,400 for 20 days at a cost of $600. The annualized interest rate can be calculated as follows:

$$\text{Annualized interest rate} = \frac{\text{Days in year}}{\text{Net period} - \text{Cash discount period}} \times \frac{\text{Cash discount \%}}{100\% - \text{Cash discount \%}}$$

$$= \frac{365}{30 - 10} \times \frac{3\%}{100\% - 3\%}$$

$$= 18.25 \times 0.030928$$

$$= 0.564, \text{ or } 56.4\%$$

By failing to take a discount, a business typically pays a high rate for use of a supplier's money—56.4 percent per annum in this case. Payment on day 10 appears to be the most logical choice. Recall, however, that payment also affects cash flows. If funds are extremely short, a small firm may have to wait to pay until the last possible day in order to avoid an overdraft at the bank.

We now turn from management of a firm's working capital to management of its long-term assets—equipment and plant—or what is called *capital budgeting*.

CAPITAL BUDGETING

Capital budgeting analysis helps managers make decisions about long-term investments. In order to develop a new product line, for example, a firm needs to expand its manufacturing capabilities and to buy the inventory required to make the product. That is, it makes investments today with an expectation of receiving profits or cash flows in the future, possibly over 5 or 10 years.

capital budgeting analysis An analytical method that helps managers make decisions about long-term investments

Some capital budgeting decisions that might be made by a small firm include the following:

- Develop and introduce a new product that shows promise but requires additional study and improvement.
- Replace a firm's delivery trucks with newer models.
- Expand sales activity into a new territory.
- Construct a new building.
- Hire several additional salespersons to intensify selling in the existing market.

More specifically, in a 2003 study by the National Federation of Independent Businesses, small business owners were asked, "In terms of dollars, what was the purpose of the largest investments made in your business over the last 12 months?" Their responses were as follows:[6]

Replacement and maintenance	45.6%
Extension of existing product or service lines	21.2
Expansion into new business areas	22.9
Safety or environmental improvement	3.5
No response	6.7

Thus, nearly half of all long-term capital investments by small companies are made for replacement and maintenance; when we add in the extension of existing product lines, we can account for two-thirds of all dollars invested by small owners. Slightly over one-fifth of all dollars are invested in new product lines and businesses.

Although an in-depth discussion of capital budgeting is beyond the scope of this textbook, in the following sections we'll discuss techniques used in making capital budgeting decisions and the capital budgeting practices of small firms. For a more detailed presentation, see a financial management textbook, such as *Foundations of Finance*.[7]

4 *Discuss the techniques commonly used in making capital budgeting decisions.*

Capital Budgeting Techniques

The three major techniques for making capital budgeting decisions involve (1) accounting return on investment, (2) payback period, and (3) discounted cash flows, either net present value or internal rate of return. They all attempt to answer one basic question: Do the future benefits from an investment exceed the cost of making the investment? However, each technique addresses this general question by focusing on a different specific question. The specific question each addresses can be stated as follows:

1. *Accounting return on investment.* How many dollars in average profits are generated per dollar of average investment?
2. *Payback period.* How long will it take to recover the original investment outlay?
3. *Discounted cash flows.* How does the present value of future benefits from the investment compare to the investment outlay?

Three simple rules are used in judging the merits of an investment. Although they may seem trite, the rules state in simple terms the best thinking about the attractiveness of an investment.

1. The investor prefers more cash rather than less cash.
2. The investor prefers cash sooner rather than later.
3. The investor prefers less risk rather than more risk.

With these criteria in mind, let's now look at each of the three capital budgeting techniques in detail.

accounting return on investment technique
A capital budgeting technique that evaluates a capital expenditure based on the average annual after-tax profits relative to the average book value of an investment

ACCOUNTING RETURN ON INVESTMENT A small firm invests to earn profits. The **accounting return on investment technique** compares the average annual after-tax profits a firm expects to receive with the average book value of the investment:

$$\text{Accounting return on investment} = \frac{\text{Average annual after-tax profits}}{\text{Average book value of the investment}}$$

Average annual profits can be estimated by adding the after-tax profits expected over the life of the project and then dividing that amount by the number of years the project is expected to last. The average book value of an investment is equivalent to the average of the initial outlay and the estimated final projected salvage value. In making an accept–reject decision, the owner compares the calculated return to a minimum acceptable return, which is usually determined based on past experience.

To examine the use of the accounting return on investment technique, assume that you are contemplating buying a piece of equipment for $10,000 and depreciating it over four years to a book value of zero (it will have no salvage value). Further assume that you expect the investment to generate after-tax profits each year as follows:

Year	After-Tax Profits
1	$1,000
2	2,000
3	2,500
4	3,000

The accounting return on the proposed investment is calculated as follows:

$$\text{Accounting return on investment} = \frac{\left(\frac{\$1,000 + \$2,000 + \$2,500 + \$3,000}{4}\right)}{\left(\frac{\$10,000 + \$0}{2}\right)}$$

$$= \frac{\$2,125}{\$5,000} = 0.425, \text{ or } 42.5\%$$

For most people, a 42.5 percent profit rate would seem outstanding. Assuming the calculated accounting return on investment of 42.5 percent exceeds your minimum acceptable return, you will accept the project. If not, you will reject the investment—provided, of course, that you have confidence in the technique.

Although the accounting return on investment is easy to calculate, it has two major shortcomings. First, it is based on accounting profits rather than actual cash flows received. An investor should be more interested in the future cash produced by the investment than in the reported profits. Second, this technique ignores the time value of money. Thus, although popular, the accounting return on investment technique fails to satisfy any of the three rules concerning an investor's preference for receiving more cash sooner with less risk.

PAYBACK PERIOD The **payback period technique**, as the name suggests, measures how long it will take to recover the initial cash outlay of an investment. It deals with cash flows as opposed to accounting profits. The merits of a project are judged on whether the initial investment outlay can be recovered in less time than some maximum acceptable payback period. For example, an owner may not want to invest in any project that will require more than five years to recoup the original investment.

payback period technique
A capital budgeting technique that measures the amount of time it will take to recover the cash outlay of an investment

To illustrate the payback method, let's assume that an entrepreneur is considering an investment in equipment with an expected life of 10 years. The investment outlay will be $15,000, with the cost of the equipment depreciated on a straight-line basis, at $1,500 per year. If the owner makes the investment, the annual after-tax profits have been estimated to be as follows:

Years	After-Tax Profits
1–2	$1,000
3–6	2,000
7–10	2,500

To determine the after-tax cash flows from the investment, the owner merely adds back the depreciation of $1,500 each year to the profit. The reason for adding the depreciation to the profit is that it was deducted when the profits were calculated (as an accounting entry), even though it was not a cash outflow. The results, then, are as follows:

Years	After-Tax Cash Flows
1–2	$2,500
3–6	3,500
7–10	4,000

By the end of the second year, the owner will have recovered $5,000 of the investment outlay ($2,500 per year). By the end of the fourth year, another $7,000, or $12,000 in total, will have been recouped. The additional $3,000 can be recovered in the fifth year, when $3,500 is expected. Thus, it will take 4.86 years [4 years + ($3,000 ÷ $3,500)] to recover the investment. Since the maximum acceptable payback is less than 5 years, the owner will accept the investment.

Many managers and owners of companies use the payback period technique in evaluating investment decisions. Although it uses cash flows, rather than accounting profits, the payback period technique has two significant weaknesses. First, it does not consider the time value of money (cash is preferred sooner rather than later). Second, it fails to consider the cash flows received after the payback period (more cash is preferred, rather than less).

DISCOUNTED CASH FLOWS Managers can avoid the deficiencies of the accounting return on investment and payback period techniques by using discounted cash flow analysis. Discounted cash flow techniques take into consideration the fact that cash received today is more valuable than cash received one year from now (time value of money). For example, interest can be earned on cash that is available for immediate investment; this is not true for cash to be received at some future date.

discounted cash flow (DCF) technique
A capital budgeting technique that compares the present value of future cash flows with the cost of the initial investment

Discounted cash flow (DCF) techniques compare the present value of future cash flows with the investment outlay. Such an analysis may take either of two forms: net present value or internal rate of return.

net present value (NPV)
The present value of expected future cash flows less the initial investment outlay

The **net present value (NPV)** method estimates the current value of the cash that will flow into the firm from the project in the future and deducts the amount of the initial outlay. To find the present value of expected future cash flows, we discount them back to the present at the firm's cost of capital, where the cost of capital is equal to the investors' required rate of return. If the net present value of the investment is positive (that is, if the present value of future cash flows discounted at the rate of return required to satisfy the firm's investors exceeds the initial outlay), the project is acceptable.

internal rate of return (IRR) The rate of return a firm expects to earn on a project

The **internal rate of return (IRR)** method estimates the rate of return that can be expected from a contemplated investment. For the investment outlay to be attractive, the internal rate of return must exceed the firm's cost of capital—the rate of return required to satisfy the firm's investors.

Discounted cash flow techniques can generally be trusted to provide a more reliable basis for decisions than can the accounting return on investment or the payback period technique.

5 *Describe the capital budgeting practices of small firms.*

Capital Budgeting Analysis in Small Firms

Historically, few small business owners have relied on any type of quantitative analysis in making capital budgeting decisions. Instead, the decision to buy new equipment or expand facilities has been based more on intuition and instinct than on economic analysis. And by those who do conduct some kind of quantitative analysis, rarely have discounted cash flow (DCF) techniques, either net present value or internal rate of return, been used.

In the study cited earlier by the National Federation of Independent Businesses, entrepreneurs were asked to indicate the method(s) they used in analyzing capital investments. The results were somewhat encouraging:[8]

Gut feel	25.3%
Payback period technique	18.7
Accounting return on investment	13.6
Discounted cash flow techniques	11.9
Combination	10.5
Other	6.1
No response	4.5
Not applicable—no major investments	2.6

Interestingly, 44 percent of the small business owners indicated that they use some form of quantitative measure (payback period, accounting return on investment, or discounted cash flow techniques) to assess a capital investment; only 25 percent of the respondents said that they use their intuition (gut feel). Furthermore, 67 percent of the company owners said that they make some effort to project future cash flows.

We could conclude that the small business owners were not very sophisticated about using theoretically sound financial methods, given that only 12 percent said they use discounted cash flow analyses. However, the cause of such limited use of DCF tools probably has more to do with the nature of the small firm itself than with the owners' unwillingness to learn. Several more important reasons exist, including the following:

- For many owners of small firms, the business is an extension of their lives—that is, business events affect them personally. The same is true in reverse: What happens to the owners personally affects their decisions about the firm. The firm and its owners are inseparable. We cannot fully understand decisions made about a firm without being aware of the personal events in the owners' lives. Consequently, nonfinancial variables may play a significant part in owners' decisions. For example, the desire to be viewed as a respected part of the community may be more important to an owner than the present value of a business decision.
- The undercapitalization and liquidity problems of a small firm can directly affect the decision-making process, and survival often becomes the top priority. Long-term planning is, therefore, not viewed by the owners as a high priority in the total scheme of things.
- The greater uncertainty of cash flows within a small firm makes long-term forecasting and planning seem unappealing and even a waste of time. The owners simply have no confidence in their ability to predict cash flows beyond two or three years. Thus, calculating the cash flows for the entire life of a project is viewed as a futile effort.

- The value of a closely held firm is less easily observed than that of a publicly held firm whose securities are actively traded in the marketplace. Therefore, the owner of a small firm may consider the market-value rule of maximizing net present values irrelevant. Estimating the cost of capital is also much more difficult for a small firm than for a large firm.
- The smaller size of a small firm's projects may make net present value computations less feasible in a practical sense. The time and expense required to analyze a capital investment are generally the same, whether the project is large or small. Therefore, it is relatively more costly for a small firm to conduct such a study.
- Management talent within a small firm is a scarce resource. Also, the owner-managers frequently have a technical background, as opposed to a business or finance orientation. The perspective of owners is influenced greatly by their backgrounds.

The foregoing characteristics of a small firm and its owners have a significant effect on the decision-making process within the firm. The result is often a short-term mind-set, caused partly by necessity and partly by choice. However, the owner of a small firm should make every effort to use discounted cash flow techniques and to be certain that contemplated investments will, in fact, provide returns that exceed the firm's cost of capital.

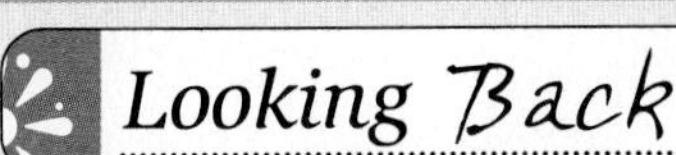

Looking Back

1 Describe the working-capital cycle of a small business.

- The working-capital cycle begins with the purchase of inventory and ends with the collection of accounts receivable.
- The cash conversion period is critical because it is the time period during which cash flow problems can arise and a firm can become illiquid.

2 Identify the important issues in managing a firm's cash flows, including the preparation of a cash budget.

- A firm's cash flows consist of cash flowing into a business (through sales revenue, borrowing, and so on) and cash flowing out of the business (through purchases, operating expenses, and so on).
- Profitable small companies sometimes encounter cash flow problems by failing to understand the working-capital cycle or failing to anticipate the negative consequences of growth.
- Cash inflows and outflows are reconciled in the cash budget, which involves forecasts of cash receipts and expenditures.

3 Explain the key issues in managing accounts receivable, inventory, and accounts payable.

- Granting credit to customers, primarily a marketing decision, directly affects a firm's cash account.
- A firm can improve its cash flows by speeding up collections from customers, minimizing inventories, and delaying payments to suppliers.
- Some small businesses speed up the cash flows from receivables by borrowing against them.
- A concerted effort to manage inventory can trim excess inventory and free cash for other uses.
- Accounts payable, a primary source of financing for small firms, directly affect a firm's cash flow situation.
- Financial management of accounts payable hinges on negotiation and timing.

4 Discuss the techniques commonly used in making capital budgeting decisions.

- Capital budgeting techniques attempt to determine whether future benefits from an investment will exceed the initial outlay.
- Capital budgeting techniques include the accounting return on investment, the payback period, and the discounted cash flow techniques.
- The accounting return on investment technique has two significant shortcomings: It is based on accounting profits rather than actual cash flows received, and it ignores the time value of money.
- The payback period technique also has two major weaknesses: It ignores the time value of money, and it doesn't consider cash flows received after the payback period.
- The discounted cash flow techniques—net present value and internal rate of return—provide the best accept–reject decision criteria in capital budgeting analysis.

5 Describe the capital budgeting practices of small firms.

- Few small firms use any type of discounted cash flow technique. In fact, the majority of small companies do not use any formal analysis whatsoever.
- The very nature of small firms may explain, to some degree, why they seldom use the conceptually richer techniques for evaluating long-term investments.

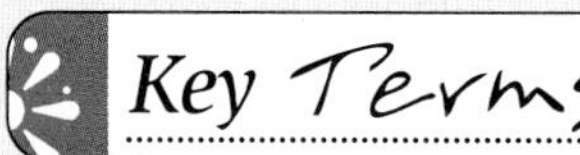

Key Terms

working-capital management, p. 481
net operating working capital, p. 481
working-capital cycle, p. 481
cash conversion period, p. 483
cash budget, p. 487
lock box, p. 492
pledged accounts receivable, p. 492
capital budgeting analysis, p. 495
accounting return on investment technique, p. 496
payback period technique, p. 497
discounted cash flow (DCF) technique, p. 497
net present value (NPV), p. 497
internal rate of return (IRR), p. 498

Discussion Questions

1. a. List the events in the working-capital cycle that directly affect cash and those that do not.
   b. What determines the length of a firm's cash conversion period?
2. a. What are some examples of cash receipts that are not sales revenue?
   b. Explain how expenses and cash disbursements during a month may be different.
3. How may a seller speed up the collection of accounts receivable? Give examples that may apply to various stages in the life cycle of receivables.
4. Suppose that a small firm could successfully shift to a just-in-time inventory system—an arrangement in which inventory is received just as it is needed. How would this affect the firm's working-capital management?
5. How do working-capital management and capital budgeting differ?
6. Compare the different techniques that can be used in capital budgeting analysis.
7. What does net present value measure?
8. Define internal rate of return.
9. a. Find the accounting return on investment for a project that costs $10,000, will have no salvage value, and has expected annual after-tax profits of $1,000.
   b. Determine the payback period for a capital investment that costs $40,000 and has the following after-tax profits. (The project outlay of $40,000 will be depreciated on a straight-line basis to a zero salvage value.)

Year	After-Tax Profits
1	$4,000
2	5,000
3	6,000
4	6,500
5	6,500
6	6,000
7	5,000

10. Why would owners of small firms not be inclined to use the net present value or internal rate of return measurements?

You Make the Call

SITUATION 1

A small firm specializing in the sale and installation of swimming pools was profitable but devoted very little attention to management of its working capital. It had, for example, never prepared or used a cash budget.

To be sure that money was available for payments as needed, the firm kept a minimum of $25,000 in a checking account. At times, this account grew larger; it totaled $43,000 at one time. The owner felt that this approach to cash management worked well for a small company because it eliminated all of the paperwork associated with cash budgeting. Moreover, it had enabled the firm to pay its bills in a timely manner.

Question 1 What are the advantages and weaknesses of the minimum-cash-balance practice?

Question 2 There is a saying "If ain't broke, don't fix it." In view of the firm's present success in paying bills promptly, should it be encouraged to use a cash budget? Be prepared to support your answer.

SITUATION 2

Ruston Manufacturing Company is a small firm selling entirely on a credit basis. It has experienced successful operation and earned modest profits.

Sales are made on the basis of net payment in 30 days. Collections from customers run approximately 70 percent in 30 days, 20 percent in 60 days, 7 percent in 90 days, and 3 percent bad debts.

The owner has considered the possibility of offering a cash discount for early payment. However, the practice seems costly and possibly unnecessary. As the owner puts it, "Why should I bribe customers to pay what they legally owe?"

Question 1 Is offering a cash discount the equivalent of a bribe?

Question 2 How would a cash discount policy relate to bad debts?

Question 3 What cash discount policy, if any, would you recommend?

Question 4 What other approaches might be used to improve cash flows from receivables?

SITUATION 3

Adrian Fudge of the Fudge Corporation wants you to forecast its financing needs over the fourth quarter (October–December). He has made the following observations relative to planned cash receipts and disbursements:

- Interest on a $75,000 bank note (due next March) at an 8 percent annual rate is payable in December for the three-month period just ended.
- The firm follows a policy of paying no cash dividends.
- Actual historical and future predicted sales are as follows:

Historical		Predicted	
August	$150,000	October	$200,000
September	175,000	November	220,000
		December	180,000
		January	200,000

- The firm has a monthly rental expense of $5,000.
- Wages and salaries for the coming months are estimated at $25,000 per month.
- Of the firm's sales, 25 percent is collected in the month of the sale, 35 percent one month after the sale, and the remaining 40 percent two months after the sale.
- Merchandise is purchased one month before the sales month and is paid for in the month it is sold. Purchases equal 75 percent of sales. The firm's cost of goods sold is also 75 percent of sales.
- Tax prepayments are made quarterly, with a prepayment of $10,000 in October based on earnings for the quarter ended September 30.
- Utility costs for the firm average 3 percent of sales and are paid in the month they are incurred.
- Depreciation expense is $20,000 annually.

Question 1 Prepare a monthly cash budget for the three-month period ending in December.

Question 2 If the firm's beginning cash balance for the budget period is $7,000, and this is its minimum desired balance, determine when and how much the firm will need to borrow during the budget period. The firm has a $50,000 line of credit with its bank, with interest (10 percent annual rate) paid monthly. For example, interest on a loan taken out at the end of September would be paid at the end of October and every month thereafter so long as the loan was outstanding.

Experiential Exercises

1. Interview the owner of a small firm to determine the nature of the firm's working-capital time line. Try to estimate the cash conversion period.
2. Interview a small business owner or credit manager regarding the extension of credit and/or the collection of receivables in that firm. Summarize your findings in a report.
3. Identify a small firm in your community that has recently expanded. Interview the owner of the firm about the methods used in evaluating the expansion.
4. Either alone or with a classmate, approach an owner of a small company about getting data on a current problem or one the company encountered at some time in the past, to see whether you would reach the same decision as the owners did.

Exploring The Web

Visit the Bank of America's Web site at **http://www.bankofamerica.com**. Click on "Small Business," then "Resource Center" and "Managing Your Finances." Then go to "Managing Your Cash Flow." Watch the video; then click on "Resources" and answer the following questions based on what you read there.

1. What is the purpose of a cash flow statement?
2. What should be included in the operating activities section of the cash flow statement? In the investing activities section? In the financing activities section?
3. What are the two methods of calculating cash flow? Briefly explain each method.

Case 22

BARTON SALES AND SERVICE (P. 567)

This case looks at the financial performance of a small air-conditioning and heating services company, with emphasis on its working-capital policies.

EVALUATING FINANCIAL PERFORMANCE

In the Spotlight

Zingerman's Delicatessen

A company must perform well financially to stay in business. Thus, failure to understand a firm's financial position can be deadly. But financial success can best be sustained within the context of a healthy business culture based on trust and integrity. Like many small business owners, Ari Weinzweig and Paul Saginaw struggle to balance financial performance and culture.

In 1982, Weinzweig and Saginaw founded Zingerman's Delicatessen in Ann Arbor, Michigan. Over the next 10 years, the deli became world famous—and then it hit a wall. Faced with either significantly changing the company or letting it stagnate, the partners came up with an ingenious strategy that has allowed them to retain the best aspects of small business life while enjoying the benefits and challenges of growth. The result is ZCoB, a group of seven small businesses in and around Ann Arbor.

Weinzweig and Saginaw had a choice. They could keep Zingerman's a small, local operation and run the risk that it would languish or atrophy. Or they could take it to the next level. But if they grew Zingerman's aggressively, they might sacrifice the very attributes that had made the deli extraordinary since its beginning—a close association with the community, intimacy with customers, team spirit among employees, and food and service of exceptional quality.

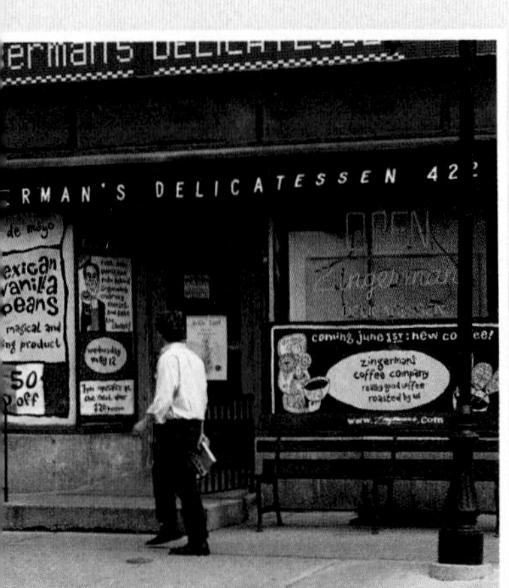

© Steven Pepple

Pastry manager Amy Emberling viewed the transformation of Zingerman's into ZCoB with misgivings. Emberling feared that the company was becoming bureaucratic and impersonal. But her fears proved to be unfounded.

Inside the company, questions about its future remain, but they seem to be manageable. "We've realized the value of living with ambiguity," says Emberling. "When something comes up, it's not always clear what the right answer is. You just have to go with the process and have faith. Mutual trust and respect play a big role. You have to operate in a world of integrity. There's a lot of integrity in this company at all levels—from the financial statements to the croissants."

That integrity and resilience will surely be tested in the years to come. Although Zingerman's has always been profitable on an operating basis, its margins have been squeezed recently by, among other things, a change of management at the deli and the expense of launching the new businesses. "There's no reason we can't earn 10% profit before tax," says Ron Maurer, ZCoB's CFO, "but it won't be easy. The question is, 'How far can we go without damaging the culture?'" Right now, the company has a goal of donating at least 10 percent of its operating profit to charitable causes, which is laudable, but that can't help but affect financial performance.

Source: Bo Burlingham, "The Coolest Small Company in America," *Inc.*, Vol. 25, No. 1 (January 2003), pp. 64–74.

Chapter 23

Looking Ahead

After studying this chapter, you should be able to

1 *Identify the basic requirements for an accounting system.*

2 *Explain two alternative accounting options.*

3 *Describe the purpose of and procedures related to internal control.*

4 *Evaluate a firm's ability to pay its bills as they come due.*

5 *Assess a firm's overall profitability on its asset base.*

6 *Measure a firm's use of debt and equity financing.*

7 *Evaluate the rate of return earned on the owners' investment.*

For a number of years, Dan had wanted to start his own business—an idea that had originated when he was in college. However, the time never seemed to be right. But then his long-time friend Hank approached him about starting a new company to provide sales training materials for companies with a large sales staff. Given Hank's experience in educational training and Dan's sales background, Dan believed they would make a good team.

So, three years ago, Dan left his sales position and began to work full-time at building the new company, Sales Unlimited. Despite some stressful times, it has gone well. Early on, the partners hired technical support and two salespersons. In addition to leading the small sales staff, Dan assumed responsibility for keeping the company's accounting records—a task for which he had no education or experience. He bought QuickBooks, an accounting software package that allowed him to keep up with the firm's accounting.

Last year, Dan and Hank decided it was time for Dan to devote all his time to sales, so they hired a bookkeeper to assume the accounting responsibilities. In time, this person took over all the accounting-related activities, including making deposits, paying suppliers, reconciling bank statements, writing payroll checks, and preparing monthly financial statements. Finally being free of the accounting responsibilities was like a breath of fresh air for Dan, as his passion was sales.

As the firm continued to grow, Dan and Hank's banker recommended that they hire an accounting firm to oversee the accounting and finance functions of the business. After interviewing several accounting firms, Dan and Hank chose a firm that seemed to fit their needs well. After the initial review, the accountant expressed some concerns. The accountant was particularly worried about the lack of internal controls, noting, "Having one person conduct all the accounting functions is asking for trouble and needs to be changed." Dan responded, "I have known the bookkeeper for years and have total confidence in his integrity. Besides, I don't want to give the impression that I do not trust him, because I do."

Dan's concern is more about not knowing how to interpret the financial statements when he receives them. He wants help interpreting what the statements say about the firm's financial performance. So, at the moment, both he and Hank are perplexed as to what they should do.

Their concerns are shared by many entrepreneurs who struggle to understand accounting matters and effectively use financial statements in managing their businesses. So, this chapter examines the basic elements of an effective accounting system. Then, suggestions are presented on how to use accounting data to draw conclusions about a firm's financial performance.

ACCOUNTING ACTIVITIES IN SMALL FIRMS

Managers must have accurate, meaningful, and timely information if they are to make good decisions. This is particularly true of financial information about a firm's operations.

An inadequate accounting system is a primary factor in small business failures. Owner-managers of small firms sometimes believe that they have less need for financial information because of their personal involvement in day-to-day operations, but they are only deceiving themselves.

Rarely are small business owner-managers expert accountants—nor should they expect to be *or even want to be*. But every one of them should know enough about the accounting process, including financial statements, to recognize which accounting methods are best for their company.

1 *Identify the basic requirements for an accounting system.*

Basic Requirements for Accounting Systems

An accounting system structures the flow of financial information to provide a complete picture of a firm's financial activities. Conceivably, a few very small firms may not require formal financial statements. Most, however, need at least monthly financial statements, which should be computer-generated. The benefits of using a computer in developing financial information are so great and the costs so low that it makes absolutely no sense to do otherwise.

Regardless of its level of sophistication, an accounting system for a small business should accomplish the following objectives:

- Provide an accurate, thorough picture of operating results
- Permit a quick comparison of current data with prior years' operating results and budgetary goals
- Offer financial statements for use by management, bankers, and prospective creditors
- Facilitate prompt filing of reports and tax returns to regulatory and tax-collecting government agencies
- Reveal employee fraud, theft, waste, and record-keeping errors

THE RECORD-KEEPING SYSTEM An accounting system provides the framework for managerial control of a firm. Its effectiveness rests on a well-designed and well-managed record-keeping system. In addition to the financial statements intended for external use with bankers and investors (balance sheets, income statements, and cash flow statements), internal accounting records should be kept. The major types of internal accounting records are as follows:

- *Accounts receivable records.* Records of receivables are vital not only for making decisions on credit extension but also for billing accurately and maintaining good customer relations. An analysis of these records will reveal the effectiveness of a firm's credit and collection policies.
- *Accounts payable records.* Records of liabilities show what the firm owes to suppliers, facilitate the taking of cash discounts, and allow payments to be made when due.
- *Inventory records.* Adequate records are essential for the control and security of inventory items. Inventory records supply information for use in making purchases, maintaining adequate stock levels, and computing turnover ratios.
- *Payroll records.* Payroll records show the total salaries paid to employees and provide a base for computing and paying payroll taxes.
- *Cash records.* Carefully maintained records showing all receipts and disbursements are necessary to safeguard cash. They provide essential information about cash flows and cash balances.
- *Fixed asset records.* Fixed asset records show the original cost of each asset and the depreciation taken to date, along with other information such as the condition of the asset.
- *Other accounting records.* Among the other accounting records that are vital to the efficient operation of a small business are the insurance register (showing all policies in force), records of leaseholds, and records of the firm's investments outside its business.

COMPUTER SOFTWARE PACKAGES Software packages can be used to generate the required accounting records. Most computer software packages include the following features:

- A checkbook that automatically calculates a firm's cash balance, prints checks, and reconciles the account with the bank statement at month's end
- Automatic preparation of income statements, balance sheets, and statements of cash flows
- A cash budget that compares actual expenditures with budgeted expenditures
- Preparation of subsidiary journal accounts—accounts receivable, accounts payable, and other high-activity accounts

In addition, numerous software packages fulfill specialized accounting needs such as graphing, cash flow analysis, and tax preparation.

Although the options are almost unlimited for accounting software programs appropriate for use in a small firm, there are several leaders in the entry-level category. Ranging in cost from $100 to $300, they include

- *DacEasy*
  http://www.daceasy.com
- *MYOB*
  http://www.myob.com
- *QuickBooks 2004*
  http://www.quickbooks.com
- *Peachtree*
  http://www.peachtree.com
- *Simply Accounting*
  http://www.simplyaccounting.com
- *NetSuite*
  http://www.oraclesmallbusiness.com

Although all these programs have been well tested and widely used, the small business owner should carefully consider the appropriateness of computer software or hardware before purchasing it. The chance of acquiring computer equipment or programs that do not fit a firm's needs is still significant.

OUTSIDE ACCOUNTING SERVICES Instead of having an employee or a member of the owner's family keep records, a firm may have its financial records kept by a certified public accountant or by a bookkeeping firm or service bureau that caters to small businesses. Very small firms often find it convenient to have the same person or agency keep their books and prepare their financial statements and tax returns.

Numerous small public accounting firms offer complete accounting services to small businesses. Such accounting firms usually offer their services at a significantly lower cost than do larger accounting firms. Besides, larger accounting firms have recently become more heavily focused on publicly traded companies, following passage of the Sarbanes-Oxley legislation, which was designed to reduce fraud in large firms. Cost is, of course, an important consideration in selecting an accountant, but other major factors, such as whether the accountant has experience in the particular industry in which the entrepreneur is operating, should play a dominant role in this decision as well.

In some areas, mobile bookkeepers also serve small firms. Bringing to a firm's premises a mobile office that includes computer equipment, they obtain the necessary data and prepare the financial statements on site. Use of mobile bookkeeping can be a fast, inexpensive, and convenient approach to filling certain accounting needs.

Alternative Accounting Options

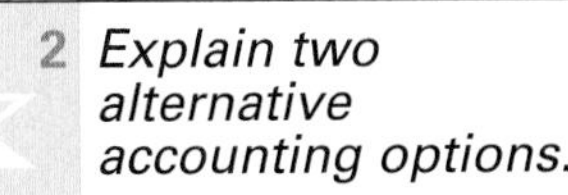
2 *Explain two alternative accounting options.*

Accounting records can be kept in just about any form as long as they provide users with needed data and meet legal requirements. Very small firms have some options when selecting accounting systems and accounting methods. Two such options—cash versus accrual accounting and single-entry versus double-entry systems—reflect the most basic issues in an accounting system.

CASH VERSUS ACCRUAL ACCOUNTING As discussed in Chapter 10, the major distinction between cash-basis and accrual-basis accounting is in the point at which a firm reports revenue and expenses. The cash method of accounting is easier to use; revenue and expenses are reported only when cash is received or a payment is made. In contrast, the accrual method of accounting reports revenue and expenses when they are incurred, regardless of when the cash is received or payment is made.

The cash method of accounting is sometimes selected by very small firms, as well as by firms with slow-moving receivables that want to help their cash flows by avoiding the payment of taxes on income not yet received. However, the cash method does not ultimately provide an accurate matching of revenue and expenses. The accrual method, although it involves more record keeping, is preferable because it provides a more realistic measure of profitability within an accounting period. The accrual method of accounting matches revenue against expenses incurred in obtaining that revenue. Alternating between a cash method and an accrual method of accounting is unacceptable, because it violates the accounting principle of consistency.

SINGLE-ENTRY VERSUS DOUBLE-ENTRY SYSTEMS A single-entry record-keeping system is occasionally still found in the very small business. It is not, however, a system recommended for firms that are striving to grow and achieve effective financial planning. A single-entry system neither incorporates a balance sheet nor directly generates an income statement. A **single-entry system** is basically a checkbook system of receipts and disbursements.

single-entry system
A checkbook system of accounting reflecting only receipts and disbursements

Most introductory accounting textbooks provide information on setting up a **double-entry system.**[1] This type of accounting system provides a self-balancing mechanism in the form of two counterbalancing entries for each transaction recorded. It can be done with the record-keeping journals and ledgers found in most office supply retail stores. However, the relatively simple accounting software programs designed for small firms are preferable.

double-entry system
A self-balancing accounting system that requires that each transaction be recorded twice

3 *Describe the purpose of and procedures related to internal control.*

Internal Accounting Controls

As already noted, an effective accounting system is vital to a firm's success. Without the information it provides, management cannot make informed decisions. However, the quality of a firm's accounting system is dependent on the effectiveness of the controls that exist within the firm. **Internal control** is a system of checks and balances that plays a key role in safeguarding a firm's assets and in enhancing the accuracy and reliability of its financial statements. The importance of internal control has long been recognized in large corporations. Some owners of smaller companies, concerned about the cost or appropriateness of a system of internal control for a small company, don't appreciate its value—but they should.

internal control
A system of checks and balances that safeguards assets and enhances the accuracy and reliability of financial statements

Building internal controls may be difficult within a small company, but it is no less important than for a large company. The absence of internal controls significantly increases the chances not only of fraud and theft but also of bad decisions based on inaccurate and untimely accounting information. Effective internal controls are also necessary for an audit by independent accountants. Certified public accountants are unwilling to express an opinion about a firm's financial statements if the firm lacks adequate internal controls.

Although a complete description of an internal control system is beyond the scope of this textbook, it is important to understand the concept. An example of an internal control is separation of employees' duties so that the individual maintaining control over an asset is not the same person recording transactions in the accounting ledgers. That is, the employee who collects cash from customers should not be allowed to reconcile the bank statement. Here are some other examples of internal control:[2]

- Identifying the various types of transactions that require the owners' authorization
- Establishing a procedure to ensure that checks presented for signature are accompanied by complete supporting documentation
- Limiting access to accounting records
- Sending bank statements directly to the owner
- Safeguarding blank checks
- Requiring all employees to take regular vacations so that any irregularity is likely to be revealed
- Controlling access to the computer facilities

The importance of developing an effective system of internal control cannot be overemphasized. Extra effort may be needed to implement internal controls in a small company, in which business procedures may be informal and segregation of duties is difficult because of the limited number of employees. Even so, it is best to try to develop such controls. An accountant may be of assistance in minimizing the problems that can result from the absence of internal controls.

EVALUATING THE FIRM'S FINANCIAL PERFORMANCE

Once an effective accounting system is in place, a firm's owner must determine how to use the data it generates most productively. Mark Twain said, "He who does not read is no better off than he who cannot read." An owner who has a good accounting system but doesn't use it is in the same situation. This section provides a framework for interpreting financial statements, designed to clarify these statements for individuals with varied accounting backgrounds and experience.

An owner needs to understand the financial effect—positive or negative—that management decisions may have. Ultimately, the results of operating decisions appear in a firm's financial statements.

Living the Dream *Entrepreneurial Challenges*

Using Internal Controls to Avoid a Costly Lesson

Allan Lichter has been co-owner of Millennium Graphics in Bridgeport, Connecticut, for 22 years. But despite all those years of experience, a lack of internal controls almost brought the firm and Lichter himself to the point of bankruptcy. Lichter tells the story in his own words—a story that's very painful for him:

> *Our accounting clerk, who had been with us for five years, started to take accounts payable checks made out to other companies for supplies they shipped to us and began to deposit them in dummy accounts she had set up at her bank under a different name. The employee was also in charge of accounts receivable as well as accounts payable, so she was able to juggle things around and make excuses to our suppliers, and they went along with it. She would answer the phone and, we were told later, make things up like she had cancer or needed an operation of some type, or had to take time off for family problems, yadda, yadda, yadda. All this was kept hidden from us because she was so smooth.*
>
> *We both trusted this employee to handle the bookkeeping. It seemed to us that everything was going along just fine. She was able to fool all of us, including our CPA.*
>
> *One day my partner just happened to pick up the phone first and a supplier who had been promised payment was on the line. He was livid about being "lied to." My partner remembered he had signed the check to cover the outstanding balance to this company only a few weeks ago and he became suspicious.*
>
> *He asked the accounting clerk to go to the check archives to see if the cancelled check had come back from the bank. When he left to go back to the production department, the clerk cleared out her desk quickly and left the building. When we realized she had left work without explanation, then found the cancelled check with a strange endorsement, we knew we had a very serious problem on our hands.*

Lichter's experience could be related by a lot of entrepreneurs. While good internal controls do not guarantee that fraud will not occur, they certainly reduce the risk substantially—and probably would have made all the difference at Millennium Graphics.

Source: Allan F. Lichter, "Bouncing Back," *New England Journal of Entrepreneurship*, Vol. 5, No. 2 (Fall 2002), pp. 9–12.

The exact methods used to interpret financial statements can vary, with the perspective of the interpreter determining what areas are emphasized. For example, if a banker and an entrepreneur were analyzing the same financial statements, they might focus on different data. But whatever perspective is taken, the issues are fundamentally the same and are captured in the following four questions:

1. Can you pay your bills as they come due? In other words, does the firm have the capacity to meet its short-term (one year or less) financial commitments?
2. Are you making a good return on your assets? There is no more important question when it comes to determining if a business is strong economically.
3. How much debt are you using, and what are the implications for the firm's future?
4. Are you getting a good rate of return on your investment? Here we want to know whether the combined effect on the owners of all the financial decisions made is positive or negative.

financial ratios
Restatements of selected income statement and balance sheet data in relative terms

Answering these questions requires restating the data from the income statement and the balance sheet in relative terms, or **financial ratios**. Only in this way can comparisons be made with other firms, with industry averages, and across time. Typically, the industry averages or norms used for comparison purposes are those published by companies such as Dun & Bradstreet, Robert Morris Associates, or Standard & Poor's.[3] Exhibit 23-1 shows the industry norms for the computer and software retailing industry for 2003, as reported by Robert Morris Associates, which compiles financial ratios for banks to use in their analyses of firms seeking loans. As shown in the table, the ratios are reported by firm size.

We can best demonstrate the use of financial ratios to evaluate a firm's performance by looking at the financial statements for Petri & Associates Leasing Company, presented in Chapter 10. For ease of reference, the firm's income statement and balance sheets are reproduced in Exhibits 23-2 and 23-3. Using these financial statements and relying on industry norms selected by the firm's management, we can answer the four fundamental questions with respect to Petri's financial performance.

EXHIBIT 23-1 | *Financial Ratios for Retail Computer and Software Stores, 2003*

	FIRM SIZE BY TOTAL ASSETS		
	Less than $500,000	**$500,000 to $2 Million**	**$2 Million to $10 Million**
Current ratio	1.0	1.4	1.2
Accounts receivable turnover	15.4	8.5	6.3
Inventory turnover*	16.2	22.9	43.9
Return on assets†	−1.53%	−6.08%	8.75%
Gross profit margin	41.2%	38.9%	29%
Operating profit margin	−0.3	−1.6	2.5
Fixed asset turnover	38.3	33.9	54.6
Total asset turnover	5.1	3.8	3.5
Debt/equity	4.5	3.1	4.1
Return on equity (before tax)	8.4%	13.4%	32.7%

*Based on cost of goods sold.
†Not reported in the RMA data, but computed by multiplying the operating profit margin times the total asset turnover.
Note: RMA cautions that the Studies be regarded only as a general guideline and not as an absolute industry norm. This is due to limited samples within categories, the categorization of companies by their primary Standard Industrial Classification (SIC) number only, and different methods of operations by companies within the same industry. For these reasons, RMA recommends that the figures be used only as general guidelines in addition to other methods of financial analysis.

Source: Adapted from *RMA 2003–2004 Annual Statement Studies*, published by Robert Morris Associates, Philadelphia, Pa. Copyright Robert Morris Associates, 2004.

Living the Dream — *Entrepreneurial Challenges*

A Cheap CEO

© Scogin Mayo

Rick Sapio keeps a sign on the wall of his office: "Profit equals revenues less expenses." The chart is a gimmick but is nevertheless important to Sapio, the CEO of Dallas-based Mutuals.com.

Sapio didn't always have that sign on the wall, and he didn't believe he needed it—or anything else—as a manifesto. When he started Mutuals.com, Sapio never really thought about keeping an eye on expenses, because he didn't have to. "I found it very easy to raise money," he says, and as the boom of the 1990s wore on and the marketplace was flush with investment capital, raising money got even simpler.

All that cash was not necessarily a good thing, Sapio admits now. "We were not accountable to being a profitable company at the beginning, and hence our energies weren't focused on looking at expenses."

During the past few years, Sapio has made some changes. His first step was learning to keep an eye on the numbers. After reading that Cisco Systems Inc. closes its books every day, Sapio took up the practice.

Now all financial transactions are entered the same day they occur, to create a real-time picture of the company's revenues and expenses. It's good discipline and surprisingly easy with today's accounting software, says Regina Lian, president of New York City's Financial Comfort, who advises small businesses on financial management.

Each day, Sapio gathers his top managers to go over the figures. Each person is responsible for updating at least one revenue item and one expense. "Every line item on our financial statement has a name next to it," Sapio says. "So, if travel's out of whack, I'll say, 'Ernie, give us a report on how we can lower travel next week.' "

Reviewing the numbers daily has forced Sapio to get serious about sticking to a budget. "If something is not on the budget, we say no to it," he says. "If we absolutely have to spend the money, then we have a line item on our P&L statement that says 'unbudgeted expense.' And we track that number."

Employees who overspend without getting prior approval can wind up paying out of their own pockets—even Sapio himself. In order to get some leadership coaching, Sapio hired a consultant, but did not have an OK from his executive team. Sapio figured the managers would approve the expense retroactively. Unfortunately for Sapio, they never came around. So when the $6,000 invoice arrived, it was Sapio's to pay.

Extreme measures? Possibly. But they've helped send a message about the firm's culture of frugality and discipline to employees. Perhaps more significantly, such strict attention to the bottom line has opened Sapio's eyes to a general organizational liability. In most businesses, Sapio says, there's one person who wastes more money than anyone else—the CEO. Sapio cites himself as the perfect "Exhibit A."

Source: Emily Barker, "Finance: Cheap Executive Officer," *Inc.*, Vol. 24, No. 4 (April 2002), pp. 38–40.

Can You Pay Your Bills?

4 *Evaluate a firm's ability to pay its bills as they come due.*

A business—or a person, for that matter—that has a large sum of money relative to the amount of debt owed is described as highly liquid (see Chapter 10). More accurately, the liquidity of a business depends on the availability to the firm of cash to meet maturing debt obligations. Measuring liquidity answers the question "Does the firm now have or will it have in the future the resources to pay creditors when debts come due?"

This question can be answered in two ways: (1) by comparing the firm's assets that are relatively liquid in nature with the debt coming due in the near term or (2) by examining the timeliness with which liquid assets, primarily accounts receivable and inventories, are being converted into cash.

The first approach to measuring liquidity is to compare cash and the assets that should be converted into cash within the year against the debt (liabilities) that is coming due and will be payable within the year. The liquid assets within a firm are its current assets, and

EXHIBIT 23-2 *Income Statement for Petri & Associates Leasing Company for the Year Ending December 31, 2005*

Sales revenue		$850,000
Cost of goods sold		550,000
Gross profit on sales		$300,000
Operating expenses:		
Marketing expenses	$90,000	
General and administrative expenses	80,000	
Depreciation expense	30,000	
Total operating expenses		$200,000
Operating income		$100,000
Interest expense		20,000
Earnings before taxes		$ 80,000
Income tax (25%)		20,000
Net income		$ 60,000

the maturing debt consists of the current liabilities shown in the balance sheet. So, to measure liquidity, we use the current ratio, discussed earlier in Chapter 10. Using the data in Exhibit 23-3, we can determine the current ratio for Petri & Associates Leasing Company:

$$\text{Current ratio} = \frac{\text{Current assets}}{\text{Current liabilities}} = \frac{\$350{,}000}{\$100{,}000} = 3.50$$

EXHIBIT 23-3 *Balance Sheet for Petri & Associates Leasing Company for December 31, 2005*

Assets	
Current assets:	
Cash	$ 50,000
Accounts receivable	80,000
Inventories	220,000
Total current assets	$350,000
Fixed assets:	
Gross fixed assets	$960,000
Accumulated depreciation	(390,000)
Net fixed assets	$570,000
TOTAL ASSETS	$920,000
Debt (Liabilities) and Equity	
Current liabilities:	
Accounts payable	$ 20,000
Short-term notes	80,000
Total current liabilities (debt)	$100,000
Long-term debt	200,000
Total debt	$300,000
Ownership equity:	
Common stock	$300,000
Retained earnings	320,000
Total ownership equity	$620,000
TOTAL DEBT AND EQUITY	$920,000

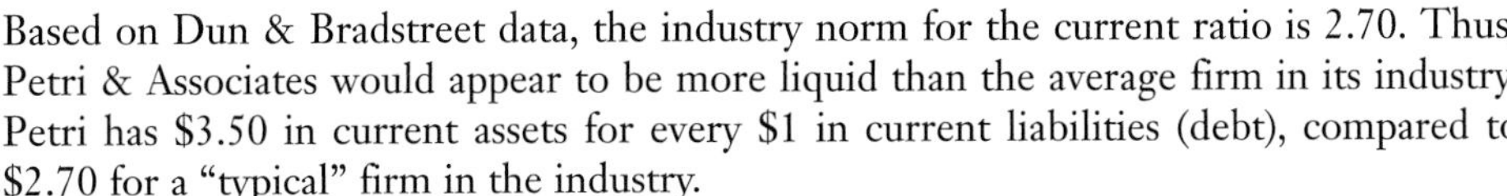

Based on Dun & Bradstreet data, the industry norm for the current ratio is 2.70. Thus, Petri & Associates would appear to be more liquid than the average firm in its industry. Petri has $3.50 in current assets for every $1 in current liabilities (debt), compared to $2.70 for a "typical" firm in the industry.

The second view of liquidity examines a firm's ability to convert accounts receivable and inventory into cash on a timely basis. The ability to convert accounts receivable into cash may be measured by computing how quickly the firm is collecting its receivables. This can be determined by measuring the number of times that accounts receivable are "rolled over" during a year, or the **accounts receivable turnover**. The accounts receivable turnover is computed as follows:

accounts receivable turnover The number of times accounts receivable "roll over" during a year

$$\text{Accounts receivable turnover} = \frac{\text{Credit sales}}{\text{Accounts receivable}}$$

If we assume that Petri & Associates' sales are all credit sales, as opposed to cash sales, the accounts receivable turnover for Petri & Associates in 2005 is 10.63 days. The computation is as follows:

$$\text{Accounts receivable turnover} = \frac{\text{Credit sales}}{\text{Accounts receivable}} = \frac{\$850{,}000}{\$80{,}000} = 10.63$$

The industry norm for accounts receivable turnover is 10.43. Thus, we may conclude that Petri & Associates is comparable to the average firm in the industry in terms of its collection of receivables.[4]

To gain some insight into the liquidity of Petri's inventories, we now need to determine how many times the firm is turning over its inventories during the year. The **inventory turnover** is calculated as follows:

inventory turnover The number of times inventories "roll over" during a year

$$\text{Inventory turnover} = \frac{\text{Cost of goods sold}}{\text{Inventory}}$$

Note that in this ratio sales are shown at the firm's cost, as opposed to the full market value when sold. Since inventory (the denominator) is at cost, it is desirable to measure sales (the numerator) on a cost basis also in order to avoid a biased answer.

The inventory turnover for Petri & Associates is calculated as follows:

$$\text{Inventory turnover} = \frac{\text{Cost of goods sold}}{\text{Inventory}} = \frac{\$550{,}000}{\$220{,}000} = 2.50$$

The industry norm for inventory turnover is 4.00. This analysis reveals a significant problem of Petri & Associates. The firm is carrying excessive inventory, possibly even some obsolete inventory. It is generating only $2.50 in sales at cost for every $1 of inventory, compared to $4.00 in sales at cost for the average firm.

Are You Making a Good Return on Your Assets?

5 *Assess a firm's overall profitability on its asset base.*

A vitally important question to a firm's investors is whether operating profits are sufficient relative to the total amount of assets invested. Exhibit 23-4 provides an overview of the computation of the rate of return on all capital invested in a firm, both by creditors and by equity investors. The total capital from the various investors becomes the firm's total assets.

A firm's assets are invested for the express purpose of producing operating profits—profits that are then distributed to creditors and stockholders. A comparison of operating profits to total invested assets reveals the rate of return that is being earned on all the firm's capital. For Petri & Associates, we compute the return on assets (discussed in Chapter 11) as follows:

$$\text{Return on assets} = \frac{\text{Operating income}}{\text{Total assets}} = \frac{\$100{,}000}{\$920{,}000} = 0.1087, \text{ or } 10.87\%$$

The firm's return on assets is less than the industry norm of 13.2 percent. For some reason, Petri & Associates is generating less operating income on each dollar of assets than are its competitors.

The owners of Petri & Associates should not be satisfied with merely knowing that they are not earning a competitive return on the firm's assets. They should also want to

Living the Dream *Entrepreneurial Challenges*

Facing the Music to Stay Profitable

Until recently, Greg Smith, president and CEO of the Petra Technology Group, based in Corning, New York, rarely examined how his company compared with the rest of the industry. Why would he? The sales and profits of the company, a $1.5 million systems integrator, had grown every year since the company's inception in 1993.

But in 1998, sales flattened. Petra faced unprofitability for the first time. Though it was easy to attribute losses to the sales slump, Smith felt there was more to the story—he just couldn't pin it down. Was he overspending in ways he couldn't see?

Smith contacted Nancy Kirby of Kirby Beals Maier, a local accounting firm. Being familiar with private company growth issues, she suggested that Smith benchmark Petra's numbers against those of other IT-services companies of the same size. Specifically, she wanted Smith to examine payroll as a percentage of sales, which is crucial in an employee-dependent services company.

Smith quickly obtained two industry studies. One was from Robert Morris Associates, and the other from the Chalfin Group Inc., a consultancy in Metuchen, New Jersey, which Smith found through an Internet search.

That was only the beginning. Armed with industry-wide information, Smith quickly saw a problem. Payroll and related costs for his 15-employee business exceeded 60 percent of company sales—a ratio the Chalfin Group generally views as a red flag for companies trying to stay in the black. "At certain points, you have to face the music to remain profitable," Smith says. Part of facing the music for Smith meant reducing his employee head count by two and using contractors instead of staff.

At Kirby's prompting, Smith also checked Petra's ratio of current assets to current liabilities. It was 0.82—too low, in her view. "He had too much short-term debt," Kirby says. Most of the short-term debt was the result of having to pay down a $100,000 line of credit every year. Smith shifted the majority of his debt from a credit line to a seven-year note. Although a small line of credit may mean future cash flow troubles, Smith isn't worried: Petra bills biweekly, and its accounts receivable turn over 10 times a year. In one study that Smith looked at, the average turnover of receivables was 5 times a year.

Smith used the numbers as guides rather than as absolutes. Most research groups recommend this approach in order to take into account the vagaries of individual businesses.

"There are so many variables," says Robert Chalfin, president of the Chalfin Group. Chalfin adds that the survey process itself often skews information in favor of profitable companies. "They're happier to talk about their results," he says.

Smith has become a lot more scrupulous in other areas as well, paying more attention to the company's weekly break-even point of $23,000 and charting sales in relation to it. He's learned that a big part of financial discipline is monitoring the simple things. "Losing money for a year is a good wake-up call," he says.

Source: Ilan Mochari, "Significant Figures," http://www.inc.com, July 1, 2000.

know *why* the return is below average. To gain more understanding, the owners could separate the return on assets into its two components: (1) operating profit margin and (2) total asset turnover. Separating the return on assets into its two factors better isolates a firm's strengths and weaknesses when it is attempting to identify ways to earn a competitive rate of return on its total invested capital.

The equation for the return on assets can be restated as follows:

$$\text{Return on assets} = \frac{\text{Operating income}}{\text{Total assets}} = \underbrace{\frac{\text{Operating profits}}{\text{Sales}}}_{\textbf{Operating Profit Margin}} \times \underbrace{\frac{\text{Sales}}{\text{Total assets}}}_{\textbf{Total Asset Turnover}}$$

operating profit margin
The ratio of operating profits to sales, showing how well a firm manages its income statement

The first component of the expanded equation, the **operating profit margin**, shows how well a firm is managing its income statement—that is, how well a firm is managing

EXHIBIT 23-4 *Return on Assets: An Overview*

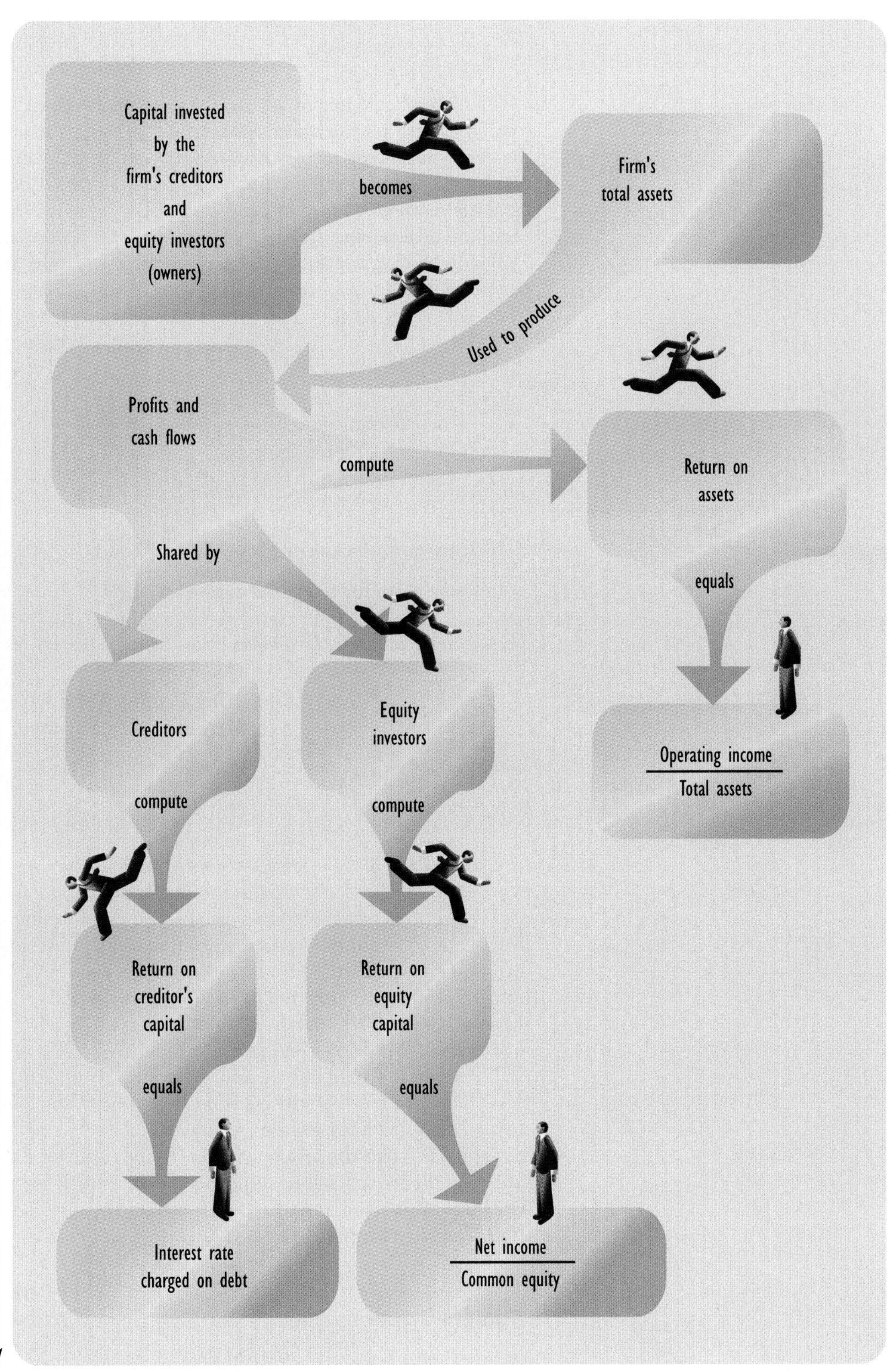

the activities that affect its income. There are five factors, or driving forces, that affect the operating profit margin and, in turn, the return on assets:

1. The number of units of product or service sold (volume)
2. The average selling price for each product or service unit (sales price)

3. The cost of manufacturing or acquiring the firm's product (cost of goods sold)
4. The ability to control general and administrative expenses (operating expenses)
5. The ability to control expenses in marketing and distributing the firm's product (operating expenses)

total asset turnover The ratio of sales to total assets, showing the efficiency with which a firm's assets are used to generate sales

The second component of a firm's return on assets, the **total asset turnover**, indicates how efficiently management is using the firm's assets to generate sales—that is, how well the firm is managing its balance sheet. If Company A can generate $3 in sales with $1 in assets while Company B generates $2 in sales per asset dollar, then Company A is using its assets more efficiently in generating sales. This is a major determinant in the firm's return on investment.

For Petri & Associates, the operating profit margin and total asset turnover can be computed as follows:

$$\text{Operating profit margin} = \frac{\text{Operating profits}}{\text{Sales}} = \frac{\$100{,}000}{\$850{,}000} = 0.1176, \text{ or } 11.76\%$$

$$\text{Total asset turnover} = \frac{\text{Sales}}{\text{Total assets}} = \frac{\$850{,}000}{\$920{,}000} = 0.92$$

The industry norms for the two ratios are as follows:

Industry norm for operating profit margin = 11%

Industry norm for total asset turnover = 1.20

Thus, comparing Petri & Associates to the industry, we have

		Operating Profit Margin		Total Asset Turnover		Return on Assets
Return on $\text{assets}_{\text{Petri}}$	=	11.76%	×	0.92	=	10.82%[5]
Return on $\text{assets}_{\text{Ind}}$	=	11.0%	×	1.20	=	13.2%

Clearly, Petri & Associates is competitive when it comes to managing its income statement—keeping costs and expenses in line relative to sales—as reflected by the operating profit margin. In other words, its managers are performing satisfactorily in controlling the five driving forces of the operating profit margin. However, Petri & Associates' total asset turnover shows why the firm is not earning a good return on its assets. The firm is not using its assets efficiently; the balance sheet is not being managed well. Petri's problem is that it generates $0.92 in sales per dollar of assets, while the competition produces $1.20 in sales from every dollar in assets.

fixed asset turnover A measure of the relationship of sales to fixed assets

The analysis should not stop here, however. It is clear that Petri's assets are not being used efficiently, but the next question should be "Which assets are the problem?" Is this firm overinvested in all assets or mainly in accounts receivable or inventory or fixed assets? To answer this question, we must examine the turnover ratio for each asset. The first two ratios—accounts receivable turnover and inventory turnover—were calculated earlier. The third ratio, **fixed asset turnover**, is found by dividing sales by fixed assets. Thus, the three financial ratios are as follows:

Turnover Ratios			Petri & Associates	Industry Norm
Accounts receivable turnover	=	$\frac{\text{Credit sales}}{\text{Accounts receivable}}$	$\frac{\$850{,}000}{\$80{,}000} = 10.63$	10.43
Inventory turnover	=	$\frac{\text{Cost of goods sold}}{\text{Inventory}}$	$\frac{\$550{,}000}{\$220{,}000} = 2.50$	4.00
Fixed asset turnover	=	$\frac{\text{Sales}}{\text{Fixed assets}}$	$\frac{\$850{,}000}{\$570{,}000} = 1.49$	2.50

Petri's problems can now be better understood. The firm has excessive inventories, as was evident earlier. Also, it is too heavily invested in fixed assets for the sales being produced. It appears that these two asset categories are not being managed well. Consequently, Petri & Associates is experiencing a lower-than-average return on assets.

We have shown how to analyze a firm's ability to earn a satisfactory rate of return on its total invested capital. To this point, we have ignored the firm's decisions as to whether to use debt or equity financing and the consequence of such decisions on the owners' return on the equity investment. So let's examine how Petri & Associates finances its assets.

How Much Debt Are You Using?

6 Measure a firm's use of debt and equity financing.

We'll return to the issue of profitability shortly. Now, however, let's consider how the firm is financed. Are the firm's assets financed to a greater extent by debt or by equity? Two ratios will be used to answer this question (although many others could be used). First, we must determine what percentage of the firm's assets is financed by total debt—with short-term and long-term debt. (The remaining percentage must be financed by equity.) As discussed in Chapter 11, the use of debt, or **financial leverage**, can increase a firm's return on equity, but with some financial risk involved. The debt ratio, which is total debt divided by total assets, was discussed in Chapter 10. The same relationship can be stated as the

financial leverage
The use of debt in financing a firm's assets

Living the Dream — Entrepreneurial Challenges

Managing by the Numbers

Dorian S. Boyland is taking care of business as he bustles about his 29,000-square-foot Honda dealership, located in Greenfield, Wisconsin. He is preparing for a grand opening, even though the store has been open since 2001.

© Todd Dacquisto

Boyland is excited about the festivities, but he intends to get a return on this investment. Make no mistake about it; he is meticulous about how he spends money, keeping advertising and sales salaries each to less than 10 percent of gross profits. No more than 10 percent of gross profits is paid to managers in commissions, and no more than 15 percent of gross profits is awarded to sales managers in commissions.

The auto dealer operates with one goal in mind: Net a 3 percent to 3.5 percent profit on sales from all seven of his auto dealerships. "I never ask how many cars we sold," says Boyland. "I ask my sales managers how much profit did we make. I operate on the premise that if I sell a car for $20,000, I know that 3 percent (or $600) of that amount is going to go to my bottom line. Now, how I get that 3 percent is how we operate the store—from the bottom up."

Boyland's cost controls are a neverending process. He abides by the book, a monthly financial analysis that is reviewed by all store managers. This information sharing allows every general manager and sales manager to critique one another, exchange ideas, and establish goals and guidelines.

Volume is very important to dealers because manufacturers expect them to achieve a certain level of market penetration. But, as Boyland sees it, "You can be No. 1 in terms of volume, but if you are constantly losing that manufacturer money, you'll be taken out of business."

It helps that Boyland is not only a respected car salesman, but also great at accounting, says Roger Cole, general manager of All Star Ford. "I have been with Dorian for the past four years. I have learned more from him during that time about how to run the store on a business basis, where it's all about percentages."

Boyland grows excited when discussing business strategies. "You have to have a passion for this business," he says. "There's a lot of money to be made and a lot of money to be lost. But whether you are selling cars or shoes, you go into business to make money. That's the bottom line."

Source: Carolyn M. Brown, "Maximum Overdrive," *Black Enterprise*, Vol. 33, No. 11 (June 2003), pp. 156–162.

debt-equity ratio, which is total debt divided by total equity, rather than total assets. Either ratio leads to the same conclusion.

For Petri & Associates in 2005, debt as a percentage of total assets is 33 percent, compared to an industry norm of 40 percent. The computation is as follows:

$$\text{Debt ratio} = \frac{\text{Total debt}}{\text{Total assets}} = \frac{\$300{,}000}{\$920{,}000} = 0.33, \text{ or } 33\%$$

Thus, Petri & Associates uses somewhat less debt than the average firm in the industry, which means that it has less financial risk.

A second perspective on a firm's financing decisions can be gained by looking at the income statement. When a firm borrows money, it is required, at a minimum, to pay the interest on the debt. Thus, determining the amount of operating income available to pay the interest provides a firm with valuable information. Stated as a ratio, the computation shows the number of times the firm earns its interest. Thus, the **times interest earned ratio** is commonly used in examining a firm's debt position. This ratio is calculated as follows:

times interest earned ratio
The ratio of operating income to interest charges

$$\text{Times interest earned ratio} = \frac{\text{Operating income}}{\text{Interest expense}}$$

For Petri & Associates, the times interest earned ratio is as follows:

$$\text{Times interest earned ratio} = \frac{\text{Operating income}}{\text{Interest expense}} = \frac{\$100{,}000}{\$20{,}000} = 5.00$$

The industry norm for the times interest earned ratio is 4.00. Thus, Petri & Associates is better able to service its interest expense than most comparable firms. Remember, however, that interest is paid not with income but with cash. Also, the firm may be required to repay some of the debt principal as well as the interest. Thus, the times interest earned ratio is only a crude measure of a firm's capacity to service its debt. Nevertheless, it gives a general indication of the firm's debt capacity.

7 Evaluate the rate of return earned on the owners' investment.

Are You Getting a Good Rate of Return on Your Investment?

The last question looks at the accounting return on the owners' investment, or return on equity, which was discussed earlier in Chapter 11. We must determine whether the earnings available to the firm's owners (or stockholders) are attractive when compared to the returns of owners of similar companies in the same industry. The return on equity for Petri & Associates in 2005 is as follows:

$$\text{Return on equity} = \frac{\text{Net income}}{\text{Common equity}} = \frac{\$60{,}000}{\$620{,}000} = 0.097, \text{ or } 9.7\%$$

The industry norm for return on equity is 12.5 percent. Thus, it appears that the owners of Petri & Associates are not receiving a return on their investment equivalent to that of owners of competing businesses. Why not? To answer this question, we have to understand the following:

1. The return on equity will increase as the difference between the return on assets and the interest rate paid for the use of debt financing increases; that is, as (return on assets − interest rate) increases, return on equity increases. But, if the difference between the return on assets and the interest rate decreases, then the return on equity will also decrease.
2. As a firm's debt ratio (total debt ÷ total assets) increases, return on equity will increase if the return on assets is greater than the interest rate, but return on equity will decrease if the return on assets is less than the interest rate.

It is important for an entrepreneur to understand the foregoing relationships. Thus, you are encouraged to return to the illustrations in Chapter 11 (pages 239–242) of the effects on an owner's return on equity (net income ÷ common equity) of (1) a firm's return on assets (operating income ÷ total assets) and (2) a firm's debt ratio (total debt ÷ total assets).

In the case of Petri & Associates, we see that the firm has a lower return on equity in part because it is not as profitable in its operation as its competitors are. (Recall that the return on assets was 10.87 percent for Petri & Associates, compared to 13.2 percent for the industry.) Also, Petri uses less debt than the average firm in the industry, causing its return on equity to be lower than that of other firms—provided, of course, that these firms are earning a return on their investments that exceeds the cost of debt (the interest rate). However, we should recognize that the use of less debt does reduce Petri's risk.

To conclude, the financial ratios used in evaluating the financial performance of Petri & Associates for 2005 are presented in Exhibit 23-5. The ratios are grouped by the issue being addressed: liquidity, operating profitability, financing, and owners' return on equity. Recall that the turnover ratios for accounts receivable and inventories are used for more than one purpose. These ratios have implications for both the firm's liquidity and its profitability; thus, they are listed in both areas.

23-5 *Financial Ratio Analysis for Petri & Associates Leasing Company*

Financial Ratios	Petri & Associates	Industry Norm
1. Firm liquidity		
Current ratio = $\frac{\text{Current assets}}{\text{Current liabilities}}$	$\frac{\$350,000}{\$100,000} = 3.50$	2.70
Accounts receivable turnover = $\frac{\text{Credit sales}}{\text{Accounts receivable}}$	$\frac{\$850,000}{\$80,000} = 10.63$	10.43
Inventory turnover = $\frac{\text{Cost of goods sold}}{\text{Inventory}}$	$\frac{\$550,000}{\$220,000} = 2.50$	4.00
2. Operating profitability		
Return on assets = $\frac{\text{Operating income}}{\text{Total assets}}$	$\frac{\$100,000}{\$920,000} = 10.87\%$	13.2%
Operating profit margin = $\frac{\text{Operating profits}}{\text{Sales}}$	$\frac{\$100,000}{\$850,000} = 11.76\%$	11%
Total asset turnover = $\frac{\text{Sales}}{\text{Total assets}}$	$\frac{\$850,000}{\$920,000} = 0.92$	1.20
Accounts receivable turnover = $\frac{\text{Credit sales}}{\text{Accounts receivable}}$	$\frac{\$850,000}{\$80,000} = 10.63$	10.43
Inventory turnover = $\frac{\text{Cost of goods sold}}{\text{Inventory}}$	$\frac{\$550,000}{\$220,000} = 2.50$	4.00
Fixed asset turnover = $\frac{\text{Sales}}{\text{Fixed assets}}$	$\frac{\$850,000}{\$570,000} = 1.49$	2.50
3. Financing		
Debt ratio = $\frac{\text{Total debt}}{\text{Total assets}}$	$\frac{\$300,000}{\$920,000} = 33.00\%$	40%
Times interest earned ratio = $\frac{\text{Operating income}}{\text{Interest expense}}$	$\frac{\$100,000}{\$20,000} = 5.00$	4.00
4. Return on equity		
Return on equity = $\frac{\text{Net income}}{\text{Common equity}}$	$\frac{\$60,000}{\$620,000} = 9.70\%$	12.5%

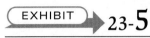

Looking Back

1 Identify the basic requirements for an accounting system.

- An accounting system structures the flow of financial information to provide a complete picture of financial activities.
- Financial reports should be computer-generated.
- The system should be accurate and thorough, allow a quick comparison of data over the years of operation, provide financial statements, facilitate filing of reports and tax returns, and reveal internal problems such as fraud and record-keeping errors.
- In addition to the balance sheet and income statement, an accounting system should provide internal records that show accounts receivable, accounts payable, inventories, payroll, cash, and fixed assets, as well as insurance policies, leaseholds, and outside investments.

2 Explain two alternative accounting options.

- Accounting systems may use either cash or accrual methods and may be structured as either single-entry or double-entry systems.
- With the cash method of accounting, transactions are recorded only when cash is received or a payment is made; the accrual method of accounting matches revenue earned against expenses associated with it.
- A single-entry system is basically a checkbook system of receipts and disbursements; a double-entry system of accounting requires that each transaction be recorded twice.

3 Describe the purpose of and procedures related to internal control.

- Internal control refers to a system of checks and balances designed to safeguard a firm's assets and enhance the accuracy and reliability of its financial statements.
- Some examples of internal control procedures are separation of employees' duties, limiting access to accounting records and computer facilities, and safeguarding blank checks.
- Building internal controls within a small business is difficult but important.

4 Evaluate a firm's ability to pay its bills as they come due.

- Liquidity is a firm's capacity to meet its short-term obligations.
- One way of measuring a firm's liquidity is to compare its liquid assets (cash, accounts receivable, and inventories) and its short-term debt, using the current ratio.
- A second way to measure liquidity is to determine the time it takes to convert accounts receivable and inventories into cash, by computing the accounts receivable turnover and the inventory turnover.

5 Assess a firm's overall profitability on its asset base.

- Operating profitability is evaluated by determining if the firm is earning a good return on its total assets, through computation of the return on assets.
- The return on assets can be separated into two components—the operating profit margin and the total asset turnover—to gain more insight into the firm's operating profitability.
- The operating profit margin is determined by dividing operating profits by sales.
- The total asset turnover is computed by dividing sales by total assets.

6 Measure a firm's use of debt and equity financing.

- The debt ratio (total debt divided by total assets) can be used to measure how much debt a firm uses in its financing mix.
- A firm's ability to cover interest charges on its debt can be measured by the times interest earned ratio (operating income divided by interest expense).

7 Evaluate the rate of return earned on the owners' investment.

- The accounting return on the owner's investment (return on equity) is measured by dividing net income by the common equity invested in the business.
- The return on equity is a function of (1) the firm's return on assets less the interest paid and (2) the amount of debt used relative to the amount of equity financing.

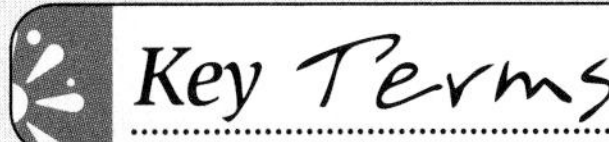

Key Terms

single-entry system, p. 508
double-entry system, p. 508
internal control, p. 508
financial ratios, p. 510
accounts receivable turnover, p. 513
inventory turnover, p. 513
operating profit margin, p. 514
total asset turnover, p. 516
fixed asset turnover, p. 516
financial leverage, p. 517
times interest earned ratio, p. 518

Discussion Questions

1. Explain the accounting concept that income is realized when earned, whether or not it has been received in cash.
2. Should entrepreneurs have an outside specialist set up an accounting system for their startup or do it themselves? Why?
3. What are the primary types of records required in a sound accounting system?
4. What are the major advantages of a double-entry accounting system over a single-entry system?
5. What is liquidity? Differentiate between the two approaches given in this chapter to measure liquidity.
6. Explain the following ratios:
   a. Operating profit margin
   b. Total asset turnover
   c. Times interest earned
7. What is the relationship among these ratios: return on assets, operating profit margin, and total asset turnover?
8. What would be the difference between using operating profit and using net income when calculating a firm's return on investment?
9. What is financial leverage? When should it be used and when should it be avoided? Why?
10. What determines a firm's return on equity?

You Make the Call

SITUATION 1

In 2005, Carter Dalton purchased the Baugh Company. Although the firm has consistently earned profits, little cash has been available for other than business needs. Before purchasing Baugh, Dalton thought that cash flows were generally equal to profits plus depreciation. However, this does not seem to be the case. The industry norms for the financial ratios and the financial statements (in thousands) for the Baugh Company, 2004–2005, follow.

Balance Sheet

	2004	**2005**
ASSETS		
Current assets:		
Cash	$ 8,000	$ 10,000
Accounts receivable	15,000	20,000
Inventory	22,000	25,000
Total current assets	$ 45,000	$ 55,000
Fixed assets:		
Gross plant and equipment	$ 50,000	$ 55,000
Accumulated depreciation	15,000	20,000
Net fixed assets	$ 35,000	$ 35,000
Other assets	12,000	10,000
TOTAL ASSETS	$ 92,000	$100,000
DEBT (LIABILITIES) AND EQUITY		
Current liabilities:		
Accounts payable	$ 10,000	$ 12,000
Accruals	7,000	8,000
Short-term notes	5,000	5,000
Total current liabilities	$ 22,000	$ 25,000
Long-term liabilities	15,000	15,000
Total liabilities	$ 37,000	$ 40,000
Total ownership equity	55,000	60,000
TOTAL DEBT AND EQUITY	$ 92,000	$100,000

Income Statement, 2005

Sales revenue		$175,000
Cost of goods sold		105,000
Gross profit on sales		$ 70,000
Operating expenses:		
Marketing expenses	$26,000	
General and administrative expenses	20,000	
Depreciation expense	5,000	
Total operating expenses		$ 51,000
Operating income		$ 19,000
Interest expense		3,000
Earnings before taxes		$ 16,000
Income tax		8,000
Net income		$ 8,000

Financial Ratios	**Industry Norms**
Current ratio	2.50
Average collection period	30.00
Inventory turnover	6.00
Debt ratio	50.0%
Return on assets	16.0%
Operating profit margin	8.0%
Total asset turnover	2.00
Fixed asset turnover	7.00
Times interest earned ratio	5.00
Return on equity	14.0%

Question 1 Why doesn't Dalton have cash for personal needs? (As part of your analysis, measure cash flows, as discussed in Chapter 10.)

Question 2 Evaluate the Baugh Company's financial performance, given the financial ratios for the industry.

SITUATION 2

The following financial statements are for the Cherokee Communications Corporation. The company provides pay phone service at many of the small convenience stores in the southwestern United States, primarily in Texas and New Mexico. The business was "meeting plan" until 2005, when a problem developed.

Balance Sheet

	2004	2005
ASSETS		
Current assets:		
Cash and cash equivalents	$ 668,778	$ 592,491
Accounts receivable	4,453,192	3,888,621
Inventories	137,036	112,699
Prepaid expenses and other current assets	411,990	407,274
Total current assets	$ 5,670,996	$ 5,001,085
Fixed assets:		
Property, plant and equipment (net)	$12,935,453	$16,466,001
Site licenses	1,941,467	3,771,571
Investments in affiliates	164,549	251,672
Total fixed assets	$15,041,469	$20,489,244
Other assets	681,754	455,488
TOTAL ASSETS	$21,394,219	$25,945,817
DEBT (LIABILITIES) AND EQUITY		
Current liabilities:		
Notes payable	$ 659,604	
Current portion of other notes payable	1,491,767	$ 3,320,197
Current portion of capital lease obligations	1,094,381	668,826
Accounts payable	310,358	835,384
Accrued telecommunications and other expenses	2,971,935	3,036,633
Income taxes payable	256,140	475,945
Total current liabilities	$ 6,784,185	$ 8,336,985
Long-term liabilities:		
Notes payable, less current portion	$ 6,605,835	$10,030,963
Capital lease obligations	780,593	56,219
Deferred income tax liability	342,359	306,021
Total long-term liabilities	$ 7,728,787	$10,393,203
Preferred stock	$ 2,400,000	$ 2,400,000
Common stockholders' equity:		
Common stock	$ 1,438,903	$ 1,438,903
Additional paid-in capital	10,630	10,630
Retained earnings	3,031,714	3,366,096
Total ownership equity	$ 4,481,247	$ 4,815,629
TOTAL DEBT AND EQUITY	$21,394,219	$25,945,817

Income Statements for Cherokee Communications, Inc.

	2004	2005
Sales revenue:		
Pay phone coin calls	$14,036,665	$17,615,059
Automated operator, routed calls	17,049,394	15,932,154
Other	505,581	1,363,738
Total revenues	$31,591,640	$34,910,951
Operating expenses:		
Telephone charges	$ 7,851,842	$ 9,078,851
Commissions	4,909,445	5,627,288
Telecommunications fees	1,821,930	1,519,095
Depreciation and amortization	4,298,090	5,353,797
Field operations personnel	2,016,935	2,988,456
Chargebacks and doubtful accounts	1,104,896	1,111,857
General and administrative expenses	5,520,405	6,435,919
Total operating expenses	$27,523,543	$32,115,263
Operating income	$ 4,068,097	$ 2,795,688
Other income (expenses):		
Interest expense	($ 1,631,416)	($ 1,816,222)
Interest income	57,278	5,069
Losses on affiliates	(34,608)	(108,556)
Unusual gains	1,160,238	27,234
Total other income (expenses)	($ 448,508)	($ 1,892,475)
Income before taxes	$ 3,619,589	$ 903,213
Provision for income taxes	1,399,140	424,831
Net income	$ 2,220,449	$ 478,382

Question 1 Using financial ratios, compare the firm's financial performance for 2004 and 2005.

Question 2 What do you think might have happened from 2004 to 2005?

SITUATION 3

Alibek Iskakov has opened a small café, Oasis, in Kokshetau, a city in Kazakhstan. A new business in operation for only a short period on a part-time basis in a less-developed country, it has small revenues. Nevertheless, ratio analysis can be used for a quick check on its status. The following amounts are given in tenge (1 dollar = 120 tenge), the Kazakhstan currency.

Balance Sheet

ASSETS	
Current assets:	
Cash	22,000
Accounts receivable	2,500
Inventories	7,300
Prepaid expenses	6,500
Total current assets	38,300
Fixed assets:	
Plant and equipment	400,000
Accumulated depreciation	(400)
Net plant and equipment	399,600
TOTAL ASSETS	437,900
DEBT (LIABILITIES) AND EQUITY	
Current liabilities:	
Accounts payable	7,000
Income tax payable	5,500
Accrued wages and salaries	7,000
Total current liabilities	19,500
Equity	418,400
TOTAL DEBT AND EQUITY	437,900

Income Statement

Sales	150,000
Cost of goods sold	80,000
Total revenues	70,000
Operating expenses:	
Selling expenses	5,000
General and administrative expenses	12,000
Other expenses	3,500
Total operating expenses	20,500
Earnings before taxes	49,500
Income tax (30%)	14,850
Net income	34,650

Source: This case was prepared by Dr. Aigul N. Toxanova and Yuliya L. Tkacheva, Kokshetau Institute of Economics and Management, Kokshetau, Kazakhstan.

Question 1 Compute the firm's accounts receivable turnover. Do you think that this ratio is relevant for this business? Why or why not?

Question 2 What is the firm's return on assets? Without the benefit of an industry norm for comparison, do you think that this is a good return on the owner's investment?

Question 3 What is the firm's return on equity? How does debt financing affect this return?

Experiential Exercises

1. Interview a local CPA who consults with small firms on small business accounting systems. Report to the class on the levels of accounting knowledge the CPA's clients appear to possess.
2. Contact several very small businesses and explain your interest in their accounting systems. Report to the class on their level of sophistication—for example, whether they use a single-entry system, a computer, or an outside professional.
3. Find out whether your public or university library subscribes to Robert Morris Associates or Dun & Bradstreet. If the library does not subscribe to either of these financial services, ask whether it subscribes to another service that provides industry norms. When you find a source, select an industry, and bring a copy of its ratios to class for discussion.
4. Locate a small company in your community that will allow you to perform a financial ratio analysis on its financial statements. You will need to decide which industry's data to use for comparative purposes and then find the norms in the library. You may need to promise the company's owners that you will change all names on statements to provide confidentiality.

Exploring the Web

1. The American Express Web site, at **http://www.americanexpress.com**, offers resources for small businesses. Click on the "Small Businesses" link and then on "Articles & Discussions." Choose the "Financial Management" link, and then, in the center of the page, click on the "More Articles, Tools and Quizzes" list arrow. Scroll down and select "Manage Your Receivables and Collections" in the TOOLS/QUIZZES section of the list, and then click "go."
   a. According to the article, what percentage of past-due accounts will never be collected?
   b. Take the quiz to test the effectiveness of your receivables policy. What areas of your receivables policy need to be improved?
   c. List 10 steps to effective collections.
   d. Read about collection laws. Jot down some laws that you were not aware of.
   e. List seven tips for avoiding overdue accounts.

2. Go to the *Inc.* magazine Web site, at **http://www.inc.com**, and use the Search feature to find the following articles. (*Note:* You may have to scroll through several pages.)
   a. Type "Forecasting" in the Search box. In the search results, locate the article entitled "Action Plan: Forecasting and Cash-Flow Budgeting." List the steps given here to create a cash flow budget.
   b. Now type "Bills" in the Search box, and locate the article entitled "Prioritizing Bills When Money Is Short." List the items that must be paid first when your business is facing a severe cash shortage.
   c. After doing a search on "Risk," locate the article entitled "Is Your Company at Risk?" List the key questions, and note which ones deal with cash flow issues.

Case 23

ARTHO, INC. (P. 570)

This case requires the student to identify a company's financial strengths and weaknesses by using financial ratios and cash flow computations across time to compare the firm's performance to that of a similar firm.

Alternative Cases for Chapter 23:

Case 10, Stegmart, p. 541
Case 11, Calvert Toyota, p. 543

Video Case 1

BOSTON DUCK TOURS

HOW PERSEVERANCE AND CREATIVITY LED AN ENTREPRENEUR TO GREAT SUCCESS

It is not uncommon for entrepreneurial ventures to meet with resistance. Even though small businesses account for more new job creation than larger established firms, many people and organizations are often reluctant to embrace entrepreneurial opportunities. Andy Wilson, founder of Boston Duck Tours, experienced this firsthand. But despite the overwhelming obstacles he faced in starting and growing his business, he persisted with a positive attitude and commitment to his idea.

After working for seven years in an investment banking firm, Wilson was no longer motivated by the suit-and-tie atmosphere of corporate America. So he left his job, bought a 90-day Greyhound Bus pass, and began touring the country. At a stop in Memphis, he was awakened by a Duck Tour being conducted outside his hotel. Intrigued, he took the tour. He didn't think any more about it until he got home to his native Boston and saw a stream of trolleys, packed with sightseers. Instantly, the Duck Tour idea came to mind.

Wilson decided to bring the Duck Tour concept to Boston and create a lively, informative, historical tour to showcase the city from both the land and the river. He invested $30,000 of his own money and then began making the rounds, seeking government permits and additional investors. He quickly encountered skepticism, and even derision, as he wended his way through a maze of nearly 100 government agencies. Because the Duck (a World War II–era amphibious vehicle) is part bus, part truck, and part boat, he had a difficult time explaining his business concept to government bureaucrats and potential investors. "The short and sweet of it is that everybody thought I was nuts because it was a new idea," said Wilson. One government official even told him that he would have better luck trying to build a skyscraper in the center of Boston Public Garden!

About to give up, Wilson decided to check out the competition before he threw in the towel. His first trolley tour, which he called "such a pathetic experience," gave him the determination to keep pushing forward. He located investors to provide the $1.25 million he required to launch Boston Duck Tours, and he began the arduous task of securing the 29 permits necessary to operate his business. He researched other Duck Tour operations that had been successful in the Midwest and formed an alliance with the operator in Branson, Missouri, to get the Ducks he needed to start the business in Boston. And he began looking for employees by running newspaper ads in the Boston Globe for Coast Guard captains.

Duck drivers (called conDUCKtors) need four licenses: a captain's license from the U.S. Coast Guard, a commercial driver's license from the state of Massachusetts, a license from the Department of Public Safety, and a sightseer's license from the city of Boston. Despite these requirements, applicants responded in droves. Determined to create a different kind of tourist attraction, Wilson decided to abandon traditional interviewing techniques. Instead, he had applicants meet with a theatrical coach who put them through theatrical skill sets. Applicants then selected items from a group of props, created a character, and put together a costume. The 45 Duck captains play characters like "Captain Courageous," a World War II radio operator downed in the South Pacific, and "Penny Wise," a Southern Belle who now drives her Duck around Boston looking for her long-lost love. The cast of conDUCKtors makes Boston Duck Tours "the best show on wheels," Wilson said.

Boston Duck Tours was only open for two months its first season. The next year, it carried almost 15 times as many passengers as it had the previous year, and tours were selling out every day. By the third year, the company was a well-established part of the city's tourism industry, and those adversaries who had made things difficult at the beginning started embracing Boston Duck Tours.

Wilson used the success of his business to strengthen his presence in the community. He got involved in local environmental groups and sponsored contests in which local schoolchildren named new Ducks. He donated one million pennies to his one-millionth passenger's charity of choice, and he gave veterans free tours during the week of Veteran's Day in honor of his father, a World War II veteran who died when Wilson was young. (The company still does that every year.)

What began as a four-Duck, 15-employee business in October of 1994 has grown to a 23-Duck, 100-employee tourism powerhouse in the Boston market. Today, over 2,700 passengers a day quack at passersby from the deck of a colorfully painted Duck, captained by an equally colorful character. And Duck Tours have hatched all over, in places like Austin,

Video material provided by Hattie Bryant, Producer of Small Business School, the series on PBS Stations, Worldnet, and the Web at http://www.smallbusinessschool.org.

Sources: http://www.bostonducktours.com; and Laura Tiffany, "Making Waves: More Than One Hundred Government Agencies Mocked Andy Wilson's Idea, but Look Who's Quacking Now," *Entrepreneur*, June 1999, p. 97.

Chicago, Dublin, Liverpool, London, Oahu, Seattle, Singapore, Tampa Bay, and the Wisconsin Dells. In 2000, Andy Wilson sold his stake in Boston Duck Tours to pursue other projects, but his management team took over and continues to build on his foundation.

Before answering the questions and working the activities, you will want to watch the Small Business School video on Andy Wilson and Boston Duck Tours. Your instructor may show the video to your class or have you view it online at http://longenecker.swlearning.com.

Questions

1. What is Andy Wilson's primary motivation for leading an entrepreneurial life?
2. What kind of entrepreneurial venture is Boston Duck Tours?
3. Describe the competitive advantage of Boston Duck Tours.
4. What characteristics of successful entrepreneurs does Andy Wilson embody?

Activities

1. Now that you are familiar with Duck Tours, do some research to determine whether there is a Duck Tour company in your city or area. If there is, make an appointment to interview the owner. Draft a set of interview questions that address the issues you learned about in Chapter 1. Here are some examples to get you started:
   - When did you get the idea for the business?
   - Why did you want to start this business?
   - What made you take the plunge into entrepreneurship?
   - What obstacles did you encounter while starting the business?
   - What competitive advantage do you have over other tourist attractions?

   Many other questions are also possible. Write a brief summary of what you learned during the interview.
2. If you do not have a Duck Tour company in your area, think about what you would need to start one. Is your town or area suited for Duck Tours? If there isn't a body of water in your city, could you still create a business based on the Duck Tour concept? Visit the Boston Duck Tours Web site at http://www.bostonducktours.com to find out more about the company and what made it a business opportunity rather than just a business idea. Write a short description (no more than a couple of paragraphs) of a unique tourism company in your city.

Video Case 2

DIVERSIFIED CHEMICAL

ETHICS FROM THE INSIDE OUT

You may recall from the video spotlight at the beginning of Chapter 2 that George Hill and Arnold Joseff found a unique way of growing their business, Diversified Chemical Technologies. What started with $4,000 in collateral and a $70,000 loan from the Small Business Administration is now a company with $70 million in annual sales; nearly 300,000 square feet of manufacturing space in Detroit and Korea; joint ventures with Xerox, Procter & Gamble, and Hong Seong; and four subsidiaries employing over 200 people, nearly a quarter of whom are chemists.

Hill and Joseff are committed to reviving abandoned buildings in blighted neighborhoods and mentoring at local schools. Their company donates to universities, provides scholarships for students studying chemistry, and underwrites the education of its employees. In addition, Hill is a member of the National Association of Black Automotive Suppliers (NABAS) and sits on DaimlerChrysler's Minority Supplier Board. In 2003, he received the Distinguished Corporate Leader Award from his alma mater, Wayne State University, for his work as a mentor and a lifetime of service to his industry.

Diversified Chemical is not just a minority-owned business; it is a business committed to developing a workforce as diversified as the products it innovates. Employees come from the United States, Asia, Europe, India, the Middle East, and Africa. The synergy of different perspectives has enabled Diversified Chemical and its subsidiaries to confidently take advantage of business opportunities and create alliances worldwide.

Without an ethical foundation, these activities and achievements would seem like nothing more than acting on the hottest trends in business. But what sets Hill and Joseff apart is that they are acting from a deeply rooted set of ethical values about how to treat people and the environment.

Before you answer the questions and work the activities, you will need to watch the videos on Diversified Chemical Technologies. You may also want to review the video spotlight that introduced Chapter 2. Your instructor may show the videos to your class or have you view them online at http://longenecker.swlearning.com.

Video material provided by Hattie Bryant, Producer of Small Business School, the series on PBS Stations, Worldnet, and the Web at http://www.smallbusinessschool.org.

Sources: "Wayne State to Honor Business Leaders for Commitment to the Community," Wayne State University news release, May 28, 2003; Brenda Schneider, "Hallmark of Black Auto Supplier Group Is Its Leadership, Community Service," *Detroit News*, May 31, 2000, http://detnews.comn/2000/detroit/6000/05/s02-65803.htm; and http://www.dow.com.

Questions

1. Based on what you saw in the videos, describe Arnold Joseff's strong underlying values.
2. Describe how Joseff sees fiscal responsibility as essential to ethical business practices.
3. Diversified Chemical Technologies operates ethically on many levels. Based on what you saw in the two videos, describe the various ways in which Diversified Chemical is an ethical and socially responsible company.

Activities

1. It is not uncommon for large corporations to have documents that provide ethical guidelines. One of the largest multinational chemical companies, Dow Chemical, is such a corporation. At the company's Web site (http://www.dow.com), you will find Dow's Code of Business Conduct (35 pages) and its Mission and Values statement (a single page). After reviewing Dow's Mission and Values statement on the Web site, draft a mission and values statement for Diversified Chemical that reflects what you have seen in the videos. (At the time of publication, there was no such document posted on the Diversified Chemical Web site.) Share your work with your classmates or study group partners.
2. Practice writing ethical guidelines for your own business enterprise. Even if you don't currently have a business concept or plan, you can still organize your thoughts on the values that will guide your future business ventures. How detailed do you want the guidelines to be? Dow's Code of Business Conduct is 35 pages; Nordstrom's fits on a 3×5 index card.
3. Once you have written down your own underlying values, indicate ways in which your business will act on them. You may find the following list of questions a good starting place for thinking about how your business will reflect your personal values:

- Will your business give to charities? If so, how will you select the groups that receive donations?
- Will you be involved in the community? In what capacity? If not, why not?
- How will you find employees? For example, will your recruitment efforts include the disabled, those of low income, minorities, and others in underrepresented groups?
- How will you manage your company's waste products? If it costs more to recycle, will you do it?
- Will you reward employees for their community involvement with nonprofit organizations and civic groups? Will you encourage your employees to become active in their communities?
- How will you determine pay levels?
- What kinds of benefits will you offer?
- Where will you locate your business? (Think back to the video: Diversified Chemical's location was guided by the founders' underlying values.)

Case 3

BIOLIFE LLC

CLEARING HURDLES

When it comes to the hurdles that every startup faces, five-year-old Biolife has already cleared a few. Its sole product—Quick Relief (QR), a patented powder that stops bleeding within seconds—is unlike anything else out there and has impressed several hard-to-impress gatekeepers, including Wal-Mart, the nation's largest retailer, and CVS Stores, the drugstore chain. Both have already given QR valuable shelf space in several thousand stores. Plus, the head athletic trainer of the Los Angeles Lakers has been seen using QR on national TV. But the hard part of CEO Doug Goodman's job is really just beginning: Now he needs to figure out the best way to convince the world to give QR a try.

It was back in 1999 that Jim Patterson and John Alf Thompson first developed QR. The two men were long-time research scientists who formed Biolife with the goal of discovering a new way to purify water. They never solved that puzzle, but one day, while working in the lab, Patterson either pricked his finger accidentally or sliced it on purpose (the story has changed several times, Goodman concedes), leading to the discovery of QR, a patented combination of resin and salt, the two components Patterson had been experimenting with at the time.

In 2002, the company sent some samples of QR to Gary Vitti, the head trainer for the Lakers. After testing it for several weeks during the off-season, Vitti used QR one day during a regular-season game, prompting the on-air announcers to wonder why Vitti was sprinkling pepper on one of his players. QR was never mentioned by name, but it was the product's first appearance on TV, and it started to create some buzz for the company, at least among sports fans. Wooing Vitti made sense, Goodman says, because the product is especially useful to the NBA, which allows only a 30-second timeout to stop a player from bleeding.

Vitti estimates that he gets around 100 requests a week from "different snake oil salesmen" hoping to get him to try out their magic potion on [Lakers players]. But there was something about QR that managed to catch his attention. At the time, he was using another product that neither he nor the players were particularly crazy about because it stung and left dark stains on the skin. "I gave this a try, and I was really surprised," says Vitti. "This one popped out because it was so different."

In fact, Vitti liked the product so much that he now has a part-time job selling QR to other trainers at the professional and college level. Goodman estimates that as many as 75 percent of the teams in the National Hockey League and NBA use QR regularly.

Without "real missionaries" like Vitti, as well as several prominent doctors on the west coast of Florida, Biolife might not have had any sales at all. In 2002, the year QR was launched, Biolife had revenue of $150,000. In 2003, after convincing more health care providers to try QR, Biolife's sales increased tenfold. The company began by training 16 pharmacists at CVS stores in the Tampa Bay area, figuring that people often ask pharmacists for medical advice. But after an initial bump in sales, interest in the product, which costs between $5 and $10 a box and comes in four different packages designed for different uses, such as Nosebleed QR, quickly died down.

The company has experimented with its packaging in an attempt to not look like a typical medical product. On the Kids QR package, for example, Goodman's eight-year-old son, Bakie, is seen riding his bike and kicking a soccer ball. Actually, all of QR's boxes feature employees or investors. On a new package of Urgent QR, an extra-strength version of the product, Charlie Entenmann (Biolife's main financial backer), 74, is shown rappelling down a mountain.

Eventually, Goodman hopes that ordinary consumers will be as enthusiastic about QR as Vitti has been. If that ever does happen, a box of QR just might replace the box of Band-Aids that most people have in the back of their medicine chests.

Questions

1. Chapter 3 discusses three types of startup ideas: Type A, Type B, and Type C. Which of these is illustrated by Biolife's startup based on its QR product?
2. Most new business ideas come from personal experience, hobbies, accidental discoveries, or a deliberate search. From which of these sources did the idea for Biolife's launch come?
3. Considering what you have learned about this startup and its development, would you say that the founders followed more of an outside-in or an inside-out approach to identify this business opportunity and launch the company? Explain your answer.
4. Conduct a SWOT analysis of the company. What do you think are Biolife's most significant strengths, weaknesses, opportunities, and threats?
5. How would you characterize the strategy that Biolife is following? Is it a cost-based or differentiation-based strategy? Or is it a focus strategy centered on one of these two fundamental strategies? Be sure to identify the facts or assumptions on which you based your conclusion.

Source: Michelle Leder, "The Problem," *Inc.*, June 2004, pp. 44–46.

Video Case 4

AUNTIE ANNE'S

BUILDING RELATIONSHIPS AS THE KEY TO SUCCESSFUL FRANCHISING—FOR BOTH FRANCHISEE AND FRANCHISOR

As you learned in the video spotlight for Chapter 4, Anne Beiler, founder and CEO of Auntie Anne's Pretzels, came from an Amish-Mennonite background. Her upbringing strongly influences how she runs her business, which currently employs over 150 people on its corporate staff and over 10,000 people in its franchise network (store owners, managers, crew members). Auntie Anne's is best described as a business format franchise because its franchisees obtain access to an entire marketing system and support network.

Auntie Anne's franchisee support network, called the franchise council, may be one factor in explaining the high demand for company franchises. Auntie Anne's franchise council system is made up of five regions, each with officers elected by the franchisees. Franchisees can address any operational aspect of the Auntie Anne's system through the regional councils. Representatives from the home office in Gap, Pennsylvania, meet yearly with the presidents of the five regions to discuss concerns and initiatives. Franchisee involvement in the regional councils is 100 percent. The council system allows franchisees to have input into all aspects of the business, from store upgrades to marketing campaigns.

To learn more about what makes Auntie Anne's Pretzel franchises unique, watch the video case for Chapter 4, and then answer the questions and work the activities below. Your instructor may show the video to your class or have you view it online at http://longenecker.swlearning.com.

Questions

1. Is an Auntie Anne's Pretzel franchise a good idea for someone with an entrepreneurial spirit? Why or why not?
2. How did FranCorp help Auntie Anne's? What role does a company like FranCorp play in the structure of franchising?
3. Today Auntie Anne's Pretzels has more than 830 stores in 43 U.S. states and 12 countries, but in 1994 the company only had 325 stores and desperately needed a cash infusion to grow. Management spent 10 months negotiating with venture capitalists, who proposed buying a 32 percent stake in the company. In the end, Anne Beiler and her management team decided not to go public. After watching the video, why do you think they made that decision?
4. How can you account for the tremendous demand for Auntie Anne's Pretzel franchises?

Activities

1. At Auntie Anne's Training Center, otherwise known as Pretzel University, new franchisees learn how to roll, twist, and bake pretzels. What other kinds of training are they required to take? Visit Auntie Anne's Web site at http://www.auntieannes.com and research the training conducted at Pretzel University. Based on the list of subjects covered, do you think you would feel confident opening your own business after completing Auntie Anne's training program? If you were to propose a new class at Pretzel University, what would it be, and why?
2. Use the InfoTrac subscription that came with your textbook to find an article by Dina Berta entitled "Auntie Anne's Latest Twist," published in *Nation's Restaurant News.* Log on to http://www.infotrac-college.com. Read the article, which describes the newest class in Auntie Anne's Pretzel University. Write two to three sentences summarizing the article.
3. After watching the video, you may come away with the feeling that Auntie Anne's offers only upside potential. But all franchising has its limitations. Read the franchising FAQs on Auntie Anne's Web site, and write down all of the costs and restrictions that are disclosed. After researching Auntie Anne's in more detail, would you be interested in becoming a franchisee? Why or why not?

Video material provided by Hattie Bryant, Producer of Small Business School, the series on PBS Stations, Worldnet, and the Web at http://www.smallbusinessschool.org.

Sources: http://www.auntieannes.com; Polly Larson, "Creating Positive Franchise Relations," *Franchising World,* September 2003, p. 5; Dina Berta, "Auntie Anne's Latest Twist: A Leadership Class," *Nation's Restaurant News,* March 1, 2004, p. 20; and "Auntie Anne's, Inc. Selects MyAdGuys' Brand Management Solution," *Internet Wire,* May 1, 2002.

Case 5

THE BROWN FAMILY BUSINESS

DEFINING WORK OPPORTUNITIES FOR FAMILY MEMBERS IN A FAMILY FIRM

For 56 years, the Brown family has operated an agricultural products business in central Texas. As Brown Bros. has grown, family leaders have attempted to preserve family relationships while operating the business in a profitable manner. At present, five members of the second generation, three members of the third generation, and one member of the fourth generation are active in the business. Other members of the family, of course, have ownership interests and a concern about the firm even though they are pursuing other careers.

In the interest of building the business and also preserving family harmony, the family has developed policies for entry and career opportunities for family members. The human resource policies governing family members are as follows:

Family Philosophy Concerning Family and Work Opportunities

1. A family working together as one unit will always be stronger than individuals or divided units.
2. Family is an "umbrella" that includes all direct descendants of P. and L. Brown and their spouses.
3. The Brown family believes that a career with Brown Bros. is only for those who
   - Believe in working for their success;
   - Believe that rewards they receive should come from the work they have done;
   - Believe in working for the company versus working for a paycheck; and
   - Believe that everyone must work to provide an equal and fair contribution for the good of the whole business.
4. While work opportunities and career opportunities with the family business will be communicated to all family members, there will be no guarantee of a job in the family business for any member of the family at any time.
5. A family member working in the family business, whether in a temporary or a long-term career position, will be offered work and career counseling by a supervisor or officer/family member (depending on the job level). However, the family member/employee is not guaranteed a job or a career position. His or her job performance and qualifications must be the primary factors in determining whether the family member will be allowed continued employment.
6. While the family business is principally agriculture-related, there are many jobs that both men and women can perform equally and safely.
7. Compensation will be based on comparable positions held by other employees.

Committee on Family Employee Development

1. Review, on an annual basis, policies for entry and recommend changes.
2. Receive notices of positions available and communicate them to all family members.
3. Review, on an annual basis, evaluations of family members' performance, training provided, outside training programs attended, and goals and development plans. Offer counseling to upper management when appropriate.
4. Committee composed of three persons—one of four Brown brothers in the business; one of seven non-operating Browns; one of the spouses of the eleven Browns. The general criteria for having a career at Brown Bros. are given in Exhibit C5-1.

Questions

1. What are the key ideas embodied in the statement of philosophy concerning family and work opportunities?
2. Evaluate each of the criteria specified for a management career in the firm. Which, if any, would you change or modify?
3. Evaluate the structure and functions of the committee on family employee development.

Source: This case was prepared by Nancy B. Upton, founder of the Institute for Family Business, Baylor University.

EXHIBIT C5-1 | *Criteria for a Career at Brown Bros.*

	Mid-Management Positions	Upper-Management Positions
Personal:		
No criminal record	Required	Required
No substance abuse	Required	Required
Education:		
High school	Required	Required
College degree (2.5 on a 4-point system)	Recommended	Required
Work experience with others:		
While completing college	Recommended	Recommended
After completing college (one to three years)	Recommended	Required

Case 6

ADGROVE.COM, INC.

RAISING CAPITAL FOR AN ADFOMEDIARY

AdGrove.com, Inc., is being founded by Amy George to assist businesses in their efforts to purchase advertising. However, launching the business will require significant capital, an amount far beyond George's capabilities. To raise the needed capital, Amy has prepared a business plan. The executive summary is provided below. (The business plan in its entirety is available at http://www.businessplans.org/AdGrove/adgro00.html.)

ADGROVE.COM, INC., EXECUTIVE SUMMARY

Buying and creating advertising in any media is a time-intensive process reflecting hours of transactions between buyers, sellers, and creative agents. For example, if a buyer wants to advertise in the radio media, he targets a few radio stations with desired listener demographics, discusses contract options with a radio account executive, bids on an ad schedule, negotiates a price, creates ad copy, approves the final ad, and pays for the service. For a skilled buyer, this entire transaction can take up to 3 weeks to complete. For a local deli or sporting goods shop with little or no demographic information, small purchasing power, and less familiarity with radio advertising, this transaction process can take more than 3 weeks and cost the small business more money per ad than large ad agencies. For the seller, in this case the radio stations, the transaction costs of dealing with such small customers can prove to be cost ineffective. AdGrove.com is an internet advertising infomediary ("adfomediary"®) that provides a one-stop shop for demographic information, ad rates, ad campaign schedule planning, ad buys, and creative development, reducing transaction time and costs for buyers and sellers of advertising spots.

The Company

AdGrove.com, Inc. ("the Company") is a C-corporation located in Austin, Texas. The Company is located on the Internet at www.AdGrove.com and is the first adfomediary® dedicated to the needs of small businesses.

Products & Services

AdGrove's featured product will be a user-friendly Internet website that provides free and fee-based services to meet the needs of its customers—advertising buyers and sellers. AdGrove's first product line will be dedicated to reaching the highly fragmented buyers and sellers of advertising space in the radio advertising sector. Qualified buyers and sellers are invited to join AdGrove.com's community as members. Membership is free and provides users access to valuable, customized services. Selling members receive opportunity to list ads, and gain access to the buying community. Buyers receive access to up-to-the minute aggregated, radio market information, ad campaign planning tools, creative services, ad space, buying discounts, monitoring services, and account management. AdGrove.com's information-rich services reduce a buyer's time while enabling the development of a cost-effective advertising strategy. In addition, AdGrove.com buyers receive unique buying discounts, usually reserved for major ad agencies and companies, and an opportunity to participate in discounted "overcapacity" ads. Adgrove.com serves as a third sales channel for radio stations, complementing their national and local sales efforts. Unlike traditional sales methods, the Internet offers radio stations access to a national market and 24-hour selling power. AdGrove.com provides radio station members with a listing and brokerage service, access to customers, on-line web advertising, and monthly value reports. These monthly AdGrove.com value reports will include buyer profiles, competitive analysis, market analysis, and savings calculated.

Market & Opportunity

AdGrove.com represents the intersection of two growing U.S. markets: advertising and business-to-business electronic commerce. The advertising industry represents a $190 billion industry and is expected to grow at 5.7% compound annual growth. The radio advertising market is a $17.7 billion sector represented by more than 12,275 radio stations in 268 major markets. Approximately 75% of radio advertising is purchased at the local level. Although there has been consolidation in the radio industry since the Telecommunications Act of 1996, the industry is still highly fragmented and growing at an 8.5% annual rate. In addition, radio stations have generally been slow to adopt Internet strategies. Business-to-business e-commerce revenues for 1998 were $17 billion and are projected to grow to $1.7 trillion by 2003. It is projected that by the year 2002 almost one-third of all business-to-business transactions will be performed via e-commerce.

Customers: As an intermediary agent AdGrove.com has two primary customers: radio stations and small business advertisers. AdGrove.com will target the top 4,000 radio stations, which represent 80% of the industry revenues. AdGrove.com will target small, high-growth businesses as its primary market. In the U.S., there are currently 24 million small businesses with approximately 885,000 new firms each year. These businesses represent 47% of all sales in the U.S. According to research, approximately 41% of small businesses are online and one in three conducts business transactions on the Internet. Each of these firms represents an average of $3.79 million annual revenues, significantly more than the $2.72 million average.

Competitors: BuyMedia.com and AdOutlet.com are websites that have launched within the last 18 months that connect buyers and sellers of radio advertising space. However, AdGrove.com is the only website with customized services and a pricing model to

Source: http://www.businessplans.org/AdGrove/adgro00.html.

EXHIBIT C6-1 | *Financial Summary and Operating Statistics*

Key Operating Statistics	Yr1	Yr2	Yr3	Yr4	Yr5
Employees	27	57	78	86	98
Financial Statistics					
Revenue	$ 53,700	$2,625,000	$12,770,000	$19,200,001	$26,900,000
Expenses	4,130,597	8,029,597	10,699,663	14,315,827	18,003,609
Net Income	−$4,076,897	−$5,404,597	$ 2,070,337	$ 4,884,174	$ 8,896,391

meet the needs of small businesses. In so doing, AdGrove.com will expand the current advertising market.

Marketing Strategy

AdGrove.com's marketing efforts are centered on strategic partnerships, an educational advertising and public relations campaign, and a regional sales force. AdGrove.com will forge a strategic partnership with the Radio Advertising Bureau, the national association that represents 4,300 radio stations and 80% of U.S. radio advertising revenues. AdGrove.com will forge an alliance with the U.S. Chamber of Commerce, the world's largest business federation, representing nearly 3 million companies, 96% of which are small businesses. AdGrove's marketing campaign will focus on driving volume to the website and converting visitors to buyers.

The Start-Up Plan

AdGrove.com will follow a three-phase start-up plan. During the first phase, the AdGrove.com team will create a demonstration site, refine product and services mix, and alpha test among focus groups of buyers and sellers. During the second phase, AdGrove.com hopes to raise the required venture funding of $2 million to launch the site. The funds will be used to finalize the development of an integrated website, negotiate strategic alliances and radio station partnership agreements, launch a marketing and sales plan, and launch the website in Austin, Texas. To meet the objectives of the first two phases, AdGrove.com will incrementally hire 16 additional staff and outsource the initial development of the website. The third phase will include a launch in 10 cities, including San Francisco, Atlanta, Washington, Seattle, Minneapolis, Boston, New York, Chicago, and Miami.

Management

AdGrove's management team has extensive experience in the marketing, Internet, and high-tech sectors. Amy George, Chief Executive Officer, has seven years of professional experience in the field of marketing for small businesses and national clients in the telecommunication, real estate, multimedia, and education industries. Alex Krishnan, Chief Operating Officer, has five years of experience in the high-tech industry in the areas of Internet strategy, program management, software design, and development. Brink Melton, Chief Technology Officer, has three years experience as a software developer and technology consultant. He has experience launching a successful technology consulting partnership dedicated to serving the needs of small businesses in Austin, TX. He is currently pursuing his MBA at the University of Texas, concentrating in information management and entrepreneurship. AdGrove.com's team of consultants are experts in the small business, radio, advertising, high-tech, and Internet start-up fields.

Financial Overview

AdGrove's five-year financials are displayed in [Exhibit C6-1]. AdGrove.com derives its primary revenue from the following sources:

- Transaction fees for brokering the sale of radio advertising spots. This is the primary revenue stream and the fee collected will be 5% of each transaction.
- Fees for value-added market research information provided to buyers.
- Advertisements and paid promotions.

Because of the high investment needs in year 1 and year 2, the Company does not achieve profitability until year 3. By year 5 revenues will grow to $26.9 million with net income of $8.9 million. The Company is seeking $2 million in first-round financing with a return on investment for investors of 70%.

Questions

1. Is the AdGrove.com executive summary more of a synopsis or a narrative?
2. If you were an investor, would the AdGrove.com executive summary spark your interest in the opportunity? In other words, would you continue reading the business plan for more details?
3. What do you like about this executive summary? What do you not like?
4. Would you suggest that George make any changes or additions to the executive summary? If so, what do you suggest?

Video Case 7

SPECIALTY CHEESE

MARKETING RESEARCH AS THE CORNERSTONE OF A SUCCESSFUL BUSINESS

According to the Agricultural Marketing Resource Center at Iowa State University, U.S. per capita cheese consumption is around 31 pounds, a figure that continues to increase because of heightened interest in ethnic cooking and the growth in specialty cheeses, among other things. The specialty cheese industry generates nearly $3 billion in annual U.S. sales, and Specialty Cheese of Lowell, Wisconsin, is constantly increasing its contribution to that total. Started by Paul and Vicki Scharfman, corporate refugees from Oscar Meyer and Colgate-Palmolive, Specialty Cheese works out of the oldest continuously operating cheese factory in the state of Wisconsin, where the number of cheese factories has plummeted from 4,000 not so long ago to 150. Even with 35 cheese types, Specialty Cheese considers itself a niche marketer threatened by rising global competition and higher selling prices.

The Scharfmans are working to manage threats to their company's marketing environment and reverse the outflow of cheese manufacturing from their state. What started with a $45,000 agricultural grant over 10 years ago has grown into a multimillion-dollar business. The Scharfmans have increased the number of employees nearly five-fold, from 24 to 110, and now boast 10 licensed cheesemakers. The company makes mostly ethnic cheeses—for example, 14 Hispanic cheeses and 7 Middle Eastern cheeses. One product alone, Just the Cheese, accounts for millions of dollars in annual sales.

This amazing growth was the result of a well-conceived marketing plan derived from a customer orientation. The Scharfmans used numerous marketing research techniques to identify markets for their products. And they always listened to what customers were telling them about their products, packaging, and promotions.

Before answering the questions and working the activities, watch the video case on Specialty Cheese. Your instructor may show the video to your class or have you view it online at http://longenecker.swlearning.com.

Video material provided by Hattie Bryant, Producer of Small Business School, the series on PBS Stations, Worldnet, and the Web at http://www.smallbusinessschool.org.

Sources: http://www.specialcheese.com; Malinda Miller, "Cheese Industry Profile," Agricultural Marketing Resource Center, Iowa State University, February 2003, revised April 2004; "Specialty Cheese Co-Op in the Works," *Food Ingredient News*, January 2004; Rick Barrett, "Wisconsin Specialty Cheese Company Takes Off," *Wisconsin State Journal*, December 12, 1996; and "The Time Is Right for Cheese," report prepared for the United States Department of Agriculture by the Food Processing Center, Institute of Agriculture and Natural Resources, University of Nebraska, Lincoln, http://www.farmprofitability.org/cheese.htm#_Toc526067524, October 2001.

Questions

1. What sources of information did the Scharfmans use to develop their marketing plan?
2. What kind of market segmentation do the Scharfmans practice? How did they identify their target markets?
3. Paul Scharfman said, "The competitive model for industry breaks down in small business. We ought to be more collaborative than competitive. . . . We try not to copy our competition but to innovate. We try to build markets. We try to work with our partners and our suppliers and our companies around us. We try to find win-wins all the time. The little local cheesemaker down the street, who's making Colby, and I—other than the fact we're both buying raw milk—might as well be in different businesses. We are not competitors." If other smaller cheesemakers are not competitors of Specialty Cheese, who is the company's competition?

Activities

1. In an interview with the *Wisconsin State Journal*, Vicki Scharfman said, "My secret fantasy is to export to Japan. They eat lots of salty snacks, and they love cheese." Use the Internet to research the Japanese cheese market and cheese varieties. A keyword search for "Japan cheese" or "Japanese cheese" should give you several places to start. Write a brief description of how the Japanese consume cheese, what kinds of cheese they normally eat, how much cheese they eat annually, etc.
2. The Scharfmans used census data to uncover target markets that matched the expertise of their company. Familiarize yourself with U.S. government census data at http://www.census.gov. If you have a business idea in mind, use this opportunity to explore the related census data. Once you are comfortable with the site, pick one of the Middle Eastern cheeses on the Specialty Cheese Web site at http://www.specialcheese.com and identify areas in the United States that constitute a substantial market for the cheese.

Case 8

SILVER ZEPHYR RESTAURANT

CHOOSING A FORM OF ORGANIZATION

Attorney Linda McGrath leaned back in her chair and surveyed her clients as they conducted several conversations simultaneously. The "Magnificent Seven," as the group had labeled itself, consisted of Alan Anderson, C.P.A.; Bill Barnes, M.D.; Carl Cochran, M.D.; Don Davis, president of Davis Petroleum Distributors, Inc.; Eilene Ellis, co-owner of the Collectors' Gift and Antique Shoppe, Inc.; Farrah F. Fischer, artist and widow of the former president of Northern Savings and Loan Association; and Gino Ginelli, managing partner of Wichita Falls Vending and Catering Company.

The group had retained Linda McGrath six weeks earlier to assist them in starting a restaurant in Wichita Falls, Texas. The idea of a new family-style restaurant with a distinctive motif had been developed by the group at a series of neighborhood dinner parties during the winter months. Linda could not help smiling as she recalled that Eilene Ellis and Bill Barnes had commented that they were the "chief engineers" of the railroad theme that the group favored.

Fortunately for the other members of the group, Alan Anderson had taken the initiative and seemingly done a thorough job. He had prepared pro forma financial data, determined the costs of various sites, and gathered preliminary bids from several contractors on the site work, paving, and restaurant facility. Alan and Don Davis had discussed the project with the executive vice president of commercial lending at Texoma Bank, and it was Alan who had suggested that Gino Ginelli was the logical person to operate the restaurant and should be included in the group.

According to Anderson's figures, the acquisition of land, building, and fixtures would require approximately $875,000 to $890,000. Further, Alan had estimated in the pro formas that working capital needs in the first two years would reach between $180,000 and $200,000. In addition, Eilene and Farrah Fischer believed that the unique furnishings and railroad memorabilia could be obtained for $125,000 to $150,000.

Based on a forecasted total requirement of $1,200,000, officials at Texoma Bank had suggested capitalization of $600,000 and were willing to loan the other $600,000 on a five-year note, floating at 3 percent above prime, assuming *unlimited* personal guarantees by all group members and their spouses. Although Alan and Don commented that they were surprised Texoma had not asked for their first-born children as further collateral, they told the group that there had been indications that the loan officers would be willing to extend the term to seven years and perhaps accept an initial debt-to-equity ratio of 1.5 to 1.

Individual Concerns

Whenever the group had met with Linda McGrath, all of the members had professed a strong desire to initiate the business. Gino, who had successfully managed a restaurant in Omaha before purchasing his present business in Wichita Falls, was particularly enthusiastic about getting back into the restaurant business. Eilene and Farrah had talked excitedly about collecting the furnishings needed to create the desired atmosphere, and Alan and Bill had always seemed solidly in favor of the venture. In fact, Alan and Bill had discussed the possibility of having a series of railroad restaurants and involving other investors if this venture was successful.

In private conversations with the attorney, however, several of the group members had expressed concern about their involvement in the project. Inasmuch as everyone agreed that Gino should have the controlling interest in the proposed business, Gino was somewhat apprehensive about the amount of initial capital required and its potential effect on the vending and catering business that he and his brother had developed and were expanding. Bill, on the other hand, expressed concern that opportunities to establish other locations might be foreclosed by Gino's reluctance or inability to expand beyond Wichita Falls.

Don, accompanied by his accountant, had asked several questions concerning the marketability and protection of minority interests in closely held companies and the tax consequences of his investment. Don and Carl Cochran were quite disturbed by the bank's requirement of unlimited guarantees by all investors. Indeed, Carl stated that he would rather invest in real estate than in restaurants but felt that he had given his word to his colleague Bill and would be horribly embarrassed to withdraw at this point. Lastly, even Alan, in spite of herculean efforts on behalf of the group, admitted to Linda that he would prefer the relative safety of a limited partnership, as he was aware of the high rate of failure among restaurants.

Legal Advice

Attorney Linda McGrath quieted the group and began to speak:

I've given the restaurant venture a lot of thought this week, as I'm sure all of you have. Based on my analysis of the situation, several alternative forms of ownership appear feasible. Each of these legal forms has certain advantages and disadvantages, and I certainly want us to explore thoroughly the pros and cons of each legal form before you reach a decision. However, before we discuss the alternatives, please let me make a few observations that I believe are germane to your decision-making process.

First, the legal form you choose must be flexible enough to include seven people. To be sure, you appear to be seven of the most congenial and compatible persons I have ever encountered, let alone represented, in a business situation. On the other hand, you must be aware that you are also seven unique individuals with different circumstances, perspectives, and perhaps objectives as they relate to the restaurant. Hopefully, we can devise a vehicle which will meet the needs of everyone, but some compromise of individual positions may be necessary to ensure the initiation of the venture.

In a similar vein, I want to emphasize the long-term nature of the commitment you are about to make. Although it is far more exciting and romantic to focus on the construction phases and gala grand opening, I believe you must adjust your thinking—particularly as it pertains to the choice of an appropriate legal form—to the long and sometimes arduous days of operating the business, and even beyond, to its termination. In other words, you have selected Gino Ginelli to manage the restaurant and are agreeable to giving him control through a majority interest. This is fine. However, we must prepare for the time when he may either wish or need to terminate his interest in the venture. How will management continuity be ensured, and how will your interests be protected? Certainly these issues should be addressed in your decision.

If Gino Ginelli is able to operate the restaurant at the levels you have projected, all of you will have opportunities to profit or, perhaps, to "capital gain." Accordingly, we need to be cognizant of marketability or transferability of interests both for those who may choose to "cash out" and for those who wish to remain. In the event additional resources are required to support this restaurant or the development of other locations, you may well need the ability to add investors to secure equity capital.

I am also compelled to say that we should prepare for termination under unfavorable circumstances. Without reflection on Gino Ginelli's abilities, I must tell you that statistics indicate that more than 50 percent of new restaurants fail within two years. This means that it would be foolish to consider only the "upside" potential of the venture and not the "downside" as well. Most of you own businesses and all of you have estates, and I believe that the liability issue must be one of your foremost considerations.

Indeed, part of the responsibility that Gino Ginelli must accept for the control or authority that he would be granted in the proposed venture is unlimited liability. Gino Ginelli understands this point and has indicated his willingness to comply with this condition. However, it seems unreasonable that the rest of you, who will not have the management control and cannot achieve as large a reward as Gino Ginelli, would be willing to risk so much by agreeing to unlimited personal guarantees. It is my belief that we definitely need to reduce your potential risk or liability through the choice of a suitable legal form, with some "bare-fisted" negotiating with Texoma Bank.

Another major point is the matter of initial investment. Once again, this is going to have to be negotiated with the financial institution, but I naturally advocate as little initial capital and as much leverage, particularly long-term debt, as possible to maximize your return on investment. Of course, there is simply no substitute for managing the assets properly, but some of the legal forms offer greater advantage and return-on-investment possibilities than others.

A final consideration involves taxation of the business and tax consequences of the venture for each of you. I'm confident that Alan Anderson would concur with the statement that tax regulations are going to affect the restaurant and you from the initial choice of organization form to its hopefully profitable conclusion and beyond. With Alan's help, I can state that we will always try to minimize the adverse effects of code regulations throughout your involvement in the venture.

In summary, I submit that you should consider carefully the following issues before selecting the most desirable legal form of organization for the restaurant:

1. *Your liability as investors*
2. *Management and control continuity*
3. *Marketability or transfer of interest*
4. *Ability to secure additional equity capital*
5. *Initial capitalization and return on investment*
6. *Taxation*

And please consider these issues while recognizing your different perspectives and the long-term nature of your commitment of resources.

Linda paused and then presented the following alternative legal forms:

The first alternative would be to incorporate, with Gino Ginelli holding 50 to 52 percent of the stock and the remaining shares divided among the other investors. All stock would be issued as Section 1244 stock. Of course, the more adventuresome among you could buy more than your pro rata share of the stock issued, if you so desired.

A second possibility would be to incorporate as a Subchapter S corporation. Again, the stock would be issued as Section 1244 stock, and the ownership percentages would be the same as with the first alternative.

A third alternative would be to form a limited partnership, with Gino Ginelli as a general partner and the rest of you choosing either limited or general status.

A fourth alternative would be to establish a limited liability company, which would allow more of you to participate in management and still have favorable liability and tax treatment.

A fifth alternative, which I believe may have real merit, would involve the creation of two or more legal entities. In other words, one company with several of you as investors might own the real estate and lease it on a long-term basis to the restaurant business, which would be owned by the remaining members of the group. The lease could be secured by the personal guarantees of the stockholders in the restaurant business.

I don't know if the idea of multiple entities appeals to you, but it seems to me that you have, in essence, three companies: a restaurant, a furnishings business, and a property company with land, building, and fixtures. We did this type of thing with the warehouse, truck fleet, and operating company of Allied Van Lines in Abilene, and it may prove to be a better match of personal interests and risk-versus-return than squeezing everything into one organization.

In any event, these are five possibilities and I'm sure others exist, so let's begin to discuss things. And, once we have reached a consensus on the appropriate legal form, we will want to consider a buy/sell agreement with a method of valuation and various funding options.

Questions

1. Evaluate the simple corporation, the Subchapter S corporation, and limited partnership options. Note the advantages and disadvantages of each.
2. Explain the nature and significance of Section 1244 stock.
3. Could a limited liability company be the answer for the "Magnificent Seven"? What would be the disadvantages of this legal form of organization?
4. Explain how the multiple entities option might be worked out, and evaluate the extent to which it might be used to meet the varied interests of the group.

Case 9

THE CHOCOLATE FARM

LOCATING ON THE WEB

Evan and Elise Macmillan really are small business people. At ages 16 and 13, respectively, they know about running and growing a successful business. They could even teach a few lessons to owners of burned-out dotcoms: Keep overhead low and don't think a Web address ensures success.

As co-founders of The Chocolate Farm—the business they started in 1999 in Denver, Colorado—they're harvesting some serious lunch money, mostly from their Web site, http://www.thechocolatefarm.com. Though their site has had more than one million visitors, Elise says they worked hard "not to get caught up in the whole Web craze" and just to offer products that would make money. "All those failed companies thought success was a sure thing if you stuck a dotcom at the end of the business's name," says Elise. "The Web is and will only continue to be a venue for conducting business, never a business model."

The Internet allows The Chocolate Farm to buck the traditional chocolate company approach of high-rent storefronts by taking orders and shipping directly to customers. "We're definitely going the low-cost route," Evan says.

The company sells recipes, animal molds, and kits showing customers how to create their own chocolate-selling business. "We don't see those who want to make chocolate as competition," Evan says. "We want to give customers choices."

The Chocolate Farm sprouted three years ago when Elise and Evan took part in an event put on by The Young Americans Education Foundation, which teaches young people about free enterprise (and the organization that lent the farm its initial $5,000). The event let young people sell products at booths, and Elise and Evan decided to sell chocolate.

The siblings did so well they started selling at weddings, parties, and banquets, giving their business a farm theme. Once they put up a Web site, the business evolved to be mainly online, where they can keep overhead low.

With a pool of 30 to 40 part-time workers, the company makes imaginative confections in a huge commercial kitchen provided by the Denver Enterprise Center—a nonprofit business incubator that's guiding the teens on running the business and outsourcing what they can't do themselves.

Today, so many orders are coming that they buy raw chocolate by the ton, and they've filled orders from as far away as New Zealand. The tepid economy hasn't dampened production. "If anything, business has gotten better. People seem to want comfort food," says Evan.

The company is private so the two won't reveal revenue, but Evan says the company has been profitable since day one and each quarter its income has doubled. Apart from that initial $5,000 business loan, all growth has been self-funded.

During the school year, the teens work part-time on the company. In the summer, they're full-time. "I think about the business a lot, and it's really cool that it's doing so well," Evan says. "But for now, school comes first."

Both say their parents are supportive and occasionally give advice and lend a hand (Mom runs another small business and Dad works in the computer industry). As for the future, it's too early to say. "I wouldn't be surprised if I study business in college," says Evan.

Source: Doug McPherson, "Truly 'Small' Business," *MyBusiness*, June–July 2002, p. 45.

Questions

1. Which, if any, of the five key location factors discussed in Chapter 9 do you believe were considered prior to making the decision to locate this venture on the Web? Explain.
2. In what additional areas could these entrepreneurs possibly obtain valuable assistance from the business incubator?
3. After visiting the Web site of this business at http://www.thechocolatefarm.com, comment on the content you found there. Is the Web business a "transaction-based" type of e-commerce? Why or why not?
4. Is this business, in your opinion, large enough to warrant a CRM system? Why or why not?

Case 10

STEGMART

PROJECTING FINANCIAL REQUIREMENTS

Angela Martin is a sophomore English major attending Central State University, a small liberal arts college in Missouri. She is president of the journalism club, which is where she first met her roommate and good friend Ashlie Stegemoller. Stegemoller is a junior computer science major. Martin and Stegemoller have been discussing the possibility of a new business venture. After months of brainstorming, they have agreed to start a venture that would offer students and local businesses help in preparing term papers and reports. Both young entrepreneurs recently attended a local seminar entitled "How to Start a New Business." From this experience, they realized the need for preparing pro forma financial statements to obtain necessary financing and also to help them better visualize the merits of the venture.

Research Findings

Research indicates an unfulfilled demand for quality report-preparation services on campus. Market projections estimate a potential volume of 19,200 reports a year from Central State's students. Additionally, there are over 100 small businesses within two miles of the university that have indicated an interest in the service.

The majority of the students at Central State University are enrolled in classes that require two or three reports each semester, ranging from 5 to 50 pages in length. The venture's secondary target market consists of businesses in the nearby city of Emmett, Missouri, which has an SMA (Standard Metropolitan Area) population of approximately 150,000. There are two office building complexes within two miles of the university, each containing over 50 small businesses.

Statement of Financial Assumptions

Drawing on their findings, Martin and Stegemoller have made the following observations:

1. Sales projections related to the preparation of student reports and term papers are based on the following assumptions:
   a. Eighty percent of the 12,000 students at the university, or 9,600 students, prepare at least two reports each 12-month period. This gives a projection of 19,200 reports (9,600 × 2 = 19,200).
   b. The firm will get 3 percent of the student market in the first year, which will increase to 5 percent and 7 percent in the following two years, respectively.
   c. Student reports will average 16 pages in length, for which the firm will receive $20 per report.
2. Revenue forecasts associated with the businesses needing the firm's services are based on the following assumptions:
   a. Sixty percent of the 100 local businesses will need at least 10 reports each 12-month period.
   b. The firm will obtain 6 percent of the business market in the first year, which will increase to 10 percent and 12 percent in the following two years, respectively.
   c. Business reports will average 30 pages in length, for which the firm will receive $40 per report.
3. On average, students will want one copy of their report in addition to the original; businesses will want five copies. The firm will charge $0.06 a page for copies.
4. Practically all copies of reports will be bound, for a charge of $1 per copy.
5. The effective income tax rate will be 20 percent.
6. The firm will extend credit to its business customers. Accounts receivable should be about 15 percent of annual business sales, and inventories should run about 12 percent of annual total sales. However, suppliers are expected to provide credit to the firm, which is estimated at 6 percent of annual sales.
7. The average cost of producing each report is estimated to be $12 in labor and $0.50 in materials.

Martin and Stegemoller have an option for a rent-free office in the university's student activities building. This arrangement was negotiated based on an understanding that they will provide the university with a special pricing schedule after 12 months of operation.

The initial operation will include two personal computers with word-processing, spreadsheet, and database software. One laser printer and two photocopying machines will also be needed. The total equipment costs will be as follows:

Computers	$12,000
Printers and copiers	$ 5,000
Total equipment costs	$17,000

The equipment will be depreciated on a straight-line basis over a five-year life expectancy.

Financing is expected to come from the following sources:

- As the founders, Martin and Stegemoller will each invest $2,000 in the business.
- Additional equity will be raised in the amount of $4,000 from an outside investor: $3,000 will be invested at startup and the remaining $1,000 at the conclusion of the first year of operations.

- The National Bank of Emmett has agreed to loan the firm $3,000, to be repaid within one year, but with the option to renew each year, provided the business is doing well. The interest rate is expected to be 9 percent.
- The $17,000 in equipment will be purchased with a down payment of $7,000; the remaining balance will be paid off at $2,000 in principal per year, plus interest due on the remaining balance at an interest rate of 10 percent.

Question

Given the above information, help Martin and Stegemoller prepare pro forma income statements, balance sheets, and cash flow statements for the first three years of their operation.

Case 11

CALVERT TOYOTA

STRUCTURING FINANCING FOR A CAR DEALERSHIP

Mike Calvert has worked for the Metro Toyota dealership in Houston, Texas, as the general manager for the past several years. Metro's present owner, Tom Gray, is interested in selling the dealership. While Calvert would like to buy the dealership, he does not have the necessary personal financing. As a result, he has approached a number of bankers to see if he could borrow the money for the purchase price. His only personal assets are shares of stock that he already owns in the dealership and some stock in a Chevrolet dealership where he had previously worked.

In an effort to secure financing to acquire the dealership, Calvert approached a banker with the following items: (1) the agreement between the seller and Calvert, the prospective buyer (Exhibit C11-1) and (2) the pro forma financial statements for the first year of operation if he acquires the business (Exhibits C11-2 and C11-3).

In order to understand how Calvert is proposing to structure the financing, you should be aware of the following:

1. There are two entities: the dealership and a real estate partnership. The dealership is the entity that will transact the day-to-day operations. The real estate partnership is a separate entity that will own the land and buildings associated with the business. Thus, the rent expense in the dealership's income statement (Exhibit C11-3) is actually the note payment to the real estate partnership. In turn, this rent income received by the partnership will be used to pay the note payments to the bank.
2. The income statement does not include a salary for Calvert.
3. Calvert will also be purchasing an insurance agency, which is not included in the financial statements. This agency will offer insurance coverage to customers. Historically, this operation has been very profitable.

Source: Interview with Mike Calvert, September 24, 2002.

Questions

1. Explain how the proposed financing for the dealership is to be structured, as represented in the agreement.
2. Is buying the dealership a good investment for Calvert? Explain.
3. If you were the banker, would you make the loan? Why or why not?
4. As the banker, how would you want to structure the loan? (Consider any problems with making the loan and how the loan could be structured to compensate for these deficiencies—if there are any.)
5. The pro forma statements prepared by Calvert assume that the note payments to the bank are amortized (equal payments each month). What changes should be made to the statements if the bank requires equal principal payments plus interest? (Assume a 12 percent interest rate.)

EXHIBIT C11-1 | *Legal Description of the Agreement*

SALES AGREEMENT

This Agreement is entered into the day and year herein below set forth by and between METRO TOYOTA, INC., a Texas corporation, hereinafter referred to as "Seller," and MIKE CALVERT TOYOTA, INC., a Texas corporation, hereinafter referred to as "Purchaser."

WHEREAS, Seller is the owner of certain assets in connection with its business in Houston, Texas; and

WHEREAS, Purchaser desires to acquire such assets from Seller upon and pursuant to the terms and conditions set forth herein;

NOW, THEREFORE, in consideration of the mutual promises, covenants, and agreements of Purchaser and Seller herein, Purchaser and Seller agree hereby as follows:

1.
Purchase and Sale

Seller hereby sells to Purchaser and Purchaser hereby purchases from Seller the following assets at the purchase price indicated:

Asset	Purchase Price
1. Accounts receivable	$ 104,000
2. Financing company receivables	$ 110,000
3. Inventory	$ 126,000
4. Parts	$ 360,000
5. Prepaid items	$ 25,000
6. Fixed assets	$ 475,000
Total	$1,200,000

Purchase Price

The purchase price for the assets set forth in Paragraph 1 shall be ONE MILLION TWO HUNDRED THOUSAND AND NO/100 DOLLARS ($1,200,000.00), which shall be allocated among the respective assets as set forth in Paragraph 1. The purchase price shall be payable as follows:

(a) At the closing, Purchaser shall pay to Seller, by cashier's or certified check, the sum of $600,000.00; and
(b) The balance of the purchase price shall be fully satisfied by Purchaser's endorsement of and delivery to Seller at the closing of the following stock certificates:
  (i) One hundred thirty thousand (130,000) shares of the common stock of Gray Taylor, Inc., evidenced by certificate number 1472.
  (ii) Sixty-five thousand (65,000) shares of the preferred stock of Gray Taylor, Inc., evidenced by certificate number 423.
  (iii) Seventy-five thousand five hundred (75,500) shares of the common stock of Metro Toyota, Inc., evidenced by certificate number 10333.
  (iv) Two hundred fifty (250) shares of the common stock of Tom Gray Management Co., Inc., evidenced by certificate number 67230.

AGREEMENT FOR PURCHASE AND SALE OF REAL PROPERTY

THE STATE OF TEXAS §
COUNTY OF HARRIS §

This Agreement for Purchase and Sale of Real Property made the day and year herein below set forth by and between GC, LTD., a Texas Limited Partnership, whose sole General Partner is TOM GRAY, hereinafter referred to as "Seller," and MICHAEL R. CALVERT, TRUSTEE, hereinafter referred to as "Purchaser."

1.
Legal Description

1.01 The property consists of that one (1) certain 4.721 acre tract of land out of the J. Walters Survey, Abstract 874, Harris County, Texas, more particularly described by metes and bounds in the attached Exhibit "A," incorporated herein for all purposes, together with all of Seller's right, title, and interest in and to adjacent streets, alleys, rights-of-way, accessions or reversions and all improvements located therein which, together, are herein designated as the "Property."

2.
Purchase and Sale

2.01 The purchase price for the property shall be the sum of THREE MILLION AND NO/100 DOLLARS ($3,000,000.00).

2.02 Seller and Purchaser hereby agree that the purchase price shall be allocated among the land and improvements as follows:

Item	Amount
Land	$ 500,000
Buildings	1,850,000
Fences	30,000
Outdoor lighting fixtures	20,000
Lifts	75,000
8,000 gallon underground storage tank	10,000
Air compressor system	15,000
Concrete paving and parking areas	500,000
TOTAL	$3,000,000

3.
Payment of Purchase Price

3.01 The sum of the TWO MILLION TWO HUNDRED THOUSAND AND NO/100 DOLLARS ($2,200,000.00) shall be payable in cash at time of closing.

3.02 The balance of the purchase price shall be evidenced by a Promissory Note executed by Purchaser and payable to the order of Seller, containing the following provision:

(a) Interest, at the same rate charged by Allied Bank of Texas, Houston, Harris County, Texas on the note to be executed by Purchaser described in Paragraph 3.03 hereof.

(b) Installments of principal and interest shall be due and payable monthly based upon a fifteen (15) year amortization with the principal balance of the Note, together with all accrued and unpaid interest thereon, being due and payable on or before the third anniversary date of the Note.

(c) Maker shall reserve the right to prepay all or any portion of the principal balance due, at any time, and from time to time, without penalty or fee.

(d) Such Note shall be secured by a Second Lien Deed of Trust to a Trustee ("Trustee") designated by Seller and shall be on State Bar of Texas form or other form mutually acceptable to Seller and Purchaser. Such Note shall be secondary, inferior, and subordinate to the First Lien Note and Deed of Trust described in Paragraph 3.03 hereof.

3.03 A portion of the cash payable at closing shall be obtained by Purchaser through a loan from Allied Bank of Texas, Houston, Harris County, Texas, which shall be secured by the vendor's lien to be retained by Seller in the Deed to Purchaser and assigned to Allied Bank of Texas, together with a First Lien Deed of Trust on the Property.

CALVERT-DAVIS REAL ESTATE PARTNERSHIP PRO FORMA BALANCE SHEET

Assets	
Land	$ 500,000
Buildings	1,850,000
Improvements	650,000
TOTAL ASSETS	$3,000,000
Liabilities	
Note payable—Allied Bank	$2,000,000
Note payable—GC, LTD.	800,000
Note payable—Calvert Toyota	200,000
	$3,000,000
Net worth	0
TOTAL LIABILITIES	$3,000,000

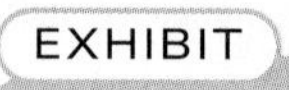

C11-2 *Calvert Toyota Pro Forma Balance Sheet*

Assets		
Cash		$ 200,000
Accounts receivable:		
Service and parts	$95,000	
Warranty claims	7,000	
PDS	2,000	
Finance co. receivables—Current	335,000	
Total receivables		$ 439,000
Inventories:		
New vehicles—Toyota	$1,500,000	
Used vehicles	200,000	
Parts and accessories	360,000	
Gas, oil, and grease	15,000	
Body shop materials	5,000	
Sublet repairs	5,000	
Work in process—labor	26,000	
Total inventories		$2,111,000
Prepaid expenses		25,000
Total current assets		$2,775,000
Fixed assets		515,000
Other assets		200,000
TOTAL ASSETS		$3,490,000
Debt (Liabilities) and Equity		
Reserve for repossession losses	$ 225,000	
Vehicle inventory financing	1,625,000	
Current portion of long-term debt	155,000	
Total current liabilities		$2,005,000
Notes payable—capital loans	$ 860,000	
Other notes and contracts	25,000	
Total long-term debt		$ 885,000
Total liabilities		$2,890,000
NET WORTH		
Capital stock		600,000
TOTAL LIABILITIES AND EQUITY		$3,490,000

C11-3 *Calvert Toyota Pro Forma Income Statement*

Total gross profit		$3,717,000
Departmental selling expenses:		
Sales commissions and incentives	$550,000	
Delivery expense	36,000	
Total selling expenses		$ 586,000
Departmental operating expenses:		
Advertising	$240,000	
Policy adjustments	20,000	
Floor plan interest	220,000	
Demos and company vehicles	50,000	
Personnel training	3,000	
Freight	3,000	
Supplies and small tools	30,000	
Laundry and uniforms	15,000	
Depreciation—equipment and vehicles	100,000	
Maintenance, repair, and rental equipment	10,000	
Miscellaneous expense	10,000	
Supervision salaries	478,000	
Salaries and wages	300,000	
Clerical salaries	180,000	
Vacation and time-off pay—production personnel	10,000	
Total operating expenses		$1,669,000
Total selling and operating expenses		2,255,000
Department profit (loss)		1,462,000
Overhead expenses:		
Rent and equipment	$420,000	
Payroll taxes	115,000	
Employee benefits	60,000	
Stationery and office supplies	30,000	
Data processing services	25,000	
Outside services	60,000	
Dues and subscriptions	12,000	
Telephone	32,000	
Legal and auditing	20,000	
Postage	3,000	
Travel and entertainment	12,000	
Heat, light, power, and water	50,000	
Other insurance	50,000	
Other taxes	25,000	
Total overhead expenses		$ 964,000
Total expenses		3,219,000
Net profit before bonuses		$ 498,000

Video Case 12

TIRES PLUS

DETERMINING THE BEST WAY TO SELL YOUR BUSINESS

As you read in Chapter 12, entrepreneurs sell their businesses for any number of reasons: They retire, the business takes an irrevocable downturn, they can't provide the necessary capital to grow the business, or they just want to cash out their investment. Tom Gegax and Don Gullett, featured in the opening spotlight in Chapter 8, owned Tires Plus in a tightly defined partnership. Over the 24 years they owned and operated the company, they never took outside investment dollars. In fact, retained earnings powered the company's entire growth from a startup to a company with 150 stores generating $220 million in annual sales.

Neither Gegax's nor Gullett's children wanted to take over the company, which motivated the founders to prepare their business for sale. Numerous management consultants warn against taking harvest strategies too casually. Owners must think about what buyers will want. Owners also need to think about the payment terms that they will accept (cash or note or other arrangement). The management team needs to be broad enough that the business is not dependent on the owners. Buyer and seller need to think of ways to encourage key managers to stay after the sale. Companies preparing to sell must also conduct due diligence on themselves (usually an attorney can help with this) and have an accountant create a set of audited financial statements dating back at least a year. One consultant recommends having 9 to 12 months' worth of cash on the balance sheet, so as not to give the appearance of a fire sale. To help with the post-sale transition, it is helpful to have documentation on all aspects of the business, from operations to human resources to accounting systems. Entrepreneurs are notorious for rolling up their sleeves and doing things themselves, but that can be a mistake when selling a business. Harvesting is a complex process, so it is a good idea to seek council. For example, investment bankers often help shepherd companies through the sales process, as in the case of Tires Plus.

After investigating other options, such as taking on outside investors, Gegax and Gullett decided that a complete sale was their best alternative to harvest the business. One month before Bridgestone/Firestone issued its historic tire recall, they sold Tires Plus to the Japanese-owned company, which merged it with its Morgan Tire unit, a 400-store chain based in Clearwater, Florida, operating under various trade names. At the time of the sale, Tires Plus had experienced years of record growth and profits.

What distinguished the sale of Tires Plus was Gegax and Gullett's continued commitment to their employees. The sale proceeds included up to $10 million paid out to many employees, including a couple dozen key employees who had been given equity in the company over the years. Loyalty bonuses were also paid to veteran employees, and severance payments were set aside for headquarters employees who either weren't offered jobs or declined positions elsewhere in the merged organization. Although not all sales transactions include such generous provisions for employees, the culture at Tires Plus was one of employee involvement and participation. According to Gegax, "The employees helped build the company."

Before answering the questions and working the activities, you need to watch the video case on Tires Plus. You may also want to review the video spotlight that introduced Chapter 8. Your instructor may show the video to your class or have you view it online at http://longenecker.swlearning.com.

Video material provided by Hattie Bryant, Producer of Small Business School, the series on PBS Stations, Worldnet, and the Web at http://www.smallbusinessschool.org.

Sources: Neal St. Anthony, "Tires Plus Sold to Florida Company," *Star Tribune*, July 7, 2000, p. 1D; Virginia Munger Kahn, "Ripe for Selling? If You're Thinking About Selling Your Business, Now Is the Time," *BusinessWeek*, July 5, 2004, p. 74; and Constance Gustke, "Back Door Plan," *Internet World*, June 1, 2001, p. 23.

Questions

1. What harvest strategies did Gegax and Gullett consider before deciding to sell to Bridgestone/Firestone/Morgan Tire?
2. How did Gegax and Gullett manage the emotional transition from being owners to being non-owners?
3. Overall, how do you think Gegax feels about the sale? Why do you think so?

Activities

1. As you saw in the video spotlight for Chapter 8, Tom Gegax and Don Gullett offered stock options to key employees so that the company would "have more people with skin in the game." Stock options are not the same as employee stock ownership programs (ESOPs). Research ESOPs using the Internet. Some sites of interest include the National Center for Employee Ownership (NCEO) at http://www.nceo.org and The ESOP Association at http://www.esopassociation.org. You may find other resources as well. The NCEO provides information on stock option purchase plans as well as ESOPs. Write a summary

of the information you find on both types of employee ownership.

2. When you finance a car, the bank writing the loan wants to know the make, model, mileage, value, and price of the car. When you finance a home (which usually is a much larger loan), the bank wants to know the price, size of the house, its features, and the amount of land and will even send an appraiser to verify that the house is actually worth the amount (or more) that you want to mortgage. Imagine that you are looking to buy a company from an entrepreneur who wants to harvest the business. Find out what kind of information the bank will need to know about the company before agreeing to finance the purchase. (Finding out this information will help you when you want to harvest a business.)

Case 13

EVERY CUSTOMER COUNTS

LOSING CUSTOMERS IS ALWAYS HARD

Maintaining good relationships with customers can be stressful for a small business. Fred is a lawyer I know who's had a successful practice for more than 25 years. When I ran into him recently, he told me he was making some changes. "I'm at a new stage of my life," he said. "From now on, I'm working only with people whom I respect and who respect me." "That's a pretty bold statement," I said. "I mean it," he said. "I just fired three clients. I sent them their files with a note saying, 'My firm will no longer represent you.' I'd had it with them. They were a constant aggravation. They didn't treat me right. They abused my office people. They took forever to pay their bills."

"How did they respond?" I asked. "One of them called me up," Fred said. "He thought it was a joke. When I told him I was serious, he asked me why. I said, 'You really don't want to know.' He insisted that he did. 'OK,' I said, 'you're a miserable person. You make everyone's life miserable, but you're not going to ruin my life anymore.' He hung up on me. It felt so good. I wished I'd done it sooner."

There was a time when I would have thought Fred was crazy. I would have said, "So what if your customers are difficult? They pay your salary. They cover your bills. They make it possible for you to remain in business. It's too darn bad if you find them aggravating. Life is full of aggravations. Get over it. Besides, keeping an old account is a lot easier than finding a new one. When you fire a difficult customer, you're just trading one set of aggravations for another."

Not that I believed in the old saying about customers' always being right. That's baloney. But I'd long felt it was important to accommodate customers even when they were wrong—for the good of the business. Lately, however, I've had a change of heart. The turning point came a few months ago, when I received a notice announcing that a fairly substantial customer was leaving my records-storage company.

Now, we don't lose many accounts, so I was curious to find out what had happened with this one. My people told me that the customer, a big law firm, had hired a new records manager, and she was impossible to deal with. Whenever she called, she would yell and scream and threaten our customer-service representatives. They'd be shaking by the time they got off the phone.

When customers abuse your employees, refuse to pay their bills, and generally take advantage of your business, you should let them go. I wanted to see for myself what was going on, so I told my accounting people to send out the standard box-removal letter, detailing the charges for permanently taking boxes out of our warehouse. I then made sure that when the records manager responded, as she undoubtedly would, her call would come to me. Sure enough, she telephoned a couple of days later, and she was furious. "How dare you send us a letter like this?" she demanded. I explained that we were simply following the terms of the contract. "I don't care what's in the contract," she said. "This is outrageous, and you can't get away with it. Who do you think we are?"

I told her we'd be glad to sit down and discuss the situation. She responded by showering me with insults. There was nothing to discuss, she said. "You'll be hearing from one of the senior partners," she fumed. "Fine," I said, "but I don't want you to call me again. I won't take your abuse on the phone, and—starting today—neither will my people." Afterward, I told my employees that they could hang up on the records manager if she called back and started to get nasty.

A senior partner did eventually contact me, and we had a pleasant-enough conversation. I asked him if he knew why his firm was dropping us. He said no but he'd investigate. When he got back to me, he indicated that the firm was reconsidering its decision. Would I be willing to meet with the office manager—that is, the boss of the records manager—who was in charge of such matters? I said, "Of course."

My sales manager, Brad, accompanied me to the meeting. The office manager turned out to be a lovely woman who said she'd like to work things out but there were a few issues we had to discuss. "Do they involve price and service?" I asked. She said yes. "We can definitely work those out," I said, "but I also have an issue." I pointed to the records manager, who was sitting next to her. "That woman has been abusive to my people," I said. At that, the records manager exploded. "Abusive!" she said. "Your people are incompetent. I've never seen such poor service."

"I'm not speaking to you," I said and turned back to the office manager. "I value all my customers very highly, but I really don't want your business unless you can assure me that this person will be civil on the telephone. If we've done something wrong, she doesn't have to be happy about it, but she can't scream and curse at my people."

The records manager started to rant again. I turned to the office manager and threw my hands up. The office manager seemed flustered. "Are you saying that you're going to fire us?" she asked. "I'm saying that the abuse has to stop immediately," I said. "You can see for yourself what we're dealing with." "Obviously, the two of you don't get along," the office manager said.

"I've spoken to this person once before today, and I can get along with almost anyone," I said. "Her behavior is simply unacceptable. If it was up to me, I'd have you pay the removal fee and call it quits right now. But I don't have to deal with you on a regular basis. Brad and our operations people do. If you can persuade him that our people are going to be treated respectfully in the future, I'll let him keep the account."

Source: Norm Brodsky, "Street Smarts: Firing Customers," http://www.inc.com/magazine/20020701/24373.html, July 29, 2004.

I excused myself, went downstairs, and waited. Twenty minutes later Brad came down. "I tried," he said. "It was hopeless. I can't believe they're keeping that woman in that job." Dropping the customer cost us about $200,000 a year in sales, but I didn't regret the decision. On the contrary, I wondered if I should have acted sooner. What if the customer hadn't sent us the withdrawal notice? How long might the abuse have continued? And how many other customers had abused my people without my knowledge? What price had we paid in terms of bad morale, low productivity, and turnover?

The experience changed the way I viewed the business. Recently, for example, I was looking into a receivables problem and discovered that part of it was due to habitual nonpaying customers. I don't mean customers who had fallen on hard times; we work with those people. I mean customers who were following a deliberate strategy of ignoring our bills and payment requests for as long as they could get away with it.

As it turned out, they were all marginal accounts (which is typical), and they were driving our accounting people up the wall. We had one collections guy who was spending hours and hours going after eight accounts that owed us $50 a month, our minimum fee, and refused to pay until we sent a warning letter. Even when we collected, the revenues from the eight accounts amounted to a paltry $400 a month, or $4,800 a year. So I announced a new policy. In the future, we'd send out no more than one warning letter to an account. The second letter would be a box-removal notice. My accounting people cheered.

Don't get me wrong. I haven't changed my principles. I still believe fervently in the importance of providing great customer service. For the vast majority of our customers, moreover, I feel nothing but warmth and gratitude, and I'd do almost anything to keep them. Nor do I have any problem with those who complain, even when their complaints are unjustified. Our goal is to have happy, satisfied customers. If one of them is unhappy or dissatisfied for any reason, we want to hear about it.

But I've learned there's a line that can't be crossed, although it took me more than 20 years to see it. When customers abuse your employees, refuse to pay their bills, and generally take advantage of you and your business, you should let them go. Life is too short, and good people are too hard to find. If you can't afford to lose the account right now, come up with a plan for replacing the business in the future.

Questions

1. How would you evaluate the customer service health of the writer's firm? Do you agree or disagree with the attitude that some customers should be let go? Why or why not?
2. Did the writer handle the customer problem well? What suggestions would you make to improve the handling of a similar situation?
3. Could CRM software assist this firm in managing accounts receivables? Be specific.
4. What psychological concepts discussed in Chapter 13 would be helpful to the writer in better understanding clients' behavior?

Case 14

LOTUS CHIPS' RECIPE FOR SUCCESS

A DASH OF DETERMINATION, A PINCH OF PASSION

Ever sit at your kitchen table with a friend, talking about a business you could start—selling the scones you make from scratch or running your own catering service? Many women have these dreams, and some act on them.

Think you could never really join these ranks? Jane Burns, 53, and Harriet Kinard, 55, of Greenwood, South Carolina, thought that too. They knew Burns's snack chips were delicious, but turning them into a business was another story. "We knew nothing about business," says Kinard.

Says Burns, "If you put both our business brains into a blue jay's head, it would fly backward."

What's their recipe for success? "Good old-fashioned horse sense and lots of hard work," says Burns. Says Kinard, "If we could do it, anybody can. We're just two good friends who had a good idea and pursued it."

Before founding Lotus Chips, Kinard and Burns had not worked full-time jobs since they became moms. "I was a homemaker and a mother, and I loved it," says Burns. She and her husband, a real estate developer, had raised three daughters. Kinard and her husband, a doctor, had raised three sons.

The women met through their children in 1980 by the pool at their country club. They became friends. Then the husbands were introduced and hit it off, too. "We led charmed lives," says Burns.

Adds Kinard, "And we never took it for granted."

But in the fall of 2000 the charm failed. In September Burns and her husband separated after 34 years of marriage. Then, in November, Kinard's husband, Ben, died of a heart attack. "We had lots of ups and downs during the months that followed—mostly downs," says Burns. Says Kinard, "We knew we needed to take positive action to lift ourselves out of our funk."

Enter Burns's chips. A creative cook who entertained regularly, Burns had found a magazine recipe for a deep-fried chip that April. "But the chips tasted really blah. So I spent a few weeks fiddling, trying to come up with something with zip." She came up with two winners: sesame chips and cinnamon-and-sugar chips.

Kinard was an enthusiastic taster. "They were unlike anything I'd ever had before," she says.

In June, Burns brought the chips to a bridge club meeting. The members loved them and asked her to bring more, in December she brought them to a family gathering where two male relatives said, "You've got to get these packaged and sold!"

Source: Adapted from Amy Gillett, "Recipe for Success," *Family Circle* (May 13, 2003), pp. 52–57. Reprinted with permission of FAMILY CIRCLE magazine.

Driving home, she began wondering, *Could I really start a business*? "I knew I had a great product. But I had no idea how to sell it."

In early January 2001 Burns approached Kinard about starting a business together. "I knew working with her would make the whole thing a lot more fun and a lot less daunting."

Kinard loved the idea. "I needed to do something productive to pull myself out of grief," she says. "And I have always loved to learn new things."

During their initial discussion over coffee and chips in Burns's breakfast nook, the women realized they knew nothing about business. Says Kinard, "My husband had always handled our finances." A call to their state health department yielded two valuable pieces of information. They wouldn't be able to make the chips in Burns's kitchen, as planned, because the kitchen has to be state certified and South Carolina does not certify home kitchens. They were also told to call the Small Business Development Center at Clemson University's extension office in Greenwood. The SBDC, a national program funded by the government and private sector, offers free counseling to small-business owners.

In February the women met with SBDC area manager Ben Smith, a former officer with Carolina First Bank. Smith told them they needed a business plan: an estimate of how much it would cost to start the business, how much product they could expect to sell and what their profit or loss would be. Their first assignment was to prepare an estimate of all their start-up costs, from buying ingredients to paying for insurance. This would help them determine how much money they would need to get started. If they needed a loan, a good business plan would help them get one. Smith also suggested they do some marketing research by visiting specialty stores to see how much similar products sold for and asking store owners if they would carry the chips.

The women decided that they could afford to fund the business themselves. The start-up costs were manageable for them: approximately $5,000. "Part of the appeal of starting a food business is that it wouldn't cost much," says Kinard. Says Burns, "We knew if it didn't work, we'd just take our ingredients and our pot and go home."

A little later the husband of a friend put Burns in touch with the manager of a local American Legion hall, who agreed to let the women use the hall's state-certified kitchen at a reasonable hourly rate. In May another family friend offered to take samples of the chips to a woman named Jean Martin, who owned two gourmet specialty shops in North Carolina. The women also brought samples to Connie Wilbum and Lynn Mathis, sisters who own a gift shop in Greenwood and who said they'd love to carry the chips.

Burns had decided to call their product China Chips, but she began worrying that people would think it was a type of Chinese food. The women asked friends and relatives to suggest other names. In October Burns's daughter Laurie called and said, "I've got it! Lotus Chips!" They liked the name immediately.

Questions

1. After evaluating the idea of these entrepreneurs against the seven "rules of thumb" outlined in Chapter 14 of the textbook, what do you believe is the level of risk for their business?
2. How well have these entrepreneurs followed the steps in the new product development process? Support your position.
3. What suggestions can you provide to Burns and Kinard about obtaining protection for the name "Lotus Chips"?
4. What other components, if any, of the "total product" have they overlooked?
5. What kind of distribution plan would you suggest for these entrepreneurs? Why?

Case 15

WACO COMPOSITES I, LTD.

PRICE CUTTING BY A COMPETITOR LEADS TO A NEW STRATEGY

A few years ago, Wayne Hampton found himself jerked into a price war. Founder of Waco Composites I, Ltd., in Waco, Texas, Hampton manufactures bulletproof panels used in hospital emergency rooms, banks, guardhouses, police stations, residential safe rooms—anywhere there's a potential security threat.

In 1999, one of Hampton's more established competitors saw the three-year-old Waco Composites as a serious threat and suddenly cut his panel prices to $13 per square foot from $15. "He was trying to starve me to death," Hampton says. Losing orders, Hampton matched the cuts—and gross profit margins fell to 18 percent from 28 percent.

A few months later, the competitor baited Hampton by slashing prices again, moving to $10.50 per square foot. Hampton knew he had two choices: Follow suit and see profits sink even lower—or find a way to differentiate his company. He picked the second option and began to introduce initiatives to enhance both product value and Waco Composites' image in the industry.

Fireproofing

Up to then, Waco Composites' fiberglass panels were no different from competitors, which made them a commodity item. Believing that fire-retardant panels would benefit his customers, Hampton hired an engineer who developed a new manufacturing process that earned Waco Composites' panels a one-hour fire rating from the American Society for Testing and Materials. What's more, this process added only pennies to company costs.

Faster Shipping

In contrast to the industry norm of product arriving within three to six weeks, Waco Composites began to ship its goods within 24 hours of receiving an order. This enabled customers to order at the last minute, keeping payables off their books longer.

Friendly, Professional Service

Customers told Hampton that competitors were perceived as unfriendly—even rude at times—and slow to provide quotes. Hampton quickly implemented formal policies to highlight his company's image of being friendly, fast and professional. For example:

- Calls are taken by real people—usually on the second ring—not an automated system.
- All price quotes are provided within an hour, compared to the several days sometimes taken by competitors.
- No profanity or slang is allowed in conversations with customers.

Some of these changes are about perceived value rather than tangible value. But that doesn't matter, Hampton says: "Perception is everything. It's as important as real value in the mind of the customer. And, unlike competitors' pricing, your company's perceived value is something that you have control over."

Questions

1. What type of elasticity of demand does this product face? Explain.
2. What is your evaluation of the competitive advantage strategy mapped out by Waco Composites? What other ideas might help the firm gain competitive advantage?
3. Do you believe the strategy being used to create a competitive advantage—without pricing as a major component—will work in this industry? Why or why not?
4. Do you think it would be feasible for Hampton to implement a variable pricing strategy? Why or why not?

Source: http://www.fasttrac.org/article.cfm?ID=244, August 26, 2004.

Video Case 16

SOLID GOLD HEALTH PRODUCTS FOR PETS

PROSPERING THROUGH CREATIVE PROMOTION

Sissy Harrington McGill, a certified nutritionist, has always loved dogs, and especially Great Danes. In 1974, she combined her passion for animals with her expertise in nutrition and launched Solid Gold Health Products for Pets. That year, McGill bought a champion Great Dane in Germany, where she discovered something unexpected: German Danes could live two to six years longer than their American counterparts. Attributing this to nutrition, she brought home samples of German dog food to be analyzed. The ingredients of the German dog food confirmed her hypothesis and motivated her to seek a license to sell the food in the United States. She started by manufacturing three tons of dog food and warehousing the food in her garage. Soon her garage held 30 tons of dog food, and by 1984 she finally moved her business out of her house.

Clearly, McGill's business did not explode overnight—after all, it took her 10 years to get out of the garage. Her company continues to grow incrementally, however, as the result of her targeted promotional strategy.

Before answering the questions and working the activities, you will need to watch the video case on Solid Gold Health Products. Be alert for the use of the various types of promotion you learned about in Chapter 16. Your instructor may show the video to your class or have you view it online at http://longenecker.swlearning.com.

Questions

1. Which promotional methods has McGill used to build her business? Be specific. Once you have a list of ways that she promoted her business, organize them into the categories discussed in the chapter: personal selling, advertising, and sales promotion.
2. What role does McGill's knowledge and expertise play in her promotional activities?
3. The objectives of advertising are to inform, persuade, and remind consumers about the existence or superiority of a firm's product or service. Which function do you think best describes the goal of McGill's advertising? Why?
4. McGill's small retail shop also offers do-it-yourself dog-washing facilities. Does this constitute a service or a promotional activity? Explain your answer.
5. Based on the promotional activities described in the video, how robust do you think McGill's promotional budget is? (Her annual sales are around $7.5 million.) How do you think McGill determines her promotional budget? Explain your answer.

Activities

1. In the video case, McGill does not mention using the Internet as one of her promotional strategies. Solid Gold does, however, operate a Web site. Visit http://www.solidgoldhealth.com and write down any types of promotional strategies you find on the site. Then search for the keywords "natural pet food" or "organic pet food" on Google or Yahoo!. Visit the Web sites of some of the competition, and compare their Internet presence to that of Solid Gold's. Then visit some online pet stores, like PETsMART, Happy Tails PetMart, and Spoiled Brats, Inc. Review the sites for various dog food promotions (coupons, rebates, contests, pop-up ads, etc.). How do the promotional strategies McGill describes in the video compare with those of other companies in her industry?
2. Review McGill's promotional techniques. How can she alter her promotional strategy to increase the number of veterinarians using and recommending her natural dog food? Design a promotional plan that will expand Solid Gold's customer base among veterinary professionals. Could McGill use the same plan to expand sales among the general population of dog and cat owners? If not, list the different promotional techniques that would be appropriate for that market.
3. Imagine that you have recently been hired by Solid Gold Health Products as a marketing manager. You are familiar with the company's text-heavy, black-and-white advertising, and you would like to experiment with other ad formats. Before you present your ideas

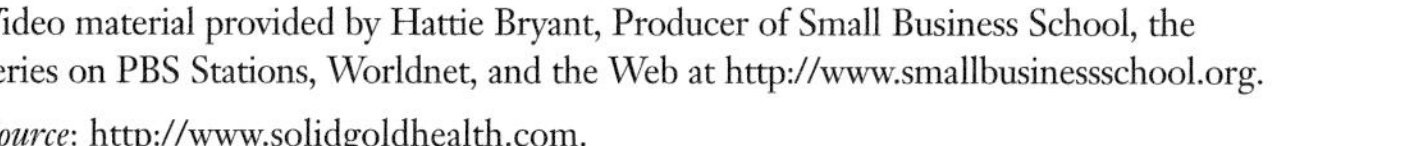

Video material provided by Hattie Bryant, Producer of Small Business School, the series on PBS Stations, Worldnet, and the Web at http://www.smallbusinessschool.org.

Source: http://www.solidgoldhealth.com.

to McGill, however, you decide to mock up some four-color (i.e., full-color) ads to show her. Create a full-page advertisement that communicates a message consistent with Solid Gold's business philosophy (see the company's Web site) but uses a flashier format. Modify this ad for Internet placement—for example, on the American Kennel Club's Web site or in its e-newsletter (see http://www.akc.org). On the back of your work, describe the various sections of each advertisement and the message you are trying to convey with the elements you have chosen. Share your ideas with your classmates.

Case 17

SUNNY DESIGNS, INC.

AN ADVENTURE IN CHINA

To strengthen their businesses, increasing numbers of entrepreneurs are expanding into the international domain. One common motivation behind such moves is the hope of achieving gains in productivity by locating factories in countries where local conditions are favorable to these operations; however, this strategy is not without its drawbacks. Consider, for example, the case of Sunny Hwang, president of Sunny Designs, Inc., a manufacturer, importer, and wholesale distributor of wooden furniture with offices in Hayward, California. Hwang tells the story in his own words.

Cheap and good has been my motto in doing business. I started my business in a flea market as a retail vendor and then soon became a jobber, then a direct importer, and finally a manufacturer. To get better value, I delved into the original source—manufacturing in China.

China is one of the best places for the manufacturing of wooden furniture due to the cheap labor, materials, and other costs. I could hire approximately 20 workers in China for the wage of 1 in the United States. The cost of lumber is about half, and rent is about 20 percent compared to the U.S. There is also reasonable infrastructure available, such as transportation, electricity, and communication.

There are many cheap products available from Chinese factories; however, the quality is greatly lacking in many cases. Therefore, low prices alone are not sufficient justification for doing business in China. As a result, I contracted with an agent who hired several inspectors to control for the quality and delivery of our furniture products. Also, I established a partnership with a local Chinese manufacturer. However, none of these individuals were able to meet our needs.

After the partnership failed, I changed my business strategy by taking charge of my own factory. I hired my nephew, who was trained in the U.S., to oversee building a new factory and take care of purchases from other Chinese factories. Because of the different culture and expectations, it was always a challenge to get along with government officials, who happen to hold most of the properties in China. They are eager to attract overseas investors, but primarily to increase job availability for the local people.

We located our factory in a town near a large city where we had negotiated favorable terms with the local government officials. However, after the company was launched, their attitudes changed. They began demanding what we considered to be unreasonable requests and would interfere with management decisions. Even purchasing lumber became difficult due to a lack of supply chains. Advance payments would be requested by the suppliers for security, which was risky because the lumber shipments would frequently be delayed and even sometimes never delivered. Within six months, the venture failed.

The previous experience, while a failure financially, did provide us a better understanding about doing business in China. This time we found an opportunity to move to a building twice as large as the first one and containing equipment that we could use. The total rent was only half the amount we had paid for the smaller building. This time we were very careful in negotiating strict terms with the government officials. Consequently, hiring qualified workers became much easier, without interference from the government officials and the local workers. Purchasing lumber also became much easier and cheaper by developing relationships of mutual trust with a limited number of agents. It takes time to acquire trust from the Chinese.

The final result has been a much-improved environment for doing business: we can now produce quality products more cheaply. It was a long and tedious journey, involving a lot of hard work, expense, and some tough lessons. But the adventure into China has proven to be a good one.

Sunny Hwang certainly recognizes the importance of knowing as much as possible about the challenges of doing business in a foreign country before getting involved there. An entrepreneur who is considering expanding into China—to connect with an outsourcing partner, to establish a production facility, or to reach a new market—should know the following key facts about the country:

- China's population of 1.3 billion people is the largest of any country in the world.
- China is the third-fastest-growing export market for small- and medium-size U.S. firms.
- Income disparities in China are great. Annual income in urban areas ranges from around $1,557 per person in Shanghai (China's wealthiest city) to the more typical $827 per year in other cities. Income in rural areas is much lower; with the average farmer earning a mere $285.
- The Chinese software market is growing at an annual rate of 30 percent.
- Use of the Internet is increasing dramatically.
- The demand for consulting services in China is increasing, especially those related to information technology.
- China has entered the World Trade Organization (WTO), a development that has raised concerns about

intellectual property protection. Many hope that its entry into the WTO will force more vigilant protection of intellectual property rights and a crackdown on counterfeiting.

- Many Chinese consumers have cell phones and regularly surf the Internet (especially in large urban centers such as Beijing, Shanghai, and Guangzhou).
- Counterfeit goods (including clothing, leather goods, software, and CDs) are readily available in China at a fraction of the cost of brand name items.
- Chinese merchants usually do business only with vendors with whom they have established relationships.

Questions

1. What is the primary force that motivated Hwang to internationalize? Did he make a good decision when he located his manufacturing facility in China? What other countries should have been considered? Why?
2. What strategy option did Hwang select for his China-based enterprise? Did he select the right strategy?
3. Given the details of the case and the key facts about China, assess the opportunities for U.S. firms in China. What features of the country should be particularly attractive to small businesses seeking to expand internationally?
4. What challenges to doing business in China did Hwang experience? Given the key facts about China, list issues that may present distinct problems for small U.S. firms doing business there.

Case 18

DOUGLAS ELECTRICAL SUPPLY, INC.

A MANAGEMENT CONSULTANT EXAMINES AN ENTREPRENEURIAL FIRM

Jim Essinger is a management consultant and training specialist from St. Louis who specializes in continuous process improvement and total quality management. Each month, he goes to Springfield, Illinois, and provides three days of training to employees of a privately owned electrical wholesaler-distributor, Douglas Electrical Supply, Inc.

Most of the employees attending this fourth session are from the Springfield branch and have either gone back to the office or to their favorite restaurants during the lunch break. Jim has noticed that one of the class members is alone in the coffee shop of the hotel where the training sessions are conducted, and he has invited the young man to join him for lunch. The nervousness of his young companion is apparent to Jim, and he decides to ask a few questions.

Jim: Tony, you seem a little distracted; is there something wrong with your lunch?

Tony: Oh, it's not that, Jim. I . . . I'm having a problem at work, and it kind of relates to the training you are doing with us.

Jim: Really? Tell me about it.

Tony: Well, as you might know, I drive a van for the company, delivering electrical products and materials to our customers.

Jim: You work at the Quincy branch, right?

Tony: Yes. I drive about 250 miles a day, all over western Illinois, making my deliveries.

Jim: I see.

Tony: About seven weeks ago, I was making a big delivery at Western Illinois University in Macomb. A lady pulled out in front of me, and I had to brake hard and swerve to miss her!

Jim: You didn't hit her?

Tony: No! She just drove off. . . . I don't think she ever saw me. Anyway, I had a full load of boxes, pipe, conduit, and a big reel of wire. The load shifted and came crashing forward. Some of it hit me hard in the back and on the back of my head.

Jim: Were you injured?

Tony: I'm not sure if I was ever unconscious, but I was stunned. Some people stopped and helped me get out of the van. I was really dizzy and couldn't get my bearings. Eventually, they called an ambulance. The paramedics took me to the hospital, and the doctors kept me for two days while they ran some tests.

Jim: Did you have a concussion?

Tony: Yes, I had some cuts and a slight concussion. My wife was really upset, and she made me stay home for the rest of the week. We have two little kids under four, and she wants me to quit and get a safer job.

Jim: She wants you to quit?

Tony: Yes! Sooner or later, all of the drivers get hit or have close calls. When you have a full load, those loads can shift and do a lot of damage. When I get in the van lately, especially when I have pipe or big reels of wire, I'm frightened. My wife is scared for me. I don't want to be killed or paralyzed, or something!

Jim: I can understand your concern, Tony. What can the company do to protect you? Can you put in some headache racks or heavy-gauge metal partitions in the van that would keep the load from hitting you if it shifts?

Tony: That's exactly what I was thinking! I've been talking with some of the other drivers during our TQM sessions. We've learned that we can get heavy-gauge partitions that would keep us safe built for about $350 per vehicle.

Jim: Good! Have you talked to management about making the modifications?

Tony: Yes, I had all the information and talked to my boss in Quincy, Al Riess. However, he hardly seemed to listen to me. When I pressed the issue, he said the company had nearly 30 vans, counting the ones in Chicago and northern Illinois, and that the company could not afford to spend $10,000 for headache racks, partitions, or anything else! Al finally said that I was just being paranoid, that I should drive more carefully, and that I should definitely stop talking to the other drivers if I valued my job.

Jim: You mean he threatened you?

Tony: You could say that. He said to keep my mouth shut and just drive . . . or else!

Jim: Tony, is there someone else you could talk to about this problem? It would seem to me that one injury lawsuit would certainly cost the company more than the modifications you're proposing.

Tony: Well, there's the problem! You know how expensive the TQM training is . . . and all of us "little people" were actually excited about TQM and continuous process improvement when the owners and you first talked to us. We believed management was changing and was really interested in our ideas and suggestions. We thought maybe they cared about us after all.

Source: This case was prepared by John E. Schoen of Baylor University.

Jim: Well, I believe the owners do want to change the culture and improve the operations.

Tony: Maybe it's different in Chicago and northern Illinois, Jim, but the guys in Peoria and Springfield are like military types and are really into control. I think they're authoritarians—is that the right term?

Jim: Yes, authoritarians, autocrats . . . .

Tony: Al Riess, my boss, is the son-in-law of Bob Spaulding, who heads our division. As you probably know, Bob has a real bad temper and nobody crosses him twice, if you know what I mean. Bob is particularly sensitive about Al—because everyone knows Al doesn't have much ability and we're losing money at the Quincy branch.

Jim: Okay, I see your problem with going to Bob. Is there a safety officer or anyone at headquarters who could logically be brought into this situation?

Tony: I don't know! The owners seem to have a lot of confidence in Bob and give him a free hand in the management of our division. No, I don't see much hope of change. It makes the TQM training pretty hollow and kind of a crock! No offense, Jim!

Jim: No, I see what you mean, Tony.

Tony: See, I have eight years invested in this company! I used to like my job and driving the van. But, now, I'm afraid, my wife is afraid . . . .

Jim: Sure, I can understand where you're coming from! Let me ask you a question. How many van drivers are there in the entire company?

Tony: I'm not absolutely sure. There are 17 drivers in our division, and I believe 13 to 15 drivers in the north. About 30 vans and drivers would be close to the correct numbers.

Jim: Are any of the drivers in a union?

Tony: None of us in this area, but all of the truck and van drivers in the north are Teamsters.

Jim: Aha! Have any of you ever talked to those drivers about this safety issue?

Tony: Oh, I see where you're coming from. . . .

Jim: Hang on! That might be your fallback position, but you won't necessarily be protected if you're regarded as a troublemaker. Let me think about ways I might be able to intercede in a functional way.

Tony: Gee, that would be great if you could. I mean we like our jobs, but we've got to be safe and we've got to be heard when it is a matter of life and death!

Questions

1. How would you describe and evaluate the leadership style of Douglas Electrical Supply?
2. What are the apparent values and assumptions of management in this business?
3. If you were asked to predict the effectiveness of this training effort, what would you say? Explain.
4. Based on this conversation, how would you size up the communication process in this business?
5. What is the proper role of a management consultant? Should Essinger try to intervene in the management process by discussing safety and personnel issues with management?

Case 19

GIBSON MORTUARY

HUMAN RESOURCE PROBLEMS IN A SMALL FAMILY BUSINESS

Gibson Mortuary was founded in 1929 and has become one of the best-known funeral homes in Tacoma, Washington. One of its most persistent problems over the years has been the recruitment and retention of qualified personnel.

Background of the Business

Gibson Mortuary is a family business headed by Ethel Gibson, who owns 51 percent of the stock. As an active executive in the business, Ethel is recognized as a community leader. She has served in various civic endeavors, been elected to the city council, and served one term as mayor.

The mortuary has built a reputation as one of the finest funeral homes in the state. The quality of its service over the years has been such that it continues to serve families over several generations. While large corporations have bought up many mortuaries in recent years, Gibson Mortuary continues to remain competitive as an independent family firm—a "family serving families." Funeral homes in general have recently become the target of public criticism, and books such as *The American Way of Death* reflect adversely on this type of business. Nevertheless, Gibson Mortuary has withstood this threat by its determined, consistent effort to provide the best possible customer service. In its most recent year, it conducted 375 funerals, which places it in the top 9 percent of all funeral homes in the nation when measured in terms of volume of business.

Ethel's son, Max Gibson, entered the business after completing military service and became general manager of the firm. He is a licensed funeral director and embalmer. Both mother and son are active in the day-to-day management of the firm.

Recruitment and Retention Problem

Perhaps the most difficult problem facing Gibson Mortuary is the recruitment and retention of qualified personnel. The image of the industry has made it difficult to attract the right caliber of young people as employees. Many individuals are repelled by the idea of working for an organization in which they must face the fact of death daily. In addition, the challenges raised by social critics reflect poorly on the industry and conveyed to many people the impression that funeral homes are profiting from the misery of those who are bereaved.

One source of employees is walk-in applicants. Also, Gibson Mortuary works through local sales representatives who often know of people who might be considering a change in their careers.

Source: Personal communication; names have been disguised.

As a small business, Gibson Mortuary presents fewer total opportunities than a larger company or even a funeral home chain. The fact that it is a family business also suggests to prospective employees that top management will remain in the family. It is apparent to all that the two top management spots are family positions. However, Ethel and Max (who is 49 years old) are the only family members employed, so there is some hope for the future for nonfamily employees.

Training Problem

Gibson Mortuary uses two licensed embalmers—Max and another individual. The pressure of other managerial work has made it difficult for Max to devote sufficient time to this type of work.

Any individual interested in becoming a licensed embalmer has to attend mortuary college (mortuary science programs are part of some community-college programs) and serve a two-year apprenticeship. The apprenticeship can be served either prior to or after the college training. Gibson Mortuary advises most individuals to take the apprenticeship prior to the college training so that they can evaluate their own aptitude for this type of career.

Gibson Mortuary prefers its personnel to be competent in all phases of the business. The work involves not only embalming, but also making funeral arrangements with families and conducting funerals and burials. However, some part-time employees only assist in conducting funerals and do not perform preparatory work.

Personal Qualifications for Employment

All employees who meet the public and have any part in the funeral service need to be able to interact with others in a friendly and relaxed but dignified manner. The personalities of some individuals are much better suited to this than those of others. Ethel describes one of the problem personalities she had to deal with as follows:

In the first place, he didn't really look the part for our community here. He was short and stocky, too heavy for his height. His vest was too short, and he wore a big cowboy buckle! Can't you see that going over big in a mortuary! He wanted to stand at the door and greet people as they came. We do furnish suits, so we tried to polish off some of the rough edges.

But he was still too aggressive. He became upset with me because I wouldn't get him any business cards immediately. One day I had to send him to the printer, and he came back and said, "While I was there, I just told them to make some cards for me. I'll pay for them myself." I said to him, "Willis, you go right back there and cancel that order! When you are eligible for cards, I'll have them printed for you." We couldn't have him at that point scattering his cards with our name all over town.

Another young applicant made an impressive appearance but lacked polish. His grammar was so poor that he lacked the minimal skills necessary for any significant contact with the public.

Two characteristics of employment that discourage some applicants are the irregular hours and the constant interruptions that are part of the life of a funeral director. A funeral director might start to do one thing and then find it necessary to switch over to another, more urgent matter. Also, some night and weekend duty in the work schedule is required.

Solving the Human Resource Problems

Although Gibson Mortuary has not completely solved its need for qualified personnel, the business is working at it. While waiting for the right person to come along, Gibson Mortuary started another apprentice prior to any college training. In addition, it is following up on a former apprentice who worked during summer vacations while attending mortuary college. The business also employs a part-time minister as an extra driver. In these ways, Gibson Mortuary is getting along, but it still hopes to do a better job in personnel staffing.

Questions

1. Evaluate the human resource problems facing this firm. Which appears most serious?
2. How can Gibson Mortuary be more aggressive in recruitment? How can it make itself more attractive to prospective employees?
3. Does the fact that Gibson Mortuary is a family firm create a significant problem in recruitment? How can the firm overcome any problems that may exist in this area?
4. Assuming that you are the proper age to consider employment with Gibson Mortuary, what is the biggest question or problem you would have as a prospective employee? What, if anything, might the Gibsons do to deal with that type of question or problem?

Video Case 20

TEXAS NAMEPLATE COMPANY

LEVERAGING THE QUALITY PROCESS

The National Institute of Standards and Technology sends out hundreds of thousands of applications for the Malcolm Baldrige National Quality Award, but merely reading over the criteria was enough to scare off all but 60 companies in 2004, and only 8 of those were small businesses with fewer than 500 employees. Similar statistics confronted Dale Crownover, owner of Texas Nameplate Company (TNC), when he applied. But he had been on the path to quality improvement long before he decided to throw his hat in the ring.

Texas Nameplate Company provides the identifying labels for all types of products, from appliances to computers to military equipment. Nameplates are stamped or etched before being sent to the company's customers, located in all 50 states and 12 foreign countries. Before Crownover took over the business from his father, TNC was a very different company. Morale was low, there were no benefits, turnover was very high, and the pay was extremely low. New faces were always on the production line. The defective part rate was crippling. The company was spending $20,000 a month, or 10 percent of sales, on bad work. Workers would just make 50 percent more than they needed to be sure that they had enough good parts to cover a customer's order. And it wasn't just a single type of nonconformance: Nameplates were cut incorrectly or missing information, holes were cut the wrong diameter or put in the wrong place, the overall dimensions were wrong. TNC had a lot of employees, but there didn't seem to be enough time to train them, particularly at the rate new employees were being brought on board. When Crownover became president in 1991, those problems were compounded by lawsuits from the city of Dallas over wastewater discharges and from the EEOC. The quality of the company's output reflected an arid organizational culture.

Shortly after taking control, Crownover had a meeting with TNC's biggest customer, General Dynamics (now Lockheed Martin). General Dynamics was implementing a vendor certification program in Statistical Process Control (SPC), and TNC would need to be certified to remain a vendor, their long relationship notwithstanding. Crownover, however, thought he knew his business and threw any correspondence related to the quality certification program in the trash. Inevitably, TNC was cut off for not complying with the SPC directive. Crownover swallowed his pride and asked for a second chance. He submitted a half-page document to General Dynamics on TNC's quality process. The version General Dynamics approved three months later covered 45 pages.

Within two years of implementing an agreed-on quality program, the company had made such a turnaround that Crownover celebrated a Zero Defects Day with his employees. In the following four years, the company nearly doubled its market share, doubled its sales growth, decreased employee turnover by 82 percent, cut its product cycle time by 61 percent, reduced its nonconformance by a third, nearly doubled the amount of product it manufactured per hour, and increased profits and decreased cost of sales each by 9 percent.

SPC was only the beginning of TNC's commitment to Total Quality Management, however. TNC went on to be ISO 9002 certified (now ISO 9001:2000), a certification granted by the International Standards Organization. TNC also applied for and won the Texas Quality Award and the prestigious Baldrige National Quality Award. Crownover continues to push forward by restructuring as a lean manufacturing operation, using Kanban production techniques for regular customers, and achieving ISO 14000 certification. To no one's surprise, Crownover applied for a second Baldrige in 2004, when he was again eligible to do so.

Before answering the questions and working the activities, you need to watch the video case on Texas Nameplate for Chapter 20. Your instructor may show the video to your class or have you view it online at http://longenecker.swlearning.com.

Questions

1. What kind of manufacturing operation is Texas Nameplate?
2. What is the role of quality in productivity measures? Describe the operational problems that led to low quality before Texas Nameplate adopted its quality control program.
3. Quality programs differ in their effectiveness. Describe the transformation that occurred and explore the reasons Texas Nameplate achieved such dramatic results.

Video material provided by Hattie Bryant, Producer of Small Business School, the series on PBS Stations, Worldnet, and the Web at http://www.smallbusinessschool.org.

Sources: http://www.baldrige.nist.gov; http://www.iso.org; Sonja Sherwood, "Living Up to the Baldrige," *Chief Executive*, July 2002, p. 16; Rick Carter, "Texas Nameplate's Texas-Sized Turnaround," *Industrial Maintenance and Plant Operation*, May 2001, p. 12; and "Winning Is Everything," *BusinessWeek*, April 26, 1999, p. F22.

4. Explain the changes Texas Nameplate has experienced in inventory control. How has it been able to make this shift?

5. Referring to both the video and the text, describe the cultural change that has taken place within the Texas Nameplate organization as a result of changes in operational practices.

Activities

1. The Malcolm Baldrige National Quality Award is the most prestigious business award in the United States. Only applications from businesses operating in the United States and its territories are considered. Go to http://www.baldrige.nist.gov to determine the criteria for winning the Baldrige. How many small businesses (fewer than 500 employees) apply each year?

2. What is ISO certification, and why is it important to businesses? Find out by researching the International Standards Organization at http://www.iso.org. What is ISO 9000? ISO 14000? Why do you think it was important for Texas Nameplate to secure certification for both families of standards? Based on your research, explain how ISO differs from the Baldrige.

3. Imagine that you are the purchasing manager for a company that buys nameplates for its line of refrigerators. Your factories are in New England, Missouri, and Montana, and you have been a customer of Texas Nameplate for years. Your boss recently talked to you about diversifying your supplier base for nameplates. You, however, prefer to concentrate your purchases with one supplier. Use the Internet to research at least three other nameplate manufacturers and find out what they offer. Write a memo to your boss listing the reasons why you are against diversifying. Include specifics about the competition where possible.

4. Imagine that you are now the boss in the scenario just presented. Write a memo to your purchasing manager about why you think that diversifying your supplier base is important. Compare Texas Nameplate (http://www.nameplate.com) to at least two other companies.

Case 21

FOX MANUFACTURING INC.

RESPONDING TO DISASTER

The end of the workday on May 12 was like any other—or so Dale Fox thought when he closed up shop for the night. But 12 hours later, an electrical fire had destroyed Fox Manufacturing Inc.'s only plant, in Albuquerque, New Mexico. The damage exceeded $1.5 million.

"It was the largest fire New Mexico had seen in years. About 37 fire trucks were at the scene trying to put out the fire. We made local and national news," recalls Fox, president of the family-owned manufacturer and retailer of southwestern-style and contemporary furniture. The fire was especially devastating since all orders from the company's three showrooms were sent to the plant. Normally, the furniture was built and delivered 10 to 12 weeks later.

Such a disaster could force many companies out of business. But just eight weeks after the fire, the first piece of furniture rolled off the Fox assembly line in a brand new plant in a new building. The company even managed to increase sales that year. And now, just three years later, the company has emerged stronger than ever. Annual sales average between $3.5 million and $5 million.

How did Fox Manufacturing manage literally to rise from the ashes? It forged an aggressive recovery plan that focused not only on rebuilding the business, but also on using the untapped skills of employees and an intensive customer relations campaign. Indeed, with more than $1 million in unfilled orders at the time of the fire, Fox offered extra services to retain its customer base. Dale Fox also took advantage of his close relationships with his financial and legal experts to help manage the thicket of legal and insurance problems that arose after the fire.

Rising from the Ashes

Recovering from this disaster, and getting the company up and running again, was a particularly grueling experience for Fox and his employees. Having to complete the monumental task in just eight weeks added to the pressure. "We had no choice," says Fox. "Because we had more than $1 million in orders, we had to get back in production quickly so we wouldn't lose that business."

Fox found himself working up to 20 hours a day, seven days a week. One of his first tasks was finding a new building to house his manufacturing facility. Remodeling the old site—and the requisite tasks of clearing debris, rebuilding, and settling claims with the insurance company—would take too long and hold up the production of new furniture. At the same time, however, he had to quickly replace all the manufacturing equipment lost in the fire. He decided to hit the road, attending auctions and other sales across the country in search of manufacturing equipment, including sanders, glue machines, molding machines, and table saws. Unfortunately, all the company's hand-drawn furniture designs and cushion patterns also perished in the fire and had to be redrawn because no backup copies existed.

Tapping Employee Talent

Although Fox initially laid off most of his hourly workers, he put the company's 15 supervisors to work building new work tables that would be needed once manufacturing resumed. They did the work at an empty facility loaned to Fox by a friend. At the same time, the company's draftsmen—working in a rented garage—started redrawing the furniture designs, this time using a computer. (It took nearly a year to redraw all the designs lost in the fire.) To check frame configurations and measurements, they had to tear apart showroom furniture. A handful of hourly employees also started tearing apart cushions to redraw the patterns.

When Fox found the new building—the former home of a beer distributor—two weeks after the fire, he started rehiring the 65-plus hourly employees to help with the remodeling. Fox knew what construction skill—carpentry, plumbing, metalworking, or painting—each had to offer because the day he laid them off he had them fill out a form listing such skills. "If I had gone through the process of having contractors bid on the work, we never would have reopened as fast as we did. Plus, our employees needed the work to feed their families," says Fox.

Within five weeks of the fire, Fox had rehired most employees. The employees, who were paid the same hourly rate they earned before the fire, proved to be competent and cooperative. Like Fox, they often worked up to 20 hours a day because they were aware of their boss's ambitious timetable for reopening.

Staying in Close Contact with Customers

Fox's salespeople started calling customers the day of the fire to explain what had happened and assure them that the company planned to bounce back quickly. Just days later, Fox's two sons called the same customers to reinforce that message and let them know that the Fox family appreciated their patience. In subsequent weeks, customers received three or four more calls or letters that updated them on the company's progress. Fox even rented billboard space in Albuquerque to advertise that the company planned to be manufacturing furniture again soon.

"If we hadn't kept in such close contact with our customers, we probably would have lost 50 percent of the orders," Fox says. But Fox's strategy paid off handsomely; the company lost less than 3 percent of its pre-fire orders. That's an amazingly

Source: Don Nichols, "Back in Business," *Small Business Report*, Vol. 18, No. 3 (March 1993), pp. 55–60. Adapted by permission of the publisher, from *Small Business Reports*, March 1993.

low percentage, especially since some customers had to wait up to 36 weeks for delivery, instead of the usual 10 to 12 weeks.

Customers had good reason to be patient: When they placed their orders, they were required to pay a 25 percent to 33 percent deposit. After the fire, as a goodwill gesture, the company agreed to pay them 1 percent per month on the deposited money until their orders were filled. To calculate his customers' interest, Fox started from the order date, not the fire date. And rather than simply deduct the interest from the final amount due, Fox wrote each customer a check, so they could see exactly how much money they had earned.

Because Fox also kept his suppliers informed, most of them continued filling the company's orders after the fire and told Fox not to worry about paying until his operation was in full swing again. "Factors were the only people we had any problem with," says Fox. "Once they found out about the fire, they wanted money that wasn't even due yet."

Relying Heavily on Professional Expertise

During a normal year, Fox pays his CPA and lawyer to handle such tasks as tax planning and consulting on leases, insurance, and operations. Together, their bills run about $25,000 to $30,000. The year of the fire, however, Fox Manufacturing's accounting bill topped $50,000; the legal bill was over $75,000. As far as Fox is concerned, it was money well spent: "Without their help, I couldn't have gotten back in business as quickly as I did."

Fox called his CPA and his lawyer as soon as he got news of the Saturday-morning fire. While the firemen battled the blaze, the three met with key management employees to develop a comeback plan. During subsequent weeks, his accountant and lawyer assumed so much responsibility for valuing lost assets and haggling with the insurance company that Fox felt comfortable leaving the city to travel around the country buying manufacturing equipment.

One early decision was to apply for a $1 million loan to buy the new building. The CPA put together all the paperwork necessary for the bank to approve it—such as a financial analysis, a cash flow statement, and profit projections. He also played a key role in helping Fox's in-house accountant determine the value of the inventory, machinery, and work in progress destroyed in the fire, which totaled about $800,000.

His involvement lent credibility to the numbers that were generated and quelled any concerns or doubts that the insurance companies had. "It was very important to have an outside CPA firm verify the numbers. If we had tried to just throw some numbers together ourselves, we could have been in over our heads in arguments with insurance companies," Fox says.

Even so, settling insurance claims was difficult, and that's where Fox's lawyer earned his money. For example, what the insurance company thought it would cost to replace the old plant was less than half of what Fox claimed. One figure over which they disagreed was the cost of replacing the electrical wiring. The insurance company estimated that it would cost $30,000; Fox and his lawyer insisted it would cost $120,000. The lawyer had a local electrician familiar with the Fox plant verify that Fox's estimate was accurate. The insurance company finally settled the claim at Fox's value.

"Dealing with the insurance company was a constant battle. There are a lot of things they won't tell you unless you bring it up," Fox warns. Indeed, it was his lawyer, not the insurance company, who pointed out that Fox was entitled to $25,000 for the cost of cleaning away debris and $2,000 to replace shrubbery that was destroyed.

And, even after they settled the claim on Fox's business-interruption insurance, it took much longer than expected to get the final $750,000 payment. Fox finally had to call his insurance company with an ultimatum: "If I didn't get the check, I told them my lawyer and I were going to Santa Fe the next day to file a formal complaint with the insurance commissioner. I got the check."

Painfully aware that another disaster could strike at any time, Fox now takes risk management to a justified extreme. He doesn't leave anything to chance and takes numerous safety precautions that will make it easier for the company to rebound should it be dealt a similar setback again. What happened to Fox Manufacturing can happen to any company—other companies would do well to follow Dale Fox's lead.

Question

What are some basic disaster precautions that Fox could have taken to minimize the loss incurred and the consequences of the disaster?

Case 22

BARTON SALES AND SERVICE

MANAGING A FIRM'S WORKING CAPITAL

The owners of Barton Sales and Service, based in Little Rock, Arkansas, are John and Joyce Barton. John serves as general manager, and Joyce as office manager. The firm sells General Electric, Carrier, and York air-conditioning and heating systems to both commercial and residential customers and services these and other types of systems. Although the business has operated successfully since the Bartons purchased it in 1996, it continues to experience working-capital problems.

Barton's Financial Structure

The firm has been profitable under the Bartons' ownership. Profits for 2003 were the highest for any year to date. Exhibit C22-1 shows the income statement for Barton Sales and Service for that year.

The balance sheet as of December 31, 2003, for Barton Sales and Service is shown in Exhibit C22-2. Note that the firm's equity was somewhat less than its total debt. However, \$10,737 of the firm's liabilities was a long-term note payable to a stockholder. This note was issued at the time the Bartons purchased the business, with payments going to the former owner.

Barton's Cash Balance

A minimum cash balance is necessary in any business because of the uneven nature of cash inflows and outflows. John explained that they need a substantial amount in order to "feel comfortable." He believed that it might be possible to reduce the present balance by \$5,000 to \$10,000, but he stated that it gave them some "breathing room."

Barton's Accounts Receivable

The trade accounts receivable at the end of 2003 were \$56,753, but at some times during the year the accounts receivable were twice this amount. These accounts were not aged, so the firm had no specific knowledge of the number of overdue accounts. However, the firm had never experienced any significant loss from bad debts. The accounts receivable were thought, therefore, to be good accounts of a relatively recent nature.

Customers were given 30 days from the date of the invoice to pay the net amount. No cash discounts were offered. If payment was not received during the first 30 days, a second statement was mailed to the customer and monthly carrying charges of 1/10 of 1 percent were added. The state usury law prohibited higher carrying charges.

On small residential jobs, the firm tried to collect from customers when work was completed. When a service representative finished repairing an air-conditioning system, for example, he or she presented a bill to the customer and attempted to obtain payment at that time. However, this was not always possible. On major items such as unit changeouts—which often ran as high as \$2,500—billing was almost always necessary.

On new construction projects, the firm sometimes received partial payments prior to completion, which helped to minimize the amount tied up in receivables.

Barton's Inventory

Inventory accounted for a substantial portion of the firm's working capital. It consisted of the various heating and air-conditioning units, parts, and supplies used in the business.

The Bartons had no guidelines or industry standards to use in evaluating their overall inventory levels. They believed that there *might* be some excessive inventory, but, in the absence of a standard, this was basically an opinion. When pressed to estimate the amount that might be eliminated by careful control, John pegged it at 15 percent.

The firm used an annual physical inventory that coincided with the end of its fiscal year. Since the inventory level was known for only one time in the year, the income statement could be prepared only on an annual basis. There was no way of knowing how much of the inventory had been used at other points and, thus, no way to calculate profits. As a result, the

EXHIBIT C22-1 | *Barton Sales and Service Income Statement for the Year Ending December 31, 2003*

Sales revenue	\$727,679
Cost of good sold	466,562
Gross profit	\$261,117
Selling, general and administrative expenses (including officers' salaries)	189,031
Earnings before taxes	\$ 72,086
Income tax	17,546
Net income	\$ 54,540

EXHIBIT C22-2 | *Balance Sheet for Barton Sales and Service for December 31, 2003*

Assets	
Current assets:	
Cash	$ 28,789
Trade accounts receivable	56,753
Inventory	89,562
Prepaid expenses	4,415
Total current assets	$179,519
Loans to stockholders	41,832
Autos, trucks, and equipment, at cost, less accumulated depreciation of $36,841	24,985
Other assets: goodwill	16,500
TOTAL ASSETS	$262,836
Debt (Liabilities) and Equity	
Current debt:	
Current maturities of long-term notes payable*	$ 26,403
Trade accounts payable	38,585
Accrued payroll taxes	2,173
Income tax payable	13,818
Other accrued expenses	4,001
Total current debt	$ 84,980
Long-term notes payable*	51,231
Total stockholders' equity	126,625
TOTAL DEBT AND EQUITY	$262,836

*Current and long-term portions of notes payable:

	Current	**Long-Term**	**Total**
• 10% note payable, secured by pickup, due in monthly installments of $200, including interest	$ 1,827	$ 1,367	$ 3,194
• 10% note payable, secured by equipment, due in monthly installments of $180, including interest	584	0	584
• 6% note payable, secured by inventory and equipment, due in monthly installments of $678, including interest	6,392	39,127	45,519
• 9% note payable to stockholder	0	10,737	10,737
• 12% note payable to bank in 30 days	17,600	0	17,600
	$26,403	$51,231	$77,634

Bartons lacked quarterly or monthly income statements to assist them in managing the business.

Barton Sales and Service was considering changing from a physical inventory to a perpetual inventory system, which would enable John to know the inventory levels of all items at all times. An inventory total could easily be computed for use in preparing statements. Shifting to a perpetual inventory system would require the purchase of proper file equipment, but the Bartons believed that that cost was not large enough to constitute a major barrier. A greater expense would be involved in the maintenance of the system—entering all incoming materials and all withdrawals. The Bartons estimated that this task would necessitate the work of one person on a half-time or three-fourths-time basis.

Barton's Note Payable to the Bank

Bank borrowing was the most costly form of credit. Barton Sales and Service paid the going rate, slightly above prime, and owed $17,600 on a 90-day renewable note. Usually, some of the principal was paid when the note was renewed. The total borrowing could probably be increased if necessary. There was no obvious pressure from the bank to reduce borrowing to zero. The amount borrowed during the year typically ranged from $10,000 to $25,000.

The Bartons had never explored the limits the bank might impose on borrowing, and there was no clearly specified line of credit. When additional funds were required, Joyce simply dropped by the bank, spoke with a bank officer, and signed a note for the appropriate amount.

Barton's Trade Accounts Payable

A significant amount of Barton's working capital came from its trade accounts payable. Although accounts payable at the end of 2003 were $38,585, the total payable varied over time and might be double this amount at another point in the year. Barton obtained from various dealers such supplies as expansion valves, copper tubing, sheet metal, electrical wire, and electrical conduit. Some suppliers offered a discount for cash (2/10, net 30), but Joyce felt that establishing credit was more important than saving a few dollars by taking a cash discount. By giving up the cash discount, the firm obtained the use of the money for 30 days. Although the Bartons could stretch the payment dates to 45 or even 60 days before being "put on C.O.D.," they found it unpleasant to delay payment more than 45 days because suppliers would begin calling and applying pressure for payment.

Their major suppliers (Carrier, General Electric, and York) used different terms of payment. Some large products could be obtained from Carrier on an arrangement known as "floor planning," meaning that the manufacturer would ship the products without requiring immediate payment. The Bartons made payment only when the product was sold. If still unsold after 90 days, the product had to be returned or paid for. (It was shipped back on a company truck, so no expense was incurred in returning unsold items.) On items that were not floor-planned but were purchased from Carrier, Barton paid the net amount by the 10th of the month or was charged 18 percent interest on late payments.

Shipments from General Electric required payment at the bank soon after receipt of the products. If cash was not available at the time, further borrowing from the bank became necessary.

Purchases from York required net payment without discount within 30 days. However, if payment was not made within 30 days, interest at 18 percent per annum was added.

Can Good Profits Become Better?

Although Barton Sales and Service had earned a good profit in 2003, the Bartons wondered whether they were realizing the *greatest possible* profit. Slowness in the construction industry was affecting their business somewhat. They wanted to be sure they were meeting the challenging times as prudently as possible.

Questions

1. Evaluate the overall performance and financial structure of Barton Sales and Service.
2. What are the strengths and weaknesses in this firm's management of accounts receivable and inventory?
3. Should the firm reduce or expand the amount of its bank borrowing?
4. Evaluate Barton's management of trade accounts payable.
5. Calculate Barton's cash conversion period. Interpret your computation.
6. How could Barton Sales and Service improve its working-capital situation?

Case 23

ARTHO, INC.

EVALUATING FINANCIAL PERFORMANCE

Paul Carey is the owner of Artho, Inc., a firm that wholesales athletic equipment. He bought the firm almost 10 years ago, after being a high school coach for 12 years. Although it has taken a lot of his time, the business requires fewer hours than the long ones he experienced in coaching. He has also found that as the owner of Artho he can continue to be actively involved in the community.

While pleased with the business and with his performance, Carey has begun to question whether he has been managing the firm's financial resources as well as he could and should. He recently attended a seminar on "Financial Management for the Nonfinancial Executive." It was an eye opener for him. He had never really understood much of what the bankers said when they talked about Artho's financial performance.

Eager to use what he had learned at the seminar to evaluate his company, Carey asked his banker to acquire financial statements on a similar company so that Carey could compare his firm's performance with that of the other company. About a week later, the banker provided financial statements for what he labeled a "comparison firm."

The financial statements for Artho, Inc., beginning in 2001 and ending in 2005, are shown in Exhibits C23-1 and C23-2. Exhibits C23-3 and C23-4 show the financial data for the comparison firm.

Questions

1. Evaluate the two firms in terms of their financial performance over time (2001–2005) as it relates to (1) liquidity, (2) operating profitability, (3) financing the assets, and (4) the shareholders' (common equity) return on investment. (Note: Using a computer spreadsheet would be extremely helpful. In fact, looking up the financial statements for these two companies at http://longenecker.swlearning.com will save you some time in doing the assignment.)
2. Compare the two firms' financial performance. Discuss the firms' differences and similarities.
3. Compute the firms' cash flows and the financing from investors from 2001 to 2005; then compare the results. (Again, the computer spreadsheet available at http://longenecker.swlearning.com will be a real timesaver in doing this exercise.)

EXHIBIT C23-1 | *Income Statements (in thousands) for Artho, Inc., 2001–2005*

	2001	2002	2003	2004	2005
Sales revenue	$2,910	$2,890	$3,295	$3,512	$3,481
Cost of goods sold	1,799	1,695	1,938	2,084	2,108
Gross profit	$1,111	$1,195	$1,357	$1,428	$1,373
Selling, general and administrative expenses	807	770	890	1,000	1,066
Depreciation	27	35	32	35	40
Operating profit	$ 277	$ 390	$ 435	$ 393	$ 267
Interest expense	20	25	17	26	42
Earnings before taxes	$ 257	$ 365	$ 418	$ 367	$ 225
Income taxes	87	124	142	125	77
Net income	$ 170	$ 241	$ 276	$ 242	$ 148

EXHIBIT C23-2 *Balance Sheets (in thousands) for Artho, Inc., 2001–2005*

	2001	2002	2003	2004	2005
Assets					
Cash and equivalents	$ 104	$ 78	$ 84	$ 80	$ 232
Accounts receivable	418	457	642	637	591
Inventories	434	583	625	635	625
Prepaid expenses	24	22	30	—	20
Other current assets	79	55	66	121	156
Total current assets	$1,059	$1,195	$1,447	$1,473	$1,624
Gross plant and equipment	$ 196	$ 220	$ 283	$ 390	$ 436
Accumulated depreciation	69	104	136	171	211
Net plant, property and equipment	$ 127	$ 116	$ 147	$ 219	$ 225
Other assets	158	173	203	243	296
TOTAL ASSETS	$1,344	$1,484	$1,797	$1,935	$2,145
Liabilities and Equity					
Notes payable	$ 8	$ 26	$ 69	$ 41	$ 86
Accounts payable	281	138	171	166	176
Taxes payable	89	81	102	48	66
Accrued expenses	—	129	140	145	169
Other current liabilities	7	6	6	6	—
Total current liabilities	$ 385	$ 380	$ 488	$ 406	$ 497
Long-term debt	115	120	145	214	285
Deferred taxes	5	—	—	5	—
Total liabilities	$ 505	$ 500	$ 633	$ 625	$ 782
Equity:					
Common stock	$ 10	$ 10	$ 10	$ 10	$ 10
Capital surplus	60	60	60	60	60
Retained earnings	769	914	1,094	1,240	1,293
Common equity	$ 839	$ 984	$1,164	$1,310	$1,363
TOTAL LIABILITIES AND EQUITY	$1,344	$1,484	$1,797	$1,935	$2,145

EXHIBIT C23-3 *Income Statements (in thousands) for the Comparison Company, 2001–2005*

	2001	2002	2003	2004	2005
Sales	$3,412	$3,941	$3,798	$4,774	$5,983
Cost of goods sold	2,050	2,337	2,245	2,805	3,470
Gross profit	$1,362	$1,604	$1,553	$1,969	$2,513
Selling, general and administrative expenses	761	922	974	1,210	1,640
Depreciation	48	60	72	84	68
Operating profit	$ 553	$ 622	$ 507	$ 675	$ 805
Interest expense	31	27	16	24	39
Earnings before taxes	$ 521	$ 595	$ 491	$ 651	$ 766
Income taxes	177	202	167	221	260
Net income	$ 344	$ 393	$ 324	$ 430	$ 506

EXHIBIT C23-4 | *Balance Sheets (in thousands) for the Comparison Company, 2001–2005*

	2001	2002	2003	2004	2005
Assets					
Cash and equivalents	$ 260	$ 291	$ 519	$ 216	$ 262
Accounts receivable	596	668	704	1,053	1,346
Inventories	471	593	615	630	931
Prepaid expenses	33	42	40	74	94
Other current assets	28	26	38	73	93
Total current assets	$1,388	$1,620	$1,916	$2,046	$2,726
Gross plant and equipment	$ 498	$ 590	$ 690	$ 923	$1,180
Accumulated depreciation	152	212	283	367	435
Net plant, property and equipment	$ 346	$ 378	$ 407	$ 556	$ 745
Other assets	139	189	195	542	580
TOTAL ASSETS	$1,873	$2,188	$2,518	$3,144	$4,051
Liabilities and Equity					
Notes payable	$ 110	$ 161	$ 228	$ 382	$ 577
Accounts payable	135	151	174	208	455
Taxes payable	42	17	38	36	79
Accrued expenses	134	139	161	345	480
Total current liabilities	$ 421	$ 468	$ 601	$ 971	$1,591
Long-term debt	69	15	12	11	10
Deferred taxes	27	30	18	18	2
Other liabilities	24	43	40	42	41
Total liabilities	$ 541	$ 556	$ 671	$1,042	$1,644
Equity:					
Common stock	$ 3	$ 3	$ 3	$ 3	$ 3
Capital surplus	94	94	94	94	94
Retained earnings	1,235	1,535	1,750	2,005	2,310
Common equity	1,332	1,632	1,847	2,102	2,407
TOTAL LIABILITIES AND EQUITY	$1,873	$2,188	$2,518	$3,144	$4,051

SAMPLE BUSINESS PLAN

appendix A

Wolf's Indoor Soccer

April 2002

1. Executive Summary

Wolf's Indoor Soccer is the only indoor soccer facility in the Benton County area. The population of Benton County is 240,000 residents. Wolf's Indoor Soccer has two professional-style, lighted fields (73' × 140'), featuring *Field Turf*® for fast-action, fun soccer. No matter what the weather conditions are, day or night, soccer players will find a safe, clean, and friendly atmosphere for soccer enjoyment.

Several divisions for youth, men, women, and coed teams provide all players—from beginners to highly skilled—the right environment for recreational yet competitive soccer. League play is continuous year round. All league participants are required to become members of Wolf's Indoor Soccer. The annual fee is $40. Team registration per session is $700. Each session has 10 games with championship awards being given to the first place team.

In addition, skills clinics are available for beginning adults and those wishing to polish their skills. The two fields can also be rented for practices, birthday parties, corporate events, preseason and post-season team parties, camps, clinics, school grad nights, fund raising tournaments, organized lacrosse and field hockey leagues and more. A soccer

Highlights

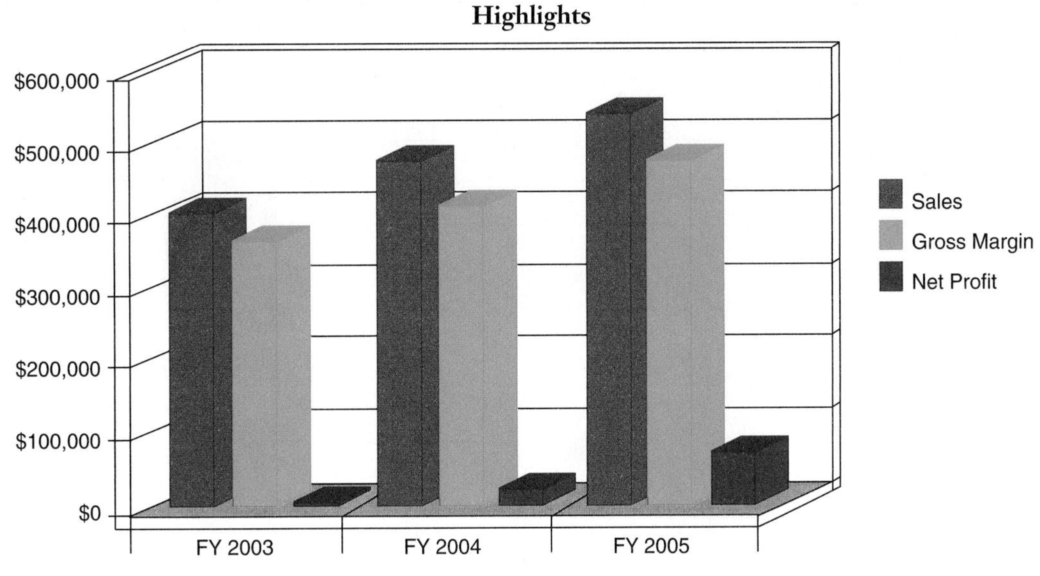

store is on site to provide leading soccer brands to players, teams, leagues and schools. The facility will also have a small cafe that will serve drinks, sandwiches, and pastry.

Wolf's Indoor Soccer projects that the center will have more than 1000 members, 30 adult teams and 30 youth teams by March of 2002.

1.1. Objectives

The objectives for Wolf's Indoor Soccer are the following:

- Build facility membership to more than 800.
- Register 30 adult and 25 youth teams by the end of first year of operation.
- Develop facility potential to be rented for special events.

1.2 Mission

The mission of Wolf's Indoor Soccer is to provide Benton County residents with a state-of-the-art soccer facility that will enable both youth and adults to enjoy the sport of soccer year round.

2. Company Summary

John Wolf has been a fixture of the county's soccer community for the past twenty years. Over the years he has coached hundreds of children. Many of his first players now have children of their own. Currently, he is the supervisor of soccer officials for Benton County area. His level of expertise in soccer has made him an important contributor to the development of the sport in Benton County. He has instant credibility with players and coaches.

Like John, Mary has been an important booster of soccer in Benton County, especially women's soccer. Mary has coached numerous girls' teams and has served as the chairperson of the Benton County Soccer Association.

The opening of Wolf's Indoor Soccer is a natural next step for this couple, who have been so important to the growth and love of soccer in the county.

Both will actively use their contacts to promote the facility to players and coaches.

2.1. Company Ownership

Wolf's Indoor Soccer is owned by John and Mary Wolf. The business will maintain a sole proprietorship status for at least the first two years of operation. The business projects that the facility will be so popular that a second indoor operation will be established in the city of Mason. At that time the business will reorganize to become an S Corporation.

2.2. Start-up Summary

The start-up cost of Wolf's Indoor Soccer is focused primarily on the field installation and the setup of the soccer store. The Wolfs will invest $60,000. In addition, the Wolfs will obtain a $100,000 loan.

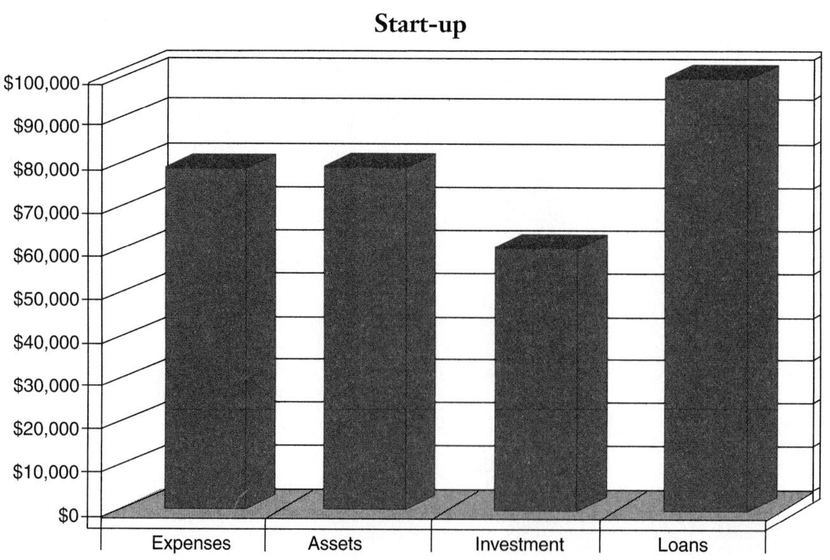

START-UP

Requirements	
Start-up Expenses	
Legal	$1,000
Brochures	$1,000
Insurance	$3,000
Rent	$5,000
Soccer Shop Setup	$10,000
Field Installation	$52,000
Cafe	$8,000
Total Start-up Expenses	$80,000
Start-up Assets Needed	
Cash Balance on Starting Date	$30,000
Start-up Inventory	$5,000
Other Current Assets	$5,000
Total Current Assets	$40,000
Long-term Assets	$40,000
Total Assets	$80,000
Total Requirements	$160,000

Funding	
Investment	
Investor 1	$60,000
Other	$0
Total Investment	$60,000
Current Liabilities	
Accounts Payable	$0
Current Borrowing	$0
Other Current Liabilities	$0
Current Liabilities	$0
Long-term Liabilities	$100,000
Total Liabilities	$100,000
Loss at Start-up	($80,000)
Total Capital	($20,000)
Total Capital and Liabilities	$80,000

2.3. Company Locations and Facilities

Wolf's Indoor Soccer is located on 9998 West 18th Street in the city of Monroe. The 30,000 foot facility is a former warehouse that will be converted into a playing facility. The location is easily accessible to all city residents. It is near Southtowne Park, which is the largest and most popular city park. This unique location is perfect. In addition, the facility has ample off-street parking.

3. Products and Services

Wolf's Indoor Soccer is an indoor soccer facility that offers league play, soccer training and a soccer shop. The facility is also available to be rented out for special events.

The following is the fee schedule:

Annual Facility Membership:	$40
Team Registration per Session:	$700
Facility Rental Fees:	Member $55–65/hr, Non-Member $80/hr
Skill Clinic Fees:	Range from $80 (per week) for children, to $400 for groups

They are led by soccer skill instructors with "A" Level Coaching Certification. The skill clinics are geared toward novices who want to improve their soccer skills.

The facility also has a soccer shop that sells the very best in soccer gear, indoor and outdoor. The shop has the best selection of turf shoes available in the city.

4. Market Analysis Summary

Soccer is a popular sport in Benton County. Currently there are 6,000 children participating in the youth soccer leagues, and 3,000 adults participating in the adult league. The number of players is growing dramatically. There are two factors that are impacting the popularity of soccer.

- The first is the large number of children in the county under the age of 12. There are approximately 30,000 children in the county under the age of 12. The projection is that the percentage of children under the age of 12 will continue to grow for the next five years. The most popular sport with this age group is soccer.

4

- The second factor is the growing number of young people between the ages of 24–35 who are participating in team sports. Participation in coed softball has increased by 20% each year for the past three years. The demand for fields has led to the county building four new playing fields this year. The adult outdoor soccer league has grown by 50% over the past two years. Currently, there are 24 adult league teams participating in the outdoor city soccer league.

4.1. Market Segmentation

Wolf's Indoor soccer will focus on the following target customers:

- Youths, ages 6–14 years of age.
- Adults, ages 24–35 years of age.

MARKET ANALYSIS

Potential Customers	Growth	2002	2003	2004	2005	2006	CAGR
Youth	12%	40,000	44,800	50,176	56,197	62,941	12.00%
Adults	10%	30,000	33,000	36,300	39,930	43,923	10.00%
Total	11.16%	70,000	77,800	86,476	96,127	106,864	11.16%

Market Analysis (Pie)

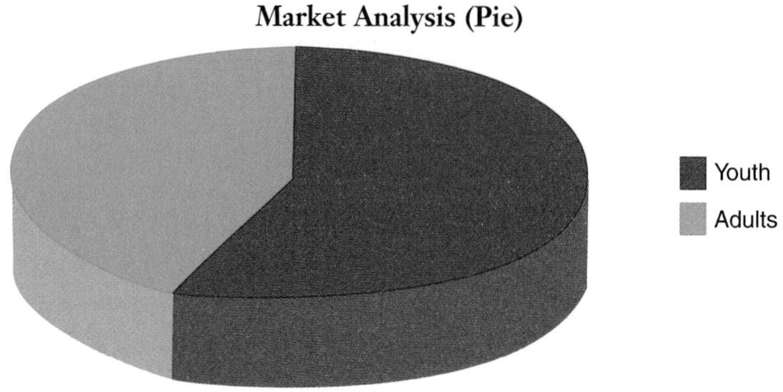

5. Strategy and Implementation Summary

Wolf's Indoor Soccer will aggressively pursue membership and team registration by discounting both the membership fee and the team fee.

- **Membership Fee:** Wolf's Indoor Soccer will offer a 25% discount on membership fees for the first six months.
- **Team Fee:** The team fee will be reduced by $100 if the team registers before the early sign-up deadline.

In addition, we will sell the facility rental potential to local schools, churches, and civic organizations.

5.1. Marketing Strategy

Marketing Programs The marketing strategy for Wolf's will differ throughout the year, depending upon demand for the facility. During the winter, when the weather is bad and most leagues play indoors, we will have to do very few marketing or advertising campaigns. During the summer, however, we must make sure that the center retains top of mind share with local recreational soccer players and parents looking for activities for their children during school holidays.

Marketing programs during the summer will consist of:

- Discounts: e.g., rent for one hour, get the second hour free.
- Advertise in the sports section of the local paper.
- Post fliers at other sports and recreation facilities.

Pricing All league participants are required to become members of Wolf's Indoor Soccer. The annual fee for individuals is $40. Team registration per season is $700.

Teams can also purchase clinics. A 1/2 day clinic that can include up to 15 people will cost $400. Children's clinics/camps will be priced at $80 for five half day sessions.

The fields will be available for rent on an hourly basis to members. Rental of a field will cost $55 per hour during the day and $65 per hour during the evenings and weekends.

5.2. Sales Strategy

Wolf's Indoor Soccer will sell the indoor facility to the current outdoor soccer teams. We will operate a booth at the city's soccer fields on the weekends for the two months before Wolf's opens. In addition, we will call the team captains and coaches directly and sell the quality and convenience of the facility. Wolf's Indoor Soccer will offer membership rates for field rental to these teams to get them in the facility. Spring is notorious for poor field conditions prior to the beginning of the soccer season.

During the first two weekends in April, Wolf's Indoor Soccer will offer free indoor soccer clinics for children and adults.

Sales Forecast The following is the sales forecast for the next three years. The clinics, cafe, and soccer shop will have direct cost of sales. The clinics will be hiring the coaches to lead the clinics. The soccer shop's direct cost will be the wholesale price of the shop's inventory.

Wolf's Indoor Soccer will make a strong push to expand league play in the summer. The summer is usually softball and baseball season and only competitive soccer teams play during the summer months. These competitive teams represent only 10% of young soccer players. The outdoor adults soccer leagues also don't operate during the summer months, leaving a large number of recreational soccer players without an opportunity to play.

The only slow period for sales will be in November and December. Though league sessions end in mid-November, December has proven to be a poor month to begin a new league session.

SALES FORECAST

Sales	FY 2003	FY 2004	FY 2005
Memberships	$42,000	$65,000	$78,000
Leagues	$185,000	$190,000	$210,000
Rentals	$43,000	$55,000	$67,000
Clinics	$38,000	$48,000	$58,000
Soccer Shop	$49,000	$54,000	$59,000
Cafe	$48,000	$54,000	$60,000
Total Sales	$405,000	$466,000	$532,000

Direct Cost of Sales	FY 2003	FY 2004	FY 2005
Memberships	$0	$0	$0
Leagues	$0	$0	$0
Rentals	$0	$0	$0
Clinics	$20,500	$21,000	$24,000
Soccer Shop	$18,500	$21,000	$23,000
Cafe	$12,000	$14,000	$16,000
Subtotal Direct Cost of Sales	$51,000	$56,000	$63,000

6

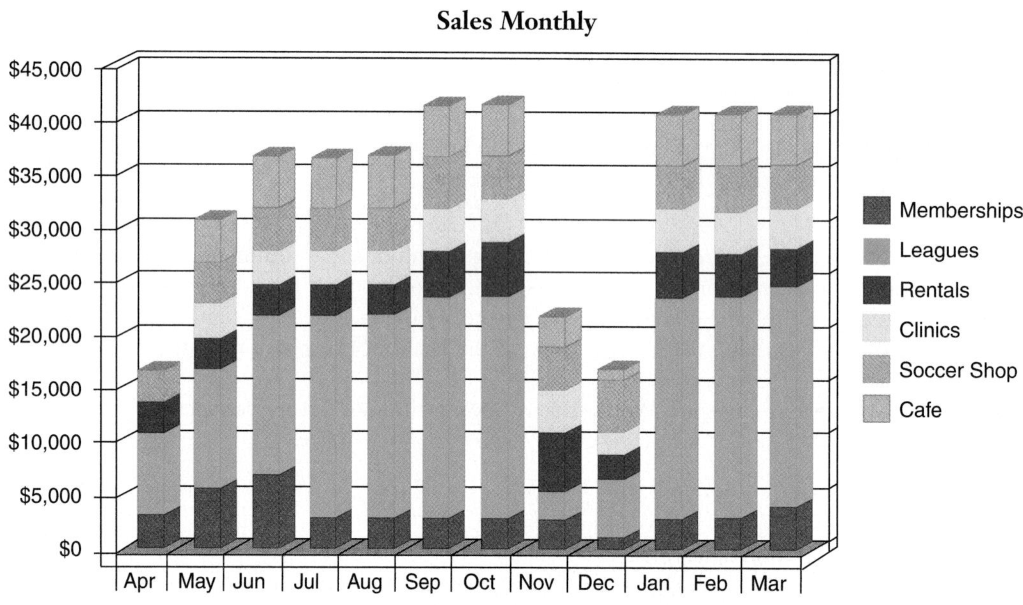

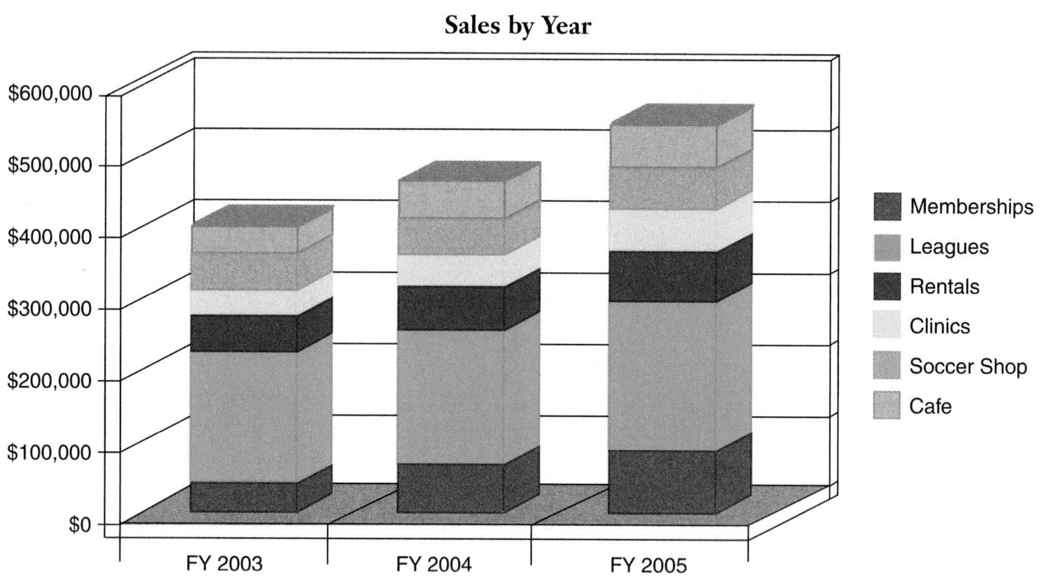

6. Management Summary

John and Mary Wolf will manage the day to day operations of Wolf's Indoor Soccer. Both John and Mary are considered very people-oriented and excellent supervisors of staff. They are familiar with every aspect of the sport and both are certified to serve as officials for indoor soccer games.

John has been instrumental in the popularity of soccer in Benton County. He was a founding member of the Benton County Soccer Council. At the time there were only a handful of people interested in the sport. Over the next five years of his leadership, the Council acquired a budget of $200,000, a staff of six and became the major catalyst for the city's new outdoor soccer facility which will be hosting this year's Region 2 regional competition.

Mary was also an important influence in the development of soccer in Benton County. Mary served as the Council's marketing and fundraising coordinator for six years. She increased donations by 15% each year over that period of time. She established the Council's marketing campaign to increase youth and adult soccer teams in Benton County.

6.1. Personnel Plan

The personnel of Wolf's Indoor Soccer are as follows:

- Manager (John Wolf);
- Asst. manager (Mary Wolf);
- Senior staff (2);
- Staff (2);
- Store staff person (1);
- Cafe staff (2).

A janitorial service will be contracted to clean the facility.
Clinic coaches will be hired, short term, as needed and paid out of clinic receipts.

PERSONNEL PLAN

	FY 2003	FY 2004	FY 2005
Manager	$33,600	$36,000	$38,000
Asst. Manager	$33,600	$36,000	$38,000
Senior Staff	$52,800	$55,000	$57,000
Staff Members	$46,800	$48,000	$50,000
Soccer Store Staff Person	$19,200	$21,000	$23,000
Cafe Staff	$28,800	$31,000	$34,000
Total People	7	7	7
Total Payroll	$214,800	$227,000	$240,000

7. Financial Plan

The following is the financial plan for Wolf's Indoor Soccer.

7.1. Break-even Analysis

The monthly break-even point is $29,856.

BREAK-EVEN ANALYSIS

Monthly Units Break-even	299
Monthly Revenue Break-even	$29,856
Assumptions:	
Average Per-Unit Revenue	$100.00
Average Per-Unit Variable Cost	$20.00
Estimated Monthly Fixed Cost	$23,885

8

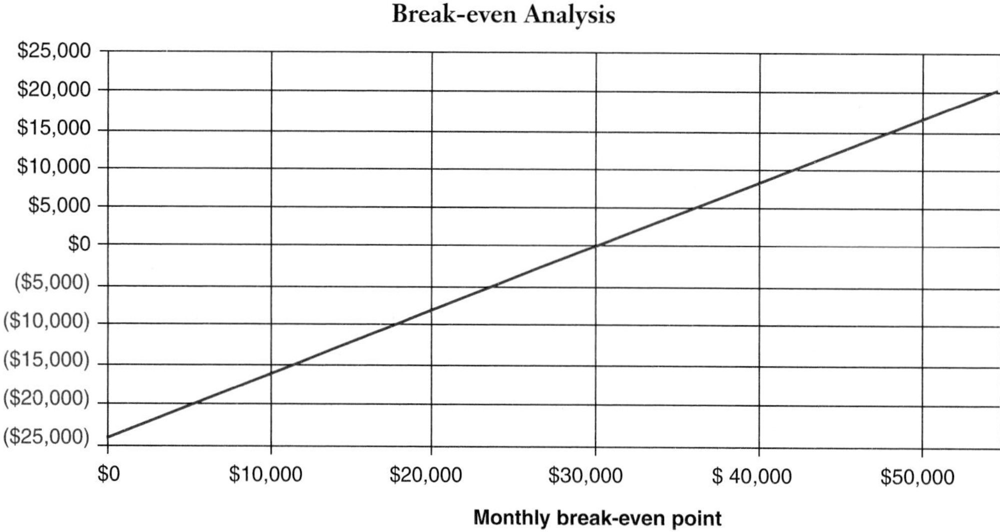

Break-even point = where line intersects with 0

7.2. Projected Profit and Loss

The following table and charts will highlight projected profit and loss for the next three years.

PRO FORMA PROFIT AND LOSS

	FY 2003	FY 2004	FY 2005
Sales	$405,000	$466,000	$532,000
Direct Costs of Goods	$51,000	$56,000	$63,000
Other Production Expenses	$0	$0	$0
Cost of Goods Sold	$51,000	$56,000	$63,000
Gross Margin	$354,000	$410,000	$469,000
Gross Margin %	87.41%	87.98%	88.16%
Expenses:			
Payroll	$214,800	$227,000	$240,000
Sales and Marketing and Other Expenses	$31,600	$33,600	$33,600
Depreciation	$6,000	$6,000	$6,000
Leased Equipment	$0	$0	$0
Utilities	$4,800	$4,800	$4,800
Insurance	$6,000	$6,000	$6,000
Rent	$48,000	$48,000	$48,000
Payroll Taxes	$32,220	$34,050	$36,000
Other	$0	$0	$0
Total Operating Expenses	$343,420	$359,450	$374,400
Profit Before Interest and Taxes	$10,580	$50,550	$94,600
Interest Expense	$9,350	$8,221	$7,063
Taxes Incurred	$369	$12,699	$26,261
Net Profit	$861	$29,630	$61,276
Net Profit/Sales	0.21%	6.36%	11.52%

9

Profit Monthly

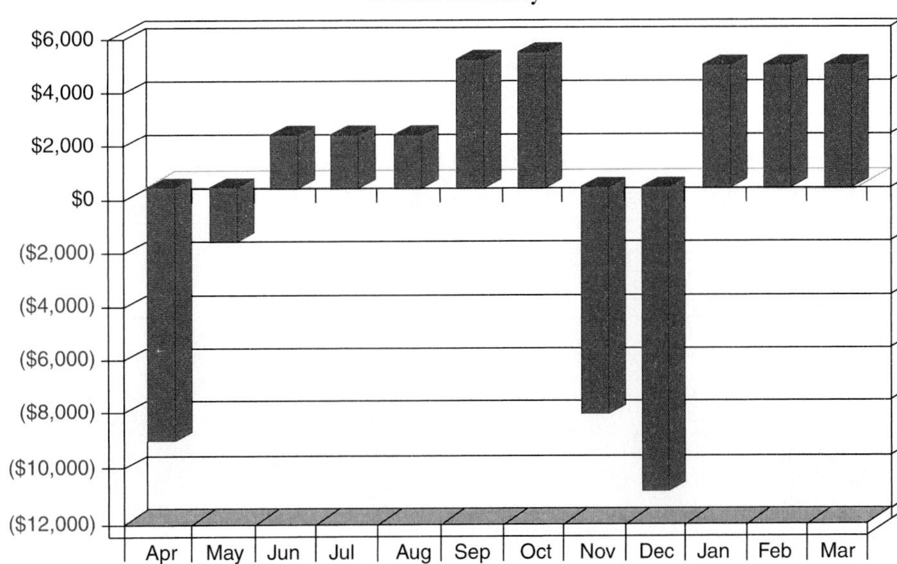

Profit Yearly

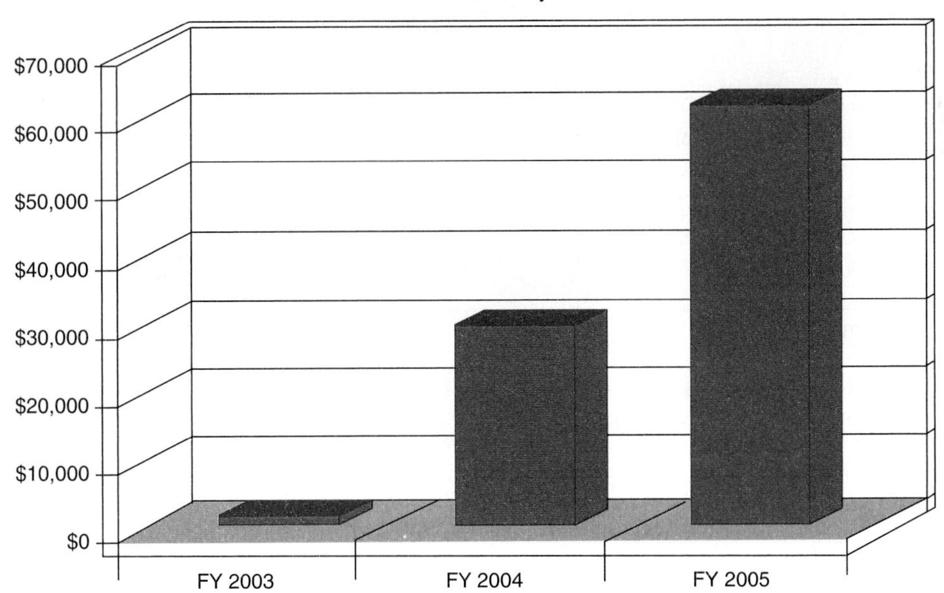

7.3. Projected Cash Flow

The following table and chart highlight the projected cash flow for three years.

PRO FORMA CASH FLOW

Cash Received	**FY 2003**	**FY 2004**	**FY 2005**
Cash from Operations:			
Cash Sales	$405,000	$466,000	$532,000
Cash from Receivables	$0	$0	$0
Subtotal Cash from Operations	$405,000	$466,000	$532,000
Additional Cash Received			
Sales Tax, VAT, HST/GST Received	$0	$0	$0
New Current Borrowing	$0	$0	$0
New Other Liabilities (interest-free)	$0	$0	$0
New Long-term Liabilities	$0	$0	$0
Sales of Other Current Assets	$0	$0	$0
Sales of Long-term Assets	$0	$0	$0
New Investment Received	$0	$0	$0
Subtotal Cash Received	$405,000	$466,000	$532,000

Expenditures	**FY 2003**	**FY 2004**	**FY 2005**
Expenditures from Operations:			
Cash Spending	$15,087	$16,979	$18,938
Payment of Accounts Payable	$369,576	$412,198	$444,721
Subtotal Spent on Operations	$384,663	$429,177	$463,658
Additional Cash Spent			
Sales Tax, VAT, HST/GST Paid Out	$0	$0	$0
Principal Repayment of Current Borrowing	$0	$0	$0
Other Liabilities Principal Repayment	$0	$0	$0
Long-term Liabilities Principal Repayment	$12,000	$11,583	$11,583
Purchase Other Current Assets	$0	$0	$0
Purchase Long-term Assets	$0	$0	$0
Dividends	$0	$0	$0
Subtotal Cash Spent	$396,663	$440,760	$475,241
Net Cash Flow	$8,337	$25,240	$56,759
Cash Balance	$38,337	$63,578	$120,336

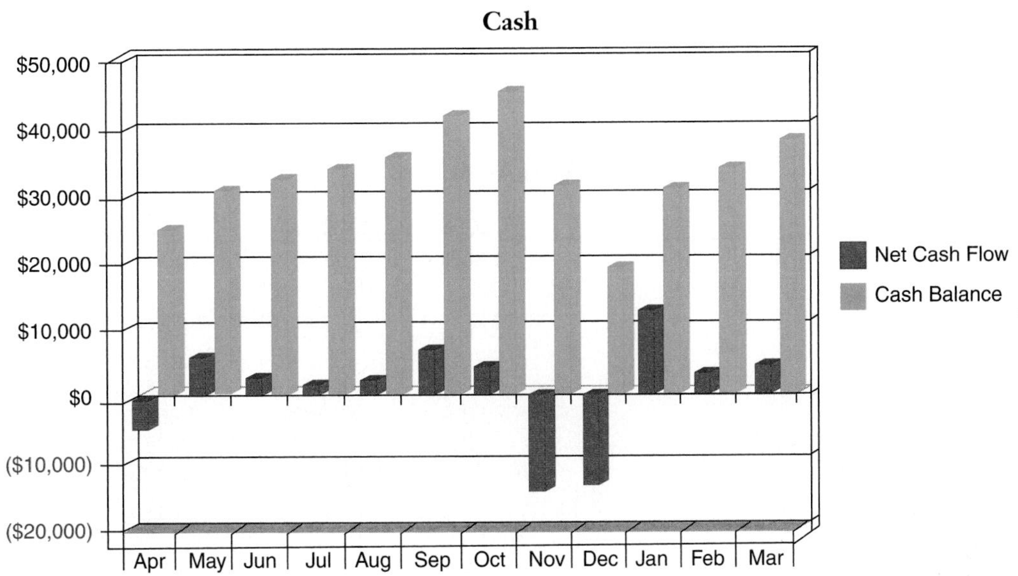

7.4. Projected Balance Sheet

The following table highlights the projected balance sheet for three years.

PRO FORMA BALANCE SHEET

Assets	**FY 2003**	**FY 2004**	**FY 2005**
Current Assets			
Cash	$38,337	$63,578	$120,336
Inventory	$4,750	$5,216	$5,868
Other Current Assets	$5,000	$5,000	$5,000
Total Current Assets	$48,087	$73,793	$131,204
Long-term Assets			
Long-term Assets	$40,000	$40,000	$40,000
Accumulated Depreciation	$6,000	$12,000	$18,000
Total Long-term Assets	$34,000	$28,000	$22,000
Total Assets	$82,087	$101,793	$153,204
Liabilities and Capital	**FY 2003**	**FY 2004**	**FY 2005**
Current Liabilities			
Accounts Payable	$13,226	$14,885	$16,602
Current Borrowing	$0	$0	$0
Other Current Liabilities	$0	$0	$0
Subtotal Current Liabilities	$13,226	$14,885	$16,602
Long-term Liabilities	$88,000	$76,417	$64,834
Total Liabilities	$101,226	$91,302	$81,436
Paid-in Capital	$60,000	$60,000	$60,000
Retained Earnings	($80,000)	($79,139)	($49,509)
Earnings	$861	$29,630	$61,276
Total Capital	($19,139)	$10,491	$71,768
Total Liabilities and Capital	$82,087	$101,793	$153,204
Net Worth	($19,139)	$10,491	$71,768

7.5. Business Ratios

Business ratios for the years of this plan are shown below. Industry profile ratios based on the Standard Industrial Classification (SIC) code 7997, Sport and Recreation Club, are shown for comparison.

RATIO ANALYSIS

	FY 2003	FY 2004	FY 2005	Industry Profile
Sales Growth	0.00%	15.06%	14.16%	15.20%
Percent of Total Assets				
Accounts Receivable	0.00%	0.00%	0.00%	5.10%
Inventory	5.79%	5.12%	3.83%	4.00%
Other Current Assets	6.09%	4.91%	3.26%	31.80%
Total Current Assets	58.58%	72.49%	85.64%	40.90%
Long-term Assets	41.42%	27.51%	14.36%	59.10%
Total Assets	100.00%	100.00%	100.00%	100.00%
Current Liabilities	16.11%	14.62%	10.84%	31.60%
Long-term Liabilities	107.20%	75.07%	42.32%	28.00%
Total Liabilities	123.32%	89.69%	53.16%	59.60%
Net Worth	−23.32%	10.31%	46.84%	40.40%
Percent of Sales				
Sales	100.00%	100.00%	100.00%	100.00%
Gross Margin	87.41%	87.98%	88.16%	0.00%
Selling, General & Administrative Expenses	87.19%	81.62%	76.64%	72.30%
Advertising Expenses	1.48%	1.29%	1.13%	2.70%
Profit Before Interest and Taxes	2.61%	10.85%	17.78%	2.60%
Main Ratios				
Current	3.64	4.96	7.90	1.23
Quick	3.28	4.61	7.55	0.83
Total Debt to Total Assets	123.32%	89.69%	53.16%	59.60%
Pre-tax Return on Net Worth	-6.43%	403.47%	121.97%	2.80%
Pre-tax Return on Assets	1.50%	41.58%	57.14%	6.90%
Additional Ratios				
Net Profit Margin	0.21%	6.36%	11.52%	n.a.
Return on Equity	0.00%	282.43%	85.38%	n.a.
Activity Ratios				
Accounts Receivable Turnover	0.00	0.00	0.00	n.a.
Collection Days	0	0	0	n.a.
Inventory Turnover	12.00	11.24	11.37	n.a.
Accounts Payable Turnover	28.94	27.80	26.89	n.a.
Payment Days	10	12	13	n.a.
Total Asset Turnover	4.93	4.58	3.47	n.a.
Debt Ratios				
Debt to Net Worth	0.00	8.70	1.13	n.a.
Current Liab. to Liab.	0.13	0.16	0.20	n.a.
Liquidity Ratios				
Net Working Capital	$34,861	$58,908	$114,602	n.a.
Interest Coverage	1.13	6.15	13.39	n.a.
Additional Ratios				
Assets to Sales	0.20	0.22	0.29	n.a.
Current Debt/Total Assets	16%	15%	11%	n.a.
Acid Test	3.28	4.61	7.55	n.a.
Sales/Net Worth	0.00	44.42	7.41	n.a.
Dividend Payout	0.00	0.00	0.00	n.a.

Appendix

SALES FORECAST

Sales	Apr	May	Jun	Jul	Aug	Sep	Oct	Nov	Dec	Jan	Feb	Mar
Memberships	$3,000	$6,000	$7,000	$3,000	$3,000	$3,000	$3,000	$3,000	$1,000	$3,000	$3,000	$4,000
Leagues	$8,000	$11,000	$15,000	$19,000	$19,000	$21,000	$21,000	$3,000	$6,000	$21,000	$21,000	$20,000
Rentals	$3,000	$3,000	$3,000	$3,000	$3,000	$4,000	$5,000	$5,000	$2,000	$4,000	$4,000	$4,000
Clinics	$0	$3,000	$3,000	$3,000	$3,000	$4,000	$4,000	$4,000	$2,000	$4,000	$4,000	$4,000
Soccer Shop	$3,000	$4,000	$4,000	$4,000	$4,000	$5,000	$4,000	$4,000	$5,000	$4,000	$4,000	$4,000
Cafe	$0	$4,000	$5,000	$5,000	$5,000	$5,000	$5,000	$3,000	$1,000	$5,000	$5,000	$5,000
Total Sales	$17,000	$31,000	$37,000	$37,000	$37,000	$42,000	$42,000	$22,000	$17,000	$41,000	$41,000	$41,000

Direct Cost of Sales	Apr	May	Jun	Jul	Aug	Sep	Oct	Nov	Dec	Jan	Feb	Mar
Memberships	$0	$0	$0	$0	$0	$0	$0	$0	$0	$0	$0	$0
Leagues	$0	$0	$0	$0	$0	$0	$0	$0	$0	$0	$0	$0
Rentals	$0	$0	$0	$0	$0	$0	$0	$0	$0	$0	$0	$0
Clinics	$1,500	$1,500	$1,500	$1,500	$1,500	$2,000	$2,000	$2,000	$1,000	$2,000	$2,000	$2,000
Soccer Shop	$1,000	$1,500	$1,500	$1,500	$1,500	$2,000	$1,500	$1,500	$2,000	$1,500	$1,500	$1,500
Cafe	$0	$1,000	$1,250	$1,250	$1,250	$1,250	$1,250	$750	$250	$1,250	$1,250	$1,250
Subtotal Direct Cost of Sales	$2,500	$4,000	$4,250	$4,250	$4,250	$5,250	$4,750	$4,250	$3,250	$4,750	$4,750	$4,750

PERSONNEL PLAN

	Apr	May	Jun	Jul	Aug	Sep	Oct	Nov	Dec	Jan	Feb	Mar
Manager	$2,800	$2,800	$2,800	$2,800	$2,800	$2,800	$2,800	$2,800	$2,800	$2,800	$2,800	$2,800
Asst. Manager	$2,800	$2,800	$2,800	$2,800	$2,800	$2,800	$2,800	$2,800	$2,800	$2,800	$2,800	$2,800
Senior Staff	$4,400	$4,400	$4,400	$4,400	$4,400	$4,400	$4,400	$4,400	$4,400	$4,400	$4,400	$4,400
Staff Members	$3,900	$3,900	$3,900	$3,900	$3,900	$3,900	$3,900	$3,900	$3,900	$3,900	$3,900	$3,900
Soccer Store Staff Person	$1,600	$1,600	$1,600	$1,600	$1,600	$1,600	$1,600	$1,600	$1,600	$1,600	$1,600	$1,600
Cafe Staff	$2,400	$2,400	$2,400	$2,400	$2,400	$2,400	$2,400	$2,400	$2,400	$2,400	$2,400	$2,400
Total People	7	7	7	7	7	7	7	7	7	7	7	7
Total Payroll	$17,900	$17,900	$17,900	$17,900	$17,900	$17,900	$17,900	$17,900	$17,900	$17,900	$17,900	$17,900

14

GENERAL ASSUMPTIONS

	Apr	May	Jun	Jul	Aug	Sep	Oct	Nov	Dec	Jan	Feb	Mar
Plan Month	1	2	3	4	5	6	7	8	9	10	11	12
Current Interest Rate	10.00%	10.00%	10.00%	10.00%	10.00%	10.00%	10.00%	10.00%	10.00%	10.00%	10.00%	10.00%
Long-term Interest Rate	10.00%	10.00%	10.00%	10.00%	10.00%	10.00%	10.00%	10.00%	10.00%	10.00%	10.00%	10.00%
Tax Rate	30.00%	30.00%	30.00%	30.00%	30.00%	30.00%	30.00%	30.00%	30.00%	30.00%	30.00%	30.00%
Other	0	0	0	0	0	0	0	0	0	0	0	0

PRO FORMA PROFIT AND LOSS

	Apr	May	Jun	Jul	Aug	Sep	Oct	Nov	Dec	Jan	Feb	Mar
Sales	$17,000	$31,000	$37,000	$37,000	$37,000	$42,000	$42,000	$22,000	$17,000	$41,000	$41,000	$41,000
Direct Costs of Goods	$2,500	$4,000	$4,250	$4,250	$4,250	$5,250	$4,750	$4,250	$3,250	$4,750	$4,750	$4,750
Other Production Expenses	$0	$0	$0	$0	$0	$0	$0	$0	$0	$0	$0	$0
Cost of Goods Sold	$2,500	$4,000	$4,250	$4,250	$4,250	$5,250	$4,750	$4,250	$3,250	$4,750	$4,750	$4,750
Gross Margin	$14,500	$27,000	$32,750	$32,750	$32,750	$36,750	$37,250	$17,750	$13,750	$36,250	$36,250	$36,250
Gross Margin %	85.29%	87.10%	88.51%	88.51%	88.51%	87.50%	88.69%	80.68%	80.88%	88.41%	88.41%	88.41%
Expenses:												
Payroll	$17,900	$17,900	$17,900	$17,900	$17,900	$17,900	$17,900	$17,900	$17,900	$17,900	$17,900	$17,900
Sales and Marketing and Other Expenses	$800	$2,800	$2,800	$2,800	$2,800	$2,800	$2,800	$2,800	$2,800	$2,800	$2,800	$2,800
Depreciation	$500	$500	$500	$500	$500	$500	$500	$500	$500	$500	$500	$500
Leased Equipment	$0	$0	$0	$0	$0	$0	$0	$0	$0	$0	$0	$0
Utilities	$400	$400	$400	$400	$400	$400	$400	$400	$400	$400	$400	$400
Insurance	$500	$500	$500	$500	$500	$500	$500	$500	$500	$500	$500	$500
Rent	$4,000	$4,000	$4,000	$4,000	$4,000	$4,000	$4,000	$4,000	$4,000	$4,000	$4,000	$4,000
Payroll Taxes (15%)	$2,685	$2,685	$2,685	$2,685	$2,685	$2,685	$2,685	$2,685	$2,685	$2,685	$2,685	$2,685
Other	$0	$0	$0	$0	$0	$0	$0	$0	$0	$0	$0	$0
Total Operating Expenses	$26,785	$28,785	$28,785	$28,785	$28,785	$28,785	$28,785	$28,785	$28,785	$28,785	$28,785	$28,785
Profit Before Interest and Taxes	($12,285)	($1,785)	$3,965	$3,965	$3,965	$7,965	$8,465	($11,035)	($15,035)	$7,465	$7,465	$7,465
Interest Expense	$825	$817	$808	$800	$792	$783	$775	$767	$758	$750	$742	$733
Taxes Incurred	($3,933)	($781)	$947	$950	$952	$2,155	$2,307	($3,541)	($4,738)	$2,015	$2,017	$2,020
Net Profit	($9,177)	($1,821)	$2,210	$2,216	$2,221	$5,027	$5,383	($8,261)	($11,055)	$4,701	$4,706	$4,712
Net Profit/Sales	−53.98%	−5.87%	5.97%	5.99%	6.00%	11.97%	12.82%	−37.55%	−65.03%	11.46%	11.48%	11.49%

PRO FORMA CASH FLOW

	Apr	May	Jun	Jul	Aug	Sep	Oct	Nov	Dec	Jan	Feb	Mar
Cash Received												
Cash from Operations:												
Cash Sales	$17,000	$31,000	$37,000	$37,000	$37,000	$42,000	$42,000	$22,000	$17,000	$41,000	$41,000	$41,000
Cash from Receivables	$0	$0	$0	$0	$0	$0	$0	$0	$0	$0	$0	$0
Subtotal Cash from Operations	$17,000	$31,000	$37,000	$37,000	$37,000	$42,000	$42,000	$22,000	$17,000	$41,000	$41,000	$41,000
Additional Cash Received												
Sales Tax, VAT, HST/GST Received	$0	$0	$0	$0	$0	$0	$0	$0	$0	$0	$0	$0
New Current Borrowing	$0	$0	$0	$0	$0	$0	$0	$0	$0	$0	$0	$0
New Other Liabilities (interest-free)	$0	$0	$0	$0	$0	$0	$0	$0	$0	$0	$0	$0
New Long-term Liabilities	$0	$0	$0	$0	$0	$0	$0	$0	$0	$0	$0	$0
Sales of Other Current Assets	$0	$0	$0	$0	$0	$0	$0	$0	$0	$0	$0	$0
Sales of Long-term Assets	$0	$0	$0	$0	$0	$0	$0	$0	$0	$0	$0	$0
New Investment Received	$0	$0	$0	$0	$0	$0	$0	$0	$0	$0	$0	$0
Subtotal Cash Received	$17,000	$31,000	$37,000	$37,000	$37,000	$42,000	$42,000	$22,000	$17,000	$41,000	$41,000	$41,000

Expenditures	Apr	May	Jun	Jul	Aug	Sep	Oct	Nov	Dec	Jan	Feb	Mar
Expenditures from Operations:												
Cash Spending	$259	$1,324	$1,396	$1,370	$1,369	$1,689	$1,503	$868	$597	$1,671	$1,521	$1,520
Payment of Accounts Payable	$20,663	$23,237	$32,519	$33,137	$32,914	$33,005	$35,728	$33,923	$28,312	$26,281	$35,583	$34,273
Subtotal Spent on Operations	$20,922	$24,561	$33,915	$34,507	$34,284	$34,694	$37,232	$34,791	$28,909	$27,952	$37,104	$35,793
Additional Cash Spent												
Sales Tax, VAT, HST/GST Paid Out	$0	$0	$0	$0	$0	$0	$0	$0	$0	$0	$0	$0
Principal Repayment of Current Borrowing	$0	$0	$0	$0	$0	$0	$0	$0	$0	$0	$0	$0
Other Liabilities Principal Repayment	$0	$0	$0	$0	$0	$0	$0	$0	$0	$0	$0	$0
Long-term Liabilities Principal Repayment	$1,000	$1,000	$1,000	$1,000	$1,000	$1,000	$1,000	$1,000	$1,000	$1,000	$1,000	$1,000
Purchase Other Current Assets	$0	$0	$0	$0	$0	$0	$0	$0	$0	$0	$0	$0
Purchase Long-term Assets	$0	$0	$0	$0	$0	$0	$0	$0	$0	$0	$0	$0
Dividends	$0	$0	$0	$0	$0	$0	$0	$0	$0	$0	$0	$0
Subtotal Cash Spent	$21,922	$25,561	$34,915	$35,507	$35,284	$35,694	$38,232	$35,791	$29,909	$28,952	$38,104	$36,793
Net Cash Flow	($4,922)	$5,439	$2,085	$1,493	$1,716	$6,306	$3,768	($13,791)	($12,909)	$12,048	$2,896	$4,207
Cash Balance	$25,078	$30,517	$32,603	$34,096	$35,812	$42,118	$45,886	$32,096	$19,186	$31,234	$34,130	$38,337

PRO FORMA BALANCE SHEET

Assets	Starting Balances	Apr	May	Jun	Jul	Aug	Sep	Oct	Nov	Dec	Jan	Feb	Mar
Current Assets													
Cash	$30,000	$25,078	$30,517	$32,603	$34,096	$35,812	$42,118	$45,886	$32,096	$19,186	$31,234	$34,130	$38,337
Inventory	$5,000	$2,500	$4,000	$4,250	$4,250	$4,250	$5,250	$4,750	$4,250	$3,250	$4,750	$4,750	$4,750
Other Current Assets	$5,000	$5,000	$5,000	$5,000	$5,000	$5,000	$5,000	$5,000	$5,000	$5,000	$5,000	$5,000	$5,000
Total Current Assets	$40,000	$32,578	$39,517	$41,853	$43,346	$45,062	$52,368	$55,636	$41,346	$27,436	$40,984	$43,880	$48,087
Long-term Assets													
Long-term Assets	$40,000	$40,000	$40,000	$40,000	$40,000	$40,000	$40,000	$40,000	$40,000	$40,000	$40,000	$40,000	$40,000
Accumulated Depreciation	$0	$500	$1,000	$1,500	$2,000	$2,500	$3,000	$3,500	$4,000	$4,500	$5,000	$5,500	$6,000
Total Long-term Assets	$40,000	$39,500	$39,000	$38,500	$38,000	$37,500	$37,000	$36,500	$36,000	$35,500	$35,000	$34,500	$34,000
Total Assets	$80,000	$72,078	$78,517	$80,353	$81,346	$82,562	$89,368	$92,136	$77,346	$62,936	$75,984	$78,380	$82,087

Liabilities and Capital		Apr	May	Jun	Jul	Aug	Sep	Oct	Nov	Dec	Jan	Feb	Mar
Current Liabilities													
Accounts Payable	$0	$2,255	$11,515	$12,141	$11,919	$11,913	$14,692	$13,078	$7,548	$5,194	$14,542	$13,232	$13,226
Current Borrowing	$0	$0	$0	$0	$0	$0	$0	$0	$0	$0	$0	$0	$0
Other Current Liabilities	$0	$0	$0	$0	$0	$0	$0	$0	$0	$0	$0	$0	$0
Subtotal Current Liabilities	$0	$2,255	$11,515	$12,141	$11,919	$11,913	$14,692	$13,078	$7,548	$5,194	$14,542	$13,232	$13,226
Long-term Liabilities	$100,000	$99,000	$98,000	$97,000	$96,000	$95,000	$94,000	$93,000	$92,000	$91,000	$90,000	$89,000	$88,000
Total Liabilities	$100,000	$101,255	$109,515	$109,141	$107,919	$106,913	$108,692	$106,078	$99,548	$96,194	$104,542	$102,232	$101,226
Paid-in Capital	$60,000	$60,000	$60,000	$60,000	$60,000	$60,000	$60,000	$60,000	$60,000	$60,000	$60,000	$60,000	$60,000
Retained Earnings	($80,000)	($80,000)	($80,000)	($80,000)	($80,000)	($80,000)	($80,000)	($80,000)	($80,000)	($80,000)	($80,000)	($80,000)	($80,000)
Earnings	$0	($9,177)	($10,998)	($8,789)	($6,573)	($4,352)	$676	$6,059	($2,203)	($13,258)	($8,558)	($3,851)	$861
Total Capital	($20,000)	($29,177)	($30,998)	($28,789)	($26,573)	($24,352)	($19,325)	($13,942)	($22,203)	($33,258)	($28,558)	($23,851)	($19,139)
Total Liabilities and Capital	$80,000	$72,078	$78,517	$80,353	$81,346	$82,562	$89,368	$92,136	$77,346	$62,936	$75,984	$78,380	$82,087
Net Worth	($20,000)	($29,177)	($30,998)	($28,789)	($26,573)	($24,352)	($19,325)	($13,942)	($22,203)	($33,258)	($28,558)	($23,851)	($19,139)

VALUING A BUSINESS

appendix B

At certain times, an entrepreneur may need to determine the value of her or his business. Despite the subjective nature of assigning value to a privately held company—that is, a firm whose stock is not traded publicly—and especially a *small* privately owned firm, there are times when the value must be estimated.

THE NEED TO COMPUTE FIRM VALUE

A variety of specific situations may call for a firm valuation, including the following:

1. An entrepreneur decides to buy a business, rather than starting one from scratch. He or she needs to know, "How much is the business worth to me, and what should I pay for it?"
2. An owner has decided to make an employee stock ownership plan (ESOP) part of the firm's retirement program (see Chapter 12). The stock has to be valued each year so that the appropriate number of shares can be contributed to the employees' retirement plan.
3. A firm is raising money from outside investors. The firm's value must be determined to establish the percentage of ownership the new investors will receive in the company (see Chapter 11).
4. One partner wants to buy out another partner or the interest of a deceased partner. The value of the business must be set so that a price can be agreed on.
5. An owner wants to exit (harvest) the business. Knowing the value of the company is essential if the business is to be sold or transferred to family members (see Chapter 12).

These are the most common reasons for valuing a business. Note that they are, for the most part, driven by external influences and exceptional circumstances. But it is a good idea to value a business on an ongoing basis—at least once a year. As a firm grows and becomes more profitable, the owner needs to know if the business is also increasing in value. In some situations, a profitable business may lose value over time. Therefore, being aware of its value is important in the management of a business. As Randall Lane said, "Knowing your net worth [value] as a private business owner provides a useful snapshot of where your company stands, what options it has, and how it can improve long-term."[1]

Terry MacRae, owner of Hornblower Yachts in San Francisco, is an advocate of regularly valuing a business. For the past 15 years, MacRae has valued his business with the help of valuation experts. In his opinion, knowing the value of your firm "keeps you out of trouble. It keeps you from being out there, believing what isn't true. And it gives you a better sense for using what resources are there. . . . It's helpful [for making] better long-term decisions."[2]

VALUATION METHODS

In valuing firms, it is important to distinguish between *firm value* and *owner value*. **Firm value**, or **enterprise value**, is the value of the entire business, regardless of how it is financed. It reflects the value of the underlying assets of the business. **Equity value**, or **owner's value**, on the other hand, is the value of the firm less the amount of debt owed by the firm. That is,

firm value (enterprise value) The value of the entire business, regardless of how it is financed

equity value (owner's value) The value of the firm less the debt owed by the firm

$$\text{Firm value} - \text{Outstanding debt} = \text{Equity value}$$

Some approaches to determining firm value focus on the left side of the equation—estimating the value of the firm as an entity. The question is, "Given the firm's assets and its ability to produce profits from these assets, what is the firm worth?" The equity value is then found by subtracting the outstanding debt from the total firm value.

Other approaches involve determining the value of the outstanding debt and the equity value separately. In those cases, firm value is found by summing the amount of outstanding debt and the equity value. While both processes produce similar results, we recommend finding the firm value and then subtracting the outstanding debt in order to determine the equity, or owner's, value.

There are three basic methods for valuing a business: (1) asset-based valuation, (2) valuation based on comparables, and (3) cash flow–based valuation. Each of these methods can be used as a stand-alone measure of firm value, but more often they are used in combination. Terry MacRae (mentioned earlier) uses all three methods when valuing his business.

Asset-Based Valuation

asset-based valuation Determination of the value of a business by estimating the value of its assets

modified book value method Determination of the value of a business by adjusting book value to reflect obvious differences between the historical cost and the current market value of the assets

replacement value method Determination of the value of a business by estimating the cost of replacing the firm's assets

liquidation value method Determination of the value of a business by estimating the money that would be available if the firm were to liquidate its assets

An **asset-based valuation** assumes that the value of a firm can be determined by examining the value of the underlying assets of the business (the left-hand side of the balance sheet). Three variations of this approach use (1) the modified book value of assets, (2) the replacement value of assets, and (3) the liquidation value of assets.

The **modified book value method** starts with the numbers shown on a company's balance sheet. These amounts are adjusted to reflect any obvious differences between the historical cost of each asset (as given on the balance sheet) and its current market value. For instance, the market value of a firm's plant and equipment may be totally different from its depreciated historical cost or book value. The same may be true for real estate. The **replacement value method** entails estimating the cost to replace each of the firm's assets. And the **liquidation value method** involves estimating the amount of money that would be received if the firm ended its operations and liquidated its assets.

Asset-based valuation is of limited worth in valuing a business. The historical costs shown on the balance sheet may be very different from the current value of the assets. The three variations to some extent adjust for this weakness, but their estimate of value has a weak foundation, as all asset-based techniques fail to recognize the firm as an ongoing business. However, the liquidation value method yields an estimate of the value that could be realized if the assets of the business were all sold separately, which is sometimes helpful information.

Valuation Based on Comparables

valuation based on comparables Determination of the value of a business by considering the actual market prices of firms that are similar to the firm being valued

earnings multiple A ratio determined by dividing a firm's value by its annual earnings; also called *value-to-earnings ratio*

A **valuation based on comparables** looks at the actual market prices of recently sold firms similar to the one being valued—either publicly traded firms (market comparables) or private firms (transaction comparables). "Similar" means that the two firms are in the same industry and are alike in such characteristics as growth potential, risk, profit margins, assets-to-sales relationships, and levels of debt financing.

For instance, one might start by finding several recently sold companies with growth prospects and levels of risk comparable to those of the firm being valued. For each of these firms, one would calculate the **earnings multiple**, or *value-to-earnings ratio*, as follows:[3]

$$\text{Earnings multiple} = \frac{\text{Firm value}}{\text{Operating income}}$$

Then, assuming that the company being valued should have an earnings multiple comparable to those of the similar firms, one would apply the calculated ratio to estimate the company's value. A novelty manufacturer and importer in Missouri, for example, was recently offered for sale at 4.9 times the firm's annual earnings (annual earnings of $45,000 × 4.9 = asking price of $220,500).[4]

This valuation method is not easy to use, as finding even one firm that is comparable in every way to the firm being valued is often difficult. It is not enough simply to find a firm in the same industry, although that might provide a rough approximation. As already noted, the ideal comparable firm is one that is in the same industry, is a similar type of business, and has a similar growth rate, financial structure, asset turnover ratio (sales/total assets), and profit margin (profits/sales). Fortunately, considerable information is published about firm sales. For instance, a publication called *Mergerstat* reports the prices of all such sales announced in the public media. Also, some accounting firms can provide information about the selling prices of comparable businesses.

normalized earnings Earnings that have been adjusted for unusual items, such as fire damage, and all relevant expenses, such as a fair salary for the owner's time

Ideally, **normalized earnings** should be used in this computation. Normalizing earnings involves adjusting for any *unusual* items, such as a one-time loss on the sale of real estate or as the consequence of a fire. In addition, normalizing earnings should include subtracting all relevant expenses, such as a fair salary for the owner's time.

Clearly, determining the appropriate earnings multiple is not an easy task either. There are two fundamental drivers of a firm's earnings multiple—risk and growth. The two are related as follows:

1. The more (less) risky the business, the lower (higher) the appropriate earnings multiple and, as a consequence, the lower (higher) the firm's value.
2. The higher (lower) the projected growth rate in future earnings, the higher (lower) the appropriate earnings multiple and, therefore, the higher (lower) the firm's value.

These relationships are presented graphically in Exhibit B-1.

In practice, earnings multiples are based primarily on conventional wisdom and the experience of the person performing the valuation. Multiples vary according to the nature of the firm. Following are some examples:

Type of Firm	Earnings Multiple
Small, well-established firms, vulnerable to recession	7
Small firms requiring average executive ability but operating in a highly competitive environment	4
Firms that depend on the special, often unusual, skill of one individual or a small group of managers	2

Earnings multiples also vary over time. In the late 1990s, firms were frequently bought and sold at seven to nine times their cash flow. In 2002, Houlihan Lokey Howard & Zukin, a Los Angeles–based investment bank, reported that firms with less than $100 million in annual sales were, on average, selling for 6.5 times cash flow. By 2003, multiples were more in the range of four to five times cash flow. For example, as shown in Exhibit B-2, in 1998 wholesaling firms, on average, sold for over eight times cash flow from operations (operating income plus depreciation expense). By 2002, multiples had declined to slightly over five times cash flow. Even so, multiples in 2002 were still higher than those in 1995. So, the same firm in the wholesaling industry with a cash flow from operations of $1 million might have sold for $8 million in 1998, but for only $5 million in 2002.[5]

Consider a real-life example. When Robert Hall, former owner of Visador Corporation, was considering selling his firm, he received an offer based on a multiple of five times the firm's operating income plus depreciation expenses.[6] The offer was presented to Hall in the following format:[7]

Company's operating income plus depreciation expense	$ 3,300,000
Earnings multiple	× 5
Firm value	$16,500,000
Outstanding debt	− 750,000
Equity value	$15,750,000

EXHIBIT B-1 *Risk and Growth: Key Factors Affecting the Earnings Multiple and Firm Value*

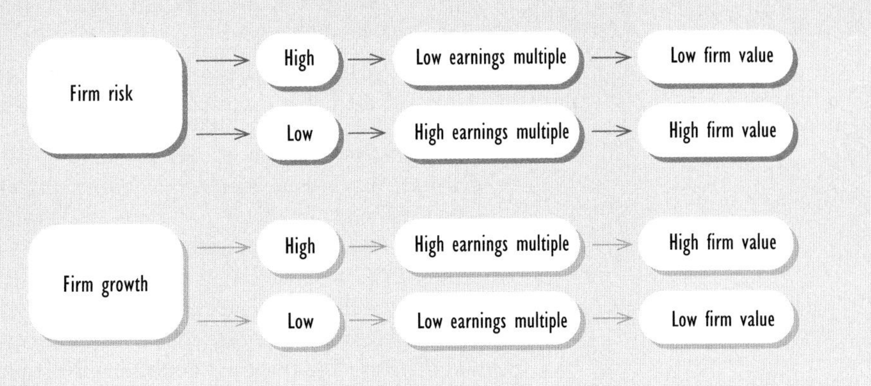

EXHIBIT B-2 *Wholesaling Industry Valuation Multiples*

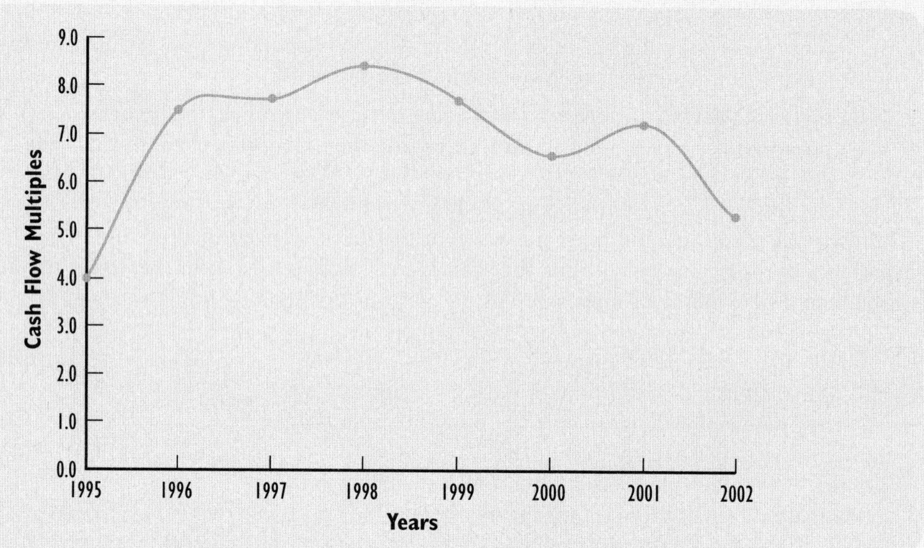

Source: Pratt's Stats from BVR, as reported in Randall Lane, "What Is Your Company Worth Now?" *Inc.*, July 2003, p. 76.

Thus, the offer for the firm was $16,500,000. To determine what Hall would receive for his ownership of the business, we subtract the $750,000 owed by the firm, to get $15,750,000.

Hall rejected the offer of $15.75 million, but made a counter-offer of $20 million for his ownership. Hall's counter-offer was accepted, which suggests that the buyer wanted the firm more than he let on initially.

The appropriateness of using earnings to value a firm is the subject of ongoing debate. Some contend that markets value a firm based on future cash flows, not reported earnings. Moreover, they argue, there are simply too many ways (within generally accepted accounting principles) to influence a firm's reported earnings, leading to material differences in valuation estimates but no difference in the intrinsic value of the firm. For these individuals, a firm's value is the present value of the firm's projected future cash flows.

Cash Flow–Based Valuation

cash flow–based valuation Determination of the value of a business by estimating the amount and timing of its future cash flows

Although not popular among smaller companies, **cash flow–based valuation**, in which a company is valued based on the amount and timing of its future cash flows, makes a lot of sense. Valuations based on earnings, although used more often, present a conceptual problem. From an investor's or owner's perspective, the value of a firm should be based on future cash flows, not reported earnings—especially not reported earnings for just a single year.

Measuring the value of a firm's future cash flows for a cash flow–based valuation is a three-step process:

Step 1. Project the firm's expected future cash flows.

Step 2. Estimate the investors' and owners' required rate of return on their investment in the business.

Step 3. Using the required rate of return as the discount rate, calculate the present value of the firm's expected future cash flows, which equals the value of the firm.

This cash flow–based approach is the most complicated of the three valuation methods discussed here; an in-depth explanation is well beyond the scope of this book. But it has one distinct advantage: A cash flow–based evaluation requires that *explicit* assumptions be made about the firm's future growth rates, its profit margins (profits to sales), how efficiently it is managing its assets (sales relative to the amount of the assets), and the appropriate discount rate (required rate of return). In contrast, a valuation based on comparables only *implicitly* considers the relationship between the multiple being used and the factors that should determine the multiple. Thus, using cash flow–based valuation requires the estimator to examine more carefully *why* the firm has value.[8]

USEFUL URLS

appendix C

Getting Started/General Information

ABCs of Small Business	http://www.abcsmallbiz.com	Articles and resources specifically for the budding entrepreneur
About.com: Small Business Information	http://sbinformation.about.com	Essential information for starting a small business; sign-up for free newsletter
BankRate.com: Small Biz Home Page	http://www.bankrate.com/brm/biz_home.asp	Advice, tips, articles, financing, and other basic startup information especially for the small home office business
Business Owner's Toolkit: Total Know-How for Small Business	http://www.toolkit.cch.com	Thousands of pages of information and tools to help one start, run, and grow a successful small business
Center for Veterans Enterprise	http://www.vetbiz.gov/start/start.htm	Startup help and services for veterans, sponsored by the Department of Veterans Affairs
MoreBusiness.com: For Entrepreneurs by Entrepreneurs	http://www.morebusiness.com	Templates, tools, how-tos, and a free newsletter
PowerHomeBiz.com	http://www.powerhomebiz.com	Information, tools, and resources for starting, managing, and growing a home business
SBA Online Women's Business Center	http://www.onlinewbc.gov/docs/starting	Special SBA Web site for women starting a small business
SBA: Minorities	http://www.sba.gov/starting_business/special/minorities.html	SBA assistance portal to federal contracting opportunities for minority-owned businesses, HUBZone empowerment contracting, small disadvantaged business certification, and 8(a) business development
SBA: Native Americans	http://www.sba.gov/starting_business/special/native.html	SBA assistance for American Indians, Alaska Natives, and Native Hawaiians to ensure that they have full and open access to business development and other tools necessary to start and expand small businesses
SBA: Startup Guide	http://www.sba.gov/starting_business/startup/guide.html	A comprehensive and easy-to-use roadmap for starting a business, with numerous electronic links for additional information
SBA: The Teen Entrepreneur Guide to Owning a Small Business	http://www.sba.gov/teens/	Web site designed by the U.S. Small Business Administration to introduce teenagers to the concept of small business ownership
SBA: Veterans	http://www.sba.gov/starting_business/special/veterans.html	SBA programs and services to help veteran entrepreneurs succeed
SBA: Women Entrepreneurs	http://www.sba.gov/starting_business/special/women.html	SBA programs and services to help women entrepreneurs succeed
SBA: Young Entrepreneurs	http://www.sba.gov/starting_business/special/young.html	A gateway to the following SBA programs for young people: Teen Entrepreneur Guide, Discover Business, YoungBiz, Kids Learning Programs, and the Center for Entrepreneurial Leadership
Small Business Notes	http://www.smallbusinessnotes.com	Pages of special interest to African American, Asian, gay and lesbian, and disabled entrepreneurs
Small Business Resource: Getting Started	http://www.reni.net/guides/getstart.asp	Startup help and click-on guide to U.S., state, and regional business resources
Startups.com.	http://www.startups.co.uk	A comprehensive reference and newsletter site devoted to small business startups in the United Kingdom
WomenBiz.gov	http://www.womenbiz.gov	Gateway for women-owned startups bidding on their first government contract

Business Plan Preparation

BPlans.com: The Business Planning Experts	http://www.bplans.com	Online resource from Palo Alto Software for self-preparers, providing advice, sample plans, and links to many consultants
Business Confidant: Your Business Planning Specialist	http://www.businessconfidant.com	Online one-stop resource, providing information on the strategic thinking, technical writing, and financial analysis needed to produce professional, investor-ready business plans
Business Plan Software . . .	http://www.planware.org	Online resource based in Ireland, featuring financial projection and cash flow forecasting software, business plan freeware, white papers, and other tools and resources
Entrepreneur.com: Solutions for Growing Businesses	http://www.entrepreneur.com	Online magazine with a site search engine to help readers find articles and tips using keywords like *business plan writing*
Good-to-Go Business Plans: Plans for Every Business	http://www.goodtogobusinessplans.com	A range of services, including business-specific templates in pre-drafted language and other tools and forms
SBA: Business Plan Basics	http://www.sba.gov/starting_business/planning/basic.html	An explanation of the basic components of a business plan, including a current and pro forma balance sheet, an income statement, and a cash flow analysis

Online Magazines, Newsletters, and Blogs

Black Enterprise: Your Online Guide to Wealth Building	http://www.blackenterprise.com	Online version of *Black Enterprise* magazine, which provides information and services for African American entrepreneurs and small businesses
Forbes.com: Small Business	http://www.forbes.com/smallbusiness	*Forbes's* online news for small businesses and entrepreneurs
Fortune Small Business	http://www.fortune.com/fortune/smallbusiness	An online, small business edition of *Fortune* magazine, which includes the FSB 100 top small businesses
Inc.com	http://www.inc.com	Online magazine for entrepreneurs, featuring "Resource Centers" with expert advice, how-to guides, *Inc.* archives, discussion boards, online polls, and "webinars" for growing a small business
Journal of Small Business and Entrepreneurship	http://www.ccsbe.org/jsbe	An academic research journal that pushes the boundaries of current entrepreneurial thought with theoretical pieces, qualitative and quantitative empirical work, and case studies
Small Business Advisor	http://www.isquare.com	Tips for marketing, accounting, etc., as well as Azriela Jaffe's weekly newsletter
Small Business Trends: The Forces Driving Small and Midsized Business	http://www.smallbusinesses.blogspot.com	Daily updates on trends that influence the global small business market
Startup Journal	http://www.startupjournal.com	The *Wall Street Journal's* online center for entrepreneurs
TrendTracker	http://trendtracker.blogspot.com	Summary of major long-term trends in the global small business market

Advocacy Groups

CFIB: Canadian Federation of Independent Business	http://www.cfib.ca	A federation of more than 100,000 independent business owners in Canada, providing lobbying at the federal, provincial, and local levels of Canada's government
Federation of Small Businesses: The UK's Leading Lobbying and Benefits Group for Small Businesses	http://www.fsb.co.uk	With over 185,000 members, the voice of small business in the United Kingdom
NFIB: The Voice of Small Business	http://www.nfib.com	The nation's largest small business lobbying group, representing its 600,000 members at the federal and state levels
SCORE: Counselors to America's Small Businesses	http://www.score.org	A nonprofit association that provides entrepreneurs with free, confidential, face-to-face, and electronic business counseling from volunteers who are experienced entrepreneurs or corporate managers/executives
United States Association for Small Business and Entrepreneurship (USASBE)	http://www.usasbe.org	An organization devoted to advancing knowledge and development through entrepreneurship education and research

U.S. and International Government

Business.gov: The Business Gateway to Federal Resources	http://www.business.gov	Official government Web site providing links to many government-related agencies that offer services and information about business development, international trade, law, and taxation, as well as downloadable government forms
Internal Revenue Service: Small Bus/ Self-Employed	http://www.irs.gov/businesses/small/index.html	The IRS's one-stop resource for small businesses and self-employed taxpayers, including an online classroom and a range of outreach products, services, forms, and information
Small Business Administration: Your Small Business Resource	http://www.sba.gov	The federal government's online business planning and finance resource center classroom and library
Small Business Consumer Centre	http://www.grants-loans.org	Canadian government–affiliated organization that offers a full range of support, advice, and advocacy for small business ventures in that country
Small Business Service	http://www.sbs.gov.uk	U.K. Department of Trade and Industry site, providing straightforward business information and access to a wide network of business support organizations in the United Kingdom
U.S. Department of Labor: Office of Small Business Programs	http://www.dol.gov/osbp	Assistance with procurement opportunities for small businesses, HUBZone businesses, and businesses owned by service-disabled veterans or women

e-Business Help

eBusiness Help Site	http://www.ebusinesshelpsite.com	How-to site for designing a home-based e-business
Seller Central	http://pages.ebay.com/sellercentral	A source for the latest tips, tools, information, and resources for building a small business on eBay
Website 101: Expanding Your Business to the Web	http://www.website101.com	Tutorials on the technical and marketing aspects of developing a Web presence
Workz.com	http://www.workz.com	In-depth articles and e-mail newsletters to help one create, manage, promote, and maintain a Web business
Yahoo! Small Business	http://smallbusiness.yahoo.com	Yahoo!'s gateway to enhancing a small business's online operations with Web hosting, business e-mail, domains, marketing tools, and other enterprise solutions

Legal Resources

Companies Incorporated	http://www.companiesinc.com	Many free educational tools, including an online learning center
FreeAdvice	http://freeadvice.com	The leading "legal advice" site for small business owners—everything from setting up a C corporation to declaring bankruptcy
SBA: Business Laws	http://www.sba.gov/starting_business/legal/buslaws.html	The SBA's online primer for understanding the legal aspects of starting and running a small business
Small Business Environmental Home Page	http://www.smallbiz-enviroweb.org	Assistance in accessing information about environmental issues and compliance
Small Business Help Center	http://www.helpbizowners.com	A wealth of information on running a small business
TannedFeet.com: The Entrepreneur's Help Page	http://www.tannedfeet.com	Comprehensive help site that includes readers' articles, business plans, and an Entrepreneurs' Forum
The Company Corporation	http://www.corporate.com	A free workbook and information on choosing the type of incorporation, the state in which to incorporate, etc.

Regional Small Business Assistance

The U.S. SBA has regional offices and state small business development centers (SBDCs). By using such search engines as Google and the appropriate keywords, you can locate state-, county-, and city-specific organizations that help small businesses in their respective regions by providing useful information and services. The following is a sample of available Web sites.

Baltimore County (Maryland) Small Business Resource Center	http://www.co.ba.md.us/-Agencies/economicdev/edd_smallbus.html	Free assistance with technical, financial, and marketing issues, including one-on-one counseling; a clearinghouse of information on a wide variety of business subjects intended to help one grow or start a small business
Central California Small Business Development Center	http://www.ccsbdc.org	A partnership between the U.S. SBA and the University of California–Merced
Florida Small Business	http://www.floridasmallbusiness.com	Online version of Florida's small business resource publication
New York City Department of Small Business Services	http://www.nyc.gov/html/sbs/home.html	NYC's portal for small business development and assistance
North Texas Small Business Development Center	http://www.ntsbdc.org	Management education to promote small business success
Office of Small Business: Small Business Development Centers of Ohio	http://www.odod.state.oh.us/edd/osb/sbdc/	A conduit to professional guidance, connecting Ohio entrepreneurs with research, financing sources, and training opportunities

Educational Institutions

Many universities have special offices devoted to developing small businesses, often in affiliation with the SBA or an SBDC. The following is a sample of available Web sites.

Small Business Advancement National Center	http://www.sbaer.uca.edu	A site sponsored by the University of Central Arkansas that increases knowledge of small business and entrepreneurship by providing business plan assistance and other aids
Turner Center for Entrepreneurship	http://www.bradley.edu/turnercenter	An SBDC based at Bradley University
University of Scranton Small Business Development Center	http:// sbdc.scranton.edu	Like other university-affiliated SBDCs, an SBDC that offers free and confidential management consulting services, as well as seminars
University of South Florida Small Business Development Center	http://www.sbdc.usf.edu	Information specific to the region, such as the impact of hurricanes on Florida's small businesses and women and minority startups

Research

Many libraries and private services provide online research guides on a variety of business and management topics related to starting a business, documenting a business plan, and the like. The following is a sample of available Web sites.

BizReference.com	http://www.bizreference.com	Comprehensive small business directory for best offers on small business Web design, development, and hosting; sample business plans; legal advice; incorporation; factoring; search engine optimization; franchise opportunities; office supplies; small business loans; and other services
Business Insurance for the Small Business Owner	http://www.insurance.ca.gov/CSD/Ins4sbo.htm	Tutorial on insuring a small business
CEOExpress	http://www.ceoexpress.com	A great collection of resources for doing business/company research
DiversityBusiness.com	http://div2000.com	The nation's primary resource portal for small businesses and large organizational buyers
EntreWorld	http://www.entreworld.org	A premier online resource for small business owners, sponsored by the Kaufman Foundation, that delivers useful information, guidance, and contacts for the entrepreneur
Factiva	http://www.factiva.com	Subscription business information research portal, sponsored by Dow Jones Reuters, providing access to monitor companies, industries, news, trends, and more
Galante's Venture Capital & Private Equity Directory	http://www.assetnews.com/products/dir/galante.htm	Directory of more than 2,200 venture capital, LBO, and mezzanine firms, allowing entrepreneurs to seek capital, research co-investors, or find new clients
MarketResearch.com	http://www.marketresearch.com	An aggregator of global business intelligence representing the most comprehensive collection of published marketing research available
Rutgers University Libraries: Business	http://www.libraries.rutgers.edu/rul/rr_gateway/research_guides/busi/business.shtml	Large university library research guide site, providing assistance in researching a variety of business and management topics, with descriptions of databases and hundreds of reference books and links to more than 3,000 selected business and management-related Internet resources
SBA: Finding Employees	http://www.sba.gov/starting_business/employees/finding.html	SBA guide providing tips on how to fill positions in a small business
SBA: Marketing Basics	http://www.sba.gov/starting_business/marketing/basics.html	Online guide that helps one learn how to determine the needs of customers through marketing research, analyze competitive advantages to develop a market strategy, and select specific markets to serve by target marketing
SBA: Taxes	http://www.sba.gov/starting_business/taxes/taxes.html	Discussions of the kinds of tax issues small businesses face
The Entrepreneur's Reference Guide to Small Business Information, 3rd ed.	http://www.loc.gov/rr/business/guide/guide2	Information about small business compiled by the Business Reference Service of the Library of Congress
Venture Economics	http://www.ventureeconomics.com	Source for global private equity intelligence, with daily news and statistics from U.S., European, and Asian private equity markets
Winspear Business Reference Library: Small Business and Entrepreneurship Information Sources	http://www.library.ualberta.ca/subject/business/smallbusiness/index.cfm	Business reference library, sponsored by the University of Alberta in Canada, providing sources of information on small business and entrepreneurship

Small Business Loans

Acción USA	http://www.accionusa.org	Mission to make access to credit a permanent resource for low- and moderate-income small businesses owners and microenterprises in the United States
BusinessTown: Finance—Getting Money	http://www.businesstown.com/finance/money.asp	Reference tools related to financing your business, including a glossary of terms
Fixed-Asset Loans for Small Businesses	http://www.sba.gov/opc/pubs/fs70.html	Explanation of the SBA's 504 loan program
Government Loans Services (SBA e-loans)	http://sba.governmentloans.com	A loan correspondent that specializes in U.S. Small Business Administration loans; certified and preferred lenders under the SBA 7a program
SBA: Financing Basics	http://www.sba.gov/starting_business/financing/basics.html	An online guide for obtaining sufficient ready capital
SBA: Financing Your Business	http://www.sba.gov/financing	Information on raising capital for a business

IT for Small Business

Small Business Computer Security Workshops	http://csrc.nist.gov/securebiz	Computer security workshops sponsored by the National Institute of Standards and Technology (NIST)
Small Business Computing: Your Online Guide to Small-Business Technology	http://www.smallbusinesscomputing.com	White papers, newsletters, and information on enterprise software and hardware for small businesses
Small Business Software Categories	http://www.business.com/directory/small_business/software	A list of vendors for small business enterprise software (office, inventory, etc.)
Small Business Webopedia by Small Business Computing.com	http://sbc.webopedia.com	Definitions of terms and concepts used by IT specialists
SmallbizTechnology.com	http://www.smallbiztechnology.com	A source of press releases and other information about technology solutions designed for small businesses

Chapter 1

1. Nicole Lewis, "Building a Growing Business," *Black Enterprise*, Vol. 33, No. 12 (July 2003), p. 35; http://www.slrcontracting.com, September 5, 2003; Fred Williams, "Inner-City Success Story," *Buffalo Niagara Enterprise*, April 28, 2003, http://www.buffaloniagara.org.
2. Leigh Buchanan, "The Heart of a Company," *Inc.*, Vol. 25, No. 6 (June 2003), pp. 74–82; Lawrence G. Prouix, "Local Drugstore Fights the Yeech! Factor," *Washington Post*, April 8, 1997, p. 209; http://www.flavorx.com, July 23, 2003; Eleni Chamis, "Pharmacists Expand Market for Flavored Medicines," *Washington Business Journal*, October 8, 2001.
3. http://www.auntieannes.com, July 25, 2003.
4. Cait Murphy, "Fortune 500," *Fortune*, Vol. 145, No. 8 (April 15, 2002), p. 94.
5. U.S. Small Business Administration, Office of Advocacy, "Small Business by the Numbers," May 2003, www.sba.gov/advo/stats.
6. Nancy M. Carter, William B. Gartner, Kelly G. Shaver, and Elizabeth J. Gatewood, "The Career Reasons of Nascent Entrepreneurs," *Journal of Business Venturing*, Vol. 18 (2003), pp. 13–39.
7. Thomas J. Stanley and William D. Danko, *The Millionaire Next Door* (New York: Simon & Schuster, 1996), p. 227.
8. "Poll: Most Like Being Own Boss," *USAToday*, May 6, 1991. For a scholarly study confirming the importance of a quest for independence as a motivational factor, see Marco Virarelli, "The Birth of New Enterprises," *Small Business Economics*, Vol. 3, No. 3 (September 1991), pp. 215–223.
9. Gangaram Singh and Alex DeNoble, "Early Retirees as the Next Generation of Entrepreneurs," *Entrepreneurship Theory and Practice*, Vol. 27, No. 3 (Spring 2003), pp. 218–220.
10. William J. Dennis, Jr., "Success, Satisfaction and Growth," *NFIB National Small Business Poll* (Washington: National Federation of Independent Business, 2001), p. 1.
11. Colleen Mastony, "Micro-entrepreneurs," *Forbes*, Vol. 162, No. 13 (December 14, 1998), p. 88.
12. Amar V. Bhide, *The Origin and Evolution of New Businesses* (New York: Oxford University Press, 2000), Chapter 1.
13. Norman R. Smith, *The Entrepreneur and His Firm: The Relationship Between Type of Man and Type of Company* (East Lansing: Bureau of Business and Economic Research, Michigan State University, 1967). See also Norman R. Smith and John B. Miner, "Type of Entrepreneur, Type of Firm, and Managerial Motivation: Implications for Organizational Life Cycle Theory," *Strategic Management Journal*, Vol. 4, No. 4 (October-December 1983), pp. 325–340; Carolyn Y. Woo, Arnold C. Cooper, and William C. Dunkelberg, "The Development and Interpretation of Entrepreneurial Typologies," *Journal of Business Venturing*, Vol. 6, No. 2 (March 1991), pp. 93–114.
14. Susan M. Walthall, "Message from the Acting Chief Counsel," *Small Business Advocate*, Vol. 20, No. 8 (November 2001), p. 3.
15. U.S. Small Business Administration, "Idaho's Small Business Person of the Year," August 6, 2003, http://www.sba.gov/id/success; Del E. Web School of Construction, "Elaine Martin," August 6, 2003, http://construction.asu.edu/banquet/wom_2002_bio; Aliza Pilar Sherman, "Wild, Wild West," *Entrepreneur*, July 2002, p. 30.
16. Aliza Pilar Sherman, "A Man's World," *Entrepreneur*, August 2003, p. 26.
17. See "Thinking About Tomorrow," *Wall Street Journal*, May 24, 1999, p. R-30; and James Worsham, "The Flip Side of Downsizing," *Nation's Business*, Vol. 84, No. 10 (October 1996), pp. 18–25.
18. Personal conversation with Jim Ruschman, June 2001.
19. Jeffry A. Timmons and Stephen Spinelli, *New Venture Creation: Entrepreneurship for the 21st Century* (New York: McGraw-Hill/Irwin, 2004), p. 332.
20. "Small Firms Make More Than Their Share of Big Inventions," *Small Business Advocate* (SBA Office of Advocacy), Vol. 22, No. 3 (March 2003), pp. 1–4.
21. Personal correspondence with Lowe's Supermarket, 2003.
22. Cited in Gary M. Stern, "Young Entrepreneurs Make Their Mark," *Nation's Business*, Vol. 84, No. 8 (August 1996), pp. 49–51.
23. J. B. Rotter, "Generalized Expectancies for Internal Versus External Control of Reinforcement," *Psychological Monographs*, 1966a. A more recent review is given in Robert H. Brockhaus, Sr., and Pamela S. Horwitz, "The Psychology of the Entrepreneur," in Donald L. Sexton and Raymond W. Smilor (eds.), *The Art and Science of Entrepreneurship* (Cambridge, MA: Ballinger, 1986), pp. 25–48.
24. Timmons and Spinelli, *op cit.*, pp. 249–255.
25. Roberta Maynard, "Sliding into Home," *Nation's Business*, Vol. 86, No. 1 (January 1998), p. 52.
26. Paul Rerucha, Letters, *Inc.*, Vol. 22, No. 16 (November 2000), p. 22.
27. Personal interview with Ed Bonneau, 2000.
28. *Ibid.*
29. Ilan Mochari, "What Would You Do Differently?" *Inc.*, Vol. 23, No. 3 (March 2001), p. 65.
30. Personal interview with Bernard Rapaport, 2000.
31. Stephen R. Covey, *The Seven Habits of Highly Effective People* (New York: Simon and Schuster, 1989), pp. 106–142.

Chapter 2

1. Max DePree, *Leadership Is an Art* (New York: Bantam Dell, 1989), pp. xvii–xviii.
2. http://www.rotary.org/aboutrotary/4way.html, October 24, 2003.
3. Leslie E. Palich, Justin G. Longenecker, Carlos W. Moore, and J. William Petty, "Integrity and Small Business: A Framework and Empirical Analysis," Proceedings of the 49th World Conference of the International Council for Small Business, Johannesburg, South Africa, June 2004.
4. Laura L. Nash, *Good Intentions Aside: A Manager's Guide to Resolving Ethical Problems* (Boston: Harvard Business School Press, 1993), p. 61.
5. Milton Friedman, *Capitalism and Freedom* (Chicago: University of Chicago Press, 1963), p. 133.
6. Jana Matthews and Jeff Dennis, *Lessons from the Edge: Survival Skills for Starting and Growing a Company* (Oxford: Oxford University Press, 2003), pp. 119–123.
7. Hattie Bryant, Producer, "Small Business School," The Series on PBS Stations, Worldnet, and the Web, http://smallbusinessschool.org.

8. Paul Cox, "CyberRebate Closure, Credit Card Firms Leave Thousands of Buyers in the Lurch," *Wall Street Journal*, May 5, 2001, p. B11a.
9. Jodie Carter, "Rolling in Dough," *Entrepreneur*, Vol. 31, No. 6 (June 2003), p. 106.
10. Jennifer Gill, "When Dot-Coms on a Deathbed Keep Hiring," *BusinessWeek*, http://www.businessweek.com, October 24, 2000.
11. Palich et al., *op. cit.*
12. Geoff Williams, "Call for Help," *Entrepreneur*, Vol. 30, No. 7 (July 2002), p. 32.
13. Harvey Meyer, "Helping Employees to Help Others," *Nation's Business*, Vol. 87, No. 3 (March 1999), pp. 48–51; Jane Larson, "2 E. Valley Businesses Win Awards," *The Arizona Republic*, June 9, 1999, p. E2.
14. Meyer, *op. cit.*, p. 50.
15. Michael Kinsman, "Corporate Caring," *San Diego Union-Tribune*, December 15, 1997, p. C-1.
16. Kenneth E. Aupperle, F. Bruce Simmons, III, and William Acar, "An Empirical Investigation into How Entrepreneurs View Their Social Responsibilities," paper presented at the Academy of Management Meetings, San Francisco, California, August 1990.
17. Priscilla Elsass, "The Cost of Illegal Business Practices," *Academy of Management Executive*, Vol. 12, No. 1 (February 1998), pp. 87–88.
18. Janet Novack, "You Know Who You Are, and So Do We," *Forbes*, Vol. 153, No. 8 (April 11, 1994), pp. 88–92.
19. This possibility is advanced by Michael Allen in "Small-Business Jungle," *Wall Street Journal*, June 10, 1988, p. 19R.
20. *Ibid.*
21. *Ibid.*
22. Justin G. Longenecker, Joseph A. McKinney, and Carlos W. Moore, "Egoism and Independence: Entrepreneurial Ethics," *Organizational Dynamics*, Vol. 16, No. 3 (Winter 1988), pp. 64–72.
23. These differences were significant at the .05 level.
24. These differences were significant at the .05 level.
25. John C. Maxwell and Jim Dornan, *Becoming a Person of Influence* (Nashville, TN: Thomas Nelson Publisher, 1997), p. 20.
26. As cited in Jeffrey L. Siglin, "Do It Right," *MBA Jungle*, November 2001, p. 69.
27. Del Jones, "Poll: More Workers Value E-Mail, Voice-Mail Privacy," *USAToday*, March 27, 2000, p. 1B.
28. "Web Use at Work Is Often Unrelated to the Job," *Wall Street Journal*, October 21, 2003, p. A24.
29. Pamela Mendels, "The Rise of the Chief Privacy Officer," *BusinessWeek*, http://www.businessweek.com, December 14, 2000.
30. Carl M. Cannon, "Ambushed," *Forbes ASAP*, February 19, 2001, p. 50.
31. Nick Wingfield and Ethan Smith, "The High Cost of Sharing," *Wall Street Journal*, September 9, 2003, p. A1.
32. Gail Edmondson, Kate Carlisle, Inka Resch, Karen Nickel Anhalt, and Heidi Dawley, "Workers in Bondage," *BusinessWeek*, No. 3709 (November 27, 2000), pp. 146–162.
33. For a general review of this topic, see Steven L. Wartick and Donna J. Wood, *International Business and Society* (Malden, MA: Blackwell, 1998).
34. Nicholas G. Moore, "Ethics: The Way to Do Business," speech given at the Sears Lectureship in Business Ethics, Bentley College, Waltham, MA, February 9, 1998.
35. *Ibid.*
36. Jan Cienski, "Faith Jostles with Profits for Some Christian Businesses," *Waco Tribune-Herald*, May 24, 1997.
37. *Ibid.;* "The Best 100 Companies to Work For," *Fortune*, Vol. 143, No. 1 (January 8, 2001), pp. 148–168.
38. Excerpt from an interview with J. C. Huizenga in "Virtuous Business and Educational Practice," *Religion & Liberty* (a publication of the Acton Institute for the Study of Religion and Liberty), Vol. 12, No. 2 (September-October 2002), p. 1.
39. John Rutledge, "The Portrait on My Office Wall," *Forbes*, Vol. 158, No. 15 (December 30, 1996), p. 78.
40. Sample codes of ethics can be obtained from the Ethics Resource Center, Inc., 1025 Connecticut Avenue, N.W., Washington, DC 22036.
41. "Discarded Tires, Once a Nightmare, Are Where Ecologists Dream to Tread," *Wall Street Journal*, April 24, 2000, p. B17; http://www.greenman.biz, September 29, 2003; http://www.rbrubber.com, September 29, 2003; http://www.regupol.com, September 29, 2003.
42. Michelle Conlin and Paul Rayburn, "Industrial Evolution," *BusinessWeek*, No. 3777 (April 8, 2002), pp. 70–72.
43. *Ibid.*
44. *Ibid.*
45. Marc Gunter, "Tree Huggers, Soy Lovers, and Profits," *Fortune*, Vol. 147, No. 12 (June 23, 2003), pp. 99–104.

Chapter 3

1. Amar Bhide, "Bootstrap Finance: The Art of Start-Ups," *Harvard Business Review*, Vol. 70, No. 6 (November-December 1992), pp. 109–117.
2. Emily Barker, "Hot Startups: The Young and the Caloric," *Inc.*, Vol. 21, No. 10 (July 1999), p. 37.
3. Jim Hopkins, "Ex-GM, Pentagon Official Scoots into Own Startup," *USAToday*, May 21, 2003, p. 7B.
4. Marc Ballon, "Hot Startups: Petal Pushers," *Inc.*, Vol. 21, No. 10 (July 1999), p. 36.
5. April Y. Pennington, "Snapshot," *Entrepreneur*, Vol. 31, No. 9 (September 2003), p. 23.
6. Donna Fenn, "Grand Plans," *Inc.*, Vol. 21, No. 11 (August 1999), pp. 44–45.
7. Nichole L. Torress, "Roamin' Holiday," *Entrepreneur*, Vol. 31, No. 9 (September 2003), p. 102.
8. Edward Clendaniel, "Greek Hero," *Forbes ASAP*, April 2, 2001, p. 24.
9. Peter Drucker, *Innovation and Entrepreneurship* (New York: HarperBusiness, 1993), p. 35.
10. Peter F. Drucker, "The Discipline of Innovation," *Harvard Business Review*, Vol. 76, No. 6 (November-December 1998), p. 149.
11. Tony Manning, *Making Sense of Strategy* (New York: American Management Association, 2001), p. 17.
12. For a rigorous study of this subject, see Suresh Kotha and Anil Nair, "Strategy and Environment as Determinants of Performance: Evidence from the Japanese Machine Tool Industry," *Strategic Management Journal*, Vol. 16, No. 7 (October 1995), pp. 497–518.
13. Jason Dean, "Recent Biotech Innovation Is a Little Fishy," *Wall Street Journal*, May 8, 2003, pp. B1, B3.
14. Robert Frank, "How Terror Fears Brought Tiny Firm to Brink of Success," *Wall Street Journal*, May 8, 2003, p. A1; Ray A. Smith, "High-Rise Is Aflame, Stairwells Are Blocked—What Now?" *Wall Street Journal*, August 21, 2003,

p. B1; Christopher McGinnis, "Your Loss?" *Entrepreneur*, Vol. 31, No. 9 (September 2003), p. 24.

15. Rona Kobell, "Funeral Industry Adapts to Change," *Houston Chronicle*, October 8, 2000, p. B7; "Business Opportunities in Space," *Fortune*, Vol. 137, No. 1 (January 12, 1998), pp. 46–47; http://www.celestis.com, January 8, 2004.
16. Michael Porter, *Competitive Advantage* (New York: Free Press, 1985), pp. 7–29.
17. Personal communication with Bill Waugh and Burger Street management; http://www.burgerstreet.com, March 15, 2004.
18. William A. Sahlman, "How to Write a Great Business Plan," *Harvard Business Review*, Vol. 75, No. 4 (July-August 1997), pp. 103–104.
19. Paul Hansen, "Big Dog Motorcycles Accelerates to $80 Million in Annual Sales, Shattering All Previous Records," press release, February 4, 2004; Karen Stevens and Dale Kurschner, "That Vroom! You Hear May Not Be a Harley," *BusinessWeek*, No. 3549 (October 20, 1997), p. 159; Lillian Zier Martell, "Wichita, Kan., Offers Tax Break to Keep Motorcycle Maker from Relocating," *Wichita Eagle*, October 20, 1999, p. C1.
20. Gary Hamel, "Strategy as Revolution," *Harvard Business Review*, Vol. 74, No. 4 (July-August 1996), p. 80.
21. http://www.starbucks.com, January 9, 2004.
22. James P. Sterba, "Here's Why Asians Are All Hopped Up About Frog Farming," *Wall Street Journal*, March 27, 2001, pp. A1, A8.
23. William M. Bulkeley, "The Competitor," *Wall Street Journal*, October 28, 2002, p. R8.
24. David Luhnow and Chad Terhune, "Latin Pop: A Low-Budget Cola Shakes Up Markets South of the Border," *Wall Street Journal*, October 27, 2003, p. A1.
25. http://www.way2coolshoes.com, August 14, 2003.
26. Gayle Sato Stodder, "New Wave," *Entrepreneur*, Vol. 25, No. 1 (January 1997), pp. 98–102.
27. Jonathan Eig, "Going Bats: Baseball, in Limiting Suppliers, Drives Many Nuts," *Wall Street Journal*, April 24, 2003, p. A1.
28. John Naisbitt, *Global Paradox* (New York: Morrow, 1994).
29. David Nasaw, "Companies Find Old News Lasts Only So Long," *Wall Street Journal*, August, 26, 2003, p. B6.
30. Amar Bhide, "How Entrepreneurs Craft Strategies That Work," *Harvard Business Review*, Vol. 72, No. 2 (March-April 1992), p. 154.
31. Christopher J. Zane, "Creating Lifetime Customers," Texas A&M University: Center for Retailing Studies, Vol. 12, No. 5 (September 2000), pp. 1–15, http://www.zanes.com/news/articles/article_detail.cfm?ArticleID=8, July 13, 2004.
32. http://www.zanes.com, January 1, 2004; Donna Fenn, "A Bigger Wheel," *Inc.*, Vol. 22, No. 16 (November 2000), pp. 78–88.
33. Porter, *op. cit.*, p. 5.

Chapter 4

1. Richard Landesberg, "A New Career for You Might Start at Franchise U.," *Success Magazine*, http://www.successmagazine.com, July-August 2000.
2. http://www.FranchiseRegistry.com/Partnership.asp, April 7, 2004.
3. See Cecilia M. Falbe and Dianne H. B. Welch, "NAFTA and Franchising: A Comparison of Franchisor Perceptions of Characteristics Associated with Franchisee Success and Failure in Canada, Mexico, and the United States," *Journal of Business Venturing*, Vol. 13, No. 2 (March 1998), pp. 151–171.
4. James H. Amos, Jr., "Trends and Developments in International Franchising," *The Franchising Handbook* (New York: American Management Association, 1993), p. 463.
5. Dennis Rodkin, "Leap of Faith," *Entrepreneur*, Vol. 26, No. 2 (February 1998), pp. 150–155.
6. Peter Weaver, "New Owners Take Stock," *Business Advisor*, January-February 2001, pp. 12–15.

Chapter 5

1. For a more complete report of this analysis, including profiles of specific family-owned firms, see Joseph Weber, Louis Lavelle, Tom Lowry, Wendy Zellner, and Amy Barrett, "Family, Inc.," *BusinessWeek*, No. 3857 (November 20, 2003), pp. 100–103.
2. For these findings and others, see William J. Dennis, Jr. (ed.), "Families in Business," *NFIB National Small Business Poll*, Vol. 2, No. 6 (2002), p. 1.
3. *Ibid.*, p. 17.
4. Khai Sheang Lee, Guan Hua Lim, and Wei Shi Lim, "Family Business Succession: Appropriation Risk and Choice of Successor," *Academy of Management Review*, Vol. 28, No. 4 (October 2003), p. 658.
5. Ramona K. Z. Heck and Greg K. McCann, "The Conclusion: Reshaping Our Vision and Ideas About Family Business," in Greg McCann and Nancy B. Upton (eds.), *The Holistic Model: Destroying Myths and Creating Value in Family Business*, p. 66.
6. Lowell J. Spirer, *The Human Factor in Starting Your Own Business* (BlueBell, PA: Lowell J. Spirer).
7. Meg Lundstrom, "Mommy, Do You Love Your Company More Than Me?" *BusinessWeek*, No. 3660 (December 20, 1999), p. 175.
8. From the Letters section of *Inc.*, Vol. 19, No. 10 (July 1997), p. 17.
9. Richard Heller, "Folk Fortune," *Forbes*, Vol. 166, No. 6 (September 4, 2000), pp. 66–69; "Create Ikea, Make Billions, Take Bus," *Fortune*, Vol. 149, No. 9 (May 3, 2004), p. 44; http://www.ikea.com, July 12, 2004.
10. Daniel L. McConaughy, "Family CEOs vs. Non-Family CEOs in the Family-Controlled Firm: An Examination of the Level and Sensitivity of Pay to Performance," *Family Business Review*, Vol. 13, No. 2 (June 2000), pp. 121–131.
11. From an advertising letter that the Wilkirson-Hatch-Bailey Funeral Home in Waco, Texas, sent out in February, 1998.
12. David G. Sirmon and Michael A. Hitt, "Managing Resources: Linking Unique Resources, Management, and Wealth Creation in Family Firms," *Entrepreneurship Theory and Practice*, Vol. 27, No. 4 (Summer 2003), pp. 341–344. These findings are consistent with the results of other recent research—see, for example, Ronald C. Anderson and David M. Reeb, "Founding-Family Ownership and Firm Performance: Evidence from the S&P 500," *Journal of Finance*, Vol. 58, No. 3 (June 2003), pp. 1301–1328.
13. John Robben, "Have Toys, Will Travel: My Father's Journey," *Family Business*, Vol. 4, No. 1 (Winter 1993), p. 63.
14. Ivan Lansberg, "Narcissism: The Hidden Cost of Success," *Family Business*, Vol. 11, No. 3 (Summer 2000), pp. 15–16.
15. W. Gibb Dyer, Jr., *Cultural Change in Family Firms* (San Francisco: Jossey-Bass, 1986), p. 22.

16. Stephanie Armour, "Couple of Heads for Business," *USAToday*, June 18, 1999, pp. 1B–2B.
17. James Samuelson, "Solomonic Solution," *Forbes*, Vol. 157, No. 5 (March 11, 1996), pp. 80–82.
18. Stephanie Armour, "More Kids Putting Parents on Payroll," *USAToday*, April 29, 1998, p. 1B.
19. Katy Danco, *From the Other Side of the Bed: A Woman Looks at Life in the Family Business* (Cleveland: Center for Family Business, 1981), p. 21.
20. John L. Ward, "Growing the Family Business: Special Challenges and Best Practices," *Family Business Review*, Vol. 10, No. 4 (December 1997), pp. 323–337.
21. Nancy Upton, *Transferring Management in a Family-Owned Business* (Washington, DC: U.S. Small Business Administration, 1991), p. 6.
22. Kenneth Meeks, "Family Business," *Black Enterprise*, Vol. 34, No. 1 (August 2003), p. 91.
23. Matthew Fogel, "A More Perfect Business," *Inc.*, Vol. 25, No. 8 (August 2003), p. 44.
24. *Ibid.*
25. Timothy Aeppel, "A Father and Son Meld New Economy and Old, and the Business Flows," *Wall Street Journal*, May 24, 2000, pp. A1, A16.
26. For a discussion of mentoring in the family firm, see John Boyd, Nancy Upton, and Michelle Wircenski, "Mentoring in Family Firms: A Reflective Analysis of Senior Executives' Perceptions," *Family Business Review*, Vol. 12, No. 4 (December, 1999), pp. 299–309.
27. For an earlier, extended treatment of this topic, see Justin G. Longenecker and John E. Schoen, "Management Succession in the Family Business," *Journal of Small Business Management*, Vol. 16, No. 3 (July 1978), pp. 1–6.
28. Colette Dumas, "Integrating the Daughter into Family Business Management," *Entrepreneurship Theory and Practice*, Vol. 16, No. 4 (Summer 1992), p. 47.

Chapter 6

1. David E. Gumpert, *How to Really Create a Successful Business Plan*, 4th ed. (Needham, MA: Lauson Publishing Co., 2003), p. 10.
2. Amar Bhide, *The Origin and Evolution of New Businesses* (New York: Oxford University Press, 2000), p. 53.
3. Gumpert, *op. cit.*, pp. 30–34.
4. http://www.royalbank.com/sme/bigidea/christinedenis.html, February 2004.
5. Bhide, *op. cit.*, p. 70.
6. Mark Stevens, "Seven Steps to a Well-Prepared Business Plan," *Executive Female*, Vol. 18, No. 2 (March 1995), p. 30.
7. Ellyn E. Spragins, "How to Write a Business Plan That Will Get You in the Door," *Inc. Guide to Small Business Management*, pp. 6–8.
8. William Sahlman, "How to Write a Great Business Plan," *Harvard Business Review*, Vol. 75, No. 4 (July-August 1997), pp. 98–108.
9. Kenneth Blanchard and Spencer Johnson, *The One-Minute Manager* (New York: William Morrow, 1982).
10. Personal conversation with Tim Smith, March 2003.
11. Rhonda M. Abrams, *The Successful Business Plan: Secrets and Strategies*, 2nd ed. (Grants Pass, OR: Oasis Press, 2003).
12. http://www.powerhomebiz.com/vol3/badbplan.htm, January 6, 2004; http://www.bpiplans.com/Articles.htm, January 6, 2004.
13. Templates to assist you in preparing a simplified business plan are available on the CD-ROM that accompanies this textbook. For additional information on business plans, visit http://longenecker.swlearning.com.
14. Jill Andresky Fraser, "Who Can Help Out with a Business Plan?" *Inc.*, Vol. 21, No. 8 (June 1999), pp. 115–117.

Chapter 7

1. Karen E. Spaeder, "Beyond their Years," *Entrepreneur*, November 2003, p. 83.
2. From the business plan of Adorable Pet Photography, http://www.bplans.com, October 27, 2003.
3. J. D. Ryan and Gail P. Hiduke, *Small Business: An Entrepreneur's Business Plan*, 6th ed. (Cincinnati: South-Western, 2003), p. 354.
4. Alan Naditz, "Desktop Sleuthing," *Independent Business*, Vol. 9, No. 1 (January-February 1998), p. 24.
5. From business plan of Fantastic Florals, Inc., http://www.bplan.com, October 30, 2003.
6. Shannon Scully, "Protecting Your Good Name," *My Business*, February/March 2002, p. 14
7. William Bak, "Read All About It," *Entrepreneur*, Vol. 22, No. 1 (January 1994), pp. 50–53.
8. Cheryl Abrams, "The Quick 'N Natural Soup Entrepreneur," *In Business*, Vol. 20, No. 3 (May-June 1998), pp. 32–33.
9. Jim Hopkins, "Entrepreneur 101: Competition," *USAToday*, February 14, 2001, p. 6B.
10. Gayle Sato Strodder, "Right Off Target," *Entrepreneur*, Vol. 22, No. 10 (October 1994), p. 56.
11. Michael Porter, *Competitive Advantage* (New York: Free Press, 1985), p. 5.
12. Joann S. Lublin, "Fountain Pen Fashion: Try 5,072 Diamonds or Abe Lincoln's DNA," *Wall Street Journal*, August 24, 2001, p. 81.

Chapter 8

1. For example, see Michael D. Ensley, Allison W. Pearson, and Allen C. Amason, "Understanding the Dynamics of New Venture Top Management Teams: Cohesion, Conflict, and New Venture Performance," *Journal of Business Venturing*, Vol. 17, No. 4 (July 2002), pp. 365–366; Elizabeth J. Teal and Charles W. Hofer, "Key Attributes of the Founding Entrepreneurial Team of Rapidly Growing New Ventures," *Journal of Private Equity*, Vol. 4, No. 2 (Spring 2001), pp. 19–31.
2. Jeffry A. Timmons and Stephen Spinelli, *New Venture Creation: Entrepreneurship for the 21st Century* (Boston: McGraw-Hill/Irwin, 2004), p. 67.
3. Simon Stockley, "Building and Maintaining the Entrepreneurial Team—A Critical Competence for Venture Growth," in Sue Birley and Daniel F. Muzyka (eds.), *Mastering Entrepreneurship: The Complete MBA Companion in Entrepreneurship* (London: Financial Times/Prentice-Hall, 2000), pp. 206–212.
4. Bridget McCrea, "Incorporating Facts," *Black Enterprise*, Vol. 33, No. 7 (February 2003), p. 40.
5. Liability insurance and other forms of protection are discussed in detail in Chapter 21. However, there are many forms of liability protection, and a full discussion of these goes beyond the scope of this text. For example, errors and omissions insurance offers coverage for damages that result

from the insured's negligence, mistakes, or failure to take appropriate action in the performance of business or professional duties. Obviously, insurance decisions can get very complicated. Experts and specific sources of information should be consulted when making these decisions.
6. Nancy Mann Jackson, "Dream Team or Nightmare Relationship," *MyBusiness*, April-May, 2003, pp. 35–37.
7. Jana Matthews and Jeff Dennis, *Lessons from the Edge: Survival Skills for Starting and Growing a Company* (Oxford: Oxford University Press, 2003).
8. W. Chris Harrison, "Form Is Everything," *E-Merging Business*, Vol. 1, No. 1 (Fall-Winter 2000), p. 198.
9. Marc Diener, "Friends Forever?" *Entrepreneur*, Vol. 31, No. 6 (June 2003), p. 77.
10. Karen Cheney, "Meet Your Match," December 15, 2001, found on http://www.quicken.com, April 14, 2004.
11. Karen Cheney, "The Perfect Partnership Plan," December 30, 2001, found on http://www.quicken.com, April 14, 2004.
12. Fred S. Steingold, *Legal Guide to Starting and Running a Small Business* (Berkeley, CA: Nolo Press, 2003).
13. Lori Ioannou, "Can't We Get Along?" *Fortune*, Vol. 138, No. 11 (December 7, 1998), p. 244[E].
14. *Ibid.*
15. http://www.irs.gov/pub/irs-soi/04al22sr.xls, July 12, 2004.
16. Laura Saunders, "Freedom Day for Small Business," *Forbes*, Vol. 163, No. 4 (February 22, 1999), pp. 128, 130.
17. For a brief description of some of the tax advantages of a limited liability corporation, see Ashlea Ebeling, "Corporate Choice," *Forbes*, Vol. 172, No. 1 (July 7, 2003), p. 126.
18. Christopher Caggiano, "Hotlinks," *Inc.*, Vol. 21, No. 14 (October 1999), pp. 72–81.
19. Dianne Cyr, "High Tech, High Impact: Creating Canada's Competitive Advantage Through Technology Alliances," *Academy of Management Executive*, Vol. 13, No. 2 (May 1999), p. 18; http://www.alitech.com, July 12, 2004.
20. Shirley Leung, "The Lure—and Danger—of Big Company Jobs," *Wall Street Journal*, September 2, 2003, p. B9.
21. Mike Hoffman, "Dear Max: Drop Dead. Love, Go Card," *Inc.*, Vol. 19, No. 5 (April 1997), p. 28.
22. Ilan Mochari, "Fishing for Big-Name Partners," *Inc.*, Vol. 22, No. 6 (May 2000), p. 163.
23. Caggiano, *op. cit.*
24. Arie Y. Lewin, "Putting the S-Word Back in Alliances," *Financial Times*, November 1, 1999, p. 12.
25. Jeffrey Shuman, Janice Twombly, and David Rottenberg, *Everyone Is a Customer: A Proven Method for Measuring the Value of Every Relationship in the Era of Collaborative Business* (Chicago: Dearborn Trade Publishing, 2002).
26. Carol Hymowitz, "How to Be a Good Director," *Wall Street Journal*, October 27, 2003, p. R1.
27. National Association of Corporate Directors, *Effective Entrepreneurial Boards: Findings from the 2001–2002 Entrepreneurial Boards Survey* (Washington, DC: National Association of Corporate Directors, 2002), p. 3.
28. Lynn Cowan, "The Board of Directors," *Wall Street Journal*, October 28, 2002, p. R6.
29. John A. Davis and Keely Cormier, *Board of Directors of the Family Firm* (Boston: Harvard Business School Publishing, 1999), p. 7; National Association of Corporate Directors, *op. cit.*, p. 9.
30. National Association of Corporate Directors, *op. cit.*, p. 17.
31. Jill Andresky Fraser, "Building the Board," *Inc.*, Vol. 21, No. 16 (November 1999), p. 132.
32. Ronald I. Zall, *A Guide for Directors of Privately Held Companies* (Washington, DC: National Association of Corporate Directors, 2003), p. 43.

Chapter 9

1. Del Jones, "California Proves Too Costly for Departing Businesses," *USAToday*, October 2, 2003, p. 1B.
2. For a more comprehensive treatment of relocation issues, see Rick Mullin, "Site Selection," *Journal of Business Strategy*, May-June 1996, pp. 26–39.
3. Gail P. Hiduke, *Small Business—An Entrepreneur's Business Plan* (Cincinnati: South-Western, 2003), pp. 133–134.
4. http://www.hatworld.com, October 3, 2003.
5. Michael Selz, "Odd Jobs," *Wall Street Journal*, May 22, 1997, p. 12.
6. Binaj Gurubacharya, "Linking Up Everest," *Waco Tribune-Herald*, March 7, 2003, p. 14A.
7. Wyoming Department of Revenue, http://revenue.state.wy.us, February 6, 2001.
8. "What Are Oregon Enterprise Zones?" http://www.econ.state.or.us/enterthezones/whatare.html, March 3, 2001.
9. Randy Fitzgerald, "It's Your Business," *Reader's Digest*, Vol. 153, No. 915 (July 1998), p. 183.
10. Debra Cash, "There's No Office Like Home," *Inc. Technology*, Vol. 20, No. 4 (1998), p. 36.
11. Nichole L. Torres, "No Place Like Home," *Start-ups*, Vol. 12, No. 9 (September 2000), p. 40.
12. John Grossman, "Meeting's at 9. I'll Be the One in Slippers," *Inc.: The State of Small Business* (Special Issue), Vol. 20, No. 7 (1998), p. 47.
13. Broderick Perkins, "Realize the Dream of a Home-Based Business," http://www.startupjournal.com, April 9, 2004.
14. Luisa Kroll, "Entrepreneur Moms," *Forbes*, Vol. 161, No. 10 (May 18, 1998), p. 85.
15. Perkins, *op. cit.*
16. Joseph C. Roetheli and Judy E. Roetheli, "The Benefits of Launching Your Business from Home," http://www.startupjournal.com, April 9, 2004.
17. Cynthia E. Griffin, "Kidding Around," *Entrepreneur*, Vol. 24, No. 9 (September 1996), pp. 56–59.
18. Michael J. McDermott, "Avoid Zoning Pitfalls When Working from Home," http://www.busop1.com/pitfall.html, September 20, 2003.
19. Leigh Buchanan, "Early to Web," *Inc.*, Vol. 24, No. 13 (December 2002), p. 84.
20. Torres, *op. cit.*
21. http://www.wemailsmiles.com, April 15, 2004.

Chapter 10

1. Jan Norman, "You're Making Sales, but Are You Making Money?" http://www.entrepreneur.com/article/0,4621,228680,00.html, March, 2004.
2. For a more in-depth presentation of the cash flow statement, see Appendix 10B at the end of the chapter.
3. Paul A. Broni, "Persuasive Projections," *Inc.*, Vol. 22, No. 4 (April 2000), p. 38.
4. Rhonda Abrams, "How Can I Make Financial Projections in My Business Plan When I Have No Solid Numbers?" *Inc.com*, September 2000.
5. Investors also look to financial projections to determine the sales level necessary for the firm to break even. A firm's

break-even point, while important from a financial perspective, is also important to pricing its products or services. The issue of pricing is discussed in Chapter 15.
6. Personal communication with Cecilia Levine, August 13, 2004.
7. Matt Ackermann, "Many Entrepreneurs Need Better Financial Planning," *American Banker*, Vol. 168, No. 189 (October 1, 2003), p. 9.
8. Scott Bernard Nelson, "Fee Agents," *Entrepreneur*, January 2003, p. 63.
9. See Chapter 23 for further discussion of the debt ratio.
10. This percentage can be found by dividing the number of days of credit the supplier is offering (30 days, in this case) by the 365 days in a year (30 ÷ 365 = 8.2%).
11. Information in this section was taken from Linda Elkins, "Real Numbers Don't Deceive," *Nation's Business*, Vol. 85, No. 3 (March 1997), pp. 51–52; and Broni, *op cit.*, pp. 183–184.
12. Broni, *op. cit.*

Chapter 11

1. "Financing Patterns of Small Firms: Findings from the 1998 Survey of Small Business Finance," SBA Office of Advocacy, Washington, DC, September 2003.
2. Mike Hofman, "The Big Picture," *Inc.*, Vol. 25, No. 12 (October 2003), p. 87.
3. Ilan Mochari, "The Numbers Game," *Inc.*, Vol. 24, No. 12 (October 2002), pp. 65–66.
4. *Ibid.*, p. 64.
5. Personal conversation with Jack Griggs, March 14, 2004.
6. To compute the $730 monthly payment, we can use a financial calculator or a computer spreadsheet.

PV (present value) = $50,000 (current loan)
N (number of payments) = 84 (7 years × 12 months = 84)
I/YR (interest rate/month) = 0.5% (6% interest rate/year ÷ 12 months = 0.005 = 0.5%)
FV (future value) = 0 (in 7 years)
PMT (payment) = $730.43

7. As discussed in Chapter 10, the ratio of current assets to current liabilities is called the *current ratio*; the ratio of total debt to total assets is called the *debt ratio*.
8. Mochari, *op. cit.*, p. 64.
9. Personal interview with Bill Bailey, former owner of Cherokee Communications, March 13, 2002.
10. Jill Andresky Fraser, "The Art of the Covenant," *Inc.*, Vol. 19, No. 8 (August 1997), p. 99.
11. For an excellent source on private equity markets, see Jeffrey Sohl, "The U.S. Angel and Venture Capital Market: Recent Trends and Developments," *Journal of Private Equity*, Spring 2003, pp. 7–17.
12. Julian Lange, Benoit Leleux, and Bernard Surlemont, "Angel Network for the 21st Century," *Journal of Private Equity*, Spring 2003, p. 18.
13. David Worrell, "Our Little Angels," *Entrepreneur*, January 2003, p. 46.
14. Jeffrey E. Sohl, "The Early Stage Equity Markets in the United States," *Venture Capital: An International Journal of Entrepreneurial Finance*, Vol. 1, No. 2 (1999), pp. 101–120.
15. John Freear, Jeffrey E. Sohl, and William E. Wetzel, Jr., *Creating New Capital Markets for Emerging Ventures*, SBAHQ-95-M-1062, report prepared for the SBA Office of Advocacy, Washington, DC, June 1996.
16. http://www.thedallasangels.com.
17. Jim Hopkins, "Corporate Giants Bankroll Start-Ups," *USAToday*, March 29, 2001, p. 1B.

Chapter 12

1. Randall Lane, "What Is Your Company Worth Now?, *Inc.*, July 2003, pp. 75, 77.
2. Nancy Mann Jackson, "The ABCs of ESOPs," *My Business*, February-March 2003, http://www.mybusinessmag.com/fullstory.php3?sid=903, May 2004.
3. *Ibid.*
4. Lisa D. Stein, presentation at the National Forum for Women in Finance, sponsored by the Financial Women's Association of New York, *Fortune*, and the Financial Executive Institute, New York, September 16–17, 1998.
5. Wayne H. Mikkelson, M. Megan Partch, and Kshitij Shah, "Ownership and Operating Performance of Companies That Go Public," *Journal of Financial Economics*, Vol. 44, No. 3 (1997), pp. 281–307.
6. Stein, *op. cit.*
7. L. Brokaw, "The First Day of the Rest of Your Life," *Inc.*, Vol. 15, No. 5 (1993), p. 144.
8. Nancy B. Upton and J. William Petty, "Funding Options for Transferring the Family-Held Firm: A Comparative Analysis," Working Paper, Baylor University, Waco, Texas, 1998.
9. The source for this information is Heritage Partners, a Boston venture capital firm, which obtained a registered trademark for a process it calls the "Private IPO®."
10. The unattributed quotes in this part of the chapter are taken from personal interviews conducted as part of a research study on harvesting, sponsored by the Financial Executive Research Foundation and cited in J. William Petty, John D. Martin, and John Kensinger, *Harvesting the Value of a Privately Held Company* (Morristown, NJ: Financial Executive Research Foundation, 1999). To acquire a copy of the book, write the Financial Executive Research Foundation, Inc., P.O. Box 1938, Morristown, NJ 07962-1938, or call 973-898-4600.
11. Jeff Bailey, "Selling the Firm—and Letting Go of the Dream," *Wall Street Journal*, December 10, 2002, p. B6.

Chapter 13

1. "What Is CRM?" http://www.hewson.co.uk/crmdefn.htm, June 5, 2004.
2. Brian Vellmure, "Let's Start with Customer Retention," http://www.initiumtech.com/newsletter_120602.htm, September 4, 2004.
3. Thomas O. Jones and W. Earl Sasser, Jr., "Why Satisfied Customers Defect," *Harvard Business Review*, Vol. 73, No. 6 (November-December 1995), p. 90.
4. Jerry Fisher, "The Secret's Out," http://www.entrepreneur.com/mag/article/0,1539,228496.html, June 8, 2004.
5. Bruce Horovitz, "Whatever Happened to Customer Service?" *USAToday*, September 26, 2003, pp. 1A–2A.
6. Melissa Campanelli, "At Their Service," *Entrepreneur*, July 2003, p. 42.
7. *Ibid.*, p. 40.
8. "Intimate Relationships in Bloom," http://www.sas.com/success/1800FLOWERS.html, June 5, 2004.
9. Charles Waltner, "New Choices for Small Business," *Informationweek*, November 27, 2000, p. 119.
10. David M. Ewalt, "CRM Race Speeds Up," *Informationweek*, March 10, 2003, p. 46.

11. Russell S. Wimer, "Customer Relationship Management: A Framework, Research Directions, and the Future," http://groups.haas.berkeley.edu/fcsuit/PDF-papers/CRM%20paper.pdf, June 8, 2004.
12. "Get to Know Your Customer Profile," http://peerspectives.org/index.peer?page=main&storyid=0035, September 4, 2004.
13. *Ibid.*
14. See, for example, Scott S. Smith, "Attention, Shoppers!" *Entrepreneur*, December 2001, http://www.entrepeneur.com/article/0,4621,294668,00.html; and "Displays Using Motion Determined to Be Most Effective in Both Product Sales and Awareness," http://www.elmedia.co.nz/Research_Data.htm, September 4, 2004.

Chapter 14

1. Debra Kahn Schofield, "Grow Your Business Slowly: A Cautionary Tale," http://www.gmarketing.com, May 14, 2004.
2. Aliza Pilar Sherman, "Parallel Universe," *Entrepreneur*, June 2004, p. 36.
3. Julie Fields, "Caught in a Candy Crunch," http://www.businessweek.com, May 20, 2004.
4. Jeffrey A. Timmons and Stephen Spinelli, *New Venture Creation: Entrepreneurship for the 21st Century* (New York: McGraw-Hill/Irwin, 2004).
5. Rebecca Quick, "As Our Reporter Said, This Apparel Web Site Was Just Way Too Hip," *Wall Street Journal*, October 25, 2000, p. B1; "Body Scanning Kiosks May Improve Clothes' Fit," *St. Louis Post-Dispatch*, October 18, 2000, p. C1.
6. Donna Boone, "Entrepreneurial Growth: Think Regional, Act Local," http://www.entreworld.com, May 20, 2004.
7. Don Debelak, "Warm Reception," *Entrepreneur*, December 2003, p. 142; Mary E. Medland, "Keeping Warm While Looking Cool," http://www.mddailyrecord.com/innovator/2003180s/html, May 21, 2004.
8. Nanci Hollmich, "Dental Appliance Ensures That You Don't Stuff Your Face," *USAToday*, May 19, 2004, p. 1B.
9. http://www.sba.gov/va/success.html, May 21, 2004.
10. Margaret Ann Miille, "A Profitable Accident," http://www.heraldtribune.com, May 20, 2004.
11. Seth Lubove, "Family Affair," *Forbes*, Vol. 170, No. 11 (November 25, 2002), p. 58; http://www.munchinine.com, May 21, 2004.
12. Geoff Williams, "Salvage Operation," *Entrepreneur*, November 2003, p. 32.
13. David J. Collis and Cynthia A. Montgomery, "Competing on Resources: Strategy in the 1990s," *Harvard Business Review*, Vol. 73, No. 14 (July-August 1995), pp. 118–128; Timmons and Spinelli, *op. cit.*
14. For example, see Richard Hall, "A Framework Linking Intangible Resources and Capabilities to Sustainable Competitive Advantage," *Strategic Management Journal*, Vol. 14, No. 8 (November 1993), pp. 607–618; Steven Maijoor and Arjen van Witteloostujin, "An Empirical Test of the Resource-Based Theory: Strategic Regulation in the Dutch Audit Industry," *Strategic Management Journal*, Vol. 17, No. 7 (July 1996), pp. 549–569; Christine Oliver, "Sustainable Competitive Advantage: Combining Institutional and Resource-Based Views," *Strategic Management Journal*, Vol. 18, No. 9 (October 1997), pp. 697–713; Thomas C. Powell and Anne Dent-Micallef, "Information Technology as Competitive Advantage," *Strategic Management Journal*, Vol. 18, No. 5 (May 1997), pp. 375–405.
15. David J. Collis, "How Valuable Are Organizational Capabilities?" *Strategic Management Journal*, Vol. 15 (Winter 1994), pp. 143–152.
16. Ian C. MacMillan, "Controlling Competitive Dynamics by Taking Strategic Initiative," *Academy of Management Executive*, Vol. 2, No. 2 (May 1988), pp. 111–112.
17. William J. Dennis, Jr. (ed.), NFIB National Small Business Poll, "Reinvesting in the Business," Vol. 3, No. 3 (2003).
18. Cora Daniels, "Etrema's Magic Metal," *Fortune*, November 10, 2003, pp. 195–196.
19. Roberta Maynard, "The Heat Is On," *Nation's Business*, Vol. 85, No. 10 (October 1997), pp. 18–19.
20. Elizabeth J. Goodgold, "Dot Your Eyes," *Entrepreneur*, February 2002, http://www.entrepreneur.com/mag/article, May 25, 2004.
21. Tahl Raz, "Not Just a Pretty Typeface," *Inc.*, Vol. 24, No. 13 (December 2002), pp. 120–122.
22. *Ibid.*
23. *Ibid.*, p. 122.
24. Maxine Lans Retsky, "The ABC's of Protecting Your Package," *Marketing News*, October 9, 1995, p. 12.
25. "Something Ventured: An Entrepreneurial Approach to Small Business Management," Episode 115, telecourse produced by INTELECOM (818-796-7300).

Chapter 15

1. Chris J. Ketron, "Paying the Price," *Inc.* "Letters to the Editor" feature, Vol. 22, No. 10 (July 2000), p. 25.
2. For an excellent discussion of price setting, see Charles W. Lamb, Jr., Joseph H. Hair, Jr., and Carl McDaniel, *Principles of Marketing*, 7th ed. (Cincinnati: South-Western, 2004), Chapter 21; Michael V. Marn, Eric V. Roegner, and Craig C. Zawada, "Pricing New Products," http://pf.inc.com/articles/2003/07/pricing.html, July 2003.
3. David Streitfeld, "On the Web, Price Tags Blur," *Washington Post*, September 27, 2000, p. A1.
4. Susan Greco, "The Fraud Bogeyman," http://www.inc.com/articles, February 1, 2001.
5. Jonathan A. Scott, William C. Dunkelberg, and William J. Dennis, Jr., *Credit, Banks and Small Business—The New Century* (Washington, DC: NFIB Research Foundation, 2003).
6. For a concise discussion of the three major reporting agencies, see Sandra Block, "Credit Report Worth a Look," *USAToday*, August 29, 2003, p. 3B.

Chapter 16

1. Barton A. Weitz, Stephen B. Castleberry, and John F. Tanner, Jr., *Selling: Building Partnerships* (New York: McGraw Hill/Irwin, 2004), Chapter 11.
2. Shannon Scully, "Why Image Matters," *My Business*, December-January 2003, p. 30.
3. http://www.flowers-partners.com, April 19, 2004.
4. George Anders, "Internet Advertising, Just Like Its Medium, Is Pushing Business," *Wall Street Journal*, November 30, 1998, p. A1.
5. Shannon Scully, "Go Fetch More Money!" *My Business*, June-July 2003, p. 41.
6. http://spamlaws.com/federal/108s877.html, April 19, 2004.
7. Melissa Campanelli, "Canning Spam," *Entrepreneur*, March 2004, p. 39.

8. http://www.webwasher.com, April 19, 2004.
9. For more details regarding domain name rules, see http://www.register.com/domain-rules.cgi.
10. Robert A. Mamis, "The Name Game," *Inc.: The State of Small Business 2000*, May 16, 2000, p. 144.
11. *Ibid.*
12. Rick Edler, "Razzle-Dazzle Makes Web Sites Great," *Inc.*, Vol. 22, No. 2 (February 2000), p. 60.
13. Ellen Neuborne, "Finding the Right Keyword," *Inc.*, Vol. 25, No. 11, (October 2003), p. 44.
14. Jefferson Graham, "For Google, Many Retailers Eagerly Jump Through Hoops," *USAToday*, February 5, 2004, p. 2A.
15. Jess McCuan, "The Ultimate Sales Incentive," *Inc.*, Vol. 26, No. 5 (May 2004), p. 32.
16. Adapted from Janet Attard, "Trade Show Dos and Don'ts," http://www.businessknowhow.com/tips/tradesho.htm, April 20, 2004.
17. Melany Klinck, "Puzzleman to the Rescue," *MyBusiness*, December-January 2003, pp. 12–13.
18. Don Debelak, "Make Your Mark," *Entrepreneur*, May 2004, p. 146; http://www.atmosklear.com. April 19, 2004.

Chapter 17

1. http://www.heritage.org/research/features/index/chapter PDFs/ExecSummary.pdf, June 4, 2004.
2. Gary A. Knight and S. Tamar Cavusgil, "Innovation, Organizational Capabilities, and the Born-Global Firm," *Journal of International Business Studies*, Vol. 35, No. 2 (March 2004), pp. 124–141; Erkko Autio, Harry J. Sapienza, and James G. Almeida, "Effects of Age at Entry, Knowledge Intensity, and Imitability on International Growth," *Academy of Management Journal*, Vol. 43, No. 5 (October 2000), pp. 909–924.
3. *Ibid.*
4. http://www.moorcrofts.com/Air%20Excellence%20Press%20Release.htm, June 4, 2004; Timothy Appel, "Two Partners Find an Unlikely New Niche Inside Commercial Jets," *Wall Street Journal*, January 15, 1999, p. B1.
5. James F. Foley, *The Global Entrepreneur: Taking Your Business International* (Chicago: Dearborn Financial Publishing, 1999), p. 5.
6. "Don't Laugh at Gilded Butterflies," *Economist*, Vol. 371, No. 8372 (April 22, 2004), pp. 71–73; Oliver Burgel, Andreas Fier, Georg Licht, and Gordon C. Murray, "The Effect of Internationalization on Rate of Growth of High-Tech Start-Ups—Evidence for UK and Germany," in Paul D. Reynolds et al. (eds.), *Frontiers for Entrepreneurship Research*, Proceedings of the 20th Annual Entrepreneurship Research Conference, Babson College, June 2002.
7. Karen E. Klein, "The Bumpy Road to Global Trade," *BusinessWeek*, No. 3702 (October 9, 2000), p. 32; http://www.sunflowerseed.com/html/company_profile.html, June 4, 2004.
8. John Grossman, "Great Leap into China," *Inc.*, Vol. 21, No. 15 (October 15, 1999), p. 29.
9. Raymond Vernon, "International Investment and International Trade in the Product Cycle," *Quarterly Journal of Economics*, Vol. 80, No. 2 (May 1966), pp. 190–207.
10. Gordon B. Baty and Michael S. Blake, *Entrepreneurship: Back to Basics* (Washington, DC: Beard Books, 2003), p. 166.
11. Rodney C. Shrader, Benjamin M. Oviatt, and Patricia Phillips McDougall, "How New Ventures Exploit Trade-Offs Among International Risk Factors: Lessons for the Accelerated Internationalization of the 21st Century," *Academy of Management Journal*, Vol. 43, No. 6 (December 2000), pp. 1227–1247.
12. Scott Doggett, "Your Company," *Los Angeles Times*, October 11, 2000, p. C6.; http://www.mssretail.com, May 7, 2004.
13. Patricia P. McDougall, Rodney C. Shrader, and Benjamin M. Oviatt, "International Entrepreneurs: Risk Takers or Risk Managers?" in Sue Birley and Daniel F. Muzyka (eds.), *Mastering Entrepreneurship* (London: Financial Times/Prentice Hall, 2000), pp. 246–250.
14. Joel Baglole, "Iceland Transforms Itself into a Hotbed of New Industries," *Wall Street Journal*, March 13, 2001, p. A21.
15. David Birch, "Thinking About Tomorrow," *Wall Street Journal*, May 24, 1999, p. R30.
16. The Boston Consulting Group/Knowledge@Wharton, "China and the New Rules for Global Business," June 2–15, 2004, http://knowledge.wharton.upenn.edu/index.cfm?fa=SpecialSection&specialId=19&CFID=64428&CFTOKEN=39263475, June 7, 2004.
17. Birch, *op. cit.*; http://www.kirkhammotorsports.com/inthepress_article12.cfm, July 30, 2004.
18. http://www.dubaiinternetcity.com/html/about_dic.htm, May 7, 2004; Hugh Pope, "Why Are the World's IBMs Putting Down Roots in the Desert? A: Dubai," *Wall Street Journal*, January 23, 2001, p. A18.
19. http://www.dubaiinternetcity.com/html/news_44.htm, May 7, 2004.
20. Automotive Parts for Manufacturers, http://www.mac.doc.gov/ceebic/countryr/Hungary/RESEARCH/Automotive%20Parts.pdf, May 7, 2004; Hungarian Country Commercial Guide: The Automotive Market, http://www.factbook.net/countryreports/hu/hu_automotivemkt.htm, May 7, 2004; John B. Cullen, *Multinational Management: A Strategic Approach* (Cincinnati: South-Western, 1999), p. 204.
21. Shrader, Oviatt, and McDougall, *op. cit.*
22. SBA Office of Advocacy, Economic Statistics and Research, "Small Business Frequently Asked Questions," http://app1.sba.gov/faqs/faqindex.cfm?areaID=24, June 7, 2004.
23. James A. Wolff and Timothy L. Pett, "Internationalization of Small Firms: An Examination of Export Competitive Patterns, Firm Size, and Export Performance," *Journal of Small Business Management*, Vol. 38, No. 2 (April 2000), p. 35.
24. Klein, *op. cit.*
25. James Flanigan, "Globalization in a Nutshell," *Los Angeles Times*, May 31, 2000, p. C1.
26. DIRECT, "DIRECT Listline," March 1, 2004, p. 3; http://www.mysimon.com, May 7, 2004; Robert Johnson, "Toy Web Site Collects Fans, Profits with Action Figures," *Wall Street Journal*, June 27, 2000, p. B2.
27. Melanie Warner, "Going Pro on eBay," *Fortune*, Vol. 141, No. 7 (April 3, 2000), pp. 250–252.
28. http://www.designerhandbagsboutique.com/content_about.htm, May 7, 2004; Maria Atanasov, "Taking Her Business on the Road," *Fortune*, Vol. 137, No. 7 (April 13, 1998), pp. 159–160.
29. Michael A. Hitt and R. Duane Ireland, "The Intersection of Entrepreneurship and Strategic Management Research," in D. L. Sexton and H. Landstrom (eds.), *The Blackwell Handbook of Entrepreneurship* (Oxford, UK: Blackwell Publishers, 2000), pp. 45–63.
30. http://www.mssretain.com/CbBackground.html, May 7, 2004; Doggett, *op. cit.*
31. U.S. Small Business Administration, "Breaking into the Trade Game: A Small Business Guide to Exporting,"

http://www.sba.gov/OIT/info/Guide-To-Exporting/all.html, June 7, 2004.

32. http://www.bluenote.net/about/index.shtml, September 13, 2004; Leslie Gourse, "Speed Kills: For Some Chains, Quality, Not Quantity, Is the Better Way," *Success*, Vol. 44, No. 8 (October 1997), pp. 98–101.
33. http://www.mooneyfarms.com/ about_us.htm, June 7, 2004.
34. *Ibid.*
35. U.S. Small Business Administration, *op cit.*, July 13, 2004.

Chapter 18

1. Julie H. Case, "The Art of Leadership," *U.W. Business* (published by the University of Washington), Spring 2003 p. 17.
2. Amar V. Bhide, *The Origin and Evolution of New Businesses* (New York: Oxford University Press, 2000), Chapter 4.
3. Jim Collins, *Good to Great* (New York: HarperCollins, 2001), p. 27.
4. Daniel Goleman, "Leadership That Gets Results," *Harvard Business Review*, Vol. 78, No. 2 (March-April 2000), pp. 78–90.
5. "Special Report: Rethinking Work," *BusinessWeek*, October 17, 1994, p. 77.
6. Jeffrey Pfeffer and John F. Veiga, "Putting People First for Organizational Success," *Academy of Management Executive*, Vol. 13, No. 2 (May 1999), p. 40.
7. William W. Horne, "Machine Maker Unhinged by Sales Emphasis," *Inc.*, Vol. 21, No. 3 (March 1999), p. 25.
8. Curtis Wozniak, "Pulling a Mandl," *Forbes*, Vol. 158, No. 10 (October 21, 1996), pp. 18–20.
9. The best-known model is found in Neil C. Churchill and Virginia L. Lewis, "The Five Stages of Small Business Growth," *Harvard Business Review*, Vol. 83, No. 3 (May-June 1983), pp. 30–50. Another study was conducted by Kathleen M. Watson and Gerhard R. Plaschka, "Entrepreneurial Firms: An Examination of Organizational Structure and Management Roles Across Life Cycle Stages," paper presented at the United States Association for Small Business and Entrepreneurship Annual Conference, Baltimore, Maryland, October 13–16, 1993.
10. Demetria Lucas, "Twin Tailors," *Black Enterprise*, Vol. 33, No. 9 (April 2003), p. 47.
11. Bhide, *op. cit.*, p. 315.
12. Personal communication from a student of one of the authors.
13. Stephen R. Covey, *The 7 Habits of Highly Effective People* (New York: Simon & Schuster, 1990), pp. 173–179.
14. Rodes Fishburne, "More Survival Advice: Communicate," *Forbes ASAP*, April 3, 2000, p. 120.
15. Jeff Bailey, "Enterprise: Peer Groups Provide Expertise Firms Lack—Organizations Like YEO Bring Owners Together to Talk and Swap Advice," *Wall Street Journal*, December 17, 2002, p. B7.
16. Grace Ertel, "An Incubator for Green Start-Ups," *In Business*, Vol. 18, No. 3 (May-June 1996), pp. 21–22.
17. Morten T. Hansen, Henry W. Chesbrough, Nitin Nohria, and Donald N. Sull, "Networked Incubators: Hothouses of the New Economy," *Harvard Business Review*, Vol. 78, No. 5 (September-October 2000), pp. 74–82.
18. http://www.score.org/success_bakers_peel.html, September 22, 2003.
19. Joanne Gordon, "Calling Dr. Demetria," *Forbes*, Vol. 165, No. 14 (June 12, 2000), p. 212.
20. *Ibid.*
21. Bengt Johannisson and Rein Peterson, "The Personal Networks of Entrepreneurs," paper presented at the Third Canadian Conference, International Council for Small Business, Toronto, Canada, May 23–25, 1984.
22. Howard Scott, "Getting Help from Your Accountant," *IB Magazine*, Vol. 3, No. 3 (May-June 1992), p. 38.

Chapter 19

1. Jim Collins, *Good to Great* (New York: HarperCollins, 2001), p. 41.
2. Rifka Rosewein, "Help Still Wanted," *Inc.*, Vol. 23, No. 5 (April 2001), p. 54.
3. Robert L. Mathis and John H. Jackson, *Human Resource Management* (Cincinnati: South-Western College Publishing, 2003), p. 147.
4. Rochelle Sharpe and Felicia Morton, "Summer Help Wanted: Foreigners Please Apply," *BusinessWeek*, No. 3691 (July 24, 2000), p. 32.
5. "Do I Know You?" *Inc. 500*, 1999, p. 211.
6. Gaylen N. Chandler and Glenn M. McEvoy, "Human Resource Management, TQM, and Firm Performance in Small and Medium-Size Enterprises," *Entrepreneurship Theory and Practice*, Vol. 25, No. 1 (Fall 2000), pp. 43–57.
7. Emily Barker, "Hi-Test Education," *Inc.*, Vol. 23, No. 10 (July 2001), pp. 81–82.
8. Shannon Scully and Lisa Waddle, "Back to School," *My Business*, September-October 2001, pp. 28–29; http://www.bookpros.com.
9. George Bohlander and Scott Snell, *Managing Human Resources*, 13th ed. (Cincinnati: South-Western College Publishing, 2004), pp. 464–465.
10. Get more information about ESOPs on the Web site of the National Center for Employee Ownership at http://www.nceo.org.
11. For more detailed information on laws protecting employees, see Bohlander and Snell, *op. cit.*
12. Robert K. Robinson, William T. Jackson, Geralyn McClure Franklin, and Diana Hensley, "U.S. Sexual Harassment Law: Implications for Small Businesses," *Journal of Small Business Management*, Vol. 36, No. 2 (April 1998), p. 7.

Chapter 20

1. Adapted from Leonard L. Berry, A. Parasuraman, and Valarie A. Zeithaml, "Improving Service Quality in America: Lessons Learned," *Academy of Management Executive*, Vol. 8, No. 2 (May 1994), p. 36.
2. Anthony W. Ulwick, "Turn Customer Input into Innovation," *Harvard Business Review*, Vol. 8, No. 1 (January 2002), pp. 91–97.
3. Diane Brady, "Why Service Stinks," *BusinessWeek*, October 23, 2000, p. 120.
4. S. Douglas Pugh, Joerg Dietz, Jack W. Wiley, and Scott M. Brooks, "Driving Service Effectiveness Through Employee-Customer Linkages," *Academy of Management Executive*, Vol. 16, No. 4 (November 2002) pp. 73–84.
5. For fuller discussion of this issue, see Mary Jo Bitner, Amy L. Ostrom, and Matthew L. Meuter, "Implementing Successful Self-Service Technologies," *Academy of Management Executive*, Vol. 16, No. 4 (November 2002), pp. 96–109.
6. Michael Hammer, "Forward to Basics," *Fast Company*, November 2002, p. 38.

7. Michael Hammer and James Champy, *Reengineering the Corporation* (New York: HarperCollins, 1994), p. 32.
8. Anne Stuart, "Going Mobile," *Inc.*, Vol. 24, No. 13 (December 2002), pp. 124–125.
9. Jay Greene, "Small Biz: Microsoft's Next Big Thing," *BusinessWeek*, April 21, 2003, pp. 72–73.
10. Jeff Bailey, "Entrepreneurs Share Their Tips to Boost a Firm's Productivity," *Wall Street Journal*, July 9, 2002, p. B-4.
11. Jeff Bailey, "Wary of Overcapacity, Small Manufacturers Are Slow to Spend," *Wall Street Journal*, September 11, 2001, p. B-2.
12. "Big Help for the Little Guy," *Fortune Technology Guide*, Vol. 142, No. 12 (Winter 2001), p. 208.
13. "E-I-E-I-E-Farming," *BusinessWeek*, May 1, 2000, p. 202.
14. Jeff Bailey, "Small Firms Enjoy the Courtship of Big Suppliers," *Wall Street Journal*, June 24, 2003, p. B-9.
15. Jeff Bailey, "Big Companies Can Provide Much-Needed Help," *Wall Street Journal*, November 4, 2003, p. B-9.
16. Roberta Maynard, "Striking the Right Match," *Nation's Business*, Vol. 84, No. 5 (May 1996), p. 19.
17. For formulas and calculations related to determining the economic order quantity, see an operations management textbook such as James B. Dilworth, *Operations Management: Providing Value in Goods and Services*, 3rd ed. (Orlando, FL: Dryden Press, 2000), pp. 416–420.

Chapter 21

1. Translated by Arthur W. H. Adkins from the Greek text of Solon's poem "Prosperity, Justice and the Hazards of Life," in M. L. West (ed.), *Iambi et Elegi Gracci ante Alexandrum Canttati*, Vol. 2 (Oxford: Clarendon Press, 1972).
2. Peter Bernstein, *Against the Gods, the Remarkable Story of Risk* (New York: John Wiley & Sons, 1998), p. 1.
3. Emmett J. Vaughan and Theresa M. Vaughan, *Fundamentals of Risk and Insurance*, 9th ed. (New York: John Wiley & Sons, 2003), p. 5.
4. *Ibid.*
5. Christopher Windham, "Self-Insurance Plans Gain as Premiums Jump," *Wall Street Journal*, December 30, 2003, p. B2.
6. Daniel Tynan, "In Case of Emergency," *Entrepreneur*, April 2003, p. 60.
7. Lara Chamberlain and William C. Dunkelberg, NFIB Small Business Economic Trends, National Federation of Independent Businesses, http://www.nfib.com/object/413117U.html.
8. Mark Hendricks, "Risky Business," *Entrepreneur*, June 2003, p. 73.
9. William J. Dennis, Jr., "Business Insurance," NFIB National Small Business Poll, Vol. 2, No. 7 (2002), p. 2.
10. Insurance Information Institute, http://www.iii.org, June 2004; Kaiser Family Foundation, http://www.kff.org, June 2004.
11. John S. de Mott, "Think Like a Risk Manager," *Nation's Business*, Vol. 83, No. 6 (June 1995), pp. 30–31.
12. Jacquelyn Lynn, "It's a Gamble," *Entrepreneur*, January 2003, p. 67.
13. Abby Livingston, "Insuring Your Earning Power," *Nation's Business*, Vol. 85, No. 4 (April 1997), pp. 75–76.

Chapter 22

1. Jill Andresky Fraser, "The Art of Cash Management," *Inc.*, Vol. 20, No. 14 (October, 1998), p. 124.
2. Accruals are not considered in terms of managing working capital. Accrued expenses, although shown as a short-term liability, primarily result from the accountant's effort to match revenues and expenses. There is little that can be done to "manage" accruals.
3. Keith Lowe, "Managing Your Cash Flow," http://www.entrepreneur.com/article/0,4621,295043,00.html, December 3, 2001.
4. S. Mayer, "How to Better Manage Your Cash Flow," http://www.entrepreneur.com/article/0,4621,312291,00.html, December 11, 2003.
5. C. J. Prince, "Catch Your Cash," *Entrepreneur*, June 2004, p. 58.
6. William J. Dennis, Jr. (ed.), *The National Small Business Poll: Reinvesting in the Business*, Vol. 3, No. 3 (2003), NFIB Research Foundation, p. 13.
7. Arthur J. Keown, John D. Martin, J. William Petty, and David F. Scott, Jr. *Foundations of Finance: The Logic and Practice of Financial Management*, 4th ed. (Englewood Cliffs, NJ: Prentice-Hall, 2003).
8. William J. Dennis, Jr., *op. cit.*, p. 11.

Chapter 23

1. See, for example, Walter T. Harrison, Charles T. Horngren, and Tom Harrison, *Financial Accounting*, 4th ed. (Englewood Cliffs, NJ: Prentice-Hall, 2004).
2. Jack D. Baker and John A. Marts, "Internal Control for Protection and Profits," *Small Business Forum*, Vol. 8, No. 2 (Fall 1990), p. 29.
3. For example, Dun & Bradstreet publishes annually a set of 14 key financial ratios for 125 types of business. Robert Morris Associates (RMA) publishes a set of 16 key ratios for over 350 types of businesses. In both cases, the ratios are classified by industry and by firm size to provide a basis for more meaningful comparisons.
4. Instead of computing the accounts receivable turnover, we could calculate the average collection period. Simply stated, if Petri & Associates turns its accounts receivable over 10.63 times in a year, then, on average, the firm collects its receivables every 34.3 days, determined by dividing 365 days by 10.63 (accounts receivable turnover).
5. When we computed Petri's return on assets earlier, we found it to be 10.87 percent. Now it is 10.82 percent. The difference is the result of rounding error.

Appendix B

1. Randall Lane, "What Is Your Company Worth Now? *Inc.*, July 2003, pp. 70–71.
2. *Ibid.*, pp. 75, 77.
3. Other ratios, besides value to earnings, that are used in valuing a firm include value to sales, value to equity book value, and value to cash flows, just to mention a few.
4. http://www.buysellbiz.com/Mid%20west%20fsbos.htm, February 4, 2004.
5. Lane, *op. cit.*, p. 76.
6. Depreciation expense was added back to operating income, since it is a non-cash expense. The resulting number is equal to the firm's cash flow from operations.
7. The numbers in this example have been changed, but they still represent the valuation process.
8. As a starting point to learn more about cash flow–based valuation, go to the Web site for this text at http://longenecker.swlearning.com and click on "Valuing the Firm."

A

ABC method a system of classifying items in inventory by relative value

acceptance sampling the use of a random, representative portion to determine the acceptability of an entire lot

accounting return on investment technique a capital budgeting technique that evaluates a capital expenditure based on the average annual after-tax profits relative to the average book value of an investment

accounts payable (trade credit) financing provided by a supplier of inventory to a given company

accounts receivable the amount of credit extended to customers that is currently outstanding

accounts receivable turnover the number of times accounts receivable "roll over" during a year

accrual-basis accounting a method of accounting that matches revenues when they are earned against the expenses associated with those revenues, no matter when they are paid

accrued expenses short-term liabilities that have been incurred but not paid

accumulated depreciation total depreciation expense taken over the asset's life

actual cash value (ACV) an insurance term that refers to the depreciated value of a property

adjusted income after-tax cash flow

advertising the impersonal presentation of a business idea through mass media

advisory council a group that functions like a board of directors but acts only in an advisory capacity

agency power the ability of any one partner to legally bind the other partners

agents/brokers intermediaries that do not take title to the goods they distribute

aging schedule a categorization of accounts receivable based on the length of time they have been outstanding

all-risk approach an approach to defining the perils covered in an insurance policy by stating that all direct damages to property are covered except those caused by perils specifically excluded

area developers individuals or firms that obtain the legal right to open several franchised outlets in a given area

artisan entrepreneur a person with primarily technical skills and little business knowledge who starts a business

asset-based loan a line of credit secured by working-capital assets

asset-based valuation determination of the value of a business by estimating the value of its assets

attitude an enduring opinion based on knowledge, feeling, and behavioral tendency

attractive small firm a small firm that provides substantial profits to its owner

attribute inspection the determination of product acceptability based on whether it will or will not work

auction sites Web-based businesses offering participants the ability to list products for bidding

average pricing an approach in which total cost for a given period is divided by quantity sold in that period in order to set a price

B

bad-debt ratio the ratio of bad debts to credit sales

bait advertising an insincere offer to sell a product or service at a very low price, used to lure customers in so that they can be switched later to a more expensive product or service

balance sheet a financial report showing a firm's assets, liabilities, and ownership equity at a specific point in time

balloon payment a very large payment that the borrower is required to make at a specified point about halfway through the term over which the payments were calculated, repaying the rest of the loan in full

banner ads advertisements that appear across a Web page, most often as moving rectangular strips

batch manufacturing a type of manufacturing operation that is intermediate (between job shops and repetitive manufacturing) in volume and variety of products

benchmarking the process of studying the products, services, and practices of other firms and using the insights gained to improve quality internally

benefit variables specific characteristics that distinguish market segments according to the benefits sought by customers

bill of lading a document indicating that a product has been shipped and the title to that product has been transferred

board of directors the governing body of a corporation, elected by the stockholders

bootstrapping minimizing a firm's investments

born-global firms small companies launched with cross-border business activities in mind

brand a verbal and/or symbolic means of identifying a product

brand image people's overall perception of a brand

brand mark a brand that cannot be spoken

brand name a brand that can be spoken

break-even point sales volume at which total sales revenue equals total costs

breakdown process (chain-ratio method) a forecasting method that begins with a larger-scope variable and works down to the sales forecast

brick-and-mortar store the traditional physical store from which businesses have historically operated

budget a document that expresses future plans in monetary terms

build-up LBO a leveraged buyout involving the purchase of a group of similar companies with the intent of making the firms into one larger company

build-up process a forecasting method in which all potential buyers in the various submarkets are identified and then the estimated demand is added up

business angels private individuals who invest in others' entrepreneurial ventures

business format franchising a franchise arrangement whereby the franchisee obtains an entire marketing system geared to entrepreneurs

business incubator a facility that provides shared space, services, and management assistance to new businesses

business interruption coverage coverage that reimburses a business for the loss of anticipated income plus continuing expenses that cannot be met because of the negative impact of a direct loss on business revenues

business model a group of shared characteristics, behaviors, and goals that a firm follows in a particular business situation

business owner's policy (BOP) a business version of a homeowner's policy, designed to meet the property and liability insurance needs of small business owners

business plan a document that sets out the basic idea underlying a business and related startup considerations

business-to-business (B2B) model a business model based on selling to business customers electronically

business-to-consumer (B2C) model a business model based on selling to final customers electronically

bust-up LBO a leveraged buyout involving the purchase of a company with the intent of selling off its assets

C

C corporation an ordinary corporation, taxed by the federal government as a separate legal entity

capabilities the integration of various organizational resources that are deployed together to the firm's advantage

capital budgeting analysis an analytical method that helps managers make decisions about long-term investments

capital gains and losses gains and losses incurred from sales of property that are not a part of the firm's regular business operations

cash-basis accounting a method of accounting that reports transactions only when cash is received or a payment is made

cash budget a planning document strictly concerned with the receipt and payment of dollars

cash conversion period the time required to convert paid-for inventories and accounts receivable into cash

cash flow–based valuation determination of the value of a business by estimating the amount and timing of its future cash flows

cash flow statement a financial report showing a firm's sources and uses of cash

cash flows from operations net cash flows generated from operating a business, calculated by adding back to operating income depreciation, deducting income taxes, and factoring in any changes in net working capital

Certified Development Company (CDC) 504 Loan Program SBA loan program that provides long-term financing for small businesses to acquire real estate or machinery and equipment

chain of command the official, vertical channel of communication in an organization

channel of distribution the system of relationships established to guide the movement of a product

chattel mortgage a loan for which items of inventory or other moveable property serve as collateral

Civil Rights Act legislation prohibiting discrimination based on race, color, religion, sex, or national origin

code of ethics official standards of employee behavior formulated by a firm

cognitive dissonance the anxiety that occurs when a customer has second thoughts immediately following a purchase

coinsurance provision the most common version of the insurance to value feature, requiring that property be insured for at least 80 percent of its value or a penalty will be applied to any covered loss

commercial general liability (CGL) coverage coverage providing payment for bodily injury and property damage for which the insured business is liable

common carriers transportation intermediaries available for hire to the general public

community-based financial institution a lender that uses funds from federal, state, and private sources to provide financing to small businesses in low-income communities

compensatory damages economic or noneconomic damages intended to make the claimant whole, by indemnifying the claimant for any injuries or damage arising from the negligent action

competitive advantage a benefit that exists when a firm has a product or service that is seen by its target market as better than those of competitors

comprehensive plan a full business plan that provides an in-depth analysis of the critical factors that will determine a firm's success or failure, along with all the underlying assumptions

consumer credit financing granted by retailers to individuals who purchase for personal or family use

content/information-based model a business model in which the Web site provides information but not the ability to buy or sell products and services

continuous quality improvement a constant and dedicated effort to improve quality

contract carriers transportation intermediaries that contract with individual shippers

control chart a graphic illustration of the limits used in statistical process control

copyright the exclusive right of a creator to reproduce, publish, perform, display, or sell his or her own works

core competencies those resources and capabilities that provide a firm with a competitive advantage over its rivals

corporate charter a document that establishes a corporation's existence

corporation a business organization that exists as a legal entity and provides limited liability to its owners

corrective maintenance repairs necessary to restore equipment or a facility to good condition

cost-based strategy a plan of action that requires a firm to be the lowest-cost producer within its market

cost of goods sold the cost of producing or acquiring goods or services to be sold by a firm

counterfeit activity the unauthorized use of intellectual property

credit an agreement between a buyer and a seller that provides for delayed payment for a product or service

credit bureaus privately owned organizations that summarize a number of firms' credit experiences with particular individuals

cross-border acquisition the purchase by a business in one country of a company located in another country

cultural configuration the total culture of a family firm, consisting of the firm's business, family, and governance patterns

culture behavioral patterns and values that characterize a group of consumers in a target market

current assets (gross working capital) assets that can be converted into cash within a company's operating cycle

current debt (short-term liabilities) borrowed money that must be repaid within 12 months

current ratio a measure of a company's relative liquidity, determined by dividing current assets by current liabilities

customer profile a description of potential customers in a target market

customer relationship management (CRM) a marketing strategy of maximizing shareholder value through winning, growing, and keeping the right customers

cycle counting a system of counting different segments of the physical inventory at different times during the year

D

debt business financing provided by creditors

debt ratio a measure of the fraction of a firm's assets that are financed by debt, determined by dividing total debt by total assets

delegation of authority granting to subordinates the right to act or make decisions

demographic variables specific characteristics that describe customers and their purchasing power

depreciable assets assets whose value declines, or depreciates, over time

depreciation expense costs related to a fixed asset, such as a building or equipment, allocated over its useful life

design patent registered protection for the appearance of a product and its inseparable parts

differentiation-based strategy a plan of action designed to provide a product or service with unique attributes that are valued by consumers

direct channel a distribution system without intermediaries

direct forecasting a forecasting method in which sales is the estimating variable

direct loss a loss in which physical damage to property reduces its value to the property owner

disability insurance coverage that provides benefits upon the disability of a firm's partner or other key employee

disclosure document a detailed statement provided to a prospective franchisee, containing such information as the franchisor's finances, experience, size, and involvement in litigation

discounted cash flow (DCF) technique a capital budgeting technique that compares the present value of future cash flows with the cost of the initial investment

distribution physically moving products and establishing intermediary relationships to support such movement

double-entry system a self-balancing accounting system that requires that each transaction be recorded twice

dual distribution a distribution system that involves more than one channel

due diligence the exercise of reasonable care in the evaluation of a business opportunity

dynamic pricing strategy charging more than the standard price when the customer's profile suggests that the higher price will be accepted

E

e-commerce the paperless exchange of business information via the Internet

e-mail promotion advertising delivered by means of electronic mail

earnings before taxes earnings or profits after operating expenses and interest expenses but before taxes

earnings multiple a ratio determined by dividing a firm's value by its annual earnings; also called *value-to-earnings ratio*

economic damages compensatory damages that relate to economic loss, such as medical expense, loss of income, or the cost of property replacement/restoration

economic order quantity (EOQ) the quantity to purchase in order to minimize total inventory costs

economic risk the probability that a government will mismanage its economy and thereby change the business environment in ways that hinder the performance of firms operating there

economies of scale efficiencies that result from expansion of production

elastic demand demand that changes significantly when there is a change in the price of the product

elasticity of demand the degree to which a change in price affects the quantity demanded

Electronic Customer Relationship Marketing (eCRM) an electronically based system that emphasizes customer relationships

employee leasing the "renting" of personnel from an organization that handles paperwork and administers benefits for those employees

employee stock ownership plans (ESOPs) plans through which a firm is sold either in part or in total to its employees

empowerment giving employees authority to make decisions or take actions on their own

enterprise zones state-designated areas that are established to bring jobs to economically deprived regions through regulatory and tax incentives

entrepreneur a person who starts and/or operates a business

entrepreneurial legacy material assets and intangible qualities passed on to both heirs and society

entrepreneurial opportunity a value-creating innovation with market potential

entrepreneurial team two or more people who work together as entrepreneurs on one endeavor

environmentalism the effort to protect and preserve the environment

equipment loan an installment loan from a seller of machinery used by a business

equity value (owner's value) the value of the firm less the debt owed by the firm

ethical imperialism the belief that the ethical standards of one's own country can be applied universally

ethical issues questions of right and wrong

ethical relativism the belief that ethical standards are subject to local interpretation

European Union (EU) an organization whose purpose is to facilitate free trade among member countries in Europe

evaluative criteria the features or characteristics of a product or service that customers use to compare brands

evoked set a group of brands that a consumer is both aware of and willing to consider as a solution to a purchase problem

exchange rate the value of one country's currency relative to that of another country

executive summary a section of the business plan that conveys a clear and concise overall picture of the proposed venture

experience curve efficiencies per-unit savings gained from the repeated production of the same good

exporting selling products produced in the home country to customers in another country

external equity capital that comes from the owners' investment in a firm

external locus of control a belief that one's life is controlled more by luck or fate than by one's own efforts

F

factoring obtaining cash by selling accounts receivable to another firm

Fair Labor Standards Act (FLSA) federal law that establishes a minimum wage and provides for overtime pay

Family and Medical Leave Act legislation that assures employees of unpaid leave for childbirth or other family needs

family business a company that two or more members of the same family own or operate together or in succession

family business constitution a statement of principles intended to guide a family firm through times of crisis and change

family council an organized group of family members who gather periodically to discuss family-related business issues

family retreat a gathering of family members, usually at a remote location, to discuss family business matters

financial leverage the use of debt in financing a firm's assets

financial plan a section of the business plan that provides an account of the new firm's financial needs and sources of financing and a projection of its revenues, costs, and profits

financial ratios restatements of selected income statement and balance sheet data in relative terms

financial statements (accounting statements) reports of a firm's financial performance and resources, including an income statement, a balance sheet, and a cash flow statement

financing costs the amount of interest owed to lenders on borrowed money

firm value (enterprise value) the value of the entire business, regardless of how it is financed

fixed asset turnover a measure of the relationship of sales to fixed assets

fixed assets relatively permanent assets intended for use in the business, such as plant and equipment

focus strategy a plan of action that isolates an enterprise from competitors and other market forces by targeting a restricted market segment

follow-the-leader pricing strategy using a particular competitor as a model in setting prices

foreign licensing allowing a company in another country to purchase the rights to manufacture and sell a company's products in international markets

formal venture capitalist individuals who form limited partnerships for the purpose of raising venture capital from large institutional investors

founder an entrepreneur who brings a new firm into existence

franchise the privileges conveyed in a franchise contract

franchise contract the legal agreement between franchisor and franchisee

franchisee an entrepreneur whose power is limited by a contractual relationship with a franchising organization

franchising a marketing system involving a legal agreement, whereby the franchisee conducts business according to terms specified by the franchisor

franchisor the party in a franchise contract that specifies the methods to be followed and the terms to be met by the other party

fringe benefits supplements to compensation, designed to be attractive and beneficial to employees

G

general environment the broad environment, encompassing factors that influence most businesses in a society

general partner a partner in a limited partnership who has unlimited personal liability

general-purpose equipment machines that serve many functions in the production process

globalization the expansion of international business, encouraged by converging market preferences, falling trade barriers, and the integration of national economies

greenfield venture a wholly owned subsidiary formed from scratch in another country

gross fixed assets original cost of depreciable assets before any depreciation expense has been taken

gross profit sales less the cost of goods sold

H

harvesting (exiting) the process used by entrepreneurs and investors to reap the value of a business when they get out of it

headhunter a search firm that locates qualified candidates for executive positions

high-potential venture (gazelle) a small firm that has great prospects for growth

home-based business a business that maintains its primary facility in the residence of its owner

I

importing selling goods produced in another country to buyers in the home country

income statement (profit and loss statement) a financial report showing the profit or loss from a firm's operations over a given period of time

indirect channel a distribution system with one or more intermediaries

indirect forecasting a forecasting method in which variables related to sales are used to project future sales

indirect loss a loss arising from inability to carry on normal operations due to a direct loss to property

industry environment the combined forces that directly impact a given firm and its competitors

inelastic demand demand that does not change significantly when there is a change in the price of the product

informal venture capital funds provided by wealthy private individuals (business angels) to high-risk ventures

initial public offering (IPO) the first sale of shares of a company's stock to the public

inspection the examination of a product to determine whether it meets quality standards

inspection standard a specification of a desired quality level and allowable tolerances

installment account a line of credit that requires a down payment, with the balance paid over a specified period of time

institutional advertising the presentation of information about a particular firm, designed to enhance the firm's image

insurance to value a common provision in property insurance policies that requires the insured to carry a minimum policy limit relative to the actual value of the property

intangible resources those organizational resources that are invisible and difficult to quantify

integrity an uncompromising adherence to doing what is right and proper

intellectual property original intellectual creations, including inventions, literary creations, and works of art, that are protected by patents or copyrights

internal control a system of checks and balances that safeguards assets and enhances the accuracy and reliability of financial statements

internal equity capital that comes from retaining profits within a firm

internal locus of control a belief that one's success depends on one's own efforts

internal rate of return (IRR) the rate of return a firm expects to earn on a project

international franchising selling a standard package of products, systems, and management services to a company in another country

international outsourcing (offshoring) a strategy that involves accessing foreign labor through contracts with independent providers

international strategic alliance a combination of efforts and/or assets of companies in different countries for the sake of pooling resources and sharing the risks of an enterprise

inventory a firm's raw materials and products held in anticipation of eventual sale

inventory turnover the number of times inventories "roll over" during a year

ISO 9000 the standards governing international certification of a firm's quality management procedures

J

Job Instruction Training a systematic step-by-step method for on-the-job training of nonmanagerial employees

job shops a type of manufacturing operation in which short production runs are used to produce small quantities of unique items

job specification a list of skills and abilities needed to perform a specific job

just-in-time inventory system a method of reducing inventory levels to an absolute minimum

K

key-person insurance coverage that provides benefits upon the death of a firm's key personnel

L

laws of motion economy guidelines for increasing the efficiency of human movement and tool design

learning effects insights, gained from experience, that lead to improved work performance

legal entity a business organization that is recognized by the law as having a separate legal existence

letter of credit an agreement issued by a bank to honor a draft or other demand for payment when specified conditions are met

leveraged buyout (LBO) a purchase heavily financed with debt, where the future cash flow of the target company is expected to be sufficient to meet debt repayments

LIBOR (London InterBank Offered Rate) the interest rate charged by London banks on loans to other London banks

licensee the company buying licensing rights

licensor the company selling licensing rights

lifestyle business a microbusiness that permits the owner to follow a desired pattern of living

limited liability the restriction of an owner's legal financial responsibilities to the amount invested in the business

limited liability company a corporation in which stockholders have limited liability but pay personal income taxes on business profits

limited partner a partner in a limited partnership who is not active in its management and has limited personal liability

limited partnership a partnership with at least one general partner and one or more limited partners

line-and-staff organization an organizational structure that includes staff specialists who assist management

line of credit an informal agreement between a borrower and a bank as to the maximum amount of funds the bank will provide at any one time

line organization a simple organizational structure in which each person reports to one supervisor

linkage a type of advertising agreement in which one firm pays another to include a click-on link on its site

liquidation value method determination of the value of a business by estimating the money that would be available if the firm were to liquidate its assets

liquidity the degree to which a firm has working capital available to meet maturing debt obligations

loan covenants bank-imposed restrictions on a borrower that enhance the chances of timely repayment

lock box a post office box for receiving remittances from customers

long-range plan (strategic plan) a firm's overall plan for the future

long-term debt loans from banks or other sources with repayment terms of more than 12 months

loss avoidance avoiding loss by choosing not to engage in hazardous activities

loss prevention stopping loss from happening

loss reduction lessening the frequency, severity, or unpredictability of losses

M

make-or-buy decision a firm's choice between producing and purchasing component parts for its products

management buyout (MBO) a leveraged buyout in which the firm's top managers become significant shareholders in the acquired firm

management plan a section of the business plan that describes a new firm's organizational structure and the backgrounds of its key players

management team managers and other key persons who give a company its general direction

market a group of customers or potential customers who have purchasing power and unsatisfied needs

market analysis the process of locating and describing potential customers

market risk the uncertainty associated with an investment decision

market segmentation the division of a market into several smaller groups with similar needs

marketing mix the combination of product, pricing, promotion, and distribution activities

marketing plan a section of the business plan that describes the user benefits of the product or service and the type of market that exists

marketing research the gathering, processing, reporting, and interpreting of market information

markup pricing applying a percentage to a product's cost to obtain its selling price

master licensee an independent firm or individual acting as a sales agent with the responsibility for finding new franchisees within a specified territory

matchmakers specialized brokers that bring together buyers and sellers of businesses

medical payments coverage coverage providing payment for injuries sustained by customers and the general public, with no fault required on the part of the insured

mentoring guiding and supporting the work and development of a new or less-experienced organization member

merchant middlemen intermediaries that take title to the goods they distribute

microbusiness a small firm that provides minimal profits to its owner

mission statement a concise written description of a firm's philosophy

modified book value method determination of the value of a business by adjusting book value to reflect obvious differences between the historical cost and the current market value of the assets

mortgage a long-term loan from a creditor for which real estate is pledged as collateral

motivations forces that organize and give direction to the tension caused by unsatisfied needs

multiple-unit ownership holding by a single franchisee of more than one franchise from the same company

multisegment strategy a strategy that recognizes different preferences of individual market segments and develops a unique marketing mix for each

N

named-peril approach an approach to defining the perils covered in an insurance policy by identifying the specific perils covered

needs the starting point for all behavior

negotiation a two-way communication process used to resolve differences in needs, goals, or ideas

net fixed assets gross fixed assets less accumulated depreciation

net income available to owners (net income) income that may be distributed to the owners or reinvested in the company

net operating working capital the sum of a firm's current assets (cash, accounts receivable, and inventories) less accounts payable and accruals

net present value (NPV) the present value of expected future cash flows less the initial investment outlay

net working capital money invested in current assets other than cash less accounts payable and accruals

networking the process of developing and engaging in mutually beneficial relationships

noneconomic damages compensatory damages for such losses as pain and suffering, mental anguish, and loss of consortium

normalized earnings earnings that have been adjusted for unusual items, such as fire damage, and all relevant expenses, such as a fair salary for the owner's time

North American Free Trade Agreement (NAFTA) an agreement that encourages free trade between the United States, Canada, and Mexico by removing trade restrictions

O

Occupational Safety and Health Act legislation that regulates the safety of workplaces and work practices

open charge account a line of credit that allows the customer to obtain a product at the time of purchase, with payment due when billed

operating expenses costs related to marketing and selling a firm's product or service, general and administrative expenses, and depreciation

operating income earnings or profits after operating expenses but before interest and taxes are paid

operating plan a section of the business plan that offers information on how a product will be produced or a service provided, including descriptions of the new firm's facilities, labor, raw materials, and processing requirements

operating profit margin the ratio of operating profits to sales, showing how well a firm manages its income statement

operations management planning and controlling the process of converting inputs to outputs

operations process the activities that create value for customers through production of a firm's goods and services

opinion leader a group leader who plays a key communications role

opportunistic entrepreneur a person with both sophisticated managerial skills and technical knowledge who starts a business

opportunity cost of funds the rate of return that could be earned on another investment of similar risk

ordinary income income earned in the ordinary course of business, including any salary

organizational culture the behaviors, beliefs, and values that characterize a particular firm

other assets assets other than current assets and fixed assets, such as patents, copyrights, and goodwill

outsourcing purchasing products or services that are outside the firm's area of competitive advantage

ownership equity owners' investments in a company, plus profits retained in the firm

P

partnership a legal entity formed by two or more co-owners to carry on a business for profit

partnership agreement a document that states explicitly the rights and duties of partners

patent the registered, exclusive right of an inventor to make, use, or sell an invention

payback period technique a capital budgeting technique that measures the amount of time it will take to recover the cash outlay of an investment

penetration pricing strategy setting lower than normal prices to hasten market acceptance of a product or service or to increase market share

percentage-of-sales technique a method of forecasting asset investments and financing requirements

perception the individual processes that give meaning to the stimuli confronting consumers

perceptual categorization the process of grouping similar things so as to manage huge quantities of incoming stimuli

peril a cause of loss, either through natural events or through the acts of people

perpetual inventory system a method for keeping a running record of inventory

personal property any property other than real property, including machinery, equipment, furniture, fixtures, stock, and vehicles

personal selling a sales presentation delivered in a one-on-one manner

personnel risks risks that directly affect individual employees, but may have an indirect impact on a business as well

physical distribution (logistics) the activities of distribution involved in the physical relocation of products

physical inventory system a method that provides for periodic counting of items in inventory

piggyback franchising the operation of a retail franchise within the physical facilities of a host store

plant patent registered protection for any distinct and new variety of living plant

pledged accounts receivable accounts receivable used as collateral for a loan

political risk the potential for political forces in a country to negatively affect the performance of businesses operating within its borders

pop-up ads advertisements that burst open on computer screens

pre-emptive right the right of stockholders to buy new shares of stock before they are offered to the public

precipitating event an event, such as losing a job, that moves an individual to become an entrepreneur

prestige pricing setting a high price to convey an image of high quality or uniqueness

preventive maintenance activities intended to prevent machine breakdowns, injuries to people, and damage to facilities

price a specification of what a seller requires in exchange for transferring ownership or use of a product or service

price lining strategy setting a range of several distinct merchandise price levels

primary data new market information that is gathered by the firm conducting the research

prime rate the interest rate charged by a commercial bank on loans to its most creditworthy customers

private carriers lines of transport owned by the shippers

private equity money provided by venture capitalists or private investors

private placement the sale of a firm's capital stock to selected individuals

pro forma statements reports that project a firm's financial condition

product a total bundle of satisfaction—including a service, a good, or both—offered to consumers in an exchange transaction

product advertising the presentation of a business idea designed to make potential customers aware of a specific product or service and create a desire for it

product and trade name franchising a franchise agreement granting the right to use a widely recognized product or name

product item the lowest common denominator in the product mix—the individual item

product life cycle a detailed picture of what happens to a specific product's sales and profits over time

product line the sum of related individual product items

product mix the collection of a firm's total product lines

product mix consistency the similarity of product lines in a product mix

product strategy the way the product component of the marketing mix is used to achieve a firm's objectives

productivity the efficiency with which inputs are transformed into outputs

products and/or services plan a section of the business plan that describes the product and/or service to be provided and explains its merits

professional employment organization (PEO) a personnel-leasing company that places employees on its own payroll and then "rents" them to employers on a permanent basis

professional manager a manager who uses systematic, analytical methods of management

profit retention the reinvestment of profits in a firm

promotion marketing communications that inform and persuade consumers

promotional mix a blend of nonpersonal, personal, and special forms of communication aimed at a target market

prospecting a systematic process of continually looking for new customers

prospectus a marketing document used to solicit investors' monies

proximate cause in the area of tort liability, a negligent act with a causal link to the damages sustained

publicity information about a firm and its products or services that appears as a news item, usually free of charge

punitive damages a form of punishment that goes beyond compensatory damages, intending to punish wrongdoers for gross negligence or a callous disregard for the interests of others and to have a deterrent effect

purchasing the process of obtaining materials, equipment, and services from outside suppliers

pure risk the uncertainty associated with a situation where only loss or no loss can occur

Q

quality the features of a product or service that enable it to satisfy customers' needs

quality circle a group of employees who meet regularly to discuss quality-related problems

R

real estate mortgage a long-term loan with real property held as collateral

real property land and anything physically attached to the land, such as buildings

reasonable (prudent person) standard the typical standard of care, based on what a reasonable or prudent person would have done under similar circumstances

reengineering a fundamental restructuring to improve the operations process

reference groups groups that an individual allows to influence his or her behavior

refugee a person who becomes an entrepreneur to escape an undesirable situation

reliability the consistency of a test in measuring job performance ability

reluctant entrepreneur a person who becomes an entrepreneur as a result of some severe hardship

repetitive manufacturing a type of manufacturing operation in which long production runs are used to produce a large quantity of a standardized product

replacement value method determination of the value of a business by estimating the cost of replacing the firm's assets

replacement value of property the cost to replace or replicate property at today's prices

resources the basic inputs that a firm uses to conduct its business

retained earnings profits less withdrawals (dividends) over the life of the business

return on assets the rate of return earned on a firm's total assets invested, computed as operating income divided by total assets

return on equity the rate of return earned on the owner's equity investment, computed as net income divided by owner's equity investment

revolving charge account a line of credit on which the customer may charge purchases at any time, up to a preestablished limit

revolving credit agreement a legal commitment by a bank to lend up to a maximum amount

risk a condition in which there is a possibility of an adverse deviation from a desired outcome that is expected or hoped for

risk control minimizing potential losses by preventing, avoiding, or reducing risk

risk financing making funds available to cover losses that could not be eliminated by risk control

risk management ways of coping with risk that are designed to preserve the assets and earning power of a firm

risk retention financing loss intentionally, through operating revenues or retained earnings

risk transfer buying insurance or making contractual arrangements with others in order to transfer risk

royalties fees paid by the licensee to the licensor for each unit produced under a licensing contract

S

S corporation (Subchapter S corporation) a type of corporation that is taxed by the federal government as a partnership

sales forecast a prediction of how much of a product or service will be purchased within a market during a specified time period

sales promotion an inclusive term for any promotional techniques other than personal selling and advertising

secondary data market information that has been previously compiled

Section 1244 stock stock that offers some tax benefit to the stockholder in the case of corporate failure

segmentation variables the parameters used to distinguish one form of market behavior from another

self-insurance designating part of a firm's earnings as a cushion against possible future losses

serendipity the faculty for making desirable discoveries by accident

Service Corps of Retired Executives (SCORE) an SBA-sponsored group of retired executives who give free advice to small businesses

service mark a brand that a company has the exclusive right to use to identify a service

7(a) Loan Guaranty Program loan program that helps small companies obtain financing through a guaranty provided by the SBA

7(m) Microloan Program SBA loan program that provides short-term loans of up to $35,000 to small businesses and not-for-profit child-care centers

short-range plan a plan that governs a firm's operations for one year or less

short-term notes cash amounts borrowed from a bank or other lending sources that must be repaid within a short period of time

single-entry system a checkbook system of accounting reflecting only receipts and disbursements

single-segment strategy a strategy that recognizes the existence of several distinct market segments but focuses on only the most profitable segment

skimming price strategy setting very high prices for a limited period before reducing them to more competitive levels

small business development centers (SBDCs) university-affiliated centers offering consulting, education, and other support to small businesses

Small Business Innovative Research (SBIR) program a government program that helps to finance companies that plan to transform laboratory research into marketable products

small business investment companies (SBICs) privately owned banks, regulated by the Small Business Administration, that provide long-term loans and/or equity capital to small businesses

small business marketing business activities that direct the creation, development, and delivery of a bundle of satisfaction from the creator to the targeted user and that satisfy the targeted user

social classes divisions within a society having different levels of social prestige

social responsibilities ethical obligations to customers, employees, and the community

sole proprietorship a business owned by one person

span of control the number of subordinates supervised by one manager

special-purpose equipment machines designed to serve specialized functions in the production process

spontaneous financing short-term debts, such as accounts payable, that automatically increase in proportion to a firm's sales

stages in succession phases in the process of transferring leadership of a family business from parent to child

stakeholders individuals who can affect or are affected by the performance of a company

statistical process control the use of statistical methods to assess quality during the operations process

stock certificate a document specifying the number of shares owned by a stockholder

strategic alliance an organizational relationship that links two or more independent business entities in a common endeavor

strategic decision a decision regarding the direction a firm will take in relating to its customers and competitors

strategy a plan of action that coordinates the resources and commitments of an organization to achieve superior performance

summary plan a short form of a business plan that presents only the most important issues and projections for the business

supply chain management a system of management that integrates and coordinates the means by which a firm creates or develops a product or service and delivers it to customers

sustainable competitive advantage a value-creating position that is likely to endure over time

SWOT analysis a type of assessment that provides a concise overview of a firm's strategic situation

T

tangible resources those organizational resources that are visible and easy to measure

tariffs taxes charged on imported goods

term loan money loaned for a 5- to 10-year term, corresponding to the length of time the investment will bring in profits

times interest earned ratio the ratio of operating income to interest charges

torts wrongful acts or omissions for which an injured party can take legal action against the wrongdoer for monetary damages

total asset turnover the ratio of sales to total assets, showing the efficiency with which a firm's assets are used to generate sales

total cost the sum of cost of goods sold, selling expenses, and overhead costs

total fixed costs costs that remain constant as the quantity produced or sold varies

total quality management (TQM) an all-encompassing management approach to providing high-quality products and services

total variable costs costs that vary with the quantity produced or sold

trade credit financing provided by a supplier of inventory to a given company

trade-credit agencies privately owned organizations that collect credit information on businesses

trade dress elements of a firm's distinctive image not protected by a trademark, patent, or copyright

trade intermediary an agency that distributes a company's products on a contract basis to customers in another country

trade mission a trip organized to help small business owners meet with potential buyers abroad and learn about cultural and regulatory obstacles in foreign markets

trademark a legal term identifying a firm's exclusive right to use a brand

transaction-based model a business model in which the Web site provides a mechanism for buying or selling products or services

transactional relationship an association between a business and a customer that relates to a purchase or a business deal

transfer of ownership passing ownership of a family business to the next generation

24/7 e-tailing electronic retailing providing round-the-clock access to products and services

Type A ideas startup ideas centered around providing customers with an existing product not available in their market

Type B ideas startup ideas, involving new technology, centered around providing customers with a new product

Type C ideas startup ideas centered around providing customers with an improved product

U

underlying values unarticulated ethical beliefs that provide a foundation for ethical behavior in a firm

Uniform Franchise Offering Circular (UFOC) a document accepted by the Federal Trade Commission as satisfying its franchise disclosure requirements

unlimited liability liability on the part of an owner that extends beyond the owner's investment in the business

unsegmented strategy (mass marketing) a strategy that defines the total market as the target market

utility patent registered protection for a new process or a product's function

V

validity the extent to which a test assesses true job performance ability

valuation based on comparables determination of the value of a business by considering the actual market prices of firms that are similar to the firm being valued

variable inspection the determination of product acceptability based on a variable such as weight or length

variable pricing strategy setting more than one price for a good or service in order to offer price concessions to certain customers

W

warranty a promise that a product will perform at a certain level or meet certain standards

Web advertising advertising appearing on the World Wide Web

Web sponsorship a type of advertising in which a firm pays another organization for the right to be part of that organization's Web page

work teams groups of employees with freedom to function without close supervision

workers' compensation legislation laws that obligate the employer to pay employees for injury or illness related to employment, regardless of fault

workforce diversity differences among employees in terms of such dimensions as gender, age, ethnicity, and race

working-capital cycle the daily flow of resources through a firm's working-capital accounts

working-capital management the management of current assets and current liabilities

Z

zoning ordinances local laws regulating land use

Index

A

B

C

D

E

T

X

Y

Z